Preface

Digital Libraries are complex and advanced forms of information systems which extend and augment their physical counterparts by amplifying existing resources and services and enabling development of new kinds of human problem solving and expression. Their complexity arises from the data-rich domain of discourse as well as from extended demands for multi-disciplinary input, involving distributed systems architectures, structured digital documents, collaboration support, human-computer interaction, information filtering, etc. In addition to the broad range of technical issues, ethics and intellectual property rights add to the complication that is normally associated with the development, maintenance, and use of Digital Libraries.

The Second European Conference on Digital Libraries (ECDL'98) builds upon the success of the first of this series of European Conferences on Research and Advanced Technology for Digital Libraries, held last year in Pisa, Italy, September 1-3, 1997.

This series of conferences is partially funded by the TMR Programme of the European Commission and is actively supported and promoted by the European Research Consortium on Informatics and Mathematics (ERCIM). The aim is to bring together the different communities involved in the development of Digital Libraries, to review progress and to discuss strategies, research and technological development (RTD) issues, as well as specific topics related to the European context. These communities include professionals from universities, research centres, industry, government agencies, public libraries, etc. One of the main objectives is to promote and sustain an international and multi-disciplinary Digital Libraries community, facilitating scientific and technological progress, enabling growth of the available infrastructure and services, increasing the dissemination bandwidth and attracting further interest, particularly from young scientists.

ECDL'98 is held in Heraklion, Crete, Greece, September 21-23, 1998, and is organised by the Institute of Computer Science (ICS) of the Foundation for Research and Technology - Hellas (FORTH) in co-operation with the Department of Computer Science of the University of Crete. It is a truly international event of a distinctively interdisciplinary nature. The international programme committee of the conference comprised 32 representatives from 13 countries. In total, 107 papers were received, a significant increase from last year, which were assigned to 56 reviewers. The significant increase in the number of paper submissions marks the growing interest that the field of Digital Libraries has attracted over the past year. Following a rigorous peer review selection process, where each paper was reviewed by at least three reviewers, 35 full papers were selected. The high quality of the submitted papers also indicates the rapid progress that is taking place in this emerging technological field. Additionally, the conference features 1 keynote speaker, 10 invited talks, 7 tutorials, 32 posters, 6 panel sessions, 2 special sessions, 13 demonstrations, and 9 DELOS Workshop papers.

We are indebted to all those who have contributed to make this conference possible. The TMR Programme of the European Commission, ERCIM, ICS-FORTH, University of Crete, and the sponsors of this conference; the international programme committee, the reviewers and the local organising committee; the invited speakers, the paper and poster presenters, the organisers and participants of tutorials, panel sessions, case studies and demonstrations, and all the conference participants.

September 1998   Christos Nikolaou and Constantine Stephanidis

Organisation

The Second European Conference on Research and Advanced Technology for Digital Libraries was organised in Heraklion, Crete, Greece by the Institute of Computer Science (ICS) of the Foundation for Research and Technology - Hellas (FORTH), in co-operation with the Department of Computer Science of the University of Crete, and with the assistance of the European Commission (TMR Programme) and the European Research Consortium for Informatics and Mathematics (ERCIM).

Programme Chair

Christos Nikolaou, University of Crete & ICS-FORTH, Greece

Programme Committee

Serge Abiteboul, INRIA, France
Robert B. Allen, Bellcore, USA
Thomas Baker, Asian Institute of Technology, Thailand
William Birmingham, University of Michigan, USA
Panos Constantopoulos, University of Crete & ICS-FORTH, Greece
Bruce Croft, University of Massachusetts, USA
Costis Dallas, Hellenic Ministry of Foreign Affairs, Greece
Edward A. Fox, Virginia Technical University, USA
Norbert Fuhr, University of Dortmund, Germany
Hector Garcia-Molina, Stanford University, USA
Keith Jeffery, RAL-CLRC, UK
Martin Kersten, CWI, The Netherlands
Judith Klavans, Columbia University, USA
Carl Lagoze, Cornell University, USA
Clifford A. Lynch, Coalition for Networked Information, USA
Jeff MacKie-Mason, University of Michigan, USA
A. Desai Narasimhalu, National University of Singapore, Singapore
Ann Okerson, Yale University, USA
Olle Olsson, SICS, Sweden
Andreas Paepcke, Stanford University, USA
Nicholas Patrikalakis, MIT, USA
Carol Peters, IEI-CNR, Italy
Jakka Sairamesh, IBM-T.J. Watson Research Center, USA
Peter Schauble, ETH Zurich, Switzerland
Hans Joerg Schek, ETH Zurich, Switzerland
Eric Simon, INRIA, France
Ingeborg T. Solvberg, University of Science and Technology, Norway
Constantine Stephanidis, ICS-FORTH, Greece
Shigeo Sugimoto, University of Library and Information Science, Japan
Costantino Thanos, IEI-CNR, Italy
Ulrich Thiel, GMD-IPSI, Germany
Stuart Weibel, OCLC, USA

Christos Nikolaou
Constantine Stephanidis (Eds.)

Research and Advanced Technology for Digital Libraries

Second European Conference, ECDL'98
Heraklion, Crete, Greece
September 21-23, 1998
Proceedings

Springer

Series Editors

Gerhard Goos, Karlsruhe University, Germany
Juris Hartmanis, Cornell University, NY, USA
Jan van Leeuwen, Utrecht University, The Netherlands

Volume Editors

Christos Nikolaou
Constantine Stephanidis
Institute of Computer Science (ICS)
Foundation for Research and Technology - Hellas (FORTH)
Science and Technology Park of Crete
GR-71110 Heraklion, Crete, Greece
E-mail: {nikolau,cs}@ics.forth.gr

Cataloging-in-Publication data applied for

Die Deutsche Bibliothek - CIP-Einheitsaufnahme

Research and advanced technology for digital libraries : second European
conference ; proceedings / ECDL '98, Heraklion, Crete, Greece, September 21 -
23, 1998. Christos Nikolaou ; Constantine Stephanidis (ed.). - Berlin ;
Heidelberg ; New York ; Barcelona ; Budapest ; Hong Kong ; London ; Milan ;
Paris ; Singapore ; Tokyo : Springer, 1998
  (Lecture notes in computer science ; Vol. 1513)
  ISBN 3-540-65101-2

CR Subject Classification (1991): H.2, H.3, H.4.3, H.5, C.2, I.7.2-3, J.1, J.7

ISSN 0302-9743
ISBN 3-540-65101-2 Springer-Verlag Berlin Heidelberg New York

© Springer-Verlag Berlin Heidelberg 1998
Printed in Germany

Typesetting: Camera-ready by author
SPIN 10692697   06/3142 – 5 4 3 2 1 0   Printed on acid-free paper

Local Organising Committee

Anastasia Anastasiadi, ICS-FORTH, Greece
Penelope Constanta, ICS-FORTH, Greece
Rena Kalaitzaki, University of Crete, Greece
Sarantos Kapidakis, ICS-FORTH, Greece
Liana Kefalaki, ICS-FORTH, Greece
Gioylh Koraoy, University of Crete, Greece
Spyros Lalis, University of Crete, Greece
Manolis Marazakis, University of Crete, Greece
Dimitris Papadakis, University of Crete, Greece
Stavros Papadakis, University of Crete, Greece
Maria Prevelianaki, ICS-FORTH, Greece
Maria Stavrakaki, University of Crete, Greece
Mixalhs Tzekakhs, University of Crete, Greece
Stella Vourou, University of Crete & ICS-FORTH, Greece

Reviewers

Serge Abiteboul, INRIA, France
Robert B. Allen, Bellcore, USA
Sophia Ananiadou, Manchester Metropolitan University, UK
Anastasia Anastasiadi, ICS-FORTH, Greece
Thomas Baker, Asian Institute of Technology, Thailand
William Birmingham, University of Michigan, USA
Vassilios Chrissikopoulos, University of Piraeus, Greece
Vasilis Christophides, ICS-FORTH, Greece
Penelope Constanta, ICS-FORTH, Greece
Bruce Croft, University of Massachusetts, USA
Costis Dallas, Hellenic Ministry of Foreign Affairs, Greece
Edward A. Fox, Virginia Technical University, USA
Norbert Fuhr, University of Dortmund, Germany
Hector Garcia-Molina, Stanford University, USA
George Georgakopoulos, University of Crete, Greece
Antonis Hatzistamatiou, ICS-FORTH, Greece
Elias Houstis, Purdue University, USA
Catherine Houstis, University of Crete & ICS-FORTH, Greece
Stelios Sartzetakis, ICS-FORTH, Greece
Keith Jeffery, RAL-CLRC, UK
Hans Joerg Schek, ETH Zurich, Switzerland
Sarantos Kapidakis, ICS-FORTH, Greece
Petros Kavassalis, MIT, USA
Martin Kersten, CWI, The Netherlands
Judith Klavans, Columbia University, USA
Carl Lagoze, Cornell University, USA
Vali Lalioti, GMD, Germany

Spyros Lalis, University of Crete, Greece
Chung-Sheng Li, IBM-T.J. Watson Research Center, USA
Clifford A. Lynch, Coalition for Networked Information, USA
Jeff Mackie-Mason, University of Michigan, USA
Manolis Marazakis, ICS-FORTH, Greece
Vaggelis Markatos, University of Crete & ICS-FORTH, Greece
A. Desai Narasimhalu, National University of Singapore, Singapore
Erich J. Neuhold, GMD, Germany
Christos Nikolaou, University of Crete & ICS-FORTH, Greece
Ann Okerson, Yale University, USA
Andreas Paepcke, Stanford University, USA
Stavros Papadakis, ICS-FORTH, Greece
Nicholas Patrikalakis, MIT, USA
Carol Peters, IEI-CNR, Italy
Manolis Prastakos, IACM, Greece
Jakka Sairamesh, IBM-T.J. Watson Research Center, USA
Peter Schauble, ETH Zurich, Switzerland
Antonis Sidiropoulos, ICS-FORTH, Greece
Eric Simon, INRIA, France
Ingeborg T. Solvberg, University of Science and Technology, Norway
Constantine Stephanidis, ICS-FORTH, Greece
Shigeo Sugimoto, University of Library and Information Science, Japan
Costantino Thanos, IEI-CNR, Italy
Ulrich Thiel, GMD-IPSI, Germany
Panos Trahanias, University of Crete & ICS-FORTH, Greece
George Tziritas, University of Crete & ICS-FORTH, Greece
Stella Vourou, University of Crete & ICS-FORTH, Greece
Pubudu Wariyapola, MIT, USA
Stuart Weibel, OCLC, USA

Sponsoring Institutions

The Second European Conference on Research and Advanced Technology for Digital Libraries
wishes to thank the following organisations for their support:

- IEEE Computer Society, USA
- Lambrakis Research Foundation, Greece
- Hellenic Telecommunication Organisation (OTE), Greece
- FORTHnet, Greece
- General Secretariat for Research and Technology, Ministry for Development, Greece
- INTRACOM, Greece
- CaberNet, UK
- Air Greece, Greece
- Swets, The Netherlands
- Ergodata, Greece

Table of Contents

Posters

Panels

Special Sessions

Delos Workshop

Demonstrations

Author Index

Intelligent Multimedia Communication

Mark Maybury[1], Oliviero Stock[2], and Wolfgang Wahlster[3]

[1]The MITRE Corporation
202 Burlington Road, Bedford, MA 01730, USA
maybury@mitre.org

[2] Istituto per la Ricerca Scientifica e Tecnologica (IRST)
via Sommarive 18, I-38050 Povo – Trento, Italy
stock@irst.itc.it

[3] German Research Center for AI (DFKI)
Stuhlsatzenhausweg 3, D-66119 Saarbruecken, Germany
wahlster@dfki.uni-sb.de

Abstract. Multimedia communication is a part of everyday life and its appearance in computer applications is increasing in frequency and diversity. Intelligent or knowledge based computer supported communication promises a number of benefits including increased interaction efficiency and effectiveness. This article defines the area of intelligent multimedia communication, outlines fundamental research questions, summarizes the associated scientific and technical history, identifies current challenges and concludes by predicting future breakthroughs including multilinguality. We conclude describing several new research issues that systems of systems raise.

1 Definition of Multimedia Communication

We define *communication* as the interaction between human-human, human-system, and human-information. This includes interfaces to people, interfaces to applications, and interfaces to information. Following Maybury and Wahlster [1], we define:

- *Multimedia* – physical means via which information is input, output and/or stored (e.g., interactive devices such as keyboard, mouse, displays; storage devices such as disk or CD-ROM)
- *Multimodal* – human perceptual processes such as vision, audition, taction
- *Multicodal* – representations used to encode atomic, elements, syntax, semantics, pragmatics and related data structures (e.g., lexicons, grammars) associated with media and modalities.

The majority of computational efforts have focused on multimedia human computer interfaces. There exists a large literature and associated techniques to develop learnable, usable, transparent interfaces in general (e.g., Baecker et al. [2]). In particular, we focus here on intelligent and multimedia user interfaces (e.g.,Maybury [3]) which from the user perspective assist in tasks, are context sensitive, adapt appropriately (when, where, how) and may:

- *Analyze* sychronous and asychronous multimedia/ modal input (e.g., spoken and written text, gesture, drawings) which might be imprecise, ambiguous, and/or partial
- *Generate* (design, realize) coordinated, cohesive, and coherent multimedia/modal presentations
- *Manage* the interaction (e.g., training, error recovery, task completion, tailoring interaction) by representing, reasoning, and exploiting *models* of the domain, task, user, media/mode, discourse, and environment.

From the developers perspective there is also interest in decreasing the time, expense, and level of expertise necessary to construct successful systems. Finally, when interacting with information spaces, there is the area of media content analysis (Maybury [4]) which includes retrieval of text, audio, imagery and/or combinations thereof.

2 Fundamental Questions

The fundamental questions mirror the above definitions:

- *Analysis:* How do we build systems to deal with synchronous and asychronous, imprecise, ambiguous, and/or partial multimedia/modal input?
- *Generation:* How do we design, realize, and tailor coordinated, cohesive, and coherent multimedia/modal presentations?
- *Management:* How do we ensure efficient, effective and natural interaction (e.g., training, error recovery, task completion, tailoring interaction styles)? How do we represent, reason, and exploit *models* of the domain, task, user, media/mode, and context (discourse, environment)?
- *Methods*: What kinds of representations and reasoning is required to enable the above. What kinds of multimedia corpora are required? What kinds of evaluation measures, metrics and methods will move this area forward?

3 Timeline

There has been interest in computer supported multimedia communication for the past three decades. We briefly characterize the major problems addressed, developments, and influence to related areas. We characterize some landmark developments using the above distinctions of analysis of input, generation of output, and interaction management.

Late 1950s
- Input/Output: Natural language interfaces (NLI) discussed at Dartmouth AI Conference. First integrated graphics/pointing system developed & deployed (SAGE) [5] [6].

1960s
- Input/Output: Laboratory investigations of VR, initial interest in NLI
- General: First Conference on Computational Linguistics [7]

1970s
- Input: Applications of NLI
- Output: Template generation systems. First speech to text systems.
- Management: focus and dialogue coherence models
- General: emerging commercial systems

1980s
- Input: Commercialization of NLI; First integrated speech and gesture (e.g., Bolt's "Put that there" [8]).
- Output: Creation of techniques for domain independent, rhetorically structured text (e.g., rhetorical schemas, communicative plans). Improved sentence/clause planning/realization. First multilingual generation systems. Automated graphics design.
- Management: User and Discourse modeling. Model-based interfaces.
- General: International workshops on user modeling, text generation, multimodal interaction (e.g., VENACO); government programs (e.g., DARPA intelligent user interface program), industrial visions of intelligent multimodal, multilingual interaction (e.g., Apple's "Phil", AT&T).

1990s
- Input: Increasing spoken language applications. More sophisticated input analysis prototypes (e.g., partial, synchronous, and ambiguous input).
- Output: Coordinated, multimodal generation prototypes. Standard reference model for presentation systems.
- Management: User adapted systems. Agents appear in commercial software (e.g., Microsoft™ Office Assistant).
- General: DARPA (e.g., Intelligent Collaboration and Visualization program (http://snad.ncsl.nist.gov/~icv-ewg/, "Communicator" spoken language architecture) and European Community Intelligent Information Interfaces (www.i3net.org) programs. First ACM international conference on intelligent user interfaces (IUI) [9]. Readings in IUI [1]. Emergence of media content analysis for new applications, e.g., news understanding, video mail and/or VTC indexing and retrieval.

4 Examples of Multimedia Information Access

Significant progress has been made in multimedia interfaces, integrating language, speech, and gesture. For example, Figure 1 shows the CUBRICON system architecture [10]. CUBRICON enables a user to interact using spoken or typed natural language and gesture, displaying results using combinations of language, maps, and graphics. Interaction management is effected via mechanisms such as a user and discourse model which not only influence the generated responses but also manage window layout based on user focus of attention.

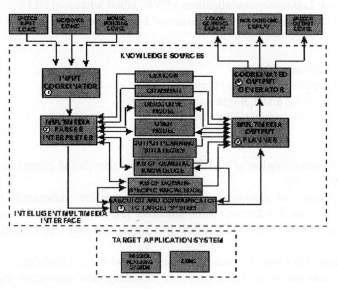

Fig. 1. CUBRICON Multimedia Interface Architecture

In a strongly related example, progress has been made in multimedia information access, integrating language, speech, and image processing, together with more traditional techniques such as hypermedia. For example, Stock et al.'s Alfresco ([11] [12]) is a system for accessing cultural heritage information that integrates in a coherent exploration dialogue a) language based acts, with implicit and explicit reference to what has been said and shown, and b) hypermedia navigation. The generation system, part of the output presentation system, is influenced by the user's interest model that develops in the course of the multimodal interaction. Another aspect developed in this system is cross-modal feedback (Zancanaro et al. [13]). The user is provided fast graphical feedback of the discourse references interpretation by the system,exploiting profitably the large bandwidth of communication we have in a multimodal system.

In a related are of media understanding [4], systems are beginning toemerge that process sychronous speech, text, and images. For example, Figure 2 shows the results of a multimedia news analysis system that exploits redundancy across speech, language (closed caption text) and video to mitigate the weaknesses of individual channel analyzers (e.g., low level image analysis and errorful speech transcription). After digitizing, segmenting (into stories and commercials), extracting (pulling out named entities [14], and summarizing into key frames and key sentences, MITRE's BNN [15], enables a user is able to browse and search broadcast news and/or visualizations thereof. A range of on-line customizable views of news summaries by time, topic, or named entity enable the user to quickly retrieve segments of relevant content.

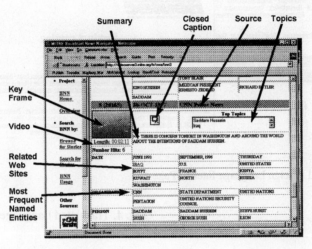

Fig. 2. Detailed Video Story Display

In terms of multilingual information access, one problem is that machine translation systems often provide only gist quality translations that, nonetheless, can be useful to end users in relevancy judgements. Figure 3 illustrates, a web page retrieved from the web by searching for German chemical companies on the web using the German word "chemie" and "gmbh". Afterretrieving German-language web site, we use a web based machine translation engine (Systran) to obtain a gist-quality translation of their chemical products (Figure 4). Note how the HTML document structure enhances the intelligibility of the resultant translation.

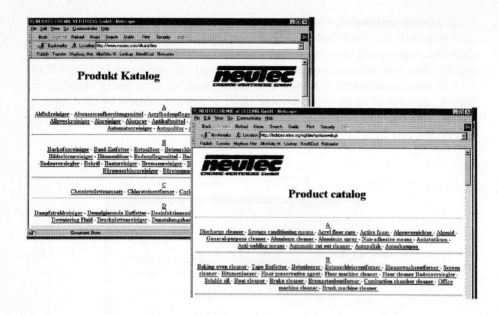

Fig. 3. Original Foreign Language Internet Page

Fig. 4. Translated Language Internet Page

5 Impediments to Progress

Research is not advancing as rapidly as possible in this area because of several impediments. These include:

1. The need for media specific and media independent representations (e.g., a graphical lexicon, syntax, semantics and perhaps even pragmatics and its relation to those in language and gesture), as well as associated tools and techniques that foster reuse and provide a shared foundation for community research.
2. The creation and sharing of resources [16], in particular Multi-* corpora, that is:
   - Multimedia content (e.g., Web, News, VTC)
   - Multimedia interaction (need for instrumentation)
   - Multiparty interaction (e.g., CSCW)

   Found data might include chat sessions and multilingual radio and television corpora and /or multilingual websites.

3. Standards and system modules for plug-and-play evaluation
    - Interfaces: distributed computing infrastructure with reusable elements including speech and language modules, user models (e.g., BGP-MS) & discourse modules, agent communication and coordination (e.g., KQML, open agent architectures)
    - Media analyzers
    - Intellectual property, e.g., ownership and distribution of media and knowledge resources

6 Major Breakthroughs Coming

In the next five years, current research will likely yield several key outcomes. Areas of expected advancement include:

- Integration of language processing and hypermedia
- Integration of multimodal processing mechanisms, e.g., image and language processing
- Increasing transition of advances in agent technology into commercial interface applications
- Transfer of HCI evaluation techniques (e.g., wizard of oz, cognitive walkthrough, task-based evaluation) to multimodal communication research.

Given advances in corpus based techniques for information retrieval and information extraction (e.g., commercial tools for proper name extraction with 90% precision and recall), and the current transfer of these techniques to multilingual information retrieval and extraction, we can expect their application to multilingual understanding. We also believe there is an equivalent opportunity for multimedia generation for other languages.

Transfer of techniques from related areas will be an important strategy. For example, researchers are beginning to take statistical and corpus based techniques formerly applied to single media (e.g., speech, text processing) and apply these to multimedia (e.g., VTC, TV, CSCW).

This work will enable new application areas for relatively unexplored tasks including:

- Multimodal/lingual information access
- Multimodal/lingual presentation generation (summarization)
- Multimodal/lingual collaboration environments

A number of fundamental issues will need to be addressed, such as those outlined below.

8

7 Role of Multiple Languages

As indicated above, multimodal interaction is the integration of multiple subfields. When extending techniques and methods to multiple languages, we have the benefit of drawing upon previous monolingual techniques that have generality. For example, many generation techniques and components (e.g., content selection, media allocation, media design) built previously for monolingual generation, can mostly be reused across languages. Analogously, interaction management components (e.g., user and discourse models) can be reused. There are, of course, many language specific phenomena that need to be addressed. For example, in generation of multilingual and multimedia presentations, lexical length affects the layout of material both in space and in time. For instance, in laying out a multilingual electronic yellow pages, space may be strictly limited given a standard format and so variability in linguistic realization across languages may pose challenges. In a multimedia context, we might need to not only generate language specific expressions, but also culturally appropriate media.

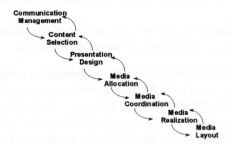

Figure 5. Generation Tasks

In making further progress in this area, there are some unique resources we might take advantage to help develop systems for multimedia information access (e.g., dubbed movies, multilingual broadcast news) that might help accelerate the development of, for example, a multilingual video corpora.

8 Systems Research

Multimedia communication systems, which incorporate multiple subsystems for analysis, generation and interaction management, raise new research questions beyond the well known challenges which occur in component technologies (e.g.,learnability, portability, scalability, performance, speed within a language processing system). These include intersystem error propagation, intersystem control and invocation order, and human system interaction.

9

8.1 Evaluation and Error Propagation

As systems increasingly integrate multiple interactive subcomponents, there is an opportunity to integrate and/or apply software in parallel or in sequence to a given information source or sink. For example, in an information access application where the user may retrieve, extract, translate, or summarize information, we have the possibility of influencing the utility of the output just by sequencing systems given their inherent performance properties (e.g., accuracy, speed). For example, we might use language processing to enhance post-retrieval analysis (extract common terms across documents, re-rank documents provide translated summaries) to hone in on relevant documents. These documents might then cue the user to effective keywords to search for foreign language sources, whose relevancy is assessed using a fast but low quality web-based translation engine. Translating content initially would have been costly, slow, and ineffective. An analogous situation arises when searching multimedia repositories. Old and new evaluation measures, metrics, and methods will be required in this multifaceted environment.

8.2 Multilingual and Multimodal Sources

New research opportunities are raised by processing multilingual and multimodal sources, including the challenge of summarizing across these. For example, what is the optimal presentation of content and in which media or mix of media? [17]. Or consider that in broadcast news spoken language transcription, the best word error rates are currently around 10% for broadcast news anchor speech. What is the cascaded effect of subsequently extracting entities, summarizing, or translating the text?

This also extends to the nature of the interface with the user. For example, applying a low quality speech-to-text transcriber followed by a high quality summarizer may actually result in poorer task performance than providing the user with rapid auditory preview and skimming of the multimedia source.

8.3 User Involvement in Process?

How should users interact with these language-enabled machines? Users of Alta-Vista are now shown foreign web sites matching their queries, with offers to translate them. When invoking the translator, however, the user must pick the source and target language, but what if the character sets and language are unrecognizable by the user? What kind of assistance should the user provide the machine and vice versa? Should this extend to providing feedback to enable machine learning? Would this scale up to a broad set of web users? An in terms of multimedia interaction, who do we develop models of interaction that adequately address issues such as uni- and multi-modal (co)reference, ambiguity, and incompleteness?

8.4 Resource Inconsistencies

Finally, with the emergence of multiple language tools, users will be faced with systems which use different language resources and models. This can readily result in incoherence across language applications, the most obvious case being when a language analysis module is able to interpret a user query containing a given word but a separate language generation module chooses a different word because the original is not in its vocabulary, resulting in potential undesired implicatures by the user. For example, if a user queries a multilingual database in English for documents on "chemical manufacturers" and this is translated into a query for "chemical companies", many documents on marketing and distribution companies would also be included. If these were then translated and summarized, a user might erroneouslyinfer most chemical enterprises were not manufacturers. The situation can worsen above the lexical level when dealing with user and discourse models which are inconsistent across applications.

9 Conclusion

We have outlined the history, developments and future of systems and research in multimedia communication. If successfully developed and employed, these systems promise:

- More *efficient* interaction -- enabling more rapid task completion with less work.
- More *effective* interaction -- doing the right thing at the right time, tailoring the content and form of the interaction to the context of the user, task, dialogue
- More *natural* interaction -- supporting spoken, written, and gestural interaction, ideally as if interacting with a human interlocutor, but taking also into account the potentially extended bandwidth of communication

Because of the multidimensional nature of multimedia communication, interdisciplinary teams will be necessary and new areas of science may need to be invented (e.g., moving beyond psycholinguistic research to "psychomedia" research). New, careful theoretical and empirical investigations as well as standards to ensure cross system synergy will be required to ensure the resultant systems will enhance and not detract from the cognitive ability of end users.

References

1. Maybury, M. T. and Wahlster, W. editors. *Readings in Intelligent User Interfaces*. Morgan Kaufmann Press. ISBN: 1-55860-444-8. (1998)
2. Baecker, R.; Grudin, J.; Buxton, W.; and Greenberg, S. second edition.*Readings in Human-Computer Interaction: Toward the Year 2000*. San Francisco: MorganKaufmann. (1995)

3. Maybury, M. T. editor. *Intelligent Multimedia Interfaces*. AAAI/MIT Press. ISBN 0-262-63150-4. (http://www.aaai.org:80/Press/Books/Maybury1/maybury.html) (1993)

4. Maybury, M. T. editor. *Intelligent Multimedia Information Retrieval*. AAAI/MIT Press. (http://www.aaai.org:80/Press/Books/Maybury2) (1997)

5. Everett, R. et al. 1957. "SAGE: A Data-Processing System for Air Defense," In Proceedings of the Eastern Joint Computer Conference, Washington, D.C., December, 1957.

6. Everett, R. et al. 1983. "SAGE: A Data Processing System for Air Defense,"*Annals of the History of Computing*, 5(4) October 1983.

7. http://www.aclweb.org/

8. Bolt, R. A.. "Put-That-There": Voice and Gesture at the Graphics Interface. *ACM Computer Graphics* 14(3): 262-270. Quarterly Report of SIGGRAPH-ACM SIGGRAPH'80 Conference Proceedings, July 14-18. Seattle, Washington. (1980)

9. http://sigart.acm.org:80/iui99/

10. Neal, J. G.; Thielman, C. Y.; Dobes, Z.;Haller, S. M. and Shapiro, S. C. Natural Language with Integrated Deictic and Graphic Gestures. In*Proceedings of the 1989 DARPA Workshop on Speech and Natural Language*, 410-423, Harwich Port: Morgan Kaufmann (1989)

11. Stock, O. and the NLP Group. AlFresco: Enjoying the Combination of NLP and Hypermedia for Information Exploration. In M. Maybury (ed.)*Intelligent Multimedia Interfaces*, AAAI Press, Menlo Park, CA. (1993)

12. Stock, O., Strapparava, C. and Zancanaro, M. Explorations in an Environment for Natural Language Multimodal Information Access. In M. Maybury (ed.) *Intelligent Mutimodal Information Retrieval*. AAAI Press, Menlo Park, Ca./MIT Press, Cambridge, MA. (1997)

13. Zancanaro, M., Stock, O. and Strapparava, C. Multimodal Interaction for Information Access: Exploiting Cohesion. In *Computational Intelligence*, 13 (4). (1997)

14. Aberdeen, J., Burger, J., Day, D.,Hirschman, L., Robinson, P., and Vilain, M. "Description of the Alembic System Used for MUC-6," Proceedings of the Sixth Message Understanding Conference. Advanced Research Projects Agency Information Technology Office, Columbia, MD, 6-8 November (1995)

15. Merlino, A., Morey, D., and Maybury, M. "Broadcast News Navigation using Story Segments", ACM International Multimedia Conference, Seattle, WA, November 8-14, 381-391. (1997)

16. First International Conference on Language Resources and Evaluation (LREC). Workshop on Multilingual Information Management, Granada, Spain. May 31-June 1 (1998)pp 68-71.

17. Merlino, A. and Maybury, M. An Empirical Study of the Optimal Presentation of Multimedia Summaries of Broadcast News. InMani, I. and Maybury, M. (eds.)*Automated Text Summarization*. (to appear)

Autonomous Search in Complex Spaces

Erol Gelenbe

School of Computer Science
University of Central Florida
Orlando, FL 32816
erol@cs.ucf.edu

Abstract The search for information in a complex system space – such as the Web or large digital libraries, or in an unkown robotics environment – requires the design of efficient and intelligent strategies for (1) determining regions of interest using a variety of sensors, (2) detecting and classifying objects of interest, and (3) searching the space by autonomous agents. This paper discusses strategies for directing autonomous search based on spatio-temporal distributions. We discuss a model for search assuming that the environment is static, except for the effect of identifying object locations. Algorithms are designed and compared for autonomously directing a robot.
Keywords Search, Optimal Strategies, Greedy and Infinite Horizon Algorithms

1 Introduction

The purpose of this research[1] is to consider general methodologies for autonomous navigation in real or virtual spaces, as a manned or autonomous vehicle, or human agent, searches for with the help of sensors. This paper describes our work on strategies for directing autonomous searches based on spatio-temporal distributions. We use the paradigm of a moving robot which searches with the aid of a "sensor". Motion here refers to displacement among web or digital library servers. A "sensor" refers to some algorithm used by the robot to exaobject the information accessible to it at a server to deterobject whether this information is worth retrieving.

Autonomous navigation in a multidimensional environment raises two main questions: (1) what is an adequate representation of the world, and (2) what should be the location of the robot(s) in this map at any given time. Given an initial location, the robot must find a continuous path in an environment, possibly through obstacles whose spatial locations are known or are being discovered. This continuous path cannot always be predeterobjectd because information about the path and the obstacles is

---

[1] This research was supported by the U.S. Army Research Office, Grant No. DAAH04-96-1-0448 (Multidisciplinary University Research Initiative on Demining).

often only incrementally available over time. The autonomous agent has to sense the contents of the "terrain" where it currently resides as well as of its immediate neighbourhood, and it must make decisions about the *"next step"* as it collects information. In [3] comparisons are made between robotic navigation and three great sailors of the past: Magellan, Columbus, and Ulysses. Magellan knows where are all the obstacles are located, and has to come up with a map of the world by navigating around the obstacles. Columbus does not know anything, and has to discover all the environment and the obstacles and, like Magellan, Columbus must create a map. Ulysses has a complete global map, but the environment changes often due to the will of the gods against Ulysses' travels; in his case we could consider that the map is composed of static and dynamic areas. In another study [18] *Clustering by discovery* is discussed. Landmarks are present in the environment considered; they can be detected by the sensors of the robot during the exploration. We define a logical road *(LR)* to be a straight line between two landmarks. The physical road *(PR)* considers the real shapes of the obstacles. During motion, the symbolic mobile "builds" a map with the landmarks already defined. There are two kinds of maps: topological maps describe the pattern of landmarks and their connections with the logical road, while metric maps give the position of each landmark in a Cartesian space. The knowledge of these two maps permits the partioning of space into clusters which depend on the scale and the environment. Clustering by discovery is then the technique for identifying clusters in a map being learned by exploration. The clustering problem consists in finding the optimized partition of a given set of points called landmarks in clusters. They change during the motion of the robot in the environment. Other studies of robotic or of animal search are listed in the bibliography. Learning models that are capable of forming a cognitive map to be used in search and navigation are discussed in [16] using either discrete elements of topographic information, or continuously available and updated information gathered during the search process. An important general issue is the coordination of multiple robots. A recent approach developed for collaboration and non-interference between agents is based on *Social Potential Fields* [23] where a global controller defines (possibly distinct) pair-wise potential laws for ordered pairs of components (i.e. robots, obstacles and objectives) of the system. The volume edited by Meyer, Roitblat and Wilson [22] presents many ideas from animal cooperation and social interaction in the design of robotic search systems.

2   A model of the environment and of robot motion

The information units we use in our research are *Scenes*; they are typically multisensory representations of the area in which objects are being
sought and localized. Each scene is "tiled" with a set of *Blocks* or locations
(x, y) which are individual units on which computation is carried out. The
Blocks' size and shape relates to the resolution with which detection and
multisensory imaging can be physically carried out, and to the resolution
with which location is feasible. Typically, multisensory data is represented
by a set of Image Blocks (IBs) which relate to the same location in the
Scene. In mathematical terms, a Scene is merely a finite, closed subset R
of Cartesian space which is augmented by information such as the known
probability of finding information at each point (or image block position)
(x, y).

   In a distributed-control framework, each robot deterobjects its movement by observing the environment at that moment and applying some
computed *control law* designed so that the system as a whole will achieve
the goals of search and detection. Our investigation will use prior information from the Scene, and local information sensed by an individual robot,
to learn in an on-line manner the next move to be made. The criterion
being optimized can be the rate at which potential object locations are
being visited. More formally, in this work we will use three specific scenes:

- Scene–1 is the currently available objective information; it is a map
  which associates with each point $(x, y) \in R$ an *a priori* probability
  $q(x, y)$ of the presence of an object, as well as the physical possibility
  (or difficulty) of moving to that point. The physical ease or difficulty
  of moving from point (x, y) to neighboring point (u, v) is represented
  by a rate $\gamma(x, y, u, v)$ – this rate will be low (or even zero) when
  this movement is laborious or impossible due to obstacles or other
  impediments, while it can be relatively high when the terrain presents
  no difficulties. An example is given in Figure 1.
- Scene–2 is the knowledge one has of reality, i.e. of the presence and
  absence of objects. It is thus the "test-bed" that one would use for
  any proposed strategy.
- Scene–3 is the map used for decision making. It contains the most recent values of the motion rates or directional field strengths $\mu(x, y, u, v)$
  which are the decision variables used by the robot.

In the approach considered in this paper, the robot must decide where to
move from its current position (x, y) at time t to some neighboring point.
It does so by calculating the rate of motion $\mu(x, y, u, v)$ from (x, y) to a

neighboring point (u, v). We will denote by $N(x, y)$ the set of neighbouring points of (x, y) of which typically there will be eight.

2.1 A simple greedy algorithm

The above discussion now leads to a simple algorithm for robot motion, assuming that the environment is static, except for the effect the robot itself has on this information due to its discovery that an object exists or does not exist after visiting a given point (x, y). The algorithm uses the *a priori* probability $q(x, y)$ that there is an object at point (x, y). This probability is only modified by the visits that the robot makes. Indeed, when (x, y) is visited, either the object is found and removed, setting $q(x, y) \leftarrow 0$, or an object is not found, leading to the same result.

The simplest algorithm we may consider is one in which the robot always moves in the direction where the probability of finding an object is greatest. This simple *"greedy" algorithm* can be expressed as:

$$\mu(x, y, u, v) = \mu_m, \quad if \quad q(u, v) = \max\{q(a, b) : (a, b) \in N(x, y)\}, \quad (1)$$
$$= 0, \; otherwise, \quad (2)$$

where μ_m is some maximum speed at which the robot can move. Note that in the case of equal values of the largest $q(u, v)$ for the immediate neighbours of (x, y), the direction of motion would be chosen at random among those neighbours for which the probability is greatest. This algorithm is fast, and can be quite effective (as the resulting simulations described next section show), and it will not trap the robot in local maxima simply because $q(x, y)$ is reduced to zero after point (x, y) is visited. Random motion when all neighbouring probabilities are equal will eventually move the robot away from a local maximum, though the escape from that area may be relatively slow and disorganized. However it does take only a local view of the search, and does not incorporate a more long range view.

The performance of the Greedy Algorithm on the hypothetical search space of Figure 1 is shown in Figure 2, and compared with a random search. In these experiments we assume that the "difficulty" of motion is the same at all points and in each direction. The measure of performance is the percentage of objects actually found. The experiment is run as follows. The probabilistic data of Figure 1 is used by the Greedy Algorithm, and the various tests reported on Figure 2 are run on *instances* or realizations of the presence of objects obtained by drawing at random the presence of an object in each location using the spatial distribution of Figure 1. We clearly see that the greedy algorithm provides a significant improvement in the rate of finding objects both with respect to a random search and with respect to a systematic sweeping search through all the servers or locations.

An obvious search strategy is a Systematic Sweep, and it is very reasonable to ask how any algorithm might perform as compared to that simple (and widely used) approach. The answer of course is simple too: this strategy which does not take into account available information about the search space will perform on the average as well as (or as poorly as) a random search in which no location is visited twice. In fact, for any given instance of a probabilistic or "actual" distribution of objects, the Systematic Sweep policy's performance, in terms of number of objects found on the average (or exactly) per unit time can be obtained by inspection from the available data, as long as the point where the search originates is known. In further work we will also consider variants of the Systematic Sweep which combine a more refined optimization technique.

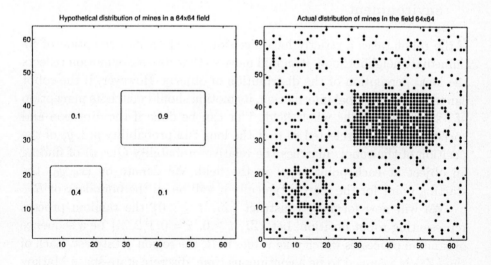

Fig. 1. Probabilistic (left) and actual (right) distribution of objects in a 64x64 field

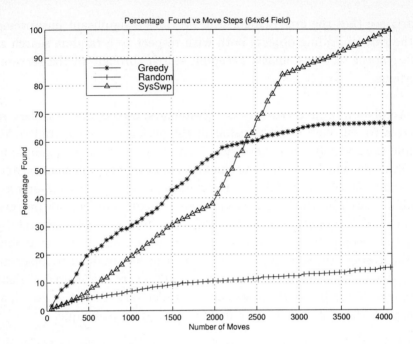

Fig. 2. Random versus Greedy and Sweep Algorithms for the field of Figure 1

3 Motion with long term objectives in a static environment

If the robot takes a strictly local decision based on its perception of its immediate neighborhood, it should move so that its overall motion reflects the local perception of the distribution of objects. However, if the robot can make use of global information, its motion should match its perception of its coverage of the whole field. This can be done if the direction and speed of motion is selected so that the long run probability $p(x, y)$ of the position of the robot, matches the relative probability $Q(x, y)$ of finding an object at each point (x, y) in the field. We denote by (x_0, y_0) the starting point for the search; typically it will be on the boundary of R.

We will now formally construct $\{Z_t, \ t \geq \ 0\}$ the random process representing robot position. Let $\{Z_t^i, \ t \geq 0, \ i = 0, 1, 2, ...\}$ be a sequence of random processes which take values in R, the region of interest. Each of the $\{Z_t^i\}$ is assumed to be a continuous time, discrete state-space Markov chain with transition rates $\mu^i(x, y, u, v)$ from state (x, y) to state (u, v), where $\mu^i(x, y, u, v) = 0$ if $(u, v) \notin N(x, y)$ so that robot motion is being constrained to take place between adjacent points in R. These processes $\{Z_t^i\}$ are constructed recursively as follows:

- $Z_0^1 = (x_0, y_0)$,
- Let $T_i = inf\{t : t > 0, Z_t^i \neq Z_0^i\}$;
- then $Z_0^{i+1} = Z_{T_i}^i$, $i = 1, 2, \ldots$.

Furthermore, let $\{S_i, \ i = 0, 1, 2, \ldots\}$ be a sequence of positive random variables representing the time spent by the robot to investigate, with its sensors, each successive position it visits. Then:

- $Z_t = Z_t^1$ for $0 \leq t \leq T_1$,
- $Z_t = Z_{T_1}^1$ for $T_1 \leq t \leq T_1 + S_1$,
- $Z_{t+\sum_{i=1}^{j-1}(T_i+S_i)} = Z_t^j$ for $0 \leq t \leq T_j, j = 2, \ldots$,
- $Z_t = Z_{T_j}^j$ for $\sum_{i=1}^{j-1}(T_i + S_i) + T_j \leq t < \sum_{i=1}^{j}(T_i + S_i)$.

In general, the $\{S_i\}$ may be doubly stochastic, and dependent on the past of the process $\{Z_t\}$, in that S_i could be some random function of the position $Z_{T_i}^i$. Thus what is being modeled is a two phase activity where a robot first starts in position (x_0, y_0) and then moves during T_1 seconds to an adjacent position, and then uses its sensors in that position during S_1 seconds to detect objects, after which it takes another T_2 seconds to move on to the next position, etc. We will denote by d_i the instant when the robot enters its $i - th$ position:

$$d_i = \sum_{j=1}^{i-1}(T_j + S_j) + T_i. \tag{3}$$

When all objects have been found, or when all the region R has been searched, or when the chances for finding new objects is considered to be minimal, the search should stop. In any case we will have $i \leq |R|$. However it will be convenient to assume that the search takes "a very long time" so that we may use convenient asymptotic techniques for the analysis of the stochastic system which is being considered.

As the robot moves and searches for objects, the probability of there being an object at a given point will change, based on whether that point has already been visited or not. The robot's object detection using its sensors will not in general be devoid of errors either, although for the sake of simplicity the present paper assumes that the robot is capable of perfect detection. Thus, once a point (x, y) has ben visited once, additional visits are superfluous from an object detection viewpoint (although they may be needed in terms of the robot's motion plan. Thus after a move to (x, y), both $q(x, y)$ and *all* the $Q(u, v), (u, v) \in X \times Y$ need to be updated,

$Q(x, y)$, which is a normalized version of $q(x, y)$ is given by:

$$Q(x, y) = \frac{q(x, y)}{\sum_{all \ (u,v)} q(u, v)}. \tag{4}$$

In this section we will design and evaluate a Simplified Infinite Horizon Optimization (SIHO) Algorithm that attempts to optimize the rate of finding objects into the "infinite horizon" at each step. The SIHO Algorithm computes the transition rates $\{\mu^i(x, y, u, v)\}$ at each $i - th$ step so that the long run probability, after the $i - th$ step, that the robot visits a point in R matches closely the probability of finding an object at that point.

Recall the structure of the process $\{Z_t, \ t \geq 0\}$. A continuous time Markov chain with rates $\{\mu^i(x, y, u, v), \ (u, v) \in N(x, y)\}$ deterobjects the motion of the robot between time d_{i-1} ($d_0 = 0$) and time $d_i + T_i$; then the robot stays at point (x_i, y_i) to search for objects during a time S_i, and then motion starts again, etc. In the following, we will be dealing with quantities subsequent to the $i-th$ step of motion, and therefore they should all be indexed by i. However, for the sake of notational simplicity, we will drop that index.

Since we will be working with the stationary probability distribution $p(x, y)$ of the robot's position, we need to make sure that the underlying stochastic process representing the motion of the robot is ergodic. This is achieved by associating positive (but sometimes very small) rates of motion at each point (x, y) for the stochastic process which represents robot motion in R. Consider a cost function which deterobjects how well the long run probability $p(x, y)$ that point (x, y) is visited during the search actually fits the known *a priori* probability that there is an object at that point:

$$C = \frac{1}{2} \sum_{all \ (x,y)} [p(x, y) - Q(x, y)]^2, \tag{5}$$

Note that $p(x, y)$ can be calculated from the previously defined quantities:

$$p(x, y) \sum_{all \ (u,v) \in \ N(x,y)} \mu(x, y, u, v) = \sum_{all \ (u,v) \in \ N(x,y)} \mu(u, v, x, y) p(u, v), \tag{6}$$

with

$$\sum_{all \ (x,y) \ in \ the \ plane} p(x, y) = 1, \tag{7}$$

under the assumption that the robot travels for a very long time around the search space. We may write (6) in matrix notation:

$$p = \mu p, \tag{8}$$

where p is the vector of stationary probabilities $p(x, y)$ and μ is the rate matrix $[\mu(x, y, u, v)]$.

The motion to the neighboring points $N(x, y)$ of the point (x, y) by choosing the direction which yields the highest rate of motion. These rates are updated using the gradient rule to obtain values of μ which yield minima of C:

$$\mu^{new}(x, y, u, v) = \mu^{old}(x, y, u, v) - \eta \frac{\partial C}{\partial \mu(x, y, u, v)}\Big|_{old} \tag{9}$$

where $\eta > 0$, and the algorithmic challenge is to carry out this computation at low cost, or to approximate it by a faster algorithm. Note that at each gradient descent step we need to compute the new value of p using the new value of μ, which is a costly $O(n^3)$ computation, though it can be accelerated because the matrix μ is sparse. Note that this approach includes in the decision, both the *expected long term behavior* of the search (via the probabilites $p(x, y)$), and the currently available information about the probability of finding objects at each point (via $Q(x, y)$). The gradient descent (9) is repeated till the point of diminishing returns is attained:

$$|\mu^{new}(x, y, u, v) - \mu^{old}(x, y, u, v)| \leq \epsilon, \tag{10}$$

for a stopping criterion $\epsilon > 0$. The resulting values $\mu(x, y, u, v)$ will then used in the following manner. The robot will move to a point $(U, V) \in N(x, y)$ such that:

$$\mu(x, y, U, V) = max_{(u,v) \in N(x,y)}\{\mu(x, y, u, v)\}. \tag{11}$$

Again, if there are several (U, V) satisfying the above relationship, then one of those should be selected at random.

When a robot visits some location (x, y) it is presumed to sense whether an object is there or not. In which case it will update the probability distribution in the following manner:

$$q^{after-visit}(x, y) \Leftarrow \text{"small} - value\text{"} \quad (e.g.\ 0.01), \tag{12}$$

since we wish to avoid unnecessary repeated visits of the robot to the same point; after a visit, either an object is detected and the work there is done, or an object is not detected so that the robot need not visit the point again. The result of detection also needs to be stored in Scene–2 which is the information one has obtained about reality. Note that after $q(x, y)$ is modified, we have

$$q'(u, v) = q(u, v), \ if \ (u, v) \neq (x, y),$$
$$q'(u, v) = q^{after-visit}(u, v), \ if \ (u, v) = (x, y).$$

Note also that <u>all</u> the $Q(u, v)$ need to be updated using (4) to the new value:

$$Q'(u, v) = \frac{q'(u, v)}{\sum_{all \ (a,b)} q(a, b)}. \tag{13}$$

Let us now turn to the computation of the gradient in (9). Of course, the computationally significant portion will be to compute the partial derivatives, and we will be making use of the cost function (5) and also of the equation for the steady-state probabilities $p(x, y)$ (6). The computationally costly portion of the algorithm is precisely (6), (13), and (14) which must be used repeatedly at each gradient descent step, and which includes the solution of linear systems of size $|X||Y| \times |X||Y|$, i.e. the size of the whole plane of motion. Fortunately this computation can be accelerated because the matrices are very sparse, since motion of the robot is only possible in adjacent directions. Note that:

$$\frac{\partial C}{\partial \mu(x, y, u, v)} = \sum_{all \ (a,b)} [p(a, b) - Q(a, b)] \frac{\partial p(a, b)}{\partial \mu(x, y, u, v)}. \tag{14}$$

We use the two system equations (6) and (7), which in matrix notation can be written as

$$[0, 0, ...0, 1] = [p_1, p_2, ..., p_n, 0] \begin{bmatrix} \mu_{11} & \mu_{12} & \cdots & \mu_{1n} & 1 \\ \mu_{21} & \mu_{22} & \cdots & \mu_{2n} & 1 \\ . & . & \cdots & . & . \\ \mu_{n1} & \mu_{n2} & \cdots & \mu_{nn} & 1 \\ \hline * & * & \cdots & * & * \end{bmatrix} \tag{15}$$

where

$$\mu_{ij} = \mu(u, v; x, y), p_i = p(u, v) \text{ and } p_j = p(x, y)$$

with

$$i = u + vw, j = x + yw \text{ and } n = wh.$$

Here w and h denote the width and height of the object field. Because each point in the plane is taken to have only 8 (and 5 or 3 at boundaries) ajacent neigbours, we have

$$\mu_{ij} = \mu(u,v;x,y) = 0, \text{if } (u,v) \notin N(x,y).$$

As we noted before the rate transition matrix is sparse. Let us denote the matrix which appears on the right-hand-side of (15) as $\mathbf{M}$. Note that the bottom row of $\mathbf{M}$ can be arbitary However to make $\mathbf{M}$ invertible, the unassigned values $*$ should be properly set. Since:

$$\mu_{ii} = - \sum_{j=1,j\neq i}^{n} \mu_{ij},$$

and by consequence the determinant of the sub-matrix

$$\mu = \begin{bmatrix} \mu_{11} & \mu_{12} & \cdots & \mu_{1n} \\ \mu_{21} & \mu_{22} & \cdots & \mu_{2n} \\ . & . & \cdots & . \\ \mu_{n1} & \mu_{n2} & \cdots & \mu_{nn} \end{bmatrix}$$

is zero: $|\mu| = 0$. Neverthless $\mathbf{M}$ has an inverse provided the $*$ are properly chosen.

Taking the derivative of (15) with respect to μ_{ij} we obtain:

$$0 = [p'_1, p'_2, ..., p'_n, 0]_{ij}\mathbf{M} + [0, ..., -p_i, ... \; p_i, ..., 0] \tag{16}$$
$$\uparrow \quad\quad \uparrow$$
$$i \quad\quad j$$

where $[p'_1, p'_2, ..., p'_n, 0]_{ij}$ denotes the derivative of $[p_1, p_2, ..., p_n, 0]$ with respect to μ_{ij}. If $[X]_{(kl)}$ denotes the (kl) element of matrix X, then

$$\frac{\partial p_\nu}{\partial \mu_{ij}} = p_i([\mathbf{M}^{-1}]_{(i\nu)} - [\mathbf{M}^{-1}]_{(j\nu)}). \tag{17}$$

For implementation purposes in relation to the field coordinates, we revert to the notation $(a,b) \to \nu$, $(u,v) \to i$ and $(x,y) \to j$ so that:

$$\frac{\partial p(a,b)}{\partial \mu(u,v;x,y)} = p(u,v)([\mathbf{M}^{-1}]_{(u,v;a,b)} - [\mathbf{M}^{-1}]_{(x,y;a,b)}). \tag{18}$$

Using (18) in (14) we obtain

$$\frac{\partial C}{\partial \mu(u,v;x,y)} = \sum_{all(a,b)} p(u,v)\,[p(a,b) - Q(a,b)]\left\{[\mathbf{M}^{-1}]_{(u,v;a,b)} - [\mathbf{M}^{-1}]_{(x,y;a,b)}\right\}. \tag{19}$$

We can now summarize the gradient based SIHO algorithm for computing the direction in which the robot moves from a given point (x, y):

1. From all the current *old* values of $\mu(a, b, c, d)$, calculate $p(x, y)$ using (6).
2. Calculate the derivative of the cost C with respect to the desired $\mu(x, y, u, v)$ for all $(u, v) \in N(x, y)$ using (19).
3. Use the gradient descent (9) to deterobject the new values of all the $\mu(x, y, u, v)$, for $(u, v) \in N(x, y)$.
4. Move in the direction (x, y) to (U, V) according to (11).

3.1 Experimental evaluation of the SIHO Algorithm

The SIHO algorithm performs well in taking advantage of the global information available about the search space. This is illustrated with some simulation results. We show an example of a probabilistically defined search space in Figure 3, which includes an "actual" field obtained by a random generation of object locations from this probabilistic data. Throughout the simulations discussed here it is assumed that once the autonomous agent reaches a location in the search space it will correctly detect or correctly reject the presence of an object (zero false alarm rate). On the Figure 3 we show simulation runs for SIHO, the Greedy Algorithm, and of the Random search. We clearly see that the rate of attaining object positions, in particular in the initial portion of the search (i.e. before each of the algorithms reaches the point of "diminishing returns"), is far greater with the SIHO algorithm than with the alternatives. SIHO will be more time consuming in computation time; however this may be a viable price to pay for the performance improvement.

It is interesting to visualize search paths in Cartesian space which are followed by the SIHO algorithm. On Figure 4 we show the *a priori* probabilistic field information of a 32 by 32 sized search space. The path followed by a robot or agent under the control of a single run of the SIHO algorithm is shown in Figure 5, where we clearly see that the SIHO algorithm does not pursue a myopic greedy approach but that the moving agent or robot actually covers the areas where the probability of finding objects is largest.

This paper contributes to the design of search strategies with probabilistic *a priori* information. However there remains much more work to do than what has been currently achieved. Issues that we are currently pursuing include the use of actual search space sensory data rather than probabilistic data to direct the search, the use of learning techniques from

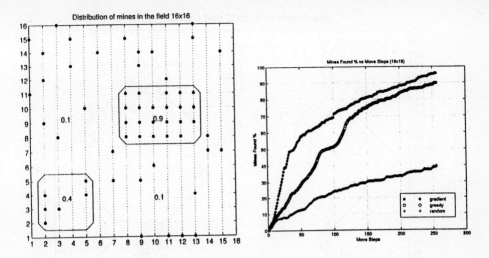

Fig. 3. "Actual" 16x16 field (left) and SIHO, Greedy, Random algorithm performance (right)

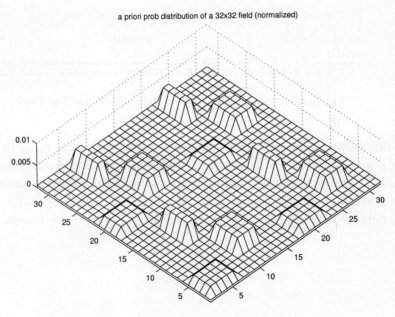

Fig. 4. A 32 by 32 Probabilistic Test Field Representation

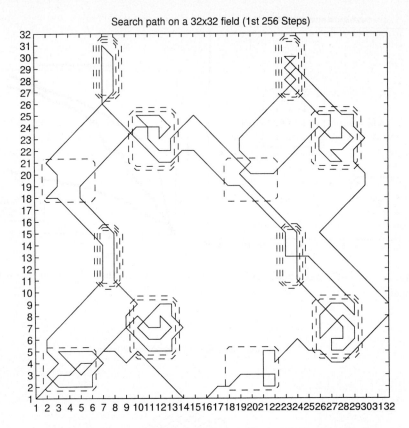

Fig. 5. SIHO Search Path on 32 by 32 Probabilistic Test Field

on-line sensory data to gather information about the field so as to direct the search, questions of false alarm rates and detection errors which will impact the search strategy, neural network approximations for computing the potential field which controls robot motion, and the use of information gradients from sensors (e.g. chemical sensors) to direct the search.

REFERENCES

1. A.C. Kamil, F. Lindstrom, J. Peters "The detection of cryptic prey by blue jays (Cyanocitta cristata): I. The effects of travel time", *Animal Behaviour* Vol. 33 (4) pp. 1068-1079, 1985.
2. J. McNamara, A. Houston "A simple model of information use in the exploitation of patchily distributed food", Animal Behaviour Vol. 33 (2), pp. 553-560, 1985.
3. C. Jorgensen, W. Hamel and C. Weisbin. "Autonomous robot navigation", *BYTE*, Vol. 11, pp. 223–235, Jan. 1986.

4. N. Rao "Algorithmic framework for learned robot navigation in unknown terrains" *Computer* pp. 37–43, 1989.

5. P. Pf. Spelt , E. Lyness and G. deSaussure. "Developpment and training of a learning expert system in an autonomous mobile robor via simulation", *Simulation*, pp. 223–228, 1989.

6. C.R. Weisbin, G. deSaussure, J.R. Einstein and F.G. Pin. "Autonomous mobile robot navigation and learning", *Computer* pp. 29–35, 1989.

7. Gelenbe E., "Random neural networks with negative and positive signals and product form solution", *Neural Computation*, Vol. 1, No. 4, pp 502-511, 1989.

8. Gelenbe E., "Stability of the random neural network model", *Neural Computation*, Vol. 2, No. 2, pp. 239-247, 1990.

9. Z. Shiller and Y.R. Gwo. Dynamic Motion Planning of Autonomous Vehicles. *IEEE Transaction On Robotics and Automation*, Vol. 7, no. 2, pp. 241–249, 1991.

10. G. Beni and J. Wang. Theoretical problems for the realization of Distributed Robotic Systems. *Proc. IEEE Int. Conf. on Robotics and Automation*, pp. 1914–1920, 1991.

11. M.J. Mataric, "Distributed approaches to behavior control", *Proc. SPIE, Vol. 1828, Sensor Fusion V*, pp. 373–382, 1992.

12. Y. Shoham and M. Tennenholtz "On the synthesis of useful social laws for artificial agent societies", *Proc. 10th National Conf. on Artificial Intelligence*, pp. 276–281, 1992.

13. S. Gross and J.L. Deneubourg, "Harvesting by a group of robots" *Proc. 1st European Conf. on Artificial Life*, pp. 195–204, 1992.

14. G. Lucarini, M. Varoli, R. Cerutti, and G. Sandini, "Cellular Robotics: simulation and hardware implementation" *Proc. IEEE Int. Conf. on Robotics and Automation*, pp. 846–852, 1993.

15. T. Ueyama and T. Fukuda. "Self-organization of Cellular Robots using random walk with simple rules", *Proc. IEEE Int. Conf. on Robotics and Automation*, pp. 595–600, 1993.

16. N. Schmajuk, H.T. Blair "Place learning and the dynamics of spatial navigation: A neural network approach," *Adaptive Behavior* Vol. 1, No. 3, pp. 353–385, 1993.

17. N. Schmajuk, A.D. Thieme, H.T. Blair "Maps, routes, and the Hippocampus: A neural network approach", *Hippocampus*, Vol. 3, No.3, pp. 387-400, 1993.

18. D. Maio, and S. Rizzi. "Map Learning and Clustering in Autonomous Systems", *IEEE Transaction On Pattern Analysis And Machine Intelligence*, Vol. 15, no. 12, pp. 1286–1297, 1993.

19. E. Hou and D. Zheng "Mobile robot path planning based on hierarchical hexagonal decomposition and artificial potential fields", *Journal of Robotic Systems*, pp. 605–614, 1994.

20. L.E. Parker "Designing control laws for cooperative agent teams", *Proc. IEEE Int. Conf. on Robotics and Automation*, pp. 582–587, 1994.

21. E. Rimon and J.F. Canny "Construction of C-space roadmaps from local sensory data: What should the sensors look for?", *Proc. IEEE Int. Conf. on Robotics and Automation*, pp. 117–123, 1994.

22. J.A. Meyer, H.L. Roitblat and S.W. Wilson (eds.) "From Animals to Animats 2: Proceedings of the Second International Conference on Simulation of Adaptive Behavior (Complex adaptive systems)" pp. 432-510. MIT Press, Cambridge, MA, 523 p., 1992.

23. J. Reif and H. Wang, "Social potential fields: A distributed behavioral control for autonomous robots", *Proc. Workshop on the Algorithmic Foundations of Robotics*, pp. 331–345, 1994.
24. S. Benhamou "Spatial memory and searching efficiency," *Animal Behaviour* Vol. 47 (6), pp. 1423-1433, 1994.

Scientific Digital Libraries in Germany: Global-Info, a Federal Government Initiative

Erich J. Neuhold and Reginald Ferber

GMD, Integrated Publication and Information Systems Institute (IPSI)
Dolivostraße 15, D-64293 Darmstadt, Germany
neuhold@darmstadt.gmd.de, ferber@darmstadt.gmd.de

Abstract. This talk will introduce and comment on the German Digital Libraries program Global-Info. It will start with a brief introduction to the way research is organized in Germany, followed by some background on ongoing and completed German projects related to Digital Libraries. Then the approach and organization of the Global-Info program are presented.

Global-Info is an interdisciplinary program that includes producers, intermediaries and consumers of scientific information. They are represented by learned societies, publishers, universities, and libraries. The program started at the beginning of this year and will run for a 6-year period with individual project durations of two to three years. A main characteristic of Global-Info is that the more specific goals and its organization will be developed by the scientific community and the publishers - i. e. the funded organizations - in a bottom up process in the course of the program.

1 Research Funding in Germany

Public research funding in Germany is organized in various ways. Universities are (except for a very few small private institutions) run by the "Länder", i. e. the sixteen single states making up the Federal Republic of Germany. This means that a good part of the research infrastructure of most universities depends on decisions made in the single states (Länder). Nationwide regulations and systems have to be based on agreements among the single states.

Additional public research funding for single projects and larger research programs on specific topics is provided through the "Deutsche Forschungsgemeinschaft" (DFG), an autonomous foundation financed to 60% by the federal government and to 40% by the "Länder". The Federal Ministry for Education, Science, Research, and Technology (BMBF) also launches funding programs. Further there are of course the programs of the European Union, several foundations and other funding institutions. Global-Info is a program of the BMBF.

2 Some German Projects Related to Digital Libraries

One of the roots of Digital Libraries is the electronic access to scientific publications. The methods used for this purpose were influenced by the traditions of the organizing groups and the technology available in the various disciplines. This means for example that in some disciplines classification schemes are important means to organize content-based access, while other disciplines prefer other methods. It also results in differences in the document formats used (like LaTeX or HTML). Parallel to the international development of scientific Digital Libraries initiatives, there have been a number of projects within the last few years that were mainly or at least partially developed in Germany. An incomplete list may be sorted according to the following criteria:

OPACs: All major scientific libraries digitized their catalogues in the past few years. Some more advanced projects are the virtual catalogues in Darmstadt (DVK) and Karlsruhe (KVK). These systems allow unified access to the catalogue information of all or at least many scientific libraries in those cities. The Karlsruhe virtual catalogue also includes the catalogues of several major national and international libraries. Other projects integrate the management of local fulltext collections, ordering of paper copies, extended search facilities, and access to relevant web resources (IBIS at the University of Bielefeld); or natural language search and interaction based on linguistic approaches (OSIRIS at the University of Osnabrück). "subito", the nationwide system for ordering paper or OCR copies of scientific articles started work at the end of 1997.

Bibliographies: There are at least two major web-based bibliography systems in Germany. The dblp server at the University of Trier for the topics "database systems" and "logic programming" includes some 81 000 browsable references to scientific articles and more than 4100 links to scientists working in these fields. The Collection of Computer Science Bibliographies in Karlsruhe (CSBK) includes some 1200 bibliographies with more than 830 000 references and some 30 000 links to fulltext documents. There are also projects to systematically collect and maintain information on electronically available journals, including information on which journals are licensed for campus access (e.g. University of Regensburg).

Repositories and Distributed Collections: Several projects were or are funded for the development of collections of scientific articles and systems to manage them (PhysDoc for physics, MeDoc for Computer Science, MathNet for mathematics, eprint for natural science and technology). In many cases these projects have additional specific research topics like brokerage and access control (MeDoc), authentification, or integration of Dublin Core Metadata (MathNet).

Search Engines: The GERHARD project offers a search engine combined with UDC classification as a browsing approach.

Specific Collections: Most of the projects mentioned up to now address one type of documents within a relatively broad subject area. In contrast to this approach there are several collections with very specific interests. The ECCC (Electronic Colloquium on Computational Complexity) at the University of Trier offers, in addition to a collection of articles, means to peer-review these articles, access to experts, and a forum for discussion in its specific domain. The Flybrain collection is an international project specialized in textual and image material on the nervous system of Drosophila. It includes images in various magnifications, 3D images, and moving images.

These examples show that there are many projects that approach different aspects of Digital Libraries. In many cases these projects are more or less isolated and not integrated into a common working environment. In some cases they were only funded for a limited period of time and are no longer maintained. Some projects are only accessible to a limited group of users from the participating institutions. In addition to such research-oriented projects there are more development and service-oriented projects that have led to operative systems at libraries and other research infrastructure units following completion.

3 The Global-Info Program

In April 1997 the BMBF published the funding program "Globale Elektronische und Multimediale Informationssysteme für Naturwissenschaft und Technik GLOBAL-INFO" ("Global Electronic and Multimedial Information Systems for Natural Science and Engineering"). According to the press release of the BMBF the program has the following characteristics: It is targeted to initiatives participating in the fundamental transition of the scientific and technical information infrastructure. The initiatives should have the goals

- to provide efficient access to the internationally available electronic and multimedia fulltext, reference, factual, and software information from the desktop computer;
- to allow a joint effort by all parties involved in the fundamental transition of the information infrastructure within a framework of international cooperation. These parties include: authors and users, learned societies, scientific associations, research institutions, scientific publishers and bookstores, scientific information centers, online providers ("Fachinformationszentren"), and libraries.

To achieve these goals, "global information systems" in the following domains were to be developed and used in international cooperation: mathematics, physics, chemistry, and computer science.

The selection of disciplines was based on an initiative that started in 1995. Several professional and learned societies ("Fachgesellschaften") in these disciplines, including DMV (Deutsche Mathematiker-Vereinigung - The German National Mathematical Society), DPG (Deutsche Physikalische Gesellschaft - The German Physical Society), GDCh (Gesellschaft Deutscher Chemiker ("Society of German Chemists")), and GI (Gesellschaft für Informatik - The German Computer Society) agreed to cooperate in the area of electronic information and communication to build a decentralized infrastructure providing at minimal cost information that was to be as complete as possible and well-structured.

Since 1995 more learned societies have joined this initiative: DGfE (Deutsche Gesellschaft für Erziehungswissenschaft ("German Educational Research Association")) DGS (Deutsche Gesellschaft für Soziologie - German Sociological Association), ITG (Informationstechnische Gesellschaft ("German Society of Information Technology Engineers")), DGPs (Deutsche Gesellschaft für Psychologie - German Psychological Society), and VDBiol (Verband Deutscher Biologen - Association of German Biologists). They all can now cooperate in Global-Info.

Global-Info sees three main types of players in the scientific information infrastructure: producers (authors, represented by learned societies and publishers), distributers (publishers and bookstores, online providers and libraries), and consumers (readers / end-users, represented by learned societies and universities). It is the goal of Global-Info to bring these players together to define their new roles in electronic information systems. In this context the Federal Ministry explicitly mentioned the fact that - due to the organization of research in Germany - most scientific publications are written and reviewed by persons employed by the state and that they are bought by state-owned libraries. The press release stated that public and private institutions would interact closely in this system and that the infrastructure should be further developed by scientific and economic initiatives and self organization. The current problems of increasing prices of scientific journals and decreasing resources for their acquisition by libraries are thus mentioned, but perspectives for solutions are left rather vague. But for projects funded by Global-Info there are clear guidelines: All participants must agree to cooperate within the projects and the projects themselves have to be "pre-competitive"; this means that Global-Info will only explore the ground for a potential market oriented development.

Altogether Global-Info can be characterized as a funding program with only few technical specifications, but with an emphasis on the organization and evaluation of a framework for the autonomous development of new paradigms in scientific electronic information supply.

3.1 Organizational Aspects

Beside these goals the types and amount of funding are defined. Sixty million DM are planned for the next six years with a funding rate of 50%. There are three types of projects:

- pilot projects ("Vorprojekte") to fund the basic needs for collaboration (including the development of further projects)
- one administration project to organize Global-Info
- the main research and development projects ("Sonderfördermaßnahmen") to be funded by Global-Info.

3.2 Pilot Projects

The deadline for the pilot project proposals was the end of July 1997. Publishers and scientific bookstores as well as universities and research institutions could apply for pilot projects if they were willing to cooperate according to the goals of the Global-Info program. For universities and research institutions there was the additional requirement that at least four different departments had to cooperate in the sense of the initiative for electronic information and communication (IuK Initiative) of the above-mentioned learned societies. One department, the library, or the computing center had to coordinate and organize the pilot project. There were some restrictions for institutions financed by the state like libraries and information centers. They were not allowed to apply for pilot projects, but they could register their interest and participate in the further process like pilot projects. However they received no funding for the pilot projects. Fifteen institutions registered in this way: six libraries, five information centers, and four research institutes.

In all twenty nine pilot projects were selected; sixteen proposed by universities, thirteen proposed by publishers. Their official start was in January 1998 but the first meeting was already at the beginning of December 1997 at the Deutsche Bibliothek in Frankfurt (Main). In the sixteen university pilot project proposals there are 82 departments involved, sixteen departments of computer science (i. e. at every university the computer science department is involved), fifteen departments for each of the disciplines of mathematics, physics, and chemistry, five departments of biology and three departments of electrical engineering. The remaining departments are each of a different discipline ranging from medicine through theology and music to photography and sports. Further, thirteen university computing centers and eleven libraries are involved. The organizing unit at the universities is in five cases a computer science department, in four cases the library, in three cases a physics department, in two cases a combined mathematics/computer science department, one chemistry department, and one computing center. Thus there is a slight emphasis on computer science departments among the overall members of participating universities, but mathematics, physics, chemistry and libraries are each nearly as often involved. Of course these numbers also reflect the founding members of the IuK initiative. Similar observations can be made for the organizing units. Here it is interesting that there is only little involvement of computing centers, whereas libraries are more strongly represented.

3.3 The Administration Project

The administration project organizes Global-Info itself. To this end the "Global-Info Consortium" was installed as a board and steering committee. It consists of five representatives of the learned societies, four representatives of the publishing houses, one representative of the libraries, and one of the online providers. There are six substitutes for these representatives. Delegates of the Federal Ministry and from the Deutsche Forschungsgemeinschaft are guests at the meetings of the Global-Info Consortium. The Consortium is supported by a secretary located at the Society of German Chemists (GDCh) at Frankfurt who also has the status of a guest at the meetings of the Global-Info Consortium.

3.4 The Main Projects

Main projects can be proposed by groups or consortia that include two or more representatives of each of the three groups involved in the publication process: authors, distributors, and users. This means that a project group has the minimal size of six participants. The maximum duration of a project is three years, the funding rate is 50%. Topics of such projects can be all technical and organizational questions with regard to the electronic publication process of textual documents or multimedia objects. This may include conversion, modeling, modularization, and quality control of documents, development of purely electronic objects, mediation of distributed sources of different types of information, electronic commerce, and archiving. The coordination of the development of different project proposals is part of the administration project. After the proposals have been coordinated they are reviewed by international experts. Finally the BMBF will decide upon the funding based on these reviews.

At first projects may be proposed by institutions from the pilot projects, from those state funded institutions that had registered their interest and in addition from some experts the Global-Info Consortium has invited to join. Later on also other institutions will be allowed to propose research and development projects.

4 The Interdisciplinary Approach of Global-Info

The very broad and interdisciplinary approach of Global-Info does not only involve scientists and institutions whose primary research is related to electronic publishing, libraries, or archiving. This approach also includes scientists and institutions that are involved in this process as authors and users. This reflects the fact that in scientific electronic publishing the classical roles of developers and users separated along the borders of the respective disciplines are widely blurred. The most prominent example for this blurring is perhaps the fact that one of the most influential standards in web publishing - HTML - was initially developed at CERN, the European Laboratory for Particle Physics. Many of the projects mentioned so far are also run by institutions that are neither computer science research institutes nor libraries and they are developed by people that are neither computer scientists nor librarians.

The idea of the Global-Info approach is to bring all these people and institutions together and use their diverse experiences in a kind of bottom up process to build a framework for scientific information and communication that fits as well as possible to the reality of working scientists. However, this approach also has its price. There is, for example, no real common theoretical background for all participants; methods familiar to one group are not known by others. Even the terminology is often not unified, i. e. different people use the same terms with different meanings in mind. Also the priorities with respect to the functionality are quite different for different groups, as are the expectations with respect to quality, reviewing, and focussed access to selected material. Thus there is much need for clarification and discussion (but often only little time). Sometimes coming to an understanding is rather slow.

5 Focal Points

To better organize the bottom up process of gathering experiences and expectations five "focal points" ("Schwerpunkte") have been defined based on the pilot project proposals:

1. Organization of content: document types, procedures, and tools for electronic publishing, transfer, storage, conversion, and indexing.
2. Networking of educational material.
3. Formal description, identification and retrieval, metadata, networking.
4. Usage of contents: alerting, awareness, information pooling, information mediation.
5. Economy models, billing (micro billing) and accounting, statistics.

Each focal point is coordinated by two members of the Global-Info Consortium, one from the universities and learned societies, and one from the publishers and database providers. In addition each focal point has selected four persons to maintain contact with the other focal points.

In addition to the rather general descriptions given above there was a list of more detailed topics given for each focal point. These lists show that there is a lot of overlap between the focal points; especially topics three and four are sometimes difficult to separate: They both focus on the aspects of indexing and retrieval. Whereas point three puts more emphasis on indexing, metadata and retrieval of single documents, point four puts more weight on the handling of whole sources (in contrast to single documents). However in practice the two issues are hard to separate.

The focal points were constituted during the kick-off meeting of Global-Info in Frankfurt. Working groups for the five focal points met and first plans were made as to how to proceed in the development of main projects. The participation in the five focal point meetings was quite different from the expressed interest in the pilot project proposals. Tab. 1 gives the respective numbers for publishers and information centers on the one hand, and for universities, research institutions, and libraries on the other.

The numbers given in Tab. 1 show that the distribution of interest within the pilot project proposals was not uniform. Whereas the universities had a slight preference for the first focal point, the publishers had a bias toward the first and last one. This reflects to some degree the traditional role of publishers: production of documents and the economic aspects of their distribution.

The number of publishers participating in the workshop sessions was close to the numbers of interested publishers from the pilot project proposals. For the universities this was quite different. There was a huge increase in participation for the focal points 2, 3, and 4, whereas for focal points 1 and 5 the numbers are comparable in both columns. For focal point two a possible reason might be that systems dealing with new methods for the supply and use of educational material can be specifically attractive to teaching members of the universities. The focal points three and four address problems of information retrieval. Such

Table 1. Interest indicated in pilot proposals vs. participation in the kick-off meetings of the focal points given for publishers and universities

Focal Point	Pilot Projects		Workshop Participation	
	Publishers	Universities	Publishers	Universities
1	12	12	12	14
2	2	8	6	18
3	6	9	6	17
4	4	7	6	25
5	8	8	9	6

Note: At the meetings also those institutions participated, that were only allowed to register their interest. Further the numbers represent institutions not persons. Many institutions were represented by several persons and hence could participate in the meetings of several focal points.

problems can on the one hand be experienced very directly when searching for scientific information on the web; on the other hand they touch current research topics like knowledge extraction (data mining, text mining, automated indexing, image processing, natural language processing), database federation, mediation of semistructured sources, and merging and presentation of IR result sets.

After their constitution at the Frankfurt workshop the working groups of the five focal points met for further meetings to discuss goals, plans, and projects. The actual way this was organized was decided by the single groups. This process of interaction, clarification, and coordination with the goal to develop common projects is still going on at the time this text is written. There are some preliminary observations that can be made: the size of the consortia planned is quite different for the five focal points. Whereas one of the groups plans to organize itself as one single consortium with more than twenty partners and more than fifteen single projects, in other focal points several consortia are planned. Up to now there seems to be only one consortium that includes members from different focal points. This is quite interesting because the original intention for the definition of the focal points was only an organizational one: To give some structure to the discussion of the very large group of participants of Global-Info. The hope of the organizers was originally that the importance of the focal points should vanish during the discussion process and give way to new and hopefully more adapted and elaborated forms of interaction between the different groups. For the moment this development seems not to take place.

The next steps envisioned by the Global-Info Consortium are the following: The first revised drafts of proposals for consortia are expected at the end of July. They will be collected and screened by September. In this phase further cooperation across the borders of the focal points can be initiated. Then the proposals will be given to international experts for review. Based on this review the BMBF will decide upon the funding. Thus the first possible starting dates will be the beginning of 1999.

6   Conclusions and Outlook

Global-Info has activated a great number of researchers, librarians, and publishers. It initiated wide interaction among different groups and disciplines; it is on the way to gathering many different ideas and initiatives in the area of the publication and use of digital scientific information. This is done in a bottom up process that often includes divergent views and approaches. To discuss and clarify these different approaches is sometimes a time and energy consuming process that requires a high degree of motivation and patience of all participants. But it also offers the chance to learn a lot about different traditions and views in other disciplines and to broaden the perspective on Digital Libraries.

However, the amount of research, prototype building, and evaluation that is necessary to build Digital Libraries that truly match how this term has been used and defined in the last few years especially in the USA ([1]) by far outstrips the potential of the German Global-Info program. For example, in our Institute IPSI we have, over the years, worked on object-oriented databases, especially oriented toward the storage of multimedia, e.g. video objects, and on the flexible management of textual data, e.g. SGML, XML, and HTML structures ([2], [3], [4], [5], [6]). We have worked on many aspects of information retrieval both for textual as well as multimedia data ([7], [8] [9], [10], [11]). To support this search for information, computer linguistics have been utilized, on the one hand for textual analysis and ontology building, on the other hand for automatic text generation to better represent search results. In electronic authoring ontology and knowledge-based approaches have been used to structure data semantically. Semantic knowledge allows for better focus in information search and retrieval but it can also be used to automatically generate layouts and data visualization. Lately, we have moved into electronic watermarking ([12]), security and privacy, and into electronic commerce where information is both the object to be bought or sold, but also the vehicle to describe things to be bought or sold ([13]).

However, despite all this effort much remains to be done. The papers presented at this conference and its predecessor ([14]) as well as the proceedings of the US digital library conferences ([15], [16]) indicate what problems remain, but also how rapidly the development of Digital Libraries of all kinds has been advancing.

References

1. Atkins, D. E.: Report of the Santa Fe Planning Workshop on Distributed Knowledge Work Environments: Digital Libraries. Available at: http://www.si.umich.edu/SantaFe/report.html
2. Böhm, K., Aberer K., Öszu, T., Gayer, K.: Query Optimization for Structured Documents Based on Knowledge on the Document Type Definition. IEEE Advances in Digital Libraries 98 (ADL 98), Santa Barbara, USA (1998) 196-205.
3. Hollfelder, S., Schmidt, F., Hemmje, M., Aberer, K.: Transparent Integration of Continuous Media Support into a Multimedia DBMS International Workshop on Issues and Applications of Database Technology (IADT'98), Berlin, Germany, July 6-9, 1998.

4. Huck, G., Fankhauser, P., Aberer, K., Neuhold, E.: Jedi: Extracting and Synthesizing Information from the Web CoopIS'98 Proceedings, (1998) IEEE Computer Society Press
5. Böhm, K., Aberer, K., Neuhold, E. J., Yang, X.: Structured Document Storage and Refined Declarative and Navigational Access Mechanisms. HyperStorM VLDB Journal, Volume 6, Number 4, (1997) 296-311
6. Klein, B., Fankhauser,P.: Error tolerant Document Structure Analysis International Journal on Digital Libraries, Volume 1 Issue 4 (1998) 344-357
7. Müller, A., Everts, A.: Interactive Image Retrieval by Means of Abductive Inference. In: Proceedings of the RIAO 97 Conference - Computer-Assisted Information Searching on Internet, Montreal, Canada, 25-27 June, 1997. Montreal: McGill University, (1997) 450-466
8. Ferber, R.: Automated Indexing with Thesaurus Descriptors: A Co-occurrence based Approach to Multilingual Retrieval. In: [14] (1997) 232-252.
9. Thiel, U., Tzeras, K.: The Search for Information in Digital Libraries. In: Proceedings of the International Symposium on Research, Development and Practis in Digital Libraries (ISDL'97) Tsukuba Science City, Japan (1997) 55-62.
10. Thiel, U., Hollfelder, S., Everts, A.: Multimedia Management and Query Processing Issues in Distributed Digital Libraries: A HERMES Perspective. To appear in: DEXA'98 Workshop Proceedings (1998).
11. Stein, A., Gulla, J. A., Müller, A., Thiel, U.: Conversational Interaction for Semantic Access to Multimedia Information. In: Maybury, M.T. (Ed.): Intelligent Multimedia Information Retrieval. Menlo Park, CA: AAAI/The MIT Press (1997) 399-421.
12. Dittmann, J., Nack, F., Steinmetz, A., Steinmetz, R.: Interactive Watermarking Environments. To appear at the IEEE Multimedia '98, Austin, Texas.
13. Tesch, T., Aberer, K.: Scheduling Non-Enforceable Contracts Among Autonomous Agents. In: Proceedings of the Third IFCIS Conference on Cooperative Information Systems (CoopIS'98) August 20 - 22 (1998) New York, USA. IEEE Computer Society Press.
14. Peters, C., Thanos, C. (Eds.): Research and Advanced Technology for Digital Libraries. First European Conference, ECDL '97, Pisa, Italy, 1-3 September, Proceedings. Lecture Notes in Computer Science, Vol. 1324, (1997) Springer.
15. Adam, N. R., Bhargava, B. K., Halem, M., Yesha, Y. (Eds.): Digital Libraries, Research and Technology Advances, ADL '95 Forum, McLean, Virginia, USA, May 15-17, 1995, Selected Papers. Lecture Notes in Computer Science, Vol. 1082, (1996) Springer.
16. Proceedings of the Third Forum on Research and Technology Advances in Digital Library, ADL '96, May 13-15, 1996, Washington, D.C. USA. (1996) IEEE Computer Society Press.

A Appendix: Web Addresses of the Institutions and Projects Mentioned (as of July 1998)

Global-Info	http://www.global-info.org
DFG	http://www.dfg.de
BMBF	http://www.bmbf.de
IPSI	http://www.darmstadt.gmd.de/IPSI
DMV	http://www.mathematik.uni-bielefeld.de/DMV
DPG	http://www.dpg-physik.de/
GDCh	http://www.gdch.de/
GI	http://www.gi-ev.de/
DGfE	http://www.educat.hu-berlin.de/dgfe
DGS	http://www.ifs.tu-darmstadt.de/rs/sozfoli.htm
ITG	http://www.vde.de/vde/html/d/fachges/itg.htm
DGPs	http://www.dgps.de/
VDBiol	http://www.uni-koblenz.de/~vdbiol/vdbiol/vdbiolweb.htm
DVK	http://www.ifs.tu-darmstadt.de/lhbgk.html
KVK	http://www.ubka.uni-karlsruhe.de/kvk.html
IBIS	http://www.ub.uni-bielefeld.de/fulltext/index.htm
OSIRIS	http://osiris1.ub.uni-osnabrueck.de/isis/demo/start.htm
subito	http://www.subito-doc.de/
dblp	http://dblp.uni-trier.de/
CSBK	http://liinwww.ira.uka.de/bibliography/index.html
PhysDoc	http://www.physik.uni-oldenburg.de/EPS/ EurophysNet/PhysDoc/query.pl.cgi
MeDoc	http://medoc.informatik.tu-muenchen.de
MathNet	http://www.math-net.de/math-net/math-net.html
eprint	http://www.physik.uni-oldenburg.de/ eprint/
GERHARD	http://www.gerhard.de/
ECCC	http://www.eccc.uni-trier.de/eccc/
Flybrain	http://flybrain.uni-freiburg.de/

Flexible and Extensible Digital Object and Repository Architecture (FEDORA)

Sandra Payette and Carl Lagoze

Department of Computer Science
Cornell University
{payette,lagoze}@cs.cornell.edu

Abstract. We describe a digital object and respository architecture for storing and disseminating digital library content. The key features of the architecture are: (1) support for heterogeneous data types; (2) accommodation of new types as they emerge; (3) aggregation of mixed, possibly distributed, data into complex objects; (4) the ability to specify multiple content disseminations of these objects; and (5) the ability to associate rights management schemes with these disseminations. This architecture is being implemented in the context of a broader research project to develop next-generation service modules for a layered digital library architecture.

1.0 Introduction

A fundamental requirement of an open architecture for digital libraries is a reliable and secure means to store and access digital content. FEDORA is a digital object and repository architecture designed to achieve these requirements, while at the same time providing extensibility and interoperability. The key features of the architecture are: (1) support for heterogeneous data types; (2) accommodation of new types as they emerge; (3) aggregation of mixed, possibly distributed, data into complex objects; (4) the ability to specify multiple content disseminations of these objects; and (5) the ability to associate rights management schemes with these disseminations.

FEDORA is positioned within a larger open-architecture framework in which the total functionality of a digital library is partitioned into a set of services with well-defined interfaces. These core services include: (1) *repository services* that provide the mechanisms for depositing, storing and accessing digital objects; (2) *index services* that provide the mechanisms for discovering digital objects; (3) *collection services* that provide the means of aggregating sets of digital objects and services into meaningful collections; (4) *naming services* that register and resolve globally unique, persistent names for digital objects; and (5) *user interface services* that provide a human gateway into the other services. The well-defined interfaces of these core services allow them to be combined with each other and other value-added services to create usable instantiations of digital libraries.

This multi-layered service structure evolves from the concepts implemented in the Dienst Architecture [9], which is the foundation for the Networked Computer Science Technical Report Library (NCSTRL) [12]. Currently, the Digital Library Research Group at Cornell University is engaged in a number of research projects to develop next-generation service modules for a layered digital library architecture. FEDORA addresses the requirements for digital objects and the repository service that provides access to them.

In this paper we describe the FEDORA architecture. Section 2 provides an overview and introduces the three logical layers of the architecture. The next three sections describe the architecture of a Digital Object: Section 3 describes the structural layer of the architecture; Section 4 describes the interface layer; and Section 5 focuses on rights management for Digital Objects. Section 6 describes the Repository, which represents the management layer of the architecture. In Section 7, we provide a practical scenario of how the architecture works, and in Section 8 we conclude and describe our future work.

2.0 FEDORA: An Overview

The FEDORA architecture describes a content container abstraction, the *DigitalObject*, and the nature of *Repositories* that provide access to these containers. We conceptualize a *DigitalObject* as having: (1) a structural kernel, which encapsulates content as opaque byte stream packages and, (2) an interface, or behavior, layer that gives contextual meaning to the data in the DigitalObject. One useful metaphor for a DigitalObject is that of a cell. At the core is a nucleus containing essential data. Surrounding this structural nucleus is a functional layer containing content *Disseminators,* components that transform core data packages into recognizable information entities such as books, multimedia encyclopedias, and the like. Both the kernel/nucleus and the content disseminators are wrapped within the cell membrane that marks its contents as a uniquely identifiable DigitalObject.

For example, a simple DigitalObject might have a structural kernel that contains a number of byte stream packages that are `gif` images and another byte stream containing Dublin Core [4] metadata. On top of this structural layer there might be an interface layer that endows the DigitalObject with book-like behavior, allowing a client to access the table of contents or a specific page. The same DigitalObject might also have descriptive metadata behavior, allowing access to bibliographic fields such as the book's author or title.

The *Repository* is the FEDORA component that provides for the management of and access to named DigitalObjects. From the perspective of the Repository, the DigitalObject is a generic opaque entity known only by its unique name. The Repository provides services to deposit, store, replicate and access DigitalObjects as generic components.

2.1 Extensibility for Types and Rights Management

The architectural layers discussed above are key to the FEDORA extensibility model. By segregating structure from interfaces, FEDORA makes it possible for DigitalObjects of extreme structural variation to present themselves to clients in a "normalized" manner. From a client perspective, the interface layer provides the means to interact with DigitalObjects through a set of behaviors that define global or domain-specific notions of "content." A set of behaviors that formally specifies the nature of a particular form of content is referred to in FEDORA as a *content type*. Content types provide the mechanisms for establishing functional equivalence among DigitalObjects with disparate internal structures. In addition, they provide a simple client-oriented interface to the object that hides the structural complexity contained within.

Extensibility of content types is of paramount importance in the repository architecture. There are already countless forms of content and new ones will continue to appear. Any viable architecture must seamlessly integrate new content forms, and the mechanisms for disseminating and presenting them. To promote extensibility, FEDORA does not predetermine any taxonomy of content types. Instead, FEDORA creates the means to link external types to DigitalObjects. The FEDORA content-type system is extensible because content types are, themselves, named entities in the digital library infrastructure that can be referenced by a unique identifier such as a Uniform Resource Name (URN).

This same extensibility model applies to rights management schemes. FEDORA's facilities for access management are inclusive rather than prescriptive - accommodating a variety of existing and new rights management schemes, rather than attempting to promulgate one global scheme.

2.2 Theoretical Foundations and Related Work

The theoretical foundations for FEDORA lie in the Kahn/Wilensky framework [7] and the Warwick Framework [8], both of which influenced the design of the FEDORA DigitalObject. FEDORA's extensibility model originates in the Distributed Active Relationship (DAR) abstraction, described by Daniel, Lagoze, and Payette[5]. DARs leverage the connectivity and computational characteristics of networked environments to create dynamic relationships between data resources. These relationships: (1) can exist between resources in different repositories, (2) can be executable, and (3) can be named entities themselves in the infrastructure.

Others are working to develop architectures and document models that support extensible document types. Monch, Drobnik and Wolfgang [11] propose a document architecture that supports the integration of new media types and formats into digital library documents. The U.C. Berkley DLI project has developed the "multivalent document model" [13] in which documents are viewed as layers of content supported by dynamically loaded behaviors. FEDORA, in contrast to these projects, is distinguished by its architectural segregation of DigitalObject structure, content-type interfaces, and mechanisms that execute content-type behavior and by its attention to rights management. FEDORA also provides the mechanisms to identify, store, and access these types in the infrastructure.

Parts of the FEDORA work are the result of a collaboration with the Corporation for National Research Initiatives (CNRI) which is implementing a Digital Object Repository for the Library of Congress Digital Library Initiative based on their Repository Access Protocol (RAP) [1]. Another related effort is the Making of America Project (MOAII) [10], which has proposed a Digital Library Service Model to support a distributed digital library of archival materials. This project, coordinated by the Digital Library Federation (DLF), is developing standards for creating and encoding digital archival objects such as books, diaries, and photographs, and is specifying a service model for each. We are collaborating with members of the DLF to demonstrate the extensibility of FEDORA by accommodating these community-specific types as they emerge.

2.3 Implementing the Architecture

FEDORA is being implemented in CORBA and Java, however we believe the abstractions and service requests we have developed to be of general applicability and to be able to transcend particular implementation technologies. We are initially using a subset of the NCSTRL collection as our testbed. By working closely with CNRI to achieve architectural convergence between the RAP and FEDORA projects, we hope to demonstrate interoperability across independently-developed repository architectures that use different underlying CORBA Object Request Brokers (ORBs).

3.0 The Structural Layer (Digital Object Structural Kernel)

The lowest layer of the Repository architecture supports examination and manipulation of the structural composition of a *DigitalObject*. At this layer we introduce abstractions and service requests to compose, manipulate and access DigitalObjects in a generic manner. The DigitalObject is an abstraction for aggregating heterogeneous data, stored as typed byte stream packages known as *DataStreams*. Structural access to this set of DataStreams is provided by a set of basic service requests, collectively known as the *Primitive Disseminator*. These service requests provide a means to operate on diverse and heterogeneous data in a consistent manner. The following architectural abstractions make up the kernel of the DigitalObject:

DataStreams
A DataStream is a typed byte stream that preserves the internal format and encoding of the type, but encapsulates it so that it can be treated generically within the DigitalObject. This distillation of data into its essential type and byte representation allows heterogeneous forms of digital content to be treated in a uniform manner,

essentially creating a state of interoperability at the level of the DigitalObject, instead of at the level of the individual content packages themselves.

Any type of data can be represented as a DataStream, and disparate forms of data can be aggregated in a DigitalObject as DataStreams. For example, the same DigitalObject can contain byte stream representations of a TIFF image of a photograph of a rare bird, a Dublin Core record describing the image, a digital audio track of the bird's song, and a geographic dataset that shows the nesting locations of the bird. At this structural layer, the contextual relationships among DataStreams are not defined. Thus, DataStreams can not be distinguished by their semantic roles such as data or metadata. These contextual relationships are defined at the interface layer, which is described in Section 4.

Primitive Disseminator

From a client perspective the DigitalObject is a sealed wrapper, known only by it unique name (e.g., a URN), that can be manipulated through a set of defined service requests. The result of any of these service requests is a *dissemination*, a view of the information contained within the DigitalObject. From the rights management perspective, which we will discuss later, the ability to obtain a dissemination can be managed via access control mechanisms.

A *Disseminator* is an abstraction for packaging a set of service requests that release disseminations from a DigitalObject. These disseminations are byte streams that may be content (e.g., a page of a book), an applet (e.g., a viewer for some content), or a mixture of both. The *PrimitiveDisseminator* is the set of service requests that is common to all DigitalObjects. (We will describe other content-specific Disseminators in Section 4). Within the kernel, the PrimitiveDisseminator provides the fundamental set of requests that allow access to the structural layer of the FEDORA architecture. These requests fall into three categories: (1) those that support the composition and manipulation of DigitalObjects, (2) those that support the access to the DigitalObject structure and its internal DataStreams, and (3) those that serve as a common mechanism for adding, discovering and invoking content-specific behavior in the context of the DigitalObject. The requests in this third category can be thought of as providing a "gateway" to the interface layer of the architecture. Table 1 lists the major service requests from the above categories, and describes their functionality.

From an object-oriented standpoint, the PrimitiveDisseminator is really the set of methods defined for the class DigitalObject. The CORBA Interface Definition Language (IDL) description of the DigitalObject can be found in [6].

Table 1. Service Requests in the PrimitiveDisseminator for a DigitalObject

For composition:	
CreateDataStream	Takes a file or a stream and transforms content into a typed DataStream which is inserted into the DigitalObject kernel.
SetAccessManager	Associates an external rights management scheme with

	the PrimitiveDisseminator by referencing an object that contains an executable. (See Section 5.0)
For structural access:	
GetDataStreams	Returns a sequence of references to DataStreams within the DigitalObject. This request exposes the number and types of contained DataStreams. The actual stream of bytes within each DataStream can be accessed, however, the request will not provide information on the meaning or the context of the data.
GetAccessManager	Returns a reference to the AccessManager component to provide manipulation of its attributes. (See Section 5.0)
Gateway to content layer:	
CreateDisseminator	Creates a content-specific disseminator for the DigitalObject by associating one or more DataStreams with a particular set of content-specific behaviors or service requests. A set of service requests that pertains to a particular content type is a named entity that can be referred to by a unique identifier (e.g., a URN).
GetDisseminators	Returns a sequence of references to Disseminators associated with the Digital Object. Once a reference to a Disseminator is obtained, it can be used to manipulate and access its internal attributes.
ListDisseminatorTypes	Returns a list of disseminator types, or content types, associated with a Digital Object. Content types are represented by a unique identifier such as a URN.
ListDisseminatorMethods	Takes a disseminator type as input and returns a list of service requests (methods) that are specific to the content type.
GetDissemination	Takes a dissemination service request as input and returns the stream of bytes produced by the invocation of that request. Essentially, returns a content-specific manifestation of DataStreams contained in the Digital Object.

Figure 1 depicts the core structure of a FEDORA DigitalObject at the kernel layer. It aggregates three byte stream data packages: a Postscript stream, a MARC record, and an Access Control List (ACL). These packages are depicted in the diagram as MIME-typed ByteStreams with no identifiable relationships among them. The PrimitiveDisseminator also resides in the structural kernel to endow the DigitalObject with its fundamental set of behaviors. As shown, the PrimitiveDisseminator is the single window into the DigitalObject kernel.

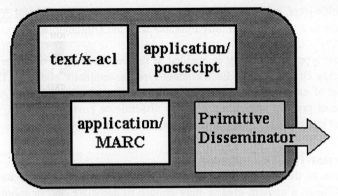

Fig. 1. Digital Object Structural Kernel

4.0 The Interface Layer (Digital Object Content-Type Disseminators)

The PrimitiveDisseminator provides service requests to interact with the DigitalObject as a structural entity. Clients, in most cases, should be insulated from the structural aspects of a DigitalObject. Instead they should interact with DigitalObjects as manifestations of well-known content forms such as a books, journals, or movies. Correspondingly, content creators should be able to restrict access to the raw byte streams of a DigitalObject by endowing it with "allowable" behaviors that represent a particular form of content (known globally or within a particular domain).

We define a *content type* as a set of service requests that specify the behaviors of a particular form of content. For example, a "book" is a content type that has operations such as getTableofContents, nextPage, or nextChapter. Similarly operations such as nextArticle and nextIssue are characteristic of a "journal".

A single DigitalObject can have multiple content types. For instance, the same DigitalObject may have a Dublin Core content type as well as a journal-article content type. In this case, a client could discover both content types and invoke the service request of either, without knowing anything about the DigitalObject's internal structure and configuration.

In fact, to reinforce the distinction between the internal structure of a DigitalObject and the content manifestations it can produce, we introduce the notion of *content-type equivalence*. Two DigitalObjects with entirely different structural compositions can have the same content types associated with them. A simple example of this can be demonstrated with the Dublin Core content type, formally represented by the service requests getDCField and getDCRecord. One DigitalObject may contain an actual Dublin Core record stored in a DataStream. Another DigitalObject may contain a MARC record and a mechanism to transform MARC into Dublin Core. Both objects could have Dublin Core content types associated with them, enabling each to produce the same output in response to the formal Dublin Core service requests. The *structure* of DigitalObjects, and the *mechanisms* for disseminating the content from structure, are opaque to a client, which only interacts with the DigitalObject through its *content types*.

Content-type functionality is enabled at the *interface layer* of the architecture by *content-type Disseminators*. Each content-type Disseminator endows a DigitalObjects with a set of extended service requests that pertain to a content type. As such, these components provide service requests to disseminate custom renderings of the data contained in the DigitalObject, without exposing its underlying structure.

The Content-Type Disseminator
In addition to the Primitive Disseminator, which is logically associated with every Digital Object, a content creator may choose to associate one or more content-type Disseminators with a DigitalObject. Each Disseminator that is associated with a Digital Object identifies a particular content type, and a set of DataStreams to be used as arguments when executing the service requests that define the type. Figure 2 depicts a DigitalObject with three Disseminators attached to it, each linking to the Datastream(s) required as input for its operations. Essentially, the DigitalObject in the figure can be treated as a book, a MARC record, or Dublin Core metadata.

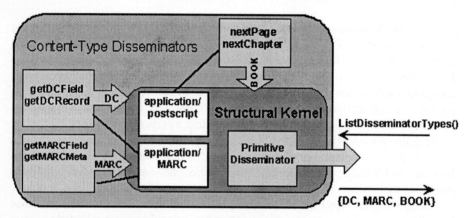

Fig. 2. A DigitalObject with three Disseminators

Clients do not speak directly to a Disseminator, instead they obtain information about content types, and initiate content-type operations, by invoking the "gateway " operations of a DigitalObject's PrimitiveDisseminator. For example, by issuing the `ListDisseminatorTypes()` request, a client can obtain a list of all content types associated with the DigitalObject (see lower right corner of Figure 2). Clients also use the PrimitiveDisseminator to invoke the service requests associated with these content types. Specifically, clients issue the `GetDissemination` request, with a content-type service request as an argument, to invoke a desired content-type behavior on a DigitalObject. This essentially creates an encapsulated service request, for example: `GetDissemination(BOOK.nextPage())`.

The service requests of particular content-types are *not* actually specified in the DigitalObject architecture; instead, FEDORA provides the *means to link to* externally-defined content types. This is intentional and a necessity for an extensible type system. The next section describes *how* content-specific types become named entities in the digital library infrastructure.

4.1 The Extensibility Model for Content Types

In the previous section we described an abstraction, the Disseminator, for associating content-type behaviors with DigitalObjects. The PrimitiveDisseminator provides the service requests for discovering the content-types associated with an individual DigitalObject. In addition, we described how a single content type (for example, Dublin Core) can be manifested in a number of structurally different DigitalObjects using different mechanisms to translate the underlying DataStreams to the disseminations of the type.

The use of external content types, however, essentially creates a "registry problem." How are these types and mechanisms uniquely named so clients can recognize and access them?

The answer to the registry problem lies in the facilities already provided by FEDORA, in conjunction with a global name service such as CNRI's Handle System [2]. Both content types and their mechanisms are, themselves, forms of content. A content type is expressed as a *signature*, the set of service requests particular to that type. A mechanism is a program or agent for executing those service requests on a set of arguments. Abstractly, both signatures and mechanisms are forms of content. As such, they can be stored and disseminated in the same fashion as any form of content, by a DigitalObject. Since a DigitalObject has a unique name (e.g., a URN) - and these names can be registered with a global naming service - content types become identifiable by the unique identifiers of the DigitalObjects that disseminate them. Thus, the registry problem is solved by using uniquely-named DigitalObjects as the means of storing and disseminating content-type signatures and mechanisms.

This section introduces two new abstractions, the *SignatureDisseminator* and the *ServletDisseminator*, to support the dissemination of content types and their mechanisms.

SignatureDisseminator

Each content type is specified as a set of service requests that operationally define it. The formal description of a set of content-type service requests is referred to as a *ContentTypeSignature*. The signature defines the name and syntax of each service request for the content type; for example, `nextPage()` and `nextChapter()` might be the simple signature for the type BOOK. To promote availability and extensibility of content types, a ContentTypeSignature is available as a dissemination of a DigitalObject, and its identity is the unique name of that DigitalObject.

A DigitalObject that contains a content-type behavior specification will have a special class of Disseminator attached to it: the *SignatureDisseminator*. This special

Disseminator is only used with DigitalObjects that release a content-type specification. It is the architectural component that enables communities to develop their own definitions of content types and make them available for general use (in conjunction with the ServletDisseminator discussed below). FEDORA defines the special SignatureDisseminator to endow a DigitalObject with the getSignature() request that returns a set of method specifications for a content type.

ServletDisseminator

The *ContentTypeServlet* is a mechanism that executes the set of content-type service requests defined by a particular ContentTypeSignature, using a specific set of DataStreams as arguments. Like the ContentTypeSignature, a ContentTypeServlet is available as a dissemination of a DigitalObject, and is identifiable by the unique name of the object that releases it.

Figure 3 shows how the ContentTypeSignature and ContentTypeServlet are used to provide content-type behavior to a DigitalObject.

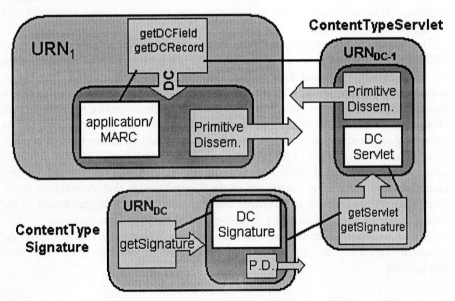

Fig. 3. Disseminator references a Servlet and Signature

In the figure, a Disseminator (labeled DC for Dublin Core) is created in the DigitalObject named URN$_1$ to endow it with Dublin Core content behavior. This is done by associating the DataStream containing the MARC record with a Disseminator that references the Dublin Core content type. In the example, the Disseminator directly references a servlet (mechanism) that converts MARC records to Dublin Core. This servlet is disseminated from the DigitalObject labeled URN$_{DC-1}$. Note that the ServletDisseminator of URN$_{DC-1}$ references another DigitalObject named URN$_{DC}$ that contains the formal ContentTypeSignature for Dublin Core. The net result is that a GetDissemination request on URN_1 activates the servlet to process the MARC record in the DigitalObject. From the client's perspective, the content type available from URN_1 is URN_{DC} and the fact that this is enabled by the mechanism URN_{DC-1} is opaque.

It should be noted that there can be a one-to-many relationship between ContentTypeSignatures and ContentTypeServlets. A single signature can be implemented by multiple servlets using different underlying techniques and data structures. For example, consider the content type BOOK. The BOOK signature may be implemented by two different ContentTypeServlets. The first servlet may fulfill the nextPage() request by performing a TIFF to GIF conversion on the DataStream that contains the TIFF image for the page. The second servlet may simply return a DataStream that contains the static GIF representation of the page. In either case, the servlet could fulfill a specified requirement that nextPage() must return a single page in the GIF format.

The CORBA IDL for each of these new abstractions - the Disseminator, SignatureDisseminator, and ServletDisseminator - can be found in [6].

4.2 Creating a Content-Type Disseminator for a DigitalObject

The book example, above, demonstrates that different implementations of the same content type may use different procedures and data formats to achieve equivalent results. To effectively incorporate a particular content-type (such as BOOK) in a DigitalObject, creators of DigitalObjects must have an easy way to assess the *data requirements* of the particular servlet that implements that content type. Accordingly, every ContentTypeServlet has an *AttachmentSpecification* to describe the kinds of DataStreams that must be present for the servlet to successfully execute.

Each ContentTypeServlet can define its own underlying data structure within the framework of the AttachmentSpecification. An AttachmentSpecification is an ordered sequence of *AttachmentStructures*. Each AttachmentStructure specifies: (1) structure identifier, which could be used to describe a role that a DataStream fulfills, (2) a MIME type for the DataStream(s), and (3) an ordinality indicator that specifies the required number of each type of DataStream.

Figure 4 shows a very simple AttachmentSpecification. In the example, the AttachmentSpecification is essentially a template for a hypothetical content type called PhotoAlbum. This type aggregates a set of images and thumbnails and allows browsing of them. Each column of the template contains instances of the data elements of the AttachmentStructure (a structure id, a MIME type, and an ordinality indicator).

52

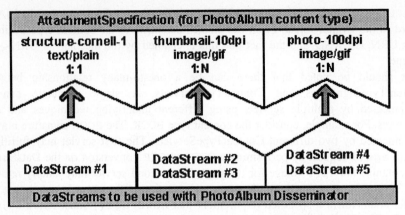

Fig. 4. Associating DataStreams with a Disseminator using the AttachmentSpecification

The above AttachmentSpecification tells a DigitalObject creator that the *first* attachment must be a single (1:1) DataStream containing a structure file that correlates thumbnail images of photographs with their respective exhibit-size images. In the example, the structure file is a domain-specific format known as `structure-cornell-1`, however, it could be a widely accepted structural metadata format. The *second* attachment must be a sequence of one or more (1:N) DataStreams of MIME type `image/gif` that will play the role of thumbnails for the photographs. The *third* attachment must be a sequence of one or more (1:N) DataStreams of MIME type `image/gif` that are the actual photographs. In this example, the author will use the structure file to correlate thumbnails to full images using the internal identifiers of the DataStreams.

This basic approach can be applied to create more complex Disseminators that operate on multiple sets of inter-related DataStreams of varying MIME types. The basic Disseminator architecture remains simple; it accommodates externally developed definitions of content types and external mechanisms for executing content-type behaviors.

We plan to develop a GUI tool that will easily allow object creators to associate Disseminators with DigitalObjects based on these AttachmentSpecifications. The CORBA IDL for the AttachmentSpecification can be found in [6].

5.0 Rights Management for DigitalObjects

We have thus far described an architecture for encapsulating data and defining content-specific interfaces for DigitalObjects. It is essential that the architecture provide facilities to protect the intellectual property that may be encapsulated in these DigitalObjects.

In FEDORA, AccessManagers are the entities that enable the association of rights management mechanisms with service requests that can be made on a DigitalObject.

Extensibility of rights management schemes is achieved in a manner similar to that already described for content types.

The AccessManager

The AccessManager is a generic component for attaching a rights management mechanism with a Disseminator linked with a DigitalObject. Each Disseminator, including the PrimitiveDisseminator, can have an AccessManager associated with it. The AccessManager associated with a Disseminator may internally provide different levels of access control for each service request defined by that Disseminator.

When the PrimitiveDisseminator has an AccessManager associated with it, structural-level service requests are processed under its control. This AccessManager may have different levels of access control for the individual operations defined by the Primitive Disseminator. For example, the service requests that allow creation and manipulation of content in the DigitalObject kernel may not be available to a general client; these will typically be reserved for those who author and manage DigitalObjects. Access to pure byte streams (DataStreams) can be provided to some or all clients; however, we believe that most clients will be interested in accessing DigitalObjects at the interface level through their content-type Disseminators. This implies that the "gateway" service requests of the Primitive Disseminator, such as ListDisseminatorTypes and GetDissemination, will be available to most access-oriented clients.

The ability to associate AccessManagers with content-type Disseminators provides an additional level of rights management. When a client invokes a service request associated with a content-type Disseminator the AccessManager is activated. The effect is that the service request is processed under the full control of the Access Manager. This control can be both at the point of invocation of a service request and at the point of transmission of the results of the service request back to the client.

For instance, using our previous Book example, an AccessManager may enforce payment of five cents per page (by interacting with some digital payment system) before invoking the getPage service request. In addition, it may apply a digital watermark to the disseminated page before it is transmitted back to the client.

5.1 Extensibility for Rights Management

To provide extensibility for rights management mechanisms, FEDORA uses the same approach as it does for content-type behaviors. Essentially, an AccessManager looks much like a Disseminator in that it has a type and a set of associated DataStreams. As with a Disseminator, these DataStreams are arguments to the execution of the AccessManager. For example, an AccessManager that provides access-control-list functionality would require a DataStream containing the ACL specific to the DigitalObject whose content we want to protect.

Like a Disseminator, an AccessManager identifies a type, the *AccessManagerType*. This type is the unique name (URN) of the DigitalObject that disseminates the mechanism to execute a particular rights management scheme. This mechanism is known as an *AccessManagerServlet*. Storing rights management mechanisms in DigitalObjects allows the use of external or third-party mechanisms for rights management. It also accommodates future extensibility allowing new rights management schemes to be created and stored in the infrastructure.

Figure 5 depicts a DigitalObject named URN_1 that has a Dublin Core (DC) content Disseminator guarded by an AccessManager. (AccessManagers are shown as 3-D boxes surrounding Disseminators.) The AccessManager is of type URN_{ACL-1}, which is an access control list scheme. This type is actually the unique name of the DigitalObject that disseminates the mechanism, the AccessManagerServlet, for the ACL scheme.

In the figure we can see that the AccessManager obtains the AccessManagerServlet from a DigitalObject named URN_{ACL-1}. This DigitalObject uses a special Disseminator, called the *AccessManagerDisseminator*, to make the ACL servlet available. Also, note that the AccessManager links to the DataStream named DS_1. This DataStream contains an access control list for DigitalObject URN_1 that is used as input to the ACL servlet. The effect is that a client invocation of either of the service requests defined for the Dublin Core content Disseminator will occur under the control of the access- control-list rights management scheme, using the ACL data contained within the DS_1 DataStream.

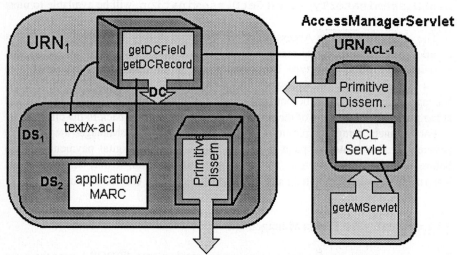

Fig. 5. Using an AccessManager with a Disseminator

6.0 The Management Layer (*DigitalObject Repository*)

Up to this point we have discussed the architecture of the DigitalObject that specifies components and service requests to manipulate and access the contents of an individual object. To provide a service context in which these DigitalObjects live, there must be an architectural layer responsible for managing DigitalObjects.

DigitalObjects cannot spontaneously create and destroy themselves; they cannot independently move themselves around in the information infrastructure; nor can they execute their content specific behaviors independently. The third layer of the FEDORA architecture provides these *object lifecycle* and *management* functions. The fundamental abstraction at this layer is the Repository itself.

The Repository

The *Repository* is the entity that provides management of and access to *contained* DigitalObjects. It also provides the environment in which ContentTypeServlets and AccessManagerServlets are executed. It is not a physical entity in which DigitalObjects actually reside. Instead, it is a service layer that presides over a logical grouping of DigitalObjects.

At the Repository level, DigitalObjects are completely opaque, meaning that there are no service requests that allow "looking into" the DigitalObject wrapper. Operations performed at this layer include moving a digital object, replicating it, deleting it, and others as described in [3]. As indicated in Figure 6, the only attribute of the DigitalObject that is visible at the Repository layer is its unique identifier, which is registered with a naming service of the digital library infrastructure. This figure also illustrates the "move" operation of a DigitalObject from one repository to another.

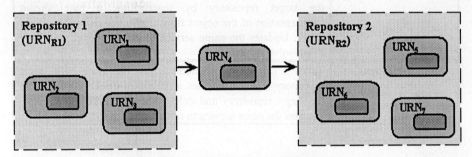

Fig. 6. DigitalObject Repositories

Containment of DigitalObjects in Repositories is facilitated by a naming service. A DigitalObject effectively does not exist in the infrastructure (i.e., it is not accessible to clients) unless it has a registered identifier such as a URN. Essentially, a DigitalObject is contained in a repository when the name service *resolves* the DigitalObject's identifier to that repository. For example, an object named URN_1 is "contained" in a repository URN_{R1}, when the name service resolves the name URN_1 to the repository named URN_{R1}. Once at the repository, client access to the requested DigitalObject is achieved through the AccessDigitalObject() request, with URN_1 as an argument.

Table 2 shows the set of Repository service requests implemented in FEDORA. We expect to add other utility-oriented operations as we continue to refine the service.

Table 2. Repository Service Requests

For Access:	
AccessDigitalObject	Takes a DigitalObject name (e.g. URN) as input, and returns a reference to a DigitalObject. This reference can be used to perform service requests on the DigitalObject via its Primitive Disseminator.
For Management:	
CreateDigitalObject	Creates a new DigitalObject, which is an empty wrapper with a PrimitiveDisseminator. Returns a reference to the DigitalObject that can be used to perform structural manipulations required to populate the empty object.
DepositDigitalObject	Takes a reference to a DigitalObject as input, and returns a unique name for that object that can then be registered with the naming service. The DigitalObject name will be registered to resolve the repository that created it.
DeleteDigitalObject	Takes a DigitalObject name as input, and removes all references to the DigitalObject from the repository, including its registration in the naming service.
ReplicateDigitalObject	Takes a DigitalObject reference and the name of a target repository as input. Creates a replica of the DigitalObject in the target repository by marshalling a byte stream representation of the object from the source repository to the target. Updates the name service to include target repository as a resolve location.
MoveDigitalObject	Takes a DigitalObject reference and the name of a target repository as input. Creates a replica of the DigitalObject in the target repository and deletes the object from its source. Updates the name service to reflect new repository location.

7.0 Putting in All Together : *Accessing a Digital Object*

We have introduced the DigitalObject as a two-layered entity, consisting of the DigitalObject structural kernel and the interface layer that exposes its content-type Disseminators. We have introduced the Repository that provides a management layer to the architecture. Once DigitalObjects are created and stored in a Repository, they can be accessed by clients. Figure 7 shows a typical request sequence for interaction with a DigitalObject once it has been accessed in a Repository. The figure assumes that the `AccessDigitalObject(URN1)` request has just been successfully completed on a Repository and the client is interacting with the DigitalObject.

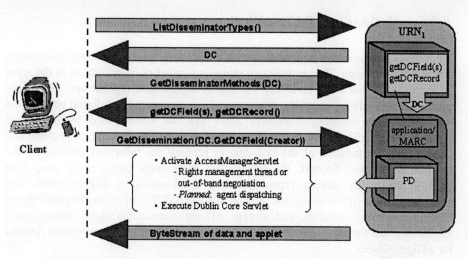

Fig. 7. Typical Client Request Sequence after Initial Access of DigitalObject

In the figure, the client is speaking directly to the PrimitiveDisseminator of the DigitalObject. First, the client issues the `ListDisseminatorTypes()` request to find out what content types are available on this DigitalObject. The PrimitiveDisseminator returns only the unique name for the Dublin Core content type, which is DC. (If there were multiple Disseminators associated with this object, a list of all the associated content types would be returned.) As in the Web, we expect that clients will be configured to internally handle a set of well-known types. In the case of a well-known type, the client can then immediately invoke a known service request on the DigitalObject; otherwise, the client can ask the object for a list of the service requests for the type. The figure depicts that later scenario, and the client issues the `GetDisseminatorMethods` request with the Dublin Core content-type name as an argument. The request returns a list of method specifications. The client decides to obtain the `Creator` element of the Dublin Core metadata and, therefore, issues a `GetDissemination` request on the object with the appropriate content-type method as an argument. When the request is received by the PrimitiveDisseminator, the AccessManager associated with the DC Disseminator is transparently activated, and the content-type service request is processed under its control. (In the figure, AccessManagers are the 3-D boxes surrounding the Disseminators.) The AccessManager may engage the client in an out-of-band negotiation, or it may dispatch an agent to perform an activity (either way it could do things like get username/password clearance, obtain payment, etc.). When the rights management engagement is successful, the AccessManager activates the DisseminatorServlet for the Dublin Core content type. The servlet operates on the MARC DataStream to extract the Dublin Core Creator, and sends this requested data, and a Dublin Core viewing applet back to the client.

8.0 Conclusions and Future Work

We have described in this paper a powerful architecture for storing and disseminating digital library content. This architecture makes a number of contributions in the areas of extensibility and interoperability for digital objects and repositories. First, the architecture cleanly separates the structure and raw data stored in a digital object from the semantically meaningful *content types* that are manipulated by clients. It accomplishes this separation through the use of servlets that are able to perform any computable manipulation of the raw data to produce the behaviors defined by the client-visible types. Second, the architecture recursively provides its own type registry, effectively storing types and their mechanisms in DigitalObjects and identifying those types using the unique names (URNs) of those DigitalObjects. Finally, it permits creation and storage of any computable rights management mechanism and the association of these mechanisms with the disseminations defined for a DigitalObject.

At the time of writing this paper, we have completed a prototype implementation of FEDORA that demonstrates the components and services described herein. We will continue to refine the architecture as we test its capabilities in a variety of contexts. In particular, we plan to test how well it accommodates a variety of community-defined content types and rights management mechanisms. Among our test cases will be the interfaces and document model in the current Dienst protocol, the archival types defined by the DLF for the MOA-2 project, and the rights management schemes developed by CNRI in its work for the Library of Congress. As mentioned earlier, we will also conduct a series of interoperability experiments with CNRI.

Since the architecture is distributed by nature, it raises a number of issues related to reliability and security. These are key challenges that we plan to investigate in the next phase of our work with FEDORA. Among the critical areas that we have identified and plan to pursue are mobile code security, rights management policy definitions, fail-safe component design, and reliable replication mechanisms.

Acknowledgements

The work described in this paper was funded by the Defense Advanced Research Project Agency under Grant No. MDA 972-96-1-006 with the Corporation for National Research Initiatives. This paper does not necessarily represent the views of CNRI or DARPA. We would like to express our gratitude to William Arms, Christophe Blanchi, and Ed Overly for their thoughtful contributions to this architecture.

References

1. Arms, William Y., Christophe Blanchi, Edward A. Overly.: An Architecture for Information in Digital Libraries. D-Lib Magazine. February 1997, http://www.dlib.org/dlib/february97/cnri/02arms1.html
2. CNRI Handle System. http://www.handle.net
3. Crespo, Arturo and Hector Garcia-Molina.: Archival Storage for Digital Libraries. ACM Digital Libraries '98. Pittsburgh, PA, June, 1998.
4. Dublin Core Metadata Element Set: Resource Page. http://purl.org/metadata/dublin_core.
5. Daniel, Ron Jr., Carl Lagoze, and Sandra Payette.: A Metadata Architecture for Digital Libraries. Proceedings of IEEE Forum on Research and Technology Advances in Digital Libraries 1998. Santa Barbara, California, April 22-24, 1998.
6. FEDORA CORBA IDL. http://www2.cs.cornell.edu/payette/papers/ECDL98/FEDORA-IDL.html
7. Kahn, Robert H., and Robert Wilensky.: A Framework for Distributed DigitalObject Services. Corporation for National Research Initiatives, http://www.cnri.reston.va.us/cstr/arch/k-w.html or hdl:cnri.dlib/tn95-01, 1995.
8. Lagoze, Carl, Clifford A. Lynch, and Ron Daniel Jr.: The Warwick Framework: A Container Architecture for Aggregating Sets of Metadata. Cornell University Computer Science Technical Report TR96-1593. June, 1996, http://cs-tr.cs.cornell.edu:80/Dienst/UI/2.0/Describe/ncstrl.cornell/TR96-1593.
9. Lagoze, Carl, Erin Shaw, James R. Davis, and Dean B. Krafft.: Dienst: Implementation Reference Manual. Cornell Computer Science Technical Report TR95-1514. http://cstr/cs/cornell.edu:80/Dienst/UI/2.0/Describe/ncstrl.cornell/TR95-1514.
10. Making of America Testbed Project White Paper. Version 1.03, March 16, 1998, http://sunsite.Berkeley.EDU/moa2/
11. Monch, Christian, Oswald Drobnik, and Johann Wolfgang.: Integrating New Document Types into Digital Libraries. Proceedings of IEEE Forum on Research and Technology Advances in Digital Libraries 1998. Santa Barbara, California, April 22-24, 1998.
12. Networked Computer Science Technical Reports Library. http://www.ncstrl.org.
13. Phelps, Thomas A. and Robert Wilensky.: Toward Active, Extensible, Networked Documents: Multivalent Architecturre and Applications. ,Proceedings of the 1st ACM International Conference on Digital Libraries. Bethesda, Maryland, March 20-23, 1996, pp. 100-108.

The Alexandria Digital Library Architecture *

James Frew[1], Michael Freeston[2], Nathan Freitas[2], Linda Hill[2], Greg Janee[2],
Kevin Lovette[2], Robert Nideffer[3], Terence Smith[4], and Qi Zheng[2]

[1] Donald Bren School of Environmental Science and Management
University of California, Santa Barbara
frew@bren.ucsb.edu
[2] Alexandria Digital Library, University of California, Santa Barbara
{freeston,nathan,lhill,gjanee,kal,zheng}@alexandria.ucsb.edu
[3] Department of Studio Art, University of California, Irvine
nideffer@arts.ucsb.edu
[4] Department of Computer Science, University of California, Santa Barbara
smithtr@cs.ucsb.edu

Abstract. Since 1994, the Alexandria Digital Library Project has developed three prototype digital libraries for georeferenced information. This paper describes the most recent of these efforts, a three-tier client-server architecture that relies heavily on a middleware layer to present a single uniform set of interfaces to multiple heterogeneous servers. These standard interfaces, all of which are implemented in HTTP, support session management, collection discovery and evaluation, metadata searching, metadata retrieval, and online holding retrieval. An XML-based metadata encoding scheme and a simple boolean query language have also been developed. The architecture described by these interfaces has been implemented at UCSB.

1 ADL Background

The Alexandria Project [1] is a consortium of researchers, developers, and educators, spanning the academic, public, and private sectors, exploring a variety of problems related to distributed digital libraries for georeferenced information.

Distributed means the library's components may be spread across the Internet, as well as coexisting on a single desktop. *Georeferenced* means that all the library's holdings are associated with one or more regions (*footprints*) on the surface of the Earth.

The centerpiece of the Alexandria Project is the Alexandria Digital Library (ADL) [2], an online information system inspired by the Map and Imagery Laboratory [3] in the Davidson Library at the University of California, Santa Barbara (UCSB). The ADL currently provides access over the World Wide Web to a subset of the MIL's holdings, as well as other georeferenced datasets.

---

* The work described herein has been supported by the NSF-DARPA-NASA Digital Libraries Initiative, under cooperative agreement NSF IR94-11330.

There have been three distinct system architectures associated with ADL since the Project's inception in 1994. The first, or "Rapid Prototype," architecture [4] employed a desktop geographic information system (GIS) as the user interface to a single ADL catalog database. The second, or "Web Prototype," architecture [5] replaced the GIS with an HTTP server, which presented a user interface of dynamically-generated HTML pages. This paper describes the third ADL architecture, as implemented in July 1998.

2   ADL Architecture Overview

The ADL architecture (Fig. 1) is a 3-tier client-server architecture:

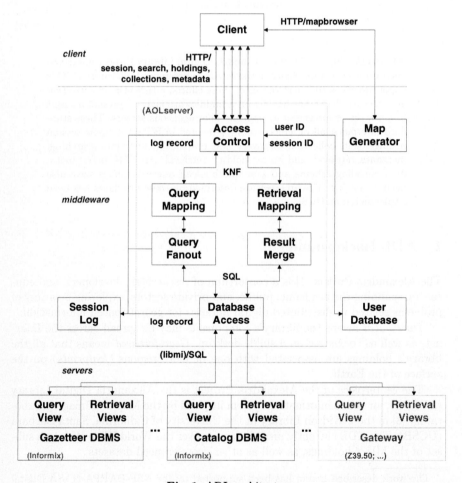

Fig. 1. ADL architecture

The crux of the architecture is a middleware layer, which maps an assortment of heterogeneous information servers (generalizations of library catalogs) into a few standard client interfaces for metadata queries, metadata retrieval, and digital holding retrieval. These interfaces are intended to be generic enough to support arbitrary clients, of which the ADL client is the first sample implementation.

3   Client

The ADL client is a graphical interface designed to support interactive queries by ADL users. The ADL client-middleware interfaces have been designed on the assumption that the ADL client is a *program*, as opposed to a human user. Specifically, the client is assumed to be capable of maintaining enough local state to support the notion of a "session," as well as supporting complex real-time user interactions (e.g. rollover help). Thus, the ADL client requires less support from the rest of the ADL architecture than did its predecessor "Web Prototype" [6] client, which was driven by server-generated HTML pages.

The current version of the ADL client is implemented entirely in Java. It is distributed as a self-installing stand-alone application, for any platform (Windows, Macintosh, Sun, SGI, etc.) supporting release 1.1 or higher of the Java Runtime Environment [7].

Further discussion of the ADL client is beyond the scope of this paper. The client is described in detail at, and may be downloaded from, `http://www.alexandria.ucsb.edu/adljigi`.

4   Client-Middleware Interface

The ADL client communicates with an ADL middleware layer via HTTP [8]. We selected HTTP as the basic protocol owing to its ubiquity, simplicity, and the ease with which current HTTP servers can be extended to support the level of functionality we require.

Each family of interfaces supported by the ADL middleware is bound to a particular URL. This eliminates the need for top-level switch logic to vector requests to the appropriate handlers, but does require that the client be aware of which URL implements which interface.

Five standard interfaces are currently supported:

1. `session`: create or terminate a logical "session" between the client and the middleware;
2. `collections`: list the library collections supported by the middleware;
3. `search`: identify library holdings that satisfy specific boolean constraints on standard high-level search-oriented metadata.
4. `metadata`: retrieve metadata for specified library holdings; and
5. `holdings`: request either a (possibly reduced-resolution) graphic representation of a specified library holding, or the holding itself.

A sixth interface, `mapbrowser`, allows a client to request a base map for a particular portion of the Earth's surface, specifying projection and feature layers (coastlines, highways, etc.). Although this service is unrelated to the contents of the library, it simplifies the development of graphical clients that display maps as navigational tools.

All ADL interfaces are implemented as HTTP GETs or POSTs to the interface's URL. By convention, the pathname portion of the URL ends with `interface/method`. Method parameters are passed according to the CGI [9] encoding conventions; they are referenced below using the format `name=value`. Except as noted, return values are provided as ASCII text (MIME type `text/plain`). An error message may be returned in lieu of whatever other return values the method supports.

4.1 Session Interface

The `session` interface establishes a logical connection between the client and the middleware that persists between HTTP transactions. Since HTTP is a stateless protocol, the client and the middleware must cooperate to preserve enough state to allow for incremental queries, user authentication, etc. In the current ADL architecture, almost all of this state is maintained by the client; the `session` interface merely allows for the assignment and de-assignment of unique *session identifiers*.

The `session` interface thus exists primarily to support tracking of system activity, especially user interactions, for evaluation purposes [10]. All ADL interfaces accept a session identifier as a parameter, so in theory any ADL system event can be traced back to the specific user responsible for it. However, the architecture is explicitly designed to not *require* this level of monitoring. In almost all cases, the behavior of an ADL interface does not change if the supplied session identifier is null or otherwise "invalid."

The session interface exposes the following methods:

1. `start` initiates an ADL session. It accepts user data and client data, and returns a unique session identifier, which may be used in any subsequent calls to ADL interfaces:
   - `user_name=name`
   - `user_pass=password`
   - `client_data=data`

   The client data is an optional, opaque string that the middleware may use to tailor its behavior to specific clients. The user name and password identify the user to the rest of the ADL system.

2. `end` terminates an ADL session:
   - `session_id=session_id`
   - `client_data=client_data`

   Although `end` is not strictly necessary, calling it allows the middleware to recycle any resources that may have been dedicated to supporting the specified session. Moreover, `end` is a POST method, and its optional contents are assumed to be client-specific session history information. These are passed by the middleware to its session logging database, for later evaluation by the ADL developers.

4.2 Collections Interface

The `collections` interface allows the client to quickly determine which library *collections* (logical groupings of library holdings) are accessible from the middleware. This interface exposes two methods:

1. `list` returns a list of simple text identifiers for all the collections that the middleware has access to. It has no arguments.
2. `scan` returns detailed metadata for a specific collection:
   - `collection_id=collection_id`

   The collection metadata are returned as XML-tagged text. Since this encoding strategy is also used by other ADL interfaces, we describe it briefly in the next section.

Metadata Format. All but the simplest metadata are encoded by the middleware with XML tags before being passed to the client. This encoding is based on two concepts: *sections* and *name-value pairs*.

Metadata are grouped into top-level sections by XML elements whose semantics are defined as part of the interface. For example, collection metadata returned by the `scan` method of the `collections` interface will always include one `BUCKET` element for each searchable parameter that the collection supports. (*Bucket* is the ADL term for a high-level searchable attribute, generally comprising the union of several more precise lower-level attributes. The current set of ADL buckets is described under "Search Buckets" below.)

Explicit name-value pairs are used to encapsulate metadata whose semantics may otherwise be opaque to ADL. Such metadata are packaged in adjacent `NAME` and `VALUE` XML elements:

```
<collection>
  <name>collection.name       </name><value>ADL Catalog</value>
  <name>collection.id         </name><value>adl_catalog</value>
  <name>collection.description</name><value>
  The Alexandria Digital Library (ADL) Catalog provides metadata for
  geospatial data (e.g., maps, aerial photographs, etc., whether in
  digital or in hard-copy form). Coverage is worldwide but primarily
  concentrated in the southern California area.
  </value>
  <bucket>
    <name>bucket.name </name><value>Geographic Locations</value>
    <name>bucket.id   </name><value>location</value>
    <name>bucket.type </name><value>map</value>
```

```
<name>bucket.scheme     </name><value>none                </value>
<name>bucket.description</name><value>
   Latitude and longitude of item's point location, or bounding
   latitudes and longitudes of item's geographical footprint
</value>
</bucket>
<bucket>
<name>bucket.name  </name><value>Format           </value>
<name>bucket.id    </name><value>format           </value>
<name>bucket.type  </name><value>tree             </value>
<name>bucket.scheme</name><value>ADL Format List</value>
<domain>
   <name>HTML </name><value>10</value>
   <name>Paper</name><value>50</value>
</domain>
<name>bucket.description</name><value>
   Format(s) in which item is available.
</value>
</bucket>
...
</collection>
```

4.3 Search Interface

The search interface allows the client to query the searchable metadata in one or more of the collections accessible to the middleware. This interface exposes two methods:

1. start initiates a query:
   - session_id=*session_id*
   - results=*max_results*
   - collections=*collection,...*
   - query=*query*

   The query is applied to each specified collection, but not in any particular order. Once max_results results have been accumulated, start will return, regardless of how the results are distributed across the specified collections. start immediately returns a *query identifier*, which is required if the query is to be terminated prematurely by stop. *Object identifiers* for individual library holdings are then streamed back to the client as the query progresses. This "two-part" return is a deliberate design choice, intended to facilitate the construction of multithreaded clients – they are free to collect the query results in parallel with other activities, once the query identifier has been retrieved.

   The form and content of a query is described in the following section.

2. stop terminates a query before it returns:
   - session_id=*session_id*

 − query_id=query_id

This provides the client with an "escape hatch" for hung or long-running queries. It is not strictly necessary to the architecture, although, like the end method in the session interface, it can be of considerable assistance to the middleware and underlying servers, by enabling them to free resources no longer required to support a particular client.

Search Buckets. The query passed to the start method specifies combinations of, and/or boolean constraints on, the ADL *search buckets*, a standard set of high-level searchable metadata. Each collection supported by the middleware must specify a mapping from its own metadata into the search bucket attributes. This mapping will almost always be many-to-one; i.e., there will inevitably be a loss of precision in querying the search buckets versus querying the collection-specific metadata directly. However, by exposing only a single high-level set of searchable metadata, the ADL middleware allows clients to be built that can both exploit search bucket semantics (e.g. spatially manipulate the "location" bucket), and search all of ADL via a single connection.

The current set of ADL search buckets is:

1. *geographic location*: latitude-longitude bounding box of the holding's footprint.
2. *type*: the "logical type" of the library holding, usually a categorization of its form (e.g., map, aerial photograph, etc.) or its content (e.g., hydrographic feature, airport, etc.)
3. *format*: the format(s) in which the library holding can be delivered, both online and offline.
4. *about (freetext)*: words from the holding's title, abstract, subject heading, index terms, keywords, etc. that indicate the topics and themes of the holding
5. *about (assigned)*: words from subject headings, index terms, and keywords that were assigned by catalogers to indicate the topics and themes of the holding
6. *originator*: words from author, investigator, publisher, and similar attributes.
7. *date range*: beginning and ending dates indicating coverage, publication, or other event relevant to the content of the holding.
8. *identifier*: any standard identifier or number (e.g., ISSN, ISBN, report number, URL) associated with the holding.

Two important design characteristics distinguish the ADL search buckets from otherwise similar "umbrella" metadata schemes such as GILS [11] or the "Dublin Core" [12]. First, the ADL search buckets have specific semantics, both in terms of constraints on their content, and in terms of how they may be searched. This allows for much more powerful searches (e.g., spatial searches against the "location" bucket) than if the buckets were only specified to contain arbitrary text. Second, the particular set of attributes comprising the ADL search buckets is intended to be optimal for digital georeferenced information (e.g., fields indicating the Earth location or digital format of the holding are far more important for *discovering* information than is the ability to easily distinguish an author from a publisher.)

KNF Query Language. The `query` passed to the `start` method is written in a simple language we call KNF ("Kevin's Normal Form"). The syntax of KNF is quite similar to the LISP programming language, and supports both method invocation and simple boolean expressions. Queries are assembled from boolean combinations of predicates, each of which is applied to a particular search bucket. For example,

```
(and
    (contains
        (rectangle
            (coord -133.1262 31.9119)
            (coord -110.6262 40.0369)))
    (or
        (overlaps
            (rectangle
                (coord -122.7626 38.3006)
                (coord -121.4461 37.3357)))
        (overlaps
            (polygon
                (coord -113.12 31.91)
                (coord -110.62 31.91)
                (coord -110.62 40.03)
                (coord -113.12 40.03)
                (coord -113.12 31.91))))))
```

specifies that the `location` bucket must contain the first rectangle, as well at least one of either the second rectangle or the polygon.

It may be helpful to think of KNF as an alternative to the `WHERE` clause in an SQL SELECT statement. To continue the analogy, the `start` method's `collections` parameter is analogous to a SELECT statement's `FROM` clause. The SELECT is implicitly the object identifiers that `start` returns.

4.4 Metadata Interface

The `metadata` interface provides access to partial and full metadata for specified holdings. A typical sequence is for the `metadata` interfaces to be invoked to evaluate the results of a `search`.

The `metadata` interface exposes two methods, both of which are passed an object identifier

– object_id=*object_id*

as their single parameter:

1. scan returns a small subset of the specified object's metadata, e.g.:

```
<doc>
  <section>scan
    <group>location
      <name>west_bounding_longitude</name><value>-115.625000</value>
      <name>east_bounding_longitude</name><value>-115.500000</value>
      <name>north_bounding_latitude<value>33.125000</value>
      <name>south_bounding_latitude<value>33.000000</value>
    </group>
    <group>title
      <name>title</name><value>
        Westmorland East; Digital Raster Graphic (DRG) Data
      </value>
    </group>;
    <group>date
      <name>begin_date</name><value>1996-05-08</value>
      <name>end_date</name><value>1996-05-08</value>
    </group>
    <group>type
      <name>type</name><value>MAPS</value>
      <name>available_as</name><value>^TIFF^</value>
    </group>
    <group>collection
      <name>collection_id</name><value>ius_catalog</value>
      <name>object_id</name><value>adl_catalog:800089</value>
      <name>parent_id</name><value>adl_catalog:909</value>
    </group>
  </section>
</doc>
```

The scan subset includes:

(a) those search buckets which are most likely to have a single, unambiguous value (location, date, type);

(b) the holding's title, which, if present, is useful for quick evaluation (but which is often absent, and therefore a poor high-level *search* term); and

(c) identifiers for the holding's collection and any parent-level metadata, as well as for the holding itself, which can be used in subsequent data or metadata retrievals.

These attributes were selected to maximize the utility of the scan metadata for quick evaluation, while minimizing the amount of per-holding information that a client must manipulate. For example, the current ADL client automatically retrieves all scan metadata for all holdings returned by the search interface.

2. full returns all available metadata for the specified holding.

As mentioned above (in "Metadata Format"), there is no guarantee that a client will be able to interpret any particular attribute in a given holding's metadata. However, the XML packaging always allows a client to unambiguously *parse* the metadata, and (for example) display it in the hierarchy implied by the nesting of the group tags.

4.5 Holdings Interface

The `holdings` interface allows the client to retrieve library holdings using their object identifiers. These identifiers are usually obtained from the `search` interface. However, since ADL object identifiers are persistent, they can be saved (or, for example, emailed to a colleague) and then passed directly to the `holdings` interface during a subsequent session.

The `holdings` interface exposes two methods, both of which are passed an object identifier

– object_id=*object_id*

as their single parameter:

1. `thumbnail` returns a reduced-resolution image rendition of the corresponding holding, if one is available. The image is returned as a MIME-typed byte stream.

   Thumbnail images are small (typically 100 by 100 8-bit pixels, compressed with GIF or JPEG) in order to minimize download time. They are intended to help a library user make quick "go/no-go" decisions about whether to pursue a (possibly much) larger, full-resolution version of the holding.

2. `access` returns a URL, from which higher-resolution versions of the holding may be retrieved.

   In earlier versions of ADL, the equivalent of `access` returned the holding itself, as a MIME-typed byte stream. The extra level of indirection was added to the current version for three reasons:

   (a) One metadata field (the URL returned by `access`) can now be used to group together a suite of high-resolution renditions of a single holding. For example, most of ADL digital holdings are available at both "full" and "browse" resolutions, where "browse" is informally defined as "big enough to make an informed decision as to whether the full resolution version is worth retrieving." Our browse image are typically about 500 by 500 pixels.

   (b) Large holdings can be moved to wherever space is available, without having to rewrite the corresponding catalog database. The `access` interface need only maintain a relatively simple mapping between object identifiers and storage locations.

   (c) All of the *distribution* restriction issues currently facing ADL are related to full-resolution holdings, not lower-resolution versions or metadata. Enforcing these restrictions in the `access` interface means we don't have to worry about them in other interfaces.

5 Middleware

The ADL middleware is responsible for implementing the client-middleware interfaces described above, and mapping them into interactions with an arbitrary number of metadata catalogs. Additionally, the middleware implements whatever access controls ADL requires.

The current ADL middleware layer is implemented by an AOLserver [13] HTTP server. All ADL-specific functionality described in this section is implemented by C functions and Tcl scripts executing in the context of the AOLserver.

5.1 Access Control

The ADL middleware supports whatever access policy is dictated by ADL. Two specific access controls are supported in the current implementation: host-based and user-based.

Host-based access control is used to refuse connections from clients that are not running at an ADL-approved Internet address. This is currently used to limit access to ADL to only those hosts connected to an IP network managed by the University of California. To this end, the access-control module maintains an explicit list of network numbers from which it will entertain connections. This mechanism is inherently unscalable, although it suffices to meet the UC-only distribution restrictions imposed by third parties on some proprietary materials in the ADL collections (e.g., commercial remote sensing imagery).

The session interface can be used to implement a crude user-based access control mechanism, simply by configuring the other interfaces so that they refuse to accept invalid session identifiers. So far, we have not seen any advantage to the easily-defeated increment of security that this would provide.

5.2 Query and Retrieval Mapping

The ADL middleware maps KNF queries and holdings requests into queries specific to the underlying ADL servers. If multiple servers, or multiple databases on a single server, must be queried, this layer handles the requisite fan-out/fan-in. Note that we currently assume that multiple databases are disjoint; thus, the fan-in process is currently simple collation, with no duplicate detection or other conflict resolution.

In the current implementation, a basic architectural assumption is that the underlying servers will expose views that are, as closely as the particular server allows, exact correlates to the ADL search buckets and metadata sections. Thus, the translation functionality of the mapping layer is currently limited to "transliterating" KNF into various dialects of server query languages (e.g., SQL).

5.3 Database Connections

The ADL middleware maintains a pool of client connections to whatever underlying servers are currently supported. The database connection layer is responsible for presenting a single functional interface to these shared connections. This serves to both localize whatever special knowledge (e.g. database client library) is needed to communicate with a particular server, and to minimize the setup or teardown time associated with making or breaking database client-server connection.

6 Servers

The ADL system currently includes two collection servers, the ADL catalog and the ADL gazetteer. Accommodating their quite different schemas has been a good test of our search bucket mapping strategy (i.e., congruent views in both the catalog and the gazetteer).

Both the catalog and the gazetteer are implemented as Informix Dynamic Server–Universal Data Option [14] databases. The only Informix-specific features that we currently exploit are the MapInfo [15] spatial data types, and their associated operators and indices, to implement the "location" search bucket.

7 Status

As of July 1998 the ADL architecture described herein is up and running on the ADL testbed system at UCSB (subject to the aforementioned access restrictions), and is also being installed at the San Diego Supercomputer Center. Access to the UCSB system is currently restricted to Internet domains controlled by the University of California.

8 Acknowledgements

We thank the staff of UCSB's Davidson Library Map and Imagery Laboratory for their support of the ADL testbed system.

References

1. Alexandria Project. http://www.alexandria.ucsb.edu
2. Smith, T., Andresen, D., Carver, L., Dolin, R., Fischer, C., Frew, J., Goodchild, M., Ibarra, O., Kemp, R., Kothuri, R., Larsgaard, M., Manjunath, B., Nebert, D., Simpson, J., Wells, A., Yang, T., Zheng, Q.: A digital library for geographically referenced materials. Computer 29:5 (1996) 54-60
3. UCSB Davidson Library Map and Imagery Laboratory. http://www.sdc.ucsb.edu
4. Frew, J., Carver, L., Fischer, C., Goodchild, M., Larsgaard, M., Smith, T., Zheng, Q.: The Alexandria Rapid Prototype: building a digital library for spatial information. 1995 ESRI User Conference Proceedings, May 22-25, 1995, Environmental Systems Research Institute, Inc., Redlands, CA (1995) http://www.esri.com/base/common/userconf/proc95/to300/p255.html
5. Frew, J., Freeston, M., Kemp, R., Simpson, J., Smith, T., Wells, A., Zheng, Q.: Alexandria Digital Library Testbed. D-Lib Magazine (July/August 1996) http://www.dlib.org/dlib/july96/alexandria/07frew.html

6. Andresen, D., Carver, L., Dolin, R., Fischer, C., Frew, J., Goodchild, M., Ibarra, O., Kothuri, R., Larsgaard, M., Manjunath, B., Nebert, D., Simpson, J., Smith, T., Yang, T., Zheng, Q.: The WWW prototype of the Alexandria Digital Library. Proceedings of ISDL'95: International Symposium on Digital Libraries, 22-25 August 1995, Japan (1995)

7. Java Runtime Environment. http://www.javasoft.com/products/jdk/1.1/jre

8. Fielding, R., Gettys, J., Mogul, J., Frystyk, H., Berners-Lee, T.: Hypertext Transfer Protocol – HTTP/1.1. RFC 2068 (January 1997) ftp://nis.nsf.net/documents/rfc/rfc2068.txt

9. NCSA HTTPd Development Team: The Common Gateway Interface. (March 1996) http://hoohoo.ncsa.uiuc.edu/cgi/

10. Hill, L., Dolin, R., Frew, J., Kemp, R., Larsgaard, M., Montello, D., Rae, M., Simpson, J.: User evaluation: summary of the methodologies and results for the Alexandria Digital Library, University of California at Santa Barbara. Proceedings of the 60th Annual Meeting of the American Society for Information Science, November 1-6, 1997, Washington, DC (1997) http://www.asis.org/annual-97/alexia.htm

11. Christian, E.: GILS: what is it? where's it going? D-Lib Magazine, (December 1996) http://www.dlib.org/dlib/december96/12christian.html

12. Weibel S., Miller, E.: Dublin Core metadata. (1997) http://purl.oclc.org/metadata/dublin_core

13. AOLserver. http://www.aolserver.com

14. Informix Dynamic Server – Universal Data Option. http://www.informix.com

15. MapInfo SpatialWare. http://www.mapinfo.com/spatialware/

A Framework for the Encapsulation of Value-Added Services in Digital Objects

Manolis Marazakis, Dimitris Papadakis, and Stavros A. Papadakis

Department of Computer Science, University of Crete
and
Institute of Computer Science, FORTH,
PO Box 1385, GR 71110 Heraklion, Greece.
e-mail: {maraz,dimpapa,spapad}@ics.forth.gr
WWW: http://www.ics.forth.gr/pleiades/projects/Aurora

Abstract. Container technology enables the encapsulation of information content together with rules and controls specifying the types of content usage permitted and the consequences of usage, such as triggering of report generation and payment. Containers have been proposed as a mechanism for securing intellectual property rights. This paper outlines other possible applications of container technology, including support for compound documents that incorporate active content, and automation of processes involving multi-party peer-to-peer interactions for the purposes of collaboration and commerce. Such value-added services are of particular interest in the context of digital libraries aiming to provide functionality extending beyond that of a simple repository of electronic documents. This paper presents the design of a container framework in the context of an architecture for network-centric applications.

1 Introduction

In the context of digital library systems and electronic documents, it has been demonstrated that container technology enables the encapsulation of information content together with rules and controls specifying the types of content usage permitted, as well as the consequences of usage (such as payment and report generation). There are proposals for using containers as a mechanism for securing intellectual property rights. This paper describes other possible applications of container technology, including support for compound documents that incorporate active content, and automation of processes involving multi-party peer-to-peer interactions for the purposes of collaboration and commerce. Such value-added services are of particular interest in the context of digital libraries aiming to provide functionality extending beyond that of a simple repository of electronic documents. Recent developments in software component frameworks contribute towards such extended functionality. With the emergence of a new generation of component-based software, such as **JavaBeans** [9], there are now powerful programming environments for building components, basic building-block components for building component ensembles, and component-based applications to address specific business requirements. Components can be combined in a variety of ways, resulting in a high degree of productivity for developers and users. A particularly important aspect is that visual application builders and scripting languages can be used for composition of components. In this setting, extensible containers become essential for managing and deploying components.

This paper presents our design for an extensible container that supports embedding of information content and executable software components, as well as support for composition of components in a distributed run-time environment. The overall aim, in the context of our ongoing work towards developing the *Aurora* architecture for network-centric applications [14], is to provide a container framework as the basis for implementing *work sessions* that combine the services of multiple autonomous providers. We focus mainly on the issue of support for highly customizable collaborative work, using configurable components.

Containers in the *Aurora* architecture encapsulate software components together with one or more information content modules, and related metadata enabling *introspection*, in other words dynamic discovery and inquiry of the container's capabilities and information content. Containers provide a framework for constructing, managing, and deploying compound documents, with the additional provision of support for active behavior. Such *active compound documents* enable several value-added services for digital objects in a digital library setting. Moreover, they provide the basis for a work session framework, by allowing external entities (such as a session manager) to establish networks of related containers in order to enact desired flows of data and events. This *service flow* paradigm is essential in the unified treatment of diverse applications.

The remainder of this paper is organized as follows. Section 2 presents our container framework design, and describes aspects of a prototype implementation. Section 3 considers applications of the container framework in providing support for value-added services for digital objects encapsulated in containers. Such objects may represent information content, as well as complete applications and computational services. Section 4 reviews related work, so as to put the presented work in perspective. Finally, Section 5 concludes the paper, and provides an outlook on the integration of technologies and services that is the overall aim of our research.

2   The Aurora Container Framework

A *component* is a software module, encapsulating application code, that can be combined with other components and a *script* to produce a a custom application environment [16]. Components execute within *containers*, which provide the run-time environment for one or more components and a range of standard management and control services for these components. A *component model* defines the guidelines that developers must adhere to, in the form of standard interfaces that enable other active components or applications to invoke its functions and access its data. Moreover, a component model defines the customizable properties exposed by components, allowing a component to be adapted to specific application requirements. Component-based application development involves selecting appropriate components and assembling them into a configuration that supports the functions required for an application.

This section is organized as follows. Section 2.1 describes the structure of containers in the *Aurora* architecture, outlining aspects of a prototype implementation. Sections 2.2 and 2.3 describe, respectively, the *uniform* management and the request control interfaces exported by *Aurora* containers. An important feature is the ability to associate metadata with the information content or services encapsulated within containers. This is discussed in Section 2.4. The uniform management interface provides operations for specifying, inspecting, and manipulating such metadata. The issue of metadata encapsulation within containers becomes particularly important in the face of recent developments related to the XML metalanguage [2], discussed in Section 2.5.

2.1 Container Structure

In the *Aurora* architecture, a *container* is an extensible shell combining application components with application-independent interfaces that support monitoring, control, and request management. The application-specific code in a container can be a front-end to information content also encapsulated in the container. It can also be a software component implementing an application function, or it can be a *wrapper* that provides a well-known interface to the services exported by a remote information resource, while hiding system-specific details of interaction. This provides the basis for uniform access to information content and services made available by diverse and autonomous providers. When a client activates a component, the container automatically allocates a thread, initiates the component's execution, and mediates all monitoring and control operations involving the component, through its uniform mangement interface. Moreover, the container mediates all interactions between the component and external entities, through its uniform request management interface.

While a software component (encapsulated in a container) remains active, it can retrieve data from an *input port* and forward data to an *output port*. Input and output are in the form of *streams*, which represent a flow of data as well as operation (action) invocations from a producer task to one or more consumer tasks. This functionality enables the combination of multiple containers in the realization of work sessions involving flows of events and data among distributed components. *Aurora* containers export a uniform *request management interface*, which enables participation in work sessions, under the supervision of a session management and monitoring service, presented in [14]. Thus, containers are the building blocks for building "bundles" of information content and active software components, as well as the building blocks for complex work sessions. Figure 1 shows the internal structure of a container.

Each container includes instrumentation for monitoring, control, and event detection and notification, which in turn is supported by instrumentation within encapsulated components. Instrumentation within components is required for

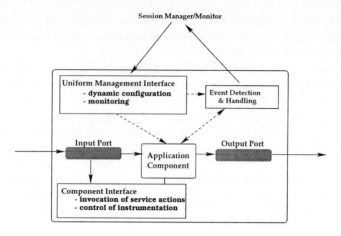

Fig. 1. Structure of *Aurora* Container.

exposing certain aspects of a component's internal state. As a minimum requirement to support composition of services using Event-Condition-Action rules [7] (expressed using the HERMES scripting language [14, 17]), each component must generate event notifications when it is activated (START event) and when it terminates either successfully (DONE event) or due to an exception (FAIL event). Optionally, a component can provide notification of the beginning and end of *phases* during its execution. The definition of phases is application-dependent, and may be nested. Notification about the beginning and end of phases may be taken into account in the specification of work sessions using the HERMES scripting language. Another important point is that upon beginning a new phase, a container may be instructed to reset a component's original communication channels settings, and, furthermore, load dynamically a new application component. These functions can be invoked via the uniform management interface exported by containers (see Section 2.2). Thus, phase transitions allow us to model run-time adaptation, which is essential for supporting dynamic and adaptive work sessions. Moreover, phase transitions allow the developer of an application component to selectively expose aspects of a component's execution flow and associated state, thus enabling detailed monitoring.

2.2 Uniform Management Interface

The *uniform* management interface of containers in the *Aurora* architecture, presented in Figure 2, supports configuration operations such as loading and unloading software components to be encapsulated in the container, starting and stopping the execution of components, enabling and disabling monitoring instrumentation, retrieving status information, and manipulating the communication channel settings for the container. The communication infrastructure of *Aurora* supports, apart from the standard request/reply mode of communication, a *publish/subscribe* mode [19]. Receivers need not be aware of who produces their data objects, and producers need not be aware of who receives their data objects. This supports flexible binding between producers and receivers, and, moreover, supports adaptation to changes that occur at run-time, as (unlike the standard request/reply mode of communication) changes of bindings only requires that receivers modify their "subscriptions". The input and output port objects within a container encapsulate the details of communication channel management. This functionality enables *external control* of containers in a man-

```
interface Container {
ErrCode LoadComponent(in string name,
            in sequence<AttrValuePair> attrs, out ComponentID cid);
ErrCode UnloadComponent(in ComponentID cid);
ErrCode StartComponent(in ComponentID cid,
        in sequence<AttrValuePair> attrs);
ErrCode StopComponent(in ComponentID cid);
ErrCode SuspendComponent(in ComponentID cid);
ErrCode ResumeComponent(in ComponentID cid,
        in sequence<AttrValuePair> attrs);
ErrCode QueryStatus(in ComponentID cid, out ComponentStatus status);
ErrCode SetMetadata(in ComponentID cid, in sequence<AttrDescr> attrs);
ErrCode QueryMetadata(in ComponentID cid, out sequence<AttrDescr> attrs);
ErrCode InitInstrumention(in ComponentID cid,
        in sequence<AttrValuePair> attrs);
ErrCode EnableInstrumention(in ComponentID cid,
        in sequence<AttrValuePair> attrs);
ErrCode DisableInstrumention(in ComponentID cid);
ErrCode ListStateVars(in ComponentID cid, out sequence<AttrDescr> vars);
ErrCode ListControlOps(in ComponentID cid, out sequence <OpDescr> ops);
ErrCode RetrieveState(in ComponentID cid, in sequence<AttrDescr> attrs,
        out sequence<AttrValuePair> state);
ErrCode SetState(in ComponentID cid, in sequence<AttrValuePair> state);
ErrCode EstablishChannel(in ComponentID src, in string subject,
        in ComponentID dest, out ChannelID chid);
ErrCode DestroyChannel(in ChannelID chid);
};
```

Fig. 2. *Aurora* Container: Uniform Management Interface.

ner that is independent of the application context in which the container is used. Another important aspect is that the application-specific code in a container can be dynamically loaded. This feature allows a container to access a resource by dynamically loading the resource's access interface. An example of such an interface is a *wrapper* that allows access to the functions provided by a legacy information system. This allows extending the functionality of a container on-demand.

Software components encapsulated in a container are expected to provide instrumentation for monitoring and control purposes. The management interface of containers provides operations for inquiring components as to what state variables and measurements they export, and what control operations they support, as well as operations to enable or disable instrumentation, and retrieve state variables and measurements. The uniform management interface enables external control of *Aurora* containers in a manner that is independent of the work session context. It is used by the *Aurora* session manager for configuration, and dynamic re-configuration, of the network of components required for a work session. It is also used by the *Aurora* monitor to control the instrumentation within application components and to retrieve, and possibly modify, the state variables made available for inspection and manipulation by these components. This is a form of *introspection*, relying again on the provision of metadata describing the exported state variable and control operations supported by the software component encapsulated within a container.

2.3   Uniform Request Management Interface

Figure 3 defines the uniform request management interface exported by containers, which allows them to perform work and interact with each other and the *Aurora* session manager in the context of a work session. It includes methods for issuing and manipulating *asynchronous* requests to other containers, as well as methods for other containers to signal the completion (successful or unsuccessful) of a previously issued request. A container can begin, abort, suspend, or resume a request. Requests are identified by *persistent* identifiers of type `RequestID`. A container (or an external entity such as the monitor) can inquire about a pending request (using the `QueryRequestStatus` method). In most of the methods of this interface, *state* related to a request is passed as an argument or returned as a result, in the form of a sequence of attribute-value pairs.

The `BeginRequest` method requires as arguments the name of the service to be invoked, a list of attribute-value pairs describing the arguments to be passed to the service, along with the identifiers for the work session and the task within the session that invokes the services. This method is *generic*, in other words the container's request management interface hides all details of how this request is to be serviced. Therefore, the *Aurora* session manager is able to manage the manage the flow of requests through this interface, without imposing any restrictions on service providers, apart from the requirement that their (proprietary) application components are registered with the *Aurora* directory service, so that the implementation of requests (through the `BeginRequest` method) is made possible.

For example (see also [14]), for a CORBA-based service the directory entry must provide an *object reference* and a specification of the input and output parameters, so that a request can be issued using the Dynamic Invocation Interface (DII). For a Web-based service that receives HTML forms to produce result HTML documents, the directory entry must define the variables embedded in the form, as well as instructions on how to extract result values from the document

```
interface TaskComponent {
ErrCode BeginRequest(in string name, in SessionID sid, in TaskID tid,
          in sequence<AttrValuePair> args, out RequestID rid);
ErrCode AbortRequest(in RequestID rid);
ErrCode SuspendRequest(in RequestID rid);
ErrCode ResumeRequest(in RequestID rid,
          in sequence<AttrValuePair> state);
ErrCode CompletedRequest(in RequestID rid,
          in sequence<AttrValuePair> state);
ErrCode AbortedRequest(in RequestID rid,
          in sequence<AttrValuePair> state);
ErrCode WaitRequest(in RequestID rid,
          out sequence<AttrValuePair> state);
ErrCode RefuseRequest(in RequestID rid);
ErrCode AcceptRequest(in RequestID rid);
ErrCode QueryRequestStatus(in RequestID rid,
          out sequence<AttrValuePair> status);
ErrCode ListRequests(in SessionID sid, out sequence<RequestID> reqs);
ErrCode GetRequest(in SessionID sid, in TaskID tid,
          out sequence<RequestID> reqs);
ErrCode GetRequestByAttributes(in SessionID sid,
          in sequence<AttrValuePair> attrs, out sequence<RequestID> reqs);
};
```

Fig. 3. *Aurora* Container: Uniform Request Management Interface.

returned by the service. Alternatively, a directory entry for a service may specify that a *wrapper* component, exporting a well-defined interface, is to be instantiated within a container. In all cases, the request management interface supported by *Aurora* containers mediates all the request and response messages targeted at a service, and a specialized component is instantiated within the container to handle the details of interacting with the target service. For a CORBA-based service, this specialized component would be responsible for issuing request, via DII, and collecting the results. For a Web-based service, a specialized component would construct an appropriate HTML form, submit it to the service, collect the resulting HTML page, and extract all result values. For service providers that export wrappers, the appropriate component would be instantiated within a container.

Since requests are asynchronous, the WaitRequest is provided to allow a component issuing a request to block waiting for a response. Another option to handle asynchronous requests is to have the component that served a request invoke a "callback" method on the component that issued the request, upon terminating the requested processing, either successfully or unsuccessfully (methods CompletedRequest and AbortedRequest, respectively). In a sense, these callback methods, together with the BeginRequest method, allow *interception* of all incoming requests and responses targeted to a service. These methods depend on the functionality of the communication ports of containers, and provide a mechanism for monitoring and enforcing terms, conditions and guarantees, as discussed in Section 3.4.

An important aspect of the request management interface of containers is that a container can browse (using method `ListRequests`) or perform searches over the pending requests in its work-list (using the methods `GetRequest` and `GetRequestByAttributes`). This provides flexibility in selecting among pending requests, and enables *late binding* of resources to tasks. A consequence of late binding is that the actual flow of control and data does not have to be fully (and statically) specified during the definition of the work session. Participants, particularly humans, are allowed to *refine* the specification by decomposing the request into further requests to other service providers. The issuer of the original request is not necessarily informed about this decomposition. A participant must explicitly accept or refuse a request (methods `AcceptRequest` and `RefuseRequest`, respectively).

2.4   Encapsulation of Metadata

Aurora is based on a two-level metadata framework, rather than assuming a single metadata standard, which defines only generic concepts (resources, events, tasks [14, 17]). This framework allows application developers and providers of information content and services to define extensible sets of application domain-specific attribute-value pairs for their offerings. The generic attribute-value format can capture application-specific details of interacting with a service that is accessible via a container.

The ability to encapsulate metadata makes containers *self-descriptive*, enabling us to design a common middleware to host active containers, in the context of work sessions [14, 17]. The uniform management interface of containers provides the operation `QueryMetadata` to inspect the metadata associated with the encapsulated information content and services. Currently, this metadata is simply a list of *attribute descriptors*, that provide, for each attribute associated with the software component encapsulated in the container, a triplet consisting of the attribute name, value type, and a text description of the attribute's semantics. The latter is intended for providing guidance to clients wishing to use the encapsulated component. Attributes may range from bibliographic and copyright information in the case of components that embody digital information content, to parameters required for accessing information and computational services. We have also started to work towards integrating XML-based metadata [2] within containers. This will enable a representation of the metadata describing a container's content (which can be an information object and/or an active software component) as a *structured document*, that can be validated and manipulated using standard-based tools. Section 2.5 presents this extension in detail.

Aurora provides a repository service for managing the metadata that enables interoperation and management of components. This repository provides a *directory* that allows providers to publish their services and resources, users and applications to locate components that satisfy their requirements, and a *binding service* for dynamic binding of resources to tasks. This is essential for dynamic environments, with evolving user needs and service offers, and enables an *open market* for service providers. The repository [14] is based on the CORBA Trader Service [3], making use of the trader's functionality to establish a federated network of autonomous cooperating directories of information related to available services. This information includes metadata for describing access methods, access control restrictions, and the service's expected behavior in terms of exception handling and performance. Once a component has been selected from the directory, via the binding service, a container is instantiated to encapsulate the component. The `SetMetadata` operation of the container's management interface enables the incorporation of a list of *attribute descriptors* within the container. At run-time, the operations `ListStateVariables` and `ListControlOperations` enable external entities (such as a service-level monitoring system) to inquire which state variables, that are exported by encapsulated components, can be inspected and manipulated at run-time.

2.5   Combining XML and Containers

The XML (eXtensible Markup Language) metalanguage [2] is a simplified subset of SGML designed to describe the markup of documents. It provides a standardized text format for describing structured data for use by WWW applications. XML documents are composed of *entities*, which are storage units containing text and/or binary data. Character streams form both a document's data and markup. *Markup*, in the form of tags, describes a document's layout and structure. Thus, XML-encoded data is self-describing. A document may optionally be associated with a *Document Type Definition* (DTD) that defines structuring rules, allowing validation of the data. A *well-formed* XML document is unambiguous, allowing standard browsing and editing tools to read the tags and construct a parse tree representing its hierarchical structure, without requiring the corresponding DTD.

Extremely diverse structured data can be encoded using standard tag sets (markup), and exchanged either between applications and clients that need to display and manipulate it, or between application servers for the purposes of automated processing [11, 10, 1]. Examples of data that can be exchanged via XML-encoded documents include purchase orders, invoices, product catalogs, sets of records retrieved from database systems, results from scientific experiments, bibliographic catalogs, and reports with embedded annotations. Since XML is a text-based format, it can be delivered via the HTTP protocol. Furthermore, XML encoding, unlike HTML, separates presentation/rendering issues from actual data content, allowing for example multiple views to be generated from the same data. Finally, the Document Object Model [30] provides a platform- and language-neutral interface allowing programs and scripts to dynamically access and update the content, structure and style of documents.

We have started work towards integrating XML-encoded metadata in our architecture. At the infrastructure level, an XML document can encapsulate metadata related to *Aurora* containers, and provide a front-end for use by both human users (mainly application developers) and programs (in particular, the *Aurora* session manager and monitor). In this approach, a structured document, that can be visualized and manipulated using standard tools, would incorporate information about the information content and software components encapsulated within the container, including information required for invocation of functions, state inspection and control. The uniform management interface of the container, via a variation of the currently supported `QueryMetadata` method, would allow a client to retrieve the entire XML document describing the container and its contents, or, more selectively, specific (named) portions of it.

In the following example, the *monitor* service and an *application developer* retrieve an XML document describing the container and its contents, each viewing the information provided in different ways. The *monitor* service acquires specific portions of the XML document in order to determine the monitoring methods exported by the component within the container. Subsequently the *monitor* service initiates one of these methods. On the other hand, the *application developer* is presented, using standard programs, with all the information carried by the XML document. Viewing this information, the *application developer* may decide to change a number of run-time parameters, in which case he explicitly feeds new values and initiates the update procedure.

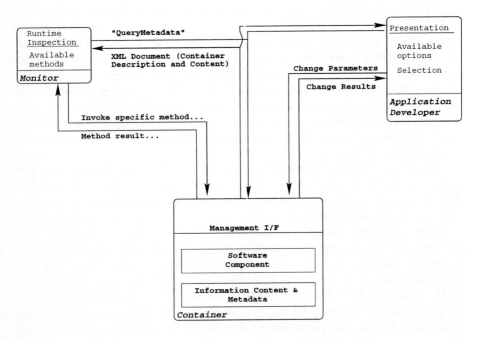

Fig. 4. XML-based container description and example usage.

At the application level, an XML document can serve as the front-end for composite services, which are supported by the *Aurora* infrastructure. In this setting, a service provider publishes a structured document describing its offerings, and through this abstraction clients can invoke composite services. The description should cover the functionality available, as well as all related terms, conditions, and guarantees. By interpreting this description, it is possible to make use of the infrastructure services. Specifically, a client could invoke a composite service via appropriate user interface abstractions, by selecting either a predefined script defining the the run-time configuration required for implementing the service or, in a more interactive setting, by dynamically defining a script for execution. Passing this script to the session manager of *Aurora* activates the process of determining the resources to be used (dynamic binding), and the process of establishing a network of containers that encapsulate the corresponding software components. Optionally, instrumentation within the components can be enabled, via the container uniform management interface, so as to allow on-line monitoring. Thus, the introduction of a structured document as interface for a composite service provides leverage in achieving on-demand configuration of components for the purposes of implementing an instance of the service. Moreover, a structured document provides an powerful interaction metaphor, particularly well-suited for collaborative applications.

3 Value-Added Services for Digital Objects

In this section, we describe examples of value-added services for digital information objects that are enabled by container technology. In our view [14, 17] several important classes of large-scale distributed applications, such as digital library systems, electronic commerce environments and scientific collaborative work environments, share key requirements with emphasis on utilizing widely distributed application components and information resources that are made available by autonomous providers. The *Aurora* architecture [14] aims for a unified treatment of the problem of supporting network-centric applications via a set of common middleware services that enable dynamic configuration and composition. The container framework presented in this paper is to serve as the basic building block for such applications, providing uniform interfaces for monitoring, control, and request management.

Section 3.1 demonstrates how container technology can be applied in producing compound documents that combine information content together with executable code to introduce active behavior. Section 3.2 focuses on the problem of electronic commerce transactions involving packages that incorporate multiple products/services offered by autonomous providers. Section 3.3 outlines an application of container technology in scientific workflow [26, 29]. These examples illustrate a long-term research goal of integrating work support technologies, such as information management, computer-supported collaborative work and workflow automation (see also [24]). From this perspective, the development of an open infrastructure, such as *Aurora*, enabling the combination of services offered by autonomous providers is seen as a major step towards realising an *information economy*, where software objects that encapsulate information content and business-oriented services play the role of goods, and agents representing clients and content/service providers play the role of trading partners. Section 3.4 pro-

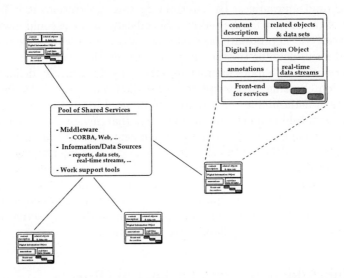

Fig. 5. Active Compound Documents in a Collaborative Work Session.

poses an application of containers as a means to not only enforce terms and conditions for access to encapsulated information content, but also to be able to provide certain service-level guarantees for encapsulated services.

3.1 Active Compound Documents

A container can encapsulate multiple modules of information content, together with a software component that mediates access to this content, optionally providing enhanced access services. Thus, a container supports a framework of *active compound documents*. A compound document can incorporate, apart from its main information content, background material to provide additional insight to the document's recipients, as well as capabilities for interaction with data and tools related with the document. Structured documents provide an powerful interaction metaphor, particularly well-suited for collaborative applications.

Containers enable *bundling* diverse information content and services, in the form of digital objects, and, by providing a management and manipulation interface, facilitate management and interaction. For example, as shown in Figure 5, using this functionality in a scientific collaboration scenario, a scientist would be able to publish a report containing an analysis of experimental data, and provide others with the ability to retrieve the data sets used in his analysis, as well as use the models (simulators or analytical tools) that he used. Moreover, others could add comments and other annotations to the report. A further capability would be to allow recipients of the report to receive updates, as well as notifications about the availability of related material. This is enabled by the publish/subscribe communication mode supported by containers, which allows "subscribers" to events related to updates and availability of new material to receive notifications without having to perform explicit polling.

3.2 Electronic Commerce

Realising complex commerce transactions among multiple trading parties involves a complex sequence of interdependent actions, spanning over a long period of time, where each action may involve interactions with information systems as well as humans. For electronic commerce to reach its full potential, it is necessary to provide an open infrastructure that supports combining functional modules developed and administered by autonomous providers. Current electronic com-

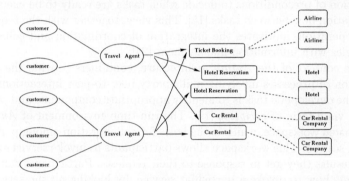

Fig. 6. An Electronic Commerce Scenario Involving Packages of Products/Services.

merce systems do not support the notion of a complex product/service package consisting of items from multiple providers. They are limited to commerce transactions over items in a single catalog or in an electronic mall that hosts multiple stores. Realising complex commerce transactions among multiple providers involves a complex sequence of actions, with interdependencies, that span over a long period of time, each action involving interactions with information systems and personnel.

As a specific example, a travel agent can arrange a complete travel package for a customer that includes flight tickets, arrangement of hotel accommodation, as well as other additional services (such as car rental and guided tours). There may be multiple offers for each negotiated item in the travel package. The customer would prefer to be contacted only when it is necessary to select among alternative arrangements, confirm reservations and provide the necessary charging information. It is also important to be able to provide notifications about the progress of customer requests. Figure 6 illustrates this commerce scenario. A scenario of this type can be implemented using the container framework presented in this paper, by encapsulating components that implement interfaces to information systems providing the required business functions (such as ticket booking). The HERMES scripting language can be used to express the required event-driven flow. The *Aurora* work session manager is responsible for interpreting the script specification in order to establish a network of cooperating components that implement the required flow of data and function invocations.

3.3 Work Sessions in Scientific Experiments

The management of work sessions involving the collection, manipulation, and management of data sets which can be generated from a large number and variety of sources, poses major challenges for current work support technologies, such as information management, computer-supported collaborative work, and workflow automation. The main objective is not necessarily to automate all tasks of the process, but rather to automate the tracking of states of tasks and to allow specification of preconditions to decide when tasks are ready to be executed and of information flow between tasks [15]. This view, together with the requirement for interoperation, motivates the integration of coordination and collaboration technologies with information management [24].

In the context of the *Aurora* architecture, containers provide the basis for automation of processes involving multi-party peer-to-peer interactions. In this setting, the developer's task is to identify appropriate components and plug them together, via a form of *scripting* [16]. The run-time environment of *Aurora* provides a shared workspace, which is the basis for collaboration among participants in a work session. This workspace allows participants to invoke services and publish the results they get in response to their requests. Participants can discover at run-time how to invoke a particular service, by looking up the service's registration entry in the directory maintained by the run-time environment. The publish/subscribe communication mode allows all "subscribers" to receive the results produced by a invoking a service. Moreover, specialized components may act as large-grain *caches* of data sets. In this case, these components become accessible by registering with the service directory and advertising their capability to provide access to data sets that have been *derived* by a sequence of manipulations on more primitive data sets.

Work sessions, leading to the realization of composite packages of information content and/services, are implemented by establishing networks of containers. Composition is made possible by interconnecting containers which encapsulate more primitive services. The uniform management interface of containers enables their inspection and external control in a manner that is independent of the work session context. Such networks of related containers can be inspected and manipulated at run-time, allowing for dynamic and adaptive modification of ongoing sessions.

3.4 Terms, Conditions, and Guarantees for Using Digital Objects

Realising an *information economy* requires mechanisms for monitoring and enforcing mutually binding terms and conditions between users and providers of information content and services, and a shift from asset management to relationship management [23]. In the *Aurora* framework, terms and conditions related to intellectual property rights for usage of information content can be combined with service-level guarantees. The metadata that can be incorporated in a container provides documentation of the terms, conditions and guarantees determined by providers of information material and services. This information can be inspected by users of containers at run-time, prior to actual usage of the encapsulated content and services. Moreover, generic enforcement mechanisms are under development [14]. In particular, the uniform request management interface of containers mediates all (asynchronous) requests arriving at the container's input port, as well as all response messages. Thus, all incoming and outgoing messages targeted at a component can be intercepted, thus providing a level of indirection necessary for performing authorization checks, logging, and any other pre-processing and post-processing actions required for enforcement of terms, conditions and guarantees.

Since a container can also host software components that implement application functions, in particular access to information and computational services, metadata can provide documentation of the expected behavior of services, in terms of exception handling behavior and expected performance. This introduces a form of *service-level agreement* [18], providing an abstraction of the expected behavior of services for individual clients or client classes. This contributes to making services more predictable, and in this sense more manageable, in the presence of inherently unreliable environments such as the Internet. It is important that the autonomy of service providers is not compromised, as a service provider is the only authority responsible for exporting an interface for use by clients and for establishing and enforcing service attributes such as reliability and performance guarantees. The *service-level agreement* abstraction hides implementation aspects, exporting only aspects related to the expected service level, together with information about how deviations from the promised behavior (such as exceptions and performance degradation) are to be handled.

4 Related Work

The notion of *contract* has begun to receive considerable attention in the context of rights management and access control [27, 22, 23], which are key issues as the interest in electronic commerce is growing [28]. Contacts provide a powerful framework for expressing and managing complex relationships between transaction participants. Container technology is the key element in InterTrust Technologies' InterTrust Commerce Platform [4]. The *DigiBox* secure container [25] enables the association of rules and controls (via cryptographic means) with information content, to specify the types of content usage permitted and the consequences of usage (such as payment and report generation). Containers are manipulated using a trusted rights protection application to make the protected content available according to its associated access control rules. Similar functionality is provided by IBM's *Cryptolope* container [8].

The multivalent document model presented in [21] is an attempt to support active and networked documents. A multivalent document is decomposed into *layers* of content, and functionality is provided by *behaviors*, which are dynamically-loaded program objects that manipulate the content. A behavior may communicate with specific layers and other behaviors in order to provide its functionality. Once built, a multivalent document can be extended by adding new layers and behaviors. This model provides a broad framework for documents that incorporate active behavior in response to user interactions, and [21] describes examples of its application, including an example of interaction with a remote service. The container framework design presented in this paper is focused on such functionality, aiming to provide a building block for network-centric applications. In our approach, containers encapsulate application components, information content and descriptive metadata, and export uniform interfaces for inspection and invocation.

An important issue for containers, especially in the context of digital library systems, is the encapsulation of metadata describing digital objects. Related work is reported in [6], which describes the Distributed Active Relationships model for representing data and metadata in digital library objects, as an extension of the Warwick Container Framework [12] which provides a unifying abstraction for handling metadata that follow diverse standards. This model explicitly expresses the relationships between networked resources and allows these relationships to be dynamically downloadable and executable. Containers are used for aggregating data sets into digital objects, with the ability to support relationships by referencing executable code that may enforce special semantics, as illustrated in a rights management scenario. This powerful abstraction has been taken into consideration in the design of *Aurora* containers. Enforcement of semantics is enabled by interception of request and response messages. Moreover, encapsulation of metadata is supported for the purposes of introspection, so that interested parties can discover at run-time what monitoring and control operations are exported by components, as well as what capabilities are offered by the components within a container.

Related research is also reported in [13], which presents FEDORA, a digital object and repository architecture designed to provide a reliable and secure means to store and access digital content. Digital objects in FEDORA are *content containers* having a structural kernel which encapsulates content as opaque byte stream packages and a behavior layer that may implement descriptive metadata as well as access functionality for the content packages. Through the structural kernel *disseminators* are used to provide a means to discover and invoke *content-specific* behavior to digital objects. Clients can discover, at run-time, the disseminators associated with a digital object as well as the methods supported by the disseminator. These methods mediate access to information content contained in the digital object. Access control is enforced by *access managers* which are activated when a disseminator is activated. Service requests targeted to the disseminator are intercepted by the access manager, which implements rights management policies. The *Aurora* container design provides introspection and interception mechanisms which can be used to implement the disseminator and access manager functionalities. The FEDORA design focuses on digital library requirements whereas the *Aurora* container design aims to provide a generic building block to be used in constructing applications by composing networks of co-operating components. The *Aurora* container design does not directly support the notion of content-type disseminations; however, it provides uniform interfaces for dynamic configuration, monitoring and control, and asynchronous request management.

We share the view presented in [5] that in an environment such as the Internet, the main integrity requirement is that the parties involved in an interaction respects *pair-wise legal agreements* with each other. Enforcing such agreements, in other words mutual respect of terms and conditions, between independent clients and providers is required for achieving meaningful business transactions, despite the limited authority of each participant. As discussed in Section 3.4, this is an essential aspect of an *information economy*, which is our long-term research goal.

5 Conclusions

This paper describes our design for a container framework that provides the following features:

- Encapsulation of self-descriptive metadata to support *introspection*, in other words allow on-line inspection of the information content and functionality that is encapsulated in the container
- Uniform monitoring and control interface to support dynamic configuration of components
- Uniform request management interface to support asynchronous requests.

The uniform interfaces for monitoring, control, and asynchronous request management are utilized by the *Aurora* work session management and monitoring infrastructure to implement composite services by combining components offered by autonomous providers. Containers provide basic building blocks for this *open* environment, addressing the problems of component configuration and on-line monitoring and control. Higher-level service in the *Aurora* architecture use these building blocks to implement applications as component configurations that support on-line inspection and manipulation [14].

As demonstrated in the previous sections, container technology is expected to play an increasingly important role as a building block for sophisticated digital library services. We consider a view of digital libraries that goes beyond that of a repository of on-line information, to provide support throughout all phases of work. As discussed in [20], users need to find, analyze, and understand information of widely diverse types. They need to re-organize the information to use it in multiple contexts, and to manipulate it in collaboration with others. This vision is incorporated in our ongoing research towards an integrated work support environment that can be seen as an *information economy*.

Towards this end, container technology contributes a framework for encapsulating value-added services in complex-structured documents, including support for active and dynamic content, as well as support for collaborative work and automated interactions with diverse services. Such capabilities broaden the scope of digital library services, and contribute towards establishing a comprehensive work coordination and collaboration environment. Our ongoing work on the *Aurora* architecture [14], which encompasses middleware services as well as demonstrator applications (see Section 3), aims to provide such a shared workspace, allowing participants to initiate work sessions and "publish" the results they get in response to their requests. Following the arguments of [24], we are working towards an open infrastructure supporting the integration of work support technologies, including information management, coordination, and collaboration, aiming for a unified treatment of diverse large-scale distributed applications.

Acknowldegements

The work presented in this paper has benefited from the advice and encouragement provided by Dr Christos Nikolaou, head of the Parallel and Distributed Systems Group (PLEIADES) of FORTH/ICS.

References

1. J. Bosak. "XML, Java, and the Future of the Web". *World Wide Web Journal*, 2(4), 1997.
2. T. Bray, J. Paoli, and C. M. Sperberg-McQueen. "Extensible Markup Language Recommendation (XML) 1.0", 1998. Available via WWW at URL http://www.w3.org/TR/1998/REC-xml.
3. "Trading Object Service Specification". In *CORBAservices: Common Object Services Specification*. Object Management Group, Framingham, Mass., 1996.
4. InterTrust Technologies Corp. "Securing the Content, Not the Wire, for Information Commerce", 1996. Available via WWW at URL http://www.intertrust.com.
5. A. Dan and F. Parr. "An Object Implementation of Network Centric Business Service Applications (NCBSAs): Conversational Service Transactions, Service Monitor and an Application Style". In *Proc. OOPSLA'97 Business Object Workshop*, 1997. Available via URL http://www.tiac.net/users/jsuth/oopsla97/.
6. R. Daniel and C. Lagoze. "Distributed Active Relationships in the Warwick Framework". In *Proc. IEEE Metadata Conference*, 1997.
7. U. Dayal, M. Hsu, and R. Ladin. "Organizing Long-Running Activities with Triggers and Transactions". In *Proceedings of the ACM SIGMOD Conference on Management of Data*, 1993.
8. H.M. Gladney and J.B. Lotspiech. "Safeguarding Digital Library Contents and Users: Assuring Convenient Security and Data Quality ". *D-Lib Magazine*, May 1997. Available via URL http://www.dlib.org.
9. JavaSoft. "JavaBeans API Specification (1.01)", 1997. Available via URL http://java.sun.com:80/beans/docs/spec.html.
10. R. Khare and A. Rifkin. "Capturing the State of Distributed Systems with XML". *World Wide Web Journal*, 2(4), 1997.

11. R. Khare and A. Rifkin. "XML: A Door to Automated Web Applications". *IEEE Internet Computing*, 1(4), 1997.

12. C. Lagoze, C.A. Lynch, and R. Daniel. "The Warwick Framework: A Container Architecture for Aggregating Sets of Metadata". Technical Report TR96-1593, Cornell Computer Science Department, 1996. Available via URL http://cs-tr.cs.cornell.edu:80/Dienst/UI/2.0/Describe/ncstrl.cornell/TR96-1593.

13. C. Lagoze and S. Payette. "An Infrastructure for Open-Architecture Digital Libraries". Technical Report TR98-1690, Cornell Computer Science Department, 1998. Available via URL http://cs-tr.cs.cornell.edu:80/Dienst/UI/1.0/Display/ncstrl.cornell/TR98-1690.

14. M. Marazakis, D. Papadakis, and C. Nikolaou. "The Aurora Architecture for Developing Network-Centric Applications by Dynamic Composition of Services". Technical Report TR 213, FORTH/ICS, 1997.

15. C. Mohan. "Recent Trends in Workflow Management Products, Standards and Research". In *Proc. NATO Advanced Institute (ASI) Workshop on Workflow Management Systems and Interoperability*, 1997. Available via URL http://www.almaden.ibm.com/cs/exotica.

16. O. Nierstrasz, D. Tsichritzis, V. deMey, and M. Stadelmann. "Object + Scripts = Applications". In D. Tsichritzis, editor, *Object Composition*. University of Geneva, 1991.

17. C. Nikolaou, M. Marazakis, D. Papadakis, Y. Yeorgiannakis, and J. Sairamesh. "Towards a Common Infrastructure to Support Large-Scale Distributed Applications". In *Proc. European Conference on Research and Advanced Technology for Digital Libraries*, 1997.

18. J. Noonan. "Automated Service Level Management and its Supporting Technologies". *Mainframe Journal*, October 1989.

19. B. Oki, M. Pfluegl, A. Siegel, and D. Skeen. "The Information Bus - An Architecture for Extensible Distributed Systems". In *Proc. ACM Symposium on Operating System Pronciples*, 1993.

20. A. Paepcke. "Digital Libraries: Searching is not Enough". *D-Lib Magazine*, May 1996. Available via URL http://www.dlib.org.

21. T.A. Phelps and R. Wilensky. "Toward Active, Extensible, Networked Documents: Multivalent Architecture and Applications". In *Proc. ACM Int'l Conf. on Digital Libraries*, 1996.

22. M. Roscheisen and T. Winograd. "The FIRM Framework for Interoperable Rights Management: Defining a Rights Management Service Layer for the Internet". In *Forum on Technology-based Intellectual Property Management*, 1997. Available via URL http://pcd.stanford.edu/rmr/commpacts.html.

23. M. Roscheisen and Terry Winograd. "A Network-Centric Design for Relationship-based Security and Access Control". *Journal of Computer Security*, 1997. Special Issue on Security in the World-Wide Web.

24. A. Sheth. "From Contemporary Workflow Process Automation to Adaptive and Dynamic Work Activity Coordination and Collaboration". In *Proc. Workshop on Workflow Management in Scientific and Engineering Applications*, 1997.

25. O. Sibert, D. Bernstein, and D. Van Wie. "The DigiBox: A Self-Protecting Container for Information Commerce". In *Proc. 1st USENIX workshop on Electronic Commerce*, 1995.

26. M.P. Singh and M.A. Vouk. "Scientific Workflows: Scientific Workflow Meets Transactional Workflow". In *Proc. NSF Workshop on Workflow and Process Automation in Information Systems: State of the Art and Future Directions*, 1996.

27. M. Stefik and J. Lavendel. "Libraries and Digital Property Rights". In *Proc. European Conference on Advanced Technologies for Digital Libraries*, 1997.
28. N. Szabo. "Formalizing and Securing Relationships on Public Networks". *First Monday*, 2(9), 1997. Available via URL http://www.firstmonday.dk/.
29. J. Wainer, M. Weske, G. Vossen, and C.B. Medeiros. "Scientific Workflow Systems". In *Proc. NSF Workshop on Workflow and Process Automation in Information Systems: State of the Art and Future Directions*, 1996.
30. L. Wood, J. Sorensen, S. Byrne, R.S. Sutor, V. Apparao, S. Isaacs, G. Nicol, and M. Champion. "Document Object Model Specification (DOM) 1.0", 1998. W3C Working Draft. Available via WWW at URL http://www.w3.org/TR/WD-DOM.

A Management Architecture for Measuring and Monitoring the Behavior of Digital Libraries

Sarantos Kapidakis[1], Sotirios Terzis[2], and Jakka Sairamesh[3]

[1] Institute of Computer Science, FORTH,
Heraklion, Crete, Greece, GR 71110
sarantos@ics.forth.gr
[2] DSG, Computer Science Department
Trinity College, University of Dublin Dublin 2, Ireland
Sotirios.Terzis@cs.tcd.ie
[3] IBM T. J. Watson Research Center
30 Sawmill, Hawthorne NewYork, 10532, USA
jramesh@watson.ibm.com

Abstract. In this paper, we investigate issues of performance management in Digital Libraries. We defined a management architecture for measuring and monitoring the behavior of digital libraries as they operate, so that we can make performance conclusions using real life digital library load. Our architecture can be easily applied on any digital library system, introducing minimal overhead to digital library performance, and requiring minimal changes to the digital library code. We implemented this architecture over a testbed of Dienst servers using real data and workload. We defined the relevant parameters for investigating the performance of the servers and we made visualization tools to study the performance results. We also demonstrated how the performance results can be used by the digital library itself, to produce advanced unattended operations, like load balancing and dynamic timeout adaptation.

1 Introduction

Digital Libraries[4] emerged to impose order in the increasing chaos of available system architectures and information formats. They are architectures for the provision of information access and management services for a controlled repository of various quality information objects such as text, audio, video, and image. Currently, there are a lot of research groups around the world investigating Digital Libraries and their associated issues [4, 9, 10, 23, 31, 17]. Their wide spread and increased popularity influences the design of future information systems.

Digital Library systems are characterized by the huge volume of information they store (e.g. the Alexandria system [7] stores gigabytes of information as satellite images and maps), by the wide distribution of their nodes (e.g. the NCSTRL-Dienst [11] system has more than 100 nodes in over 15 countries covering most of the U.S. and Europe) and by the fact that they often integrate existing collections of information over the *World Wide Web* (e.g. the Infobus [18] that connects systems like Altavista, the Alexandra system [7] and the university of Michigan digital library system [2]). These characteristics make those systems especially changeable and have profound influence on their performance. As a result, mechanisms for the dynamic adaptation of the system to the constantly changing operation environment are required.

In the development of Digital Library systems various models have been deployed. For example, the Stanford's [18] view of digital libraries is as a shared information bus that connects various information sources. On the other hand, the Michigan's [2] view is of a collection of collaborating agents. The common denominator in all these different views is that a digital library system consists of a number of servers, spread over the Internet, that interact with each in order to service user requests. In processing a request a server might invoke a number of external programs. All the communication between the servers is done with the use of the World Wide Web's protocol, *HTTP*. This is the system model for our investigation.

Our primary goal is to define an architecture for monitoring and measuring the performance of Digital Libraries. This architecture should be based on the model presented above and should allow us to monitor system's behavior as it operates, since it will be the base for the dynamic behavior adaptation mechanisms, such as load balancing, dynamic timeout adaptation and support for quality of service searching and retrieval [24, 25]. A secondary but equally important goal is that the monitoring architecture should be easy to apply in any Digital Library system and should be easily acceptable by the users. This means that the architecture should (a) impose minimal overhead to the system's performance and (b) require minimal changes to the system's code.

Considerable work has been done in the area of performance management and monitoring in distributed systems [26, 8, 20, 13, 22, 16]. Besides this research work, a series of commercial products for distributed systems performance management is also available [1, 15, 21, 19, 3]. Of particular interest in our case is the work in on-line performance monitor [26], since our goal is to design a performance monitor that (a) will not interfere in the system's operation (external monitor) and (b) will monitor the system in operation. Additionally, performance monitors deploy various semantic models on their operation according to [8] and can be classified based on that as *program profiling* (e.g. Parasight [1]), *event based* (e.g. Pablo [20]), *information modelling based* (e.g. the performance monitor described by Snodgrass in [22]). In our case the most appropriate approach seems to be the *event based* since according to our system model the actions of interest are component invocations and message exchange. Although past research work addressed most of the main issues in performance management, the use of a current commercial product is not encouraging because they (a) are proprietary and (b) are limited only to some hardware and software platforms. Also, the development of the Universal Measurement Architecture *UMA* [29], an X/Open standard (implementation available by Amdahl [30]), although it deals with the problem of hardware and software incompatibilities, does not deal with the problem of proprietary technology.

We developed a performance management architecture for the monitoring and measuring of digital libraries. We implemented this architecture over a testbed of Dienst servers using NCSTRL data. We defined the relevant parameters for investigating the performance of the servers (total response time, local/remote service time, etc). Besides them, performance parameters for the operating system overheads and the WWW interface time were also defined. We conducted a performance study on our testbed using some special visualisation tools that we also implemented. The performance study was based on the tracking of request execution by monitoring the system and led to the proposal of some modifications on the design and implementation of the Dienst system. In order to demonstrate how the performance architecture can be the base for dynamic behavior adaptation we designed and implemented some demonstrating request (load) balancing strategies for distributed searching over a network of servers. According to these strategies a server, using local observations, can forward a request to the *least loaded* (faster) server from the pool of those where the requested information is available (replicated). We also built a load balancing testbed for experimentation, to demonstrate the extensibility of our architecture. Finally, we investigated other application of our architecture like mechanisms for dynamic timeout adaptation during distributed searching.

In section 2 we present our performance analysis and architecture and in section 3 we discuss interesting applications of performance monitoring and supporting tools. In section 4 we describe the Dienst system and in section 5 we describe the analysis of the Dienst operation, and explain how we did performance monitoring on Dienst. In section 6 we present the results from using our implementation, in section 7 we present our extensions to Dienst, as a consequence of the performance monitoring, and we conclude in section 8.

2 Performance analysis and architecture

In this section, we discuss the management architecture that we designed. We implemented and used this testbed for investigating mechanisms for distributed performance monitoring and demonstrating applications like load balancing requests in order to improve search response time.

We defined the minimum server functionality to support a management architecture for monitoring and measuring. We developed a simple user interface (html based) to monitor the performance variables. We also developed a new Java based user interface, which can selectively display graphically some of the performance variables as they change in real-time (i.e. new requests are coming).

We developed a simple client-server architecture model for performance management of the digital library. This model is based on ideas from SNMP based performance management in networks and distributed systems. We developed mechanisms for measuring the delays in the various components of the digital library system. We have broken down the performance monitoring architecture into five main elements:

- We define and name the performance parameters (of various software modules and components) for the various tasks performed by the server when servicing a user request. Each performance monitor keeps a list of well-defined parameters, which it updates based on every request it processes.
- We measure and store the performance parameters, by developing a Measurement System for updating and storage. We developed mechanisms to measure the variables for every request generated. A measurement process (daemon) updates the performance variables and stores their current values, averages and variances in a database.
- We define a protocol to retrieve the performance parameters. The parameter database is managed by a process, called database manager process (DMP), which returns the variables and values in the database.
- We use tools to visualize the performance parameters.
- We, optionally, extend the digital library protocol, to retrieve and report the performance parameters. We developed a simple message protocol to monitor and debug the server. The new protocol consists of a simple addition to the current server protocol.

Only the first and last steps are digital library specific and must be designed and implemented differently for each system. All others do not need to change!

A performance variable is associated with each task (or function) that we wish to measure. For example, we measure the time spent by a server while searching its local database.

In order to define the performance parameters, we first analyze the digital library system to find and clearly define all procedures of interest, which we call *components*. Although different components may overlap, we must specifically locate their starting and ending times. Figure 1 indicates a possible relation for some components and their starting and ending times.

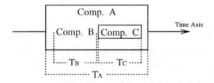

Fig. 1. Relation of example components $(T_A > T_B + T_C)$

The performance monitor captures the time spent by the server while performing the various tasks of a user request. The entry and exit time of components are recorded, as illustrated in Figure 2.

Each server sends two messages to the performance monitor: the first message when the task begins, and the second just before it finishes. This is done for every task we measure. The messages are sent through a socket to the performance monitor. *These are the only changes that are needed on the server!* This way, the changes to the code of the digital library are minimal, and do not compromise

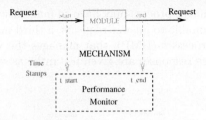

Fig. 2. Messages passed by components, to the performance monitor

its functionality and complexity. Additionally, the digital library performs as minimal additional work as possible, and does not sacrifice its performance, as only some extra messages are sent, and separate processes take care of the rest of the procedure. Finally, the digital library does not depend on the existence or the operation of the performance monitor.

In our architecture, the performance monitor can accept many connections, for retrieving performance parameters of the digital library system, as seen in figure 3. This way, others, like system administrators and users interested in the system performance, as well as the digital library itself, can ask for the performance of the system. Using the appropriate requests, we can retrieve specific or all performance variables from the performance monitor.

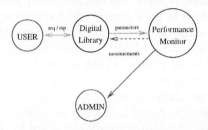

Fig. 3. Interaction with the performance monitor

The way that the performance monitor communicates with the rest of the world, does not specify its internal structure and its evolution. In its simpler form, it could be a single-threaded process. A system with two manager processes, which, technically, can be different processes or just threads, is more functional: The first process captures the messages, time-stamps them and passes them to the second process through an open pipe. The second process computes the difference between the time-stamps and updates the corresponding variables. It also computes the mean and variance. This way the first process is always unloaded and can process requests instantly, so that the added time-stamps are accurate. Of course, if the digital library system has the ability to provide satisfactorily accurate time-stamps with negligible performance cost, the first process can be eliminated.

As the second manager process may have to make heavy computations, and during this time it is unable to answer requests, a third manager process, called Database Manager Processes (DMP), that manages the variable database, ensures that performance responses are given instantly, as seen in figure 4.

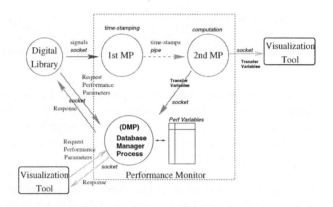

Fig. 4. Internal structure of the performance monitor

The second manager process still makes all its heavy calculations, and when new results are available, it sends the updates to all processes connected it it, such as the DMP, which is then responsible for answering requests from the outside world. Performance tools can be easily connected now: tools that poll for new values can connect to the DMP, and tools that passively wait for updates when they are available can connect to the second manager process!

Using this architecture, we can also build a self adapting digital library system, a system where the digital library, just like any other process, asks for its own performance, as seen in figure 4, and can take decisions that depend on the past performance. Now, the digital library can adapt to the performance conditions (e.g. the timeouts), and can explore new alternatives (e.g. load balancing)!

3 Applications and supporting tools

Some of the performance monitoring applications include performance visualization, load balancing, dynamic adaptation of timeouts and quality of service guarantees.

3.1 Visualization of Performance

The performance parameters are useful to administrators, to monitor the performance of the network and their systems, to detect problems and to make appropriate decisions to improve the performance. Also, the performance parameters are useful to users, to see the performance of their system and adjust their actions or expectations. In any case, visualization tools are needed to present the performance behavior to humans. Some of the different ways that users can see the performance parameters, are:

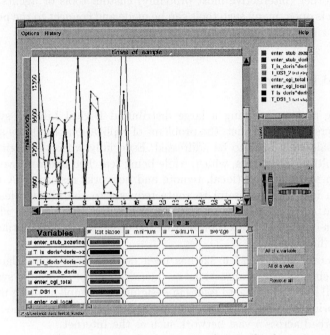

Fig. 5. Our performance visualization tool

- Using the performance log files directly. Our performance monitor keeps logs, if configured to do so, in many files in html format, with links between them (like from one digital library component to another, following the execution path), so that users can use them offline to process the parameters and see the flow of information and to follow process or parameters relations, using the links. Although this is very helpful for statistics and post-mortem debugging, this was not the main goal of our monitor.
- Using a WWW browser and performance monitoring requests, users can see current values of the performance parameters. The performance monitor accepts http requests for performance and formats and sends the reply in html format, so that the user can use his familiar WWW browser to utilize the monitor. The replies have a strict structure, so that they are easily parsable by programs, too.
- Using a graphics tool users can see the parameters as they change. We built a graphical visualization tool, as shown in figure 5, that can connect at the performance monitor and get the current system performance and display it. In this tool, every request creates a new set of points. The tool has a

Java based user interface, can selectively display some of the performance variables as they change in real-time (i.e. new requests are coming), and can also read the performance monitor log files and display the past values of the performance variables, while appending the new requests to the picture.

– Using other (interactive most probably) custom tools or agents. Since our system is open, many such tools can be made and connect to the performance monitor (possibly, at the same time, too).

3.2 Load balancing

In creating and maintaining a large distributed Digital Library system with many servers on the Internet, the problems of replication of indexes and objects and load balancing need to be addressed. Especially when the digital libraries contain multimedia objects, which, while being searched and retrieved by users, will use up many system (local, remote and network) resources. A measure of the system load is very useful to route requests to the idle (or least loaded) servers that contain the relevant objects. We expect that servers will *replicate* information objects or indexes of information objects in order to utilize network resources efficiently.

Considerable work[5, 27, 6, 32] has been done in developing algorithms for load balancing jobs or transactions or queries in large computer systems, but very few[14] have investigated issues in designing and implementing mechanisms for monitoring performance and load balancing jobs in distributed computer systems spread across a vast network such as the Internet.

Load balancing is possible only when replication is used. The replication can be based on political and/or technical reasons or, in the best case, on past performance statistics from server load and network conditions.

Our performance monitoring system can also be used for load balancing: since the performance measurements are known to the performance monitor, the digital library server can ask for these measurements and decide where to send its requests. The load balancing may refer to requests that access indexes (mostly search queries) and/or to requests that access objects (objects retrieval). There can be advantages in both cases: the use of indexes is more dense, while objects may be bigger. The mechanisms for load balancing is the same for both cases! We provide the mechanisms for load balancing, a good testbed for developing, debugging and evaluating policies.

We neither developed efficient policies nor built a specific policy into our system. We did try an indicative policy, that gave acceptable results, in order to demonstrate the functionality of our system. Good policies may depend on geographical data, connectivity, reliability requirements, data distribution and replication, user requirements and even on legal issues and individual cooperations and deals. We provide the testbed to experiment with such algorithms.

In order to visualize the load balancing status and effectiveness, we also made a load balancing monitor tool, as shown in figure 6.

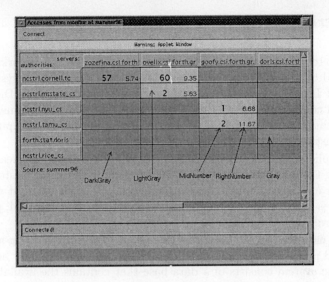

Fig. 6. Load balancing visualization tool

3.3 Dynamic adaptation of timeouts

When a process waits for another (remote) process to finish, it never knows for how long it should wait, not even if the process is still working, or is unable to return its result, because of the high diversity of system heterogenicity and network bandwidth. A good estimation of the amount of the time to wait, the *timeout period*, can improve the response time with minimal (or the desired degree of) information lost. In most systems, the timeout periods are predefined constants!

In [25], we propose novel timeout adaptation mechanisms which set timeouts for distributed searching in a dynamic fashion by estimating the round-trip delays to various digital library servers and defining appropriate wait intervals.

3.4 Quality of Service

Quality of Service guarantees can only be given when we have an estimate of the current network performance. Thus, our architecture is a prerequisite for that. As a first step, we only show the expected performance to the users, by estimating the expected performance of the available operations (like the transfer time of files) from past history. For this functionality, we also used an external tool that monitors all TCP/IP packets from the local network to all destinations, keeps statistics and provides available bandwidth information, on request.

Our mechanisms can be used for full quality of service support, according to the desired levels of service. To support many levels of quality of service, the past and current performance is used and many possible scenarios can be evaluated.

4 Description of Dienst usage

In order to test our ideas, we need to implement them on a real, working system. We applied our ideas at the NCSTRL[12] based Digital Library system, which consists of Dienst servers distributed across the Internet. Each Dienst server manages a collection of computer science technical reports (documents) owned by organizations such as computer science departments and computer science research institutions.

We applied our performance management architecture for measuring and monitoring the operation of the NCSTRL[1] based digital library system: we conducted our experiments over a testbed of Dienst[12] servers. Dienst was chosen, because it is used in NCSTRL and connects sites all over the world, providing a good natural testbed for distributed testing on digital libraries.

Dienst uses the WWW protocols (mainly HTTP) for searching and presentation, and provides transparent distributed search and document access. Each node of the system consists of a data base that contains the available objects, a WWW server that handles all incoming Dienst requests, Dienst CGI stubs that are called by the WWW server and a Dienst server, that is called by the CGI stubs. Dienst servers manage three basic library services: (a) repositories of multi-format technical reports; (b) indexes of the technical reports collection and search engines for these indexes; (c) distributed search and retrieval.

The operation of a Dienst server is as follows: a user submits a keyword search query[2] to one of the Dienst servers. The Dienst server initiates a search request to the other Dienst servers, responses are collected, and the user is presented with the search results. More details on the organization and operation of the NCSTRL system are given in [12].

We defined the performance variables which capture the delays experienced by each user request as they propagate through the components of Dienst. The components, for example, include the delays in WWW interface to Dienst, local Dienst server processing, network delays and remote processing of the user requests.

Our experience with Dienst shows that it is good, portable, easy to use and manage software, but it is slow and its distributed structure is complex. It is not a professional tool, but we would recommend it for most installations for its modularity and adaptability. Nevertheless, it has obvious scaling limitations!

To overcome bad network connectivity and delays, Dienst divides the servers into regions and is using *Backup Index Servers*, contacted when the Dienst server fails to respond in time and additionally introduced (statically assigned) *Regional Meta Servers* and *Merged Index Servers* (Regional Index Servers), which keep a replica of the indexes of the other regions. To improve scalability and performance, an entirely new architecture is needed, without so strong statically assigned roles, based on performance facts and not speculations!

---

[1] NCSTRL stands for Networked Computer Science Technical Report Library.

[2] In this paper, request, search request, query, all mean the same.

5   Dienst Analysis and Performance Monitoring

The user communicates directly with one Dienst server, and when he issues a Dienst request, this server decides where to forward the split subqueries. Each server is responsible for searching its own local Database. Each Dienst request goes through many stages, as seen in figure 7, where most of them are trivial components, but may introduce significant overhead.

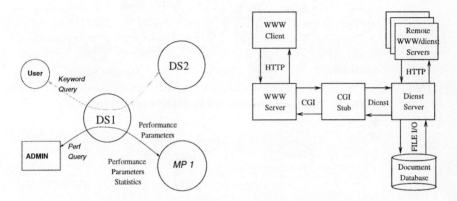

Fig. 7. The user and system view of the stages of a query

We formulated a mathematical model of the operation of the Dienst servers in servicing a request. We model the time spent in "important" components of the Dienst server, as seen in figure 8. The model also takes into consideration the maximum timeout periods involved. With this model we can better understand procedures and the relationships between the components, prove properties about components and their execution, express results precisely, and trace problems. For more information on the mathematical model, see [28].

According to our performance architecture, our model for performance monitoring on Dienst is simple, and illustrated in figure 9. The performance requests also use the native Dienst model: they can be sent to a Dienst server, and this server decides where to forward the split subqueries. Each server is also responsible to communicate with its own performance monitor to retrieve performance parameters.

By using our performance monitoring system on Dienst, we studied the Dienst protocol and program and located inefficiencies. We also studied the log files, to better explore the flow of information. We propose improvements, such as a new protocol for server communication and timeouts. We extented Dienst architecture to perform load balancing and proceeded to an implementation, which was used for experimentation and to get example results.

In order to have a user friendly way to access the performance requests and to be able to ask the Dienst server itself for them, we extended the Dienst

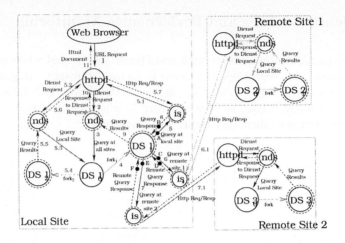

Fig. 8. The processes involved in a query processing

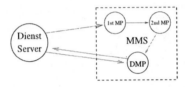

Fig. 9. The Dienst performance management system

protocol by adding new Dienst performance requests. These requests just call the appropriate request from the performance monitor and redirect their output:

`Dienst/Stat/2.1/Print-Local-Parameters`
   for retrieval of all parameters local to this host only and
`Dienst/Stat/2.1/Print-Parameters`
   for retrieval of all parameters of all hosts.

The performance requests can be asked like all others requests, directly on WWW or from links in the dienst interface. Users can continue using only original Dienst requests, and the performance monitor is invisible to them! The requests return simple html tables, as in figure 10, that can be shown directly to the user, or parsed by programs. More complex requests can always be answered directly by the performance monitor.

6 Experimental results

Here we describe a session where we experimented by monitoring the performance of three Dienst servers (DS1, DS2 and DS3), to interpret the results we get. We defined a few variables and monitored them. Dienst requests (keyword based) were sent to one server (DS1) and the performance variables were monitored for each request and the statistics computed. Figure 10, displays an instance of the output of the performance monitor, as will be explained later:

Print Parameters

Performance Parameters of Dienst Server 3

Parameter	Calls	RSP	Min	Max	Total	Mean	Std Dev
T_{DS1_2}	5	0.617	0.574	0.677	3.162	0.632	0.039
T_{nds}^{local}	5	1.219	1.219	2.138	8.959	1.791	0.426

Performance Parameters of Dienst Server 2

Parameter	Calls	RSP	Min	Max	Total	Mean	Std Dev
T_{DS1_2}	5	0.42	0.406	0.477	2.197	0.439	0.03
T_{nds}^{local}	5	0.796	0.69	1.682	6.456	1.291	0.502

Performance Parameters of Dienst Server 1

Parameter	Calls	RSP	Min	Max	Total	Mean	Std Dev
T_{DS1_1}	5	15.16	15.16	17.776	80.873	16.174	0.964
T_{DS1_2}	5	0.608	0.608	1.016	3.758	0.751	0.159
$T_{is_{Server3}}^{Server1->Server3}$	5	11.527	11.527	13.968	62.964	12.592	0.879
$T_{is_{Server2}}^{Server1->Server2}$	5	9.782	8.784	11.97	50.698	10.139	1.156
$T_{is_{Server1}}^{Server1->Server1}$	5	10.553	2.062	11.793	36.841	7.368	4.716
T_{nds}^{local}	5	1.295	1.053	2.367	7.859	1.571	0.581
T_{nds}^{total}	5	15.735	15.735	18.085	84.807	16.961	0.888
$T_{is_{Server3}}$	5	5.424	5.424	7.651	32.408	6.481	0.804
$T_{is_{Server2}}$	5	3.289	2.989	5.032	19.182	3.836	0.785
$T_{is_{Server1}}$	5	4.507	3.987	5.976	23.343	4.668	0.805

NCSTRL-ERCIM
ERCIM This server operates at Institute of Computer Science Technical Report Library at Server 1.
Send email to terzis@csi.forth.gr

Fig. 10. Web based User Interface to monitor the performance variables

The performance variables capture delays in the following components: (a) local search response time; (b) local index database processing time; (c) remote processing time of the index database; (d) remote search response time (includes network delay+remote processing time).

For each performance variable, the following are observed. `Calls`: Number of requests (measurement points), `RSP`: current value of the variables (last request response time), `Min`: minimum value of the variable, `Max`: maximum values of the variable, `Total`: aggregate of the measurements, `Mean`: Total divided by the number of requests, `Std Dev`: Standard Deviation of variable values.

In the figure 10, 5 requests were generated at Dienst server 1. The requests were routed to the remote Dienst servers 2 and 3 for a search in their index files. The request is also routed locally for a search in the local index file (of Dienst server 1).

The parameters for Dienst server 2 and 3 are simply the remote search response times for both servers. There are two variables per remote server. T_{DS1_2} is the time taken to perform a search in the index file for the user request. The average time is 0.632 seconds. T_{nds} is the time taken for the overall operation before the reply is sent back to Dienst server 1, which initiated the request.

The parameters for Dienst server 1 represent the following:

- Response time of request from Dienst server 1 forwarded to Dienst server 3 ($T_{is_{server3}}^{Server1->Server3}$) is an average of 12.592 seconds for the 5 requests generated. This time is the sum of the rountrip network delay and the remote processing time of the request. Similarly for remote Dienst server 2 and the local search response time.

- Remote request response time for Dienst server 3 is represented by $T_{is_{server3}}$. The mean is 6.481 seconds. This includes the remote request processing time and the operating system overheads. Similarly for Dienst server 2 and 1 (local).

- Remote request processing time for Dienst server 3 is shown in the first table of the figure (T_{nds}^{local}). This is the time taken to search the index database at the remote server T_{DS1_2} and some overhead.

- Total request response time, T_{nds}, is the sum of all delays in collecting the responses. This is 16.961 seconds for the 5 requests that were generated.

Network delay between two Dienst servers can be computed by simply subtracting the Remote request response time between two servers (stored in the remote database) from the remote request processing time (stored in the local database).

6.1 Locating inefficiencies via Monitoring

The Performance Monitoring was used in profiling Dienst search queries and for studying the effect of parameters on their response time. The parameters studied are divided into two categories: (a) those that depend on the configuration of the Dienst server (e.g. index database size); (b) those that depend on the machine that hosts the server (e.g. memory size, cpu speed, etc) and the network delay (latency) to reach the server.

The testbed consists of four Dienst servers:

[1.] a Sun4c workstation with 48M memory and SunOS 4.1.2
[2.] an Alpha workstation with 32M memory and Digital Unix V3.2
[3.] an Alpha workstation with 64M memory and Digital Unix V3.2
[4.] a Sun4c workstation with 16M memory and SunOS 4.1.3.

The two sun machines have the same index database (4644 words). The first Alpha machine indexes 10979 words and the second 20222 words. The load was heavy and artificially created. The load is generated by a perl script which submits keyword queries to the one of the Dienst servers. Even from our testing measurements, it became apparent that the performance of the Dienst version 4.1.4, that we tested, is seriously affected by:

- Machine load (and other machine properties).
  The first observation was that the high resource consumption of the current Dienst implementation imposes a limit on the rate of requests it can service. This request rate limit depends on the machine configuration (mostly the

memory), and thus, factors that affect them, like the index database size and the complexity of the queries.

We can see the difference of request processing time over machine memory size:

Sun4c, Memory Size in MB	16	48
Request Processing Time	4.657s	0.638s

Also, a request that searches only one database needed 1.16 seconds when the database was on a different machine that was easily accessed (on the same local network) and 2.95 seconds when the call was to the same machine (to the local database), even though that the databases had the same content and there is no network latency involved: the overhead that was introduced by creating a new process on the non idle machine is high!

The continuous forks of Dienst (one for every request to the Dienst server) and the fact that it is written on a scripting language, perl, significantly affects the system overhead.

– Data Base size.

It seems that the decision of Dienst to hold the whole index database in memory, creating huge processes and swapping them out of the memory affects seriously its performance. In the following table we see the size of the Dienst process and a typical request processing time as a function of the size of the index:

Words in Index DB	2,327	5,326	10,797	77,105
MB of Dienst process	9.5	9.7	10.6	13.6
Request processing time	1.5s	2.2s	4.9s	6.4s

– Request complexity.

Different types of queries need different processing time. Dienst seems to optimize queries up to 2 keywords, sacrificing performance on the other, more rare cases.

– Network delays.

Typically, the most significant part of the request's time is the network latency, and is non flexible! The exact percentage of the Network Latency to the total request servicing time (as shown in the table below) depends on other factors, and mainly the index database size. It takes an index database almost seven times bigger in order to make the network latency part non-dominant in request servicing time.

Words indexed	10,979	77,105
Network Latency ÷ Total execution	70%	35%

The percentage of the Network Latency depends, also, on the network "distance" of the server initiating the request and the server servicing it. For example the use of a remote server instead of a local, added about 12 more seconds of the Network Latency time, as measured at that time.

– Timeout setup.

The values of the different timeouts on the Dienst protocol also affect its performance. A long timeout value not only increases delays, but also may let Dienst processes compute results that nobody is waiting for.

7 Applications of Performance Monitoring on Dienst

Using this simple performance architecture in our testbed, we measured the delays in various components of Dienst, such as local processing of the user request, network round-trip delays when the request is sent to the remote sites for processing, and remote site processing delays. Each server keeps statistics such as averages and variances of each performance variable that is defined. For the sake of simplicity, these variables are common for all kinds of queries. In general, simple queries need very small computational time when compared to the more complex multiple-keyword or form based query. Keeping track of variables for each kind of request is computationally intensive.

An application of the performance architecture, that is used to propose Dynamic Adaptation of Timeouts, based on the history the performance monitor keeps for the response time of each Server, can be found in [25]. Here we will present an application on load balancing.

Some advantages of performance load balancing are that there is no need for apriori network knowledge, especially when nodes are setup for the first time, and can lead to better performance, with dynamic system reconfiguration, as the system always adapts to the changing environment. Also, leads to a simpler system structure, where there is no need for explicit specialized roles such as Merged Index Servers and Backup Index Servers, and provides better reliability when servers are down, as others are automatically the next choice.

Load balancing can refer to retrieval of either indexes or data. In our implementation we only performed load balancing on indexes. To avoid lengthy computations on the Dienst server, the Dienst protocol has to be further extended to get precalculated results, like the ordered list of servers to query.

Some disadvantages and problems of load balancing is that the network conditions change continuously, and performance data based on non current information are partially useful. In a few circumstances, there may be no previous history and the decision will be almost random! Finally, there may be unpredictable response time from factors that are not easily detected, like from a dependency on query complexity.

We built the mechanisms, but in order to test them we also need policies.

Here we describe some implementation details in our load balancing experiments: We set up 8 servers, divided into 4 sets, each set has 2 servers that have identical content. The four servers at FORTH are pseudo-remote. This means that they add a random delay to each response so that their response time is similar to the really remote servers. Also, there is partial overlap on the content of the different sets of servers. The server sets and locations were:

UoCrete-Greece	FORTH-Greece_1
UoColumbia-USA	FORTH-Greece_2
FORTH-Greece_3	FORTH-Greece_4
GMD-Germany	CNR-Italy

Here are a few simplifications that were used by our policy: When a digital library node holds data for many publishers, we assume that all questions to the publishers are independent. When a server can provide multiple publishers the performance of the server depends on all the publishers in question and the total load assigned to the node. For more detailed results, see [28].

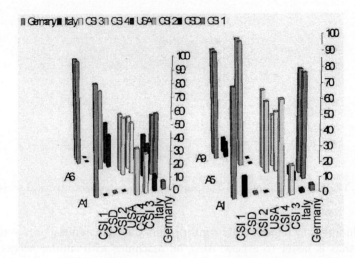

Fig. 11. Load Balancing Experiment Results

In figure 11 we present two different experiments. In both experiment we show the distribution of the same set of requests to the 8 servers of our testbed. The set used consisted of 50 requests and was submitted twice. The requests were selected such that they simulate the Cornell University Dienst server load. More details about the experimental procedure can be found in [28]. It is important to notice that changes in network and machine load are depicted in the distribution of the requests. For example, looking at the pair of the Italy and Germany servers, which are identical, we see that in the first experiment the network latency and thus the response times of both servers were almost the same the requests were distributed almost evenly between the two. On the contrary, in the second experiment the network latency to Italy was significantly higher than the that for Germany. Thus, the response times of the Germany server were constantly lower, so the request were almost all routed to the Germany server. A similar case is with the pair of the CSI 3 and CSI 4 servers, but in this case the difference is not due to network latency but because of other machine load that was introduced.

The exact point where the change in the environment (network and machine) and thus to the response time takes place can be better seen by analysing the request distribution between the pairs of identical servers: the plateaux in figure 12 represent the periods where the respective server was *not preferred*. So, by looking at the pair CSI3 - CSI4, we see that in the begining both servers are equally preferred, at some point in the middle the CSI 4 server was preferred mostly, due to busrts of load that were introduced to CSI 3. When this external (to digital library system) activity resumed both servers became equally preferred again. On the other hand, the concurrent plateaux in the Gremany-Italy pair show a period during which both servers were anavailable.

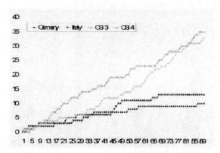

Fig. 12. Analysis of request distribution between pairs of identical servers

Concluding, our experiments confirm that the most requests are sent to the machine that is faster to access. Also, on machines with similar access time, a possible external load on a machine can change the target of most requests!

8 Conclusions

In this paper, we provide a management architecture for measurement and monitoring digital library, which we applied to Dienst servers. We defined relevant performance parameters which capture the time spent in the various phases of a request as it propagates through the system. We used these parameters for demonstrating query load balancing so as to improve the overall request response time. In addition, we designed algorithms for adaptive timeouts in distributed searches.

The performance monitoring can be used in the digital library systems, to improve on the design, behavior and scaling and adaptive mechanisms and Quality of Service. Our architecture gives a better knowledge of the time taken by the various tasks of the digital library servers and helps in understanding and using this knowledge in applications like Load balancing user queries to servers. Our emphasis is on portable mechanisms, not results: In order to get meaningful results, we must use the performance monitoring on the regular digital library usage! Especially for load balancing, more realistic data distributions must be used, as no natural data distributions currently exists. Using these mechanisms, sophisticated policies can be exercised.

For the future, we would like to get performance monitoring results for load balancing on real data. We also want to design mechanisms for user level analysis (session, account, access patterns), to examine compatibility with the Universal Measurement Architecture and to find better policies for load balancing and timeouts. Finally, we would like to experiment with more complex performance processing algorithms that take into account empirical observations, like that predictions do vary with the time and the day.

9 Acknowledgements

We would like to thank Christos Nikolaou[3] for his many suggestions and support in this work. We would also like to thank Carl Lagoze[4] for bringing us to the problems associated with performance of distributed searching over a large number of servers. Finally, we should thank Antonis Hatzistamatiou and George Sapunjis for the implementation of the visualization tools.

References

1. Ziya Aral and Ilya Gertner, *Non-intrusive and interactive profiling in Parasight*, Proceedings of the ACM/SIGPLAN PPEALS, p. 21-30, July 1988.
2. Daniel E. Atkins, *The University of Michigan Digital Library Project: The Testbed*, D-Lib Magazine, July/August 1996.
3. *Continuous Profiling Infrastructure*, Product Description, Digital Equipment Corp., June 1997.
4. *Digital Libraries*, special issue, Communications of the ACM, 38(4), April 1995.
5. D. Ferguson and L. Georgiadis and C. Nikolaou, "Satisfying Response Time goals in a Transaction Processing System," *Proceedings of the Conference on Parallel and Distributed Information Systems*, 1993.
6. D. Ferguson, J. Sairamesh and R. Cieslak, "Black Holes, Sacrificial Lambs, and a Robust Approach to Transaction Routing," *Proceedings of the International Conference on Parallel and Distributed Computing*, 1995.
7. James Few, Michael Freeston, Randall B. Kemp, Jason Simpson, Terence Smith, Alex Wells and Qi Zeng, *The Alexandria Digital Library Testbed*, D-Lib Magazine, July/August 1996.
8. Weiming Gu, Jeffrey Vetter and Karsten Schwan, *An Annotated Bibliography of Interactive Program Steering*, SIGPLAN Notices, September 1994.
9. M. A. Hearst, *Research in Support of Digital Libraries at Xerox PARC*, D-Lib Magazine, May 1996.
10. J. L. Klavans, *New Center at Columbia University for Digital Library Research*, D-Lib Magazine, March 1996.
11. Carl Lagoze and Jim Davis, *Dienst: An Architecture for Distributed Documents Libriaries*, Communications of the ACM, 38(4), April 1995, p. 47.
12. C. Lagoze, E. Shaw, J. R. Davis and D. B. Krafft, *Dienst: Implementation Reference Manual*, TR95-1514, Cornell University, May 5th, 1995.
13. Frank Lange, Reinold Kroeger and Martin Gergeleit, *JEWEL: Design and Implementation of a Distributed Measurement System*, IEEE Transactions on Parallel and Distributed Systems, Volume 6, No 2, May 1992.

---

[3] Christos Nikolaou is the head of the Parallel and Distributed Systems Group - PLEIADES, ICS-FORTH.

[4] Carl Lagoze is with the Department of Computer Science, Cornell University, New York.

114

14. M. Litzkow, M. Livny, and M. W. Mutka, "Condor - A Hunter of Idle Workstations," *Proceedings of the 8th International Conference of Distributed Computing Systems,* pp. 104-111, June, 1988.
15. *Managing Application Performance with TME10*, Technical White Paper, Tivoli Systems, 1996.
16. B. P. Miller, M. D. Callaghan, J. M. Cargille, J. H. Hollingsworth, R. B. Irvin, K. L. Karavanic, K. Kunchithapadam and T. Newhall, *The Paradyn Parallel Performance Measurement Tools*, IEEE Computer, 28 (11), November 1995.
17. C. Nikolaou, S. Kapidakis and G. Georgianakis, *Towards a Paneuropean Scientific Digital Library*, TR96-0167, Institute of Computer Science - FORTH, May 1996.
18. Andreas Paepcke, *Summary of Stanford's Digital Library Testbed Design and Status*, D-Lib Magazine, July/August 1996.
19. *POLYCENTER Performance Advisor for Unix*, Product Description, Computer Associates, Digital Equipment Corp., 1996.
20. D. A. Reed, R. J. Noe, K. A. Shields and B. W. Schwartz, *An Overview of the Pablo Performance Analysis Environment*, Department of Computer Science, University of Illinois, Urbana Illinois, November 1992.
21. *Resource Management Facility*, IBM Corp., June 1995.
22. Richard Snodgrass, *A Relational Approach to Monitoring Complex Systems*, ACM Transactions on Computer Systems, Volume 6, No 2, May 1988.
23. Chris Rusbridge, *The UK Electronic Libraries Programme*, D-Lib Magazine, December 1995.
24. J. Sairamesh, S. Kapidakis and C. Nikolaou, *Architectures for QoS based Retrieval in Digital Libraries*, Workshop on Networked Information Retrieval, SIGIR'96.
25. J. Sairamesh, S. Kapidakis, S. Terzis and C. Nikolaou, *Performance Framework for QoS based Searching and Retrieval in Digital Libraries*, TR97-0204, Institute of Computer Science - FORTH, August 1997.
26. Beth A. Sroeder, *On-Line Monitoring: A Tutorial*, IEEE Computer, June 1995.
27. A.N. Tantawi and D. Towsley, "Optimal Static Load Balancing in Distributed Computer Systems," *Journal of the ACM*, April, 1985, pg. 445-465.
28. S. Terzis. *Performance Monitoring in Digital Library Systems* Master thesis, TR97-0210, Institute of Computer Science - FORTH, October 1997.
29. *UMA Technical Information*, Performance Management Working Group, March 1994.
30. *A+UMA Performance Data Manager Technical Overview*, Amdahl Corp., October 1996.
31. I. H. Witten, S. J. Cunningham and M. D. Apperley, *The New Zealand Digital Library Project*, D-Lib Magazine, November 1996.
32. Phillip S. Yu and Avraham Leff and Yann-Hang Lee, "On Robust Transaction Routing and Load Sharing," *ACM Transactions on Database Systems*, pg. 476-512, sept. 1991.

Building **HyperView** Wrappers for Publisher Web Sites

Lukas C. Faulstich[*,1], Myra Spiliopoulou[2]

[1] Institut für Informatik, Freie Universität Berlin,
<http://www.inf.fu-berlin.de/~faulstic>
[2] Institut für Wirtschaftsinformatik, Humboldt-Universität zu Berlin,
<http://www.wiwi.hu-berlin.de/~myra>

Abstract. Electronic journals are becoming a major source of scientific information. Researchers interested only in certain topics do not have time to scan all possibly relevant journals on a regular basis. A digital library can assist them by providing a uniform, search-able interface for electronic journals. To this purpose, a catalogue of metadata on the available journals such as authors and titles of articles must be established by the digital library. If there is no cooperation with journal publishers, this metadata must be extracted from the publishers' Web Sites, overcoming the intrinsic heterogeneity problems.

Within the framework of the ongoing Natural Sciences Digital Library project at the Free University of Berlin, we have designed a wrapper-mediator mechanism that copes with the heterogeneity problems of automatic metadata acquisition. It is based on our generic HyperView methodology for integration of Web Sites. From this methodology it inherits two elegant and effective features. First, the structure of the publisher site is specified with abstract graph-schemata, instead of being hard-coded in scripts for data acquisition. Second, a powerful view concept based on declarative graph-transformation rules is used for information extraction.

1 Introduction

The number of electronic journals is rapidly increasing. Publishers currently offer several thousand electronic journals. For researchers, the advent of online journal editions has made life much easier since all information is reachable immediately from the own desktop. On the other hand, this huge amount of heterogeneously structured information makes conventional methods for dealing with it such as book-marking and browsing of publisher Web Sites inadequate.

University libraries have started to provide access to electronic journals. In most cases, however, these are essentially collections of links to the journal home pages at the publishers' Web Sites. In some cases, these links are also included in the library catalogs. Examples for electronic journal link collections are (among many others) the Stanford University Libraries [27], Simon Fraser University

* Supported by the German Research Society, Berlin-Brandenburg Graduate School on Distributed Information Systems (DFG grant no. GRK 316)

Electronic Library in Computing Science [25], and the Electronic Journals collection [29] at the Stony Brook University Libraries.

In the case of the *Elektronische Zeitschriftenbibliothek* [28] at the University of Regensburg, a search-able catalogue of electronic journals is provided. It allows to focus the search to certain scientific disciplines or to journals available in print at a specific Bavarian university library. For each journal, links to the journal home page, to the catalogue entry, as well as an indicator about the electronic availability of the full text are presented.

The DBLP computer science bibliography maintained by Michael Ley [19] offers tables of contents of many conference proceedings as well as of about 150 computer science journals. For some journals, links to the electronic editions of the articles are provided. Each author name occurring in these tables of contents is linked with the bibliography of this author. However, most publishers do not provide metadata. So, the majority of the bibliographic data for journals has to be entered *manually by librarians* into a database. The HTML pages of this service are generated in advance as a materialized database view.

Another service that relies mostly on manually entered bibliographic information is the British "national information service for the higher education community" BUBL [6]. BUBL provides search-able abstracts and tables of content for about 200 journals. Unfortunately, links to the corresponding electronic journal editions are missing, and only links to publisher home pages are provided.

There are other projects which import the full text of articles into the digital library, thus supporting search facilities on these articles. JSTOR [16] is an archival project for older volumes of journals which are scanned, indexed using text recognition software, and stored in image form. A search-able WWW interface to these journals is available to the participating universities.

In the DeLIver [24] project, publishers provide articles of selected electronic journals in SGML form. These articles are stored in the digital library and indexed using so-called *concept spaces*, thus supporting advanced search facilities. In contrast to this close cooperation, only minimal cooperation of the publishers is assumed in our DigLib project.

From all these projects we can see that catalogues of electronic journals which go beyond collections of hyper-links require the acquisition of metadata on the included journals. In the cases we have seen, this is still done manually by librarians. If publishers do not provide this information, active methods for gathering metadata from the available WWW sources are needed.

In principle, all information needed for a catalogue of electronic journals is present at the publisher's Web Site. However, the form of this information varies extremely: it depends on the overall design of a site, on the policy of updating or dynamically generating pages and of displaying new data. To correctly design a mechanism importing metadata from a publisher's site, those particularities must be taken into account. On the other hand, a generic method is necessary to describe the site and the import activities it calls for at an abstract level. Otherwise, any change in a site would break the existing import scripts and require costly re-implementation.

In this study, we present a mechanism for the import of bibliographical data into the local repository of a digital library. We use an adaptive import scheduling strategy which estimates the publication dates of new journal issues. At each estimated due day, the "HyperNavigator" is triggered to import bibliographical data on the new issue by navigating the publisher's Web Site. The HyperNavigator is a module based on our HyperView methodology for wrapping and integrating heterogeneous Web Sites. It is based on high-level declarative view specifications and a demand-driven materialization strategy. Its formal framework is the subject of a companion paper [11]. Here we demonstrate how our methodology can be applied to the problem of wrapping publisher Web Sites.

Our import mechanism for bibliographical data is used in the Natural Sciences Digital Library project (Free University Berlin), which we describe in Section 2. The import scheduling strategy is discussed in Section 3. In Section 4, we present the HyperNavigator, first as a generic architecture and then in the context of our project. Related work is presented in Section 5. We conclude our study in the last section.

2   Overview of the DigLib Project

The DigLib project at the Free University Berlin establishes a digital library for the natural sciences. This will enable the university library to provide Web-based access to electronic journals and university publications like dissertation theses and technical reports. Within the framework of DigLib, a search-able catalogue of electronic journals is being developed. The contents of the journals are accessible at the site of their publishers, reachable by links kept in the catalogue. The current DigLib prototype provides only links to journal home pages.

2.1   Why using the HyperView methodology in DigLib?

By applying the HyperView methodology to wrap publisher Web Sites, we can provide not only links to the current issues, but also links to articles together with bibliographic data such as the titles and authors. These data can become part of the catalogue. Furthermore, we can use HyperView to wrap existing search facilities of the publisher Web Sites in order to support distributed full-text search on abstracts or even articles. Hence, the user may issue content-related queries on the catalogue and obtain links to relevant journal issues and articles.

The information retained on each electronic journal must be automatically extended, as new issues appear. The publication data on these new issues should be incorporated into the catalogue and become available to the users for querying. This raises the issue of discovering when a new issue of a journal becomes available at the publisher's Web Site, and the challenging issue of importing metadata on it to the local repository containing our catalogue.

These Web Sites are intrinsically heterogeneous in their structure and in the way they are updated. For example, one publisher may decide to keep each volume of a journal on a separate page, while another places all issues of the journal on a single page. Some publishers provide links to the current issue of a journal, others require the user to pick the newest issue from a list of all issues. If a link to the current issue exists, its target URL may be constant or variable etc. etc. Since the target size of the DigLib corpus will exceed the one thousand journals from many different publishers, we have to provide a solution for automatic metadata import in spite of that heterogeneity. The solution we propose in Section 4 is based on the HyperView methodology.

2.2 The Architecture of DigLib

The abstract architecture of DigLib is shown in Fig. 1. It can be seen as a configuration of the generic "Warehouse for Internet Data" (WIND) architecture presented in [10]. The WIND architectural model foresees a set of local repositories, in which database objects and textual documents from heterogeneous sources can be stored. In the framework of DigLib, only one relational database system (RDBMS) is needed.

This RDBMS stores the search-able catalogue of bibliographic records together with other, administrative data like user profiles. The end-user interface for query formulation is a HTTP server. The PHP server-side HTML embedded scripting language [23] is used for database access. An extended interface is foreseen for the librarian, for operations like insertion of new journals and registration of users.

The Repository Manager coordinates the maintenance of the catalogue data and of the user profiles in the RDBMS. One of its services is the Import Scheduling Service ("ISS"), which periodically schedules the import of the latest journal issues. The import itself is performed by the HyperNavigator. The HyperNavigator has two levels: the publisher-specific HyperView wrappers and the publisher-independent mediator. The mediator guarantees access transparency, in that all access requests performed by the Repository Manager refer to journals without knowledge of their actual HTML representation. The activation of the wrapper responsible for each publisher is performed internally by the mediator.

2.3 The Modules Responsible for Information Import

As new journal issues become available at the publishers' sites, we need to import their description in our local repository. We have designed an "Import Scheduling Service" (ISS). The ISS selects daily the journals of which the latest issue should be imported, and puts them into a ToDo list. This list is processed by the HyperNavigator, which inserts the descriptions of the new issues into a private relation. At some off-peak hour, this relation is used to update the DigLib catalogue. This approach ensures that the activities of preparing and performing the import do not affect the availability of database tables used by other services.

An overview of the import mechanism is depicted in Fig. 2. The ISS and the HyperNavigator are described in the next sections.

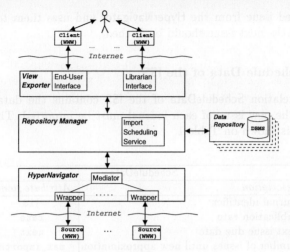

Fig. 1. The DigLib architecture

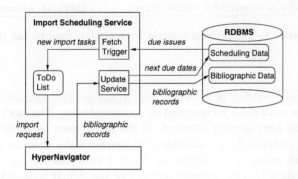

Fig. 2. The import activities in DigLib

3 The Import Scheduling Service

The Import Scheduling Service deals with a specialized instance of the *material-ized view maintenance* problem. In the terminology of [30], a publisher Web Site wrapped by the HyperNavigator can be seen as a *query-able source* on which a view is established using an *eager* approach. In our case, changes in the source can be detected relatively efficiently, since journal issues appear with a known frequency and form a running sequence. Therefore we can estimate the best time for polling a source and have to watch only a limited number of HTML pages for discovering new journal issues. For a detailed overview on the general problem of materialized view maintenance see [14].

The Import Scheduling Service (cf. Fig. 2) consists of two (sub)services: (i) The "fetch trigger" identifies the journals, whose next issue should be fetched, and inserts them into a ToDo list. (ii) The "update service" obtains data on each newly imported issue from the HyperNavigator and uses them to compute the date at which the next issue should be fetched.

3.1 The Schedule Data of the ISS

The private relation ScheduleData of the ISS contains the data necessary to decide when the new issue of each journal must be imported. The signature of ScheduleData is shown on Table 1.

ScheduleData	
Description	*Attribute name*
Journal identifier	jid
Publication rate	rate
Next issue due date	next
Number of issues until new approximation	max_imports
Counter of issues until new approximation	count_imports
Minimum delay encountered thus far	min_delay
Days in advance for import start	days_in_advance

Table 1. The internal relation ScheduleData used by the ISS

The journal identifier is a foreign key to the journal entries in the DigLib catalogue. The rate must be specified on an annual basis. The next date specifies the day of the next import attempt. If the given next is already past upon insertion, the "fetch trigger" will place the journal right into the ToDo list.

The second group of attributes in Table 1 concerns the approximation of the next due date by the "update service" of the ISS. If no exact next date is provided by the publisher, next is incremented after each import by 1 year / rate days. This estimation can be subject to errors so that either the import is attempted too early and has to be repeated, or it is too late, and users have to wait unnecessarily long for the new issue.

The ISS therefore follows a conservative strategy in the sense that next is adjusted by the ISS days_in_advance days before the actual date of publication. The ISS keeps a min_delay statistic and re-adjusts its approximation after max_imports. The librarian may prevent this readjustment by setting the value of max_imports to NULL.

3.2 Importing Journals using the ToDo List

The "fetch trigger" of the ISS inserts into the ToDo list an entry for each new issue to be fetched by the HyperNavigator. Each entry is comprised by the journal identifier jid, a priority value, and access information for the new issue. This access information is obtained from the DigLib catalogue and consists of publisher, journal URL, number and volume of the current issue. The priority is computed from statistics kept in the catalogue. It takes into account the number of users registered with DigLib for notifications on this journal and and the number of requests for the journal.

If the new issue has not yet appeared or the available time span for the import run is over, the import fails and the journal remains in the ToDo list. In this case, its priority is increased. Otherwise, the journal is removed from the list and the publication data are inserted into the private relation of the HyperNavigator. The jid is also returned to the "update service" of the ISS which uses this information to compute the next due date for this journal.

3.3 Computing the Due Date of the Next Issue

For each new issue imported, the "update service" of the ISS resets the next and current_issue values of the journal. If the value of max_imports is set, we first compute the minimum delay encountered thus far and increase the counter of the issues imported till now. We then increase the value of next by the publication period of the journal, as computed from the journal's annual rate.

Thereafter, we test whether max_imports have already been performed. If yes, then it is time to readjust the next value against the min_delay encountered thus far. This implies shifting the next by as many days as the min_delay, so that premature attempts to import the issue are avoided in the future. If it is likely that the journal appears earlier than assumed by next, the administrator may specify that the next is shifted backwards by a number of days_in_advance. Once a satisfactory approximation of next is reached, the days_in_advance should be reset to zero. Hence, the new value of next is set by shifting the old one forward by min_delay days and backward by days_in_advance.

3.4 Obtaining Notifications from the Publishers

The ISS is designed to cope with the delivery of new issues, for which no exact publication date is available. If the publisher can provide this information, the ISS must replace the next date of the affected journals. For the delivery of this information, two different scenarios are possible: (i) If the publisher actively delivers this date, e.g. via a eMail service, then the ISS must be extended by a module receiving and processing such notifications. Alerting services based on other technologies [9], e.g. channels, may be used as well. (ii) If the publisher just announces the date passively on its Web pages, then the HyperNavigator can be used to poll the publisher site for this information.

4 The HyperNavigator

4.1 The HyperView Approach

The HyperView methodology is intended for the integration of well-known Web sources and the acquisition of information from them. We used it in the framework of DigLib to build the HyperNavigator, our module for the import of journal metadata from the Web Sites of the publishers.

The HyperView approach is based on the architecture shown in Fig. 3. Each Web Site is encapsulated in a site-specific wrapper. Information from different wrappers is integrated in a mediator. From the conceptual viewpoint, we use different levels of abstraction to model Web Sites. These levels are reflected by the layers of our architecture. The HTML layer models single HTML pages, the ACR layer the abstract structure of each Web Site, and the database layer the integrated domain-oriented view of all Sites.

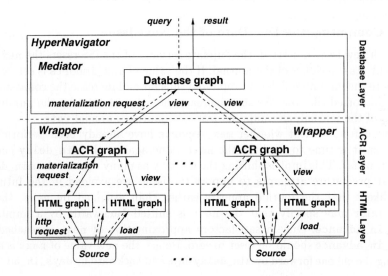

Fig. 3. The layers of the HyperNavigator

Each layer consists of labeled directed graphs which are conceived as abstractions of the graphs in the preceding layer. Each graph conforms to a given graph schema. Inter-layer edges connect abstract data items with the data items from which they abstract. Thus, a large layered data graph is formed.

The layered design is intended to provide transparency and encapsulate site-specific constructs. The graph of each of the higher layers is computed as a view of the layer immediately below it. These views are defined by declarative graph-transformation rules which are invoked on demand to materialize new graph elements at the higher layer, by matching graph elements and thus extracting information from the lower layer. On the HTML layer, HTML pages are loaded, parsed, and represented as directed labeled graphs on demand.

In the current prototype for the DigLib project, the information in the HyperNavigator database layer is computed in response to queries from the import scheduling service and inserted into the relational database system of DigLib.

4.2   Modeling Web Sites

When setting up an HyperView system, two kinds of schemata must be developed: a global, domain-oriented schema for the database layer, and for each Web Site a site-specific *Abstract Content Representation* (ACR) schema. The ACR schema reflects the logical schema of the underlying Web Site. HTML pages are modeled by a common generic schema.

A set of site specific rules has to be defined which is used to match the data contained in these HTML graphs and to create an intermediate data layer conforming to the ACR schema of the source.

Another set of rules has to be defined which restructures the information stored in the ACR graphs and to integrate it on a third layer into a common graph database conforming to the database schema. In DigLib, the database schema defines concepts for electronic journals, volumes and issues of journals, and articles, along with their usual attributes.

The advantage of using rules for information extraction compared with other more character-oriented techniques proposed in the literature (see Section 5) lies in the fact that its rules are declarative, easy to maintain, and (to some extend) robust against minor deviations and restructurings of pages. If structural changes in the Web Sites break the existing views, it is often sufficient to change only the rules for the ACR graph, without affecting the higher layers.

The HyperNavigator Database schema. In order to wrap Web Sites for electronic journals, we first have to set up a database schema, as shown in Fig. 4, which models the domain of electronic journals independently of the heterogeneous structure of the publisher Web Sites.

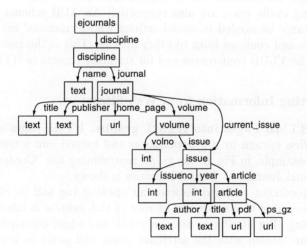

Fig. 4. ejournal database schema

We categorize all electronic journals by discipline. Each journal consists of several volumes, each having a number of issues. Each issue contains several articles, for which the authors, title, and links to the PostScript/PDF version are retained. It should be stressed that this is a preliminary schema that will further evolve during the lifetime of DigLib. A more complex schema graph, probably containing cycles, can be modelled as easily.

ACR Schema of an Example WWW Source. For each Web Site, an ACR schema has to be developed which reflects the conceptual structure of this Site. In this paper we present as example the Link information service <http://link.springer.de> of the Springer-Verlag Berlin Heidelberg New York. It provides several houndred electronic journals grouped by scientific discipline into so-called "online libraries". Each journal has a home page and a "Contents" page listing each volume together with the issues belonging to this volume. For each issue there is a table of contents, where the authors and title of each article can be found, across with links to the abstract and to the full paper in PostScript and PDF format.

The conceptual structure of the Springer-Verlag server is depicted in the ACR schema of Fig. 5. Note that this schema only models information related to electronic journals. Other data made available by the server need not to be modeled.

Each node of the ACR schema models a class of pages or page fragments. The edges correspond to hyper-links between pages or to part-of relations between page fragments. Due to structural differences between journals published by the German and the American branch of Springer-Verlag, we had to establish a separate subschema for the journals appearing in the American branch, whose nodes are indicated by the suffix " _us".

This example ACR schema has a simple tree structure. More complex structures, including cyclic ones, are also supported. An ACR schema with cycles would for instance be needed to model articles whose citations' list is electronically available and contains links to other articles. This is the case for articles published in the VLDB conferences and for scientific reports in HTML format.

4.3 Extracting Information from Web Sites

Parsing of HTML Pages into HTML graphs. HTML pages are analyzed in the HyperView system by a generic parser and turned into a tree-structured graph. As an example, in Fig. 6, the graph representing the "Contents" page of the International Journal on Digital Libraries is shown.

Each subdocument enclosed between an opening tag and its closing counterpart is represented as a subtree. The root of this subtree is labeled with the name of the tag. Tag attributes are converted into edges emanating from the root, which are labeled with the attribute name and point to a node labeled with the attribute value. The content of the subdocument is represented as a sequence of children nodes containing either untagged text (called PCDATA in

125

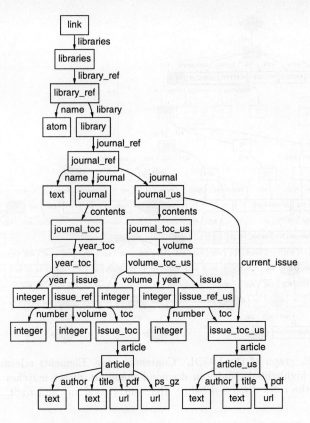

Fig. 5. ACR schema for Springer-Verlag. American journals indicated by suffix "_us".

HTML terminology) or root nodes of further tagged subdocuments. From the root node, numbered *#(i)* edges are pointing to these children nodes.

Defining a View over the HTML Graphs. We now describe the establishment of the ACR graph over the HTML pages of a Web Site. Each ACR graph is a view defined by a set of rules developed and maintained by the DigLib administrator. In the case of the Springer-Verlag, the complete ruleset consists of 15 rules; we explain two of them in detail.

As mentioned before, the "Contents" page of a journal lists all available issues, ordered by year. Suppose that the HyperNavigator has already loaded this page and there is a journal_toc node with a *source* edge pointing to the root node of this page in the ACR graph. The internal HTML representation of this page (with some icons and navigational links omitted) has been shown in Fig. 6.

Rule get_year_toc shown in Fig. 7 computes a *year_toc* edge leading from the journal_toc node to a new year_toc node in the ACR graph which corresponds to a page fragment listing all journal issues for a particular year. In the

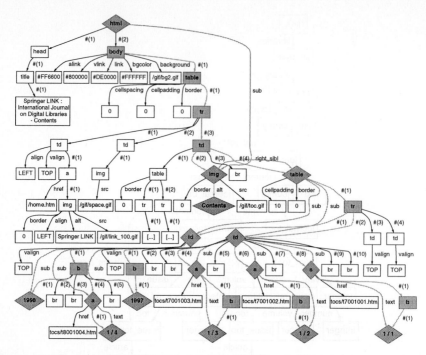

Fig. 6. HTML graph of the IJODL "Contents" page. Elements relevant to rule application are highlighted. Nodes in diamond-shape are direct matches for the nodes occurring in the rules discussed below. Relevant virtual *sub* and *right_sibl* edges are included.

existing HTML graph of the content page, the rule matches a path from the root <html> node to a <td> tag which contains a string matching a year number Year. This path follows derived *sub* edges expressing a logical subnode relation. This relation is implemented by alternative rules, depending on the type of the source node. Another derived edge, *right_sibl*, allows direct access to the right sibling of a node. A link to this <td> node and an year attribute with value Year is added to the new year_toc node then.

The second rule, get_issue_ref, computes an *issue* edge from the year_toc node (created by rule get_year_toc) to a issue_ref node with volume number Volume and issue number Number as matched by the HTML part of the rule. A *source* edge points to the anchor containing a hyper-link to the table-of-contents page of that issue. Further similar rules can be used now to follow this link, match entries for articles and their components, and extract information on author, title, and links to the abstract and the full document in PostScript or PDF format.

Defining a View over the ACR Graphs. We describe now how we establish the database graph over the ACR graphs of different publisher Web Sites. The

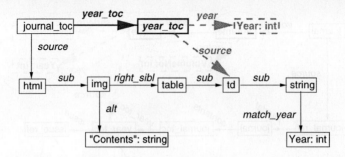

Fig. 7. Rule get_year_toc. **Notation** (also used for the other rules): (i) the upper part relates to the result graph of the view (here: the ACR graph), the lower part to the source graph (here: an HTML graph). (ii) Existing graph items to be matched are shown with normal-width (black) lines. (iii) Graph items which are materialized by the rule on demand are shown with bold (red) lines and boldface (red) font. (iv) Additional graph items produced as a side-effect of the rule are shown with bold dashed (green) lines and boldface (green) font.

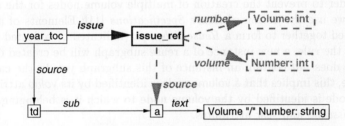

Fig. 8. Rule get_issue_ref

database graph is a view defined by a set of publisher-specific rules. From the ruleset for the ACR graph of the Springer-Verlag, we select the rule get_issue as an example. This rule is shown in Fig. 9.

In the ACR subschema for the German branch of Springer-Verlag, issue_ref nodes are organized by year. In the database graph, we have issue nodes organized by volume. The purpose of the rule get_issue is to map the issue_ref nodes to issue nodes.

Note that the issues comprising a volume of a journal are not necessarily identical with the issues having appeared in a certain year. Some journals may have two or more volumes per year. Volumes may start at any time of the year. With our graphical notation, this fact is specified in an intuitive way.

For a given journal node, the corresponding "Contents" page (represented by the journal_toc node) is found. For each issue_ref node that belongs to volume *VolumeNo*, has number *IssueNo*, and can be reached through a year_toc node for year *Year*, the rule creates a volume node and an issue node in the database and supplies them with the attribute values of *VolumeNo*, *IssueNo*, and *Year*.

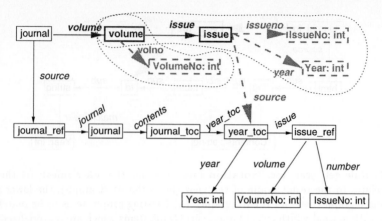

Fig. 9. ACR rule get_issue. Notation: *Reuse Subgraphs* are indicated by dotted loops.

In order to prevent the creation of multiple **volume** nodes for the same *VolumeNo*, we use the notion of *Reuse Specifications* [11]: Elements of a rule can be grouped together to form a *Reuse Subgraph* (indicated by a dotted loop). On applying the rule, a new instance of a reuse subgraph will be created only if the database does *not* contain an instance of this subgraph yet. In the case of rule get_issue, this implies that a **volume** node is identified by its *volno* attribute, and a **issue** node is identified by the **volume** node to which it is belonging, together with its *issueno* and *year* attributes.

Querying the HyperNavigator. The HyperNavigator provides a simple graph-based query language which is used to specify the information to be imported into the DigLib catalogue. A query is a rule that does not produce new graph elements, but just returns for each match a binding for the variables occuring in the rule. HyperView rules can be supplied with arbitrary computable constraints on the variables in order to restrict the set of matches. For each admissible match, we return the variable, or – in the case of the digital library – insert it as a new tuple into the database of the DigLib server. In the case of a stand-alone HyperView server which has a user interface of its own, rules will be used to generate HTML pages which contain the results of a query in a generic or customized format.

In Fig. 10 we show an example of a query retrieving volume, issue number, and title of all articles containing the word "metadata" in their title and having appeared after 1996 in any computer science journal on "Digital Libraries" (string in the journal name).

In DigLib, we use information from the digital library database to formulate import queries that avoid unnecessary page accesses. In particular, the publisher, the URL of a journal and the volume and number of the last imported issue are given as parameters. Hence, the HyperNavigator does not have to navigate from

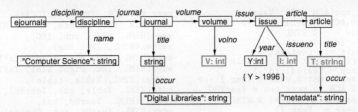

Fig. 10. Example Query: all articles on "metadata" having appeared in a computer science journal on "Digital Libraries" after 1996. The vertices corresponding to the retrieved attributes are shown in boldface.

the publisher's home page to the journal page but can access it directly in order to check for a new issue.

Fig. 11 shows the import query for the next issue of the Intl. Journal on Digital Libraries. From the scheduling data in the catalogue we know that the current issue is the 4th one of the 1st volume. The Import Scheduling Service reads this information and passes it to the **HyperNavigator** when establihing the **ToDo** list (see subsection 3.2). The result of this query is inserted by the **HyperView** into the DigLib catalogue.

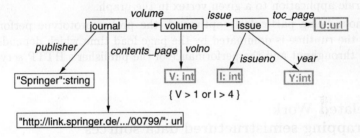

Fig. 11. Import Query for the next issue of the IJODL

4.4 Implementation of the **HyperNavigator**

A prototype of the **HyperNavigator** has been implemented in SWI Prolog. Schema and instance graphs are stored in the Prolog fact database. We implement **HyperView** rules as Prolog predicates by using a special syntax for expressing rules. This special syntax is translated into plain Prolog code by a preprocessor.

For rule **get_year_toc** (depicted in Fig. 7), this syntax and the result of the translation are shown in Fig. 12.

The prolog predicate for a rule can be registered with a schema graph by specifying that it is to be used to materialize edges with a certain label in an instance graph of this schema.

```
get_year_toc(ACR, TOC, Year):--         get_year_toc(ACR, TOC, YearTOC):-
    TOC @ ACR: journal_toc ->               edge(ACR, TOC, source, Root @ HTML),
    source = _ @ HTML ->                    edge(HTML, HTML, sub, IMG),
    sub = Img: img -> [                     vertex(HTML, IMG, img),
        alt =  'Contents',                  edge(HTML, IMG, alt, 'Contents'),
        right_sibl = _ : table ->           edge(HTML, IMG, right_sibl, Table),
        sub = YearNd: td ->                 vertex(HTML, Table, table),
        sub-> match_year = Year ] -->       edge(HTML, Table, sub, YearNd),
    TOC @ ACR -> year_toc = YearTOC ->      vertex(HTML, YearNd, td),
    [  source =  YearNd @ HTML,             edge(HTML, YearNd, sub, String),
       year =  Year ]).                     edge(HTML, String, match_year, Year),
                                            add_vertex(ACR,YearTOC,year_toc),
                                            add_edge(ACR,TOC,year_toc,YearTOC),
                                            add_edge(ACR,YearTOC,source,YearNd@HTML),
                                            add_edge(ACR,YearTOC,year,Year).
```

Fig. 12. Prolog notation and translation for rule get_year_toc

Once there is a request for edges with that label emanating from a certain source node, the Prolog fact database will be queried first. If this fails, each predicate registered for that kind of edge is called in turn to materialize the requested edges. This approach overcomes the inefficiencies inherent to most graph-rewriting techniques by always applying rules only on demand, and focusing the rule application to a given vertex in the graph.

Without being particularly optimized, the prolog prototype performs fast enough: the runtime is dominated by the page load time which depends on the network throughput and the performance of the publisher's HTTP server.

5 Related Work:
Wrapping semistructured data sources

In digital libraries, wrappers are used mostly to adapt an existing search facility of a source to a certain search protocol, say, Z39.50 [20]. However, little has been reported about the use and construction of WWW wrappers in the field of digital libraries.

In the Stanford Digital Library Project, wrappers (here called "proxies") are used to access distributed, autonomous services, but also for providing metadata on attribute sets of search proxies [5]. The actual construction of wrappers is not covered in this work. For building WWW wrappers, the WebExtractor [15] (discussed below) has been developed in the context of this project.

In the German MeDoc [8] project, publisher servers are wrapped in order to support a common search protocol and to provide term frequency profiles which are used to preselect sources for distributed queries. Due to the close cooperation with publishers in this project, these wrappers did not have to be built on top of WWW sources.

Wrappers for WWW sources have to provide three functionalities: navigation, information extraction, and information integration. In the HyperView system, these aspects are combined into a seamless graph-based approach.

Web query languages, such as WebSQL [21], W3QS [17], WebLog [18], and WebOQL [2] focus primarily on ad-hoc queries. With the exception of WebOQL, they all ignore the syntactical structure of HTML pages and consider only the included hyper-links. Still, these approaches provide valuable insight into the navigational aspect of Web Site wrapping.

InfoExtractor [26], a tool developed by INRIA/Bull, and the Web Extractor [15] built by the TSIMMIS [13] group at Stanford both use a hierarchy of regions defined by regular expressions to analyze the structure of a document and extract parts of it as result. These methods are completely character-oriented and do not take advantage of the structure provided by the HTML syntax. This makes it difficult to write wrappers that are robust with respect to reordering of page elements or small variations in the HTML text.

The wrapper generation toolkit [3] of Ashish and Knoblock works in a semi-automatic way by presenting guesses on the structure and interesting regions of example pages to the user. Again, this tool is character-oriented and sensitive to details of the HTML code. Furthermore, the issue of Web navigation is not covered.

NoDoSE [1] aims at extracting structured data from semistructured text documents in general, not only for HTML pages. The user has to decompose hierarchically an example document and specify the type of data to be extracted from each part, with respect to a user supplied object-oriented schema. The system comprises a mining component which supports this decomposition by inferring grammar rules.

The YAT [7] system is a tool for specifying data conversions. The YAT data model represents documents by ordered labeled trees which can be linked by references. Tree models form an instantiation hierarchy. YATL is a declarative, rule based language featuring pattern matching and restructuring operators. Each rule matches one or more (sub-)trees and produces a new tree. Currently, the major limitation of YAT is its missing support for incremental data conversion on demand. This means that all data has to be imported and converted once, making it less suitable for Web views. Furthermore, pattern matching across hyper-links which is important for Web Site navigation is not supported.

EDITOR is a procedural language [4] for extraction and restructuring of text from arbitrary documents. It combines a set of elementary text manipulation commands with loop constructs. This approach seems to be quite low-level imposing negative consequences for the legibility and maintenance of EDITOR programs. EDITOR is used in the context of the ARANEUS project which provides a tool box for the management of data from the Web. The EDITOR language is used for extracting data from semistructured HTML pages which are modeled in the hierarchical ("page-oriented") ARANEUS Data Model (ADM). The language ULIXES is used to specify and navigate within the link structure of the pages and to build nested-relational views over the extracted data. The generation of Web pages from these views is specified in the language PENELOPE. Compared to the seamless, graph-based HyperView approach, ARANEUS uses three different languages and different data models (ADM, relational) within the same system.

Strudel [12] is a system for the management of Web Sites. It assumes the underlying data to be available in a graph representation, but does not deal with the construction of wrappers which could retrieve this data from external Web Sites.

6 Conclusion and Outlook

The increasing number of electronic journals calls for effective access. Digital libraries can meet this demand by establishing search-able catalogues integrating the bibliographic data of electronic journals and providing uniform access to the articles stored at heterogeneous publisher Web Sites.

In this paper we deal with the problem of metadata acquisition for such a catalogue, in the context of the ongoing Natural Sciences Digital Library project at the Free University of Berlin. We propose an adaptive import strategy implemented in the Import Scheduling Service.

The HyperNavigator is triggered by the Import Scheduling Service in order to carry out the metadata import. It is based on the HyperView methodology for establishing views over heterogeneous Web Sites. The main advantages of our methodology are its graph-based approach and the uniform use of views defined by declarative rules at all levels of the system.

We have demonstrated the feasibility of this approach for the *Link* information service of the Springer-Verlag publishing house. We have presented the required schemata and have discussed detailed examples of the rules defining the views. We have also covered briefly the implementation of the HyperNavigator.

We are currently integrating the HyperNavigator with the DigLib server being under development. An interesting extension of this work is to use the Hyper-Navigator for wrapping also the existing search interfaces of publisher WWW servers, thus supporting distributed full-text retrieval.

Acknowledgments: We wish to express our special thanks to Ulf Leser, Agnes Voisard, Jana Lewerenz, and Daniel Faensen for their helpful suggestions and comments on this paper.

References

1. B. Adelberg. NoDoSE: A tool for semi-automatically extracting semi-structured data from text documents-brad adelberg. In *SIGMOD Conference 1998*, 1998.
2. G. Arocena and A. Mendelzon. WebOQL: Restructuring documents, databases and webs. In *Proc. of 14th. Intl. Conf. on Data Engineering (ICDE 98)*, 1998.
3. N. Ashish and C. Knoblock. Wrapper generation for semi-structured internet sources. In *Proc. Workshop on Management of Semistructured Data*, Tucson, 1997.

4. P. Atzeni and G. Mecca. Cut & paste. In *PODS'97*, pages 12–15, Tucson, Arizona, 1997.

5. M. Baldonado, C.K. Chang, L. Gravano, and A. Paepcke. The stanford digital library metadata architecture. *International Journal on Digital Libraries*, 1(2):108–121, 1997.

6. BUBL (British National Information Service for the higher education community). <http://bubl.ac.uk/admin/purpose.htm>.

7. S. Cluet, C. Delobel, J. Siméon, and K. Smaga. Your mediators need data conversion! In *SIGMOD Conference 1998*, pages 177–188, 1998.

8. M. Dreger et al. Medoc information broker - harnessing the information in letera-ture and full text databases. In N. Fuhr J. Callan, editor, *Proc. SIGIR workshop on Networked Information Retrieval*, 1996.

9. D. Faensen, A. Hinze, and H. Schweppe. Alerting in a digital library environment – do channels meet the requirements. In *ECDL'98*, 1998.

10. L.C. Faulstich, M. Spiliopoulou, and V. Linnemann. WIND: A warehouse for internet data. In *Advances in Databases – Proceedings BNCOD 15*, number 1271 in LNCS, pages 169–183. Springer, 1997.

11. Lukas C. Faulstich. Integrating web sites using HyperView. Submitted for publi-cation., 1998.

12. Mary Fernandez, Daniela Florescu, Jaewoo Kang, Alon Levy, and Dan Suciu. Catching the boat with Strudel: experiences with a web-site management system. In *SIGMOD*, pages 414–425, 1998.

13. H. Garcia-Molina, J. Hammer, K. Ireland, Y. Papakonstantinou, J. Ullman, and J. Widom. Integrating and accessing heterogeneous information sources in TSIM-MIS. In *AAAI Symposium on Information Gathering*, pages 61–64, 1995.

14. A. Gupta and I. S. Mumick. Maintenance of materialized views: Problems, tech-niques and applications. *IEEE Quarterly Bulletin on Data Engineering; Special Issue on Materialized Views and Data Warehousing*, 18(2):3 – 18, 1995.

15. J. Hammer, H. Garcia-Molina, J. Cho, R. Aranha, and A. Crespo. Extracting semistructured information from the web. In *Proc. Workshop on Management of Semistructured Data*, Tucson, 1997.

16. JSTOR. <http://www.jstor.org/>.

17. D. Konopnicki and O. Shmueli. W3QS : A system for WWW querying. In *ICDE'97*, pages 586–586, April 1997.

18. L. V. S. Lakshmanan, F. Sadri, and I. N. Subramanian. A declarative language for querying and restructuring the Web. In IEEE, editor, *RIDE'96*, pages 12–21. IEEE Computer Society Press, 1996.

19. M. Ley. Die Trierer Informatik-Bibliographie DBLP. In *GI Jahrestagung 1997*, pages 257–266, 1997. <http://dblp.uni-trier.de>.

20. C.A. Lynch. The Z39-50 information retrieval protocol: An overview and status report. *ACM Computer Communication Review*, 21(1):58–70, 1991.

21. A. O. Mendelzon, G. A. Mihaila, and T. Milo. Querying the World Wide Web. *International Journal on Digital Libraries*, 1(1):54–67, 1997.

22. P. Merialdo P. Atzeni, G. Mecca. To weave the web. In *VLDB '97*, pages 206–215, 1997.

23. PHP3 manual. <http://www.php.net/manual/>, 1998.

24. B.R. Schatz, W.H. Mischo, T.W. Cole, J.B. Hardin, A.P. Bishop, and H. Chen. Federating diverse collections of scientific literature. *IEEE Computer*, 29(5), 1996.

25. Simon Fraser University Electronic Library in Computing Science. <http://fas.sfu.ca/projects/ElectronicLibrary/Collections/CMPT/>.

26. D. Smith and M. Lopez. Information extraction for semi-structured documents. In *Proc. Workshop on Management of Semistructured Data*, Tucson, 1997.

27. Stanford University Libraries – Electronic Journals Collection. <http://www-sul.stanford.edu/collect/ejourns.html>.

28. Elektronische Zeitschriftenbibliothek, Universität Regensburg. <http://www.bibliothek.uni-regensburg.de/ezeit/ezb.phtml>.

29. Stony Brook University Libraries – electronic journals. <http://www.sunysb.edu/library/ldeljour.htm>.

30. J. Widom. Research problems in data warehousing. In *4th International Conference on Information and Knowledge Management*, pages 25 – 30, 1995.

The Application of Metadata Standards to Video Indexing

Jane Hunter[1], Renato Iannella[2]

[1]CITEC, 317 Edward St, Brisbane, Qld, 4001, Australia.
Phone +61 7 3365 4310, Fax +61 7 3365 4311 jane@dstc.edu.au

[2]DSTC Pty Ltd, The University of Queensland, Qld, 4072, Australia.
Phone +61 7 3365 4310, Fax +61 7 3365 4311 renato@dstc.edu.au

Abstract. This paper first outlines a multi-level video indexing approach based on Dublin Core extensions and the Resource Description Framework (RDF). The advantages and disadvantages of this approach are discussed in the context of the requirements of the proposed MPEG-7 ("Multimedia ContenDescription Interface") standard. Finally a hybrid approach is proposed based on the combined use of Dublin Core and the currently undefined MPEG-7 standard within the RDF which will provide a solution to the problem of satisfying widely differing user requirements.

1. Introduction

With the enormous growth in digital audiovisual information on the Internet, there is a corresponding need for tools which enable fast and efficient indexing, querying, browsing and delivery of audiovisual data. The development of content-based metadata standards for audiovisual data will greatly simplify the development of multimedia capable search engines on the World Wide Web.

Dublin Core was designed specifically for generating metadata for textual documents. Although a number of workshops have been held to discuss the applicability of Dublin Core to non-textual documents such as images, sound and moving images, they have primarily focused on extensions to the 15 core elements through the use of sub-elements and schemes specific to audiovisual data, to describe bibliographic-type information rather than the actual content.

The objective of the proposed MPEG-7 ("Multimedia Content Description Interface") standard is to specify a standard set of descriptors and description schemes for describing the content of audiovisual information. The MPEG-7 work group expects to issue a Call for Proposals in October 1998.

This paper first outlines a multi-level video indexing approach based on Dublin Core extensions and the Resource Description Framework (RDF). The advantages and disadvantages of this approach are discussed in the context of the requirements of the proposed MPEG-7 standard. Finally a hybrid approach is proposed based on the combined use of Dublin Core and the currently undefined MPEG-7 standard within the RDF which will provide a solution to the problem of satisfying widely differing user requirements.

2. Video Indexing

Typically the indexing of a news/current affairs program consists of the following steps:
1. Segment the video hierarchically into sequences, scenes, and shots. (A *shot* is a continuous sequence of frames captured from one camera. A *scene* is composed of one or more shots which present different views of the same event, related in time or space. A *segment* is composed of one or more related scenes.)
2. Describe the complete video - bibliographic information (title, creator, dates, subjects, item numbers, publisher details, names, synopsis etc.) plus format, framerate, duration etc
3. Describe each sequence - id, start time/frame, end time/frame, brief textual summary
4. Describe each scene - id, start time/frame, end time/frame, brief textual summary, transcript (ideally derived from a closed caption decoder)
5. Describe each shot - id, start time/frame, end time/frame,keyframe (first frame of the shot, ideally derived from an automatic shot detection algorithm)

2.1 Example of News Clip Indexing

Below is an example of the indexed breakdown of a 52 second news clip on the political situation in Cambodia. It was recorded from a news broadcast by SBS, Australia's National Multicultural Broadcaster. Consequently the images below are copyright SBS and should not be reused without the permission of SBS.

This news clip is the third sequence in a 30 minute news show. It is broken into 4 scenes, each of which contains a number of shots. Associated with each scene is an ID, a brief description, its duration (SMPTE time codes) and its associated transcript. Associated with each shot is an ID, a brief description, the start time code and a GIF image which is the first frame (keyframe) from that shot.

Sequence #3

Scene#3.1 - Introduction by Indira Naidoo
Duration = 19:31:24;1 - 19:31:35;25 (12secs)
Transcript = "One of Cambodia's leading democracy campaigners Sam Rainsy has criticised the Australian government's response to the political crisis in his country. He says Australia must get more involved in Cambodia."

Shot#3.1.1
Introduction by Indira
Naidoo
19:31:24;1

Scene#3.2 - Sam Rainsy arrives in Australia
Duration = 19:31:36;1 - 19:31:53;25 (18secs)
Transcript= "Known as a fighter of corruption and an opponent of Hun Sen, Sam Rainsy arrived with one message about Australia's response to the crisis." "Not strong enough. I hope it will be clearer in the next few days."

Shot#3.2.1	**Shot#3.2.2**
Arrival at Airport	Interview with Sam Rainsy
19:31:36;1	19:31:46;1

Scene#3.3 - Footage of grenade attack
Duration = 19:31:54;1 - 19:32:03;25 (10secs)
Transcript = "Sam Rainsy knows the violence of political life in Cambodia. Four months ago, 16 of his supporters were killed in a grenade attack near Phnom Penh."

Shot#3.3.1	**Shot#3.3.2**	**Shot#3.3.3**
People running from explosion	Woman carrying injured child	Policeman covering corpse
19:31:54;1	19:31:57;1	19:32:00;1

Scene#3.4 - Katherine McGrath outside Parliament House, Canberra
Duration = 19:32:04;1 - 19:32:16;25 (12secs)
Transcript = "Today in Canberra, the Government defended its performance, saying it's absolutely determined to work with Asean countries to see a return to democracy in Cambodia."

Shot#3.4.1
Katherine McGrath outside
Parliament House.
19:32:16;1

3. Extensions to Dublin Core for Moving Images

The elements of Dublin Core are: Title, Creator, Subject, Description, Publisher, Contributor, Date, Type, Format, Identifier, Source, Language, Relation, Coverage and Rights. The semantics of these attributes are described in [1].

The following is the list of sub-elements at the time of writing this paper. This list is still under development by the Dublin Core community.

- Title.Main ,Title.Alternative
- Creator.PersonalName, Creator.PersonalName.Address, Creator.CorporateName, Creator.CorporateName.Address
- Publisher.PersonalName, Publisher.PersonalName.Address, Publisher.CorporateName, Publisher.CorporateName.Address
- OtherContributor.PersonalName, OtherContributor.PersonalName.Address, OtherContributor.CorporateName, OtherContributor.CorporateName.Address
- Date.Created, Date.Issued, Date.Available, Date.Acquired, Date.DataGathered, Date.Accepted, Date.Valid
- Relation.IsPartOf, Relation.HasPart, Relation.IsVersionOf, Relation.HasVersion, Relation.IsFormatOf, Relation.HasFormat, Relation.References, Relation.IsReferencedBy, Relation.IsBasedOn, Relation.IsBasisFor, Relation.Requires, Relation.IsRequiredBy
- Coverage.PeriodName, Coverage.PlaceName, Coverage.T, Coverage.X, Coverage.Y, Coverage.Z, Coverage.Polygon, Coverage.Line, Coverage.3D
  The semantics for these attributes are described in [2].

3.1 Moving Image Resources Workshop Recommendations

The Resource Discovery Workshop: Moving Image Resources [3], examined Dublin Core's potential use for describing moving images resources, tested it against a variety of examples, and critically reviewed its application. It concluded that the Dublin Core model could be used to describe moving image resources given some provisos and solutions to the problems listed below:

- Dublin Core terminology is not sufficiently intuitive for non-library trained researchers and non-specialists to use. To overcome this, ample qualifiers (i.e. long definitive lists of sub-elements and Schemes) should be provided.
- Dublin Core has difficulty satisfying the widely differing needs of both non-specialist interdisciplinary searchers and specialist users.
- *DC.Publisher* requires a large number of sub-elements for moving image resources, including place.
- To overcome the problem of separating primary from secondary creators, *DC.Creator* and *DC.Contributor* should be combined into *DC.Creator* with a large number of clearly specified sub-elements indicating the role.

- Differentiating between original works, various manifestations during production and digital surrogates and each of their respective *DC.Creator*, *DC.Publisher*, *DC.Date* values is a major problem.
- *DC.Coverage* shouldn't be used at all since it can't be used consistently to contain concepts of place and duration. Place can be allocated to either *DC.Subject* (provenance) or *DC.Publisher* (place of release) and duration (running time) can be allocated to *DC.Format*.
- Only *DC.Description*, the free text description does not potentially require some kind of sub-element or Scheme, apart from the suggestion that censorship board classification should go here.

A summary of the outcomes of this workshop can also be found at [4].

3.2 Proposed Dublin Core Extensions for Multilevel Searching

The Moving Image Workshop focused primarily on the semantics of what bibliographic data should be put in which Dublin Core element. Defining what to put where and the lists of sub-elements and Schemes required to satisfy different communities' semantical needs is best left to the specialists themselves.

A major but different type of problem identified by the workshop is the one of satisfying the differing needs of non-specialist interdisciplinary searchers and specialist users. Some users require only very basic information whilst others require detailed interpretive descriptions at a very low level. One of the most problematic issues with trying to apply a "core" data set to something as complex as film or video, is that even summary information can typically include a brief interpretative description of every shot, a full cast and credits list, details of awards and copyright details and detailed technical information often running to many hundreds of lines of data entry. The Moving Image Resources Workshop identified a need for some distinction between 'core' and 'full' data sets for moving image resources. In many cases archival catalogue records are so detailed that they provide a surrogate to actually viewing the resource. This can be particularly important where viewing might endanger a fragile original or for academic researchers who may not need to view a film but do need to find detailed information about it.

The following section describes a solution to this problem through the use of optional extensions to certain Dublin Core elements. This approach provides multiple levels of descriptive information. The top level can be used for non-specialist inter-disciplinary searching. The lower levels can be used for fine-grained discipline-specific searching. The elements discussed are Type, Description, Format, Relation and Coverage.

3.2.1 DC.Type
This defines the category of the resource. For the sake of interoperability, *Type* should be selected from a hierarchy of enumerated lists. For example:

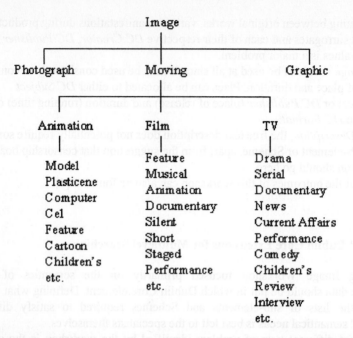

The structured lists above enable the genre of the complete clip/document to be specified. In addition, there is a need to be able to specify parts and sub-parts of complete clips/documents.

Generally film and video documents can be broken down into the following parts: sequences, scenes, shots, frames. Each sequence consists of a number of contiguous scenes. Each scene consists of a number of contiguous shots. Each shot consists of a number of contiguous frames. Each frame can be subdivided into regions representing actors or objects. This hierarchy of enumerated types also defines the rules for valid Relations between Types i.e. *IsPartOf* and *HasPart*.

- Sequence
  - Scene
    - Shot
      - Frame
        - Object/Actor/Person

Some examples of Types based on the enumerated lists above are:

- DC.Type = "Image.Moving.Film.Documentary.sequence.scene"
- DC.Type = "Image.Moving.TV.News.sequence.scene.shot.frame"

3.2.2 DC.Description

Currently within Dublin Core, this represents a textual description of the content of the resource. It is usually an abstract in the case of document-like objects or a textual content description in the case of visual resources. In reality, the description can be any media type e.g. text, image, audio, video, or a URI.

In the newsclip indexing example described in <u>Section 2.1</u>, the complete sequence/clip, the scenes and the shots possess a textual description. In addition, scenes possess a transcript and shots possess a keyframe. This paper proposes that each *DC.Type* possess an associated set of allowable descriptors which are specified as subelements to the *DC.Description* element.

For example if DC.Type = "Image.Moving.TV.News.Scene" then valid descriptors are Description.text and Description.transcript. If DC:Type = "Image.Moving.TV. News.Scene.Shot" then valid descriptors are Description.text and Description. keyframe. If DC.Type = "Image.Moving.TV.News.Scene.Shot.Frame" then valid descriptions are Description.text and Description.histogram which is a colour histogram of the frame.

In addition, the valid format of the content of a particular description type must match a value from the IMT (Internet Media Type) Scheme. For example the value of Description.keyframe value must be one of the IMT image formats: image/gif, image/jpeg, etc.

Alternatively, the actual content can be a value taken from an enumerated list or controlled vocabulary specified by a given Scheme. For example, Camera Motion must be selected from one of: *dolly forward, dolly back, truck left, truck right, pan left, pan right, tilt up, tilt down, zoom in, zoom out, stationary*. Camera Distance must be one of: *close-up, medium shot* or *long shot*. Camera Angle must be either *low, high* or *eye-level*. Opening and Closing transitions can only be one of: *cut, fade, wipe* or *dissolve*.

Table 1 below illustrates the proposed hierarchical structure and examples of associated permissable descriptors and formats. This approach is suffiently flexible to allow particular communities and working groups to define their own rules on combinations of descriptors and descriptor schemes.

Table 1. Resource Types and Permissable Descriptor Types and Formats

DC.Type	DC.Description	Allowable Formats
Image.Moving.*	DC.Description.Text	Text
Image.Moving.*. sequence	DC.Description.Text	Text
Image.Moving.*. sequence.scene	DC.Description.Text	Text
	DC.Description.Script	Text
	DC.Description.Transcript	Text
	DC.Description.EditList	Text
	DC.Description.Duration	secs, frames
	DC.Description.StartTime	secs, frame no, SMPTE
	DC.Description.EndTime	secs, frame no, SMPTE
	DC.Description.Keyframe	JPEG, GIF
	DC.Description.Locale	Text
	DC.Description.Cast	Text

	DC.Description.Objects	Text
Image.Moving.*. sequence.scene.shot	DC.Description.Text	Text
	DC.Description.Duration	secs, frames
	DC.Description.StartTime	secs, frame no, SMPTE
	DC.Description.EndTime	secs, frame no, SMPTE
	DC.Description.Keyframe	JPEG, GIF
	DC.Description.Camera.Dist	Controlled vocab.
	DC.Description.Camera.Angle	Controlled vocab.
	DC.Description.Camera.Motn	Controlled vocab., line
	DC.Description.Lighting	Controlled vocab.
	DC.Description.OpenTrans	Controlled vocab.
	DC.Description.CloseTrans	Controlled vocab.
Image.Moving.*. sequence.scene.shot. frame	DC.Description.Text	Text
	DC.Description.Image	JPEG,GIF
	DC.Description.Timestamp	secs, frame no, SMPTE
	DC.Description.Colour	Histogram, Text
	DC.Description.Anno.Text	Text
	DC.Description.Anno.Posn	Point, Area, Object-Id
Image.Moving.*. sequence.scene.shot. frame.object	DC.Description.Text	Text
	DC.Description.Position	Point
	DC.Description.Shape	Polygon
	DC.Description.Trajectory	Line
	DC.Description.Speed	Pixels/frame
	DC.Description.Colour	Histogram, Text
	DC.Description.Texture	Tamura,SAR feature vector
	DC.Description.Volume	3D polygon
	DC.Description.Anno.Text	Text
	DC.Description.Anno.Posn	Point, Area

3.2.3 DC.Format

This represents the data format of the resource and can be used to identify the software and possibly hardware that might be needed to display or operate the resource. For the sake of interoperability, Format should be selected from an enumerated list that is currently under development in the Dublin Core workshop series. The kinds of information which will be stored in this element include:

Format.video.type = 35mm film, VHS etc.
Format.video.colourdepth = 256

Format.video.length = 31 mins.
Format.video.codec = MJPEG, MPEG1, MPEG2, AVI, QT, etc.
Format.video.framerate = 25
Format.video.resolution, Format.video.width, Format.video.height
Format.sound, Format.sound.channels, Format.sound.samplerate

3.2.4 DC.Relation
For video, we need to be able to describe parts of complete videos or clips such as: *sequences, scenes* and *shots*. The Relation subelements *HasPart* and *IsPartOf* provide this facility. For example the Relation values for scene3 would be:
Relation.HasPart Content= shot3.1, shot3.2, shot3.3
Relation.IsPartOf Content= sequence3
The hierarchy of parts and sub-parts will impose rules on the use of the*HasPart* and *IsPartOf* subelements. Clearly shots can be parts of scenes but not vice versa.

3.2.5 DC.Coverage
For moving image data, the proposal is to use the Coverage element to describe the temporal location of clips, scenes, shots etc. within a larger video segment. The format of the time value may be a frame number, SMPTE time code or time from the start.
Coverage.t.min scheme=SMPTE content="09:45:23;14"
Coverage.t.max scheme=SMPTE content="09:45:32;1"
In addition, the Coverage subelements, Coverage.x, Coverage.y, Coverage.z, Coverage.line, Coverage.polygon and Coverage.3D can be used to describe the spatial locations, motion and shapes of objects/actors within a frame. Detailed descriptions of these subelements, as determined by the Coverage Working Group can be found at [5].

4. Application of Dublin Core Extensions to News Clip Indexing

The following section provides an example of how Dublin Core, with the extensions described above, could be applied to index the news clip described in Section 2.1.
The news clip chosen is the third sequence in a 30 minute TV news program. This particular sequence contains 5 scenes, each of which contains a number of shots. Only the Dublin Core elements for Scene 3.3 and Shot 3.3.2 are described. The descriptions for the other scenes and shots can easily be deduced from this example.

Complete News Program
Title = SBS World News
Creator = Special Broadcasting Service
Publisher = Special Broadcasting Service
Contributor.Presenter = Indira Naidoo
Description.text = "Major world news events of the day"

Date = 1998-02-20
Type = "Image.Moving.TV.news"
Format.type = VHS
Format.length = 30 mins
Identifier = "http://www.dstc.edu.au/videos/98-02-20.mpg"
Language = en

Sequence#3

Subject = "Cambodia -- Politics and government; Cambodia -- History; Australia -- Foreign relations -- Australia"
Description.text = "Cambodia's democracy campaigner, Sam Rainsy, criticises Australia's response to his country's political crisis"
Contributor.Reporter = "Catherine McGrath"
Type = "Image.Moving.TV.news.sequence"
Format.length = 62 secs
Coverage.t.min scheme=SMPTE content= 19:31:24;1
Coverage.t.max scheme=SMPTE content= 19:32:26;1
Relation.IsPartOf = Complete News Program
Relation.HasPart = scene3.1, scene3.2, scene3.3, scene3.4, scene3.5

Scene#3.3

Description.text ="Footage of grenade attack."
Description.transcript = "Sam Rainsy knows the violence of political life in Cambodia. Four months ago, 16 of his supporters were killed in a grenade attack near Phnom Penh."
Type = "Image.Moving.TV.news.sequence.scene"
Format.length = 10 secs
Coverage.t.min scheme=SMPTE content= 19:31:57;1
Coverage.t.max scheme=SMPTE content= 19:32:07;1
Relation.IsPartOf = sequence3
Relation.HasPart = shot3.3.1, shot3.3.2, shot3.3.3

Shot#3.3.2

Description.keyframe = shot3.3.2.gif
Description.text = "Woman carrying injured child"
Type = "Image.Moving.TV.news.sequence.scene.shot"
Format.length = 3 secs
Coverage.t.min scheme = SMPTE content = 19:31:57;1
Coverage.t.max scheme = SMPTE content = 19:32:00;1
Relation.IsPartOf = scene3

4.1 The Resource Description Framework

The Resource Description Framework (RDF) [6] is a specification currently under development within the W3C Metadata activity [7]. RDF is designed to provide an infrastructure to support metadata across many web-based activities. It is the result of a number of metadata communities bringing together their needs to provide a robust and flexible architecture for supporting metadata on the Internet and WWW. It's design has been heavily influenced by the Warwick Framework work [8].

RDF will allow different application communities to define the metadata property set that best serves the needs of each community. It will provide a uniform and interoperable means to exchange the metadata between programs and across the Web. RDF will also provide a means for publishing both a human-readable and a machine-understandable definition of the property set itself.

RDF is still under development but to date the following documents have been released for public comment:

- A public draft of the RDF Model and Syntax Specification (released Feb. 16 1998) [9].
- A public draft of the RDF Schema work-in-progress (released April 10 1998) [10].

RDF uses XML (eXtensible Markup Language) [11], as the transfer syntax in order to leverage other tools and code bases being built around XML. For example, SMIL (Synchronized Multimedia Integration Language) [12], a language for specifying Web-based Multimedia presentations, is encoded in XML.

We have chosen to use the RDF syntax for encoding video metadata because it provides a model for defining relationships between resources. This is illustrated below. The layered video structure is supported by defining RDF Sequence collection nodes within each DC:Relation:HasPart and a separate RDF:Description for each element of the Sequence collection. The indentations contribute to the readability and ease of understanding of the video structure.

More examples of the use of RDF syntax to encode Dublin Core metadata can be found at [13].

4.2 Dublin Core Example in RDF

Below are a series of RDF-encoded metadata descriptions for the different levels of the video clip. Each RDF description points to the corresponding actual content via the *About* value, which is a URL.

The difficulty with continuous media is that there is currently no standard way of pointing to a particular portion of an audio or video file, using a URL. Qualifying information that needs to be able to be specified in a URL referring to video or audio content includes:

- a specific time offset into a video/audio
- a specific time range within a video/audio

- a specific label within a video/audio where the label is resolved to a position and duration within the video/audio by some other service

Simpson-Young and Yap [14] propose a number of alternative approaches to solving this problem. Ideally one would be able to specify sequence#3 by something like:
http://www.dstc.edu.au/videos/98-02-20.mpg#start=00:54:24.01&end= 00:56:32.24
For the following examples we assume that each#*fragment* specified can be resolved to the appropriate time offset and duration and thus we refer to sequence#3 by:
  "http://www.dstc.edu.au/videos/98-02-20.mpg#seq3"

The RDF metadata for the URL "http://www.dstc.edu.au/videos/98-02-20.mpg" is shown below.

```
<?xml:namespace ns="http://www.w3c.org/RDF/" prefix="RDF"?>
<?xml:namespace ns="http://metadata.net/DC/" prefix="DC"?>

<RDF:RDF>
  <RDF:Description About="http://dstc.com/98-02-20.mpg">
    <DC:Title>SBS World News</DC:Title>
    <DC:Creator>Special Broadcasting Service</DC:Creator>
    <DC:Subject>News, Current Affairs</DC:Subject>
    <DC:Description>Major world news events</DC:Description>
    <DC:Publisher>Special Broadcasting Service</DC:Publisher>
    <DC:Contributor.Presenter>Indira Naidoo
                            </DC:Contributor.Presenter>
    <DC:Format DC:Scheme="IMT">video/mpg</DC:Format>
    <DC:Type>Image.Moving.TV.News</DC:Type>
    <DC:Language>en</DC:Language>
    <DC:Date>1998-05-12</DC:Date>
    <DC:Format.Length>30 mins</DC:Format.Length>
    <DC:Relation.HasPart>
      <RDF:Seq>
        <RDF:LI Resource="http://dstc.com/98-02-20.mpg#seq1"/>
        <RDF:LI Resource="http://dstc.com/98-02-20.mpg#seq2"/>
        <RDF:LI Resource="http://dstc.com/98-02-20.mpg#seq3"/>
        <RDF:LI Resource="http://dstc.com/98-02-20.mpg#seq4"/>
        <RDF:LI Resource="http://dstc.com/98-02-20.mpg#seq5"/>
        <RDF:LI Resource="http://dstc.com/98-02-20.mpg#seq6"/>
        <RDF:LI Resource="http://dstc.com/98-02-20.mpg#seq7"/>
      </RDF:Seq>
    </DC:Relation.HasPart>
  </RDF:Description>
</RDF:RDF>
```

The RDF metadata for the URL "http://www.dstc.edu.au/videos/98-02-20.mpg#seq3" is shown below. Similarly, the metadata for the scenes and shots can be deduced from these examples.

```
<?xml:namespace ns="http://www.w3c.org/RDF/"prefix="RDF"?>
<?xml:namespace ns="http://metadata.net/DC/"prefix="DC"?>
<RDF:RDF>
  <RDF:Description About= "http://www.dstc.edu.au/videos/98-02-
20.mpg#seq3">
     <DC:Type>Image.Moving.TV.news.sequence</DC:Type>
     <DC:Description.text>"Cambodia's democracy campaigner,
  Sam Rainsy, criticises Australia's response to his
  country's political crisis." </DC:Description.text>
     <DC:Subject>Cambodia -- Politics, Government,
  History</DC:Subject>
     <DC:Contributor.Reporter>Catherine  McGrath
  </DC:Contributor.Reporter>
     <DC:Format.Length>90 secs</DC:Format.Length>
     <DC:Coverage.t.min DC:Scheme="SMPTE">
  19:31:24;1</DC:Coverage.t.min>
     <DC:Coverage.t.max DC:Scheme="SMPTE">
  19:32:54;1</DC:Coverage.t.max>
     <DC:Relation.HasPart>
       <RDF:Seq>
         <RDF:LI Resource="http://www.dstc.edu.au/videos/  98-
  02-20.mpg#scene3.1"/>
         <RDF:LI Resource="http://www.dstc.edu.au/videos/  98-
  02-20.mpg#scene3.2"/>
         <RDF:LI Resource="http://www.dstc.edu.au/videos/  98-
  02-20.mpg#scene3.3"/>
         <RDF:LI Resource="http://www.dstc.edu.au/videos/  98-
  02-20.mpg#scene3.4"/>
         <RDF:LI Resource="http://www.dstc.edu.au/videos/  98-
  02-20.mpg#scene3.5"/>
       </RDF:Seq>
     </DC:Relation.HasPart>
  </RDF:Description>
</RDF:RDF>
```

5. Audio Metadata

So far, only visual and textual indexing have been considered, but audio also constitutes a major source of indexing information. Speech recognition can enable keyword queries on videos without the need for transcripts. By providing an example of a particular speaker's speech, speaker recognition enables users to perform queries such as: "Find all videos of Pamela Anderson speaking". Music recognition can enable the retrieval of videos containing a particular tune by humming or whistling. Audio cues such as silence, music and volume can be used to assist with the video segmentation. The downside of including this audio information is that it adds even further complexity to the already complex video metadata.

Figure 1 below illustrates how the soundtrack adds more layers to the already hierarchical video structure. Now the video consists of both temporally parallel and sequential components.

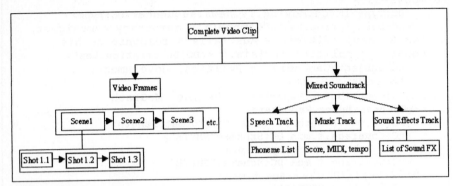

Fig. 1. Multilayered Hierarchical Structure of a Video Clip

The sound track plays back in parallel with the playback of the video frames. The soundtrack may consist of a large number of individual sound tracks mixed together. Typical types of soundtracks include : speech, music, sound effects, live, mixed. If the individual speech, music and sound effects tracks are not available, then mixed sound tracks can potentially be seperated into speech, music and sound effects tracks. Each of these individual sound tracks can be described using their own domain-specific descriptors and descriptor schemes and if required can be segmented into scenes and shots. For example the speech track may be described by a list of phonemes and their durations or phone lattices. A music track may be described by a score, MIDI file, melodic contour, frequency contour, tempo or amplitude envelope. A sound effects track may be described by a list of sound effect objects.

Because audio is such a complex data structure in its own right, this paper will not attempt to describe the possible DC:Description subelements and formats corresponding to each of the five types: mixed, speech, music, soundeffects, live. However it will briefly discuss the various approaches for including the audio metadata within the complete video metadata to enable cross-modal searching.

5.1 Adding Audio Metadata Using RDF

So far all of the video structures have been temporally sequential. The inclusion of audio metadata adds the requirement for temporal parallelism. RDF only provides three types of collections :*sequence, bag* and *alternatives. Sequence* can be used to specify ordering between collection members e.g. temporal, importance, alphabetical. *Bag* implies that all of the members are of equal importance. *Alternatives* implies there is a choice between members. Since there is no specific *Parallel* element for describing such temporal relationships, the next best alternative is to use the Bag element and to specify temporal locations and durations using DC.Coverage.t.min and

DC.Coverage.t.max. The ability to specify synchronisation between specific components is not supported without further subelements.

Below is a simple example which illustrates how to specify the temporal relationships and metadata of both audio and video components using RDF. The descriptions can be specified using Dublin Core, as shown above, or any other domain-specific metadata format.

```
<?xml:namespace ns="http://www.w3c.org/RDF/" prefix="RDF"?>
<?xml:namespace ns="http://metadata.net/DC/" prefix="DC"?>

<RDF:RDF>
    <RDF:Description About="http://www.dstc.edu.au/videos/98-
02-20.mpg">
        <DC:Title>SBS World News</DC:Title>
        <DC:Creator>SBS</DC:Creator>
        <DC:Subject>News, Current Affairs</DC:Subject>
        <DC:Description>Major world news events of the
day.</DC:Description>
        <DC:Publisher>SBS</DC:Publisher>
        <DC:Format DC:Scheme="IMT">video/mpg</DC:Format>
        <DC:Type>Image.Moving.TV.News</DC:Type>
        <DC:Language>en</DC:Language>
        <DC:Date>12/05/98</DC:Date>
        <DC:Format.Length>30 mins</DC:Format.Length>
        <DC:Relation.HasPart>
            <RDF:Bag BAGID="CompleteVideo">
            <RDF:LI Resource=
"http://www.dstc.edu.au/videos/98-02-20.mpg#sndtrack1"/>
            <RDF:LI Resource=
"http://www.dstc.edu.au/videos/98-02-20.mpg#sndtrack2"/>
            <RDF:LI Resource=
"http://www.dstc.edu.au/videos/98-02-20.mpg#sndtrack3"/>
            <RDF:LI Resource=
"http://www.dstc.edu.au/videos/98-02-20.mpg#sndtrack4"/>
            <RDF:LI Resource=
"http://www.dstc.edu.au/videos/98-02-20.mpg#videopart"/>
            </RDF:Bag>
        </DC:Relation.HasPart>
    </RDF:Description>
  </RDF:RDF>
```

The metadata for the URL "http://www.dstc.edu.au/videos/98-02-20.mpg#videopart" is as for the example in Section 4.2.

6. The Pros and Cons of Using Dublin Core and RDF for Video Metadata

The advantages of a pure Dublin Core approach include:

- It provides both 'core' and 'full' data descriptions to satisfy a range of user groups' needs.
- It enables searching across different media types and can exploit all of the work already done on Dublin Core metadata generation and Dublin-Core based indexing and search tools.
- It inherits the advantages associated with Dublin Core - simplicity, semantic interoperability, scalability, international consensus and flexibility. (Though it could justifiably be argued that the proposed extensions for video destroy the simplicity.)

The advantages associated with using RDF syntax for encoding the Dublin Core metadata are:

- It allows labelled directed graphs to be built which support the hierarchical containment structure of video.
- It is encoded in XML (eXtensible Markup Language) which is based on SGML and is better able to support multimedia than HTML.
- It can leverage off other tools and code bases being built around XML e.g. SMIL (Synchronized Multimedia Integration Language) [12], a declarative language for describing Web-based multimedia presentations. (SMIL describes how the various components are to be combined temporally and spatially to create a presentation.)
- It is both human-readable and machine-readable.
- It provides a container for different communities' metadata schemes.

Dublin Core was designed to do high-level interdisciplinary searching for complete textual documents across heterogeneous databases and schemas. It provides a simplified set of 15 elements which enables searching across the WWW. Dublin Core was not designed to provide metadata at a low level such as scenes and shots. Consequently there are a number of disadvantages associated with using Dublin Core for describing complex video documents. These include:

- The loss of simplicity.
- The need for a great number of sub-elements (especially within the Description element), Schemes and rules.
- There is no way to specify fine-grained synchronization between the different components i.e. explicit durations or absolute and relative offsets.
- The entanglement of semantics and structure between Dublin Core and RDF. There is no clear delineation between semantics in Dublin Core and video structure in RDF.

The last issue of separation of structure from semantics is problematic. For the sake of simplicity, it would be better if the two components could be separated. But the relation-ships between elements is often an important part of the metadata and thus the structural descriptions need to be integrated with the semantic descriptions as part of the metadata. This can lead to messy, complex metadata that is not easily read.

The above exercise also revealed a number of limitations associated with using RDF to contain Dublin Core video metadata descriptions. These include:

- It is unclear whether RDF permits nested collections i.e. collections within collections, as illustrated in the RDF code below.
- It is unclear how or if RDF allows pointers to metadata (i.e. another rdf file) rather than a resource (e.g. an mpg file)
- RDF does not provide *Par* or Parallel-type Collections in which each of the components are replayed in parallel.
- RDF doesn't support the specification of fine-grained synchronization between elements i.e. explicit durations or temporal offsets, as illustrated below.

```
<DC:Relation.HasPart>
  <RDF:Par BAGID="CompleteVideo">
      <RDF:LI ID="SoundTrack1"
      Resource="http://www.dstc.edu.au/music/opening.wav"
      RDF:DUR="6.0s"
      RDF:BEGIN="ID(VideoPart)(BEGIN)+1.8s"/>
      <RDF:LI ID="SoundTrack2"
      Resource="http://www.dstc.edu.au/audio/intro.aiff"
      RDF:DUR="4.0s"
      RDF:BEGIN="ID(VideoPart)(BEGIN)+2.8s"/>
       <RDF:LI>SoundTrack3</RDF:LI>
      <RDF:LI>SoundTrack4</RDF:LI>
      <RDF:LI ID=VideoPart>
        <RDF:Description>
          <RDF:Seq BAGID="VideoSequences">
           <RDF:LI>Sequence1</RDF:LI>
           <RDF:LI>Sequence2</RDF:LI>
           <RDF:LI>Sequence3</RDF:LI>
           <RDF:LI>Sequence4</RDF:LI>
           <RDF:LI>Sequence5</RDF:LI>
           <RDF:LI>Sequence6</RDF:LI>
           <RDF:LI>Sequence7</RDF:LI>
          </RDF:Seq>
        </RDF:Description>
      </RDF:LI>
  </RDF:Bag>
</DC:Relation.HasPart>
```

7. Current State of MPEG-7

The objective of MPEG7 [15] is to provide standardized descriptions of audiovisual information to enable it to be quickly and efficiently searched. MPEG-7, formally called `Multimedia Content Description Interface', will standardize:

- A set of description schemes and descriptors, and

- A language to specify description schemes, i.e. a Description Definition Language (DDL)

MPEG-7 will address the coding of these descriptors and description schemes. The combination of descriptors and description schemes shall be associated with the content itself, to allow fast and efficient searching for material of a user's interest. AV material that has MPEG-7 data associated with it, can be indexed and searched for. This `material' may include: still pictures, graphics, 3D models, audio, speech, video, and information about how these elements are combined in a multimedia presentation (`scenarios', composition information).

The development of the MPEG-7 standard is still at a very early stage with the Call for Proposals being scheduled for October 1998 and the Draft International Standard not expected to be published until July 2001. But given the overlap in objectives between MPEG-7 and Dublin Core, it makes sense for the MPEG-7 community to be aware of the work of the Dublin Core community and vice versa, to ensure compatibility, interoperability and mappability where possible.

7.1 Hybrid Approach

Minimalists from the Dublin Core community will undoubtedly be offended by the proposal to extend Dublin Core to such fine-grained descriptions as outlined above. A hybrid proposal based on RDF would overcome such criticisms but still exploit the valuable aspects of Dublin Core. RDF was designed to provide a container for different metadata formats. The proposal is to use RDF to contain both Dublin Core and MPEG7 descriptions of the same content.

Dublin Core can be used to describe audiovisual documents as a whole and to enable searching for complete audiovisual documents i.e. search and query at a high level on the 15 core elements. For example; "Find all video clips on Boris Yeltsin". This would perform a text search on the 15 core elements for the string "Boris Yeltsin".

MPEG7 can be used to provide a detailed hierarchical description of the content. The MPEG7 data can be used to enable low level content-based querying such as; "Give me close-up shots of Boris Yeltsin walking in front of the Kremlin". Since large components of the Dublin Core work do satisfy the MPEG7 requirements, it makes sense to exploit these aspects in MPEG-7. The exercise above has shown that Dublin Core, with extensions (particularly domain-specific qualifiers in the Description field), could form a basis for MPEG-7.

The advantages of the hybrid approach are:
- Existing Dublin Core text-based search engines can still be used to search across heterogeneous media types.
- It satisfies the original intention of Dublin Core to provide a core description and not to replace specialized cataloguing methods.
- Existing catalogues such as US MARC can be mapped to Dublin Core.
- MPEG-7 can be developed independently to provide low level fine-grained content-based querying.

- The easy integration of other developing metadata standards such as PICS (Platform for Internet Content Selection) [16] for classifying audiovisual content.
- SMIL (Synchronized Multimedia Integration Language) can also be used for combining separate audiovisual documents into a synchronized multimedia presentation.

```
<?xml:namespace ns="http://www.w3c.org/RDF/" prefix="RDF"?>
<?xml:namespace ns="http://metadata.net/DC/" prefix="DC"?>
<?xml:namespace ns=http://mpeg.org/mpeg7 prefix="MPEG7"?>
<RDF:RDF>
  <RDF:Description About=  "http://www.dstc.edu.au/videos/98-
02-20.mpg">
    <DC:Title>SBS World News</DC:Title>
    <DC:Creator>Special Broadcast Service</DC:Creator>
    <DC:Subject>News, Current Affairs</DC:Subject>
     <DC:Publisher>SBS</DC:Publisher>
    <DC:Contributor.Presenter> Indria Naidoo
                        </DC:Contributor.Presenter>
    <DC:Format DC:Scheme="IMT">video/mpg</DC:Format>
    <DC:Type>Image.Moving.TV.News</DC:Type>
    <DC:Language>en</DC:Language>
    <DC:Date>1998-05-01</DC:Date>
    <DC:Format.Length>30 mins</DC:Format.Length>
    <MPEG7:Duration>1400</MPEG7:Duration>
    <MPEG7:Camera.Angle>close-up</MPEG7:Camera.Angle>
    <MPEG7:Locale>Gore Hill Studios</MPEG7:Locale>
  </RDF:Description>
</RDF:RDF>
```

8. Future Work

Future Work includes:
- Extending Reggie, the DSTC Metadata Editor, [17] to generate video metadata. This entails enabling the entry of metadata for multilayered, hierarchical structures. It also requires the definition of a new schema file and the validation of combinations of DC.Type, DC.Description types and DC.Description content.
- Integrating the scene change detection software, closed caption decoder and video replayer and annotator into Reggie.
- Submitting a proposal based on Dublin Core and RDF to the MPEG-7 standards committee.
- Building a WWW video search engine based on the metadata repository generated by Reggie.
- Building mappings between high level semantic queries and low level features stored within the video metadata, for specific domains or communities.

Figure 2 illustrates the proposed system setup. Most of the components are available but their integration and enhancements to satisfy certain video requirements are still being carried out.

Output from a TV or VCR is fed into a Closed Caption decoder to generate the transcript. Video output is also fed into an MPEG1 video capture card. The MPEG1 file is input into automatic scene change detection software to generate JPEGimages which represent the key frames which occur at the scene changes.

Extensions will be made to the existing DSTC Metadata Editor, Reggie, to enable the generation of standardized metadata descriptions, in RDF format, for each MPEG1 video clip. Reggie will provide the user interface for the user to specify the hierarchical video structure, metadata values and dynamic links and to store all of this in a single standardized RDF machine- and human-readable format.

The generated RDF files are stored in a metadata repository on the HTTP server and the MPEG1 files are stored on the continuous media server. Video delivery is performed via the DSTC's SuperNOVA architecture [18] which provides end-to-end QoS management and streaming video which adapts dynamically to the available bandwidth.

Fig. 2. System Architecture

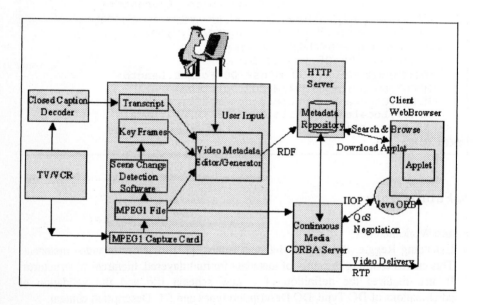

9. Conclusions

With the addition of certain video-specific sub-elements, Dublin Core metadata encoded in RDF (with the addition of timing controls), will satisfy the requirements for indexing most moving image resource types. However this is not what Dublin Core was designed for. It was designed to provide a very simple core of 15 descriptive elements. Minimalists in the Dublin Core community would be horrified at the thought of using Dublin Core extensions to describe something as detailed as an object's texture in a particular frame of a movie.

However, the exercise above shows that the Dublin Core extensions proposed, could provide a good basis for MPEG7. In addition, RDF (with some extensions) provides an ideal infrastructure for describing video using a combination of both Dublin Core (for the high level description) and MPEG7 (for the lower level fine-grained descriptions). The advantages of this approach are many: the output is both machine and human readable; multilayered and hierarchical structures are supported and most compellingly, the work already done on Dublin Core, RDF and XML based metadata tools can be exploited.

Acknowledgements

The authors wish to acknowledge the use of material belonging to SBS, Australia's National Multicultural Broadcaster. The authors also wish to acknowledge that this work was carried out within the Cooperative Research Centre for Research Data Networks established under the Australian Government's Cooperative Research Centre (CRC) Program and acknowledge the support of the Distributed Systems Technology CRC under which the work described in this paper is administered and the Queensland Government's CITEC.

References

1. 'Description of Dublin Core Elements', http://purl.oclc.org/metadata/dublin_core_elements.
2. Guenther R., 1997, 'Dublin Core Qualifiers/Substructure',
    http://www.loc.gov/marc/dcqualif.html.
3. Duffy C. and Owen C., 1997a., 'Resource Discovery Workshops: Moving Image Resources'
    http://pads.ahds.ac.uk/padsUserNeedsMetadataWorkshopsFilm.html.
4. 'A Practical Implementation of the Dublin Core',
    http://ahds.ac.uk/public/metadata/disc_11.html.
5. Ad Hoc Working Group – Coverage Element, 1997, 'Dublin Core Element: Coverage',
    http://www.sdc.ucsb.edu/~mary/coverage.htm.
6. 'W3C RDF Activity', http://www.w3.org/RDF.
7. 'W3C Metadata Activity', http://www.w3.org/Metadata.
8. Lagoze, C., C.A. Lynch and R. Daniel, 1996, "The Warwick Framework: A Container Architecture for Aggregating Sets of Metadata" ,
    http://cs- tr.cs.cornell.edu:80/Dienst/UI/2.0/Describe/ncstrl.cornell/TR96-1593
9. 'W3C Working Draft of the RDF Model and Syntax Specification', 1998,
    http://www.w3.org/TR/WD-rdf-syntax.
10. 'W3C Working Draft of the RDF Schema work-in-progress', 1998,
    http://www.w3.org/TR/WD-rdf-schema.
11. 'EXtensible Markup Language (XML)', 1998, http://www.w3.org/XML/.
12. 'Synchronized Multimedia Integration Language', W3C Working Draft, 1998,
    http://www.w3.org/TR/WD-smil.

13. E. Miller and R. Ianella, 'Dublin Core Examples in RDF', 1998, http://www.dstc.edu.au/RDU/RDF/dc-in-rdf-ex.html.
14. B. Simpson-Young and K. Yap, 'An Open Continuous Media Environment on the Web', AusWeb'97, 1997, http://ausweb.scu.edu.au/proceedings/simpson-young/paper.html.
15. 'MPEG-7 Starting Points and FAQs', 1998, http://www.mpeg.org/~tristan/MPEG/starting-points.html#mpeg7.
16. 'PICS (Platform for Internet Content Selection)', http://www.w3.org/PICS/.
17. 'Reggie, the DSTC Metadata Editor', http://metadata.net/dstc/.
18. 'The SuperNOVA Project', http://www.dstc.edu.au/SuperNOVA/.

Search and Progressive Information Retrieval from Distributed Image/Video Databases: The SPIRE Project

Vittorio Castelli, Lawrence D. Bergman,

Chung-Sheng Li, and John R. Smith *

IBM Thomas J. Watson Research Center,

P.O. Box 704, Yorktown Heights, NY 10598

Email: {csli,vittorio,bergman}@watson.ibm.com

Abstract. In this paper, we describe the architecture and initial implementation of a content-based retrieval mechanism from heterogeneous image archives. In particular, we propose an architecture to produce local representation of the images stored in heterogeneous archives and a progressive framework that reorganizes the images into a hierarchical representation based on a multiresolution decomposition and an abstraction pyramid. Search operations can rely on this representation and be performed in a hierarchical fashion, thus significantly reducing the total amount of data that need to be processed. Dramatic speedup has been achieved for many search operations, such as template matching, texture feature extraction, and histogram extraction.

Keywords: image databases, satellite imagery, content-based retrieval.

1 Introduction

The emergence of a global trend towards pervasive computing, coupled with the ever decreasing cost of fast storage media and of powerful processors, has fostered the development of publicly accessible large digital libraries containing videos, images, audio and text data. The intended audiences range from the public at large, that can now access videos, photographic images, audio and text on line, to very specialized users, belonging to both the scientific community and the scholars in the humanities.

* This work was funded in part by NASA/CAN contract no. NCC5-101.

The amount of data stored in digital libraries is growing at an exponential rate, and the currently existing storage and retrieval infrastructures are not adequately scalable. Thus, the need for new methods and infrastructures for storing, automatically indexing, and efficiently retrieving the information from the repositories, arises naturally.

Content-based search has emerged in recent years as a widespread paradigm for retrieving information from digital libraries. In general, the *content* of an image or video segment can be specified at three different levels of abstraction, namely, *pixel* level, *feature* level, and *semantic* level. The existing systems supporting content-based search usually rely on low-level image features such as shape, color histogram, and texture to perform images or video indexing. Prominent examples for photographic images include the MIT PhotoBook [15], IBM QBIC [14], VisualSeek from Columbia University [18], and the Multimedia DataBlade from Informix/Virage [2]. Content-based search techniques have also been applied to medical images [8] and video clips [22, 20, 1]. While the research community has proposed solutions to numerous difficult problems, there are still several outstanding issues. In particular, there is the need for a general architecture that can support the search and retrieval of images or video from heterogeneous distributed archives across the Internet/Intranet, and of a progressive framework which allows hierarchical indexing and retrieval of images and videos.

In this paper, we describe an architecture and the initial implementation of a progressive framework to store and retrieve image and video data from a collection of heterogeneous archives. The framework is extensible in that it allows the search constraints to be specified at one or more abstraction levels. The proposed architecture is scalable thanks to a progressive approach, in which a hierarchical scheme is used to de-correlate and reorganize the information contained in the images at multiple abstraction levels. As a result, search operators can be selectively applied to small portions of the data, the search space can be pruned accordingly, and the remaining results can be progressively analyzed in further detail. This technique achieves a significant speedup over more conventional implementations. The speedup factor for template matching (the search operator at the raw pixel level) and classification (the search operator at the semantic level) is more than 20 times. A 400% to 800% speedup has also been achieved for texture extraction and matching (the search operator at the feature level).

2 Preliminaries

The retrieval paradigm described in this paper relies on the concept of query objects (also called *target* objects). We distinguish between *simple* and *composite* objects. In the case of images, simple objects are connected regions that are homogeneous with respect to some specific characteristics. Composite objects are sets of simple objects satisfying a number of spatial or temporal constraints.

Simple objects of an image or video database can be defined and referred to at different abstraction levels.

1. *Raw Pixels*: At the lowest abstraction level, object are simply aggregations of raw pixels from the image into a connected region.
2. *Feature*: The next higher abstraction level for representing images is at the feature level. An image feature is here defined as a distinguishing primitive characteristics or attribute of an image [16], usually numeric (scalar or vector) or categorical. Example of features are luminance, shape descriptors, and gray scale texture. Such features are natural, as they correspond immediately to visual appearance of an image. Other features, such as amplitude histogram, color histogram, and spatial frequency spectra, are in a sense artificial, as they are usually obtained from specific complex manipulations of an image, and cannot be immediately associated with visual cues. Objects at the feature level are created by segmenting the image into regions with homogeneous features. For example, in the described system, texture vectors are first extracted from overlapping moving windows of fixed sizes, associated with the centers of the windows, and finally segmented using the algorithm described in [21].
3. *Semantic*: This is the highest abstraction level at which a content-based search can be performed. Semantic information from an image is usually extracted from a pre-trained classifier or supplied through human interpretation. For satellite images, this information could include the type of land cover of a specific area such as water, forest, or urban.

In our case, we can operate on both indexed objects and objects extracted at run-time. Spatial indexing is performed using R-Trees [7], while high-dimensional indexing relies on a proprietary scheme.

The search is usually based on a *similarity* comparison rather than on exact match, and the retrieved results are ranked according to a *similarity index*, e.g., a *metric*.

The comparison between raw-data objects is done in a pixel-by-pixel fashion. Commonly used similarity measures include the correlation coefficient and the L^p distances. Comparison at the pixel level is very specific, and therefore is only used when a relatively precise match is required. Similarity search in the feature space thus consists of comparing the target feature vector with the feature vectors stored in the database. Again, L^p distances and the weighted Euclidean distance are commonly used measures of similarity. The class of a semantic object is a categorical variable. The natural distance measure between categorical variables is the 0-1 distance, defined as $D(X,Y) = 0$ if $X = Y$, $D(X,Y) = 1$ otherwise. More complex distance metrics are defined trough a (necessarily symmetric) matrix $D = [d_{i,j}]$, where $d_{i,j} = d_{j,i}$ is the distance between an object of class i and an object of class j.

3   System Architecture

The current architecture of the system, shown in Fig. 1, consists of a of Java clients, HTTP servers, connection managers, and cliettes which consisting of a client process that interacts with the Java client and server process that interacts with the search engine. A heterogeneous environment can consist three different types of image archives: (1) image files that are connected directly to the web server, (2) images that are stored in the local file systems with pointers stored in a catalog which is exposed to the web server, (3) images that are stored directly in the database as binary large object (or BLOB). A catalog which has one entry for each image is built for all the images stored in the heterogeneous data archives. When a new image is inserted in the database, it is compressed using a scheme called "S-F Graph" [17, 19], combining a multi-resolution decomposition with a spatial segmentation of the image. From each level of the multi-resolution pyramid, the system automatically extracts, indexes an stores a semantic and a feature level description.

In principle, each image object includes both image data and access method, unless it is stored in a well-known image format such as JPEG, TIF, or GIF (where the standard defines the access method). Consequently, it is usually necessary to access the meta-data that describes the access method of the image before the image data can be accessed. Therefore, we rely on the assumption that the databases connected to the web servers are compliant to Common Object Request Broker Architecture (CORBA) and can thus be accessed through Internet Inter-ORB Protocol (IIOP).

This architecture is currently evolving: we are in the initial stages of a NASA-sponsored project called "NASA Earth Sciences Information Partners (ESIP) Program" (http://saturn.gsfc.nasa.gov/), aimed at building a working prototype federation of data providers and scientific data users. Among the responsibilities of the award recipients is the definition of an inter operability protocol; thus, our architecture and its interfaces will be modified to comply with the recommendations of the federation.

The search is session-based. When a java client is downloaded from the server, a connection request is sent to the connection manager. The connection manager ([13]) is responsible for allocating a client sub-session on one of the distributed servers, and the selection of the server is based on the current loading condition.

Each cliette session consists of two sub-sessions: one is responsible for interacting with the java client and keeping the query state, the other is responsible for interacting with the search engine and keeping the temporary query results. The client sub-session and the server sub-session are concurrent processes. A query queue exists between the client sub-session and the server sub-session so that the java client can submit multiple queries concurrently.

Queries are constructed and parsed syntactically at the client using a drag-and-drop interface. This interface also allows the definition of new objects and features. After being specified and syntactically analyzed, the query is sent to the client session on the server. The client sub-session places the query into a message queue for the server sub-session. A query usually involve both meta-data search and image content search. The server sub-session parse the query string into a script consisting of a set of SQL statements and content-based search operators. Search on the meta-data is performed by the database engine, while the image

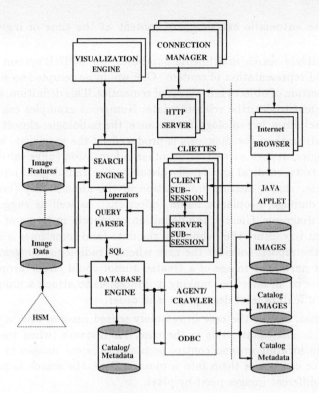

Fig. 1. Architecture of the system.

content search is performed by the content search operators. Usually the meta-data search serves as a pruning mechanism, to achieve maximum reduction of the search space during the first stages of the query execution process. The content-based search engine also accesses the feature descriptors as well as the raw pixels of an image region in order to compute the final results.

The results of the search are rendered by the visualization engine. The results of both search and rendering are stored into the query result cache, and made available to subsequent queries. Thus, successive refinements of the query are possible without the need for establishing another session with the search engine.

4 The Progressive Framework

4.1 Motivation

The heart of the search and retrieval paradigm implemented in our system is the progressive framework, which combines data representation with search opera-tions. The main motivation for the development of the progressive framework is the richness of non-structured data (such as images and video), and especially of scientific data, which requires more advanced content-specifications method-ologies than those usually found in current image-retrieval systems, and which prevents the automatic extraction of content at the time of ingestion in the database.

To effectively search multimedia databases, the SPIRE system relies on an object-based representation of content. One would be tempted to state that the correct definition of objects is in terms of semantics. This definition, nevertheless, is not sufficient to describe scientific data. Numerous examples can be found in different disciplines. In radiology, for instance, the radiologist almost never makes the diagnosis; rather, the diagnosis is produced by the specialist, who relies on the radiological report as well as on other information (physical examination, laboratory tests, medical and family history). The radiological report contains location, size, shape, texture information of the abnormality (bone fracture, soft tissue damage, neoplastic lesion, infections), as well as suggestions for a differential diagnosis. Clearly, the definition of objects in terms of semantics is not sufficient to capture the richness of the data (and sometimes is not available even from the report: consider the case where a radiologist suggests that what is seen in a particular image of a treated tumor could either neoplastic tissue or scar tissue or an infection, making it impossible to attach a unique semantic label), and a feature level description is in order.

Sometimes, as it is the case in remotely sensed images, even a feature-level description is inadequate: this is the case, for instance, when the scientist is interested in locating ground control points in different images in order to superimpose or composite them into a mosaic. Here, the search is performed by comparing different images pixel-by-pixel.

Simple objects can be defined simultaneously at different abstraction levels. A geologist analyzing resistivity data acquired from a well bore (data that are usually displayed as images) could potentially ask the repository to return all the portions of images containing limestone with texture similar to a specified example. Here, the object must be specified simultaneously at the semantic and at the feature level: there can be other strata with similar texture to the example, but that are not made of limestone. At the same time, the limestone at different depths (and, of course, at different geographical locations) display significant variations in texture (which reflect into different porosity properties).

Simple objects (i.e., connected regions which are homogeneous with respect to a set of characteristics specified at one or more abstraction levels) are not sufficient to support an extensible search framework.

For example, consider the detection of the so-called "bright points" on the solar corona using images acquired with the SOHO instruments. Bright points are, as the name suggests, small bright areas, easily visible in the images acquired with the Extreme ultraviolet Imaging Telescope (EIT), and differ from other similar phenomena by their association with a very orderly, persistent magnetic field, which confines the hot plasma. These magnetic fields are easily detected visible using photospheric magnetograms, acquired with a different instrument. The magnetogram represents data from a deeper layer within the sun than the one imaged by the EIT instrument. Thus, bright points are defined in terms of two simple objects specified at the feature level (bright areas in the EIT data and magnetic fields in the photospheric magnetogram data) which are related by a positional constraint (i.e., they are at the same location, but at different "depths").

More complex objects can require more complex definitions: consider again a case involving solar data. The scientist is now looking for Coronal Mass Ejections (CME), which are violent eruptive phenomena. A CME appears as a sudden brightening of a bright spot, immediately followed by appearance of one or two dark spots near the brightening spot (the hot plasma gets concentrated from the darkening areas to the brightening spot), and finally a "shock wave" can be observed, that extends to the entire surface of the sun within a few hours. The definition of CME involve a set of simple objects (a bright spot, a brightening spot, and one or two darkening areas) related by spatial and temporal constraints (the bright spot is followed by a brightening spot in the same position, the darkening areas are adjacent to the brightening spot, darkening occurs slightly after the brightening, the darkening areas are essentially always larger in size than the brightening spot).

From the simple examples discussed above, it is apparent that we cannot support complex, interesting queries by just relying on pre-extracted information. The search engine can be used in a research or in a specialistic operational environment only if it allows the easy definition of new features and object types. At the same time, efficiency in processing the queries is an essential component in an interactive environment.

To achieve flexibility without sacrificing efficiency, we have combined data representation with query scheduling and data analysis within a unified search framework, whose components are described in the following sections.

4.2 Data Representation

In order to facilitate progressive operations, each image or video in the heterogeneous archives is processed through the following steps.

- *transformation*: Possible transformations include Karhunen-Loeve transformation (or singular value decomposition), discrete cosine transform, subband coding, discrete wavelet transformation (which is a special case of subband coding), and other transformations. For images in our repository, we use a scheme based on the combination of spatial decomposition and wavelet packet decomposition, called S-F Graph [17, 19]. As a byproduct, a multiresolution representation of the data can be easily reconstructed from the transform. Reorganization of the original images using one of the above linear transformation allows the concentration of the different types of information contained in the original images into selected regions of the transform.
- *partition*: After partitioning, the data is (logically or physically) reorganized to facilitate the access during the execution of the query. Each transformed coefficient by itself could form a partition. However, the partitioning/grouping of the transformed image or video should take into consideration the optimal granularity for delivering progressive output results.

- *feature extraction and segmentation*: To create a feature level representation of the data, the individual levels of the multi-resolution pyramid are processed to extract features (where the term feature here refers to a numeric quantity). For each application domain, the most commonly used features (such as texture, color or spectral histogram, and shape information) are identified, pre-extracted, and indexed. In some instances, e.g., for texture, the literature contains numerous heterogeneous features set. Our system includes a facility for comparing the discriminatory capabilities of different feature sets for the purpose similarity searches [9]. Each image is segmented into regions of homogeneous features, each individual region is represented as an object and indexed in the database. The segmentation is currently performed using the MMAP algorithm described in [21].

  The system also allows the user to define new types of feature objects by specifying positive and negative examples. In this case, the segmentation and the object extraction are performed at query execution time. Positive and negative examples are used to construct on-the-fly a metric for searching the feature space. Different approaches are implemented in the system, including linear superposition of weighted Euclidean distances and a method based on multidimensional scaling [12]. When defining objects through examples, the user can visualize how well different portions of images match the current definition by asking the system to produce a Match Score Image [4], where the similarity score is represented as transparent color overlayed on a gray scale representation of the target image. New features can be defined while specifying a query, through a facility in the client interface [3] that reveals to the user the functionalities implemented in our image processing library.
- *semantic content extraction*: To create a semantic level representation of the data, the most commonly used semantic objects are pre-extracted and indexed. In the case of satellite images, we automatically classify the individual pixels using the digital numbers from the different spectral bands into the 9 classes of the USGS Level-1 Land Usage/Land Cover classification taxonomy. This taxonomy provides a coarse division into rather different classes, and can be used either by very unsophisticated user to ask general questions, as well as by very advanced users (who would be interested in a more refined taxonomic classification) to quickly prune the search space. Adjacent pixels belonging to the same class are then grouped together into semantic objects, that are indexed and stored together with domain-specific attributes.

4.3 Processing the query

When the user issues a query, a schedule is generated, statically or dynamically, which assigns a processing sequence of the partitions to the transformed attributes (or its derived features), based on the required operations. The general framework is described in [10]. In practice, a composite object (or a query) can be represented as a graph where the nodes are the component objects and the edges represent the relations. Objects and relations can be either crisp (for instance, semantic objects, and adjacency relations), or fuzzy (e.g.,a forest can be partially an evergreen and partially a deciduous forest if the two types of trees are intermixed, and relations such as "near" are intrinsically fuzzy). To simplify the framework, degrees of similarity are treated within the system as fuzzy membership, thus, for instance, the system operates on similarity scores computed at the feature level as if they were degrees of membership. Pre-extracted and indexed objects are easier to retrieve than objects extracted at query execution time using pre-extracted features, which in turn are easier to retrieve than objects computed entirely during the query execution. Crisp objects are more effective in pruning the search space than fuzzy objects when the usual definition of fuzzy AND as the minimum of the membership functions is adopted. Similarly, sharp relations are more effective in pruning the search space than fuzzy relations. Finally, some heuristics are built into the system that estimate which types of objects and which relations are in general more efficient in pruning the search space. Using all the above information, the system produces a query execution schedule that minimizes the search time by efficiently pruning the search space. More details are available in [11]

4.4 Using the multiresolution approximations

Texture features are used for content-based search at the feature level. Texture extraction is usually time-consuming, as this operation has to be applied to all the regions of all the images in the database. Also, similarity searching in the texture domain is tantamount to performing nearest neighbor queries in high-dimensional spaces, a notoriously difficult problem [6]. Finally, sometimes the user can define during the construction of a query new texture feature that the system has to extract while performing the search.

The multiresolution representation of the data can significantly help in increasing the speed of the search process, through the algorithm described below. This algorithm applies both when the features are pre-extracted and when they are computed during the execution of the query.

1. Divide the transformed images into regular or irregular regions at each resolution according to the boundaries extracted by edge detection or image segmentation. We assume that the segmentation at each resolution is similar. As a result, a $B \times B$ block at level 0 corresponds to a $B/2 \times B/2$ block at level 1, and corresponds to a $B/4 \times B/4$ block at level 2.

2. Compute the texture feature vector of each region at the Lth resolution level for each block of the image. L is the starting (or the coarsest) resolution of the image that the progressive image retrieval algorithm is applied.

3. Compute the texture feature vector of each block of the target template at the Lth resolution level.

4. Compute the similarity between the blocks in the target template and the blocks from the image at resolution level K. The candidate regions of blocks are then sorted according to a distance metric between the feature vectors of the target template and that from the image.

---

5. The feature vector of those regions at resolution level $L-1$ are then computed and compared to those extracted from the target template at the same level.
6. This process is continued until level 0 of the image is reached.

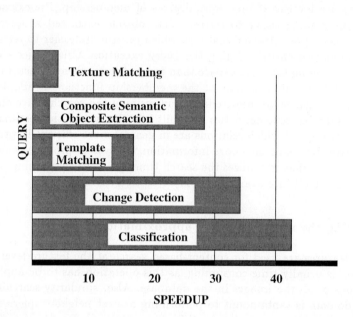

Fig. 2. Speedup in user time for different content-based queries, achieved using a progressive implementation of the search operators, over the corresponding traditional implementation. In each case, the speedup has been obtained as the ration of the user times for the classical implementation and the progressive implementation of the query. User times were measured with the `time` UNIX command.

A similar algorithm, called progressive classification [5], has been devised to extract semantic (ground cover) information from multispectral satellite images. Here the benefits are twofold: not only the speed of the operation is significantly higher than in the classical implementation, where each pixel at full resolution is individually labeled, but also the accuracy of the result, measured in terms of probability of classification error, is improved (this theoretical result is actually corroborated by experimental evidence). Figure 2 shows the speedups achieved for several simple content-based queries.

5 Summary and future work

In this paper, we presented an architecture to perform progressive content-based search from federated image archives. Different database systems and different image/video storage formats can be used in a heterogeneous archive environment. A local representation of each image is constructed in order to facilitate the search. Objects at both the semantics and the feature levels are extracted. In addition, a hierarchical representation is constructed for each image. Consequently, content-based search operations can be applied hierarchically and resulting in a significant speedup.

We are in the preliminary stages of several pilot projects which will investigate the applicability of our technology to different fields, ranging from environmental epidemiology, to solar images analysis, to petroleum engineering, to marine geology, to medical images. In all of these cases, the studies will be conducted in cooperation with domain experts. The early results suggest that the framework we have developed has a very wide applicability to those domains where large amounts of scientific heterogeneous data exist, where conventional techniques do not provide the expressive power required by the investigators.

Acknowledgments

The authors would like to thank Col. Chacko, Dr. Yan Briant, Dr. Peter Tilke, Dr. Barbara Thompson, Dr. Loey Knapp, Dr. Nand Lal, Dr. Christopher Small, Dr. Suzanne Carbott, Dr. Jonathan Patz, Dr. Subhash Lele, Dr. Gregory Gurry Glass for their comments and suggestions, and for defining applicability scenarios for our technology.

References

1. F. Arman, A. Hsu, and M.Y. Chiu. Image processing on compressed data for large video database. In *Proc. ACM Multimedia 93*, pages 267–272, 1993.

2. J. R. Bach, C. Fuller, A. Gupta, A. Hampapur, B. Horowitz, R. Humphrey, and R. Jain. The virage image search engine: An open framework for image image management. In *Proc. SPIE - Int. Soc. Opt. Eng.*, volume 2670, Storage and Retrieval for Still Image and Video Databases, pages 76–87, 1996.

3. L. Bergman, J. Schoudt, V. Castelli, L. Knapp, and C.-S. Li. Asimm: A framework for automated synthesis of query interfaces for multimedia databases. In *Proc. SPIE - Int. Soc. Opt. Eng.*, volume 3229, pages 264–275, 1997.

4. Lawrence D. Bergman and Vittorio Castelli. The match score image: A visualization tool for image query refinement. In *Proc. SPIE Photonic West - Int. Soc. Opt. Eng.*, To appear 1998.

5. Vittorio Castelli and oth. Progressive search and retrieval in large image archives. *IBM Journal of Research and Development*, to appear.

6. V. Dasarathy, Belur, editor. *Nearest Neighbor Pattern Classification Techniques*. IEEE Computer Society, 1991.

7. A. Guttman. R-trees: a dynamic index structure for spatial searching. *SIGMOD Record*, 14(2):47–57, June 1984.

8. T. Y. Hou, P. Liu, A. Hsu, and M. Y. Chiu. Medical image retrieval by spatial feature. In *Proc. IEEE Intern. Conf. System, Man, and Cybernetics*, pages 1364–1369, 1992.

9. Chung-Sheng Li and Vittorio Castelli. Deriving texture feature set for content-based retrieval of satellite image database. In *Proc. of the IEEE Int. Conf. on Image Proc.*, pages 567–579, Santa Barbara, CA, Oct 26-29 1997.

10. Chung-Sheng Li, Vittorio Castelli, and Lawrence D. Bergman. Progressive content-based retrieval from distributed image/video databases. In *Proc. of 1997 IEEE Int. Symp. on Circuits and Systems: ISCAS97*, volume 2, pages 1484–87, Hong Kong, 9-12 June 1997.

11. Chung-Sheng Li, Vittorio Castelli, Lawrence D. Bergman, and John R. Smith. Sproc: Fast algorithm for sequential processing of composite objects retrieval from large image/video archives. In *Proc. SPIE Photonic West - Int. Soc. Opt. Eng.*, San Jose, CA, Jan 24-30 1998.

12. Chung-Sheng Li, John R. Smith, and Vittorio Castelli. SSTIR: Similarity search through iterative refinement. In *Proc. SPIE Photonic West - Int. Soc. Opt. Eng.*, San Jose, CA, Jan 24-30 1998.

13. Y.-H. Liu, P. Dantzig, C. E. Wu, J. Challenger, and L. M. Ni. A distributed web server and its performance analysis on multiple platforms. In *Proc. ICPADS*, pages 665–672, Hong Kong, 1996.

14. W. Niblack, R. Barber, W. Equitz, M. Flickner, E. Glasman, D. Petkovic, P. Yanker, C. Faloutsos, and G. Taubin. The QBIC project: Querying images by content using color texture, and shape. In *Proc. SPIE - Int. Soc. Opt. Eng.*, volume 1908, Storage Retrieval for Image and Video Databases, pages 173–187, 1993.

15. A. Pentland, R.W. Picard, and S. Sclaroff. Photobook: Tools for content-based manipulation of image databases. In *Proc. SPIE - Int. Soc. Opt. Eng.*, volume 2185, Storage and Retrieval for Image and Video Databases, pages 34–47, February 1994.

16. W. Pratt. *Digital Image Processing*. John Wiley, New York, second edition edition, 1991.

17. J.R. Smith and S.-F. Chang. Frequency and spatially adaptive wavelet packets. In *Proc. of 1995 IEEE Intern. Conf. Acoust. Speech Signal Proc.*, pages 2233–2236, Detroit, MI, May 1995.

18. J.R. Smith and S.-F. Chang. Visualseek: A fully automated content-based image query system. In *Proc. 4th ACM Multimedia Conf.*, pages 87–98, Boston, MA, USA, 18-22 Nov 1996.

19. J.R. Smith and S.-F. Chang. Joint adaptive space and frequency basis selection. In *Proc. IEEE Int. Conf. Image Processing*, Santa Barbara, CA, October 1997.

20. S. W. Smoliar and H. Zhang. Content based video indexing and retrieval. *IEEE Multimedia*, 1(2):62–72, Summer 1994.

21. Norbert Strobel, Chung-Sheng Li, and Vittorio Castelli. Texture-based image segmentation and mmap for digital libraries. In *Proc. of the 1997 IEEE Int. Conf. on Image Processing*, volume I, pages 196–199, Santa Barbara, CA, Oct 26-29 1997.

22. H. Zhang and S. W. Smoliar. Developing power tools for video indexing and retrieval. In *Proc. SPIE - Int. Soc. Opt. Eng.*, volume 2185, Storage and Retrieval for Image and Video Databases, pages 140–149, Feb 1994.

Improving the Spatial-Temporal Clue Based Segmentation by the Use of Rhythm

Walid Mahdi[1], Liming Chen[1] and Dominique Fontaine[1]

[1] TRANSDOC Project, Laboratoire HEUDIASYC
umr cnrs 6599 Centre de Recherche de Royallieu
Universite de Technologie de Compiègne
BP 20529 - 60205 Compiègne cedex, FRANCE
fax : (33) 3-44-23-44-77
{mahdi, chen, fontaine}@hds.utc.fr
http://transdoc.ibp.fr

Abstract. Video is a major media in the society of information under way. Unfortunately, the full use of this media is limited by the opaque character of the video which prevents content-based access. In this paper we improve our previous spatial temporal clues-based semantic video segmentation technique, and propose the use of the rhythm within a video to more precisely capture temporal relations within a scene and between scenes in a video. Preliminary evidence based on a 7 minutes video shows that our spatial temporal clues-based segmentation technique coupled with the rhythm consideration fully detect the narrative structure of a video.

1 Introduction

With ever increasing computing power and data storage capacity, the potential for large digital video libraries is growing rapidly. These libraries will have thousands of hours of video which will be made available, via the wide area networks, to users upon requests [7][15].

In order to enable content based access of digital video libraries, the information embedded within the video must be first segmented, then indexed and searched with satisfactory recall and precision.

The majority of existing automatic content-based segmentation of video consist of segmenting the video into shots which are separated by cuts, and their detection is based on objective visual primitives such as color [16], image correlation and 3D hints [3]. The shot represents the fundamental unit of manipulation of the video. Thus, by detecting the shot boundaries, it's possible to create indexes and to develop users' browsing tools to enable navigating and searching. Unfortunately, the representation by shots of a video document does not well describe its narrative and visual contents.

Indeed, the results from a user's query of interest to a video library is a set of non continuous time shots. Moreover, browsing thousands of shots contained in a video document *(3225 shots in Octobre of S.M. Eisenstein* [4], *500 to 1000 shots in a normal film* [1]*)*, presents a greater challenge for the user during his linear navigation and search for any particular video segment. Whereas the granularity of the information content is such that a one half-hour video may have tens semantically separate units, that each one of them corresponds to a scenario of the story board of the film.

Many approaches are proposed to improve search and discovery in the video medium. Their main ideas consists of partitioning video data into small clips of « *meaningful* » data. A manual segmentation into 1600 « *video clips* » of 45-hour library is considered by the *Informedia Project* [6]. Mills imposes a fixed segmentation into clips on the video data [10]. Strict alternate shots are detected and combined into scenes by the method of Faudemay [7]. Another *a priori* model, has been proposed for news broadcasts [17] to extract certain specialized semantic elements of the video sequences.

For a digital video library, a priori model or a manual segmentation may not be practical. We previously proposed a new automatic technique for the semantic video segmentation purpose, using the spatial temporal clues extracted from the video shots. The experimental evidence we conducted on 7 minutes video showed that our prototype reached a success segmentation rate up to 89% as compared to a manual segmentation by an expert. In this work, we improve our previous technique, and propose the use of the rhythm within a video to more precisely capture temporal relations within a scene and between scenes in a video. Preliminary evidence applied to the same 7 minutes video shows that our new automatic segmentation technique, which combine the spatial temporal clues and the consideration of the rhythm within a video fully captures the underlying narrative structure, avoiding the drawback of our previous segmentation which leads sometimes to one shot scenes.

The rest of the paper is organized as follows. We first study in section 2 the structure of the video data which is defined by three levels : shot, scene and sequence. Section 3 briefly recalls the spatial-temporal video model that we have proposed [8]. We also highlight the limit of this spatial-temporal model which sometimes leads to scenes formed by one shot. In section 4, we define the rhythm in a video and give several criteria based on statistic measures for shots clustering. In section 5, we present our new video segmentation method which combines the use of rhythm with the spatial-temporal clues based segmentation method. The experimental results that we have driven on a 7 minutes video selected from the CD-II Movie « *Dances With Wolves* » is then presented in section 6. Section 7 summarizes our work and also gives some indications for further work.

2 Video Structure

A video program such a motion pictures, TV movies, etc., has a story structure and organization. This story structure is defined by the following levels : narrative sequence, scene and camera shot **Fig. 1** show this structure. A camera shot is a set of *"continuous frames representing a continuous action in time or space"*. It reflects a fragment of the story units and represents the fundamental unit of production of video. A scene is a dramatic unit composed of a single or several shots. It usually takes place in a continuous time period, in the same setting, and involves the same characters. At the higher level, we have the narrative sequence, which is a dramatic unit composed of several scenes, all linked together by their emotional and narrative momentum [4][5].

During the montage, which "refers to the editing of the film, the cutting and piecing together of exposed film in a manner that best conveys the intent of the work" [5], two narrative sequences are linked together by an effect of transition such as dissolves or fades and two shots are linked by cuts. Consequently, this « *temporal delimitation of sequences* » criterion must be integrated in any model of segmentation of video stream into semantic units.

To convey parallel events in a scene, shots of the same person or same settings, taken from the same camera, at the same location, are repeated, alternated or interleaved by other shots with different contents. Most often, the similarities of contents are shown through similar visual characteristics of the composition of frames in the shots.

To further regroup the shots into semantic units and offer a better organization of the video. Many semantic elements of the video sequences were explored. We have previously used in [8] a spatial-temporal clue for segmentation into semantic units.

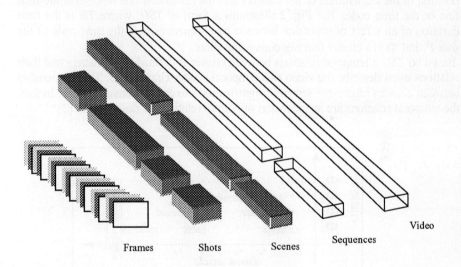

Frames   Shots   Scenes   Sequences   Video

Fig. 1. Video structure

Video is also characterized by a rhythm. In fact certain editors produce rhythmical effects when the duration of successive shots is practically, or alternatively practically close ; in certain cases it is even identical. The shots regrouped by the rhythmical effects belong generally to the same scene. More over, the shots which don't respect the general rhythm of the shots that precede or follow it, frequently carries an important information like a scene changement [1].

3   The Spatial-Temporal Clue Based Segmentation Method

We presented in [8] a new video segmentation method based on spatial temporal clues extracted from video shots previously segmented. The similar shots are clustered together and a new representation of the video data as a Time-space Graph *(TSG)* is produced. The *TSG* graph is based on the detection of shots boundaries and a strategy of clustering of video shots [12][13]. Each cluster regroups a set of similar shots and represents a fragment of a semantic unit [14]. Two shots are clustered together if the distance of similarity between them is less than a predefined threshold. The similarity is based on visual primitives such as colors, image correlation, optic flow, 3D hints, etc. Furthermore, the clustered shots must be in the same sequence to keep semantic clustering. A sequence as described in [4], is linked to another one by an effect of transition *(dissolve, ...)* to tell the spectator that a break in the narration of the history is occurred. The process of clustering is applied to each sequence separately. When all shots of a sequence are clustered a new *clustering* of sequence's shot is throw out.

A Time-Space Graph (*TSG*) is then created as a new description model of the video stream. The vertical axis represents the spatial distribution of shots, the position of the cameramen or the clusters and the horizontal one represents the time line or the time code. The **Fig. 2** illustrates a form of *TSG*, where *TR* is the time duration of an effect of transition between two sequences, t_i is the time code of the shot P_i and Φ_i is a cluster that regroups some shots.

Based on *TSG* a temporal relations between cluster is defined. The clusters and their relations ships describe the video as a temporal cluster Graph *TCG*. The relationship between clusters must have semantic signification's to extract semantic units. In fact, the temporal relations are an extension of Allen's relations as described in [2].

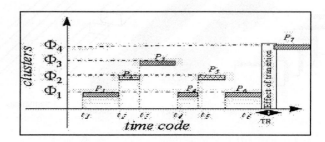

Fig. 2. Description of video data as TSG graph.

For the moment, four types of relations between clusters are used : *Meets, Before, During* and *Overlaps*. The two first ones describe a sequential relation between two clusters. Therefore, they have only one parameter that represents the delay τ of succession between them. The *Meets* relation is generated between two clusters that are included in the same sequence, and no delay separates these two clusters. The *Before* relation describes a transition of sequences. Each member of this relation is included in a different sequence, then in a different semantic unit. The delay parameter represents the time duration of the effect of transition that links the two sequences together. *During* and *Overlaps* are used when two clusters intersect in the time (**Fig 3.,4.**). They describe that their members are included in the same semantic unit. The time code of all shots of the left cluster of a *During* relation defines its parameters (**Fig. 3**). For an *Overlaps* relation its parameters are defined by the time code of all shots of its right member in intersection with its left member. In addition, the last parameter of this relation is the time code of the first shot of the right member which is not in intersection with the left member (**Fig. 4**).

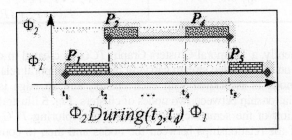

Fig. 3. During relation generated from the TSG graph.

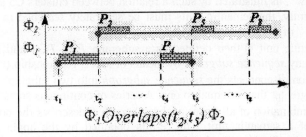

Fig. 4. Overlaps relation generated from the TSG graph.

The succession and the intersection between two members of a temporal relation is determined by the space-time distribution of their shots (*STG*). **Fig. 3** and **Fig. 4** illustrate two examples of *During* and *Overlaps* relations.

As consequences of the previous definitions, these extended temporal relations define a set of temporal constraints which must be satisfied. **TABLE I** summarizes all of these temporal constraints associated with the temporal relations, where t represents the time code of a shot, T the time duration of a shot and τ the time duration of the effect of montage that links a shot to its successor (if *"cut"* then $\tau = 0$ else $\tau \neq 0$).

Table I. Table of temporal relations constraints

Temporal relations	Temporal constraints
Φ_1 Meets Φ_2	$P_n^1.t + P_n^1.T = P_1^2.t - 1$
Φ_1 Before (τ) Φ_2	$P_n^1.t + P_n^1.T + \tau = P_1^2.t - 1$
Φ_2 During $(P_1^2.t,...,P_i^2.t,...P_{i+1}.t)$ Φ_1	$P_n^1.t + P_i^1.T \leq P_i^2.t - 1$ && $P_i^1.t + P_i^1.T \geq P_n^2.t - 1$
Φ_1 Overlaps $(P_1^2.t,...,P_i^2.t,...P_{i+1}.t)$ Φ_2	$P_1^1.t + P_1^1.T \leq P_i^2.t - 1$ && $P_n^1.t + P_n^1.T \geq P_i^2.t - 1$ && $P_n^1.t + P_n^1.T \leq P_{i+1}^2.t$

Consequently, a Temporal-Clusters Graph (*TCG*) is created in order to get a new representation of the video stream carrying out these temporal relationships. In such a *TCG*, a node is associated with each cluster, and an edge is drawn for each temporal relationship between two nodes of clusters. **Fig. 5** illustrate a form of *TCG*. The extraction of the semantic units consists of exploring *TCG* according to the semantic of the relationships between the nodes and then to combine the selected nodes together into a new unit. Extracting semantic units of a video document is equivalent to analyze the four types of temporal relation : *Before, Meets, Overlaps* and *During*. The *Before* relation divides the *TCG* into so called *"sequence subgraphs "*, as illustrated by such a relation between clusters C5 and C7 of **Fig. 5**. Consequently, the semantic units must be separately searched in each *"sequence subgraph"* of *TCG*.

A semantic unit is then defined as a subgraph Γ of *TCG* and it is obtained by dividing any *sequence subgraph* by means of *Meets* relationship (the elimination of this relation disconnects the *sequence subgraph* into two subgraphs). The size of Γ could be greater than or equal to one. A series of continuous shots that are obtained by the combination of all nodes of the subgraph Γ describes the boundaries and the content of a semantic unit. The results obtained by the application of the this method, on a 7 minutes video from the CD-II Movie « *Dances With Wolves* » are presented in the section 6 by the **Table I**. It's showed that this technique reached a success segmentation rate up to 89% as compared to a manual segmentation by an expert. Nevertheless, the actual version of the prototype (*VTRM*)[9] that implements the spatial-temporal clue based segmentation method, considers sometimes that nodes of *TCG* which is connected by the *meet* type temporal relation, and having size then 2, as an independent scene. This consideration may deform the semantic reality. To solve this problem we consider that is essential to apply another tool which allow to restore the complete area semantic of those nodes type.

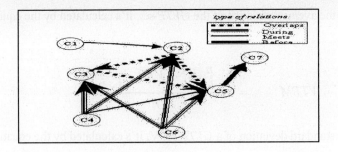

Fig. 5. An example of TCG graph which generated automatically.

4 The Rhythm Based Segmentation

To explore the rhythm effects of a video sequences, we propose a measure to detect the change or maintenance of the rhythm. This measure is based on a statically method of distribution ; which is the *"Gaussian law of distribution"*[11]. For the application of this method we firstly tacked it for granted that the shot duration follows a normal law of distribution. We shall proceed first, by giving the flow of our rhythm based segmentation method.

Assume there are N shots, $\varphi = \{P_1, P_2, \dots\dots, P_i, P_{i+1}, \dots P_N\}$. Every shots P_i ($1 \leq i \leq N$) is characterized by its time duration T_i and its time code (starting time) t_i. Assume also that $VTP_{i, i+1}$ is the duration's variation between the shots P_i and P_{i+1} (that is $VTP_i = |P_i - P_{i+1}|$). So, to the set of shots φ, we associate a set of the duration variations between the shots P_i and P_{i+1} (with P_i, $P_{i+1} \in \varphi$).

Suppose that the n $(n>2)$ first successive shots have very close rhythm, in other words the variations $VTP_{1, 2} \dots\dots VTP_{n-1, n}$ are practically equal.

Let $GP = \{P_1, P_2, \dots\dots, P_n\}$ and $GVTP = \{VTP_{1, 2} \dots\dots VTP_{n-1, n}\}$. We define $F(GP)$ and $L(GP)$ as two functions which return respectively the first and the last shot belonging to GP. A shot P_i ($n+1 \leq i \leq N$) is added to GP if, and only if, it satisfies the two following conditions *(a) and (b)*:

(a) -The temporal continuity condition:

The addition of the shot P_i to GP, must guarantees the temporal-continuity between the shots P_j $(P_j \in GP)$,that is :

$$\forall P_j, P_k \in GP \ (j \neq k, \ P_j \neq 1 \ and \ P_j \neq n) \ \exists P_k, \ P_j.t = P_k.t + 1 \ and \ P_i.t = P_{L\,(GP)}.t + 1.$$

(b) -The aggregation condition basing on the rhythm :

$$| \ VTP_{L\,(GP)\,,\,i} - VTPM | < \alpha * \delta$$
with:

- *VTPM* is the average variation of the *GVTP* set, it's calculated by the equation *(1)*.

$$VTPM = \frac{\sum_{i=1}^{n-1} VTP_{i,i+1}}{n}.$$ (1)

- δ is the standard deviation of a *GVTP* set V, it's calculated by the equation *(2)*.

$$\delta = \sqrt{\frac{\sum_{i}^{n-1} \left(VTP_{i,i+1} - VTPM \right)^2}{n}}.$$ (2)

- α is a coefficient that characterize the interval *[VTPM - α δ, VTPM+ α δ]* among them we obtain a membership probability p of shots P_i to be into this interval. In fact, if we are a set $GVTP_i$ rhythm variation presented by the surface Π of the **Fig. 6**, we obtain with α = 2.5 a rate of successful aggregation practically equal to 96 %.

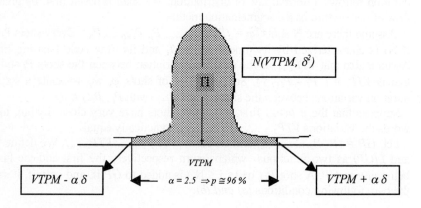

Fig. 6. The density function curve of an Normal Low

If the shot P_i doesn't satisfy one of the aforementioned conditions, a new *GP* set is formed by at least three shots that follow immediately after P_i, and the comparison process is launched again. The results obtained by the application of the rhythm based segmentation method, on a video sequence selected from the CD-II Movie « *Dances With Wolves* » and the variation curve of this sequence are presented in the section 6 respectively by the **Table II**. and the **Fig. 7**.

5   The Coupling Of The Spatial-Temporal Clue Based Segmentation With The Rhythm Based Segmentation

The coupling goals are to increase the rate successful of the results obtained by the application of the spatial-temporal clue based segmentation. Particularly we have to treat the one-shot formed sub-graphs (scenes formed by one shot). Call up that the extraction of the semantic units consists of exploring *TCG* according to the semantic of the relation ships between the nodes. The rhythm based segmentation method aims to combine the nodes formed by one shot remaining after the application of the temporal-continuity operator [8] with the other nodes that immediately precede or follow it. Of course the temporal continuity condition must be respected. The coupling of the two segmentation methods is achieved as follows :

Assume that after the application of the spatial-temporal clue based segmentation method, we obtain the set Γ of scenes, $\Gamma = \{S_1, S_2, \ldots\ldots S_N\}$ with each S_i containing more than two shots, and $\chi = \{P_i, \ldots P_j\}$ with $i \neq j$ and $\forall P_i \in \chi$, $\neg \exists\, S_i \in \Gamma$ such $P_i \in S_i$. We may consider every S_i as a GP_i set of shots as already defined in the previous section. The way the GP_i set is formed, makes the following algorithm easy to apply :

Algorithm :

1-   Initially, there are n set of scenes, $GP_1 = S_1, \ldots\, GP_n = S_n$, every GP_i is formed out of a temporal-continuous set of shots.

2-   If $\chi \neq \{\,\}$ then
    2.1. Select a shot $P_i \in \chi$.
    2.2. /* *verification of the temporal-continuity between the fist or the last shot of GP_j and the shot P_i* */
    Look for a GP_j set of shots, such $P_i.t = P_{F(GPj)}.t - 1$ or $P_i.t = P_{L(GPj)}.t +1$.
    2.3. Else (*if not step 2.2*) go to step 2.

3-   Else(*if not step 2*) then go to step 7.

4-   4.1. Calculate the duration variation set *GVTP* corresponding to the GP_j set.
    4.2. Calculate the average variation *VTPM* corresponding to the *GVTP* set.
    4.3. Calculate the standard deviation δ corresponding to the *GVTP* set.

5- /* *testing if the aggregation condition basing on the rhythm is satisfied* */
    If $|\,VTP_{L\,(GPj)\,or\,F(GPj),\,i} - VTPM\,| < \alpha * \delta$ then

    5.1. /* *add the shot P_i to the set GP_j*/ $GP_j = GP_j + \{P_i\}$;
    5.2. /* *remove the shot P_i from the set χ*/ $\chi = \chi - \{P_i\}$;
    5.3. Go to step 2.

6- Else (*not step 5*)
    6.1. If we don't reach the end of the set χ then go to step 2.

178

6.2. else (*not step 6.1.*), if ∀ *GP_j*, *GP_j* has not been modified, then go to step 7.

6.3. else (*not step 6.2.*), if ∃ *GP_j*, *GP_j* has been modified, then go to step 2.

7- Stop.

6   Experimental Results

In order to show the efficiency of coupling model for the semantic segmentation purpose, we have experienced it on a small video sequence composed of 8575 frames (*from 1690 to 10263*). This sequence has been selected from the CD-II Movie « *Dances with Wolves* » and segmented into 67 shots by the method of 3D hints [3].

The obtained results are compared to those obtained respectively by the spatial-temporal clue based segmentation, the rhythm based segmentation and the ones based on a manual segmentation. **Table II** shows the different results.

The analysis of the result obtained by the rhythm based segmentation shows that this method solely, doesn't provide an interesting result comparing to the results obtained by the one based on a manual segmentation. In the same way, the result obtained by the spatial-temporal clue based segmentation presents the inconvenience of the numerous scenes formed by one shot. The coupling method of segmentation when applied on the aforementioned sequence shows a rate of successful segmentation equal to 100%.

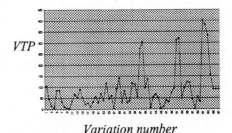

Variation number

Fig.7. The rhythm variation curve :
Each point of the curve correspond to the
difference duration between two shots . So the
variation (or the point) number 1 is equal to
| p₁.T -p₂.T |.

TABLE II. Experimental results

METHODS	RESULTS
Expert results	Scene 1 :shot 1............shot29 Scene 2 : shot 30 Scene 3 :shot 31.........shot 51 Scene 4 : shot 52 Scene 5 : shot 53........shot 67
Spatial temporal clue based segmentation method	Scene 1 :shot 1............shot27 Scene 2 : shot 30 Scene 3 :shot 33.........shot 47 Scene 4 : shot 52 Scene 5 : shot 53.........shot 67 Each shot of 28,29, 31, 32, 48, 49, 50 and 51 is considered as a scenes constituted by one shot.
Rhythm based segmentation method	Set 1 : shot 1......................shot 29 Set 2 : shot 30 Set 3 : shot 31.....................shot 34 Set 4 : shot 38.....................shot 61 Set 5 : shot 62.....................shot 64 Set 6 : shot 65 Set 7 : shot 66....................shot 67
Coupling method (α = 2.5)	Scene 1 :shot 1................shot29 Scene 2 : shot 30 Scene 3 :shot 31................shot 51 Scene 4 : shot 52 Scene 5 : shot 53................shot 67

7 Conclusion

The video analysis framework and coupling techniques proposed in this paper have contributed to more precisely extraction of scenes and story units in a video avoiding the drawback of our previous segmentation. We have successfully segment story units which represent distinct events or locales from a 7 minutes video of CD-II Movie « *Dances with Wolves* » film and the results are promising. We also are able to decompose the video into the hierarchy of story units, clusters of similar shots and shots at the lowest level. The combination captures the important relation ships within scenes and between scenes in a video. Thus allowing the analysis of the underlying story structure without any priori knowledge. Currently we are testing the proposed technique segmentation on entire « *Dances with Wolves* » film and on different programming types. We will further evaluate the performances, promises and limitations of such analysis.

References

1. Aigrain, P. , Joly, P., Lougueville, V. "Medium Knoledge-based Macro-Segmentation of Video into Sequences." *Proc. IJACI Workshop on intelligent Multimedia Information Retrieval*, ED. Mark Maybury, Montreal (1995).
2. Allen, J. F. "Maintaining Knowledge about Temporal Intervals." *CACM* (1983), *Vol. 26*, pp. 832-843.
3. Ardebilian, M., Tu, X.W., Chen, L. and Faudmay, P. "Video segmentation Using 3-D Hints Contained in 2-D Images." *Proc. SPIE (*1996).
4. Aumont, J., Marie, M. "l'Analyse de films." *édition Nathan Université* (1988), Chap. 2.
5. Chandler, D. "The Grammar of Television and Film." UWA (1994) (http://www.aber.ac.uk/~dgc/gramtv.html).
6. Christel, M. G., Winkler, D. B. and Taylor, C. R., "Improving Acess to a digital Video Library." In *Human-computer interaction : INTERACT97, the 6th IFIP Conference on Human-Computer Interaction* (Sydney, Australia July 14-18, 1997).
7. Faudmay, P., Chen, L., Montacité, C., Tu , X., Ardebilain, M., Floch , J. "Multi-Chanel Video Segmantation." *Proc. SPIE* (1996).
8. *Hammoud, R., Liming, C., Fontaine, D., " An extensible spatial-temporal model for semantic video   segmentation".1st Int.forum on multimedia on image Processing (IFMCP 98), Anchorage, alaska, 10-14 mai 1998.*
9. Hammoud, R. I., "La Segmentation de la Video Basée sur les Indices Spatio-Temporels." *Université de Technologie de Compiègne, D.E.A., C.D.S.* (Septembre, 1997).
10. Mills, M., Cohen , J. et Wong, Y. Y., "A Magnifier Tool for Video Data." *Proc. of CHI '92* (May, 1992), 93-98.
11. *Sabin,.L, M, "Statistique : concepts et méthodes" édition Masson (1993), chap6, pp 216.*
12. *Minerva M. yeng, Boon- lock yeo, "Time-constrained clustering for segmentation of video into story units", In proceeding of ICPR, pp 375-380 1996 (IEEE press).*
13. *Minerva M. yeng, Boon- lock yeo and Bede Liu, "Extracting story units from long Programs for video browsing and navigation" In proceeding of Multimedia , June pp 296-305, 1996 (IEEE Press).*
14. *Minerva M. yeng, Boon- lock yeo , Wayne Wol and Bede Liu, " Video browsing using clustering and scene transition compressed sequences", In proceeding of Multimedia computing and networking, SPIE Vol2417, pp 399-413, sans jose, calif.*
15. Smith, M. A. and kanada , T., "Video Skimming for quick Browsing based on Audio and Image Characterization." Submitted to the Special Issue of the *IEEE TRANSACTIONS ON PATTERN ANALYSIS AND MACHINE INTELLIGENCE on Digital libraries: Representation and Retrieval* (1995). Also as Technical Report CMU-CS-95-186

16. Swain, M.J and Ballard, D.H, "Color Indexing." *Inter. J.of C. Vision, Vol. 7 (* No. 1,1991), 11-32.
17. Zhang, H., Gong, Y. and Smoliar, S., "Automatic Parsing of News Video." *Proc. of IEEE conference on Multimadia Computing and Systems,* Boston (1994).

Multilingual Information Retrieval
Based on Document Alignment Techniques

Martin Braschler[1]*, Peter Schäuble[2]

[1] Eurospider Information Technology AG
Schaffhauserstr. 18, CH-8006 Zürich, Switzerland
braschler@eurospider.ch
[2] Swiss Federal Institute of Technology (ETH)
CH-8092 Zürich, Switzerland
schauble@inf.ethz.ch

Abstract. A multilingual information retrieval method is presented where the user formulates the query in his/her preferred language to retrieve relevant information from a multilingual document collection. This multilingual retrieval method involves mono- and cross-language searches as well as merging their results. We adopt a corpus based approach where documents of different languages are associated if they cover a similar story. The resulting comparable corpus enables two novel techniques we have developed. First, it enables Cross-Language Information Retrieval (CLIR) which does not lack vocabulary coverage as we observed in the case of approaches that are based on automatic Machine Translation (MT). Second, aligned documents of this corpus facilitate to merge the results of mono- and cross-language searches. Using the TREC CLIR data, excellent results are obtained. In addition, our evaluation of the document alignments gives us new insights about the usefulness of comparable corpora.

1 Introduction

We present a multilingual information retrieval method that allows the user to formulate the query in his/her preferred language, in order to retrieve relevant documents in any of the languages contained in a multilingual document collection. This is an extension to the classical Cross-Language Information Retrieval (CLIR) problem, where the user can retrieve documents in a language different from the one used for query formulation, but only one language at a time (see e.g. [11]). The multilingual information retrieval problem we tackle is therefore a generalization of CLIR.

---

* Part of this work has been carried out during the author's time at the National Institute of Standards and Technology NIST

184

There is a growing need for this general type of multilingual information retrieval, e.g. in multilingual countries, organizations and enterprises. In the future, multilingual information retrieval will also play an important role in the World-Wide Web, whose yearly growth is around 50% for English documents, and more than 90% for non-English documents.

Our approach to multilingual information retrieval is corpus-based, using so-called document alignments. The alignment process associates documents that cover similar stories. This leads to an unidirectional mapping between texts in different collections. The following is an example of such a pair of aligned documents, taken from the French-German SDA alignments (see below). Shown are the titles of the two texts. As can be seen, they clearly cover the same event.

Table 1. Example of an alignment pair

Condor-Maschine bei Izmir abgestürzt: Mutmasslich 16 Tote. (Condor plane crashed near Izmir: probably 16 dead)
Un avion ouest-allemand s'écrase près d'Izmir: 16 morts. (A Western German plane crashes near Izmir: 16 dead)

The individual collections in different languages and the mapping given by the alignments together form a *multilingual comparable corpus*. A related resource would be a *parallel corpus*. In such a parallel corpus, the paired documents are not only similar, but high-quality manual translations. One of the benefits of the presented method is the excellent availability of comparable corpora as opposed to rare and expensive parallel corpora.

Using a derived comparable corpus, the system accomplishes multilingual IR by doing pseudo (local) feedback (see [14]) on sets of aligned documents. We show how this process can easily be combined with a dictionary based approach to the translation problem. We present some excellent results obtained on the collections used for the TREC-6 CLIR track (see Appendix A) for the two language pairs English-German and French-German. The English-German run is within a few percentage points of the best runs reported for TREC, including those using full machine translation, while the French-German run clearly outperforms the other runs reported for this language combination.

We further use the alignments to extend the classical CLIR problem to include the merging of mono- and cross-language retrieval results, presenting the user with *one* multilingual result list. In this case, the alignments help overcome the problem of different RSV scales. This more general problem will also be investigated in the CLIR track for the upcoming TREC-7 conference.

Related work on alignment has been going on in the field of computational linguistics for a number of years. However, most of this work relies on parallel corpora and aligns at sentence or even word level. Usually, the amount of data processed is also smaller by several magnitudes. For an example of sentence alignment, see e.g. [3].

Other corpus based approaches to cross-language IR have been proposed in the past, including the use of similarity thesauri (see e.g. [10] and [12]) and LSI (see [5]).

Our approach is based on document/document similarities, whereas the similarity thesaurus approach and LSI approach are based on term/term similarities, with the similarity thesaurus working in a dual space, and LSI using a low-dimensional vector space obtained by singular value decomposition. On the other hand, the similarity to the Ballesteros/Croft approach [1] is only superficial. While they perform feedback before or after translation, using only a dictionary to translate the query, in our case the feedback takes place on a set of aligned documents, effectively producing the translation *itself*. A comprehensive overview of cross-language IR approaches can be found in [6].

The remainder of the paper is structured as follows: section 2 discusses the approach for computing alignments. Section 3 discusses methods for evaluating the alignments and section 4 shows the application of alignments in a CLIR system. Section 5 closes the paper by giving a summary and an outlook.

2 Document Alignment

2.1 Using Indicators for Alignment

Alignments are produced by using so-called "*indicators*" to find similarities between pairs of documents from the collections involved. Indications of such a similarity include:

- The documents share common proper nouns (the spelling of names in similar languages is often quite stable).
- The documents share common numbers (numbers are largely language independent).
- If the documents have compatible classifiers assigned, these can be used.
- The same story is usually published on similar dates by news agencies. Thus, dates can be used as indicators.
- A lexicon can be used to translate terms between the languages. Words shared by both documents are then an indication of similarity.

Only the last class of indicators (lexicon-translated terms) needs a linguistic data resource (the lexicon).

The basic concept underlying the alignment process is to use texts from the first collection as queries and run them against the documents from the other collection, thus retrieving their most similar counterparts. These pairs of similar documents give then a mapping between the two collections.

Following is a list of main differences between straightforward retrieval and the strategies used in this paper:

1. Elimination of terms based on frequency rather than stopword lists
2. Extracting indicators from the query
3. Thresholding/Query length normalization
4. Date normalization
5. Use of sliding date windows

2.2 Producing the Alignments

Alignments were produced for both English AP to German SDA texts (AP–SDA alignment) and French SDA to German SDA texts. While SDA texts in German and French are not direct translations, the *"coverage overlap"*, i.e. the portion of topics shared between the two collections, is much higher, making them easier to align. Additionally, SDA texts in both languages have manually assigned classifiers that are compatible. This greatly simplifies alignment. Because the two collections are similar enough, it is possible to align them using *no* linguistic resource.

For aligning English AP and German SDA, we use medium-frequency terms as indicators, eliminating both terms with very low and very high frequency. This is similar to using a list of "stopwords" for retrieval, with two main differences: first, not just words from the high-frequency end of the spectrum but also those from the opposite end get eliminated, and second, the list of eliminated words is much larger. The reason for this is that high-frequency terms (occurring in 10% of all documents) don't help to discriminate between similar and non-similar documents. Low-frequency terms (occurring in only one or two documents) are too likely to give purely random associations. Similar observations have been documented repeatedly in the literature (e.g. [2], [8]).

The processed AP documents are converted into queries and "transferred" into the target language (i.e. German). The necessary effort for this "translation" step varies greatly depending on how similar the collections are. AP and SDA are too far apart to align them based solely on proper nouns and numbers, so use of a lexicon of some sort is necessary to bridge the language gap. We used a wordlist (very simple form of dictionary) to avoid the need of acquiring a costly dictionary. Such a wordlist was assembled from various *free* sources on the Internet. All those sources provided very simplistic lists of translations, without extra information as to part of speech, frequency of different translations, etc. The lists also contain a fair number of misspellings and questionable translations. The combined list with English - German translations is quite big. It contains 141,240 entries (85,931 unique "head" entries), most of them of the form "word - word", but some of them phrases and even full sentences.

Using a "noisy" wordlist instead of a high-quality machine-readable dictionary is less of a restriction than might be expected. The collections used for the experiments contain thousands of documents. Doing sophisticated syntactic and semantic analysis on them, such as part-of-speech tagging and word-sense disambiguation, would be very time consuming. Oard and Hackett [7] report that machine-translating the entire SDA and NZZ collections into English took two months of computing time running *six* computers (most of them SPARC 20 workstations) in parallel. We believe that the alignment process is much more tolerant to translation errors than direct query or document translation for information retrieval, so that this kind of effort can be avoided.

In case of multiple translations, a word was replaced by all possible alternatives. This is because the list contains no extra information and no context analysis takes place. Words missing from the list were omitted, unless they begin with a capital letter. Words starting with capital letters were treated as potential names and were transferred "as-is" into the resulting query.

For running the queries against the other collection, two further major modifications were needed: thresholding (including query length normalization) and normalizing by date distance.

News agencies tend to publish stories about the same events on or near the same date. The likelihood of a good match is higher if the dates of the documents of a potential pair are close to each other. *Date normalization* boosts the similarity score of such documents, through dividing the raw alignment score by the logarithm of the distance in days between the two texts.

Thresholding is needed for making a decision based on the retrieval score as to whether the two texts should form a pair. Because AP and SDA are quite different, there is no good counterpart for a lot of the documents, and no pair should be produced. To make scores of individual pairs more comparable, the score is normalized with the query length to give a final score. With our weighting scheme not guaranteeing an upper bound on the score, this is however still not an ideal solution, and thresholding remains an issue that requires further work. Possible approaches to thresholding include setting a single fixed threshold which is applied to all queries, or using the observation that the ratio of documents that have good counterparts remains roughly constant from day to day and filtering out the best portion of pairs that fulfill this criterion.

2.3 Visualization of Alignments

Alignments, and the impact of date normalization and thresholding on them, can be visualized as follows (see Figure 1): Pairs of aligned documents are plotted as dots in a plane spanned by two time axes. The x-axis represents all AP-documents from 1988, sorted by date. The y-axis stands for the SDA documents of the same year, also in date order. The graph in the upper left corner shows alignments without either date normalization or thresholding. As would be expected, a lot of dots fall into the diagonal, as the dates of the documents making up the corresponding pair are close. However, a fair number of dots are scattered all over the plot. When a threshold is applied that filters out roughly two thirds of the pairs, the diagonal remains well represented. However, the dots outside the diagonal are still quite evenly distributed, even though the graph is sparser (upper right graph). The lower left graph shows the situation if date normalization is switched on. This graph is without thresholding. The dots are now drawn much closer to the diagonal. If date normalization and thresholding are combined, a thick diagonal emerges, and the dots get sparser the farther they are from the diagonal (lower right graph). This is the desired effect.

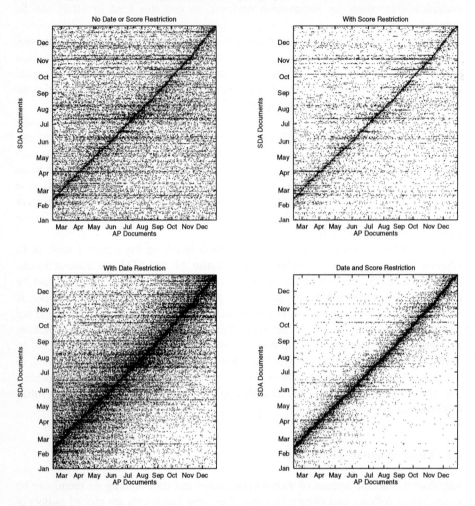

Fig. 1. Effects of date normalization and thresholding

These preceding observations lead to a possible optimization: as most pairs produced lie in a fairly narrow band around the diagonal, the alignment can be computed using a sliding "*date window*", which restricts the document search space drastically. Instead of searching for a match in the whole 3 years of SDA for every AP document, just documents inside a date window a few days wide are considered. This speeds things up dramatically, by up to two orders of magnitude. Searches take place on a series of overlapping small subcollections as the date window shifts over the collection. Experiments indicated that a window of 15 days is a good choice. If the collections are more similar, much narrower date windows are possible. Note that some desirable matches (background stories, periodic events) may be missed using this strategy. Graphically, this corresponds to eliminating all dots outside of a small band around the diagonal from the lower right graph in Figure 1.

The alignment pairs produced are *not* reversible. Several English AP documents may be aligned to the same SDA text and not all SDA documents are member of a pair. This is a consequence of different amounts of coverage of the same events by the two news agencies, and therefore hard (and probably not desirable) to avoid. If alignments in the opposite direction are needed, the roles of the AP and SDA documents must be swapped, and the pairs recomputed.

Aligning the whole AP and SDA takes roughly a week using a single SPARCstation 5. Small changes, like eliminating debugging information, could easily reduce this time significantly. The alignment process is also parallelizable, with different computers working on different parts of the collections. And, most importantly, if date windows are used, old alignments could be kept without recalculation when the collections have new documents added. Aligning a new day's worth of news stories would only take a few minutes this way.

2.4 Aligning More Similar Collections

Aligning the French and German SDA texts gives insights into possible simplifications when the two collections are more similar than English AP and German SDA. The SDA texts also have *manually* assigned classifiers that are language-independent. The classification is rather rough (some 300+ different classifiers, mostly just country codes), but nevertheless helpful.

As no wordlists like those used for the AP-SDA alignment could be found for German-French, the SDA-SDA alignment works *without* any lexicon. This would not have been possible, had the two collections been more different. This demonstrates, however, that it is possible to produce alignments without the use of *any* linguistic data resource, provided the collections are similar enough.

Beyond using the classifiers, the SDA-SDA alignment relies only on matching proper nouns (i.e. names) and numbers as indicators. This way a document matches a query if it shares at least one classifier and any proper noun/number. Identification of proper nouns works by looking at capitalization of words.

The higher similarity of the two collections allows choosing a narrower date window than for SDA–AP alignment; experiments gave the best results for a window of only one day (i.e. same-day matches only). Thresholding didn't give consistent improvements for SDA-SDA, probably because as many good as bad pairs were filtered. This demonstrates again the need for a better thresholding strategy.

3 Evaluation of Alignments

3.1 General-purpose vs. Application-specific Evaluation

Evaluating document-level alignments can have fundamentally different goals. On one hand, one can assess how many of the pairs produced consist of documents that are really related to each other (i.e. "good alignments"). This is a general point of view - the quality of the alignments is judged without any particular application in mind. An alternative is to evaluate the performance of a specific application that uses the alignments. In our case, this means using them for cross-language information retrieval. Concentrating on one application has the drawback of losing generality, however the danger of "overtuning" the alignment process to theoretical goals that have no merit in practice is avoided. In this paper, both ideas are investigated. Quality assessment independent of a specific application will be discussed in the following, whereas an evaluation of the alignments for use in CLIR can be found in section 4.

3.2 Judging the Quality of Alignment Pairs

To evaluate the quality of the alignments independent of a specific application, a *sample* of the pairs was judged for "quality". This is similar to doing relevance assessments to evaluate retrieval runs. There exist however the following major differences:

- It is not immediately clear how to judge the "quality" of a pair. Defining the alignment task as "finding the most similar counterpart in the other collection" means that a human judge would have to read the *entire* collection to make sure no more similar text exists. This is clearly impractical. When the criterion is relaxed to "find a good (i.e. similar) counterpart in the other collection", looking at the two documents that form the pair is sufficient.
- It is also unclear on how to quantify how good a match is. When doing relevance assessments for documents returned by a retrieval system, there is a comparably short query against which a human judge can compare the documents. For assessing alignments, this "query" is a whole document, and much less focused. It seems harder to make a "yes/no" decision. As a consequence, a five-class scale was used (see Table).
- The human judge has to read through two documents per judgment instead of one as for relevance judgments, with the query changing for every pair. There is also no ranking available to form the sample, so the sample must be quite large in order to get reliable statistics. This means more work for the judge.

Table 2. Classes used for judgment of alignment pairs

Class 1	Same story	Two documents cover exactly the same story/event (e.g. the results of the same candidate in the same primary for the US presidential election)
Class 2	Related story	Two documents cover two related events (e.g. two different primaries for the US presidential election)
Class 3	Shared aspect	Two documents address various topics, but at least one of them is shared (e.g. update on US politics of the day, one item is about the upcoming presidential election)
Class 4	Common terminology	Two documents are not really related, but a significant amount of the terminology is shared (e.g. one document on the US, the other on the French presidential election)
Class 5	Unrelated	Two documents have no apparent relation (e.g. one document about the US presidential election, the other about vacation traffic in Germany)

A 1% random sample of the final (i.e. after thresholding) pairs of the AP-SDA alignment was judged with respect to these five classes. The results were as follows:

Table 3. Results from evaluation of a 1% random sample

1% sample:	852 out of 85125 pairs	
Class 1:	327	38.38%
Class 2:	174	20.42%
Class 3:	16	1.88%
Class 4:	123	14.44%
Class 5:	212	24.88%

Which classes are considered to be good alignments will likely vary with the intended application. When used for extraction of linguistic information, like term associations or translations, a high quality of alignment is probably needed, so that maybe only pairs from classes 1 and 2 would be acceptable. The proportion of "success" of the alignment process would then be 58.8 ± 3.3% (95% confidence interval). This seems a bit low, so that AP and SDA are probably too dissimilar for such use. For application in a CLIR system, pairs from classes 1 through 4 are likely to help for extracting good terms. The proportion of success is then 75.1 ± 2.9%, and some very good results are obtained when the alignments are used for retrieval (details on this follow in the next section).

4 Applications of Alignments for IR

4.1 Cross-Language Retrieval Using Document Alignments

We now describe how we use the alignments to build a system for multilingual information retrieval . Such a system is comparably simple and very inexpensive, as very few linguistic resources were used for aligning the documents. It is also fairly independent of specific language combinations, as long as suitable collections for aligning can be found.

A surprisingly simple strategy was used that can be derived as follows: In case the two collections to be searched were parallel, i.e., real translations of each other, it would be possible just to search the collection that corresponds to the language of the query, and return a result list produced by replacing every found document by its counterpart in the other collection. This is of course not a very interesting case, as the collection to be searched is seldom available in translated form. We therefore replace the requirement for a parallel corpus with one for a comparable corpus. This requirement can be met in a lot of interesting real-world applications. One such example is the alignment of English AP and German SDA, allowing one to search the SDA texts in English.

First, the user's query is run against the source collection, thus obtaining a ranked list. Instead of replacing the found documents by their translations, the document-level mapping produced by the alignment process is used to replace them with their most similar counterparts from the other collection, if available. This produces a new result list containing documents in the target language. Because a lot of documents are not part of an alignment pair, however, they would never be retrieved using this strategy.

This problem was approached by using a pseudo *relevance feedback* (in this case *local feedback*) (see e.g. [4], [14]) loop *after* the replacement step (but *before* a search in the target language takes place) . A certain number of the highest ranked documents are *assumed* relevant and terms are extracted from these documents that are thought to represent them well. These terms form a query used for a new search. Because the documents are already in the target language, so is the query produced. This is fundamentally different from the approach in Ballesteros/Croft [1], where feedback is used before or after the translation. In our feedback takes place on a set of aligned documents and is used to *produce* the translation *itself*. Unlike in usual applications of relevance feedback, the new terms cannot be combined with the original query because their languages don't match. Only terms coming from the feedback process form the new query.

This simple strategy works surprisingly well for certain queries. It fails however if the initial query doesn't retrieve any relevant documents. This can be amended by combining the strategy with a dictionary translation of the query. The same wordlist used for producing the alignments can be used for a *crude* word-by-word translation of the query. Such translations normally have problems, even if the dictionary is of high quality. Translations are often very ambiguous, and including many extraneous wrong translations hurts retrieval performance a lot. Another problem is missing entries from the dictionary, because the query term is inflected or because even the base form itself is absent.

Therefore, simple word-by-word replacement with all possible translations usually doesn't perform well and is less appropriate than for computing alignments. Additional efforts are needed, like using part-of-speech, sense disambiguation, lexically correct word normalization etc. It is however easily possible to *combine* such a simple dictionary translation with the relevance feedback process described above. Instead of deleting the original query before feedback, it can be replaced with such a "pseudo-translation". Because the terms get reweighted in the feedback process, even the problem of assigning weights to the two sources of information (dictionary vs. alignments) is automatically taken care of. The alignments as additional source of information help lessen the mentioned translation problems.

In case the collection to be searched is not aligned, two independent aligned collections can be used to produce the query. The aligned collections are then only used for the transfer of the query into the target language, whereas the search takes place on the third collection.

4.2 Results on the TREC-6 CLIR Collection

Results for the strategies just described on the TREC-6 CLIR collection are presented in the following: Figure 2 shows a comparison of using alignments alone, using a dictionary pseudo-translation and then using both methods *combined*, i.e. doing initial retrieval using a dictionary translation, and then improving this translation using the alignments, as outlined above. The collection being searched is a combination of both German SDA and NZZ, and therefore a superset of the one that was aligned to English AP or French SDA. This makes the results directly comparable to the ones reported by participants of the TREC-6 CLIR task. The full topic statements were used for all runs, and the evaluation used relevance assessments for 21 queries. Some caution is appropriate with regard to the scope of the conclusions because this was the first year with a CLIR task at the TREC conference, and the size of the query set was rather small.

The left graph shows a comparison of doing English-German CLIR using the alignments, the wordlist or the combination of both. The combination gives by far the *best* result, improving the dictionary-only run by a massive 62% in terms of average precision. The combined run achieves not quite 60% of the monolingual baseline. This is a substantial drop, but due to the fact that the baseline is very high (it outperforms the German monolingual runs reported for TREC-6), the result is still within 5% of the best TREC-6 English-German runs. This is an excellent result, as those were using full machine translation of the documents or the queries.

The graph on the right compares the monolingual baseline with cross-language runs coming from French and English. The French-German run produces slightly better results than the English-German. This is remarkable because of the much simpler alignment process. It shows that when very similar collections are available for alignments, a system without *any* lexicon-like data resource can be built. This French-German run outperforms all of the few TREC-6 runs reported for this language combination by a wide margin.

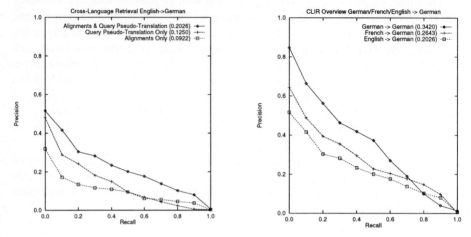

Fig. 2. Recall/precision graphs showing results of cross-language retrieval using document-level alignments

4.3 Merging the Results of Mono- and Cross-Language Searches

Merging the results of a mono-language search and of one or several cross-language search(es) is a non-trivial problem for two reasons. First, the Retrieval Status values $RSV_i(q,dj)$ of the different search methods i are on different scales. Second, the numbers of relevant documents in the different languages are unknown. It is possible that the same number of relevant documents exist in each language; but is also possible that all relevant documents are in a single language.

To cope with the merging problem we suggest linear transformations of the Retrieval Status Values. For instance, assume that the document d_j has been retrieved by method i because it is in language i, then its retrieval status value $RSV_i(q,d_j)$ is mapped to a common scale $RSV(q,d_j)$ in the following way:

$$RSV(q,d_j) := \alpha_i + \beta_i * RSV_i(q,d_j). \tag{1}$$

The parameters α_i and β_i are determined by means of aligned documents and a least square fit which minimizes the sum of the squares of the error of aligned pairs. For instance, assume that d_j and d_k were aligned because d_j covers a story in language h and d_k covers the same or a similar story in language i. These two documents obtained the scores $RSV_h(q,d_j)$ and $RSV_i(q,d_k)$. Because they were aligned, they should be mapped to similar scores,

$$\alpha_h + \beta_h * RSV_h(q,d_j) \approx \alpha_i + \beta_i * RSV_i(q,d_k) \,, \tag{2}$$

or in other words: the square of the difference

$$\Delta_{jk}^2 := (\alpha_h + \beta_h * RSV_h(q,d_j) - \alpha_i - \beta_i * RSV_i(q,d_h))^2 \tag{3}$$

should be minimized, which is achieved by a least square fit. The advantage of this approach is that not only relevant but also irrelevant pairs of aligned documents are used for merging. Of course, non-aligned documents can also be mapped to the common scale using the mappings that were determined by means of the aligned pairs. Results of future experiments will show which percentage of documents have to be aligned in order to accomplish merging the search results in this way.

5 Summary and Outlook

We present a method for computing a document-level mapping between texts from different collections written in different languages and propose techniques for evaluating such a *document-level alignment*. The alignments are then used for building a cross-language information retrieval system, and the results of this system using the TREC-6 CLIR data are given. We also show how to use the alignments to extend the classical CLIR problem to a scenario where mono- and cross-language result lists are merged.

The alignment process is very modest in terms of the resources used; it needs neither expensive hardware nor costly high-quality linguistic resources. It should also be easy to adapt it for a dynamic environment where documents are constantly added to the collections. In such a case, thanks to using date windows, the alignments could be extended without the need to discard old pairs.

Use of the alignments for CLIR gives excellent results, proving their value for real-world applications. Applications for alignments other than CLIR, such as automatic dictionary extraction, thesaurus generation and others, are possible for the future. The question of how well the findings apply to a range of different collections remains open; however, the fact that AP and SDA are quite dissimilar gives hope that a lot of data can be aligned. The methods shown should also be fairly easily adaptable to other language pairs, as long as some conditions can be met (e.g. similar collections or wordlist available).

There is much room for improvements in the alignment process. Indications are that it is crucial to extract the right pieces of the documents, such as by filtering out terms with high and low frequency. This idea could be carried further by using the similarity of the best matching passage between two documents, or by using a summarization step and then comparing the summaries. First experiments with fixed-length passages showed a prohibitive increase in computational complexity, though.

Perhaps the most interesting issue is the integration of more or better linguistic resources. The alignment process should take advantage of such resources, while still remain usable if they are unavailable. With hopefully more linguistic tools becoming affordable, there should be considerable potential in such enhancements.

6 Acknowledgments

Thanks go to the whole NLPIR group at NIST for help, especially Donna Harman and Paul Over for numerous valuable discussions of the experiments presented. Work leading to some aspects of these experiments began earlier at the information retrieval group at ETH; thanks go to Páraic Sheridan.

References

1. Ballesteros, L., Croft, B. W.: Phrasal Translation and Query Expansion Techniques for Cross-Language Information Retrieval. In: Proceedings of the 20th Annual International ACM SIGIR Conference on Research and Development in Information Retrieval, (1997) pages 84-91
2. Crestani, F., van Rijsbergen, C. J.: Information Retrieval by Logical Imaging. In: Journal of Documentation (1994)
3. Gale, W. A., Church, K. W.: A Program for Aligning Sentences in Bilingual Corpora. In: Computational Linguistics, 19(1) (1993) 75-102. Special Issue on Using Large Corpora I.
4. Harman, D. K.: Relevance Feedback and Other Query Modification Techniques. In: Frakes, W. B., Baeza-Yates, R.: Information Retrieval, Data Structures & Algorithms, Prentice-Hall (1992) pages 241-261
5. Landauer, T. K., Littman, M. L.: Fully Automatic Cross-Language Document Retrieval using Latent Semantic Indexing. In: Proceedings of the Sixth Annual Conference of the UW Centre for the New Oxford English Dictionary and Text Research, (1990) pages 31-38.
6. Oard, D. W.: Cross-Language Text Retrieval Research in the USA. Presented at: 3rd ERCIM DELOS Workshop, Zurich, Switzerland (1997)
   Available from http://www.clis.umd.edu/dlrg/filter/papers/delos.ps.
7. Oard, D. W., Hackett, P.: Document Translation for Cross-Language Text Retrieval at the University of Maryland. To be published in: Proceedings of the Sixth Text Retrieval Conference (TREC-6) (to appear)
   Available from http://trec.nist.gov/pubs/trec6/papers/umd.ps.
8. Qiu, Y.: Automatic Query Expansion Based on A Similarity Thesaurus. PhD Thesis, Swiss Federal Institute of Technology (ETH), Zurich, Switzerland (1995)
9. See http://www.sda-ats.ch
10. Schäuble, P.: Multimedia Information Retrieval. Kluwer Academic Publishers (1997)
11. Schäuble, P., Sheridan, P.: Cross-Language Information Retrieval (CLIR) Track Overview. To be published in: Proceedings of the Sixth Text Retrieval Conference (TREC-6) (to appear)
12. Sheridan, P., Ballerini, J.-P.: Experiments in Multilingual Information Retrieval using the SPIDER system. In: Proceedings of the 19th Annual International ACM SIGIR Conference on Research and Development in Information Retrieval, (1996) pages 58-65

13. Voorhees, E. M., Harman, D. K.: Overview of the Sixth Text Retrieval Conference (TREC-6). To be published in: Proceedings of the Sixth Text Retrieval Conference (TREC-6) (to appear)
14. Xu, J. and Croft, B. W.: Query Expansion Using Local and Global Document Analysis. In: Proceedings of the 19th Annual International ACM SIGIR Conference on Research and Development in Information Retrieval, (1996) pages 4-11.

Appendix

Used Resources

All alignment experiments were carried out by modifying components of the PRISE, a public domain information retrieval system developed at the National Institute of Standards and Technology (NIST). The experiments used the text collections from cross-language task of the TREC-6 ([11], [13]) conference. These collections (see Table 1) consist of documents in English, German and French. Although both the French and some of the German texts are from SDA, they are *not* direct translations of each other. They are written by different people independently and produced by different editorial offices [9]. While AP and SDA are both news wires, NZZ is a newspaper, and differs both in style and the dates covered. As it is important that the collections used for alignment are as similar as possible, the NZZ texts didn't seem to be suited for alignment as well as the rest of the collections. They were therefore excluded from the alignment process. They were however used for the CLIR experiments.

Table 4. Details for the document collections used

Collection	Language	Dates Covered	Size (MB)	# Docs
AP (Associated Press)	English	mid-Feb 1988 to end of 1990	741 MB	242,918
SDA (Schweizerische Depeschenagentur)	German	Jan 1988 to end of 1990	332 MB	185,099
NZZ (Neue Zürcher Zeitung)	German	Jan 1994 to end of 1994	194 MB	66,741
SDA (Schweizerische Depeschenagentur)	French	Jan 1988 to end of 1990	252 MB	141,656

Experimental Studies on an Applet-Based Document Viewer for Multilingual WWW Documents – Functional Extension of and Lessons Learned from Multilingual HTML

Shigeo Sugimoto[1], Akira Maeda[2], Myriam Dartois[1], Jun Ohta[1],
Shigetaka Nakao[1], Tetsuo Sakaguchi[1], Koichi Tabata[1]

[1] University of Library and Information Science
Tsukuba, Ibaraki, Japan
{sugimoto, myriam, jun, nakao, saka, tabata}@ulis.ac.jp
[2] Nara Institute of Science and Technology
Ikoma, Nara, Japan
aki-mae@is.aist-nara.ac.jp

Abstract. The World Wide Web (WWW) covers the globe. However, the browsing functions for documents in multiple languages are not easily accessed by occasional users. Functions to display and input multilingual texts in digital libraries are clearly crucial. Multilingual HTML (MHTML) is a document browser technology for multilingual documents on the WWW. The authors developed a display function for multilingual documents based on MHTML technology and extended it to text inputs in multiple languages for off-the-shelf browsers and sample applications. This extension creates an environment for digital library end-users, wherein they can view and search multilingual documents using any off-the-shelf browser. This paper also discusses the lessons learned from the MHTML project.

Keywords: Multilingual Document Browsing, Off-the-Shelf WWW Browsers, Multilingual Texts Display and Input, Text Retrieval in Multiple Scripts

1   Introduction

The Internet and the World Wide Web (WWW) represent a very important infrastructure for digital libraries. English is widely accepted as the common language on the WWW for global communication, but there are still many documents on the Web written in non-English languages. Functions for accessing information in foreign languages as well as English are crucial for the WWW and digital libraries. A working group co-funded by ERCIM and NSF has been working on defining the technologically important aspects of building a multilingual information access environment[5]. Since libraries are inherently multilingual, library information systems have to include multilingual library information. For library information systems handling Chinese, Japanese, and Korean (CJK) texts, the display and input functions for a large set of characters containing non-standardized characters is a key technology for building a digital library.

The WWW and Mosaic were great breakthroughs for accessing information on the Internet. They respectively introduced a hypertext system on the Internet and a unified user interface for information access tools provided on the Internet. Current WWW technologies provide us with various elaborate features, such as digital video and audio interfaces and animation. Those technologies played an important role in promoting research and development of digital libraries since they helped many people understand the importance of the digital library. The authors consider that the most important aspects of digital libraries are their ubiquity and low cost. Since digital library users are widely spread over the Internet, a user can access a digital library from different environments, and the digital library provides for casual users who cannot afford an expensive user environment.

Browser technology for documents in multiple languages is an important tool for accessing information on the Internet and for digital libraries. There are browsers that can process multilingual documents[9][15]. However, even though Unicode has been employed as the primary character code standard on the WWW, it is not easy for the occasional user to set up his/her browser for browsing documents written in a foreign language or in multiple languages. WebFonts[2] is a promising technology for browsing documents in foreign languages because the set of fonts required to view a document is automatically loaded in the client. However, input functions for foreign language texts are not included.

The authors have been working on a browser technology called Multilingual HTML (MHTML) to display multilingual documents on an off-the-shelf WWW browser, even if the browser does not have the fonts required to display the documents[6][7][13]. Since the document-browsing function is realized as a Java applet, users only need an off-the-shelf browser which is capable of running Java applets. We applied MHTML technology to a gateway service to view foreign documents and to a multilingual electronic text collection of folktales[3][4]. We extended MHTML to achieve a text input function in multiple languages. We implemented a Japanese text input server which sends a user interface applet to input Japanese words/characters from a remote client without any Japanese functions. We also applied the extended MHTML to text retrieval systems.

This paper describes the extension of MHTML and the overall MHTML project in order to discuss crucial issues for MHTML in connection with digital libraries. We first describe the background issues of multilingual document access on the WWW from the viewpoint of digital libraries. We then explain the basic concept of MHTML technology and its application systems. In addition, we describe the extension of MHTML for text input and text search functions and the experimental application systems of the extended MHTML, which include an online public access catalog system (OPAC) and an SGML-based full text retrieval system. We also offer a brief description of previously developed application systems. And finally, we discuss the lessons learned from MHTML.

2 Background Issues: Display and Input of Texts in Multiple Languages

The most basic functions required to access information on the WWW are the display of HTML documents and the inputting of text from a client. However, these functions are not always provided on the client for texts in foreign languages. The MHTML project was initially started to realize a light, easy-to-use, ubiquitous environment for browsing WWW documents written in multiple languages on an off-the-shelf WWW browser. We first developed a viewing function to display multilingual documents on clients where fonts for multilingual texts were not necessarily installed. We realized that even if a standard character code set for multilingual texts was widely accepted, it is not practical to assume that the end users of digital libraries can afford a complete set of fonts for the code set.

The text input function is as crucial as the display function for browsing documents in multiple languages. The text input function is generally defined as a mapping to a character code or a code string from the user's action on an input device, i.e., a single keystroke, a combination of keystrokes, a sequence of keystrokes, or a mouse click. Since inputted texts are usually displayed on a screen, text input requires a display function as well. In the case of an ordinary Japanese text input function, for example, a Japanese word or phrase expressed in phonetic characters (Hiragana, Katakana, or alphabets) is converted to the appropriate Japanese word or phrase expressed in Kanji, Hiragana, Katakana, and/or alphabets. The phonetic expression in alphabets is transliteration, which can be inputted from an ordinary ASCII keyboard. The mapping function can be located in the client or in a server connected via a network, but the font has to be locally provided. Moreover, users have to set up their local environments in accordance with the requirements for inputting texts, such as connection to the mapping function and font installation. It is difficult for an end user who only occasionally accesses foreign documents to set up his/her environment.

Since every library has materials written in foreign languages, a library information system (LIS) has to manage bibliographic data and/or electronic texts written in foreign languages. The LIS must provide functions to display and input multilingual texts on any client, since the user can access library information not only from a terminal located in the library but also from a client in his/her home or office. In addition, it has to handle characters not included in any industrial standard character code set, since those standards do not contain characters which are rarely used but are required to encode historical documents. For example, the cataloging rule of the National Center for Science Information Systems of Japan (NACSIS) states that "if a Kanji found in any bibliographic data is not included in the Japanese standard character code sets, the character should be encoded based on an identification number given by major large

Kanji dictionaries"[16]. (One of the dictionaries, the Daikanwa Jiten, contains approximately 49,000 characters[8].) In addition, ideographic characters are extensible. Microsoft Word can display a smiley symbol as a character. An author may invent a new character and use it in his/her work. In Japanese systems, this non-standard character problem has generally been solved by assigning a code to a new character and locally defining a glyph for the new character in the local font file. This newly-added character is called Gaiji in Japanese. A Gaiji is only effective in a system or systems where its code and glyph are shared. In a server-client system, the server and its clients have to share codes and glyphs for a set of Gaijis in order to display them on the screen. However, it is not easy to maintain a set of Gaijis in a distributed environment since the client is not always working with a single server. Thus, Gaiji is a significant problem for network communication.

3 MHTML

3.1 Basic Concepts

Figure 1 shows the outline of the display mechanism of MHTML. An MHTML server fetches an HTML document and converts it into an MHTML object that contains a source text string and a minimum set of font glyphs. As shown in Fig. 2, the MHTML object contains a source text string, a minimum set of font glyphs, and a header. The character codes of the source text string are internalized to the object so that the codes are effective only in the object. (Not all tags contained in the source text string are internalized, since they are used by the applet to interpret the text.) The server sends the client an MHTML viewer applet, which fetches the MHTML object from the server and displays the source text contained in the object. The applet renders the source text string on the client using the glyphs contained only in the object. The language repertoire of the server primarily depends on the set of fonts stored in the font bank; conversion of documents into the ISO-2022-JP-2[12] standard is usually straightforward.

As described previously, browsing technologies that require no local fonts are advantageous for displaying foreign characters and non-standard characters on a remote client. We compared MHTML with the following three technologies that require no fonts on the client.

1. Page Image Conversion (GIF image): Converts a source document into a set of page images. A page image is created by a capturing tool on UNIX, which produces a GIF image.
2. Character to Inline Image Conversion by String (CII/S): Converts each set of continuous Japanese characters (i.e. string) into an inline image and an associated IMG tag, and creates an HTML text containing only ASCII characters and a set of inline images. (Note: The maximum string length is 30.)
3. Character to Inline Image Conversion by Character (CII/C): Converts every Japanese character into an inline image and an associated IMG tag, and

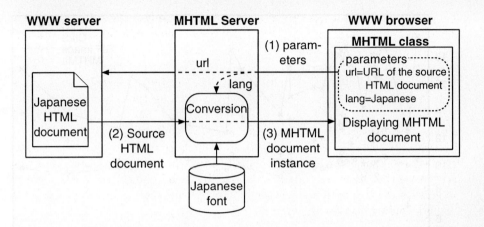

Fig. 1. MHTML system overview

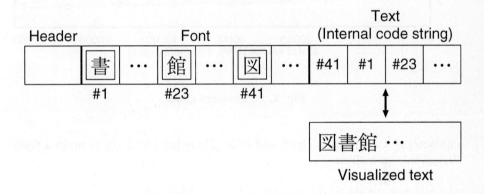

Fig. 2. Object definition

creates an HTML text containing only ASCII characters and a set of inline images.

We measured the sizes of data converted from 30 Japanese academic articles published in HTML (shown in Fig. 3), where the X- and Y-axes indicate the source document size and the ratio between the size of the converted data and its source data. This graph demonstrates the advantage of MHTML. In addition, since an MHTML object is sent in one connection, the expense of creating a connection between a server and a client is quite low. The disadvantage of MHTML is the expense of sending an applet. However, since the applet is cached on the client, the expense is reduced if the user repeatedly accesses foreign documents.

MHTML also has the advantage that it can display a document which contains non-standard characters such as Gaiji. An MHTML server can display any

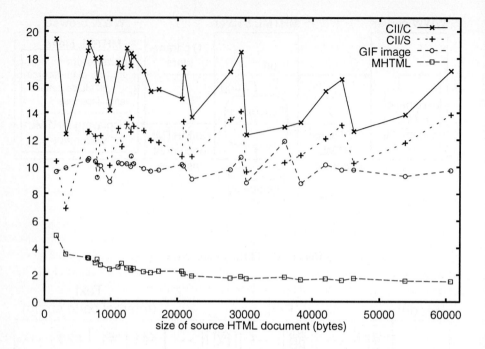

Fig. 3. Performance graph

character if it is given its glyph and code. There are two ways to make a Gaiji displayable on a client:

1. Add new glyphs to the font file in the font bank, or
2. Add a new font file containing glyphs for a set of Gaijis to the font bank.

3.2 Previous Works on MHTML

(1) Gateway Server[17]

We implemented a gateway server. The server receives the URL of a document from a client, fetches the document from the document server, converts the document into an MHTML object, and sends the object to the client with an MHTML viewer applet. Figure 1 shows a gateway server for Japanese documents. The gateway server implemented in ULIS has fonts for Japanese, Simplified Chinese, Traditional Chinese, Korean, Thai, Western European, Cyrillic, and Greek. The gateway also accepts multilingual scripts encoded in ISO-2022-JP-2. The major difficulty that beset the authors during the development of the gateway server was the evolution of HTML. The set of HTML tags which are accepted by the gateway includes the basic tags to display texts and define links, but does not includes those for images, tables, frames, and input.

(2) Japanese Folktales Collection in Multiple Languages[18]

MHTML technology is useful for developing a user interface for a multilingual electronic text collection on the Internet. The authors applied MHTML to develop the user interface for a multilingual electronic text collection of Japanese folktales[3][4]. The tales were taken from Japanese old tales and rewritten by volunteer authors. Each tale is written in one or more languages, including English, Japanese, French, and Spanish. Figure 4 shows a view of the user interface, which displays the folktale written in Spanish, Japanese, and Chinese in parallel. In this example, three MHTML viewer applets are embedded in a table.

4   Extension of MHTML – Text Input

4.1   Requirements to Text Input Function

Text search is a primary function for information access, such as text searches in a database and in a document displayed on the screen. The text input function in multiple languages is indispensable for realizing the text search function in multiple languages. By slightly extending the MHTML technology, we gained a framework for text input in multiple languages in an off-the-shelf browser. Based on that framework, we developed a Japanese text input function for an off-the-shelf browser running on a client which has no Japanese text environment.

As described in section 2, text input is a mapping from an action on an input device (or devices) of a client to a character code (or sequence), and is usually displayed on the client. It is not necessary to provide a special keyboard to input non-alphabetical texts such as Chinese, Japanese, Korean, and Thai. For example, we can type a Japanese word in a transliterated form using the English alphabet, which is called Romaji. A text string in the transliterated form is sent to a conversion function that maps the source string into a string encoded in Japanese characters. This conversion function is located either in the client or in a remote server; the client must have a local environment for the text input function and a set of Japanese fonts. For languages with not many characters, e.g. CJK, a virtual keyboard, a keyboard displayed on the screen that gives the mapping to physical keys from virtual keys, is useful.

The authors applied MHTML technology to solve this problem. Figure 5 shows an outline of a Japanese text input server based on MHTML. The Japanese input server was implemented using text input software called wnn[11] and a user interface applet defined based on the extended MHTML. The text input server (TI server) is located between the client and the WWW server which provides service to the client. The TI receives a Japanese word written in transliterated form and produces a list of Japanese words. (See note.) Figure 5 depicts the interaction between the user and the TI server. This interaction is required to choose an appropriate Japanese word (or phrase) from the list of words. Figure 6 shows a text input applet to input Japanese texts, which was designed as part of the user interface of an OPAC system described in the next section; the WWW server in Fig. 5 is an OPAC server. This text input applet has a

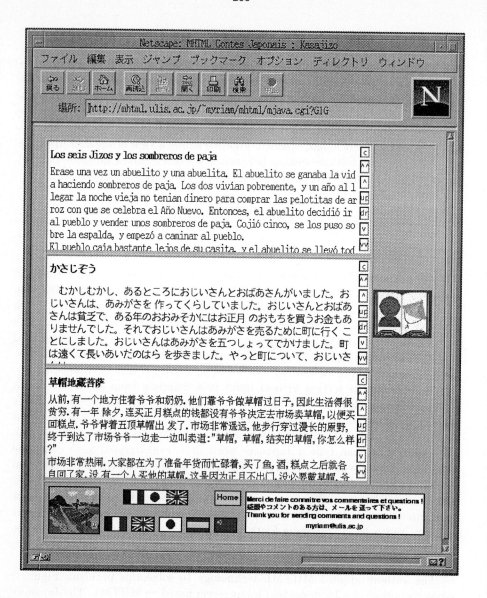

Fig. 4. An old tales page

text input field for typing a Japanese word or phrase in transliterated form. The CONVERT button is used to send the inputted string to the Japanese text input server. A list of words is returned from the TI server and is displayed on the left of the input field. A word selected from the list by a mouse click is displayed in the top line. Users can append additional words/characters to form a complete word or phrase for retrieval. The SUBMIT button is used to send the character code string displayed in the top line to the OPAC server, which uses the string for retrieval. The Japanese texts displayed on the applet are sent as an extended MHTML object. Figure 7 shows the structure of the extended MHTML object. The extended MHTML object contains an identifier of character encoding and character codes in addition to the components of the basic MHTML object shown in Fig. 2. A source character code string can be reproduced from an extended MHTML object by replacing every character in the internalized text string with its corresponding source character code. The character encoding identifier is required to make the reconverted text conform with the ISO-2022-JP-2 standard. Conversion to Unicode is also possible.

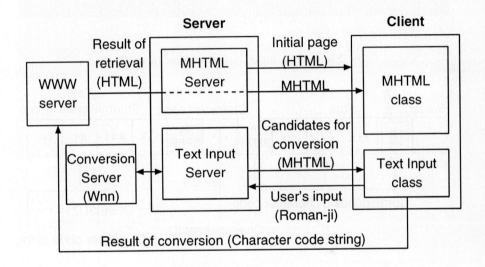

Fig. 5. Text input system outline

(**Note**: Japanese characters include Hiragana, Katakana, and Kanji. Both Hiragana and Katakana are a set of phonetic characters. Every Hiragana character has a corresponding Katakana character, and vice versa. Kanji, which was originally a Chinese character, is ideographic. A single Kanji may have more than one pronunciation, and a group of Kanjis may have the same pronunciation. Therefore, the transliterated form can be mapped to more than one Japanese word expressed in Japanese characters, making it somewhat ambiguous.)

4.2 Examples of Extended MHTML Applications

4.2.1 A Simple OPAC System

Figure 8 shows the user interface of an OPAC. The user interface consists of two windows. The top window, which is obtained using the same applet as in the previous examples, displays the retrieval result. The bottom window, which

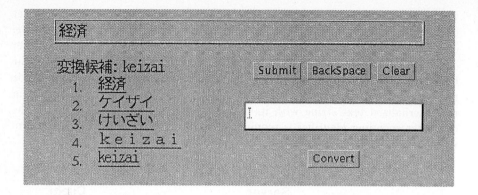

Fig. 6. Text input system window image

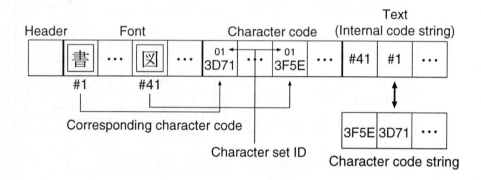

Fig. 7. Extended MHTML definition

is described in the previous section, receives and displays the word or phrase to be used as a search term. The catalog records are written based on SGML. Since this is a very simplified example, the search term given is used for a full text search in the whole OPAC database. This user interface can be extended to implement more elaborate search commands.

4.2.2 An SGML-based Text Retrieval System[10]

We experimentally developed an SGML-based text retrieval system designed to receive texts encoded in multiple scripts. It can currently store and retrieve Japanese and ASCII texts, and it is extensible to texts scripted in any character codes. Its user interface was designed using MHTML in order to provide users with ubiquitous accessibility to texts scripted in multiple languages.

Figure 9 shows the outline of the system configuration. It receives text encoded in a regional standard and converts it into the ISO-2022-JP-2 standard. The text is converted into a Unicode-based text to create the index, and the

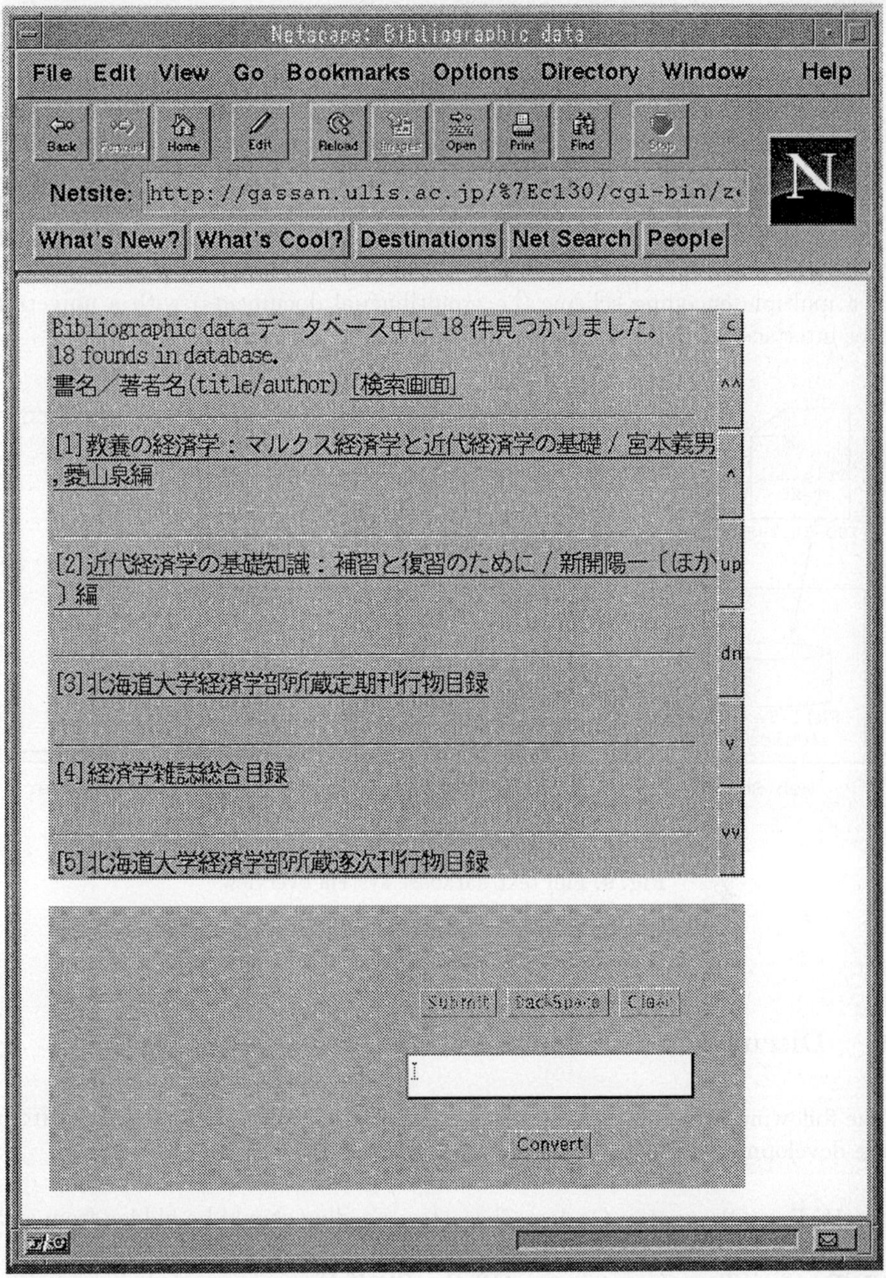

209

Netscape: Bibliographic data

File   Edit   View   Go   Bookmarks   Options   Directory   Window   Help

Back Forward Home   Edit Reload Images Open Print Find Stop

Netsite: http://gassan.ulis.ac.jp/%7Ec130/cgi-bin/z

What's New?   What's Cool?   Destinations   Net Search   People

Bibliographic data データベース中に 18 件見つかりました。
18 founds in database.
書名／著者名(title/author) [検索画面]

[1]教養の経済学：マルクス経済学と近代経済学の基礎 / 宮本義男, 菱山泉編

[2]近代経済学の基礎知識：補習と復習のために / 新開陽一〔ほか〕編

[3]北海道大学経済学部所蔵定期刊行物目録

[4]経済学雑誌総合目録

[5]北海道大学経済学部所蔵逐次刊行物目録

Submit   BackSpace   Clear

Convert

Fig. 8. OPAC interface image

text is also stored as is. The ISO-2022-JP-2 standard has multiple character code spaces for character sets of regional languages and defines the switching protocol between the spaces. This feature is convenient for use with an existing document encoded in a regional standard in the internationalized environment. However, this encoding scheme makes the text retrieval function complex. Since the flat character space given in Unicode makes the text retrieval function simple, Unicode is employed as the basic encoding scheme to build the index. The index is created based on N-gram, and its user interface is created using extended MHTML. Thus, this system provides a framework for retrieving texts encoded in a multiple encoding scheme (i.e., multilingual documents) with a universal user interface for retrieval.

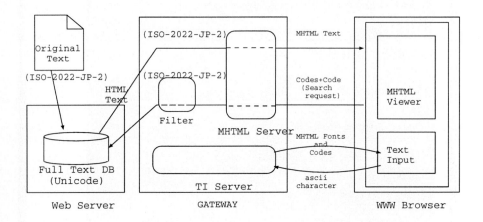

Fig. 9. Full text database system overview

5   Discussions – Lessons Learned from MHTML

The following list summarizes the most significant lessons that we learned from the development of MHTML technology and its applications.

1. **Hiding Character Codes**: Character encoding should be hidden from end users.
2. **Foreign Text Input in an Off-the-Shelf Environment**: It is crucial to provide end users with not only a display function but also a text input function for a foreign language or multiple languages. Both functions must work on an off-the-shelf environment for users without special settings.
3. **Universality**: Users should be able to access digital libraries from various locations, including offices, homes, and libraries.

4. **Extensibility to Non-standard Characters**: Extensibility to non-standardized characters and Internet-usability of the characters are crucial for digital libraries, especially for the humanities and CJK texts.

5. **Performance and Customizability**: Customizability to enhance performance is required to promote the use of MHTML.

Hiding Character Codes

The end user need not be aware of the character codes of a document that he/she is browsing. However, a user of an off-the-shelf WWW browser who wishes to view foreign (i.e., non-English) documents must know how to select a character encoding parameter and a set of fonts available on the browser. It is crucial to hide the character codes from the end user because character codes have no meaning to the user, and also because the difference in character code sets between a server and a client tends to be a hidden barrier for the user to access a service given by the server.

Foreign Text Input in an Off-the-Shelf Environment

The server-client model separates the user interface (i.e., input/output) from the processing function. However, since the user interface software on a client tends to depend on the environment of the client, the user must set up the client environment in accordance with the requirements of the server. The text input function is one of the most basic functions of the user interface but it also requires this kind of local setting on the client. The text input function for CJK is a typical example, since it has to handle thousands of different characters on a system environment which is primarily designed based on European alphabets, e.g., keyboards and operating systems.

The concept of the text input server is an extension of the common concept of Japanese text input systems. This extension was straightforward but created significant differences between the input functions. In the case of a conventional text input server, since the character codes are passed between the client and the server, the codes must be interpretable on both sides. However, with MHTML, the client does not need to interpret the source character code, since every character is presented on the client as a graphical entity directly by the server. The difference is obvious in the case of inputting and outputting a Gaiji. A Gaiji is usually defined and registered in each machine, so the code assigned to the Gaiji has no meaning on other machines.

Universality

The WWW and its browsers are ubiquitous resources for global information access. We can access any web page that requires no plug-in software from anywhere on the Internet. However, missing fonts are a primary barrier to universal information access for a user who wishes to access non-English documents. Universality is an essential aspect of digital libraries since a user should be able to access a digital library from anywhere on the Internet. However, it is obviously absurd to restrict information stored in digital libraries to characters in English alphabets.

Extensibility to Non-Standard Characters

It is a good idea to input queries in a transliterated form and convert them into original forms to search texts in non-English languages. However, transliteration is not ideal for searching a text database that contains ideographic characters, such as CJK texts, because there are lots of distinct words whose transliteration into alphabets are identical, or synonyms. Also, since each ideographic character contains meaning in itself, a text written in transliterated form loses the meaning. As described previously, a large Kanji dictionary contains 49,000 characters, while the primary and auxiliary Japanese standard sets define about 12,000 characters in total. In addition, document authors may invent new characters. These characters, like Gaiji, need not be included in any industrial standard character set but they should be usable in a text accessible and searchable via the Internet. As mentioned above, a Gaiji can be displayed and inputted on a Web browser and given to a text retrieval system through the browser. If a document provider who wishes to publish a document which contains a Gaiji adds a glyph for the Gaiji to the local font file and an entry in a dictionary for a text input server, the Gaiji can be used along with standard characters in a distributed environment. This feature is helpful for publishing electronic texts of historical materials and also for building a bibliographic database for those materials.

Performance and Customizability

Since the MHTML applet is designed to be independent of any specific language, it has no built-in font glyphs in its class definition written in Java. Since applets are usually cached in a client, the loading time of the MHTML applet is negligible if the user fetches MHTML objects repeatedly. However, the glyphs are not cached even if the user accesses documents in the same language. We can improve the caching effect for repeated access to documents in a single language by putting all the character glyphs of the language in an applet, if the character set is small. However, CJK has many characters, and so it is impractical in that particular case to include all of the font glyphs defined in the standard character set. It would be advantageous to put a set of very frequently used characters included in the large character set into an applet, for example Hiragana and a small set of basic Kanji in Japanese.

Miscellaneous

The applet used in the old tales system is the same as the one used in the gateway system. The TI applet reuses classes designed for the former system to show Japanese texts, i.e. the fields for fixed strings and a list of words. Thus, we were successful in reusing the classes developed for MHTML. Reusability of classes is very important for future extension of MHTML applets. It would be advantageous to organize classes of MHTML as user interface widgets to build user interfaces. A simple user interface building tool was used in the old tales system to build up the user interface.

Human resources, especially native speakers and/or language specialists, are key factors in developing multilingual services. Distributing the MHTML server over the Internet is helpful for expanding the language and character repertoires. The MHTML server software is downloadable from the HTML homepage. As of the end of April 1998, it had been downloaded to more than 100 sites. The Japanese old tales collection, which started in French, English, and Japanese, is being expanded by volunteers to Spanish, German, Korean, and Chinese.

6 Conclusion

The technology implemented as MHTML is quite simple. The research into MHTML was started to realize a simple, light, easy-to-use, and inexpensive environment to read and write foreign texts in the WWW environment. The functions implemented in the research have proved the feasibility of such an environment. We believe that the framework achieved in MHTML has the potential to change the paradigm of text input and output in a distributed environment.

- The client can hide the document character codes. The end-user wants to read and write the characters and not worry about the character codes on his/her machine.
- Limitation of a character code set given by an industrial standard can be removed for communication between the server and the end-user. The character set used to display and input texts for server-user communication can be extended server by server. A Gaiji is no longer an illegal character for a remote user.

The authors applied MHTML technology to build user interfaces for an electronic text collection, an OPAC, and a full-text retrieval system. They are also collaborating with the Dublin Core internationalization group[1] to apply MHTML to a multilingual user interface for a metadata database. These application systems require simplified text-based user interfaces. MHTML requires fonts to extend the language repertoire. Fonts from public domain are required to extend services to not-for-profit organizations.

References

1. Baker, T.; Dublin Core in Thai and Japanese: Managing Universal Metadata Semantics, Digital Libraries, no.11, pp.35-47, 1998 (in Japanese)
2. Chase, B., et al.; Web Fonts, W3C Working Report Draft, July 1997; http://www.w3.org/TR/WD-font-970721
3. Dartois, M., et al.; A multilingual electronic collection of folk tales for casual users using off-the-shelf browsers, D-lib magazine, 1997, http://www.dlib.org/dlib/october97/sugimoto/10sugimoto.html

4. Dartois, M., et al.; Building a multi-lingual electronic text collection of folk tales as a set of encapsulated document objects: An approach for casual users to browse multi-lingual documents on the fly, Proceedings of ECDL'97, pp.215-231, 1997

5. Klavans, J. and Schauble, P.; NSF-EU Multilingual Information Access, CACM, vol.41, no.4, p.69, 1998

6. Maeda, A., et al.; Viewing Multilingual Documents on Your Local Web Browser, CACM, vol.41, no.4, pp.64-65, 1998

7. Maeda, A., et al; A Multilingual HTML Document Browsing System for Clients without Multilingual Fonts, Transactions of IPSJ, vol.39, no.3, pp.802-809, 1998 (in Japanese)

8. Morohashi, T. (ed); Daikanwa Jiten, Daisyuukan (in Japanese)

9. Mukaigawa, S. Izumi, N.; Design and Implementation of Internationalized WWW Browser — i18n Arena, Proceedings of Japan WWW Conference '95, 1995 (in Japanese)

10. Nakao, S., et al.; A System for Building a Full-Text Multilingual Database Accessible from any WWW Browser, Technical Report of Japan Society of Information and Knowledge, 1998 (in Japanese)

11. Nishikimi, M., et al.; Realization of Multilingual Environment, Prentice Hall Japan, 387p., 1996 (in Japanese)

12. Ohta, M. and Honda, K.; ISO-2022-JP-2; Multilingual Extension of ISO-2022-JP, RFC 1554, 1993

13. Sakaguchi, T., et al.; A Browsing Tool for Multi-lingual Documents for Users without Multi-lingual Fonts, Proceedings of DL'96, pp.63-71, 1996

14. The Unicode Consortium; The Unicode Standard, Ver.2.0, Addison-Wesley, 1996

15. Yergeau, F., et al.; Internationalization of the Hypertext Markup Language, RFC 2070, 1997

16. Standards for Bibliographic Information (User Manual for Catalog System: Database), NACSIS, 1991 (in Japanese)

17. Multilingual HTML Homepage, http://mhtml.ulis.ac.jp/

18. Multilingual Oldtales Collection Homepage, http://www.DL.ulis.ac.jp/oldtales/

SIS - TMS : A Thesaurus Management System for Distributed Digital Collections

Martin Doerr[1] and Irini Fundulaki[1]

[1] Institute of Computer Science, Foundation for Research and Technology - Hellas, Science and Technology Park of Crete, Vassilika Vouton, P.O. Box 1385, GR 711 10, Heraklion, Crete, Greece
{martin, fundul}@csi.forth.gr

Abstract. The availability of central reference information as thesauri is critical for correct intellectual access to distributed databases, in particular to digital collections in international networks. There is a continuous raise in interest in thesauri, and several thesaurus management systems have appeared on the market. The issue, how to integrate effectively such central resources into a multitude of client systems and to maintain the consistency of reference in an information network has not yet been satisfactorily solved. We present here a method and an actual thesaurus management system, which is specifically designed for this use, and implements the necessary data structures and management functions. The system handles multiple multilingual thesauri and can be adapted to all semantic thesaurus structures currently in use. Consistency-critical information is kept as history of changes in the form of backward differences. The system has been installed at several sites in Europe.

1 Introduction

Modern information systems typically consist of a number of autonomous information sources and provide access to huge amounts of heterogeneous information. To overcome the difficulties of handling a multitude of heterogeneous interfaces and data structures, free-text search engines are widely used. They provide access under least assumptions and hence are ultimately limited in precision and recall. In particular they do not solve per se the problem of appropriate terminology and multilinguality for search request formulation.

Besides database federations with integrated schemata, the use of thesauri and other kinds of reference information, so-called "authorities", have been successful means to improve access to "verbose" (texts, [1], [2], [3], [4]) and "non-verbose" data (images, data records etc. [5] [6]) residing in multiple heterogeneous and possibly multilingual information sources. (By "verbose" we mean a text large enough such that one can sufficiently conclude with statistical methods on its contents).

One may distinguish three kinds of use of authorities (compare [7], [8], [9]):

– Guide the user from his/her naïve request to the use of an set of terms optimal for his purpose and for the characteristics of the target information source. If the respective knowledge about the target is not explicit or implicit in the thesaurus, the results are limited. If the targets are many, it is not practical.
– Expand naïve user terms or the terms optimal for the purpose of the user into sets of terms optimal for each different information source. In the case of full-text retrieval, this may mean to produce a weighted list of possible common words for the user's concept. For structured database queries, this may mean to select only the closest term in use on that system [10]. Still the degree of matching between the requested terms and the used terms are undefined.
– Classify all information assets of a certain collection with controlled vocabulary from a specific thesaurus. Together with the above measures., a well defined matching of query terms and target terms [10] can be achieved.

The above holds for monolingual sources using the same or different thesauri, or multilingual sources, as long as appropriate transitions, translations or correlations can be established. The focus of this paper is to present methods and an actual system suited to store, maintain and provide access to knowledge structures that are in use or needed for these three tasks and the respective auxiliary system interfaces.

The creation of multilingual thesauri is a crucial problem in this context, because traditional human editing is extremely labor-intensive [11]. We restrict ourselves in this paper to the support of this process by a central data management system. The application of statistical methods, computational linguistic methods, elaborate CSCW means and their combination for efficient production of multilingual thesauri are subject of the recently started Term-IT project (TELEMATICS project LE4-8356).

The simultaneous and remote access to hundreds or even thousands of target systems requires the complete integration of thesaurus tools in a wide area information environment. For optimal results, the terms used for asset classification, in the search aid thesaurus and in the experts' terminology should be consistent. This led us to the vision of a three level architecture of components cooperating within an information environment: vocabularies in local databases, local thesaurus management systems of wider use and central term servers for retrieval support.

Typically, local databases have a more or less idiosyncratic way to enforce vocabulary control. For reasons of standardization of format and centralization of handling, we foresee an independent thesaurus manager to which the vocabularies of several local databases are loaded, and in the sequence organized as thesauri ("authorities") by an expert, following variations of the ISO2788 semantic structure. In addition, standard external vocabularies can be loaded. These authorities may be specific to one database, a user organization, or a whole language group. The local vocabularies and terms already used for classification may need updating with changes done at the thesaurus manager.

Search agents or user interfaces for information retrieval need knowledge of the authorities in local use, at least of the higher level terms, or knowledge about the language in case of free text search. Therefore they must communicate with one or more term servers, which hold-released versions or extracts of the local authorities.

Moreover, a term server must be fed with equivalence expressions between the meaning of terms in different authorities, either by an expert team or by linguistic methods and subsequent human control. These expressions are used to replace the terms in a user request with more or less equivalent terms of the target system - automatically or in a dialogue with the user. As equivalence expressions are difficult to produce, term servers containing different translations may be cascaded to make multistep replacements, e.g. Finnish to English, English to Greek, etc. Of course precision will suffer.

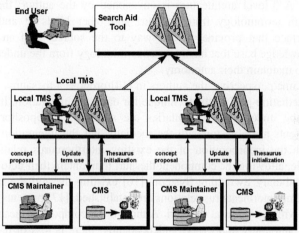

Fig. 1. 3-level terminology service

This three stage architecture ideally reflects the practice and needs of classification, expert agreement, user organization and search aids. It is a fully scalable solution which has already been partially realized in the AQUARELLE [12], [13] project and system. The methods and system development we present in the following are targeted to be components of such an environment and architecture. The work presented here is outcome of a series of cooperations with libraries, museums and cultural bodies, but of other domains as well.

1.1 Thesaurus Management Systems

The use of thesauri for classification and information access in global information spaces becomes complex due to the large number of existing or needed thesauri; a fact that is justified by existence of multiple thesaurus providers from different scientific backgrounds with different practices, aspects and history. Multi-thesaurus systems have been proposed in order to provide access to information sources in global spaces classified with multiple and possibly interconnected thesauri.

The basic research issues associated to multi-thesaurus systems are

– the maintainance of the autonomicity and independent evolution of the component vocabularies
– the incorporated methodology for the treatment of interthesaurus links and
– the role of the system in a retrieval process.

[8] and [11] propose the construction of a multi-thesaurus system that incorporates multiple interlinked thesauri. [8] proposes SemWeb, "an open multilingual, multifunctional system for integrated access to knowledge about concepts and terminology". A 3-level architecture is envisioned by the author: the incorporated sources contain terminology from thesauri and other kinds of authority data; a common interface that provides a gate-way to the sources and an evolving and integrated knowledge base that incorporates terminology from the underlying sources, that are able to maintain their autonomy.

Under the same perspective, the authors in [14] propose a thesaurus federation that draws upon mediation [15] as the technique for database integration. In the mediator, metadata of the underlying vocabularies are stored in a repository. The actual thesaurus contents are not stored in the mediator but the integration of thesauri is perceived with the incorporation of the existing interthesaurus relations in a term mapper module, allowing the component thesauri to maintain their autonomy.

In the "Vocabulary Switching System" [16] existing thesauri are incorporated in the system but no interthesaurus relations are established. [17] presents an example of this approach with agricultural thesauri. Although the component thesauri are able to maintain their autonomy and evolve independently, there is loss of recall during the retrieval process. The retrieved items are only those indexed with the thesaurus used for retrieval, and in order to ensure recall, either the user must manually incorporate search terms from other thesauri, or the underlying sources must be classified in multiple vocabularies, a time consuming process that requires extensive knowledge of the incorporated terminologies.

Authors in [18] propose a method for the construction of an interlingua to reduce the established mappings between the component thesauri in a multi-thesaurus system to about one per term.

Merging thesauri is another approach to the construction of a multi-thesaurus system. During a merging procedure, a single thesaurus is built from a set of others. Terms referring to the same concept are identified and federated into a unique concept, and consequently all inconsistencies are identified and resolved either automatically or semi-automatically. Work in thesauri merging has been performed by [19], [20], [21] and [22]. Merging is only appropriate for a homogeneous environments because of the intellectual and coordination problems it raises.

In [23] the authors point out that the difficulty of locating the appropriate terms hinders query formulation and indexing of a collection. A number of thesaurus management systems offer only flat lists of selected terms from which the user can choose one, which are not ideal if the number of choices is large. Direct access to the contents of a thesaurus is also provided, but this is considered not to be useful to users who are not aware of the structured vocabulary. In addition to the above, navigation in a hypertextual format is supported with the use of the broader/narrower relations of terms that can be proved slow if multiple levels of the hierarchies must be traversed to access the desired terms. A rather interesting work on a hypertextual interface is presented by the authors in [24]. The user can move at will in a hypertextual ordered space, selecting terms for immediate use or for subsequent searches without leaving the thesaurus or going into separate search mode.

A number of commercial thesaurus management systems have been produced to assist users in the development of structured vocabularies. Some have been developed as modules of complete indexing and retrieval systems while others can be acquired and used independently of any software. Nearly no one has a client-server architecture. Some of the most interesting thesaurus management systems are the Thesaurus Construction System (TCS)(http://www.liu-palmer.com/), the MultiTes (http://www.cris.com/~multites), the STRIDE(http://www.questans.co.uk/),the STAR/Thesaurus(http://www.cuadra.com/) and the LEXICO/2 systems (http://www.pmei.com/lexico/lexico.html). To our knowledge the majority of the existing commercial thesaurus management systems are compatible with the ANSI/NISO standards, support the evolution of multiple monolingual and multilingual vocabularies (TCS, MultiTes), provide consistency mechanisms to check for reciprocal relations, duplicate terms and non-consistent cross-references (MultiTes, LEXICO2) and support batch and/or interactive editing of thesaurus contents. An interesting feature of some of the systems such as STRIDE, and the STAR/Thesaurus is the maintenance of a log of the transactions, although it is not completly clear how this information is represented and eventually stored. Another interesting feature is the ability to create user defined relations (MultiTes). Although this feature adds great flexibility to the system, the absence of consistency control on the created relations creates difficulties in their maintenance. Most of the systems support many formats for the representation of information, mostly textual and/or hypertextual and only few provide graphical interfaces.

2 Requirements for Thesaurus Management

We roughly divide the requirements into those for (1) interaction with the thesaurus contents except manipulations, (2) maintenance, i.e. the manipulation of the contents and the necessary and desirable support of associated work processes, and finally (3) analysis, i.e. the logical structure needed to support (1), (2), and the thesaurus semantics in the narrower sense.

Interaction needs. The interaction needs with the thesaurus contents split into man-machine interfaces and interfaces to other systems. Most literature concentrates on the first point. In [9], [11] we have pointed out the relevance of system interfaces as well. Besides literature and experience with users of our systems, we refer here to [25] and related user meetings organized by the Museum Documentation Association, UK, the Getty Information Institute, CA, and the AQUARELLE project [26].

The most prominent human interaction is the identification of concepts for retrieval purposes. Without going into details, strategies can be:

- Linguistic - search by noun phrases, words, part of words or misspelled words. Often however similar concepts do not have terms of any linguistic similarity, e.g. "knife" and "dagger".
- Hierarchical – search by narrowing down from broader notions of the same nature, e.g. "sword" –> "foil", or navigational in nearby branches as "red" – "pink (color)", "small" – "large".
- Associative – search by related notions or characteristic context, e.g. "bridges" – "bridge construction", "baby" – "dolls".

The next step is the understanding of the concepts and matching against what he/she had in mind. As well, he/she has to verify, if the concepts found are the best choice within the given vocabulary. Understanding is supported by explanations ("scope notes"), multimedia examples, or schematic presentations and the term environment of associative and hierarchical links.

Effective interaction is a problem of presentation and of semantic analysis. Most views should be available as text and graphics. Semantic views must be very flexible. They must render good overviews of local environments which show many kinds of relations, and "global" overviews which show few kinds of semantic relations at a time. Disorientation must be avoided during navigational access, e.g. by global views and by logging previous steps/paths. Furthermore, interaction speed is crucial, as users may easily give up if response is too slow.

Last, construction, maintenance and quality control of thesauri requires a different kind of access, characterized by global views on certain properties, missing properties, conflicting declarations, statistics and transaction information. Questions of completeness and clear distinction between concepts are important as well.

System interfaces may serve the following purposes:
- Enabling term browsing as search/classification aid from within an external GUI.
- Automatic term expansion/translation for retrieval mechanisms.
- Term translation/replacement in order to update obsolete classification terms in some information base.
- Term verification for vocabulary control within an external application.

This requires an API and a client-server architecture. As thesauri are central resources, the capability to communicate on low bandwidth over WAN is important. The API functions needed are very simple. Up to now, such interfaces are subject to customization, but they could easily be standardized and make the use of thesauri in actual application significantly easier. Interfaces of the first two types have been developed and experimented with in the AQUARELLE project. The authors currently engage in experimentation with the other interface types.

Maintenance needs. One can roughly distinguish between maintenance of semantic structure and workflow support. Semantic structures have primarily to be maintained by interactive data entry facilities, that easily allow to manipulate hierarchical structures and other links, preserving constraints as connectivity, referential integrity, anticyclicity etc.

Market systems and most literature so far do not deal with the problems that arise, when a thesaurus is developed outside of the databases which use its terms for classification. The ISO2709 has a link for the case, when a concept is split into siblings. Such isolated semantics do not provide a solution. The basic problem is that vocabularies of hundreds of thousands of terms cannot be compared by hand with millions of data records in order to migrate to the new edition.

There must be a notion of a release and the effective changes between releases as analyzed in the following chapters. The current practice to backtrack modification dates for that purpose is not satisfactory.

The process of gathering concepts from users and experts, quality control and their embedding in a large thesaurus can be rather complex. Distant users and experts need to communicate and make thousands of small agreements [11]. Much work and research is needed on this field, which is out of the scope of this paper.

Requirements of Analysis. As follows from the above, the conceptual model of a thesaurus management system needs a great flexibility. All modern systems allow for adding user defined semantic relations. To our opinion, this is not enough. Rather all of the following aspects have to be considered and made configurable to a certain degree:

- logical and linguistic links within and between thesauri, as BT, UF, equivalence etc. (see below), which are relevant for query processing
- rules for dynamic concept formation (e.g. combine "factories" with process terms)
- context associations to assist browsing (e.g. the ISO2709 "subdivisions", in which database field the term is used, how many items it classifies).
- explanations as scope notes, , source references and multimedia [27] for human understanding
- migration information between releases
- workflow information about proposals, decisions, term status, persons and groups involved, following steps, "todo" etc.

Obviously, this is open ended, and we shall describe in the following which choices we have made in our systems for the time being.

3 The SIS-TMS

The SIS-TMS is a multilingual thesaurus management system and a terminology server for classification and distributed access to electronic collections following the above analysis. The its distinct features are its capability to store, develop, display and access multiple thesauri and their interrelations under one database schema, to create arbitrary graphical views thereon and to specialize dynamically any kind of relation into new ones. It further implements the necessary version control for a cooperative development and data exchange with other applications in the environment.

It originates in the terminology management system (VCS Prototype) developed by ICS-FORTH in cooperation with the Getty Information Institute in the framework of a feasibility study. It was enhanced within the AQUARELLE project, in particular by the support of multilinguality. An earlier version is part of the AQUARELLE product [26]. A full product version will be available summer '98.

The SIS-TMS is an application of the *Semantic Index System* (described below), a general purpose object-oriented semantic network database, product of the ICS-FORTH with client-server architecture.

3.1 The Semantic Index System

The Semantic Index System (SIS) [28], a product of the Institute of Computer Science-FORTH, is an object oriented semantic network database used for the storage and maintenance of formal reference information as well as for other knowledge representation applications. It implements an interpretation of the data model of the knowledge representation language TELOS [29] omitting the evaluation of logical rules. A formal treatment of this data model can be found in [30].

The structures and the modeling constructs of SIS allow the representation of complex thesaurus structures in an elegant and compact way. SIS attributes referring to entities are implemented as bi-directional, directed, typed links. We model terms, descriptors, persons, sources etc as entities. Hence for all of them vocabulary control and referential integrity is enforced automatically throughout the system. There is no need to make special arrangement for multi-valued relations, as broader terms, related terms, synonyms etc. Multiple instantiation is used besides others to organize terms by semantic and administrational criteria, to organize workspaces and to view multiple thesauri once together, once separate. Metamodels are used to annotate consistency constraints to be enforced by the application. The dynamic schema of SIS allows a graceful evolution of thesauri into richer knowledge bases. Finally, the system is highly optimized for fast referential access.

3.2 Thesaurus Structures

Assumptions on Concepts. According to [7] one of the major purposes of a thesaurus is to "provide a map of a given field of knowledge, indicating how *concepts* or ideas about concepts are related to one another, which helps an indexer or a searcher to understand the structure of the field.

We distinguish concepts from terms, in contrast to IS2788. Cognitive scientists have proposed several definitions for the notion of "concept" (e.g. [31]). According to one point of view, a concept is perceived as a set of entities, called "concept instances" characterized as such by common agreement rather than formal reasoning on the properties that characterize an individual entity as an instance of a concept. We adopt this view for thesauri, considering a concept as a notion by which some people agree to refer in a well defined manner to a set of real world objects with the same properties, without necessarily defining properties. Consequently, certain semantic relations between concepts are interpreted as relations between sets as will be presented below. For more details see [22], [10].

Following ISO2788, we regard terms as nouns or noun-phrases, by which groups of people use to refer to certain concepts in a certain context. Due to varying groups and contexts, concepts and terms are related many to many.

Modelling Thesaurus Notions. The SIS-TMS schema is extensible at run-time. New semantic relations can be created or existing ones can be specialized. The current conceptual model of the SIS-TMS for the representation of multiple interlinked thesauri incorporates the thesaurus notions and intrathesaurus relations of the ISO2788 for monolingual thesauri and an extended version of the ISO5964 interthesaurus relations [10]. In prototype versions, this schema has been extended for the ULAN and TGN, vocabularies of the Getty Information Institute and the Library of Congress Subject Headings. We mainly use ISO2788 terminology for the names of the classes and relations in the SIS-TMS schema. In the manner of semantic networks, these names are directly presented in the user interface together with the respective data and read quite naturally (See fig. 5, left window).

We model *Preferred Terms* for indexing and *Non-Preferred Terms* as synonyms and entry points for the user. In addition, *Non-Preferred Terms* may be used for full-text retrieval. We adopt the notion of *Descriptor* of the Art & Architecture Thesaurus [34] according to which: "a descriptor is the term that uniquely identifies the concept". Hence a *Descriptor* is a term and a concept identifier in double nature. All other terms, preferred or not, are related to the concept and not further described, as we are not interested in linguistics.

As the *concept* is identified by a *descriptor*, i.e. by a linguistic expression that best expresses the common understanding of experts or public and it must be unique within the context in which it has been defined, it may not be exactly the word an expert uses. For instance, "pink (color)" and "pink (vessel)" would be good descriptors, but experts would say "pink" in both cases. In the SIS-TMS, all terms and descriptor names are enforced to be unique throughout the database. Terms may be multiply related to different concepts (*Descriptors*), but if a good term appears to conflict with a descriptor, the descriptor has to be renamed, i.e. usually extended for disambiguation.

Concepts carry all the intra and interthesaurus relations that make up the semantic structure of the thesaurus contents, they carry the administrational information, and they can be described by scope notes and understood language independently.

Figure 2 shows the isA hierarchy of the *SIS-TMS* Classes of thesaurus notions. We use in the following "abstract" for classes which are not directly instantiated, and "abstract hook" for abstract classes, which are designed to be superclasses of classes in future extensions. "ThesaurusNotion" is the abstract root. "ThesaurusExpression" is the abstract hook for terms, person names, date expressions etc. "ThesaurusConcept" is the abstract hook for concepts in the above sense, persons, places etc. "HierarchyTerm" is the class for concept in the above sense, those that can be generalized or specialized into broader/narrower meaning. It combines *Node Labels*, or "guide terms" and descriptors. We do not distinguish functionally between both (see e.g. [32]). "AlternativeTerm" is the complement of "Descriptor". "Topterm" are those having no broader terms. "ObsoleteDescriptor" are abandoned concepts (sometimes thesauri decrease, e.g. in favor of dynamic concept formation) and finally "ObsoleteTerm" are deleted noun-phrases. The latter two serve version management for referential integrity incremental update.

Intrathesaurus Relations. The semantic relations in a thesaurus can be divided into intrathesaurus relations within a coherent terminological system and interthesaurus relations between independent terminological systems. They are used to represent relationships between concepts and between concepts and terms, i.e. from the class HierarchyTerm to the class HierarchyTerm or Term.

The intrathesaurus relations identified by ISO2788 are: the *hierarchical relationships,* distinguishing a systematic thesaurus from an unstructured list of terms (glossary or dictionary), associating concepts bearing broader/narrower meanings, identified by the *BT(broader term)* relation, the *associative relationships*, relating concepts that are not members of an equivalence set nor can they be organized in a hierarchy, identified by the *RT (related term)* relation, and finally the *equivalence relationship* established between preferred and non-preferred terms, considered to refer to the same concept, and it is identified by the *use* and its inverse *UF* (used for) relations. As it does not distinguish between terms and concept, and we reinterpret these relations as the link between the conceptual and linguistic level. We refer in the following their functional role and specializations.

BT is used for semantic generalization or specialization of query terms. From a knowledge representation approach, the *BT* relation carries isA semantics, and a query term may be expanded by its narrower terms, if we ask for objects of this kind. Consequently SIS-TMS enforces that all HierarchyTerms have a broader Term except for TopTerms, and that the BT relation is acyclic. A Term may have multiple broader terms in the sense of multiple supersets. Thesaurus maintainers may distinguish between the main and alternate broader terms.

RT is used for the detection of relevant concepts by users. It plays a role like a general attribute category in KR systems. Dozens of useful specializations can be found, as the "subdivisions" of ISO2709, whole-part relations, and rule-related relations. In the latter case, machine interpretation may occur. *Art & Architecture Thesaurus* team has identified more that 20 different meanings of the RT relation.

UF (use for) can be used by users as entry points in a thesaurus. Actually most thesauri distinguish the *ALT* relation to preferred terms from the *UF* to non-preferred terms. The EET (European Education Thesaurus) [33] consequently regards any translation of a concept to some language as a kind of UF.

In SIS-TMS, *hierarchical association, equivalence association* and *associative relation* are modeled as metacategories of intrathesaurus links. These generic categories group and control the specialization of relations to preserve compatibility and to maintain the related global consistency rules. I.e. the application code can refer to those for constraint enforcement and for export of data in a compatible format. Hence the application code is robust against extensions. User defined extensions as the above mentioned specializations of *BT, RT,* and *UF* links are substantial for specific applications and the maintenance of their logical consistency, as well as for the conceptual evolution of thesaurus structures into knowledge bases despite format standardization.

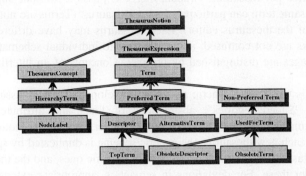

Fig. 2. IsA hierarchy of the SIS-TMS Classes of thesaurus notions

Other systems allow for new user defined links, but do not relate them to existing semantics and hence do not automatically imply standard conformant viewing, handling and constraint enforcement. Specialization of relations is a distinct feature of the SIS-TMS.

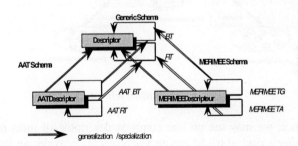

Fig. 3. Subschema Creation per Thesaurus

Representing Multiple Interlinked Thesauri. A challenge in the SIS-TMS was the development of the conceptual model to incorporate multiple interlinked thesauri under one database schema. For the development of the currently implemented conceptual schema two approaches were studied. The problems is, how to distinguish between the work of each thesaurus editor on one side, on the other side to see the common things as common without running continuously search routines, and on the third side to get a global view on how the different thesauri fit together. For more details see [11].

According to the second, a global name space is made up for all terms and concepts of one language. For each thesaurus, a separate schema is generated. Due to multiple instantiation in SIS, these schemata can overlap conflict-free on the data. The system tables stay limited per thesaurus. Gradual merge is possible without duplicating the records, as the same term can participate in any thesaurus. (Terms are not regarded as the invention of the thesaurus editor). Each thesaurus may have different semantic structures. Links are not confused, as they belong to individual schemata. Terms of different languages are distinguished by prefixes. Concepts of an interlingua can be dealt likewise.

On top of this world, one generic schema is developed as superclasses to provide global views. "Supercategories", abstractions of links and attributes from the individual schema as presented in the previous chapter, provide the notion of global semantics. For each new thesaurus, the generic schema is duplicated by specialization of its generic classes and relations into thesaurus specific ones, and the thesaurus data are loaded under these. For deviations in semantics, appropriate extensions can be made. This model results in a large schema. As an SIS schema is declarative, and not by storage allocation, no space is wasted. We selected this novel approach.

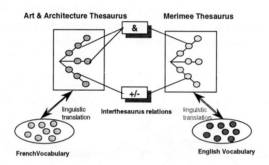

Fig. 4. Multilingual relations

As a consequence, we may see on one common descriptor all links made by other thesauri, achieving a kind of trivial merge. Each schema provides an isolated view of one thesaurus, and the generic schema a unified view of all. Basically, each thesaurus is handled as an annotation, an *opinion* of a group on a common term and concept space. This method can be elaborated into much more sophistication [11].

Interthesaurus Relations. The interthesaurus relations modeled in the SIS-TMS are an extended version of the ISO5964 links as presented in [10]. Those refined relations are the outcome of a discussion that took place in the framework of the AQUARELLE project between experts in multilingual thesaurus creation and ICS-FORTH, the provider of the multilingual thesaurus management component used in the project. The specific problem was to embed a system of multiple independent thesauri in different languages into a system for access to heterogeneous databases containing objects of material culture, supporting automatic term expansion/translation under a Z39.50 protocol. The conclusion of this discussion was that ISO5964 does not define precise enough semantics for that purpose.

We define the following relations: *exact equivalence, broader equivalence, narrower equivalence, inexact equivalence, union* and *intersection* of concepts. A detailed presentation of the semantics of above relations are presented in [10]. These links are from concept to concept (HierarchyTerm), and should not confused with linguistic translations, which use any suitable word from the other language rather than the specific thesaurus descriptors.

Obviously equivalence relations are opinions of one group, or at least under the responsibility of one group. Of course, good teams seek advice from each other. But the geographical distance and other local needs hinder synchronous updates. We therefore foresee different equivalence relations for group A from Thesaurus A to B, than for group B from B to A. If group A or B withdraws a concept, it remains marked as obsolete in the database, giving the other group a chance to redirect their links later. New concepts are marked as new, and should not be referred to until released. Suitable permissions can be set up in the SIS-TMS, so that such a database can be maintained cooperatively without conflicts through the net.

3.3 Maintaining consistency between CMS and the TMS

In the environment presented in section 1 we foresee, that Collection Management Systems (CMS) such as digital libraries, library systems, museum documentation systems and others draw their classifation vocabulary from a Local Thesaurus Management Systems (TMS) which is a shared resource. The contents of the Local Thesaurus Management Systems have been initialized from the contents of the local CMS. The CMS needs continuously new terms, and incorporates classification terms in its records, eventually in central lists as well. The CMS can also propose new terms to the TMS. The TMS will be updated with new terms from many sides, and old concepts and terms may be renamed, revised and reorganized.

The essential problem is to ensure and maintain consistency between the contents of the vocabularies in the underlying CMS and the contents of the Local Thesaurus Management Systems. It can be regarded as a heterogeneous database problem with vertical distribution, classified data records on one side, semantic term structures on the other, and the shared identifiers both sides communicate on are the descriptors. Descriptors, i.e. concepts for classification, may be renamed, and the identity is lost. One could use system identifiers, numbers, instead, but this is the same impractical in distributed environments. Further, existing CMS do not necessarily have foreseen system identifiers for terms. Even the term codes the AAT uses are not preserved from version to version. The solution is simple: there are no global persistent identifiers. Instead, a history of identifiers is kept for each concept from release to release in the TMS. A CMS must note, with which release its terms agree. With this knowledge, concepts can permanently and automatically be identified between all systems in such a federation.

Further, abandoned concepts must be marked. In this case, an expert has to find in the records of the CMS which other concept applies in each case. Ideally, there should be links that indicate all shifts of the scope of concepts from version to version. Thesaurus editors are however not used to do so. At least all new descriptors mark an environment of concepts, where concepts may have changed scope or have been refined. As the respective updates in the CMS have to be done by hand, they are time consuming, and immediate consistency between CMS and the TMS is not possible. Suitable interface software cans speed-up the process of updating the CMS. The CMS does not need any knowledge of the semantic links in the TMS.

Finally, Term Servers or other TMS should to be kept up-to-date with data of a local TMS. Even though a thesaurus is a central resource, it changes slowly, and therefore it is practical to have local copies around. Term Servers, as described above, should combine different local authorities and in addition maintain interthesaurus links between those. Therefore, incremental updates have to be foreseen, even more, as authorities can be very large.

For each part of an authority, which is to be shared with another term base, only one management system must be the master. The master maintains as well the richest semantics, the others (slaves) may or may not keep reduced schemata. Nevertheless, the slaves may make references to the imported data. Therefore, as above, concepts cannot just be withdrawn. Beyond the above measures for communicating updates on concepts, all semantic descriptions have to be transferred. As those are attached in our system to the descriptors, it is sufficient for incremental updates to mark descriptors of the master which encountered a change in their attached information, and to transfer all the attached information to the slaves. Following these considerations, we have implemented the version control in the SIS-TMS.

Version Control and Data Consistency. The purpose of the version control is the information of thesaurus editors about previous discussions and states, and the capability to incrementally update another CMS or term server with the changes done in the TMS. Thesaurus releases are created at a slow rate, months or years. A rollback features is therefore not necessary, backups are sufficient for that purpose. Individual changes can be withdrawn at any time. A function is however provided, which inserts the latest changes into the last release for "last minute changes".

Consequently, the idea of the SIS-TMS implementation is to keep in the database only the least versioning information for the above purposes as *backward differences* for scalability reasons. All other version data may be put in history logs in future versions. Versioning is based on releases rather than dates. The "current" release is being edited, and no history of changes is kept within it. Rather, the results of individual changes are merged. In contrary to version control systems, always the current version is displayed together with all registered backward changes per entity. The latter can be filtered out. Under this perspective, we register whether

– a descriptor has been introduced (a new concept is described)

– an existing descriptor has been abandoned (the concept is regarded inappropriate for classification or should be composed dynamically from other concepts)

– an existing descriptor is renamed

– any semantic information around a descriptor has changed.

We distinguish between operations on released concepts and on unreleased. In the unreleased, the user can introduce descriptors, which are classified as *"new descriptor"*. He/she can perform all operations on descriptors and undo them.

The operations on released concepts are constraint, because they contain data that have been communicated to other systems and may have been used for indexing. Introduction of descriptors as well as deletions are not permitted. A descriptor can be abandoned by the following procedure: It is classified as *"obsolete descriptor"* and its *broader/narrower* associations to the others are deleted but it remains a member of the term list of its hierarchy, retaining the context in which it has been defined. Further, the "gap" in the hierarchie is "closed" by drawing *BT* relations between the narrower terms of the *obsolete* descriptor and its broader terms. We do not constrain any changes in the associated information, semantic and administrational links and attributes, as this is not necessary to keep other systems up-to-date or to avoid daggling references.

If editors regard the noun phrase, which identifies a descriptor, as inappropriate for the semantics of the concept, or it is going to cause name conflicts, it can be renamed. Renaming an object in SIS does not alter its system identifier and its properties remain attached to it. SIS-TMS maintains uniqueness of all term-names in the system. Whereas ALT and UF terms can be deleted at any time. Released descriptor names, which come out of use, become "obsolete terms". Further, for each release, links are maintained where the names have gone to. The complete algorithm is not trivial, as within one release all rename actions must be merged in order to be unique, and obsolete names may be reused as ALT or UF terms. Currently, following the AAT philosophy, we do not allow a concept (descriptor) to refer another descriptor as UF, but we expect in that case, that the respective descriptor is renamed to disambiguate it from the other concept.

3.4 Interaction in the SIS-TMS

The user interacts with the SIS-TMS via its graphical user interface, that provides *unconstrained navigation* within and between multiple interlinked thesauri. The user can retrieve information from the SIS-TMS knowledge base using a number of predefined, configurable queries and accept the results either in *textual or graphical form.*

The implemented predefined queries support access to the semantic and managerial relations of a term and to the contents of a hierarchy or facet. It has been considered by thesaurus users that the graphical presentation of the broader term relations is an essential requirement for thesaurus interfaces. The SIS-TMS not only provides such graphical representations but an essential feature is its ability to represent in a single graph any combination of relationships in arbitrary depth. (See fig 5, central window). A very efficient graph-layout algorithm allows the display of large structures in real time. A "global view" window is used to zoom in any part of a larger graph.

Therefore the user is able to view, in a single graph, all relations pertaining to a term. The existence of multiple broader terms introduce no difficulty to such graphical presentations. These graphs are of particular interest to authority providers since they represent in an compact way all the necessary relations for the detection of inconsistencies. The development group of the French MERIMEE thesaurus has already mentioned the easiness of identifying inconsistencies using the graphical representations of the SIS-TMS in contrast to scanning textual presentations.

The SIS-TMS graphical user interface does not need customization if a thesaurus is loaded in the knowledge base. The implementation of the predefined queries uses the generic schema presented previously and is therefore thesaurus independent . Consequently, if a thesaurus is loaded in the SIS-TMS knowledge base, it can be immediately queried without any customization of the predefined queries.

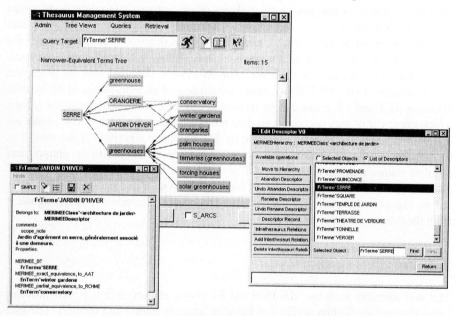

Fig. 5. SIS-TMS User Interface, Browser and Data Entry facility.

The loading of thesauri and term lists compliant with the ISO2788 and ISO5964 principles is performed by means of an input module. In the near future, we intend to develop a generic import tool that accepts as input thesauri described in other formalisms besides the above. The SIS-TMS has an output module that exports term lists. A flexible report writer that will be implemented in the near future.

The maintenance of thesaurus contents in the SIS-TMS is performed either with the import module supporting batch updates in the information base in form of tagged text files or interactive updates through the *Entry Forms*.

We distinguish *primitive* and *complex* operations: the former are the *creation, deletion, renaming, classification* (assignment to a class), *generalization* (assignment to a superclass) and *attribute assignment* (creation of a link) and the latter are defined on the basis of more than one primitive operation.

The updates in the SIS-TMS are performed through the *Entry Forms* in a task-oriented way.(See fig 5, right window). A task is defined by a set of *objects*, which can be updated with this task, and a set of operations, which can be performed on these objects. Tasks can be configured at run-time. This approach results in a *logical partition* of the contents of the information base for user, which can be used to organize access permissions, in particular for the cooperative work on interlinked thesauri. The following groups of tasks have been set-up SIS-TMS:
– on the organizational part of a thesaurus
– on the contents of a thesaurus and
– on administrative information of a thesaurus.

Tasks concerning the organizational part of a thesaurus are performed on facets and hierarchies, which can be created, deleted, renamed as long as the defined consistency constraints are preserved. Contents tasks manipulate terms and semantic links and maintain the version control as described above. Administrative tasks concern the updates on the literary warrants (source references where a term is used) and editors responsible for changes of the thesaurus contents.

4 Experience and Conclusions

The SIS-TMS is a refinement of the VCS Prototype, a terminology management system developed by FORTH in cooperation with the Getty Information Institute in the framework of a feasibility study. Based on the evaluation of this prototype and new requirements, a new version of the system and the Semantic Index System server formed for the terminological system in the AQUARELLE system. In the sequence, installations have been made at thee French, Greek and Italian Ministry of Culture, the RCHME Thesaurus Group and the MDA. Further, the system has been used for access to digital libraries and traditional library systems in Greece.

The experience at these installations confirms the need to take thesauri out of the local databases, and to install systems, which allow to keep the use of terms consistent with evolving authorities. All these organizations maintain a series of databases, either under separate local responsibility or under central administration, with which they need to communicate terminology. Our vision of a three level architecture fits very well there. The AQUARELLE access system demonstrated strikingly the need to provide translation capabilities between different thesauri, as we provide, and not only uniform multilingual thesauri in interlingua. Further the value of real-time flexible graphics was intensely appreciated by all users. It could be demonstrated, that certain structural properties and associated quality issues can only be controlled by graphics. The data entry system proved to be appropriate. Further enhancement is needed in the report writing: users like to print out thesauri in a book-like form. More experimental results will be available at the end of the AQUARELLE project.

We have the impression that integrated terminology services in distributed digital collections are going to become an important subject, and that the SIS-TMS provides a valuable contribution to that. It solves a major problem, the consistent maintenance of the necessarily central terminological resources between semiautonomous systems. The terminological bases themselves need not be internally distributed, as the access needs low bandwidth, read-only copies can easily be sent around at the given low update rates, and term servers can be cascaded. In the near future, we shall further enhance the functionality of this system to make its usability as wide as possible. In parallel, we engage and are looking for projects that integrate terminology services. Whereas there exist several standards for thesaurus contents, no one has so far tried to standardize the three component interfaces: (1) Term Server to retrieval tools, (2) TMS to CMS, (3) TMS to Term Server. As in a distributed information system many components from many providers exist, we are convinced that these three interfaces must become open and standardized, to make a wide use reality.

5 References

1. Jaana Kristensen, Expanding end-user's query statements for free text searching with a search-aid thesaurus. *Information Processing and Management*, 29(6):733-744, 1993.
2. A. Spink, Term Relevance Feedback and Query Expansion: Relation to Design. *Proceedings of the 17th Annual International ACM SIGIR Conference on Research and Development in Information Retrieval*, pp. 81-90, 1994.
3. Spink A., Goodrum A., Robins D., & Mei Mei Wu. "Elicitations during information retrieval: Implications for IR system design." In *Proceedings of the 19th Annual International ACM SIGIR Conference on Research and Development in Information Retrieval*, (pp. 120-127). Konstanz:Hartung-Gorre, 1996.
4. Brajnik G., Mizzaro S., & Tasso C., "Evaluating user interfaces to information retrieval systems: A case study on user support." In *Proceedings of the 19th Annual International ACM SIGIR Conference on Research and Development in Information Retrieval* (pp. 128-136). Konstanz:Hartung-Gorre 1996.
5. P. Constantopoulos and M. Doerr, An Approach to Indexing Annotated Images, Multimedia Computing and Museums, Selected Papers from the *Third International Conference on Hypermedia and Interactivity in Museums*, by David Bearman, pp. 278-298, San Diego-CA, USA, October 1995.
6. A.F. Smeaton and I. Quigley. Experiments on using Semantic Distances between Words in Image Caption Retrieval. *Proceedings of the 19th Annual International ACM SIGIR Conference on Research and Development in Information Retrieval*, pp. 174-180, Zurich, August 1996.
7. D. J. Foskett. Thesaurus. In *Readings in Information Retrieval,* eds. K. Sparck Jones and P. Willet, publisher Morgan Kaufmann, 1997.
8. D. Soergel. "SemWeb: Proposal for an open, multifunctional, multilingual system for integrated access to knowledge about concepts and terminology." *Advances in Knowledge Organization,* 5, pp.165-173, 1996.
9. M. Doerr. Authority Services in Global Information Spaces. *Technical Report, ICS-FORTH/TR-163*, Institute of Computer Science-FORTH, 1996.
10. M. Doerr and I. Fundulaki. A proposal on extended interthesaurus links semantics. *Technical Report* ICS-FORT/TR-215, March 1998.

11. M. Doerr, "Reference Information Acquisition and Coordination", in: "ASIS'97 -Digital Collections: Implications for Users, Funders, Developers and Maintainers", *Proceedings of the 60th Annual Meeting of the American Society for Information Sciences,* " November 1-6 '97, Washington, Vol.34. Information Today Inc.: Medford, New Jersey, 1997. ISBN 1-57387-048-X.

12. V. Christophides, M. Doerr and I. Fundulaki. The Specialist seeks Expert Views-Managing Folders in the AQUARELLE project. Selected Paper from the *Museums and the Web, MW97*, eds. D. Bearman, J. Trant.

13. M. Doerr, I. Fundulaki "The Aquarelle Terminology Service", ERCIM News Number 33, April1998, p14-15

14. R. Kramer, R. Nikolai, C. Habeck. Thesaurus federations: loosely integrated thesauri for document retrieval in networks based on Internet technologies. In *International Journal on Digital Libraries* (1), pp. 122-131, 1997.

15. G. Wiederhold. Interoperation, mediation and ontologies. In Proceedings of the International Symposium on Fifth Generation Computer Systems (FGCS94), Workshop on Heterogeneous Cooperative Knowledge-Bases (ICOT), Japan, December 1994, W3, pp.33-48.

16. R. Niehoff and G. Mack. The Vocabulary Switching System. In *International Classification*, 12(1):2-6, 1985.

17. A. Stern and N. Richette. On the construction of a super thesaurus based on existing thesauri. In Tools for Knowledge Organisation and the Human Interface. Vol. 2, pp. 133-144, 1990.

18. H. H. Neville. Feasibility study of a scheme for reconciling thesauri covering a common subject. In *Journal of Documentation*, 26(4), pp. 313-336, 1970.

19. R. Rada. Connecting and evaluating thesauri: Issues and cases. *International Classification*, 14(2), pp. 63-69, 1987.

20. R. Rada. Maintaining thesauri and metathesauri. International Classification, 17(3), pp. 158-164, 1990.

21. C. Sneiderman and E. Bicknell. Computer-assisted dynamic integration of multiple medical thesauruses. *In Comp. Biol. Med.*, 22(1), pp.135-145. 1992.

22. M. Sintichakis and P. Constantopoulos, A Method for Monolingual Thesauri Merging, Proc. of the 20th International Conference on Research and Development in Information Retrieval, ACM SIGIR, July 1997,Philadelphia, PA, USA.

23. S. Bechhofer and C. Goble. *Art Position Paper* - The Need for Structured Terminology. Medical Informatics Group, University of Manchester, March 1997.

24. E. H. Johnson and P. A. Cohrane. A Hypertextual Intefrace for a Searher's Thesaurus, Grainger Engineering Library Information Center, University of Illinois, June 1995.

25. Getty Information Institute (1995) Request for Comment Issued for the New Vocabulary Coordination System for the Getty Information Institute Authorities. Santa Monica, CA. (http://www.gii.getty.edu/gii/newsarch.html#article6).

26. A. Michard, G. Pham-Dac, Descriptions of collections and encyclopaedias on the Web using XML. To be published in *Archives and Museums Informatics*, Kluwer Pub., 1998.

27. The AQUARELLE project, TELEMATICS Application Program of the European Commission, Project IE-2005 1996.

28. P. Constantopoulos and M. Doerr. The Semantic Index System - A brief presentation.

29. J. Mylopoulos, A. Borgida, M. Jarke, M. Koubarakis, Telos: Representing Knowledge about Information Systems, *ACM Transactions on Information Systems,* October 1990.

30. A. Analyti and P. Constantopoulos and N. Spyratos. "On the Definition of Semantic Networks Semantics", *Technical Report*, Institute of Computer Science-FORTH, ICS/TR-187, February 1997.
31. R. S. Michalski. Beyond Prototypes and Frames: The Two-Tiered Concept Representation. *Categories and Concepts, Theoretical Views and Inductive Data Analysis*, eds. I. Mechelen, J. Hampton, R. Michalski, P. Theuns, 1993
32. D. Soergel. The Arts and Architecture Thesaurus (AAT)-A critical appraisal. *Technical Report*, College of Library and Information Sciences, University of Meryland, 1995.
33. C. Roulin. Sub-Thesauri as part of a metathesaurus. *In International Study Conference on Classification Research, Classification Research for knowledge representation and organisation*, pp. 329-336. Elsevier, 1992.
34. Introduction to the Art & Architecture Thesaurus. Published on behalf of The Getty Art History Information Program, Oxford University Press, New York, 1994.

Parallel Text Alignment

Charles B. Owen
Michigan State University
cbowen@cse.msu.edu

James Ford, Fillia Makedon, Tilmann Steinberg
Dartmouth Experimental Visualization Laboratory
6211 Sudikoff Laboratory, Dartmouth College
Hanover, NH 03755
{jford, makedon, shadows}@cs.dartmouth.edu
http://devlab.dartmouth.edu/

Abstract: Parallel Text Alignment (PTA) is the problem of automatically aligning content in multiple text documents originating or derived from the same source. The implications of this result in improving multimedia data access in digital library applications range from facilitating the analysis of multiple English language translations of classical texts to enabling the on-demand and random comparison of multiple transcriptions derived from a given audio stream, or associated with a given stream of video, audio, or images. In this paper we give an efficient algorithm for achieving such an alignment, and demonstrate its use with two applications. This result is an application of the new framework of Cross-Modal Information Retrieval recently developed at Dartmouth.

1 Introduction

1.1 Media Synchronization and Cross Modal Information Retrieval

Multiple Media Correlation is the theory and implementation of algorithms dealing with the synchronization, compression and correlation of two or more media data streams of the same or differing modalities. Owen [1] has presented a new model for multiple media stream correlation and illustrated its use in the context of several applications, including text-to-speech synchronization, slides-to-video presentation synchronization, text-to-text stream synchronization, and other multiple media correlation paradigms. This paper focuses on text-to-text synchronization. Most common approaches to media data analysis are "monomedia" approaches in that they involve the query and retrieval of information within one modality, such as searching for an audio segment within an audio database or a video frame within a video database. Such content-based browsing of multimedia data information can benefit from the additional information of any known transcript data [2]. Simultaneous analysis of multiple modalities can discover useful relationships between media objects, thus enhancing the power of queries usually based on a single type of media object or modality. *Multiple media analysis* derives hidden information that facilitates the retrieval of information across modalities. *Multiple media correlation* is a specific category of multiple media analysis that computes temporal and spatial relationships between two or more media objects. One example is the correlation of lip motion in video image data to speech audio: the audio provides clues to the motion of the lips. If the spatial synchronization between the two streams is found (where the moving lips are located in the video), then the audio can be used to predict the lip motion, thus allowing joint audio-video data compression [3].

This paper describes an application of *cross-modal information retrieval*, (CMIR), a new multimedia information retrieval framework which enables the querying of one modality (e.g., textual transcript) to access information in another modality (e.g., speech or an alternative textual transcript). The prerequisite for CMIR is the existence or derivation of synchronization information that will enable location of the desired result in the target media, given its location in the query media, for two or more different but related media streams.

Some early projects related to CMIR investigated alignment of newly recorded voice audio to degraded voice audio in motion picture dubbing [3,4]. There has been considerable work on searching for speech content at Cambridge University [5], at the Swiss Federal Institute of Technology [6], and at the Informedia Project at Carnegie Mellon University [7]. The type of *media synchronization* presented here should not be confused with the conventional multimedia topic of synchronization [8] which is concerned with the synchronized presentation of content.

1.2 Computed Intra-Language Alignment and the *HEAR HOMER* Project

An interesting problem in media synchronization is the alignment of common language content, a problem that is closely related to the alignment of differing language translations or content. In case of aligning different language translations, there has been considerable work, some of which uses lexical information [2, 9, 10]. *Parallel text alignment (PTA)* is the term used to denote the alignment of multiple same-language translations which are derived or based on the same document. Thus, PTA provides different parallel textual presentations (streams) of the same content. An automatic alignment among parallel texts is a mapping of content in one text to content in another wherein the subjects of the mapping are translations of the same range in the original text. Discovery of the alignment between the texts allows random access of information "across" different textual streams, enables comparative analysis of translation style and semantics and the retrieval of content and metadata attached to the translation content from the translations based on a search of an original document or an alternative translation. Figure 1 gives an intuitive explanations of the PTA concept.

As opposed to *intra-language alignment*, which is the alignment of two documents in the same language, an example of *cross-language alignment* is the alignment of two documents that are not in the same language, such as Spanish to English. This paper specifically addresses the problem of *computed intra-language alignment*.

Most previous work in parallel text alignment has focused on cross-language applications. The problem of intra-language alignment is new and was discovered as a part of the *HEAR HOMER* project at the DEVLAB [11], an ongoing digital library project at Dartmouth to study how ancient historical and literary text can be improved via a multimodal retrieval reference system for ancient texts. The goal is to introduce new tools which facilitate the analysis of ancient texts and discover new user interfaces that improve the data access of contextually relevant materials, such as different translations, images of museum objects, commentaries from rare books, audio clip-commentaries by experts, maps, slides, or video segments. This type of meta-information is usually divorced from the ancient texts; making it easily available to users not only brings such texts to life after thousands of years, but also provides a powerful educational mechanism for studying diverse materials.

Many translations of Homeric poems (such as the *Odyssey* and *Iliad*) exist and are studied routinely by scholars. Of particular interest is the question of how two or more translators chose to present the same original text. Presentation choice varies considerably: some translators choose to translate the content line-by-line, in a literal form, while others preserve the poetic structure, but feel no need to correspond verse-for-verse and thus often increase or decrease the number of lines considerably (George Chapman for example). Still others translate the poems as prose, a more free-form interpretation (Butler for example).

Some common problems facing users of ancient texts concern data access: (a) the lack of integrated systems that allow comparisons of original texts and multiple translations; (b) the lack of accurate and fast query support mechanisms to allow multimedia information retrieval using simple phrases; (c) the lack of robust tools to query metadata attached to original materials, such as text-to-speech retrieval tools that can work with parallel text alignment tools to enable someone to ask, "what does Homer say on this...." and hear it, i.e., retrieve speech from translation Y while querying translation X.

An obvious question is: why not just align the Homeric translations to the original Greek? There are several reasons why an English-to-English alignment is more desirable than synchronization to original language. Synchronization to ancient Greek is not well understood at this time; many synchronization language combinations exist, but little work has been done on ancient Greek. In any event, Greek base texts do not represent the only application for this technology: synchronization of translations of works that are not based on Greek present the same problems. An English-to-English solution can address all of these issues without requiring a large group of two-language systems. Furthermore, an English-to-English alignment has no intermediate document and, therefore, computes a single level synchronization function. If two translations are aligned to an original document, synchronization between the translations must be a composition of the alignment for one and the inverse alignment for the other, potentially compounding synchronization errors and granularity.

This paper presents a solution for the intra-language parallel text synchronization problem. The solution is based on the algorithm described in Section 3.1.2 and the general model for multiple media correlation. An interesting characteristic of this work is that the solution is not restricted to pair-wise application—simultaneous N-way alignment of multiple documents is also possible. The utility of N-way alignment is an open question and deserves further study.

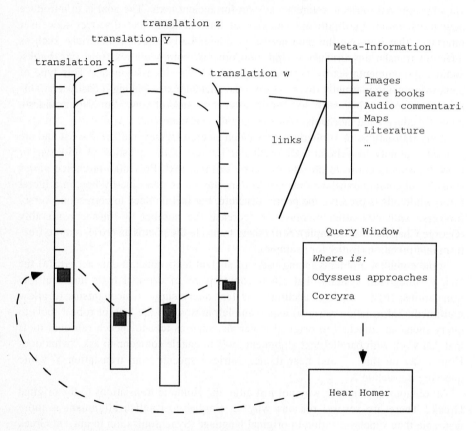

Fig. 1. The *HEAR HOMER* system architecture

Intra-language parallel text alignment has many additional applications aside from scholarly study. Computed synchronization data among parallel texts allows for cross-modal retrieval of content, the searching of one text for content in another. As an example, translators independently translate or modify names. Samuel Butler does not use the name *Pallas* in his translation of Homer's *Odyssey*, though George Chapman uses this name routinely in place of *Minerva*. A search for Pallas in the George Chapman translation can be converted to a Samuel Butler result wherein the alternative name is used, but the person intended is the same.

Owen [12] describes the Xtrieve cross-modal information retrieval system, a system supporting this type of query. Other possibilities include the alignment of multiple textual narratives describing the same sequence of images—a picture tour of the Louvre museum for example. The relation of tours by a curator and by an art historian is useful to a Louvre museum web site administrator who wishes to present the two alternative views in parallel.

Figure 1 outlines the functionality of the *HEAR HOMER* system. Queries in the *HEAR HOMER* query window are used to locate appropriate segments of ancient text translations. Precalculated alignments between different translations allow these segments to be mapped to corresponding segments in other translations; using expert-supplied links, they can also refer to relevant annotative materials (meta-information). Different types of information can be linked at appropriate locations in a translation "stream" so that users have the option to, for example, (a) see an interactive map of the conjectured locations of a story, (b) see images of related museum objects with annotations explaining them, (c) see images from paintings in later times (e.g., the Renaissance) that depict the particular scene described in an ancient text, (d) see images of the geophysical setting of the scene, as it is today or as it is conjectured (in other words bring the story back to life), (e) find links to literature through the centuries, such as making meaningful links to Shakespeare, (f) find meta-notes from rare books or drawings from rare books, or glossary information, and so on.

Section 3 describes the general problem formulation. Section 4 then describes the media element comparison method and Section 5 the MRG construction strategy. Section 6 discusses experimental evaluation of the approach. Section 7 discusses some additional issues and future research directions. Section 2 describes related work in the field of parallel text alignment.

2 Related work

Though the alignment of intra-language content is new, it is closely related to cross-language alignment. There has been considerable work in this area including work with domain knowledge (lexical information) and without [2, 9, 10, 13].

The system described in this paper uses WordNet, a large, existing, linguistic knowledge base for scoring word similarity. Rigau and Agirre use WordNet in conjunction with a cross-lingual dictionary to build a cross-language lexicon for information retrieval and alignment [14]. Other researchers have focused on discovering this knowledge directly from the text data.

Fung and McKeown [15] use Dynamic Time Warping (DTW), a causal alignment technique to align feature vectors of words in alternative translations based on the restrictive assumption that translated terms will be approximately the same distance apart. Best matching word vectors indicate related terms. These terms are used to create anchor points between the documents that are traced on a 2D diagram with a shortest line to compute the alignment.

Kabir, in an earlier DEVLAB project, determined points of similarity among documents using many simultaneous tools including synonyms and problem specific knowledge hints such as equivalent names [16]. These points are used to construct a line aligning the texts.

A common focus of many of the parallel text approaches is the location of features that indicate specific alignment points. These features include character n-grams, matching words, or related sentences and paragraphs. The technique described in this paper seeks to υσε all non-syntactic words in the documents as features rather than attempting to discover a limited set of important words.

Given varying granularities (characters, words, sentences, etc.) of feature vectors, computation of a best alignment path varies from the simple shortest line approach described above to image-based approaches advocated by Church [10]. The image-based approaches construct a *dot plot*, a square image of size $(n_1+n_2)^2$. Feature correspondences are plotted in this image and line detection is used to find a path. Church plots coincidental characters in an attempt to discover a lexicon with no examination of the actual words. Fung and Church apply the same technique to matching word pairs with more general results, particularly when one of the languages is non-Roman [17]. These approaches will always suffer from quadratic scaling problems in that they are based on image sizes that are $\Omega(n_1 n_2)$.

Detailed comparison of this work to cross-language alignment results is difficult. Cross-language alignment evaluation is typically performed on literal translations with known alignments, such as the official record of the European Parliament. Results are described at varying granularities. It is most common that the results are a presentation of the discovered lexicon, a graphical representation of alignment, or cross-language retrieval statistics on standard databases. Section 6.2 presents some example results from other systems for comparison.

3 Problem formulation

The Parallel Text Alignment problem is an application of the Multiple Media Correlation framework developed at Dartmouth which involves the spatial and temporal synchronization of two or more media streams. In the PTA application, the two streams are text of the same language. In the more general version of the multiple media correlation problem, we could have the alignment of, for example, an audio with a video stream, or an audio with a text stream, and so on.

3.1 Algorithms for Multiple Media Correlation

3.1.1 The Multiple Media Correlation model
The general algorithm presented is an N-way solution for causal and spatial normalization of N weighted, additive media representation graphs. This is a very general solution and can be applied to a large variety of problems. Enhancements of the algorithm demonstrate that causal variations, Markovian representations, and ranked result formulations are easily accomodated.

Media Synchronization

Some applications, such as audio and video, are inherently synchronized, typically a result of simultaneous, synchronized acquisition. Inherent synchronization does not imply implicit synchronization. Timing errors during acquisition might require explicit alignment. Close-caption video can be considered inherently synchronized from the application point of view; however, this synchronization did not always exist and had to be created at some point. Usually, the captioning is based on known script material and aligned by hand by an operator. During live broadcasting, "on-the-fly" generation of captioning suffers in quality due to the increased complexity of the task and the latency of the operator.

Media representation graphs

Media representation graphs (MRGs) are a powerful and very general model for media objects. Causal media element models can be converted directly into MRGs by simply converting the elements into a sequential list of vertices, each vertex representing a media element.

Notation

In this article an MRG instance is notated as μ_i. Vertices in the graph are considered to be indexed in an arbitrary order such that $\mu_i(s)$ represents a single vertex in the MRG.. Directed edges in the graph are represented as (s_1, s_2). The set of vertices reachable from vertex $\mu_i(s)$ is denoted $\mu_i(s).reachable$. Edges are weighted. A path in an M.RG is represented using the function $\tau(s), s = 1, ..., S$, wherein s and S are integers and the function τ a mapping from an integer causal index to a vertex index. The usage is equivalent and will be clear in context.

Index s=1 denotes the unique start vertex for a MRG; end vertices in MRGs are optional and their indices must be specifically specified. Comparison of N MRG elements will be assumed to produce a real value result.

A *supervertex n* refers to an ordered list of vertex indices such that one index for each MRG is included, effectively the cross product of all constituent MRG vertices. A path that normalizes all of the MRGs will visit a vertex in each graph for each value of s. The list of vertices visited simultaneously in this way for one value of s is a supervertex. A *supergraph M* is a graph where each vertex is a supervertex.

A path exists from one supervertex to another if and only if paths exist between all vertices that are elements of the supervertex. A synchronized transition from coincident vertices to coincident vertices assumes the path exists in all MRGs under normalization. The weight of an edge in the supergraph is the sum of all of the weights of the constituent edges.

General MRG object correlation

An optimum correlation is defined to be the set of valid, complete paths in the constituent MRGs and a path length S such that the sums of the path edge weights in all constituent MRGs and the supervertex comparison scores are minimized.

A requirement for solution existence is the existence of a path in the supergraph from the start vertex to an end vertex. Such a path is not guaranteed to exist by the existence of such paths in the constituent MRGs. If valid paths in the first graph have an even, valid paths in the second graph an odd number of vertices, the supergraph of these two graphs has no reachable end vertex.

3.1.2 N-way weighted MRG normalization Algorithm

The computation of an optimal solution for multiple media correlation is closely related to the shortest path in the supergraph. This leads to the following trivial solution algorithm:

```
// Trivial solution to general N-way weighted MRG
normalization problem

construct supergraph G from all constituent MRGs

// add vertex correlation scores to edge weights

for all (v1, v2) ∈ G.E such that v2 = v do

    w(v1, v2) <-- w(v1, v2) + w(v2)

compute single-source shortest paths from start vertex
of G // e.g. using Dijkstra's algorithm

select the end node with the shortest path
```

This first algorithm is rarely practical in media applications because of the typically large size of the MRGs, with vertex counts in the hundreds of thousands. The supergraph size, as the product of the constituent graph sizes, commonly is on the order of billions of vertices. Also, in many applications an entire MRG may not exist at any one time.

The actual algorithm is simply an alternative approach to single-source shortest-paths that has been modified to match the multiple media correlation problem specification, but proceeds *synchronously*, computing candidate paths that are all the same length at any point in time. Also, the active vertex list provides a tool that will be used for controlling the search space that will actually be accessed.

```
// N-way weighted MRG normalization
```

• Constrained shortest path algorithm
• Does not build supergraph
• Maintains a tree of supergraph paths
• All candidate paths are the same length (or done)
• Execution time $O((V_s+E_s)V_s \log V_s)$ — however, common cases yield better performance
• Supports pruning strategies

Performance

Since all paths are simple, the number of executions of the *while* body is clearly bounded by the number of vertices in the supergraph. Each algorithm step iterates over the set of active vertices and tests all reachable vertices. Hence, the worst case time bound for the algorithm is $O((V_s+E_s)V_s\log V_s)$, which is very slow relative to that of Dijkstra's algorithm. However, several special problem instances will yield much better performance, and this large bound assumes the entire search space will be examined, which in practical applications is not the case.

3.1.3 Strategies for performance

The performance of the above algorithm is asymptotically dependent upon the size of the MRGs. Any decrease in the size of these graphs will significantly increase performance. The most common reduction in size is the merging of parallel, identical paths. This is a common reduction when speech is involved, since many words have common prefix and suffix elements. Other likely possibilities for decreasing MRG size include decreasing the media element space to a smaller number of items (by using a more compact or less redundant representation), increasing the causal duration of media elements, or limiting the spatial resolution of selection (spatial resolution translates into parallel paths in the MRG).

Pruning strategies

The search space quickly expands to include a significant percentage of the active space in the supergraph. Some significant limit on this search space is not only required for efficient performance, but logical — it is not necessary that all of the search space be searched at all times.

A common approach is to apply a pruning heuristic, which eliminates paths from consideration after each step of the algorithm based on the path weight. The idea is to eliminate unlikely paths; there are several approaches to determine which paths to prune.

The first approach is to apply *proportional pruning*, removing all vertices *a* in *active* whose weight surpasses the minimum weight multiplied by a parameter $\beta > 1$. However, it was discovered in experimentation that path weights increase monotonically by an expected amount in each algorithm step, due to the additive nature of the model. Thus, an *additive pruning factor* is more sensible than a multiplicative factor. In this method, the weight of a vertex is compared to the *sum* of the minimum weight and a parameter $\beta > 0$.

The third approach, called *ranked pruning*, simply prunes all but the α least weight paths. This has been found to be more applicable to media normalization problems than proportional or additive pruning. Media normalization problems have a unique characteristic in that the pruning parameter determines the coverage of the search space that can be active at any time, effectively lower-bounding the search range for the application.

A logical enhancement is to also prune the search tree recursively. In practice, the tree tends to collapse to a single path relatively quickly, yielding a tree that consists of a long list with a tree at the end of it. *Path compression* can further reduce the memory usage of such a search tree, either by flushing the list to disk as it develops, or applying compression/redundancy reduction techniques.

3.2 Parallel Text Alignment Formulation

Let μ_1 and μ_2 be two translations of an original (and potentially unknown) document μ_0. These translations may be literal, implying close local relationships to the original document, or not. This paper will use as examples two translations of *The Odyssey* by Homer. Many translations of *The Odyssey* exist. The translations that will be described are by Samuel Butler and George Chapman [18, 19]. The Chapman translation is a literal line-by-line transformation of the ancient Greek. The Butler translation is a highly embellished prose translation. Table 1 is an example from Book 1 of *The Odyssey* illustrating the differences in the translation approaches. (The George Chapman translation is in verse form. It is presented here without the line breaks specified by Chapman in order to permit columnar presentation of the material.) The example selection was chosen from a computed alignment using the techniques described in this paper.

Table 1 also illustrates many of the problems associated with this application. Though these passages are discussing the same topic, they differ considerably. The Chapman version is considerably longer than the Butler version. Even names, an expected alignment point, have been found to change. Butler refers to Minerva, Chapman to Pallas. These differences are common throughout the books. Indeed, it has been found that hand-alignment of these translations is quite difficult.

In spite of these differences, both translations are related to the same source material and do share many common words and names. Some of these terms have been underlined in the table. In addition, the similarity is increased when synonym relationships, such as that of "sire" and "father", are taken into account.

This document set is meant as an example only. The concepts and algorithms presented in this paper are completely general and applicable to a large class of translation problems.

3.3 Solution granularity

The problem solution is assumed to have some granularity. An exact word-for-word alignment between two documents is not possible due to the large variation in approach. Also, any variation in length seems to limit that possibility. Synchronization is desired for presentation, retrieval, and study of these documents. It is unlikely that any of these functions are necessary at the word level. More likely, an alignment that allows for good contrast of lines, sentences, paragraphs, or stanzas is more appropriate semantically.

Normalization of the causal ordering of the words in the documents under alignment is the first step in the alignment process. From this computed normalization the inter-media synchronization can be readily computed. The best normalization is one that brings related words as close as possible to each other in the normalized

Butler Translation:

Then Minerva said, "Father, son of Saturn,
King of kings, it served Ægisthus right,
and so it would any one else who does as
he did; but Ægisthus is neither here nor
there; it is for Ulysses that my heart
bleeds, when I think of his <u>sufferings</u> in
that lonely <u>sea-girt</u> island, far away, poor
man, from all his friends. It is an island
covered with forest, in the very middle of
the sea, and a <u>goddess</u> lives there,
daughter of the magician <u>Atlas</u>, who looks
after the bottom of the ocean, and carries
the great columns that keep <u>heaven</u> and
<u>earth</u> asunder".

Chapman Translation:

Pallas, whose eyes did sparkle like the
skies, answer'd: "O Sire! Supreme of
Deities, <u>Ægisthus</u> past his fate, and had
desert to warrant our infliction; and
convert may all the pains such impious
men inflict on innocent sufferers to
revenge as strict, their own hearts eating.
But, that Ithacus, thus never meriting,
should suffer thus, I deeply suffer. His
more pious mind divides him from these
fortunes. Though unkind is piety to him,
giving him a fate more <u>suffering</u> than the
most unfortunate, so long kept friendless
in a <u>sea-girt</u> soil, where the sea's navel is a
sylvan isle, in which the <u>Goddess</u> dwells
that doth derive Her birth from <u>Atlas</u>, who
of all alive the motion and the fashion
doth command with his wise mind, whose
forces understand the inmost deeps and
gulfs of all the seas, who (for his skill of
things superior) stays the two steep
columns that prop <u>earth</u> and <u>heaven</u>".

Table 1. Two translations of Homer's Odyssey

coordinate system. [12] describes how the Xtrieve cross-modal information retrieval system makes uses of retrieval granularity in relation to text-to-text alignment in order to present logical retrieval units.

3.4 Monotonicity and endpoint constraints

An important assumption is that a normalization should be monotonic, presenting the same content in the same basic order. This does not imply strict monotonicity in word order. The Table 1 examples include the phrases "heaven and earth" and "earth and heaven". However, the general order of presentation for all of the translation content is monotonic. Since granularity at the word level is not considered to be important, an alignment that places "heaven and earth" and "earth and heaven" next to each other will be more than sufficient. The only known work in parallel-text alignment that does not assume monotonicity is the Smooth Injective Map Recognizer (SIMR) system by Melamed [20]. SIMR allows small local groups of size k, $6 < k < 9$, to be non-monotonic, primarily in support of local word order variations. The approach presented in this paper could be modified to allow local non-monotonicity using a post-processing phase that determines the local window match terms.

It is assumed that both translations begin and end together, implying the endpoint constraint. The Chapman translation does have additional "arguments" (short poetic introductions) prepended to the translation which do not relate to the Butler translation. These are clearly indicated and are simply omitted from the synchronization process.

4   Media element comparison

Application of the algorithm of Section 3.1.2 requires definition of a media element comparison function ρ, a function that compares media elements corresponding to vertices in a media representation graph and computes a score for the match. Lower value scores indicate better matches than higher values. Perfect alignment of identical words should, ideally score a match of zero.

The first question is: what media elements to choose? Though the obvious choice seems to be words, this is not the only option. Church advocates aligning at the character level, basically, the discovery of common n-grams between the texts [10]. Bonhomme and Romary are examples of the more common opposite extreme, the alignment of multi-word units, typically sentences or paragraphs [9]. Much of that work has focused on cross-language applications and testing on large, highly literal translation corpuses. Classics translations tend to have less sentence and paragraph correspondence due to the varied approaches to translation: prose, lyric, or verse. Also, discovery of sentence and paragraph structure is difficult in many applications due to loss of punctuation or uncertainty about sentence structure [21]. Examination of the types of texts required for the *HEAR HOMER* project indicates word-based alignment will be more effective. Direct correspondence between sentences or between paragraphs/stanzas seem to be rare.

4.1   Windowed text comparison

Strict word alignment is very difficult to do. The simple example of word order reversal leads to an unsolvable problem, if one assumes alignment monotonicity. What is preferred is a means of scoring this alignment well, even if the words do not align strictly.

Figure 2 illustrates two segments of text. Forcing the word correspondences to align perfectly in this figure would be very difficult. In the left translation there are only two words between "sufferings" and "lonely", while in the right translation there are seven between the best related matches. The words in between do not match well or are syntactic terms (which will be ignored due to application of a stop-list [22]).

An alternative view of Figure 2 would be to think of the edges as rubber bands, pulling the translations into a warping which minimizes the total tension. This is, indeed, the model that is used in this work. A word $\mu_1(s_1)$ in media object μ_1 is compared to a *window* surrounding the point s_2 in media object μ_2. A fixed range parameter w sets a window width $2w+1$ such that words within the window are indexed by s_w in $[s_{2-w}, s_{2+w}]$. Each word $\mu_2(s_w)$ is compared to $\mu_1(s_1)$ using a distance measure $d(\mu_1(s_1), \mu_2(s_w))$. This measure will be referred to as the *word score* and will be discussed in the next section. The word score is weighted using an energy function

$e(\alpha) = (s_w - s_2)^2 / (w+1)^2 (\xi_{\varnothing})$ where $\xi_{\varnothing}$ is the weight for a null match, the score for words which do not match at all. The minimum adjusted score is the winner. This example assumes two media objects under correlation. However, the problem is easily extended to N objects simply by adding all of the scores from each combination $\{1, i\}, i = 2,..., N$.

Fig. 2. Word comparisons as a rubber band.

The combination of the word score and the energy function is referred to as the *window score*. Figure 3 is a plot of the window score equation assuming pair-wise comparison and a single matching term. The plot assumes the match term is moved back and forth in one document relative to the other by a distance plotted as word distance. In this figure the window parameter is set to $w=5$. The curve within the match range is parabolic, approaching the value of $\xi_{\varnothing}$ at the end of the window, where the worst case score is limited to $\xi_{\varnothing}$.

This approach is asymmetrical in that every word in μ_1 will participate in the window score, while only selected choices in μ_i, $i > 1$ will participate. However, this is rarely an issue in practice. Figure 4(a) shows two text segments. The bar represents a rubber band. As the two text segments are moved relative to each other, the rubber band is stretched. The important observation is that if μ_i is assumed to be the left text, the rubber band attachment will be "sea-girt" on the left and find "sea-girt" in the window on the right as long as the distance between the words is within the match range. If μ_i is assumed to be the right text segment instead, the same rubber band with the same stretch characteristics will attach to "sea-girt" on the right and find "sea-girt" in the window on the left. However, "soil" would not participate in the score if μ_i is the text on the left, because words in μ_i all match to other words in μ_2. Effectively, the word could be omitted and the match remain the same. But, if "soil" does participate in a score assuming the alternative application of the window, there would have to be a word in the window range on the left it matched against, which would have been found when that word was indexed by s_1 with μ_i on the left, *assuming that word did not find a better alternative.*

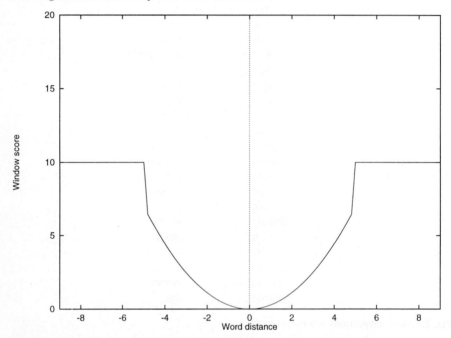

Fig. 3. Plot of window score for pair-wise alignment and a single matching term.

Figure 4(b) shows a example where the two cases will differ. If the window is applied to the right text segment, only one rubber band will exist, attaching to only one of the matching elements. If the window is applied to the segment on the left, both occurrences of "sea-girt" will cause rubber bands, the effect being a bit stronger pull for this media segment (a lower score over the segment). This is rarely an issue, since it requires more than one occurrence of matching words in a small window range (typically five or less), a relatively rare occurrence. Also, both cases *favor matching of these text segments*, the desired result.

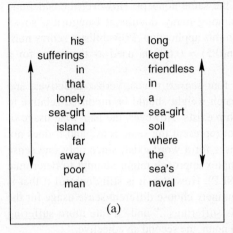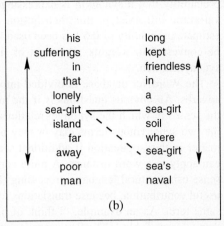

(a)   (b)

Fig. 4. Window match characteristics as alignment moves.

4.2 WordNet and word comparison

The window score mechanism described above assumes a mechanism for generating a word score for pair-wise word comparisons. The most obvious word score is 0 for exact matches. The score for an exact match is denoted ξ_{exact}. However, it has been found to be very common that translators will vary considerably in word usage. For cross-language applications, this variation is taken care of by the existence or discovery of a cross-language translation dictionary. For English-only applications another approach is required.

The word scoring approach is based on the WordNet lexical database of the English language [23, 24]. WordNet is an on-line implementation of a *linguistic network*, creating a structure for determining relationships between and information about words. WordNet supports many such relationships.

The primary relationship of value in word comparison beyond simple equality is *synonymy*, similarity of meaning. Two words are considered to be related through synonymy if one of the words has the other as a member of its synonym list. Since WordNet is structured as a semantic net, all synonym relationships are reciprocated. If β is a synonym of α, then α is a synonym of β. The synonym relationship in this application is a symmetrical relationship.

The word score for synonym relationships in this application, $\xi_{synonym}$ should not be 0, since an exact match should be favored over an approximate match. A synonym relationship is not a guarantee of identical usage. "Race" and "run" are synonyms, but "race" may be a noun usage implying an event, in one document and "run" a verb implying moving quickly, in the other document. If a probabilistic view of the problem is taken, an exact match could be considered a probability 1 match. A detailed study of the use of synonyms in translation documents could assess a probability that a synonym is expressing the same concept. However, considerable variation will exist in this distribution among many document categories, so an estimate probability of 0.5 has been used in this application. Probabilistic scores must be converted to weights. A weight of $-\ln(0.5) = 0.693$ is used as the score for a synonym match.

The WordNet database is divided into four *senses*: nouns, verbs, adjectives, and adverbs. An obvious questions is if the match weight should be modified relative to the senses in which the synonym relationship exists. However, the pair-wise usage of the two synonymous terms may or may not represent the same sense and it does not matter in this application if additional senses for a word exist, since only one sense can apply to a word instance. A more complex approach might attempt to determine sense using natural language processing (NLP). However, it is still doubtful if that is useful contribution, because translations routinely choose different sense usage for the same term. As an example, "I think of his sufferings..." and "a fate more suffering than..." from Table 1. The first usage is as a noun, the second an adjective.

A *morphological relationship* between two words is a relationship through modification of a base word. The most common example is the addition of "s" to the end of a word to form a plural. WordNet supports morphological relations as part of the database front-end processing, rather than as a component of the database itself. The morphological analysis tool is applied to each term during search to determine if each is a base term in the database. The same tool is applied in the problem solution described here to discover morphological relationships between comparison terms.

The score, ξ_{morph}, for a morphological relationship was selected as 0.693, the same as for a synonym relationship. While it may appear that a morphological relationship is a stronger relationship than synonymy, this is not necessarily the case in application. Clearly, a plural and singular application do not mean the same thing in all cases. Some words have multiple alternative bases. The bases for "axes" are "ax" and "axis". Also, the WordNet morphological rules are limited in that they are context-free and do not have knowledge of special terms, proper names, etc.

The score for a bad match, $\xi_{\emptyset}$ should be a larger positive value. A probabilistic approach to the problem would be that two words that do not match at all have a probability of 0 of alignment. However, this is not at all the case. The probability that two words will align should be non-zero, because words that do not have relatives in the alternative document must still exist in-line. They are aligning to other, non-matching words because they have been chosen by the translator as part of a concept. Hence, $\xi_{\emptyset}$ should be larger than ξ_{exact} and $\xi_{synonym}$, but not infinity. The score chosen in this work has been $\xi_{\emptyset} = 10$. This score was selected as a compromise between a maintaining a large margin over the scores ξ_{exact}, $\xi_{synonym}$, and ξ_{morph} and maintaining reasonable total path scores. As long as this score is considerably larger than ξ_{exact}, $\xi_{synonym}$, and $\xi_{synonym}$, the value of $\xi_{\emptyset}$ becomes inconsequential, since any larger value will simply scale all path totals identically.

4.3   Stop-list application

Syntactic words such as "and", "the", and "do" are not present in the WordNet database. Syntactic terms convey little information, are not semantically meaningful, and are effectively *noise* in the alignment process. However, the non-existence of a word in the database does not indicate insignificance—proper names are highly significant, but also not present. The solution to this problem is to apply a "stop-list", a list of 571 common English syntactic words ignored in the matching process. The stop-list used in this application is based on that of the Smart system [22].

5   Media representation graph

A textual document is a sequential list of words. However, what does it mean to align two or more text documents? Clearly, the alignment cannot be simply word-to-word since the document lengths may vary. Some mechanism is required that will allow for causal warping of the documents relative to each other.

The rate of progression through a text document relative to a causal warping function can be varied in two ways: repeating words or skipping words. Word repetition assumes that $\tau_i(s_1) = \tau_i(s_j)$, $\forall\ 1 < j < r$ for some range $s_j \in [s_1, s_1 + r]$, that the causal normalization function maps a sequential range of casual normalization variables to the same word. Skipping words assumes that some words do not exist in the domain of τ_i. Skipping words is not considered an effective approach, because skipped words do not participate in alignment at all. A skipped-words approach was implemented as an earlier result, but is not presented here. The approach presented in this section models causal warping entirely through the repetition of words.

Figure 5 illustrates a simple causal MRG with words associated with the vertices. Loop-back edges model the repetition of words. Stop-list terms are omitted from the MRG completely and do not participate in the normalization process. Since conversion of a document to an MRG with application of a stop-list is a transformation operation, not an equivalence operation, an index for each word is also associated with the vertex. This index allows for the conversion of the computed normalization to word document synchronization information. Additional document content not directly related to the body of the text, such as titles, credit information, and front matter, is also omitted.

A supergraph in the presence of these two example causal document MRGs is illustrated in Figure 6. Loop-back edges have been omitted from this supergraph even though they are implied by the existence of loop-back edges in all constituent MRGs. As discussed in [12], loop-back edges in the supergraph are never elements of an optimal solution because optimal solutions are simple paths in the supergraph. Repeating a supergraph vertex simply extends the match length and a shorter path with a weight less than or equal to that of a path including supergraph vertex repetition will always be selected. One path has been highlighted in Figure 6. This is the best path through this supergraph section.

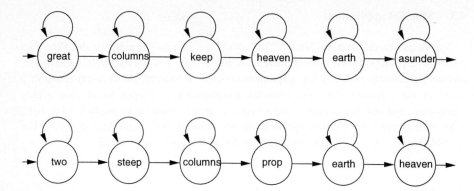

Fig. 5. Document media representation graph.

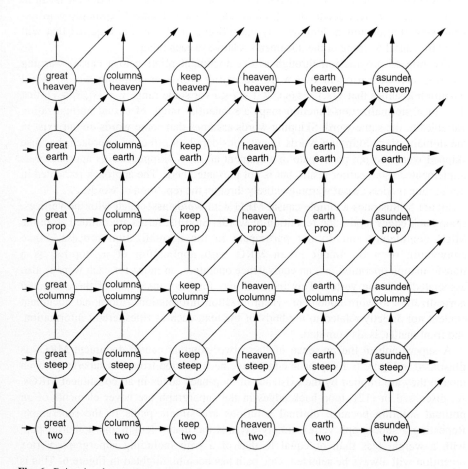

Fig. 6. Pair-wise documents supergraph

The number of vertices and edges in the supergraph is $O(\Pi_{i=1 \ldots N} c_i)$, where c_i is the number of non-stop-list words in document μ_i. Clearly, it is not practical to construct the supergraph. The *Odyssey* Book 1 synchronization problem would require a 3,265,763 vertex supergraph, and the alignment of the book of *Genesis*, described in Section 6, would require a supergraph with 178,371,808 vertices. A practical solution to this problem requires application of the algorithm of Section 3.1.2, which does not build the supergraph, and a pruning strategy as described in [12]. Section 6 discusses how the effectiveness of the pruning parameter is assessed. Should an insufficient pruning parameter be selected, the best path could be pruned early, and a sub-optimal solution selected.

6 Evaluation

This section describes techniques and criteria for the evaluation of parallel intra-language text alignment. The system described in this paper has been implemented and all of the evaluation tests described in this section are based on this implementation. The implementation parameterization consists of a word window size of $w=5$, match scores of $\xi_\mu=10$, $\xi_{exact} = 0$, $\xi_{synonym} = 0.693$ and $\xi_{morph} = 0.693$. The window width parameter was determined experimentally though range testing. The pruning parameter was set to 1000.

Evaluation of parallel text alignment is complicated by the lack of ground-truth data. Any known correct alignment is based on either literal translation or hand-marking. This work is the first known attempt to establish test criteria and test data for intra-language text alignment. Two evaluation strategies are applied to the determination of match accuracy: comparison with reference alignments and subjective evaluation of alignment quality. An additional evaluation criteria is retrieval efficacy, the ability to search one translation and find the appropriate result in another, but no known reference corpus exists to support such an evaluation.

6.1 Subjective evaluation and an example

Subjective evaluation is the simple examination of the program results by a human operator. The author and several other users have viewed the Homeric alignment and feel it is accurate at a granularity of twenty words or better.

6.2 Comparison to reference data

A more quantitative evaluation can be achieved by comparing the computed results to known mark points. An example dataset with multiple translations and known mark points is the Bible; many different translations of the Bible exist, some from earlier translations (King James Version, KJV, and Revised Standard Version, RSV) and some from original text (New International Version, NIV). The verse and chapter structure enforce a fixed alignment among the different translations that can be used as a reference for evaluation.

The system was evaluated using several books of the Bible. Each word pair (w_1, w_2), representing the computed alignment between two non-stop-list words in the synchronization result, was converted to a relative verse number (v_1, v_2). A relative verse number is simply a sequential numbering of all verses in a document instance. The verse number corresponding to a word instance is determined by the relative verse in which the word is located. A verse distance $\varepsilon = v_2 - v_1$ is computed. This error indicates a distance between the ideal placement of the word and the computed placement in verse units. As mentioned before, word-for-word synchronization means very little. Verse sizes are a relatively small unit and highly indicative of content structure.

The effectiveness of the Bible as an alignment test might be questioned because of the presumed literality of translations. There is considerable commonality among all of the translations considered here, but there are also considerable differences. As an example, Genesis 42:26 is translated as "And they laded their asses with the corn, and departed thence." (KJV), "they loaded their grain on their donkeys and left." (NIV), and "Then they loaded their asses with their grain, and departed." (RSV). All three translations vary in content within a verse. In some cases, verses are omitted from the later translations due to better knowledge of original texts and content is added as new texts become available.

Table 2 presents results for several book/translation combinations. Each combination listed includes percentages for error ranges of -2 to +2 verses. The word counts listed in the table column "Aligned Words" are after application of the stop-list. The "Max Rank" column will be discussed in the next section. An additional column, the "RMS Error" column lists the square root of the average squared character error distance (root-mean-squared or RMS error), where a character error distance is defined as the distance in characters from the first letter of the word to the correct verse. This error measure has been included primarily for comparison with related work, where RMS error measures are common. Note, however, that the RMS error will be increased in this result due to the word-based alignment. An error distance will always be multiples of the length of words (plus any inter-word spacing). This result has been adjusted to omit the SGML markup between verses, since that quantity would be an additive amount and is not related to the alignment process.

As can be seen, the synchronization result matched the known correct result very closely. The most common error is a one verse error. The balanced error distribution (similar positive and negative verse error measures) is a result of the symmetrical nature of the algorithm application. One verse errors are typified by "hang-over", the overlap of one verse alignment with another. The small RMS error values are an indication that this "hang-over" is usually small, often only one or two words. An example is the alignment of the beginning of Matthew 2:13 (KJV): "And when they departed, behold, the angel of the Lord appeareth...". In the NIV translation, this example overlaps the last word of Matthew 2:12 (NIV): "...by another route. (13) When they had gone, and angel...". It is interesting to observe that "route" would be expected to match the last word of Matthew 2:12 (KJV): "way". However, "way" is a stop-list term. Often the overlap occurrences are due to a final word in a verse matching not only the corresponding word in the alternative verse, but also the first one or more words of the next verse. This behavior is due to the loop-back edges in the MRG which allow words to repeat if necessary to slow the presentation relative to the alternative translation.

Bible Book	Versions	Aligned Words	
Genesis	KJV, NIV	14,142	12,604
Genesis	KJV, RSV	14,142	12,728
Matthew	KJV, NIV	8,226	7,294
Matthew	NIV, KJV	7,294	8,226
Matthew	KJV, RSV	8,226	7,004
Ruth	KJV, NIV	911	811

Bible Book	Error					RMS Error	Max Rank
	-2	-1	0	+1	+2		
Genesis	0.01%	3.3%	93.6%	3.1%	0%	5.7	277
Genesis	0%	1.8%	97.1%	1.1%	0%	3.2	142
Matthew	0.02%	3.8%	92.7%	3.4%	.03%	5.6	159
Matthew	0.01%	3.4%	93.2%	3.4%	0.02%	7.7	129
Matthew	0%	3.3%	94.5%	2.2%	0%	5.0	134
Ruth	0%	5.2%	92.7%	2.1%	0%	6.6	140

Table 2: Evaluation results for Bible books

As mentioned earlier, it is difficult to compare the results for intra-language alignment directly with those for cross-language alignment. However, it is useful to examine how those approaches are evaluated and relate them to the results presented in this work.

The Melamed Smooth Injective Map Recognizer (SMIR) system was tested on Canadian government data that has been hand-aligned by a panel of 8 judges (the Hansard corpus) [20]. The translations are very literal. Errors are quoted in paragraphs, a somewhat less restrictive alignment criteria than the verse measure presented in this paper. The quoted errors for two databases are 1.3% and 1.8% assuming knowledge of bitext correspondences (lexical domain knowledge). Considering that a paragraph granularity is considerably larger than a verse granularity, the results in Table 2 are quite comparable.

Melamed quotes character RMS error distances [13]. It is curious that error reporting in characters has become popular, since it is not indicative of alignment at a meaningful granularity. The quoted RMS errors range from 5.7 characters for literal French/English translations of parliamentary debates to 20.6 for literal translations of technical reports. Church aligns at the character level and quotes an RMS error of 57 characters, based on the Hansard corpus [10]. The results in Table 2 are clearly comparable to these results.

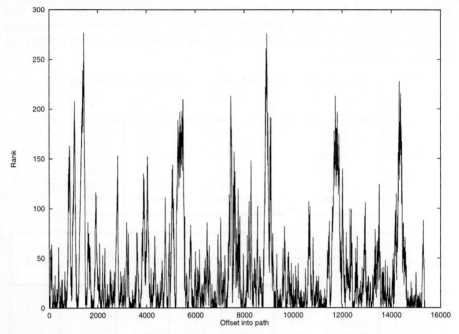

Fig. 7. Best path rank plot for Genesis KJV to NIV alignment.

6.4 Pruning strategy evaluation

The efficient performance of this algorithm is dependent upon use of a pruning strategy. In the evaluation, the pruning width was set to a fixed value of 1000. This parameterization limits the search space for the Genesis KJV/NIV alignment to no more than 15,359,000 supervertices. This is about 8.4% of the available space. Is it effective to so severely limit the search space?

The implementation was instrumented to record the weight rank for every vertex in the search tree for each tree depth s. During the back-tracking phase the maximum (worst case) rank is recorded and is presented in Table 2. Since this rank is typically less than a fourth of the pruning parameter value, it is unlikely that a better path was pruned. A worst case path of 277 indicates that the pruning parameter could be set to any greater value and the path would not be pruned. Figure 7 is a plot of the rank for the Genesis KJV/NIV best computed normalization path. This plot is indicative that the rank does not exhibit asymptotic growth over time.

6.5 Execution performance

The algorithm execution time is dependent upon the pruning parameter value and the size of the texts. The implementation discussed in this paper is highly instrumented and not optimized. Even so, this implementation is able to process approximately 5 synchronization tree levels per second of CPU time on a 275MHz DEC Alpha processor. This is equivalent to 50,000 media element comparisons per second. This places alignment times for the larger documents in the half hour range. Shorter documents are a bit faster due to the logarithmic factor in the asymptotic running time. (The log factor in the implementation is due to the determination of a supervertex visit using red-black trees [25]). Since alignment computation is a one-time process for a set of texts, longer computation times are not considered a serious factor.

Two implementations of the algorithm of Section 3.1.2 exist. A completely general implementation is used in this application. The text-to-speech application presented in [12] uses an implementation that has been optimized to take advantage of the synchronous nature of that application. Several system engineering level modifications to that implementation led to performance improvements in excess of 100 to 1. It is strongly believed that similar performance improvements could be gained in the general implementation.

Memory usage is based on the same parameters. The size of the synchronization tree is bounded by the pruning parameter. In practice, the tree is even smaller due to decreasing tree width for depths less than s at any point in the algorithm execution. Using the entirely general directed graph and tree class libraries supplied by the ImageTcl multimedia development environment, the largest problem required about 100MB of memory during execution [26]. Most memory was used for recording execution statistics, and optimizations are expected to decrease usage considerably.

7 Concluding remarks

Experimentation with parallel texts and the application of multiple media correlation has resulted in a solution for a general class of problems in intra-language alignment. In the process several interesting issues have arisen that have great potential for future work. Post-processing alignment data in search of a locally non-monotonic alignment is one such issue. The section also discusses N-way alignment and extension of this work to cross-language alignment.

7.1 N-way alignment

The experimental results described in this paper assume pair-wise alignment of parallel texts. However, since the algorithm of Section 3.1.2 is a general N-way solution, the extension of the results in this paper to 3-way or more alignment is trivial. N-way text alignment advantages need to be researched further and constitute an element for future work. It is expected that an *N*-way alignment will favor terms co-located in all texts, effectively giving them stronger rubber bands to pull the alignment.

It is expected that the pruning parameter will have to be increased for *N*-way applications. Also, the performance will be affected by the 2^{N-1} out-degree of the supergraph vertices. It is doubtful that problem instances beyond 3-way can be efficiently solved.

7.2 Cross-language parallel text alignment

The focus of this work has been entirely on intra-language alignment. This focus was driven by large digital library projects in the Classics, such as the *HEAR HOMER* project, and a perception that intra-language alignment had been overlooked by the parallel text research community. However, the general techniques described here are entirely applicable to cross-language application. A cross-lingual WordNet database can be built using techniques described by Rigau and Agirre [14]. An interesting future project currently being considered is the alignment to ancient Greek, another useful element for the *HEAR HOMER* project.

7.3 Conclusion

The alignment of parallel texts provides a new technology that directly impacts digital library multimedia data access. The reason is that parallel texts can represent a variety of things, from parallel translations in the classics, to parallel annotations of commercial product parts, to parallel medical explanations. The use of this technology has been demonstrate on a large scale using classical texts from Homer and from the Bible. This technology is being derived from the Multiple Media Correlation framework and an energy minimization model which make this approach to parallel text alignment unique. The use of windowed word comparisons is also a new approach to the problem of local non-monotonicity in translations. A media element must be chosen, in this case significant words. A method for building a media representation graph (MRG) for a problem instance is devised with vertices having associated words and word indexes and a media element comparison strategy is devised which is based on windowed word comparisons. The implementation uses Dartmouth's multimedia prototyping system, ImageTcl, and the standard ImageTcl media correlation tools. The automatic synchronization of parallel texts also provides a new mechanism for indexing and cross-modal retrieval.

This work is unique in that it provides powerful computed Intra-language alignment solutions which are particularly useful to experts in classic literature who are interested in studying how different translators interpreted the same original text. Its impact on educational uses of digital libraries in the classroom or other educational settings, such as museums, has already been tested at Dartmouth and in a joint project with the University of Athens.

References

1. Owen, C.B. and Makedon, F.: Cross-Modal Retrieval of Scripted Speech Audio. In: Proc. of SPIE Multimedia Computing and Networking, San Jose, CA (1998) to appear
2. Dagan, I., Pereira, F., and Lee, L.: Similarity-Based Estimation of Word Cooccurrence Probabilities. In: Proc. of the 32nd Annual Meeting of the Assoc. for Computational Linguistics, ACL'94, New Mexico State University, Las Cruces, NM (1994)
3. Chen, T., Graf, H.P., and Wang, K.: Lip Synchronization Using Speech-Assisted Video Processing. IEEE Signal Proc. Letters 2 (1995) 57-59
4. Bloom, P..J.: High-Quality Digital Audio in the Entertainment Industry: An Overview of Achievements and Challenges. IEEE ASSP Magazine 2 (1995) 2-25
5. Brown, M.G., Foote, J.T., Jones, G.J.F., Spärck Jones, K., and Young, S.J.: Video Mail Retrieval by Voice: An Overview of the Cambridge/Olivetti Retrieval System. In: Proc. of the ACM Multimedia '94 Workshop on Multimedia Database Management Systems, San Francisco, CA (1994) 47-55
6. Ballerini, J.-P., Büchel, M., Domenig, R., Knaus, D., Mateev, B., Mittendorf, E., Schäuble, P., Sheridan, P., and Wechsler, M.: SPIDER Retrieval System at TREC-5. In: Proc. of TREC-5 (1996)
7. Hauptmann, A.G., Witbrock, M.J., Rudnicky, A.I., and Reed, S.: Speech for Multimedia Information Retrieval. In: Proc. of User Interface Software and Technology UIST-95, Pittsburg, PA (1995)
8. Gibbs, S., Breiteneder, C., and Tsichritzis, D.: Modeling Time-Based Media. The Handbook of Multimedia Information Management. Prentice Hall PTR (1997) 13-38.
9. Bonhomme, P., and Romary, L.: The Lingua Parallel Concordancing Project: Managing Multilingual Texts for Educational Purposes. In: Proc. of Language Engineering 95, Montpellier, France (1995)
10. Church, K.W.: Char_Align: A Program for Aligning Parallel Texts at the Character Level. In: Proc. of the 30th Annual Meeting of the Assoc. for Computational Linguistics, ACL'93, Columbus, OH (1993)
11. Makedon, F., Owen,, M., and Owen, C.: Multimedia-Data Access Remote Prototype for Ancient Texts. In: Proc. of ED-MEDIA 98, Freiburg, Germany (1998)
12. Owen, C.B.: Multiple Media Correlation: Theory and Applications. Ph.D. thesis, Dartmouth College Dept. of Computer Science (1998)
13. Melamed, I.D.: A Portable Algorithm for Mapping Bitext Correspondence. In: Proc. of the 35th Conference of the Assoc. for Computational Linguistics, ACL'97, Madrid, Spain (1997)
14. Rigau, G., and Agirre, E.: Disambiguating Bilingual Nominal Entries Against WordNet. In: Proc. of the Workshop on the Computational Lexicon, ESSLLI'95 (1995)
15. Fung, P., and McKeown, K.: Aligning Noisy Parallel Corpora Across Language Groups: Word Pair Feature Matching by Dynamic Time Warping. In: Proc. of the 1st Conf. of the Assoc. for Machine Translation in the Americas, AMTA-94, Columbia, Maryland (1994)
16. Kabir, A.S.: Identifying And Encoding Correlations Across Multiple Documents. DEVLAB Research Report, Dartmouth College (1997)
17. Fung, P., and Church, K.W.: K-vec: A New Approach for Aligning Parallel Texts. In: Proc. of the 15th Int. Conf. on Computational Linguistics COLING'94,,Kyoto, Japan, (1994) 1096-1102
18. Homer: The Odyssey. Translated by Samuel Butler.
19. Homer: The Odyssey. Translated by George Chapman.
20. Melamed, I.D.: A Geometric Approach to Mapping Bitext Correspondence. Report 96-22, IRCS (1996)

21. van der Eijk, P.: Comparative Discourse Analysis of Parallel Texts. Unpublished manuscript (1994)
22. Salton, G.: Introduction to Modern Information Retrieval. McGraw-Hill Computer Science Series, New York (1982)
23. Richard Beckwith, George A. Miller, and Randee Tengi. Design and Implementation of the Wordnet Lexical Database and Searching Software. Report, Princeton University Cognitive Science Laboratory (1993)
24. Miller, G.A., Beckwith, R., Fellbaum, C., Gross, D., and Miller, K.: Introduction to WordNet: An On-line Lexical Database (revised). CSL Report 43, Princeton University Cognitive Science Laboratory (1993)
25. Cormen, T.H., Leiserson, C.E., and Rivest, R.L.: Introduction to Algorithms. MIT Press, Cambridge, MA (1990)
26. Owen, C.B.: The Imagetcl Multimedia Algorithm Development System. In: Proc. of the 5th Annual Tcl/Tk Workshop'97, Boston, MA (1997) 97-105

An Analysis of Usage of a Digital Library

Steve Jones, Sally Jo Cunningham, Rodger McNab

Department of Computer Science
University of Waikato, Hamilton, New Zealand
Telephone: +64 7 838 4021 Fax: +64 7 838 4155
E-mail: {stevej, sallyjo, rjmcnab}@cs.waikato.ac.nz

Abstract. As experimental digital library testbeds gain wider acceptance and develop significant user bases, it becomes important to investigate the ways in which users interact with the systems in practice. Transaction logs are one source of usage information, and the information on user behaviour can be culled from them both automatically (through calculation of summary statistics) and manually (by examining query strings for semantic clues on search motivations and searching strategy). We conduct a transaction log analysis on user activity in the Computer Science Technical Reports Collection of the New Zealand Digital Library, and report insights gained and identify resulting search interface design issues.

1 Introduction

There is extensive literature on transaction log analysis of OPACs (see [12] for an overview). However, only recently have these techniques has been applied to digital libraries—likely because many digital libraries have only just attained a usage level suitable for log analysis [8]. Since log analysis provides insight into user search behaviour it is useful in the design and evaluation of query interfaces. Transaction log analysis, as applied to OPACs, has yielded a diversity of results; it appears difficult to generalize about information seeking and search behaviors for all users at all times. Instead, the primary utility of these analysis techniques lies in the production of detailed descriptions of the behavior of a given group of users, on a single retrieval system, for a particular document collection. In this paper we have suggested ways that these fine-grained details can then be used to tailor our system to its target user group.

We apply transaction log analysis techniques to the New Zealand Digital Library (http://www.nzdl.org), focussing in this paper on the Computer Science Technical Reports (CSTR) collection. The CSTR contains nearly 46,000 publicly available computing-related technical reports harvested from over 300 research institutions from around the world. Two principles of our digital library architecture are to make

Domain code and country	Accesses N	%	Domain code and country	Accesses N	%
ar Argentina	74	0.26	lk Sri Lanka	16	0.06
at Austria	151	0.53	mx Mexico	69	0.24
au Australia	1308	4.61	my Malaysia	286	1.01
be Belgium	185	0.65	nl Netherlands	259	0.91
br Brazil	480	1.69	no St. Pierre & Miquelon	63	0.22
ca Canada	1307	4.61	nz New Zealand	1957	6.90
ch Switzerland	89	0.31	ph Philippines	65	0.23
de Germany	3102	10.94	pl Poland	83	0.29
dk Denmark	143	0.50	pt Portugal	237	0.84
es Spain	559	1.97	ru Russia	197	0.69
fi Finland	918	3.24	se Sweden	310	1.09
fr France	1381	4.87	sg Singapore	274	0.97
gr Greece	231	0.81	si Slovenia	335	1.18
hk Hong Kong	124	0.44	th Thailand	246	0.87
id Indonesia	128	0.45	tw Taiwan	193	0.68
ie Ireland	309	1.09	uk United Kingdom	1051	3.71
il Israel	185	0.65	uy Uruguay	66	0.23
it Italy	662	2.33	za South Africa	77	0.27
jp Japan	822	2.90	Other countries	567	2.00
kr South Korea	1224	4.32			
arpa	20	0.07	mil	51	0.18
com	3406	12.01	net	1197	4.22
edu	3515	12.39	org	170	0.60
gov	267	0.94			

Number of searches: 29,041   Time span: 30 April 1996 - 2 July 1997

Table 1. Computer Science Technical Report (CSTR) usage statistics by domain

a minimum of assumptions about conventions adopted by document repositories, and to avoid manual document processing. Since the CSTR collection is based on a large, diverse set of document repositories, we cannot rely on the presence of bibliographic metadata. The collection is not formally catalogued; however, the full texts of the documents are extracted and indexed. The primary access mechanism for the collection is thus an unfielded keyword search. Both ranked and Boolean querying are supported.

In the following section we describe how the data has been collected, and some demographic details of the users are presented. The usage logs are automatically processed by software which extracts specified summary statistics, and it is this data that we analyze in section 3. A manual analysis of the logs is presented in section 4. In section 5 we summarise our observations.

2 Data Collection

All user activity within the NZDL is automatically logged, and although actions can be associated with particular user identifiers, users themselves remain anonymous. The data that we consider here was collected in an 61 week period from April 1996 to July 1997. More than 30000 queries were recorded and analysed for the period in question.

User activities are time-stamped and include: query text, query options, documents viewed and the size of result sets. Query options include type (Boolean or ranked), stemming, case sensitivity, term proximity (within the same report, same page or first page), the maximum number of documents to return and the number of returned documents to display on each page of results. The log records the number of resulting documents that the user chooses to view for each query, as well as the location of those documents in the result list. Data from local users is not included in this analysis.

2.1 User demographics

Since users of the CSTR do not register for this database, the only information held on an individual's use is the IP address of the machine through which the collection was accessed. While this prevents us from incorporating detailed user demographics into the transaction log analysis, the design decision has had two practical advantages: users can immediately begin searching without spending time registering or verifying their account (an important consideration, given that this user group appears to prefer brief interactions with search systems); and anonymous access assures users of their privacy, so that user interest profiles specific to given individuals cannot be developed (again, a matter of concern for users of digital libraries [13]).

Examination of the search access by domain code (see Table 1) indicates that the heaviest use of the collection comes from North America, Europe (particularly Germany and Finland), as well as the local New Zealand community and nearby Australia. As expected for such a collection, a large proportion of users are from educational (.edu) institutions; surprisingly, however, a similar number of queries come from commercial (.com) organizations, perhaps indicating that the documents are seeing use in commercial research and development units.

3 Analysis of summary statistics

The raw data from the transaction logs is automatically processed and collated into tables of summary data. In this section we discuss a selection of this data.

	Boolean as default 46 week period	Ranked as default 15 week period	Total 61 week period
Number of queries	24687	8115	32802
Boolean queries	16333 (66.2%)	2693 (33.2%)	19026 (58%)
Ranked queries	8354 (33.8%)	5420 (66.8%)	13774 (42%)

Table 2. Frequency of Boolean and ranked queries

No. of terms in query	0	1	2	3	4	5	6	>6
Frequency (total=32796)	492	8788	11095	6505	2926	1477	692	821
Percentage	1.5	26.79	33.83	19.83	8.92	4.50	2.11	2.5

Table 3. Distribution of the number of terms in queries

3.1 User Acceptance of Default Settings

The logs reveal that users rarely amend default settings for query and result display options. With respect to query type (Boolean or ranked), only 33% of queries use non-default settings (see Table 2). This is consistent regardless of the default setting. Also, only 21% of queries changed the default term proximity setting. Default settings for case-sensitivity and stemming were changed even less frequently-in only 5% and 6% of queries respectively. The default result set size was changed in only 10.5% of user queries.

There are two possible interpretations of these observations. First, the default settings may be appropriate to the requirements of the majority of users. However this hypothesis is confounded by the fact that users tend to accept the default query type even though this default varied over the observation period. The second interpretation, that users tend to accept whatever defaults are set is, we believe, more likely. Consequently care must be taken to ensure the efficacy of those settings. Given the reluctance of searchers to use Boolean operators and the relatively small number of terms appearing in most queries (see section 3.2), we have settled on ranked querying as a default. Firstly, ranked queries are simpler to form, and the presence of the occasional extraneous Boolean operator in a ranked query often does not materially affect the result list (we also automatically detect and flag this situation as an error). Additionally, the ranking technique returns documents only partially matching the query, which often provides a richer set of hits than the full-match required by Boolean searching-and thus provide greater return for the short, simple queries preferred by users. Similarly, by setting query term stemming and

	Boolean as default 46 week period	Ranked as default 15 week period	Total 61 week period
Number of Boolean queries containing			
intersection	3731 (22.8%)	1178 (43.7%)	4909 (25.8%)
union	345 (2.1%)	122 (4.5%)	467 (2.5%)
negation	181 (1.1%)	35 (1.3%)	215 (1.1%)
compound expressions	682 (4.2%)	187 (6.9%)	869 (4.6%)

Table 4. Frequency of operators in Boolean queries

case insensitivity as the defaults, the system can partially compensate for brief queries through a de facto query expansion.

It is less clear what setting should be used as a default for term proximity. The CSTR interface supports three levels of proximity: query terms must appear within the same document, within the same page, or on the first page. The latter option is used mainly to force an approximation of title and author searching in the collection, as the documents are not formally catalogued and restricting the search to the first page is likely to pick up this sort of information. Currently, we set the proximity default at the whole document level, again to return as large a set of hits as possible. In practice, it is unclear whether this setting returns too many false drops; an additional user study is needed to confirm this default setting.

3.2 Query Complexity

The CSTR collection supports both ranked and Boolean querying (including intersection, union and negation operators and compound expressions formed through inclusion of parentheses). Queries tend to be short and simple-the average number of search terms in a query is 2.5 and just under 80% of queries contained one, two or three terms (see Table 3). Given this extreme query brevity the choice of each search term becomes crucial. We are investigating techniques to support users in selecting terms which accurately and concisely represent their information needs [11]

Just over a quarter of Boolean queries contained at least one intersection operator, only 2.5% contained at least one union operator and only 1% included the negation operator. Only 4.5% of Boolean queries contain compound expressions. By far the majority of Boolean queries use no Boolean operators at all (see Table 4). Consequently we might surmise that the underlying search engine need not be further optimised to process complex queries.

Number of Queries Issued in a User Session	Frequency % of Sessions
0	21.51
1	34.45
2	17.23
3	9.49
4	6.09
5	3.83
6	2.28
7	1.51
8	1.20
9	0.54
10	0.49

Table 5. Frequency of queries issued in user session

We might expect the target users of the CSTR (computing researchers) to be conversant with Boolean logic, yet they appear unwilling to apply it when searching. One explanation for this observation is that Boolean logic is ill-suited to specifying queries for information retrieval. Another is that the Boolean query language provided is too complex or restrictive to allow users to effectively specify queries. The literature suggests that difficulties with textual Boolean query languages are common [2, 3, 6]. Users must remember the appropriate symbols or keywords for the Boolean operators. There is a conflict between the inclusive AND of the English language and the exclusive AND of Boolean logic. Similarly, OR tends to be exclusive in English, but inclusive in Boolean logic. Also, textual Boolean query languages use a wide and inconsistent variety of representations for the operators. All of these issues lead users to produce erroneous queries or avoid Boolean expression if at all possible.

However, the use of Boolean expressions can support expressive and powerful querying. There is evidence to suggest that other presentations of the Boolean query model can be effective [5, 7]. For this reason we are investigating alternative interface metaphors for Boolean querying [9].

3.3 User Sessions

Approximately a fifth (21.51%)of all user sessions were visits to the NZDL WWW pages which did not entail the submission of a query. Just over a half (51.68%)of all sessions included submission of only one or two queries. Slightly more than a fifth (21.69%) included submission of three, four, five or six queries, and 5.12% included seven or more. These figures are shown in Table 5. From these figures it appears that many users are prepared to expend little effort in the development of sequences of queries to focus in on their topic of interest. Given that few, short queries resulting in

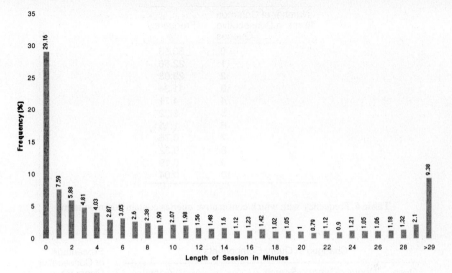

Fig. 1. Distribution of user session lengths

no documents being viewed are most common, we assume that a substantial portion of users end a session without having met their information seeking needs. We will need to carry out further investigation to determine just why so many users seem to abandon their query process prematurely.

The length of user sessions was also recorded. 29.16% of sessions lasted less that one minute (see Fig. 1). We assume that in these instances, users are merely investigating the NZDL rather than intending to undertake some querying activity. Over half (54.34%) of user session have duration of five or fewer minutes, and two thirds (66.43%) have a duration of ten minutes or less. Some users have long sessions, which leads to an average session length of 10.83 minutes. The length of session and number of queries submitted might be dependent on the user interface and facilities provided by the NZDL, or it might be the case that users make rapid judgements about whether to persevere with the use of such an on-line retrieval system. If this is the case then we must provide for immediate, effective searching.

3.4 Query Refinement

Analysis of users' consecutive queries reveals interesting aspects of query refinement behaviour. A set of 6680 user sessions was analysed and contained a total of 13650 queries. The majority (66.37%) of queries issued by users have at least one term (a word or phrase) in common with the previous query (see Table 6). These figures discount the first query issued by a user. Most often, consecutive queries have one or two terms in common (22.56% and 23.08% respectively). A further 11.34% have three terms in common and 9.39% have four or more in common. This high

Number of Common Terms in Consecutive Queries	Frequency %
0	33.53
1	22.56
2	23.08
3	11.34
4	4.71
5	2.22
6	1.15
7	0.76
8	0.32
9	0.19
10	0.04

Table 6. Frequency with which consecutive queries contain common terms

Changes to Query Components						Percentage of Consecutive Query Pairs With Change
Query String	Query Terms	Query Type	Search Granularity	Stemming	Case Sensitivity	
√	√					60.68
						13.75
√						5.66
		√				3.66
√	√	√				3.44
			√			2.72
√	√		√			2.56
√		√				1.19
√	√	√	√			1.03
					Other	5.31

Table 7. Frequency with which refinements are made within consecutive queries

incidence of term overlap implies that refinement is a common activity. Given that the average number of terms within a query is 2.5, and only a fifth of queries contain four or more terms, we believe that query refinement occurs in small incremental steps. User are likely to make minor changes by adding a new term, or altering the existing terms.

We can look more closely at exactly how queries are refined. In addition to query terms, the logs record how the attributes of consecutive queries change. These include the type of query (Boolean or ranked), the granularity of the search (document level, page level and so on), and the use of stemming and case-sensitivity. Most commonly it is only the terms within the query which are altered. This occurs

Changed Query Attribute	Percentage of Consecutive Query Pairs With Change
Query String	76.94
QueryTerms	69.46
Query Type	11.74
Search Granularity	8.75
Stemming	3.38
Case Sensitivity	1.35

Table 8. Frequency with which refinements are made within consecutive queries (including changes to more than one attribute)

in 60.68% of cases. The remaining 39.32% of cases contain a variety of combinations of attribute refinement. These are shown in Table 7. We have made a distinction between a query string and the terms within a query. The query string represents the query terms exactly as entered by the user. The query terms are extracted from this string for processing. Two different query strings may contain the same terms, but in a different order. In fact, this was the only change in 5.66% of cases. This may be explained by users amending term ordering in the belief that it would affect the results returned by ranked queries.

As we have noted, users rarely change default settings. This is reflected in the frequency with which settings were changed between consecutive queries. In 3.66% of cases the query type was changed but all other aspects of the query, including the query string and terms, remained the same. We might expect the query string and terms to change because of the insertion or removal of Boolean operators. This perhaps reveals a lack of understanding on the part of users, or in all of these cases only a single query term was involved. This remains to be investigated. In 3.44% of cases a change of query type was accompanied only by a change in query string and terms, which is what we might expect if these are multiple term queries. In 2.72% of cases the search granularity was the only attribute which was changed. An insignificant number of cases involved changes to only the case-sensitivity or stemming.

Table 8 shows the percentage of cases in which each of the attributes changed between consecutive queries, including when they changed in conjunction with other attributes. It is worth noting that in 13.75% of cases no aspects of the query changed. That is, exactly the same query was successively submitted. We believe that this is due to the effects of response time. For complex queries, or at times of heavy server loading, the response time might have been such that the users were unsure if their query had been successfully submitted, and tried again.

Overall, although query refinement is a common activity, the nature of refinement is very basic. Users of the CSTR tend to focus on amending query terms rather than attributes of a query. It is possible that the user interface mechanisms for making such changes are not sufficiently evident or intuitive, and we shall investigate this

Maximum number of documents to be returned	RANKED		BOOLEAN		TOTAL	
	Frequency	%	Frequency	%	Frequency	%
50	5515	95.61	2293	77.36	7808	89.42
100	54	0.94	176	5.94	230	2.63
200	42	0.73	162	5.47	204	2.34
500	157	2.72	333	11.23	490	5.61

Table 9. Frequency with which result list size options are selected

Documents viewed per query	RANKED		BOOLEAN		TOTAL	
	Frequency	%	Frequency	%	Frequency	%
0	3700	64.2	1909	64.4	5609	64.2
1	1103	19.1	573	19.3	1676	19.2
2	404	7.0	204	6.9	608	7.0
3	192	3.3	107	3.6	299	3.4
4	143	2.5	61	2.1	204	2.3
5	65	1.1	36	1.2	101	1.2
6	40	0.7	20	0.7	60	0.7
7	30	0.5	12	0.4	42	0.5
8	19	0.3	7	0.2	26	0.3
9	16	0.3	6	0.2	22	0.3
10	16	0.3	4	0.1	20	0.2
11-67	40	0.7	25	0.8	65	0.7

Table 10. Distribution of the number of documents viewed per query

through observational analysis of users. Few users consulted the on-line help documentation-just over 6% of user sessions contained accesses to help-which reinforces the notion that functionality must be as immediately and intuitively accessible as possible.

3.5 Result Viewing

In almost 90% of queries the default result set size of 50 documents was retained (see Table 9). Intermediate sizes of 100 and 200 were each requested in approximately 2.5% of queries, and a size of 500 was requested in almost 6% of queries. Again users seem content with default settings. However, we find a distinction when ranked and Boolean queries are considered separately. 95.6% of ranked queries, but only 77.4% of Boolean queries used the default setting. A substantial number of users

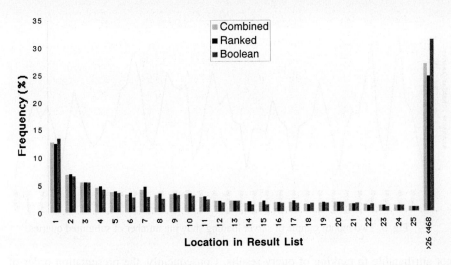

Fig. 2. Distribution of the result list location of viewed documents

require larger result sets to be returned when Boolean queries are used. With reflection, with seems sensible. Ranked queries imply that the most useful documents will be presented first, and consequently there may be little need to look past the first 50 resulting documents. With Boolean queries there is no ranking of the result set, and therefore users might retrieve and be more prepared to browse larger result sets to find interesting documents.

Disappointingly, the majority of queries (64.2%) do not lead to users viewing document content (see Table 10). Just over 19% of queries result in the viewing of one document, 12.7% result in the viewing of two, three or four documents, with around 4% resulting in the viewing of 5 or more. The distributions of the number of documents viewed for ranked and Boolean queries are very similar. The document summaries provided in query result lists appear to effectively support users in determining that they are *not* interested in particular documents. However, the queries that users form may be too simplistic to produce result lists which appropriately match their needs. Alternatively, the results returned may not be displayed at the appropriate granularity. For example, an uninteresting document title may hide the presence of a highly relevant subsection within the document. We are investigating the effects of passage level indexing and retrieval for this collection [14].

When users do view documents they are most likely to view those which are at the start of the result list (see Fig. 2). 12.7% of all viewed documents were located at the first position in the result list. The next most common location was the second position (6.8% of viewed documents). Nearly three- quarters (73.2%) of all documents retrieved were in the first 25 positions in the list. The similar document viewing distribution between ranked and Boolean queries implies that the effect is

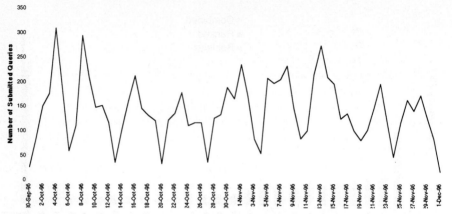

Fig. 3. Two month sample of server loading showing number of submitted queries

not attributable to ranking of query results. Consequently, the presentation order of result sets lists must be carefully considered.

3.6 Server Loading

Fig. 3 shows a representative two month extract of the logs from 30 September 1996 to 1 December 1996. The number of queries issued on each day in this period is shown. A pattern for access over each week can clearly be seen, and is repeated throughout the full logs. Each vertical bar is placed at a Monday (in New Zealand, the location of the NZDL server). The peaks and troughs of the graph correspond directly to weekdays and weekends. Although a reduction in usage might be expected throughout the weekend, access from North America on Friday (New Zealand Saturday) ensures that there is only one day per week when usage substantially drops. Such information can support planning of system maintenance and upgrading to cause minimum disruption to globally distributed users.

4 Manual analysis of transaction logs

To gain a finer grained appreciation of the types of searches that users conduct, the 30,000 queries were manually examined. While statistical analysis gives broad overviews of trends in usage, these summary tables cannot convey details of the semantic intent of the user queries. In this section, we discuss more qualitative information garnered from the transaction logs.

4.1 Spelling issues

Mis-spellings are relatively rare in the search terms; only approximately 240 of the searches contained incorrectly spelled words or typographical errors (although since the unusual number of acronyms in the computing field sometimes makes it difficult to determine whether a term is mis-spelled or mis-typed, this estimate should be regarded as a lower bound). The major problem detected with spelling was that few users took into account the differences between UK and American spellings when constructing their queries. While these differences may only cause minor losses in recall or precision for some disciplines, in computing the affected words are sometimes crucial parts of descriptive phrases: for example, "information seeking behavior/behaviour", or "data visualization/visualisation". Interestingly, some users appear to attempt to perform their own stemming, rather than setting the stemming option in the search interface (for example, searching for "chain & topology & algebrai & simpli").

Another difficult issue with computing terms is that many product names, protocols, program names, and so forth contain special characters. The underlying search engine for the CSTR collection, like many retrieval engines, strips special characters and retains only alphanumerics. While this situation is not problematic in many disciplines, for computing it means that, for example, it is difficult to locate documents about the language "C++" as distinct from the language "C". Additionally, it is unclear to users how they should represent strings containing special characters: for example, should they type "modula-3", "modula 3", or "modula 3"? Since most users do not read the system documentation, they must discover by trial and error that "modula-3" and "modula 3" map to the same internal query string.

4.2 Sub-collection choice

The New Zealand Digital Library architecture is designed as a collection of collections; rather than a single, homogenous digital library covering all subjects, it is instead seen by the users as a set of sub-collections each focussing on a different subject area. At the startup query page, the user must select the sub-collection to search as s/he enters the initial query. The transaction log was examined for indications that users were inappropriately searching the CSTR collection-that is, directing a query to the CSTR when another sub-collection would have been more suited to filling the user's apparent information need. Since computing is very much an applied field, it is difficult to categorically state that a given query is categorically not related to computer science; for example, the query "berrypicking" may refer to a particular model of the interaction between a user and an information retrieval system, and "snake" appears as a technical term in a surprising number of in theoretical computing and computer vision documents. However, upon examination of the logs we noted 149 queries that appeared highly unlikely to be pertinent to the CSTR collection. These queries fell into three categories: the searcher (not unnaturally) appeared to believe that a service with the title "New Zealand Digital Library" would contain general information about New Zealand ("kiwi bird", "1080 poison" [a possum poison very much in the news in NZ at that time]); the user believed that the digital library was a general search engine ("Anarcist [sic] cook book", "the civil war of america", "gay marriage"); or the search seemed to be aimed at retrieving documents held in the Gutenberg or Oxford Text Initiative collections ("Animal Farm by George Orwell", "I Know Why The Caged Bird Sings", "social satire").

Evidence for the first two cases is supported by noting a similar set of off-target queries having been posed to the CSTR reference librarian, who fielded requests for help from patrons having difficulty locating information in the CSTR collection [4]. The latter problem-users selecting the wrong sub-collection to search-appears to be due at least in part to the fact that the CSTR collection is pre-selected as the default in the radio button list of sub-collections on the initial query screen. Additionally, if the user pages back to the initial query screen after performing a query, then the default is automatically reset to the CSTR-and the user must notice this and change the target collection again. Currently, the CSTR is the largest sub-collection in the NZDL, and consequently receives the lion's share of usage. As the other collections grow, this problem in locating a relevant collection may be expected to grow as well, necessitating a re-design of the initial system page to direct users to appropriate document sets.

A further problem may that users simply do not understand the differences between the documents covered in each of the sub-collections. In addition to the 149 queries that were almost certainly not applicable to the CSTR, others were noted that seemed more appropriately directed at the NZDL's two sub-collections that include popular computing topics rather than to the more strictly academically focussed CSTR ("Microsoft Access 7.0", "pentium processor"). Again, this misunderstanding of the CSTR focus is supported by reference help requests for information on current popular computing topics [4]. This problem indicates a need to include more information on sub-collection focus in the initial system page, rather than storing these details in subsidiary information pages (as is currently the case).

4.3 Additional search strategies

As noted in the introduction, the CSTR collection is uncatalogued; users are limited to keyword searches. The system documentation suggests work-arounds for approximating some types of fielded searches (for example, limiting a search on an author's name to the first page, as most technical reports list the authors there). As noted in the previous section, few users consult the documentation or use the "first page only" option. However, examination of the logs reveals a significant number of queries that appear to be attempting to search on what would, in a formally catalogued system, be fielded document access points: author names, full document titles, technical report numbers, date of publication, author contact details (institute, email address), and journal or proceedings title. Users searching under publication details (such as journal or proceedings name) appear not to realize that the CSTR contains unpublished technical reports, and that these searches would be better directed to a different sub-collection containing a bibliography of published works.

Again, only an approximate measure of the number of appearances of these types of search can be taken; for example, it can be difficult to distinguish an uncapitalized author's name from a lowercase acronym, and some searches are undoubtedly intended as keyword searches for mention of a technique ("texture Fourier" is most likely intended to retrieve documents on the use of Fourier transforms in recognizing/rendering textures, rather than papers by Fourier). Given these caveats, roughly 17% of searches appear to include a name in the search string-a significant minority. Informal discussions with local (New Zealand) users indicates that some searches are indeed intended to retrieve documents where referenced individual is an author, while other searches take advantage of the fact that the entirety of the document is indexed and are attempting to locate matches in the reference sections-thereby retrieving documents that cite that author. In either case, the simple keyword search approach appears in some cases to be insufficiently precise, as evidenced by successive queries presenting the name in different formats (apparently in an attempt to guess the "correct" form in the collection index).

A handful of queries appeared to recognize that although by far the majority of documents in the CSTR are in English, the collection also contains technical reports in other languages. These user sessions included queries in German, sometimes with German translations of queries following the English terms ("heterogenous databases", "heterogene datenbanken"). Our current strategy for dealing with a multi-language document collections includes a multilingual interface (with help screens and query construction pages available in five languages); however, the NZDL does not currently support language-specific stemming over more than one language per collection, and does not permit the restriction of queries to a single language (primarily because the CSTR documents are not tagged by language). These issues remain to be incorporated into our digital library architecture.

5 Summary

The target user group for the CSTR collection-computer science researchers-might be expected to exhibit a propensity towards active exploration of new software and its functions. However, we have observed that the majority of users discriminate little when provided with tailorable querying options. Most accept the default settings, regardless of what those settings are. Very few investigate the system through supporting online documentation, or by experimentation with alternative settings and actions. Since this user group might be considered a 'best case' group for voluntary investigation of software this low level of interaction with the system indicates that initial default settings must be given full consideration.

Overall, user sessions are very short, few queries are submitted in those sessions, and the queries themselves are very simple. This strongly suggests that users wish to invest minimal time and effort in forming detailed specifications of their information needs. When refinement to queries does occur, users tend to make relatively small changes, most likely to involve addition or rearrangement of query terms. Little investigation of result sets occurs. Most user queries do not result in documents being viewed or retrieved, and it seems that users focus on only the first few returned documents. Consequently we must support users in converging rapidly on effective query terms and search options. Precision might be emphasised over recall in retrieving documents given that exploration of result sets appears to be minimal.

Many users seem to be familiar with fielded searching, as evinced by their attempts to use cataloguing information such as title or author in their keyword searches. We should be working towards capitalizing on this familiarity by focussing on soft-parsing or heuristic techniques for extracting bibliographic information from uncatalogued documents [1].

References

1. Bollacker, K.D,, Lawrence, S.,, Giles, C.L.: CiteSeer: an Autonomous Web Agent for Automatic Retrieval and Identification of Interesting Publications. *Proceedings of the Second International Conrerence on Autonomous* Agents, Minneapolis, St. Paul, May 9-13, (1998).
2. Borgman, C.L.: The User's Mental Model of an Information Retrieval System: an Experiment on a Prototype Online Catalog. *International Journal of Man-Machine Studies*, 24, 1 (1986) 47-64.
3. Borgman, C.L.: Why Are Online Catalogs Still Hard to Use? *Journal of the American Society for Information Science*, 47, 7 (1996) 493-503.
4. Cunningham, S.J.: Providing Internet Reference Services for the New Zealand Digital Library: Gaining Insight Into the User Base for a Digital Library. *Proceedings of the 10th International Conference on New Information Technology*, (1998) 27-34.
5. Davies, T., Willie, S.: The Efficacy of a Venn-based Query Interface: an Evaluation. In *Proceedings of QCHI95 Symposium*, Bond University, Queensland, Australia, August, (1995) 41-50.
6. Greene, S.L., Devlin, S.J., Cannata, P.E., Gomez, L.M.: No IFs, ANDs or ORs: a Study of Database Querying. *International Journal of Man-Machine Studies*, 32, 3, (1990) 303-326.
7. Halpin, T.A: Venn Diagrams and SQL Queries. *The Australian Computer Journal*, 21, 1, (1989) 27-32.
8. Jansen, B.J., Spink, A., Saracevic, T.: Failure Analysis in Query Construction: Data and Analysis from a Large Sample of Web Queries. *Proceedings of ACM Digital Libraries '98*, Pittsburgh, (1998) 289-290.
9. Jones, S., McInnes, S.: A Graphical User Interface for Boolean Query Specification. *Working Paper 97/31*, Dept. of Computer Science, University of Waikato, New Zealand, (1997).
10. McNab, R. J., Witten, I. H., Boddie, S. J.: A Distributed Digital Library Architecture Incorporating Different Index Styles. *Proceedings of the IEEE Forum on Research and Technology Advances in Digital Libraries*, Santa Barbara, CA, April, (1998) 36-45.

11. Nevill-Manning, C.G., Witten, I.H., Paynter, G.W.: Browsing in Digital Libraries: a Phrase-based Approach. *Proceedings of ACM Digital Libraries '97*, Philadelphia, (1997) 230-236.
12. Peters, T.A.: The History and Development of Transaction Log Analysis. *Library Hi Tech* 42 (11:2), (1993) 41-66.
13. Samuelson, P. Legally Speaking: Encoding the Law into Digital Libraries, *Communications of the ACM* 41, 4, (1998) 13-18.
14. Williams, M.: An Evaluation of Passage-Level Indexing Strategies for a Full-Text Document Archive. *LIBRES* 8, 1, (1998). Electronic publication, available at http://aztec.lib.utk.edu/libres/libre8n1/.

Illustrated Book Study:
Digital Conversion Requirements of Printed Illustrations

Anne R. Kenney, Louis H. Sharpe II, and Barbara Berger
Cornell University Library and Picture Elements, Inc.

ark3@cornell.edu, lsharpe@picturel.com, beb1@cornell.edu

Abstract. Cornell University Department of Preservation and Conservation and Picture Elements, Incorporated have undertaken a joint study for the Library of Congress to determine the best means for digitizing the vast array of illustrations used in 19th and early 20th century publications. This work builds on two previous studies. A Cornell study [1] characterized a given illustration type based upon its essence, detail, and structure. A Picture Elements study [2] created guidelines for deciding how a given physical content region type should be captured as an electronic content type. Using those procedures, appropriate mappings of different physical content regions (representing instances of different illustration processes) to electronic content types are being created. These mappings differ based on the illustration type and on the need to preserve information at the essence, detail, or structure level. Example pages that are typical of early commercial illustrations have been identified, characterized in terms of the processes used to create them (e.g., engraving, lithograph, halftone) and then scanned at high resolutions in 8-bit grayscale. Digital versions that retain evidence of information at the structure level have been derived from those scans and their fidelity studied alongside the paper originals. Project staff have investigated the available means for automatic detection of illustration content regions and methods for automatically discriminating different illustration process types and for encoding and processing them. A public domain example utility is being created which automatically detects the presence and location of a halftone region in a scan of an illustrated book page and applies special processing to it.

1.0 Introduction

Cornell University Library's Department of Preservation and Conservation and Picture Elements, Incorporated have undertaken a joint study for the U.S. Library of Congress to determine the best means for digitizing the vast array of illustrations found in 19th and early 20th century publications. This project is intended as the first step in the development of automated means for detecting, identifying, and treating each illustration process type in an optimal manner to create electronic preservation images. The technology does not currently exist to do this. In fact, no thorough attempt has been made to even characterize all of the features of importance for illustrations produced by a given production process, from the point of view of high-fidelity digital image capture.

The Illustrated Book study has a number of key objectives:

1. Select representative samples of relief, intaglio, and planographic illustration processes prevalent in book production in the 19th and early 20th century.

2. Characterize the key attributes of different illustration process types by subjective examination, identifying significant informational content for each type at three levels: essence, detail, and structure (see below).

3. Develop appropriate mapping of illustration content types to electronic content types that preserve their essential features to an appropriate degree.

4. Investigate methods for automatic detection of illustration content regions.

5. Investigate automatic methods to discriminate different illustration process types.

6. Investigate methods for processing different illustration process types.

7. Create an example utility for halftone detection and processing.

8. Report project results to the Library of Congress and to the broader preservation community.

As a result of this study, detailed guidance will be available on the best electronic imaging approaches to digitally preserve the range of book illustrations typically found in commercial publications from the past two centuries. The groundwork also will have been laid for further development that could lead to fully automated processing of such illustrations for the highest possible fidelity. This automated processing will be exceptionally useful during the next decade as cost-effective, high-quality production scanning will be needed to capture these materials for preservation in electronic libraries.

2.0 Project Methodology

2.1 Selecting Sample Pages

An advisory committee of Cornell curators, faculty, and other experts in printmaking and the graphic arts played a critical role in the selection process. Project staff consulted a number of extremely useful publications [3-5] in assembling a group of books and journals containing known illustration types. From this grouping, the advisory committee chose examples that best represent the range of printmaking techniques prevalent in the 19th and early 20th century commercial book trade. Twenty-two illustrations were selected from Cornell University Library's holdings (chart below includes 9 representative samples from this group). These included wood cuts, engravings, etchings, half-tone letterpress, dry-point, mezzotint, photogravure, lithographs, collotypes, and an Anastatic print. All examples appeared in bound volumes, either as separate plates or as illustrations on a text page, and they varied in size, level of detail, and sophistication of technique.

2.2 Characterizing the Attributes of Different Illustration Process Types

Determining what constitutes essential information is a subjective decision that must be based on a solid understanding of the nature and significance of the material to be converted. Advisory committee members participated in this process at Cornell. They characterized the key attributes of printed versions of the different illustration processes, and assessed the significant informational content that must be conveyed by an electronic surrogate to support various research needs. They were also asked to reflect on the intended uses of the sample documents in the context of their having been issued as part of larger published works rather than as individual pieces of art.

Three levels of presentation were determined:
- *essence*: representing what the unaided eye can detect at normal viewing distances.
- *detail*: representing the smallest significant part typically observable close up or under slight magnification, e.g., five times.
- *structure*: representing the process or technique used to create the original. The level required for a positive identification of the illustration type will vary with the process used to create it. For instance, it is easy to make a positive identification of a woodcut or a halftone with the unaided eye. The telltale "black lace" of an

aquatint, however, may only be observable at magnification rates above 27x.

The assessment process was well documented, and the table located at the end of this paper was created.

2.3 Mapping Illustration Process Types to Electronic Content Types

Once the various illustration process types have been characterized subjectively, one can then define their attributes objectively, e.g., by measuring the spatial extent of the finest lines or the tonal range of the subtlest contrast features. The next step involves translating the objective measurements of the original illustration into similar assessments that pertain directly to the electronic version. Digital imaging is a process of representing an original document by sampling and mapping it as a grid of uniform dots or picture elements (pixels). Each pixel is assigned a tonal value and represented as a digital number.

The appropriate mapping of illustration process types to electronic content types is being addressed according to:

1. the "process" used and its corresponding telltale structural attributes, and, more importantly,
2. the identification of generic graphic attributes that affect digital (as opposed to analog) conversion. These include, but are not limited to: key feature shape, size, spacing, uniformity and smoothness; tonality variation across fine features; scale size of textures; printing process used; screen size and angle; and so on.

2.4 Digitizing Sample Pages

The project team is assessing how resolution, bit depth, compression, and, to a lesser degree, image processing and enhancement, work together to replicate in the digital image the significant informational content of the original source documents.

Each sample page was scanned at a variety of resolutions with 8-bit grayscale data captured. Grayscale data is essential to reproduce the subtleties of tonality inherent in many of the illustration types. It also permits accurate representation of fully bitonal features (having little tonality) when the feature size decreases toward the size of the image sampling function. Grayscale images allow various techniques used by skilled illustration artisans to have the intended tonal effects. For example, grayscale can preserve the modulation of the acid bite in an etching or the variation of the depth of a gouge in an engraving. Grayscale further permits the production of reduced-resolution images from a high-resolution original by means of accurate scaling algorithms.

All illustrations were captured at a fixed spatial resolution of approximately 24 dots per millimeter (600 dots per inch) with an attempt made to capture the entire page which incorporates the illustration. These *full* view images were captured on a PhaseOne PowerPhase camera back having a 7072 pixel moving tri-linear color CCD array. A Hasselblad camera body and Zeiss lenses were used, with a TG-1 filter intended to produce a photopic-like response from the array's wavelength characteristics and the tungsten lighting (using ENH-type reflector bulbs). A color balanced grayscale output was created by the PhaseOne system from the red, green, and blue inputs.

For some finely inscribed images, a high magnification was used to capture close-up views of their structure. These *zoom* images were captured on a Kodak Ektron 1400 series camera, having a 4096 element moving linear grayscale CCD array. Nikon 35 mm enlarging lenses and extension tubes were used.

It was determined that in most cases the *full* view images successfully represented the structure of the different illustration processes. A set of images at several lower spatial resolutions was created from these source images by a process of bi-linear interpolation. These images were then used by members of the advisory committee to determine minimum spatial resolutions for preserving the structure and the detail characteristics of the different illustration processes. The lower resolution images derived from the full images also formed the starting point for investigations into the image processing techniques best suited to preserving the essence of each illustration type for access purposes.

2.5 Evaluating Sample Images

The advisory committee that assisted in identifying the distinguishing characteristics of the originals was also involved in assessing the digital surrogates at three levels of view. These levels are being evaluated as follows:

- *Essence*: A judgment on how well the electronic version has captured essence is based on a side-by-side examination of the original and a printed facsimile produced from the digital file at normal reading distance, viewed by the unaided eye.
- *Detail*: An assessment of detail capture is based on how well on-screen and printed versions of the digital images can represent the smallest significant part of the original as viewed close up and/or under slight magnification, e.g., five times.
- *Structure*: Both on-screen and printed facsimiles of the digital images are being assessed to determine the extent to which they can convey the information necessary to distinguish one illustration process type from another. This assessment involves viewing the originals under various levels of magnification and comparing them to full resolution on-screen images at 1:1 or 2:1.

While *detail* and *structure* relate to the objective fidelity of a digital representation at different magnifications, the *essence* characteristic is a subjective evaluation of the psycho-visual experience a reader has at normal viewing distance in the context of a page.

Digital requirements for the *essence* view were based on what a person with 20/20 vision could expect to discern at a normal reading distance of 16". According to optometrists', such a person can distinguish a small letter "e" which subsumes 5 minutes of arc at that distance. The "e" comprises five parts, each of which represents 1 minute of arc. A minute of arc represents 1/60 of a degree, or .01667 degrees. To determine the size of the smallest feature discernible at 16", the following formula is used: $x/16 = \tan(.01667)$; so $x=.004656$ inches. This means that a person with 20/20 vision can detect features as fine as $1/215^{th}$ of an inch (118 micrometers) at a 16" distance.

These human visual capabilities suggest that a reasonable requirement for preserving the essence on a page is to have one to two pixels span the finest perceivable feature. If one dot were used to cover that distance, the resolution required to capture such detail would equal 1/.004656, or 215dpi. If two dots were used to span that distance, the resolution required to capture such detail would equal 215 x 2, or 430 dpi. We suspect that the needed resolution to consistently represent the essence of a page lies somewhere between these two [6].

Digital requirements for the *detail* view were pegged at 5x magnification. If the human eye can discern 215 dpi at normal reading distance, then a detail view would represent 5 times 215, or 1075 dpi. The project staff and advisory committee will assess how well these mathematical projections translate into visual realities.

Digital requirements to reflect the *structure* view were determined by measuring the finest features associated with each of the illustration process types, which for all but the finest of them (collotype, photogravure, and mezzotint) measured 0.04mm or greater. Again, assuming that one to two dots are required to span the finest feature, we can calculate the resolution needed to preserve structural information in the digital surrogate. In some cases, the resolution requirements for both detail view and structural view are the same. These mathematical projections will be confirmed and/or modified by the advisory committee at its third meeting (scheduled for August 1998). They can also be used to project costs and times associated with the capture and delivery of such views.

From this assessment process will come recommendations for the digital conversion requirements for the broad range of illustration types found in 19th and 20th century publications. These recommendations will be verified by scanning additional sample illustrations using the available scanning equipment located in the Department of Preservation and Conservation, Cornell University Library.

2.6 Investigating Methods for Automatic Detection of Illustration Content Regions

Many approaches to segmentation of mixed content pages have been published in the open literature as part of the domain of research referred to as document understanding. Picture Elements is investigating the approaches other researchers have taken in identifying graphic illustration regions within a book page image by performing a detailed survey of the literature. These methods are being evaluated for their robustness when faced with the varieties of illustration process types prevalent in commercial publication from the past two centuries. This step of the investigation is simply concerned with the detection of illustrations of any type, not the discrimination of one type from another.

2.7 Investigating Automatic Methods to Discriminate Different Illustration Process Types

Given a set of appropriate mappings of illustration process types to electronic content types, the next step is to discriminate among those illustration types that require different electronic treatments. By studying the statistical and morphological details of the various illustration types which must be discriminated, characteristic signatures in the electronic images of the captured example pages are being sought that allow for the classification of a given illustration's type with some degree of accuracy. Although these methods will not be implemented in software during this project, the methods used will be designed with such a future implementation in mind.

2.8 Investigating Methods for Processing Different Illustration Types

The most appropriate electronic treatment of a given illustration type has two components. The first is the set of parameters that describe the electronic image (such as spatial resolution, grayscale bits per pixel, and so on). The second component comprises any additional processing that must be applied to that electronic image to place it into final form for either viewing on a computer monitor or for printing. These two destinations will likely require different processing steps. These processes might include:

- *Inverse Halftoning.* Conversion of halftone dots (at some screen spacing) from one electronic image (at some spatial resolution) into multitonal pixel values (at possibly yet another spatial resolution). The original electronic image for this process might be either a binary image or a multitonal image.

- *Thresholding.* Conversion of a multitonal image to a bitonal image based upon either the brightness at a given picture element (global or adaptive level thresholding) or upon the presence of edges of sufficient strength (edge thresholding).

- *Smoothing.* Modification of edge boundaries in a bitonal image to reduce edge raggedness, such as might have been produced by the illustration process, the printing process (paper texture or ink spreading), the digitization process, or the thresholding process.

- *Low-Pass Filtering.* Modification of a multitonal image via a convolution kernel to reduce its apparent resolution by removing data at higher spatial frequencies. Sometimes used to remove Moiré patterns or other scanning artifacts.

- *Edge Enhancement Filtering.* Modification of a multitonal image via a convolution kernel to increase the energy of data at higher spatial frequencies. Sometimes used to enhance "muddy" or blurred originals.

- *Halftoning (or re-halftoning).* Conversion of a multitonal image to a bitonal image in such a manner as to retain the impression of multiple tones.

- *Compression.* Insofar as compression may be lossy, it also constitutes a processing step that may affect the image's appearance in useful or non-useful ways. Appropriate compression types will vary with the electronic image type and its "texture." For example, halftoned representations of multitonal data may require JBIG compression to achieve a sufficiently small compressed size.

- *Scale-to-Gray.* When high-resolution bitonal images are destined for a lower-resolution presentation (as on a video monitor), this process moves information from the spatial domain to the tone domain to preserve legibility.

For each distinguishable class of illustration type (each member of which shares a set of attributes measurable in the originally captured electronic image), a set of appropriate processing steps is being identified both for the final printable image and for the final screen-viewable image. Sample processed images will be created for those processing chains that can be created with off-the-shelf imaging tools without additional programming.

2.9 Creating an Example Utility for Halftone Processing

Halftones are particularly difficult to capture in digital format, as the screen of the halftone and the grid comprising the digital image will often conflict with one another, resulting in distorted digital image files exhibiting Moiré patterns. A method for satisfactorily converting halftones is most pressing, as the halftone letterpress process became one of the most dominant illustration types used in commercial book runs beginning in the 1880s.

This project will result in the development of a practical, working utility to detect the presence and location of a halftone region on a page (known to contain a halftone) and appropriately process that halftone region independently from its surrounding text. The design goal for the utility is to process a stream of book page images containing three types of information:

1. text-only pages, where the utility does nothing;
2. halftone-only pages, which the utility processes in various ways, and
3. pages containing halftone regions in addition to text, where the utility identifies the halftone regions (by bounding rectangles), and processes the halftone regions in various ways.

Since this utility will not be embedded inside a specific scanner, but will run externally on a UNIX server, it may be used on data from any scanner that can supply the appropriate raw bit stream (e.g., unprocessed grayscale of a sufficient spatial resolution).

The utility will be developed on one of the Library of Congress' RS/6000 servers by remote access over the Internet. Testing will be performed on that machine. Testing at Cornell will either be performed via remote Internet access to the Library server or by porting the developed software to an appropriate UNIX machine (also Internet accessible) at Cornell. The utility will be released into the public domain under the BookTools Project (http://www.picturel.com/booktools).

Two separate utilities are being developed: find_ht and un_ht:
- *find_ht* accepts a single page grayscale image file as input and returns a description of a bounding rectangle for the largest halftone region found. As an additional input it can accept a list of several rectangle descriptors which define keep-out areas. This feature can be used (through multiple calls to find_ht) to iteratively find all halftone regions on a page.
- *un_ht* accepts a single page grayscale image file and the coordinates of a bounding rectangle as input. It applies the processes that are appropriate to the attributes of the halftone and retains key structural information. The result is an output image file containing a processed version of the image data found within the specified rectangular area of the input image.

2.10 Testing and Verifying the Process

Cornell University Library Department of Preservation will test and evaluate the prototype utility for halftone processing against documents containing a range of halftones, from 70 line to 175 line screens placed at varying angles on the page. The pages will be taken from both serial and book publications; some will be represented as separate plates and others within a page of text; and they will date from the 1880s to 1940s. The results of this process will be compared to those obtainable using the halftone processing developed by Xerox Corporation and incorporated into the XDOD scanning system used extensively at Cornell in the brittle book conversion projects.

2.11 Preparing and Distributing the Final Report

A detailed report will be prepared by December 1998 that summarizes all the findings and includes example images. This report will be in electronic form for dissemination over the Internet. A loose-leaf volume incorporating a set of printouts also will be delivered to the Library of Congress.

3.0 Conclusion

This study will produce a number of important results. The means for characterizing the key features of book illustrations as they pertain to digital image capture will be developed and guidelines for assessing conversion requirements recommended. This is especially critical for publications from the mid-19th century to the mid-20th century which were printed on paper that has become brittle. These volumes must be copied to preserve their informational content, and by defining preservation quality requirements for electronic conversion, digital imaging can become an attractive alternative to conventional means of reformatting, such as microfilming and photocopying. The guidelines for conversion requirements for the range of book illustration types may be used immediately by cultural institutions in stipulating digital capture requirements in Requests for Proposals for outsourced conversion projects.

The basic groundwork for preparing an automated method for detecting and processing different illustration types will be completed, and an example utility for processing halftones developed and tested. The halftone processing utility in particular will be a most welcome addition in the preservation tool kit. Based on Cornell's experience in outsourcing conversion efforts, one of the major difficulties encountered has been in the capture of halftone information. Many of the digital files for halftone pages received from outside vendors exhibit Moiré patterns, and the pages containing halftones must be reconverted in-house and treated in a one-by-one fashion. Obviously the ability to automate their treatment in a manner to ensure full informational capture that is free of distortion would be of tremendous benefit to cultural repositories that are converting late 19th century and early 20th century materials.

Since the halftone utility addresses a vertical slice of the more general problem of distinguishing and appropriately processing a wide range of illustrations, it will likely not perform properly when presented with other illustration types. Nonetheless, this work lays the groundwork for characterizing and processing other graphic illustration types. Some of these may exhibit halftone-like attributes, such as line engravings and etchings that are produced using a fine and highly regular pattern of lines or hatch marks, and it may be possible to extend the automated utility in a future project to include them. Beyond the scope of this present project, the intent is to later develop additional utilities for processing the remaining illustration types.

This project also facilitates a shift in thinking about how to create the highest possible image quality for a given collection. This new capture architecture has the appropriate raw grayscale or color data collected from any scanner whose document handling capabilities suit the peculiarities of a particular item, such as a bound volume, a 35mm slide, or a 40 inch wide architectural drawing. The scanner choice can be made on the basis of its physical suitability and the quality of its raw image data, without regard to any special processing needs associated with the source document itself. All special processing and manipulation of raw data from these various sources is then performed in an off-line, largely scanner-independent manner by a centralized server we might call a post-processing server. In this way we are not constrained by the variable and inconsistent processing offered within the many different scanners which are needed to overcome the physical peculiarities of each item in a collection. This work will be particularly important in developing the means for capturing bound volumes without having to resort to disbinding or to the creation of photo-intermediates. This work will benefit cultural institutions inaugurating digital imaging projects involving a range of source documents, including the bound illustrated book.

Table 1. Common Book Illustrations of the 19th and 20th Centuries. See on-line supplement for images that represent essence, detail, and structure at: http://www.library.cornell.edu/preservation/illustratedbookstudy/illusbooktable.htm

ILLUSTRATION TYPE	PREVALENCE	ILLUSTRATION CHARACTERISTICS	CHARACTERISTICS OF SPECIFIC EXAMPLE
RELIEF PRINTING	Most Common Method of this Era	• Raised print surface: "white" surface removed to leave "black" printing surface • Matte or glossy paper; separate plate or presented in text; little to no tonal variation	
Wood Engraving[8]	1400s- Present	• Created along the end grain of wood • Technique permits finer detail than woodcut • Line width varies. • Ink appears darker around edges • Illustration varies depending upon where it is in the press run.	• Typical of 1860s school • Carefully tooled • Presented on text page • Matte paper
Halftone[9]	1880s-Present	• Photo-mechanical reproduction process • Regularly spaced dots of variable sizes • Ridges of ink along dot edges • Poor reproduction of detail	• 166 screen ruling at 45 degrees • Halftone of a painting • Presented on text page • Glossy paper
INTAGLIO PRINTING		• Recessed print surface: "black" areas removed to create grooves to hold ink • Tonal variation created by groove depth; separate plate or presented in text	
Steel Engraving[10]	1820s-Present	• Grooves or pits are scribed into steel surface. • Lines are fine, uniform, smooth, and parallel, with crisp edges that tend to be pointed at the end.	• Typical example • Presented on text page • Matte paper

INTAGLIO PRINTING	1400s-Present	• Recessed print surface: "black" areas removed to create grooves to hold ink • Tonal variation created by groove depth; separate plate or presented in text	
Copper Engraving[11]	1700-1880s	• Lines are fine, uniform, smooth, and parallel, with crisp edges that tend to be pointed at the end. • Softer than steel; large print runs show signs of plate wear, with loss of fine lines	• Topographical scene • Separate plate; no plate mark • Matte paper, covered with protective sheet
Etching[12]	1600s-1880s	• Wax or gelatin covered plate etched, then dipped in acid. • Lighter lines than engraving, width varies as result of acid dips	• Separate plate; plate mark is present • Matte paper
Photogravure[13]	1880s-	• Photo-mechanical reproduction process • Varied amounts of ink on page offers excellent reproduction of detail, good tonal variation • Irregular aquatint grain or very fine screen pattern of soft, ragged dots	• Representation of photograph, reproduced in warm brown tone • Separate plate; plate mark present • Matte paper, covered with protective sheet
Mezzotint[14]	1780s-1870s	• Tonal engraving method in which the plate surface is covered with closely placed dots. The serrations are then burnished so that they hold large or small amounts of ink.	• Typical example • Separate plate; plate mark present • Matte paper, covered with protective sheet

PLANOGRAPHIC PRINTING		• Flatness of both paper and ink, wide tonal variation possible.	
Lithograph[15]	1820s-Present	• Image drawn directly on the printing surface • Drawing substance must be greasy • Fixed to the printing surface by sponging with gum arabic and weak acid	• Two-stone lithograph; light blue-green under-layer • Separate plate, no plate mark • Matte paper
Collotype[16]	1870s-1910	• Photomechanical reproduction process • Telltale random and fine cracks (reticulation). • Process is used where accuracy of tone is important; excellent detail rendering	• Collotype of an engraving • Reticulation apparent • Printed on separate paper, trimmed, and pasted into the book • Glossy paper, covered with protective sheet

References

1. Kenney, Anne R. and Chapman, Stephen: Digital Imaging for Libraries and Archives. Cornell University Library, Ithaca, New York (1996)
2. Picture Elements, Inc.: Guidelines for Electronic Preservation of Visual Materials, Library of Congress Preservation Directorate, Washington, D.C. (1995)
3. Reilly, James M.: Care and Identification of 19th-Century Photographic Prints, Eastman Kodak, Rochester, New York (1986)
4. Wakeman, Geoffrey: Victorian Book Illustration, Newton Abbot, Norwich, Great Britain (1973)
5. Gascoigne, Bamber: How to Identify Prints, Thames and Hudson, New York, New York (1986)
6. Brenni, Vito J.: Book Illustration and Decoration, A Guide to Research, Greenwood Press, Westport, Connecticut (1980)
7. Wandell, Brian A.: Foundations of Vision, Sinauer Associates, Inc., Sunderland, Massachusetts (1995) Wandell makes reference to studies showing that, at high ambient light levels, the highest detectable spatial frequency is 50 to 60 cycles per degree (cpd). Since there are 60 minutes of arc in one degree of arc, this says we need two digital samples (one for the black bar of the cycle and one for the white bar of the cycle) in one minute of arc or 120 of them in one degree of arc. This is reasonably consistent with the optometrists' metric, which is based on visual perception under normal light conditions.
8. Shakespeare, William: Shakspere's songs and Sonnets, S. Low, London, England (1875?), 26
9. Harper's magazine, New York, (v. 99 ,1899) 55
10. Rogers, Samuel: Italy; a poem , E. Moxon, London, England (1854) 79
11. Russell, William S: Pilgram memorials, and Guide to Plymouth, Crosby and Ainsworth, Boston, Massachusetts (1866) 80
12. Hamerton, Philip G: Chapters on animals, Seeley, Jackson, and Halliday, London, England (1883) 144
13. Earland, Ada: Ruskin and his circle, Hutchinson & Co., London, England (1910) frontispiece
14. Cellini, Benvenuto: The Life of Benvenuto Cellini, John C. Nimmo, London, England (1896) frontispiece
15. Valentine, David T.: History of the City of New York, Putnam, New York, New York (1853) 183
16. Piozzi, Hester Lynch: Dr. Johnson's Mrs. Thrale: autobiography, letters, and literary remains of Mrs. Piozzi, Foulis, Edinburgh, Scotland (1910) 89

Structuring Facilities in Digital Libraries

Peter J. Nürnberg[1], Uffe K. Wiil[2], and John J. Leggett[3]

[1] Department of Computer Science, Aarhus University,
Ny Munkegade 116, Bldg 540, DK-8000 Århus C, Denmark
pnuern@daimi.aau.dk
[2] Department of Computer Science, Aalborg University Esbjerg,
Niels Bohrs Vej 8, DK-6700 Esbjerg, Denmark
ukwiil@aue.auc.dk
[3] Center for the Study of Digital Libraries, Texas A&M University,
College Station, TX, 77843-3112, USA
leggett@csdl.tamu.edu

Abstract. Digital libraries offer much promise for patrons and many challenges for system designers and implementers. One important issue that faces digital library system designers is the type of support provided to patrons for intellectual work. Although many researchers have noted the desirability of robust hypermedia structuring facilities in digital library systems, this research has tended to focus on navigational hypermedia (primarily used for associative storage and retrieval) only. Many other types of hypermedia, such as spatial, issue-based, and taxonomic, have been ignored. We briefly review some of our experiences with building digital library systems and discuss some of the lessons we learned from our initial prototypes. We then present a scenario of digital library work that illustrates many of the kinds of tasks we have observed users of our systems perform. We use this scenario to suggest a potential area of improvement for current hypermedia support in digital library systems and discuss some of our initial work in this area. Finally, we present some directions of future work and some concluding remarks.

1 Introduction

Libraries are much more than physical collections of data. They are institutions that filter and select information based on space, cost, and quality criteria; professionals that generate metadata about their collections and offer support to their patrons; social organizations that provide the basis for collaborative work; and, much more. The degree to which *digital libraries* can and will assume these and other roles has been and continues to be the subject of much research [8, 15, 16, 25, 29, 34]. Above all, it is clear that digital libraries are much more than electronic collections of data – they are virtual analogs to the complex organizations that are physical libraries [21, 28, 46].

We can call the software and hardware parts of a digital library a *digital library system*. In this paper, we examine one technology – hypermedia – that has received much attention in discussions about digital library systems [3, 7, 39,

43, 45, 47]. Despite the recognition that hypermedia has received to date in this area, current work has tended to focus heavily on only one particular type of hypermedia structure, namely, navigational. Navigational hypermedia structures are mostly suited for supporting associative storage and retrieval. Several other types of hypermedia structures suited to supporting other problem domains have been reported upon, e.g.: spatial [23], which focuses on supporting information analysis tasks; issue-based [27, 44], which focuses on supporting argumentation and capture of design rationale; and, taxonomic [33, 35, 36], which focuses on supporting classification tasks. All of these types of structure share certain basic notions, although each also has its own specialized and tailored abstractions. Despite the potential usefulness of these structures for digital library patrons, little work has been done to date on providing this kind of support within digital library systems. We argue that digital library system designers should extend the navigational hypermedia facilities in many digital library systems to include tailored structural abstractions such as those found in found in spatial, issue-based, taxonomic, and other kinds of hypermedia.

The remainder of this paper is structures as follows. Firstly, we consider the current state of hypermedia support in digital library systems. Secondly, we discuss some of our own past work in this area, and describe some of the lessons we have learned from our experiences. Thirdly, we present a scenario of digital library use, distilled from our experiences with users of our systems. This scenario illustrates a recurrent need for the kinds of flexible structure management provided by various kinds of hypermedia systems. Fourthly, we consider the notion of *structural computing*, or generalized hypermedia, and describe its implications for digital library system design. Finally, we present some of our work in applying structural computing principles to digital library system design, describe directions of future work, and provide some concluding remarks.

2 Hypermedia and Digital Libraries

In this section, we look at the role hypermedia currently plays in digital library system design. We first examine the type of hypermedia most often provided in a digital library setting and the problem domain it was designed to address. We then consider open hypermedia systems, which represents one of the most commonly accepted ways in which to provide this hypermedia functionality.

2.1 Traditional Hypermedia Problem Domain

The first hypermedia researcher is generally taken to be Vannevar Bush, who, in 1945, described the problem of information overload and one possible method for coping with it [4]. He proposed an information structuring system called the Memex ("memory extender") that would allow its users to associate arbitrary pieces of information and navigate over these associations. Bush reasoned that since people used associations to store and retrieve information in and from their own minds, a machine that provided this ability would be useful for storing and retrieving information in and from external sources. He realized that alongside organization schemes built on community conventions (such as alphabetization, Library of Congress classification, etc.), people often retrieved (or found) information by navigating through information spaces using arbitrary and idiosyncratic associations. The Memex would allow such idiosyncratic associative structures to be created, stored, and then retrieved at a later time during navigation of the information space. These developments later led to many *navigational hypermedia* systems, starting in the early 1960's (e.g., NLS [6]) and continuing through to today (e.g., the WWW [2]). All navigational hypermedia systems primarily focus on addressing the problem of *associative storage and retrieval*.

The case for powerful navigational hypermedia in digital library systems has been made by a number of researchers [3, 7, 16, 39, 43, 45]. Most of these researchers have noted the usefulness of associative structures in locating tasks performed by patrons. Such structures can help patrons find information they might otherwise have missed. They are also useful as a kind of metadata, since they are a form of implicit commentary or annotation on the associated data that can help patrons understand this data more fully. In most hypermedia systems designed for supporting digital libraries, structure is stored separately from data, allowing patrons to make private associations or selectively view the associations provided by the library.

2.2 Traditional Open Hypermedia Systems

One approach to providing navigational hypermedia within a digital library is to integrate a (traditional) open hypermedia system (OHS) into the digital library system. An OHS is one that provides navigational hypermedia facilities to an open set of (often third-party) clients orthogonal to their data storage machanisms [5]. The advantages of providing navigational hypermedia through an open system as opposed to within a closed, monolithic one are well documented [26, 37]. One of these advantages is that an OHS does not modify the data over which it defines its structure – data may and often are managed by entities other than the OHS. Instead, the OHS publishes an interface that allows arbitrary clients that manipulate arbitrary data to make use of structuring facilities, including persistent structure storage. Note that the term *open* in this context has a quite specific meaning. A hypermedia system may be open in the traditional sense of the word if it allows arbitrary clients to interact with it through a published interface. However, it may not be an open *hypermedia* system if it does not provide structuring facilities over arbitrary data types handled by the client. An example of such a system is the WWW. Although a WWW server may interact with an open set of browsers, such browsers may only take advantage of the structure inherent in the markup of HTML files. Traditional WWW servers cannot define structures over arbitrary data types. For example, it is not possible for a WWW server to store a link between frames in two mpeg movies. Thus, the WWW is an open system, but not an OHS. Building a digital library system with integrated open hypermedia support allows new clients that handle arbitrary data types to be added to the digital library system and still take advantage of existing hypermedia functionality. Some examples of traditional OHS's are Chimera [1], DHM [10], Microcosm [5], and SP3/HB3 [19]. All of these systems have integrated numerous clients, both third party and specially built. Additionally, many of these systems have been integrated (in different ways and to different degrees) with the WWW, providing external structure storage to WWW browsers in a way that does not modify the data (unlike traditional HTML markup). Some of these experiments have been reported in [9, 13]. Fig. 1 illustrates a common generic OHS architecture.

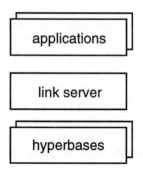

Fig. 1. A generic open hypermedia system architecture. The *link server* provides navigational hypermedia services to an open set of clients, called *applications*. In turn, these link servers use the services of an open set of persistent structure stores, called *hyperbases* (hypermedia databases [41, 42, 49]).

3 Experiences

In this section, we briefly review some of our own experiences with building digital library systems, especially focusing on the provision of hypermedia functionality within these systems. We begin by introducing the kinds of collections we have used to populate our digital library testbeds. We continue by providing an overview the SP3/HB3 environment and its applications to supporting our digital library efforts. We conclude by pointing out some of the key lessons we learned from our experience. More complete treatments of our prototypes and experiences to date are available in [32, 33, 47].

3.1 Botanical Collections

For several years, we have worked together with botanical taxonomists to build a digital library of herbarium collection data. This work has gone on in cooperation with collection managers and botanical taxonomists at the Texas A&M

University herbarium, which contains over 250,000 dried plant specimens, and with members of the Flora of Texas Consortium, who are seeking to distribute a collection of nearly 6000 taxonomic records defined over 1,000,000 specimens.

For reference, we present a short description of the botanical taxonomic problem. The object of botanical taxonomic classification is the taxonomy. A taxonomy consists of taxa, which themselves consist of other taxa or plant specimens. Taxa are composed in a hierarchic fashion. That is, the taxonomy itself may be viewed as a tree, with specimens at the leaves. Taxa at different levels in the tree have different names, such as family, genus, species, etc.

We have noticed a number of interesting characteristics of the botanical classification work that occurred over our digital library collections and over botanical collections in general. We mention three of these here, concentrating on the implications for any system that is designed to support such work.

1. *Different groups of taxonomists impart different characteristics to identical taxa.* Even if two groups of taxonomists agree on the definition of a taxon in terms of its subtaxa, supertaxon, and component specimens, they may disagree on other attributes of the taxon, such as its name. Such debates are viewed as important intellectual work by taxonomists. This implies the need for treating taxa as first-class entities in the system, allowing them to carry arbitrary attribute/value pairs, be versioned, locked for collaborative work sessions, etc.

2. *Different groups of taxonomists produce different taxonomies, even if the specimen set examined is identical.* Groups in which particular specialists work on a given taxon may show more detail in the expansion of that taxon, or different groups may use different measures of similarity when composing taxa, weighting various types of evidence differently. This implies the need for versioning (with respect to taxonomic authority) for the taxonomies generated over the given specimen data.

3. *The products of botanical classification work are often full taxonomies, not simply revisions to existing taxonomies.* Whether updates or new revisions, products are viewed as closed and well-defined entities, representing the opinion of a particular group at a specific time. These static snapshots of work belie the complexity of botanical classification work, however. New evidence, analysis methods, and interpretations are constantly being introduced. The practice of generating these static snapshots comes from the limitations of non-electronic media. However, such closed products are useful for consumption by others. Ideally, authors should view their collective product as open, while readers should be able to view some closed subset of this work. This implies the need for computation of structure that can generate such closed products dynamically.

3.2 SP3/HB3

SP3/HB3 [19] is an OHS developed at Texas A&M University in the mid 1990's. Roughly speaking, its architecture corresponds to the one shown in Fig. 1, with the addition of another type of architectural entity called a metadata manager. Metadata managers are architectural peers of the link server, mediating interactions between applications and hyperbases. Like the link server, they also provide specialized and tailored abstractions to their clients. Unlike the link server, however, they derive their specialized abstractions from the data abstractions provided by the hyperbase. The link server, on the other hand, builds upon the structural abstractions of the hyperbase.

HB3 is the name of the hyperbase in the SP3/HB3 environment. It is implemented on top of a relational database management system (DBMS). The latest instance of HB3 was built on top of the Illustra DBMS [14], although previous versions resided on top of other DBMS's. HB3 provides its clients with generic data and navigational structural abstractions. These abstractions may be tagged with arbitrary attribute/value pairs. It also provides basic concurrency, access, and version control mechanisms for both data and structure objects.

The Link Services Manager (LSM) is the SP3/HB3 link server. It provides basic link authoring and browsing functionality to an open set of clients through a simple API. Applications wishing to use these services must register with an instance of the LSM and communicate (and respond to) various requests through a proprietary protocol.

Several metadata managers for SP3/HB3 have been built. Of particular importance to this discussion is the TaxMan, which is a metadata manager that serves botanical taxonomic abstractions described above such as taxon and specimen. Since these abstractions are derived from the generic data abstractions, they are first-class system entities that may carry arbitrary attributes, be versioned, locked, etc. The TaxMan also implements various computations over its abstractions, such as generating the closed sets of taxa as described above.

As with metadata managers, several applications have been implemented or integrated into SP3/HB3. One of these is the TaxEd, which allows the authoring and browsing of taxonomies, specimen records, etc. TaxEd uses the facilities of the TaxMan to provide its users with taxonomic abstractions. Additionally, TaxEd participates in the LSM link services protocol, allowing arbitrary associative linking among taxonomic objects handled by different TaxEd instance and even arbitrary objects handled by any other SP3 application.

3.3 Lessons

The three implications of botanical classification work practices for system design we discussed above evolved over time. Our first prototypes did not provide sufficient flexibility. As our understanding of the problem domain increased, TaxMan became more complex. It became increasingly apparent that TaxMan resembled the LSM in many ways. Both provided a type of first-class structure over a data set (taxa and links, respectively). Both used partitioning and grouping mechanisms to effect closure of their structure spaces (taxonomies and contexts). Both used computations over structure to generate new structures dynamically or to perform other tasks (such as finding all taxa without specimen records in a taxonomy or all dangling links in a context). Most importantly, both shared "structure" specific problems, such as keeping consistent pointers to versioned data, providing structure-specific access control in the form of reference permissions, etc. However, there was very little reuse between TaxMan and LSM.

One reason for this is the location of the tailoring of abstractions for these two entities. As stated above, HB3 is implemented on top of a DBMS, which means that ultimately, HB3 views all persistent abstractions as database records. It provides a generic data abstraction derived from these records, which it then serves to clients such as the TaxMan. It also provides a closed set of specializations of this generic data abstraction in the form of navigational hypermedia abstractions, which are then used by the LSM. HB3 provides versioning, concurrency, and access control for both data and structure abstractions. Many of the policies for providing this advanced functionality for structure abstractions were geared to navigational structure, and thus not reusable in general for the taxonomic structure served by TaxMan.

In order to maximize the amount of reuse, we need to introduce the concept of "generic structure". Generic structure is a specialization of generic data that can be further refined into abstractions suitable for other problem domains, such as associative storage and recall or classification. We discuss this idea further in Sec. 5.

4 Scenario of Digital Library Use

In this section, we consider a scenario of digital library use. We base this scenario on our experiences with the users of our digital library and hypermedia system prototypes, many of whom are botanical taxonomists. In this scenario, we describe another similar kind of classification work called linguistic reconstruction. In this task, linguists try to deduce the grammar and vocabulary of a language by examining its descendant languages. They often do this by comparing these descendants and interpolating the characteristics of a common ancestor. For example, if one examines the vocabularies of English, German, Danish, and Swedish, one notices a number of similarities. From these similarities, it is possible to construct the vocabulary of some common ancestor, which in this case might be called Proto-Germanic. In addition to using strictly linguistic data to perform reconstructions, historical and archeological data can often be helpful as well. In the example above, we can confidently posit that Proto-Germanic existed, since we can find archeological evidence for a single group of tribes that settled (many of) the regions in which English, German, Danish, and Swedish are spoken today. Although we can compare Danish and Chinese and reconstruct a common ancestor, this makes little sense based on historical evidence. Reconstructions can be applied to any sets of languages, even to reconstructed languages themselves. The resulting language "family tree" looks very much like the taxonomies discussed above built by botanical and other taxonomists.

Introduction. *Marge, Maggie, and Lisa are linguists. They are attempting to reconstruct Proto-Indo-European (PIE) from Latin, Greek,* and Sanskrit. One key issue they need to resolve is how these languages are related. One possibility is that all three languages diverged from PIE at about the same time. Another possibility is that some pair of these languages (say, for example, Latin and Greek) have an intermediate common ancestor which should first be reconstructed and then compared to the remaining language (in this case, Sanskrit) to generate PIE. Marge, Maggie, and Lisa decide they can only resolve this issue by learning more about the period of history during which PIE is posited to have existed (c. 3000 BC).

Associative Storage and Retrieval. They begin by consulting various historical and archeological texts. They can search not only the texts themselves, but also the associations between various facts built up by previous researchers. By browsing these associations, they are able to find more material and understand more connections than would have been possible in the same time using only the texts themselves. They annotate the historical and archeological (digital or digitized) texts with their observations and make additional associations, all within their own workspace. Because of the remoteness of this period of history, no clear picture emerges as to the history of the PIE and its speakers. Instead, they learn of many different hypotheses concerning this period of history.

Information Analysis. Marge, Maggie, and Lisa continue by considering the data they gathered from their initial investigations. At first, they do not have a clear overview or understanding of the problem space. They use the information analysis tools provided by the digital library system to organize their thinking on the relevant historical data. Over time, they develop an initial understanding of the problem space.

Argumentation Support. Once they understand enough of the problem space to begin their work, Marge, Maggie, and Lisa use on-line tools provided by their digital library system to argue the merits of the various positions presented in these works. The digital library system allows them to capture the issues and evidence presented during their analysis and helps them structure their reasoning. After analyzing the evidence, they reach the conclusion that one hypothesis is most likely, one is plausible, and the others may be discounted.

Classification. Instead of building a PIE language family tree from scratch on paper, Marge, Maggie, and Lisa download the PIE language family tree maintained by the library that represents the most current thinking on the history of Latin, Greek, and Sanskrit. They make various updates to this community taxonomy in their private workspace. They create another version of this workspace to illustrate how their results would differ under the historical hypothesis they found plausible but less likely.

5   Structural Computing and Digital Libraries

In this section, we introduce the notion of structural computing, or generalized hypermedia, and its possible role in future digital library system design, analogous to our analysis of the connections between navigational hypermedia and current digitial library system design above. We first consider a number of problem domains in addition to associative storage and retrieval that are mentioned in the scenario above, and review some of the different types of hypermedia abstractions and systems proposed to support tasks in these domains. We then analyze component-based open hypermedia systems in terms of their abilities to provide this wide range of abstractions to applications.

5.1   Additional Hypermedia Problem Domains

The first part of the scenario above describes the use of structures found in navigational hypermedia systems that are used for associative storage and retrieval tasks. As discussed above, the usefulness of supporting navigational structures in digital library systems is well-established. Our scenario continues by describing several other types of tasks carried out by the characters, each of which calls for the support of other types of structural abstractions. Nürnberg et al. [31] have used the term *structural computing* to denote a generalized approach to applying hypermedia structuring concepts to an open set of problem domains. Below, we look at three problem domains that characterize some of the other types of tasks presented in the scenario and describe the structural computing abstractions (or, in these cases, non-navigational hypermedia abstractions) that have been proposed to help users perform tasks in these domains.

Information Analysis and Spatial Hypermedia. Marshall and Shipman [23] note that *information analysts* faced with the task of organizing and understanding large amounts of data develop structures over this data over time. As their understanding of the information space changes, the structures they use to characterize the space also change. Systems designed for such analysts are required to support emerging, dynamic structures that avoid the problems associated with premature organization and formalization, as discussed, e.g., by Halasz [12] and Marshall et al. [24]. Marshall and Shipman have proposed *spatial hypermedia* to meet these requirements. Spatial hypermedia systems allow users to represent pieces of information as visual "icons". Analysts can represent relationships among objects implicitly by varying certain various visual attributes (color, size, shape) of the icons and by arranging the icons in arbitrary ways in a 2.5 dimensional space. A spatial parser can then recognize the spatial patterns formed by these icons. Examples of such spatial structures might be lists of red rectangles that contain text or piles of blue ovals that contain images. Both the user and the system can use the structures recognized by this parser to support the task of analysis. For example, the system may recognize some particular type of structure as occurring frequently and conclude that it represents a meaningful abstraction to the analyst. It may then prompt the analyst to recognize this type of structure formally, perhaps by naming it. This formal recognition may allow additional functionality to be provided, such as searches for instances of the structure in the space or replacement of the structure with a new visual symbol that may be "expanded" into its constituent parts.

The second part of the scenario above describes the use of more structures built by the patrons themselves over the data in the digital library. In this case, we could imagine a spatial hypermedia information analysis tool as acting as a kind of analog to large working table in a reading room of a physical library on which patrons can organize and arrange the material of the library, except that the materials may remain available to other patrons and their analysis can be supported by computer-based algorithms and tools.

Argumentation Support and Issue-Based Hypermedia. McCall et al. [27] describe community *argumentation support* systems in the context of capturing design rationale. In contrast to the information analysis domain described above, which must support personalization, here the focus is on a unified community understanding of an information space. Systems designed to support participants in a joint decision process or an argument must support simultaneous structure and data creation operations. Argumentation spaces consist of typed data nodes that represent issues to be discussed, positions with respect to issues, evidence that argues for or against a position, and other such entities. Many *issue-based hypermedia* systems provide tools that allow formal reasoning operations to be performed over the structures built, such as finding circular arguments [27]. Argumentation structures are like spatial ones in that they often serve the role of helping users develop an understanding of a space. However, unlike spatial structures, issue-based structures must be persistent and have first-class status.

In the third part of the scenario above, the patrons move their "reading room" material to a more formal system, in which structure is built up explicitly between items instead of implicitly through spatial arrangement. An issue-based hypermedia system would provide patrons not only with a tool for organizing library materials, but "value-added" formal reasoning tools as well. As above, this can be done without affecting the availability of these materials.

Classification and Taxonomic Hypermedia. We described one instance of the *classification* problem (namely, botanical classification) above. As is the case for information analysts, taxonomists must be able to build and express their own idiosyncratic understandings of the information space. This must be done in parallel with the development of a communal understanding among several people, as is the case in argumentation support systems. Systems designed to support classification tasks have many of the same requirements as spatial hypermedia systems. Additionally, they require the ability to tailor different views of the space to match the different understandings represented by different users and community conventions. Parunak [35, 36] and Nürnberg et al. [32, 33] have proposed *taxonomic hypermedia* to meet these requirements. Generic taxonomic hypermedia is built over a set of samples, each containing, for example, text descriptions, images, and movies of a plant for botanical taxonomists, or grammar and vocabulary descriptions for linguists. These samples can be grouped into taxa, which themselves may be further grouped into supertaxa. Unlike spatial hypermedia structures, which are usually non-persistent and not treated as first-class objects by the system, taxa must be persistent and able to be named, described, tagged with various attributes, versioned. Taxonomic hypermedia systems must support the addition of new samples; the ability to comment on samples, taxa, or other comments; and, the ability to redefine the taxa to which samples and other taxa belong. Additionally, they must support the ability to change the "view" of the taxonomic space, which may entail re-parenting records, changing the visibility characteristics of certain comments, and/or other actions.

In the final part of the scenario, the patrons use a taxonomic hypermedia system to formulate and express their findings. This taxonomic system provides versioning and collaborative work support, both of which have been described as necessary components of digital library systems in general [11, 19, 38, 50] and of taxonomic systems in particular [32, 33]. Of course, the percentage of patrons performing linguistic reconstructions may not be very high, but classification is a very common task, even for people whose "normal" intellectual products are not expressed as taxonomies. Much intellectual work in many fields concerns dividing problem spaces, classifying problem instances, and describing prototypic examples of problems, solutions, or data.

Summary. Of course, many non-hypermedia systems have also been designed to address the work practices mentioned above. One advantage of addressing them within the context of hypermedia systems, however, is that they all share a need for flexible structuring mechanisms and policies, with the result that they all can benefit from the kinds of support that hyperbase systems and structural computing environments can provide, as we learned with our early TaxMan experiences described above. In the next section, we describe some of these kinds of infrastructure and how they can support systems like those mentioned above.

5.2 Component-Based Open Hypermedia Systems

A hypermedia system enables its users to build and manipulate structure over some set of data. If it is to support a wide range (or open set) of problem domains, however, it is not sufficient for the system to provide only some sufficiently "powerful" or "expressive" set of structural abstractions to developers of new applications. Instead, the system must allow some basic set of core abstractions to be tailored to abstractions well-suited to particular problem domains. Spatial hypermedia application designers, for example, should not be forced to develop their systems in an environment that provides only navigational structural abstractions such as "link" and "node". Instead, they should be able to extend the basic structural abstractions provided by the environment into ones suitable for spatial hypermedia applications, such as "icon", "space", and "arrangement".

In our previous work (and in any traditional OHS), facilities for managing navigational structure cannot be easily leveraged to manage non-navigational structure. In order to support new structural abstractions within an OHS environment, one is forced essentially to "reinvent" basic structure management facilities for each new set of abstractions added (i.e., for each new problem domain addressed). Although it is certainly possible to design and implement navigational, spatial, issue-based, taxonomic and other kinds of hypermedia systems independently, doing so requires much wasted effort.

A component-based OHS (CB-OHS) is essentially an OHS that contains an extensible set of structure servers [30]. Each structure server can be viewed independently as a kind of OHS, in that it provides its structuring facilities to an open set of clients (over arbitrary data types). However, the difference between a CB-OHS and a traditional OHS is that the former serves an open set of structure facilities. Contemporary CB-OHS's provide generic structure management (structural computing) functionality that can be specialized to provide support for specific kinds of structure (such as navigational or spatial). This allows both re-use of common functionality and an extensible platform to which new kinds of tailored structure servers may be added. A generic CB-OHS architecture is shown in Fig. 2.

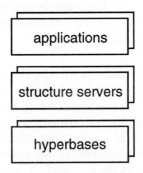

Fig. 2. A generic component-based open hypermedia system architecture. Note the replacement of the link server of a traditional OHS with a new open layer of structure servers.

Two examples of CB-OHS's are HOSS [33] and HyperDisco [48]. As with the traditional OHS's, these systems have been integrated with third party and specially built clients. Additionally, new structure servers have been implemented alongside traditional link servers. For example, HOSS has implemented servers of navigational, spatial, and taxonomic structure. In addition to both of these systems, the Open Hypermedia Systems Working Group (OHSWG) (see http://www.csdl.tamu.edu/ohs/) has begun definition of interface standards for different types of structure servers. Many of the most well-known OHS's and both CB-OHS's mentioned above are represented in the OHSWG by researchers who have committed to implementing or conforming to applicable

OHSWG component-based interfaces for providing structure facilities. Additionally, the OHSWG plans to deliver the first of these specifications as proposals to the World Wide Web Consortium (W3C) and the Internet Engineering Task Force (IETF) by the end of 1998.

6 Current Work

In this section, we discuss Construct, a new public domain CB-OHS that is natively compliant with OHSWG (de facto) standards, reference models, and reference architectures. Construct builds upon previous work done at Texas A&M University (e.g., [17, 19, 33, 40, 41]), Aalborg University (e.g., [48, 49, 51]), and Aarhus University (e.g., [9–11]). Various components of Construct are currently under development at Aarhus University and Aalborg University Esbjerg in the Coconut and Fasit projects of the Danish National Center for IT Research. In the remainder of this section, we first provide a brief overview of the project and its history. Then, we examine each architectural layer more closely.

6.1 Overview

Construct consists of a number of distributed hyperbases and structure servers. Applications (both legacy and custom made) access the different types of hypermedia services provided by the different types of structure servers. Both hyperbases (called hyperstores in Construct) and structure service components are comprised of different layers of functionality (see Fig. 3).

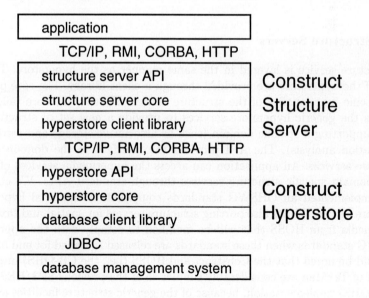

Fig. 3. Architectural layers of Construct.

Communication between components occurs in potentially many different ways. Structure service components can receive hypermedia requests from applications (or from encapsulating components acting on behalf of applications) encoded using different technologies and (de facto) standards (TCP/IP, Java RMI, CORBA, and HTTP). Likewise, communication between structure services and hyperstores can occur using the same technologies and (de facto) standards. As of May 1998, Construct supports communication using ASCII streams over TCP/IP, Java RMI, and tunnelling through HTTP. Support for CORBA and potentially other technologies and (de facto) standards will be provided in future versions.

6.2 Hyperstore

A hyperstore provides persistent structure (and optionally data) storage to other entities in the environment. Each hyperstore is implemented on top of a database management system (DBMS) that is accessed from the Database Client Library through JDBC drivers. The Construct Hyperstore server is currently running on top of Oracle. We are in the process of evaluating various public domain persistent stores with the intent of porting the hyperstore to such a store in early 1999. The Database Client Library implements basic storage and retrieval services to be used by the Hyperstore Core. The Hyperstore Core implements core hypermedia services (such as objects, attributes, behaviors and relations), and core collaboration services (such as nested transactions, concurrency control, notification control, access control, and version control) using the services of the underlying DBMS. The hyperstore services are provided through the hyperstore API.

6.3 Structure Servers

A structure service is layered in the same manner as the hyperstore. The services of the hyperstore are provided through a client library. The core provides the specific functionality of the structure service. That is, the core tailors and extends the generic hyperstore services to provide a new set of structure services supporting a specific domain (such as associative storage and retrieval or information analysis). The API provides the interface to the domain specific structure services. An application can access the hypermedia services of one or more domain specific structure services through standard APIs. We currently have implemented an OHSWG standards compliant navigational hypermedia structure server. We are also porting structure servers for spatial and taxonomic hypermedia from HOSS that will be modified to comply with the appropriate OHSWG standards when these standards are released (planned for end of 1998). It should be noted that the Construct and HOSS (i.e., the CB-OHS) implementations of TaxMan are considerably simpler than the previous SP3/HB3 (traditional OHS) implementation, because of the generic structure facilities available in the Construct and HOSS backends.

6.4 Applications

A number of applications have been integrated into or specially written for HOSS and HyperDisco and are now available for Construct. A complete description of these applications is available in the sources cited above. Some of the applications we have found most useful are the integrations of XEmacs and the Netscape and Microsoft WWW browsers. These are general purpose tools useful both in a digital library setting and elsewhere. With respect to applications more specifically aimed at digital libraries, we are porting the HOSS TaxEd client described above to Construct. We plan to continue to use the botanical collections over which TaxEd operates as testbeds for our work, but now concentrate on orchestrated, integrated delivery of multiple types of structural computing services alongside the taxonomic and navigational services reported in the source cited above.

7 Future Work

One obvious area for future work is to develop more structure servers that serve structural abstractions tailored to new hypermedia problem domains, as well as applications that take advantage of these new abstractions. As with all problem domains discussed above for which hypermedia systems and/or structure servers have been developed, this is a problem rooted in observing work practices. From a hypermedia perspective, this involves identifying the structural abstractions used by people performing work (in this case, in the digital library). We expect to find opportunities for defining new structure servers as our base of experience with digital library patrons grows. Clearly, at least structure servers that manage bibliographic metadata should be built. Although such metadata can be (and usually is) managed by non-hypermedia systems, developing metadata servers as instances of structure servers offers proven and integrated ways to handle integrity, versioning, concurrency, and similar problems familiar from other hypermedia domains.

Another interesting area for future work concerns hypermedia awareness on the part of the operating system. Though "hypermedia operating system" work is still immature, there have been some preliminary investigations reported in [33]. Hypermedia operating systems are potentially of interest to digital library system designers. The motivation for considering structure awareness at the operating system arises primarily from the observation of the changing nature of the way in which application-level computing environments are built. Many traditional operating system designs arose from observations of the computing environments of three and four decades ago. However, modern computing environments have much different characteristics. As just one example, consider that it is increasingly more common for code and data to be physically distributed and fetched on demand. In such an environment, does virtual locality provide a good measure of semantic locality? Estimating semantic locality is key to efficient memory management algorithms. Previous observations based on contiguous code and data spaces of centralized, monolithic processes do not apply as straightforwardly in modern computing environments. Consider that an operating system that was aware of hypermedia structures between data items would have more available information to deduce semantic distances than simply information about proximity in the virtual address space. Nürnberg et al. [33] consider other possible advantages of structure awareness at the operating system that concern functionality other than memory management such as access control, network management, and the operating system user interface. Some related work has been carried out in the operating systems field concerning the use of semantic locality for file replication [18, 22], although this work does not use explicit hypermedia structure as its measure of locality. The presence of this work, however, does indicate room for improvement of the policies of current operating systems based on increasingly less valid characterizations of modern operating environments. If a digital library system is to provide comprehensive structuring facilities to its users, and if such structures represent common paths and patterns of access, it seems logical to investigate the possibility of using this information wherever possible in the system to provide a more efficient environment for the digital library patron.

8 Conclusions

Digital libraries will be more than simply electronic stores of information. They will be powerful resources for knowledge workers in the next century, acting as virtual places in which patrons will gather to use the digital library materials and interact with one another to carry out intellectual work. Critical to these digital libraries will be digital library systems that will enable users to work effectively and efficiently. In this paper, we have considered a scenario of work carried out in a digital library to demonstrate the usefulness of comprehensive structuring facilities provided by several different types of hypermedia. We then considered the implications for digital library system architectures, arguing that component-based open hypermedia systems that can provide these comprehensive facilities more effectively than traditional open hypermedia systems. We also described some of our current work in this area and directions for future work.

Digital library research has long been acknowledged as an inherently interdisciplinary undertaking. In this paper alone, in which we have focused only on hypermedia structuring facilities, we have highlighted the need to synthesize the results from fields as diverse as human-computer interaction, computer-supported collaborative work, hypermedia, and operating systems in order to address the issues surrounding the design and implementation digital library systems. We believe any successful attempt to address digital library systems will require the broad kind of interdisciplinary cooperation we have described here, and that component-based open hypermedia systems provide a good platform for developing and experimenting with more powerful, flexible, and useful digital library systems.

Acknowledgements
The work presented in this paper was partially funded by the Danish National Center for IT Research project 123 (Coconut).

References

[1] Anderson, K. M., Taylor, R. N., and Whitehead, E. J. 1994. Chimera: Hypertext for heterogeneous software environments. *Proceedings of the European Conference on Hypertext '94* (Edinburgh, Scotland, Sep), 94-107.

[2] Berners-Lee, T., Cailliau, R., Luotonen A., Nielsen, H. F., and Secret A. 1994. The World Wide Web. *Communications of the ACM 37* (8) (Aug), 76-82.

[3] Bieber, M., and Vitali, F. 1997. Toward support for hypermedia on the World Wide Web. *IEEE Computer 30* (1) (Jan), 62-70.

[4] Bush, V. 1945. As we may think. *Atlantic Monthly 176* (1) (Jul), 101-108.

[5] Davis, H., Hall, W., Heath, I., Hill, G., and Wilkins, R. 1992. Towards an integrated information environment with open hypermedia systems. *Proceedings of the 1992 European Conference on Hypertext (ECHT '92)* (Milano, Italy, Dec), 181-190.

[6] Engelbart, D. C. 1962. Augmenting human intellect: A conceptual framework. Stanford Research Institute Technical Report AFOSR-3223, Contract AF 49(638)-1024, (Oct) Palo Alto, CA.

[7] Fox, E. A., Akscyn, R. M., Furuta, R. K., and Leggett, J. J. 1995. Introduction to special issue on digital libraries. *Communications of the ACM 38* (4) (Apr), 23-28.

[8] Graham, P. 1995. The digital research library: Tasks and commitments. *Proceedings of the Second Symposium on Digital Libraries (DL '95)* (Austin, TX, Jun), 49-56.

[9] Grønbæk, K., Bouvin, N. O., and Sloth, L. 1997. Designing Dexter-based hypermedia services for the World Wide Web. *Proceedings of the Eighth International Hypertext Conference (Hypertext '97)* (Southampton, UK, Apr), 146-156.

[10] Grønbæk, K., and Trigg, R. H. 1994. Design issues for a Dexter-based hypermedia system. *Communications of the ACM 37* (2) (Feb), 40-49.

[11] Grønbæk, K., Hem, J. A., Madsen, O. L., and Sloth, L. 1994. Designing Dexter-based cooperative hypermedia systems. *Communications of the ACM 37* (2) (Feb), 64-74.

[12] Halasz, F. 1988. Reflections on NoteCards: Seven issues for the next generation of hypermedia systems. *Communications of the ACM 31* (7) (Jul), 836-852.

[13] Hall, W., Carr, L., and De Roure, D. 1995. Linking the World Wide Web and Microcosm, Presented at the BCS workshop on New Directions in Software Development, (Wolverhampton, UK, Mar).

[14] Illustra Information Technologies, Inc. 1995. *Illustra User's Guide.* Oakland, CA: Illustra Information Technologies, Inc.

[15] Kacmar, C., Jue, D., Stage, D., and Koontz, C. 1995. Automatic creation and maintenance of an organizational spatial metadata and document digital library. *Proceedings of the Second Symposium on Digital Libraries (DL '95)* (Austin, TX, Jun), 97-105.

[16] Kacmar, C., Hruska, S., Lacher, C., Jue, D., Koontz, C., Gluck, M., and Weibel, S. 1994. An architecture and operation model for a spatial digital library. *Proceedings of the Symposium on Digital Libraries (DL '94)* (College Station, TX, Jun), 156-162.

[17] Kacmar, C. J., and Leggett, J. J. 1991. PROXHY: A Process-Oriented Extensible Hypertext Architecture. *ACM Transactions on Information Systems 9* (4) (Oct), 399-419.

[18] Kuenning, G. and Popek, G. 1997. Automated hoarding for mobile computers. In *Proceedings of the Sixteenth ACM Symposium on Operating System Principles (SOSP-16)* (Saint Malo, France, Oct).

[19] Leggett, J. J., and Schnase, J. L. 1994. Viewing Dexter with open eyes. *Communications of the ACM 37* (2) (Feb), 76-86.

[20] Levy, D. M. 1995. Cataloging in the digital order. *Proceedings of the Second Symposium on Digital Libraries (DL '95)* (Austin, TX, Jun), 31-37.

[21] Levy, D. M., and Marshall, C. C. 1994. What color was George Washington's white horse? *Proceedings of the Symposium on Digital Libraries (DL '94)* (College Station, TX, Jun), 163-169.

[22] Matthews, J., Roselli, D., Costello, A., Wang, R., and Anderson, T. 1997. Improving the performance of log-structured file systems with adaptive methods. *Proceedings of the Sixteenth ACM Symposium on Operating System Principles (SOSP-16)* (Saint Malo, France, Oct).

[23] Marshall, C. and Shipman, F. 1995. Spatial hypertext: designing for change. *Communications of the ACM 38* (8), 88-97.

[24] Marshall, C. C., Shipman, F. M., and Coombs, J. H. 1994a. VIKI: spatial hypertext supporting emergent structure. *Proceedings of the ECHT '94 European Conference on Hypermedia Technologies* (Edinburgh, Scotland, Sep), 13-23.

[25] Marshall, C. C., Shipman, F. M., and McCall, R. J. 1994b. Putting digital libraries to work: Issues from experience with community memories. *Proceedings of the Symposium on Digital Libraries (DL '94)* (College Station, TX, Jun), 126-133.

[26] Meyrowitz, N. 1989. The missing link: Why we're all doing hypertext wrong. *The Society of Text*, The MIT Press, 107-114.

[27] McCall, R., Bennett, P., D'Oronzio, P., Ostwald, J., Shipman, F., and Wallace, N. 1990. PHIDIAS: Integrating CAD graphics into dynamic hypertext. *Proceedings of the First European Conference on Hypertext (ECHT '90)* (Versailles, France, Nov), 152-165.

[28] McKnight, C. 1995. Digital library research at Loughborough: The Last fifteen years. *Proceedings of the Second Symposium on Digital Libraries(DL '95)* (Austin, TX, Jun), 65-70.

[29] Miksa, F. L., and Doty, P. 1994. Intellectual realities and the digital library. *Proceedings of the Symposium on Digital Libraries (DL '94)* (College Station, TX, Jun), 1-5.

[30] Nürnberg, P. J., Leggett, J. L., and Wiil, U. K. 1998. An agenda for open hypermedia research. To appear in *Proceedings of the Ninth ACM Conference on Hypertext (HT '98)* (Pittsburgh, PA, Jun).

[31] Nürnberg, P. J., Leggett, J. J., Schneider, E. R. 1997. As we should have thought. *Proceedings of the Eighth ACM Conference on Hypertext (HT '97)* (Southampton, UK, Apr), 96-101.

[32] Nürnberg, P. J., Schneider, E. R., and Leggett, J. J. 1996a. Designing digital libraries for the hyper-literate age. *Journal of Universal Computer Science 2* (9).

[33] Nürnberg, P. J., Leggett, J. J., Schneider, E. R., and Schnase, J. L. 1996b. HOSS: a new paradigm for computing. *Proceedings of the Seventh ACM Conference on Hypertext (HT '96)*, (Washington, DC, Mar), 194-202.

[34] Nürnberg, P. J., Furuta, R. K., Leggett, J. J., Marshall, C. C., and Shipman, F. M. 1995. Digital libraries: Issues and architectures. *Proceedings of the Second Symposium on Digital Libraries (DL '95)*, (Austin, TX, Jun), 147-153.

[35] Parunak, H. 1993. Hypercubes grow on trees (and other observations from the land of hypersets). *Proceedings of the Fifth ACM Conference on Hypertext (HT '93)* (Seattle, WA, Nov) 73-81.

[36] Parunak, H. 1991. Don't link me in: Set based hypermedia for taxonomic reasoning. *Proceedings of the Third ACM Conference on Hypertext (HT '91)* (San Antonio, TX, Dec), 233-242.

[37] Pearl, A. 1989. Sun's link service: A protocol for open linking. *Proceedings of the Second ACM Conference on Hypertext (Hypertext '89)* (Pittsburgh, PA, Nov), 137-146.

[38] Pettengill, R., and Arango, G. 1995. Four lessons learned from managing World Wide Web digital libraries. *Proceedings of the Second Symposium on Digital Libraries (DL 95)* (Austin, TX, Jun), 177-180.

[39] Schnase, J. L., Leggett, J. J., Metcalfe, T., Morin, N. R., Cunnius, E. L., Turner, J. S., Furuta, R. K., Ellis, L., Pilant, M. S., Ewing, R. E., Hassan, S. W., and Frisse, M. E. 1994a. The CoLib project: Enabling digital botany for the 21st century. *Proceedings of Symposium on Digital Libraries (DL '94)* (College Station, TX, Jun), 108-118.

[40] Schnase, J. L., Leggett, J. J., Hicks, D. L., Nürnberg, P. J., and Sánchez, J. A. 1994b. Open architectures for integrated, hypermedia-based information systems. *Proceedings of HICCS '94* (Maui, HI, Jan).

[41] Schnase, J. L., Leggett, J. J., Hicks, D. L., Nürnberg, P. J., and Sánchez, J. A. 1993. HB1: Design and Implementation of a Hyperbase Management system. *Electronic Publishing – Origination, Dissemination 6* (1) (Mar), 35-63.

[42] Schütt, H. A., and Streitz, N. A. 1990. HyperBase: A hypermedia engine based on a relational database management system. *Hypertext: Concepts, Systems, and Applications. Proceedings of the European Conference on Hypertext* (France, Nov.), A. Rizk, N. Streitz, and J. Andre, Eds. Cambridge University Press, Cambridge, UK, 95-108.

[43] SIGLINK. 1995. Special Issue on Digital Libraries. C. Kacmar, Ed. *SIGLINK Newsletter 4* (2) (Sep), 2-28.

[44] Smolensky, P., Fox, B., King, R., and Lewis, C. 1988. Computer-aided reasoned discourse or, how to argue with a computer. *Cognitive Science and its Application for Human-Computer Interaction*, R. Guindon, Ed. Ablex, Norwood, NJ, 109-162.

[45] Stotts, D., Smith, J., Dewan, P., Jeffay, K., Smith, F. D., Smith, D., Weiss, S., Coggins, J., and Oliver, W. 1994. A patterned injury digital library for collaborative forensic medicine. *Proceedings of the Symposium on Digital Libraries (DL '94)* (College Station, TX, Jun), 25-33.

[46] Sugimoto, S., Gotou, S., Zhao, Y., Sakaguchi, T., and Tabata, K. 1995. Enhancing usability of network-based library information system – experimental studies of a user interface for OPAC and of a collaboration tool for library services. *Proceedings of the Second Symposium on Digital Libraries (DL '95)* (Austin, TX, Jun), 115-122.

[47] Wiil, U. K. 1998. Evaluating HyperDisco as an infrastructure for digital libraries. *Proceedings of ACM Symposium on Applied Computing '98 (SAC '98)* (Atlanta, GA, Feb).

[48] Wiil, U. K., and Leggett, J. J. 1997. Workspaces: The HyperDisco Approach to Internet Distribution. *Proceedings of the Eighth ACM Conference on Hypertext (HT '97)* (Southampton, UK, Apr), 13-23.

[49] Wiil, U. K. 1993. Experiences with HyperBase: A Multiuser Hypertext Database. *SIGMOD RECORD 22* (4) (Dec), 19-25.

[50] Wiil, U. K., and Leggett, J. J. 1993. Concurrency control in collaborative hypertext systems. *Proceedings of the Fifth ACM Conference on Hypertext (HT '93)* (Seattle, WA, Nov), 14-24.

[51] Wiil, U. K., and Leggett, J. J. 1992. Hyperform: Using Extensibility to Develop Dynamic, Open and Distributed Hypertext Systems. *Proceedings of the 1992 European Conference on Hypertext (ECHT '92)* (Milan, Italy, Nov), 251-261.

E-Referencer: A Prototype Expert System Web Interface to Online Catalogs

Christopher S. G. Khoo[1], Danny C. C. Poo[2], Teck-Kang Toh[2], Soon-Kah Liew[1],
and Anne N. M. Goh[1]

[1]Centre for Advanced Information Systems
School of Applied Science
Nanyang Technological University
Singapore 639798
assgkhoo@ntu.edu.sg
[2]Dept. of Information Systems
School of Computing
National University of Singapore
Singapore 119260
dpoo@comp.nus.edu.sg

Abstract. An expert system Web interface to online catalogs called E-Referencer is being developed. An initial prototype has been implemented. The interface has a repertoire of initial search strategies and reformulation strategies that it selects and implements to help users retrieve relevant records. It uses the Z39.50 protocol to access library systems on the Internet. This paper describes the design of E-Referencer, and the development of search strategies to be used by the interface. A preliminary evaluation of the strategies is also presented.

1 Introduction

An expert system Web interface to online catalogs called E-Referencer is being developed. An initial prototype has been implemented and is accessible at the URL *http://islab.sas.ntu.ac.sg:8000/E-Referencer/*. It uses the Z39.50 Information Retrieval protocol to communicate with library systems on the Internet. This paper describes the design of E-Referencer and the effort to develop effective search strategies for it. A preliminary evaluation is also presented.

An effective search interface is an important component of a digital library. A digital library can adopt two main retrieval approaches:

1. Best match retrieval, which outputs a ranked list of documents or records, with the closest match at the top of the list
2. Boolean retrieval, which retrieves records that match criteria specified using Boolean operators.

Although we feel that it is desirable for a search interface to offer both retrieval approaches, we have concentrated our effort on the second approach since most library systems are still using Boolean retrieval.

It is well-known that users have difficulty specifying their queries using Boolean expressions. They also lack much of the knowledge and skills needed to search online databases and online library catalogs effectively.

We are developing an expert search interface to encapsulate some of the knowledge and searching expertise of experienced librarians. The interface processes the user's natural language query, selects a suitable search strategy and formulates an appropriate search statement to send to the library system. Based on the user's relevance feedback on the search results, it selects a strategy for reformulating the search.

Our goal is to develop an interface that will search multiple online catalogs, integrate the records returned by the various library systems, and rank the records before displaying them to the user. However, the current implementation connects to one library system at a time and does not rank the records retrieved.

Although the focus of the current development effort is on present day library systems, we intend to adapt the system to search other types of databases and digital libraries.

2 Background and Previous Work

Several researchers have investigated the problems users experience when searching present-day online catalogs [1-4], as well as the search strategies that experienced librarians use [5-10].

For example, users have difficulty matching their search terms with those indexed in the online catalog. They have difficulty coming up with synonyms as well as broader and narrower terms related to their topic. Cousins found that many subject queries were not expressed at the level of specificity that was appropriate or suitable for searching the online catalog [11].

Users also do not know how to broaden a search when too little or nothing is retrieved, or to narrow a search when too much is retrieved. Hildreth pointed out that "to optimize retrieval results in subject searching, more than one search approach may have to be employed in the overall search strategy. ... Conventional information retrieval systems place the burden on the user to reformulate and re-enter searches until satisfactory results are obtained" [12].

Borgman said that most of the improvements to online catalogs in recent years were in surface features rather than in the core functionality [13]. She indicated that online catalogs "were designed for highly skilled searchers, usually librarians, who used them frequently, not for novices or for end-users doing their own searching."

Khoo and Poo described five types of knowledge that experienced librarians use when searching the online catalog [14]:

- knowledge of the nature and structure of catalog records
- knowledge of the thesaurus system used to index library materials

- knowledge of the search language of the system
- knowledge of search strategies, and when and how to apply them
- general knowledge as well as subject knowledge.

Attempts to develop expert system interfaces to online catalogs include the system developed by Drabenstott and her colleagues [15-17] and that by Chen [18-19].

Drabenstott has developed a prototype online catalog that uses search trees or decision trees that represent how experienced librarians select a search strategy and formulate a search statement. The decision tree is represented as a flowchart. In an evaluation using a small database of 15,000 records, she found that the decision trees were more effective than selecting a search strategy at random.

Decision trees are relatively rigid and the selection process proceeds in one direction. Adding new search strategies to the model may not be easy because it necessitates changes to other parts of the model. It may not be easy to customize the model for particular users and user groups. Processing of the user query can only go forward following the direction indicated by the flow chart, i.e. it cannot backtrack unless explicitly indicated in the flowchart and cannot test a few search strategies before selecting one (i.e. search backwards).

Chen's system [18-19] was developed as part of his dissertation and was an ambitious one, with many search strategies and knowledge bases. The evaluation was carried out with a very small database of 300 records. It is not clear whether similar or better results can be obtained with a much simpler system.

3 System Design and Implementation

The approach we use in developing E-Referencer is that of rapid prototyping and incremental development. We first implement a prototype using simple-minded strategies specified by an experienced librarian (one of the authors). We then carry out experiments to evaluate the prototype and compare its performance with that of experienced librarians. From this, we identify how the prototype is deficient, how it can be improved and what additional strategies are required. This cycle of incremental development and testing also ensures that our interface will be spare, and will not be bloated with knowledge bases and rules that do not really improve effectiveness.

The system design is based on the following assumptions and principles:

- The library systems accessed are Boolean retrieval systems, implying that the interface has to convert the user's query to a Boolean search statement.
- The interface should accept natural language queries from the user, eliminating the need for the user to learn Boolean logic.
- The interface should not badger the user with many questions, and should not present long lists of items for selection. Otherwise the user will lose patience and give up.
- The interface (Z39.50 client) communicates with the library system (Z39.50 server) over the Internet. Therefore, the amount of data transferred should be kept

User

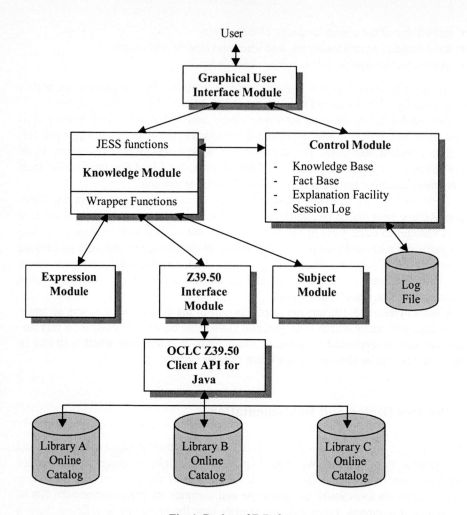

Fig. 1. Design of E-Referencer

to a minimum. The interface should not request a large number of records for further processing since this will slow down the response time.

- The interface should not overload the library system by sending a large number of trial query formulations or query formulations with a large number of terms to process.
- The interface should be flexible and easily customizable for different users or user groups.

The overall design of the interface was described in [20], and is illustrated in Fig. 1. A prototype has been implemented as a Java applet which can be loaded using a Web browser that supports Java 1.1.

The interface makes use of the OCLC Z39.50 client API written in Java (available at *http://www.oclc.org/z39.50/*), and the stemming program based on Porter's algorithm [21] available at the *Glasgow IDOM - IR Resources* Web site (URL *http://www.dcs.gla.ac.uk/idom/ir_resources/linguistic_utils/*).

For the expert system, we make use of the Java Expert System Shell (Jess) (available at *http://herzberg.ca.sandia.gov/jess/*). *Jess* supports the development of rule-based expert systems coupled with code written in Java. *Jess* is a clone of the popular expert system shell *C Language Integrated Production System* (CLIPS) [22], which interprets facts and rules written in a subset of the CLIPS language. In E-Referencer, the search strategies are written as Jess rules. Useful functions for connecting to and searching the Z39.50 server, stemming, etc., are implemented as Jess functions through the use of Jess "wrappers".

The interface has the following modules:

1. The *Graphical User Interface Module* handles the interaction between the user and E-Referencer.
2. The *OCLC Z39.50 Client API* provides functionality for connecting to, searching and retrieving information from the various library systems that support the Z39.50 protocol.
3. The *Z39.50 Interface Module* is developed as a "wrapper" for the OCLC Z39.50 Client API, to enable it to interact with the rest of E-Referencer.
4. The *Expression Module* provides functions for manipulating a search expression, e.g. removing stopwords, converting a search expression to reverse polish notation, removing AND and OR operators from an expression, inserting AND and OR operators between query keywords, etc. The various functions can be called by a search strategy.
5. The *Subject Module* handles the reformulation of the initial search query into a new search query by analyzing the terms found in the records retrieved by the initial search.
6. The *Control Module* is the heart of the expert system. It controls and calls the various functions of the system using a script. It has the following components:

   - A *Knowledge Base* of search strategies in the form of rules specified in JESS script.
   - A *Fact Base* which stores the intermediate search results and information needed to select the next search strategy. A new strategy is selected by evaluating the rules (from the Knowledge Base) against the facts (in the Fact Base).
   - An *Explanation Facility* for explaining why and how certain strategies were chosen.
   - A *Session Log* that keeps a permanent record of all the search results and strategies used. The Log is used to analyze the performance of E-Referencer.

7. The *Knowledge Module* contains wrapper functions for integrating the expert system scripts of the Control Module with the other modules of E-Referencer. This is necessary since the other modules such as the Expression Module, Subject Module and the Z39.50 Interface Module are all in Java code and they have to interact with the Control Module which selects and executes the appropriate search and reformulation strategies based on the rules in the Knowledge Base.

The intelligence in E-Referencer lies mostly in the search strategies coded in the system as well as the rules for selecting an appropriate search strategy. The search strategies can be divided into two categories:

- initial search strategies – the procedures used to convert the user's natural language query statement to an appropriate Boolean search statement
- reformulation strategies – the procedures used for reformulating a search statement based on the results of the previous search statement.

Currently, a simple decision tree is used for selecting a search strategy. However, we plan to develop weighted production rules ("If .. then …" rules) for selecting a search strategy. This gives greater flexibility in 2 ways:

- the system can use a mixture of forward and backward chaining to find the best strategy (i.e. forward and backward search)
- a machine-learning facility can be developed to train the system on a test collection to find the best weights to assign to individual rules.

4 Search Strategies and Selection Rules

4.1 Initial Search Strategies

Initial Strategy 1 (keyword/phrase search in all fields) is a simple-minded procedure that removes stopwords, stems the remaining words, and searches for the words in all searchable fields in the library database. Word adjacency is preserved. Punctuation marks and stopwords are replaced with the Boolean AND, but the words in between are retained as phrases. More details are given in Table 1.

Initial Strategy 2 (subject headings search) attempts to identify appropriate Library of Congress (LC) Subject Headings to use. We initially tried two approaches for identifying LC Subject Headings automatically. The first approach was to identify the best matching headings – the shortest subject heading-subdivision(s) that contains the highest number of query words. The second approach was to identify exact matches – the longest subject heading(s) for which all the words in the heading were found in the user query. Both approaches were found to be ineffective. More details are reported in [23].

We are currently investigating a third approach in which a shortlist of subject headings is displayed for the user to select. All subject headings as well as "non-preferred terms" from the LC Subject Headings list that begin with any one of the query keywords are displayed for the user to select. If a non-preferred term is selected, it is replaced with the valid subject heading when the formal query statement is formulated by the interface. This third version of *Initial Strategy 2* is the one that is evaluated in this paper.

A *subject heading search* strategy has two advantages compared with *keyword search*:

Table 1. Initial Strategy 1: Keyword/Phrase Search in All Fields

---

0. User enters query. Example query:

   expert systems in library reference service

1. Remove stopwords at the beginning and end of the user's query statement. Replace other stopwords and punctuation with Boolean AND:

   expert systems AND library reference service

2. The words between the Boolean ANDs are assumed to be linked with the adjacency operator (i.e. intended to be searched as a phrase):

   expert systems AND library reference service

3. Stem the words and add a truncation sign at the end of every word:

   expert? system? AND librar? refer? servic?

4. Formulate a search statement to carry out a keyword search in all fields:

   find expert? system? AND librar? refer? servic?

---

1. If a non-preferred term in the LC Subject Headings list is selected by the user, the interface can use the LC "see" reference to identify the valid heading. This procedure helps to identify synonyms and related terms that may not contain any of the user's keywords. The interface can also use the selected LC heading to automatically identify narrower terms to include in the search.
2. If the interface needs to broaden the search subsequently, the interface can use the LC Subject Headings thesaurus structure to identify broader terms to use.

4.2 Reformulation Strategies

After the initial strategy is executed, E-Referencer displays the first 20 titles retrieved and prompts the user to indicate which titles are useful. (We believe that the user can comfortably consider 20 titles. Also, librarians can usually decide how to reformulate a search after examining fewer than 20 records.)

After the user has indicated which records are relevant, the interface will execute one of the reformulation strategies. A reformulation strategy may modify the previous search statement or construct an entirely new search.

Three types of reformulation strategies are used:

1. broadening strategies
2. narrowing strategies
3. relevance feedback strategies.

322

Table 2. Broadening and narrowing Strategies

Broadening Strategies

Strategy 1: Convert adjacency operators to Boolean ANDs.

Strategy 2: Search each keyword individually to identify keywords not found in the database. Remove such keywords from the search statement.

Strategy 3: Select every combination of 3 keywords. AND the keywords in each combination. Link the combinations with Boolean OR.

Strategy 4: Select every combination of 2 keywords. AND the keywords in each combination. Link the combinations with Boolean OR.

Strategy 5: Convert ANDs to ORs.

Strategy 6: Prompt user to enter synonyms and related terms for each keyword.

Strategy 7: Use a broader subject heading (not currently implemented)

Strategy 8: Use stronger stemming (not currently implemented)

Narrowing Strategies

Strategy 1: Convert one of the OR operators to AND, and execute the search. Replace the OR operator, convert a different OR operator to AND, and execute the search. Do this for each of the OR operators in turn. Combine all the search sets using OR.

Strategy 2: Convert one of the AND operators to an adjacency operator, and execute the search. Replace the AND operator, repeat the procedure for each of the other AND operators in turn. Combine all the search sets using OR.

Strategy 3: Ask the user for additional keywords to AND to the search.

The broadening strategies and narrowing strategies are given in Table 2, and relevance feedback strategies are described in Table 3.

A *broadening strategy* modifies the previous search statement to make it less constrained. The new set of records retrieved will be a superset of the earlier result set. Clearly this kind of strategy is appropriate when no record is retrieved, or when most of the records retrieved are relevant and the user wants to get more records.

A *narrowing strategy* modifies the previous search statement to reduce the number of records retrieved. The set of records retrieved will be a subset of the earlier result

Table 3. Relevance Feedback Strategies

A. The following terms are extracted from the 20 records displayed to the user:

- unstemmed keywords in the title fields
- stemmed keywords in the title fields
- subject heading—subdivisions
- main subject headings (ignoring the subdivisions)
- all combinations of 2 terms (i.e. 2 subject headings, 1 subject heading +1 keyword,
- 2 keywords, etc.)

B. The following statistics are calculated for each of the terms extracted in Step A:

- no. of relevant records containing the term
- no. of non-relevant records containing the term
- % of relevant records containing the term
- % of non-relevant records containing the term

C. The following scores are calculated for each of the terms extracted in Step A:

- no. of relevant records containing the term
- no. of relevant records – no. of nonrelevant records
- no. of relevant records / (no. of nonrelevant records + 0.5)
- % of relevant records containing the term
- % of relevant records – % of nonrelevant records
- % of relevant records / (% of nonrelevant records + 5%)

---

set. A narrowing strategy is appropriate when too many records are retrieved, and the user wants to reduce the set to those records that are more likely to be relevant.

A *relevance feedback strategy* analyzes the content of the records retrieved and attempts to identify keywords and subject headings that are likely to retrieve relevant documents. Generally, if a keyword or a subject heading (or some combination of them) occurs in most of the records found relevant by the user and occurs in few non-relevant records, then it is likely to retrieve other relevant records.

The first step in the relevance feedback strategies is to compile a list of terms found in the 20 records displayed to the user (see Table 3 for more details). For each term, the system computes the following statistics:

1. number of relevant records (i.e. records marked relevant by the user) containing the term
2. number of non-relevant records (records marked non-relevant by the user) containing the term

3. percentage of relevant records containing the term
4. percentage of non-relevant records containing the term.

The terms are then scored according to one of the formulas:

1. no. of relevant records
2. no. of relevant records – no. of non-relevant records
3. no. of relevant records / (no. of non-relevant records + 0.5)
4. % of relevant records
5. % of relevant records – % of non-relevant records
6. % of relevant records / (% of non-relevant records + 5%).

We carried out preliminary experiments to find out which formula will identify the best term to use. A qualitative analysis of the results gave us the following insights:

1. Formulas 5 and 6 are not effective when there is only 1 non-relevant record (or a small number of non-relevant records). This is because the *% of non-relevant records* factor in the formulas places too much weight on the single non-relevant record.

2. Formula 2 is effective in distinguishing relevant from non-relevant records only in the set of records retrieved in the initial search. For example, if the interface retrieved 100 records, 20 of which are presented to the user for relevance judgments. then this formula can identify terms that distinguish relevant from non-relevant records in the remaining 80 records retrieved. The terms identified may not be useful in retrieving relevant records from the whole database!

3. Formula 1 is the most effective formula for identifying terms that can be used in formulating a new search statement. Formula 4 gives the same results as formula 1.

4. It is desirable to assign different weights to the different types of terms extracted from the records displayed to the user. For example, subject headings should be weighted higher than single keywords. Combinations of 2 terms should be weighted higher than single terms. The weighting scheme we have developed is given in Table 4. The weights are somewhat arbitrary, but they indicate the order of importance of the types of terms.

5. If there is only 1 relevant document, it is difficult to identify which term in the record is important to the search topic. Our weighting scheme results in subject headings being selected over keywords, and this appears to be an appropriate strategy.

6. If few records are retrieved in the initial search, it is difficult to identify the appropriate terms to use for reformulating the search. The interface should automatically apply a broadening strategy to retrieve more records for relevance judgment.

7. Sometimes, 2 or more terms have the same score. The system then has to select a Boolean operator to combine the terms. In the context of E-Referencer, it is appropriate to use the Boolean AND to combine the terms, because if no record is re-

trieved, E-Referencer automatically broadens the search by converting the Boolean AND to OR.

8. It is sometimes desirable to use the NOT operator to reject a term in the new query formulation. If there are more than 2 non-relevant records, and a particular term occurs in all the non-relevant records but occurs in none of the relevant records, then it is desirable to "NOT" the term from the search.

9. For this study, we extracted subject headings with and without subdivisions for consideration. However, we did not extract the subdivisions separately. We noted that in some cases it was desirable to extract the subdivisions for consideration. For example, "Decision-making" is a subject heading, but it can also be a subdivision as in "Investments—Decision making". If the user is looking for books on decision making, it may be desirable to search for "Decision making" as a subdivision as well as a subject heading.

For the purpose of evaluation, we manually simulated the following relevance feedback procedure:

1. When many records are retrieved in a search (more than 40), formula 2 is used to identify the terms to use for reformulating the search. The terms identified are then ANDed to the previous search query to narrow the search.

2. Otherwise, formula 1 is used to identify the terms to use for constructing a completely new query.

In either case, the weighting scheme described earlier is used to modify the scores after formula 1 or 2 is applied.

Table 4. Weighting for Different Types of Terms during Relevance Feedback

Type of term	Weight
Unstemmed keyword	1
Stemmed keyword	1.5
2 adjacent keywords	1.7
Subject heading with subdivision(s)	2
Subject heading without subdivision	2.5
Combination of 2 keywords not adjacent	2
Combination of subject heading and keyword	3
Combination of 2 subject headings	4

Table 5. Decision Tree for Selecting a Reformulation Strategy

Condition 1	Condition 2	Strategy
0 record retrieved	Query contains only 1 word (after removing stopwords)	Broadening strategy 6: Prompt user to enter synonyms and related terms
	Query contains 2 or more words	Broadening strategies, tried in the order given in Table 2 until at least 1 record is retrieved
20 or fewer records retrieved (all displayed to the user)	All records are relevant	Relevance feedback strategy
	All records are not relevant	Broadening strategies, tried in the order given in Table 2
	Some records are relevant, some are not	Relevance feedback strategy
More than 20 records retrieved	All records are relevant	Display 20 more records
	All records are not relevant	Narrowing strategy
	Some records are relevant, some are not	Relevance feedback strategy

4.3 Rules for Selecting a Reformulation Strategy

The rules currently used to select a reformulation strategy are listed in Table 5. Note that when the initial strategy fails to retrieve any record, broadening strategies are tried in the order listed in Table 2 until at least one record is retrieved.

5 Evaluation of the Search Strategies

5.1 Initial Search Strategies

The purpose of the evaluation is to gain some insight into how the initial strategies can be improved and which strategy is effective in which situation. This will help us to formulate rules for selecting a search strategy.

The evaluation was based on 12 queries selected from among those submitted by university staff and students for literature searches. Table 6 gives an example of a query, and lists the 12 topics used.

The queries contain the sections *topic*, *description* and *keywords*. However, the expert system made use of the words given on the topic line only. We have not yet found an effective way for the expert system to make use of the words in the other 2 sections.

The queries were selected to cover a range of subjects. The library system at one of the campuses of the Nanyang Technological University (NTU), Singapore, was used

Table 6. Titles of Sample Queries

Example Query

No: D97-4
Topic: Face recognition
Description: Use computer through camera to capture and recognize human faces. These would be useful for law enforcement & security.
Keywords: face, frontal, profile

List of Query Topics

Query No.	Topic
A96-7	Digital library projects
A96-14	Cognitive models of categorization
A97-16	Internet commerce
B97-1	Making a framework for surveying service quality in academic libraries
B97-3	Looking to do a comprehensive literature review of the Sapir-Whorf Hypothesis
D96-2	Software project management
D96-16	Decision under uncertainty
D97-1	Thermal conductivity of I.C. Packaging
D97-2	Fault-Tolerant Multiprocessor Topologies
D97-4	Face recognition
D97-7	A study on computer literacy and use by teachers in primary schools
N97-13	Expert systems in library reference service

---

in the evaluation. This library serves the Engineering, Management and Communication Studies schools, and is thus weak on the Social Sciences, Humanities and Pure Sciences. There is at least one record in the library database that is relevant to each query.

We compared the searches performed by the expert system using *Initial Strategies 1* and *2* with those carried out by an experienced librarian (one of the authors). Two sets of relevance judgments were obtained – from a lecturer and a graduate student at NTU Division of Information Studies. The judgments were made based on the users' written descriptions of their information needs.

We were trying different search strategies, and it would be difficult to get the original requestors to provide relevance judgments repeatedly over a period of time. At this early stage of system development, useful insights for improving the system can be obtained even if the relevance judgments are not provided by the original requestors.

The 2 judges were asked to indicate whether the records retrieved were relevant, marginally relevant or not relevant. For this evaluation, records that were judged to be marginally relevant were considered to be non-relevant. The precision measure (proportion of records retrieved that are relevant) was calculated for the first 20 records displayed. (The expert system currently displays only 20 records to the user for relevance judgment.) The mean precision for the 2 sets of relevance judgments was then calculated for each query. The results are given in Table 7.

For both *Initial Strategy 1* and *2*, if the strategy does not retrieve any record, then broadening strategies are tried in the order listed in Table 2 until a non-null set is obtained. (This process is transparent to the user.) The search result evaluated was the first non-null set retrieved by the interface.

Initial Strategy 2 has not been implemented in E-Referencer yet. It was manually simulated for evaluation. One of the researchers reviewed the shortlist of subject headings and selected those that appeared to be appropriate for the query. The selected subject headings were entered into E-Referencer, and *Initial Strategy 1* was applied. This meant that the selected subject headings were searched as keywords in all fields. This seems desirable because some records in the library database (e.g., books on order, new arrivals and dissertations) are without LC subject headings.

Table 7 shows that the average precision was 0.36 for *Initial Strategy 1*, 0.52 for *Initial Strategy 2* and 0.54 for the librarian's final search strategy. The average number of relevant records retrieved was 3.0 for *Initial Strategy 1*, 4.7 for *Initial Strategy 2* and 6.0 for the librarian's search.

Initial Strategy 2 worked surprisingly well, and was clearly more effective than *Initial Strategy 1*. However, *Initial Strategy 2* often requires the user to scan a long list of subject headings, most of which are not relevant. We hope to develop a method for picking out the more likely subject headings so that the user is presented with a shorter list to consider.

Both strategies performed worse than the librarian. However, the evaluation was not really fair to the expert system. The librarian executed several search statements, and continually refined the search after examining records retrieved by earlier search formulations. The search set evaluated was the final set obtained by the librarian. On the other hand, the search set from the expert system that was evaluated was the first non-null set retrieved.

The purpose of the initial strategy is to obtain a few relevant records so that a reformulation strategy can refine the search. From that perspective, the initial strategies were succesful. *Initial Strategy 1* succeeded in retrieving at least one relevant record for 10 of the 12 queries. *Initial Strategy 2* retrieved at least one relevant record for all the queries.

Initial Strategy 1 failed to retrieve any relevant record for query B97-3 ("Looking to do a comprehensive literature review of the Sapir-Whorf Hypothesis") and query D97-7 ("A study on computer literacy and use by teachers in primary schools"), which are long queries containing many words. The search strategy that eventually retrieved a non-null set was *Broadening Strategy 3* ("Select every combination of 3 terms"). This strategy resulted in long but unsuccessful search statements. For exam-

Table 7. Results for the Initial Strategies

Query No.	Search by Librarian			Search by Expert System Using *Initial Strategy 1*			Search by Expert System Using *Initial Strategy 2*		
	No. Displayed	No. Relevant	Precision	No. Displayed	No. Relevant	Precision	No. Displayed	No. Relevant	Precision
A96-7	17	6	0.35	4	0.5	0.13	9	5	0.55
A96-14	3	2	0.67	20	1	0.05	20	1	0.05
A97-16	20	7.5	0.38	4	1	0.25	4	1	0.25
B97-1	13	7	0.54	20	3	0.15	20	1.5	0.08
B97-3	4	3.5	0.88	2	0	0.00	2	2	1.00
D96-2	20	14	0.70	11	10.5	0.95	20	16.5	0.83
D96-16	20	9	0.45	20	9	0.45	20	12	0.60
D97-1	20	5	0.25	3	1.5	0.50	13	3.5	0.27
D97-2	6	6	1.00	5	3.5	0.70	2	2	1.00
D97-4	15	5	0.33	8	2	0.25	20	7	0.35
D97-7	14	2.5	0.18	19	0	0.00	19	4	0.21
N97-13	5	4	0.80	4	3.5	0.88	1	1	1.00
Average	**13.1**	**6.0**	**0.54**	**10**	**3.0**	**0.36**	**12.5**	**4.7**	**0.52**

Note:
1. The figures given for *No. Relevant* and *Precision* are the average for 2 sets of relevance judgments by 2 persons.
2. The evaluation is based on the first 20 records retrieved. E-Referencer currently displays only 20 records for relevance judgment.

example, the query "Looking to do a comprehensive literature review of the Sapir-Whorf Hypothesis" resulted in the following search statement:

find (look? and comprehens? and literatur?) or (look? and comprehens? and review?) or (look? and comprehens? and sapir-whorf?) or (look? and comprehens? and hypothesi?) or (look? and literatur? and review?) or (look? and literatur? and sapir-whorf?) or (look? and literatur? and hypothesi?) or (look? and review? and sapir-whorf?) or (look? and review? and hypothesi?) or (look? and sapir-whorf? and hypothesi?) or (comprehens? and literatur? and review?)
...

One way of handling long queries is to eliminate words with high document frequencies, because such words tend to be unimportant words. We found that eliminating high frequency words will be effective for the first query but not the second query. For the second query, the word "computer" is important even though it has a high document frequency.

Another way to manage long queries is to find the number of records retrieved by each combination of three words, and then eliminate those combinations retrieving a high number of records. This approach will be explored in the future.

Table 8. Results of the Relevance Feedback Strategy

Query No	Search by Expert System Using *Initial Strategy 1*			Result after Relevance Feedback		
	No. Displayed	No. Relevant	Precision	No. Displayed	No. Relevant	Precision
A96-14	20	1	0.05	20	2	0.10
A97-16	4	1	0.25	9	2	0.22
B97-1	20	1	0.05	7	2	0.29
D96-2	11	10	0.91	20	1	0.05
D96-16	20	14	0.70	20	16	0.80
D97-1	3	2	0.67	20	1	0.05
D97-2	5	5	1.00	2	1	0.50
D97-4	8	2	0.25	2	2	1.00
N97-13	4	3	0.75	4	3	0.75
Average	**10.6**	**4.3**	**0.51**	**11.6**	**3.3**	**0.42**

Note:
1. The figures given for *No. Relevant* and *Precision* are based on relevance judgments by 1 person
2. The evaluation is based on the first 20 records retrieved.

5.2 Evaluation of the Relevance Feedback Strategy

We evaluated the relevance feedback procedure described earlier (at the end of Section 4.2). *Initial Strategy 1* (keyword/phrase search in all fields) was used to obtain the set of records for relevance judgments. The relevance feedback strategy was then applied to the first 20 records displayed to the user. For this evaluation, we made use of relevance judgments from only 1 of the judges. The results are given in Table 8.

The search results worsened after relevance feedback. The average number of relevant records retrieved dropped from 4.3 to 3.3. The precision also dropped from 0.51 to 0.38.

The result was particularly bad for query D96-2. The precision plummeted from 0.91 to 0.05. This suggests that when the precision is very high, as in this case, a broadening strategy should be used instead of relevance feedback. If query D96-2 is excluded from the calculation, then the average precision and number of relevant records retrieved did not decrease with relevance feedback, but they did not improve either.

More work needs to be done to develop a more effective relevance feedback strategy.

6 Conclusion and Future Work

Two initial search strategies for use in an intelligent Web interface to online catalogs were studied. *Initial Strategy 1* searches the user's query words in all fields. *Initial Strategy 2* identifies all subject headings that begin with any 1of the user's keywords and presents the list to the user to select. If the initial search strategy does not retrieve any record, then broadening strategies are applied until at least 1 record is retrieved. The evaluation based on 12 queries suggests that both strategies are generally effective in helping users retrieve some relevant records.

Initial Strategy 2 (the subject headings approach) works particularly well, but more work is needed to develop a method to pick out the more likely subject headings to present to the user. Otherwise, the user may be overwhelmed with a long list of subject headings, most of which are not relevant.

We investigated 6 formulas for identifying appropriate terms to use for reformulating the search after relevance feedback. Several insights were obtained from a qualitative analysis of the results. The procedure of extracting terms from records judged relevant by the user, scoring the terms using *Formula 1* (number of relevant records containing the term), and then selecting the terms with the highest scores appear to work best. *Formula 2* (number of relevant records containing the term minus the number of non-relevant records containing the term) can be used when the initial search retrieves a large set of records. In this case, the terms with the highest score for *Formula 2* can be used to identify the subset of records that are more likely to be relevant. It is also desirable to weight the different types of terms. Subject headings should be weighted higher than single keywords, for example. Unfortunately, we did not find an improvement in the search results after applying this strategy.

This study has several limitations:

- the sample of queries was very small
- relevance judgment was not performed by the same people who submitted the queries
- the queries were collected from requests for literature searches, and while they reflect real user needs, they may not be typical of queries entered in online catalogs.

The purpose of the experiments was to help us develop search strategies for use in the interface and identify major problems. The next evaluation will involve real users of online catalogs.

Development work in progress includes:

- developing rules for selecting the initial and reformulation strategies
- developing a machine-learning procedure to adjust the weights of the rules based on a test collection of queries and relevance judgments
- developing a method for ranking the records retrieved
- constructing a word association file based on term co-occurrence in a library database. This will then be used for automatic query expansion
- developing different search strategies and selection rules for different user groups.

References

1. Dalrymple, P.W.: Retrieval by Reformulation in Two Library Catalogs: Toward a Cognitive Model of Searching Behavior. J. Amer. Soc. Inf. Sci. 14 (1990) 272-281
2. Ensor, P.: User Practices in Keyword and Boolean Searching on an Online Public Access Catalog. Inf. Tech. Libr. 11 (1992) 210-219
3. Lancaster, F.W., Connell, T.H., Bishop, N., McCowan, S.: Identifying Barriers to Effective Subject Access in Library Catalogs. Libr. Reso. Tech. Serv. 35 (1991) 377-391
4. Markey, K.: Subject Searching in Library Catalogs: Before and After the Introduction of Online Catalogs. OCLC Online Computer Library Center, Dublin, OH. (1984)
5. Connell, T.H.: Subject Searching in Online Catalogs: Metaknowledge Used by Experienced Searchers. J. Amer. Soc. Inf. Sci. 46 (1995) 506-518
6. Fidel, R.: Searchers' Selection of Search Keys: I. The Selection Routine. J. Amer. Soc. Inf. Sci. 42 (1991) 490-500
7. Fidel, R.: Searchers' Selection of Search Keys: II. Controlled Vocabulary or Free-Text Searching. J. Amer. Soc. Inf. Sci. 42 (1991) 501-514
8. Hsieh-Yee, I.: Effects of Search Experience and Subject Knowledge on the Search Tactics of Novice and Experienced Searchers. J. Amer. Soc. Inf. Sci. 44 (1993) 161-174.
9. Shute, S.J., Smith, P.J.: Knowledge-Based Search Tactics. Inf. Proc. Manag. 29 (1991) 29-45.
10. Spink, A., Saracevic, T.: Sources and Use of Search Terms in Online Searching. In: ASIS '92: Proceedings of the 55th ASIS Annual Meeting, Vol. 29. Learned Information, Medford, NJ (1992) 249-255
11. Cousins, S.A.: In Their Own Words: An Examination of Catalogue Users' Subject Queries. J. Inf. Sci. 18 (1992): 329-341

12. Hildreth, C.: Beyond Boolean: Designing the Next Generation of Online Catalogs. Libr. Trends 35 (1987) 647-667
13. Borgman, C.L.: Why are Online Catalogs Still Hard to Use? J. Amer. Soc. Inf. Sci. 47 (1996) 493-503
14. Khoo, C., Poo, C.C.D.: An Expert System Front-End as a Solution to the Problems of On-line Catalogue Searching. In: Information Services in the 90s: Congress Papers. Library Association of Singapore, Singapore (1991) 6-13
15. Drabenstott, K.M.: Enhancing a New Design for Subject Access to Online Catalogs. Libr. Hi Tech, 14 (1996) 87-109
16. Drabenstott, K.M., Weller, M.S.: Failure Analysis of Subject Searches in a Test of a New Design for Subject Access to Online Catalogs. J. Amer. Soc. Inf. Sci. 47 (1996) 519-537
17. Drabenstott, K.M., Weller, M.S.: The Exact-Display Approach for Online Catalog Subject Searching. Inf. Proc. Manag. 32 (1996) 719-745
18. Chen, H.: An Artificial Intelligence Approach to the Design of Online Information Retrieval Systems. Ph D. Dissertation, New York University (1989)
19. Chen, H.: Knowledge-Based Document Retrieval: Framework and Design. J. Inf. Sci. 18 (1992) 293-314
20. Khoo, C.S.G., Poo, D.C.C.: An Expert System Approach to Online Catalog Subject Searching. Inf. Proc. Manag. 30 (1994) 223-238
21. Porter, M.F.: An Algorithm for Suffix Stripping. Program 14 (1980) 130-137
22. CLIPS: A Tool for Building Expert Systems. URL http://www.ghg.net/clips/CLIPS.html (1997)
23. Khoo, C.S.G., Poo, D.C.C., Liew, S.-K., Hong, G., Toh, T.-K.: Development of Search Strategies for E-Referencer, an Expert System Web Interface to Online Catalogs. In: Toms, E., Campbell, D.G., Dunn, J. (eds.): Information Science at the Dawn of the Millennium: Proceedings of the 26th Annual Conference of the Canadian Association for Information Science. CAIS, Toronto (1998)

The Planetary Data System - A Case Study in the Development and Management of Meta-Data for a Scientific Digital Library

J. Steven Hughes and Susan K. McMahon

Jet Propulsion Laboratory, California Institute of Technology, Pasadena, CA 91109, USA
Steve.Hughes@jpl.nasa.gov, Susan.McMahon@jpl.nasa.gov

Abstract. The Planetary Data System (PDS) is an active science data archive managed by scientists for NASA's planetary science community. With the advent of the World Wide Web, the majority of the archive has been placed on-line as a science digital library for access by scientists, the educational community, and the general public. The meta-data in this archive, primarily collected to ensure that future scientists would be able to understand the context within which the science data was collected and archived, has enabled the development of sophisticated on-line interfaces. The success of this effort is primarily due to the development of a standards architecture based on a formal model of the planetary science domain. A peer review process for validating the meta-data and the science data has been critical in maintaining a consistent archive. In support of new digital library research initiatives, the PDS functions as a case study in the development and management of meta-data for science digital libraries.

1 Introduction

The Planetary Data System (PDS) [1] is an active science data archive, managed by scientists for NASA's planetary science community, that has been in operation since March, 1990. Envisioned as a long term archive, the PDS early on developed a standards architecture for both the science data and the meta-data necessary for understanding the context under which the data were captured, as well as interpreting diverse storage formats in which the data were stored. This standards architecture includes a formal model of the planetary science domain, a standard grammar for encoding the information, and a standard language represented in the Planetary Science Data Dictionary. This standards architecture has been used to create a high quality science data archive of about five terabytes that is distributed on Compact Disk (CD) media. The meta-data in this archive, even though collected to ensure the usability of the science data for future scientists, has also allowed the majority of the archive to be made available through the World Wide WEB (WEB) as a digital library. The implementation of this archive as an on-line digital library provides an instructive case study in the development and management of meta-data for digital libraries.

In the following we will give a brief history of the PDS covering the early development of the standards architecture, the meta-data model, and describe how the meta-data in the archive has had a significant positive impact on the ability to support on-line search and access via the Web. In addition, several "lessons learned" regarding the development and management of meta-data will be discussed.

2 Overview of the PDS

In 1986 the Committee on Data Management and Computing (CODMAC) issued a report [2] that explored management approaches and technology developments for computation and data management systems designed to meet future needs in the space sciences. This effort resulted from prior observations that a wealth of science data would ultimately cease to be useful and probably lost if a process was not developed to ensure that the science data were properly archived. In particular it was proposed that the data be transferred to stable media, and that sufficient meta-data be included to ensure that future users of the data would be able to correctly interpret the data formats as well as understand the context under which the data were collected.

After the development of a successful prototype, the PDS was funded in 1987 and work started on modeling the entities within the planetary science domain. Using formal modeling techniques, the team developed data structure charts that described in detail the data sets within the planetary science community and other related entities including missions, spacecraft, instruments, target bodies, measured parameters, and bibliographic references. For example, in Figure 1, the instrument entity had sufficient detail so that a user of the system would have a good understanding of the instrument's operation without having to go to an instrument design document. If more detail was needed, the model allowed references to supporting documents using bibliographic citations. An example of a science data set is the collection of about 50,000 Mars images returned by the Viking Orbiter spacecraft in 1976. An individual image within this data set is called a data set granule.

An additional design goal was to allow sophisticated searches for the data using catalogs. In particular, the scientists wanted the capability to find data sets through relationships with other entities. For example, using relationships between data sets, spacecraft, and instruments, scientists wanted the ability to identify the images that had been captured using a specific filter, on a specific camera type, and on a specific spacecraft. A simplified entity model showing these relationships is given in Figure 2.

The PDS went on-line in 1990 with about 75 data sets in its archive. A high level data set catalog allowed the searching and ordering of any data set in the archive through an on-line interface with 88 user views. To bring data into the archive, the PDS developed a data ingestion procedure that included a formal peer review process. The peer review committee included peer scientists who reviewed the science data and collected meta-data for validity and usability

```
Level Group/Element Structure
-----------------------------------------

1 spacecraft instrument identification group
    2  instrument identification
    2  instrument name
    2  spacecraft identification
    2  instrument type
1 instrument description
1 scientific objectives summary
...
1 filter group
    2  filter name
    2  filter number
    2  filter type
...
1 instrument optics group
    2  optics description
...
```

Fig. 1. Data Structure Chart for Science Instrument

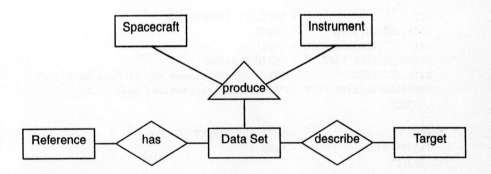

Fig. 2. Simplified Entity Model

while technical staff members reviewed the data for adherence to the standards architecture. The PDS currently has about 350 peer-reviewed data sets in its archive, with another 150 waiting the completion of peer review. The standards architecture and procedures, including the peer review process, are documented in three volumes: the Data Preparation Workbook [3], the Standards Reference [4], and the Planetary Science Data Dictionary (PSDD) [5]. The heart of the standards architecture was, and continues to be, the Planetary Science Data Dictionary.

3   The Data Dictionary

The original data structure charts used to model the entities in the planetary science domain were the basis for what was to become the Planetary Science Data Dictionary (PSDD). Meeting as a committee, a group of scientists and technical staff defined a data element for each attribute (element) that described an entity in the data structure charts. For each attribute, the team: created a name that conformed to a nomenclature standard, wrote a definition, assigned a data type, and either identified a range of values for numerical attributes or collected a set of possible values for enumerated attributes. They also created object classes by grouping the data elements by entity. Figure 3 shows the meta-data collected for a Mars image data set using the Data Set Object.

```
OBJECT                        = DATA_SET
   DATA_SET_ID                = "VO1/VO2-M-VIS-5-DIM-V1.0"

   OBJECT                     = DATA_SET_INFORMATION
      DATA_OBJECT_TYPE        = IMAGE
      DATA_SET_RELEASE_DATE   = 1991
      PRODUCER_FULL_NAME      = "ERIC ELIASON"
      DATA_SET_DESC           = "This digital image map of Mars is a ..."
      CONFIDENCE_LEVEL_NOTE   = "All of the corrections made ..."
   END_OBJECT
      ...
   OBJECT                     = DATA_SET_TARGET
      TARGET_NAME             = MARS
   END_OBJECT
      ...
END_OBJECT
```

Fig. 3. Data Set Object

The initial release of the PSDD contained 455 data elements. It should be noted that where the development of the original data structure charts focused on detailed specification of attributes for each entity, the development of the data dictionary focused on generalization where similar attributes from different entities were merged into one data element. The level of generalization was continually debated in the committee with scientists typically arguing toward specification and data modelers arguing toward generalization.

The PSDD continues to grow as new data sets are ingested into the archive. In particular, a new instrument typically requires a new set of data elements to describe the resulting data. The process of adding data elements for new instruments and the resulting data is viewed positively since the principal investigator or his team is able to define the domain of discourse for all similar instruments and data that might be archived in the future. However, there is a need to control the wholesale proliferation of new data elements. Typically a committee will first determine what existing data elements can be used, sometimes after proposing minor changes to the definition. The attempt is to define new data elements only for truly new characteristics or concepts. For example, the Viking Orbiter camera images were described with about 35 data elements. The Voyager camera images also required about 35 data elements, the majority of which had been used by Viking. The Galileo camera images, however, used the Voyager data elements and added over 60 more. As a more extreme example, the Magellan Synthetic Aperture Radar (SAR) used relatively few existing data elements and required the addition of over 100 new data elements. Figure 4 shows a meta-meta-data object used for ingesting new data elements into the data dictionary.

```
OBJECT                    = ELEMENT_DEFINITION
  NAME                    = TARGET_NAME
  DESCRIPTION             = The target_name element identifies ...
  UNIT                    = N/A
  VALID_MAXIMUM           = N/A
  VALID_MINIMUM           = N/A
  MAXIMUM_LENGTH          = 30
  MINIMUM_LENGTH          = 1
  STANDARD_VALUE_SET      = {MERCURY, VENUS, MARS, ...}
  ...
END_OBJECT                = ELEMENT_DEFINITION
```

Fig. 4. Element_Definition Object

The PSDD currently contains over 1075 data elements and provides the primary domain of discourse for the Planetary Science Community. For example, before the PDS, the term spacecraft_id could have been a number, acronym - VO1, or a name - Viking Orbiter 1. It is now clearly defined as an acronym. In addition, the definition of the data element target_name with a standard values set has limited the number of new aliases for target bodies. The PDS also adheres to standards set by international standards organizations. The International Astronomical Union (IAU) gazetteer is used as the standard for planetary feature names and the Systeme Internationale table of standard units is used as a basis for units of measurement.

4 The Data Model

As described previously, a formal model of the planetary science domain resulted from the original data structure charts that described the entities within the planetary science community [6]. This model, described in the PSDD, was easily translated to the relational model for subsequent implementation in a relational database management system. The resulting database supported very complex searches for data sets. For example, a scientist could query for data sets that had been created using selected filters and detectors on specific instruments at a specific time.

It soon became apparent, however, that the task of collecting the data necessary to populate this model was problematic for two primary reasons. The first reason was that the scientists soon felt that the effort needed for collecting and organizing the information as required by the model was not worth the benefit of being able to find the data using sophisticated queries. This reasoning was supported by the then valid argument that the majority of the science users would not use the catalog to find the data in the first place. Most were familiar with the community and they knew where to go or who to ask to find the data. Any users unfamiliar with the community could be referred to a knowledgeable individual for help.

The second reason was that in certain areas the model was too rigid and too complex. In particular, since a "black box" instrument model had been developed based on the relatively few instruments known at the time, new types of instruments did not always fit the model well. As a simple example, cameras have an optics section where magnetometers have none. In using the instrument model to describe a magnetometer, the optics section of the model had to be NULLed out. Situations such as this led many to feel that the instrument model was too camera specific.

Realizing that a meta-data collection and model-fitting bottle-neck existed, that the existing users did not need a sophisticated search capability, and that the volume of data to be ingested into the archive was rapidly increasing, the PDS decided to streamline the model for the data set catalog. In particular, much of the information that had been captured as discrete data elements was aggregated into simple text descriptions. For example, the ten data elements that described the optics section of an instrument were eliminated. If the instrument had optics, they were described in a subsection of the instrument description. However, data elements such as instrument_name, instrument_type, and instrument_desc that identify or describe the instrument were retained. In addition, data elements that show a relationship to other entities were also retained. For example, instrument_host_id is used in the instrument model to link the instrument to the instrument host (spacecraft).

It is important to point out that the streamlining only occurred at the high- or data set-level in the model. Specifically the mission, spacecraft, instrument, and data set models were streamlined to use more text, greatly simplifying the meta-data collection and manipulation for these entities. In regard to the requirement that sufficient meta-data exist for future users to understand the science context, the peer review process was modified to ensure that any useful information that might have been lost by the elimination of data elements was included as text in descriptions. This meta-data continued to be included on the archive media.

At the detailed- or individual granule level, however, the model remained relatively complex. In fact, the amount of meta-data captured at the detailed level has significantly increased as data from more complex instrumentation has been ingested. To enable this increase in complexity, the meta-data model at this level has been kept flexible, allowing the addition of data elements as needed. The Galileo image example previously mentioned is a good example of the need for additional keywords to handle basically similar but more complex instrumentation and processing. This flexibility however necessarily complicates the development of generic catalogs for searching data sets at the granule level.

5   The Language

During the design phase of the PDS, the model for the planetary science community had been captured in a data dictionary. The need for a language to represent the model and to capture meta-data for the archive resulted in the development of the Object Description Language (ODL), a language consisting of "keyword = value" (keyword/value) statements. The primary requirements for this language were flexibility, simplicity in meta-data representation, and readability by humans as well as machines. Each keyword represents an attribute (element) in the original data structure charts and was defined as a data element in the data dictionary.

The need for the aggregation of keyword/value statements to describe entities resulted in the addition of a grouping mechanism where the statements were grouped into objects bracketed by "OBJECT=entity" and "END_OBJECT" statements. Using this capability, an object class was created for each entity in the model. These were included as a core part of the PDS standards architecture. A formal grammar was defined for the language and several language parsers were developed.

A mandatory requirement for the ingestion of a data set into the PDS archive is that the meta-data describing the data set, its component granules and the associated spacecraft, instrument, mission, and other related entities, be captured in ODL using standard models. This information is then written into ASCII text files (called labels) and written with the data onto the archive volume, which is typically Compact Disk (CD) media. Once an archive volume has been reviewed and archived, the meta-data can be extracted for use in catalogs, inventories, and other specialized search aids. Figures 3 and 5 illustrate portions of labels for an image data set and one of its images respectively.

```
DATA_SET_ID             = "VO1/VO2-M-VIS-5-DIM-V1.0"
SPACECRAFT_NAME         = {VIKING_ORBITER_1, ...}
TARGET_NAME             = MARS
IMAGE_ID                = MG88S045
SOURCE_IMAGE_ID         = {"383B23", "421B23", ...}
INSTRUMENT_NAME         = {VISUAL_IMAGING_SUBSYSTEM ...}
NOTE                    = "MARS DIGITAL IMAGE ...

OBJECT                  = IMAGE
    LINES               = 160
    LINE_SAMPLES        = 252
    SAMPLE_TYPE         = UNSIGNED_INTEGER
    SAMPLE_BITS         = 8
    SAMPLE_BIT_MASK     = 2#11111111#
    CHECKSUM            = 2636242
END_OBJECT
```

Fig. 5. Image Label

The PDS has found that translation of ODL to other languages has been relatively easy. In particular, meta-data in ODL is currently translated to SQL insert statements to load a relational database for the data set catalog. In addition, meta-data in ODL, being object based, has been readily converted to other object-oriented representations.

6 Categories of Meta-data

Early in the standards development, the PDS determined that there were many categories of meta-data required for a long term archive. Although not clearly identified in the early design of the system, the continued use of the meta-data in the archive has necessarily resulted in an informal categorization of the meta-data collected. At the highest level, these categories have been loosely described as structural and catalog.

6.1 Structural Meta-Data

Structural meta-data typically refers to information about how the entity is represented on the archive media. Within the structural category, there are roughly three subcategories. The first of these is the meta-data required to understand the data representation as written by the hardware on the media. For example, the PDS is often required to archive data for machine architectures that no longer exist and for which there are no resources for conversion. In such cases the raw data are simply copied to the archive media and described sufficiently so that future users can successfully interpret the representation. An example is the use of Binary Coded Decimal (BCD), a format that is seldom used for scientific data but which was actually found in an older science data set. The second category includes meta-data typically associated with a computer's file system, such as file name, record type, and record size. Finally, there is the meta-data needed to describe the structure of the data as organized by the data producer. For example, a typical Viking Orbiter image is stored as a raster image of 800 lines by 800 line-samples of 8 bits each.

6.2 Catalog Meta-Data

The catalog category includes meta-data useful for identifying the data, or describing the context within which the data were captured and processed and how they are to be interpreted for science. It is especially useful for building catalogs and inventories. Within this category there are again three subcategories. First, "identification" meta-data is used to identify the object being described and to identify other related objects. For example, a Viking Orbiter image has a unique image_id, is related to the data set within which it is contained through a data_set_id, and is related to the instrument that captured it through an instrument_id. The second category of meta-data describes context. For example, the Viking Orbiter image includes exposure_duration and filter_name as data elements to describe the instrument state at the time the image was taken. Notice that these keywords are actually detailed instrument attributes but are included as image meta-data since their values are specific to the image. Finally, other "property" meta-data may be collected to describe modeled aspects of a data set granule. For instance, if an image is a part of a digital map, then map projection attributes such as projection_type and resolution are included.

7 Lessons Learned

7.1 The Importance of a Formal Model

The existence of a formal model for the planetary science domain was critical for the development of a long term science data archive. As mentioned previously, the primary reason for the model was to support the collection of meta-data for the archive so that future users would know the context within which the data were taken.

The availability of a formal model also made the development of sophisticated on-line interfaces relatively easy. Without this model the search capabilities would have been essentially limited to free text searches across the textual descriptions. Figure 6 shows an example of an early Web interface to the data set catalog. This interface provides listings of data sets grouped by selected keywords. By clicking on the link, a dynamic list of data sets is generated, ordered by attribute.

At the detailed- or data set granule-level, comprehensive models for the data were developed using all the information available. New attributes were added as

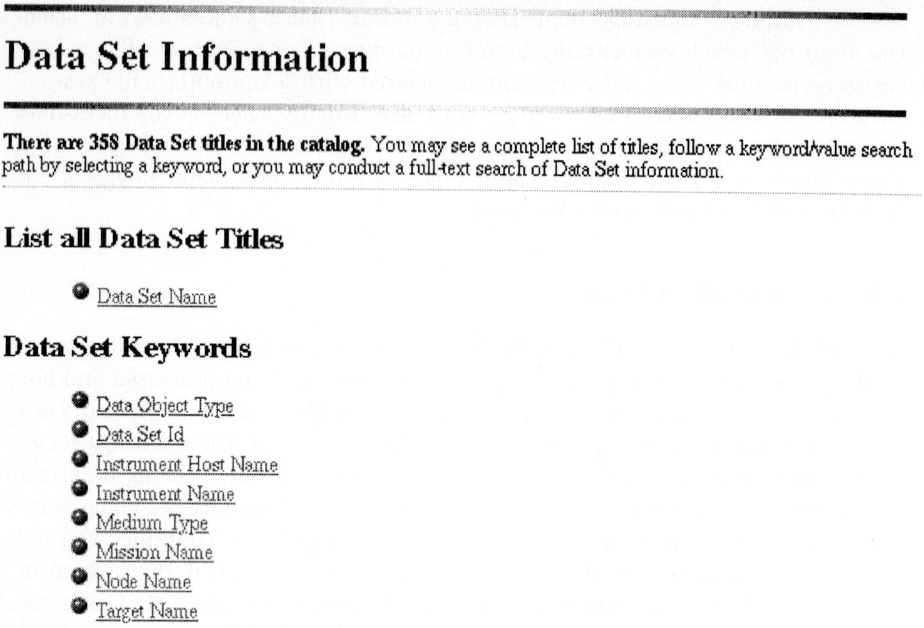

Data Set Information

There are 358 Data Set titles in the catalog. You may see a complete list of titles, follow a keyword/value search path by selecting a keyword, or you may conduct a full-text search of Data Set information.

List all Data Set Titles

- Data Set Name

Data Set Keywords

- Data Object Type
- Data Set Id
- Instrument Host Name
- Instrument Name
- Medium Type
- Mission Name
- Node Name
- Target Name

Fig. 6. Data Set Catalog Interface

needed. Again, even though the primary purpose of the meta-data was to support future users, interface developers never complained about too much meta-data being available for searching purposes. Figure 7 shows an example of an interface to the Viking image catalog. The user enters constraints for the search and the system responds with a list of matching browse images, image attributes, and selection buttons for ordering.

Most important, however, was the fact that without the model the consistency of the meta-data could not have been maintained. The standard models guided the collection of the meta-data and allowed the development of software to perform syntactic and semantic validation. In particular, the data dictionary was used by the software to validate data elements and their values.

7.2 The Model Fitting Problem

The most difficult part of developing a digital archive is the collection, model fitting, and validation of the meta-data. In fact, a major part of the PDS budget is used to support this effort. Where the actual science data require a certain level of effort for collection and validation, familiarity with the data makes this task manageable. The collection of meta-data, however, is typically a research task requiring access to a variety of information sources. In the PDS community this could be instrument designers, spacecraft developers, mission planners, navigation experts, software developers, as well as the principal investigators.

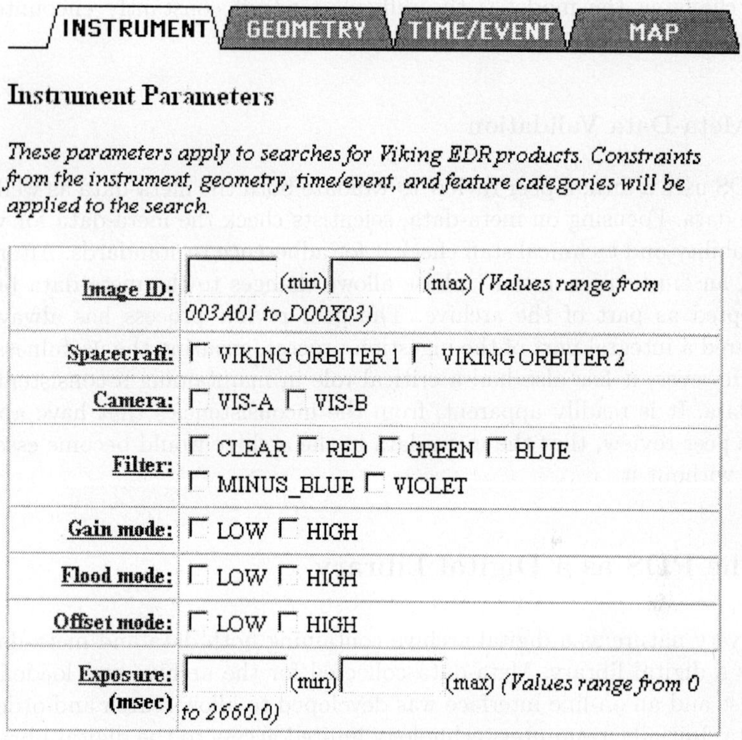

345

Instrument Parameters

These parameters apply to searches for Viking EDR products. Constraints from the instrument, geometry, time/event, and feature categories will be applied to the search.

Image ID: [ ] (min) [ ] (max) *(Values range from 003A01 to D00X03)*

Spacecraft: ☐ VIKING ORBITER 1 ☐ VIKING ORBITER 2

Camera: ☐ VIS-A ☐ VIS-B

Filter: ☐ CLEAR ☐ RED ☐ GREEN ☐ BLUE ☐ MINUS_BLUE ☐ VIOLET

Gain mode: ☐ LOW ☐ HIGH

Flood mode: ☐ LOW ☐ HIGH

Offset mode: ☐ LOW ☐ HIGH

Exposure (msec): [ ] (min) [ ] (max) *(Values range from 0 to 2660.0)*

Fig. 7. Viking Image Catalog Interface

Once the data has been collected, it must be modified to fit the existing models. A simple example would be the collection of date-time information and conversion to a standard format to ensure consistency and ease of use, such as yyyy-mm-ddThh:mm:ss.sss. A more complex example would be the ingestion of data from a new source, such as a rover on the surface of a planet. For those navigation models developed for instruments either in flight or stationary on a surface, a new navigation model had to be developed for an instrument moving on a surface. In summary, making the collected meta-data fit an existing model versus changing the model is the difficult tradeoff constantly encountered in ingestion.

7.3 Meta-Data Validation

The PDS uses a formal peer review to validate both the meta-data as well as the science data. Focusing on meta-data, scientists check the meta-data for validity and usability and technical staff check it for adherence to standards. After a peer review, an "in lien resolution" phase allows changes to the meta-data before it is accepted as part of the archive. The peer review process has always been considered a integral part of the ingestion process, ensuring the usefulness of the data. However, it has also had a critical role in maintaining a consistent set of meta-data. It is readily apparent, from the inconsistencies that have appeared despite peer review, that the meta-data in the archive would become essentially useless without it.

8 The PDS as a Digital Library

By its very nature as a digital archive containing both data and meta-data, the PDS is a digital library. Meta-data collected for the archive was loaded into a database and an on-line interface was developed to allow search and ordering of the data. Initially, computer technology limited access to the digital library to a relatively small group of users.

As technology has progressed, however, new and more powerful user interfaces have been developed. With the advent of the Web and the development of Web interfaces [7], the PDS found that its customer base grew dramatically. However, the meta-data model changed little to meet the new interface requirements. The majority of changes were syntactical as opposed to semantic.

The PDS is a collection of federated, heterogeneous nodes that are distributed geographically. These nodes focus on different science disciplines and have implemented dissimilar data management systems locally. The PDS standards architecture alone forces a commonality across the system. Based on this architecture, a federation of search aids, such as catalogs and inventories, have been developed to give users the ability to search and access the entire archive without knowledge of its distributed nature. Figure 8 shows a hierarchy of the search aids available.

At the highest level, the Distributed Inventory System (DIS) allows users to search for either archived or pending data sets, or any resource that supports the use of the data. Twenty attributes are available for constraining the searches, including data type, time, and related missions, instruments, spacecraft, and target bodies. At the data set level, the data set catalog allows the search and ordering of archived data sets. The detailed level has several sophisticated catalogs for individual granule searching, including map-based search for images. If not available through a catalog interface, the majority of the remaining archive is available on-line either as CD volumes or in disk farms.

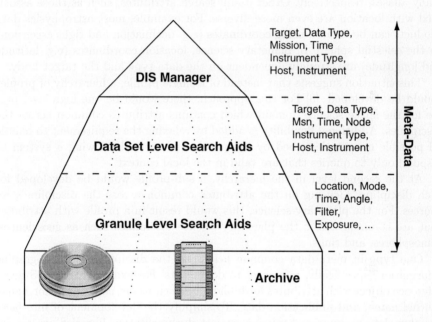

Fig. 8. Search Aid Hierarchy

9 Current Research

The PDS is currently working with other digital libraries in the space science community to provide seamless access to hundreds if not thousands of space science data resources. The goal is to support interoperability across diverse and distributed science data systems as well as provide access for the broader science community, the educational community, and the general public. To support this effort, the concepts, standards, and protocols that have resulted from digital library research are being considered, such as the widely used Z39.50 protocol.

Of particular interest are the BIB-1 and GEO-1 profiles for the library and geospatial domains. Since a profile describes the meta-data available in a digital library, it allows federated, heterogeneous systems to be integrated using the Z39.50 protocol. However, because of the size of the BIB-1 and GEO-1 profiles and the requirement that to be integrated, a system must fully support the profile, a variation of this approach is being considered for the space science domain. In particular, a cursory review of the high level meta-data across the three primary disciplines within space science, namely astrophysics, space physics, and planetary science, has revealed that only about ten attributes are similar across all three disciplines. The most common attributes are those associated with time and target body, and even in these two cases, there are differing formats and many aliases, respectively. Other useful search attributes, such as those associated with location are even more diverse. For example, most astrophysics data products can be located using coordinates (e.g. declination and right ascension) on the celestial sphere. In planetary science, location coordinates (e.g. latitude and longitude) are strongly dependent on the data type and the target body.

This situation suggests that instead of a single profile, a hierarchy of profiles should be developed. [8] For this approach, there would be one high-level profile for the space science domain which contains attributes common across the disciplines. Additional flexibility is added by relaxing the requirement to handle all possible queries described by the profile and instead allowing a system to respond only to queries that are valid in the local context.

At the second level in the hierarchy, a sub-profile would be developed for each discipline, focusing on the attributes common across the discipline's resources. For the planetary science, this would result in a profile with attributes that are common across the planetary science disciplines such as geosciences, atmospheres, and rings.

One type of meta-data common across all the disciplines is bibliographic information, specifically, references to documents. For example, the PDS has a reference object with attributes for bibliographic citations, such as author_name, journal_name, and publication date. To simplify the development of interfaces to other data systems and mission project documentation libraries, we are interested in international standards such as Dublin Core.

Across the space science community, meta-data has been stored in a variety of formats. As the individual systems are integrated, a common language must be used for expressing meta-data for inter-system communication. XML is being considered for this purpose. In particular the capability to structure the responses from a query so that they can be parsed for further processing is a critical component in the plan. It is expected that the categorization and formal modeling of meta-data within each system, and its representation in languages such as XML, will play an important part in the success of catalog interoperability.

10 Conclusion

The PDS, as a science data archive, developed a model of the planetary science domain that includes spacecraft, instruments, missions, target bodies, references, data sets, and data set granules. It was developed using a formal methodology for modeling entities and their relationships within a domain. This model is a fundamental part of the PDS standards architecture and is described in the Planetary Science Data Dictionary. Its function is to capture the meta-data needed to understand the instruments that captured the science data, the formats used to store the data, and the mission objectives for getting the data, so that scientists will be able to intelligently use the data in the future. The meta-data is validated in a peer review and is extracted for catalogs, inventories, and other on-line search aids.

The existence of the formal model and the collected meta-data has allowed the PDS to easily develop on-line catalogs and access tools. The conversion of the meta-data from ODL format to other models and languages has been easy because of the existence of the model and the consistency of the meta-data. The hard problem continues to be the collection, organization, and validation of the meta-data. With the advent of the Web, the PDS has placed the majority of the archive on-line resulting in a scientific digital library that supports the science community, the educational community, and the general public.

Given past experiences, the PDS is well situated for developing interfaces that allow access to the PDS archive via standardized protocols such as Z39.50, standard languages such as XML, and standard interfaces now being considered for globally accessible digital libraries.

11 Acknowledgements

The research described in this paper was carried out by the Jet Propulsion Laboratory, California Institute of Technology, under a contract with the National Aeronautics and Space Administration.

The authors would also like to acknowledge our current sponsor, Joe Bredekamp in NASA's Office of Space Science, and the PDS Central and Discipline Node staff, both past and present, who have worked hard to make the PDS a model science data system.

References

[1] Russell, C. T., et al.: Special Issue: Planetary Data System. Planetary and Space Science. Pergamon, Vol. 44, No. 1(1996)
[2] Arvidson, R.A., et al. Issues and Recommendations Associated with Distributed Computation and Data Management Systems for the Space Sciences. National Academy Press (1986)
[3] Planetary Data System Data Preparation Workbook. JPL Internal Document, JPL D-7669, Part 1. Jet Propulsion Laboratory (1993) Also accessible at http://pds.jpl.nasa.gov/prepare.html
[4] Planetary Data System Standards Reference. JPL Internal Document, JPL D-7669, Part 2. Jet Propulsion Laboratory (1995) Also accessible at http://pds.jpl.nasa.gov/prepare.html

350

[5] Planetary Science Data Dictionary Document. JPL Internal Document, JPL D-7116. Jet Propulsion Laboratory. Also accessible at http://pds.jpl.nasa.gov/prepare.html
[6] Hughes, J.S., Li, Y.P.: The Planetary Data System Data Model. Proceedings of Twelfth IEEE Symposium on Mass Storage Systems (1993) 183–189
[7] Hughes, J.S., Bernath, A.M.: The Planetary Data System Web Catalog Interface - Another Use of the Planetary Data System Data Model. Proceedings of the Fourteenth IEEE Symposium on Mass Storage Systems (1995) 263–273.
[8] Plante, R.L., McGrath, R.E., and Futelle, J.: A Model for Cross-Database Searching of Distributed Astronomical Information Resources. National Center for Supercomputing Applications. University of Illinois, Urbana-Champaign, White Paper.

Performing Arts Data Service –
An Online Digital Resource Library

Stephen Malloch, Carola Boehm, Celia Duffy, Catherine Owen, Stephen Arnold[1],
Tony Pearson

Performing Arts Data Service,
Gilmorehill Centre for Theatre Film and Television,
University of Glasgow,
G12 8QF
http://pads.ahds.ac.uk
info@pads.ahds.ac.uk
[1]Department of Music,
14 University Gardens,
University of Glasgow,
G12 8QF
S.Arnold@music.gla.ac.uk

The Performing Arts Data Service (PADS) aims to support research and
teaching in UK Higher Education by collecting and promoting the use of digital
data relating to the performing arts: music, film, broadcast arts, theatre, dance.
The PADS is one of 5 service providers of the Arts and Humanities Data
Service (AHDS) which will provide a single gateway for arts and humanities
scholars wishing to search for datasets across various discipline areas. Data is
indexed with Dublin Core metadata, will interoperate with other databases
within the AHDS and beyond using Z39.50, and will be available via the Web.
The diversity of data with which the PADS must deal is a major issue, and any
information system for such a service must support text based, visual/image,
time-based and complex data, and offer appropriate access over wide area
networks. This paper focuses on the system requirements of such a system and
briefly describes one implementation of those requirements.

1 Introduction

The Performing Arts Data Service (PADS) is one of a syndicate of five Service
Providers appointed by the Arts and Humanities Data Service (AHDS)[1], funded by
the Joint Information Systems Committee (JISC)[2] of the UK's Higher Education
Funding Councils, and is based at the University of Glasgow. The AHDS's mission is
to co-ordinate access to, and facilitate the creation and use of, electronic resources in
the arts and humanities by offering a range of services.

The AHDS will provide a single gateway for arts and humanities scholars wishing to search for datasets across various discipline areas. Other service providers include: the History Data Service, The Archaeology Data Service, the Oxford Text Archive and the Visual Arts Data Service.[1] The service providers' databases will interoperate with other databases within the AHDS and beyond via Z39.50 [3], and searching will be available via the Web. In order to achieve meaningful search results, data from all the service providers is indexed with Dublin Core metadata.

The Performing Arts Data Service's role within this framework is to support research and teaching in UK Higher Education by collecting and promoting the use of digital data relating to the performing arts: music, film, broadcast arts, theatre and dance. The PADS differs from the other service providers in that it has a particular concern with data consisting of time-based media.

Data relating to Performing Arts is by nature diverse: everything from purely text based (scripts, stage directions) to visuals/images (musical scores, artwork, photographs) to the intrinsically time-based (recordings of live performances, film, video, radio broadcast and multimedia compositions). Any information system for dealing with this range of material must be able to store complex and composite data, cope with a multitude of single documents, and offer intelligent, user-friendly and controlled access over wide area networks.

This is no small task; however, the University of Glasgow has already proven experience in this area of work, notably through two recent projects. The (Scottish Higher Education Funding Council funded) NetMuse Project [4] was a project developing web-based music courseware for delivery over the ATM based Scottish Metropolitan Area Networks (MAN's). This included development of a Java based audio player[5] for streaming full CD quality music, further developed as part of the SMaTBaM! project (Serving Massive Time Based Media)[6]. The SMaTBaM project researched storing, retrieval and delivery of complex and time-based media and was designed specifically to benefit the work of the PADS.

The SMaTBaM! project researched and set up a prototype of a system which would be suitable for the PADS, including the means of delivery of time based data as well as the storage and retrieval issues. (Its work contributes significantly to this paper.) This prototype has now been scaled up and forms the basis of the PADS system which is described later in this paper.

This paper will focus on the general information systems requirements for storage and retrieval of diverse, complex and multimedia data over the web. Additionally, it will briefly describe the implementation of this system at the PADS and highlight some of its important features.

[1] See http://www.ahds.ac.uk/ for URL's to other service provider.

2 Information System Requirements for Performing Arts Data on the Web

Data relating to the performing arts are, as stated above, by nature diverse and have specific requirements which have only been dealt with to a limited extent in past projects. For example, the inherent character of time-based content and the provision of real-time access in high quality provides problems that only high performance servers and networks can cope with, and creates archiving problems that cannot be dealt with the traditional relational database model or catalogue systems.

Though much archival material to be stored and distributed will always be simple data types - such as text, image, audio or video - rather than more complex or composite types of data, appropriate mechanisms for searching and standards for exchanging information efficiently are still needed. Furthermore, structures and models are needed to fulfill the needs of the more complex relationships between these types of data.

The use of digital data resources to facilitate research and teaching in the performing arts has to define methods of storing and distributing complex time-based data to be able to serve quality and quantity information across wide area networks. The important issues here can be split into five areas which shall be considered in more detail:

1. the nature of the data
2. metadata
3. preservation issues
4. delivery issues
5. interoperability.

2.1 Nature of data in relation to Performing Arts

A collection dealing with Performing Arts related data consists of both secondary resources (materials 'about' the performing arts which may include moving image and sound-based media) and primary resources (the digitised multimedia objects themselves). A service such as the PADS should aim to facilitate the access of both primary and secondary resources – where possible real-time access to data, including sound and moving images, is desirable.

It is also desirable for a collection to be expandable by the inclusion of data from other collections holding resources in the same field whilst maintaining a single gateway for accessing the data. This distributed resource environment lets other collection holders keep and maintain their collection in their own repository, while access is handled by a central access point.[2]

---

[2] The National Preservation Office of the National Library of Australia has made this 'distributed responsibility' one of its "Statement of Principles of Preservation of and Long-Term Access to Australian Digital Objects". See http://www.nla.gov.au/npo/natco/princ.html.

A performing arts resource collection encompasses a wide range of different disciplines, from the disciplines of music and film to dance, theatre and the broadcasting arts [7].

The resources as a whole can be characterised as

- being made out of different types of data
- containing differing complexities of data
- possessing different relationships
- being time-based in their nature.

Different Types of Data. As with all multimedia related systems, all the "usual" data types are involved from sound, video, text, image and binaries. Storing them in a certain way provides us with a more complex entity of data types: html, sgml, mpeg, wav, gif, jpeg, java, etc. It is certain that these data formats will evolve further in number and content. The use of different formats in a system should therefore be a means but not a solution. In other words, to minimise the danger of storing data in standards that might not be supported in the future, much thought should go into separating the content of a resource from its presentations. For an example of the separation of content resource and various representational views, one might think of a picture stored in the highest resolution possible in a central resource archive, and its compression to a lower quality for web use. One would still be able to provide a higher quality resource to appropriate users; or an even lower quality one if required by copyright restrictions.

To be able to store a resource in the highest quality possible, combined with the ability to convert it into formats suitable for a certain purpose, or added formats in the future, is to provide an open and flexible system with maximum compatibility in the long term.[3]

Differing complexity of data. While video and images might be stored largely as single binary data-objects, music, theatre and the broadcasting arts could involve the storing and accessing of highly structured data, presenting complex objects or 'composite objects'.[4]

In some cases, it might be hard to distinguish which is the original resource, and which is a composite part of it. If one accepts the fact that the content of a resource

---

[3] In the computing world, this separation of content and representation has one of its object-oriented manifestations in the Model-View-Controller paradigm. The model being the content, the data, or a knowledge domain, the view being one possible presentation of it. The controller can be seen as the gadget maintaining the connection between the model and the view. One musical note, for instance, could be depicted in a system by an internal, proprietary data structure. To this note, one or more views can be "plugged in" as for instance a midi representation, a sound representation, a graphic representation. Devising new views is thus independent of the content. See also [8].

[4] Elementary or simple objects are objects made out of one entity or one binary (e.g. text files, bitmaps, wave files, midi files). Composite objects consist of a number of elementary (or other composite) objects, for instance a music data structure. Complex objects are objects with attributes, that change in size.

might be of complex or composite nature, then the step towards devising a way to store it as such is not far. Technologies are needed that offer the ability to depict, represent, access, store and manipulate complex structures in their complex "Gestalt". A broadcasting feature, as one resource, might encompass video data, sound data, and text data and still be one work of art.

We should accept the fact that our future data might not remain in its binary form and much of our present resources have never been in the "Gestalt" of one entity. Java Applets, Web-objects and other distributed object environments are already being used by artists to create works made out of many components and having many facades. Also, the existing resources, which have been traditionally stored as metadata in catalogues, while their real content is being stored as artefacts in shelves, cassettes, or discs, are often not just one entity. In trying to devise resource systems of the next decade, it would be illogical to diminish the resources and their "real-life" manifestation by disregarding their composite character.

Different Relationships. Assuming that we have objects stored in a persistent way, the access and search results are influenced by the context these objects are in. The mapping of content and context into a digital world means defining and storing different kinds of relationships between objects.[9][10] Relationships can be of numerous variety. For example, five relationships already widely used in information systems are: *inclusion, inheritance, association, attributes* and *web links.*

Inclusion. One object is included in another object (e.g. a file in a folder, a certain sound used in a composition, a note in a bar)

Inheritance. One object inherits the characteristics of another object (e.g. all Bach's works have a BWV, so each single work inherits the attribute BWV-verzeichnis-number of the Bach Works Object; or, all service provider users have read rights, these might be inherited down towards the developers of collections, who also have write rights; or, as a third example, all sounds stored at high quality inherit the characteristic of being served out over ATM network only).

Association. One object is associated with another object (e.g. Mendelssohn's composition "Fingal's Cave" is associated with the geographical rock formation of Staffa. Another example would be that two pages can be associated with each other in form of a sequence. One page should follow the other in a certain context as for instance a book, course, slide show, score etc.).

Attributes. An object contains certain attributes, or certain characteristics which describe its state of being or its internal structure (e.g. all objects in the PADS archive have the attribute Dublin Core, where the Dublin Core object itself has 15 further attributes defining the elements of the Dublin Core).

Web Links. Web-links can be thought of as being a realisation of a certain kind of association. The publication of these resources involves the presenting of one resource via different types of other resources or one resource related to others. For instance, a computer-music piece may exist as a sound file, presenting the first recorded performance, and be archived as the code of the computer program itself and the secondary information associated with the resource.

Time-Based Data. Storing and accessing time-based media requires special attention in storage and delivery of the objects. Solutions are needed to store information in its inherent complex form on the server side, to transmit these information packages in real-time with high-quality over a wide-area network, and to provide a user interface able to access and use the resources intelligently.

For a high-quality service four types of time-based material, all requiring real-time access, can be identified 1) large binary data objects, such as sound or video – a stream of binary data 2) subsets of large binary data objects: playing just a part of a sound or video 3) two or more parallel large binary objects: such as multiple synchronised audio streams or 'lip sync' in film and TV where sound and vision tracks are often recorded on different media 4) complex objects: such as MAX music scores, more complex Java applications, sound-sound combinations or multiple, logically independent streams of arbitrary type.[11]

2.2 Metadata – Dublin Core in Relation to Performing Arts

During 1997, the PADS engaged in various activities to investigate and debate how best to facilitate resource discovery in an on-line setting. Specifically, we looked at the Dublin Core metadata standard[5] and how it could be applied as a tool to describe the time-based (sound and image) data resources that are the special responsibility of the PADS. We have subsequently applied the Dublin Core to our pilot collections (both sound and moving images).

The initial PADS work,[6] which formed part of a series of activities in all the arts and humanities discipline areas represented by the Arts and Humanities Data Service (AHDS), was conducted under the auspices of the AHDS and the UK Office for Library and Information Networking[7], with funding from the Joint Information Systems Committee of the UK's Higher Education Funding Councils (JISC). The aim of the series was to explore how different subject domains both describe and search for electronically held information and to evaluate the usefulness of the Dublin Core as a common set of concepts shared across disciplines that may be used in the construction of the AHDS's integrated catalogue.

Metadata can be defined as the descriptive information by which users locate resources - a sort of electronic catalogue card. The Dublin Core aims to provide users with a way of determining context, subject, intellectual rights and, crucially for the

---

[5] http://purl.org/metadata/dublin_core
[6] http://www.pads.ahds.ac.uk/padsMetadataWorkshopCollection
[7] http://ukoln.ac.uk/

performing arts and time-based media, the type of resource required. Even by taking a simplified distillation of the Dublin Core elements, for example creator and subject, a user can locate a specific object with reasonable accuracy. But the ability to specify what type of object, for example a moving image file, a sound clip or an animated 'gif', facilitates real primary resource location, previously a hit and miss affair. (For example, users searching for a music resource need to be able to specify whether they need a sound recording or a score of the work.)

One of the attractions of the Dublin Core metadata set is its simplicity and ease of use - the Dublin Core was originally intended to be used by non-specialist authors to describe World Wide Web documents. However, the AHDS workshop series[8] and other initiatives from the library and information community have proposed some fairly complex and lengthy qualifiers and amendments to some of the definitions. The PADS held two workshops in April-May 1997, inviting participants with a cross-section of expertise and interest in moving image and sound resources from both service provider communities (libraries and archives) and user communities (UK academics in performing arts disciplines). The groups examined the potential use of the Dublin Core for describing time-based resources, tested it against a variety of examples and critically reviewed its application. The findings from the workshops, which have been borne out by subsequent pilot applications to PADS data, were that the Dublin Core can function adequately, but we have some reservations over certain of its elements. The PADS's recommendations about the use of various elements of the Dublin Core and proposed qualifying statements which are appropriate to moving image and sound resources are documented in the workshop reports.[9] We are still learning from our experience in applying the Dublin Core to our collections - and, most importantly, we anticipate learning from our users' experiences too.

2.3 Preservation Issues

Whilst digital resources present some advantages regarding preservation, namely that of loss-less digital transfer between media, they also pose new problems – particularly the rapidly changing world of storage media formats. As the paper published by the JISC/British Library Workshop of the 27th and 28th November 1995 at the University of Warwick [12] states, there are three types of digital resource preservation: medium preservation, technology preservation and intellectual preservation.

"The problem, and what is new about preservation in the electronic environment, is that electronic information must now be dealt with separately from its medium. This can be illustrated by an analogy ...[I]f a book is placed on a closet shelf, and the closet door is closed for 500 years, then at the end of that time one can, broadly speaking, open that door and read the book. With an electronic resource one does not have that confidence after ten years, and for several reasons." [13]

---

[8] http://ahds.ac.uk/public/metadata/discovery.html
[9] http://www.pads.ahds.ac.uk/padsMetadataWorkshopCollection

In the case of having digital resources as the resource itself (not only having records or catalogues describing it) we have, as mentioned above, the content and the representation of that content. The content is the resource itself, the viewers are the means for the user to see or access this resource. An example would be a piece of digitally stored music "viewed" with a Netscape sound player, or a Real-Audio streaming player, or a CD player. The content of the music seemingly does not change. The viewers, or in other words, the representations, do change.

In devising systems in which the rapid changes of technologies will not make the means of viewing information obsolete, we need to implement a separation of content and view as much as possible. The traditional technique of archivists was the "refreshing" of digital information by copying it into a new standard, a new media, or a new format or "migrating" it from one hardware/software configuration to another.[14, 15, 16] Both techniques can be lossy and time consuming. In adapting systems with the separation of content and viewer, combined with the ability of plugging in new viewers, a maximum of independence of technology change is achieved, while the resource is digitally stored in the highest quality possible and remains so. If compression methods are needed to solve any storage shortages, then a lossless compression method, or a compression method with the least loss, should be used.

In the present era of distributed digital resources on the web, the storage format that will enable the most efficient delivery is often used. This results in using compression methods that would be unacceptable for academic research or cultural heritage preservation. Delivery means and storage means will have to be separated in digital archives and libraries if we are to move into the era of using digital resource preservation as a means to archive cultural heritage. Even if this seems an unrealistic viewpoint from today's standpoint, we will have to deal in future with digital artefacts that cannot be reconstructed into their original quality because they were originally stored in lossy compressed formats. Taking museums and archives for a model, their main aim is to preserve the artefacts as well as possible, and most of the financial expenditure of museums is allocated to this preservation of cultural heritage.

The third preservation requirement specified in the paper published by the JISC/British Library is *intellectual preservation*. This addresses the integrity and authenticity of the information as originally recorded. The JISC/British Library Workshop summed up the changes a digital resource may undergo:

1. Accidental change (data loss during transfer, accidents during updating, saving the wrong version)
2. Intended change - well meaning. New versions or drafts (authorial texts, legislative bills); structural changes (updating books in print or a telephone directory); interactive documents, (hypertexts with note-taking capabilities)
3. Intended change – fraud. E.g. political papers, laboratory notebooks, historical rewriting, legal documents, contracts.

This preservation aspect deals with security, versioning and copyright issues and an information system must be able to handle these issues. An archived digital resource must be secure from unwanted changes, therefore a secure rights administration scheme is required (ideally on the level of user, groups and object collections). The digital resource may change over time, in which case a versioning scheme will be required. Copyright of a digital resource must be securely presented, either by imprinting the copyright information on the resource itself, or by attaching it in a secure manner.

To sum up: in order to guarantee a high quality of digital resource preservation a system design should: a) *separate content from representation;* b) *separate storage from delivery*, and if needed use different storage formats from delivery formats; c) use *lossless compression* methods for storing, where possible; d) implement *secure rights administration*; d) cope with *versioning* over time if required.

2.4 Delivery Issues

For a number of reasons the traditional 'downloading' method of file transfer (e.g. ftp) is inadequate for moving large amounts of multimedia data around the inter/intranet. Time taken to download, having to download a whole file before listening/watching and reservations of copyright holders concerned about digital copying of material have all led to the concept of 'streaming' media.

Digital audio and video data fit well the model of a stream of binary information which is fed to some type of decoder before recreating the original sound/picture. Streaming mechanisms allow the music or video to begin quickly (after a buffer has downloaded), they don't require large amounts of disk space on the client side and they never result in a pure digital copy of the data being created. The popularity of streaming is clearly visible in the number of RealPlayer, LiquidAudio, Shockwave etc. plugins which have been downloaded from the Internet in recent years.

There are two generic issues relating to delivery of time-based media which give rise to a host of specific questions, namely *Quality of Service* and *bandwidth*.

Quality of Service (QoS). Arguably the most important aspect required when dealing with time based media. If the meaning of the data in question relies on its time-based nature then there must be some way to ensure that meaning is effectively communicated (i.e. data is delivered within the specified time-frame) otherwise the meaning of the data is lost.[10]

Bandwidth. Perhaps the most obvious feature of multimedia data, especially video, is the sheer quantity of data and hence bandwidth required. Table 1 shows some data rates for selected common digital audio and video formats[17]. As the speed of the existing internet for non-time based use (e.g. general web searching/browsing) currently shows, there is a distinct shortage of bandwidth for current purposes alone, never mind the potentially vast amounts of audio and video data just waiting for the day it can be streamed at high quality.

---

[10] Even the argument that "infinite bandwidth" will become available does not contradict this idea, as infinite bandwidth would simply be the means of implementing QoS.

Table 1. Data Rates for Selected Media Formats

Standard or Format.	Bandwidth Range (bps = bits per sec)
TV and video data	
PAL	400.2 Mbps (580x575px, 50fps)
NTSC	209.5 Mbps (600x485px, 30fps)
ITU-R 601	140-270 Mbps (320x480px)
MPEG-1	1.2–2.0 Mbps (352x240px, 30fps)
MPEG-2	4-60 Mbps 1.5 Mbps (VHS, 352x240px) 5-6Mbps (b'cast, 1440x1152px) 7Mbps (studio, 1920x1080px)
H.320 H.261	RealVideo 1.0 28.8kbps (newscast) 55kbps (full motion) 100kbps ("near" NTSC)
Audio data:-	
ISO audio Layer 1 Layer 2 Layer 3	MPEG 1 Audio Philips DCC 192kbps MUSICAM 128kbps ASPEC 64 kbps

The other issues relating to delivery – which must take bandwidth and QoS into account - are *network technologies, network protocols, compression/quality, access tools* and *"network philosophy"*.

Network Technologies. The most common networks in use today are 10Base-T Ethernet, 100Base-T Ethernet, FDDI, token ring and ATM; running over fibre optic or twisted pair cables. Raw bandwidth is a combination of the physical medium and networking technology used. 10Mbps Ethernet is perhaps the most established technology for office/campus LAN's, 100Mbps Ethernet is becoming more common, and 155Mbps ATM networks are quite widely deployed e.g. the UK Metropolitan Area Networks (MAN's).

Network Protocols. Although network protocols are often independent of the underlying technology, the two are not necessarily entirely dissociated. ATM, for example, does not follow the OSI model [18] which makes its applicability to IP traffic more difficult; also, IP switching hardware routes IP packets by examining the IP header deeper down the packet, and by identifying 'flows' of packets.[19]

As for time based protocols, the internet has long used TCP and UDP over IP for most needs: neither of which are particularly suited to time-based media. TCP (Transport Control Protocol), for example, is commonly known as a 'reliable' protocol since all packets will eventually arrive, however, packets may arrive out of order and dropped packets will need re-transmitted resulting in delays unacceptable for real time data. UDP (User Datagram Protocol) is often used for network video streaming as occasional dropped packets are sometimes less important than timely delivery of the next packet. (e.g. better to drop a frame of video and go to the next one than to freeze the picture and get each frame right.) New protocols are in development in an attempt to address the needs of time-based data: *RTP, RTCP, RSVP* and *RTSP*.

RTP. The Real-time Transport Protocol provides support for applications with real-time properties, including timing reconstruction, loss detection, security and content identification. A supporting protocol *RTCP* – Real-time Transport Control Protocol – is also under development, though RTP can be used without RTCP. RTP can be used over a variety of protocols, and often uses UDP. RTP is currently also in experimental use directly over AAL5/ATM.[20]

RSVP. 'Resource Reservation Protocol' is a network control protocol designed to allow Internet applications to obtain QoS measures for their data generally by reserving resources along the data path(s). The RSVP working group of the IETF (Internet Engineering Task Force) is developing an Internet standard specification for RSVP which is a component of the future "integrated services" Internet, which will provide both best-effort and real-time qualities of service.[21]

RTSP. Also under development is the Real Time Streaming Protocol (RTSP). An application layer protocol, RTSP is designed specifically for streaming audio and video and intends to provide a framework for interoperability between streaming client-server applications from different vendors.[11]

Table 2. Network technologies and protocols

OSI Layer	OSI Layer Name	Examples
4	Transport	TCP, UDP, RTP, RTCP
3	Network	IP, RSVP
2	Data Link	Ethernet 802.1p 802.1Q; Gigabit Ethernet 802.3z/ab
1	Physical	10BaseT, FDDI

Also worth mentioning here is IPv6 (Internet Protocol version 6 - RFC1883) the so-called "next-generation" IP protocol. IPv6 will expand the IP addressing system to allow a much greater number of addresses and will introduce features such as flow labelling, hierarchical routing, and security. When IPv6 is finally implemented it is likely to be of some benefit for time-based media, but this is not imminent.

---

[11] See, http://www.realaudio.com/prognet/rt/

362

Compression/Quality of Media. Although the argument that "infinite bandwidth" will become available is sometimes used in debates about time-based media over the web, it is fairly safe to assume that many streams of broadcast quality, uncompressed video (up to 400Mbps of bandwidth) shall not be moving round the internet for a considerable number of years yet. *Compression*, as well as real-time network protocols, will therefore play a part in any current media serving solution, and has a direct effect on quality and bandwidth issues.

Although audio requires less bandwidth than video, it is perhaps more demanding of compression techniques and network performance for high quality streaming since the slightest glitch is very noticeable, whereas video is more tolerant of occasional dropped frames. The Moving Pictures Expert Group[12] have developed a number of compression standards for audio and video. The MPEG-2 video standard has been designed for broadcasting and should meet all high quality demands; MPEG-1 audio – whilst not CD quality - uses compression techniques similar to consumer MiniDisc (Sony) and DCC (Digital Compact Cassette - Philips) and should be adequate for most higher quality audio needs. Echoing the preservation issue, material can be archived in its highest quality format offline and encoded with a chosen compression format for delivery at a lower bitrate.

Access tools. At this point in time access to streaming media is only available via proprietary servers and players which do not interoperate. Some form of interoperation will be useful as (or if) and when media servers (and available bandwidth) become common place. E.g. a single client that could receive streams from Sun Media Centres, SGI MediaBase servers and RealPlayer servers. RTSP based solutions will perhaps change this situation someday.

Network 'Philosophies'. The final point to note when considering the delivery of time-based media is that the Internet (and indeed the Intra-net) is not a static entity but continually evolving as new technologies are developed and implemented. This area is defined by both competing manufacturers and design philosophies.

One design 'philosophy' debate which has been argued over since the Internet began is that of connection-orientated networking versus connection-less networking. This can be seen currently in the competition between Gigabit Ethernet and ATM for high bandwidth backbones. Since the design philosophy of the Internet has always been to keep the network simple and put the complexity into the end systems, it would not be too surprising if Gigabit Ethernet eventually dominates since ATM is an inherently connection-orientated system (the internet is generally considered connection-less). ATM has, however, proved itself to be highly successful at reliably and satisfactorily delivering time-based media.[13]

---

[12] http://drogo.cselt.stet.it/mpeg/

[13] See, for instance, [22] where a conductor in Bonn held a rehearsal with musicians in Geneva connected via ATM audio and video codecs. A much more demanding scenario is hard to imagine: real-time, duplex transmission of audio and video, playing a modern piece of music

Relative newcomers to the philosophical debate include IPv6, and protocols such as RTP, RTCP, and RSVP. RSVP is interesting in this context since it also (slightly) subverts the purist connection-less paradigm by implying that routers must have some knowledge of state of connections. These new protocols are yet to prove themselves for the purpose of reliable and satisfactory networked delivery of time-based data.

Cable modems are another area where much research and development is going on – since cable is a significant market – and ATM could play an important role here.

2.5 Interoperability

A key element of the PADS service is to provide interoperability with other collection holders within the AHDS, and a decision was taken by the AHDS to use the Z39.50 protocol for this. However, we shall consider here the general systems requirements of digital multi-media collections. These types of collection already exist, for example: broadcasting stations, music/video archives, record companies and libraries.

These collections are stored in different storage mediums and formats, ranging from simple file systems, to relational database management systems to the growing number of object-oriented database management systems.[23, 24, 25] In addition, a large number of music catalogues in a variety of formats has to be also made accessible.

Between library and library-like catalogues, an implementation of the Z39.50 protocol (version 3, 1995) will be sufficient. For interfacing catalogues with relational databases, there will need to be a Z39.50 - SQL interface. There are very few relational database vendors who have implemented a Z39.50 support; one reason being that their "interoperability protocol" has been SQL, which has been universally accepted and implemented by almost all major database vendors.

Discussions have already taken place to extend the Z39.50-1995 protocol with SQL.[14] From here it is logical step and a matter of time to stay interoperable with the present database generation which is based on object-oriented technologies, and has defined an object query language (OQL) and an object definition language (ODL).[15] With the prospective widespread use of digital libraries, object-oriented database management systems will become a major mean of storing, accessing and using complex, multimedia data objects.[16]

Assuming a basic interoperability of different collections holding digital, multimedia objects, the underlying transfer protocol will have an influence on the

---

with unpredictable timing. The fact that this was possible at all shows what other technologies and protocols have to compete with.

[14] See Proposal for SQL Access in Z39.50: Z39.50/SQL+, http://www.dstc.edu.au/DDU/research_news/reports/zproposal.html. It should be noted that although such plans are being discussed elsewhere, the AHDS' plans are limited to procuring specific interfaces between collection holders and Z39.50.

[15] ODMG 2, http://www.odmg.org/

[16] See [26, 27, 28] which have been influenced largely by projects in cooperation with the Library of Congress.

performance, the quality and the representation means of the objects to be delivered. Using a stateless protocol, such as HTTP (v1.0), means that only one object can be delivered per session. Thus the connection closes after each document is delivered, losing all the information of the former session.

In devising a secure and distributed system, with collections stored in different locations, access handled from a central gateway and user access in the best case being controlled to a point of write, read and execute rights of single objects and collections, stateless protocols can be a problem. Solutions lie in the underlying existence of user rights management, such as a database management system able to control the access of many users in dependency of objects or collection of objects, or/and the use of a stateful protocol.

3 PADS Systems Architecture – an Implementation of the System Requirements

Having considered the system requirements of an information system for Performing Arts data on the web, we shall briefly give an overview of one implementation of these requirements. Namely, the current system architecture in use at the PADS.

There are three principle components to the PADS system architecture: the underlying hardware (servers and networking); and the two key software components: "MediaBase" and "Hyperwave Information Server".

The hardware consists of two Silicon Graphics Origin200 servers. One is configured as a "media server" running MediaBase[17] software and is designed to meet the needs of the delivery issues highlighted above. Networking is provided through 100Mbps Ethernet ports and 155Mbps ATM connections.

Although MediaBase includes a database system for keeping track of low level 'metadata' (relating to format, file size, location etc) and a web gateway for browsing and searching media files directly, the 'real' metadata storage is done in the second server which runs Hyperwave Information Server.

3.1 Hyperwave Information Server

Hyperwave Information Server (Hyperwave)[18] is a relatively new product originally developed at the University of Graz in Austria, an has many features which lend itself to a digital resource library such as the PADS.

Hyperwave consists of three 'layers' of software: the *protocol* conversion layer, the *session* layer and the *database* layer. The protocol layer interprets incoming protocols to Hyperwave's own protocol – allowing Hyperwave to be accessed through a wide range of different gateways including HTTP, telnet and Z39.50. The

---

[17] http://www.sgi.com/Products/WebFORCE/Products/Mediabase.html
[18] See, http://www.hyperwave.de/

session layer communicates with the database, retaining state information and parallelising client requests. The database layer is where actual documents, links and meta-information are stored; this layer is fully indexed for searching purposes.

The database at the heart of the Hyperwave system is object orientated, allowing the storage of all kinds of objects themselves as well relationships, attributes and links between objects.

Hyperwave also allows storage of 'remote' objects e.g. storage of metadata relating to an object which is physically held elsewhere. This is in fact how time-based media data is stored at the PADS. E.g. a movie's metadata – title, director, cast, format (in Dublin Core fields of course) – is held within Hyperwave but the actual object is stored in the MediaBase server: simply clicking on a link starts the file streaming from MediaBase to the client.

Other features worth highlighting include: the ability to have different 'views' of the same object; secure user and group rights administration – with Unix-like permissions down to the object level – allowing remote administration of certain collections for example; gateways to SQL databases, allowing them to be 'hooked up' while still providing a single interface to the end user.

More details of the PADS system architecture can be found via the web pages: http://pads.ahds.ac.uk/ and in the online documentation for the SMaTBaM! project[6].

4 Conclusion

This paper has described the general information systems requirements of Performing Arts related data on the web, and concludes that such a system should: cope with complex and composite objects, support a range of relationships between objects, separate content from presentation, separate storage from delivery, use lossless storage where possible, provide a framework for dealing with time-based media, cope with versioning and changes to objects, provide secure rights administration, support stateful connections and interoperate with other relevant collections. One implementation which seeks to meet as many of these requirements as it can is the system currently being implemented at the Performing Arts Data Service.

References

[1] http://www.ahds.ac.uk/, July 1997
[2] http://www.jisc.ac.uk/, July 1997
[3] http://lcweb.loc.gov/z3950, July 1997
[4] http://www.netmuse.gla.ac.uk/, July 1997
[5] S. Malloch, S. Arnold, T. Pflicke, "Using Java to stream audio over ATM", Proceedings of the ICMC, Thessaloniki, 1997
[6] http://www.music.gla.ac.uk/HTMLFolder/Research/SMaTBaM.html, July 1997

[7] http://www.music.gla.ac.uk/HTMLFolder/Research/smatbam-private/categories.html, July 1997

[8] Jacco van Ossenbruggen: Music in Time-Based Hypermedia: http://www.cs.vu.nl/~jrvosse/Papers/echt94/html/index.html, July 1997

[9] Relationship Service Specification for distributed objects, (OMG) ftp://www.omg.org/pub/docs/formal/97-12-16.pdf, July 1997

[10] Laboratory for Advanced Information Technology: the Knowledge Interchange Format, KIF, http://www.cs.umbc.edu/kse/kif/kif101.shtml, July 1997

[11] Scott Flinn, Coordinating Heterogeneous Time-Based Media Between Independent Applications, http://www.cs.ubc.ca/spider/flinn/publications/mm95/scheduler.html, July 1997

[12] http://www.ukoln.ac.uk/, July 1997

[13] Commission on Preservation and Access and The Research Libraries Group, Inc., "The Challenge of Archiving Digital Information:" http://www.rlg.org/ArchTF/, July 1997

[14] http://www.nla.gov.au/nla/staffpaper/preserve.html, July 1997

[15] Bibliography of Resources Related to Preservation of Digital Resources: http://www.oclc.org/oclc/research/9448or/9448toc.htm, July 1997

[16] Long Term Preservation Of Electronic Materials: http://ukoln.bath.ac.uk/fresko/warwick/intro.html, April 1997

[17] M. McCutcheon, M. R. Ito, G. W. Neufeld, "Video and Audio Streams Over an IP/ATM Wide Area Network" UBC Transport Encoded Video over IP/ATM Project, Technical Report 97-3, June 97. http://www.ncstrl.org:3803/, April 1997

[18] A. Tanenbaum "Distributed Operating Systems" p44, Prentice Hall International Editions, New Jersey 1995.

[19] RFC's and hardware relating to IP switching: http://www.ipsilon.com/products/specifications.htm#HWPROC, April 1997

[20] C. Liu, Multimedia Over IP: RSVP, RTP, RTCP, RTSP, http://www.cis.ohio-state.edu/~cliu/, July 1997

[21] RFC1633, http://ds.internic.net/rfc/rfc1633.txt, April 1997

[22] D. Konstantus, Y. Orlarey et al "Distributed Music Rehearsal" Proceedings of the ICMC, Thessaloniki, 1997.

[23] Time-Warner Pathfinder Personal Edition, http://pathfinder.com/@@5cnHOgcAhVYFFeXJ/welcome/, July 1997

[24] Chicago Tribune's Metromix, http://www.metromix.com/, July 1997

[25] Liberation (Libraries: Electronic Remote Access to Information Over Networks), http://www.iicm.edu/liberation, July 1997

[26] Kahn/Wilensky, "A Framework for Distributed Digital Object Services, http://www.cnri.reston.va.us/home/cstr/arch/k-w.html, July 1997

[27] Daniel Lagoze's Dienst/NCSTRL http://cs-tr.cs.cornell.edu:80/Dienst/UI/1.0/Display/ncstrl.cornell/TR96-1593, July 1997

[28] "The Warwick Framework A Container Architecture for Aggregating Sets of Metadata." http://cs-tr.cs.cornell.edu:80/Dienst/UI/1.0/Display/ncstrl.cornell/TR96-1514, July 1997

Learning User Communities for Improving the Services of Information Providers

Georgios Paliouras,* Christos Papatheodorou,+ Vangelis Karkaletsis,*
Costantine Spyropoulos,* Victoria Malaveta+

* Institute of Informatics and Telecommunications,
+ Division of Applied Technologies,
National Centre for Scientific Research (NCSR) "Demokritos",
15310, Aghia Paraskevi, Attikis, GREECE
*Tel: +301-6503196, Fax: +301-6532175,
*E-mail:{paliourg, vangelis, costass}@iit.demokritos.gr
+ Tel:+301-6503287, E-mail:{papatheodor,victoria}@leucippus.nrcps.ariadne-t.gr

Abstract. In this paper we propose a methodology for organising the users of an information providing system into groups with common interests (communities). The communities are built using unsupervised learning techniques on data collected from the users (user models). We examine a system that filters news on the Internet, according to the interests of the registered users. Each user model contains the user's interests on the news categories covered by the information providing system. Two learning algorithms are evaluated: COBWEB and ITERATE. Our main concern is whether meaningful communities can be constructed. We specify a metric to decide which news categories are representative for each community. The construction of meaningful communities can be used for improving the structure of the information providing system as well as for suggesting extensions to individual user models. Encouraging results on a large data-set lead us to consider this work as a first step towards a method that can easily be integrated in a variety of information systems.

1 Introduction

The separation of "wheat from hay" on the Internet is becoming increasingly important as the amount of information available electronically becomes unmanageable for its non-expert receivers. As a result, a number of service providers have appeared recently in the market to help Internet users separate the information they need out of the plethora of information on the net. The simplest form of such a service is a search engine, which matches user-specified keywords to documents related to these keywords through word indices. The capabilities of such a search engine are restricted both in terms of the complexity of the search pattern and also in terms of the relevance of the information that gets retrieved. The overflow of information demands more advanced techniques. It is not the amount of information that gives the value, but access to the required information at the right time and in the most suitable form.

In this paper we examine the exploitation of user modelling techniques for the customisation of information to the needs of individual users. More specifically, we propose a methodology for organising the users of an information providing system into groups with common interests (*communities*). The communities are built from data collected from the users (*user models*). Each model contains the user's interests on the news categories covered by the information providing system. These interests are expressed by the user during his/her registration to the information system. The user model can be modified by the user at any point in time, reflecting changes of interest on the news categories.

The task of building user communities from user models can be seen as a data mining task, since we are looking for interesting patterns within a database, i.e., the user models. For this reason the type of method that is applicable to this problem is the method used mainly in data mining: *unsupervised learning*. In this paper we examine two unsupervised learning techniques, COBWEB [10] and ITERATE [3] and evaluate them on the task of building user communities. Both learning algorithms belong in the conceptual clustering family which is particularly suitable to symbolic training data, as it is the case here, where the users express their preferences on the news categories covered by the information system.

The resulting communities can be used to improve the services provided by the information system. However, this can be done effectively only when the generated communities are meaningful, that is if they contain those sets of preferences that are representative for the participating users. Ideally we would like to be able to construct a prototypical model for each community, which is representative of the participating user models and significantly different from the models of other communities. Such communities can be used to:
-   re-organise the structure of the information system, e.g. re-define the hierarchy of news categories,
-   suggest extensions to individual user models, e.g. news categories that are not selected by a user, but which are popular within his/her community,
-   support the expansion strategy for the service, e.g. include new sources of information for popular news categories.

A sound and objective method for characterising communities is highly desirable, in order for the system designer to use the clustering results. This is a major problem in statistical clustering methods. That's why we examine the use of a metric to decide which categories are representative for the community. This metric was used to evaluate the results of the application of the two learning algorithms in a large dataset of 1078 user models which was given to us by an Internet information provider.

Section 2 of the paper takes a broader view of user modelling in order to position our problem within this research domain, explains how machine learning techniques can be exploited in user modelling and describes the two learning algorithms and their applicability to our problem. Section 3 discusses the problem of constructing meaningful communities and introduces a metric for the characterisation of the generated community descriptions. Section 4 presents the setting of an experiment for the application of the two learning algorithms and discusses the experiment results.

Section 5 presents briefly related work and section 6 describes ongoing work and introduces our plans for future work.

2 Research Background

2.1 User Modelling

User Modelling technology aims to make information systems really user-friendly, by adapting the behaviour of the system to the needs of the individual. The importance of adding this capability to information systems is proven by the variety of areas in which user modelling has already been applied: information retrieval, filtering and extraction systems, adaptive user interfaces, student modelling.

Information retrieval and filtering systems aim to deliver to the user those documents that are relevant to his/her information requirements, whereas information extraction systems aim to deliver specific facts from those documents. *NewT* is a system that helps the user filter Usenet Netnews [13] according to his interests. Brajnik and Tasso [5,6] present the exploitation of the user modelling shell UMT in the prototype information-providing *system Tourist Advisor (TA)*. Kay [12] describes the *Movie Advisor* project, which operates on a database of movie descriptions, suggesting movies that should appeal to a specific user. *Doppelgänger* [15] is a user modelling system that gathers sensor data about users, makes inferences on those data and makes the results available to applications. *Firefly*'s agent software (see *http://www.firefly.com*) groups users preferences based on their similarities in order to suggest buying opportunities to specific customers based on their similarity to other customers. *Fab* [1] is a filtering system that recommends items similar to those a given user has liked in the past, and items liked by users whose interests are similar to those of a given user. *UMIE* [2] is a Web-based prototype user modelling component *(see http://www.iit.demokritos.gr/UMIE)*, that filters the data extracted from an information extraction system according to the users models.

Adaptive user interfaces are implemented exploiting user models which contain information about the typical use of the system by each user. These user models differ from those in information filtering and retrieval, because they contain mainly procedural information, specifying how the system is used by each user. Substantial effort has been made to automate the adaptation of user interfaces to the user. This is usually achieved by monitoring the use of the system by the user, e.g. [7, 8, 12, 15].

This paper focuses on information retrieval and filtering systems, but the methodology that we propose is directly applicable to other systems that incorporate user models.

A user model consists mainly of the individual preferences of the user. Furthermore, it may contain personal information about the user, such as his/her age, occupation, etc. The latter type of information is not directly necessary for the adaptation of the system to the user, but may be used to categorise the user into a *stereotype*, which in turn allows the system to anticipate some of the user's behaviour. Stereotypes have been introduced in [19], as a means of organising the users of the system into meaningful groups. For instance, a stereotype might state that "young people are interested in sports news." Thus, a stereotype characterises groups of users, with common preferences. The characterisation of the group is based on personal information included in the models of the participating users.

Personal information about the users of a system is not always available and therefore the construction of user stereotypes may not be possible. In that case, the organisation of users into groups with common interests can still be useful. Such a group of users is termed a *user community* and corresponds to a stereotype missing personal information. Clearly, the loss of information in the transition from stereotypes to communities is not without cost. A stereotype can be used to predict the preferences of a user, even when he/she has not explicitly stated any of them. This is not possible with communities, which can only be used to extend/modify an existing user model. Despite that, user communities can be used in several ways to improve the quality of service provided by the information system.

2.2 Learning from user models

Machine learning methods have been applied to user modelling problems, mainly for acquiring models of individual users interacting with an information system, e.g. [4, 9, 17]. In such situations, the use of the system by an individual is monitored and the collected data are used to construct the model of the user, i.e., his/her individual requirements.

We are concerned with a higher level of generalisation of the users' interests: the construction of user communities. This task requires the application of learning techniques to user models, which are assumed to have been constructed by a separate process, either manual or automatic. Fig. 1 illustrates the two different levels of learning in user modelling. In the lower part of the graph, user models are constructed from individual user queries and at the higher level, the user models are used to build communities.

The choice of learning method depends largely on the type of training data that are available. The main distinction in machine learning research is between *supervised* and *unsupervised* learning methods. Supervised learning requires the training data to be preclassified. This usually means that each training item (*example*) is associated with a unique label, signifying the category in which the item belongs. In our case, this would mean that each user model must be associated with a category label out of a set of possible categories that have been defined beforehand. Given these data, the learning algorithm builds a characteristic description for each category, covering the examples of this category, i.e., the users belonging to the category, and only them, i.e., none of the users of other categories. The important feature of this approach is that the category descriptions are built conditional to the preclassification of the examples in the training set. In contrast, unsupervised learning methods do not require preclassification of the training examples. These methods form clusters of examples, which share common characteristics. When the cohesion of a cluster is high, i.e., the examples in it are very similar, it is labelled as a category.

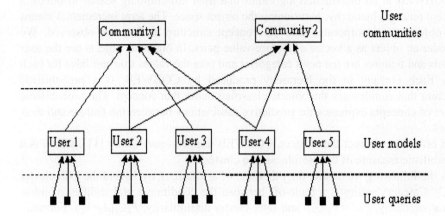

Fig. 1. Two levels of user-model construction

Supervised learning seems most appropriate for the construction of user stereotypes, i.e., the characteristic description of user groups based on personal information about the users. In contrast, the construction of user communities is a typical unsupervised learning task. In our work, we have chosen to concentrate on the construction of user communities, since the collection of personal information about an information system on the Internet is problematic. The construction of stereotypical descriptions for the communities, if personal information is available, is a straightforward task for the common supervised learning algorithms, e.g. C4.5 [16] and AQ15 [14].

Unsupervised learning tasks have been approached by a variety of methods, ranging from statistical clustering techniques to neural networks and symbolic machine learning. In this work, we have opted for the symbolic learning methods, because we are interested in the comprehensibility of the results. The branch of symbolic machine learning that deals with unsupervised learning is called *conceptual clustering* and two popular representatives of this approach are the algorithms COBWEB and ITERATE. These two algorithms are briefly described in the following subsection.

2.3 Learning algorithms

The two algorithms that we use in this work perform *conceptual clustering*. Conceptual clustering is a type of learning by observation that is particularly suitable for summarising and explaining data. *Summarisation* is achieved through the discovery of appropriate clusters, which involves determining useful subsets of an object set. In unsupervised learning, the object set is the set of training examples, i.e.

each object is an example. *Explanation* involves *concept characterisation*, i.e., determining a useful concept description for each class.

COBWEB is an incremental algorithm that uses hill-climbing search to obtain a concept (cluster) hierarchy, partitioning the object space. The term incremental means that objects are incorporated into the concept structure as they are observed. We consider an object as a vector of feature-value pairs. In our case, objects are the user models and features are the news categories and take the values true and false for each user. Each concept in the hierarchy produced by COBWEB, is a probabilistic structure that summarises the objects classified under that concept. The probabilistic nature of concepts expresses the predictive associations between the feature and their values.

In order to construct the clusters, COBWEB uses *category utility* [11], which is a probabilistic measure of the usefulness of a cluster.

In the following we denote the j-th value of a feature A_i by V_{ij} and the k-th cluster by C_k. Category utility is a trade-off between the conditional probabilities of intra-cluster similarity, $P(A_i=V_{ij}|C_k)$, and inter-cluster dissimilarity, $P(C_k|A_i=V_{ij})$. Formally the category utility for a cluster k is defined as:

$$CU_k = P(C_k)\left[\sum_i\sum_j P(A_i=V_{ij}|C_k)^2 - \sum_i\sum_j P(A_i=V_{ij})^2\right] \tag{1}$$

and for the whole set of objects:

$$CU = \frac{\sum_{k=1}^{n} CU_k}{n}, \tag{2}$$

where n is the number of clusters in a partition.

CU represents the increase in the expected number of feature values that can be correctly guessed:

$$P(C_k)\sum_i\sum_j P(A_i=V_{ij}|C_k)^2 \tag{3}$$

given a partition $(C_1,C_2,...,C_n)$, over the expected number of correct guesses with no such knowledge:

$$\sum_i\sum_j P(A_i=V_{ij})^2 \tag{4}$$

COBWEB incorporates objects into the concept hierarchy using the following four clustering operators:
- placing the object in an existing cluster,
- creating a new cluster,
- combining two clusters into a new one (merging) and
- dividing a cluster (splitting).

Given a new object, the algorithm applies each of the previous operators and selects the hierarchy that maximises category utility. COBWEB is an efficient and flexible algorithm. The complexity of the incorporation of an object in a hierarchy is quadratic to the nodes of the derived hierarchy. Since the size of the hierarchy is log-linearly related to the size of the object set, COBWEB is scalable to large training sets. The algorithm can also deal with missing feature values. However, COBWEB depends on its incremental character, i.e. it is dependent on the order of the observed objects.

In ITERATE the problem of the order-dependence is dealt by an object ordering strategy called ADO (Anchored Dissimilarity Ordering). ITERATE is not incremental and does not produce a concept hierarchy, but a flat partition of the objects. It starts by generating a tree, which is then flattened into a set of cohesive and maximally distinct clusters. However ITERATE is a descendant of COBWEB and inherits several of its features, e.g. the probabilistic structure of the concepts, and the category utility measure.

ITERATE has three primary steps:
- classification tree generation from a set of objects,
- partition of the tree to extract a set of clusters and
- iterative redistribution of the objects among the clusters to achieve a new set of maximally separable clusters.

During the first step, ITERATE produces a classification tree using the category utility measure similarly to COBWEB. The differences between the two methods are the following:
- ITERATE does not utilise the merging and splitting operators of COBWEB and
- if a node of the tree contains one or more objects, it sorts them using ADO scheme in order to obtain a maximally dissimilar ordering among the objects.

In the second step, ITERATE extracts an initial partition structure by comparing the category utility of the clusters, CU_k along a path in the classification tree. For every path from the root to a leaf of the tree, the algorithm computes the category utility of each cluster. While this measure increases, the algorithm goes on to the next cluster of the path. At the cluster for which the measure value drops, the algorithm inserts its previous cluster to the initial partition list. In this manner ITERATE ensures that no concept subsumes another and maximises cluster cohesion.

In the final step, ITERATE redistributes the objects to the clusters of the initial partition (derived in step 2), until the *category match* measure is maximised for each object. During this process, some clusters may be merged and thus the initial partition is improved. The category match metric measures the increase in the expected predictability of cluster C_k for the feature values present in data object d. Formally category match is defined as:

$$CM_{dk} = P(C_k) \sum_{i,j \in \{A_i\}_d} \left(P(A_i = V_{ij} | C_k)^2 - P(A_i = V_{ij})^2 \right) \tag{5}$$

The category utility measure of a given cluster, is a sum of the category match measures of the objects in the cluster.

3 Construction of meaningful communities

The clusters generated by the application of the two learning algorithms to the data collected from the users (user models), represent the user communities. The question that arises is whether there is any meaning in the derived communities. Since there is no personal information available about the users, the construction of stereotypical descriptions for the communities is not possible. The only information available is the set of preferences of the users in each community. Thus, the natural way to construct meaningful communities is by trying to identify sets of preferences that are representative for the participating users. Ideally we would like to be able to construct a prototypical model for each community, which is representative of the participating user models and significantly different from the models of other communities.

The construction of prototypical models for the communities is a problem in itself. We specify a metric to decide which are the representative news categories for each community of news readers. This metric measures the increase in the frequency of a category within a community, as compared to the default frequency of the category in the whole data set. The frequency of a category corresponds to the proportion of users that are interested in this category. In [3] the increase in frequency was used as an indication of the increase in the predictability of a feature within the community. Given a category c, with default frequency f_c, if the frequency of this category within a community i is f_i, the metric is defined as a simple difference of the squares of the two frequencies:

$$FI_c = f_i^2 - f_c^2 \tag{6}$$

FI stands here for Frequency Increase. Clearly, when FI_c is negative there is a decrease in frequency and the corresponding category is not representative for the community. The definition of a representative news category for a community, is simply that $FI_c > \alpha$, where α is the required extent of frequency increase. If $\alpha > 0$ then the requirement is that the frequency of a category within a community has increased, in comparison to the frequency in the initial dataset. The question that arises is how large the increase should be in order for the category to be considered as a characteristic one for a community.

In order to see the impact of the parameter on the characterisation of the communities, we propose to vary α and measure the following two properties of the generated community descriptions:

- *Coverage:* the proportion of news categories covered by the descriptions. Some of the categories will not be covered, because their frequency will not have increased sufficiently.
- *Overlap:* the amount of overlap between the constructed descriptions. This is measured simply as the ratio between the total number of categories in the description and the number of distinct categories that are covered.

In the following section, we evaluate the results of the two learning algorithms in a case study for the construction of meaningful communities. More specifically, we measure the coverage and overlap properties of the generated community descriptions, varying α values.

4   Case Study

4.1   Experimental setting

We applied the two learning algorithms on the task of constructing user communities for a news-filtering system. This system collects information from various sources in the Internet and forwards it to its users, according to their user models. The news articles are organised by the information provider into 24 news categories, e.g. sports, computers, etc., which are further divided into 239 subcategories, e.g. sports/football, sports/volleyball, etc. During his/her registration, each user specifies a subset of these categories, which correspond to his/her personal interests. This personal list of news categories constitutes the user model, which determines what news he/she receives. The user model can be modified by the user at any point in time, reflecting changes of interest.

The dataset for the experiment contained 1078 user models, with an average of 5.4 news categories and 17.4 subcategories specified in each model. These user models formed a set of training examples for the learning algorithms. Each example was represented as a binary feature vector, which specified which news categories the user was interested in. In other words, each bit in the vector corresponded to a category and was "on" if the user was interested for this category and "off" otherwise. Given these training examples, the two algorithms constructed groups of users with common interests.

The two-layered organisation of news categories in the system suggested two different test cases: one using the 24 general categories and one using their subcategories. Unfortunately, the ITERATE algorithm could not handle the size of the dataset, when considering the 239 subcategories.[1] For this reason, we only examined the first of the two test cases, the results of which are presented in the following section.

---

[1] We are currently examining whether this is due to the design of the algorithm or its implementation. If the former case is true, ITERATE is not scalable to training sets with a large number of descriptive features.

376

4.2 Results

In the first experiment, the COBWEB algorithm was applied on the small data set, i.e., the one with the 24 news categories. The generated concept hierarchy consisted of 699 nodes, of which the first three layers are presented in Fig. 2. An important property of the tree in Fig. 2 is the balanced split of objects in different branches. The nodes in the same level of the tree cover subsets of the data set that are of comparable size. Therefore the underlying concepts are of similar strength.

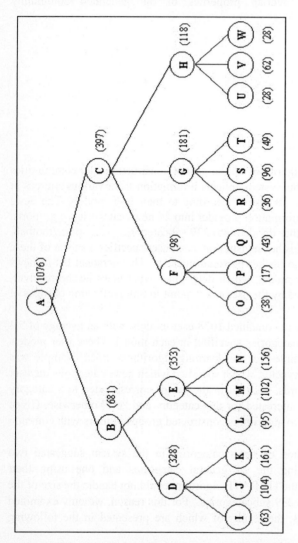

Fig. 2. The top three layers of the concept hierarchy produced by COBWEB. Node A is the root of the hierarchy, covering the whole dataset. The numbers in brackets correspond to the number of objects covered at each node.

We chose to examine only the top three levels of the tree generated by COBWEB, because the number of clusters generated by ITERATE is comparable to the second and third levels of the COBWEB tree. ITERATE generates 11 classes in the second step, i.e., as the initial partition of the object space. The final partition, which is constructed by ITERATE contains only two clusters and is therefore of limited use.

ITERATE's partition of the data set into the 11 clusters is as follows:
C1 (34), C2 (88), C3 (167), C4 (5), C5 (129), C6 (247), C7 (122), C8 (62), C9 (67), C10 (59), C11 (98),
where the number in brackets corresponds to the number of objects in each cluster. The majority of clusters are of comparable size, with the exception of a very small one, C4, and four large clusters: C3, C5, C6 and C7.

As mentioned in section 3, we use the FI_c measure in (6) in order to construct meaningful communities from the generated clusters.

Ideally, we would like to acquire descriptions that are maximally distinct, i.e., minimise the overlap, and increase coverage. Fig. 3 and Fig. 4 show how the two measures vary for different sizes of α, for COBWEB and ITERATE. In the case of COBWEB, we examined two different partitions of the objects, corresponding to the second and the third level of the concept hierarchy, i.e., nodes {**D, E, F, G, H**} and {**I, J, K, L, M, N, O, P, Q, R, S, T, U, V, W**}.

Fig. 3 shows that the coverage of the two algorithms varies in a similar manner as the value of α increases. As expected, the larger the value of α the fewer the categories that are covered by the clusters. In the case of COBWEB, the coverage on the second level of the hierarchy is consistently lower than that on the third level. The reason for this is that the concepts on the third level are more specialised than those on the second. The frequency of the categories in the more specific clusters, is higher than in the more general ones.

Fig. 4 depicts the amount of overlap between the community descriptions for the two algorithms. It becomes clear from those results that the larger the number of the communities, the larger the overlap between their descriptions. Thus, there is a trade-off between coverage and overlap, as the number of communities increases. In the case of the 15 different clusters, the extent of the overlap is significantly higher than in the other two cases. The 5-cluster case in COBWEB gives the best results in terms of the distinctness in the descriptions.

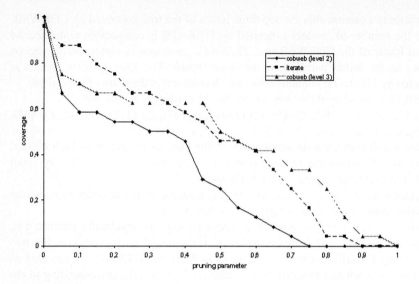

Fig. 3. Results on the coverage of news categories for the two algorithms. On the x axis, the value of the pruning parameter α is changed from 0 to 1 at an increment of 0.05.

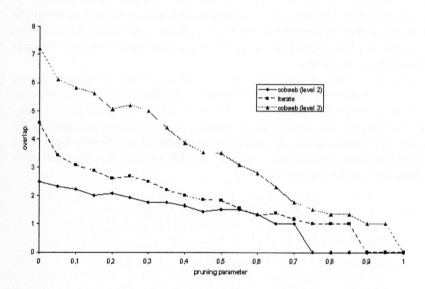

Fig. 4. Results on the overlap between community descriptions as α varies.

In the final step of our work we looked at the actual community descriptions in the manageable case of the 5 clusters generated by COBWEB. For $\alpha=0.5$, a set of very concise and meaningful concept descriptions were acquired. Table 1 lists the news categories for the 5 clusters, together with their FI_c values.

Communities **E**, **G** and **H** are well-separated, corresponding to a group of people interested in the Internet, another who are interested in Economics and a third interested in computers. Group **F**, consists of people interested mainly in economics and finance, but also in computers. Some interest in computers is to be expected from the users of a system on the Internet. Finally, cluster **D** serves as a "miscellaneous" category and does not seem to be homogeneous. The main similarity between the people in **D**, is that they are very specific in their choices, resulting in user models that are empty, i.e., most categories are not of interest to the user.

Table 1. Descriptions for the 5 categories generated on the second level of the concept hierarchy

D	E	F	G	H
	Internet (0.55)	Economic Indicators (0.73)	Economic Indicators (0.58)	Computers (0.53)
		Economics & Finance (0.68)	Economics & Finance (0.61)	
		Computers (0.6)		
		Transport (0.53)		
		Financial Indicators (0.5)		

An obvious problem with the descriptions in Table 1 is that a large number of news categories are not covered. In general, these are the categories that are chosen by either too few or too many users. In the former case the algorithms choose to ignore them during learning and in the latter case, they correspond to such general interests, that they are difficult to attribute them to particular communities. Filtering out these two types of category is a positive feature of the FI metric. Coverage can increase, by moving selectively at lower levels of the COBWEB hierarchy. For instance, the children of node **H** give meaningful and concise communities, corresponding to categories that are related to computing, e.g. electronics, networks, telecommunications. However, this is not the case for all of the five communities in Table 1. For instance, the children of node **E** do not provide further meaningful subgroups in the community. The ability to select nodes in different levels of the concept hierarchy is an important advantage of the COBWEB algorithm. Arguably, this selection is done automatically by the ITERATE algorithm, using the category utility metric. However, in our case ITERATE did not provide meaningful and concise communities.

5   Related work

This paper presents a methodology for the exploitation of user modelling technology in information providing services. There are two main approaches: community and stereotype modelling. The choice depends mainly on the type of information that is available. Community modelling does not require system-independent information. This is important, because such information is often not available, e.g. in WWW applications it is impossible to have personal information about all people who access a site. The lack of system-independent information, in our case study, led us to follow the community modelling approach.

However, there are cases where system-independent variables are also included in a community-based system. This is the case in [15] where both types of variables are treated in the same manner by the system. In our case, the communities include only system-dependent variables, since the registered users do not provide any personal information either explicitly or implicitly. We have to note that this is the case with most information providing services.

Although community modelling has the advantage that it does not require system-independent information, it should be stressed that communities cannot replace stereotypes. No suggestions can be made about a new user, unless he/she explicitly states some of his/her interests. The work presented in [1] pays particular attention to that fact and distinguishes between two types of community-based system. In the first type the user specifies some of his interests, whereas in the second the system builds the user model gradually, since there is no initial information about the user. The news filtering system used in our experiment belongs to the first type, since the user during his/her registration has to specify the interesting news categories. The latter type of system cannot classify a new user into any of the communities and can therefore not provide any user-specific behaviour.

Concerning the construction of user communities there are two main approaches. In the first one the user models themselves are used to reason about the interests of a new user. For instance, we could search for an old user B who shares most of his interests with the interests of the new user A and then use the user model of B to suggest extensions to the model of A. This type of reasoning is called *case-based* and does not involve any learning, in the sense of drawing general rules from the data. The algorithm that is mostly used for this type of reasoning is called k-nearest-neighbour. The information systems that are based on this approach are called *recommender or collaborative filtering systems* [18].

The second approach for constructing user communities is to perform some kind of clustering, using either a standard statistical method, such as a hierarchical clustering algorithm or a neural network. Although clustering seems a computationally expensive task compared to the case-based approach, this is not a real problem since communities change far less often than individuals. On the other hand, clustering is a necessary task according to the objectives of the work presented in this paper. As we mentioned in the introduction, the resulting communities can be used to improve the services provided by the information system. However, this can be done effectively, only when the generated communities are meaningful. That's why we examined the use of a metric (i.e. the Frequency Indicator) to decide which categories are representative for the community. Although the clustering approach is used for the construction of communities [15], this is the first time, as far as we know, that the clustering algorithm results are evaluated in order to generate meaningful community descriptions.

6 Conclusions

In this paper we have presented a methodology for constructing user communities. These communities can be used to improve the exploitation of an information system by its users. The construction of the communities was achieved by elaborating unsupervised learning techniques. In particular, we used two conceptual clustering algorithms: COBWEB and ITERATE. Our main concern is whether meaningful communities can be constructed. This is a major problem in statistical clustering methods, the results of which are usually hard to interpret. A sound and objective method for solving this problem is highly desirable, in order for the clustering results to be of practical use for the service provider. This issue forms the motivation of our research work. We examined the use of a metric in order to decide which categories are representative for a community. We evaluated the results of the two learning algorithms, based on that metric, in a case study.

Our results are very encouraging, showing that useful information can be extracted about the use of an information system, through the characterisations of the generated community descriptions. We consider this work as a first step towards a method that can easily be integrated in a variety of information systems, in order to provide the required insight into the use of the system.

A further direction of interest is the use of machine learning to construct user stereotypes, when personal information is available. The conceptual relationship between stereotypes and communities suggests that some of the work presented in this paper will also be of use there. However, as mentioned above, learning user stereotypes is primarily a supervised learning task, due to the assumed dependence between user groups and their personal characteristics.

Concluding, we believe that the task of constructing user communities for information systems is of great practical use and it is also a technically challenging matter. Despite the encouraging results presented in this paper, we would like to evaluate our methodology on other systems as well. So, we have already started to validate the proposed methodology, in the recently established information providing system of the NCSR "Demokritos" Library.

Acknowledgements

We would like to thank Prof. Biswas for supplying the ITERATE code and the GMD machine learning group for their public version of COBWEB. We are also grateful to the Internet service provider, who prefers to remain anonymous, for the large dataset we used in our experiments.

References

1. Balabanovic, M. and Shoham, Y.: Content-Based, Collaborative Recommendation. Communications of the ACM 4 (1997) n. 3 66-72
2. Benaki, E., Karkaletsis, V. and Spyropoulos, C. D.: Integrating User Modelling Into Information Extraction: The UMIE Prototype. Proceedings of the User Modelling conference UM'97 (1997) 55-57
3. Biswas, G., Weinberg, J. B. and Fisher, D.: ITERATE: A Conceptual Clustering Algorithm for Data Mining. IEEE Transactions on Systems, Man and Cybernetics 28 (1998) 100-111
4. Bloedorn, E., Mani, I. and MacMillan, T. R.: Machine Learning of User Profiles: Representational Issues. Proceedings of the National Conference on Artificial Intelligence (AAAI) (1996) 433-438
5. Brajnik, G. and Tasso, C.: A Shell for Developing Non-monotonic User Modeling Systems. International Journal of Human-Computer Studies 40 (1994) 31-62
6. Brajnik, G., Guida G. and Tasso, C.: User Modelling in Intelligent Information Retrieval. Information Processing and Management 23 (1987) 305-320
7. Brusilovsky, P., Schwarz, E.: User as Student: Towards an Adaptive Interface for Advanced Web Applications. Proceedings of the User Modelling conference UM'97 (1997) 177-188
8. Chin, D.N.: KNOME: modelling what the user knows. In: Kobsa, Wahster (eds): User models in dialog systems. Springer-Verlag, Berlin (1989) 74-107
9. Chiu, P.: Using C4.5 as an Induction Engine for Agent Modelling: An experiment of Optimisation. Proceedings of the User Modelling conference UM'97 (1997) Workshop on Machine Learning for User Modelling
10. Fisher, D. H.: Knowledge Acquisition via Incremental Conceptual Clustering. Machine Learning 2 (1987) 139-172
11. Gluck, M. A. and Corter, J. E.: Information, Uncertainty and the Utility of Categories. Proceedings of the Seventh Annual Conference of the Cognitive Science Society. Lawrence Erlbaum Associates (1985) 283-287
12. Kay, J.: The um Toolkit for Cooperative User Modelling. User Modeling and User Adapted Interaction, 4 (1995) 149-196
13. Maes, P.: Agents that Reduce Work and Information Overload. Communications of the ACM 37 (1994) n. 7 31-40
14. Michalski, R. S., Mozetic, I., Hong, J. and Lavrac, N.: The Multi-Purpose Incremental Learning System AQ15 and its Testing Application to Three Medical Domains. Proceedings of the National Conference on Artificial Intelligence (AAAI) (1986) 1041-1045
15. Orwant, J.: Heterogeneous Learning in the Doppelgänger User Modeling System. User Modeling and User-Adapted Interaction 4 (1995) 107-130
16. Quinlan, J. R.: C4.5: Programs for Machine Learning. Kaufmann (1993)
17. Raskutti, B. and Beitz, A.: Acquiring User Preferences for Information Filtering in Interactive Multi-Media Services. Proceedings of the Pacific Rim International Conference on Artificial Intelligence (1996) 47-58

18. Resnick, P. and Varian, H.R.: Recommender Systems. Communications of the ACM 4 (1997) n. 3 56-58

19. Rich, E.: Users are Individuals: Individualizing User Models. International Journal of Man-Machine Studies 18 (1983) 199-214

Soft Navigation in Product Catalogs

Markus Stolze

IBM Research Division, Zurich Research Laboratory, CH-8803 Rüschlikon,
Switzerland
mrs@zurich.ibm.com

Abstract. Current electronic product catalogs support only Hard Navigation in the product list. Products or product categories are displayed only if they match a criterion that a user has specified explicitly as a constraint or implicitly by following a navigation link. Hard navigation is problematic if users want to express soft preferences instead of hard constraints. Users will make sub-optimal buying decisions if they mistake soft preferences for hard requirements and focus only on products that match all their preferences.

Soft Navigation is an alternative means to navigate product catalogs. Users express preferences which are used to evaluate products and display them in such a way that higher-scoring products are more visible than lower-scoring products. This paper presents a product scoring catalog (PSC) that supports soft navigation and allows users to express preferences and rate their importance by following a set of rules. The paper closes by outlining possible extensions to PSC and indicating research issues related to soft navigation product catalogs.

1 Introduction

Electronic product catalogs can be regarded as a special type of digital library. The "documents" in these digital libraries are the product descriptions, which will often contain structured information describing the product features. Usually, shoppers "retrieve" product descriptions by iteratively navigating the product-feature space.

Typical electronic shops let shoppers browse their catalogs in a hierarchical way. For example, a shopper looking for a new notebook computer in the electronic catalog of PC-Zone (http://www.pc-zone.com/) has to navigate to the catalog information in a hierarchical manner. After navigating from the main page to the section on notebooks, a shopper has to decide whether he or she wants to view the notebooks in the "active color notebooks" section or those in the "passive color notebooks" section. In the "passive color notebooks" the processor type has to be selected. After this a list of 3 to 15 notebooks with the requested display and processor is displayed.

This method of catalog navigation works well if the two main requirements a shopper has are a certain display type and certain processor type, and the former requirement is more important than the latter. It does not work well for

shoppers whose main requirement is, for example, a display size of at least 14".
In this case the customer has to navigate to all individual product descriptions
in the hierarchy, collect the information about screen sizes, and make a manual
selection.

Filtering catalogs such as the Visa Shopping Guide solve the sequence problem. These catalogs allow shoppers to enter constraints on product features in
any order and use these constraints as filters for the list of all products. Shoppers are supplied with an initial filtering form that lists all available features
and possible values (Fig. 1). Pressing the "Find It" button gets them to the list
of notebooks that satisfy the constraints (Fig. 2). If users want to revise their
requirements they use the browser "Back" button to return to the filtering form.

Another problem arises if users want to express their preference for a product
with certain features, but that they would also consider products without such
features. For example, a shopper might be looking for a notebook with build-in
CD, but he or she might also be willing to consider notebooks without it if these
notebooks offer other advantages. In a case like this where shoppers express soft
preferences instead of hard requirements, hierarchical catalogs and filtering catalogs both break down because they support only *hard navigation*. Both interpret
user statements about preferred product features as hard constraints that must

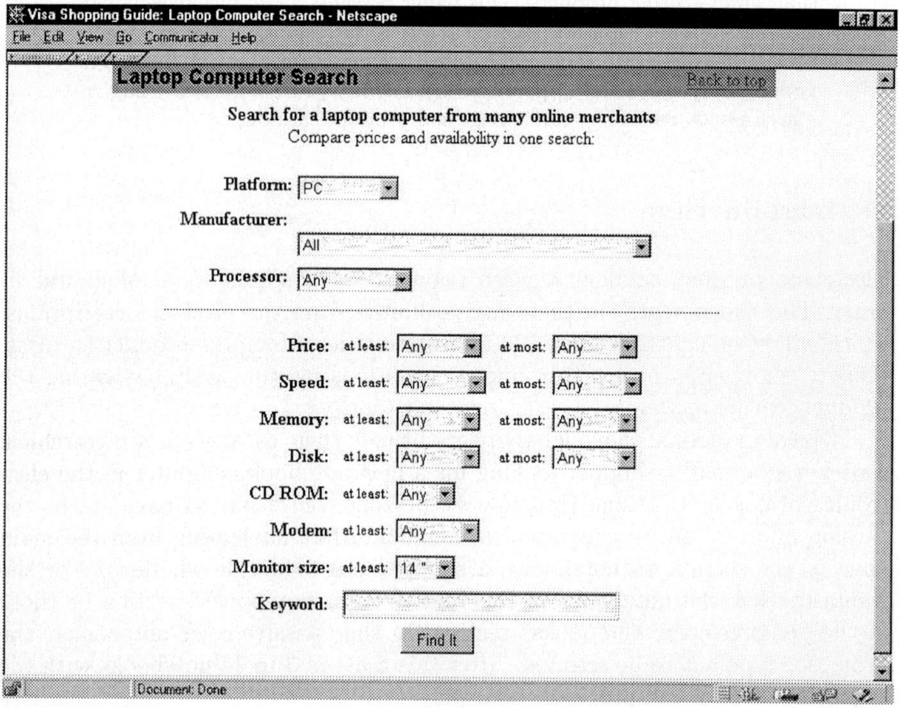

Fig. 1. Visa Shopping Guide feature-based filtering for notebooks

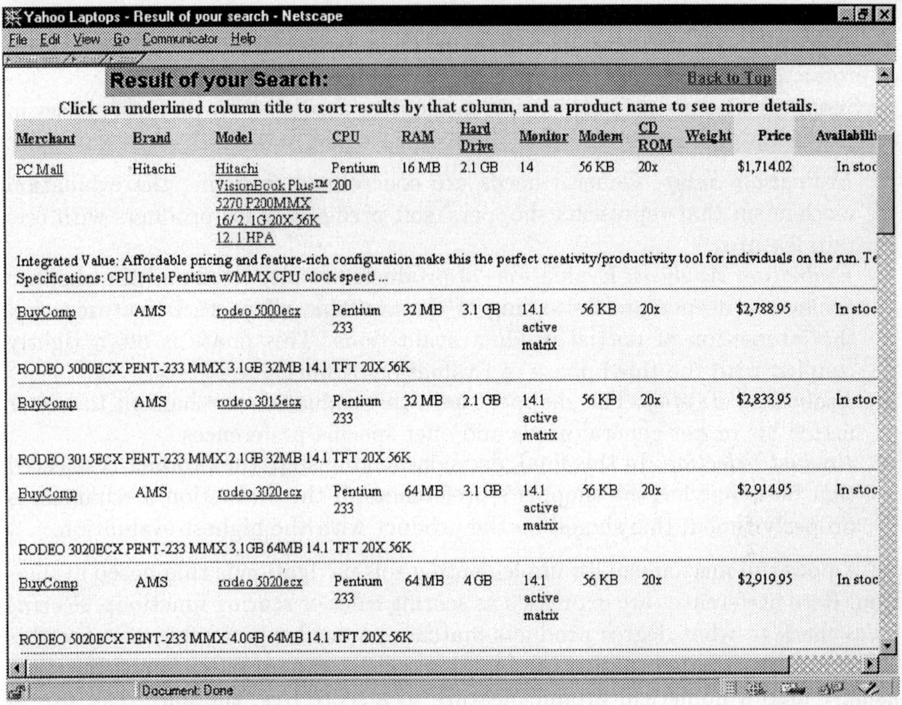

Merchant	Brand	Model	CPU	RAM	Hard Drive	Monitor	Modem	CD ROM	Weight	Price	Availabili
PC Mall	Hitachi	Hitachi VisionBook Plus™ 5270 P200MMX 16/2.1G 20X 56K 12.1 HPA	Pentium 200	16 MB	2.1 GB	14	56 KB	20x		$1,714.02	In stoc
Integrated Value: Affordable pricing and feature-rich configuration make this the perfect creativity/productivity tool for individuals on the run. Te Specifications: CPU Intel Pentium w/MMX CPU clock speed ...											
BuyComp	AMS	rodeo 5000ecx	Pentium 233	32 MB	3.1 GB	14.1 active matrix	56 KB	20x		$2,788.95	In stoc
RODEO 5000ECX PENT-233 MMX 3.1GB 32MB 14.1 TFT 20X 56K											
BuyComp	AMS	rodeo 3015ecx	Pentium 233	32 MB	2.1 GB	14.1 active matrix	56 KB	20x		$2,833.95	In stoc
RODEO 3015ECX PENT-233 MMX 2.1GB 32MB 14.1 TFT 20X 56K											
BuyComp	AMS	rodeo 3020ecx	Pentium 233	64 MB	3.1 GB	14.1 active matrix	56 KB	20x		$2,914.95	In stoc
RODEO 3020ECX PENT-233 MMX 3.1GB 64MB 14.1 TFT 20X 56K											
BuyComp	AMS	rodeo 5020ecx	Pentium 233	64 MB	4 GB	14.1 active matrix	56 KB	20x		$2,919.95	In stoc
RODEO 5020ECX PENT-233 MMX 4.0GB 64MB 14.1 TFT 20X 56K											

Fig. 2. Resulting filtered product list from Fig. 1

be satisfied and not as soft preferences that the user would like to have satisfied. Hard navigation catalogs use constraints to filter out the products that do not satisfy the given constraints.

Hard navigation catalogs can be problematic if shoppers remain unaware of the fact that through their navigation actions they might be excluding entire groups of products from view. For example, shoppers using the hierarchical notebook catalog will miss an interesting offer if they focus exclusively on the passive color notebooks section, without realizing that there is an active color notebook available with specifications that are very similar to those of a notebook they are considering buying. Similar problems will occur in filtering catalogs if shoppers do not select constraints in the sequence of importance or if they use the filtering mechanisms to express preferences (Steiger and Stolze 1997).

2 Soft Navigation

When using Soft Navigation, users express preferences of various strengths for product features instead of hard filtering constraints. The stated preferences are used to evaluate and sort products so that the higher-scoring products are at the top of the product list and those that match few preferences move down the list. This way, products become gradually less visible the lower their scoring is, because usually only the top part of the product list is displayed and the viewing of products lower down on the list requires scrolling.

Shoppers who use soft navigation catalogs go through four distinct phases in their decision process:

1. *Evaluation Setup:* General needs are concretized to define the evaluation mechanism that represents shoppers' soft preferences for products with certain features.
2. *Evaluation Analysis:* Evaluations of products are inspected and the shopper achieves a deeper understanding of the available offers, their features, and the interaction of partial product evaluations. This phase is often tightly coupled with the third phase of Evaluation Tuning.
3. *Evaluation Tuning:* The shopper tunes the evaluation mechanism to better match his or her general needs and offer-specific preferences.
4. *Product Selection:* In this final, decision-making step, the product is selected that best matches the shopper's preferences. If the evaluation mechanism is properly tuned, this should be the product with the highest evaluation.

A powerful mechanism for implementing soft navigation is rule-based evaluation. Here preferences are expressed as scoring rules or scoring functions. *Scoring rules* check to what degree products match a particular preference and use this to compute a base score. Scoring functions also compute base scores, but they usually map a numerical product feature to a score (e.g. the hard-disk size in GB to the HD scoring ranging from 1 to 100). The importance of preferences is expressed in mix rules. Mix rules combine base scores by creating weighted averages. Scores of more important preferences will receive more weight and therefore contribute more to the overall product score. Mix rules can also use combined scores that have been computed by other mix rules as their input. Thus, the overall score is computed through a hierarchical combination of base scores in a scoring tree (Fig. 3).

The scoring tree is a means for shoppers to assign importance to product features in a hierarchical top-down way. To express their preferences, shoppers will usually modify an existing scoring tree by editing, removing, or adding rules. After each modification of the scoring tree, the product scores are recomputed and the sorted product list is adjusted accordingly. The scoring tree is translated internally into a MAUT additive value function (Keeney and Raiffa 1993) that ranges over all leaf notes of the scoring tree (i.e. the scoring rules and the scoring functions). The weight for each leaf note is the product of all weight arcs leading to the leaf note. For example, in Fig. 3 the weight of the Modem Rate scoring rule is $0.1 \times 0.2 = 0.02$.

In a given scoring tree the scores for a product are computed according to the following two rules:

Rule 1. If the score SM is a mix scoring, then the value of that score is the weighted sum of all sub-score values.

Rule 2. If the score SR is a rule score or a function score, then the associated rule or function is used to compute the associated scoring value.

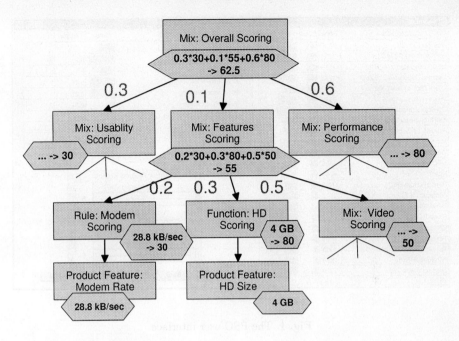

Fig. 3. Scoring tree for evaluating notebooks. Links are labeled with weights of mix rules. Feature values and scoring values for one product example are given in diamonds

3 Product Scoring Catalog

The product scoring catalog (PSC) is a Java-based prototype of an online catalog supporting soft navigation. The prototype was developed at the IBM Research Laboratory in Zurich by the e-business solutions group.

3.1 Shopper's View

The PSC user interface consists of three main areas (cf. Fig. 4). The *product list* occupies the left half, the *scoring tree* is in the upper right part, and the *edit panel* is in the lower left. Figure 4 is a screen shot from a sample application that supports the selection of notebooks. The list on the left shows the offered notebooks. For each of the notebooks the price and the overall scoring is listed. Information in the scoring column is coded as a number between 0 and 100 and as a horizontal bar. In Fig. 4 the product list is sorted by score; it can also be sorted by the values in other product list columns by pushing the column header.

The *scoring tree* describes how products are evaluated. Elements in the scoring tree can be one of four different types: Mix rule (M), scoring rule (R), scoring function (F), and product features that are referenced by the rules (document icon). Scoring rules and scoring functions describe how to score products with

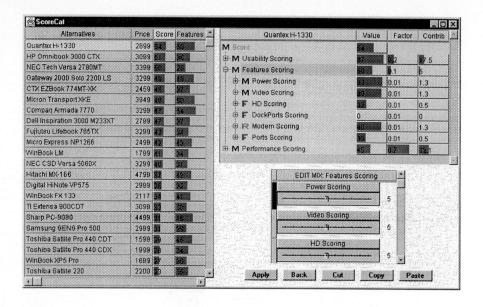

Fig. 4. The PSC user interface

respect to a base preference, mix rules describe the relative importance of base preferences. The columns in the scoring tree display the element names and their values for the product selected in the product list. Thus, the values in the scoring tree explain how the overall scoring of the selected product is computed. If the shopper selects an element in the scoring tree, all its subelements are shown. The rightmost column in the product list displays its range of values and the element is displayed in the *edit panel*. Rules from the scoring tree can be edited, copied and pasted into the tree again. This way the scoring tree can be changed to model the shopper's preferences.

Products in the product list and rules in the scoring tree can be linked to Web pages containing detailed information on products, product features and evaluation rules. Shoppers will use the individual product pages to order the item that best matches their preferences.

Support for Evaluation Setup. Evaluation setup in the context of PSC is the initial configuration of the evaluation tree. Currently PSC does not support an individualized evaluation tree setup. A predefined evaluation tree is automatically loaded from the server from which the applet originated when PSC is started. From a user's perspective, the evaluation setup step is skipped and users immediately jump to the evaluation analysis and evaluation tuning. Support for the scoring function configuration based on shopper needs is less important for products such as notebooks for which it is relatively easy to obtain an evaluation tree that represents the needs of a typical shopper. For domains in which there is considerable variety in the individual needs and preferences, a specific setup phase will be necessary. We are planning to support this through an initial configuration dialog.

Support for Evaluation Analysis. PSC offers two main ways for shoppers to analyze the space of available offers and to investigate the evaluation profile of a given product. To analyze the space of available offers, shoppers can select a score or a product feature in the evaluation tree and the product list will display the corresponding information for each product. To investigate the evaluation profile of a given product, it is selected by the shopper in the product list. As a result, the second column of the evaluation tree will display the scores and feature values for any visible elements of the evaluation tree.

Informal usability studies indicate that first-time users are easily overwhelmed by the amount of information and possibilities for evaluation analysis. During evaluation analysis, users spend most of their time exploring the branches of the tree and analyzing the distribution of scoring values and feature values. In some situations users did not realize that it would be more useful in the current state of analysis to focus on a candidate product and to analyze its evaluation profile. After the session, users felt that they had probably found the most appropriate notebook, but they were not absolutely sure.

Support for Evaluation Adaptation. In PSC users adapt the scoring function by performing one or more of the following four actions:

1. Modify the relative importance of subevaluations in a mix rule by setting the sliders appropriately.
2. Modify the evaluations of scoring rules by setting the sliders of rule clauses appropriately.
3. Modify the function text of a scoring function.
4. Rearrange the evaluation tree through cut, copy, and paste of evaluation tree elements.

Currently, PSC does not support directly the introduction of new evaluation tree elements, but this function can be emulated by copying, pasting, and modifying existing tree elements. In our informal usability studies we observed that users tend to focus on actions 1 and 2. Usually they did not modify the tree structure, even when this would have been appropriate. None of the users tried to modify scoring rule conditions or bodies of evaluation functions. The most frequently requested additional functionality was support for requirement-based filtering.

Support for Product Selection. Product selection in PSC is done by double-clicking on a product in the product list. This links to a detailed information page on that product, usually including ordering details.

3.2 Merchant's View

For a merchant to offer a PSC-based cataloging service, the merchant has to place the PSC applet on a page, supply it with a product definition file with structured product descriptions and with a scoring tree definition file with the descriptions of scoring rules. The merchant should also make sure that web pages referenced by PSC elements contain the appropriate information. The files with product definitions and scoring tree definition are loaded by the applet when a user views the corresponding page.

4 Related Work

PSC supports soft navigation by supplying users with an editable evaluation tree that implements a MAUT additive value function. PersonaLogic and Rosewitz and Timm's Sales Assistance System (Rosewitz and Timm 1998) are two systems that also support soft navigation. The two tools differ from PSC in their underlying evaluation mechanisms and the evaluation phase they focus on.

The PersonaLogic tool uses CGI forms for system-user interaction and focuses mainly on the initial phase of evaluation setup. PersonaLogic leads users through a sequence of question forms that determine preferred and required product feature values. The answers are used in a CSP-based mechanism (Guttman *et al.* 1998) to evaluate and rank offers. PersonaLogic includes only limited support for Evaluation Analysis and Evaluation Tuning. Shoppers cannot inspect why a given product received a certain evaluation. For tuning the evaluation mechanism, part of the setup process has to be replayed and the questionnaire forms adapted accordingly.

Rosewitz and Timm's Sales Assistance System, like PersonaLogic, is based on CGI technology. Initially, users are presented with a flat list of preference settings that they can either choose directly or through a separate question-and-answer dialog. Once the preferences have been set, users can visit the product evaluation page and see the evaluations that have been computed by the underlying fuzzy function mechanism. The Sales Assistance System, like PersonaLogic, mainly supports the Evaluation Setup phase. The Evaluation Analysis and Evaluation Tuning phases are less well supported, as users cannot inspect why a given product received a certain score, nor do they have a way to inspect or change the fuzzy functions used to compute the evaluation.

In our opinion, the two tools discussed above are best suited for supporting first-time users to perform simple preference-based selection tasks. For these tasks the low interactivity offered by CGI forms is sufficient and users will not need to explore in detail why the system rated a certain product higher than another.

The other end of the complexity continuum is occupied by tools for decision analysis such as ExpertChoice (http://ahp.net) and LogicalDecisions (www.LogicalDecisions.com). Apart from the pure analysis functionality, the tools include support for decision problem structuring and elicitation of probabilities, value functions, value weights, and risk preferences. They also include functionality to support advanced sensitivity analysis. Decision analysis is an academic field in its own right (Clemen 1996), and decision analysis tools are meant for use by professional decision analysts (Buede 1996).

PSC tries to walk the line between a simple online buying support such as PersonaLogic and complex decision-making support tools such as LogicalDecisions. PSC's goal is to supply shoppers with all the functionality that helps them make informed and confident shopping decisions, but shield them from the complexities of unconstrained decision analysis. PSC facilitates the assignment of weights to product preferences by presenting the evaluation mechanism as a hierarchical scoring tree that comes with pre-set weights. More elaborate techniques for weight elicitation exist. For example, the Analytical Hierarchical Process (Saaty 1980) and ISMAUT (Anandaligam and White 1993; D'Ambrosio and Birmingham 1995) use pairwise comparison of product to deduce weights indirectly. These techniques will be useful in domains where shoppers have problems assigning numerical weights to product feature preferences, but are able to express global preferences for one product or another.

Other techniques can also be used to facilitate the entry and the modification of preferences. Configuration mechanisms (Mittal and Frayman 1989) can be used to reduce the complexity of creating personalized scoring trees. Critiquing agents (Fischer *et al.* 1993) and visualization techniques (Rao *et al.* 1995) can be used to educate users and make them aware of potential problems in their product analysis. Apart from improving the support for product selection based on product features, shoppers should also be supported in performing "merchant brokering" (Guttman *et al.* 1998) and decide where to buy the desired product. In this context shopping robots similar to Jango (www.jango.com) can help users identify inexpensive merchants and Recommender Systems techniques (Resnick and Varian 1997) can be used to "automate the word of mouth" and help shoppers learn from the experiences of other shoppers.

In parallel with increasing the support for shoppers, the support for merchants should also be improved. Mechanisms for personalization (Bayers 1998) can help merchants target their offerings better to the needs of individual customers. Mechanisms for intelligent integration of information (Genesereth *et al.* 1997) can be used to make it easier for merchants to link their offerings into exciting marketplaces. Soft navigation should also be extended so that merchants can offer configurable products. Catalogs that work with configurable products exist (e.g. the Dell site for computer configuration: www.dell.com), but these catalogs do not offer support for generating and comparing alternative configurations.

The product catalogs to be maintained by merchants can be regarded as digital product information libraries. It is therefore not surprising that many of the issues addressed by digital library research such as meta level content descriptions, content editing tools, intellectual property, and payment (Adam and Yesha 1996) are also relevant for the development of tools that help merchants create, maintain, and market product information.

5 Discussion: Implications for Merchants and Information Providers

One of the most frequently asked questions with respect to soft navigation catalogs is whether merchants want to encourage shoppers to do comparison shopping. We think the answer is 'Yes' for the following four reasons:

1. Merchants have an interest in soft navigation catalogs because they allow the online offering of more expensive technical products that attract shoppers who like to make decisions based on product features and price. Our current prototype PSC is best suited for frequent users for whom it makes sense to learn to use the interface and the rule syntax. Nevertheless, we are certain that it is possible to extend PSC so that it can also be used by first-time users without shielding them from explanations why products score the way they do. We assume that shoppers, when shopping for more expensive products, will favor catalogs that offer soft navigation because this offers shoppers more freedom to express their preferences and more support in identifying the product that best matches the stated preferences. Of course this does not necessarily mean that merchants who offer these catalogs will necessarily get more business. In the electronic world of online auctions and shopping robots, nothing will keep shoppers from finding out whether other shops offer the same product at a better price. But providers of catalogs have the opportunity to shape substantially the product configurations and the kinds of services people will request.

2. Merchants have an interest in soft navigation catalogs because they change shoppers' mind sets from shopping for the cheapest product to shopping for the product that best matches the shopper's needs and budget constraints. This is a mind set that allows merchants to explain non-price-related advantages of products and will lead to a win-win situation for shoppers and merchants (Guttman *et al.* 1998). Soft navigation helps users identify the products that best match a detailed preference profile. Selling well-matched products is attractive for merchants because these products will be valued higher by shoppers, which makes it easier for merchants to justify a higher price. This way soft navigation catalogs create an incentive for merchants to market products targeted towards specific shopper preferences. This will create a movement towards higher product differentiation and a counter-movement to the generally feared commoditization of electronically offered products.

   Soft navigation catalog users are not necessarily consumers. A likely class of users are brokers who have to prove (sometimes required by law) that they are giving "best" advice. When using soft navigation catalogs, proving "best" advice will be much easier because user preferences can be stored together with the proposed list of products. Merchants with well-targeted products will find this better than a "rational" approach to brokering because it will guarantee them more business through brokers that might otherwise focus less on client preferences.

3. Merchants and producers have an interest in soft navigation catalogs because they open up new ways to learn about consumer preferences. Knowing the rules consumers use for making buying decisions will be very valuable for determining product marketing strategies and for validating inventory decisions and product development priorities. Merchants and producers can analyze the data to find out which special features of products have to be stressed more, and they can investigate to what degree the products in their product portfolio support the features that consumers are asking for. The information about user preferences can also be used for better-targeted product presentation and advertisements.

4. Merchants and information providers have an interest in soft navigation catalogs because they offer new opportunities to market information. Soft navigation catalogs work best with high-quality, comprehensive product information and personalized scoring rule sets. Currently, the information required by soft navigation catalogs is produced by various sources:

   - Producers create data sheets of their products.
   - Independent organizations such as Consumer Reports and magazines such as Byte perform product tests and publish articles that help consumers match product features to consumer needs.
   - Specialized news groups and organizations such as the Better Business Bureau (http://www.bbb.org/) and ConsumerRatings.com will contain information on customer satisfaction ratings. In particular the news groups will also describe additional rules for evaluating products.

Creating digital libraries that organize the access to these heterogeneous catalog data sources seems like an interesting challenge for digital library techniques. Information economies (Sairamesh *et al.* 1996) could be built around this product information, which would handle translation, aggregation, and billing services. The challenge will be to devise schemes that make the handling of information sources easy for users and attractive to information providers and information conditioners.

References

Adam, A., Yesha, Y.: Electronic Commerce and Digital Libraries: Towards a Digital Agora. ACM Computing Surveys **28** (1996) 818–835

Anandaligam, G., White, C. C.: A Penality Function Approach to Alternative Pairwaise Comparison in ISMAUT. IEEE Trans. Systems, Man and Cybernetics **23** (1993) 330–333

Bayers, C.: The Promise of One-to-One (a Love Story). Wired **6** (1998) 130–134, 184–187

Buede, D.: Decision Analysis Software Survey. ORMS Today Online Editions **23** (1996), No. 4: www.lionhrtpub.com/orms/orms-8-96/buede.html

Clemen, R. T.: Making Hard Decisions: An Introduction to Decision Analysis. Wadsworth Publishing Co., Belmont, CA (1996)

D'Ambrosio, J. G., W. P. Birmingham, W. P.: Preference Directed Design. J. Artificial Intelligence in Engineering Design, Analysis and Manufacturing (AI EDAM) **9** (1995) 219–230

Fischer, G., Nakakoji, K., Ostwald, J., Stahl G., Sumner, T.: Embedding Critics in Design Environments. The Knowledge Engineering Rev. J. **8** (1993) 285–307

Genesereth, M. R., Keller, A. M., Duschka, O. M.: Infomaster: An Information Integration System. In: Proceedings 9th Conference on Management of Data (SIGMOD-9) Tucson, AZ, May 1997, pp. 539–542

Guttman, R., Moukas, A., Maes, P.: Agent-Mediated Electronic Commerce: A Survey. Knowledge Engineering Review (June 1998), in press

Keeney, R. L., Raiffa H.: Decision Making with Multiple Objectives: Preferences and Value Tradeoffs. Cambridge University Press, Cambridge, UK (1993)

Mittal, S., Frayman, F.: Towards a Generic Model of Configuration Tasks. in: Proceedings of 11th IJCAI (1989) pp. 1395–1401

Rosewitz, M., Timm, U.: Electronic Sales Assistance. CHI'98 Workshop on Beyond Internet Business-as-Usual, Los Angeles, CA (1998)
See http://www.zurich.ibm.com/~pst/chi98

Rao, R., Pedersen, J., Hearst, M., Mackinlay, J., Card, S., Masinter, L., Halvorsen. P.-K., Robertson, G.: Rich Interaction in the Digital Library. CACM **38** (1995) 29–39

Resnick, P., Varian, H. R.: Recommender Systems. CACM **40** (1997) 56–58

Sairamesh, J., Yemini, Y., Ferguson, D. F., Nikolaou, C.: A Framework for Pricing Services in Digital Libraries. In: Research and Advanced Technology for Digital Libraries. C. Peters and C. Thanos, Eds., First European Conf. ECDL '97, Pisa, Italy. Lecture Notes in Computer Science, Vol. 1324 (Springer, Berlin Heidelberg, 1997), p. 181 k

Saaty, T. L.: The Analytic Hierarchy Process. McGraw Hill, New York (1980)

Steiger, P., Stolze, M.: Effective Product Selection in Electronic Catalogs. In: Proceedings Human Factors in Computing Systems Conf. (CHI'97), Atlanta, GA (1997) pp. 291-292

Mixing and Merging for Spoken Document Retrieval

Mark Sanderson[1] and Fabio Crestani[2]

[1] CIIR, Computer Science Department
University of Massachusetts
Amherst, MA, 01007 USA
sanderso@cs.umass.edu
[2] Department of Computing Science
University of Glasgow
Glasgow G12 8QQ, Scotland
fabio@dcs.gla.ac.uk

Abstract. This paper describes a number of experiments that explored the issues surrounding the retrieval of spoken documents. Two such issues were examined. First, attempting to find the best use of speech recogniser output to produce the highest retrieval effectiveness. Second, investigating the potential problems of retrieving from a so-called "mixed collection", i.e. one that contains documents from both a speech recognition system (producing many errors) and from hand transcription (producing presumably near perfect documents). The result of the first part of the work found that merging the transcripts of multiple recognisers showed most promise. The investigation in the second part showed how the term weighting scheme used in a retrieval system was important in determining whether the system was affected detrimentally when retrieving from a mixed collection.

1 Introduction

Over the past few years the field of Information Retrieval (IR) has directed increasing interest towards the retrieval of spoken documents. Much, if not all, of the work published so far has concentrated on the use of Speech Recognition (SR) systems that identify either sub-word units (i.e. syllables [14] or phonemes [3]) or words from a limited vocabulary (i.e. the work of Jones et al [6]). Little has been published on the use of large vocabulary continuous SR systems. However, in recent years this type of system has become sufficiently accurate with a large enough vocabulary that its application to IR is feasible.

In 1997 IR and SR received a boost when the 6th Text Retrieval Conference (TREC-6) ran a Spoken Document Retrieval (SDR) track. As part of this track, a test collection of spoken documents, the SDR collection, was created: providing a common test bed for IR and SR researchers. At TREC-6 a number of presentations of work on the SDR collection were made [5]. This paper contains the work presented by the Glasgow IR group (briefly described in [2]) in addition to other work completed more recently. It starts with an introduction to the SDR collection and the evaluation schemes used to measure retrieval effectiveness on it. This is followed by a description of the experiments conducted for TREC and the results gained from them. Next the paper describes an investigation into the issue of retrieval from a mixed collection before, finally, concluding.

2 The SDR collection

The SDR collection was created for the TREC-6 SDR track. It is composed of stories taken from the Linguistic Data Consortium (LDC) 1996 Broadcast News corpora. The collection consists of 1451 stories representing about 50 hours of recorded material. A story (document) is generally defined as a segment of news material with the same content or theme. Segmentation of the stories is performed by hand. Notice that a story is likely to involve more than one speaker and contain background music, noise, etc. The collection also comes with 49 *known item queries* (known as topics in TREC), i.e. queries for which there is only one relevant document in the collection.

The collection is supplied in a number of forms:

- digitised recordings of the broadcasts;
- detailed hand-generated transcriptions used in speech recogniser training and for speech recognition scoring containing such things as detailed timing information for the occurrence of each word. (This form of the collection should not be regarded as perfect, as there are a number of errors such as spelling mistakes.);
- the detailed transcripts with most of the recogniser training data removed leaving just a text document. Retrieval on this version of the collection provided a standard against which retrieval on the recognised collections was compared.
- automatically generated transcripts produced by a recogniser when applied to the digitised recording. A standard transcript, generated by a large vocabulary SR system from NIST/IBM, was provided with the collection to allow researchers who do not have their own recogniser a chance to experiment on such a collection. In addition to this transcript, Glasgow was given access to one produced by the Speech Group at the University of Sheffield using their Abbot large vocabulary (about 60,000 words) continuous SR system [8].

The evaluation schemes used with the SDR collection are:

- *mean rank*, i.e. the rank at which the known item was found, averaged over the queries. The smaller the number, the more effective the run;
- *mean reciprocal*, i.e. the reciprocal of the rank at which the known item was found averaged over the queries. A larger value implies better effectiveness. The mean has the range $[0, 1]$.
- *number of queries where the relevant document is found in the top n rank*, where n is 1, 5, or 10.

These measures (inevitably) have advantages and disadvantages. The mean rank may appear to be a fair measure, but a few bad retrievals easily skew the mean. For example if 48 of the 49 queries' known items were retrieved at rank position 1 but the 49th query was retrieved at rank 700, the mean rank would be 15. The mean reciprocal is not affected by this problem, but it also has drawbacks in that it is sensitive to small changes in high rank position. For example, the difference between the reciprocal of rank positions 1 and 2 is 0.5 whereas the difference between positions 4 and 5 is ten times smaller. Notice that mean reciprocal is the same as average precision when there is only one relevant document per query. The number of queries within rank position (hereby indicated as $q.w.r.p.$) is probably the easiest measure to understand and although small changes in rank position might not be reflected by it, this is most likely unimportant. The latter two measures are the ones used in the experiments presented in this paper.

3   Introduction to the experiments

A number of experiments were conducted on the SDR collection, these were used to explore different aspects of the retrieval of spoken documents. The main aim of the experiments was to find the method that produced the best effectiveness for retrieving from spoken documents. This involved comparing the effectiveness of retrieval on the two recogniser transcripts available, exploring the use of recogniser word likelihood estimates, and discovering the value of retrieving from a "merged" collection: one composed of the output of more than one speech recogniser. A second aim of the experiments was to make an initial exploration of the retrieval of so-called "mixed collections": those composed of documents resulting from different sources (e.g. speech recognition, hand transcription, optical character recognition, etc). Given the SDR collection's relative "youth" and subsequent low use, a final aim of the experiments was to examine how good it was for the task it was designed for. Observations on this aspect are made through the paper.

All of these experiments were conducted on the TREC-6 SDR collection along with the Abbot generated transcript. The SIRE systems [9] was used as the experimental retrieval system. Unless otherwise stated, throughout the experiments, the system was configured to use a $tf * idf$ weighting scheme [4]: document and query words had their case normalised, stop words were removed, and stemming (using Porter) was performed. A brief explanation of the $tf * idf$ weighting scheme is reported in section 3.1.

The two recognisers vs. the hand transcription

The initial experiment was to discover which recognised transcript produced the best retrieval effectiveness and how different that effectiveness was from that obtained using the hand-transcribed version. Using SIRE in its standard set up, it was found that across all evaluation measures, the Abbot transcript was better than NIST/IBM, in fact retrieval from the Sheffield transcript was almost as good as retrieval from the hand transcription (a strong indication of the utility of using this type of SR system). It is worth noting, however, that the SDR retrieval tasks are rather easy, as even on the poorest configuration, for 41 of the 49 known item queries, the item was retrieved in the top ten.

The differences between the two recognisers were attributed to differences in their accuracy. An analysis of the Word Error Rate (WER) was performed on the Abbot and NIST/IBM transcripts, the results of which are shown in the following table. Unlike a classic WER that is computed over all words, this rate was calculated for the SDR query words (after stop word removal) as well. As can be seen, from table 1 the Abbot transcripts were more accurate than NIST/IBM.

Table 1. Word Error Rates (%) for the two recognisers used.

	Stop Words	Query Words	Other Words
Abbot	40.3	33.1	39.7
NIST/IBM	49.4	45.5	49.0

Table 2 reports a comparison of the effectiveness of the three different SR systems using the same weighting scheme; as it can be seen Abbot performs better than NIST/IBM for lower values of the q.w.r.p.

3.1 Additional recogniser output

Unlike the transcript available from NIST/IBM, the transcript available to us from Abbot contains a value attached to each word that is an indication of Abbot's "confidence" of recognising a word. It was speculated that this additional information might be incorporated in a term weighting scheme to improve retrieval effectiveness: i.e. words that had a higher confidence value were more likely to be correctly recognised and, therefore, should be assigned a high term weight.

The value attached to a particular word in a document was regarded as a probability indicating the likelihood of that word being spoken in that document. This required the values to be mapped into the range $[0, 1]$. A number of different mappings were used, as reported in [1], and the retrieval results were compared with those obtained by discarding this additional information. This probability was incorporated into a tf weight to produce a probabilistic term (ptf) weight. Therefore, given a document d_i represented by means of a number of index terms (or words) t_j, the $tf * idf$ weighting scheme is defined as:

$$tf * idf(d_i) = \sum_{j=1}^{n} tf_{ij}(C + idf_j)$$

Table 2. Comparison of effectiveness for three different SR systems.

Hand trans. with tf_idf_porter_stop	
Mean reciprocal	0.704332
q.w.r.p. = 1	27
q.w.r.p. *leq* 5	43
q.w.r.p. *leq* 10	46
NIST/IBM rec. with tf_idf_porter_stop	
Mean reciprocal	0.610862
q.w.r.p. = 1	23
q.w.r.p. *leq* 5	38
q.w.r.p. *leq* 10	41
Abbot rec. with tf_idf_porter_stop	
Mean reciprocal	0.690164
q.w.r.p. = 1	31
q.w.r.p. *leq* 5	36
q.w.r.p. *leq* 10	41

where tf_{ij} is the frequency of term t_j in document d_i, idf_j is the inverse document frequency of term t_j, and C is a constant that is set experimentally to tailor the weighting schema to different collections. The values of tf_{ij} and idf_j are defined as follows:

$$tf_{ij} = K + (1 - K)\frac{freq_i(t_j)}{maxfreq_i}$$

where K is a constant that need to be set experimentally and $maxfreq_i$ is the maximum frequency of any term in document d_i, and

$$idf_j = \log \frac{N}{n_j}$$

where N denotes the number of documents in the collection and n_j the number of documents in which the term t_j occurs. This weighting scheme has been used extensively in the experiments reported in this paper.

The $ptf * idf$ uses the probabilities given by Abbot to evaluate $freq_i(t_j)$ as:

$$freq_i(t_j) = \sum_{d_i} Prob(t_j)$$

We used this new values of frequencies in the above tf formula to produce so called ptf values to be used in the $ptf * idf$ weighting scheme.

The experiment to examine if the ptf weight would improve effectiveness was a simple comparison between a retrieval system using a $tf * idf$ weighting scheme against the $ptf * idf$ scheme. As can be seen in the following table, the comparison showed the *ptf* weighting scheme to be inferior to the simpler *tf∗idf*. Although not shown in table 3, a number of transformations were used to map the likelihood values into a probability, all other mapping produced worse retrieval effectiveness than the scheme shown here.

Table 3. Results of experiments using *ptf ∗ idf* weighting.

Abbot rec. with ptf_idf_porter_stop	
Mean reciprocal	0.665091
q.w.r.p. = 1	29
q.w.r.p. *leq* 5	35
q.w.r.p. *leq* 10	41

An analysis was conducted to see why the additional likelihood data was detrimental to effectiveness. It was realised that the likelihood value attached to a particular word was generally higher the longer a word was. Therefore, the likelihood data should have been normalised to the length of the word, measured in letters or duration to speak it. However, a variation of this technique has already been tried by Siegler et al [10] with no success. It would appear that the reason for the lack of utility of this data remains to be discovered.

4   Experiments with merged collections

The previous section presented an investigation of the use of probabilities assigned by Abbot to words in the transcription. This work led us to consider if there was some other way of generating confidence values to assign to recognised words. The two speech transcripts (NIST/IBM and Abbot) were quite different from each other as the following example illustrates.

NIST/IBM:

```
..I will talk about blacks and winds we
eventually go wrong a of the tough
question who he hid...
```

Abbot:

```
..we talked about blanks and whites we
eventually get around to the tough
question his own unions say well....
```

Hand generated transcript:

```
..when we talk about blacks and whites we
eventually get around to the
tough question some of you are...
```

It was realised that by using a simple strategy of concatenating the documents of the two transcripts, one would effectively produce a collection with word confidence information. If, for example, the two documents fragments shown above were concatenated, the correctly recognised word "question" would occur twice, but the incorrectly recognised word "winds" would only occur once. Through use of a tf weighting scheme, "question" would receive a higher weight than the word "winds". It was decided to test if this strategy of concatenation, or merging, of the documents improved retrieval effectiveness.

Of course, such a merged collection would contain two separate hypotheses on what was spoken and would therefore, contain more correctly (and incorrectly) recognised words. Regardless of the tf producing confidence values for words, the mere presence of the extra words might, on their own, improve retrieval effectiveness and it was decided that this should also be tested.

Table 4 shows the results of retrieval on the merged collection using a $tf * idf$ weighting scheme, as can be seen when compared to the retrieval results presented in the previous tables, the merged strategy was slightly better (on three of the four measures), though very similar, to retrieval on the Abbot transcripts. From this result it would appear that merging the good transcript with the poorer has not reduced effectiveness and possibly improved it.

Table 4. Results of experiments the merged collection using $tf * idf$ weighting.

Merged with tf_idf_porter_stop	
Mean reciprocal	0.699470
q.w.r.p. $= 1$	30
q.w.r.p. leq 5	41
q.w.r.p. leq 10	42

Notice, the utility of merged collections was also investigated by two other groups at TREC-6: Siegler et al and Singhal et al [11]. Both were merging the NIST/IBM standard transcript with the output of their own SR systems. Both reported similar results on merging to those made here: marginal improvements in effectiveness were found.

A further experiment using the merged collection was to try to discover if any benefit from it was from the larger vocabulary within it or from the (presumably) better tf weights resulting from the combination of the two recogniser hypotheses. To discover this, SIRE was re-configured to ignore tf weights and use only idf term weighting when retrieving. As can be seen in table 5, retrieval experiments were conducted on the merged collection and its two component collections. Here, in contrast to the previous experiment, effectiveness from the merged collection was similar but slightly worse than effectiveness on the Abbot transcript. Perhaps this indicates that removal of tf weights from the merged collection was detrimental, but, the differences are so small that nothing conclusive was drawn from this result.

Table 5. Results of experiments the merged collection using *idf* weighting.

Merged with idf_porter_stop	
Mean reciprocal	0.593621
q.w.r.p. = 1	24
q.w.r.p. *leq* 5	35
q.w.r.p. *leq* 10	37
NIST/IBM rec. with idf_porter_stop	
Mean reciprocal	0.587153
q.w.r.p. = 1	24
q.w.r.p. *leq* 5	35
q.w.r.p. *leq* 10	37
Abbot rec. with idf_porter_stop	
Mean reciprocal	0.606046
q.w.r.p. = 1	23
q.w.r.p. *leq* 5	38
q.w.r.p. *leq* 10	40

5 Experiments with mixed collections

One other area of investigation afforded by the SDR collection was an opportunity to investigate the retrieval of documents from a mixed collection: one composed of both hand-transcribed and recognised documents. Here the focus was on whether one type of document (transcribed or recognised) was more likely to be retrieved over the other and to discover if such a preference was affected by the term weighting scheme used.

5.1 Previous work

There appears to be little previous work on the topic of retrieving from mixed document collections. Researchers have, however, investigated the manner in which retrieval functions are affected by errors in recognised documents.

Concentrating on documents recognised by an OCR system, Taghva et al [13] and Singhal et al [12] both found that OCR error did not impact on effectiveness greatly, but found that existing schemes for ranking documents could be adversely affected by recognition error. Singhal et al reported that if the OCR system they were using incorrectly recognised a letter in a word (e.g. "systom" for "system"), this would result in a word that was likely to be rare and, therefore, have a high *idf*. Due to the manner in which document rank scores are calculated in the vector space model, the presence of a number of such "error words" in a document would result in its being ranked lower than it if it were without error. Buckley presented an alteration to the vector space model that addressed this problem. Tahgva et al found a similar form of problem with the length normalisation part of the INQUERY term weighting scheme. If an OCR system incorrectly recognised an image as being a textual part of a document, a large number of extra 'words' were introduced and the length of said document was increased by a large amount.

This research has shown how recognition error can adversely affect the ranking of documents. Although the research presented examined OCR, one can imagine similar types of problems arising in speech recognition: incorrectly recognising a word as another; or trying to recognise a sound that is not speech. In the context of mixed document retrieval, documents containing these errors are likely to cause similar ranking problems to those reported in the research presented above. However, other forms of error may affect retrieval in the context of a mixed document collection and, therefore, an experiment was conducted to investigate this.

5.2   The experiments

To conduct the investigation the hand-transcribed and the Abbot recognised collections were combined into a single collection of 2902 documents. (The Abbot transcript was used, as it was more accurate than the NIST/IBM.) A retrieval experiment was conducted the measurement of which concentrated on where in the ranking the hand-transcribed and recognised documents were to be found. To establish this, two measures of retrieval effectiveness (using mean reciprocal) were made, one based on the location of the relevant hand-transcribed documents and one on the location of the relevant recognised documents. Any difference between these two measures was taken to indicate the different rank positions of the two document types.

The configuration of the first experiment used *tf* * *idf* weighting. Results of this experiment are shown in the following table 6.

Table 6. Results of retrieval experiments using *tf* * *idf* weighting.

	Hand Rel.	Abbot Rel.
Mean reciprocal	0.591955	0.380770

As can be seen, there is a large difference between the two figures. This result was interpreted as showing that the hand-transcribed documents were being retrieved in preference to the recognised. It was speculated that the reason for this difference was caused by the terms in the recognised documents generally having a smaller tf than that found in the hand-transcribed documents. In other words, a query term found to occur five times in the hand-transcribed version of a document might only be correctly recognised twice in the spoken version. Therefore, the term in the recognised document would have a lower tf than in the transcribed document and this would lower the relevance score assigned to the recognised document. In order to test this speculation the first experiment was repeated using just idf weighting. The results of this are shown in table 7. As can be seen, the difference between the two figures was much smaller, indicating that it was the differences between the tf weights that caused the preference of retrieving the hand-transcribed documents.

Table 7. Results of retrieval experiments using idf weighting.

	Hand Rel.	Abbot Rel.
Mean reciprocal	0.479931	0.496340

Clearly these results reveal a shortcoming of the $tf * idf$ weighting scheme we have adopted within our IR system. We suspect, however, that this may be a problem for many such weighting schemes as most make the implicit assumption that term frequencies within the documents of a collection are distributed similarly across that collection. A means of handling this situation may be sought in the work of Mittendorf [7] who has examined the issue of retrieval from corrupted data.

6 Conclusions and future work

The work presented in this paper was very much an initial foray into the field of IR using large vocabulary SR. However, we feel that the experimental results presented here give an indication to some of the issues and potential solutions in this area.

First, the utility to IR of large vocabulary continuous SR systems like Abbot has been demonstrated through the retrieval results gained on the SDR collection. However, results as good as these may not be entirely fair as very few of the queries in SDR had words outside Abbot's vocabulary (whether these queries were created with the vocabularies of SR systems in mind is unknown). More "realistic" queries containing many proper nouns might produce different results and require an alternative approach: for example, an SR system using both word and sub-word unit recognition; or an IR system using a query expansion technique to expand, from a text corpus, unrecognised query words with those in the SR system's vocabulary (using, for example, Local Context Analysis [15]).

From the experimental results, it is clear that more work is required if the use of likelihood values will improve retrieval effectiveness. More promising is the use of merged collections that showed some slight improvement in effectiveness. Finally, the experiments on mixed collections showed that care must be taken in selecting a weighting scheme that handles the different term occurrence statistics of documents taken from different sources.

References

1. F. Crestani and M. Sanderson. Retrieval of spoken documents: first experiences. Research Report TR-1997-34, Department of Computing Science, University of Glasgow, Glasgow, Scotland, UK, October 1997.
2. F. Crestani, M. Sanderson, M. Theophylactou, and M. Lalmas. Short queries, natural language and spoken document retrieval: Experiments at Glasgow University. In *Proceedings of TREC-6*, Gaithersburg, MD,USA, November 1997. In press.
3. C. Gerber. The design and application of an acoustic front-end for use in speech interfaces. M.Sc. Thesis, Department of Computing Science, University of Glasgow, Glasgow, Scotland, UK, February 1997. Available as Technical Report TR-1997-6.
4. D. Harman. Ranking algorithms. In W.B. Frakes and R. Baeza-Yates, editors, *Information Retrieval: data structures and algorithms*, chapter 14. Prentice Hall, Englewood Cliffs, New Jersey, USA, 1992.
5. D. Harman, editor. *Proceedings of the Sixth Text Retrieval Conference (TREC-6)*, Gaithersburg, MD, USA, November 1997. (In press.).
6. G.J.F. Jones, J.T. Foote, K. Spark Jones, and S.J. Young. Video mail retrieval using voice: an overview of the Stage 2 system. In *Proceedings of the MIRO Workshop*, Glasgow, Scotland, UK, September 1995.
7. E. Mittendorf and P. Schauble. Measuring the effects of data corruption on information retrieval. In *Proceedings of the SDAIR 96 Conference*, pages 179–189, Las Vegas, NV, USA, April 1996.
8. T. Robinson, M. Hochberg, and S. Renals. The use of recurrent networks in continuos speech reognition. In C.H. Lee, K.K. Paliwal, and F.K. Soong, editors, *Automatic Speech and Speaker Recognition - Advanced Topics*, chapter 10, pages 233–258. Kluwer Academic Publishers, 1996.
9. M. Sanderson. System for information retrieval experiments (SIRE). Unpublished paper, November 1996.
10. M.A. Siegler, M.J. Witbrock, S.T. Slattery, K. Seymore, R.E. Jones, and A.G. Hauptmann. Experiments in spoken document retrieval at CMU. In *Proceedings of TREC-6*, Gaithersburg, MD, USA, November 1997.
11. A. Singhal, J. Choi, D. Hindle, and F. Pereira. AT&T at TREC-6: SDR Track. In *Proceedings of TREC-6*, Washington DC, USA, November 1997.
12. A. Singhal, G. Salton, and C. Buckley. Lenght normalisation in degraded text collections. Research Report 14853-7501, Department of Computer Science, Cornell University, Ithaca, NY, USA, 1995.
13. K. Taghva, J. Borsack, and A. Condit. Results of applying probabilistic IR to OCR. In *Proceedings of ACM SIGIR*, pages 202–211, Dublin, Ireland, 1994.
14. M. Wechsler and P. Schauble. Speech retrieval based on automatic indexing. In *Proceedings of the MIRO Workshop*, Glasgow, Scotland, UK, September 1995.
15. J. Xu and W.B. Croft. Query expansion using local and global document analysis. In *Proceedings of ACM SIGIR*, pages 4–11, Zurich, Switzerland, August 1996.

An Integrated Approach to Semantic Evaluation and Content-Based Retrieval of Multimedia Documents

A. Knoll[2], C. Altenschmidt[3], J. Biskup[3], H.-M. Blüthgen[1], I. Glöckner[2], S. Hartrumpf[4], H. Helbig[4], C. Henning[1], R. Lüling[5], B. Monien[5], T. Noll[1], and N. Sensen[5]

[1] University of Technology RWTH Aachen
[2] University of Bielefeld
[3] University of Dortmund
[4] University of Hagen
[5] University of Paderborn

Abstract. We present an overview of a large combined querying and retrieval system that performs content-based on-line searches in a large database of multimedia documents (currently text, tables and colour images). Queries are submitted as sentences in natural language and are transformed into the language of the target database. The documents are analyzed semantically for their information content; in a data fusion step the individual pieces of information extracted from these documents are aggregated into cognitively adequate result documents.

There is no pre-indexing necessary when new documents are stored into the system. This retains a high degree of flexibility with respect to the questions that may be asked. It implies, however, that both huge amounts of data must be evaluated rapidly and that intelligent caching strategies must be employed. It is therefore mandatory that the system be equipped with dedicated high-speed hardware processors.

The complete system is currently available as a prototype; the paper outlines its architecture and gives examples of some real sample queries in the knowledge domain of weather data documents.

1 Introduction

Due to the increasingly comfortable electronic authoring and publishing tools available today, knowledge is more and more represented in documents containing text, pictures and audiovisual information. While the automatic search for keywords in textual databases (e. g. HTML documents) is straightforward, the automatic indexing of pictures with respect to their semantic content is a very difficult issue. Furthermore, simple keyword search does not meet the average user's need for precise retrieval. Thus, the detection of information and its human-readable preparation becomes a central point of interest for multimedia documents. Tools are needed that analyze the content of a large number of documents and make possible

- the submission of content-related questions,
- the fast detection of interesting information,
- the association, interpretation and cognitively adequate presentation of the detected information.

The *HPQS* (High Performance Query Server) presented in this paper is a coherent architecture for such a tool. It implements the whole process from accepting queries in natural language to analyzing, summarizing and presentation of information.

There are a number of systems offering parts of the functionality of the HPQS. QBIC [10] and VIR [29] realize content-based retrieval in picture databases (on the *image signal level*, not, however, on a *symbolic level*). QBIC extracts information about color, texture and the shape of parts of the picture. For a given picture, the VIR systems performs a search through an image database and selects similar pictures in terms of color distribution and other parameters. Some other systems [1] [2] demand special input such as sketches. An overview of early systems is presented in [23]. IRIS [22] and MediaMiner [7] offer a content-based picture-search that is based on the input of keywords. All pictures are indexed when they are stored into the database. They can only be accessed using the given keywords.

The HPQS system goes far beyond the scope outlined above:

- *Natural language* (NL) *queries* are interpreted semantically using a number of problem independent databases and databases that model the target application domain;
- Semantic information extracted from various source documents is aggregated using *fuzzy data fusion algorithms*;
- A *mediator* caches meta data information that is extracted from mass data and uses it for further requests, if possible;
- A *parallel media server* stores and delivers mass data information and performs search operations on these mass data items;
- *Dedicated high speed hardware* processors perform selected search operations on mass data items that demand large computational power.

To realize these basic characteristics the system consists of the five main modules shown in Figure 1:

Natural Language Interface: Questions are posed in natural language. From the query an Intermediate Semantic Representation (ISR) is constructed.

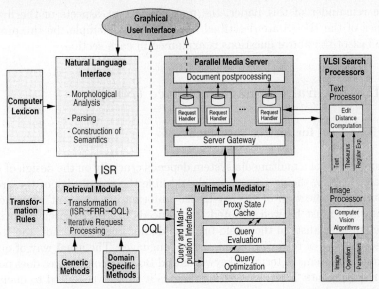

Fig. 1. Architecture of the High Performance Query Server

Retrieval Module: From the ISR representations an FRR (**F**ormal **R**etrieval **R**epresentation) is constructed. It makes use of transformation and interpretation knowledge. The FRR is transformed into ODMG-OQL requests. Information is fused using novel methods from fuzzy set theory.

Multimedia Mediator: The multimedia mediator structures and mediates the available mass data by storing, evaluating and creating additional *meta data*. OQL queries are processed with the help of the parallel server.

Parallel Server: The parallel server manages and delivers all available mass data. Additionally, time-consuming evaluation methods that work on the mass data information (e. g. image processing) can be initiated by the multimedia mediator and are performed by the parallel server.

Search Processors: Selected algorithms with high computational complexity for image processing and full-text retrieval are implemented as dedicated coprocessors which are integrated into the parallel server using standard PCI interfaces.

An example knowledge area was selected to demonstrate the performance of the HPQS: the domain of weather data documents, i.e. satellite images, tables in numerous different formats and textual weather reports. This domain can in principle be replaced with every other domain. Examples of questions that can be handled are the following:

- *Which was the warmest town in Germany yesterday?*
- *There were how many sunny days in Berlin in the last month?*
- *Show me pictures of cloud formation over Bavaria during the first week of August!*

In the remainder of this paper, the most important aspects of the five main modules of the HPQS are described. As a running example the the processing of the last of the above questions is explained in each section.

2 The natural language interface (NLI)

2.1 The case for an NL interface

The acceptance of a multimedia system depends crucially on the design of its user interface. Ideally, the user interface should hide the complexity of the program, thus providing the view of an easy-to-use "information assistant". Furthermore, the interface must be well adapted to the needs of average users who may be competent specialists in their field but who do not know or do not want to learn the peculiarities of retrieval techniques or languages. The usual way of querying information systems in terms of keywords and Boolean connectives does not meet these requirements. For the following reasons it is not well suited to querying in a multimedia domain either:

- *Absence of keywords.* First of all, there are obviously no *words in the images* being searched for and hence keyword matching is not possible. In our framework, descriptors are assigned automatically (on demand) by means of application-dependent methods operating on the multimedia documents. These image analysis methods typically provide *much more* than keywords; e. g. local relations between regions of interest can be computed along with a description of the regions themselves. This relational information plays an important role in image interpretation. It may make a difference to users planning their vacation in Italy whether "there are clouds" in the current weather image or whether "there are clouds in Italy". Keywords and boolean connectives, however, are obviously not sufficient for expressing such structured, model-based information.
- *Semantic querying.* Keywords with Boolean connectives are a rather cumbersome way of specifying a user's search request. Even in the textual case, users are seldom interested in documents in which only some search keywords happen to occur. Put succinctly, texts are more to humans than a set or distribution of word occurrences; they are pieces of natural language with an associated *meaning* and informational content which may or may not fulfill the user's information needs. Ideally, users should be permitted to query an information system on this level of meaning.
- *Intuitive interface.* Another problem with the usual query interfaces is their lack of user-friendliness. Although some of these interfaces (e. g. GLIMPSE, see [26]) offer powerful querying mechanisms like approximative search, regular expression search, adjacency operators, and search in specific document fields, most users are presumably not capable of taking full advantage of these features because they do not know when to apply them. By contrast,

natural language provides an intuitive interface because everybody knows how to use his native language without effort. Therefore, providing an NL front-end not only relieves the user from learning yet another querying language, but also removes technical barriers in accessing the more advanced features of an information retrieval system.

2.2 The NatLink interface

The NL interface NatLink (**natural language interface to knowledge**) aims at constructing of adequate semantic representations for a broad class of acceptable queries and texts in general. In contrast to many other linguistic formalisms, emphasis is laid on the semantic acceptability of NL input, not on its grammaticality. In particular, the robustness issue plays an important role. This includes the proper treatment of unknown words, elliptic sentences, and slightly ungrammatical sentences.

Robustness of NL analysis conflicts to some extent with the goal of generating expressive and deep semantic representations. For example, if a word is not found in the computational lexicon, morphologic analysis and syntactic context will usually provide very shallow information about the semantics of the given word. In the approach taken here, the depth of semantic analysis dynamically adapts to the syntactic and semantic information being available, resulting in a trade-off between robustness and depth of semantic representations.

A prerequisite of this approach is that the target formalism supports semantic representations on different levels of granularity or specificity. MESNET (see [16, 20]), a multilayered extension of semantic networks, has been designed to fulfill these requirements. Due to its multidimensional structure of classificatory knowledge, it is also possible to handle generic and individual concepts in MESNET as well as intensional vs. extensional aspects of meaning. MESNET has shown to be useful as

- the semantic representation for computational lexica ([27, 28]);
- the target language for NL analysis ([18, 19]);
- the basis for a translation into formal queries to information retrieval systems ([17]).

The natural language input[1] is analyzed by NatLink (see Figure 2) according to the principles of the *word-class controlled functional analysis* (WCFA, see [18, 19, 15]). Like other word-oriented approaches (e. g. [9], [6]), WCFA supports incremental parsing which improves the system's robustness.

The *word class functions* (WCFs), which WCFA is based on, roughly correspond to the traditional parts of speech but are usually more fine-grained. They

---

[1] Currently, the natural language used is German. The examples in this paper are translated.

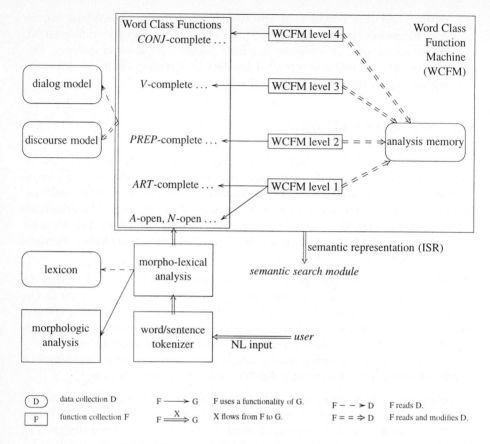

Fig. 2. Architecture of NatLink's WCFA implementation

comprise common nouns, proper nouns, interrogative determiners, interrogative pronouns, etc. All morpho-syntactic and semantic word information relevant to the analysis process is stored in the computational lexicon using typed feature structures. The lexicon is hierarchically structured, which ensures reusability, consistency, and extensibility of information by means of multiple inheritance with defaults (see [13, 14]).

WCFA parsing is *expectation-oriented*. After morphologic and lexical processing of a word, an "opening act" is performed which generates syntactic and semantic expectations (valency, agreement, etc.). The WCF also specifies "completing acts", which perform the saturation or refinement of the expectations stipulated during the opening act. When performing a "closing act", the analysis of the current constituent is completed and may then be used by the WCFA parser to fill other expectations.

Semantic representations of so-called *semantic kernels* (e. g. for noun phrases, prepositional phrases) are constructed as soon as possible during analysis in order

415

to resolve syntactic ambiguities in an early processing phase. Semantic kernels constitute the minimal units which a semantic representation can be assigned to in the course of incremental parsing. An example of an ISR expression, which is passed on to the next component (the semantic search module) as NatLink's analysis result, is shown in Figure 3.

One central problem in constructing semantic representations for NL sentences is the disambiguation of different kinds of ambiguities as the system should infer the true meaning the user had in mind. NatLink uses hybrid disambiguation methods (see for example [30]) that use symbolic knowledge (e. g. interpretation rules for prepositions) and subsymbolic knowledge (e. g. frequency statistics semi-automatically generated from NL corpora).

The WCFA parser is *modularly structured* in that the process of NL analysis is decomposed into four different levels, roughly corresponding to elementary nominal phrases, complex nominal phrases, elementary propositions, and complex propositions. It covers a large fragment of German syntax relevant to natural language access to databases. The lexicon contains a considerable percentage of German lexemes that occur frequently in the given application domain. In the next project phase, lexical and grammatical coverage will be extended and NatLink will be equipped with an appropriate dialog model.

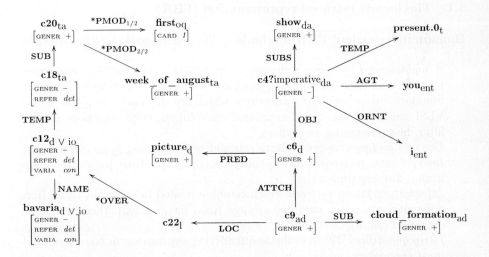

Fig. 3. Simplified ISR expression (in graphical form) generated by NatLink for the query: *Show me pictures of cloud formation over Bavaria in the first week of August!* (*Zeige mir Aufnahmen von Wolkenbildung über Bayern in der ersten Augustwoche!*)

3 The Retrieval-Module

Information retrieval (IR) differs from database querying not only in that the objects involved are far less structured, but also by the fact that with IR the relevance of an object with respect to a given query must be treated as an inherently gradual relation. With NL input, there are additional sources of gradual information, i.e. the inherent fuzziness or vagueness of natural language concepts has to be dealt with on the query side. On the interpretation side, knowledge about the constituting features of the concepts in the query is often incomplete. This results in a partial mismatch between the semantic representation of the question and the target concept. Instead of postulating "crisp" methods using Boolean evaluations, it seems more natural to represent such knowledge by fuzzy rules and judge the degree of applicability of these rules by means of gradual evaluations.

Consequently, the well-structured view of the multimedia system provided by the mediator component (see below) must be complemented by powerful means for representing vague queries and gradual search results. In order to meet these requirements, a formal retrieval representation (FRR) was developed, which extends the object query language by connectives from fuzzy logic and operators for information aggregation and data fusion.

3.1 The formal retrieval representation (FRR)

Domain independent FRR methods —The generic part of FRR comprises:

- *A sophisticated text-search module*, which builds on the very fast implementation of edit-distance matching provided by the VLSI text search processors.
- Standard *image processing primitives* which are also partly implemented in VLSI hardware, e.g. two-dimensional convolution, edge detection, median filter, histogramming and others;
- *Discrete and parameterized fuzzy sets* and corresponding *fuzzy connectives*;
- *Interpolation methods* which estimate a continuous-time parameter curve from a discrete time-series;
- *Information fusion methods* which combine related information taken from different sources (e.g. weighted average, fuzzy integral, and other data fusion operators [25, 5]).
- *Fuzzy quantifiers* [12] to evaluate quantifying expressions in NL queries (*almost everywhere, never,...*);

FRR hence provides domain-independent search methods for all considered multimedia formats, as well as fuzzy information combination operators. These are the focus of our work because they are a prerequisite of

- The evaluation of complex NL queries involving expressions of quantification, comparison, or other types of aggregation;

– The processing of NL queries which refer to an underlying *domain model*.

In the meteorological domain, for example, users are typically interested in certain weather conditions in a specified local and temporal region. Weather conditions, however, are *not fully specified by any single document* in the database; for example, satellite images provide the required data on cloudiness, while ground temperature readings can be obtained from temperature maps. In addition, more than one document may describe the same aspect of a weather situation. Therefore, operators for information combination are required which establish content-related links between the available documents and allow for the fusion of (possibly conflicting) information extracted from several document sources. These tasks are crucial to the management of the various levels of abstraction within our system.

Special emphasis has been laid on an adequate treatment of fuzzy quantification. This is because the "modes of combination" of natural language, i.e. the various ways in which concepts might be interrelated, are by no means restricted to the Boolean connectives *and, or* and *not*. Unlike those, NL offers a variety of (more subtle) aggregation operators, among which *fuzzy quantifiers* (like *many, few,...*) are of particular relevance due to their abundance in NL queries. The meaning of NL queries depends heavily on these quantifying expressions, as witnessed for example, by the different meaning of *there are few clouds over Italy* vs. *there are lots of clouds over Italy*, which both could be part of queries submitted to our system. In addition, fuzzy quantifiers are an important research topic because they form a class of powerful yet human-understandable operators for information aggregation.

In order to adequately cover the meaning of these fuzzy quantifiers, an axiomatic approach to fuzzy quantification has been developed [12] which builds on the novel concept of a Determiner Fuzzification Scheme (DFS). DFS theory overcomes several limitations of existing approaches to fuzzy quantification (e.g. [33, 8]). It is the first theory to model fuzzy quantifiers of *arbitrary dimension*, it is not limited to absolute (*at least n,...*) and proportional (*most,...*) quantifiers; it is not limited to finite universes of discourse; and, most importantly, it is *based on a rigid axiomatic foundation*. The theory has been fully implemented and is used in the HPQS system for interpreting quantifiers in NL queries, and for various purposes of information aggregation. An example will be given below.

Domain dependent methods —In addition to the generic part of FRR, domain-specific methods must be implemented which provide for an operational interpretation of natural language domain concepts based on the raw document data (or intermediate search results). These domain methods can build on generic FRR methods for text and image search provided by the FRR.

The prototypical implementation in the meteorological domain serves to validate the fuzzy search mechanism. These sample evaluation methods include:

- Cartographic projections of the specific image classes under consideration;
- Access to temperature readings in false-colour ground-temperature maps;
- Objective ("more than 20° Celsius") and subjective ("warm") classification of temperatures;
- Estimation of cloud-top height and cloud density in satellite images;
- Estimation of degrees of cloudiness.

Combined with the generic FRR methods described above, temperatures and degrees of cloudiness can be interpolated; average, minimal and maximal values can be determined; evaluations can be aggregated across time and space using fuzzy quantifiers etc. As the user queries are matched against a weather model which combines information extracted from related documents, selection or rejection of a document under a given query may depend on the information provided by other documents. By considering these content-related links between associated documents, a much finer-grained and purposive search can be achieved than is possible with standard methods.

3.2   Query translation step

The retrieval module translates ISR query representations generated by the NL interface into FRR queries, which are then passed to the mediator module for evaluation. The translation process includes

- *Normalization*: mapping of terms to their database correlates (e.g. of names of cities to geographic identifiers);
- *Anchoring in discourse situation* (e.g. resolution of temporal deictic expressions like "today");
- *Default assumptions* whenever needed, e.g. in order to limit the scope of a region search to Europe;
- *User interaction* to validate decisions on alternative interpretations.

The transformation is accomplished by application-specific transformation rules which construct the query FRR from the ISR graph. The premise part of each transformation rule specifies the structure of subgraphs to which the rule applies (e.g. temporal or local specifications, domain concepts). The consequence parts of the rules provide the corresponding FRR expressions from which the query FRR is constructed.

3.3   Query execution step

For performance reasons, the FRR methods are implemented and actually executed in the lower layers of the system, namely on the parallel media server and (whenever possible) on VLSI hardware. In order to enable remote access to these methods, they are wrapped into corresponding classes and methods of the mediators object-oriented database schema. The retrieval module is shielded from the intricacies of remote query execution: in order to invoke an FRR operation, it simply invokes an OQL query to the mediator module, which then caters for the remote (and possibly parallel) execution of the corresponding FRR operation. NL queries are usually decomposed into a sequence of such mediator queries.

3.4 Example of semantic search in HPQS

In order to show how a semantic search based on interrelated documents is actually performed in HPQS, we consider the sample query: *Show me pictures of cloud formation over Bavaria during the first week of August!* This query requests weather images C from the database with an associated date $C.date$ in the first week of August 1997 subject to the condition $R(C)$

    C witnesses a weather situation of cloud formation over Bavaria.

While the user simply requests *documents* of the database (in opposition to question-answer systems and expert systems), the condition R refers to an underlying *domain model* (in this case, of meteorology) in which the concept of "cloud formation" over some specified region may be given a procedural interpretation.

Considering a single image C is not sufficient to compute $R(C)$ because "formation" is essentially a matter of change and thus can only be judged relative to other images (in this case, images of relevance to the weather situation *before* $C.date$). Therefore, at least the weather image immediately preceding C must be taken into account. The task of detecting the relevant documents is decomposed as follows: "cloud formation" in a given local region is interpreted as a strong increase in cloudiness in that region in two consecutive weather maps. The system thus scans through the sequence of images in the specified time interval (first week of August 1997). For each image C under consideration, it firstly determines the predecessor image P. The following operations are then applied to C and P :

a) Compute estimates C_1 = C.cloudiness(), P_1 = P.cloudiness() of the density of low clouds in C and P;

b) Compute the fuzzy evaluations (grey-value images)
C_2 = C_1.sunny().negation(), P_2 = P_1.sunny();

c) Transform the results into the cartographic projection of the region B under consideration – in this case, B = Bavaria, yielding
C_3 = C_2.germanyProjection(), P_3 = P_2.germanyProjection();

d) Combine C_3 and P_3 *relative to the given region* B by applying a suitable fuzzy quantifier $\mathcal{M}(\geq 70\%)$ to form the gradual result
$$R = \min\{\,\mathcal{M}(\geq 70\%)(B, C_3),\ \mathcal{M}(\geq 70\%)(B, P_3)\,\}.$$

R is the fuzzy conjunction of the conditions that at least 70 % of Bavaria are sunny in the predecessor image P and that more than 70 % of Bavaria are cloudy in the current image C (for details on the underlying theory of fuzzy quantification and the definition of $\mathcal{M}(\geq 70\%)$, see Glöckner [12]).

Intermediate results of the search process are shown in Figure 4. As indicated by the search results obtained from real data in Figure 5, the system detects images in which there is a clearly visible increase in cloudiness.

C_1 C_2 C_3

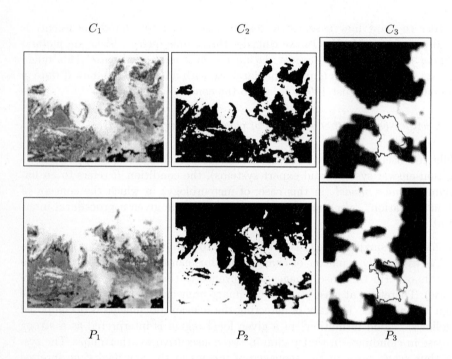

P_1 P_2 P_3

Fig. 4. Intermediate search results (C image under consideration, P predecessor of C)

4   Multimedia Mediator

The paradigm of a *mediator* was first advocated by G. Wiederhold [31]. The HPQS' Multimedia Mediator, or MMM for short, distributes an OQL query to the external sources making the best possible use of their parallelism and translates return values to the format specified in the query for a uniform presentation. Within the HPQS we have only one external source, namely the Parallel Server (see below).

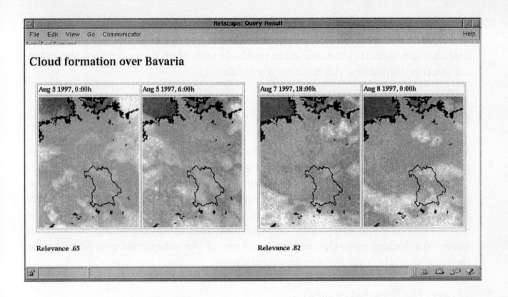

Fig. 5. Detected documents (relevant segments)

4.1 Architecture

Figure 6 illustrates the MMM's overall architecture. The core of the mediator is based upon an object-oriented database. The database consists of a *Multimedia Schema* defined by a mediator administrator and a *Proxy State* for external multimedia items conforming to the schema.

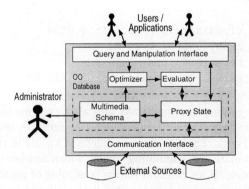

Fig. 6. Architecture of the MMM

Users or applications can query the proxy state as well as manipulate data by communicating with a *Query and Manipulation Interface*. Such requests are passed to the database, possibly after having been improved by an *Optimizer*.

Most operations on proxy objects have to be reflected to the multimedia items they represent. This reflection is performed by a *Communication Interface*, which contains specialized communication methods such that it can contact the external sources containing the multimedia items.

4.2 Optimizing queries

The optimizer is based on query transformations. In general this transformation process translates a single query into two passes with several subqueries. When the subqueries of the first pass are evaluated, they produce all necessary parameters for retrieving the data under consideration from the external sources. After actually retrieving these data, another query is evaluated in the second pass, which combines the subqueries' intermediate results for answering the original query. We demonstrate the evaluation of one of the subqueries generated by the retrieval module from the sample question:

```
select ImageAndRelevance(
  image: I,
  relevance: BAY.rateGreaterEqual(0.7,
          I.cloudiness().sunny().negation().germanyProjection())))
from I in q_138
```

where the objects in the set q_138 represent image files stored on the parallel server together with the required operations cloudiness, sunny, negation, and germanyProjection. Each of these specific operations performs some image processing and returns the processed image. The query is thus translated into a series of subqueries:

```
R1: select I.P_cloudiness() from I in q_0138
R2: select I.P_sunny() from I in R1
R3: select I.P_negation() from I in R2
R4: select I.P_germanyProjection() from I in R3
```

These queries are evaluated sequentially and after each evaluation the resulting parameter lists are sent to the parallel server in order to retrieve the required attributes. rateGreaterEqual is a method defined locally in the mediator. Thus, we can finally evaluate the combining query, which is identical to the original query in our example. If an external source is capable of parallel processing, like the HPQS' Parallel Server, the parameter lists returned by the subqueries are sent to the source as a set, so the source can execute one method on several lists of parameters in parallel.

In order to reduce communication overhead and avoid expensive external computations the mediator can materialize query results and intermediate results for future use, i.e. for each retrieved multimedia item a *proxy object* is created which contains or points to the retrieved value. Then this proxy object can be used for evaluation of further queries referencing it.

When materializing values, we have to deal with several problems, including the choice of a *materialization strategy*, i.e. under which conditions to materialize an object, assumptions on *incomplete knowledge*, i.e. in case of set values whether to evaluate under the closed world assumption or a partial open world assumption, and the choice of *refreshment strategies*. A more detailed discussion of these topics is beyond the scope of this paper but can be found in [3] and [4].

5   The parallel media server

The main task of the parallel server is firstly to manage the mass data that is stored in the HPQS, and secondly to perform search operations on these mass data items. As the execution of search operations is the most time-consuming operation of the request processing, the introduction of parallelism promises a substantial cut in the overall response time of the system. Furthermore, the server is scalable and can be expanded if necessary.

The parallel server stores objects on distributed disks, delivers objects, inserts new objects, and deletes objects. Since these are also the typical tasks of a WWW server, its communication channels are based on the HTTP protocol. The parallel server can apply search methods and other procedures *directly* and simultaneously on different mass data items. There are two main interfaces with the other modules in the HPQS:

- The parallel server interacts with the mediator. The latter can put, delete and receive data items from the parallel server. Additionally, the interface enables the mediator to start the parallel execution of methods on the parallel server.
- The parallel server also interacts with the hardware search processors. The server feeds data into the search processors and receives the results of the operations that are forwarded to the mediator. Thus, the search processors act as clients of the parallel server, which itself is a client of the mediator.

5.1   Structure of the server

The server is mainly constructed as a parallel WWW-Server that also executes methods on data items. Figure 7 shows the architecture of the server, which is composed of the data management unit and the execution unit. Each incoming request is examined and then processed by the appropriate unit, both of which share the same object database.

The *data-management unit* consists of a dispatcher and a couple of worker processes on each processor node. The dispatcher examines the incoming requests and decides by which node the request is to be processed. The appropriate

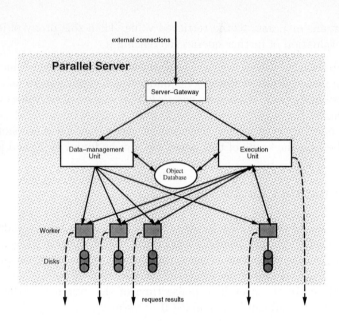

external connections

Parallel Server

Server–Gateway

Data–management Unit

Execution Unit

Object Database

Worker

Disks

request results

Fig. 7. The structure of the parallel server system

workers then parse the request and perform the necessary disk accesses. Since there are several workers on each node, requests can be processed in parallel on each node. The *execution unit* first schedules the jobs which are necessary for processing the request. The jobs are then executed on the appropriate nodes; the results are collected and sent back.

There are several problems with designing such a combined data storage and processing server as efficiently as possible. One problem arises from the question of data placement: which data should be stored on the disk of which node? The disks are the slowest part in the parallel server and each disk can only provide one access per time unit. It is therefore important to distribute the data over the disks in such a way to allow as many accesses to different disks in parallel as possible.

The main idea of the data distribution is to place data items that are often accessed simultaneously on different disks. We achieve this goal by analyzing the access pattern of the past and by using a graph-theoretic model in order to determine the distribution [24].

Another problem arises from the scheduling of the methods. These jobs should be distributed over the nodes as evenly as possible to make sure that they can be finished as early as possible. Nonetheless, each job needs special data and should be executed on the node which stores most of these data. This problem can be formalized into a new scheduling problem not examined so far. It turns out that even the special case with only two possible processing nodes is NP-hard. We have therefore developed heuristics which solve the scheduling problem in a fast and efficient way.

5.2 Processing of the example request

The example requests resulting from the sample question leads to a couple of method invocations on the parallel server. On each picture that has to be investigated for the selected week a number of operations have to be executed. Table 1 shows the times that are needed for one execution of each of these functions.

Method	Avg. time [s]
mefExtFilteredFindLowClouds	14.2
ociExtSunny	0.3
fiExtNegation	0.2
germanyProjection	4.0

Table 1. Execution times of methods invoked by the sample question

The total sequential processing time of the methods for this request is $(14.2 + 0.3 + 0.2 + 4.0) \cdot 56$ s $= 1047.2$ s (≈ 18 minutes), assuming that there are 56 relevant images which have to be examined. Using the parallel server with n nodes, each of the methods can be executed on all 56 images in parallel. So the total processing time would be $\lceil \frac{56}{n} \rceil \cdot 18.7$s. Assuming that there are 8 computing nodes, this results in a total time of ≈ 2.2 minutes. These times apply to the software solution without the VLSI search processors.

6 Search Processors

To ensure acceptable response times for the HPQS, basic and frequently used algorithms for image processing and full text retrieval will be implemented in dedicated processors. The image processing algorithms contain 2-dimensional and weighted median filtering as well as histogramming. The text algorithm allows approximate (fuzzy) full text search based on a dynamic programming procedure.

The dedicated processors are located on an add-on card. Integrated into the parallel server they communicate with the host CPUs via a PCI interface. The host CPUs perform the pre- and postprocessing functionality with low computational complexity but with a high grade of flexibility for the special processors.

The image processor component for 2-dimensional filtering provides different window sizes. Through the application of new resource-sharing concepts [32] a flexible trade-off between throughput rate and chip real estate is possible. The solution for the weighted median filtering component is based on the odd/even-transposition algorithm [21]. Beyond flexible window sizes it features efficient implementations for different throughput rates through the use of a bit-serial approach. The histogramming component achieves a high throughput rate through the use of histogram value partitioning and a dedicated synchronous full-custom memory based on the 3-transistor DRAM cell.

The text processor will be a solution optimized for approximate (i.e. fault tolerant) full text search. Therefore, the underlying basic algorithm was extended to enable the processing of language specific and special characters as well as wildcards and multi token words. The main part of the processor is a systolic array of processing elements with a throughput of more than 130 Mill. characters per second and a computational power of nearly 17 Bill. operations per second.

The work on the dedicated processors follows a special design style. Components critical to time, area, and especially power consumption are assembled as highly optimized full-custom macros by a datapath generator [11]. Starting from a VHDL description of the component's signal flow graphs, this datapath generator assembles the macro layouts from abutment cells. These abutment cells are derived automatically from a library of a very few handcrafted and optimized leaf cells. This exploits the inherent regularity and locality typical for signal flow graphs of digital signal processing for the optimization of chip area, throughput rate and especially power consumption. Moreover, the automation offers the possibility for effectively optimizing the signal flow graph by simply modifying the VHDL description. By contrast, irregular control logic is implemented using a common semi-custom design style.

7 Conclusions

We have presented the prototypical implementation of a complex digital library system whose search and presentation capabilities reach beyond current systems. The user input is assigned a semantic interpretation. This enables a fine grained and precise search if methods are available in the specific knowledge domain that analyze documents for their semantic contents and produce result documents utilizing data fusion.

The system is fully operational with some limits on the classes of questions that it can be asked; the data sets it works on are already on the order of several Gigabytes of text and image data. The response time for answering questions covering up to 100 colour images is currently on the order of a few minutes. The latter will drop to fractions of a second once the hardware processors currently under development become available.

Lines of future research are the analysis of video and audio documents so as to include them in the search process, the optimization of the mediator and the database as well as the generation and presentation of the result documents.

Acknowledgement —The authors wish to acknowledge the valuable contribution Volker Jentsch made by establishing this research group.

References

1. A. Del Bimbo, M. Campanai, and P. Nesi. A three-dimensional iconic environment for image database querying. *IEEE Trans. on Software Eng.*, 19(10):997–1011, October 1993.

2. A. Del Bimbo and P. Pala. Visual image retrieval by elastic matching of user sketches. *IEEE Trans. on Patt. Anal. and Mach. Intell.*, 19(2):121–132, February 1997.

3. J. Biskup, J. Freitag, Y. Karabulut, and B. Sprick. A mediator for multimedia systems. In *Proceedings 3rd International Workshop on Multimedia Information Systems*, Como, Italia, Sept. 1997.

4. J. Biskup, J. Freitag, Y. Karabulut, and B. Sprick. Query evaluation in an object-oriented multimedia mediator. In *Proceedings 4th International Conference on Object-Oriented Information Systems, Brisbane, Australia*, Berlin, Nov. 1997. Springer.

5. I. Bloch. Information combination operators for data fusion: a comparative review with classification. *IEEE Transactions on Systems, Man, and Cybernetics*, 26(1):52–67, 1996.

6. Norbert Bröker, Udo Hahn, and Susanne Schacht. Concurrent lexicalized dependency parsing: The ParseTalk model. In *Proceedings of the 15th International Conference on Computational Linguistics (COLING 94)*, 1994.

7. IBM Corp. http://www.software.ibm.com/data/mediaminer/immn0b15.html.

8. D. Dubois and H. Prade. Fuzzy cardinality and the modelling of imprecise quantification. *Fuzzy Sets and Systems*, 16:199–230, 1985.

9. Michael Eimermacher. *Wortorientiertes Parsen*. PhD thesis, TU Berlin, Berlin, 1988.

10. M. Flickner, H. Sawhney, W. Niblack, J. Ashley, Q. Huang, B. Dom, M. Gorkhani, J. Hafner, D. Lee, D. Petkovic, D. Steele, and P. Yanker. Query by image and video content: The QBIC system. *IEEE Computer*, 28(9), September 1995.

11. Michael Gansen, Frank Richter, Oliver Weiß, and Tobias G. Noll. A datapath generator for full custom macros of iterative logic arrays. *Proceedings of the IEEE 1997 International Conference on Application Specific Systems, Architectures, and Processors*, pages 438–447, July 1997.

12. Ingo Glöckner. DFS – an axiomatic approach to fuzzy quantification. Technical Report TR97-06, Technische Fakultät, Universität Bielefeld, 1997.

13. Sven Hartrumpf. Redundanzarme Lexika durch Vererbung. Master's thesis, Universität Koblenz-Landau, Koblenz, June 1996.

14. Sven Hartrumpf. Partial evaluation for efficient access to inheritance lexicons. In *Proceedings of the 2nd International Conference on Recent Advances in Natural Language Processing (RANLP-97)*, pages 43–50, Tzigov Chark, Bulgaria, September 1997.

15. Hermann Helbig. Syntactic-semantic analysis of natural language by a new word-class controlled functional analysis. *Computers and Artificial Intelligence*, 5(1):53–59, 1986.

16. Hermann Helbig. Der MESNET Primer – Die Darstellungsmittel der Mehrschichtigen Erweiterten Semantischen Netze. Technische Dokumentation, FernUniversität Hagen, Hagen, Germany, January 1997.

17. Hermann Helbig, Carsten Gnörlich, and Dirk Menke. Realization of a user-friendly access to networked information retrieval systems. In *Proceedings of the AAAI Spring Symposium on Natural Language Processing for the World Wide Web*, pages 62–71, Stanford, CA, 1997.

18. Hermann Helbig and Sven Hartrumpf. Word class functions for syntactic-semantic analysis. In *Proceedings of the 2nd International Conference on Recent Advances in Natural Language Processing (RANLP-97)*, pages 312–317, Tzigov Chark, Bulgaria, September 1997.

19. Hermann Helbig and Andreas Mertens. Word Agent Based Natural Language Processing. In Loe Boves and Anton Nijholt, editors, *Proceedings of the 8th Twente Workshop on Language Technology – Speech and Language Engineering, Twente, 1 and 2 December 1994*, pages 65–74, Enschede, 1994. Universiteit Twente, Fakulteit Informatica.

20. Hermann Helbig and Marion Schulz. Knowledge representation with MESNET: A multilayered extended semantic network. In *Proceedings of the AAAI Spring Symposium on Ontological Engineering*, pages 64–72, Stanford, CA, 1997.

21. Christiane Henning and Tobias G. Noll. Architecture and implementation of a bitserial sorter for weighted median filtering. *Proceedings of the 1998 Custom Integrated Circuits Conference, Santa Clatra, CA*, May 1998.

22. T. Hermes, C. Klauck, J.Kreyß, and J. Zhang. Image retrieval for information systems. In *Proc. SPIE's Symp. on Electronic Imaging*, San Jose, February 1995.

23. S. Iyengar and R. Kashyap. Special section on image databases. *IEEE Trans. on Software Eng.*, 14(5):608–688, May 1988.

24. Jörg Jensch, Reinhard Lüling, and Norbert Sensen. A data layout strategy for parallel web servers. In *Proceedings of EuroPar '98*, 1998.

25. A. Knoll, R. Schröder, and A. Wolfram. Fusion of data from fuzzy integral-based active and passive colour stereo vision systems for correspondence identification. In *Proceedings of the VIII European Signal Processing Conference (EUSIPCO-96)*, Trieste, Italy, Sept. 10-13 1996.

26. U. Manber and S. Wu. GLIMPSE: A tool to search through entire file systems. Tr 93-34, Department of Computer Science, University of Arizona, Tucson, Arizona, 1993.

27. Marion Schulz. *Eine Werkbank zur interaktiven Erstellung semantikbasierter Computerlexika*. PhD thesis, FernUniversität Hagen, Hagen, 1998.

28. Marion Schulz and Hermann Helbig. COLEX: Ein Computerlexikon für die automatische Sprachverarbeitung. Informatik-Bericht 210, FernUniversität Hagen, Hagen, Germany, December 1996.

29. Virage Inc. http://www.virage.com.

30. Stefan Wermter, Ellen Riloff, and Gabriele Scheler, editors. *Connectionist, Statistical, and Symbolic Approaches to Learning for Natural Language Processing*, volume 1040 of *LNAI*. Springer, Berlin, 1996.

31. G. Wiederhold. Mediators in the architecture of future information systems. *IEEE Computer*, 25(3):38–49, 1992.

32. Wolfgang Wilhelm and Tobias G. Noll. A new mapping technique for automated design of highly efficient multiplexed fir digital filters. *Proceedings of the IEEE International Symposium on Circuits and Systems*, pages 2252–2255, June 1997.

33. L.A. Zadeh. A computational approach to fuzzy quantifiers in natural languages. *Comput. and Math.*, 9:149–184, 1983.

Taiscéalaí: Information Retrieval from an Archive of Spoken Radio News

Alan F. Smeaton[1], M. Morony[2], Gerard Quinn[1], and Ronan Scaife[2]

[1] School of Computer Applications, Dublin City University,
Glasnevin, Dublin 9, IRELAND
asmeaton@CompApp.DCU.ie
[2] School of Electronic Engineering, Dublin City University,
Glasnevin, Dublin 9, IRELAND

Abstract. In this paper we describe Taiscéalaí, a web-based system which provides content-based retrieval on an up-to-date archive of RTÉ radio news bulletins. Taiscéalaí automatically records and indexes news bulletins twice daily using a stream of phones recognised from the raw audio data. A user's typed query is matched against fixed length windows from the broadcasts. A user interface allows the news bulletins most likely to be relevant to be presented and the user to select sub-parts of the bulletins to be played. Many of the parameters we have chosen to use such as the size and amount of overlap of windows and the weighting of phones within those windows, have been determined within the framework of the TREC Spoken Document Retrieval track and are thus well-founded. We conclude the paper with a walkthrough of a worked example retrieval and an outline of our plans for extending Taiscéalaí into an integrated digital library for news.

1 Introduction

A digital library is basically a collection of information to which people require access for a variety of purposes. The information may be distributed in nature, may be of any kind of digital media, may be interconnected and linked into a "web" or perhaps consist of independent information objects and may support different kinds of access and retrieval paradigms. Access mechanisms for information stored as text are well established and information retrieval has been the subject of much research over the last 4 decades. Work on access mechanisms for information stored as digital audio, image or digital video has only recently been possible and is now being pursued with vigour by the research community.

Content-based access to spoken audio information is a desirable technology as part of a digital library because there is a wealth of information available to us only in audio format. Obvious examples are radio broadcasts but audio also forms an important component in retrieval from video.

Audio information can be very difficult to analyse because of speaker differences, various types of background noises, the fact that speech is continuous and the fact that the quality of some audio information, e.g. a telephone interview broadcast over the radio, can be quite poor. In developing a system to perform retrieval from digital audio information we have bypassed some of these problems by using a source, radio news bulletins, where the quality of studio broadcast is normally good. Radio news bulletins, however, still present some challenges in that they can be interspersed with telephone and non- studio outside interviews, there are normally a number of different newsreaders (in our case about 10) who speak in continuous speech, and there may be many more correspondents who will report on individual stories. Thus content-based retrieval from spoken radio news bulletins is a task with many problems as we shall see.

Content-based access to radio news bulletins must be done by processing the raw speech into some form since newsreaders do not read from a complete script but from a series of individual stories which are swapped around and changed right up to the last minute and even during a broadcast. Furthermore, in our application the actual scripts are not kept in electronic format for subsequent archiving and hence content retrieval. Thus we are faced with having to process the recorded audio data if we want to do content-based processing of news bulletins.

In this paper we describe Taiscéalaí (Taiscéalaí is a word play on the Irish words "taisce" meaning a collection, store or hoard and "scéalaí" meaning news stories), an operational information retrieval system for an archive of radio news bulletins which is automatically updated with daily bulletins. In section 2 we look at other work on information retrieval from spoken documents, including the work done in TREC by ourselves and others, and we outline the approach to spoken document retrieval that we have taken. Section 3 presents a high level view of our speech processing and in section 4 we outline how we index and retrieve segments of an audio broadcast. Section 5 contains a walkthrough of a retrieval session using our system and in section 6 we present our conclusions and plans for integrating Taiscéalaí with other news sources.

2   Information Retrieval from Spoken Documents

Information retrieval from spoken documents is very different to retrieval from text, not just because of the medium and the errors inherent in any speech recognition system but because audio is a continuous stream rather than broken up into marked discrete units such as documents, sections or paragraphs. Most information retrieval on text is performed on sets of individual documents which are regarded as being independent of each other. If the documents are large then they may be broken down into smaller logical units for retrieval such as sections or chapters.

In most applications where spoken audio is recorded, natural boundaries between independent elements of the audio such as stories in a news bulletin do not form an inherent part of the audio itself and individual units are concatenated together without markup or significant pauses. For example, in an audio recording of a play, drama or soap opera the audio would not necessarily contain indicators of scene changes; in a recording of a business meeting there is no clear and consistent indicator of movement from one agenda item to the next; in a radio news bulletin there is no indicator of the boundary between one story and the next although an individual bulletin will contain a relatively small number of stories. This would be analogous to concatenating individual text documents together and removing markup indicators such as title fields or authornames. In an ideal world we would like to have some audio indicator between story bounds in a broadcast radio news bulletin but this is not the case and so we are faced with a problem. As an aside, a consequence of the current fad within TV production with digital effects is that our local TV station has introduced an auditory "whoosh" effect between story bounds in TV news bulletins which would make story bound detection easier but this is not used in radio.

One of the first spoken document retrieval systems was developed at ETH Zürich and is reported in [8]. Here a recogniser was developed for Swiss-German radio news broadcasts which recognised sub-word units of pronunciation called phones. Broadcasts were divided into fixed length overlapping windows which were indexed by triphones or triples of adjacent phones. User queries were turned into triphones and the matching function between query and broadcast triphones catered for phone recognition errors. This work has acted as a model for our own developments and broadly speaking we have extended this by developing our own recogniser for Irish radio news broadcasts, determined our own window size, overlap and weighting parameters using the TREC environment, and we have developed a different kind of interface allowing users to choose their own segments of a broadcast to be played.

Significant interest in information retrieval from spoken documents has been nurtured by the organisers of TREC-6 [3] and TREC-7 during 1997 and 1998 who have developed a specialist track on this topic. A corpus of US radio and TV news broadcasts was made available to participants as raw audio data (.WAV format), as a ground truth transcript and in the format output from an IBM speech recognition system, i.e. including recognition errors. In the TREC task the data corresponded to complete news broadcasts and the boundaries between news stories were marked up manually. In an operational news speech retrieval system such as our own, news story boundaries are not normally part of the audio and it is extremely difficult without extensive post-processing on the recognised speech to automatically detect shifts in topic representing changes in the stories being broadcast. Like the work at ETH, our approach to hanlding the fact that a single broadcast contains multiple concatenated stories is to divide the entire broadcast into fixed length overlapping windows and to treat each window as an independent document for indexing and retrieval in a traditional information retrieval approach.

There is a lot of justification for using triphones as the indexing units for speech broadcasts. As part of the phone recognition process the context in which each phone occurs, i.e. the most likely phone preceding and following a given phone, can be modeled as we have done in our recogniser instead of trying to recognise each phone in isolation. This means that there is a natural appeal of grouping of phones into triples, not just within words but across word boundaries as well. Using individual phones would be equivalent to retrieving text based on matching individual letters in queries and documents and using biphones does not fully take advantage of the context in which a phone occurs.

Recently, a significant justification for using triphones as a representation for audio broadcasts has been reported by Ng and Zue [6] who indexed an archive of spoken news bulletins by monophones, biphones and triphones, and ran a series of retrieval experiments measuring retrieval effectiveness against the basic unit of representation. Their results confirmed a triphone representation of query and broadcast to yield the most effective retrieval performance.

In the Taiscéalaí system, audio recordings are made direct from a radio connected to a PC, using a cron script to record for 10 minutes daily at 13:00 hours, and for 7 minutes nightly at 00:00 hours, 7 days a week. The midday bulletin varies in length between 7 and 9 minutes on weekdays, and between 5 and 7 minutes at weekends; the midnight bulletin generally lasts around 5 minutes. The vagaries of the PC clock, and slight variations in the times at which bulletins begin, together with the variation in the lengths of bulletins, necessitated the development and inclusion of a trimming procedure which pares away extraneous material surrounding a news bulletin such as commercials, signature tune, etc. This, and the process we use to analyse speech, is described in the following section.

3 Speech Processing Techniques

Modern approaches to automatic speech recognition are firmly based on statistical pattern recognition techniques. The most widely used technique is Hidden Markov Modelling (HMM), which uses probabilistic finite-state automata (HMMs) to model the objects to be recognised. These may be words, or in our case the individual sounds or phones of which words are made up. A HMM comprises a number of states connected by arcs, each state being characterised by a probability density describing the likelihood of particular feature vectors appearing while in that state, the arcs defining possible state-to-state transitions, and probabilities attached to the arcs. The state distribution parameters and transition parameters for a HMM must be estimated from large amounts of training-data and once a set of models has been trained, any new utterance may be recognised by finding the sequence of HMMs that provides the most probable match to the feature-vectors representing the utterance.

Building a recogniser from scratch is highly labour-intensive, but there are several packages available to reduce the scale of the task. We used HTK, developed by Cambridge University Engineering Department and available under license from Entropic, to develop the recognition system used in Taiscéalaí. The task for the speech recognition side of our work was to build a fully automated system for recording, trimming, and transcribing news bulletins, so that trimmed bulletins and aligned transcriptions could be passed to the indexing and retrieval module on a daily basis for indexing and addition to the search archive.

24 hours of recorded bulletins were used for training HMMs. 86% of the training data is studio-quality speech read by newsreaders (52%) or correspondents (34%). The remaining 14% of the data is made up of telephoned reports, outdoor reports or interviews affected by environmental noise such as traffic noise. 10% of the total training-data is telephone bandwidth, and 4% is full-bandwidth data affected by environmental noise or reverberation.

10 different newsreaders are represented in the training data, and somewhere between 15 and 20 regular correspondents. Some 65% of the data is from male speakers, and 35% from females. 90% of the data is from speakers with a form of pronunciation that could be described as standard for the Republic of Ireland. Regional accents from both Ireland and the North of Ireland are fairly well represented among the correspondents. There is a small amount of speech (well below 5% of the total) from outside Ireland and Northern Ireland, most of it Southern British English.

The fact that the data consisted of bulletins of 5 to 10 minutes duration necessitated a two-stage approach to our task [1]. The first requirement was a procedure for trimming recorded bulletins and dividing them into manageable sections for processing; "manageable" here means in effect "not longer than about 20 seconds". The sections were also classified at this stage into one of four types – studio quality speech, telephone-bandwidth speech, full bandwidth speech affected by environmental noise, or non-speech (applause, cheering, etc.).

A Gaussian classifier was used as the basis of the first stage processing. The classifier employed 14 features, extracted for a 32 ms window applied every 16 ms, extracting features such as the log power, log power above 4 kHz, estimate of background noise level calculated over 15 frame windows centred on the current frame and the 3rd, 4th, 8th and 16th cepstral coefficients derived from the Fourier log magnitude spectrum. More details on this can be found elsewhere [5]. We used 50 complete news bulletins to train the classifier, labeled by hand using Entropic's WAVES package and the 14-feature analysis vectors were derived and collected into class-samples.

Once classification is effected, all pre- and post-bulletin material is discarded, and within the bulletin proper, all silence and breath segments of whatever audio-type are reclassified simply as pauses which we use in displaying the results of a search. A multi-pass procedure is then used to find the longest pauses on which to break the bulletin into segments in such a way as to ensure that no segment in the final outcome is longer than 20 seconds. This first stage processing of bulletins takes about one third of real time, most of this being taken up by feature-extraction; classification and segmentation proper together take only about 10% of real time.

Training for the second-stage procedure was based on 12,000 utterances sectioned out by hand from the 24 hours of training bulletins. These utterances were then transcribed by an audio- typist to produce English text. A pronunciation dictionary was used to enable HTK to train phonetic HMMs from the acoustic data and associated textual transcription, the word-level transcriptions produced by the audio typist being converted automatically to phonetic transcriptions by means of the dictionary. We used a pronounciation dictionary derived originally from the online Carnegie Mellon University (CMU) dictionary. We put the CMU dictionary through successive transformations to make it suitable for use in an Irish context including the following:

- we corrected some entries with the uniquely Irish pronunciation for words like O'Reilly (*ou-r-ai-l-ii*), O'Mahony (*ou-m-aa-h-ax-n-ii*) and McKeown (*m-ax-k-y-ou-n*).
- we corrected others for the Hiberno-English rather than American pronunciation of words like nuclear (*n-uu-k-l-i-axxr* to *n-y-uu-k-l-ii-axr*) and multi (*m-uh-l-t-ai* to *m-uh-l-t-ii*).
- we added the most commonly-occurring words, such as place and person names not already in the dictionary such as Taoiseach (*t-ii-sh-ax-k*), Tánaiste (*t-oo-n-ax-sh-t-ax*) and Fianna Fáil (*f-ii-ax-n-ax-f-oi-l*) by processing the last 18 months text from the Irish Times newspaper finding words not in the dictionary but in the newspaper.
- non-rhotic pronunciations of words with *r* were added to accommodate British (Anglo-English) accents and so "card" has an entry (*k-aa-d*) in addition to (*k-aa-r-d*).

At the time of writing our dictionary contains some 160,000 entries, including multiple pronunciations.

It was a priority for us to develop a recogniser that worked in reasonable time, and while HTK made possible the development of recognisers with impressive degrees of accuracy, recognition times using the most accurate systems were far too slow for our immediate purposes (well in excess of 100 times slower than real time). Various methods were tried for speeding up recognition times as we now describe.

It is possible to build simple phone recognisers which run in real time on any reasonably fast machine. By a simple phone recogniser is meant one which builds models of the phones of the language disregarding the immediate contexts in which the phones occur; 40 or 50 models are then generally adequate to cover all the sounds involved. However, since the acoustic realisation of a phone is critially dependent on the phones adjacent to it, much greater accuracy can be achieved by modelling triphones, that is, phones conditioned on the sounds that precede and follow. This leads, however, to very much more complex systems and to increases in recognition times, especially if one also models contexts that include word-boundaries as we have done.

To reduce the number of models in our system, we used decision-tree clustering [12], allowing several similar sound-classes to share a single set of model parameters where appropriate. A distinction then comes into play between logical models or classes as the names of wholly specific sounds, and physical models as the actual HHMs used to represent the logical models. Generally we wish to retain specific class names in order to keep the connectivity between context-dependent logical models explicit, while having a single physical model represent several classes allows a single score for that model to be propagated to all the classes that share it.

Our principal tack in attempting to reduce recognition time was to simplify our phonetic modelling. Whereas it is common practice to use context-dependent (usually three-state) triphones to model the sounds of the language, we used three state models only where it seemed absolutely crucial to do so, given our knowledge of acoustic phonetics. Whereas each state in a triphone-model is conditioned on the identities of both the preceding and following phones, we made the first state of almost all models, both two and three state models, contextually dependent only on the preceding phone, and the last state similarly dependent only on the following phone. The only exceptions were the schwa vowel (the vowel in "the" and "a"), and h when it occurred between voiced sounds (as in "so high", "ahead"). For all other vowels, and for y, only the central state was made sensitive to both left and right contexts. The stops p, t and k occurring before vowels had their initial state sensitive only to the preceding context, and both their second and final state sensitive only to the following context.

The early stages of building our recogniser involved training simple phone models. Once context-dependency was introduced, and context-dependent single gaussian HMMs had been trained, the HMMs were 'dismembered', each state of each initial HMM becoming a stand-alone one-state HMM in its own right. After two reestimations of these one-state HMMs, clustering of models took place in accordance with the prescriptions outlined in the previous paragraph, leading to a system with 2,700 physical models and almost 50,000 logical models (this may be compared with our most accurate (but extremely slow!) system's 27,000 physical and 100,000 logical models). The 2,700 physical HMMs were further refined by mixture-splitting and reestimation, and at the end of training each 'sub-phonic' class was represented by an 8-mixture Gaussian with diagonal covariances.

During recognition, scoring in the sense of calculating likelihoods from mixture gaussians was restricted to the 2,700 physical models, likelihood scores being propagated from physical models to all the logical models which share them. We achieved a large reduction in memory-use by dispensing with the logical-physical distinction in respect of the 37,000 logical triphones of vowels other than schwa, redefining the transition network in terms of their physical models where appropriate, thus reducing the number of logical classes to less than 12,000 which was significant, and had no impact on accuracy. The reduction was possible because the sounds affected – vowels other than schwa – retained the physical vs logical distinction with respect to their first and final subphonic states; thus the vowel a appearing between k and t as in "cat" is represented by three sub-phonic classes k-$a1$, k-$a2$+t, and $a3$+t, and since clustering never combines triphones of different vowels, the middle triphone is recoverable by virtue of its central element alone, regardless of the precise form of the physical model that represents it.

The speech recognition process we developed transcribes in a little under 18 times real time though needless to say, increased recognition speed was purchased at the cost of significant degradation in accuracy. To put this recognition time into context, the IBM speech recogniser used to generate the transcript used in TREC-6 runs at 40 times real time on a large IBM mainframe, the

Dragon/UMass recogniser used in TREC-6 runs at 80 times real time on a 200 MHz PC while the University of Sheffield recogniser used by Sheffield and the University of Glasgow in TREC-6 runs at 5 times real time, though this was a cut down version developed in order to handle the volume of information that needed recognition for the TREC task. All our speech processing takes place on a PC with a Pentium Pro 180 MHz processor, running Linux.

4 Indexing Radio News Broadcasts for Retrieval

The RTÉ Radio 1 news broadcasts are captured, trimmed and transcribed into phones as described in the previous section and the stream of triphones representing each "window" is sent for indexing. Broadcasts are also automatically converted into RealAudio format for low bandwidth playback over the internet using our RealAudio server, and the original WAV format of the captured audio is then discarded.

Using the timing tags which form part of the phoneme transcription we divide each broadcast into overlapping windows and we treat each as an indexable "document" of triphones. During playback of any section of the archive we would like to have some context into which we can set our search terms and this could be implemented by playing back some short buffer before search term occurrences. However, multiple occurrences of search terms adjacently or in close proximity will cause more than 1 window to become highly scored and the system or the user would be faced with choosing between them. To address this we developed a series of term (triphone) weighting functions which pay importance not only to the occurrence of a query triphone but also to the position of that triphone within each window.

A variety of formulae were evaluated on the TREC-6 spoken document retrieval data [3] in a large series of experiments we carried out post-TREC. Our results in the official TREC-6 task (once a bug had been fixed) were comparable to other reported approaches [9]. Our subsequent results are even more improved and will be reported elsewhere [7]. These experiments on the TREC data set have guided us in the development of techniques and settings for our operational audio retrieval system and constitute the closest approach we have taken to "evaluating" the performance of the Taiscéalaí system. The three triphone weighting formulae we concentrate on are termed pyramid, middle tower and equal weights and are shown in Figure 1.

Pyramid assigns most importance to triphones in the middle of each window with sliding scales each side, middle tower assigns the greater importance to triphones in the middle third of each window while equal weights ignores positional occurrences of triphones. For each of these we varied the window size, overlap and parameters such as the "height" of the pyramid and middle tower using the TREC-6 spoken document data represented exactly as in our Taiscéalaí system.

One of the criticisms of the TREC-6 spoken document retrieval track was the way in which it was evaluated. The task is referred to as "known item retrieval" where each topic is contrived in such a way that there is one and only one

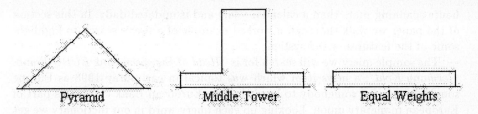

Fig. 1. Weighting formulae used

relevant story and the task is to find this single item at as high a rank position as possible. In TREC-6, retrieval effectiveness was computed as a single figure, the mean reciprocal rank position which is the average of the reciprocals of the rank positions of the relevant stories, over all topics. This favoured systems which find the relevant items at rank position 1 with a sliding scale as the relevant item is located further down the rankings. An alternative measure proposed by Schäuble is the sorted rank order, a graph of the rank positions of the known items sorted left-to-right in increasing rank position. This measure has the advantage that nothing is hidden behind averages over the different topics.

In evaluating the series of weighting functions for the positional occurrence of query triphones within windows we used mean reciprocal rank position and sorted rank order as evaluation measures and our best performances were obtained with a middle pyramid weighting on 30 second windows, overlapped by 10 seconds with triphones in the middle given a weight of 10 times those at the start and end. The stream of phones for each broadcast are turned into windows with weighted triphones and indexed by our text search engine [4]. The text of a user's query is turned into a phone representation by a dictionary lookup and triphones, including cross-word triphones, are generated as a set of search terms. Each 30 second window in the archive is scored as the sum of the $tf \times IDF$ weighted search triphones occurring within it.

For presenting the results of a search to a user we initially developed a system which ranks the windows and presents the top-10 but we also have a Java interface which computes scores for bulletins, and the highest scored bulletin is presented. This contains a graphical indication of the distribution of window scores throughout the bulletin as well as an indication of the type or class of broadcast (in studio, telephone interview, etc.) at various stages. The system allows the user to manually select any segment of the broadcast to be played, the selected segment is retrieved and created as a RealAudio file and playback on the user's machine is initiated. A worked example is illustrated in the next section.

5   The Taiscéalaí Retrieval System

The Taiscéalaí retrieval system for spoken radio news bulletins is operational on an archive of over 4,500 minutes of audio news since 26 April 1997 (almost 80 hours spanning more than a calendar year) and is updated daily. In this section of the paper we walk thorough a worked example of a user's search to highlight some of the features of the system.

The sample query we will search for is *"Head of European bank EURO France Germany Kohl"*, a news item which was topical in early May 1998 as Europe sought to appoint somebody to head the new European Bank created as part of European monetary union. Looking up each query word in our dictionary we get the phonemic translation shown in Table 1 which illustrates 2 pronunciations each for of the words "European", "EURO" and "Kohl", and 3 pronunciations for "Germany":

Table 1. Phonetic translation of search Terms

Query Word	Phoneme Translations
head	*h-e-d*
of	*ax-v*
	o-v
European	*y-oo-r-ax-p-ii-ax-n*
	y-uu-r-ax-p-ii-ax-n
bank	*b-a-ng-k*
EURO	*y-oo-r-oH*
	y-uu-r-ou
France	*f-r-a-n-s*
Germany	*jh-axx-m-ax-n-ii*
	jh-axxr-m-ax-n-ii
	jh-ur-m-ax-n-ii
Kohl	*k-oH-l*
	k-ou-l

From these phonemes are generated a set of triphones which are used as the search query. Each of the 30 second windows in the archive is assigned a score and then the top-ranked bulletins are retrieved and presented. Figure 2 shows a screendump where the user is displaying a time series of window scores for the bulletins ranked 6th (18 May 1998) to 8th (03 May 1998).

If we examine the time series presented for the bulletins we note a series of "spikes" on each which correspond to pauses in the audio of greater than 0.45 seconds in duration, and the height of these spikes is proportional to their length. These are provided as they are sometimes good indicators of story bounds which can help the user in selecting parts of the broadcast to be played. The parts of the x-axis for each bulletin marked in red corresponds our recogniser determining a telephone or outside broadcast while the yellow corresponds to an in-studio newsreader. The time series display indicates the regions of the broadcast where query triphones occur in the recognised transcript and it is around these "plateaus" that the user selects parts of the broadcast to be played. In the screendump the user has selected a portion of the broadcast ranked 8th

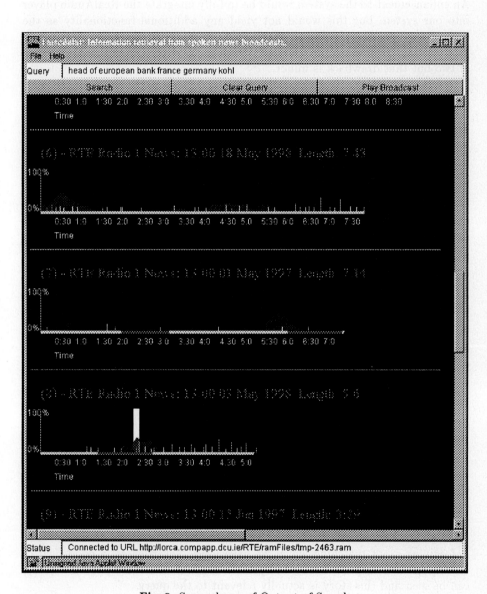

Fig. 2. Screendump of Output of Search

from about 2:20 to 2:25. This is then pulled from the archive and created as a temporary RealAudio file and played for the user using their RealAudio player. An enhancement to the system would be to fully integrate the RealAudio player into our system but this would not yield any additional functionality as the present arrangement of using an outside plug-in works satisfactorily. The overall user interface might be more coherent if we had one overall control panel instead of two but that drawback is minor.

A transcript of the selected broadcast is shown below:

More details have emerged of the bitter row between France and other European Union heads of government over the appointment of a President to the European central bank

The stream of phones recognised by our recogniser (artificially broken into words for readability) is:

m oo r — d ii d t ei l z — h a v — ax m a l axxr jh d t - ax v - dh a v — b i t axr - r ax r ou v - b ax t w ii n d - f au n t s - ax n d - uh dh axr — y uu r ax p ii ax n d - y uu n y ax n - h a d z - ax v — k o v axr m ax n d s k - o v axr - dh ii - i t p oi n n t m ax n d — ax v - o t - k r e z ax d ax n t - t uu - dh ii - y uu r ax p ii ax n - s a n t r o l - b a ng k

while the correct phonetic transcription should be:

m oo r - d ii t ei l z - h ax v - ax m axxr jh d - ax v - dh ax — b i t ax r - r au - b ax t w ii n - f r a n s - ax n d - uh dh axr — y uu r ax p ii ax n - y uu n y ax n - h e d z - av - g uh v axr m ax n t - ou v axr - dh ii - ax p oi n t m ax n t — ax v - ax - p r e z ax d ax n t - t uu - dh ii — y uu r ax p ii ax n - s e n t r ax l - b a ng k

Some recognition errors are apparent. 22 of the 28 words in the segment are either correct or have just one error in which an incorrect phoneme but of the same class as the correct one, has been used, such as *a* or *o* for *ax*, or *k* for *p*. This suggests that we further explore a similarity function which accounts for matches between phonemes in the same class rather than the strict and unforgiving exact matching which we have used. Nevertheless, a good deal of overlap between triphones derived by the recogniser and those from the query, can be seen and this story is actually relevant to the query.

The system described here is available for public use at `http://lorca.compapp.dcu.ie/RTE/java/` but requires support for the JDK1.1 AWT available in the HotJava browser and also in Netscape 4.05 preview release 1. The search system which retrieves a ranked list of windows as opposed to bulletins and does not require Java support is at http://lorca.compapp.dcu.ie/RTE/

6 Conclusions and Future Integration into a Digital Library

Broadcast radio news is a timely medium for news dissemination and like most news it has value when it is archived and is searchable retrospectively. However, because the utterances spoken by a newsreader are not normally read directly from an electronic format which is saved we are faced with having to use speech recognition with its inherent problems, in order to access broadcast bulletins by content. To deliver an audio news service and allow more effective processing of its content we could couple a text based newswire such as Reuters or the New York Times News service to a speech generator but speech synthesis still smacks of being artificial and people like to hear natural and familiar voices reading them their news. Thus, even though there are many difficulties in using it, we are faced with recording and using the actual broadcast audio, especially from archives, if we want to allow content manipulation.

The present version of Taiscéalaí is operational but the quality of retrieval could be improved by basing the retrieval on phoneme classes rather than exact matches between triphones. At present, recognition errors such as k-r-e-z-ax-d-ax-n-t for "president" are propagated through to retrieval and this leads to the inadvertent retrieval of "mondegreens", words or phrases which sound alike but which are totally different such as "A girl with colitis goes by" and "A girl with kaleidoscope eyes" or "Gladly the cross-eyed bear" and "Gladly the cross I'd bear". This is something we would evaluate in a TREC setting first, before transferring results to the operational system. We would also like the system to automatically suggest a portion of the broadcast for playback based on the time series scores and the presence of pauses. This may need some smoothing on the curve of window scores and we are looking at smoothing functions to do just this. This would remove the burden of having to select segments of broadcasts for playback and take users back to the "just-click-on-it" approach.

One of the great appeals of a digital library apart from its distributed nature, is the fact that many different information sources, possibly in different media, are combined into one unified, one-stop library. In a related project we have developed a cluster-based search system for the archive available from an online newspaper [10]. It is our intention to integrate this newspaper news archive with a news broadcast news archive into a single system where, for example, OOV words for the speech recognition can be determined automatically from the newspaper and flagged for an administrator to handle, or where the news of some local time period or window (as determined from the newspaper text) can be used to help with the speech recognition by reducing the size of the possible vocabulary. There are many such ways in which two news sources can be inter-twined.

What we have done in our work with Taiscéalaí is that we have made capture, processing, indexing, archiving and searching, operational and live on real and continuously updated data, with a search on an up-to-date archive of news broadcasts offered to the public. We look forward to extending this functionality into other areas.

Acknowledgments: The work reported in this paper was supported by FORBAIRT under the Strategic Research Program grant ST–96–707.

References

1. Bakis, R., Chen, S., Gopalakrishnan, P., Gopinath, R., Maes, S. Polymenakos, L.: Transcription of Broadcast News – System Robustness Issues and Adaptation Techniques. In: Proceedings of the ICASSP **1** (1997) 711–714
2. Gauvain, J.L., Adda, G., Lamel, L., Adda-Decker, M.: Transcribing Broadcast News Shows. In: Proceedings of the ICASSP **1** (1997) 715–718
3. Harman, D.K., Voorhees, E.M.: Proceedings of the Sixth Text Retrieval Conference. (in press) (1998) Available at http://trec.nist.gov/
4. Kelledy, F., Smeaton, A.F.: TREC-5 Experiments at Dublin City University: Query Space Reduction, Spanish Stemming and Character Shape Coding. In: Proceedings of the Fifth Text Retrieval Conference (TREC-5), Voorhees, E.M. and Harman, D.K. (Eds.), NIST Special Publication 500-238 (1997) 57–64
5. Morony, M.: Description of the Speech Processing Used in the Taiscéalaí System. Available at http://lorca.compapp.dcu.ie/RTE/technical.html (1998)
6. Ng, K., Zue, V.W.: An Investigation of Subword Unit Representations for Spoken Document Retrieval. Poster presented at SIGIR97, available at http://www.sis.lcs.mit.edu/kng/papers/sigir97.ps (1997)
7. Quinn, G.: Experiments on the Performance of a Retrieval System for Radio News (in preparation), (1998)
8. Schäuble, P., Weschler, M.: First Experiences with a System for Content Based Retrieval of Information from Speech Recordings. In: Proceedings of the IJCAI Workshop on Intelligent Multimedia Information Retrieval. Available at http://www-ir.inf.ethz.ch/ISIR-Papers.html (1995)
9. Smeaton, A.F., Kelledy, F., Quinn, G.: Ad hoc Retrieval Using Thresholds, WSTs for French Mono-Lingual Retrieval, Document-at-a-Glance for High Precision and Triphone Windows for Spoken Documents. In: Proceedings of the Sixth Text Retrieval Conference. Voorhees, E.M. and Harman, D.K. (Eds.) (in press) (1998) Available http://trec.nist.gov/
10. Smeaton, A.F., Burnett, M., Crimmins, F., Quinn, G.: An Architecture for Efficient Document Clustering and Retrieval on a Dynamic Collection of Newspaper Texts. In: Proceedings of the BCS-IRSG Colloquium, Springer Workshops in Computing (in press) (1998)
11. Woodland, P.C., Gales, M.J.F., Pye, D., Young, S.J.: Broadcast News Transcription Using HTK. In: Proceedings of the ICASSP **1** (1997) 719–722
12. Young, S.J., Odell, J.J., Woodland, P.C.: Tree-Based State Tying for High Accuracy Acoustic Modelling. In: Proceedings of the ARPA Workshop on Human Language Technology (1994)

Semantic Structuring and Visual Querying of Document Abstracts in Digital Libraries

Andreas Becks[1], Stefan Sklorz[1], Christopher Tresp[2]

[1] Lehrstuhl für Informatik V, RWTH Aachen, Ahornstraße 55, 52056 Aachen, Germany
{becks, sklorz}@informatik.rwth-aachen.de
[2] LuFG Theoretische Informatik, RWTH Aachen, Ahornstraße 55, 52056 Aachen, Germany
chris@cantor.informatik.rwth-aachen.de

Abstract. Digital libraries offer a vast source of very different information. To enable users to fruitfully browse through a collection of documents without necessarily having to state a complex query, advanced retrieval techniques have to be developed. Those methods have to be able to structure information in a semantic manner. This work presents some first steps in semantically organizing thematically pre-selected documents of a digital library. The semantic structure of the document collection will be expressively visualized by the proposed system. We illustrate our ideas using a database of medical abstracts from the field of oncology as a walking example.

1 Introduction

The success of digital libraries does not only depend on the provision of a large amount of heterogeneous information. It is also necessary to offer expressive and intuitive interfaces for searching documents. In some domains, such as medicine, the user is interested in finding information where the relevance of documents cannot be measured superficially by using key word systems. Rather relevance has to be estimated on a deeper knowledge level. Furthermore, if an information need can – for some reason – hardly be formulated using key words it should be possible to 'explore' the collection by browsing through the stored items. The goal of this work-in-progress is to provide an interface to document collections which offers a semantically structured map of documents, enabling easy and intuitive access to the content of digital libraries. There are two basic demands to be addressed: applying semantic criteria for assessing inter-document similarity as well as structuring the collection and visualizing the result.

Relating to the first demand, conventional retrieval systems use syntactic techniques based on some sort of lexical matching rather than applying background knowledge from the field of interest. The vector space model [18, 21], which is one of the best-known retrieval models, compares term vectors according to their similarity, e.g. by applying a cosine measure. The term vectors consist of real-valued components describing the weight of the corresponding terms of the indexing vocabulary.

Although this model achieves a quite acceptable retrieval quality for some applications it lacks semantic justification. An attempt to alleviate this shortcoming was made in [7], where 'latent semantic indexing' is introduced. This approach considers the correlation structure of terms and documents in order to obtain a more reliable indexing of documents. 'Latent semantic indexing' offers an improvement in the general setting but is not sufficient to allow for modeling of deeper semantic contexts which play a role in special purpose collections. The same holds for thesaurus based approaches as described in [5].

In the context of more specialized document collections elaborated knowledge-based approaches become important. Two examples of works concerning very domain specific methods of semantic retrieval are [4], where a system for searching in usenet newsgroup files is introduced and discussed, and [9], a work dealing with semantic software retrieval. Broader approaches of semantic information retrieval models are based on terminological (or description) logics [16, 22]. These works allow the definition of concepts and relationships between concepts in order to express background knowledge and thus to incorporate explicit semantics into information retrieval. In this work we will use a multi-valued terminological logic developed by the authors in order to take linguistic vagueness, inherent in the medical terminology, into account and to support the concept of similarity in an adequate way.

The second field of works deals with structuring a document collection and visualizing the result. Here the main idea is to detect document clusters where the objects (documents) within the clusters are very similar regarding a certain measure of similarity. The basis for this approach is the cluster hypothesis by van Rijsbergen [19] which states that 'closely associated documents tend to be relevant to the same requests'.

An alternative way of accessing documents based on clustering is proposed in [6]. The main idea of this so-called scatter/gather browsing is to provide an iteration of two steps for browsing through a document collection. In a first step documents are grouped according to dominant key words (scatter phase). The user then can chose interesting groups which are combined afterwards (gather phase). These phases are repeated until the user switches to a focussed search. Scatter/gather allows a dynamic structuring but the criteria for grouping the documents are very superficial. Furthermore, there is no intuitive representation of the documents' relationships. In [1] a combination of document clustering and visualization is proposed which aims at a better identification of relevant documents in query result sets. The basis for this approach is the vector space model. Using the cosine measure the similarity of all pairs of documents from the top ranking list of the result set is calculated. This relationship is then visualized in a 2D or 3D-space. Another very promising work is [15] which uses a self-organizing feature map (SOFM) [12] in order to generate a map of documents where documents dealing with similar topics are located near each other. Unfortunately, again the similarity is measured using statistical information. In this case short word contexts are used. For gaining a deeper, semantic comparison this approach is not suitable.

Our idea is now to combine some of our works in order to overcome the limitations discussed in this section. Besides using a multi-valued description logic as mentioned above we apply a visualization technique for interpreting SOFMs. The former was exemplarily used for representing vague medical knowledge, the latter for data mining purposes, i.e. visual clustering of numerical feature patterns and the extraction of fuzzy terms which describe the clusters discovered. In this work we extend our methods for the purpose of semantic structuring of document databases. We show that an interaction of the adapted components will result in a powerful new approach in the field of semantic information structuring. Beyond this, we gain a new view on the techniques involved which finally shows how completely different approaches can work together synergetically.

2 A Semantic Map of a Document Collection – An Overview

2.1 Accessing a Semantic Map of Documents – The System's Interface

The following scenario will illustrate our idea of a semantic retrieval system with an interactive user interface for structuring complex information. One of the user groups drawing a remarkable effort from information provided by well-organized libraries is the one of medical scientists. Consider a specialist in the field of oncology who contacts a digital library. A section of this document collection could contain document abstracts, e.g. from a journal (a real world example for a database containing medical document abstracts is given by the *Journal of Clinical Oncology*[1]). The physician is interested in the immediate finding of articles where relevance is defined by the semantic similarity to some kind of prototype abstract delivered by the specialist.

A well equipped and powerful system should be able to compare the content of the abstracts regarding their semantics, i.e. it should compute a degree of similarity based on background knowledge rather than on simple heuristics. Since a huge number of general knowledge about the domain is necessary, e.g. knowledge about taxonomies, the use of knowledge based procedures becomes important to overcome the limitations of simple syntactic comparison. Given a degree of similarity which the input prototype abstract shares with each document from the database under consideration there are two ways of accessing relevant documents: A simple approach is to compute a ranking of all abstracts corresponding to the given one. One disadvantage of this procedure is that the specialist does not receive any information about the degree of similarity that two other abstracts have. Only the input abstract is compared with all others.

A more expressive approach is to visualize the similarity of all pairs of abstracts. The proposed system generates a map where each abstract from the database is represented as a point and semantically similar abstracts are grouped as neighbored points. This leads to clusters in an image. By clicking on a point which represents an abstract the expert now directly receives the corresponding object. For example, see figure 1 which shows a "map of abstracts": The dark borders separate fields of similar abstracts. The brighter the borders are the more similar the fields of abstracts are.

---

[1] The Journal of Clinical Oncology is © by the American Society of Clinical Oncology. A number of abstracts from this journal is available at http://www.jcojournal.org.

Starting point for navigating through the library's content can be a prototype abstract fed into the system. The input abstract will be associated with a certain point in the map (marked by a circle in figure 1). The corresponding area of objects contains related documents. It is now possible to browse through the relevant part of the collection separated by the borders in order to find similar abstracts. Future works include the generation of expressive field descriptions as an alternative anchor for searching.

input: prototype abstract

field of abstracts
dealing with
similar topics

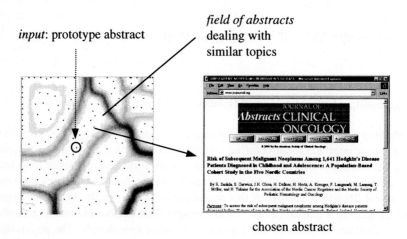

chosen abstract

Fig. 1. Selecting abstracts from a map

2.2 Realizing a Semantic Map of Documents – The System's Components

This section presents our suggestion for the overall structure of the proposed system (see figure 2). In order to receive a powerful and close-to-reality way of calculating the resemblance of abstracts, a knowledge representation system based on many-valued logic can be applied which we have introduced in [26]. Here the structure and rough interaction of all components of the system will be presented. The following sections will describe the single steps more detailed.

First, the system receives the different abstracts, which are indexed using a knowledge representation language for vague concepts. As we have pointed out in [2] the abstracts can be processed using natural language processing in combination with some knowledge bases. A system that automatically translates medical findings into the formal representation used in this paper is presented in our work [27]. The abstracts will be enriched with semantic information from the knowledge bases, e.g. information about class membership regarding terms defined in a concept base.

The next step includes the similarity calculation between each pair of abstracts. Therefore, some measure of similarity has to be applied giving information about the relevance of statements that are equal or unequal to some degree or even not comparable. The measure uses information provided by the knowledge bases. This results in a similarity matrix where the overall similarity of each pair of abstracts is calculated.

The resulting matrix of similarity degrees is not intuitively comprehensive and therefore cannot serve as an adequate user interface. At this point, the application of clustering methods should help to divide similar from more different abstracts. The calculated clusters can be visualized using a visualization technique presented in our work [24]. This technique is based on Kohonen's self-organizing feature maps (SOFM) [12]. Clustering methods need a vector of features for each object (object vectors) to find clusters of similar objects. Surprisingly, the similarity matrix itself is unfit to serve as these vectors since it is highly redundant and its dimensionality (i.e. the number of it's rows and columns) grows linearly with the number of abstracts compared. Therefore, we first arrange all the objects in an m-dimensional space where m is chosen to gain maximum benefit for the clustering method. The coordinate vector of each object in this space is then taken as object vector (i.e. each dimension of the space represents one virtual feature) and fed into the clustering algorithm.

Now the clustering task is solved with the help of the SOFM neural network and the received map can be visualized. The advantage of this approach is the delivery of an interactive selection of abstracts by choosing points in the visualization. This is a very intuitive way to provide an intelligent access to the abstracts.

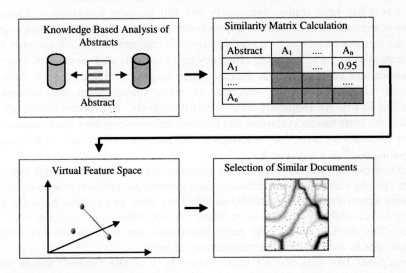

Fig. 2. The overall structure of the system

Within the next two sections the components for the proposed system will be discussed in more detail. Section 3 deals with issues regarding the semantic representation and comparison of medical document abstracts. Section 4 presents methods for structuring and visualizing the documents' space. We conclude this paper by summing up the results and pointing to some topics of our ongoing research.

3 Comparing Abstracts Using Background Knowledge

In this section we discuss the steps for gaining an expressive semantic representation of medical document abstracts and for assessing their similarity. Firstly, we present our approach for describing the documents. This description has to be powerful enough to serve as a basis for a knowledge based comparison of documents. After that we sketch the process of indexing which requires some natural language processing. Finally, we introduce a knowledge based measure of similarity for comparing the indexed documents. The result of the last step is a similarity matrix which serves as the basis for structuring the abstract collection. Due to the scope of this paper the basic ideas of the methods are presented. For a deeper discussion we refer to further literature on the topics.

3.1 Representing Medical Abstracts

Finding information in texts, such as medical abstracts, is a major field of research in information retrieval. Because of the variety of possibilities to express the same meaning with different lexical and syntactical phrasing, the problem of how to represent a text has been studied intensively and still is under examination. There are different approaches to achieve an improvement of the recall associated with a query. Besides text searching systems, reaching from simple methods which use stop word elimination to improve searching efficiency up to sophisticated methods of computer linguistics, one can find various documentation languages. These serve as meta-formalisms which describe the semantics of texts. Classification and thesauri, as described in [3], are frequently used standard methods. The former assign texts to classes, the latter handle synonyms and relations between concepts. Such methods are useful for indexing texts, but, nevertheless, are not powerful enough to be used for comparing texts on a semantic level.

To improve the performance of text classification systems, knowledge representation systems can be of use. Terminological knowledge representation systems [17] are very expressive and semantically sound. They offer an excellent basis for comparing texts merely in an knowledge based manner, rather than applying pure heuristics. This section shows how these formalisms can serve to do well-founded comparisons in order to measure the similarity of texts.

Disciplines like medicine are characterised by a certain "vague" notion, which means that medical facts can only be expressed insufficiently using a crisp logical representation. This implies that classical description logic based systems are not suitable for this kind of knowledge. There are only a few approaches dealing with representation of vague knowledge. In [30] a term subsumption language is extended using concepts of many-valued logic. Another well-elaborated approach is [25]. In the context of vagueness inherent to medical terminology both works are not sufficiently expressive. The first uses multi-valued predicates only on the level of atomic concepts, the second lacks the possibility to express linguistic hedges [32].

In our work [26] basic concepts of a more expressive representation language and fundamental patterns of reasoning for vague concepts are introduced. The proposed system is a terminological one, which means that it consists of a formalism called TBox for defining concept knowledge, and a language for filling the concepts and their relations with real world objects. The latter formalism is an assertional component called ABox. Table 1 shows an extract of the formal syntax and semantics of the TBox formalism. The notion of classical hybrid systems is extended by the introduction of the so-called VBox which serves to define vague attribute values. Those attributes are represented as fuzzy sets [31] on a concrete domain.

Table 1. An extract from the formal syntax and semantics of the TBox formalism

Syntax	Semantics
$C_1 \leq$ anything	Introduction of the primitive concept C_1 as a subset of the *universe of discourse*, denoted by Δ_C :
	$Inc[C_1, \Delta_C] =_{def} 1$,
	where Inc: $F(\Delta) \times F(\Delta) \to [0,1]$ denotes a fuzzy inclusion, e.g. *Lukasiewicz's* inclusion, and $F(\Delta) =_{def} \{\Phi \mid \Phi: \Delta \to [0,1]\}$.
$C_1 \leq T$ or $C_1 := T$	Introduction of the defined concept C_1 (necessary or sufficient condition, respectively) where C_T denotes the concept defined by the Term T:
	$Inc[C_1, C_T] =_{def} 1$.
$R: C_1 \times C_2$	Introduction of the role R as a fuzzy binary relation between the two (fuzzy) concepts C_1 and C_2, $R: C_1 \times C_2 \to [0,1]$, with
	$\mu_R(x,y) =_{def} \begin{cases} \geq 0 & \text{, if } \mu_{c1}(x) > 0 \wedge \mu_{c2}(y) > 0 \\ = 0 & \text{, otherwise.} \end{cases}$
$CON: C_1 * G[C_1]$	Introduction of the feature connection CON between the concept C_1 and the concrete fuzzy set domain $G[C_1]$ of this concept, $CON: X \to F(G[C_1])$, where $X =_{def} \{ x \mid x \in \Delta_{C1} \wedge \mu_C(x) > 0 \}$ denotes the instances of C_1.
$\neg C_1$	The concept operator $\neg$ calculates the negation of a concept. We use the Lukasciewicz negation : $\forall d \in \Delta_{C1}: \mu_{\neg}(d) =_{def} 1 - \mu_{C1}(d)$
$C_1 \sqcap ... \sqcap C_n$ $C_1 \sqcup ... \sqcup C_n$	The concept operator $\sqcap$ ($\sqcup$) combines a finite number of concepts $C_1, ..., C_n$ using a T-norm τ (co-T-norm σ):
	$\forall d \in \Delta_C: \mu_{and}(d) =_{def} \tau (\mu_{C1}(d),..., \mu_{Cn}(d))$ or $\forall d \in \Delta_C: \mu_{or}(d) =_{def} \sigma (\mu_{C1}(d),..., \mu_{Cn}(d))$, respectively.
restrict (CON,F_1)	Restriction of possible attribute values of a feature connection CON to the attribute value F_1. CON(d) denotes the feature value of d assigned by the feature connection CON:
	$\forall d \in \Delta_C: \mu_{restrict}(d) =_{def} Inc[CON(d),F_1]$

The language proposed in the cited work can be used for indexing medical abstracts. To illustrate this, consider the following example taken from an abstract of the *Journal of Clinical Oncology*:

(1) Patients who survive Hodgkin's disease at a young age are at very high relative risk of subsequent malignant neoplasms throughout their lives.

To keep the example simple, assume the following alternative sentence:

(2) High aged patients surviving cancer are not very likely to bear subsequent diseases.

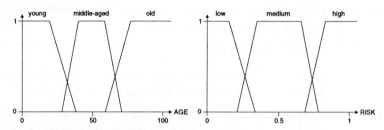

Fig. 3. Visualization of vague features

The two sentences can now be represented as follows. The fundamental conceptual knowledge has to be defined in the TBox, which contains at least the following concept and role definitions and feature connections:

- Primitive concepts "HUMAN" and "RISK" have to be introduced. Furthermore, the concept "LYMPHOGRANULOMATOSIS" as a sub-concept of "CANCER" and "DISEASE" must be defined.
- Necessary roles to be defined include SURVIVES: HUMAN × DISEASE as well as RELATED_WITH: ANYTHING × ANYTHING.
- To associate concepts with vague attributes, feature connections like AGED: HUMAN * AGE[HUMAN] and HAS_INTENSITY: PHENOMENON * INTEN-SITY[PHENOMENON] are necessary. The feature connection HAS_FORM: DISEASE * FORM[DISEASE] associates diseases with (not necessarily) vague attribute values.

Some vague features defined in the VBox are shown graphically in figure 3. Medical abstracts can be seen as concrete knowledge about objects of the real world and are thus represented in terms of an ABox as demonstrated in table 2. To summarize, we use a terminological knowledge representation system which enables vague concept interpretations, allows relationships with uncertain structure between concepts and introduces vague features. The background knowledge is implemented using the language provided by the TBox for concepts – which may be defined as vague ones (see section 3.3) – and the VBox for vague features, respectively. The ABox formalism is used for indexing the abstracts.

Table 2. Indexing texts using ABoxes. The asterisks indicate that the corresponding strings relate to objects. The double colon (::) marks object introductions

Abox A_1 for Sentence (1)	ABox A_2 for Sentence (2)
HODGKIN_DISEASE* :: LYMPHOGRANULOMATOSIS	DISEASE* :: DISEASE
	CANCER* :: CANCER
NEOPLASM* :: DISEASE	PATIENT* :: HUMAN; RISK* :: RISK
PATIENT* :: HUMAN ; RISK* :: RISK	AGED (PATIENT*, OLD)
AGED (PATIENT*, YOUNG)	SURVIVES (PATIENT*, CANCER*)
SURVIVES (PATIENT*, HODGKIN_DISEASE*)	HAS_FORM (DISEASE*, SUBSEQUENT)
	HAS_INTENSITY (RISK*, LOW)
RELATED_WITH (PATIENT*, RISK*)	RELATED_WITH (RISK*, DISEASE*)
HAS_INTENSITY (RISK*, HIGH)	
RELATED_WITH (RISK*, NEOPLASM*)	

3.2 Indexing Medical Abstracts

One key problem is how to extract relevant information (concepts and instances) from a textual source, in this case medical abstracts that are written down in medical terminology. Overall, this problem belongs to the complex domain of natural language processing (NLP). An interesting idea of how to connect knowledge representation with language processing is originated by [29] and adapted for our approach.

In [27], we have presented a medical terminus parser, i.e. a parser which copes with specific characteristics of the medical terminology (medical findings in the example used in the cited paper). This special NLP method is characterized by

a) a more weight carrying semantic component instead of a very elaborated syntactic component. The input is very often wrapped into *telegram style* sentences and therefore is not subject to conventional syntactic rules of well formed expressions,

b) the need for elaborated special domain knowledge within a supporting knowledge base.

During the process of verifying the syntax, a rule of the underlying grammar is applied if both the syntax is accurate and there is a semantic correlation to corresponding knowledge in a knowledge base. In the case of medical findings the telegram style does not allow a complete verification of the syntax. Nevertheless, the idea to couple syntax and semantic analysis remains fruitful. In the processing of medical document abstracts analyzing the syntax serves as a stronger filtering mechanism.

A further problem addresses the intensive use of vague linguistic notions in medical terminology. It is plausible to use our special knowledge representation formalism to handle this kind of vague knowledge. The analysis of medical texts is done by using the formalism as follows: Medical statements of an abstract are translated into ABox objects within a component for medical terminology processing. For example, descriptions like 'slight elongation of the liver' are transformed into an ABox instance of the general concept liver connected with the corresponding modified feature SLIGHT(ELONGATION) where SLIGHT is defined in the VBox. Details of the applied medical terminus parser are given in [27].

3.3 A Knowledge-based Measure of Similarity

Now the degree of similarity of the two ABoxes can be computed by comparing the features connected with a concept c and the matching roles in each box. First of all, we describe the major steps to compare single constructs from each ABox. Then a measure for computing the degree of similarity of the two ABoxes, representing the abstracts, will be presented briefly. This measure delivers the values for the necessary similarity matrix.

Vague features, represented as fuzzy sets, can be compared using a reciprocal fuzzy measure of inclusion, such as

$$incl(A,B) =_{def} inf\{ min(1,1-A(x)+B(x)) \mid x \in U\} \qquad (1)$$

for arbitrary fuzzy sets A and B, defined on universe U. The measure of equality of two vague attributes F_1 and F_2 may then be defined as

$$F_1 \approx F_2 =_{def} incl(F_1,F_2) \; et_f \; incl \; (F_2,F_1), \qquad (2)$$

where et_f denotes a fuzzy conjunction. The choice of this measure is not compelling, other measures of equality based on fuzzy connectives can be used. Which of these are suitable in a concrete modelling task cannot be decided *a priori*. Figure 4 illustrates two fuzzy sets representing vague features which share some objects to a certain degree and therefore can be regarded as similar to a certain degree.

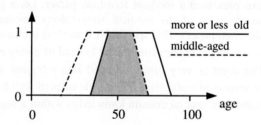

Fig. 4. Fuzzy sets representing similar vague features

Note that besides comparing attributes, i.e. vague features, and roles it is possible to measure the similarity of concepts itself. Using the definition of concepts from the knowledge base the subsumption relations of the conceptual knowledge can be computed which will produce a "vague" subsumption network with the edges between concepts being weighted to their degree of similarity (cf. [26]). Concepts, e.g. lymphoma (tumour attacking the lymph gland), can be described by introducing their specific (possibly vague) characteristics. Thus, lymphoma could be characterised by their degree of malignity and histological and cytological criteria. A simple definition of the concept "tumour" could be given as follows:

tumour := lump ⊓ restrict (degree_of_malignity, high).

This leads to a point where certain concepts are recognized as more similar than others. Figure 5 visualizes the numerical similarity value between different concepts. Note, that the semantics underlying this hierarchy are in some way different from networks displaying an 'is-a' hierarchy.

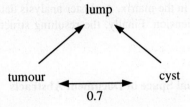

Fig. 5. Vague network of concepts

Now pairs of objects have to be compared. Obviously, in our simple example we have pairs like HAS_INTENSITY (RISK*, HIGH) − HAS_INTENSITY (RISK*, LOW) or AGED (PATIENT*, YOUNG) − AGED (PATIENT*, OLD), which can be compared using the ideas shown above. In order to get a single degree of similarity, denoted by α with $\alpha \in [0,1]$, the following procedure has to be applied: Let $B_{max} =_{def} \min(|A_1|, |A_2|)$ denote the maximal number of comparable constructs, i.e. concepts which have a semantic relation, where $|A_i|$ denotes the cardinality of ABox A_i. Choose the ABox with minimal cardinality, say A_1. For $1 \leq i \leq B_{max}$ choose construct κ_i^1 from ABox A_1 and choose a comparable construct for κ_i^1, say κ_i^2. Then, compute the degree of similarity for κ_i^1 and κ_i^2, denoted by α_i, and if there is no matching construct, set $\alpha_i =_{def} 0$, respectively. The degree of similarity of A_i and A_2, i.e. the similarity of the related abstracts, is defined as

$$\alpha =_{def} \frac{\sum \alpha_i}{\max(|A_1|, |A_2|)}. \tag{3}$$

By applying this procedure to every pair of abstracts, we obtain a similarity matrix for the abstracts in the database. The advantage of this knowledge based comparison is that the resulting degree of similarity is more comprehensible for the user than a pure heuristic measure can ever be. There are several approaches, cf. [10], which use semantic networks as a basis for comparison. Although the loss of the ability to compare concepts in a semantic way is a drawback, the basic concepts proposed here can be combined with those heuristic methods working on semantic networks. Thus, an expressive measure of similarity can be achieved which can now directly be used to calculate a matrix of similarity as a basis for clustering the documents regarding to their semantic resemblance. This matrix represents the overall similarity of each pair of documents abstracts.

4 Structuring and Visualizing a Collection of Documents

Up to this point we have computed a similarity matrix on the basis of a knowledge based measure of similarity. The next step is constructing a virtual multi-dimensional feature space in which representatives for document abstracts are placed according to the similarity information in the matrix. A cluster analysis detects the structure of this space and reduces its dimension. Finally, the resulting structure information will be visualized.

4.1 Generating a Virtual Space of Document Abstracts

We use an unsupervised learning algorithm for detecting clusters in the feature space, realized by a self-organizing feature map (SOFM). This model of a neural network offers three advantages in order to achieve our goal of an interactive retrieval interface: First of all, SOFMs map high dimensional feature vectors into a two dimensional grid structure, preserving most topological information. This means that all vectors in the grid are ordered according to their similarity in the feature space. Second, the model's ability of generalizing the input patterns enables the association of *a priori* unknown vectors in a useful manner. This characteristic enables the retrieval of relevant abstracts using a prototype document as described in section 2.1. The third reason for choosing the SOFM model is that it serves as the basis for our powerful visualization technique which leads to the proposed interactive interface.

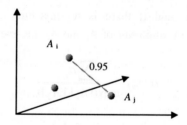

Fig. 6. Abstract representatives in an Euclidian Space

As discussed in section 2.2 the matrix of similarity values is no suitable input for the clustering method due to its high dimensionality and redundancy. The solution is to transform the matrix in an m-dimensional feature space which is done by using a modified version of the 'FastMap' algorithm [8]. In [2] we have described this step more detailed. The result of the transforming process is an m-dimensional Euclidean space containing document abstract representatives (figure 6), which are called object vectors in the following. The distance of each pair of 'abstracts' is the reciprocal measure of similarity, i.e. distance$_{ij}$=(1/similarity$_{ij}$)-1 for abstract representatives A_i and A_j.

4.2   Mapping the Virtual Space of Document Abstracts into two Dimensions

In the previous section we have discussed the possibility to represent each abstract by an m-dimensional object vector. Now, our visualization technique [24] will be introduced based on Kohonen's SOFM. This technique enables the grouping of similar abstracts and furthermore provides a simple access for selecting abstracts. The idea is that the SOFM orders the object vectors. Hence, the abstracts are ordered in such a way, that similar object vectors lie near each other in a two dimensional grid. Then, our visualization technique shows borders between them if they form clusters in the input space (cf. figure 1). Before explaining our method in more detail, we briefly present the idea of Kohonen in order to provide a general understanding of the concept of self-organizing feature maps.

SOFM maps a set of object vectors from the space $\mathbb{R}^m$ to a two dimensional grid structure of units without losing too much topological information. The mapping is thereby realized by an unsupervised learning algorithm. There are no connections between the single units in the grid. But the object vectors x are handed over directly to every unit. Therefore, each unit i at the position (i_1, i_2) in the grid contains m weighted connections to the m components of the object vectors and receives an m-dimensional weight vector m_i that describes the strength of these connections. Depending on an object vector x and m_i, each unit i calculates an output $\eta_i(x, m_i)$. The output function η defines a distance measure between x and m_i – for example the Euclidian distance. During the learning process, a single unit will be determined for each object vector x at each time, where the unit's vector m is most similar to x. Such a unit is called the *cluster center* of the considered object vector. The major advantage of the SOFM is gained by the observation that after the learning process the relative positions of different cluster centers towards each other in the grid show the similarity between corresponding object vectors. Furthermore, the positions of all vectors m_i are ordered in the grid according to their similarity. Therefore we can expect that the cluster centers are arranged in the same regions of the grid, if the corresponding object vectors form clusters in the input space. But without knowledge about cluster membership of the object vectors, it is difficult to identify those regions in the grid. This problem will be solved in the following section.

4.3   Visualizing the Structure of the Abstracts' Space

We have developed a graphical method which directly uses the properties discussed above in order to solve the described problem. This is done by calculating a value for each grid point (i_1, i_2) which exhibits the greatest similarity of the vector m_i of unit i and all object vectors $x_1, x_2, ..., x_n$ according to

$$P[i_1][i_2] = \min_{1 \leq k \leq n}\{\eta_i(x_k, m_i)\}. \tag{4}$$

Thus, we gain a matrix P. We can use this matrix to visualize the clusters in the input space by determining for each value in P a gray level or a color, e.g. through a linear function that maps the minimum value to white and the maximum value to black. In such a display of the matrix P, it is possible to detect regions in the SOFM that are separated by large numbers in P and correspond to clusters in the input space.

This interpretation seems to be evident, if we consider that the density of the vectors m_i of a trained SOFM reflects the density of the object vectors used for training according to theoretical studies described in [20] and [13], for example. Following this assumption, the vectors m_i in each of the separated regions will be close to each other. In contrast, the empty space between clusters in the Euclidian input space representing the "virtual" space of abstracts will only be represented by few vectors m_i in the SOFM. Reconsidering the way the matrix P is calculated, it is obvious that these few vectors are finally responsible for the formation of the dark boundaries in the graphical display of P. Thus, the cluster structure in the set of object vectors can be visualized.

Similar graphical approaches [11,14,28] which use the SOFM for clustering as well, display the distances between the weight vectors m_i of neighboring units. For example, this can be done by calculating the distance between each pair of vectors m_i and m_j, if their corresponding units i and j are adjacent in the two dimensional grid structure of the SOFM. The average of all distance values computed for a single unit could be assigned to the unit under consideration in order to determine a gray level or a color to be displayed similar to the P-matrix display described above. The graphical display received in this way is comparable to the one gained by the P-matrix, if most of the weight vectors m_i are very similar or almost equal to the object vectors. In contrast, P still provides good results, if the vectors m_i are uniformly distributed in those subspaces of the input space which correspond to the clusters to be discovered. In [23] this property is used for an automated extraction of fuzzy terms in order to describe the discovered clusters. Here we need this quality to gain a maximum benefit from the SOFM's generalization ability when mapping prototype abstracts onto our 'map of abstracts'.

To summarize this section, the SOFM in conjunction with our visualization technique allows us to determine clusters of object vectors and, hence, clusters of abstracts in a graphical way. Furthermore, we can select abstracts by clicking on a single point in the visualization, i.e. on a P-matrix position, since each position corresponds to an object vector according to the calculation of P and the fact that each object vector represents an abstract. We have already shown this idea in an exemplary fashion in illustration 1.

5 Conclusion

The idea of this paper was to present a new approach in semantic organizing and visual querying of document bases. As an example we used medical document abstracts, but the methods proposed here are not limited to this special kind of documents. By combining semantics and clustering of document collections we try to achieve a powerful interface for interactively browsing through specialized branches of digital libraries. For this, we have extended and adapted some of our works from the fields of knowledge representation and data mining and combined them in order to gain synergy effects. Furthermore, this study irradiates our preceding works in a new light.

This approach offers a very powerful way of evaluating the relevance of documents regarding a prototype document. The evaluation process bases on semantic techniques of comparison rather than on simple heuristics and is suitable for special purpose databases. The query interface proposed here is a graphical one, i.e. users can choose documents by clicking on representatives in an intuitively structured 'map of documents'. Future works include the generation of expressive logical field descriptions, characterizing the content of a field in the visualized map of documents. These descriptions can then serve as 'labels' for each area of interest and, furthermore, they offer a basis for key word search to allocate certain fields of documents. The key word search should be supported using information provided by the knowledge base.

The presented idea is a starting point in building a system for semantic information structuring. The different components were introduced, their characteristics were pointed out and their cooperation was sketched. We believe that these ideas are some first steps in solving the problem of semantic structuring and visual querying of document collections and will be of a high value for working with digital libraries.

Acknowledgement. This work was partially supported by the DFG Graduierten-kolleg "Informatik & Technik", RWTH Aachen.

References

1. Allan, James, Leouski, Anton V., Swan, Russell C.: Interactive Cluster Visualization for Information Retrieval. Tech. Rep. IR-116, Center for Intelligent Information Retrieval, University of Massachusetts (1997)
2. M. Baumeister, A. Becks, S. Sklorz, Ch. Tresp, U. Tüben: Indexing Medical Abstract Databases. Proceedings of the European Workshop on Multimedia Technology in Medical Training, ABI, Bd. 20, Aachen, Germany (1997)
3. M. Burkart: Dokumentationssprachen. In Bruder et al.: Grundlagen der praktischen Information und Dokumentation, München (1990)
4. R. Burke, K. Hammond, V. Kulyukin, S. Lytinen, N. Tomuro, S. Schoenberg: Question Answering from Frequently-Asked Question Files: Experiences with the FAQ Finder System. The University of Chicago, Technical Report TR-97-05 (1997)
5. Chen, Hsinchun. Collaborative Systems: Solving the Vocabulary Problem. IEEE Computer, May (1994)
6. Cutting, D.R., Karger, D.R., Pedersen, J.O., Tukey, J.W. Scatter/Gather: A Cluster-based Approach to Browsing Large Document Collections. Proc. of the 15th Annual Int. ACM SIGIR Conf. on Research and Development in Information Retrieval, Copenhagen (1992)
7. Deerwester, Scott, Dumais, Susan T., Harshman, Richard. Indexing by Latent Semantic Analysis. Journal of the Society for Information Science, 41(6), 1990, pp. 391-407
8. Faloutsos, Lin: Fastmap: A Fast Algorithm for Indexing, Data-Mining and Vizualization of Traditional and Multimedia Datasets. Proceedings of the Int. Conf. on Management of Data (SIGMOD'95); 2(24), June 1995
9. M.R. Girardi, B. Ibrahim: An approach to improve the effectiveness of software retrieval. Proceedings of the 3rd Irvine Software Symposium, Irvine, California (1993)

10. K. Hammond, R. Burke, C. Martin, S. Lytinen: FAQ Finder: A Case-Based Approach to Knowledge Navigation. AAAI Spring Symposium on Information Gathering from Distributed, Heterogeneous Environments, Stanford, CA. (1995)

11. J. Iivarinen, T. Kohonen, J. Kangas, S. Kaski: Visualizing the clusters on the self-organizing map. Proc. of the Conf. on AI Research in Finland, Helsinki (1994), pp. 122 - 126

12. T. Kohonen: Clustering , Taxonomy and Topological Maps of Patterns. Proceedings of the 6th Int. Conf. on Pattern Recognition, München (1982)

13. T. Kohonen: Self-Organizing Maps. Springer, Berlin, 2nd Edition (1995)

14. M. A. Kraaijveld, J. Mao, A. K. Jain: A nonlinear projection method based on Kohonen's topology preserving maps. IEEE Transactions on Neural Networks, Vol. 6, pp. 548 - 559

15. K. Lagus, T. Honkela, S. Kaski, T. Kohonen: Self-Organizing Maps of Document Collections: A New Approach to Interactive Exploration. Proc. of the Second International Conference on Knowledge Discovery and Data Mining, AAAI Press, California (1996)

16. Meghini, Carlo, Straccia, Umberto: A Relevance Terminological Logic for Information Retrieval. Proceedings of the 19th Annual International ACM SIGIR Conference on Research and Development in Information Retrieval, Zürich, Switzerland (1996)

17. B. Nebel: Reasoning and Revision in Hybrid Representation Systems. Springer (1990)

18. V. Raghavan, S. Wong: A Critical Analysis of Vector Space Model for Information Retrieval. Journal of the American Society for Information Science, 37(5), 1986

19. C.J. van Rijsbergen: Information Retrieval. 2nd edition, Butterworths, London (1979)

20. H. Ritter: Asymptotic level density for a class of vector quantization process. IEEE Transactions on Neural Networks, Vol 2, 1991

21. G. Salton (Ed.): The SMART Retrieval System – Experiments in Automatic Document Processing. Prentice Hall, New Jersey (1971)

22. Schmiedel, Albrecht: Semantic Indexing Based on Description Logics. In: Reasoning about Structured Objects: Knowledge Representation Meets Databases, Proc. of 1st Workshop KRDB '94. Saarbrücken, Germany (1994)

23. S. Sklorz, M. Mücke: A Hybrid Approach for Medical Data Analysis. Proceedings of the 5th European Congress on Intelligent Techniques and Soft Computing (EUFIT'97), Volume 2, Aachen, Germany, September (1997)

24. S. Sklorz: A Method for Data Analysis based on Self Organizing Feature Maps., Proceedings of the World Automation Congress (WAC '96), Vol.5 TSI Press Series, 611-616, ISBN 1-889335-02-9, Albuquerque, USA (1996)

25. Straccia, Umberto: A Fuzzy Description Logic. In: Proceedings of AAAI-98 (1998)

26. C. Tresp, A. Becks, R. Klinkenberg, J. Hiltner: Knowledge Representation in a World with Vague Concepts, In: Intelligent Systems: A Semiotic Perspective, Gaithersburg (1996)

27. C. Tresp, U. Tüben: Medical terminology processing for a tutoring system. International Conference on Computational Intelligence and Multimedia Applications (ICCIMA98), Monash Univ., Australia (1998)

28. A. Ultsch, H. Simon: Exploratory Data Analysis: Using Kohonen Networks on Transputers. Technical Report, No. 329, University of Dortmund (1989)

29. M. Schröder: Erwartungsgestützte Analyse medizinischer Befundungstexte. Ein wissensbasiertes Modell zur Sprachverarbeitung. Infix DISKI, Sankt Augustin (1995)

30. J. Yen: Generalizing Term Subsumption Languages to Fuzzy Logic. In: Proceedings of IJCAI-91, Sydney, Australia (1991)

31. L.A. Zadeh: Fuzzy Sets. In: Information and Control, 8, 1965

32. L.A. Zadeh: A fuzzy-set-theoretic interpretation of linguistic hedges. Journal of Cybernetics, 2:4-34, 1972

Documentation, Cataloging, and Query by Navigation: A Practical and Sound Approach

F.J.M. Bosman[1], P.D. Bruza[2], Th.P. van der Weide[3], and L.V.M. Weusten[4]

[1] Department of Information Systems, University of Nijmegen, Toernooiveld, NL-6525 ED Nijmegen, The Netherlands `robb@cs.kun.nl`
[2] `bruza@icis.qut.edu.au`
[3] `tvdw@cs.kun.nl`
[4] Department of Letteren, University of Nijmegen NL-6525 ED Nijmegen, The Netherlands

Abstract. In this paper we discuss the construction of an automated information system for a collection of visual reproductions of art objects. Special attention is payed to the economical aspects of such a system, which appears to be mainly a problem of data entry. An approach is discussed to make this feasible, which also strongly provokes consistency between descriptions.

Another main target of such a system is the capability for effective disclosure. This requires a disclosure mechanism on descriptions which is easy to handle by non technical users. We show the usefulness of query by navigation for this purpose. It allows the searcher to stepwise build a query in terms of (semi-)natural language. At each step, the searcher is presented with context sensitive information.

The resulting system is described and we discuss an experiment of its use.

1 Introduction

It is typical for a department of History of Art to administer a large collection of reproductions of art objects. For example, the Department of History of Art of the University at Nijmegen, The Netherlands has a collection of about 60,000 slides depicting art objects, covering all areas of art, and originating worldwide. The purpose for having such large collections is to allow both students and teachers to quickly and efficiently find slides they need as a support during teaching activities. Traditionally, card indexes are used to provide access into the slide collection through a number of keys. Usually, an index on author name, and an index on artwork topic are available.

Such a manual disclosure mechanism has several drawbacks. First, the procedures for cataloging are rather laborious and time consuming for the documentalist. Second, iconographic indexing is a subjective activity. As a result, the classification of the documentalist might be quite different from that of a searching person. For example, it may occur that a searcher will search in vain for a slide depicting merchants in the category *trade* , while these images are stored in the category *professions*.

The need for automation has been largely recognized these days. This has led to a number of approaches, which all seem to have their own intrinsic limitations. For example, in 1976 Bildarchiv Foto Marburg started with the disclosure of its large arthistorical photocollection. This gave them a restraining lead: the available software at that time did not focus as much on retrieval as it did on data-input, resulting in a well filled database with inferior query-possibilities. Other institutions spent a lot of time developing a very detailed description-format, demanding a too time devouring research for each description, resulting in a too low processing rate.

The Odilon project started as a cooperation between the Department of History of Art and the Department of Computing Science, both at Nijmegen. It was continued in the Odilon for Windows project, a cooperation with Fratelli Alinari in Florence, Italy for disclosing a part of their enormous collection. This has resulted in a new, Windows based, implementation of Odilon.

First a thorough analysis of the situation in the slide library was performed, not only from a technical point of view, but also from a economical, and, last but not least, a cognitive point of view. A first conclusion was that a hypertext-like approach could meet the objectives of the different areas of competence, provided an improved mechanism for disclosure would be used. This mechanism should be easy to use for all categories of searchers, and help them to find their way through a vast amount of information. Secondly, if being user friendly is considered to be a critical success factor, being *input friendly* directly addresses "le raison d´être" of the system. Filling the system with input data is the main cost factor, in which face all other costs vanish to nothing.

The program resulting from the Odilon project has been tested extensively by the Department of Art History, since its first running prototype in 1991. At the moment, more than 80% of the slide descriptions have been entered into the system. Experiences of documentalists are promising. Furthermore, students as well as teachers and researchers of History of Art are more and more basing their haunt for pictorial information on Odilon.

The structure of the paper is as follows. In section 2, the architecture of Odilon is presented. Section 3 introduces two disclosure mechanisms for subject classification; ICONCLASS and *HyperIndex*, the indexing technique based on so-called index expressions. Both are part of Odilon. In section 4, we discuss the HyperIndex in Odilon and the experiences so far, from a practical point of view. Section 5 contains a number of conclusions, and gives guidelines for further research.

2   The architecture of Odilon

The intention of the slides library is to provide images and information of art objects. Note that several slides can be available for the same art object, to show its different aspects. The slides are used both by scholars and professors. They can be used for research and for preparing lectures. The library is also available for non-educational purposes such as advertisements and public relations.

2.1 System approach

In the manual system, slides were described by indexcards. In order to make the enormous amount of information contained in the existing slide catalog easier and better accessible, it was decided to build an automated information system. Globally, this information system is aimed at two distinct targets:

1. to relieve the documentalist from laborious, time consuming cataloging and maintenance tasks.
2. to provide an effective disclosure mechanism.

These requirements had to be satisfied, taking into account the system as used before the introduction of the automated system. That is, positive elements of the former catalog had to be preserved, while the negative elements were to be eliminated. This resulted in some additional requirements regarding the automated information system:

- The system should let the documentalist record the slide descriptions from their index cards. This suggests maintaining the fields slide number, date, subject, technique, material, size, artist and place, which were recorded on the indexcards.
- Information should be entered using a system dictionairy to avoid synonyms and spelling errors. This will result in a standard language with a predetermined terminology to yield homogeneous and consistent information. Menu options should be used where possible to provide the documentalist and searchers with easier and faster access to the data.
- When users are consulting the information system, they should be able to refine and join previous selections.
- The not standardized classification on topics should be replaced by the ICONCLASS system ([Waa85]). This system is described in section 3.1.
- To prevent tampering with important information, there has to be a priority distinction between the documentalist and other users. Only the documentalist will be allowed to add new slide descriptions or to change incorrect descriptions. Obviously, all users must be able to consult the information system.

3 Classification

When cataloguing artobjects or visual reproductions of artobjects, it is desirable to be able to classify the subject descriptions. It is as least as likely that a searcher would want to find a painting of *sunflowers* (subject) as a painting with *oil on canvas* (technique). Traditionally, keywords were used to accomplish this. In this section we discuss two different ways to classify subject discriptions.

3.1 ICONCLASS

ICONCLASS is a standardized, well documented system for classifying representations. The term ICONCLASS is derived from **Icon**ographic **class**ification.

ICONCLASS has been designed as a framework for characterizing and searching art objects independent from any language. Subjects, themes, and motifs in the art of the Western world can be classified. In ICONCLASS nine *Main Divisions* form the basic classification. Each division has a number of subclasses; subclasses have subclasses of their own etc.

Basic principles of classification

ICONCLASS provides a collosal potential for classifying art objects. For example a representation of *children playing in a park* may be classified by:

- Main division: Society, civilization, culture.
- Primary subdivision: Recreation, amusement.
- Secondary subdivision: Recreation.
- Tertiary subdivision: Enjoying nature.

In order to make this classification manageable, a coding scheme for classes is introduced (see Figure 1). The position of each class within its superclass is coded by an according single letter or digit. The code which identifies a specific class is obtained by concatenating the codes from the classification path. For the example described above, this would lead to 43B1.

The combination of digits and letters, indicating together an iconographic item is called a *notation*. This results in such notations as 11Q7612 (=christmas), 25H213 (=river), or 34B11 (=dog).

Note that the secondary subdivisions are not indicated by digits but by letters in their alphabetical order. This has three advantages:

- more subdivisions: 25 secondary subdivisions can be distinguished instead of 9. (The letter J is not used)
- greater legibility of notations.

Problems with ICONCLASS

Describing representations, from its very nature, depends on the interpretation of the person involved. As with each characterization mechanism, a description shows only some aspects of the object. Which aspects are recognized depends on the point of view of this person at that very moment. The main challenge of Information Retrieval is to try to overcome the problem of vague descriptions and vague queries as good as possible. For ICONCLASS this problem manifests itself as follows:

1. Imagine a slide depicting a painting of a man walking through a field with his dog and a flock of sheep. The following classes may be used to characterize this slide: (1) 25F (=animals), (2) 25F2 (=mammals), (3) 25H

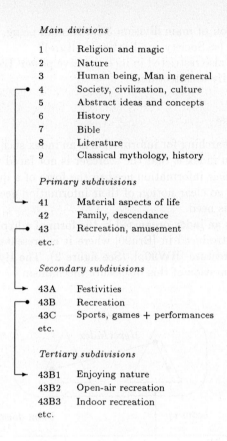

Main divisions

1	Religion and magic
2	Nature
3	Human being, Man in general
4	Society, civilization, culture
5	Abstract ideas and concepts
6	History
7	Bible
8	Literature
9	Classical mythology, history

Primary subdivisions

41	Material aspects of life
42	Family, descendance
43	Recreation, amusement
etc.	

Secondary subdivisions

43A	Festivities
43B	Recreation
43C	Sports, games + performances
etc.	

Tertiary subdivisions

43B1	Enjoying nature
43B2	Open-air recreation
43B3	Indoor recreation
etc.	

Fig. 1. The hierarchical structure of ICONCLASS

(=landscapes), (4) 34 (=man and animal), (5) 34A (=taming and training of animals), (6) 34B11 (=dog), (7) 34C (=protection of animals), (8)
43B1 (=enjoying nature), (9) 46A14 (=farmers), (10) 46A8 (=unusual manners of living), (11) 47I221 (=herding), or (12) 35 (= pastorals, Arcadian
scenes). It is clear that for both the documentalist and the searcher a choice
of classification is usually hard to make.

2. The hierarchical structure of ICONCLASS makes a hierarchical use of the
   class structure most appropriate. This way of working may lead to problems, as it is not always clear a priori in what subclass a term should be
   located. This problem has been recognized, and led to the production of an
   (automated) index system for the use of ICONCLASS. This index provides
   a translation of terms to classes in some specified context. This, however,
   does not solve the problem metioned above. For example, when trying to
   find all slides of an artwork depicting a *baby*, the user is confronted with
   the following dilemma: what is the relevant context? In other words, is baby

a subclassification of main division 3 (= Human being, man in general), or main division 4 (= Society, civilization, culture)?

3. ICONCLASS is also restricted in its expressive power. For example, it cannot be used to classify architecture.

3.2 HyperIndices

A useful aid when searching for information is an index such as found in a book. The advantage of an index is that the searcher is not faced with the problem of having to express their information need in the form of a query. Also, for those searchers who have no clear notion of their information need, an index is often helpful to clarify this need.

A HyperIndex is an index organized in the form of a hypertext. This form of index is formally introduced in [Bru90] where it is presented in the framework of a two level architecture [BW90b]. (See figure 2). The HyperIndex in Odilon is the first implementation of this disclosure mechanism.

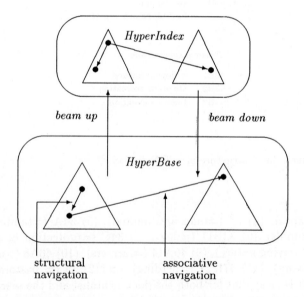

Fig. 2. The Architecture of Two Level Hypermedia

The HyperBase can be understood as hypermedia as is typical in current systems [Con87,SK89], but which is fragment based with a strong emphasis on the notion of a *view*.

The HyperIndex forms the top level of the architecture. It is a hypertext of index terms which index the underlying HyperBase. The feature of the HyperIndex is its structure. (See figure 3). The structure provides the opportunity to browse through the index terms in an organized fashion. This facet not only facilitates information retrieval but can guide a possibly distracted or lost searcher. The basis of the organized search capability is the fact that any focus (the current index term being scanned by the searcher), can be *refined* (context contraction) or *enlarged* (context extension). Figure 4 shows two examples of refining. In this figure we see that a node consists of a number of entries where all entries represent indexing information. The first entry represents the current focus of the user in the HyperIndex, and the other entries are *buttons* which can be activated to refine ($\triangle$) or enlarge ($\triangledown$) the current focus. By enlargement or refinement, the button activated becomes the new focus.

When an index term is found which describes the information need, the objects from the underlying HyperBase which are characterized by this index term can be retrieved and examined. This operation is referred to as a *beam down* because the searcher is transferred from the HyperIndex to a view at the HyperBase level which is constructed from the relevant objects. Navigating through the HyperIndex and retrieving information in the above way has been coined *Query By Navigation* [BW90b].

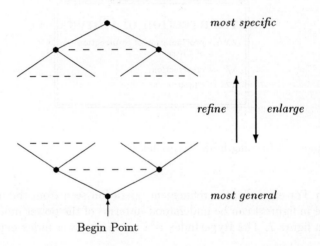

Fig. 3. Conceptual View of a HyperIndex

The index terms in the HyperIndex have the form of so called *index expressions* [Bru90,BW90a]. In contrast to keywords or term phrases index expressions have a structure (see figure 5). This figure also shows that the relationships between terms are also modeled. These relationships are termed *connectors*, or *operators*, which are basically restricted to prepositions. Figure 6 shows some of the allowable connectors and the relationship types that denote.

From the structure of an index expression the so called power index expression can be derived. This is a lattice-like structure which supports Query by

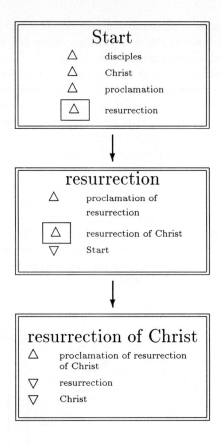

Fig. 4. Example of Refining in the HyperIndex

Navigation. For example, the refinement operation seen from the user interface perspective in figure 4 can be understood in terms of the power index expression depicted in figure 7. The HyperIndex is a union of power index expressions.

3.3 The Derivation of Index Expressions from Title Descriptions

An important process in constructing the HyperIndex is the derivation of index expressions from the slide titles. As there are 60,000 slides in the slide library it is not practically feasible to do this manually. A transducer was therefore implemented that translates a title description into an index expression. From the resultant index expressions the power index expressions are then generated resulting in the HyperIndex.

It has been observed in [BW91,B98] that titles of documents, section subsections and figures often have a form very similar to that of index expressions. This similarity becomes even more evident when articles such as the and a are

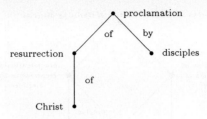

Fig. 5. Example Index Expression Representation

Connector	Rel. Type	Examples
of	possession action-object	castle of queen pollination of crops
by	action-agent	voting by students
in, on, *etc.*	position	trees in garden
to, on, for, in	directed assoc- iation	attitudes to courses research on voting
with, ·, and	association	Napoleon with army fruit · trees
as	equivalence	humans as searchers

Fig. 6. Connectors and their associated Relationship Types

removed. The first phase of the transducer was to remove such articles. For example,

On the rejection of the mitre and of the crosier by Saint Bruno

results in

On rejection of mitre and of crosier by Saint Bruno

While removing articles the transducer also checks for so called connector irregularities. This occurs when there are two or more connectors between terms. As there may only be one such connector, the transducer chooses the first. On the other hand, if there are no connectors between two successive terms, a null connector is inserted. Furthermore, connectors at the beginning of the descrip-

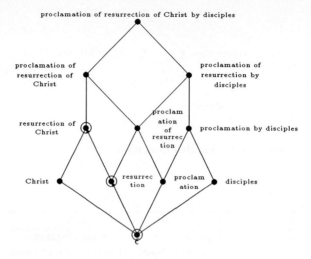

Fig. 7. Refinement within a lattice structure

tor are removed. The running example after connector irregularities have been resolved looks like the following:

rejection of mitre and crosier by Saint · Bruno

The problem remains to detect the underlying structure. This is achieved by employing a two level priority scheme in relation to the connectors. This priority scheme was a result of the observation that some connectors bind terms more strongly. The connectors deemed to bind most strongly are ·, and, with and of. These connectors have therefore priority 0. In terms of figure 6 the first three of these connectors form the *association* term relationship type. On the case of the connector of, we found it particularly binding in the context of a *possession* relationship type. The remaining connectors all receive priority 1 because we observed no consistent behavior which could form the basis of criteria which would lead to more priorities.

The connector priorities are used to derive an underlying tree structure in the descriptor. This structure is built up as the descriptor is scanned left to right. The heuristic used is that the tree is *deepened* if a high priority connector is detected, otherwise it is *broadened* at the root.

Figure 8 shows the successive build up of the structure derived from the running example. Up to the point of parsing by the structure developed thus far would be two levels deep as both and and of have priority 0. When by is parsed the tree is broadened at the root. Thereafter no broadening occurs.

The transducer turned out to be surprisingly good. In a test of more than a thousand descriptions parsed, less than ten percent needed manual intervention. These were mostly descriptions that weren't in the passive form, for example,

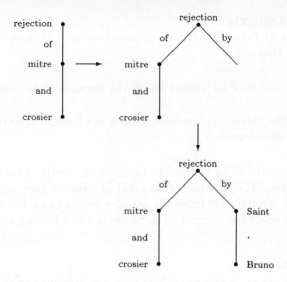

Fig. 8. Build up of index expression structure

Saint Bruno rejects mitre and crosier instead of Rejection of mitre and crosier by Saint Bruno.

We were fortunate that the languages used in title descriptions (Dutch, German, English, French and Italian) all have connectors embedded in them in the form of prepositions and basically for this reason the transducer worked equally effectively for all languages. Note, however, that automatic derivation of index expressions from titles in languages such as Finnish would not have been possible using the above scheme, because such languages do not contain prepositions.

Finally, the two level priority scheme generally produced good structures, where "good" means that a large percentage of the index (sub)expressions generated from these structures for the HyperIndex were meaningful.

4   The Odilon HyperIndex system

4.1   Effectiveness of HyperIndex

This section reports a study carried out with Odilon to investigate the effectiveness of the HyperIndex. One aim was to gather information which could be used to improve the HyperIndex implementation. Query by navigation seems to be a useful concept from a technical point of view, but how effective is it in practice? Therefor the effectiveness of the HyperIndex was compared with ICONCLASS. This was done by comparing the results of searchers using either ICONCLASS or HyperIndex to answer a number of questions. In order to do this formal criteria are needed. For more information, see [BBB91].

Effectiveness criteria

Given that n is the set of found slidenumbers, and N is the set of relevant slidenumbers, then

Recall : The recall of an answer set is the fraction of relevant slidenumbers retrieved.

Precision : The precision of an answer set is the fraction of retrieved slidenumbers that are relevant.

Two other criteria can be used to measure the result of both ICONCLASS and HyperIndex: The number of **Logical decisions** (see section 4.1) by a searcher and the number of times the searcher wants to see the slides belonging to the current selection, referred to as **Show** in the following text.

The user interface

An important facet of indexes is how they are displayed to the user, because this is a factor to their effectiveness. When the users enter the HyperIndex they are presented with a screen like that depicted in figure 9.

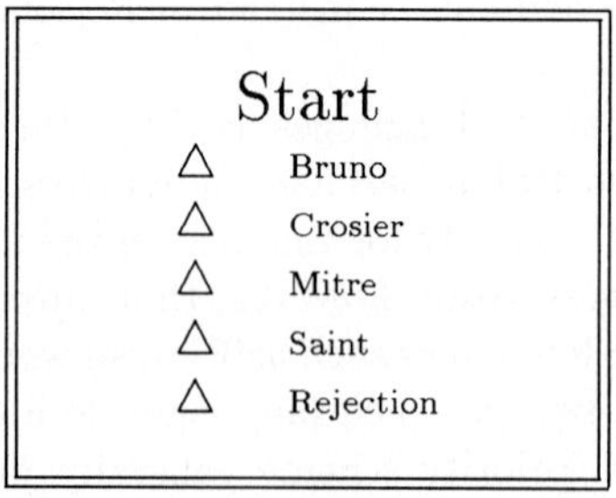

Fig. 9. Example start node of the HyperIndex

The first screen is the gateway into the HyperIndex. All terms in the HyperIndex will be directly accessible from this screen. To facilitate easy access to descriptions the *Finder* was implemented using the word wheel technique. Users are presented with a window in the screen where they can type in a keyword. After typing the first letter a pop up window appears showing all keywords beginning with that letter arranged in alphabetical order. As the searchers continue to type, the entries in the pop up window are adjusted accordingly. At any time the searchers can choose a keyword in the pop up window thus avoiding further typing. This choice becomes the begin point for Query by Navigation [BW90b]. From any focus in the HyperIndex the user can navigate to more specific indexing information (refining), or to more general information (enlarging).

Database content

The total number of slides in the database for the experiment described below was 437. 153 of these were architecture slides, having no ICONCLASS. Leaving 284 to select from by using ICONCLASS. The 437 slide subject descriptions were used to build the HyperIndex. The resultant HyperIndex contained 2434 entries of which 650 were keywords. This means that the starting screen (see figure 9) contained 650 entries.

The users

Three groups of users were identified in this experiment. The first group consisted of art historians who used the ICONCLASS system. It was decided to use only art historians for this part of the experiment, because as stated before ICONCLASS users need at least some knowledge of both art and ICONCLASS to use it effectively. The second group also consisted of art historians. This group used the HyperIndex system. In the third group computer scientists with little or no knowledge of art history, used HyperIndex. The motivation to let both art historians and computer scientists test HyperIndex was twofold. First it would test the effectiveness of HyperIndex in regard to naive (in the art history sense) searchers. Secondly, as the computer scientists have knowledge of mathematical structures, it would be tested if they use this knowledge and thus navigate more effectively over the HyperIndex structure than the art historians.

Experimental procedure

The objective of the experiment was to test how effective searchers could satisfy predefined information needs using either ICONCLASS plus other available avenues, or HyperIndex.

Experimental environment

The log file for each HyperIndex user consisted of instances of each of the following events:

- Starting a new session by selecting a keyword in the Finder.
- Each new selected focus.
- Each view of the current selection (**Show**).

For ICONCLASS users the recorded events were:

- Each class selected.
- Each view of the current selection.

Each instance in the log file is called a **Logical decision**.

Interpretation of experimental data

First, the sequence of actions by a searcher cannot be classified as correct or incorrect; in fact most of the searcher's actions are not known to the system.

Considerable time may elapse between two recorded actions: the searchers, may be reading information on the screen, may be confused, or may be consolidating their knowledge. This will influence their next action, but is not recorded in the log file. As a consequence it is not sure if the users know what they are doing, or at least think they do, or if they are just guessing their next action.

What can be measured easily is how the set of slidenumbers found by the searcher compares to the ideal set of slidenumbers for a particular question, recall and precision, as well as the number of logical decisions and shows.

Performance of art historians
Question 1: Find slides depicting the Annunciation.
This question was expected to be easy with both ICONCLASS and HyperIndex. For HyperIndex this turned out to be true. All searchers selected *Annunciation* and found all slides. Some refined their choice to see if more slides would turn up. This points to a lack of mathematical knowledge, as this obviously cannot lead to more hits. ICONCLASS worked not as well as thought. Annunciation is indeed a class, but a large number of users did not find the path to it.
Question 2: Find three slides depicting flowers.
This question was a little harder for both. All HyperIndex users selected *flowers*, but only one slide could be found this way. A path had to be found to *Sunflowers* to find the other slides. Not all users managed to do this. ICONCLASS proved to be not suited for this type of question at all. All slides in the relevant set were paintings with ICONCLASS *Still-live*, while the searchers selected classes within *Nature* etc.
Question 3: Find slides with French city-views by Van Gogh.
This question, again, was not an easy one. Most slides could be found by starting HyperIndex with *Paris*, and using the lattice structure to arrive at *Arles*. ICONCLASS users had to find ICONCLASS *City-view*. Both methods let to almost equal Recall results.
Question 4: Find a slide depicting an equestrian statue of Aurelius.
An easy one for HyperIndex. All subjects chose either *Equestrian statue*, *Aurelius* or, showing their knowledge of the matter, *Marcus* to find the requested slide. None of the ICONCLASS searchers succeeded. Due to the obscure classification, *Traffic on land*, they searched confused until forced to give up (The average searcher gave up after 15 Logical decisions).
Question 5: Find slides depicting harvest scenes.
Two slides of the relevant set were easily found with both methods. ICONCLASS has a class *Harvest*, which takes a while to find though, and with HyperIndex a searcher can select *Harvest*. The third slide gave trouble in both methods. A *Mower* in a cornfield has been given ICONCLASS *Landscapes*. None of the ICONCLASS users found this slide. HyperIndex users could find it by browsing through the index and selecting *Harvester*.
Question 6: Find slides depicting Greek Gods.
This question and the next proved to be real trouble makers for HyperIndex searchers, while they are both easy enough for ICONCLASS. ICONCLASS *Clas-*

sical Mythology reveals almost all slides of the relevant set. HyperIndex can only be used to select one God after another, because no links consist between individual Gods.

Question 7: Find slides depicting the passion of Christ
Again, an easy problem to solve with ICONCLASS by selecting *Passion of Christ*. HyperIndex users had to select every single element of the passion, which can only be done if the searchers have knowledge to help them chose.

Question 8: Find slides depicting Mary.
A hard question for both methods. Who would find a slide depicting Mary on *flight into Egypt*, without being an expert on this matter. ICONCLASS users were able to find most requested slides, but a number of them did not chose *Madonna* as a second class after finding ICONCLASS *Mary* first.

Table 1 in Appendix A summarizes the effectiveness of art historians using ICONCLASS.

Performance of the computer scientists

Table 3 in Appendix A summarizes the effectiveness of computer scientists searching in the HyperIndex. It does not significantly differ from the art historians (see table 2 in Appendix A). The supposition that the computer scientists would make better use of the underlying structure is partially confirmed. In question 3, all computer scientists began to search with the term *Paris* because they lacked the knowledge to begin with city names such as *Arles*. From the focus *Paris* it was possible to navigate to *Arles* by refining *Paris* to *view of Paris*, enlarging this to *view* and refining again to *view of Arles*. This last focus could be enlarged to *Arles* which characterized quite a few of the relevant slides. The art historians tended to use their knowledge of painting and began searches with the names of places where Van Gogh painted whilst in France. They therefore navigated less.

Overall performance

ICONCLASS has an average Recall of 0.64, for this 9.8 Logical decisions were needed. Precision is 0.88. Show is used 3.2 per question. Problems occurred with questions 2 and 8. These questions very much show the limitations of ICON-CLASS. If it is not perfectly clear to which class a piece of art belongs or more classes are appropriate, and no alternative avenue is at hand, it is indeed very hard to find the wanted information. The users of ICONCLASS showed they had the following problems:

- For religious subjects it is not clear whether to look in main division 1: *Religion and Magic*, or in division 7: *The bible*.
- Users do not know what subclasses they can expect within a division or class.
- Users sometimes have no idea what ICONCLASS is appropriate for a subject. For example: An equestrian statue of Aurelius turns out to be of ICON-CLASS *Traffic on land*.

– Painted objects are not classified as objects as such, but as the paintings ICONCLASS. For example: A Painting of Van Gogh with Sunflowers has ICONCLASS: *Still-live*.

HyperIndex has an average Recall of 0.68. To achieve this, 6.0 Logical decisions are made. Precision is 0.91 and Show is used 3.0 times. The users of HyperIndex showed they had the following problems:

– Some users do not see the fact that by only refining they will not find more answers, resulting in more Logical decisions and Shows.
– Users often do not use the refinement and enlargement possibilities to go from one topic to another. They see a certain term within their current focus, leave the index and start with this term from scratch.
– Users forget which points have already been visited.
– Users arrive at a certain point which does not give them the desired result, and they don't know where to go from there.

First consider the problem of *disorientation*. Since the HyperIndex system does not have a linear structure but lets users move up and down the lattice, it can be difficult to ascertain the layout of the structure. Users become disoriented in that they do not know where they are in the information space and do not know how to get at some place they believe exists.
It appears that some of the difficulties that searchers have in maintaining their orientation while using the HyperIndex system, could easily be overcome by implementing a *history* function. This addition allows the user at any given focus in the HyperIndex to see the used path to that focus. Users will thus be able to recall the items which detracted them from the main search path, they can decide to select any old focus from the history and make this the current focus.

From the results of the experiment it is perfectly clear that one type of question is particularly hard to answer with HyperIndex. Questions which can only be answered by browsing through the itemindex to find items which are applicable yield a low to very low Recall. This problem too can be easily overcome. The searcher should not have to browse through the entire itemindex, but have all applicable items grouped together to chose from. Grouping can be done by adding a cross-reference to the HyperIndex. The searchers can now use associative navigation to provide answers to their information need.

The second experiment
How would the changes in the system effect the results of searchers using these changes to find answers to the questions of the first experiment? A second test was performed using the same slidedatabase and experimental procedure as before. Two Computer scientists were selected to participate. The searchers used the same HyperIndex system as in the first experiment. Added were the history function and the cross-references needed to answer the questions.

Interpretation of new experimental data

Since this experiment was done only to test the additions to the system, only three questions were of particular interest; questions 6, 7 and 8, which in the first experiment were hard to answer using HyperIndex. The other questions were needed to compare results to the first experiment. The results for these questions should not differ from the first experiment.

As predicted, the searchers had much better results for questions 6, 7 and 8. (see table 4 in Appendix A). Selecting all cross-references, however, drove up the number of Logical decisions and Shows. The history function was seldom used. This is probably due to the relative short search paths which had to be used and therefore the ease with which searchers can find each focus again by selecting the same term.

4.2 Later Additions

To provide searchers with direct access to the visual reproduction of the artobjects in their selection an imagemodule was added to Odilon. A thumbnail image is now displayed with the object data and the searcher can also switch to a fullscreen image.

The first version of Odilon used a staightforward implementation of the HyperIndex. A disadvantage was that the HyperIndex may grow alarmingly, because of the possibly huge number of subexpressions. A recent Master's thesis project resulted in an implementation for dynamic generation of the HyperIndex. This resulted in a marginal overhead during query by navigation, while saving almost 75% diskspace [H97].

The high number of Logical decisions and Shows for HyperIndex, resulting from the addition of cross-references can be brought down by splitting them into two relationship types: A term cross-reference relation, which still allows *Mary* and *Madonna* to be related. The second is an ISA relation. For example, *Hercules* ISA *God*. This allows the HyperIndex searcher to refine the focus *God* to *Hercules*, but focus *God* will also show all *Hercules* related slides in the selection.

5 Conclusions

The fact that computer scientists results did not differ significantly from those of Art historians demonstrates one of the advantages of HyperIndex over ICONCLASS, where domain knowledge is needed in order to use it as an effective disclosure system. The experiments showed that ICONCLASS is especially suited searching classes of objects, while HyperIndex performs very well on searches for objects which can be in different classes. To state this differently, ICONCLASS is a semantic, HyperIndex a syntactic disclosure system. Some disadvantages of HyperIndex stem from the fact that it is derived from an automatic syntactic process. The index expression *Announcement of birth of Christ* will never be related to the expression *Mary*, even though the two are highly related. This is because the index expression transducer is a syntactic analyzer which cannot make the connection to *Mary*. The documentalist, however, would most certainly make this connection. This is the strength of semantic classification, although it is a manual process. HyperIndex doesn't have to stay far behind though in answering semantic queries. Some problems can be solved by manually adding new links. Only once has the relation between *Announcement of birth of Christ* and *Mary* to be added to link all current and future occurrences of both expressions. Adding too many links can however turn against the searchers in the long run; Just as large software programs with many jumps can turn into "spaghetti" code, so a HyperIndex system can turn into a swamp of meaningless, obscure connections and references. The HyperIndex system, therefore, must allow editing and deleting manually added links easily.

References

[B98]   F. Berger. Navigational Query Construction in a Hypertext Environment. Phd Thesis, Department of Computer Science, University of Nijmegen 1998.

[BB91]   R. Bosman and R. Bouwman. The Automation and Disclosure of a Slides Library. Master's thesis, University of Nijmegen, Nijmegen, The Netherlands, April 1991.

[BBB91] R. Bosman, R. Bouwman, and P.D. Bruza. The Effectiveness of Navigable Information Disclosure Systems. In G.A.M. Kempen, editor, *Proceedings of the Informatiewetenschap 1991 conference*, Nijmegen, The Netherlands, 1991.

[Bru90] P.D. Bruza. Hyperindices: A Novel Aid for Searching in Hypermedia. In A. Rizk, N. Streitz, and J. Andre, editors, *Proceedings of the European Conference on Hypertext - ECHT 90*, pages 109–122, Cambridge, United Kingdom, 1990. Cambridge University Press.

[BW90a] P.D. Bruza and Th.P. van der Weide. Assessing the Quality of Hypertext Views. *ACM SIGIR FORUM (Refereed Section)*, 24(3):6–25, 1990.

[BW90b] P.D. Bruza and Th.P. van der Weide. Two Level Hypermedia - An Improved Architecture for Hypertext. In A.M. Tjoa and R. Wagner, editors, *Proceedings of the Data Base and Expert System Applications Conference (DEXA 90)*, pages 76–83, Vienna, Austria, 1990. Springer-Verlag.

[BW91]   P.D. Bruza and Th.P. van der Weide. The Modelling and Retrieval of Documents using Index Expressions. *ACM SIGIR FORUM (Refereed Section)*, 25(2), 1991.

[Con87] J. Conklin. Hypertext: An Introduction and Survey. *IEEE Computer*, 20(9):17–41, September 1987.

[H97]   E. Hebing Implementation of Hyperindices. Master's thesis, University of Nijmegen, Nijmegen, The Netherlands, June 1997 (in Dutch).

[SK89]   B. Schneiderman and G. Kearsley. *Hypertext Hands-On!* Addison-Wesley, Reading, Massachusetts, 1989.

[Waa85] H. van der Waal. *ICONCLASS an iconographic Classification System*. North-Holland, 1985. Completed and edited by L.D.Couprie, E.Tolen and G.Vellenkoop.

A   Experiment results

Question	Recall	Precision	Logical decisions	Show
1	0.56	1.00	11.6	2.4
2	0.30	0.70	12.4	2.8
3	0.69	0.40	10.4	4.3
4	1.00	1.00	∞	∞
5	0.55	1.00	11.0	2.8
6	0.77	0.98	4.2	4.0
7	1.00	1.00	5.4	1.4
8	0.26	0.98	8.4	2.8
Average	0.64	0.88	9.8	3.2

Table 1. Experiment results of art historians using ICONCLASS

Question	Recall	Precision	Logical decisions	Show
1	1.00	1.00	1.8	1.6
2	0.65	1.00	13.0	2.8
3	0.71	0.61	6.2	3.1
4	1.00	1.00	2.6	1.4
5	0.80	1.00	3.4	2.2
6	0.43	0.92	7.6	5.2
7	0.30	0.94	9.0	5.4
8	0.54	0.84	4.4	2.4
Average	0.68	0.91	6.0	3.0

Table 2. Experiment results of art historians using HyperIndex

Question	Recall	Precision	Logical decisions	Show
1	1.00	1.00	1.3	1.3
2	0.75	1.00	11.2	2.5
3	0.82	0.56	5.1	4.2
4	1.00	1.00	3.0	1.3
5	0.88	1.00	3.0	3.5
6	0.44	0.69	7.5	4.8
7	0.16	1.00	8.0	4.5
8	0.35	0.93	3.5	2.4
Average	0.68	0.90	5.3	3.1

Table 3. Experiment results of computer scientists using HyperIndex

Question	Recall	Precision	Logical decisions	Show
1	1.00	1.00	1.5	1.0
2	0.75	1.00	8.5	3.0
3	0.73	0.58	6.3	3.6
4	1.00	1.00	2.5	1.5
5	0.88	1.00	2.5	2.0
6	0.92	0.93	24.0	20.0
7	0.57	1.00	18.5	14.0
8	0.61	0.97	2.0	2.0
Average	0.81	0.94	8.2	5.8

Table 4. Second experiment results of computer scientists using HyperIndex

Signature File Methods
for Semantic Query Caching

Boris Chidlovskii[1] and Uwe M. Borghoff[2]

[1] Xerox Research Centre Europe, Grenoble Laboratory
6, Chemin de Maupertuis, F–38240 Meylan, France
childovskii@xrce.xerox.com
[2] Institut für Softwaretechnologie, Fakultät für Informatik
Universität der Bundeswehr München, D-85577 Neubiberg, Germany
borghoff@informatik.unibw-muenchen.de

Abstract. In digital libraries accessing distributed Web-based bibliographic repositories, performance is a major issue. Efficient query processing requires an appropriate caching mechanism. Unfortunately, standard page-based as well as tuple-based caching mechanisms designed for
conventional databases are not efficient on the Web, where keyword-
based querying is often the only way to retrieve data. Therefore, we
study the problem of semantic caching of Web queries and develop a
caching mechanism for conjunctive Web queries based on *signature files*.
We propose two implementation choices. A first algorithm copes with the
relation of semantic containment between a query and the corresponding
cache items. A second algorithm extends this processing to more complex cases of semantic intersection. We report results of experiments and
show how the caching mechanism is successfully realized in the Knowledge Broker system.

1 Introduction

Digital libraries operating in a networked environment process user queries by
contacting heterogeneous Web repositories that provide bibliographic data in
particular domains. Such systems invoke so-called *wrappers* to convert user queries
into the target query language, and to control the return flow of data from these
servers [19–21]. As data are transferred over the network in HTML/XML format,
the wrappers also extract answer documents from the retrieved HTML/XML
files before they report the final answers (often locally pre-filtered) to the user.

As in any client-server system, high performance in such a networked digital library is often reached by efficient utilization of computational storage resources at the client sites. In the networked environment, where data from remote
servers are brought to clients on-demand, local client memory is largely used to
cache data and minimize future interaction with the servers. This data caching
is particularly important in Web-based digital libraries, as network traffic and
overloaded servers can lead to long delays in answer delivery. As standard page
caching is not possible on the Web, and tuple-caching has certain limitations,

much effort has been spent to cache user queries and corresponding answers (instead of pages or tuples) for possible future reuse [4, 9, 13].

Query caching is particular advantageous when the user of a digital library refines a query several times, for example, by adding or removing a query term. In this case, many of the answer documents may already be cached and can be delivered to the user right away.

A typical query to a Web data repository is a conjunction of terms. Each term in the query is a keyword, possibly negated with the operator NOT, and applied to one or more attributes (title, author, etc.). In most Web repositories allowing the search over the site contents, the operator NOT is equivalent to AND NOT to force a query to contain at least one non-negated term.

Semantic caching. Semantic caching manages the client cache as a collection of semantic *regions*; access information is managed and cache replacement is performed at the unit of semantic regions [9]. Semantic regions group together semantically related documents covered, for example, by a user query.

Each semantic region has a constraint formula which describes its contents, a region signature, a counter of tuples in the contents, a pointer to the set of actual tuples in the cache, and the additional information that is used by the replacement policy to rank the regions. Like a query, any region formula is a conjunction of terms.

When a query is posed at a client, it is split into two disjoint pieces: (1) the portion of the answer available in the local cache, and (2) a *remainder* query, which retrieves any missing information from the server. If the remainder query is not null (i.e., the query asks for some documents that are not cached so far), the remainder query is sent to the server for further processing [5].

A semantic model for query caching mechanisms in a client-server architecture was discussed in [9]. Query caching in heterogeneous systems was discussed in [13], where it is reduced to a Datalog query evaluation, which, however, may by computationally hard. Intelligent query caching is also used in the SIMS project [4], where some important principles for any intelligent caching mechanism were developed. These principles are: 1) a query cache should process both containment and intersection cases; 2) a cache item should not be large; 3) a cache item should have a simple formula to avoid too complex reasoning on the query remainders.

Semantic caching versus page and tuple caching. In a standard client-server architecture the transfer units between servers and clients are pages or tuple sets, unlike in a networked digital library. *Page caching* mechanisms assume that each query posed at the client can be processed locally and be broken down to the level of requests for individual pages. Then, if a requested page is not present in the client cache, a request for the entire page is sent to the server. Such a query processing is improper in a Web-based digital library, where keyword-based querying is often the only way to retrieve data and where the data organization at the servers is completely hidden from the clients.

With *tuple caching*, the cache is maintained in terms of individual tuples or documents, allowing a higher degree of flexibility than pure page caching. On the Web, tuple caching is possible though not very attractive, as there is no way to inform the servers about qualified tuples in the client cache. Moreover, clients can not detect whether their local caches provide a complete answer to the queries. As a result, clients are forced to ignore their cache entries while performing the query. Once the query is sent to the server and all qualifying tuples are returned, the clients detect and discard the duplications.

Our contribution. In this paper, we develop a new mechanism for caching Web queries which is based on so-called *signature files*. Each semantic region in the cache is associated with a signature. For a user query, the signature is created in a similar way and verified against the region signatures stored in the cache. The proposed caching mechanism includes a procedure that identifies all cache items qualified for the query, i.e., it detects which cache items can be re-used immediately, and which missing information must be requested from the servers.

This mechanism has three main advantages. First, it processes both critical cases in the same elegant way, 1) when a query is contained in the cache, or 2) when it intersects some regions. As a result, the proposed mechanism avoids most cases of tuple duplications, and has a moderate storage requirement. Second, it supports efficient reporting of partial answers and generating of query remainders. Finally, it provides a simple solution for the region coalescing and the replacement policy.

Although the main motivation and the targeted use of our proposed algorithms are Web-based digital libraries, we point out that the presented approach can be easily generalized to full-fledged distributed database environments.

The remainder of the paper is organized as follows. Section 2 introduces the signature file methods and discusses the cache architecture based on semantic region signatures. Section 3 studies the semantic containment between a query and semantic regions. The first caching algorithm is presented. In Section 4, we develop a second algorithm which covers the semantic intersection too. Results of experiments with the caching algorithms are reported in Section 6. Section 7 discusses some open issues and concludes the paper.

2   Signature Files and Cache Architecture

Signature files were originally designed for the retrieval of full-text fragments containing query words [10,11]. Consequently, signature files where used in a variety of applications, including navigation in OODBS, indexing of Prolog items, and multimedia office management [11,12,15]. The best known technique uses the superimposed coding to associate each semantic region with a formula in the conjunctive form. Each term in a region formula is assigned a term signature represented as a binary sequence of ones and zeros. The region signature is generated by superimposing (bit-wise OR-ing) all term signatures generated from the region formula. Figure 1.a shows the signature generation for the semantic

Region formula: "query ∧ caching"

Term signatures:

query	0010 0010 1000
caching	0100 0100 0001

Region signature: 0110 0110 1001

a)

Queries	Query Signatures	Results
1) Web	1000 0001 1000	no match
2) caching	0100 0100 0001	region containment
3) query ∧ caching	0110 0110 1001	equivalence
4) Web ∧ query ∧ caching	1110 0111 1101	query containment
6) false ∧ drop	0110 0110 1001	false drop

b)

Fig. 1. a) Region signature construction; b) Sample queries and their signatures

region "query ∧ caching". For a user query – which is also a conjunction – all terms are assigned signatures and superimposed onto a query signature in a way similar to regions. Then, the query signature is matched against each region signature in the signature file to provide a partial answer and construct the query remainder.

The two caching algorithms proposed in this paper work with different semantic relations between semantic regions and the query. The first caching algorithm copes with *semantic containment* between the query and a region, where one contains the other. The second caching algorithm described in Sect. 4 extends this processing to the more frequent and complex cases of *semantic intersection*, when neither region contains the query nor vice versa. We begin with the semantic containment which consists of three cases. Query Q is *equivalent* to a region R if their formulas are equivalent. A region R *contains* query Q if the query formula can be obtained from the region formula by dropping one or more terms. In this case, the answer to the query is a proper subset of the region contents. Inversely, the semantic region R is contained in a query Q if the region formula can be obtained from the query by dropping one or more query terms. The region containment implies that the answer is a superset of the region contents. In any of the three cases described above, the region R is *qualified* for query Q.

Let S_Q and S_R denote a query signature and a region signature, respectively. With the bit-wise comparison of the signatures, the semantic containment is detected as follows:

Region containment, $S_Q \subset S_R$: for each bit in the query signature set to one, the corresponding bit in the region signature is also set to one (see Query 2 in Fig. 1.b).

Equivalence, $S_Q = S_R$: the region and query signatures have the same bits set to one (see Query 3 in Fig. 1.b).

Query containment, $S_Q \supset S_R$: for each bit in the region signature set to one, the corresponding bit in the query signature is also set to one (see Query 4 in Fig. 1.b).

A signature file eliminates most, but not all of the regions which are not qualified for the query. Query 6 in Fig. 1.b represents a false drop. *False drops* are semantic regions where the signatures are qualified for the query, but they should not have qualified. False drops are eliminated by further comparing the query with the regions. If false drops are numerous, the performance degrades dramatically.

Much work has been done on minimizing the false drop probability [14, 12]. It has been shown that in order to minimize the false drop probability, the expected number of zeros and ones in a signature must be the same [12]. When the length of the signatures increases – for the same number of distinct keywords in a region or query formula – the density of ones in the signatures decreases. The chance of getting false drops will decrease correspondingly. However, the storage overhead increases. If the signature length is F bits and the maximal number of terms in the query is t, the optimal number k_{opt} of bits set to one in a term signature is given as

$$k_{opt} = \frac{F \cdot \ln 2}{t}. \tag{1}$$

In information retrieval, the signature file method is a compromise between conventional inverted file and full-text scanning methods. The advantage of the method over an inverted file method lies in its moderate storage overhead. The storage overhead is some 10-20% for signature files compared to 100% and more for inverted files. On the other hand, the retrieval speed of the signature file method is higher than in the case of full scanning of text blocks, but lower than in the case of inverted files [15].

In semantic caching of Web queries, the number of terms in a query or region formula can vary. Still, the number remains small when compared to the number of words in a text block. Consequently, the signature storage overhead is again reduced when compared to the signature methods used in information retrieval. When different regions intersect and tuple duplicates are stored, unfortunately, there is another source of storage overhead in the case of semantic caching. In Sect. 4, we discuss this problem in some detail.

Cache organization. To process a query faster, our cache architecture maintains region signatures separately from region contents (see Fig. 2). Apart from a signature, each entry (region) in the signature part contains the region formula, the counter of tuples, the link to the corresponding region contents, and the value of a replacement function. Qualified regions are detected in the signature part. Once a semantic region is qualified for a full or partial answer, tuples in the region contents that match the query are reported to the user.

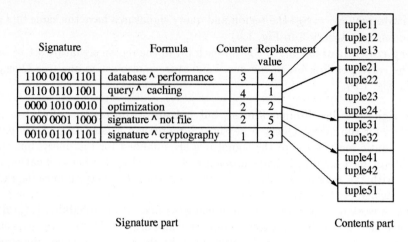

Signature	Formula	Counter	Replacement value
1100 0100 1101	database ∧ performance	3	4
0110 0110 1001	query ∧ caching	4	1
0000 1010 0010	optimization	2	2
1000 0001 1000	signature ∧ not file	2	5
0010 0110 1101	signature ∧ cryptography	1	3

Signature part   Contents part

Fig. 2. Cache architecture

Negation. Any region formula contains keywords as well as their negations. To provide a smooth processing for queries with negations, signatures for a keyword and its negation can be related. A negated term is coded as a signature with a bit-wise negation of the basic term signature. However, as the number k of bits set to one in a term signature is much smaller than the signature length F, this would result in $F - k$ bits set to one in the negated term signature. Therefore, this solution would have a considerably higher false drop probability, for any region's formula containing the negated term. To avoid this problem, we treat a keyword and its negation (and their signatures) as two independent terms, with k bits set to one in both signatures.

3 A Simple Caching Algorithm

The first algorithm processes three cases of the semantic containment, namely, (1) equivalence, (2) query containment, and (3) region containment. If the query is equivalent to a region in the cache, the query answer coincides with the region contents. If a region contains the query, the complete answer can also be produced from the region contents, with the query formula used as a filter. Moreover, if two or more regions contain the query, any of them can produce the answer. To reduce the filtering overhead, the algorithm selects and filters the region where the content has the smallest number of tuples. In the case of region containment, the algorithm extracts a partial answer from the region contents and generates the query remainder which is then sent to the server. If several regions are contained in the query, any or all of them can produce the partial answer. As the number of such regions can be huge, the algorithm selects the top m regions with a maximal number of tuples.

If no semantic containment is detected, the cache is not used at all, and the initial query is sent to the server. When an answer to this query is received, a new cache region is created. If the cache space is already used up, one or several "old" regions are released. As the basic replacement strategy, we use the well-known LRU ("least recently used"). The strategy is appropriate for the Web, where searching is always coupled with navigation and discovery. Typically, a new query refines a previous query [22].

With the algorithmic framework described above, three important issues require further analyses, namely, the construction of region remainders, region coalescing and cache region replacement.

3.1 Constructing query remainders

Assume that m semantic regions, $R_1, \ldots, R_m$, are contained in the query. Although the query remainder Q_r can be constructed as $Q_r = Q - R_1 - \ldots - R_m = Q \wedge \neg R_1 \wedge \ldots \wedge \neg R_m$, such a constraint formula, after simplification, can contain disjunctions, and may not be appropriate for a server that accepts conjunctive queries only. For example, for the query a and the region $a \wedge b \wedge c^1$, the constraint formula $a - a \wedge b \wedge c$ results in the following disjunction formula:

$$a - a \wedge b \wedge c = a \wedge \neg(a \wedge b \wedge c) = a \wedge \neg b \vee a \wedge \neg c.$$

To distinguish the regions which drive the query remainder to a conjunctive form from those which do not, we introduce a difference measure between the query and the region formulas. The *difference* is defined as the number of terms in the region formula not presented in the query. This definition splits the set of regions $R_1, \ldots, R_m$ into groups, where all regions in a group differ in l terms from the query, $l = 1, 2, \ldots$. In the example given above, the region formula $a \wedge b \wedge c$ has a two-term difference from the query a. Note, however, that the case $l = 0$ is also valid. When a query and a region are equivalent, or when a region contains a query, the difference is zero, and, correspondingly, the query remainder is null.

As stated in the following theorem, the difference measure allows us to guarantee that regions with one-term difference preserve the conjunctive form of the query remainder.

Theorem 1. *Assume a cache containing m region formulas have one-term differences, say $a_1, a_2, \ldots, a_m$, from a query formula Q. Then, the query remainder Q_r is $Q \wedge \neg a_1 \wedge \neg a_2 \wedge \ldots \wedge \neg a_m$.*

Proof. Let $\mathcal{E}$ denote the set of all possible query terms. As all m regions contain the query, we can denote the region formulas, without loss of generality, as $Q \wedge a_1, Q \wedge a_2, \ldots, Q \wedge a_m$.
Then we obtain:

$$Q_r = Q - (Q \wedge a_1) - \ldots - (Q \wedge a_m) = Q \wedge (\mathcal{E} - a_1 - \ldots - a_m) =$$

$$= Q \wedge (\mathcal{E} \wedge \neg a_1 \wedge \ldots \wedge \neg a_m) = Q \wedge \neg a_1 \wedge \ldots \wedge \neg a_m \square$$

---

[1] We use characters from the beginning of the alphabet to denote query terms.

3.2 Region coalescing

As we have explained before, when a query and a region are equivalent, or when a region contains a query, the query remainder is null. The query is not sent to a server but processed locally. The cache contents are kept unchanged. The region providing the answer to the query updates the replacement values (see Sect. 3.3).

In the region containment case, i. e. when a query contains a region, the query remainder is not null, and, moreover, it is a complement to a semantic region R (see Fig. 3.a). When an answer to the query remainder Q_r is received, there are two strategies to add the answer to the cache. With the *no-coalescing* strategy, a new cache region is created for the query remainder. This implies that smaller regions appear in the cache. However, such regions may result in the degradation of the cache reuse. With the *coalescing* strategy, no new cache region is added; instead, region R's contents are extended with the answer to the remainder. The region formula R is substituted (relaxed) with Q.

Obviously, both strategies require the same cache space to store tuples. Still, the coalescing strategy appears to be preferable. First, it uses only one region instead of two. Furthermore, if m semantic regions, $R_1, \ldots, R_m$, yield the region containment (see Fig. 3.b), the coalescing strategy is even more advantageous. The query remainder $Q_r = Q - R_1 - \ldots - R_m$ is a complement to the union of the regions. Here, the coalescing strategy will keep a single region (with formula Q), instead of m individual regions $R_1, \ldots, R_m$, and the query remainder. As regions $R_1, \ldots, R_m$ may contain tuple duplications, the coalescing strategy provides better storage utilization, both for the signature parts and for the content parts of the cache.

3.3 Replacement strategy

As the cache space is a scarce and limited resource, the cache may discard the least recently used regions to free space for new regions. The standard LRU strategy was designed for the replacement of pages or tuples in the cache. It acts upon objects of the same size, that is, the replacement unit is one page or one tuple.

In the query caching case, the situation is different. When a region R qualifies for a query, the involvement of the region in the answer can vary. If the query contains the region – as depicted in Fig. 3.a – the region contents is *completely* involved in responding, as all tuples from the region contents appear in the answer. By contrast, if the region contains the query (see Fig. 3.c), the region involvement is *partial*, as only some of the tuples in the region match the query.

Therefore, the replacement function should take into account the *region involvement* in the answer of the query. If the region involvement is complete, the new replacement value for the region is "the most recent one", as in the case when the answer to the query is shipped from the server. If the region involvement is partial, and there are tuples in the region contents not matching

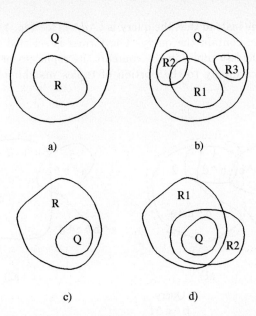

a)   b)

c)   d)

Fig. 3. Semantic containment cases: a) Single region containment; b) multiple region containment; c) single query containment; d) multiple query containment

the query, the change of the replacement value toward "the most recent one" depends on how large the portion of the matched tuples is.

The region involvement can be measured as $p = T_Q/T$, where T_Q is the number of tuples appearing in the answer to the query, and where T is the total number of tuples in R's contents.

Without loss of generality, we assume that "the most recent value", V_{top}, is incremented by one, each time a new query is issued. If the current replacement value of region R is V_R, $V_R < V_{top}$, and the region involvement is p, we calculate a new replacement function as $V_R' = V_R + (V_{top} - V_R) \cdot p$. If $p = 1$, then $V_R' = V_{top}$. If $p = 1/2$, then $V_R' = (V_{top} + V_R)/2$. Note, that this replacement function can be implemented for any region in the cache, whether the region qualifies for the query or not. If a region does not qualify for the query, and, therefore, its involvement p is zero, the region replacement value is kept unchanged.

Example 2. The cache contains three regions with formulas $a \wedge b \wedge c$, $b \wedge d$ and $d \wedge \neg a$. Figure 4.a1 shows the regions with their replacement values (assuming $V_{top} = 6$). Assume a new query is d. The second and third regions yield the query containment. As both region formulas differ from the query formula in one word only (b for the second region and $\neg a$ for the third one), the generated query remainder is given as $d \wedge a \wedge \neg b$. Once the complete answer is produced, the second and third region, as well as the query remainder are substituted with one region with formula d (Fig. 4.a2). Its replacement value is $V_{top} = 7$.

Now we assume instead that the query is $b \wedge d \wedge f$ (see Fig. 4.b1). Two regions, $b \wedge d$, and $d \wedge \neg a$, contain the query. The former is selected as the answer to the query, as it has less tuples in the contents. Its replacement value is updated (from 3 to 4) accordingly to the portion of tuples matching the query in the region contents.

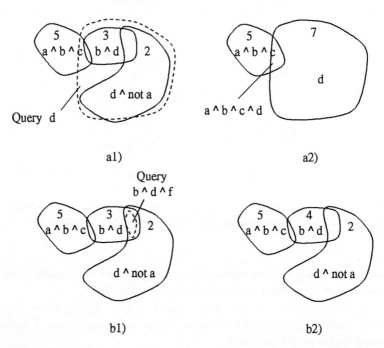

al)   a2)

b1)   b2)

Fig. 4. Region coalescing examples: a1) Query $Q = d$ is issued; a2) Regions coalesced after the query; b1) Query $Q = b \wedge d \wedge f$ is issued; b2) Regions updated after the query

Caching algorithm 1. *Input*: cache with semantic regions and query Q.
Output: answer to Q and the cache updated.

1. Verify the query signature against all region signatures in the cache.
2. $S_Q = S_R$: If there is a region which formula is equivalent to the query, return the region contents as the query answer. Update the replacement function value of the region and stop.
3. $S_Q \supset S_R$: If one or more regions contain the query, choose the region with the minimal cardinality. Scan tuples in the region contents and return ones matching the query. Update the replacement function value of the region and stop.
4. $S_Q \subset S_{R_i}$: If several regions are contained in the query, choose top m regions, $R_1, \ldots, R_m$, with the maximal cardinality. Return all tuples from the

regions contents of $R_1, \ldots, R_m$, discarding duplications. Construct the query remainder as follows:
- Set the query remainder to query Q.
- For each region R_i providing the region containment, calculate the difference between the region formula and the query. If the difference is one term a_i only, constrain the query remainder with $\neg a_i$.

Send the query remainder to the server. When the answer is received, replace regions $R_1, \ldots, R_m$ with one region Q. Put V_{top} as the replacement value for Q and stop.
5. Otherwise, send query Q to the server. Once the answer is received, create a new region for Q in the cache. To free space for the region, remove the regions with the least replacement values, until query Q fits the cache.

4 The Advanced Caching Algorithm

The caching algorithm described in the previous section efficiently manages the semantic containment and equivalence cases. However, it does not manage the more frequent and complex case of semantic intersections. In a semantic intersection, a region can produce a portion of the answer, but it neither contains nor is contained in the query.

Example 3. Assume, the cache contains region R_1 with formula "query $\wedge$ caching" and query Q is "optimal $\wedge$ query" (see Fig. 5.a). Since there is no containment, Algorithm 1 does not exploit R_1 for the partial answer, although the tuples in the region contents matching the formula "optimal $\wedge$ query $\wedge$ caching" match also the query. Moreover, when Algorithm 1 receives the answer to query Q from the server, it creates a new semantic region R_2 with the same formula "optimal $\wedge$ query" (see Fig. 5.b). Two semantic regions R_1 and R_2 contain tuple duplicates, which match their intersection formula "optimal $\wedge$ query $\wedge$ caching". In other words, in the semantic intersection cases, Algorithm 1 retains a low cache use and a high tuple duplication level.

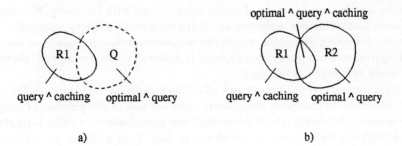

Fig. 5. Semantic intersection example

In this section we develop an advanced caching algorithm which, besides the containment cases, also processes the semantic intersection. This helps to improve cache utilization and to reduce tuple duplications.

The intersection of a semantic region R and a query Q is given by the intersection of their formula : $R \cap Q$. Given the region signature S_R and the query signature S_Q, we use their signature intersection $S_Q \cap S_R$, which is obtained by bit-wise AND-ing of S_Q and S_R. Then, for a signature S, the signature cardinality $|S|$ denotes the number of bits set to one in the signature.

In the semantic intersection of a semantic region R and a query Q, we distinguish two cases:

Complement: $Q \cap R = \emptyset$; the formula intersection is null. For instance, query $a \wedge b$ is a complement to the region $a \wedge \neg b$. Consequently, the region contains no tuples to answer to the query. However, in the complement case, the region coalescing is possible. For the query and region above, the coalescing would result in one region with formula a.

Intersection: The $Q \cap R \neq \emptyset$; the formula intersection is not null. There are two following sub-cases:

  - Query and region formulas have some common terms appearing in the intersection (in Example 2, region "query $\wedge$ caching" and query "optimal $\wedge$ query" have term "query" in common).
  - Query and region formulas have no common words. For instance, region a and query b have no common terms, but their intersection $a \wedge b$ is not empty, and, therefore, the region can contribute to the partial answer.

Semantic intersection in signature files. If the query Q and a region R have some common terms, their signatures have bits set to one which correspond to signatures of the common terms. The more terms formulas Q and R have in common, the larger the number of bits jointly set to one. The semantic intersection of Q and R could be measured as the number $|S_Q \cap S_R|$ of corresponding bits set to one in both signatures. Unfortunately, this is not always true. For example, even though the signature intersection of a region with formula a and a query b may have no bits set to one, the region with formula a might indeed have tuples matching the formula $b \wedge a$.

In the remainder of this section, we show how the signature file method allows for an efficient detection of region intersections with the query. Moreover, it supports partial answer deliveries and helps constrain the query remainder. Note that the following discussion about the semantic intersection assumes that neither equivalence nor query containment is detected in the cache, and, therefore, the query remainder is not null.

As in semantic containment, not all of the regions intersecting with the query can contribute to the query remainder; again because of the problem of conjunctive queries. To detect the regions that can contribute to a valid formula, we use again term differences, as introduced in Sect. 3. In addition, we make use of Theorem 1, which, while proven for the semantic containment only, also applies to the case of semantic intersection. We argue as follows: if a cache contains m

regions where the corresponding formulas are not contained in the query Q, but have one-term differences, say $a_1, a_2, \ldots, a_m$, the query remainder Q_r can be constructed as $Q \wedge \neg a_1 \wedge \neg a_2 \wedge \ldots \wedge \neg a_m$.

To use the theorem, we must revise one step in the proof which differentiates the semantic intersection from semantic containment. Indeed, with the semantic intersection, no region is contained in the query, and, therefore, no region formula can be presented as $Q \wedge a_i$. For the case $m = 1$, we have $Q_r = Q - R_1 = Q - Q \wedge R_1$. The constraint formula $Q \wedge R_1$ has one-term difference from query Q too, but is contained in Q. Hence, it can be represented as $Q \wedge a_1$. Therefore, $Q_r = Q \wedge \neg a_1$. The case $m > 1$ of the proof is derived in a similar way.

Example 4. As region "caching $\wedge$ query" has one-term difference from the query "optimal $\wedge$ query", the region can report the portion "optimal $\wedge$ query $\wedge$ caching" to the user and construct the query remainder "optimal $\wedge$ query $\wedge \neg$ caching". Similarly, the region with formula a has one-term difference from query b. Therefore, the portion $a \wedge b$ is reported, and the query remainder is set to $b \wedge \neg a$.

This feature of semantic regions with one-term difference from the query in constraining the query remainder leads us to a double-scan evaluation of the query against the cache contents. The first, fast scan over the region signatures identifies all regions with one-term difference in order to quickly construct the query remainder and to produce the first partial answer. The second, slow scan checks whether other intersection cases can enrich the partial answer. The two scans over the region signatures differ in the filtering function applied to the region signatures.

Each region R filtered during the first scan should have at most one-term difference from the query. Therefore, if the region signature has $|S_R|$ bits set to one, and its intersection with the query signature has $|S_R \cap S_Q|$ such bits, the difference between the two numbers should be at most k bits, where k is the number of bits set to one in a term signature. The following theorem states this fact explicitly.

Theorem 5. *If region R has one-term difference from query Q, then*

$$|S_R \cap S_Q| \geq |S_R| - k. \tag{2}$$

The first scan verifies the condition (2) on the region signatures. If the condition holds for a region signature, the region formula is checked for a one-term difference. As in the case of semantic containment, a false drop appears if condition (2) holds but the region formula does not provide a one-term difference. In Sect. 5, we report the results of some experiments and show that the number of false drops when verifying the condition (2) can be kept small through some appropriate choices of signature file parameters, calculated using formula (1).

The second scan detects regions where the corresponding formulas differ in two and more terms. These regions do not qualify to constrain the query remainder. By analogy with one-term difference, a region R where the corresponding formula differs in $l, l \geq 2$ terms from the query, satisfies the condition

$$|S_R \cap S_Q| \geq |S_R| - k \cdot l. \tag{3}$$

However, this condition can not be used to full extent for the second scan. First, the condition (3) loses its importance for increasing values of k. In fact, a typical Web query or region formula has an average of three or four terms. Condition (3) is often reduced to a simple $|S_R \cap S_Q| \geq 0$. This would sweep all the region signatures, resulting in a large number of false drops, and a high filtering overhead. Second, regions differing in two or more terms from the query, usually contribute much less to the answer than regions with a one-term difference. Third, the tuples they contribute will be duplicated in the answer to query remainder, as their formulas were not excluded from the remainder. Therefore, the second scan can be omitted for some of the Web-based data repositories. For instance, if we know that regions with two-term difference contribute less than 1% to the partial answer (the Library of Congress discussed in Sect. 5 is such a repository), the query processing can stop after the first scan.

If the regions with two-term difference appear to be useful for partial answers, we consider two options for the second scan:

- $|S_R \cap S_Q| \geq |S_R| - 2k$: this option fetches mainly the regions with two-term difference from the query. Therefore, some regions differing in more terms will not be fetched.
- $|S_R \cap S_Q| \geq 0$: all region formulas satisfy this option, yielding to numerous false drops. However, *all* tuples in the cache matching the query are retrieved.

In most cases, the first option is more preferable as it provides a good tradeoff between the number of false drops and the number of tuples retrieved. The second option can be used if the cache space is very small, or if the application is keen to retrieve all tuples from the cache matching the query.

Region coalescing and region replacement. The semantic intersection gives a new extension to the coalescing strategy. The strategy can coalesce the query and a region when their unified formula is a conjunction. For instance, it can coalesce query $a \wedge b$ and the region $a \wedge \neg b$ in one region. Three conditions are sufficient: 1) the region has a one-term difference, say a_1, from the query; 2) symmetrically, the query has a one-term difference, say a_2, from the region; 3) a_1 is a negation of $a_2{}^2$.

The replacement policy, as designed for the semantic containment, remains the same for the semantic intersection. When a new query is issued, any semantic region in the cache has its replacement value updated, i. e. towards V_{top}, proportionally to the region involvement in the answer.

The second caching algorithm covers both relations between the query and semantic regions, that is, the semantic containment, as discussed in Sect. 3, and the semantic intersection, as discussed above. Moreover, the algorithm does not distinguish between regions providing the query containment and semantic intersection. Both cases are processed uniformly.

---

[2] Note, however, that a_1 and a_2 have independent signatures due to the cache architecture (see Sect. 2).

Caching algorithm 2. *Input*: cache with semantic regions and query Q.
   Output: answer to Q and the cache updated.

1. (*First scan*) Check the query signature against the region signatures in the cache.
2. $S_Q = S_R$: if there is a region which formula is equivalent to the query, return the region contents as the answer. Update the replacement value of the region and stop.
3. $S_Q \cap S_R = S_R$: if one or more regions contain the query, choose the region with the minimal cardinality. Scan the region contents and return the tuples matching the query. Update the replacement value of the region and stop.
4. $|S_Q \cap S_R| \geq |S_R| - k$: Identify all regions, say $R_0, \ldots, R_m$, $m \geq 0$, with one-term difference from the query. Return the tuples matching the query in the semantic regions of $R_0, \ldots, R_m$, discarding duplications. Construct the query remainder Q_r as follows:
   - Set the query remainder to query Q.
   - For each region R_i, $i = 0, \ldots, m$, calculate the difference a_i from the query and constrain the query remainder with $\neg a_i$.
   Send the query remainder to the server.
5. (*Second, optional scan*) Scan the region signatures with the condition T, where T is a choice between $|S_R \cap S_Q| \geq |S_R| - 2k$ and $|S_R \cap S_Q| \geq 0$. For each region R fetched, check the $Q \cap R$ formula intersection. If the formula is not null, report the tuples from the region contents matching the query.
6. When the answer to the query remainder Q_r is received, update the cache as follows.
   - If regions $R_{i_1}, \ldots, R_{i_p}$ contain the query, replace them with a new region with formula Q.
   - If a region R is complement to query Q and formula $R \cup Q$ is a disjunction, substitute R and Q with a new region.
   - Otherwise, add a new region to the cache with the formula Q_r.
   Update the replacement values for all regions contributed to the partial answer.

Example 6. Assume the cache contains the regions with formulas $a \wedge b$, $c \wedge d \wedge \neg e$, and the user query be $b \wedge c$; Figure 6.a shows the regions with their replacement values (assuming $V_{top} = 7$) and the query. The first scan detects that the region $a \wedge b$ has a one-term difference from the query and can constrain the query remainder Q_r which is $b \wedge c \wedge \neg a$. All tuples from the region contents matching the query report their partial answer. The second scan detects the semantic intersection for region $c \wedge d \wedge \neg e$. The region contents is scanned and tuples matching this query complete the partial answer.

   Once the answer to the query remainder Q_r is received, a new region with the formula $c \wedge d \wedge \neg e$ is created. The replacement value is set to $V_{top} = 8$. Also, both regions $a \wedge b$ and $c \wedge d \wedge \neg e$ have their replacement values updated, in proportion to their contribution to the answer (see Fig. 6.b).

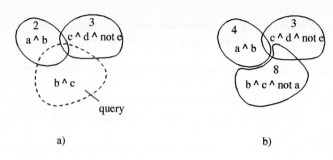

Fig. 6. Region coalescing for the semantic intersection: a) Query $c \wedge d$ is issued; b) after the query has been issued

5 Experiments

We have conducted a number of experiments to test the caching algorithms developed in the paper. As a Web information server, we have used the Library of Congress (about 6.3 million records) with the search page available at http://lcweb.loc.gov/. The search page supports one to three terms in the query; the first term must not be negated, while others can. Since no full-text retrieval is available, tuples are rather small with respect to the cache size. For any query, terms were randomly chosen from a dictionary containing some 80 terms in the field of computer science; these terms were taken from the Yahoo Classifier.[3]

Any query in the experiments contained one to three terms, with an equal probability for each case. If a second or third term was included, it was negated in one of three cases. Each algorithm tested in the experiments started with an empty cache and used the first queries just to fill it. Once the cache becomes full, the main parameters of the cache were evaluated during a series of s sequential queries. The main parameters, including values for F and k of the signature generation, are reported in Table 1.

Table 1. Experiment parameters

Parameter	Description	Value
S	Cache size	256k-1024k
F	Number of bits in signature	48-96 bits
k	Number of set bits for simple word	5-10 bits
s	Length of query series	100

In the experiments we have tested three main parameters:

Cache efficiency: the average portion of the answer provided from the cache. For one query, the efficiency is evaluated as r_c/r_t, where r_t is the total number

---

[3] http://www.yahoo.com/Science/Computer_Science/.

of answer tuples, and r_c is the number of the answer tuples retrieved from the cache. For a series of s queries, the cache efficiency is the mean of individual query efficiencies.

Duplication ratio: for one query it is evaluated as $(S - S_d)/S$, where S is the total cache size and S_d is the cache size when all tuple duplications are removed.

False drop ratio: the average number of false drops per query, taken over a series of s queries.

We have tested the following algorithms: Algorithm 1 (Sect. 3) and Algorithm 2 (Sect. 4, with the first scan only) combined with the coalescing[4] and no-coalescing strategies; in the graphs, they are named Coal-1, NoCoal-1, Coal-2 and NoCoal-2; The algorithms are tested over the parameters : (1) signature length F and the number k of bits set to one in a term signature; (2) cache size.

The following graphs summarize the experiment results.

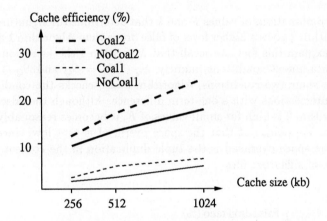

Fig. 7. Cache efficiency experiments

The cache efficiency grows almost linearly for all combinations, as the cache size increases (see Fig. 7). The efficiency is higher using Algorithm 2 as semantic intersection is more frequent than semantic containment. Similarly, the coalescing strategy works better than the no-coalescing strategy.

The duplication ratio graphs (see Fig. 8) demonstrate the difference between the coalescing and no-coalescing strategies. The ratio is higher applying the no-coalescing strategy which keeps different regions for queries which may semantically intersect. Algorithm 2 is slightly better – with respect to minimizing tuple duplications – than Algorithm 1 because it also detects query complements (though, this rarely happens).

---

[4] In all tests, the coalescing strategy was adopted so that regions are coalesced if the new region size is not superior to 10% of the total cache size.

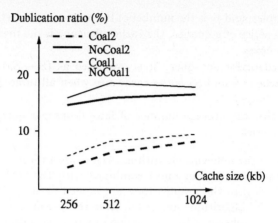

Fig. 8. Tuple duplication ratio in the cache

For all combinations of values F and k that determine the signature construction, Algorithm 2 gives a higher level of false drops than Algorithm 1 as shown in Fig. 9. To explain this fact, we recall that Algorithm 1 checks region signatures for two containment conditions, namely, $S_Q \cap S_R = S_Q$ and $S_Q \cap S_R = S_R$. Besides the same two conditions, Algorithm 2 also checks the condition (2) to detect all intersections with a one-term difference. Although the false drop ratio using Algorithm 2 is high for small values of F, it becomes reasonably low when F increases. We point out that the space overhead is kept low, since the main source of the space overhead is the tuple duplication in the content parts, and not the size of signature files.

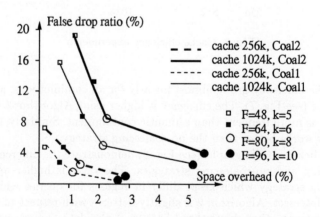

Fig. 9. False drops versus the space overhead

Our main conclusions from the experiments can be summarized as follows:

1. Algorithm 2 provides both a higher cache efficiency and a lower duplication ratio, when compared to Algorithm 1. The false drop ratio in Algorithm 2 is higher, but the difference is small. It can be neglected when using a slightly enlarged signature length.
2. The coalescing strategy is always better than the no-coalescing strategy when looking at the tuple duplications and the number of regions in the cache.
3. The experiments demonstrated the difference between the two major sources of space overhead in the cache, namely, the use of signature files and tuple duplications. For typical Web queries, the signature files do not occupy much space, allowing control of the false drop ratio by the appropriate values of F and k. However, tuple duplications can considerably reduce the cache efficiency. It is extremely worthwhile to reduce the duplication ratio.

6 Conclusion and Open Issues

We have presented a new caching mechanism for conjunctive Web queries as realized in the Knowledge Broker system [3]. The mechanism is based on signature files and allows for an efficient reuse of already obtained answers. Two caching algorithms were presented that cope with the relations of semantic containment as well as semantic intersection between a user query and the semantic regions, respectively.

The basic query model covers conjunctive queries only. With the superimposed coding used in signature files, the model cannot be extended to process disjunctive queries directly in the cache. Such a query must be split into conjunctions beforehand. A further analysis of signature file methods to overcome this problem is a real challenge.

The caching mechanism works efficiently for a single Web repository. In the case of a large set of different, possibly heterogeneous Web repositories, the cache management becomes more complicated. The attempt to put an additional constraint like "server=<repository-name>" does not solve the problem. It would change the query processing completely: the key element in the proposed caching mechanism is based on a one-term difference between the query and the semantic regions! Our plans are to study this problem so that we can adopt the signature method properly.

References

1. S. Adali, K. S. Candan, Y. Papakonstantinou, V. S. Subrahmanian. Query Caching and Optimization in Distributed Mediator Systems. In *Proc. SIGMOD '96 Conf.*, pp. 137–148, 1996.
2. R. Alonso, D. Barbara, H. Garcia-Molina. Data Caching Issues in an Information Retrieval System. In *ACM TODS* **15**: 3, 359–384, 1990.
3. J.-M. Andreoli, U. M. Borghoff, R. Pareschi. Constraint-Based Knowledge Broker Model: Semantics, Implementation and Analysis. In *Journal of Symbolic Computation* bf 21: 4, 635–667, 1996.

498

4. Y. Arens and C. A. Knoblock. Intelligent Caching: Selecting, Representing, and Reusing Data in an Information Server. In *Proc. CIKM '94 Conf.*, Gaithersburg, MD, pp. 433–438, 1994.

5. U. M. Borghoff, R. Pareschi, F. Arcelli, F. Formato. Constraint-Based Protocols for Distributed Problem Solving. In *Science of Computer Programming* 30, 201–225, 1998.

6. M. J. Carey, M. J. Franklin, M. Livny, E. J. Shekita. Data Caching Tradeoffs in Client-Server DBMS Architectures. In *Proc. SIGMOD '91 Conf.*, pp. 357–366, 1991.

7. C.-C. K. Chang, H. Garcia-Molina, A. Paepcke. Boolean Query Mapping Across Heterogeneous Information Sources. In *IEEE TOKDE* **8**: 4, 1996.

8. C.-C. K. Chang and H. Garcia-Molina. Evaluating the Cost of Boolean Query Mapping. In *Proc. 2nd ACM Int'l. Conf. on Digital Library*, 1997.

9. S. Dar, M. J. Franklin, B. Jonsson, D. Srivastava, M. Tan. Semantic Data Caching and Replacement. In *Proc. 22nd VLDB Conf.*, Bombay, India, pp. 330–341, 1996.

10. C. Faloutsos. Signature files: Design and Performance Comparison of Some Signature Extraction Methods. In *Proc. SIGMOD '85 Conf.*, pp. 63–82, 1985.

11. C. Faloutsos and S. Christodoulakis. Signature Files: An Access Method for Documents and Its Analytical Performance Evaluation. In *ACM TOIS* **2**: 4, 267–288, 1984.

12. C. Faloutsos and S. Christodoulakis. Description and Performance Analysis of Signature File Methods for Office Filing. In *ACM TOIS* **5**: 3, 237–257, 1987.

13. P. Godfrey and J. Gryz. Semantic Query Caching For Heterogeneous Databases. In *Proc. 4th KRDB Workshop on Intelligent Access to Heterogeneous Information*, Athens, Greece, pp. 6.1–6.6, 1997.

14. H. Kitagawa, J. Fukushima, Y. Ishikawa and N. Ohbo.. Estimation of False Drops in Set-valued Object Retrieval with Signature Files. In *Proc. 4th Int'l. Conf. FODO '93*, Chicago, IL. Springer-Verlag, LNCS **730**, 146–63, 1993.

15. D. L. Lee, Y. M. Kim and G. Patel. Efficient Signature File Methods for Text Retrieval. In *IEEE TOKDE* **7**: 3, 423–435, 1995.

16. A. Y. Levi, A. Rajaraman, J. .J. Ordille. Quering Heterogeneous Information Sources Using Source Descriptions. In *Proc. 22nd VLDB Conf.*, Bombay, India, pp. 251–262, 1996.

17. P. T. Martin and J. I. Russell. Data caching strategies for distributed full text retrieval systems. In *Information Systems* **16**: 1, 1–11, 1991.

18. A. Paepcke, S. B. Cousins, H. Garcia-Molina, et al. Towards Interoperability in Digital Libraries: Overview and Selected Highlights of the Stanford Digital Library Project. In *IEEE Computer Magazine* **29**: 5, 1996.

19. Y. Papakonstantinou, A. Gupta, H. Garcia-Molina, J. Ullman. A Query Transaction Scheme for Rapid Implementation of Wrappers. In *Proc. DOOD'95 Conference*. Springer-Verlag, LNCS **1013**, 161–186, 1995.

20. Y. Papakonstantinou, H. Garcia-Molina, J. Ullman. MedMaker: A Mediation System Based on Declarative Specifications. in *Proc. ICDE'96 Conf.*, pp.132–141, 1996.

21. Ch. Reck and B. König-Ries. An Architecture for Transparent Access to Semantically Heterogeneous Information Sources. In *Proc. Cooperative Information Agents*. Springer-Verlag, LNCS **1202**, 1997.

22. A. Yoshida. MOWS: Distributed Web and Cache Server in Java. In *Computer Networks and ISDN Systems* **29**: 8–13, 965–976, 1997.

Introducing MIRA: A Retrieval Applications' Development Environment

José M. Martínez, Jesús Bescós, and Guillermo Cisneros

Grupo de Tratamiento de Imágenes, E.T.S.Ing.Telecomunicación, Universidad
Politécnica de Madrid, Cuidad Universitaria s/n, E-28040 Madrid, Spain,
{jms, jbc, gcp}@gti.upm.es,
WWW home page: http://www.gti.ssr.upm.es/

Abstract. MIRA (Multimedia Information Remote Access) is an implementation of a generic Application Development Model, demostrat-
ing the scalability of such Model. MIRA allows session management and
common working space (desktop) paradigms, allowing not only to retrieve information but also to have facilities for further handling of such
information. The MIRA Tele-research application was based on specifications from Museum curators. Hence, MIRA is currently the basis of
the BABEL network, which joins a number of Museums and Libraries.

1 Introduction

MIRA[1] (Multimedia Information Remote Access) is an implementation of a
model [1] intended to develop novel applications directed to multimedia information retrieval through telecom networks. The model (see Figure 1) allows the
development of client applications using a Functional Core that provides a wide
variety of common functional services. Once its functional services [2] are available at the Information and Service Provider sites, several applications can be
easily developed on top of them. Several heterogeneous storage systems can provide information to the Funcional Core by means of the development of gateways
conforming a Storage and Retrieval API. Application development and information provision can be done independently, and are automatically integrated (that
is, new applications are able to access existing information providers, and new
information providers may give information to existing applications) by means
of the common Funcional Core.

As WWW [3], the MIRA (Multimedia Information Remote Access) Information System addresses the problem of *multimedia data transfer* making possible
the dialogue with different information providers through a common information retrieval system. Nevertheless, some specific user groups required further
features not available in WWW environments, such as the need for the session
and common working space (desktop) paradigms, security, user management,
information filtering, and service handling. This allows to retrieve information
from different sources in a common session, and to have facilities for further study

---

[1] MIRA 1.0 ©Universidad Politécnica de Madrid, IPR M-47412 (20-06-1996).

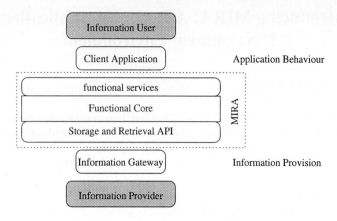

Fig. 1. Application Development Model

and analysis of the information retrieved, in a service environment. Moreover, the current focus of MIRA is the access to information stored in general storage systems mainly structured and supported by a Relational Database Management System (RDBMS), not just static information (e.g., HTML pages).

One of the aforementioned specific user groups has been Museum curators. Hence, MIRA is currently the software platform installed in the Museums and Libraries joined to the BABEL network [4] and the Tele-research client application can be downloaded by free from http://www.gti.ssr.upm.es/babel/. Its main objective is the provision of common (homogeneous) integrated access to the heterogeneous Museums' databases, providing a desktop paradigm for performing research sessions.

The paper is structured as follows: first the MIRA Functional Core is presented, together with a description of the funcional services provided for application development; then the gateway (Storage and Retrieval Module) to the different information providers (eg., databases) is described as well as the steps required to provide information to the Functional Core (and through it to the applications); finally the Tele-research application is presented.

2 MIRA Functional Core

From a functional point of view the Functional Core offers two interfaces. The first, facing the client application developer, offers a services API that includes both management (Service Engine) and data (Information Engine) services; communication services are used by the Functional Core but are not directly available to the application developer in this implementation. Management services are fully implemented in the server, and they are available via a low level application protocol (Management Transfer Protocol) laid over the Communication Services (a TCP channel, in this case). Most data services are implemented in the server (the client is only in charge of user session management), and are available through a proprietary high level application protocol (Data Transfer Protocol) laid on top of the management one.

The second interface, to the storage system, consists of a set of services that The Functional Core will use; these services are implemented in the Storage and Retrieval component of the information gateway.

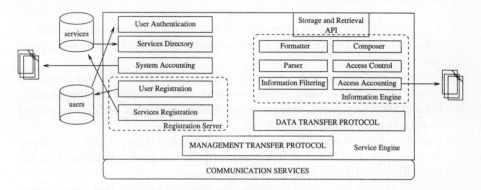

Fig. 2. MIRA Functional Core diagram

From an operational point of view (see Figure 2), each server host runs a service server (which implements the Service Engine), which integrates and channels user requests to an information server (which implements the Information Engine), linked to a particular storage system. As the system foresees the existence of multiple hosts, distributed management (users, security, accounting,...) is globally controlled by a System Service server.

Once described the location and relationships among the involved servers, we will next deepen into the functional organisation of each server, the particular services that they offer, and how they do it.

2.1 MIRA Service Engine

The main role of this component is to support the management functionality required to provide a service in a networked environment. For this purpose, first it deals with user and services registration, authentication, accounting, etc. Second, it makes use of basic communication services (IP support) to provide transfer protocols that will transport management and information data.

Each Service Server is able to operate standalone (just this server together with a set of clients); that is, to maintain its own users and services in order for the user to avoid connection to the overall system when only local data is required. Anyway, as explained in the introduction to this section, MIRA achieves global service management via the existence of a unique central Service

Server, what we have called a System Service Server. Hence, the system does not require each local server to carry out management tasks, although this feature is available (eg., for optional local management).

Service Engine modules We can identify a set modules within the Service Engine (see Figure 2), each in charge of specific tasks whose conjunction results in the offered services.

- User Registration, which allows to manage user related operations, that is, registration and deletion, and modification of specific attributes (e.g., password, profile).
- Servers Registration, which allows to register new Service Servers (intended to provide access to a new storage system), and to remove existing ones.
- Servers Directory, which maintains descriptions and other useful data related to each storage system linked to the overall system.
- User Authentication, which accesses to the user database, checks for authentication, and returns a user ticket which is afterwards sent, included into the Data Transfer Protocol, in any further request.
- System Accounting, which maintains log files that register first service operations such as a login, a password modification, or a registration, and then information operations, performed by the associated Information Engine.

Service Engine Services Attending to their functionality, and in order to avoid this maybe confusing name, we will refer to them as Management Services. We can group them into three different categories:

- Servers Management Services
  These services deal with the installation, configuration, and update of the servers that support the service environment. Access to them is provided through a set of administration tools, either locally launched (via UNIX shells), or remotely controlled (through a client application). We can group these services as follows:
  - System Management, which include services to install the System Server and register Service Servers.
  - User Management, in charge of user registration and users' parameters monitoring.
  - System Accounting, oriented to registration of service events, the basics to generate the log files to build accounting reports.
  - Server Management, that includes installation of each new Service Server (attached to an Information Server, which provides access to a Storage System), collection of information describing the added site, control of access levels to it,...
  - Service Accounting, which allow to define for each Information Engine a mask with the information services whose log is required to compose the designed reports; hence, logging of non required operations is avoided.

- Access Management Services

  These services allow a client to enter the System and launch an specific service. We can classify them as follows:

  - Client Registration, which perform authentication related tasks for a registered user that accesses via a client terminal. For this purpose, it makes use of the start-up services (see below) that return the ticket (user profile) attached to each user at registration.
  - Directory, intended to access the information maintained in the Servers Directory, in this case the information describing each storage system.
  - Start-up, in charge of the initialisation of both, the communication channel to the queried server, and the server itself.

2.2 MIRA Information Engine

The main role of this component is to offer a global data abstraction for a user accessing the Information System. The implementation of the two models required to achieve such a goal has been based on the following guidelines:

- Common Data Model: we selected a specific and simple common Document Model or Document Architecture [5] with basic content, structure, presentation, manipulation, and representation sub-models. Regarding content, we took into account the inclusion of text and long text fields, images, video-clips, and audio sequences. Structure was split into a common part -hierarchical and basic spatial relationships uniquely defined for each storage system, and hence only exchanged once, via a configuration file (see section 3.1)- and a specific part -links among internal content, and to other documents-; according to the content of the analysed databases, definition of inter-media temporal relationships was not included. Presentation was not defined inside the document, and it currently depends on the client application (e.g., *card oriented* in the case of the Tele-research one). In the same way, manipulation is currently defined by the client application. Current implementations are directed towards achieving compatibility with today's de factos standards (specifically HTML[6] and MHEG[7]).
- Common Query Model: due to the fact that both the set of valid values for some fields (thesaurus[2]) and the searching structures of the targeted databases were highly different (even when all were museums databases), it was decided to establish just a Common Query Mechanism. That means a common query language (SQL extended to take into account free search and hierarchical search capabilities), and a common graphical methodology that made up each database searching structure to guide the composition of individual per-database queries (not a single query internally parsed and translated to all the targeted databases). Hence, although this approach did

---

[2] In MIRA Configuration Files (see section 3.1), thesaurus is restricted to the hierarchical thesaurus. Nevertheless, here thesaurus refers to the more general, and correct, meaning of *closed set of valid values for a field*.

not provide a full abstraction of the searching process, it covered the aim to introduce a great level of homogeneity.

The abstraction achieved has been reinforced by the agreement (user requirements) on a single Graphical User Interface which, based on the aforementioned common models, provides a *unique manual* to search in all databases (Common Query Mechanism), and an effective global abstraction for the resulting documents (Common Data Model). Moreover, as data objects are referenced via unique identifiers, it is foreseen the provision of a Virtual Search Access Point, a database populated with information from different storage system (upon agreement on a common minimum set of fields, and associated thesaurus, for searching) that will allow for simultaneous searching with the same single query.

The adaptation of the information structures of every particular storage system to these models, is performed in the Storage & Retrieval module via a configuration file (see section 3.1)

Information Engine modules As for the Service Engine, we can distinguish several modules within the Information Engine (see Figure 2).

- The Parser, which extracts the client request from the Data Transfer Protocol, interprets it, and launches the chain of tasks that fulfils the required service.
- The Composer, which talks to the storage system via the Storage and Retrieval API in order to compose a requested document (still coded in an internal format)
- The Formatter, which translates the information provided by the Composer to the Common Data Model, finally represented via the appropriate formal representation language, a proprietary ASCII coded set of rules for the first implementations. As mentioned before, the designed document model clearly distinguishes the common structure from the specific one and the content. These specific parts are really formatted according to the defined common structure.
- Access Control, which checks the requestor's profile and provides the *source mask*, to perform the information filtering on behalf of the source [8]. This mask, defined by the Information Provider, controls the information fields that the user is allowed to access. Apart from this mask, the system considers two other ones: the *user mask*, that restricts the source mask according to user preferences; and the *terminal mask*, that restricts the source mask according to client terminal capabilities.
- Information Filtering, which merges the source, the terminal and the user mask to compose the final information filter, applied before each searching and document composition operation.
- Access Accounting, which creates access log files which afterwards are used by the Service Engine to perform access reports that may be used for statistics, billing, and other service level tasks.

– Session Manager, which maintains the parameters required for user session tracking, saving, deletion,... This module is currently the only one not fully implemented in the server; information (preferences, pointers to selected results, etc.) is locally stored in the client in order to save network resources.

Information Engine Services The internal modules just defined for the Information Engine co-ordinate their operation to offer a set of services. We have grouped them under different groups, according to the functionality they cover:

– Session Services

A session is the context into which an information access service is instantiated. The underlying functionality is responsible for maintaining state information during the user session, hence avoiding retransmission for each service invocation. State information deals with user identity, access level, session language, terminal, history,...

The main part of MIRA Session Services are implemented in the client side of the Information Engine. Available services include:

- Session initialisation and termination, which respectively correspond to the login and logout operations, centrally controlled by the System Service Server.
- System description, which informs the application about the servers available according to the profile that the user shows.
- Maintenance of personal textual annotations, introduced via a notepad window of the application.
- Maintenance of a personal results set, composed by the Unique Identifiers of the desired objects.
- Maintenance of a history of the desired queries, so that the user can keep track of the searching process.
- Maintenance of user preferences related to the overall system behaviour. Some of these preferences, the ones related to general information filtering, are considered for the composition of the user mask.

– Browsing Services

Two complementary methods are available when browsing information: searching and navigation. The first allows a somehow more direct access, but it is only really effective if we have a previous knowledge of what we are looking for. On the other hand, navigation allows a more free and intuitive browsing, but needs additional support (at application and GUI levels) for avoiding the "lost in hyperspace" and "loss of homogeneity or incoherence of obtained information" phenomena.

The following searching services provide the Common Query Mechanism, but do not directly solve the *unique query for multiple database* search problem:

- Get available and independent storage systems (eg. databases). This service is provided synchronously to the session initialisation.
- Get available entries (eg., tables) of a particular storage system.
- Get field values (eg., columns) of a particular entry.

- Get a query form: returns a query composition form, that after user edition is converted to an Object Specification (a query). This service is currently fully implemented in the client side.

Regarding navigation functionality, it is provided by just one service, the *resolve link*, which maps a Link Specification to an Object Specification that can be directly transfered to the retrieval services.

- Retrieval Services

Retrieval involves two consecutive steps offered by the correspondent services:

- Resolution: an Object Specification (really a query to the database) is mapped to a set of Unique Identifiers (UIDs).
- Access: returns the Object whose UID is provided, either complete, or filtered by any of the available customisation services (see below).

- Customisation Services

As aforementioned, three masks are provided to the Information Filtering module. Hence, three services are available to set their values:

- The source or information provider mask is used to control user access level; it is composed in the application by matching the user profile (received at login time) with the access profile associated to each available information unit of a storage system (coded in its Configuration File, later explained in section 3.1).
- The terminal mask is automatically extracted by the application, according to the measured availability of resources on a particular terminal. However, its recommended values can be modified by the user.
- The user mask is the result of the restrictions that the user applies over the source mask and the terminal mask. The application allows to carry out this operation, selecting (from the available fields left by the two mentioned masks) the fields that should appear in the object's label, in its short description, and in the full object information.

3 The MIRA Storage & Retrieval module

The Storage & Retrieval Module acts as a gateway to the different storage systems, providing a database abstraction to the Information Engine, the one that definitely dialogues with all the storage systems.

In order to design it for each database, first it is necessary to define both the local searching structure that will support the general search services, and the basic object structure as well as its associated hyperweb structure (intra-document and inter-document relationships); these features will have to be mapped onto the generic document model. The client accesses the search structure via the search support services; the object structure is defined via a Matrix Map [9], consisting of a set of structured pointers to the actual data.

As most of these services are usually static (their output does not vary often during exploitation of the information source), they are defined via configuration files that the client application should interpret. Then, during operation, other dynamic tasks, like listing the current available list of values for a specific field, translation of the supported query languages, or effective retrieval of object components matching the provided Matrix Maps, are carried out via the use of the services (functions) available through the Storage & Retrieval API. Table 1 compiles these services, the ones that the gateway programmer should provide to the Information Engine.

Table 1. MIRA Storage and Retrieval API.

Group	Services	MIRA
Session support	storage open	storage login
	storage close	storage logout
		get languages
Search support	storage entries	get configuration file
(for query edition)	storage fields	get configuration file
	storage values	list of terms
Search	storage search	query hits (in MQL)
		query identifiers (in MQL)
	storage translate	translate (private)
Navigation	storage resolve link	resolve related objects
Retrieval	storage resolve	(private)
	storage retrieve object types	get configuration file
	storage retrieve matrix map	get configuration file
	storage access fields values	retrieve card
		retrieve raw text
		retrieve image
		retrieve audio
		retrieve video

In the light of the above, the gateway development comprises two steps: first, the creation of the configuration files; and, then, the implementation of the Storage & Retrieval services listed in Table 1. Both steps are closely related, because, as we will see in the following section, this file acts as a data template that should be coherent with the object structure returned by the retrieval services.

Finally, regarding access control, the only identification information that the storage system receives with each operation is the user profile, returned by the Service Engine during authentication (see section 2.1). This is so in order to reduce the complexity in the access to the storage system, that should only deal with types of users (a set of profiles). Of course, this implies that the Information Provider relies on the Service Engine to cover all security aspects. Therefore, as the Service Engine is managed by the Service Provider, if it is not the same organization as the Information Provider, both entities must reach an agreement on security and explotation of the information.

3.1 The Configuration File

The storage system Configuration File (SSCF) allows to accommodate each storage system particularities within the MIRA Common Data Model and Common Query Mechanism. This file is currently manually written, following a quite simple syntax; afterwards, a MIRA utility (the make_cnf program) is used to generate the run-time SSCFs (one for each available language in the storage system).

The SSCF is divided in four sections:

- LANGUAGES: indicating the languages available for the storage system. This does not usually mean that the actual data are available in several languages; it just means that the searching keywords (e.g., field names) can be retrieved in these languages.
- ENTRIES: defining the search structure, that is, a set of hierarchically organised groups of available fields to search for, a set of trees of fields (we call each tree, an *entry* of the searching structure). Each field should belong to one of the types identified in Table 2. The information provider is free to select the way to organise the available searching fields, and the labels attached to identify each field, each entry, each group, each sub-group, etc. These will be the labels later shown to the user in order to guide the searching process.
- QUERY LANGUAGES: defining the optional alternative query languages intended for a professional user used to work with the native query language of a storage system. This automatically bypasses the Common Query Mechanism.
- DOCUMENT: defining the documents' structures. As an entry includes a particular subset of the entry fields, each entry could define a different document structure, that is, different content that may or not be organised in a similar way.

Searching Structure As it was previously outlined, the Searching Structure is defined in the ENTRIES section of the SSCF. Each element (i.e., line) of this section includes the storage system language-independent reference to it (only if it identifies an actual field), the element search type (see Table 2), the associated permission level (see section 2.1), and the presentation labels in the supported languages. At this point, notice that the definition of a specific search type does not imply that it is supported: this depends on the particular implementation of the Storage & Retrieval module.

The Information Provider can define several entry points (an element with type ENTRY_LIST in Table 2), each of one defining a different way to search either the overall storage system, or a specific part of it.

For example, in the case of a museum database, we may have a global entry to search through the whole database, and one entry for each department (allowing a more detailed search, as there are fields which may make sense only in one department). Also a management entry (with fields like date of acquisition, type of acquisition, price, etc) with special access permission could be considered. One could finally imagine each entry as a different view, a different database table, or even a different database, all part of a single storage system. Notice that we can achieve multiple ways to access the stored data without modifying anything from the actual databases.

Table 2. Search Types.

ENTRY_LIST	starts a search structure
LIST_OF_ITEMS	groups several search fields
TEXTUAL_FIELD	selection of several terms from a list and combine them with OR
DATE_FIELD	date field
INTERGER_FIELD	integer numerical field
DECIMAL_FIELD	real numerical field
THESAURUS_OR	hierarchical thesaurus, combined with OR in the last level
THESAURUS_AND	hierarchical thesaurus, combined with AND in the last level
FREE_TEXT_SEARCH	free search of textual fields

Document Structure The document structure is also defined in the last part of the SSCF. As explained before, the DOCUMENT section of this file intends to accommodate the particular field composition of a document to the generic rules that define the MIRA Common Data Model. For this purpose, the SSCF defines at least one document template, that can be assigned to one or more entries (i.e., views of the storage system)

Each element (i.e., field information) of the DOCUMENT section is composed by: a component type (see Table 3), that indicates the constraints that will control its presentation; three composition flags, that control the presence or not of this field into the Full Document, the Descriptor and/or the Label objects); a transfer mode flag, which indicates whether the field value attached to the document is either the actual data, or a reference to it; a permission level (see section 2.1), used to filter information according to the user profile; finally, the presentation labels in the supported languages. All these information fields should be ordered matching the result returned by the *retrieve card* service.

3.2 The MIRA Query Language

The MIRA Query Language (MQL) follows a simple syntax, defined in order to easily translate the query composed in the *Query Edition Window* of the Tele-research Application to an SQL like sentence. This translated query is the input that the Information Engine provides to the Storage & Retrieval module,

Table 3. Components Types.

CARD	starts a presentation object definition and links it to an entry point
LINK_TO_ENTRY	allows to link the object definition to additional entry points
LIST_OF_ITEMS	groups several search fields
TEXTUAL_FIELD	short text (presented in a line, in the Teleresearch Application)
DATE_FIELD	date
INTERGER_FIELD	integer numerical field
DECIMAL_FIELD	real numerical field
LONG_TEXT	preformatted ASCII text (not in Descriptors or Label Objects)
IMAGE_THUMBNAIL	image for navigation (only one in a document)
IMAGE_MINIVIEW	image (not in Descriptors or Label Objects)
IMAGE_FULLVIEW	image (not in Descriptors or Label Objects)
VIDEO	video (not in Descriptors or Label Objects)
AUDIO	audio (not in Descriptors or Label Objects)

which should translate it into the specific query language of the attached storage system.

In fact, MQL's body is just an SQL WHERE clause, extended to allow also support for hierarchical thesaurus and free text search in the same query. In this case, the MQL string header starts with a '0' character. Other header numbers correspond to the alternative query languages described in the corresponding section of the SSCF.

4 The MIRA Tele-research Application

The first application designed to test MIRA System capabilities was a tele-research application, originally intended for museum curators. From the user point of view, the application allows to access available databases, independently of their data structure, via a common interface. This section aims to give a brief description of the functionality achieved in the application.

4.1 The application flow

The application behaviour is mainly based on a series of user requirements generated during the first phases of the RACE RAMA Project [10]. These were later modified and optimised to conform the actual MIRA Tele-research Application.

The application flow begins with the login process, shown to the user via a blank screen with a login dialog. The entered login-password is sent to the Service Server whose IP address is defined in the application *server.cnf* client configuration file. This server manages authentication, and, if successful, returns, via the Management Protocol, first the user profile, and then the list of storage systems that this user is allowed to access.

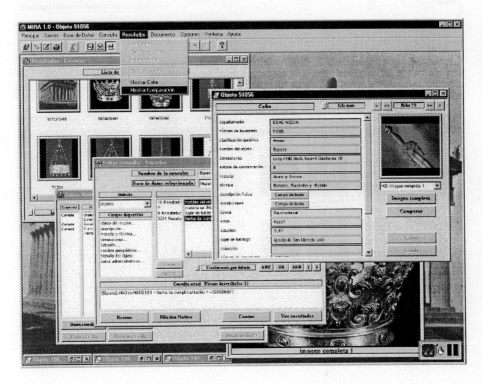

Fig. 3. The Teleresearch multi-document Application

Once the login is accepted, a Multi-Document Interface (MDI) Windows Application is presented (see Figure 3). If the user does not have any saved sessions, a new one is automatically and transparently created (notice that the client is responsible for user session management); the user is then prompted to choose the targeted storage systems among those listed as accessible. This is just a guidance to the first search, that is, new targets can be selected later on. After the selection, a session window appears (see Figure 4a), in charge of showing a summary of all the composed queries (no one at the beggining of the application), providing the means to create and edit them, and to watch their respective result sets. If the user had previous sessions saved, a selection dialog is automatically displayed. Once selected a session, its corresponding session window (usually not empty in this case) is directly presented.

When the user decides to create/edit a query directed to a particular storage system (by default, the first targeted), the application first asks the corresponding Information Engine for the associated SSCF (see section 3.1). This file will

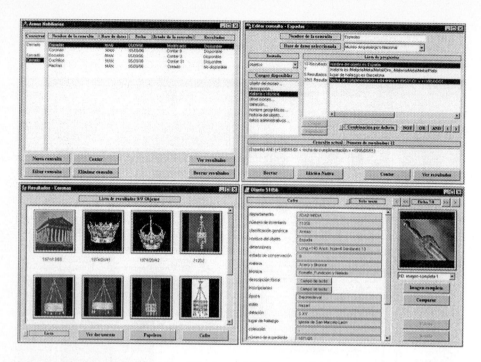

Fig. 4. Teleresearch Application Windows: (a) Session (b) Query (c) Results (d) Document

not be reloaded until a new session is started. The application reads the database structure from its SSCF and deploys it on a query window (see Figure 4b). Then, the user can start composing the desired query: as a specific search field is selected, field values are retrieved from the database, to allow for value selection. Depending on the field type, a different selection dialog is automatically displayed. Once values are selected, the composed question is added to a question list. A question is an OR combination of values from a single field. Its use was highly advised by the end users in order to achieve simplicity, scalability, and reusability of the final query, as the list of questions allows to keep track of the searching process, to refine a result set before downloading a significant amount of data (the user can ask for the count on a single question), and to compose (via their proper combination with logical operators) a wide variety of complex queries related to a common topic.

Once a query is finished and sent, the Information Engine answers with a list of descriptors (by default, a label, a thumbnail image, and just a few fields describing the full object) of all the cards that fulfil the request. A new results window (see Figure 4c) starts then displaying the retrieved descriptors as they arrive, so that the user can navigate among them, and select the ones really desired. The user can customise the fields that will compose the descriptor (label, thumbnail image or not, and short information fields), according to previous database knowledge, or to network efficiency considerations. In fact, these preferences modify the user mask (see section 2.2), which is sent to the Information Engine on every information request.

From these descriptors the user is able to ask for full information. As a document is requested, the application gets its content from the Information Engine, reads the database object structure from the SSCF, and combines both to show a document window (see Figure 4d) that controls the presentation and subsequent requests of all document content: textual and numerical fields, images, long texts, audio and video sequences, and lists of related objects through which the user can navigate.

All the aforementioned operations can be carried out for every targeted storage system exactly in the same way. Differences apply to the actual set of searching fields, and to the resulting content, but not to the searching mechanism, or to the visual layout of the final documents. The session window will keep track of all the composed queries and will allow the user to access the corresponding query window, and results window. Document windows, instead, do not directly show any reference to the storage system they come from; they conform the final product of the user research, an homogeneous information package.

Besides, the application shows a wide set of helping tools, like session handling routines, a session notepad, put-aside results set (a folder that keeps database independent pointers to the descriptors of selected documents), image, sound, and video viewers, basic image enhancement operations, a user-to-administrator messaging system, etc. Altogether achieve a common working space (desktop) to search among all targeted storage systems.

Finally, regarding customisation, we distinguish between terminal customisation (default values that control the application behaviour and presentation), and information customisation (the ability to change the user mask, one of the three elements involved in the Information Engines customisation services).

Notice that this is a session based application. Once the user has finished a working session, the application prompts for saving it. In this case, all composed queries and their current status, along with pointers to the results kept in the put-aside box, and terminal oriented preferences, are saved. The user can then start working on from this point at a later time.

5 Conclusions

This paper has presented the (Multimedia Information Remote Access), an implementation of the Information System Model described in [1]. This Model is based on a Functional Core which is the key item in an Application Development Support System to ensure scalability in any further implementation. The Funcional Core of the Model is based on an Information Engine and a Service Engine. MIRA fully implements the Information Engine and implements a reduced set of the Service Engine functionalities, the ones enough for the system to have a consistent service management.

Several applications can be developed on top of the MIRA Functional Core in order to provide access to databases plugged in via Retrieval Modules (gateways).

The MIRA Teleresearch application is currently working in Internet, providing session management as well as common working space (desktop) paradigms, allowing not only to retrieve information but also to have facilities for further study and analysis of the information retrieved.

Acknowledgements: The authors wish to thank to the Comisión Interministerial de Ciencia y Tecnología of the Spanish Goverment for its partial support to this work. We also wish to thank Museo Arqueológico Nacional of Madrid for having allowed the use of its database contents in this paper.

References

1. Martínez, J.M., Bescós, J., Cisneros, G.: Developing multimedia applications: system modeling and implementation. Multimedia Tools and Applications **6 (3)** (1998) 239–262.
2. Martínez, J.M., Bescós, J., Cisneros, G.: Functional services for application development. Video Techniques and Software for Full-Service Networks. SPIE Proc. Vol. 2915. SPIE, Boston (1996) 147–158.
3. Berners-Lee, T., Cailliau, R., Luotonen, A., Nielsen, H., Secret, A.: The World Wide Web. Communications of the ACM **37 (8)** (1994) 76–82.
4. Cisneros, G., Martínez, J.M., Bescós, J.: The BABEL project: a museums and libraries network. Proceeding of Museums and the Web (1998).
5. Steinmetz, R., Narhstedt, K.: Multimedia: computing, communications and applications. Prentice-Hall (1995).
6. Raggett, D.: HTML 3.2 Reference Specification - W3C Recommendation.
7. Meyer-Boudnik, T., Effelsberg, W.: MHEG explained. IEEE Multimedia **2 (1)** (1995) 26–38.
8. Loeb, S.: Architecting personalized delivery of multimedia information. Communications of the ACM **35 (12)** (1992) 39–50.
9. Smith, K.: Accessing multimedia network services. IEEE Communications Magazine (may, 1992) 72–80.
10. Cisneros, G., Delclaux, A.: RAMA: Remote access to museum archives. Information Services and Use **14 (4)** (1994) 171–181.

Interacting with IDL: The Adaptive Visual Interface

M. F. Costabile, F. Esposito, G. Semeraro, N. Fanizzi, S. Ferilli

Dipartimento di Informatica, Università di Bari
Via Orabona 4, 70125 Bari, Italy
{costabile,esposito,semeraro,fanizzi,ferilli}@di.uniba.it

Abstract. IDL (Intelligent Digital Library) is a prototypical intelligent digital library service that is currently being developed at the University of Bari. Among the characterizing features of IDL there are a retrieval engine and several facilities available for the library users. In this paper, we present the web-based visual environment we have developed with the aim of improving the user-library interaction. The IDL environment is equipped with some novel visual tools, that are primarily intended for inexperienced users, who represent most of the users that usually access digital libraries. Machine Learning techniques have been exploited in IDL for document analysis, classification, and understanding, as well as for building a user modeling module, that is the basic component for providing IDL with user interface adaptivity. This feature is also discussed in the paper.

1 Introduction and motivation

The rapid advance of computing power and networked connectivity is determining increasing attention on interconnected digital libraries, and on all functions they must support in order to cope with the wide variety of users who access, retrieve, and display information from such systems, and also with the nature of the stored information, that is distributed on various sources which differ in type, form and content. Users need to easily understand the kind of objects they have access to, how they can retrieve and organize them along ways that permit to make rapid decisions on what is relevant and which patterns exist among objects. Users also need to manipulate the retrieved information in order to incorporate it in their specific tasks. As a consequence, digital libraries must provide enhanced user interfaces that support this intensive interaction between users and information.

In this context, conventional interfaces, based on the view of information retrieval as an isolated task in which the user formulates a query against a homogeneous collection to obtain matching documents, are completely out of date. Indeed, this view does not correspond to the reality of users working with both digital and physical libraries for several reasons. For example, users are often unable to formulate specific questions, and they realize what they are trying to ask and how to ask it by browsing the system. This process has been called *progressive querying* in [9] and *iterative query refinement* in [24]. Moreover, users often consult multiple sources with different contents, forms, and methods of access.

Several authors agree that users interacting with a huge amount of (unknown and various) information find extremely useful some *meta-information* on the following different aspects of the stored data [24]: 1) *content*, that is, what information is stored in the source; 2) *provenance*, which refers to how the information in the source is generated and maintained, whether it is a public source or a personal archive, how frequently it is maintained, etc.; 3) *form*, i.e. the schemes for the items in the source, including their attributes and the types of values for these attributes; 4) *functionality*, that concerns the capability of the access services, such as the kinds of search supported with their performance properties; 5) *usage statistics*, that is statistics about source usage, including previous use by the same user or other ones.

IDL (Intelligent Digital Library), is a prototypical intelligent digital library service that is currently being developed at the University of Bari [11; 28]. Among the characterizing features of IDL there are a retrieval engine and several functionalities that are available to the library users. IDL exploits machine learning techniques (hence the adjective "intelligent") for document analysis, classification, and understanding, as it has been already discussed in previous works [12; 15; 29].

One of the goals of our work is to investigate effective ways for endowing the interaction environment with appropriate representations of some meta-information, particularly about content, in order to provide users with proper cues for locating the desired data. The various paradigms for representing content range from a textual description of what is stored in the information source to structured representations using some knowledge representation language. Our choice is to exploit visual techniques, whose main advantage is the capability of shifting load from user's cognitive system to the perceptual system.

We describe the web-based visual environment we have developed for IDL, in order to improve the user-library interaction. We will essentially focus the presentation on some novel visual tools which allow the representation of meta-information that can facilitate the users in retrieving data of interest. Moreover, we will discuss the user modeling module, that is the basic component for providing user interface adaptivity. This feature is achieved by automatically classifying the user exploiting machine learning techniques based on decision trees.

The paper is organized as follows. An overview of the main features and architecture of IDL is in Section 2. Section 3 presents the visual interaction environment of IDL, while Section 4 illustrates how the adaptivity of the interface is achieved through machine learning techniques. Related work is reported in Section 5, while Section 6 concludes the paper and outlines the future work.

2 IDL: a general view

According to Lesk, "a digital library is not merely a collection of electronic information" [19]. It is "a distributed technology environment that dramatically reduces barriers to the creation, dissemination, manipulation, storage, integration and reuse of information by individuals and groups" [18].

On the ground of this definition, we developed IDL as a prototypical digital library service, whose primary goal is to provide a common infrastructure that makes easy the process of creating, updating, searching, and managing *corporate* digital libraries. Here, the word *corporate* means that the different libraries are not necessarily perceived by the user as a single federated library, as in the Illinois Digital Library Initiative Project [27]. Nevertheless, all the libraries share common mechanisms for searching information, updating content, controlling user access, charging users, etc., independently of the meaning and the internal representation of information items in each digital library.

Indeed, IDL project focuses on the development of effective *middleware services* for digital libraries, and on their interoperability across heterogeneous hardware and software platforms [3].The main features of IDL are strictly related to the library functions of 1. collection, 2. organization, 3. access:

1. support for information capture - supervised learning systems are used to overcome the problem of setting cheaply and effectively information items free of the physical medium on which they are stored;
2. support for semantic indexing - again, supervised learning systems are used to automatically perform the tasks of document classification and document understanding (reconstruction of the logical structure of a document), that are necessary steps to index information items according to their content;
3. support for content understanding and interface adaptivity - IDL provides users with an added value service, which helps novice users to understand the content and the organization of a digital library through a suitable visual environment, and supports skilled users (supposed to be familiar with the digital library) in making an easy and fast retrieval of desired information items by means of an appropriate interface modality. As to the interface adaptivity, it is achieved through automated user classification based on machine learning techniques.

IDL is a digital library service. Its architecture is the typical client/server architecture of a hypertextual service on the Internet. More specifically, the current version of IDL adopts a *thin-client stateful* architecture [21]. In such a model, the application runs with only one program resident on the personal computer of the user: a Web browser. Moreover, there is no need of storing data locally, therefore no DBMS is present on the client-side of the architecture. This justifies the attribute *thin-client* given to that model.

Data are simply *grabbed* from the library host, and then presented to the user through HTML screens. These screens are dynamically generated by means of Java applets, since their content must *mirror* the current content of the repository in the library host or simply they must be generated according to the user choices. Furthermore, the architecture is called *stateful* since it is characterized by the presence of a *Learning Server* that, besides the other services related to document management, is able to infer *interaction models* concerning several classes of users from data collected in *log files* and managed by the *IDL Application Server*. A description of how the IDL Learning Server performs this task is given in Section 4.

The reasons that led us to adopt a thin-client stateful architecture, rather than a *fat-client* model, are several:

- the cost of using IDL is just that of a telephone call to the Internet Service Provider (ISP), and not to the remote host of the library, for users that do not have a permanent Internet connection;
- there is no software - to be downloaded, maintained, updated - on the PC of the user, with the exception of the client browser system;
- there is no need to download/upload data from/to the server of the library;
- the user can enter IDL from any personal computer connected to Internet through either a permanent or a dial-up connection.

A thorough description of the architecture of IDL is reported in [28].

IDL is programmed in several languages, ranging from C, C++ to Java, and it exploits the various services offered by the World Wide Web.

3 Web-based interaction environment of IDL

In this section we present the interaction environment of IDL, to which remote users may have access on the WWW. Such an environment has evolved with respect to the web interface described in [28], and has been enriched with some new visual tools, namely the *topic map* and the *tree-based interface*, that have been incorporated, in order to help a wide variety of users to search, browse, and select information from the library sources.

The first interface developed was essentially *form-based*, and allowed users to carry out the following general activities: 1) creation/deletion of a digital library; 2) management of specific digital libraries; 3) browsing/querying of a selected digital library.

The above activities can be performed by three different kinds of persons, that interact with IDL according to the different role they play in the system and, as a consequence, according to the different access rights they own. Thus, we can identify and define a hierarchy of roles, whose prerogatives range from the mere usage of the digital libraries (e.g., querying and/or retrieving by content the documents they are interested in) up to the global management of the whole corporate system, possibly performing structural modifications in it.

At the top level of this hierarchy we find the *Library Administrator*, who is unique and is at the head of the system in its entirety. The Administrator's fundamental task consists in managing and supervising the access to the various libraries involved in the system. The Administrator, in particular, is the only person who has the power of allowing a new library to join the service, or, conversely, of eliminating an already existing one (activity 1. above).

Each digital library involved in the system has its own manager, which constitutes the second role in the hierarchy and is called *Library's Custodian* or *Librarian* (in the whole paper we suppose the user is male). Each Librarian is responsible for his own digital library, and receives from the Library Administrator a proper password, by which he is able to enter the system in order to perform his tasks. This is necessary for the sake of security since Librarians have the power of modifying both the content and the structure of the libraries they manage, i.e. to add, delete or update not only documents belonging to any class in the library, but even the classes themselves, with all their search indexes (*attributes*) or the definition of each search index.

At the bottom of the hierarchy we find the *Generic User* (user for short), who is any person entering the system through Internet with the aim of consulting the available digital libraries. The user can query the library in a number of ways, in order to retrieve the documents he is interested in. Then, if it is the case, the user can display/view, in a digital format, any of the found documents. Of course, the user cannot change anything in the system, except for local copies of the documents. Each user will automatically get a personal identification code when having access to the system for the first time, and this id will identify such a user in all the future interaction sessions.

Even though the form-based interface is Web-based and turns out to be powerful and flexible in that it permits a search by a combination of index fields, it is more appropriate for users who are already acquainted with the library structure and also have some information about the library content. By observing casual users interacting with our prototype, we realized that often users performed queries whose result was null, just because they did not have any idea of the kind of documents stored in the library. Therefore, we decided to enrich the IDL interaction environment by developing some novel visual tools, that aim at allowing users to easily grasp the nature of the information stored in the available sources and the possible patterns among the objects, so that they can make rapid decisions about what they really need and how to get it.

3.1 The topic map

One of the new features of the IDL environment, that users appreciate most, is the possibility of getting a rapid overview of the content of the data stored in a library through the *topic map*. Such a visualization is actually an *interactive dynamic map* (interactive map for short), as it has been proposed in [33]. An interactive map gives a global view of either the semantic content of a set of documents or the set of documents themselves. The semantic content reflects the topics contained within the set of documents and the way they are organized to relate to each other; it is represented by a thesaurus that is built automatically from a full-text analysis.

Interactive maps exploit the metaphor of exploring a geographic territory. A collection of topics, as well as a collection of documents, is considered to be a geographical territory that contains resources, which metaphorically represent either topics or documents; maps of these territories can be drawn, where regions, cities, and roads are used to convey the structure of the set of documents: a region represents a set of topics (documents), and the size of the region reflects the number of topics (documents) in that region. Similarly, the distance between two cities reflects the similarity relationship between them: if two cities are close to each other, then the topics (documents) are strongly related (for example, documents have related contents).

Topic maps are very effective since they provide an overview of the topics identified in a collection of documents, their importance, and similarities and correlations among them. The regions of the map are the classes of the thesaurus, each class contains a set of topics represented by cities on the map. Roads between cities represent relationships between topics. In this way, topic maps provide at a glance the semantic information about a large number of documents. Moreover, they allow users to perform some queries by direct manipulation of the visual representation.

Document maps represent collections of documents generated from a user query, that may be issued on the topic map by selecting regions, cities, and roads. The cities of these maps are documents, and they are laid out such that similar or highly correlated documents are placed close to each other.

In order to generate the topic map in IDL, we need to identify the set of topics or descriptors defining the semantic content of the documents stored in one of the corporate digital libraries; such topics constitute the library *thesaurus*. There are several thesauri used in the information retrieval literature; most of them are built manually and their descriptors are selected depending on specific goals. An example is the Roget's thesaurus, that contains general descriptors. When building the library thesaurus, we have used standard techniques, also taking into account the type of documents currently stored in the library [32].

In AI_in_DL, one of the libraries in the current IDL prototype for which we provide a topic map, the documents are scientific papers that have been published in the journal IEEE Transactions on Pattern Analysis and Machine Intelligence (pami), in the Proceedings of the International Symposium on Methodologies for Intelligent Systems (ismis), and in the Proceedings of the International Conference on Machine Learning (icml). Therefore, we have used the INSPEC thesaurus containing specific terms in the field of Artificial Intelligence. This thesaurus contains 629 keywords, that are either single words or expressions made up of more words (up to five).

We have represented documents and keywords (topics) by vectors, that is a common practice in information retrieval [17; 25]. The coordinates of the document vectors and those of the topic vectors are computed in the following way: the coordinate d_i of the vector representing document D is 1 if the topic T_i was found in D, and 0 otherwise; the coordinate t_i of the vector representing topic T is 1 if document D_i contains T, and 0 otherwise.

A number of correlations can be easily computed from these vectors, and then visualized in the topic or document map. In particular, for the topic map we are interested in the number of documents to which a topic is assigned (the so called term frequency), and also in the correlation between pairs of topics, that is the number of documents to which both topics of the pair are assigned. Moreover, clustering techniques are applied to the descriptors of the thesaurus in order to generate classes of similar descriptors, that will be visualized close together in a region of the topic map. Like in [25; 33], the similarity between two topics is computed by the following formula:

$$Sim \, (T_i, \, T_k) = NT_iTk \, / \, (NT_i + NT_k - NT_iT_k)$$

where:

NT_iT_k is the number of documents to which both topics T_i and T_k are assigned,

NT_i is the number of documents to which topic T_i is assigned,

NT_k is the number of documents to which topic T_k is assigned.

The thesaurus is then partitioned in a set of classes A_1, A_2, ..., A_p, where each A_i contains descriptors that are similar, and p is a user-settable parameter. In the AI_in_DL library of the current IDL prototype, p has been set to 5, and the partition has been computed very simply. As centroid of each one of the five classes, we have chosen the five topics in our thesaurus with maximum term frequency; they are: *learning, classification, framework, noise,* and *training.* For any other topic in the thesaurus, by using the above formula we have computed its similarity with the centroid of each class, and we have assigned the topic to the class with the highest similarity. Then, we have added a sixth class, that is the special class "miscellaneous", gathering topics dissimilar to any other topic.

Two remarks are worth making about the generation of the library thesaurus and its class partitioning. The first is that, if the documents stored in the library were of general nature, we could have used other well-known techniques for building the thesaurus as well as for computing the relevance of documents with respect to topics. In our current research, the main interest is in effectively representing the topics and the related documents once a classification has been somehow performed, rather than in identifying new document classification techniques, for which we rely on already ascertained research.

The other remark is that the generation of the thesaurus is computationally expensive, but it needs to be performed only once from scratch. If the number of documents is large, it is unlikely that a new document will change the classes of the thesaurus. Therefore, adding a new document to the initial collection will only imply the re-computation of the correlations. The classes will be re-computed only after adding a large number of documents.

3.2 Interacting with the topic map

As already mentioned, our design of topic maps borrows some ideas from the interactive maps proposed in [33]. However, in the IDL environment we have used some color-based coding techniques and added several widgets to that initial design, that make more effective the overall visualization and provide adequate mechanisms for flexible interaction in a data intensive context, such as that one of an online digital library.

In the IDL topic map, cities represent topics of the thesaurus, and a region represents a set of topics, i.e., the topics in a class Ai. The distance between two cities reflects the similarity relationship between them: if two cities are close to each other, then the topics are strongly related. As a novel feature, we have adopted a color-based technique to code the importance of a topic, that depends on the number of documents that topic has been assigned to. Therefore, the rectangle used to represent a city will be drawn in an appropriate color.

Fig. 1 shows the topic map for the AI_in_DL library of the current version of IDL. As we can see, there are six regions on the map, in which topics are concentrated around the region centroid. Topics are visualized in ten colors, that range from light blue to red, where light blue is used to represent the less important topic, and red the most important one (unfortunately colors are not distinguishable in the grey level figures included in this paper). The color scale reproduced in the widget with label TOPICS shown at the top left corner in Fig. 1 has two important functions: 1) it shows the used colors and the progression from the less to the most important one (the less important is on the left of the scale, represented by the lower column); 2) it is a very useful interaction mechanism, that works as a range slider [30], giving users the possibility of quickly filtering the information on the map. Indeed, the user can filter out from the map the less important topics by simply moving the slider from left to right with the mouse. Such kind of filters is very useful, especially when the map is

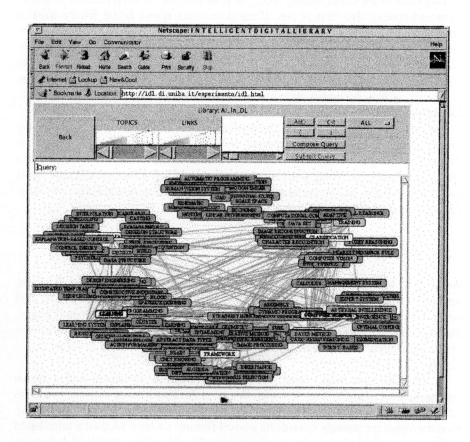

Fig. 1. Topic Map

very cluttered up, as it often happens in digital libraries that, by definition, contain huge information. Fig. 2 is similar to Fig. 1, but the TOPICS range slider has been moved of 3 positions to the right, thus eliminating less important topics (and all their links); the resulting map is much less cluttered.

A similar color-based technique has been adopted for coding a relation between pairs of topics through a road (i.e., a link) connecting two topics on the map. In our design, the link between two topics has a different color, depending on the importance of the link, that is the number of documents assigned to both linked topics. The colors are similar to those used for the topic importance and a similar widget with label LINKS, also visible in Fig. 1, is used to act as a filter on the map. This reduces the number of links shown on the map, so that users may concentrate on the most important links.

The topic map is visualized in a small window on the screen; hence, in a general

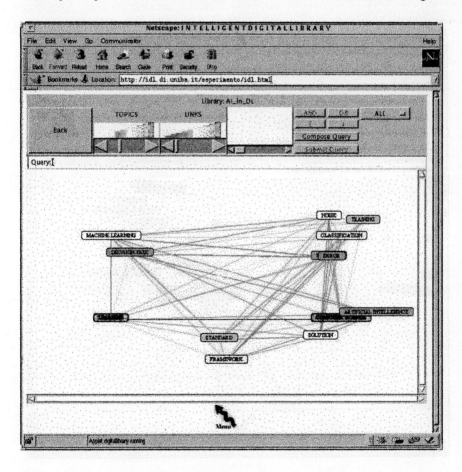

Fig. 2. A topic map in which less important topics have been hidden in order to make it less cluttered

overview many topics are hidden. A zoom mechanism is essential for allowing users a proper browsing. We designed a widget which is capable of giving a feedback about what portion of the map is currently zoomed with reference to the whole map, in a way that is similar to a moving lens. Such a widget is located next to the LINKS widget in the area above the map. It is made of two rectangles, a black one which represents the whole map and a red one, that indicates the portion of the map currently visualized. In the situation in Fig. 1, the whole map is shown, so that the border of the red rectangle overlaps the border of the rectangle representing the whole map. By shifting to right the slider below this rectangle, it is possible to reduce the area of the graph that will be visualized. If we look at Fig. 3, we see that the range slider has been shifted to right, and consequently the red rectangle is much smaller than the rectangle representing the whole map. Indeed, the topic map now visualizes a zoomed portion of the whole map shown in Fig. 1. As indicated by the red rectangle

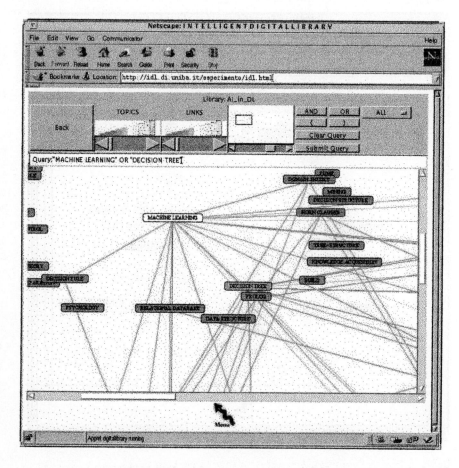

Fig. 3. A zoomed portion of the topic map with the composition of a query

in the widget, the visualized area is part of the top left region of the map in Fig. 1. The topics of such a region are now much better visible than in Fig. 1, and the red rectangle provides a useful feedback of where we are in the context of the whole map. The user can browse the zoomed map and visualize the area of interest by acting on the scroll bars at the bottom and at the right of the window showing the topic map.

Fig. 3 also illustrates the query facility that has been implemented in the topic map. We allow users to perform some queries by direct manipulation of the map. In the area above the topic map, we see six buttons next to the zoom widget. Such buttons, together with the pull down menu, are used for performing a query. Comparing this area with the same area in Fig. 1, we see that in Fig. 1 only the button "Compose Query" is enabled. By clicking on this button, the user can compose a query. Indeed, all the other buttons are now enabled, and the user can compose the query by simply clicking on a topic in the map to select it and on the buttons "AND", "OR", "(", ")", if they are needed. The pull-down menu to the right of the buttons is to be used for choosing the document class to be queried. The default item is "All", standing for all classes. The classes are listed in a pull-down menu, since they can be modified by the Librarian and the menu is dynamically generated.

During its composition, the query is shown in a proper area, as we can see in Fig. 3, where the string "MACHINE LEARNING" OR "DECISION TREE" is visible between the widget area and the map. Such a string is also editable. The user is interested in retrieving all documents containing any of the above mentioned keywords. The user can now submit the query by clicking on the button "Submit Query". The results will be visualized in a document map where the documents are shown through icons whose color indicates the relevance of the retrieved documents concerning the query, in a way similar to what has been done for the topics. By clicking on a document icon, the user can see the details of that document.

3.3 Tree-based interface

The tree-based interface provides another visual modality to both browse IDL and perform queries. The user navigates into IDL along a tree structure, starting from the root and expanding the tree step by step, so that at each node of the tree the user can make a decision whether to further explore that path or not.

Initially, the system shows the root tree, namely the root node IDL. By selecting each node, a pop-up menu appears with two items: the first item explodes the selected node, the second item provides an explanation of the meaning of the node, in order to orient the user in his choice. When expanding the root node IDL, its offsprings will show the digital libraries available in IDL.

Node IDL in Fig. 4 is not expandable anymore; the expandable nodes are shown in a blue rectangle with the label inside. If the user now selects another node among those that are still expandable, the pop-up menu appears again and the user can explode the selected node. Fig. 4 shows a situation in which the user has expanded the node AI_in_DL. In this way he has implicitly selected such a library, and the classes of documents have been displayed as a further level of the tree. Then, the user has selected the class "icml" and expanded this node, so that all available indexes on this class of documents are now displayed. The user may now perform a query by entering appropriate values for one or more of such indexes. The search values are input through a pop-up window, that appears once the user clicks on a specific index node. Once the user has inserted the search values for the selected indexes, he can now submit the query by clicking on the button "Submit" at the bottom right corner of the window.

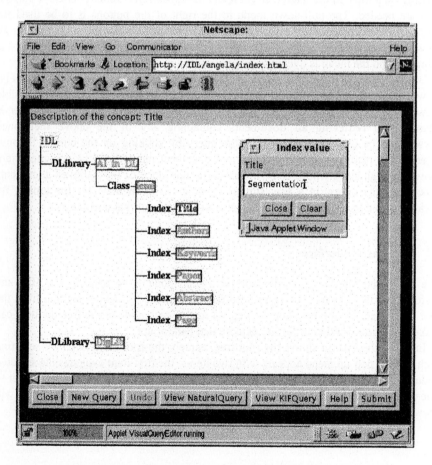

Fig. 4. Query submission with search values for Title index

Several options are available for improving the usability of this interface. As an example, the query can be visualized differently by clicking on some buttons at the bottom of the window. Such a query visualization is a useful feedback for the user.

The three different interfaces above, namely the form-based, the topic map, and the tree-based, make up the IDL interaction environment. Thanks to the IDL adaptivity feature, that will be described in the next section, the system proposes to the users the interface that it considers the more appropriate for them. Of course, users have the freedom to shift anytime to another interface, at will.

4 Interface adaptivity through IDL Learning Server

A fundamental problem to cope with when developing a system exploited by several users is to make it *adaptive* to the various kinds of users that can be recognized, with the aim of improving the overall *usability* of the system. A prototype of an intelligent component, working in a client/server way and able to automatically classify a user, is currently embedded in the Application Server of IDL. In the overall architecture of IDL, such a prototype is part of the *Learning Server*.

IDL Learning Server can be defined as a suite of learning systems that can be exploited concurrently by clients for performing several tasks, such as document analysis/classification/understanding and inference of user models. Here we focus on this last task, intended as the task of inferring user profiles by means of supervised learning methods.

In fact, each user of a system has special capabilities, skills, knowledge, preferences and goals. This is particularly true in the case of a service meant to be publicly available on the WWW like IDL. The reasons why users consult IDL can be the most disparate ones, from real needs of bibliographic search to checking the orthography of a word. After all, each user has his own profile, thus, when using the system, he will behave differently from any other user. Of course it is impossible, even for an intelligent system, to recognize each single user in order to adapt its behavior to him. Nevertheless, it is desirable that an intelligent system is able to understand which kind of user it is interacting with and tries to help him by making the accomplishment of his goal easier (through contextual helps, explanations, suitable interactions modalities etc.). As a consequence, one of the main problems concerns the definition of classes of users meaningful for the system, and the identification of the features that properly describe each user and characterize the kind of interaction.

As to the task of inferring user models, the main function of the Learning Server is to automatically assign each IDL user to one of some predefined classes, on the ground of information drawn from real interaction sessions with IDL. In the literature of human-computer interaction, this activity is known as interaction modeling [2]. This approach takes advantage of Machine Learning methods [20], since interaction modeling can be cast as a supervised learning problem by considering some user interactions with IDL as training examples for a learning system, whose goal is to induce a theory for classifying IDL users.

The classification performed by the learning server can be exploited in several ways. In IDL, it is used to associate each class of users with an interface being adequate to the user's degree of familiarity with the system, aiming at speeding up the process of understanding the organization and the content of the chosen digital library and properly assisting the user in retrieving the desired information.

Among all the possible IDL generic users, we defined three classes of users, namely *Novice*, *Expert* and *Teacher*. It is possible that, during the time, the user acquires familiarity in the use of the system, that must be able to track out potential changes of the class the user belongs to. This problem requires the ability of the system to register and identify the user. Each new user is required to fill in a digital form with personal data, and after that he receives an identity code - User ID - that he will use whenever he will enter IDL again. Correspondingly, IDL Application Server provides to create and associate each User ID with a log file, in which all the interactions of that user with IDL are stored.

Examining the data stored in the log file generated for each user during the interaction session, it is possible to extract some characteristics useful to recognize the users. Most of the identified characteristics turned out to be application dependent, while only few turned out to be system dependent. For instance, relevant characteristics are those concerning the way in which users exploit the capabilities of IDL search engine, such as date and time of session beginning, class of documents chosen, search indexes chosen, criterion for sorting the search results, number of documents obtained as results of the search, types of errors performed during the interaction with IDL.

Data stored in the log files are then exploited to train a learning system in order to induce a decision tree and a set of rules that makes up the theory used by the system to autonomously perform a classification of the users interacting with IDL.

Fig. 5 illustrates IDL Learning Server that, when a user connects to IDL, consults the available rules and compares them to the set of characteristics extracted from the log file. Fig. 6 shows the scheme of IDL Learning Server, that is based on C4.5/C4.5RULES [23]. It has been customized in order to work in a batch way to infer the classification theory from the log files, concerning the set of users whose

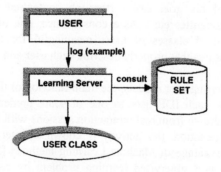

Fig. 5. IDL Learning Server

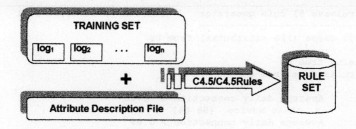

Fig. 6. The scheme of IDL Learning Server

interactions are selected to train the system. Furthermore, we are currently investigating the possibility of using incremental learning systems [13] that avoid the drawback of starting over from scratch the learning process each time new log examples become available.

A preliminary experiment concerning the classification of IDL users consisted in collecting 500 examples of interactions and generating from them a training set for the system component C4.5. As previously told, we identified three fundamental classes of users, namely Novice, Expert and Teacher. Each log file is used to draw the values taken by the attributes that describe user interactions. We considered 126 attributes. Therefore, each training example is made up of a set of 126 values and is labeled with one of the three classes Novice, Expert, Teacher. The details of the classification experiment are in [14] and not reported here for lack of space.

The system component C4.5RULES examines the decision tree produced by C4.5 (depicted in Fig. 7) and generates a set of production rules (Fig. 8) of the form L $\rightarrow$ R, where the left-hand side L is a conjunction of boolean tests, based on the attributes, while the right-hand side R denotes a class. One of the classes is also designated as a default, in order to classify those examples for which no rule's left-hand side is satisfied. Rule generation is done with the aim of improving the comprehensibility of the induced results. Indeed, in our experiment, C4.5RULES

```
C4.5 [release 5] decision tree generator  Sun Jun  2 16:04:09 1997
--------------------------------------------------------------------
Read 500 cases (126 attributes) from DF.data
Decision Tree:
  Average daily connection <= 0.09 : Novice (67.0)
  Average daily connection > 0.09 :
  | Freq of BadQuery on class Springer of DB AI_in_DL > 0.5 : Expert (122.0)
  | Freq of BadQuery on class Springer of DB AI_in_DL <= 0.5 :
  |  |    Freq of BadQuery on class Pami of DB AI_in_DL <= 0.5 : Teacher
(244.0)
  |  |    Freq of BadQuery on class Pami of DB AI_in_DL > 0.5 : Expert (67.0)
Tree saved
```

Fig. 7. The decision tree induced by C4.5

```
C4.5 [release 5] rule generator        Sun Jun  2 16:04:20 1991
----------------------------------------
Read 500 cases (126 attributes) from DF
---------------
Processing tree 0
Final rules from tree 0:

Rule 1:    Average daily connection <= 0.09
           -> class Novice  [98.0%]
Rule 4:    Average daily connection > 0.09
           Freq of BadQuery on class Springer of DB AI_in_DL > 0.5
           -> class Expert  [98.9%]
Rule 3:    Average daily connection > 0.09
           Freq of BadQuery on class Pami of DB AI_in_DL > 0.5
           -> class Expert  [98.8%]
Rule 2:    Average daily connection > 0.09
           Freq of BadQuery on class Pami of DB AI_in_DL <= 0.5
           Freq of BadQuery on class Springer of DB AI_in_DL <= 0.5
           -> class Teacher  [99.4%]
Default class: Teacher
```

Fig. 8. The rules induced by C4.5RULES

produced only 4 rules from the 7-node decision tree, that seem to be more *readable* than the original tree-structured classification model. After the training phase, whenever any user accesses IDL through a client, the log file generated during the interaction session is exploited to provide a new example that the learning server will classify on the ground of the inferred rules. The way in which rules are consulted by the learning server (and the existence of the classification rules itself) is completely transparent for the user.

On the ground of the performed user classification, the Learning Server selects a distinct type of visual user interface, regarded as the proper one for that group of users. Specifically, the Learning Server *prompts* any user recognized as a member of the class *Novice* with the topic map interface, while the tree-based interface is proposed to a user in the class *Expert* and *Teacher* users have the form-based interface as their default.

The main idea underlying the mapping between user classes and types of interfaces is that users being unfamiliar with the system need an environment that allows them to preliminarily understand the content of a (probably unknown) digital library, just like a fellow that goes into a library for the first time, while *skilled* users are supposed to already know both the organization and the type of content in the digital library, thus they wish for a powerful tool that allows them to speed up the process of search and retrieval of the specific data they are looking for. Furthermore, the choice performed by the Learning Server is not constraining for the user, who is allowed to opt for another interface whenever he wants.

The system is able to follow up the user's evolution since a single user is classified whenever he enters IDL. Thus, after a certain number of interactions, it is foreseeable that IDL will propose a different interface to the same user. In particular, we found that, after an average number of 25 interactions, the 30% of novice users were shifted to an upper class.

5 Related work

Research on digital libraries has recently received a great impulse, mainly due to the great breakthrough of the Internet and the World Wide Web.

As a consequence, the main digital library research projects share the key issue of providing users with efficient tools to "search and display desired selections from and across large collections" [26], "locate and access desired information" [1]. Furthermore, that issue was already described in the National Science Foundation Announcement about Research on Digital Libraries [22], that gave rise to the Digital Library Initiative, sponsored by NSF, ARPA and NASA (for more details, visit the URL: http://www.grainger.uiuc.edu/dli/national.html).

The IDL visual interaction environment has been influenced by these guidelines and also by recent research on information visualization, which turned out to be a way of improving the intensive interaction between users and information [4; 6; 10; 16]. In [24], a variety of studies, tools, and systems developed at Xerox PARC illustrates the style of rich interaction that users will have with digital libraries. The work proposed in this paper is a contribution in that direction.

The proposed approaches of performing queries by visual means capitalize on some previous work on visual query systems [5; 8]. In [7], a framework for multiparadigmatic visual access to databases, exploiting form-based, diagram-based, and icon-based paradigms, has been proposed. That interface also presents some adaptivity features, and proposes to the users the most appropriate visual interaction paradigm on the basis of a stored user model, even if the users always have the possibility of shifting to a different paradigm. However, user classification and modeling do not exploit machine learning techniques, that appear very appropriate for this task, as it has been shown in this paper.

The topic map and the tree-based interface have been designed with the aim of assisting those users who are unable to formulate specific questions, and that can realize what they really want and how they can retrieve it only by browsing the system. The process of formulating a query progressively, i.e. step by step, by first asking general questions, obtaining preliminary results, and then revisiting such outcomes to further direct the query in order to extract the result the user is interested in has been called *progressive querying* in [9]. The idea is similar to the *iterative query refinement* in [24]. It is an interesting feature a query system should have, and it has been exploited by the visual query tools implemented in IDL.

The interactive dynamic maps proposed in [33] were the main source of inspiration for the topic map, as we have described in Section 4. However, in the IDL environment we have improved the visualization by exploiting some color-based coding techniques and added several widgets with the aim of providing interaction mechanisms suitable for a data intensive context, such as that one of online digital libraries. Furthermore, in our system the topic map allows users to perform queries by direct manipulation, a facility that was not very well developed in [33].

The interaction through the topic map is in accordance with Shneiderman's Visual Information Seeking Mantra "Overview first, zoom and filter, then details on demand" [31]. We have implemented mechanisms for zooming and filtering working on the overview provided by the topic map. Once some documents have been retrieved, a simple click on a icon in the document map will provide detailed information on that document, up to a complete view of the whole document.

6 Conclusions and future work

Online digital libraries pose several demands due to the large number and variety of its users, and also to the nature of the stored data, that is distributed on autonomous information sources that differ in content, form, and type. One of the consequences is that digital libraries must be equipped with environments that permit a new style of rich interactions with such information-dense systems. The work presented in this paper is a contribution in this direction. More specifically, we have provided the digital library service with a web-based environment that allows the users to visualize some meta-information about the document contents in order to facilitate the task of retrieving documents of interest.

We are aware that usability is an extremely important requirement for applications having a large variety of users, such us online digital libraries. We already performed some usability evaluation, by observing a restricted sample of users interacting with the IDL prototypes developed so far and recording the main difficulties they had. The new visual tools incorporated in the IDL environment were developed in order to cope with some problems we noticed novice users had. Such users were mainly students of our undergraduate courses. We plan to conduct accurate usability testing with a larger sample of users, with different background and expertise.

As a further step to user modeling, we are going to design a framework that allows us to add information about user's topics of interests to the log files. Such additional information items will allow the IDL learning server to infer user profiles that will be profitably exploited both by personalized components for information filtering and by modules based on *push* technology.

As to the learning server, in the next future we intend to complete its development in order to integrate inductive reasoning capabilities in first-order logic.

Acknowledgments. The authors would like to thank M. Santoro and M. Zagaria for their precious collaboration in designing the Java applets of the visual environment. This work was partially funded by a MURST grant for the INTERDATA Project.

References

1. Adam, N. R., and Yesha, Y.: Guest Editors' Introduction, Special Section on Digital Libraries. IEEE Transactions on Knowledge and Data Engineering, 8 (1996) 513-514.
2. Banyon, D., and Murray, D.: Applying User Modeling to Human-Computer Interaction Design. Artificial Intelligence Review, 7 (1993) 199-225.
3. Bernstein, P. A.: Middleware: A Model for Distributed System Services, Communications of the ACM, 39(2) (1996) 86-98.
4. Card, S., Eick, S. G., and Gershon, N.: Information visualization, CHI97 Tutorial Notes, Atlanta, GA (1997).
5. Catarci, T. and Costabile, M.F., (eds.): Special Issue on Visual Query Systems. Journal of Visual Languages and Computing, 6 (1) (1995).
6. Catarci, T., and Cruz, I.F.: Special Issue on Information Visualization. ACM Sigmod Record, 25 (4) (1996).
7. Catarci, T., Chang, S.K., Costabile, M.F. , Levialdi, S. and Santucci, G.: A Graph-based Framework for Multiparadigmatic Visual Access to Databases. IEEE Transactions on Knowledge and Data Engineering, 8 (1996) 455-475.
8. Catarci, T., Costabile, M.F. , Levialdi, S. and Batini, C.: Visual Query Systems for Databases: A Survey. Journal of Visual Languages and Computing 8 (2) (1997) 215-260.
9. Chang, S.K., Costabile, M.F., and Vairo, M.: VR Queries and their Transformations in a Progressive Querying Environment. In: Proceedings of the International Workshop IDS'96, Edinburgh, July 8-10th, 1996, Springer (1996).
10. Cruz, I.F.: Taylorable information visualization. ACM Computing Surveys, 28A(4) (1996).
11. Esposito, F., Malerba, D., Semeraro, G., Antifora, C. D., and de Gennaro, G.: Information Capture and Semantic Indexing of Digital Libraries through Machine Learning Techniques. In: Proceedings of the 4th International Conference on Document Analysis and Recognition (ICDAR'97). IEEE Computer Society Press, Los Alamitos, CA (1997) 722-727.
12. Esposito, E., Malerba, D., Semeraro, G., Fanizzi, N., and Ferilli, S.: Adding Intelligence to Digital Libraries: IDL. In: Proceedings of the IJCAI-97 Workshop W3 "AI in Digital Libraries - Moving from Chaos to (More) Order", Nagoya, Japan (1997) 23-31.
13. Esposito, E., Malerba, D., Semeraro, G., and Ferilli, S.: Knowledge Revision for Document Understanding. In: Ras Z. W. and Skowron A. (eds.), Foundations of Intelligent Systems. 10th International Symposium, ISMIS'97, Charlotte, NC, USA, October 1997. LNAI 1325. Springer (1997) 619-628.
14. Esposito, E., Semeraro, G., Abbrescia, L., Fanizzi, N., Ferilli, S., and Lops, P.: Un learning server per l'induzione delle regole di classificazione degli utenti in un sistema di biblioteche elettroniche su internet. In: Proceedings AI*IA Workshop on Machine Learning, Turin (1997) 118-121 (also available in English as LACAM Internal Report).
15. Esposito, F., Malerba, D., Semeraro, G., Fanizzi, N., and Ferilli, S.: Adding Machine Learning and Knowledge Intensive Techniques to a Digital Library Service. Journal of Digital Libraries, Springer (1998) to appear.
16. Gershon, N., and Brown, J. R.: Special Report on Computer Graphic and Visualization in the Global Information Infrastructure. IEEE Computer Graphics and Applications, 16(2) (1996) 60-75.
17. Larson, R.R.: Evaluation of retrieval techniques in an experimental on-line catalog. JASIS, 43 (1991) 34-53.
18. Lesk, M.:The Digital Library: What is it? Why should it be here? Source Book on Digital Libraries. Technical Report TR 93-35, Virginia Tech, Dept. of Computer Science, Blacksburg, VA. Edited Volume (Ed. E. A. Fox). (1993).

19. Lesk, M.: Practical Digital Libraries: Books, Bytes, and Bucks. Morgan Kaufmann, San Francisco, CA (1997).
20. Moustakis, V. S., and Herrmann, J.: Where Do Machine Learning and Human-Computer Interaction Meet?. Applied Artificial Intelligence, 11 (1997) 595-609.
21. McChesney, M. C.: Banking in Cyberspace: An Investment in Itself. IEEE Spectrum, February (1997) 54-59.
22. NSF Research on Digital Library Announcement NSF 93-141 (1993).
23. Quinlan, J. R.: C4.5: Programs for Machine Learning. Morgan Kaufmann (1993).
24. Rao, R., Pedersen, J.O., Hearst, M.A., Mackinlay, J.D., Card, S.K., Masinster, L., Halvorsen, P.-K., and Robertson, G.G.: Rich interaction in the digital library. Communications of the ACM, 38 (4) (1995) 29-39
25. Salton, G., and McGill, M.J.: Introduction to Modern Information Retrieval, New York, NY, McGraw-Hill (1983).
26. Schatz, B., and Chen, H.: Building Large-Scale Digital Libraries. IEEE Comp., 29(5) (1996) 22-26.
27. Schatz, B., Mischo, W. H., Cole, T., W., Hardin, J., B., Bishop, A., P., and Chen, H.: Federating Diverse Collections of Scientific Literature. IEEE Comp., 29(5) (1996) 28-36.
28. Semeraro, G., Esposito, F., Malerba, D., Fanizzi, N., and Ferilli, S.: Machine Learning + On-line Libraries = IDL. In: C. Peters C. and Thanos C. (eds.), Research and Advanced Technology for Digital Libraries. First European Conference, ECDL'97, Pisa, Italy, Sept. 1997. LNCS 1324. Springer (1997) 195-214.
29. Semeraro, G., Esposito, F., Malerba, D., Fanizzi, N., Ferilli, S., and Lops, P.: IDL: A Prototypical Intelligent Digital Library Service. In: M. Lenzerini (ed.), AI*IA 97: Advances in Artificial Intelligence, Roma, Italy, Sept. 1997. LNAI 1321. Springer (1997) 447-450.
30. Shneiderman, B.: Dynamic queries for visual information seeking, IEEE Software, 11(6) (1994) 70-77.
31. Shneiderman, B.: The eyes have it: A task by data type taxonomy for information visualization, Proceedings of 1996 IEEE Symposium on Visual Languages, Boulder, Colorado, Sept. 1996, IEEE Computer Society Press, Los Alamitos, CA (1996) 336-343.
32. Soergel, D.: Thesauri for knowledge-based assistance in searching digital libraries, First European Conference, ECDL'97, Tutorial Notes, Pisa, Italy (1997).
33. Zizi, M., and Beaudouin-Lafon, M.: Hypermedia exploration with interactive dynamic maps. International Journal on Human-Computer Studies, 43 (1995) 441-464.

Evaluating a Visual Navigation System for a Digital Library

Anton Leouski and James Allan

Center for Intelligent Information Retrieval
Department of Computer Science
University of Massachusetts
Amherst, MA 01003   USA

leouski@cs.umass.edu, allan@cs.umass.edu

Abstract. In this paper we investigate a general purpose interactive information organization system. The system organizes documents by placing them into 1-, 2-, or 3-dimensional space based on their similarity and a spring-embedding algorithm. We begin by designing a method for estimating the quality of the organization when it is applied to a set of documents returned in response to a query. We show how the relevant documents tend to clump with each other in space. We proceed by presenting a method for measuring the amount of structure in the organization and we explain how this knowledge can be used to refine the system. We also show that increasing the dimensionality of the organization generally improves its quality. We introduce two methods for modifying the organization based on the information obtained from the user and show how such feedback improves the organization. All the analysis is done off-line without direct user intervention.

1   Introduction

An important part of a digital library is the ability to access the stored information effectively. Methods for interactive information presentation and organization have been getting much attention in recent years. In this paper we present a non-interactive approach for evaluating a graphical document organization system. This is a general purpose tool that could find important applications in the context of digital libraries when it is necessary to locate what one is interested in rapidly or to assess the content of a document group quickly. Our study of this system in an information retrieval setting is motivated by automatic search and retrieval being an important way of accessing the content of a digital library and also by the large amount of readily available experimental data.

An information retrieval system places retrieved documents in a list in the order they are most likely to be relevant: the first document is the best match to the user's query, the second is the next most likely to be helpful, and so on. We are interested in situations where this simple model breaks down – where the user is unable to find enough relevant material in the first ten retrieved documents.

In particular, we are interested in helping a searcher find all of the relevant material in the ranked list without forcing him or her to wade through all of the non-relevant material. We believe that in this case an information organization technique that arranges the retrieved data and reveals how individual documents relate to each other will help the user to isolate relevant material quickly.

In this study we investigate an interactive visualization technique where retrieved documents are placed in 3-dimensional space and positioned according to the similarity among them [5]. To begin with, the documents are represented as vectors of terms, the vector size is equal to the vocabulary size of the retrieved set. Each retrieved document's vector defines a point in a high dimensional space. The distances between these points and their relative position are strong indicators of the similarity among the corresponding documents. Unfortunately, it is difficult to visualize objects in more than three dimensions. To display the points properly and show the relationships to the user we need to reduce the number of dimensions to 1, 2, or 3. There are many different algorithms that do dimensionality reduction. We use spring-embedding in our system.

The following questions are investigated in this study:

- The Cluster Hypothesis of Information Retrieval states that "closely associated documents tend to be relevant to the same requests." [20, p.45]. In our experiments we found continued support for the hypothesis' truth in retrieved documents – relevant documents tend to appear in close proximity to each other, often forming tight "clumps" that stand apart from the rest of the material. Is the observed separation between relevant and non-relevant a natural attribute of the visualization?
- Feedback techniques enhance the separation between relevant and non-relevant documents and visualizations can capitalize on that improvement. If a searcher expends the effort to mark some documents as relevant and others as non-relevant, can the separation between the two sets be enhanced – among both the marked documents and the unmarked part of the retrieved set?
- Is a high dimensional visualization more useful than a low dimensional one for the purpose of isolating the relevant documents? That is, is a 2-D picture more helpful than its 1-D counterpart; is 3-D better than 2-D? The documents exist in an extremely high-dimensional space (e.g., thousands of dimensions). When these configurations are forced down into 2 or 3 dimensions for the purpose of visualization, some documents are shown "nearby" when they are actually unrelated. We expect that visualizing in extra dimensions will show the relationships among documents more accurately and the relevant documents will be better isolated from non-relevant ones.

We begin by discussing related studies in clustering and visualization. In Section 3 we briefly summarize the visualization technique at the core of our system and proceed to define evaluation metrics used in this work in Section 4. Section 5 describes the experimental setup and we conclude with discussion of the results in Section 6 and plans for future work.

2   Related Work

The Cluster Hypothesis was originally conceived as applying to an entire collection where it holds for only some collections [21]. There is strong evidence, however that the hypothesis is valid within a set of documents retrieved in response to a query. Two decades ago, Croft showed that the top-ranked documents usually contained a "best" cluster – one that had most of the relevant documents [10]. More recently Hearst and Pedersen showed the same effect by using Scatter/Gather to cluster the top-ranked documents presented to searchers [14].

2.1   Textual Presentations

The Scatter/Gather interface [14] presents the document clusters as text. It groups the documents into five (or another preselected number) clusters and displays them simultaneously as lists. On a large enough screen, the top several documents from each cluster are clearly visible. Another text-based visualization is presented by Leouski and Croft [16]. Their method is similar to the one used by Scatter/Gather, but the number of clusters is based on a similarity threshold. Their display looks more like a standard ranked list because they can have an arbitrarily large number of clusters (limited only by the size of the retrieved set).

2.2   Graphical Presentations

It is very common for clusters to be presented graphically. The documents are usually presented as points or objects in space with their relative positions indicating how closely they are related. Links are often drawn between highly-related documents to make the fact that there is a relationship clearer.

2-D Visualization Allan [1, 2] developed a visualization for showing the relationship between documents and parts of documents. It arrayed the documents around an oval and connected them when their similarity was strong enough. Allan's immediate goal was not to find the groups of relevant documents, but to find unusual patterns of relationships between documents.

The Vibe system [11] is a 2-D display that shows how documents relate to each other in terms of user-selected dimensions. The documents being browsed are placed in the center of a circle. The user can locate any number of terms inside the circle and along its edge, where they form "gravity wells" that attract documents depending on the significance of that terms in that document. The user can shift the location of terms and adjust their weights to better understand the relationships between the documents.

3-D Visualization High-powered graphics workstations and the visual appeal of 3-dimensional graphics have encouraged efforts to present document relationships in 3-space. The LyberWorld system [15] includes an implementation of the Vibe system described above, but presented in 3-space. The user still must select terms, but now the terms are placed on the surface of a sphere rather than the edge of a circle. The additional dimension should allow the user to see separation more readily.

Our system is similar in approach to the Bead system [8] in that both use forms of spring embedding for placing high-dimensional objects in 3-space. The Bead research did not investigate the question of separating relevant and non-relevant documents. Figure 1 shows sample visuals of our system (they are explained in more detail in later sections).

2.3 Evaluation of Presentation

In their user study, Hearst and Pederson [14] showed that users are able to choose the cluster with the largest number of relevant documents using the textual summaries Scatter/Gather creates. This analysis does not apply in our situation, as we neither create clusters nor create any textual representations.

Our approach to evaluation carries some similarity to predictive evaluation (e.g., see Card and Moran [7]): we define a precise task (the rapid identification of relevant material) and we evaluate the system particularly for this task. We also assume a set of possible strategies for the user. However, instead of predicting the actual time that is required to execute the task using the system, we estimate the *ability* of the system to *support* the task.

3 Spring-Embedder

In order to display high-dimensional vectors, they have to be approximated by vectors in a smaller number of dimensions. We used a spring-embedding approach [12]. Our choice was rather arbitrary and any other technique (e.g., Linear Programming) is entirely possible.

The idea of spring-embedder is simple but elegant: Consider a set of points in a high-dimensional space and a function that defines the distance between two points. We will call this high-dimensional space t-space, where t is the actual dimension of the space. Consider also a low-dimensional space where this point set is going to be visualized e.g., 1, 2, or 3 dimensions. We call this space v-space (as in visualization). The algorithm creates a point configuration in v-space space that "mimics" the configuration in t-space – it attempts to preserve the relative distances and positions of the points in t-space. Generally, it is impossible to reproduce the same configuration *exactly* in low dimensions.

Each object in t-space is modeled with a steel ring in v-space. The rings repel each other with a constant force: the rings are pushing away from each other and the system is striving to break apart. The "break-away" does not happen because the rings are inter-connected with springs. The force constant of a spring is proportional to the original distance between points in t-space. This way a "mechanical" model is created. Left to itself the model oscillates and assumes an "optimal" final state. If two points were very close to each other in t-space, the corresponding rings are connected with a very strong spring, and they are very likely to end up close to each other. On the other hand, the rings that correspond to pairs points that are far apart have a weak link and the general repulsive force among the rings will push them apart.

Although ring placements may vary widely across oscillations, the final configuration does not usually depend on the original ring locations and these locations are randomly selected. For N objects there are $(N^2 - N)/2$ springs. If all springs are presented in the model, all rings are connected very strongly and the final configuration tend to resemble a tight "soccer-ball." To prevent this from happening and to reduce computational expense, we impose a limit on the inter-point distances in t-space. If a distance between two points in t-space exceeds a predefined threshold, such points are consider to be infinitely far apart and the corresponding rings are not connected with a spring. Indeed, this allows us to model a situation when two documents are said to be different, when at the same time they have some terms in common.

Unfortunately, selecting the right threshold is a difficult task. Changing the threshold value adds or removes springs in the model and can have a dramatic effect on visualization. This leads us to another question that we investigate in this study:

- For N objects there are $(N^2 - N)/2$ springs, so there are $(N^2 - N)/2$ different threshold values as each threshold allows an additional spring into the model. In the absence of any information, a threshold has to be chosen randomly across all $(N^2 - N)/2$ values. How much effect has a threshold value on the final configuration? How can we select the "best" threshold value, or at least limit our choice only to "good" thresholds?

4 Evaluation Method

Our proposed visualization analysis is task-oriented. For this study we define the task as *fast identification of relevant material*. Given that the user already knows some of the relevant documents, the question is: how fast could he or she identify the rest of the relevant documents from the visual image created by the system? There are two main components to this problem. First, there is the spatial configuration of the points representing the retrieved data – the amount of structure in the image, the separation between relevant and non-relevant objects. Second, there is a question of how the user goes about finding the relevant information – the user's strategy. Both of these aspects are the variables in the evaluation.

4.1 Spatial Properties

The system used in this study represents documents with objects that are floating in space. These objects form visual patterns. We are interested in spatial properties of these patterns and require some evaluation technique to quantify these properties. This section discusses what kind of properties we are interested in, establishes requirements for the evaluation technique, and suggests some statistics that might be of use. Specifically:

- Do the spatial locations appear to be random, or are they clustered? A spatial point pattern that exhibits some structure provides potentially more information than a set of randomly scattered objects. We require a statistical test to determine if the spatial pattern shows any structure.
- If the spatial pattern shows any structure, what is the extent of the structure? We require a way to quantify the amount of "clumpiness" in the point pattern. Such a statistic is crucial for this study: different observers would disagree as to the amount of structure in the point pattern. Further, the process of obtaining such judgments would be enormously expensive.
- Suppose the objects in question are of different type, e.g. relevant and non-relevant documents. Given that we do not define any cluster boundaries, how can we measure the separation between objects of different type? How can we evaluate the "purity" of the spatial structure?

In the following sections we introduce a function K that serves to measure the amount of spatial structure. We also show how the ideas behind the K function could be used to extend and adapt the notion of precision to analyze the quality of these structures.

4.2 K Function

The theory of point fields (i.e., point processes) [9, 19] introduces a simple and efficient technique for measuring spatial dependencies between different regions of a point pattern[1]. Consider a set of points in a d-dimensional space and a distance function on this space. Suppose λ is the number of points in a unit volume of space, or the *intensity* of the point field. Let $N(h)$ be the number of extra points within a distance h of a *randomly* chosen point. Then Barlett [6] defines the K function as

$$K(h) = \lambda^{-1}E(N(h)), \quad h \geq 0 , \tag{1}$$

where $E(\cdot)$ is the expectation operator on the point field. In other words, the K function is the average number of points in the point field within distance h of any point in this field, normalized by the number of points in a unit volume of space. Practically, it measures a local concentration of points, or what part of the point field on average is within distance h of any point in the point field. Ripley [17, 18] shows that the K function has properties that make it an effective summary of spatial dependence in a point field over wide range of scales.

The main application of the K function is to test if a point field exhibits any structure [19, p. 224]. Indeed, $K(h)$ is proportional to the number of points

---

[1] Random point fields are mathematical models for irregular "random" point patterns. We will use this terminology to describe the location pattern of objects corresponding to the retrieved documents.

at most h away from an arbitrary point. If this number is unusually high, we find many points in close proximity of every given point – i.e., we have clumps or clusters of points in the point field. If the number is low, we have few points in close proximity – i.e., we have gaps in the field. Because of the expectation operator in (1) these conclusions apply "on average" to the whole point field. Therefore, the K function should not be much affected by outliers. The function does not explicitly depend on point locations, making it independent of the shape of the point field.

The K function is just a metric for comparing one point field to another. To decide if the the point field has clusters, we compare this field to some configuration that is known not to have clusters. Generally, a completely random arrangement of points with neither clumps nor gaps is selected. This configuration of points is called a "random point field."

It is customary [9] to model this random point field with a Poisson point field, a configuration where a point is equally likely to occupy any location in the space of the field. The only condition is that no two points can occupy the same location in space. The K function for a d-dimensional Poisson field is defined as

$$K_{Poisson}(h) = \frac{\pi^{d/2} h^d}{\Gamma(1 + \frac{d}{2})} \tag{2}$$

It is also customary to use the following statistic $L(h)$ instead of $K(h)$:

$$L(h) = \sqrt[d]{K(h) \frac{\Gamma(1 + \frac{d}{2})}{\pi^{d/2}}}, \text{ note that } L_{Poisson}(h) \equiv h \tag{3}$$

When $L(h)$ is greater than $L_{Poisson}(h) \equiv h$, there are clumps in the point field; $L(h) < h$ implies gaps in the configuration.

The test variable

$$\tau = \max_{h \leq h_0} |L(h) - h|, \tag{4}$$

is used to test the amount of structure in the point fields, here h_0 is the upper bound on the interpoint distance. The outcome of the test is based on comparing τ with its table values [19, p. 225].

To compute the values of the K function the expectation operator in (1) is replaced with an empirical average over the N given points:

$$\hat{K}(h) = \hat{\lambda}^{-1} \sum_{i=1}^{N} \sum_{j=1}^{N} I(\|s_i - s_j\| \leq h)/N, \quad i \neq j, h \geq 0. \tag{5}$$

Here $\hat{\lambda} = N/v$ is the estimator of the intensity, v is the volume that contains the point field, s_i is the location of the ith point, and $I(x)$ is the indicator function: 1 if x is true, 0 otherwise.

4.3 Average Spatial Precision

Evaluation using recall and precision has a long history in Information Retrieval. Using the same ideas that are behind the K function we define a spatial statistic that closely resembles precision. We call this measure *spatial precision*.

Suppose we have a point field Ω_R – a set of points representing the retrieved documents. As defined by our task, some of the relevant documents are known to us, some of them are not. We are interested in how fast we could find the unknown relevant documents. We select three subsets of the point field:

- $\Omega_{KR} \subset \Omega$ – points that represent known relevant documents.
- $\Omega_{UR} \subset \Omega$ – points that represent unknown relevant documents.
- $\Omega_{UN} \subset \Omega$ – points that represent unknown non-relevant documents.

Let us define $N(r; \Omega_{KR}, \Omega_{UR}, \Omega_{UN})$ as the proportion of the documents of set Ω_{UR} among documents of both Ω_{UR} and Ω_{UN} that are at least as close to an arbitrary document of set Ω_{KR} as are the closest r documents of set Ω_{UR}. Then the spatial precision is defined as:

$$P(r; \Omega_{KR}, \Omega_{UR}, \Omega_{UN}) = E(N(r; \Omega_{KR}, \Omega_{UR}, \Omega_{UN})) \tag{6}$$

For example, pick a random known relevant document and from its location start to grow a d-dimensional sphere. Let it grow until it includes two unknown relevant documents. $P(2; \Omega_{KR}, \Omega_{UR}, \Omega_{UN})$ is the expected fraction of the unknown documents inside the sphere that are relevant. There is a particular similarity with a ranked list: given a starting point we move away from it, marking documents as we encounter them, recreating the ranking. Instead of moving in one direction, as in ranked list, we move out in all directions simultaneously. It is can be thought of as traversing a "multidimensional" ranked list. One difference is that we have several starting points that we are equally likely to choose from (i.e., members of Ω_{KR}). In this case we average the performance over all these starting points.

The *average spatial precision* is then obtained by averaging $P(\cdot)$ in (6) over the set of possible values for r:

$$\bar{P}(\Omega_{KR}, \Omega_{UR}, \Omega_{UN}) = E(P(r; \Omega_{KR}, \Omega_{UR}, \Omega_{UN})) \tag{7}$$

To compute $\bar{P}$ we replace the expectation operator in (7) with an empirical average:

$$\bar{P}(\Omega_{KR}, \Omega_{UR}, \Omega_{UN}) =$$

$$\frac{1}{|\Omega_{UR}|} \sum_{i=1}^{|\Omega_{UR}|} \frac{1}{|\Omega_{KR}|} \sum_{\forall k \in \Omega_{KR}} \frac{i}{i + \sum_{\forall n \in \Omega_{UN}} I(||k - n|| \le \rho_{i,k})}, \tag{8}$$

where $\rho_{i,k}$ is such that

$$\sum_{\forall r \in \Omega_{UR}} I(||k - r|| \le \rho_{i,k}) = i \tag{9}$$

The average spatial precision $\bar{P}$ (a function) is a generalization of "conventional" average precision (a number). The conventional definition of the average precision assumes given sets of relevant and non-relevant documents (Ω_{UR} and Ω_{UN}). It also assumes a starting point for the computation: the top of the ranked list (Ω_{KR}). In the following text unless otherwise noted we use term "precision" to mean the average spatial precision.

4.4 User's Strategy

As we mentioned at the beginning of this section, the evaluation analysis requires some assumptions about the user's strategy or how the user is looking for the relevant material. It is impossible to define the degree of separation between the relevant documents and the non-relevant documents without assuming some searching strategy first. Generally, the strategy is rather intuitive and goes unspecified. For example, consider a linear separation test – two sets of points in 2-dimensions are considered well-separated if it is possible to draw a straight line between them. Here the assumed strategy is "draw the line; consider all the points that are on one side of the line."

We have assumed a particularly user's strategy when we defined the average precision. We assumed that the user begins from an arbitrary known relevant document and looks at the closest unknown document. He or she then proceeds to the next closest document and so on. In other words, the unknown documents are reordered based on their proximity to the starting point. Average precision serves as the measure of the visualization effectiveness. It characterizes not only the spatial configuration presented by the visualization but also the user's strategy. Some experiments to validate the suggested strategy are clearly needed. This was not done for this paper.

Note that this strategy depends to some degree upon the visualization we have described. Other presentation approaches might require a different model of interaction.

5 Experiments

For this study we used TREC ad-hoc queries with the corresponding collections and relevance judgments [13]. Specifically, TREC topics 251-300 were converted into queries and run against the documents in TREC volumes 2 and 4 (2.1GB). Our intent was to study the effect that different types of queries have on the result. For each TREC topic we considered four types of queries: (1) the title of the topic; (2) the description field of the topic; (3) a query constructed by extensive analysis and expansion [3]; and (4) a query constructed from the title by expanding it using Local Context Analysis (LCA) [22].

The top 50 documents for each query were selected. Because each query behaved differently, there were four different ranked lists for each topic. We are interested in situations when there was not *enough* relevant material in the top ten documents. We ignored each run that contained too many relevant documents – it is a success already and the visualization is unnecessary. We also discarded complete failures, or runs that had just a few relevant documents. We are interested in how the visualization changes when the user's feedback about both relevant and non-relevant documents is provided. A small amount of either relevant or non-relevant data renders such analysis uninteresting. Therefore, the lists with fewer than 6 relevant documents in the top 50 or fewer than 3 or greater than 9 relevant documents in the top 10 were discarded. This resulted in 20 queries for title-only version, 24 for the description queries, 26 for the full versions, and 17 for the expanded title version.

We also collected the same data using a different set of queries on a different collection. We used TREC topics 301-350 to create the queries and ran the queries against TREC volumes 4 and 5 (2.2GB). Again four different types of queries were constructed: (1) the title of the topic; (2) the title and the description field of the topic; (3) the full version constructed by expansion [4]; and (4) the expanded version of title query. The same restrictions were imposed on the retrieved set. This resulted in 25, 27, 25, and 22 queries of each type, respectively.

5.1   Vector Generation and Embedding

For each document we created a vector V such that v_i was a $tf \cdot idf$ weight of the ith term in the document. For each query this resulted in a set of vectors in t-space, where t is the size of the vocabulary of the top 50 retrieved documents (about 3000 words in most cases).

The t-dimensional vectors were embedded in 1-, 2-, and 3-dimensional space using the spring-embedder described in Section 3. Distance between vectors was measured by the sine of the angle between the vectors. The embedded structure depended on the number of springs among objects. This number is determined by a threshold: a maximum distance between documents at which the corresponding objects are connected with a spring. For a set of 50 objects there are 1225 different spring configurations, and therefore, 1225 different embeddings.

Figure 1 shows several presentations of the 50 documents retrieved in response to a representative query. Figures 1a and 1b show that the relevant documents (dark spheres) are very well separated from the non-relevant documents (light spheres) in both 2- and 3-D embeddings of the visualization.

5.2   Threshold Selection

Nothing in the spring-embedding approach suggests a way of choosing one threshold value over another (i.e., one embedding over another). In the absence of the information we would have to randomly select one structure to show to the user. We analyze system performance by averaging precision over all possible values of threshold.

We also determine what is the probability of randomly selecting a "good" threshold value. For all queries in question and for all possible spatial embeddings (for all threshold values) we count the number of of times each average precision value occurs and normalize them over the total number of embeddings. This gives us probability distribution for precision values. If we take this distribution, fix some value of the precision ($prec_0$), and add all the values in the distribution for each point that exceeds $prec_0$, we compute the probability for an arbitrary selected spatial configuration among all possible embeddings (remember, that the embeddings vary because of the threshold) to exceed $prec_0$, or $P(prec|prec > prec_0)$

Our hypothesis is that embeddings with high spatial structure will have high precision score. Here we rely on the Cluster Hypothesis: if the spatial structure has clusters, it is likely that these clusters are "pure" clusters of relevant documents. The clusters of non-relevant documents are also possible, but "mixed" clusters are less likely. As an alternative to selecting the threshold value randomly, we choose an embedding with $\tau = \max(L(h) - h)$ in the top 20% of the values ranging over all threshold values.

5.3   Warping

One hypothesis of this work was that if the system had information about the relevance or non-relevance of some documents, it could adjust the visualization to emphasize the separation between the two classes. To this end, we implemented a form of relevance feedback to create a new set of vectors.

A subset of the 50 documents being used was presumed known and marked as relevant or not using the TREC relevance judgments. We experimented with the subsets of different sizes. The known relevant documents were averaged to create a representative relevant vector, V_R. Similarly, the remaining known non-relevant documents were averaged to create a representative non-relevant document, V_N. With $\Delta V = V_R - 0.25 \cdot V_N$, each known relevant vector was modified by adding ΔV to it and the known non-relevant vectors were modified by subtracting ΔV. Any resulting negative values were replaced by zero.

This approach is very similar to relevance feedback methods traditionally applied in Information Retrieval, but rather than modifying the query, the relevant documents themselves are modified to be brought "closer" to each other.

The vectors were modified in t-dimensional space and the entire set of 50 was then embedded in 1-, 2-, and 3-dimensional space as described previously. The hope was that unjudged relevant documents would move towards the known relevant, and unjudged non-relevant would shift towards the known non-relevant.

Figure 1c shows how the warping process can improve the separation between relevant and non-relevant documents. It shows the same documents as those in Figure 1b, but with space warping added. The relevant and non-relevant documents are still grouped apart from each other, but the location of the groups is much more easily recognizable – particularly since 10 of the documents in the presentation have already been judged.

5.4   Restraining Spheres

An advantage of a ranked list is the direction it implies: the user always knows where to start looking for relevant information (at the top of the list) and where to go to keep looking (down the list). We observed that the space warping, however effective it is in bringing together relevant documents, tends to "crowd" the objects, making the whole structure more compact and not easily separable. We developed a small modification to the warping approach that enhances separation among documents. At the same time this technique creates a general sense of direction on the object structure.

During spring-embedding, judged relevant documents were forced to lie inside a small sphere. Similarly, judged non-relevant documents were forced into another sphere positioned apart from the first one. The rest of the documents were allowed to assume any location *outside* of these spheres. In other words, we took the spring-embedded structure by the judged documents and "pulled it apart".

Figures 1d shows the effect of restraining spheres. In this particular case, the simple warping would probably be useful, but the location of unjudged relevant documents is even more obvious since the documents have been stretched.

6 Results and Analysis

We begin by assuming that the user has identified two documents: one relevant and one non-relevant. (We believe this is a reasonable strategy and almost always could be done by looking at the titles in the ranked list.) For simplicity, let us assume the user identified the highest ranked relevant and the highest ranked non-relevant document. We evaluate how quickly the user would be able to find the rest of the relevant documents starting from the known relevant one using the spatial information.

6.1 Threshold Selection

In the absence of any other information, a threshold value would have to be chosen randomly. Limiting our choice to the embeddings with spatial structure (τ) in the top 20% has proved very effective. The average precision across all "eligible" threshold values was significantly increased by 17.2% ($p_{t-test} < 10^{-5}$). The solid line on Figures 2a and 2b show how the threshold selection procedure increases the probability of randomly choosing a high quality spatial structure without any information supplied by the user. The effect is also consistent across relevance feedback methods. Note that there is almost no change in maximum and minimum values of precision. It means the method does not limit our choices of quality on the spatial structure: it just makes it more probable we will select a "good" one.

6.2 Comparison to Ranked List

Table 1 shows average precision values for different query sets in different dimensions. (Recall that spatial precision is used.) The ranked list is treated as an embedding in 1-dimension where each document is positioned on a line according

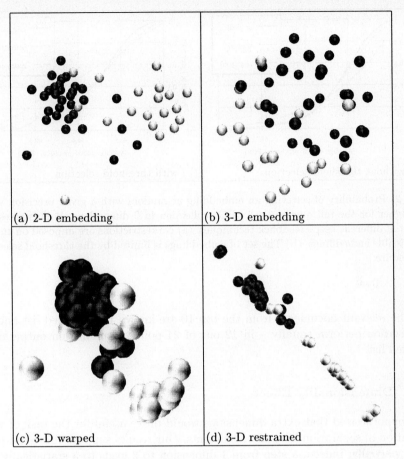

Fig. 1. Visualization of retrieved documents for one of the queries. Both 2- and 3-space embeddings are shown, plus two variations on the 3-space. Relevant documents are shown as black spheres; non-relevant as grey.

to its rank value. In this table, the numbers for the ranked list are always better than the numbers for the embedded structures. However, there are several important points to consider. First, the precision numbers for spatial embeddings are averaged across many different configurations. If only the best possible precision value is considered for each query, the precision numbers are about 75-80% (20% higher than for the ranked list). Second, the threshold selection procedure significantly improves the result. Third, the actual numbers are not that different. For example, compare the first and the last columns with numbers. For each query we are considering 50 documents. There are 18 relevant documents on average. A difference of 6% means that the user will consider one extra non-relevant document before finding all the relevant ones. Last, in this experiment we assumed that only the top ranked relevant document is known. Table 3 shows that when

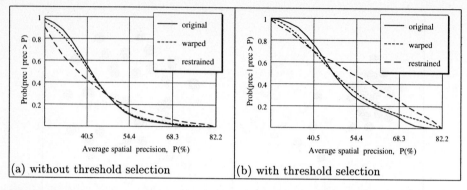

Fig. 2. Probability of selecting an embedding at random with a given precision value or higher for the full queries on TREC5 collection in 2 dimensions. It illustrates the effect of different user's feedback techniques. (a) No restrictions are imposed on the set of possible embeddings. (b) The set of embeddings is limited by the threshold selection procedure.

all the relevant documents from the top 10 are known both ranked list and visualization perform equally – in 12 out of 24 points visualization outperforms ranked list.

6.3 Dimensionality Effect

We hypothesized that extra dimensions would prove useful for the task of visualization of separation between documents. Our results support this hypothesis only partially. Indeed, a step from 1 dimension to 2 leads to a statistically significant jump of 23.1% in precision ($p < 10^{-5}$). The difference between 2- and 3-dimensional embeddings is 1.1%, and this result, however consistent, is not significant. (It is significant by the sign test, but not by the t-test. The cut-off value of $p = 0.05$ is used in both tests.)

Figure 3 shows how an increase in dimensionality of embedding leads to a general growth in precision. It is difficult to see, but the maximum precision value for 1-D is higher than for 2-D or 3-D. It means that a better separation between relevant and non-relevant documents could be achieved in 1-dimension than in 2- or 3-dimensions. However, to randomly select a high precision structure in 1-dimension is extremely difficult.

6.4 Interactive Embedding

We studied how the quality of the visualization changes as the system is supplied with more and more relevance information. Given the first relevant/non-relevant pair of documents, we use it to warp the embedding space and apply the restraining spheres. Then we add the information about the next relevant/non-relevant

Table 1. Visualization quality evaluation of different query sets in different dimensions. Percent of average precision is shown. The first column is for the system's ranked list. The second column is for the original structure in t-dimensional space. The third column shows the result of spring-embedding. The last column is for embedding with threshold selection done by τ measure. The relevance judgments for two documents are known to the system – the top ranked both relevant and non-relevant documents.

Queries		Rank List	t-D space	Embedding w/o threshold selection			Embedding w/ threshold selection		
				1-D	2-D	3-D	1-D	2-D	3-D
TREC5	Title	63.0	43.8	38.0	41.8	41.8	42.5	58.2	59.1
	Desc.	54.7	42.1	39.2	42.1	42.1	41.0	51.3	52.2
	Full	58.4	53.1	45.3	46.3	46.7	47.0	49.9	50.9
	Exp. Title	66.6	60.0	46.6	48.5	48.5	49.0	57.3	59.7
TREC6	Title	58.8	52.1	44.7	47.5	47.8	46.9	57.6	59.9
	Desc.	57.7	48.2	39.8	44.0	44.6	41.7	54.8	55.3
	Full	68.6	53.9	42.5	48.8	49.5	43.4	57.9	59.4
	Exp. Title	64.3	52.0	42.3	45.5	45.9	44.0	55.9	59.0

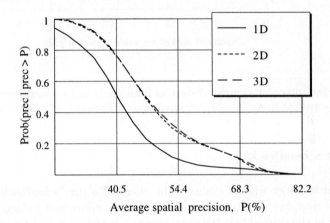

Fig. 3. Probability of selecting an embedding with a given precision value or higher for the full queries on TREC5 collection. The effect of different dimensions on the original embedding is illustrated. The set of embeddings is limited by the threshold selection procedure. The values on X-axis are averaged over the query set.

pair. And so on. Table 2 and Figure 4 illustrate how the average precision increases as more data become available to the system. We show the average precision computed starting from five top ranked relevant documents. The warping does not have any effect after the first two steps. The restraining spheres keep pulling the documents apart; however, their influence is also diminishing.

Table 2. Average precision computed starting from the first 5 relevant documents. The retrieved documents from TREC5/full queries are embedded in 2 dimensions. The first column of numbers is for the case when no feedback has been yet received.

Type of feedback	Number of pairs judged				
	0	1	2	3	5
warping	49.3	50.5	51.4	51.4	51.5
restraining	49.3	49.9	51.4	52.3	53.4

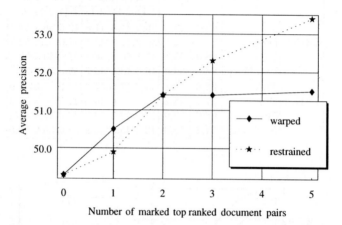

Fig. 4. Average precision computed starting from the first 5 relevant documents. The retrieved documents from TREC5/full queries are embedded in 2 dimensions.

6.5 User's Feedback

Our second strategy was to evaluate the effect of a user's feedback on the visualization. Suppose the user extended his or her effort and judged the top 10 documents in the ranked list. We are interested in how fast it is possible to identify the rest of the relevant material starting from the known relevant documents. We compare the effects warping and restraining have on this task.

From Table 3 we conclude that warping did not do as well as we expected. It increased average precision by 1.1% consistently, but not significantly ($p_{sign} <$ 0.02 and $p_{t-test} < 0.37$). It actually *hurt* precision in 3D. The effect of warping together with restraining was more profound and nearly always beneficial. The procedure significantly increased precision by 7.4% ($p_{sign} < 0.001$ and $p_{t-test} <$ 0.037).

Figures 2a and 2b show that feedback techniques increase the probability of selecting an embedded structure with high precision value. The growth is observed both with and without threshold selection, but with threshold selection the difference between restrained and original cases is more prominent.

Table 3. Relevance feedback effect on different queries in different dimensions. Percent of average spatial precision is shown. The threshold selection procedure was applied.

Queries		Rank List	Embedded in	Original	Warping	Restraining
TREC5	Title	46.8	1-D	35.7	36.2 (+1.3%)	31.5 (-11.7%)
			2-D	47.3	48.9 (+3.3%)	40.7 (-14.0%)
			3-D	48.4	50.3 (+3.9%)	40.2 (-17.0%)
	Desc.	40.8	1-D	38.6	39.8 (+3.3%)	37.1 (-3.1%)
			2-D	48.5	48.8 (+0.6%)	49.6 (+2.2%)
			3-D	49.6	48.3 (-2.5%)	47.3 (-4.5%)
	Full	43.1	1-D	41.9	42.4 (+1.2%)	47.3 (+12.8%)
			2-D	45.9	47.1 (+2.8%)	52.0 (+13.4%)
			3-D	46.1	47.0 (+2.0%)	47.5 (+3.0%)
	Exp. Title	42.5	1-D	42.4	42.7 (+0.6%)	51.7 (+22.1%)
			2-D	46.2	46.8 (+1.4%)	54.4 (+17.8%)
			3-D	46.6	46.2 (-0.8%)	52.4 (+12.5%)
TREC6	Title	50.6	1-D	42.9	45.0 (+4.8%)	45.7 (+6.6%)
			2-D	53.6	53.9 (+0.7%)	57.4 (+7.2%)
			3-D	55.9	55.4 (-0.9%)	58.9 (+5.5%)
	Desc.+Title	45.7	1-D	37.6	38.8 (+3.2%)	43.8 (+16.6%)
			2-D	49.8	51.0 (+2.4%)	56.2 (+13.0%)
			3-D	51.3	50.9 (-0.8%)	56.4 (+9.9%)
	Full	53.1	1-D	36.3	37.4 (+2.9%)	44.5 (+22.5%)
			2-D	46.6	47.0 (+0.7%)	55.3 (+18.5%)
			3-D	48.9	47.5 (-2.8%)	54.0 (+10.5%)
	Exp. Title	53.7	1-D	39.1	38.7 (-0.9%)	42.5 (+8.9%)
			2-D	48.4	49.7 (+2.8%)	56.0 (+15.7%)
			3-D	50.6	50.0 (-1.1%)	56.5 (+11.7%)

We also observed a strong effect that poorly formulated and ambiguous queries have on feedback. The restraining spheres largely decreased the precision of the embeddings generated for documents retrieved by the title queries on TREC5 collection. Expanding the "bad" queries (see "TREC5/Exp. Title" row in Table 3) to eliminate the possible ambiguity seems to alleviate the problem. The TREC6 title queries were created to be of higher quality and ranked better.

6.6 Best Case Analysis

We have also done some "best case" analysis, when instead of averaging precision over the set of possible embeddings we considered the structure with highest precision. In this case the values are about 15-20 points higher than in the average case and the system beats ranked list hands down. There are good embeddings out there – it is just difficult to find them.

7 Conclusion

In this paper we presented a non-interactive analysis of graphical interface for an information retrieval system that might be part of a digital library. Such analysis could help the researcher to isolate what part of the performance in a system-user pair is attributed to the visualization as compared to the user's skill. It could help the researcher to form an objective opinion of the system's abilities, generate clear expectations of the system performance in real life situations. We envision this approach as a companion to a user study – clearly stated hypotheses about the system actions should lead to a more accurate and potentially more productive user study.

- It has been known for at least two decades that the Cluster Hypothesis is true within the top-ranked retrieved documents. Although the system used in this study does not explicitly generate clusters, we show that the objects representing relevant documents tend to group together. Each query has, on average, about 18 relevant documents in the top 50. If the documents are randomly scattered in space, one would expect an average precision be about 27.8%. The average precision value around 50% speaks of clustering among relevant documents.

- In the context of our visualization, we confirmed the hypothesis that relevance feedback methods can improve separation between relevant and non-relevant documents. Figure 1 shows an example of how these methods can have a significant influence on the embedding structure.

- We have hypothesized that an extra dimension is always helpful for visualization. Our results support this hypothesis only partially. There is a clear advantage in using higher dimensions over 1-D. However, there is almost no improvement in adding an extra dimension to a 2-D visualization.

- We have introduced an evaluation technique to assess the system's performance off-line. That allowed us to collect a large amount of data to make statistically significant claims about the system's quality without requiring an extensive user study.

  However, we made an important assumption that a clear separation between relevant and non-relevant material will help the user to find the relevant material. This assumption is rather intuitive, but nevertheless a user study is necessary for its validation.

  We have also made some assumptions about the user's search strategy. An alternative strategies could result from observations of real users. Our analysis allows us to compare different strategies and select the best one for the visualization.

- The Cluster Hypothesis also helped us to select good embedding structures. As a result we show that embeddings with high clumpiness value τ tend to have higher precision.

- The "best case" analysis shows that the suggested visualization has a very high potential. It seems to be worthwhile to attempt a deeper investigation in how to make the threshold selection process more robust.

– The suggested visualization method in its current state (no robust threshold selection procedure) works on average just about as well as a ranked list for finding relevant documents. In another study [4] most of the users loved this visualization: they found it intuitive and fun to use. That study also found no difference in precision between ranked list and 3-D visualization. We provide additional support that suggests visualization is neither better nor worse than a ranked list. In this study we showed that although the visualization does not help, it at least does not hinder the actual effectiveness of the system and it has much potential to be better.

7.1 Future Work

In this study we considered only two classes of documents: relevant and non-relevant. This was caused by the lack of data of any other kind. We are looking into extending our approach into situations when the user places the relevant documents into multiple classes. That task is modeled after the interactive TREC task of "aspect retrieval."

We are planning to do more work to investigate different user strategies before attempting a real user study. The user study is an important final test of our hypotheses. We are also interested in visualizations that show how new documents relate to previously known material.

In this study we assumed that the user has already found some of the relevant documents (e.g., by means of the ranked list). We plan to look into the problem of helping the user to establish these first relevant documents. One way is to check the "clumpiest" areas of the visualization.

Acknowledgments

We would like to thank Russell Swan for the preliminary work on the 3-D spring embedder evaluated in this study.

This material is based on work supported in part by the National Science Foundation, Library of Congress and Department of Commerce under cooperative agreement number EEC-9209623. This material is also based on work supported in part by Defense Advanced Research Projects Agency/ITO under ARPA order number D468, issued by ESC/AXS contract number F19628-95-C-0235. Any opinions, findings and conclusions or recommendations expressed in this material are the authors' and do not necessarily reflect those of the sponsor.

References

1. J. Allan. *Automatic Hypertext Construction*. PhD thesis, Cornell University, January 1995. Also technical report TR95-1484.
2. J. Allan. Building hypertext using information retrieval. *Information Processing and Management*, 33(2):145–159, 1997.

3. J. Allan, J. Callan, B. Croft, L. Ballesteros, J. Broglio, J. Xu, and H. Shu. Inquery at TREC-5. In *Fifth Text REtrieval Conference (TREC-5)*, pages 119–132, 1997.
4. J. Allan, J. Callan, W. B. Croft, L. Ballesteros, D. Byrd, R. Swan, and J. Xu. Inquery does battle with TREC-6. In *Sixth Text REtrieval Conference (TREC-6)*, 1998. Forthcoming.
5. J. Allan, A. Leouski, and R. Swan. Interactive cluster visualization for information retrieval. Technical Report IR-116, CIIR, Department of Computer Science, University of Massachusetts, Amherst, 1996.
6. M. S. Barlett. The spectral analysis of two-dimensional point processes. *Biometrika*, 51:299–311, 1964.
7. S. Card and T. Moran. User technology: from pointing to pondering. In Baecker, Grudin, and B. an Greenberg, editors, *Readings in Human-Computer Interaction: towards the year 2000*. Morgan Kaufmann, 1995.
8. M. Chalmers and P. Chitson. Bead: Explorations in information visualization. In *Proceedings of ACM SIGIR*, pages 330–337, June 1992.
9. N. A. C. Cressie. *Statistics for Spatial Data*. John Willey & Sons, 1993.
10. W. B. Croft. *Organising and Searching Large Files of Documents*. PhD thesis, University of Cambridge, October 1978.
11. D. Dubin. Document analysis for visualization. In *Proceedings of ACM SIGIR*, pages 199–204, July 1995.
12. T. M. J. Fruchterman and E. M. Reingold. Graph drawing by force-directed placement. *Software–Practice and Experience*, 21(11):1129–1164, 1991.
13. D. Harman and E. Voorhees, editors. *The Fifth Text REtrieval Conference (TREC-5)*. NIST, 1997.
14. M. A. Hearst and J. O. Pedersen. Reexamining the cluster hypothesis: Scatter/gather on retrieval results. In *Proceedings of ACM SIGIR*, pages 76–84, Aug. 1996.
15. M. Hemmje, C. Kunkel, and A. Willet. LyberWorld - a visualization user interface supporting fulltext retrieval. In *Proceedings of ACM SIGIR*, pages 254–259, July 1994.
16. A. V. Leouski and W. B. Croft. An evaluation of techniques for clustering search results. Technical Report IR-76, Department of Computer Science, University of Massachusetts, Amherst, 1996.
17. B. D. Ripley. The second-order analysis of stationary point processes. *Journal of Applied Probability*, 13:255–266, 1976.
18. B. D. Ripley. Modelling spatial patterns. *Journal of the Royal Statistical Society*, 39:172–192, 1977.
19. D. Stoyan and H. Stoyan. *Fractals, Random Shapes and Point Fields*. John Willey & Sons, 1994.
20. C. J. van Rijsbergen. *Information Retrieval*. Butterworths, London, 1979. Second edition.
21. E. M. Voorhees. The cluster hypothesis revisited. In *Proceedings of ACM SIGIR*, pages 188–196, June 1985.
22. J. Xu and W. B. Croft. Querying expansion using local and global document analysis. In *Proceedings of the 19th International Conference on Research and Development in Information Retrieval*, pages 4–11, 1996.

Visualizing Document Classification:
A Search Aid for the Digital Library

Yew-Huey Liu[1], Paul Dantzig[1], Martin Sachs[1], Jim Corey[2], Mark Hinnebusch[2]
Marc Damashek[3] and Jonathan Cohen[3]

[1] IBM T.J. Watson Research Center
30 Saw Mill River Road, Hawthorne, NY 10532
[2] Florida Center For Library Automation
2002 NW 13 Street, Suit 320 Gainsville, FL 32609-3478
[3] U.S. Department of Defense
9800 Savage Road, Ft. Meade, MD 20755-6000

Abstract. The recent explosion of the internet has made digital libraries popular. The user-friendly interface of Web browsers allows a user much easier access to the digital library. However, to retrieve relevant documents from the digital library, the user is provided with a search interface consisting of one input field and one push button. Most users type in a single keyword, click the button, and hope for the best. The result of a query using this kind of search interface can consist of a large unordered set of documents, or a ranked list of documents based on the frequency of the keywords. Both lists can contain articles unrelated to user's inquiry unless a sophisticated search was performed and the user knows exactly what to look for. More sophisticated algorithms for ranking the relevance of search results may help, but what is desperately needed are software tools that can analyze the search result and manipulate large hierarchies of data graphically. In this paper, we present a language-independent document classification system for the Florida Center for Library Automation to help users analyze the search query results. Easy access through the Web is provided, as well as a graphical user interface to display the classification results.

1 Introduction

The need to process large growing collections of electronic documents has become an everyday challenge as the Web continues to grow at exponential speed. Searching and browsing are the two resource discovery paradigms mostly used to access these vast amounts of information [1]. Efficient searching and retrieval are achieved using numerous sophisticated automatic indexing and storing techniques. Unless users know exactly what they are searching for with very specific search keywords, the result lists will surely contain unrelated documents. Browsing through the results becomes a very time-consuming, tedious job. Even with a sophisticated search engine using various refinement techniques, natural language, query expansion [2, 3] or pre-categorized directories (such as Yahoo), the result lists can still contain more information than a user can handle. Various ranking algorithms for the result lists have been researched extensively over the past few years in areas such as probability and other mathematically related fields.

Despite all the efforts, it is still not enough even with better ranking algorithms. Thus, the major focus has been on the post-processing of the web search results. The advantage of post-processing is that a much smaller amount of data is processed compared to the entire web. A particular concern is the speed of the clustering algorithm and the way of presenting the data [4]. Various techniques are used to represent the hierarchy of the clustering, such as cone trees, hyperbolic trees, bulleyes or perspective walls.

Digital Library represents a tightly coupled Web environment; helping users to better interpret their search result is important to the success of Digital Library.

Document classification and clustering techniques have long been an area of interest in Information Retrieval [5, 6], but have been primarily used for improving the effectiveness and efficiency of the retrieval process. Use of the same technologies to automate browsing discovery paradigms has been explored by Maarek, etc [7]. The "Librarian's Assistance" tool they presented provides assistance in organizing sets of documents by contents. It takes inputs as unstructured set of textual objects and automatically generates a hierarchy of document clusters with which the user can interact. The primary use for their tool is the visualization of underlying structures for explanatory purposes. Their clustering process is based upon pairwise similarity between documents, which is itself inferred from a profile of representative indices for each document. Multiple-word indices that represent lexical affinities are used.

In addition, the Scatter/Gather - a cluster-based document browsing method developed at Xerox Palo Alto Research Center [8] is an alternative to ranked titles for the organization and viewing of retrieval results. The idea is to create a table of contents that changes along with a user's growing understanding of what kinds of documents are available and which are more relevant to the user's interests. The search results from any standard search engine are partitioned into k clusters. Each cluster is presented to the user with the most frequently used words in the cluster, as well as the most typical documents. The user may select (gather) one or more clusters and either display all the document titles in those clusters or ask the system to scatter the clusters again, i.e. to partition the selected subset into other k clusters. For each iteration the clusters become smaller and smaller and, hopefully, more and more interesting.

All these tools are designed to give users an overall understanding of the information corpus. They are useful in navigating and narrowing in a specific area. But the relevance information of individual documents is missing. Some search engines provide a graphical interface that shows the frequency of the search keyword and where in the document they occur. However, there is currently no tool that combines the clustering algorithm with a visualization tool and relevance information in a compact way.

A novel vector-space language-independent N-gram technique [9] for classifying documents, known as *Acquaintance*, has been used by U.S. Department of Defense to classify large quantities of electronic documents. Together with *Parentage*, another novel approach of clustering documents and displaying results in graphic format, they provide users a set of tools for document classification and clustering. They are built on the Apple Macintosh as a stand-alone document classification workstation where all the data resides locally. A user gathers his/her own data and invokes *Acquaintance* to analyze them, and then use *Parentage* to display and manipulate the results.

In an on-going joint Digital Library project between IBM and the Florida Center for Library Automation, Acquaintance and Parentage present a promising technique to help its library users to classify and cluster results of searches on it's large digital library collection. But the original design of *Acquaintance* and *Parentage* does not fit well with the distributed nature of the current digital library design where documents are kept on a large server with huge disk spaces, while clients access the Digital library through standard Web browsers.

To take advantage of the power of the server, an IBM SP system, we have redesigned the architecture and transformed the technique into a distributed client/server environment. Computationally intensive tasks are done on the server side, while simple graphic manipulation is done through the Web browser using a Java applet.

Our implementation are carried out in three phases. In the first phase, a traditional search is done before the classification program is called to analyze the search results. This phase is called *"search results narrowing"*. The second phase is called *"search by document contents"*, which uses an existing document to retrieve similar documents inside the digital library collection. The last phase allows a user to input a document outside the digital library collection and find similar documents. This last phase is called *"search by unknown"*.

In this paper, we present our server/client architecture. The detailed design and implementation are focused on the first phase - *search results narrowing*. Our design does not depend on the specific search engine of Florida digital library system. A Z39.50 compliant client interface can be used to handle other search engines if they are Z39.50 compliant.

2   Classification Technologies

In this section, we present the major technologies used at the server to classify a set of documents and convey the similarity among documents graphically. A complete classification process includes four steps; N-gram process, clustering by document similarity, graphic representation of document similarity, and highlights (index terms) listing generating.

2.1   N-Gram Technology

The document-classification process is based on the use of N-gram statistics. N-gram-based representations for documents have several distinct advantages for various document processing tasks [10]. First, they provide a more robust representation in the face of grammatical and typographical errors in the documents. Second, they are robust in the presence of garble such as may occur in a document created by Optical Character Recognition (OCR). Third, N-gram representations require no linguistic preparations such as word-stemming or stopword removal. Thus they are ideal in situation requiring multi-language operations.

An N-gram is an N-character slice of a longer string. An N-gram length is chosen. For example, N=5 is an appropriate choice for English documents. The analysis process scans the document, 1 character at a time, and counts the number of each N-gram found in each document. After normalization to the total number of N-grams in the document, this set of numbers (the N-gram frequency distribution) is considered to be a vector characterizing the contents of the document. An additional N-gram vector (the centroid) is calculated for the entire set of documents. After normalization, the centroid vector is subtracted from the N-gram vector of each document. Subtracting the centroid removes the effect of the ordinary words of the language and the words common to the set of documents so that the subsequent analysis emphasizes what is unique about each document relative to all the documents in the set. The dot product of two document vectors is a scalar whose value is determined mainly by those N-grams which have high frequencies in both documents. The dot product of the vectors is thus a measure of the similarity of the two documents. The algorithm is described in more detail below.

The algorithm begins by stepping through the text, moving one character at a time. From each N-gram, a hash function generates a value that is treated as an address in a document vector, and the contents of that vector address are incremented by one. When all of the N-grams in the document have been processed, the document vector is normalized by dividing the frequency count of N-grams at each vector address by the total number of N-grams in the document. Once all the documents are characterized by normalized document vectors, a centroid vector is calculated based on the normalized frequency for each N-gram in all of the documents. This centroid vector is subtracted from each of the document vectors when gauging similarity among documents by using geometric techniques. Two major algorithms used in computing N-gram scores are *"Recursive Hashing Functions for N-grams"* and *"Computing Similarity Scores"*.

Recursive Hashing Functions for N-grams. Theoretically, applying N-gram technology to a document which has A possible alphabets could produce A^n distinct N-grams. In reality, normal text contains far fewer (English text seems to contain on the order of 10^5 5-grams - much smaller than the possible $27^5 \approx 1.4 \times 10^7$). For this reason, it is practical to accumulate the counts very quickly using a hash table. Using this method, an N-gram g_j is mapped to a table address $k(g_j)$ using some easily computed hash function k, which possesses pseudo-random properties including the mapping of all N-grams to a compact range of integers in a somewhat uniform fashion.

Consider a text sample of length S with symbols(bytes) $s_1, s_2, ..., s_S$, the jth N-gram g_j is the N-long subsequent of the text centered about the jth character.

$$g_j = \left(s_{j-(n-1)/2}, s_{j-(n-1)/2+1}, ..., s_{j-(n-1)/2+n-1}\right) \qquad (1)$$

The hashing function used in our design is

$$k(g_i) = \left[\sum_{k=0}^{n-1} \rho_k Ord(s_{j-(n-1)/2+k})\right] mod M \qquad (2)$$

where $\rho_0, \rho_1, ..., \rho_{n-1}$ are distinct large primes, M is the hash table size, and $Ord(\bullet)$ gives the numerical value of its character argument. While not necessarily optimal, this hash function does possess the virtue of speed, since the multiplication can be carried out using look-up tables already reduced by the modulus. We have chosen a power of 2 for the modulus in the interest of speed.

Computing Similarity Scores. Once documents are characterized by normalized document vectors, the resulting vector-space model permits the use of geometric techniques to gauge similarity among the documents. When comparing a set of document vectors to a set of reference vectors, the cosine of the angle between each document vector and each reference vector, as viewed from the centroid, is computed using the equation:

$$S_{mn} = \frac{\sum_{j=1}^{J}(X_{mj} - \mu_j)(Y_{nj} - \mu_j)}{\sqrt{\sum_{j=1}^{J}(X_{mj} - \mu_j)^2 \sum_{j=1}^{J}(Y_{nj} - \mu_j)^2}} = cos\theta_{mn} \qquad (3)$$

where m=1,...,M, n=1,..., N

Where the vector $X_m, m \in 1...M$ are the M document vectors, the vectors $Y_n, n \in 1...N$ are the N reference vectors in a J-dimensional space and (is the centroid vector.

A cosine value of 1.0 indicates that the document and reference vectors are perfectly correlated (or identical), a value of minus 1.0 means that they are perfectly anticorrelated (or anththethcal), and a measure of 0.0 means they are uncorrelated (or orthogonal).

2.2 Clustering by Document Similarity

Once the similarity is calculated, a set of documents can be divided into classes by putting documents that have a similarity score above a predefined threshold in the same class. Each class thus consists of a set of documents, which are related to each other but have no relationships (above the threshold) to documents in other classes. Each class is further processed to distinguish strongly interconnected documents by forming clusters. The clustering algorithm uses a novel length-2 path distance and a cluster distance based both on within-cluster averages and between cluster averages.

The algorithm is agglomerative, meaning that each document begins as its own cluster and that, in subsequent steps, those smaller clusters are joined to form larger ones. Also, like other clustering approaches, it tries to join the closest documents first, deferring consideration of more distant connections. In contrast to nearly all other agglomerative procedures, the order of joining is determined not by cluster closeness directly, but by the length of the joining edge.

Length-2 Path Distance. The length between two documents, i and j, is based both on the similarity score between them and on the similarity score of edges that might join them through a third document. Finding the length-2 contributions requires finding each document k such that k has a similarity score greater than the pre-defined threshold to both documents i and j.

Cluster Radius and Inter-cluster Separation. Both cluster radius and inter-cluster separation are based on averages of the squares of document distances. The cluster radius is the average over all pairs of documents within that cluster. The inter-cluster separation is average over all pairs of documents, one document drawn from each cluster.

2.3   Graphic Representation of Document Similarity

To help a user understand the similarity between documents, a graphic interface is used. Each document is represent by a vertex, and similarity score between two documents is represented by weighted link between vertices. No link between two vertices means the similarity score is below the pre-defined threshold. An incremental arrangement method is used to draw a graph to convey similarity between documents. The vertices are positioned so that the greater the similarity between two documents, the closer they appear on the screen.

A method known as *multi-dimensional scaling* is used to assign a vertex position on a two-dimensional numeric scale. The target distance between two vertices is calculated based on the proposed algorithm by Kamada and Kawai [11]. The distance between two vertices is defined as the minimum weight that can be accumulated by traversing a path from one vertex to the other. The linear network distance is derived by analogy to a resistive electrical circuit. In this analog, a weighted undirected graph is modeled as a network of fixed conductance, with vertices in the network corresponding to vertices of the graph and each graph edge represented by a conductance equal to the edge weight connecting the appropriate pair of vertices. The edge weights are assumed nonnegative. With this analogy in mind, the graph distance between two vertices is defined to be the total resistance between the corresponding network vertices.

2.4   Highlights - Document Index Terms

To help the user understand why certain documents are in a class or cluster, a set of index terms (Highlights) is generated. Highlight lists are displayed alongside the vertices representing the class or cluster.

To produce index terms of a document without using a stop list, stemmer or other language and domain-specific components, we use N-gram counts [12] to extract highlights by comparing with its "background". A background serves to characterize the "average" text in the corpus against which highlights will be formed. This background is built at the initial classification time using the entire result lists as its base. The general method of extracting highlights using the N-gram scoring method descried earlier is summarized as the following:

1. Each word in a document that contains an N-gram exceeding the pre-set threshold is extracted. The score of that N-gram is assigned to its center character. Contiguous words will be extracted as phrases if appropriate. If the characters on either side of a space jointly contribute to a significantly scoring N-gram, the contiguous words are treated as a single highlight (phrase). Setting the character score threshold is discussed in next paragraph.
2. Each extracted word or phrased is given a score based on the scores of its contained characters. Extracted words and phrases are merged into a list. The scores of each occurrence are combined to get a total score for each entry.
3. The collection of extracted words and phrases is sorted by score to obtain the list of highlights.

Setting the Character Score Threshold. The selection of words is based on selecting significant-scoring characters, which is, in turn, based on comparison to a threshold. The system is given a threshold of δ standard deviations by the system administrator. The score threshold τ is then set using the first two sample moments of the character scores.

$$\tau = m_1 + \delta m_2 \tag{4}$$

where

$$m_1 = \frac{1}{S}\sum_{j=1}^{S} Z_j \ \ and \ \ m_2 = \sqrt{\frac{1}{S}\sum_{j=1}^{S}(Z_j - m_1)^2} \tag{5}$$

Typically, δ is chosen in the neighborhood of 2.

3 Florida Center For Library Automation

The Florida Center For Library Automation (FCLA, http://www.fcla.edu) provides computer services that assist the university libraries of the State University System (SUS) of Florida in providing students and faculty with electronic access to scholarly materials. The State University System of Florida consists of ten universities, twelve off-campus centers, seven agriculture research and education centers, as well as sixty-nine county cooperative extension programs located throughout the state. The software system that provides online access

562

to the collections of all SUS libraries is known as LUIS (Library User Information Service). LUIS also provides gateway services to research materials all over the world. The Bibliography database (NOTIS System) contains 23 million records, in which about 20% have on-line electronic documents. A 4-node IBM SP system with a terabyte of RAID Disks is used to store these on-line electronic documents. These electronic documents are in HTML format, Postscript format, plain ASCII format, or Adobe PDF format.

4 Architecture of the Classification Server and Its Web Clients

In the FCLA system, the user first performs a search on the NOTIS bibliography database. The search result list includes the IDs of the documents. This list is then forwarded to the Document Classification Server (DoCS) on the SP to perform the classification analysis. Figure 1 shows how the system is deployed at FCLA.

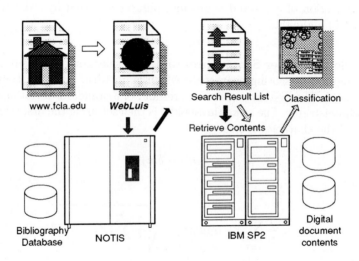

Fig. 1. System deployed in FCLA

Since the document classification algorithms are all computationally intensive processes, users might spend considerable time waiting for the process to finish. To improve the response time, the result list is forwarded to the DoCS as soon as the search is completed at the bibliography database server. Pre-classification results are stored and forwarded to users as soon as users click the *"Classifying the result list"* button. If a user does not choose to do the classification, the result will be purged in 15 minutes to free up space. If user later decides to do the classification, the process will be started again from the beginning.

At the Web client side, a Java Applet is loaded and started as soon as the *"Classifying the result list"* button is clicked. The Java Applet makes a direct connection with the DoCS server and requests the graph file representing the classification results. Using the information in the graph file, the Java Applet provides the user the ability to examine and understand the classification result graphically.

4.1 The Server Architecture

To classify users' search results, our document classification server (DoCS) sits on the SP system and waits for any classification request from a user. As soon as the server receives the list containing results of a search, a server thread is dispatched to execute the classification algorithm. Figure 2 shows requests between a web client and the server.

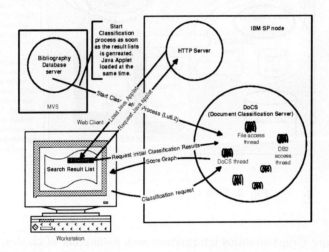

Fig. 2. DL Web Architecture

There are four types of thread in the server. The first one is the communication thread which listens on requests coming from the bibliography server as soon as the search results are available following a user's key-word search request. The current implementation can serve either TCP request or SNA requests. The second thread is the *file access thread*, which retrieves the electronic contents of all the documents and its corresponding metadata information based on the result list. The current implementation supports the UNIX filesystem and the IBM DB2 database. Once the information is extracted from the underlying document management system, it is handed to the third thread - the *Classification thread*. This thread does the basic four steps of the classification technique previously discussed. The classification results are cached by the main thread and are identified by unique search IDs. A fourth thread is invoked dynamically per user request. Upon receiving the unique search ID from a user, the thread finds the classification results and generates a *Score Graph* for the client. The N-gram score for each document is not forwarded to the client. The scores are cached for further processing of the same document sets. Figure 3 shows the interaction between these four types of server threads.

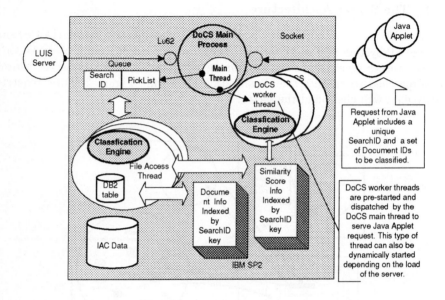

Fig. 3. Four types of the server threads

The *Score Graph* contains information such as number of classes, number of clusters per class, member listing of each class, member listing of each cluster, x and y axes of each document in the graph, similarity score between two related documents and highlight lists for every class and cluster.

Except for the fourth type of thread, all the threads are started at initialization time and stay up for the duration of the service. An initialization file is used to configure the server, such as how many threads and what type of thread is needed. In addition, several threshold parameters for the classification algorithm are defined in the initialization file.

To support phase II - *Search by document content* and phase III - *Search by unknown*, a fifth optional thread is used to calculate N-gram score for each document. This is done at the document load time. In additional to loading the metadata of each document, each document's N-gram score vector is calculated and saved. These N-gram score vectors are used to calculate the similarity score among the input documents and the digital library collection to find similar documents.

The Z39.50 Client Interface. To support different search engines, our server uses Z39.50 server/client protocol to handle results from a search. An optional Z39.50 communication thread can be used to accept Z39.50 compliant search results and forward them to our classification thread.

4.2 The Java Client

The Java applet is started as soon as users click the "classification" button on their search result screen.

Each keyword search has a unique search ID. This ID is used to identify the result of the classification. Since the classification process has been performed before the user's request classification, results are available almost immediately. A score graph is sent and is processed by the applet. A graph is displayed initially by a square vertex representing an individual class. Each class vertex is labeled with a class highlight (index term). The user can choose classes to expand in order to examine the complex relationship among documents in a class. The user can either select one class at a time or work with all classes at once. Users can also display the document source by clicking its corresponding vertex.

The user can choose to highlight just the vertices in one cluster, and display highlight lists for that cluster. Class highlight lists and cluster highlight lists can help user decide which class or cluster is more relevant to his/her search. These highlight lists are generated at initialization time. Highlights lists for single documents can be requested from the server as an additional processing request.

Figure 4 shows the screen snapshot of the Java applet display.

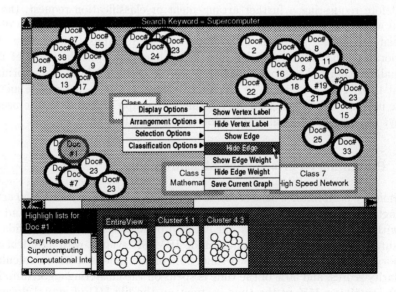

Fig. 4. Screen Snapshot of the Java Applet display

The top portion of the Java applet display shows document classification graphically with a floating menu providing various types of control. There are four major menu options; display, arrangement, selection and classification. The display option, as listed in Figure 3, controls how the information is displayed. For example, edges can be labeled by edge weight, which shows the similarity N-gram score between two documents. The second option controls how the selected vertices are arranged. The third option controls how vertices are selected. There are also two addition local browser windows that can be invoked through this option. One window is for the original search result lists arranged by the original ranking order. The second window is for the result list arranged according to classes and clusters. Each document listed in these two local browser windows is numbered according to the original search lists order. Clicking on these two windows will highlight the corresponding vertex (or vertices) on the main Java graphic window. For example, clicking on a cluster ID will highlight all the vertices belonging to that cluster.

The last option allows user to issue additional classification requests on a subset of the document corpus. Only this option requires communication with server for additional processing. Member vertices in a cluster are arranged by proximity, the physical distance shows the relevance between two documents. Users can manually chose vertices in the graph and request arrangement by considering only the proximity of these selected vertices even if they belong to different clusters.

The lower left corner in Figure 3 displays the first 4 index items in the highlight list of a selection item. The highlight lists can be requested for a class, a cluster, a single vertex, a group of vertices, or a edge. The edge highlight list is equal to the index terms common to the two vertices connected by the edge.

Before requesting a further arrangement or classification request, the user might want to save the original graph for future reference. The lower right display is used for such a purpose. There are at most 5 graphs that can be stored temporarily, and can be recalled at a later time. Since the Java applet is not normally authorized to store information on the client machine, the information about these graphs is stored in the memory and can use considerable memory. If the user chooses not to save the intermediate graph information, the user can always request the original graph information from the server.

4.3 Preliminary Performance Measurement

Preliminary performance measurement shows that for a list containing 50 articles of length 2-10K bytes, the total classification takes about 30 seconds and for a list with 300 similar size articles, the entire process takes about 90 seconds. The measurement was taken on a single node IBM SP system with 128M of main memory. Among the total elapsed time, 35% of the time is spent on calculating similarity scores, and 50% of the time is spent on the clustering algorithm. Most of the remaining 15% of the time is spent on the file I/O of actual document contents.

The same classification process took 4 minutes and 9 minutes respectively on the Macintosh workstation.

5 Conclusions and Future Work

We have designed and implemented a document classification system that can improve document discovery and retrieval compared to using the similarity search ranking algorithm alone. Our sophisticated visualization tool helps users interact with the classification result without losing the relevancy information.

In the future, we will do more performance measurements and improve the performance by distributing workload among a cluster of nodes in the IBM SP system to increase throughput, and explore the parallel N-gram processing and clustering algorithm.

References

1. Bowman, C.M., Danzig, P.B., Manber, U., Schwartz, M.F.: Scalable Internet: Resource discovery. Communication of the ACM, **37(8)**, (August 1994).
2. Efthimiadis, E. N.: User Choices: A New Yardstick for the Evaluation of Raking Algorithms for interactive Query Expansion. Information Processing and Management, **31(4)**, (1995) 604–620
3. Chang, C., Hsu, C.: Customizable Multi-Engine Search Tool with Clustering. Proceeding of the Sixth International World Wide Web Conference, Santa Clara, CA, USA, April 7-11, 1997
4. Hearst, Marti A.: Interfaces for Searching the Web. Special Report Article in Scientific America, **3**, (1997)
5. Voorhees, E.: The Effectiveness and Efficiency of Agglomerative Hierarchic clustering in Document Retrieval. Ph.D. thesis, Cornelle University, (1986)
6. Willett, P.: Recent Trends in hierarchic document clustering: a critical review Information Processing and Management,**24(5)**, (1988), 577–597
7. Maarek, Y.S., Wecker, A. J.: The Librarian's Assistant: Automatically Assembling books into Dynamic Bookshelves Proceeding of RIAO'94, Intelligent Multimedia, Information Retrieval Systems and Management, New York, NY, (1994)
8. Hearst, Marti A., Pedersen, Jan O.: Reexamining the Cluster Hypothesis: Scatter/Gather on Retrieval Results. Proceedings of SIGIR'96, (1996)
9. Damashek, Marc,: Gauging similarity with N-Grams: Language independent categorization of text Science, **267**, 843–848, (10 February 1995).
10. Cavnar, William B.: N-Gram-Based Text Categorization. Proceeding of the Third Symposium on Document Analysis and Information Retrieval. University of Nevada, Las Vegas, 1994, 161–176
11. Kamada T., Kawai, S.: An Algorithm for Drawing General Undirected Graphs. Information Processing Letters, **31(1)**, 12 April 1989, 7–15
12. Cohen, J.,: Highlights: Language and domain-independent automatic indexing terms for abstracting Journal of the American society for information science. **46(3)** 162–174, (1995)

A Linguistically Motivated Probabilistic Model of Information Retrieval

Djoerd Hiemstra

University of Twente,
Centre for Telematics and Information Technology,
The Parlevink Language Engineering Group
P.O. Box 217, 7500 AE Enschede, The Netherlands
hiemstra@cs.utwente.nl
http://www.cs.utwente.nl/~hiemstra/

Abstract. This paper presents a new probabilistic model of information retrieval. The most important modeling assumption made is that documents and queries are defined by an ordered sequence of single terms. This assumption is not made in well known existing models of information retrieval, but is essential in the field of statistical natural language processing. Advances already made in statistical natural language processing will be used in this paper to formulate a probabilistic justification for using tf×idf term weighting. The paper shows that the new probabilistic interpretation of tf×idf term weighting might lead to better understanding of statistical ranking mechanisms, for example by explaining how they relate to coordination level ranking. A pilot experiment on the Cranfield test collection indicates that the presented model outperforms the vector space model with classical tf×idf and cosine length normalisation.

Keywords: Information Retrieval Theory, Statistical Information Retrieval, Statistical Natural Language Processing

1 Introduction

There are three basic processes an information retrieval system has to support: the representation of documents, the representation of a user's information need and the comparison of these two representations. In *text* retrieval the documents and the information need are expressed in natural language. Although text retrieval got by far the most attention in the information retrieval community, so far the success of natural language processing techniques was limited. Most of the effort in the field of text retrieval was put in the development of statistical retrieval models like the vector space model (proposed by Salton et al. [11]), the classical probabilistic model (proposed by Robertson and Spark Jones [7]) and more recently the inference network model (proposed by Croft and Turtle [3]).

The application of natural language processing techniques in combination with these models has solid but limited impact on the performance of text retrieval[1] [13]. The research does however provide little insight to the question *how* to use natural language processing. Natural language processing modules are usually considered as preprocessing steps, that is, they are not included in the model itself. This paper attempts to formulate a model that captures statistical information retrieval and statistical natural language processing into one unifying framework. It is the model itself that explicitly defines how documents and queries should be analysed. This seems a rather trivial requirement, but we claim that this is not the general idea behind the existing models for information retrieval. The (implicit) assumption made by these retrieval models is that some procedure, either manual or automatic, is used to assign index terms to documents. It is the result of this procedure that can be reflected by the model, not the procedure itself.

This paper is organised as follows. In section 2 the basic linguistically motivated retrieval model will be presented. Section 3 will give a new probabilistic interpretation of tf×idf term weighting by using estimation procedures developed in the field of statistical natural language processing. Finally, section 5 will present conclusions and plans for future work. These plans include the development of a model for phrases and the development of a model for cross-language information retrieval.

2 The Basic Retrieval Model

This paper defines a linguistically motivated model of full text information retrieval. The most important modeling assumption we make is that a document and a query are defined by an ordered sequence of words or terms.[2] This assumption is usually not made in information retrieval. In the models mentioned in the introduction documents and queries are modeled as unordered collections of terms or concepts. In the field of statistical natural language processing the word order assumption is essential for many applications, for instance part-of-speech tagging, speech recognition and parsing. By making the 'ordered sequence of terms assumption'

---

[1] Retrieval performance is usually measured in terms of precision (the fraction of the retrieved documents that is actually relevant) and recall (the fraction of the relevant documents that is actually retrieved).

[2] In the linguistically motivated model *terms* and *words* are equivalent, both expressions will be used in this paper. A classical index term that consists of more than one word will be called a *phrase*.

we will be able to use advances already made in statistical natural language processing. In this section we will define the framework that will be used in the subsequent sections to give a probabilistic interpretation of tf×idf term weighting.

2.1 The sample space

We assume that a collection consist of finite number of textual documents. The documents are written in a language that exist of a finite number of words or terms.

Definition 1 Let P be a probability function on the joint sample space $\Omega_D \times \Omega_T \times \Omega_N$. Let Ω_D be a discrete sample space that contains a finite number of points d such that each d refers to an actual document in the document collection. Let D be discrete random variable over Ω_D. Let Ω_T be a discrete sample space that contains a finite number of points t such that each t refers to an actual term that is used to represent the documents. Let T be a discrete random variable over Ω_T. Let N be a discrete random variable over the sample space Ω_N. N will refer to the user's information need.

We will typically use the probability distribution $P(D|N)$ to rank documents given an information need. The random variable D will refer to an abstract representation of a document rather than to its physical representation which is modeled by index terms T.

We did not define the complete sample space Ω_N. The information need N is internal to the user and it is not known how it relates to other information needs. In practice we will usually only consider the conditional probability of terms and documents given one information need N, that is, in practice the model will be defined for one information need only.

2.2 Modeling documents and queries

A query and a document will be modeled as compound events. A compound event is an event that consists of two or more single events, as when a die is tossed twice or three cards are drawn one at a time from a deck [6]. In general the probability of a compound event does depend on the order of the events. For example a document of length n will be modeled by an ordered sequence of n random variables $T_1, T_2, \cdots, T_n$. The probability of the ordered sequence will be defined by $P(T_1, T_2, \cdots, T_n|D)$. Most practical models for information retrieval assume independence between index terms. This leads to the following model of documents.

$$P(T_1, T_2, \cdots, T_n | D) = \prod_{i=1}^{n} P(T_i | D) \tag{1}$$

Note that the assumption of independence between terms in documents does not contradict the assumption that terms in documents have a particular order. The independence assumption merely states that every possible order of terms has the same probability. It is made to illustrate that a simple version of the linguistically motivated model is very similar to existing information retrieval models. In the near future we hope to publish a version of the model in which the independence assumption does not hold: a model that uses phrases.

A query of length l will be modeled by an ordered sequence of l random variables $T_1, T_2, \cdots, T_l$. The probability of the ordered sequence will be defined by $P(T_1, T_2, \cdots, T_l | N)$. This probability can be viewed at as describing the process of a user formulating a query of length l, beginning with the word T_1 and ending with the word T_l. Unlike the modeling of documents, queries will not be modeled by assuming independence between query terms. Instead the query will get a probability of 1 if the user formulates only one query and some smaller probability if the user formulates more than one query. In a practical information retrieval system there should be some kind of interactive process between system and user in which one or more queries with corresponding probabilities are defined.

Analogous to a user formulating a query, equation 1 can be viewed at as the author of a document D writing a document of length n, beginning with the word T_1 and finally ending with the word T_n.

2.3   The matching process

The matching process is modeled by the joint probability measure $P(D, N, \mathcal{T})$ in which $\mathcal{T}$ will refer to the compound event $T_1, T_2, \cdots T_l$. The following conditional independence assumption is made:

$$P(D, N | \mathcal{T}) = P(N | \mathcal{T}) P(D | \mathcal{T}) \quad , \mathcal{T} = (T_1, T_2, \cdots T_l) \tag{2}$$

By definition 1 terms are mutually exclusive and therefore two compound events are mutually exclusive if they differ in at least one of the single events. This means that it is possible to sum over all possible compound events T to determine the ranking of documents given an information need (see e.g. Wong and Yao [16]).

$$P(D|N) = \sum_{T} P(T|N)P(D|T) \quad , T = (T_1, T_2, \cdots T_l) \qquad (3)$$

All compound events that were not formulated as a query by the user will have zero probability $(P(T|N) = 0)$, so in practice it is sufficient to use equation 3 for the formulated queries only. In order to use the independence assumption of equation 1 we should rewrite $P(D|T)$ in equation 3 by applying Bayes' rule.

$$P(D|T_1, T_2, \cdots, T_l) = P(D)\frac{P(T_1, T_2, \cdots, T_l|D)}{P(T_1, T_2, \cdots, T_l)} \qquad (4)$$

$$= P(D)\frac{\prod_{i=1}^{l} P(T_i|D)}{P(T_1, T_2, \cdots, T_l)} \qquad (5)$$

Equation 4 is the direct result of applying Bayes' rule. Filling in the independence assumption of equation 1 leads to equation 5. It seems tempting to make the assumption that terms are also independent if they are not conditioned on a document D. This will however lead to an inconsistency of the model (see e.g. Cooper's paper on modeling assumptions for the classical probabilistic retrieval model [2]). Since $\sum_d P(D = d|T) = 1$ we can scale the formula using a constant C such that $\frac{1}{C} = \sum_d P(D = d, T)$.

$$P(D|T_1, T_2, \cdots, T_l) = C\, P(D) \prod_{i=1}^{l} P(T_i|D) \qquad (6)$$

Equation 3 and 6 define the linguistic motivated statistical retrieval model if we assume independence between terms in documents.

3 Estimating the probabilities

The process of probability estimation defines how probabilities should be estimated from frequency of terms in the actual document collection. We will look at the estimating process by drawing a parallel to statistical natural language processing and corpus linguistics.

3.1 Viewing documents as language samples

The general idea is the following. Each document contains a small sample of natural language. For each document the retrieval system should build a little statistical language model $P(T|D)$ where T is a single event. Such a language model might indicate that the author of that document used a certain word 5 out of 1000 times; it might indicate that the author used a certain syntactic construction like a phrase 5 out of 1000 times; or ultimately indicate that the author used a certain logical semantic structure 5 out of 1000 times.

One of the main problems in statistical natural language processing and corpus linguistics is the problem of sparse data. If the sample that is used to estimate the parameters of a language model is small, then many possible language events never take place in the actual data. Suppose for example that an author wrote a document about *information retrieval* without using the words *keyword* and *crocodile*. The reason that the author did not mention the word *keyword* is probably different from the reason for not mentioning the word *crocodile*. If we were able to ask an expert in the field of *information retrieval* to estimate probabilities for the terms *keyword* and *crocodile* he/she might for example indicate that the chance that the term *keyword* occurred is one in a thousand terms and the chance that the term *crocodile* occurred is much lower: one in a million. If we however base the probabilities on the frequency of terms in the actual document then the probability estimates of low frequent and medium frequent terms will be unreliable. A full text information retrieval system based on these frequencies cannot make a difference between words that were not used 'by chance', like the word *keyword,* and words that were not used because they are 'not part of the vocabulary of the subject', like the word *crocodile*. Furthermore there is always a little chance that completely off the subject words occur like the word *crocodile* in this paper.

We believe that the sparse data problem is exactly the reason that it is hard for information retrieval systems to obtain high recall values without degrading values for precision. Many solutions to the sparse data problem were proposed in the field of statistical natural language processing (see e.g. [5] for an overview). We will use the combination of estimators by linear interpolation to estimate parameters of the probability measure $P(T|D)$.

3.2 Estimating probabilities from sparse data

Perhaps the most straightforward way to estimate probabilities from frequency information is maximum likelihood estimation [6]. A maximum likelihood estimate makes the probability of observed events as high as possible and assigns zero probability to unseen events. This makes the maximum likelihood estimate unsuitable for directly estimating $P(T|D)$. One way of removing the zero probabilities is to mix the maximum likelihood model of $P(T|D)$ with a model that suffers less from sparseness like the marginal $P(T)$. It is possible to make a linear combination of both probability estimates so that the result is another probability function. This method is called linear interpolation:

$$P_{li}(T|D) = \alpha_1 P_{mle}(T) + \alpha_2 P_{mle}(T|D), \quad 0<\alpha_1,\alpha_2<1 \text{ and } \alpha_1+\alpha_2=1 \quad (7)$$

The weights α_1 and α_2 might be set by hand, in which case we would choose them in such a way that $\alpha_1 P_{mle}(T = t)$ is smaller than $\alpha_2 P_{mle}(T = t|D)$ for each terms t. This will give terms that did not appear in the document a much smaller probability than terms that did appear in the document. In general one wants to find the combination of weights that works the best, for example by optimising them on a test collection consisting of documents, queries and corresponding relevance judgements.

Table 1. frequency information

N_q	the number of queries formulated for the information need at hand
N_d	the number of documents in the collection
$tf(t,d)$	*term frequency:* the number of times the term t appears in the document d.
$df(t)$	*document frequency:* the number of documents in which the term t appears.

Table 1 lists the frequencies that are used to estimate the probabilities of the model. Two frequencies are particularly important, the term frequency and the document frequency. The term frequency of a term is defined by the number of times a term appears in a document and can be viewed at as local or document specific information. Given a specific document many terms will have a frequency of zero, so the term frequency suffers from sparseness. The document frequency of a term is defined by the number of documents in which a term appears and can be viewed at as global information. (Sometimes document frequency is referred to as collection frequency.) The document frequency of a term will never be zero, because by definition 1, terms that do not appear in any document will not be included in the model. The sparseness problem can be avoided by estimating $P(T|D)$ as a linear combination of a probability model based on document frequency and a probability model based on term frequency as in equation 10:

$$P(\mathcal{T}|N) = \frac{1}{N_q} \quad , \mathcal{T} = (T_1, T_2, \cdots, T_l) \tag{8}$$

$$P(D = d) = \frac{1}{N_d} \tag{9}$$

$$P(T_i = t_i | D = d) = \alpha_1 \frac{df(t_i)}{\sum_t df(t)} + \alpha_2 \frac{tf(t_i, d)}{\sum_t tf(t, d)} \tag{10}$$

Note that term frequency and document frequency are not derived from the same distribution. Although the term frequency can also be used to compute global information of a term by summing over all possible documents, this information will usually not be the same as the document frequency of a term, more formally: $df(t) \neq \sum_d tf(t, d)$.

3.3 Relation to tf×idf

The use of term frequency and document frequency to rank documents was extensively studied, especially by Salton et al. for the vector space model [10]. They argued that terms appearing in documents should be weighted proportional to term frequency and inversely proportional to the document frequency. They called weighting schemes that follow this approach *tf×idf* (term frequency × inverse document frequency) weighting schemes and the application in a model of information retrieval the *term discrimination model*. The combination of tf×idf weights and document length normalisation gave the best retrieval results on several test collections, but they were not able to justify their approach by probability theory (which is not a prerequisite for using it in the vector space model anyway):

> ... *The term discrimination model has been criticised because it does not exhibit well substantiated theoretical properties. This in contrast with the probabilistic model of information retrieval* ...

The lack of theoretical justification of tf×idf weights did not keep developers of the probabilistic model and the inference network model from using them. Robertson et al. [8] justified the use of term frequency in the probabilistic model by approximating a ranking formula that is based on the combination of the probabilistic model and the 2-poisson model. There is however a more plausible probabilistic justification of tf×idf weighting which can be justified by the linear interpolation estimator of equation 10. This can be shown by rewriting. Multiplying the ranking formula defined by equation 6, 9 and 10 with values that are the same for each document will not affect the final ranking, so we can multiply the ranking formula by $df(t)$ and α_2 as follows:

$$P(D = d|T_1 = t_1, \cdots) \propto \prod_{i=1}^{n} (\alpha_1 \frac{df(t_i)}{\sum_t df(t)} + \alpha_2 \frac{tf(t_i, d)}{\sum_t tf(t, d)}) \; \text{[by eq. 6,9 and 10]}$$

$$\propto \prod_{i=1}^{n} (\alpha_1 \frac{1}{\sum_t df(t)} + \alpha_2 \frac{tf(t_i, d)}{\sum_t tf(t, d) \cdot df(t_i)}) \quad [\times \prod_{i=1}^{n} \frac{1}{df(t_i)}]$$

$$\propto \prod_{i=1}^{n} (\frac{\alpha_1}{\alpha_2 \sum_t df(t)} + \frac{tf(t_i, d)}{df(t_i)} \cdot \frac{1}{\sum_t tf(t, d)}) \quad [\times \prod_{i=1}^{n} \frac{1}{\alpha_2}]$$

The resulting formula can directly be interpreted as tf×idf weighting with document length normalisation, because:

$\dfrac{\alpha_1}{\alpha_2 \sum_t df(t)}$ is a small constant for any document d and term t

$\dfrac{tf(t_i, d)}{df(t_i)}$ is the tf×idf weight of the term t_i in the document d

$\dfrac{1}{\sum_t tf(t, d)}$ is the inverse length of the document d

Any monotonic transformation of the document ranking function will produce the same ranking of the documents. Instead of the product of weights we could therefore also rank the documents by the sum of logarithmic weights [7]. The result would be an additive model, which is more in correspondence with the way in which the existing models mentioned in the introduction usually are presented.

On first glance the constant $\alpha_1/\alpha_2 \sum_t df(t)$ seems to have little impact on the final ranking. But in fact, different values of α_1 and α_2 will lead to different document rankings. In section 3.5 we will show some effects of different values of α_1 and α_2 on the ranking of documents, especially for short queries.

Document length normalisation which is made explicit by $1/\sum_t tf(t, d)$ is also defined by the estimator of equation 9. The a priori relevance of a document estimated as in equation 9 can be defined by any other estimator, e.g. by using approaches as described by Singhal et al. for the vector space model [12].

3.4 A new informal definition of tf×idf weighting

Equation 10 gives rise to a new informal definition of tf×idf weighting. Giving an informal definition after the formal definition seems a bit useless, but we believe that it will help to understand what exactly makes tf×idf weighting successful. The classical definition of tf×idf weighting can be formulated as follows:

Definition 2 The weight of a term that appears in a document should increase with the term frequency of the term in the document and decrease with the document frequency of the term. Terms that do not appear in a document should all get the same weights (zero weights).

An alternative definition is based on equation 10. If we assume that $\alpha_1 \, df(t_i)/\sum_t df(t)$ is much smaller than $\alpha_2 \, tf(t_i, d)/\sum_t tf(t, d)$ then it can be formulated as follows:

Definition 3 The weight of a term that appears in a document should increase with the term frequency of the term in the document. The weight of a term that does not appear in a document should increase with the document frequency of the term.

An example may clarify the implications of both definitions. Suppose the user formulates the query *information retrieval* and there is no document in the collection in which the terms *information* and *retrieval* both appear. Furthermore suppose that the term *information* is much more common, i.e. has a higher document frequency than the term *retrieval*. Now the system will rank documents containing k occurrences of the term *retrieval* above documents containing k occurrences of the term *information*. The classical explanation would be as follows:

Explanation 1 The query term *retrieval* matches better with documents containing *retrieval* than the query term *information* matches with documents containing *information*, because *retrieval* has a higher inverse document frequency than *information*.

The alternative explanation would be that:

Explanation 2 The query term *information* matches better with documents not containing *information* than the query term *retrieval* matches documents not containing *retrieval* because *information* has a higher document frequency than *retrieval*.

There is no a priori reason to prefer one explanation above the other. However, the idea of definition 3, that global information is only used to weight terms of which there is no local information, might lead to better understanding of probabilistic term weighting in text retrieval.

3.5 The problem of non-coordination level ranking

There is a well known problem with statistical information retrieval systems that use tf×idf weighting: sometimes documents containing n query terms are ranked higher than documents containing $n + 1$ query terms. We will call this problem the *problem of non-coordination level ranking* in which the *coordination level* refers to the number of distinct query terms contained in a document. A coordination level ranking procedure will always rank documents containing $n + 1$ query terms above documents containing n query terms even if the top documents have little evidence for the presence of $n + 1$ query terms and lower-ranked documents have a lot of evidence for the presence of n terms.

According to studies of user preferences and evaluations on test collections the problem of non-coordination level ranking becomes particularly apparent when short queries are used [9]. In a lot of practical situations short queries are the rule rather than the exception, especially in situations where there is no or little user training like with Web-based search engines. For some research groups, the importance of coordination level is the reason for developing ranking methods that are based on the lexical distance of search terms in documents instead of on document frequency of terms [1, 4]. However, as pointed out by experiments of Wilkinson et al. [15], some tf×idf measures (e.g. like the measure proposed by Robertson et al. [8]) are more like coordination level ranking than others (e.g. like the measure proposed by Salton et al. [10]). Wilkinson et al. showed that weighting measures that are more like coordination level ranking perform better on the TREC collection, especially if short queries are used.

Following the results of Wilkinson et al. it might be useful to investigate what exactly makes a weighting measure "like" coordination level ranking. The following example may provide some insight. Suppose the user enters a small query of only two terms a and b. As in the previous example a might be the term *information* and b might be the term *retrieval*. Furthermore suppose that the document d_1 contains a lot of evidence for term a and no evidence for the term b; and that document d_2 contains little evidence of both terms. It can be shown that document d_1 will have a lot of evidence for a and none for b if $tf(a, d_1)$ is high, $tf(b, d_1) = 0$ and the length of d_1 is short. Document d_2 contains little evidence of a and b if $tf(a, d_2) = tf(b, d_2) = 1$ and if d_2 is a long document. The length of a document will be defined by $l(d) = \sum_t tf(t, d)$. Now the following equation defines the requirement for coordination level ranking, that is, the similarity of document d_1 to the query $a\ b$ should be smaller than the similarity of document d_2 to the query. The left hand side of the equation contains the similarity of the query compared to document d_1 and the right hand side contains the similarity of the query to document d_2. The similarities are defined by the ranking formula introduced in section 3.3 with $c = \alpha_1/\alpha_2 \sum_t df(t)$.

$$(c + \frac{tf(a,d_1)}{df(a)l(d_1)})(c+0) \; < \; (c + \frac{1}{df(a)l(d_2)})(c + \frac{1}{df(b)l(d_2)})$$

$$c^2 + \frac{c\ tf(a,d_1)}{df(a)l(d_1)} \; < \; c^2 + \frac{c}{df(a)l(d_2)} + \frac{c}{df(b)l(d_2)} + \frac{1}{df(a)df(b)l(d_2)^2}$$

$$\frac{c\ tf(a,d_1)}{df(a)l(d_1)} - \frac{c}{df(a)l(d_2)} - \frac{c}{df(b)l(d_2)} \; < \; \frac{1}{df(a)df(b)l(d_2)^2} \qquad (11)$$

$$\vdots$$

$$c \; < \; \frac{l(d_1)}{l(d_2)(tf(a,d_1)df(b)l(d_2) - df(b)l(d_1) - df(a)l(d_1))}$$

Equation 11 shows that we can rewrite the requirement for coordination level ranking as a requirement for the constant c. If c is small enough than the problem of non-coordination level ranking will never occur. By changing the value of c the ranking formula can be adapted to different applications. If we are developing a Web-based search engine we might choose a relatively small value for c, but if we are developing a search engine for evaluation in TREC [14] we might choose a higher value of c. For the Web-based search engine we might define a collection specific lower bound of c by keeping track of the collection extrema like maximum term frequency and document frequency ($maxtf$ and $maxdf$) and maximum and minimum document lengths ($maxl$ and $minl$). If we fill in these extrema and the definition $c = \alpha_1/\alpha_2 \sum_t df(t)$ in (11) then the lower bound will be defined as follows on the ratio between α_1 and α_2.

$$\frac{\alpha_1}{\alpha_2} \; < \; \frac{minl \cdot \sum_t df(t)}{maxl \cdot (maxtf \cdot maxdf \cdot maxl - maxdf \cdot minl - minl)} \qquad (12)$$

Equation 12 defines a ranking formula that always produces coordination level ranking for queries of two words. For longer queries the bound will be lower and for queries with unrestricted length only $\alpha_1 = 0$ will guarantee coordination level ranking.

3.6 A plausible explanation of non-coordination level ranking

The arguments in the previous section showed the following. The smaller the value of the constant c, the more the ranking formula will behave like coordination level ranking. It is good to note that most tf×idf measures defined for the existing models of information retrieval include constants for which the arguments introduced above also hold (for instance the "+0.5" in the Robertson/Sparck Jones formula [7, 8]). However, the classical definition of tf×idf weighting (definition 2) does not give a plausible explanation of why and when non-coordination level ranking does happen. Using the new definition 3 and the fact that c is defined by the ratio $\frac{\alpha_1}{\alpha_2}$ we can give the following explanation of non-coordination level ranking when tf×idf weights are used.

Explanation 3 Non-coordination level ranking occurs if query terms that do *not* appear in a document are weighted too high compared to query terms that *do* appear in a document.

According to definition 3 terms that do not appear in a document are weighted proportional to the document frequency. If we choose a relatively high value for the constant α_1 then query terms that do not appear in a document will be weighted too high, possibly causing non-coordination level ranking.

4 A Pilot Experiment

There remains an important question: How does the model perform in an experiment with a test collection? The following pilot experiment is relatively weak because we used a relatively outdated test collection and compared the new model with a relatively outdated vector space weighting scheme. The results are however promising. The next step will be evaluation in this years Text Retrieval Conference TREC-7 [14].

4.1 Experimental results

In the experiment we implemented a linguistically motivated probabilistic retrieval engine and a standard vector space engine. Both engines used the same tokenisation and stemming of the words in the documents. As a test collection we used the Cranfield collection which was also used extensively in early experiments with the vector space model [10]. Table 2 lists the non-interpolated average precision averaged over 225 queries of the Cranfield collection for different values of α_1 and α_2.

Table 2. experimental results on the Cranfield collection

weight	avg. precision
$\alpha_1 = 0.05$ $\alpha_2 = 0.95$	0.3904
$\alpha_1 = 0.1$ $\alpha_2 = 0.9$	0.4016
$\alpha_1 = 0.2$ $\alpha_2 = 0.8$	0.4141
$\alpha_1 = 0.4$ $\alpha_2 = 0.6$	0.4249
$\alpha_1 = 0.6$ $\alpha_2 = 0.4$	0.4297
$\alpha_1 = 0.8$ $\alpha_2 = 0.2$	0.4325
$\alpha_1 = 0.9$ $\alpha_2 = 0.1$	0.4311
$\alpha_1 = 0.95$ $\alpha_2 = 0.05$	0.4252

To evaluate how our weighting scheme performs relatively to other tf×idf weighting schemes with document length normalisation we implemented the vector space model with tfc.nfx weighting as proposed by Salton and Buckley [10]. The non-interpolated average precision averaged over 225 queries of this system was 0.4032 on the Cranfield collection.[3] The linguistically motivated system performs better for quite a wide range of different values of α_1 and α_2. Experiments with the TREC collection, have to determine if the difference in performance is in fact a property of the respective ranking strategies.

4.2 Coordination level ranking

The Cranfield collection is a small collection (1398 documents) with a relative large number of queries (255 queries). Cranfield has the following collection extrema: The smallest document is 18 words long, the longest 354 words. The maximum term frequency is 28 and the maximum document frequency 729. Following the arguments of the previous section it is possible to calculate a lower bound on the ratio between α_1 and α_2 that will define coordination level ranking given a query of length 2. This leads to a lower bound of 0.000525 on the ratio between α_1 and α_2 which corresponds roughly to $\alpha_1 = 0.0005$ and $\alpha_2 = 0.9995$. Although correct, the lower bound introduced by equation 12 is obviously not very useful for identifying proper values for α_1 and α_2. There are several reasons that might explain why the system performs optimally for much higher values of α_1:

1. Coordination level ranking does not lead to good average precision on the Cranfield collection.

[3] Salton and Buckley [10] report a 3-point interpolated average precision of 0.3841. Our version of their system reaches a 3-point interpolated average precision of 0.4204 which is probably due to the use of a stemmer.

2. The system does produce coordination level ranking, but the bound on the ratio between α_1 and α_2 is too low to be of any use.
3. The system does produce coordination level ranking, but the bound is not useful because the collection does not have very small queries (the average query length is about 9.5 words).

Additional experiments have to point out which reason or reasons actually explain the experimental results the best.

5 Conclusion and Future Plans

This paper presented the linguistically motivated probabilistic model of information retrieval. Using estimation by linear interpolation which is often used in the field of statistical natural language processing we were able to present a probabilistic interpretation of tf×idf term weighting. We showed that this new interpretation leads to better understanding of the behaviour of tf×idf ranking. In a pilot experiment we showed that a system based on the derived model performs better on the Cranfield collection than a system based on a standard vector space model using classical tf×idf weights and cosine document length normalisation.

This paper did not present the linguistically motivated model for information retrieval in its full strength. Although we claim that the most important modeling assumption of the model is that documents and queries are defined by an ordered sequence of terms, the assumption is not essential for the claims made in this paper. In future papers we will investigate two major information retrieval issues that require natural language processing techniques. The first issue is the use of phrases in information retrieval. The second issue is the problem of cross-language information retrieval.

Acknowledgements

I would like to thank the following people for their support. Franciska de Jong, Paul van der Vet and Wilbert Kallenberg for general advice; David Hawking of the Australian National University for his advice on coordination level ranking. Wessel Kraaij of The Netherlands Organisation for Applied Scientific Research (TNO) for discussions on information retrieval.

References

1. C.L.A. Clarke, G.V. Cormack, and E.A. Tudhope. Relevance ranking for one to three term queries. In Proceedings of RIAO'97, pages 388–400, 1997.
2. W.S. Cooper. Some inconsistencies and misidentified modeling assumptions in probabilistic information retrieval. ACM Transactions on Information Systems, 13:100–111, 1995.
3. W.B. Croft and H.R. Turtle. Text retrieval and inference. In P. Jacobs, editor, Text-based Intelligent Systems, pages 127–156. Lawrence Erlbaum, 1992.
4. D. Hawking and P. Thistlewaite. Relevance weighting using distance between term occurrences. Technical Report TR-CS-96-08, The Australian National University, August 1996. http://cs.anu.edu.au/techreports/.
5. C. Manning and H. Schütze, editors. Statistical NLP: Theory and Practice, draft. http://www.sultry.arts.su.edu.au/manning/courses/statnlp/, 1997.
6. A.M. Mood and F.A. Graybill, editors. Introduction to the Theory of Statistics, Second edition. McGraw-Hill, 1963.
7. S.E. Robertson and K. Sparck Jones. Relevance weighting of search terms. Journal of the American Society for Information Science, 27:129–146, 1976.
8. S.E. Robertson and S. Walker. Some simple effective approximations to the 2-poisson model for probabilistic weighted retrieval. In Proceedings of the SIGIR'94, pages 232–241, 1994.
9. D.E. Rose and C. Stevens. V-twin: A lightweight engine for interactive use. In Proceedings of the 5th Text Retrieval Conference TREC-5, pages 279–290. NIST Special Publications, 1997.
10. G. Salton and C. Buckley. Term-weighting approaches in automatic text retrieval. Information Processing & Management, 24(5):513–523, 1988.
11. G. Salton and M.J. McGill, editors. Introduction to Modern Information Retrieval. McGraw-Hill, 1983.
12. A. Singhal, C. Buckley, and M. Mitra. Pivoted document length normalization. In Proceedings of the SIGIR'96, pages 21–29, 1996.
13. T. Strzalkowski and K. Sparck Jones. Nlp track at trec-5. In Proceedings of the 5th Text Retrieval Conference TREC-5, pages 97–101. NIST Special Publications, 1997.
14. E.M. Voorhees and D.K. Harman. Overview of the 6th text retrieval conference. In Proceedings of the 6th Text Retrieval Conference TREC-6. NIST Special Publications, 1998.
15. R. Wilkinson, J. Zobel, and R. Sacks-Davis. Similarity measures for short queries. In Proceedings of the 4th Text Retrieval Conference TREC-4, pages 277–286. NIST Special Publications, 1996.
16. S.K.M. Wong and Y.Y. Yao. On modeling information retrieval with probabilistic inference. ACM Transactions on Information Systems, 13:38–68, 1995.

The *C-value/NC-value* Method of Automatic Recognition for Multi-word Terms

Katerina T. Frantzi[1] and Sophia Ananiadou[1] and Junichi Tsujii[2]

[1] Dept. of Computing and Mathematics, Manchester Metropolitan University, Chester Str., Manchester, M1 5GD, U.K.
[2] Dept. of Information Science, University of Tokyo, Hongo 7-3-1, Bunkyo-ku, Tokyo 113, Japan

Abstract. Technical terms (henceforth called simply *terms*), are important elements for digital libraries. In this paper we present a domain-independent method for the automatic extraction of multi-word terms, from machine-readable special language corpora.
The method, (*C-value/NC-value*), combines linguistic and statistical information. The first part, *C-value* enhances the common statistical measure of frequency of occurrence for term extraction, making it sensitive to a particular type of multi-word terms, the nested terms. The second part, *NC-value*, gives: 1) a method for the extraction of term context words (words that tend to appear with terms), 2) the incorporation of information from term context words to the extraction of terms.

1 Introduction

Terms, the linguistic representation of concepts [25], are important elements for digital libraries. Rapid changes in many specialised knowledge domains (particularly in areas like computer science, engineering, medicine etc.), means that new terms are being created all the time, making important the automation of their retrieval.

Many techniques for multi-word automatic term recognition (ATR) move lately from using only linguistic information [2, 1, 3], to incorporating statistical as well. Dagan and Church, [7], Daille et al., [8], and Justeson and Katz, [18], Enguehard and Pantera, [11], use frequency of occurrence. Daille et al., and Lauriston, [21], propose the likelihood ratio for terms consisting of two words. For the same type of terms, Damerau, [9], proposed a measure based on mutual information (MI). Those of the above methods that aim to multi-word terms which may consist of more than two words, use as the only statistical parameter the frequency of occurrence of the candidate term in the corpus. A detailed description and evaluation of previous work on multi-word ATR can be found in [16].

The method we present and evaluate in this paper extracts multi-word terms from English corpora combining linguistic and statistical information. It is divided into two parts: 1) the *C-value*, that aims to improve the extraction of nested multi-word terms [12], and 2) the *NC-value* that incorporates context information to the *C-value* method, aiming to improve multi-word term extraction in general [15, 14]. The first part, *C-value* has been also used for collocation extraction [13]. The second part incorporates a method for the extraction of term context words, which will be also presented and evaluated in this paper.

Since ATR methods are mostly empirical, [19], we evaluate the results of the method in terms of precision and recall, [27]. The results are compared with those produced with the most common statistical technique used for ATR to date, the frequency of occurrence of the candidate term, which was applied on the same corpus.

2 The *C-value* Approach

This section presents the *C-value* approach to multi-word ATR. *C-value* is a domain-independent method for multi-word ATR which aims to improve the extraction of nested terms. The method takes as input an SL corpus and produces a list of candidate multi-word terms. These are ordered by their *termhood*, which we also call *C-value*. The output list is evaluated by a domain expert. Since the candidate terms are ranked according to their termhood, the domain expert can scan the lists starting from the top, and go as far down the list as time/money allow.

The *C-value* approach combines linguistic and statistical information, emphasis being placed on the statistical part. The linguistic information consists of the part-of-speech tagging of the corpus, the linguistic filter constraining the type of terms extracted, and the stop-list. The statistical part combines statistical features of the candidate string, in a form of measure that is also called *C-value*.

Subsections 2.1 and 2.2 describe and justify the linguistic part and the statistical part of the method. Subsection 2.3 describes the algorithm. In subsection 2.4 we apply the method to a medical corpus and present the results. Subsection 2.5 evaluates the results.

2.1 The Linguistic Part

The linguistic part consists of the following:

1. Part-of-speech information from tagging the corpus.
2. The linguistic filter applied to the tagged corpus to exclude those strings not required for extraction.
3. The stop-list.

Tagging.
Part-of-speech tagging is the assignment of a grammatical tag (e.g. noun, adjective, verb, preposition, determiner, etc.) to each word in the corpus. It is needed by the linguistic filter which will only permit specific strings for extraction.

The linguistic filter.
It would be 'very desirable' for a method to be able to extract all types of terms

(e.g. noun phrases, adjectival phrases, verbal phrases, etc.). In such a case the linguistic filter would not be needed. This approach has not yet been followed by us or by any other researchers in ATR. The reason is that the statistical information that is available, without any linguistic filtering, is not enough to produce useful results. Without any linguistic information, undesirable strings such as *of the, is a*, etc., would also be extracted.

Since most terms consist of nouns and adjectives, [26], and sometimes prepositions, [18], we use a linguistic filter that accepts these types of terms.

The choice of the linguistic filter affects the precision and recall of the output list. A number of different filters have been used, [3, 8, 7, 18]. A 'closed' filter which is strict about the strings it permits, will have a positive effect on precision but a negative effect on recall. As an example, consider the filter that Dagan and Church use, [7], the $Noun^+$. This filter only permits sequences of nouns, and as a result produces high precision since noun sequences in an SL corpus are the most likely to be terms. At the same time, it negatively affects recall, since there are many noun compound terms that consist of adjectives and nouns, which are excluded by this filter.

An 'open' filter, one that permits more types of strings, has the opposite effect: negative for precision, positive for recall. An example of such a filter is that of Justeson and Katz, [18]. They extract noun phrases of the form
$((Adj|Noun)^+|((Adj|Noun)^*$
$(NounPrep)^?)(Adj|Noun)^*)Noun$. The above filter would extract more terms than the $Noun^+$ one, since terms that contain adjectives and prepositions are also extracted, but it also extracts more non-terms. It extracts terms like *tetracyclines for ocular rosacea, scotomas in low vision, coloboma of retina*, but it also extracts non-terms like *strabismus in children, composition of tears, therapy of strabismus, sensory aspects of strabismus*.

The choice of the linguistic filter depends on how we want to balance precision and recall: preference on precision over recall would probably require a closed filter, while preference on recall would require an open filter.

We are not strict about the choice of a specific linguistic filter, since different applications require different filters. We will present our method combined with each of the 3 filters,

1. $NounNoun^+$,
2. Adj^*Noun^+,
3. $((Adj|Noun)^+|((Adj|Noun)^*$
   $(NounPrep)^?)(Adj|Noun)^*)Noun$,

and see how the results are affected. We will also take the results of our method using each of these filters, and compare them with the results from frequency of occurrence when combined with these filters.

The stop-list.
A stop-list for an SL in ATR is a list of words which are not expected to occur as term words in that domain. It is used to avoid the extraction of strings that

are unlikely to be terms, improving the precision of the output list. When used in previous approaches, it is not clear how it is constructed, [6, 11]. Our stop-list consists of 229 function and other content words, picked from a sample of our corpus (1/10). The words that are included in the stop-list exhibited high frequencies in that sample of the corpus. Some examples are: *great, numerous, several, year, just, good*, etc.

We should note the fact that because a word has not appeared as a term-word of a specific domain in the past does not guarantee that it will not do so in the future. Consider for example the word *optical*, which is relatively new in computer science. If it were a stop-list word, then terms like, *optical character, optical character recognition, optical character reader, optical laser disc, optical mouse* would have been missed when they first appeared in the domain. The choice of using a stop-list is again a matter of balance between precision and recall. A stop-list benefits precision but could leave out terms that contain 'unexpected' words.

2.2   The Statistical Part

The *C-value* statistical measure assigns a termhood to a candidate string, ranking it in the output list of candidate terms. The measure is built using statistical characteristics of the candidate string. These are:

1. The total frequency of occurrence of the candidate string in the corpus.
2. The frequency of the candidate string as part of other longer candidate terms.
3. The number of these longer candidate terms.
4. The length of the candidate string (in number of words).

We will now examine each of these parameters. The frequency of occurrence of the candidate string in the corpus is, as we have seen, the measure which has been used for multi-word ATR until now. In this case, the termhood of a string equals its frequency of occurrence in the corpus

$$termhood(a) = f(a) \tag{1}$$

where
a is the candidate string,
$f(a)$ its frequency of occurrence in the corpus.

As a statistical measure for ATR, the frequency produces good results since terms tend to occur with relatively high frequencies. For example, in our 800,000 word eye-pathology corpus, *optic nerve* appeared 2,084 times, *Descemet's membrane* 1,666 times, *basal cell carcinoma* 984 times, etc. Of course not all terms exhibit high frequencies: *stromal necrosis, epithelial oedema*, and *congestive glaucoma* appear only 3 times each. Low frequency events cause problems for statistical approaches.

Since frequency produces relatively good results, and since its application to corpora is simple, why are we not satisfied with using just that and look for something more?

Consider the string *soft contact lens*. This is a term in ophthalmology. A method that uses frequency of occurrence would extract it given that it appears frequently enough in the corpus. Its substrings, *soft contact* and *contact lens*, would be also extracted since they would have frequencies at least as high as *soft contact lens* (and they satisfy the linguistic filter used for the extraction of *soft contact lens*). However, *soft contact* is not a term in ophthalmology.

A quick solution to this problem is to extract only a substring of a candidate term if it appears a sufficient number of times by itself in the corpus (i.e. not only as a substring). Then, in order to calculate the termhood of a string, we should subtract from its total frequency its frequency as a substring of longer candidate terms

$$termhood(a) = f(a) - \sum_{b \in T_a} f(b) \qquad (2)$$

where
a is the candidate string,
$f(a)$ is its total frequency of occurrence in the corpus,
T_a is the set of candidate terms that contain a,
b is such a candidate term,
$f(b)$ is the frequency of the candidate term b that contains a.

However, the problem is not totally solved. Consider the following two sets of terms from computer science.

real time clock	floating point arithmetic
real time expert system	floating point constant
real time image generation	floating point operation
real time output	floating point routine
real time systems	

Both of these two sets contain *nested terms*. We call *nested terms* those that appear within other longer terms, and may or may not appear by themselves in the corpus. The first set contains the term *real time* and the second the term *floating point*. Except *expert system*, all of the other substrings, *time clock, time expert system, time image generation, image generation, time output, time systems, point arithmetic, point constant, point operation, point routine*, are not terms. So substrings of terms may or may not be terms themselves. Also, terms that are substrings do not have to appear by themselves in a text. As a result, a measure like formula 2 would exclude terms if these have been only found as nested, or if they are not nested but present a very low frequency.

So, could we avoid the extraction of substrings that are not terms, and at the same time extract those substrings that are terms?

Simply by looking at the above two sets of examples, we might suspect that *real time* and *floating point* are terms. The indication is that *real time* appears in every term of the first set, and *floating point* in every term of the second. We have no such indication for *time clock, time expert system, time image generation, image generation, time output, time systems, point arithmetic, point constant, point operation, point routine*.

Because *real time* appears in 5 longer terms, and *floating point* in 4 longer terms, this means that both show 'independence' from the longer terms they appear in. This is not the case for *time clock*, which only appears in one term. The higher the number of longer terms that our string appears as nested in, the more certain we can be about its independence.

The last parameter in the *C-value* measure is the length of the candidate string in terms of number of words. Since it is less probable that a longer string will appear f times in a corpus than a shorter string[3], the fact that a longer string appears f times is more important than that of a shorter string appearing f times. For this reason, we incorporate into the measure the length of the candidate string.

Since the maximum length terms can not be nested in longer terms, and some strings are never found as nested anyway, we distinguish two cases

1. If a is a string of maximum length or has not been found as nested, then its termhood will be the result of its total frequency in the corpus and its length.
2. If a is a string of any other shorter length, then we must consider if it is part of any longer candidate terms. If it appears as part of longer candidate terms, then its termhood will also consider its frequency as a nested string, as well as the number of these longer candidate terms. Though the fact that it appears as part of longer candidate terms affects its termhood negatively, the bigger the number of these candidate terms, the higher would be its independence from these. This latter number moderates the negative effect of the candidate string being nested in longer candidate terms.

The measure of termhood, called *C-value* is given as

$$C\text{-}value(a) = \begin{cases} log_2|a| \cdot f(a) & \\ & a \text{ is not nested,} \\ log_2|a|(f(a) - \frac{1}{P(T_a)} \sum_{b \epsilon T_a} f(b)) & \\ & otherwise \end{cases} \quad (3)$$

where
a is the candidate string,
$f(.)$ is its frequency of occurrence in the corpus,
T_a is the set of extracted candidate terms that contain a,
$P(T_a)$ is the number of these candidate terms.

It is obvious that *C-value* is a measure based on the frequency of occurrence of a. The negative effect on the candidate string a being a substring of other longer candidate terms is reflected by the negative sign '−' in front of the $\sum_{b \epsilon T_a} f(b)$. The independence of a from these longer candidate terms is given by $P(T_a)$. That the greater this number the bigger its independence (and the opposite), is reflected by having $P(T_a)$ as the denominator of a negatively signed fraction.

---

[3] This is based on the assumption that the probability of occurrence of the word a in the corpus is independent from the probability of occurrence of any other word in the corpus, which is not always true, [10].

The positive effect of the length of the candidate string is moderated by the application of the logarithm on it.

2.3 The Algorithm

In this subsection we describe the steps taken in the *C-value* method to construct a list of candidate terms from a corpus.

Step 1
We tag the corpus. As mentioned earlier, we need the tagging process since we will use a linguistic filter to restrict the type of terms to be extracted.

Step 2
This stage extracts those strings that satisfy the linguistic filter and frequency threshold. The terms will be extracted from among these strings. The maximum length of the extracted strings depends on:

1. The working domain. In arts for example, terms tend to be shorter than in science and technology.
2. The type of terms we accept. Terms that only consist of nouns for example, very rarely contain more than 5 or 6 words.

The process of finding this maximum length is as follows: We attempt to extract strings of a specific length. If we do not find any strings of this length, we decrease the number by 1 and make a new attempt. We continue in this way until we find a length for which strings exist.

At this point, extraction of the candidate strings can take place. Initially, a list of strings of each length is created, i.e. a list for the bigrams, a list for the trigrams, etc. Here, we remove the word tag, thereby preventing more than one tag for the same word[4]. The lists contain the strings with their frequency of occurrence.

The lists are then filtered through the stop-list and are concatenated. The longest strings appear at the top, and decrease in size as we move down, with the bigrams being at the bottom. The strings of each length are ordered by their frequency of occurrence.

Step 3
This is the stage where the *C-value* for each of the candidate strings is evaluated. *C-value* is calculated in order of the size of the strings, starting with the longest ones and finishing with the bigrams. The *C-value* for the longest terms is given by the top branch of formula 3.

We set a *C-value* threshold, so that only those strings with *C-value* above this threshold are added onto the list of candidate terms. For the evaluation of *C-value* for any of the shorter strings, we need two more parameters (their frequency as part of longer candidate terms, and the number of these longer candidate terms).

---

[4] We will provide examples in the next subsection.

To obtain these two parameters, we perform the following:

For every string a, that it is extracted as a candidate term, we create for each of its substrings b, a triple $(f(b), t(b), c(b))$,

where

$f(b)$ is the total frequency of b in the corpus,

$t(b)$ is the frequency of b as a nested string of candidate terms,

$c(b)$ is the number of these longer candidate terms.

When this triple is first created, $c(b) = 1$ and $t(b)$ equals the frequency of a. Each time b is found after that, $t(b)$ and $c(b)$ are updated, while $f(b)$, its total frequency, does not change.

$c(b)$ and $t(b)$ are updated in the following manner:

$c(b)$ is increased by 1 every time b is found within a longer string a that is extracted as a candidate term.

$t(b)$ is increased by the frequency of the longer candidate term a, $f(a)$, every time b is found as nested. If $n(a)$ is the number of times a has appeared as nested, then $t(b)$ will be increased by $f(a) - n(a)$.

Now in order to calculate *C-value* for a string a which is shorter by one word, we either already have for it a triple $(f(a), t(a), c(a))$ or we do not. If we do not, we calculate the *C-value* from the top branch of formula 3. If we do, we use the bottom branch of formula 3.

In that case, $P(T_a) = c(a)$ and $\sum_{b \epsilon T_a} = t(a)$.

After the calculation of *C-value* for strings of length l finishes we move to the calculation of *C-value* for strings of length $l - 1$. This way it is evident whether the string to be processed has been found nested in longer candidate terms.

At the end of this step, a list of candidate terms has been built. The strings of the list are ranked by their *C-value*.

An example on how *C-value* works can be found in [12].

2.4 The Application on a Medical Corpus

The corpus consists of eye-pathology medical records. Initially we had to delete all the fields with the personal details of each record (i.e. name, address, age, etc.). From each record two fields were kept: the diagnosis and the description of the disease, resulting in a corpus of 810,719 words in upper case. The size is enough for our statistical processing, since it is an SL corpus rather than a GL one. Lehrberger points out that 'lexical restrictions may consist of the exclusion of large parts of the total vocabulary of the language due to restricted subject matter', [22].

The corpus contains orthographical mistakes, e.g. *trabenular* instead of *trabecular*, *meshwrk, meshowrk, mehswrok* instead of *meshwork* etc. It also shows inconsistencies as in the following two cases:

1. The use of hyphens. The same term appears with or without a hyphen or even as one word: *vitreoretinal* and *vitreo-retinal, superonasal,*

supero-nasal, and *supernasal, serofibrinous, sero-fibrinous,* and *sero fibrinous.* The use of a hyphen, as we have seen, is a general problem of term recognition (i.e. variation).

2. The single quotes (' and '). These are used sometimes to enclose a term or even a part of a term. For example *naevoid cells* and *'naevoid cells', 'naevoid' cells, V-shaped perforation,* and *'V'-shaped perforation, basaloid cells,* and *'basaloid' cells.* In most of these cases we removed the single quotes.

We tagged the corpus with Brill's rule-based part-of-speech tagger, [4, 5]. Before tagging, the corpus had to be tokenised following the Penn Treebank Tokenisation, [23]. Punctuation had to be separated from the words, and the corpus placed in a one-sentence-per-line format.

Sample of the corpus before the tokenisation, after the tokenisation but before the tagging, and after the tagging can be found in [16].

The tagged corpus is ready for the extraction of candidate strings that are selected by the linguistic filter, the frequency threshold and the stop-list. In order to check the performance of *C-value* with various filters, we extract 3 lists of candidate strings, using the 3 following filters we mentioned in subsection 2.1. The maximum length strings we extract consist of 5 words.

The frequency threshold used for the 3 lists extracted by those filters, is 3, i.e. only strings with frequency of occurrence of 3 or more are extracted. The stop-list was constructed by examining a sample of the corpus (1/10 of its size) and consists of 229 word.

At this stage, these three lists are those that would be produced using the 'traditional' statistical measure for multi-word ATR, i.e. frequency of occurrence plus a linguistic filter. We will use these three lists to compare the performance of the *C-value* list with that of pure frequency of occurrence.

The *C-value* algorithm is applied to each of the three lists. We set the value of the *C-value* threshold 0, i.e. strings with *C-value* greater than 0 will be included in the final list. The strings with a *C-value* of 0 are those found *only* as nested in *one* longer candidate term.

For each of the input lists (i.e. for each of the linguistic filters), one *C-value* list is produced. The strings within each list are ranked according to their *C-value*, ready for evaluation by the domain-expert.

2.5 Evaluation

ATR techniques are mostly based on frequency, since terms tend to appear with high frequencies, [7, 18]. *C-value* also uses the parameter of frequency. However, there are terms that appear with very low frequencies: *toxoplasmic choriorenititis, vernal conjunctivitis, zoster keratitis,* all appear only once. Since *C-value* uses a frequency filter, it will not extract these terms. In order to be able to extract low frequency terms, we should not use a frequency threshold. This is possible[5], but it will increase the manual intervention of the domain expert, who

---

[5] Then, what *C-value* would aim to do is a re-ranking of the list, moving the real terms closer to the top of the list.

evaluates the produced list to extract the 'real' terms. The list would then be a lot longer: in our corpus, the strings with frequency greater than 2 (in the list of the 2nd linguistic filter) are 2,956. If we include also those with frequency 2, they become 5,560. And if we also include those with frequency 1 the number rises to 16,688. For this reason a frequency threshold is used. If however, the application requires higher recall and permits lower precision, the frequency threshold can be removed, or moved to lower values.

We will now evaluate the results of *C-value* in terms of precision and recall and compare them with those of frequency of occurrence.

There exists a lack of formal or precise rules which would help us to decide between a term and a non-term. Domain experts (who are not linguists or terminologists) do not always agree on termhood. Given this fact, we talk about 'relative' rather than 'absolute' values of precision and recall, in comparison with the alternative proposed method of frequency of occurrence. We will compare the results of the *C-value* method and the method that uses frequency of occurrence, using the three linguistic filters described before.

We calculate precision for each of the three linguistic filters, and compare them with the corresponding result of frequency of occurrence. Since *C-value* is a method to improve the extraction of nested terms, the comparison is made for this category of terms. We also calculate the overall values of precision (over the whole lists).

If we wanted to calculate the absolute value for recall, a domain expert would have had to find all the multi-word terms from the corpus (or a sufficiently large sample of it), and then we would have had to check whether these terms had been extracted by *C-value*. Given the time-consuming nature of this task, we decided to calculate recall with respect to frequency of occurrence, which we used as the baseline method.

Table 1 shows the precision for

1. the candidate terms that have also appeared as nested,
2. the candidate terms that have only appeared as nested,
3. all the candidate terms,

extracted by *C-value* and by frequency of occurrence, using the three linguistic filters. For the first case, the results show that, using *C-value*, precision increases by 6% for the first filter, 7% for the second, and 8% for the third filter. The precision using the third filter is only 1% less than that of the first filter. This shows that with the *C-value* method we can use an open linguistic filter without losing much precision.

For the second case, using the *C-value* method, precision increases by more than 31% for the first filter, 38% for the second, and 31% for the third filter. The precision for the second and third filters are even greater than that of the first. This strengthens the point that with *C-value* we have the freedom to use a more open linguistic filter that extracts more types of terms.

For the third case, the differences are not as impressive as before, due to the fact that there are candidate terms that have never been found as nested, and as such, they are treated by *C-value* in a similar way to frequency (the only difference being the incorporation of the length of the candidate term). These candidate terms moderate the increase we have on precision for the nested terms when using *C-value*.

		1st filter	2nd filter	3rd filter
also	*C-v*	40.76%	44.18%	39.58%
nested	freq	34.4%	37.59%	31.96%
only	*C-v*	50%	60%	54.54%
nested	freq	18.57%	22%	12.91%
	C-v	38%	36%	31%
all	freq	36%	35%	30%

Table 1. Precision: *C-value* vs Frequency

C-value is an additional filter to that of frequency of occurrence, and as such, the maximum recall it can reach is that of frequency of occurrence. Table 2 shows recall compared with frequency of occurrence, for the three linguistic filters. It provides both the overall recall, and the recall for the first 25% of extracted candidate terms. We see that with the *C-value* filter, recall falls less than 2% with the first linguistic filter, and around 2.5% with the second and third linguistic filters. However, regarding the first part of the lists, recall does not fall at all when using the first linguistic filter, and increases by 1% and 1.5% when using the second and third linguistic filters respectively. This shows exactly that *C-value* 'attracts' real terms more than pure frequency of occurrence, placing them closer to the top of the extracted list.

interval	1st filter	2nd filter	3rd filter
overall	98.22%	97.41%	97.47%
first 25%	100%	101.13%	101.41%

Table 2. Recall: *C-value* vs frequency.

3 Incorporating Context Information

In this section we incorporate context information into ATR. Subsection 3.1 provides the rationale for using context information. Subsection 3.2 provides a description of the proposed method to extract term context words and to assign them a weight of 'importance'. The application of the method to our medical corpus and its evaluation is presented in subsection 3.3. Subsection 3.4 describes *NC-value*, an extension to *C-value* which uses context information for the extraction of multi-word terms. In subsection 3.5 we evaluate the results of *NC-value* on our medical corpus, and compare *NC-value* with *C-value* and frequency of occurrence.

3.1 Context Information

We often use the environment of a word to identify its meaning. In automatic systems the information used for disambiguation is restricted mainly to surface criteria as opposed to semantic, discourse and pragmatic information. Lexical information from the context of words has been used for the construction of thesaurus dictionaries [17]. In that case, the context of a word provides clues to its meaning and its synonyms. Grefenstette's system, SEXTANT, uses local lexical information to acquire synonyms. Words that are used in a lexically similar way are candidates to be synonymous. The nouns, adjectives and verbs from the context of the examined word are used to give hints for its meaning.

Regarding term recognition, Sager, [24], stated that terms are strict about the modifiers they accept:

> "Extended term units are different in type from extended word units in that they cannot be freely modified. There is a very limited range of qualifiers which can be used with the term 'heat transfer'; the word 'heat wave' can be modified by such hyperbolic expressions as 'suffocating' or 'never ending' and a great number of other qualifiers. Extended terms are linguistic representations of essential characteristics whereas in words such collocations are inessential in that they can be omitted without affecting the denotation of the head of the nominal group as a lexeme." [24]

Since extended term units differ from extended word units as far as modification is concerned, we could use information from the modifiers to distinguish between terms and non-terms. Thus, if *consistent* is an adjective that tends to precede terms in medical corpora, and it occurs before a candidate term string, we could exploit this information for the benefit of term recognition. Besides adjectives and nouns, we can expand the use of modifier types to verbs that belong to the environment of the candidate term: the string *show* of the verb *to show* in medical domains is often followed by a term, e.g. *shows a basal cell carcinoma*. The string *called* of the verb *to call*, and the form *known* of the verb *to know*, are often involved in definitions, e.g. *is known as the singular existential quantifier* and *is called the Cartesian product*. We will use the three part-of-speech elements also used by [17] to obtain information about the termhood of a candidate string, when they either precede or follow it. These are

1. nouns (*compound cellular naevus*),
2. adjectives (*blood vessels are present*), and
3. verbs (*composed of basaloid papillae*).

3.2   The context weighting factor

Here we describe a method to create a list of 'important' *term context words* from a set of terms extracted from a specialised corpus. By term context words we mean those that appear in the vicinity of terms in texts. These will be ranked according to their 'importance' when appearing with terms.

The context words we treat are adjectives, nouns and verbs that either precede or follow the candidate term.

The criterion for the extraction of a word as a term context word is *the number of terms it appears with*. The assumption is that the higher this number, the higher the likelihood that the word is 'related' to terms, and that it will occur with other terms in the same corpus. Term context words for a specific domain/corpus are not necessarily the same for another domain/corpus. For this reason, we relate term context words to a specific corpus. For example, the words *present, shows, appear, composed* tend to appear with terms in our medical corpus, but may have different meaning if found in a different domain, e.g. mathematics.

We can express the above criterion more formally with the measure

$$Weight(w) = \frac{t(w)}{n} \tag{4}$$

where
w is the context word (noun, verb or adjective) to be assigned a weight as a term context word,
$Weight(w)$ the assigned weight to the word w,
$t(w)$ the number of terms the word w appears with,
n the total number of terms considered.

The purpose of the denominator n is to express this weight as a probability: the probability that the word w might be a term context word. We will elaborate on this point in the following subsection.

3.3   Evaluation

The context weighting factor is a measure that gives the probability for a context word to appear with terms, by expressing the percentage of terms that the context word has appeared with. This measure is in line with the definition of probability of an event as given in probability theory, [20].

Despite its validity as a probability measure, we believe that it could be strengthened if we (somehow) include information not only from terms but from non-terms as well. In other words, we should consider the number of terms that a candidate context word appears with, as well as the number of non-terms. The second number should negatively affect the degree by which the candidate context word is a term context word. This parameter has not been incorporated in the current measure.

Let us now consider the type of words that we treat as candidates for term context words. In line with Grefenstette, [17], we use nouns, adjectives and verbs that appear in the candidate term's environment. Our choice is also influenced by Sager, [24], who states that terms are strict in the modifiers they accept. However we believe that further investigation of the following issues may improve the extraction of term context words:

1. Some of the above three lexical categories (nouns, adjectives, verbs) may be more important for termhood information. For example, it could be the case that nouns give more information about the termhood of a candidate term than verbs.
2. Some of the above three lexical categories (nouns, adjectives, verbs) may be more important when they either precede or follow the candidate string. For example, it could be the case that verbs that precede the candidate string are more important than verbs that follow it.

We evaluate the list of the term context words produced by the weighting measure. With this evaluation, we want to establish to what degree the extracted term context words relate to terms. We create a list of context words using the above measure and a set of terms from our corpus. Then, we establish the relationship of the extracted words to

1. another set of terms that does not overlap with the one used to create the list of context words,
2. a set of non-terms.

The words in the list of term context words are ordered by the proposed measure. We will consider three different sets from this list to establish the above mentioned relationship:

1. A set taken from the top of the list.
2. A set taken from the middle of the list.
3. A set taken from the bottom of the list.

Our aim is to establish that the first set shows greater association to terms than the third set, and smaller association to non-terms than the third set. Ideally, the second set's results should be in the middle.

We first take a list of terms from our corpus. We use the list extracted by *C-value*. We extract 200 'real' terms[6] from this list. Using these terms and formula 4 we create the list of term context words.

The 200 verified terms comprise the 20% of terms that have been extracted. We will see how the remaining 80% of terms of the *C-value* list associate with the term context words extracted. We will also see the association of non-terms from the *C-value* list with these term context words.

---

[6] Terms extracted and verified by a domain expert.

We extract three sets of term context words from the top, the middle and the bottom of the list, each set consisting of 20 words. These sets can be found at [16]. We obtain the number of terms each context word appears with, and we then sum them up obtaining the total number of terms for each set of context words. The percentage of terms over terms plus non-terms for each set is given in table ??. We can see that the top set is associated with 12% more terms than the middle one and 21% more terms than the bottom one.

	top set	middle set	bottom set
terms	56%	44%	35%

Table 3. Context words relating to terms.

Our proposed measure for the extraction of term context words accomplishes its purpose, which is to assign high values to words that tend to appear with terms. We therefore use it to extract term context words that will then be used to improve the extraction of terms.

3.4   NC-value

In this subsection we present the method we call *NC-value*, which incorporates context information into the *C-value* method for the extraction of multi-word terms. Assuming we have a corpus from which we want to extract the terms, we divide the algorithm into three stages.

First stage
We apply the *C-value* method to the corpus. The output of this process is a list of candidate terms, ordered by their *C-value*.

Second stage
This involves the extraction of the term context words and their weights. These will be used in the third stage to improve the term distribution in the extracted list. In order to extract the term context words, we need a set of terms, as discussed in the previous section. We have chosen to keep the method domain-independent and fully-automatic (until the manual evaluation of the final list of candidate terms by the domain-expert). Therefore, we do not use any external source (e.g. a dictionary) which will provide us with the set of terms to be used for this purpose. We use instead the 'top' candidate terms from the *C-value* list, which present very high precision on real terms. We expect to find non-terms among these candidate terms that could produce 'noise', but these non-terms are scarce enough not to cause any real problems. We have chosen to accept a small amount of noise, i.e. non-terms, for the sake of full automation. These

'top' terms produce a list of term context words and assign to each of them a weight following the process described in the previous section.

Third stage

This involves the incorporation of context information acquired from the second stage of the extraction of multi-word terms. The *C-value* list of candidate terms extracted during stage one is re-ranked using context information, so that the real terms appear closer to the top of the list than they did before, i.e. the concentration of real terms at the top of the list increases while the concentration of those at the bottom decreases. The re-ranking takes place in the following way: Each candidate term from the *C-value* list appears in the corpus with a set of context words. From these context words, we retain the nouns, adjectives and verbs for each candidate term. These words may or may not have been met before, during the second stage of the creation of the list with the term context words. In the case where they have been met, they retain their assigned weight. Otherwise, they are assigned zero weight. For each candidate term, we obtain the context factor by summing up: the weights for its term context words, multiplied by their frequency appearing with this candidate term.

For example, assume that the candidate word W appears 10 times with the context word c_1, 20 times with the context word c_2, and 30 times with the context word c_3. Assume also that the weight for c_1 is w_1, the weight for c_2 is w_2, and the weight for c_3 is w_3. Then, the context factor for W is:
$10 \cdot w_1 + 20 \cdot w_2 + 30 \cdot w_3$

The above description is the second factor of the *NC-value* measure which re-ranks the *C-value* list of candidate terms. The first factor is the *C-value* of the candidate terms. The whole *NC-value* measure is formally described as

$$NC\text{-}value(a) = 0.8\,C\text{-}value\ (a) + 0.2 \sum_{b \in C_a} f_a(b) weight(b) \qquad (5)$$

where
a is the candidate term,
C_a is the set of distinct context words of a,
b is a word from C_a,
$f_a(b)$ is the frequency of b as a term context word of a,
$weight(b)$ is the weight of b as a term context word.

The two factors of *NC-value*, i.e. *C-value* and the context information factor, have been assigned the weights 0.8 and 0.2 respectively. These have been chosen among others after experiments and comparisons of the results, as we will discuss in the following section.

3.5 Evaluation

The top of the list produced by *C-value* is used for the extraction of term context words, and the list produced by *C-value* is re-ranked by *NC-value*. However, *NC-value* can be viewed independently from the *C-value* in the sense that in the above sentence we can substitute *C-value* with a different method for the extraction of terms. That is, the proposed method for incorporating context information can be applied to other approaches for term extraction, i.e. frequency of occurrence.

Let us now consider the creation of the list with the term context words, to be used by *NC-value*. The top candidate terms from the *C-value* list are used[7], since these show high precision on real terms. It is expected that among those terms there will be some non-terms as well. This is unavoidable since we have chosen to keep this process fully-automatic. Full-automation can be sacrificed for the sake of 'correctness' in different applications. In that case, a domain expert would have to check the top of the *C-value* list, that will be used for the extraction of the term context words, and remove the non-terms. The process after this would remain the same.

Regarding the weights 0.8 and 0.2 that have been assigned to *C-value* and the context factor in the *NC-value* measure, these were chosen among others after a series of experiments. The combination 0.8–0.2 gave the best distribution in the precision of extracted terms.

Regarding the evaluation of the results, we carried out tests using the *C-value* list produced by the linguistic filter which includes the preposition 'of'. We chose this filter as it was the most open among the three used, and as such it was the most flexible, accommodating many domains.

The *NC-value* list can be found in [16]. The evaluation will be in terms of precision only. The recall of the *NC-value* list is the same to that of the *C-value* list, since *NC-value* re-ranks the *C-value* list without adding or deleting any candidate terms. As such, the recall of the *NC-value* list is 97.47% (with respect to the real terms extracted by the method based on frequency of occurrence).

The overall precision is the same for the *C-value* list, i.e. 31%. What is different is the distribution of terms in the extracted list. Table 4, and table 5, show the precision and accumulative precision of the *NC-value* list, in comparison with the corresponding *C-value* and frequency of occurrence for the intervals of the ordered candidate terms in the lists. The intervals have been chosen so as to have approximately the same number of n-grams among the lists of the three methods.

The first column in table 4 shows the three methods used. The remaining columns show the precision for each method within the specified intervals. For example, the precision of the *NC-value* for the first interval [top to 40] is 75.70%. The same format is used in table 5, where the accumulative precision is presented.

From the above, we observe that *NC-value* increases the concentration of real terms at the top of the list. More precisely, we observe that *NC-value* brings a 5% increase in precision for the first two intervals.

For the third interval we see a small drop in precision, which is even smaller for the fourth interval. These drops are expected and are desirable due to the increase of precision for the first two intervals. The drops seem smaller than the increases for the first two intervals just because the third and fourth intervals contain a large number of strings.

---

[7] The first 5% extracted candidate terms were used for these experiments.

	[top–40]	(40–10]	(10–4)	[4–bottom]
NC-value	75.70%	36.08%	26.41%	25.60%
C-value	70.84%	31.31%	27.11%	25.56%
frequency	69.62%	31.64%	24.94%	25.44%

Table 4. Precision: *NC-value*, *C-value* and frequency.

	[top–40]	(top–10]	(top–4)	[top–bottom]
NC-v	75.70%	46.14%	32.80%	31.15%
C-v	70.84%	42.24%	33.04%	31.15%
freq	69.24%	41.70%	33.50%	29.70%

Table 5. Accumulative precision: *NC-value*, *C-value* and frequency.

4 Conclusions

This paper presented and evaluated the *C-value/NC-value* domain-independent method for the semi-automatic extraction of multi-word terms from special language English corpora. We showed two main points:

1. Using more statistical information than the pure frequency of occurrence of candidate terms, improves the precision of the extracted nested multi-word terms, with a slight only loss on recall.
2. Using information from the context of the candidate terms, improves their distribution in the extracted list, i.e. real terms tend to appear closer to the top, while non-terms concentrate closer to the bottom of the list.

We note here that this work was tested in only one corpus. This corpus consisted of medical records and belongs to a specific text type that covers well-structured texts. Although we have shown that the method performs well for this text type of corpora, we are cautious in making this claim for other types of special language corpora, before conducting appropriate experiments.

5 Acknowledgments

We thank Dr. Tom Sharp for providing us with the corpus, and Dr. Michael Florin and Az Bakar for evaluating the extracted lists of candidate terms.

References

1. Ananiadou, S.: A Methodology for Automatic Term Recognition. Proceedings of the 15th International Conference on Computational Linguistics, COLING'94, (1994) 1034–1038
2. Ananiadou, S.: Towards a Methodology for Automatic Term Recognition. University of Manchester Institute of Science and Technology (1988)
3. Bourigault, D.: Surface Grammatical Analysis for the Extraction of Terminological Noun Phrases. Proceedings of the 14th International Conference on Computational Lingustics, COLING'92, (1992) 977–981
4. Brill, E.: A simple rule-based part of speech tagger. Proceedings of the 3rd Conference of Applied Natural Language Processing, ANLP'92, (1992)
5. Brill, E.: A Corpus-Based Approach to Language Learning. Ph.D. Thesis, Dept. of Computer and information Science, University of Pennsylvania (1993)
6. Dagan, I., Pereira, F., Lee, L.: Similarity-Based Estimation of Word Cooccurence Probabilities. Proceedings of the 32nd Annual Meeting of the Association for Computational Linguistics, ACL'94, (1994) 272–278
7. Dagan, I., Church, K.: Termight: Identifying and Translating Technical Terminology. Proceedings of the 7th Conference of the European Chapter of the Association for Computational Linguistics, EACL'95, (1995) 34–40
8. Daille, B., Gaussier, E., Langé, J.: Towards Automatic extraction of Monolingual and Bilingual Terminology. Proceedings of the 15th International Conference on Computational Linguistics, COLING'94, (1994) 515–521
9. Damerau, F.J.: Generating and Evaluating Domain-Oriented Multi-Word Terms from Texts. Information Processing & Management 29 (1993) 433–447
10. Dunning, T.: Accurate Methods for the Statistics of Surprise and Coincidence. Computational Linguistics 19 (1993) 61–74
11. Enguehard, C., Pantera, L.: Automatic Natural Acquisition of a Terminology. Journal of Quantitative Linguistics 2 (1994) 27–32
12. Frantzi, K.T., and Sophia Ananiadou, S., Tsujii, J.: Extracting Terminological Expressions. The Special Interest Group Notes of Information Processing Society of Japan, 96-NL-112, (1996) 83–88
13. Frantzi, K.T., Ananiadou, S.: Extracting Nested Collocations. Proceedings of the 16th International Conference on Computational Linguistics, COLING'96, (1996) 41–46
14. Frantzi, K.T., Ananiadou, S., Tsujii, J.: Automatic Term Recognition using Contextual Cues. Proceedings of the 2nd Workshop on Multilinguality in Software Industry (MULSAIC'97), 15th International Joint Conference on Artificial Intelligence, IJCAI'97, (1997) 73–79
15. Frantzi, K.T.: Incorporating Context Information for the Extraction of Terms. Proceedings of the 35th Annual Meeting of the Association for Computational Linguistics (ACL) and 8th Conference of the European Chapter of the Association for Computational Linguistics (EACL), (1997) 501–503
16. Frantzi, K.T.: Automatic Recognition of Multi-Word Terms. Ph.D. Thesis, Manchester Metropolitan University Dept. Of Computing & Mathematics, in collaboration with UMIST Centre for Computational Linguistics, (1998)
17. Grefenstette, G.: Explorations in Automatic Thesaurus Discovery. Kluwer Academic Publishers, (1994)
18. Justeson, J.S., Katz, S.M.: Technical terminology: some linguistic properties and an algorithm for identification in text. Natural Language Engineering 1 (1995) 9–27

19. Kageura, K., Umino, B,: Methods of Automatic Term Recognition -A Review-. Terminology **3** (1996) 259–289
20. Larson, H.J., Larson, J.: Introduction to probability theory and statistical inference. Wiley series in probability and mathematical statistics, Wiley, New York, Chichester (1982)
21. Lauriston, A.: Automatic Term Recognition: performance of Linguistic and Statistical Techniques. Ph.D. Thesis, University of Manchester Institute of Science and Technology (1996)
22. Lehrberger, J.: Sublanguage analysis. Analyzing language in restricted domains, Ralph Grishman and Richard Kittredge (editors), Lawrence Erlbaum, **2** (1986) 19–38
23. Penn: Penn Treebank Annotation. Computational Linguistics **19** (1993)
24. Sager, J.C.: Commentary by Prof. Juan Carlos Sager, Actes Table Ronde sur les Problèmes du Découpage du Terms, Montréal, 26 aouũt. Guy Rondeau, AILA–Comterm,Office de la Langue Francaise, Québec, (1978) 39–74
25. Sager, J.C., Dungworth, D., McDonald, P.F.: English Special Languages: principles and practice in science and technology. Oscar Brandstetter Verlag KG, Wiesbaden, (1980)
26. Sager, J.C.: A Practical Course in Terminology Processing. John Benjamins Publishing Company, (1990)
27. Salton, G.: Introduction to modern information retrieval. Computer Science, McGraw-Hill (1983)

Comparing the Effect of Syntactic vs. Statistical Phrase Indexing Strategies for Dutch

Wessel Kraaij[1] and Renée Pohlmann[2]

[1] Institute of Applied Physics
Netherlands Organisation for Applied Scientific Research (TNO)
Delft
The Netherlands
kraaij@tpd.tno.nl
[2] Utrecht Institute of Linguistics OTS
Utrecht University
Utrecht
The Netherlands
Renee.C.Pohlmann@let.uu.nl
http://www-uilots.let.uu.nl/~uplift

Abstract. In this paper we describe the results of experiments contrasting syntactic phrase indexing with statistical phrase indexing for Dutch texts. Our results showed that we at least need a compound splitting algorithm for good quality retrieval for Dutch texts. If we then add either syntactic or statistical phrases, performance generally improves, but this effect is never statistically significant. If we compare syntactic vs. statistical phrase indexing, syntactic phrases are slightly superior to statistical phrases, particularly at high precision. At higher recall levels syntactic and statistical phrases are equally effective. However, since a compound splitting algorithm requires a dictionary and knowledge about constraints on compound formation, a purely non-linguistic indexing strategy, with or without phrases, does not seem to be very effective for Dutch.

1 Introduction

It is common practice in Information Retrieval (IR) to use phrases as indexing terms in order to enhance precision. The basic idea behind phrase indexing is that phrases characterize document content more effectively than single word terms. When a single word index is used, a query containing the phrase *information retrieval* will also match with documents containing only *information* or *retrieval*. If *information retrieval* is recognized as a unit, however, these matches may be avoided or given a much lower score (depending on the matching strategy). Different strategies have been used to identify suitable phrases for indexing, the most important distinction being between strategies based on statistical co-occurrence data and strategies based on linguistic processing. So far, both types of strategies have proven to be successful in improving retrieval effectiveness (cf. e.g. [5] and [15]), but comparisons between the two approaches have not been able to show much difference between them (cf. e.g. [6], [13] and, more recently, [9] and [11]).

In [12] we reported on the results of our experiments with syntactic phrase indexing for Dutch monolingual retrieval. These experiments showed that it is possible to improve retrieval effectiveness for Dutch texts by using syntactic information to create complex index terms. In this paper we will describe the results of a complementary experiment with phrases based on statistical co-occurrence data. The rest of this paper is organized as follows: In section 2 we will summarize our earlier experiment with syntactic phrases. In sections 3 and 4 we will present the results of our experiments with statistical phrases and in section 5 we will formulate our conclusions and give some directions for further research.

2 Syntactic Phrase Experiment

The experiments described in [12] were inspired by similar work for English by Strzalkowski (cf. [14]). Strzalkowski uses a statistical IR system extended with an NLP module which extracts phrases from both queries and documents in addition to single word terms. To create a uniform representation for semantically similar but syntacticly different constructions, e.g. *retrieval of information* vs. *information retrieval*, the phrases are normalized as head-modifier pairs. Strzalkowski's NLP module generates parse trees for entire sentences and extracts the following head-modifier pairs from these structures:

1. a head noun of a noun phrase and its left adjective or noun adjunct
2. a head noun and the head of its right adjunct
3. the main verb of a clause and the head of its object phrase
4. the head of the subject phrase and the main verb

We used the same basic design for our experiments with syntactic phrase indexing. We extended the TRU vector space retrieval engine [1] with an NLP module consisting of the Multext part-of-speech tagger [2], a stemmer based on the CELEX lexical database [3] and the Patz'er NP-parser [18]. We evaluated a number of indexing strategies using different criteria for the extraction of head-modifier pairs from the texts and for the addition of phrase constituents as separate index terms. Our parser, however, does not generate parse trees for entire sentences but only identifies and assigns structure to noun phrases. We therefore only used a subset of the types of head-modifier pairs that Strzalkowski uses (i.e. categories 1 and 2). Like Strzalkowski, we experimented with using corpus statistics to assign head-modifier structure to ambiguous noun phrases. We collected frequency information for unambiguous head-modifier pairs in our corpus and used this information to select the most probable structure in case of ambiguity. We also experimented with assigning a default structure to ambiguous noun phrases. Figure 1 gives an example of head-modifier pair extraction from a complex NP.

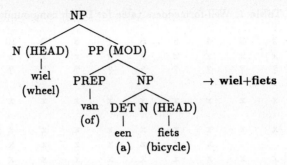

Fig. 1. head-modifier pair extraction from NP with PP modifier

In Dutch, compound nouns are usually written as a single orthographic unit, e.g. *levensverzekeringsmaatschappij* (life insurance company). As a result of this, compound constituents would normally not be treated as separate index terms by our basic retrieval engine. Earlier research in our project on stemming algorithms [10] indicated that splitting up compounds in queries and using the constituents for query expansion improves recall. We therefore incorporated a compound splitter in our NLP module and experimented with adding compound constituents as separate index terms and reducing complex compounds to head-modifier pairs. Figure 2 gives an example of head-modifier pair extraction from a complex compound.

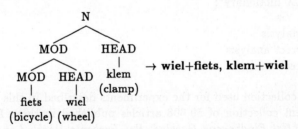

Fig. 2. head-modifier pair extraction from complex compound

The compound splitter was originally developed by Vosse [19] as part of a spelling checker. The splitter will try to split a compound into its components (stems) working from left to right on the basis of a well-formedness table for Dutch compounds and a lexicon. The lexicon used is again CELEX. The well-formedness table used by the splitter is reproduced in Table 1 below (cf. [19] p. 65), 'x' means that a combination is allowed and '?' that a combination is doubtful but not always disallowed.

Apart from the well-formedness table a number of simple heuristics are used to avoid unwanted or unlikely analyses, e.g. compounds analyzed as consisting

Table 1. Well-formedness table for Dutch compounds

WF	1	2	3	4	5	6	7	8	9	10
1	x	x	x	x	x	x	x	x	x	x
2	?	?	?	?	?	?	?	?	?	?
3										
4	x	x	x	x	x	x	x	x	x	x
5										
6	x	x	x	x	x	x	x	x	x	x
7			x	x	x	x	x	x	x	x
8	x	x	x	x	x	x	x	x	x	x
9										
10										
11	x	x	x	x	x	x	x	x	x	x
12	x	x	x	x	x	x	x	x		
13										

1 = verb (stem), 2 = verb (infinitive), 3 = verb (any other form), 4 = noun (stem), 5 = noun (diminutive singular), 6 = noun (plural), 7 = noun (diminutive plural), 8 = adjective (stem), 9 = adjective (any other form), 10 = adverb, 11 = number, 12 = preposition, 13 = rest (pronouns, interjections ...)

of a large number of two- or three-letter words. If the splitter is unsuccessful, the word is left unchanged. The following results were obtained with the compound splitter using a random sample of approximately 1,000 compounds not included in the CELEX dictionary[1]:

- 5% no analysis
- 3% incorrect analysis
- 92% correct analysis

The test collection used for the experiments described in this paper consists of a document collection of 59,608 articles published in three Dutch regional newspapers (*Het Eindhovens Dagblad, Het Brabants Dagblad* and *Het Nieuwsblad*) from January to October 1994 and 66 queries and relevance judgements. The queries were formulated by test subjects recruited among staff and students of Utrecht University. Test subjects also performed the relevance judgements for their queries. Our test collection previously consisted of 36 queries and relevance judgements. We conducted a new user experiment and extended the number of queries to 66. The results quoted in this paper were obtained with the larger test corpus and therefore differ slightly from those published in earlier work (cf. [10] [12]). Some general statistics for the document collection are given in Table 2 below.

We used 4 different measures to evaluate retrieval performance for the experiment. These measures are: average precision, ap5-15 (precision at 5, 10 and

---

[1] Some frequent compounds are included in the CELEX dictionary.

Table 2. Document collection statistics

Total number of documents	59,608
Total number of words (tokens)	26,585,168
Total number of terms (types)	434,552
Max number of words per document	5,979
Av. number of words per document	446
Max number of terms per document	2,291
Av. number of terms per document	176

15 documents retrieved, averaged), R-recall (recall at R, where R is the number of relevant articles for a particular query) and recall1000 (recall at 1000 documents retrieved). We used the so-called *pooling method*[2] to compute the number of relevant articles per query. We also performed statistical significance tests to establish whether the differences between values are significant or should be attributed to chance. The design chosen for these statistical tests is based on [16] and [17]. Details on the statistical tests can be found in the appendix.

The results of our experiment indicated that adding head-modifier pairs to the index can improve retrieval effectiveness. The best overall results (16% improvement in average precision, 15% improvement in ap5-15, 22.7% improvement in R-recall and 16.8% improvement in recall1000, compared to the performance of our basic retrieval engine) were obtained by adding all noun-noun and noun-adjective head-modifier pairs from complex NPs (including complex compounds) to the index while, at the same time, adding all constituents as separate index terms.

We decided that it would be interesting to compare the results obtained in the syntactic phrase indexing experiment with results obtained using statistical phrases for indexing. As discussed in section 1 above, most researchers so far have found little or no difference in performance between linguistic and statistical phrase indexing methods for English test corpora. We wanted to see whether this result would also hold for our Dutch test corpus.

3 Statistical Phrase Experiment I

Our statistical phrase experiment was modeled on similar experiments by the SMART group with the TREC test collection [4]. Their definition of a statistical phrase is "any pair of adjacent non-stopwords which occurs in more than 25 documents of the TREC 1 document set". Because our document collection is significantly smaller than the TREC 1 collection (60.000 vs. 211.000 documents) we experimented with different document frequency thresholds for the statistical phrases. We set the threshold at 1-10, 15, 20 and 25. 3 turned out to be the best option for our corpus. We decided to take a system version with stemming but

---

[2] See [7] p. 9 *ff*.

610

without proper name recognition[3] (vBase) as a starting point for our statistical phrase experiments. In Table 3 the results of our experiment are summarized. For reference, the results for vTRU (the TRU vector space engine with no extensions at all) and vBase+prop (a version with proper name recognition) are also shown. vSyn is the best syntactic version of our previous experiments as described in section 2 above[4]. The percentages indicate improvement/decrease compared to the performance of the baseline (vBase).

Table 3. Evaluation measures averaged over queries

version	avp	% change	ap5-15	% change
vTRU	0.282	− 9.0	0.431	− 0.9
vBase	0.310		0.435	
vBase+prop	0.311	+ 0.3	0.437	+ 0.4
vStat	0.323	+ 4.2	0.451	+ 3.7
vStat+weight	0.327	+ 5.6	0.451	+ 3.7
vSyn	0.370	+ 19.2	0.496	+ 14.0

version	R-recall	% change	recall1000	% change
vTRU	0.311	− 6.4	0.785	− 8.2
vBase	0.333		0.855	
vBase+prop	0.336	+ 1.0	0.865	+ 1.2
vStat	0.345	+ 3.6	0.862	+ 0.9
vStat+weight	0.352	+ 5.9	0.863	+ 0.9
vSyn	0.382	+ 14.8	0.917	+ 7.2

It is immediately clear that the performance of the statistical version, although it is slightly better than vBase, is no way near the performance of the syntactic version. Decreasing the weight of the statistical phrases (vStat+weight), a common strategy in experiments with phrase indexing, slightly improves results for average precision and R-recall but the difference with vSyn is still considerable[5].

We decided to do a detailed per query analysis to find out what caused this difference in behaviour between the syntactic and the statistic versions. We identified queries that performed much better or worse than average for the different evaluation measures and system versions and we subsequently looked at these queries in detail. We produced lists which contained the scores and rank for each relevant and non-relevant document retrieved (cut-off at 200), the query terms that matched and their weight and the rank assigned to documents by the

---

[3] Our proper name recognition algorithm simply glues adjacent words with capitals together. The statistical phrase algorithm should also find the most frequent multi word proper names.
[4] Referred to as vAP1 in [12].
[5] And statistically significant, i.e. they are never in the same equivalence class, cf. the appendix for the results of statistical tests.

reference version. These lists made it easy to inspect the effect of individual query terms and phrases.

This detailed analysis revealed that compound splitting was probably responsible for most of the difference between the statistical and syntactic versions and that phrases only played a secondary role. Recall that, unlike the statistical versions, our syntactic version not only adds phrases but also splits up compounds in both queries and documents (see section 2 above). Compound constituents turned out to be very good search terms for quite a number of queries. Query 55, for example, contains the compound *theatervoorstelling* (theater performance). Of the 128 relevant documents for this query, 40 only contain (one of) the compound constituents *theater* or *voorstelling* but not the compound.

Furthermore, the compound splitting strategy has a secondary effect of emphasizing the compounds in queries and documents. Every compound is effectively doubled (they occur once as a compound but also as separate constituents). Although the results of our previous experiments with syntactic phrase indexing indicated that this effect is not solely responsible for improved performance[6], we decided to run a second experiment with statistical versions, which split up compounds as well as add phrases, so that we could compare the two strategies for phrase indexing and separate out the effect of adding phrases more accurately.

4 Statistical Phrase Experiment II

In this second experiment we tested two new statistical versions, one version (vStat+split) which besides adding statistical phrases also splits up compounds and, in order to separate out the effect of "compound doubling" as described in section 3 above more clearly, we also tested a second variant (vStat+replace) where compounds are *replaced* by their constituents[7]. We also added two new versions without phrases, one with compound doubling (vBase+split) and one with compound replacement (vBase+replace). Table 4 gives the results for this second experiment.

The results of the second experiment confirm our hypothesis that compound splitting is crucial for good quality retrieval for Dutch. Compound splitting alone (with or without doubling) is clearly responsible for most of the improvement in retrieval performance. Emphasizing compounds without adding phrases (vBase+split) always has a positive effect, especially at higher recall levels. Adding syntactic phrases (vSyn) always improves performance compared to vBase+split (although the difference is never statistically significant). The statistical versions with compound splitting (vStat+split and vStat+replace) are much better than the versions without splitting. In most cases, their performance is now comparable to the syntactic version. If we look at high precision

---

[6] In [12] we compared versions which only split up compounds with versions which also add phrases. The best phrase version (also used in this experiment) clearly outperformed the best split version.

[7] Although we later found that some compounds are still doubled because vStat+replace reunites the constituents in the statistical phrase formation process.

Table 4. Evaluation measures averaged over queries

version	avp	% change	ap5-15	% change
vBase	0.310		0.435	
vStat	0.323	+ 4.2	0.451	+ 3.7
vBase+split	0.364	+ 17.3	0.483	+ 11.0
vStat+split	0.363	+ 17.0	0.466	+ 7.1
vSyn(+split)	0.370	+ 19.2	0.496	+ 14.0
vBase+replace	0.349	+ 12.7	0.482	+ 10.8
vStat+replace	0.365	+ 17.6	0.481	+ 10.5

version	R-recall	% change	recall1000	% change
vBase	0.333		0.855	
vStat	0.345	+ 3.6	0.862	+ 0.9
vBase+split	0.376	+ 13.1	0.905	+ 5.9
vStat+split	0.380	+ 14.4	0.904	+ 5.8
vSyn(+split)	0.382	+ 14.8	0.917	+ 7.2
vBase+replace	0.366	+ 10.0	0.897	+ 4.9
vStat+replace	0.372	+ 11.7	0.902	+ 5.5

(ap5-15), however, the difference between the syntactic version and the two new statistical versions is more prominent (but not statistically significant).

A preliminary conclusion might be that statistical phrases mainly have an effect at higher recall levels, whereas syntactic phrases improve both (high) precision **and** recall. We assume that the higher precision of the syntactic version is caused by the more controlled method of phrase formation. A possible explanation for he difference in performance between vStat+split and vStat+replace at high precision might be a weighting effect. Additional index terms make a document (or query) longer, which results in lower weights for each index term because of our retrieval engine's cosine document length normalization. This has the effect of a deterioration of precision for queries where the additional phrases do not result in extra matches.

5   Conclusions and Further Plans

Our experiments have shown that compound splitting is essential for good quality retrieval of Dutch texts. If we assume a baseline of compound splitting and add either syntactic or statistical phrases, performance generally improves, but this effect is never statistically significant. If we compare syntactic vs. statistical phrase indexing, syntactic phrases are slightly superior to statistical phrases, particularly at high precision. At higher recall levels syntactic and statistical phrases are equally effective. However, since compound splitting requires at least a dictionary and knowledge about constraints on compound formation, a purely non-linguistic indexing strategy, with or without phrases, does not seem to be very effective for Dutch.

In a new experiment we intend to investigate whether an extension of the scope of syntactic analysis to larger units than noun phrases would lead to further improvements. Our results seem to indicate that our method to integrate phrases in the vector space index, i.e. by simply adding them to the document term vectors, might not be ideal. Document length normalization has the effect of a deterioration of precision for queries where the additional phrases do not result in extra matches. Since we have also seen that downweighting phrases can help to improve average precision (see section 3), we also intend to experiment with separate indexes for single words and phrases (cf. [11] for an example of such an approach) so that we can control these effects more precisely.

References

1. IJsbrand Jan Aalbersberg, Ewout Brandsma, and Marc Corthout. Full text document retrieval: from theory to applications. In G.A.M. Kempen and W.A.M. de Vroomen, editors, *Informatiewetenschap 1991, Wetenschappelijke bijdragen aan de eerste STINFON-Conferentie*, 1991.
2. Susan Armstrong, Pierrette Bouillon, and Gilbert Robert. Tools for part-of-speech tagging. Multext project report, ISSCO, Geneva, 1995.
3. R. H. Baayen, R. Piepenbrock, and H. van Rijn, editors. *The CELEX Lexical Database (CD-ROM)*. Linguistic Data Consortium, University of Pennsylvania, Philadelphia (PA), 1993.
4. C. Buckley, G. Salton, and J. Allan. Automatic retrieval with locality information using SMART. In Donna Harman, editor, *The First Text REtrieval Conference (TREC-1)*, pages 59–73. National Institute for Standards and Technology, 1993. Special Publication 500-207.
5. C. Buckley, A. Singhal, M. Mitra, and (G. Salton). New retrieval approaches using SMART:TREC4. In Donna Harman, editor, *The Fourth Text REtrieval Conference*. National Institute for Standards and Technology, 1996. Special Publication 500-236.
6. J. L. Fagan. *Experiments in Automatic Phrase Indexing for Document Retrieval: A Comparison of Syntactic and non-Syntactic Methods*. PhD thesis, Cornell University, Ithaca NY, CS Department technical report 87-868, 1987.
7. Donna Harman. Overview of the first Text REtrieval Conference (TREC-1). In Donna Harman, editor, *The First Text REtrieval Conference (TREC-1)*, pages 1–20. National Institute for Standards and Technology, 1993. Special Publication 500-207.
8. William L. Hays. *Statistics for the Social Sciences*. Holt, Rinehart and Winston, London, 1978.
9. David A. Hull, Gregory Grefenstette, B. Maximilian Schulze, Eric Gaussier, Hinrich Schütze, and Jan O. Pedersen. Xerox TREC-5 site report: Routing, filtering, NLP and Spanish tracks. In Donna Harman and Ellen Voorhees, editors, *The Fifth Text REtrieval Conference (TREC-5)*. National Institute for Standards and Technology, 1997. Special Publication 500-238.
10. Wessel Kraaij and Renée Pohlmann. Viewing stemming as recall enhancement. In Hans-Peter Frei, Donna Harman, Peter Schauble, and Ross Wilkinson, editors, *Proceedings of the 19th ACM-SIGIR Conference on Research and Development in Information Retrieval (SIGIR96)*, pages 40–48, 1996.

11. Mandar Mitra, Chris Buckley, Amit Singhal, and Claire Cardie. An analysis of statistical and syntactic phrases. In L. Devroye and C. Chrisment, editors, *Proceedings of RIAO'97*, pages 200–214, 1997.

12. Renée Pohlmann and Wessel Kraaij. The effect of syntactic phrase indexing on retrieval performance for Dutch texts. In L. Devroye and C. Chrisment, editors, *Proceedings of RIAO'97*, pages 176–187, 1997.

13. Gerard Salton, Chris Buckley, and Maria Smith. On the application of syntactic methodologies in automatic text analysis. *Information Processing & Management*, 26(1):73–92, 1990.

14. Tomek Strzalkowski. Natural language information retrieval. *Information Processing & Management*, 31(3):397–417, 1995.

15. Tomek Strzalkowski and Jose Perez Carballo. Natural language information retrieval: TREC-4 report. In Donna Harman, editor, *The Fourth Text REtrieval Conference (TREC-4)*. National Institute for Standards and Technology, 1996. Special Publication 500-236.

16. Jean Tague-Sutcliffe. *Measuring Information, An Information Services Perspective*. Academic Press, San Diego (CA), 1995.

17. Jean Tague-Sutcliffe. A statistical analysis of the TREC-3 data. In Donna Harman, editor, *Overview of the Third Text REtrieval Conference (TREC-3)*, pages 385–398. National Institute for Standards and Technology, 1995. Special Publication 500-225.

18. Joost van Surksum and Jan Willem den Besten. Patz'er - een patronenzoeker voor Nederlandstalige teksten. TNO-TPD/Hogeschool Enschede, november 1993.

19. T. G. Vosse. *The Word Connection*. PhD thesis, Rijksuniversiteit Leiden, Neslia Paniculata Uitgeverij, Enschede, 1994.

Appendix A: Statistical Significance Tests

The design chosen for the statistical analysis is a repeated measures single factor design, sometimes also referred to as randomized block design (see, for instance, [8], chapter 13). This design has the advantage that the query (or subject) effect is separated from the system effect. We know that different queries will render different results so if we separate this effect from the system effect we are able to single out the factor we are interested in. The statistical model for the randomized block design can be summarized as follows:

$$Y_{ij} = \mu + \alpha_i + \beta_j + \epsilon_{ij} \tag{1}$$

Y_{ij} represents the score (e.g. average precision) for system variant i and query j, μ is the overall average score, α_i is the effect of the ith system, β_j is the effect of the jth query and ϵ is the random variation about the average.

The H_0 hypothesis which is tested by an analysis of variance (ANOVA) is:

The averages of the observed statistic are equal for all system versions, i.e. the system effect (α) is zero.

If this hypothesis is falsified, we can conclude that at least one pair of averages differs significantly. T-tests are subsequently applied to determine which pairs of system versions really show a significant difference. Tables 5, 6, 7 and 8 present the results of the ANOVAs that were run on the data.

Table 5. ANOVA table average precision

Source	DF	Sum of Squares	Mean Square	F val
system	9	0.5311	0.0590	6.3349
queries	65	28.3105	0.4355	46.7565
error	585	5.4494	0.0093	
total	659	34.2910		
s.e.d. (systems): 0.0168				

Table 6. ANOVA table average precision at 5, 10 and 15 documents retrieved

Source	DF	Sum of Squares	Mean Square	F val
system	9	0.3208	0.0356	2.8349
queries	65	50.0273	0.7697	61.2041
error	585	7.3565	0.0126	
total	659	57.7046		
s.e.d. (systems): 0.0195				

Table 7. ANOVA table R-recall

Source	DF	Sum of Squares	Mean Square	F val
system	9	0.3367	0.0374	3.8909
queries	65	24.3800	0.3751	39.0073
error	585	5.6251	0.0096	
total	659	30.3418		
s.e.d. (systems): 0.0171				

Table 8. ANOVA table recall at 1000 documents

Source	DF	Sum of Squares	Mean Square	F val
system	9	0.8992	0.0999	11.3027
queries	65	9.9526	0.1531	17.3223
error	585	5.1710	0.0088	
total	659	16.0227		
s.e.d. (systems): 0.0164				

The most important figures in the ANOVA tables are the F-values in the rightmost column, which represent the quotient of the variance in measurements which can be attributed to the effect we are interested in (Mean Square system or query) and the variance due to chance (Mean Square error). This quotient is dependent on the degrees of freedom (DF) of the variables in the model, i.e. number of system versions and queries $-$ 1. Because the F values exceed $F_{.99;9,585}$[8] $= 2.48$, we may conclude that the system effect is significant at the 0.99 level for all ANOVAS, This means that we can reject the hypotheses that the system effects of the corresponding measures are equal to zero with a certainty of 99%. The query effect is also clearly significant for all evaluation measures. The F-values exceed $F_{.99;65,585} = 1.55$. This justifies the choice for a randomized block design where the query effect is separated from the system effect.

Because the ANOVA shows that there are significant differences between system versions, it is necessary to do multiple pairwise comparisons to detect which specific versions are concerned. We have used T-tests to identify significant differences between specific versions. The standard error of difference (s.e.d.) values rendered by the ANOVA are used to discriminate significantly different versions in the following way:

$$| \bar{x}_1 - \bar{x}_2 | > 2 \times s.e.d. \tag{2}$$

The results of the T-tests are given in Tables 9, 10, 11 and 12 below. In these tables system versions have been divided into equivalence classes indicated by numbers.

---

[8] The standard value for significance level $1-0.01$ and the degrees of freedom.

Table 9. Equivalence classes avp

system	avp		
vSyn	0.370	1	
vStat+replace	0.365	1	
vBase+split	0.364	1	
vStat+split	0.363	1	
vBase+replace	0.349	1 2	
vStat+weight	0.327	2 3	
vStat	0.323	2 3	
vBase+prop	0.311	3 4	
vBase	0.310	3 4	
vTRU	0.282	4	

Table 10. Equivalence classes ap5-15

system	ap5-15		
vSyn	0.496	1	
vBase+split	0.483	1 2	
vBase+replace	0.482	1 2	
vStat+replace	0.481	1 2	
vStat+split	0.466	1 2 3	
vStat+weight	0.451	2 3	
vStat	0.451	2 3	
vBase+prop	0.437	3	
vBase	0.435	3	
vTRU	0.431	3	

Table 11. Equivalence classes R-recall

system	R-r		
vSyn	0.382	1	
vStat+split	0.380	1	
vBase+split	0.376	1 2	
vStat+replace	0.372	1 2	
vBase+replace	0.366	1 2 3	
vStat+weight	0.352	1 2 3	
vStat	0.345	2 3 4	
vBase+prop	0.336	3 4	
vBase	0.333	3 4	
vTRU	0.311	4	

Table 12. Equivalence classes recall1000

system	r1000		
vSyn	0.917	1	
vBase+split	0.905	1	
vStat+split	0.904	1	
vStat+replace	0.902	1	
vBase+replace	0.897	1 2	
vBase+prop	0.865	2 3	
vStat+weight	0.863	3	
vStat	0.862	3	
vBase	0.855	3	
vTRU	0.785	4	

Reduction of Expanded Search Terms for Fuzzy English-Text Retrieval

Manabu Ohta[1], Atsuhiro Takasu[2], and Jun Adachi[2]

[1] Graduate School of Engineering, University of Tokyo, Tokyo 113-8654, Japan
[2] Research & Development Department, National Center for Science Information Systems (NACSIS), Tokyo 112-8640, Japan

Abstract. Optical character reader (OCR) misrecognition is a serious problem when OCR-recognized text is used for retrieval purposes in digital libraries. We have proposed fuzzy retrieval methods that, instead of correcting the errors manually, assume that errors remain in the recognized text. Costs are thereby reduced. The proposed methods generate multiple search terms for each input query term by referring to the confusion matrices, which store all characters likely to be misrecognized and the respective probability of each misrecognition. The proposed methods can improve recall rates without decreasing precision rates. However, in English fuzzy retrieval, occasionally a few million search terms are generated, which has an intolerable effect on retrieval speed. Therefore, this paper presents two heuristics to reduce the number of generated search terms by restricting the number of errors included in each expanded search term while maintaining retrieval effectiveness.

1 Introduction

Some digital libraries enter a large number of printed documents into a database as document images and, at the same time, compile full-text databases by OCR scanning their text parts [1]. In this case, however, the recognition errors that the OCR process inevitably produces must be handled. Conventionally, all the errors are corrected manually after OCR scanning and the text is then entered into a full-text database. However, the manual post-editing is expensive, especially for a large-scale database. Therefore, we have proposed fuzzy retrieval methods, which assume that errors remain in the recognized text and have shown that excellent retrieval effectiveness was achieved in retrieval of both English-text and Japanese-text [2, 3]. The proposed methods do not correct any errors included in the OCR-recognized text but make allowance for them in the retrieval process. The cost of constructing a database is thus considerably reduced.

An example of a retrieval method specifically designed to handle such text is to cluster similar characters into a representative character to avoid retrieval failure [4]. This method can decrease retrieval omissions if clusters of characters are well formed, although the characters classified in one cluster cannot be distinguished from each other, which leads to the other problem of retrieval noise. Another example of such error-tolerant retrieval methods is based on approximate string matching. Lopresti et al. introduced new versions of several information retrieval (IR) models by combining approximate string matching and fuzzy logic [5, 6]. They examined the effects of various kinds of simulated OCR noise on the performance of the models and showed good recall rates. Inevitably, however, such sub-string-based models also result in lower precision rates.

On the other hand, one of our proposed methods applies confusion and expanded confusion matrices, which expand a query term into multiple search terms that are matched against recognized text containing OCR errors. The confusion matrix stores characters that are likely to be substituted when a particular character is misrecognized, and the respective probability of each occurrence. The expanded confusion matrix stores all characters likely to be missed, inserted, combined, or decomposed along with their respective probabilities. The query term expansion of the proposed method improves recall rates and also maintains high precision rates because the expanded search terms are narrowed down to those whose validity values are greater than a given threshold. Those validity values are calculated for each expanded search term candidate by referring to the confusion and expanded confusion matrices. However, the number of expanded search terms increases exponentially with the length of the query term and, in some cases, more than a million terms are generated even after evaluation by validity values. This is a major flaw of the proposed method. Some heuristic rules that are different to validity values are needed to overcome this inefficiency of retrieval speed, without decreasing retrieval effectiveness. Therefore, this paper presents two heuristics to reduce the number of expanded search terms while maintaining retrieval effectiveness by restricting the number of errors included in each candidate for expanded search terms.

The following Sect. 2 describes the algorithm of the proposed fuzzy English-text retrieval method and Sect. 3 shows the retrieval effectiveness and number of expanded search terms obtained through preliminary experiments for method performance. Section 4 presents two heuristics to reduce the number of expanded search terms and shows the experimental results indicating the performance of these heuristics when applied to a full-text search of English academic articles. Conclusions and future work are given in Sect. 5.

2 Algorithm of the Proposed Method

2.1 English-Text OCR Errors

To clarify English-text OCR errors from a practical standpoint, we carried out a preliminary experiment in which 80,985 characters were read from scientific articles in English to determine the most common types of errors. Both edited (error-free) and recognized text for comparison of these articles were obtained from Elsevier Electronic Subscriptions (EES), which offers electronic versions of Elsevier's paper journals. Resultant categories are as follows:

Table 1. Types of English-text OCR errors[†]

Error Type	Number of Occurrences	Occurrence Frequency (%)
Substitution	232	40.1
Missing	68	11.7
Insertion	60	10.4
Combination	167	28.8
Decomposition	38	6.6
Other	14	2.4

[†]Results of a preliminary experiment in which 80,985 characters were read

1. Character substitution: any non-original character that has been substituted for an original character. If n ($n \geq 2$) non-original characters have been substituted for the same number of original characters, n character substitutions are assumed to have occurred independently. For example, "C" can be substituted for "c", "l" for "i", and "t" for "f".
2. Character missing: any original character that has been missed. For example, "3-D" can be recognized as "3D" because "-" was missed.
3. Character insertion: any non-original character that has been inserted. This type of error is caused by spacing errors and undesired marks on document images, with the inserted character most typically being a space or a punctuation mark. For example, "object" can be recognized as "ob,ject" owing to the insertion of ",".
4. Character combination: two or more original characters that have been combined to form a non-original character. For example, "ri" can be recognized as "n", "te" as "k", and "li" as "h".
5. Character decomposition: an original character that has been decomposed into two or more non-original characters. For example, "m" can be recognized as "tn" or "rn".

Table 1 summarizes the resultant occurrence frequencies for each type of English-text OCR error, where the error type *Other* represents errors not categorized in the above types. The *Other* types of error include bursty errors such as "RCOnStMCdOn" for the original "reconstruction". As the occurrence frequency for *Other* types is negligibly small, the other five categories addressed in the following sections account for about 97% of OCR's recognition errors.

2.2 Outline of the Proposed Method

In this paper a search refers to a full-text search in which OCR-recognized text is stored as a long string of English characters.

The proposed method is a full-text search method, which applies confusion and expanded confusion matrices in which all characters likely to be misrecognized, and the respective probability of each misrecognition, are stored. Prior to

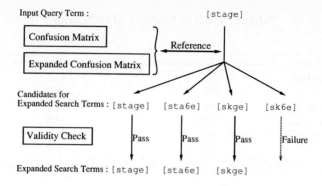

Fig. 1. Diagram of the query term expansion process

each search to retrieve an input query term, these matrices expand the query term into multiple search terms that are matched against recognized text containing OCR errors. As shown in Fig. 1, if the input query term is "stage", the applicable confusion and expanded confusion matrices suggest the following character substitutions: "6" for "g" and "k" for "ta". In this expansion process, each candidate for the expanded search term is assigned a validity value based on error-occurrence probabilities. Only those candidates with validity values greater than a given threshold are output as expanded search terms. The confusion and expanded confusion matrices are constructed beforehand by comparing OCR-recognized text with corresponding error-free edited text supplied as a training set. Therefore, the proposed method can be applied to any kind of OCR system as long as a training set is supplied.

2.3 Validity Evaluation Algorithm

Conviction Degree of a Character. Here, a finite character set is defined as $\Sigma = \{C_1, C_2, ..., C_{all}\}$. If any original character C_x is denoted A_x and its associated non-original substitutional character C_y is denoted B_y, the probability that any B_y can be regarded as A_x is represented by $P(A_x|B_y)$, which is calculated using Bayes' theorem, i.e.,

$$P(A_x|B_y) = \frac{P(A_x)P(B_y|A_x)}{\sum_{z=1}^{n} P(A_z)P(B_y|A_z)}, \tag{1}$$

where $P(A_x|B_y)$ is referred to as the conviction degree of a character.

Confusion Matrix. The confusion matrix is designed solely to handle the substitution errors that occur most frequently and, as shown in Fig. 2, contains original characters A_x, their associated non-original substitutional characters B_y, and their conviction degrees, $P(A_x|B_y)$.

B_y = Non-original interchanged character C_y

	B_1	B_2	B_3	......
A_1	$P(A_1/B_1)$	$P(A_1/B_2)$	0	
A_2	0	$P(A_2/B_2)$	0	
A_3	0	$P(A_3/B_2)$	$P(A_3/B_3)$	
⋮				

A_x = Original character C_x

Fig. 2. Structure and contents of the confusion matrix

Expanded Confusion Matrix. The expanded confusion matrix has a structure similar to the confusion matrix for substitution errors, and is actually a combination of four analogous matrices designed to handle the other four types of error.

Figures 3(a) and (b) show the matrices for missing and insertion errors, where virtual characters V_m and V_i are defined as representing non-original and original characters B and A, respectively. Such definitions make these matrices analogous to the confusion matrix, and therefore allow the same validity algorithm, independent of the types of error. Figures 4(a) and (b) show the matrices for combination and decomposition errors in which, for the same reason, $a_x = (A^{i-1}A^i)_x$ and $b_y = (B^{i-1}B^i)_y$ are defined as two continuous original and non-original characters, respectively. In addition, the conviction degree (probability) that a non-original character B_y can be regarded as a combined error caused by a_x, $P(a_x|B_y)$ is stored in the matrix for the combined characters. Similarly, the conviction degree that a non-original character string b_y can be regarded as a decomposed error caused by an original character A_x, $P(A_x|b_y)$ is stored in the matrix for the decomposed characters.

Conviction Degree of a Character String. If OCR-recognized text is assumed to include only substitution errors, the probability that any expanded search term is correct is assumed to be the product of the probabilities that each character in the character string is correct. More specifically, for any string of original (error-free) characters with length n, $A^{012...n}$, and similarly for non-original (recognized) characters, $B^{012...n}$, the probability that character string $B^{012...n}$ matches character string $A^{012...n}$ is expressed as

$$P(A^{012...n}|B^{012...n}) = P(A^0|B^0)P(A^1|B^1)...P(A^n|B^n), \qquad (2)$$

624

(a) Missing character matrix

	A_1	A_2	A_3	......
V_m	$P(A_1/V_m)$	$P(A_2/V_m)$	$P(A_3/V_m)$	

V_m = Virtual character corresponding to original missed character A_x

(b) Inserted character matrix

	B_1	B_2	B_3	......
V_i	$P(V_i/B_1)$	$P(V_i/B_2)$	$P(V_i/B_3)$	

V_i = Virtual character corresponding to non–original inserted character B_y

Fig. 3. Structure and contents of matrices for (a) missing and (b) inserted characters

where $P(A^{012...n}|B^{012...n})$ is defined as the conviction degree of the character string.

However, when taking account of the other types of error, i.e., missing, insertion, combination and decomposition errors, the conviction degree of a character string is calculated in a slightly different manner. That is, when the expanded confusion matrix generates expanded search terms from an input query term, the characters do not always have a one-to-one correspondence since ambiguities in character spacing are allowed. Figure 5 diagrammatically shows how the conviction degree is calculated for each type of error handled by the expanded confusion matrix. As shown in Fig. 5, the conviction degree of a missed, inserted, combined, or decomposed character, i.e., P_m, P_i, P_c, or P_d, is specifically calculated and then handled exactly like that of a substituted character, so (2) can still be applied.

- In the case of including a missing error.
  It should be noted that P_m cannot be directly determined from (1). That is,

$$P_m = P(A_x|V_m) \cdot P_{miss}, \tag{3}$$

where $P(A_x|V_m)$ is stored in the matrix for missing characters as shown in Fig. 3(a) and P_{miss} is the probability that a missing error occurs; i.e., from Table 1,

$$P_{miss} = \frac{68}{80,985} \doteq 0.00084 . \tag{4}$$

P_{miss} must be included in (3) because V_m in the recognized text is a virtual character and therefore does not actually exist.
- In the case of including an insertion, combination, or decomposition error: P_i, P_c, or P_d, is directly derived from the matrix for inserted, combined, or decomposed characters, respectively.

(a) Combined character matrix

	B_1	B_2	B_3	......
$a_1 =$ $(A^{i-1}A^i)_1$	$P(a_1/B_1)$	$P(a_1/B_2)$	$P(a_1/B_3)$	
$a_2 =$ $(A^{i-1}A^i)_2$	$P(a_2/B_1)$	$P(a_2/B_2)$	$P(a_2/B_3)$	
$a_3 =$ $(A^{i-1}A^i)_3$	$P(a_3/B_1)$	$P(a_3/B_2)$	$P(a_3/B_3)$	
⋮				

$a_x = x$- th combination of original character string $A^{i-1}A^i$

(b) Decomposed character matrix

	$b_1 =$ $(B^{i-1}B^i)_1$	$b_2 =$ $(B^{i-1}B^i)_2$	$b_3 =$ $(B^{i-1}B^i)_3$	......
A_1	$P(A_1/b_1)$	$P(A_1/b_2)$	$P(A_1/b_3)$	
A_2	$P(A_2/b_1)$	$P(A_2/b_2)$	$P(A_2/b_3)$	
A_3	$P(A_3/b_1)$	$P(A_3/b_2)$	$P(A_3/b_3)$	
⋮				

$b_y = y$- th combination of non-original character string $B^{i-1}B^i$

Fig. 4. Structure and contents of matrices for (a) combined and (b) decomposed characters

3 Method Performance

3.1 Experimental Conditions

To clarify the abilities and problems of the proposed method, its full-text search performance was evaluated in terms of both retrieval effectiveness and the number of expanded search terms. And the following experiments were performed on the text data obtained from Elsevier Electronic Subscriptions (EES) because we wanted to measure the performance of the proposed method applied to practically available OCR-recognized text data, instead of simulated noisy text data prepared only for measurement. The following experimental conditions were used in the evaluation and were also applied to the experiments in Sect. 4.

1. Two sets of text were chosen for the evaluation of full-text search performance. The first set was a training set itself that was used to construct the confusion and expanded confusion matrices, and was actually text data of about 80 kilobytes collected from *Artificial Intelligence*, August 1995 to May 1996. The other set was a test set of about 50 kilobytes of text data that was collected from *Cognition*, from September 1995 to June 1996 and was completely different to the training set.
2. The OCR system employed was determined to have a recognition accuracy of 99.1% by calculation on the training set.
3. Performance was determined based on the retrieval of 50 randomly selected nouns contained in the training or test set, respectively[1]. Plurals were ignored. The following retrieval effectiveness and number of expanded search terms are the average values for the 50 terms.
4. All candidates for expanded search terms were given conviction degree P values as applicable. They were narrowed down to those that satisfied the retrieval condition, $P \geq$ threshold.

---

[1] Some examples of the query terms are "estimation", "flow", and "image".

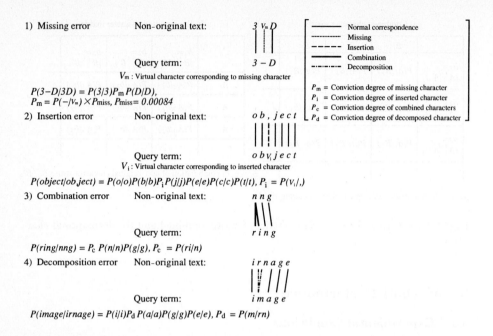

1) Missing error   Non-original text: $3\ V_m\ D$

                        Query term: $3 - D$

V_m : Virtual character corresponding to missing character

$P(3-D/3D) = P(3/3)P_m P(D/D),$
$P_m = P(-/V_m) \times P_{miss}, P_{miss}= 0.00084$

2) Insertion error   Non-original text: $o\ b\ ,\ j\ e\ c\ t$

                        Query term: $o\ b\ v_i\ j\ e\ c\ t$

V_i : Virtual character corresponding to inserted character

$P(object/ob\,ject) = P(o/o)P(b/b)P_i P(j/j)P(e/e)P(c/c)P(t/t), P_i = P(V_i/,)$

3) Combination error   Non-original text: $n\ n\ g$

                        Query term: $r\ i\ n\ g$

$P(ring/nng) = P_c\ P(n/n)P(g/g), P_c\ = P(ri/n)$

4) Decomposition error Non-original text: $i\ r\ n\ a\ g\ e$

                        Query term: $i\ m\ a\ g\ e$

$P(image/irnage) = P(i/i)P_d\ P(a/a)P(g/g)P(e/e), P_d = P(m/rn)$

Legend:
——— Normal correspondence
·········· Missing
– – – Insertion
——— Combination
–·–·–·– Decomposition

P_m = Conviction degree of missing character
P_i = Conviction degree of inserted character
P_c = Conviction degree of combined characters
P_d = Conviction degree of decomposed character

Fig. 5. Diagram showing how the conviction degree is calculated by using the expanded confusion matrix

5. The retrieval effectiveness refers here to the recall and precision rates in terms of a full-text search for strings, which are calculated by using (5) and (6), respectively.

6. All uppercase characters were transformed into the corresponding lowercase characters beforehand (normalization). Word extraction was undertaken by using 17 kinds of delimiters such as spaces.

$$\text{Recall (\%)} = \frac{\text{Number of appropriate results retrieved by the proposed method}}{\text{Number of actual character strings satisfying input query}} . \quad (5)$$

$$\text{Precision (\%)} = \frac{\text{Number of appropriate results retrieved by the proposed method}}{\text{Number of all results retrieved by the proposed method}} . \quad (6)$$

3.2 Retrieval Effectiveness

Figure 6 shows the relationship between retrieval effectiveness and the threshold for P, which was determined by varying the threshold value and calculating the

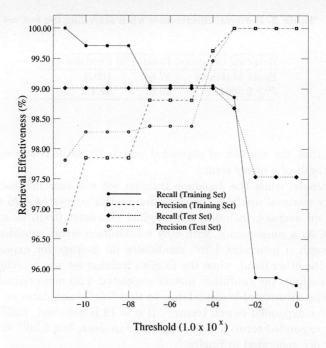

Fig. 6. Effect of threshold for P on retrieval effectiveness

Table 2. Retrieval effectiveness when searching the training set

Retrieval Condition	Recall (%)	Precision (%)
Exact Matching	95.73	100.0
$P \geq 0.0001$	99.05	99.63

resulting recall and precision rates. Validity evaluation using P made it possible to gain high recall rates at the cost of a slight decrease of precision rates. For later discussion, the optimal threshold was determined to be 0.0001. The reason for this was that when the threshold value, 0.0001, was applied, both recall and precision rates were over 99%, as shown in Fig. 6. Tables 2 and 3 show the resultant retrieval effectiveness at the optimal threshold for the training and test sets, respectively. In Tables 2 and 3, the retrieval condition *Exact Matching* means that misrecognized text is searched by an original query term without any query term expansions.

3.3 Number of Expanded Search Terms

The previous section showed that the proposed method improved retrieval effectiveness. However, a major bottleneck for implementation of the proposed

Table 3. Retrieval effectiveness when searching the test set

Retrieval Condition	Recall (%)	Precision (%)
Exact Matching	97.54	100.0
$P \geq 0.0001$	99.01	99.47

method is that the number of expanded search terms increases exponentially with the length of a query term.

For example, when the Japanese training set was searched using the proposed fuzzy retrieval method, the confusion matrix suggested 1.26 non-original characters on average, including the original character itself, as substitutable candidates. As a consequence, with only substitution errors considered, a query term of length n generates 1.26^n candidates on average for expanded search terms. On the other hand, when the English training set was searched using the proposed method, the confusion matrix suggested 5.50 non-original characters on average as substitutable candidates, so that 5.50^n candidates on average are generated for expanded search terms [2]. If $n = 10$ is assumed, $1.26^{10} \approx 10$ candidates for expanded terms are generated in Japanese, but $5.50^{10} \approx 25,000,000$ candidates are generated in English[3].

Figure 7 shows that large numbers of expanded search terms were generated when allowing for substitution, missing, insertion, combination, and decomposition errors. More specifically, Fig. 7 shows that an input query term was expanded to about 170,000 search terms in the training-set retrieval and about 93,000 terms in the test-set retrieval, respectively, even though the optimal threshold, 0.0001, was applied to narrow the expanded search terms.

4 Reduction of the Number of Expanded Search Terms

4.1 Proposed Heuristics

About 170,000 expanded search terms, the number shown in Sect. 3.3, is intolerable in practice because of its effect on retrieval speed. Therefore, this paper presents two heuristics for validity checks of the expanded search terms, which are totally different to the conviction degrees, in order to reduce the number of terms. The presented heuristics are applied in addition to evaluation by conviction degrees. Note that the retrieval effectiveness, especially the recall rate,

[2] The difference in these numbers between English and Japanese languages is highly dependent on the character sets. The Japanese language has about 3,000 characters in daily use and as a result very sparse confusion and expanded confusion matrices are generally obtained compared with English.

[3] In practice, a validity check is applied to those candidates by evaluating their conviction degrees, and the number of expanded search terms is therefore not as large as mentioned above.

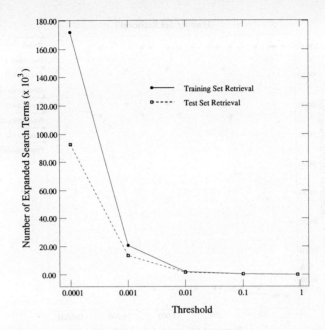

Fig. 7. Effect of threshold for P on the number of expanded search terms

which has been achieved by the proposed method can be sacrificed if the number of expanded search terms is reduced arbitrarily. Therefore, this paper proposes the following two heuristics and shows their influence on both retrieval effectiveness and the number of expanded search terms with experimental results. Both these heuristics restrict the errors included in each expanded search term to less than a given number.

- Heuristic 1:
  Independent of the length of a query term, only those expanded search terms including at most x errors are generated[4].
- Heuristic 2:
  Only terms with at most a given number of errors, proportional to the length of a query term, are generated. More precisely, when $n \cdot y \leq m < (n + 1) \cdot y$ holds true, only terms with at most n errors are generated, where m is the length of a query term and y is a parameter that determines the proportion of errors.

---

[4] Although one misrecognized character is counted as one error as for substitution, missing, insertion, and decomposition errors, two continuous characters causing a combination error are counted as one error.

Training Set Retrieval

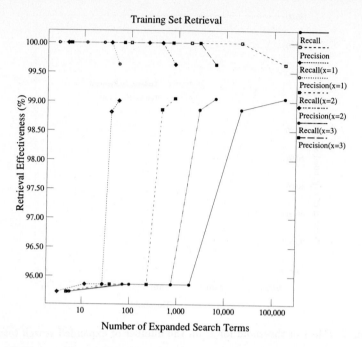

Fig. 8. Effect of heuristic 1 when searching the training set

4.2 Effect of Heuristics

Heuristic 1. Figures 8 and 9 show the retrieval effectiveness and corresponding numbers of generated terms when searching the training and test sets by adopting heuristic 1 and varying x from 1 to 3, respectively. Those lines simply marked as *Recall* and *Precision* in these figures show the results when no heuristics were applied.

Figures 8 and 9 show that the highest recall rates and the lowest precision rates were obtained when the optimal threshold, 0.0001, was applied. Figure 8 also shows that heuristic 1 reduced the number of generated terms to 56.24. Heuristic 1 also decreased the recall rate from 99.05% to 99.01% or by about 0.04% when $x = 1$ was applied to training-set retrieval. The following misrecognition existing in the training set caused this fall in the recall rate.

– "problem" → "pmblen˜"

A candidate for expanded search terms, "pmblen˜", includes a combination error of "ro" → "m" and a decomposition error of "m" → "n˜". So the condition of $x = 1$ rejects this candidate although its conviction degree is 0.002517 and exceeds the threshold of 0.0001.

Figure 9, on the other hand, shows that heuristic 1 reduced the number of generated terms to 52.66 without decreasing retrieval effectiveness when $x = 1$ was applied to test-set retrieval.

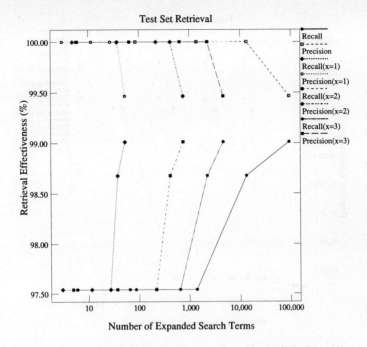

Fig. 9. Effect of heuristic 1 when searching the test set

Heuristic 2. Figures 10 and 11 show the retrieval effectiveness and corresponding numbers of generated terms when searching the training and test sets by adopting heuristic 2 while varying y from 1 to 15, respectively. These figures show the results when $y = 5, 10, 15$ and also when no heuristics were applied.

The highest recall rates and the lowest precision rates were obtained when the optimal threshold, 0.0001, was applied. Heuristic 2 reduced the number of generated terms to 56.24, but also decreased the recall rate from 99.05% to 99.01% or by about 0.04% when $y \geq 14$ was applied to training-set retrieval. On the other hand, heuristic 2 reduced the number of generated terms to 52.66 without decreasing retrieval effectiveness when $y \geq 13$ was applied to test-set retrieval. Note that the conditions $y \geq 14$ and $y \geq 13$ in training-set and test-set retrieval, respectively, mean the same as the condition of $x = 1$ when adopting heuristic 1.

4.3 Overall Evaluation

Heuristic 2 was proposed because we expected that the errors included in each expanded search term increased proportionally to the length of a query term. Experimental results, however, indicated that the recall rate of more than 99 % was retained even when the search was narrowed to those terms with no more than one error independent of their length. In other words, sufficient retrieval

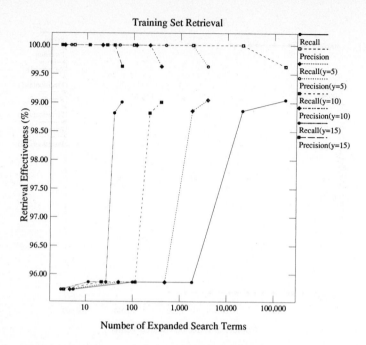

Fig. 10. Effect of heuristic 2 when searching the training set

effectiveness can be obtained if heuristic 1 is applied with the condition $x = 1$. At the same time, it is clear that the proposed heuristics have a considerable effect on reducing the expansion of search terms because the experiments showed that both heuristics reduced the number of generated terms from about 170,000 to 56.24 in training-set retrieval and from about 93,000 to 52.66 in test-set retrieval.

The parameters x and y generally need to be determined by similar experiments on training sets to those described in Sect. 4.2. However, our experiments suggest that expanding a long query term into terms with more than two errors is not realistic, and that applying heuristic 1 with the condition $x = 1$ is a reasonable approach for both retrieval speed and effectiveness. The experiments showed that $x \geq 2$ in the case of heuristic 1 and $y \leq 6$ in the case of heuristic 2 were necessary to avoid falls in retrieval effectiveness in training-set retrieval. However, as many as 845 and 2,009 terms were generated when $x = 2$ and $y = 6$ were applied, respectively.

5 Conclusions and Future Work

Two heuristics were proposed that reduced the number of generated search terms expanded from a query term in English-text fuzzy retrieval by restricting the number of errors included in each expanded term. The performance of these heuristics was experimentally evaluated by determining retrieval effectiveness

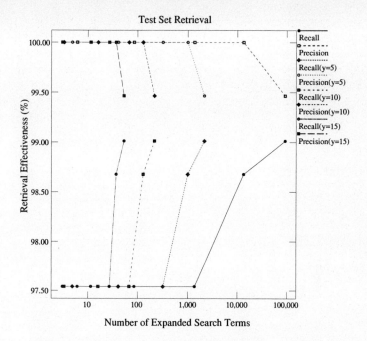

Fig. 11. Effect of heuristic 2 when searching the test set

such as recall and precision rates, and the number of generated terms. Experimental results indicated that about 100,000 terms, which passed a validity check by conviction degrees, were narrowed to about 50 with only a slight fall of recall rates when expansion was restricted to terms with no more than one error. For future work, we intend to apply a preliminary reduction to the retrieval space before applying the proposed methods because, even after applying the proposed heuristics, about 50 times as much retrieval cost is needed compared to searching a query term without expansion, which is still not a negligible cost.

References

1. Fujisawa, H., Marukawa, K.: Full-Text Search and Document Recognition of Japanese Text. Proc. SDAIR'95, Las Vegas, Nevada, USA (1995) 55–80
2. Ohta, M., Takasu, A., Adachi, J.: Retrieval Methods for English-Text with Misrecognized OCR Characters. Proc. ICDAR'97, Ulm, Germany (1997) 950–956
3. Ohta, M., Takasu, A., Adachi, J.: Probabilistic Retrieval Methods for Text with Miss-Recognized OCR characters. Proc. IROL'96, Taejon, Korea (1996) 35–41
4. Myka, A., Güntzer, U.: Fuzzy Full-Text Searches in OCR Databases. Advances in Digital Libraries (1995) 87–100
5. Lopresti, D.: Robust Retrieval of Noisy Text. Proc. ADL'96 (1996) 76–85
6. Lopresti, D., Zhou, J.: Retrieval Strategies for Noisy Text. Proc. SDAIR'96, Las Vegas, Nevada, USA (1996) 255–269

Internet Publications: Pay-per-Use or Pay-per-Subscription?

Roberto Zamparelli

Human Communication Research Centre, 2 Buccleuch Place, EH9 1PE, Scotland, GB
roberto@cogsci.ed.ac.uk

Today, the prevailing philosophy for the electronic transmission of copyrighted material is *pay-per-use*, whose main features are:

1. The user pays a fee for each item obtained, part of which goes as royalties to the item's creator.
2. Legal users who give away unauthorised copies to other users, for free or for a fee, are prosecuted according to law.
3. Each item purchased is registered and typically protected by encryption or other devices, to make unauthorised copying more difficult.

In this poster, I claim that a pure pay-per-use model of electronic information dissemination is not sustainable, as it runs contra current social and technological trends, and that an alternative model, *pay-per-subscription* is superior. By "pay-per-subscription" I mean an abstract model where:

1. The authorship of some work is registered.
2. A user is allowed to download for private use any copyrighted item a 'virtual library' has in store, any number of times, against payment of an flat, periodical subscription rate to the library.
3. The subscription also gives right to a range of inherently inalienable (non-transferable) services.
4. The author of a work given to the virtual library is rewarded in proportion to the number of times his or her work is downloaded by different users.

The argument is that, with the current American-lead trend toward a more restrictive interpretation of what counts as *duplication* (as opposed to *broadcasting*, see [2, 1]) and with communication globalization, enforcing copyright restriction will be either impossible or politically unsound, unless it goes with a reduction of the *motivation for copying* on the user's side [3]. But this is precisely the effect that a pay-per-subscription model can obtain: after paying the fee, a user will not copy illegally simply because *copying legally is easier*. In the simplest such model, after paying their fee, the users would have access to the whole library collection; in a more complex model there may be several levels of subscription; even in this case, unauthorised duplication should arguably be less commercially damaging than in a pure pay-per-use scenario.

Two main problems must be solved to obtain a workable pay-per-subscription model.

1. How to prevent unauthorised library-license transmission (a user's using another user's library license).
2. How to insure financial coverage for the works which are made available, and appropriate distribution of revenues.

I argue that the solution to the first problem lies in: **(i)** anchoring the library fees to intrinsically non-transferable services (loan of objects, personal services, installation assistance for software, etc.); **(ii)** customising the material received by a user and stressing the social appeal of customisation, which can in fact be seen as a type of encryption that acts on the *desirability* of goods; **(iii)** adopting mixed pay-per-view/pay-per-subscription systems and delaying the distribution of more recent material.

As for second problem, various possibilities are discussed, i.e. **(iv)** 'smart' advertising (e.g. accessing past material with today's ads), **(v)** multi-level subscription fees and**(vi)** taxation schemes.

References

[1] White House Information Infrastructure Task Force. Intellectual property and the national information infrastructure. the report of the working group on intellectual property rights. Technical report, 1995. http://www.uspto.gov/web/offices/com/doc/ipnii/.
[2] Pamela Samuelson. Alert stop the clinton copyright grab! the administration's white paper on intellectual property in the digital era is a wholesale giveaway of the public's rights. *Wired*, 4(1), 1996. http://www.wired.com/wired/whitepaper.html.
[3] Roberto Zamparelli. Copyright and global libraries: Going with the flow of technology. *First Monday*, 2(11), November 1997. http://www.firstmonday.dk/issues-/issue2_11/index.html.

Statistical Identification of Domain-Specific Keyterms for Text Summarisation

Budi Yuwono[1] and Mirna Adriani[2]

[1] Graham Technology Plc., 41 Carlyle Avenue, Hillington, Glasgow G52 4XX, Scotland
[2] Department of Computing Science, University of Glasgow, Glasgow G12 8QQ, Scotland

We believe that in order to be useful a text summarisation technique must be domain dependent, in that the resulting summary must cover the important aspects and concepts specific to the subject matter's domain. The main problem with a typical domain-dependent text summarisation technique is the cost of acquiring and hand-coding the required domain-specific knowledge into the system, e.g., in the form of phrase-structure templates. To solve this problem, we propose a solution which uses automatically retrieved sample documents as the source of the domain-specific knowledge, and extracts the knowledge in the form of keyterms. These keyterms represent the key aspects and concepts (terminology) relevant to the input document. The sample documents are retrieved from a collection, called **base collection**- containing documents of various topics, based on their similarity with the input document. The input document is then summarised by extracting a number of sentences containing the keyterms.

Our text summarisation technique is based on the statistical distribution of words among documents in the base collection, within individual documents, and among sentences in the input document. In particular, statistically-based formula are employed for scoring each of the candidate sample documents, keyterms, and key sentences. Our technique makes use of standard word or term distribution parameters that are commonly provided or can be easily obtained through the use of modern text retrieval systems.

Given a text document as input, the technique performs the following four steps. In **step one**, all terms in the input document are ranked based on their tf^*idf[1] weights. The top c_1 terms are then taken as the input document's keyterms. In **step two**, documents in the base collection are ranked based on the sum of the c_1 keyterms contained in each document. The top n documents are then taken. In **step three**, domain-specific keyterms are extracted from the previous n documents and the input document. All terms in these $n+1$ documents are ranked based on their weights computed in a similar manner as in step one. The top c_2 terms are then taken as the domain-specific keyterms representing aspects or concepts of common interest to the $n+1$ documents. Finally, in **step four**, all sentences in the input document are ranked based on their relevance scores with respect to the above c_2 keyterms. The scores are computed using a similar formula as in step two, only that sentences are treated in the stead of

---

[1] Salton, G., and McGill, M.: An Introduction to Modern Information Retrieval. New York, McGraw-Hill (1983).

documents. The top m sentences are then taken to form the summary, where m is the maximum number of sentences wanted in the summary. The resulting m sentences are then ordered according to their relative positions with each other in the input document. By preserving the relative positions of the sentences, the resulting summary can reflects the original document's argumentative structure better.

Evaluating the goodness of a text summary is a difficult task because such a judgement varies widely among different readers depending on the individual reader's interest, knowledge about the subject domain, and purpose of reading. In order to minimise the subjectivity of the evaluation, we propose a more author centred, in contrast to reader centred, evaluation method. By author centred means that all of the document's themes, which are indicated by the author using the document's rhetorical structure, are of equal importance to be included in the summary. More specifically, in each paragraph of the document there is a nucleus sentence which states the main proposition or argument of the paragraph. We call such a sentence a **theme sentence**. We use evaluation aspects called informativeness and indicativeness. **Informativeness** is defined as whether or not a key sentence is a theme sentence conveying a valid proposition in the document. **Indicativeness** is defined as whether or not a key sentence indicates the subject matter discussed in the input document, particularly, in terms of the concept or concepts involved. Ideally, a good key sentence is both informative and indicative. We measure the informativeness of a text summary by dividing the number of informative sentences with the number of sentences in the summary. Whereas indicativeness is measured by dividing the number of paragraphs represented or indicated by the summary with the total number of paragraphs in the input documents.

We have conducted series of experiments using 2,330 news-wire articles as the base collection, and 20 input documents chosen randomly from a pool of 822 magazine articles. The result of our first series of experiments demonstrates that the indicativeness of the resulting summaries correlate positively with the number of keyterms used. Beyond a certain point, increasing this number further decreased the informativeness of the resulting summaries. This indicates that more keyterms can reveal more about the content of the input document, but with less coherence. The result of another series of experiments shows that the average indicativeness is not affected by the percentage of relevant documents retrieved from the base collection (precision) in the technique's step two. This is as expected because indicativeness, as defined previously, does not depend on the domain specific knowledge, but document specific knowledge instead. On the other hand, the precision affects the average informativeness, as more relevant documents increase the scores of the more domain specific, as opposed to document specific, keyterms. In general, the results of our experiments demonstrate that the proposed technique is sufficiently robust and input-source independent. The technique can be easily tailored to suit different users or user communities by installing a base collection of the user's preference.

The STACS Electronic Submission Service

Jochen Bern, Christoph Meinel, and Harald Sack

FB IV, Lehrstuhl für theoretische Informatik,
Universität Trier, D-54 286 Trier, Germany
{bern,meinel,sack}@Uni-Trier.DE
http://www.informatik.uni-trier.de/TI/

1 Problems in Electronic Conference Submission

One very popular software used to handle electronic conference submissions was written by the SIGACT Electronic Publishing Board. It was first used for the FOCS '95 conference, and later for a range of conferences including COCOON, FOCS, PODC, SODA, SPAA, STOC, and WDAG, staying basically unchanged.

Another conference in computer science that uses electronic submission mechanisms is the Symposium on Theoretical Aspects in Computer Science. STACS is an international conference covering all aspects of Theoretical Computer Science. It has proven to be - together with ICALP - the main European exchange place for ideas in this area. The program committee is internationally of top rank, the number of submissions is high (typically 100 to 140 papers), and the acceptance rate is low. Researchers come from all over the world to attend.

Our experience is that the problems in the design of conference submission services can be grouped into the following categories:

- **User Interface Problems** — First and foremost, selection of (a) **portable file format(s)** for submitted papers would be desirable; Failing that (e.g., PostScript), portability problems should be reported to the submitter **in an intelligible error message.** Next, steps have to be taken to ensure **reliable and unaltered delivery** of submissions. Finally, the whole workflow needs to be **intuitive and "familiar"** to the submitter.
- **Security Related Problems** — Conference announcements nowadays are put onto the WWW and, thus, can be found with search engines, so submission services may be accessed by more people than the attendees. A conference submission service needs to enforce a strict deadline. Consequently, malevolent manipulation is a serious threat and, besides the need for **privacy in submitter-service communications,** there is a need for reasonable protection against **denial of service attacks.** Where this cannot be achieved, we have to ensure that there are means to **trace the source of possibly malevolent manipulation** as far back as possible.
- **Problems in Further Processing** — Organizer, referees, and publisher have requirements on the **metadata** collected along with the submissions, which has to be taken into account in the design of the service. An issue of special importance for conference submissions, as these are usually collated into a single publication, is whether the format of the submissions allows **combination of submitted papers into a single document.**

2   The STACS Submission Service

Most of the user interface is based on email and does not require users to be known beforehand. In order to make a submission, users request an identification (called *ticket*) for the paper to be transmitted, then send a PostScript file with prepended metadata in ASCII, and receive a first analysis in reply.

If this first analysis does not suffice, the user can then request a complete log of the PostScript interpreter (ghostscript) and / or retrieve *pictures* of single pages. The rationale in offering pictures is that their content **is completely environment independent** (barring multicolor issues). ghostscript is by far the most popular, stable, and forgiving PostScript interpreter available. We expect users to be widely familiarized with its warnings and error messages, making the logfiles a usable means for debugging to them.

After having assessed the suitability of the submitted PostScript, the user will finally issue either a SUBMIT command or a DELETE instruction.

Intruders are prevented from guessing a ticket by use of a random number of considerable length. In addition, we would like to have the legitimate traffic encrypted. As a compromise, we made the use of the most common cryptographic toolkit, PGP, optional.

A security precaution against service denial attacks is that we require users to retrieve a ticket *before* they are allowed to send data. The email requesting a ticket won't contain any information besides the reply address, and need not be stored. Thus, in order to clog the disks with fake data, a perpetrator needs to obtain the issued tickets first, which means that the email address is "live" and owned (legally or illegally) by him.

As soon as a paper is SUBMITted, the server software will assign a submission number, watermark the PostScript with the number, and send a notification to the server maintainer and the organizer (as well as the submitter).

3   Relevance to Digital Libraries

It is highly desirable to make documents available electronically some time ahead of the advent of digital libraries to facilitate the conversion of recent, hence popular, works. In the case of nonportable (resp. not-quite-portable) formats, submission of documents to conferences is an important point of verification because of the time constraints and the large number of relatively different and physically remote sites (submission service, organizers, referees). Automated verification of documents upon submission will greatly cut down on the problems incurred later, not to mention encourage use of "benign" tools and formats among authors.

At the same time, the interface between authors and submission service is the easiest place to collect and verify metadata on the documents, too. Introduction of properly constructed questionnaires presented to the authors might well be the method of choice to prevent the electronic documents from turning out to be legacy data in terms of metadata availability.

Integrating Article Databases and Full Text Archives into a Digital Journal Collection

Anders Ardö, Franck Falcoz, Tove Nielsen, and Salam Baker Shanawa

Technical Knowledge Center & Library of Denmark, DTV
P.O. Box 777, DK-2800 Lyngby, Denmark
and@dtv.dk, http://www.dtv.dk/it/

Extended Abstract

The aim of DTV's Article Database Service (DADS) is to offer our end users a whole new generation of library services with integrated search and browse facilities, a common user interface and direct electronic document delivery – all accessible from their own desks. The system should handle bibliographic data, including abstracts as well as articles in full text and table–of–contents data.

Using an electronic article database service users can access a particular article or journal within seconds rather than hours or days typical for paper based collections. Large collections of material can be searched simultaneously and retrieved instantly. There is also the possibility for active dissemination of information based on "interest profiles" of users, ie current awareness services.

Technical design considerations of the DADS system include:

- Integration of data (full text documents, bibliographic records and table–of–contents data) from different vendors and information sources
- Common user interface for searching and browsing
- Simultaneous searching in multiple heterogeneous databases
- Integrated ordering and delivery of documents
- Accessibility 24 hours a day, 7 days a week, 365 days a year
- The system should be based on open standards, wherever possible
- Support of multiple hardware platforms and operating environments.

Organizing, indexing and providing access to material from different information providers becomes a major task. One of the key concepts in this respect is metadata (as it always have been). In order to integrate metadata from different providers we needed a metadata format that could include all of the different bibliographic data extracted from the different data sets plus locally generated information. We looked at several different standard metadata formats such as MARC [1] and Dublin Core [2]. None of those formats could meet our requirements. Besides that there is also a risk of losing data in case of mapping to and from any standard metadata formats. Our decision was to define our own metadata format which fulfills our requirements and design it so it is easy to export records in the standard formats mentioned above (with some loss of information).

The implemented system is based on the use of open international standards, wherever possible. The most important standards used in the system are:

- TCP/IP, as an underlying communications protocol (Internet standard)
- HTTP and HTML for the user interface (WWW)
- Z39.50 [3] for database access
- PDF as storage format for full text documents

We have found that the imported data sets often contain duplicate article records with the same or slightly varying information. Within one data set, these records are usually errors or updates to previous records. Between data sets, they are just two different records describing the same article (e.g. an Elsevier article also cataloged by INSPEC). For duplicates within one data set, only the latest, most up to date record should be kept, ie we de–duplicate records within one data set. For duplicates between data sets, the amount and the quality of information in each record varies and we cannot decide to keep just one. Our approach is to load each data set in a separate database (and sometimes on a separate server) and do a virtual merge which does not actually merge records but simply mark them as duplicate records. Our Web to Z39.50 gateway [4] can then detect these duplicate records and do the merge on the fly. The goal of this virtual merging is twofold: one to present only the preferred version of an article record in cases of duplicates and, secondly for articles with full text, to propagate the full text link to all records of that article.

The system is developed towards a distributed solution, in which important databases and services can be duplicated and thus end user availability will be increased. The on–line storage is backed up by a large tape–robot in order to allow fast restoring of data and short down–times in case of hardware failure.

The first version of DADS (with search, view and order) was opened locally for our university campus February 1998. The second version with added features like journal browse, search history and "personal shelves" for searches, journals and articles was released in July 1998.

Status (May 1998): The system include more than 6000 journals, 2000 conference proceedings, books, and reports giving some 3.800.000 bibliographic records (INSPEC: 2.180.000, SwetScan: 1.670.000, Elsevier: 74.000, Academic Press: 28.800). There are 130.000 articles available in full text. New material and new publishers are constantly added.

This project is supported by the Danish Ministry of Education under the program "Danmarks Elektroniske Forskningsbibliotek". The project was initiated by Lars Björnshauge, Mogens Sandfær and Annette Winkel Schwartz at DTV. We also want to thank the many colleagues at DTV who has actively participated in the development and testing of the system.

References

1. Library of Congress: MARC standards (http://lcweb.loc.gov/marc/)
2. Stuart L Weibel and Eric J Miller, 1996. Dublin Core Element Set Reference Page (http://purl.oclc.org/metadata/dublin_core/)
3. Library of Congress: The Z39.50 document (http://lcweb.loc.gov/z3950/agency/document.html)
4. EUROPAGATE consortium, Europagate – Welcome (http://europagate.dtv.dk/)

Alerting in a Digital Library Environment
Do Channels Meet the Requirements?

Daniel Faensen, Annika Hinze, and Heinz Schweppe

Institute of Computer Science, Freie Universität Berlin, Germany
{faensen,hinze,schweppe}@inf.fu-berlin.de

Keywords: digital libraries, push technology, alerting, channel, CDF, Netcaster

An Alerting Service (AS) informs its clients about new information provided by several suppliers. Special interests of clients can be defined as profiles. In the context of digital libraries, suppliers are the *providers* of *documents*. Providers are typically scientific publishers. In this paper we assume, that the providers are known to the clients. A general model and architecture of an Alerting Service is given in [1]. Channel technology has been developed for broadcast of news and continous streams of data like stock rates. For the digital library enviroment a finer granularity in profile definition than for common broadcasting is needed. In contrast to broadcast services, publishing events of multiple providers have to be presented to each client in a uniform way.

In this summary we evaluate how the two competing approaches of Channel technology, Netscape's Netcaster [3] and Microsofts Active Channels [2] meet these requirements.

To satisfy user's needs events have to be filtered by more or less complex profiles, e. g. a set of documents (like journals), a list of keywords (selected arbitraryly or from a thesaurus) or a query in a full-fledged query language like STARTS [4]. An easy-to-use and powerful profile definition language is one requirement for an AS. The second is a unified view, that means splitting the $n : m$-relationship between providers and clients.

The use of both technologies strongly depends on how the contents is to be filtered, i.e. how the user profile is to be defined. As a concrete example for the comparison we take te electronic publication of scientific journals.

The most remarkable difference between Microsoft Active Channels and Netscape Netcaster is (i) the necessary efford to implement a channel and (ii) the flexibility the technology offers. While a CDF file is quickly written only few program logic can be added. Netcaster Channels give the programmer a much more flexible tool. However, the implementation effort required by Netcaster is much higher then by Active Channel. In our architecture channels can be used at two communication pathways: (i) as a tool for information providers to notify the alerting service about the occurance of new objects and (ii) to push profile-filtered collections of new objects from alerting service to users. For the latter case both technologies revealed to be adequate. For the first case the use of channel technology strongly depends on the complexity of the profiles. In a simple TOC service where the alerting service only acts as a mediator between user

	TOC	Profile definition by				
		Subject	arbitrary keywords		sophisticated	
			metadata	FT	related doc.	weight
alert between — AS - U	stat./dyn.	dyn.	dyn.	dyn.	see discussion	
coopP - AS	easy	provider supplied[1]	provider supplied	external		
ncoopP - AS	special[2]	external[3]		external		
profile stored at	U or AS	U or AS	U or AS	AS[4]	U or AS	AS

Evaluation of the use of CDF as technology to implement a digital library alerting service with respect to the way content (journals and journal articles) should be filtered. For details see text.

Legend:
AS - U: way of sending the notification from alerting service to user
coopP - AS: support of communication between information providers and alerting service
ncoopP - AS: including of non-cooperative providers
TOC – The user will be informed on the Table Of Contents of newly published issues of journals she is interested in
FT – keywords are matched against FullText
U – user / user side
AS – alerting service
coopP – cooparative provider
ncoopP – non-cooparative provider
stat./dyn. – CDF file is hold statically respectively generated dynamically

and provider, channels can easily be implemented on the provider side. If profiles become more complex, responsibility for the provider increases. She has to add appropriate metadata to the channel items since querying is done against them. If queries have to be posed against the whole objects (e.g. full texts) the provider channel can still be used to notify the alerting service which in turn initiates a query against the provider's database using its search interface. Providers without such an interface cannot be supported. Non-cooperating providers, i.e. those which don't want or are not able to implement channels, in each case have to be queried in a periodically.

More problems remain with channel technology: A supplier does not keep track of the state of individual clients. Therefore alerting events may get lost or the same data may be offered several times to the same client depending on the mode and frequency of his interaction with the alerting service.

This study resulted from the designing phase of a project that implements an alerting service for the digital library of the Freie Universität Berlin. Our next step is the implementation of the service.

References

[1] D Faensen and A Hinze and H Schweppe: *Alerting in a Digital Library Environment – Do Channels Meet the Requirements?* Preprint tr-b-98-08, FB Mathematik, FU Berlin, 1998, at `ftp://www.inf.fu-berlin.de/pubs/tr-b-98-08.ps.gz`

[2] Microsoft: *Webcasting in Microsoft Internet Explorer 4.0 White Paper* (1997) at `http://www.eu.microsoft.com/ie/press/techinfo-f.htm?/ie/press/whitepaper/pushwp.htm`

[3] Netscape Communications Corporation: *Netcaster Developers Guide* at `http://developer1.netscape.com/docs/manuals/netcast/devguide`

[4] L Gravano, K Chang, H García-Molina, C Lagoze, and A Paepcke. STARTS: Stanford proposal for internet meta-searching. In J Peckham, editor, *SIGMOD 1997, Proceedings ACM SIGMOD International Conference on Management of Data, May 13-15, 1997, Tucson, Arizona*, volume 26 of *SIGMOD Record*, pages 207–218, june 1997.

NAIST Digital Video Library: Tools for Restructuring Video Data for the Content Based Information Retrieval - A Representative Image of Shot Concept for the Internet

Yukiko Kawasaki, Rei Suzuki, and Hideki Sunahara*

Nara Institute of Science and Technology, 8916-5, Takayama,
Ikoma, Nara 630-0101, Japan

Nara Institute of Science and Technology started services of a digital library system for campus use since April 1996. This system includes the function to access the digital video data. However, this function just provide showing video data on the terminals. In order to make the digital video library more useful to browse and retrieve, we proposed a new structure of the digital video data.

There are a lot of elements relating to the video media, such as representative frames of each topics, the sound information which is accompanied with such the representative frame, the text information which explains about the contents, and so on. A new structure extracts some elements from the digital video data before storing the video data in the database(Fig.1(left)). This structure provides a useful function in order to retrieve, browse and edit the target data in the digital library systems for the Internet(Fig.1(right)).

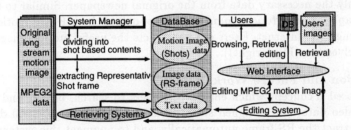

Fig. 1. system managers database(left side) and query(right side) architecture

We use following two terms: "shot"and "RS-frame"(Representative frame of Shot). *Shot* is a short sequence of the stream. A long video stream is composed of a large number of topics. For example, a news program about 30 minutes length includes a number of different topics of few minutes. Therefore, a motion video stream can be divided into a number of shots of about only a few minutes stream depending on the contents. Users can get the target scene directly by searching with shots without playing the video long stream consecutively. *RS-frame* is a representative frame of shot, which is selected from the shot properly. It is used to retrieve and browse the shots efficiently in addition to text

* yukiko-k@is.aist-nara.ac.jp, ray@itc.aist-nara.ac.jp, suna@wide.ad.jp

data. Various ways of automatic detection of a frame with a telop which usually appears each of the headlines in a news program are studied [1] [2]. However, RS-frame is not a frame with a telop but a representative frame selected from the shot. User can efficiently retrieve and browse the target scene with RS-frame.

Matching with users still image

Using the RS-frame, users can retrieve motion image data not only with a text but also with a frame. On the pattern matching for frame retrieval, users can use not only frames in the servers database but also frames users still image for the Internet. To get the matching between similar frames of the user and RS-frames of the server, user should input the URL of the users still image(Fig.2).

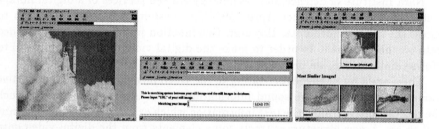

Fig. 2. users' still image(left), Web interface(center), and the result matching(right)

Scrapbook of motion image

People usually make a newspaper scrapbook according to his/her interests . They choose only the necessary data from the original newspaper. Similar to the hand made scrapbook, we propose to make a scrapbook of the MPEG2 motion image data through the Internet. Users can constructs the useful motion image library of themselves own(Fig.1(right)).

Conclusion and Future Work

We proposed a concept which enables the users to search, browse and edit the digital video data, and designed some parts of that system. We will develop a way to extract the RS-frame automatically, and to augment this system to multimedia.

Acknowledgment We extend special thanks to Prof.Yuji Oie, Ms.Mika Ito and members of minato laboratory whose contribution made this paper a possibility.

References

1. Takashi YAHATA, Akihiro SUGANO, Shinji SHIMOJO, Shojiro NISHIO, Hideo MIYAHARA, "Design of a TV News Database for News-On-Demand Systems," IEICE Technical Report DE95-50, pp.1-8,1995-10
2. Y.ARAKI,Y.SUGIYAMA, N.ISHIKAWA, T.TERANISHI and M.SAKURAI," Indexing and Classification of News Video Articles by Speech, Character and Image Recognition," IEICE PRMU96-93-103, pp.31-38,1996

LIBERATION: A Value-Added Digital Library

Robert Stubenrauch[1], Barbara Vickery[2], Ato Ruppert[3]

[1] JOANNEUM RESEARCH, Schießstattgasse 4a, A-8010 Graz, Austria
Robert.Stubenrauch@joanneum.ac.at
[2] University of Nottingham Library, University Park, Nottingham NG7 2RD
Barbara.Vickery@nottingham.ac.uk
[3] Library of Freiburg University, Werthmannplatz 2, D-79098 Freiburg i. B., Germany
ruppert@ub.uni-freiburg.de

1 Objectives

Within the framework of university settings the basic goal of LIBERATION was to add as much value to existing electronic publications from the scientific domain as possible by fully exploiting the sophisticated structuring and knowledge management features provided by an advanced underlying information management system. In that way all affected groups of users, from the production end (scientific publishers) through distributors (university libraries) to the consumers' end (student, scientists), should benefit significantly and the roles of information producers and consumers would blend to a large degree.

2 Technical Approach

The technical approach was to customise the Knowledge Management system Hyperwave which resulted in a fully Web compatible digital full-text library with the list of features including the following:

- a highly flexible GUI, consistent over complete library;
- hierarchically structured, modular content encourages re-usage of material;
- dynamically generated navigation facilities make hard-coded links unnecessary;
- implicit structure of content reduces maintenance effort significantly;
- arbitrary document formats, including multimedia
- meta-data of arbitrary type; actually employed is the Dublin Core scheme;
- powerful search: full-text and meta-data search; scope selection; iterative search;
- subscription to periodically performed individual searches; results sent via email;
- server clustering: search across server boundaries; central pool of user accounts;
- separation of content, meta-data and links increases modularity and re-usability;
- encourages private compilations of existing material ("personal views");
- user may annotate any document privately, publicly or group-specific;
- access restriction controlled via hierarchic user groups;
- various charging models, from pay-per-view to a number of simultaneous users;

3 Content and Usage

Within LIBERATION the focus concerning content is on computer science and applications though some significant collections have been incorporated from the domains of philosophy and theology. Material has been contributed from a number of science and educational publishers from within and outside the project consortium, in English and German. Naturally, research reports and theses produced locally have also been used. The users typically are student classes and individual scientific users such as lecturers. In one case, the system's annotation facility was used as a platform for a structured group discussion in the framework of a seminar.

The material is currently structured hierarchically by the type of material but can additionally be organised in arbitrary other hierarchic manners. Volume-wise the shared digital library of the three sites at Nottingham, Freiburg and Graz contains about 60 volumes of publications. The number of individual "atomic" documents (such as individually accessible HTML pages) is about 200.000.

4 Conclusions and Future

At the time being, pilot projects using the system are still ongoing but preliminary evaluations suggest that from the technical point of view the list of issues to be considered for future developments - most of which will go beyond the scope of the project LIBERATION - should include the following items:
- integration of online catalogues and digitised archives;
- provision of tools for maintenance and incorporation of existing material;
- integration of communication tools, synchronous as well as asynchronous.

From the business point of view it will be essential to develop a model that exploits and markets the value that is *added* by such a system to "plain" electronic publications. Technology will have to provide inexpensive means to integrate existing electronic resources on a broad basis.

However, for various reasons it is getting increasingly difficult to integrate high-quality content on a large-scale basis and thus reach a critical mass of material which, however, is necessary to attracts users. Therefore, in addition to collect original material on locally maintained servers it will be necessary to provide tools to incorporate remote resources but nevertheless offer comfortable ways to "personalise" the access to and the usage of such material in order to truly *work* with it and put it in individual contexts. This is a direction that will be taken by potential follow-up projects employing LIBERATION as a starting point.

5 Facts

The project runs from May 1996 to November 1998 and is funded by the EC (Telematics Applications Programme, Libraries Sector). Partners are: IICM (Austria); Library of Univ. of Nottingham (UK); Library and IfI, Freiburg Univ. (Germany); BIFAB, Addison-Wesley, Springer-Verlag (all: Germany). The system can be run on Windows NT and common Unix platforms. Both end users and system administrations can fully access the system through standard Web browsers of the 4th generation.
The full paper of this extended abstract is available at:
http://www.iicm.edu/stubenrauch/ECDL98.
The project Web site is located at http://www.iicm.edu/liberation or http://www.lib-online.com.

A Methodology to Annotate Cultural Heritage Digital Video

Claudia Di Napoli[*], Mario Mango Furnari[*], Francesco Mele[+], Giovanni Minei[+]

[*]C.N.R. - Istituto di Cibernetica, Via Toiano, 6 70082 Arco Felice (Naples) - ITALY
[+]Microgravity Advanced Research Support Center, Via Tavernola, 80144 - Naples - ITALY
[*]{C.Dinapoli,mf}@cib.na.cnr.it
[+]{mele,minei}@mars.unina.it

The goal of our work is to provide a well-structured methodological approach for annotating digital video in the domain of cultural heritage, taking into account that the methodologies and technologies currently available do not allow to make the annotation process completely automatic. In the proposed approach an interaction with the user that decides both the video segments to be annotated, and the set of labels to be associated to a segment is always required. This approach uses a predefined set of categories (*world-view*), hierarchically structured, which classifies the *video subjects* describing the contents shown in a video. This approach leads both to a way of integrating heterogeneous sources of information, and to structure information in such a way to retrieve video segments through a simple query language.

The *world-view* ([1], [2]), in the annotation process, is a hierarchy of classes representing a *view* of a particular knowledge domain, where each class is represented by a relation c of arity n (the number of attributes). The hierarchy comes from relations between pair of classes where a class A is a subset of a class B if the set of attributes of A is contained in the set of attributes of B. The world-view is defined as: $Wv=(A, C, R, S)$, where $A=\{at_1, at_2, ..., at_m\}$ is a set of m attributes (where m is the arity of the relation which represents the lowest class in the hierarchy); $C=\{c_1, c_2, ..., c_n\}$ is the set of the relation names (i.e. class names); $R=\{r_1, r_2, ..., r_n\}$ is a set of the relations which represent classes where $r_i=c_i(\cup_s at_s)$ and s is the arity of the relation; $S=\{r_s \prec r_t, r_f \prec r_q,...,\}$ is a set of relations between pairs of the relations r_i where the $r_i \prec r_j$ means that the set of attributes of the relation r_i is included in the set of attributes of the relation r_j.

An instance of a class with name c_x is represented as: $class(obj, c_x)$, $at_1(obj, val\_at_1)$, $at_2(obj, val\_at_2)$,..., $at_n(obj, val\_at_n)$, where $c_x \in C$, $at_1, at_2, ..., at_n \in At$, and val_at_1, $val\_at_2, ..., val\_at_n$ are the attribute values of the object uniquely identified by obj. It is not necessary to specify the relations $at_i(obj, val\_at_i)$ for all the class attributes, while the relation $class(obj, c_x)$, that expresses which class (or even subclass) obj belongs to, is mandatory.

The video annotation methodology we propose consists of associating video segments to strings of symbols (nouns of video subjects), usually suggested by the linguistic comment of the video, and also of associating contexts to these segments. A context represents the logical or the physical location of the selected video segment. The annotation process is represented as: $An=(F, Sg, Sn, Ar)$ where $F=\{f_1, f_2, ..., f_n\}$ is the set of frames which constitute the video; $Sg=\{sg_1, sg_2, ..., sg_n\}$ is a set of video segments $sg_i(k, j)=\cup_h f_h$ where $h=k, ..., j$, and k and j represent respectively the start and the end index of the segment sg_i; $Sn=\{sn_1, sn_2, ..., sn_n\}$ is a set of video subject names; $Ar=\{a_1, a_2, ..., a_n\}$ is a set of relations $a_i=ar_i(sn_i, s_i, sc_i)$ where $sn_i \in Sn$, $s_i \in Sg$, and $sc_i \in Sn$ with sc_i representing the video segment context. The operation of annotating a video segment, represented by a_i, is collocated in the world-view making it corresponding to a particular class, called video_subj.

To complete the video annotation we propose to associate video subjects to classes belonging to the given world-view or to class attributes. This operation is represented as: $Ac=(Wv, Oc, Oat)$, where $Wv=(A, C, R, S)$ is a world-view; $Oc=\{o_1, ..., o_n\}$ is the set of relations $o_i=ro_i(obj_i, c_i)$ where $c_i \in C$ and obj_i are identifiers of video subject instances; $Oat=\{oa_1, ..., oa_n\}$ is the set of relations $oa_i=roa_i(obj_i, val\_at_i)$ where val_at_i is the value of the attribute $at_i \in A$ and obj_i are identifiers of video subject instances as before. The world-view we consider is a hierarchy whose root (level 0) is the video class, so all the video subjects which compose the video belong to this class. Furthermore this class has a set of attributes which provides the first level of description of a video segment. The first level in the hierarchy (level 1) is represented by the video_head e video_subj subclasses, where video_head refers to the technical data associated to the video. Of course it is essential to enrich the hierarchy (i.e. to build more levels in the hierarchy) in order to provide a query language for retrieving video segments, but the annotation process is always possible even with a hierarchy of level 1 (the depth of the hierarchy depends on the expertise level and/or on the objectives of the user who is in charge of the annotation process).

The resulting hierarchical structure allows to use a specific query language to retrieve information related to the recorded video subjects. A query is represented in the form of Horn clauses whose body is a logical conjunction of relations which can be of the following types: class(Obj, Class_name), at_i(Obj, At_i_value), UopV where U and V can be constants or variables and op=$\{<, >, =, \geq, \leq, \neq\}$, rel($x_i$) where rel can be any kind of relation (not included in the world-view), as the ones that could be present in an external relational database, provided that some x_i are variables shared with at least one of the variables of the relations class, at_i, and op.

References

1. Alon Y. Levy, Anand Rajaraman, Joann J. Ordille, Query-*Answering Algorithms for Information Agents,* Proceedings of the Thirteenth National Conference on Artificial Intelligence (AAAI-96), Portland, OR, 1996.
2. Alon Y. Levy, Anand Rajaraman, Joann J. Ordille, *Querying Heterogeneous Information Sources Using Source Descriptions,* Proceedings of the 22th VLDB Conference Mumbai (Bombay), India, 1996.

BALTICSEAWEB – Geographic User Interface to Bibliographic Information

Sauli Laitinen and Anssi Neuvonen

VTT Information Service, Box 2000, FIN-02044 VTT, Finland

Abstract. Geographic user interfaces has been created to bibliographic information on environmental conditions of the Baltic Sea in a project, BALTICSEAWEB, within the Libraries sector of the EU Telematics Applications Programme. Two versions of map-based search interfaces have been developed which allow searches made in a database of more than 11 000 bibliographic records. The searches can be modified by using a WWW based search form. In addition a number of original documents have been made available in electronic form so that the user can not only retrieve bibliographic records but also original documents. BALTICSEAWEB offers environmental information on the Baltic Sea through a user-friendly and well structured geographical interface. The home page of the project can be found at URL http://www.baltic.vtt

1 Introduction

A digital library is being developed containing documents on environmental conditions of the Baltic Sea. Nominated contact libraries in each of the countries around the Baltic Sea select and catalogue documents to a centralized bibliographic database, which currently contains more that 11 000 references since 1970. Also original documents have been converted into electronic form and linked to the database so that the user can in many cases retrieve not only literature references but also the full text documents.

The information system was initiated in the late 70'ies under auspices of the Baltic Marine Environment Commission, the Helsinki Commission to offer a concise source of information about the findings related to the Baltic Sea. The early version of the database was used to compile printed bibliographies and the database was also made available on traditional online services. Later on access was provided by a form-based www interface on the Internet.

A development project, BALTICSEAWEB, was started in the 1997 within the Libraries sector of the EU Telematics Application Programme for further development of the information system. The aim of the project was to provide users with original documents in electronic form and to develop a geographic user interface to allow searches made using a map. In addition to linking original documents to bibliographic information the project has provided a demonstrator with two versions of map-based user interfaces. Functional requirements were defined by interviewing users and the demonstrator system has been validated by selected users.

2. Geographical user interfaces

The geographical user interfaces developed within the BALTICSEAWEB project are a dynamic Java-applet with scaleable map and a solution with a more static clickable map. Owing to varying quality of Internet services among the users both versions of the geographic user interface as well as a simple search form are being offered in the operational phase.

The clickable Baltic Sea area map is implemented with standard (static) html-pages. The Baltic Sea area is divided into 15 sub-regions according to scheme used by the Baltic Marine Environment Commission. By clicking the map the user can limit the search to concern a selected region only and add specificity to the search by using additional search parameters such as subject headings or free text keywords.

The more sophisticated geographical user interface which allows free area selection is implemented with a Java-applet (Fig. 1). The user can select multiple regions, cities or monitoring stations from the map. The map also allows zooming. After combining different search criteria the user then either submits the query or goes to an advanced search form, where the selected criteria have been automatically transferred.

Fig. 1. Geographic user interface allows drawing an area with the mouse and selecting specific regions, e.g. cities rivers and bays to combine them for a search.

Implementing Powerful Retrieval Capabilities in a Distributed Environment for Libraries and Archives[1]

Chrisa Tsinaraki, George Anestis, Nektarios Moumoutzis, Stavros Christodoulakis

Laboratory of Distributed Multimedia Information Systems and Applications (MUSIC)
Technical University of Crete
P.O. Box 134, GR, 73100 Chania, Greece
e-mail: {chrisa, ganest, nektar, stavros}@ced.tuc.gr

An on-line distributed environment, which was implemented in the context of the VENIVA project for historical libraries and archives is presented here. Emphasis is given in the presentation of the powerful search capabilities provided to the end-users, which are typical for the end-users (either researchers or ordinary people) of any Digital Library environment.

The information managed resides in a number of different relational databases in one or more institutions (i.e. Libraries and Historical Archives). The end-user of the system uses a WWW client to pose traditional boolean queries, similarity queries or complex queries containing both boolean and similarity terms on the contents of the databases. In the case of similarity queries, the end-user can also select the evaluation formula used to rank the objects that the system returns as the answer to his query. This gives a flexibility to experiment with alternative retrieval models without starting the implementation from scratch. A *Graphical Query Editor* is used in order to construct the queries.

The innovative aspect of this work is that the similarity queries are translated by an appropriate component of the server into a series of traditional SQL queries, so that there is no need to have separate systems to support the various services offered. Only a standard relational DBMS (Database Management System) is used in the core of the system. The software layer that has been implemented on top gives all the additional flexibility. The implementation is based on a sound and flexible mathematical retrieval model.

The framework, which supports queries containing both boolean and similarity terms in the context of VENIVA, is based on a powerful mathematical tool for the description of similarity queries and different evaluation models. It has been implemented on top of a relational DBMS as a distributed system. This framework aims to integrate *Information Retrieval System (IRS)* techniques on top of traditional relational DBMS. In particular, a mathematical model for the description of Information Retrieval Systems based on different fuzzy models has been developed [1].

The framework has been implemented [2] on top of a relational DBMS as a distributed system. The general architecture of this system is shown in Fig. 1. *Schema editor* is a graphical tool, which is used to define the mapping between fuzzy relations and relational tables. It is also responsible to create the relational tables that are used to store the fuzzy relations corresponding to similarity queries. The mappings are then stored in the *Map File*. Based on these mappings, the *Retrieval Engine* is able to translate retrieval requests from any *Application* into SQL queries sent to the *Relational DB* and give back the results

---

[1] Support for this work was provided by the VENIVA (VENetIan Virtual Archive) ESPRIT project (EP N° 20638)

to the *Application* when requested. The *Retrieval Engine* is also responsible for decomposing a retrieval request in a series of INSERT statements to populate the tables used to store the queries. The current implementation supports the Microsoft Access DBMS and offers queries in conjunctive normal form.

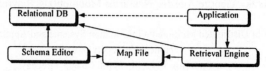

Fig. 1. System Architecture

The procedure we follow in order to use the framework has the following steps:
- Using Schema Editor, on a relational database, the schema of the IRS is defined. Namely there are defined entity sets, relationship sets and fuzzy attributes.
- Retrieval Engine is started, taking as input the schema of the IRS that was created in the previous step using Schema Editor.
- The application that offers the user interface for the formation of the queries and submission is created. The application communicates with Retrieval Engine and sends queries to it. In addition, the application takes care of the presentation of the results to the user. The application implemented in the context of VENIVA is the Graphical Query Editor.

We have presented here the flexible search capabilities provided in the context of the VENIVA project. These services are implemented on a homogenized schema based on popular standards for the description of the contents of Libraries and Historical Archives. The advanced Information Retrieval capabilities supported are built on top of existing relational database technology which has been properly extended to support ranking of objects with different evaluation formulas. The presented approach provides a practical methodology for publishing the contents of historical institutions to the broad public using existing mature technologies such as WWW and Relational DBMSs.

Future research will focus on the integration of relevance feedback techniques so that the end-user can refine his query based on the investigation of the objects that meet his needs. Moreover, support for textual attributes will be integrated with thesauri and special access methods.

References

[1] N. Moumoutzis: "The Design of a System Supporting the Development of Interactive Geographical Applications", MEng Thesis, Department of Electronic and Computer Engineering, Technical University of Crete, Chania, 1998.
[2] G. Anestis: "Design and Implementation of a Boolean and Similarity Retrieval System on top of Relational Database Management Systems", Diploma Thesis, Department of Electronic and Computer Engineering, Technical University of Crete, Chania, 1997.
[3] K. Beard, V. Sharma: "Multidimensional ranking for data in digital spatial libraries", International Journal on Digital Libraries, vol. 1, number 2, pp 153-160, September 1997.
[4] S. DeFacio, A. Daoud, L. A. Smith, J. Srinivasan: "Integrating IR and RDBMS Using Cooperative Indexing" In Proceedings of the 18th ACM SIGIR International Conference on Research and Development in Information Retrieval, 1995, pp 84-92.

[5] S. Dessloch, N. Mattos: "Integrating SQL Databases with Content-specific Search Engines", Proceedings of the 23rd VLDB Conference Athens, Greece, 1997, pp 528-537.

[6] R. Fagin: "Combining Fuzzy Information from Multiple Systems", Proceedings of the 15th Symposium on Principles of Database Systems, Montreal, Canada, June 1996, pp 216-226.

[7] D. A. Grossman, O. Frieder, D. O. Holmes, D. C. Roberts: "Integrating Structured Data and Text: A Relational Approach", Journal of the American Society of Information Science, vol. 48, no. 2, February 1997.

[8] L. Gravano, H. Garcia-Molina: "Merging Ranks from Heterogeneous Internet Sources", Proceedings of the 23rd VLDB Conference Athens, Greece, 1997, pp 196-205.

[9] L. Haas, D. Kossmann, E. Wimmers, J. Yang: "Optimizing Queries across Diverse Data Sources", Proceedings of the 23rd VLDB Conference Athens, Greece, 1997, pp 276-285.

[10] J. Hammer, M. Breunig, H. Garcia-Molina, S. Nestorov, V. Vassalos, R. Yerneni: "Template-based wrappers in the TSIMMIS system", In Proceedings of the 1997 ACM SIGMOD International Conference on Management of Data, pp 532-535.

[11] G. Hjaltason., H. Samet: "Ranking in Spatial Databases", Proceedings of 4th Symposium on Advances in Spatial Databases (SSD '95), Lecture Notes in Computer Science No. 951, Springer-Verlag, 1995, 83-95.

[12] Ad Hoc Commission on Descriptive Standards, "ISAD(G): General International Standard Archival Description"

[13] Working Group on the General International Standard Bibliographic Description set by IFLA, "International Standard Bibliographic Description", 1977

[14] H. V. Jagadish, A. O. Mendelzon, T. Milo: "Similarity-Based Queries", in proceedings of the 14th Symposium on Principles of Database Systems, San Jose CA, USA, 1995, pp 36-45.

[15] Joon Ho Lee, "Properties of Extended Boolean Models in Information Retrieval", In Proceedings of the 17th ACM SIGIR International Conference on Research and Development in Information Retrieval, 1994, 182-190.

[16] R. Kruse, J. Gebhardt, F. Klawonn: "Foundations of Fuzzy Systems", John Wiley & Sons Ltd., ISBN 0-471-94243-X, 1994

[17] C. Lynch, M. Stonebraker: "Extending User-Defined Indexing with Applications to Textual Databases", Proceedings of the 14th VLDB Conference Los Angeles CA, USA, 1988, pp 306-317.

[18] Avram, Henriette D. The MARC pilot project: final report on a project sponsored by the Council on Library Resources, Inc. Washington: Library of Congress, 1968.

[19] M. Persin: "Document Filtering for Fast Ranking", ", In Proceedings of the 17th ACM SIGIR International Conference on Research and Development in Information Retrieval, 1994, pp 339-348.

[20] G. Schmidt, T. Ströhlein: "Relations and Graphs", Springer-Verlag, ISBN 3-540-56254-0, 1993.

[21] G. Shalton: "The use of Extended Boolean Logic in Information Retrieval", In Proceedings of the 1984 ACM SIGMOD International Conference on Management of Data, pp 277-285.

[22] G. Shalton: "Automatic Text Processing", Addison-Wesley, Reading, MA, 1989

[23] V. Vassalos, Y. Papakonstantinou: "Describing and Using Query Capabilities of Heterogeneous Sources", Proceedings of the 23rd VLDB Conference Athens, Greece, 1997, pp 256-265.

[24] W. Moen, M. Tucker, "A Guide to Global Z39.50"

OWL-Cat: A Web-Based OPAC Appealing End-Users to Exploit Library Resources

Silvana Mangiaracina, Stefano Ferrarini, Maria Grazia Balestri

CNR Area della Ricerca di Bologna, Biblioteca, via Gobetti 101,
40129 Bologna, Italy
{mangiaracina, ferrarini, balestri}@area.bo.cnr.it

Databases have always been the most appropriate tool to catalogue library items, but their most important feature, to instantly retrieve sets of data which satisfy search criteria, has often represented an awkward task to be accomplished, depending on the different kinds of query languages, which vary with hardware and software architecture. WWW browsers and the development of the Internet have offered Information specialists a unique opportunity both to facilitate end-users in the search and retrieval process and to remove barriers which have always separated local from remote resources.

At the crossover point between libraries' supply and users' requests, Web-based OPAC's allow not only the location of items which are physically owned by the library, but also access to remote resources (either full-text documents or databases, free and fee-based, or selected links relevant to the library community) and actually display or retrieve them on the desktop of any registered user.

Indexing digital resources also means recording type of data which require appropriate database fields such as MARC 856, designed to accommodate URL (Uniform Resource Locator) addresses, as well as others which contain information accessible only to authorized users. This will allow librarians to distribute the appropriate data in a more timely and secure manner than alerting different classes of users on 'bits and pieces' of information at any occurring change (e.g. URL changes, passwords and so on), therefore saving time to implement other specific features. Grouping resources from different points of view or grouping users with different interests for current awareness purposes, in order to implement all kinds of alerting services would have been previously inconceivable for librarians, because of the enormous amount of work involved. Also, from the librarian point of view, the crucial task of updating the catalogue must be as smooth and quick as possible, and find in the OPAC interface a valid companion to normalize data.

The structure and functionalities of OWL-Cat (Online Web Library–Catalogue Access), a tool designed to interface DBMS *Basis Plus* and its Library Management Module *Techlib Plus ver. L1G.2* to the World Wide Web are described. The functionalities and new services of OWL-Cat have been implemented at the CNR Research Area Main Library in Bologna.

658

OWL-Cat features include:
- Providing help to the less experienced user, who had previously achieved negative results, by presenting him/her valid alternatives to run a successful search.
- Helping the librarian to make use of advanced features to correct record orthography and consistency, and to normalize data in authority files.

A number of issues have been identified in designing a Web library-gateway:
1. the librarian need not worry about maintenance of the interface;
2. checking data consistency should be carried out by the system;
3. the system should be able to autonomously manage different user categories, priorities, authorizations, validations and so on.

The most interesting and innovative features of OWL-Cat are:

User Interface. Querying by forms and by browse. OWL-Cat offers two ways for formulating searches: fill-in forms and browse lists. There are two kinds of forms, simple and advanced. This is to take into account both low-frequency user and more sophisticated user. Search results are "short" or "detailed" lists of retrieved items. Users can then navigate through related information of interest displayed in the result lists (i.e. co-authors, series titles, publisher, subjects and so on). This nonlinear search will also avoid the problem of a too narrow strategy or misspelling or truncation errors.

OWL-Cat also builds browsing lists which will help the final user home in on his/her needs and to locate relevant resources. Browsing activity is a way for rapidly scanning all the content of interest in the library in a systematic, and eventually, exhaustive manner, as an alternative to inputting data in search forms. OWL-Cat browsing lists (subjects, publishers, series titles, corporate, conference and personal author lists) help users to shape one's own mental representation of the whole library content, which, in turn, can be continuously re-organized on the basis of user preference.

Browse lists are periodically created. OWL-CAT autonomously queries the whole database on behalf of the user and organizes query results in HTML pages. Furthermore, precompiled queries launched by hotlinks in browse lists increase system performance, and also filter generic queries which overload Web gateway traffic and absorb excessive machine resources.

Resources of resources: URL browse list. OWL-Cat provides the possibility of automatically generating electronic journal information pages from information gathered in database records. The URL browse list is created by querying all the records that have a MARC 856-like, not empty, field. It then provides timely access to Table of Contents, abstracts and full-text electronic journals. In some cases, the database record will contain other related information such as limitations of online subscription, type of subscription (i.e. abstract only, full-text), username and password, notes, plus, of course, URLs. OWL-Cat takes care of delivering this "confidential" information only to authorized users on the basis of a multi-user policy

At the librarian's ease, a process of URL checking is launched, which allows further correction of the database. OWL-Cat provides the librarian with a very easy tool to authorise/remove classes of users to/from different services.

Towards a Framework for Building Collaborative Information Searching Systems

B. Trousse, M. Jaczynski and R. Kanawati
INRIA Sophia-Antipolis, ACTION AID
2004 route des lucioles
BP 93, 06902 Sophia Antipolis
e-mail: {trousse,jaczynski,kanawati}@sophia.inria.fr

1   Introduction: Collaborative Information Searching

If the World Wide Web (the web for short), should become the world wide digital library, not only effective and efficient information searching techniques are needed, but also an adequate collaboration support that enable people to cooperate and collaborate in locating relevant information just as they do in physical libraries. Collaboration support is required during information searching as well as for sharing results of previous searching process. Collaborative information searching (CIS) can be either *direct* or *indirect*. In direct collaboration, people communicate directly, in synchronous or asynchronous manner, in order to show one another where to go to find a given information or simply to send to one another the required information. In indirect collaboration information gathered from previous information searching process conducted a user are used to help other users in their searching activities. Recommender systems are an example of indirect *CIS* systems. In this work we address the problem of providing a framework that facilitates the design and the implementation of various *CIS* applications. An overview of this framework, called, *Broadway*Tools* is presented in the next section.

2   Our CIS project: Broadway*Tools

Our approach consists on providing a set of object-oriented reusable components (or tools) that implements main services required for *CIS*. Today, *Broadway*Tools* provides four groups of tools set:

- *Server tools*: these include a recommendation server, a user profile and session manager server, a page information server, and an annotation server. The recommendation server computes the advice using case-based reasoning techniques [Jac97]. The user profile server stores the user Ids and their profiles. The page information server analyses the content of pages to extract relevant data such as the title, the headers and the keywords. Finally, the annotation server is used to retain textual annotations linked to Web pages.

- *Graphical interface tools*: We have defined some tools used to build graphical interfaces modules such as toolbars : a toolbar is a Java applet that displays a set of buttons to quickly access some exported functions.

– *Service tools*: These services represent some tools used to build modules operating between theses graphical interfaces and the servers. We provide four tools : the robots, the loggers, the HTTP proxy, the watchers, and the event dispatcher. The robots are used to navigate the Web automatically. The loggers can record a set of selected types of events for further analysis. The HTTP proxy is used to manipulate HTML pages before the users are able to display them and also to improve page access efficiency with a central cache. This proxy tool is based on the Jigsaw http server developed by the *W3C*[1] (World Wide Web Consortium) in which we have defined specific resource filters. A watcher is an applet used in combination with the proxy to get information about the users's activity inside their web browser. Finally, the event dispatcher allows asynchronous communications between the different modules, without a direct connection from the event providers to the event consumers.

– *Database persistence tools*: All the servers are persistent and we use the ObjectStore PSE tool to store data in local files or in a remote object oriented database. We have defined other tools above PSE to facilitate the integration of the persistence.

In order to build a concrete *CIS* application from our framework, the application developer has two man tasks to do:

– *Specialization*: this is an optional phase. Object components provided by *Broadway*Tools* can be used in their default implementation or specialized to realize application specific version of the service they provide.

– *Integration*: this task concerns the development of useful interfaces and tools generating the specific events to be taken into account by different (specialized) servers for the concrete application.

The *Broadway*Tools* frameworks has served to develop an web browsing advisor, called *Broadway*. The Broadway system is described in [JT98] (also presented in this book).

References

[Jac97] M. Jaczynski. A framework for the management of past experiences with time-extended situations. In *proceedings of CIKM'97*, pages 32–39, Las Vegas, Nevada, November 1997.

[JT98] M. Jaczynski and B. Trousse. WWW assisted browsing by reusing past navigations of a group of users. In *Proceedings of the European Workshop on Case-based Reasoning*, LNCS/AI, Dublin, Iraland, September 1998. Springer-Verlag.

---

[1] http://www.w3c.org

Toward a New Paradigm for Library Instruction in the Digital Library

Verlene J. Herrington

AG Communication Systems, 2500 W. Utopia Rd,
Phoenix, Arizona 85072-2179
herringv@agcs.com

Hypertext and the Internet have dramatically altered the world of information access. The digital library does not focus on ownership and holdings, but strives for instant global access to information. Text is no longer merely linear discourse; hypertext is branching, linking, interactive discourse with no absolute beginning or end, no boundaries and no permanence. Technology has thrust the library into the Information Age, but models of service delivery have not changed, especially in the area of library instruction. Academic librarians must examine their beliefs and values regarding the purpose and value of library instruction.

Over 30 years ago, Thomas Kuhn wrote The Structure of Scientific Revolutions and coined the phrase "paradigm shift". Kuhn theorized that science may encounter a law so significantly different that a discipline is forced to alter its worldview or paradigm of its environment. A paradigm describes everything which the science is based on--all of its laws, beliefs, procedures and methods. Until Kuhn, science was thought to be built on an accumulation of all that had been learned over history with each new law adding to the mass of scientific knowledge, not radically changing it. It has been 500 years since Gutenberg's printing press altered the paradigm of the world forever. Likewise, hypertext and the Internet are radically transforming the worldview of global information access, electronic publishing, scholarly collaboration, and resource sharing.

Although technology has changed the "look" of the library, there has been no major paradigm change in the area of library instruction--mainly because the underlying belief structure remains the same. A paradigm implies shared assumptions, concepts, values and practices--a shared view of the world. The current model of library instruction is based on the belief structure that the library is so complex that the library user cannot access the information and remediation is needed. The library system is deficient, as well as the library user. The current model is not linked to the primary mission of the library, but is linked to the goal of teaching. This model is based on negative beliefs and a deficit model: compensatory instruction is needed because of the library system's failure.

A new model of library instruction assumes just the opposite: the library system is easy to use and there is no need for library instruction or even printed materials. This model carries positive assumptions about the library and the library user. Library users are not helpless and dependent--they are in control. They want a system which is easy to use and transparent. They do not want complicated instructions or lectures. The hectic world of today calls for information to be easy to access, fast and complete. Library users want to interact with the library, as they interact with a Sega or a Nintendo. Library users want information at the point of need, not when the instructional librarian schedules a class to present predetermined information.

The new model does not propose the elimination of instructional librarians, but suggests that instructional librarians focus on designing user-friendly interfaces, and not on teaching. If library instruction evolved out of a need, the solution is to eliminate the need. Instructional librarians should focus on human factors research as it applies to system design and information access.

Ontobroker in a Nutshell

Dieter Fensel, Stefan Decker, Michael Erdmann, and Rudi Studer

University of Karlsruhe, Institute AIFB, 76128 Karlsruhe, Germany
Email: {decker, erdmann, fensel, studer}@aifb.uni-karlsruhe.de,
http://www.aifb.uni-karlsruhe.de/WBS/broker

The World Wide Web (WWW) provides huge amounts of information in informal and semi-structured representations. This is one of the key factors that enabled its incredible success story. The representation formalisms are simple and retain a high degree of freedom in how to present the information. However, freedom in information representation and simple representation formalisms cause serious bottlenecks in accessing information from the web. We designed and implemented some tools necessary to enable the use of ontologies [2] for enhancing the web. We developed a broker architecture called *Ontobroker* [1] with three core elements: a query interface for formulating queries, an inference engine used to derive answers, and a webcrawler used to collect the required knowledge from the web. The strength of our approach is the tight coupling of informal, semiformal and formal information and knowledge. This supports their maintenance and provides a service that can be used more generally for the purpose of knowledge management and for integrating knowledge-based reasoning and semiformal representation of documents.

The query formalism is oriented toward a frame-based representation of ontologies that defines the notion of instances, classes, attributes and values. The structure of the query language can be exploited to provide a tabular query interface as shown in Figure 1 which asks for the researchers with last name Benjamins and their email addresses. We also need support for selecting classes and attributes from the ontology. To allow the selection of classes, the ontology has to be presented in an appropriate

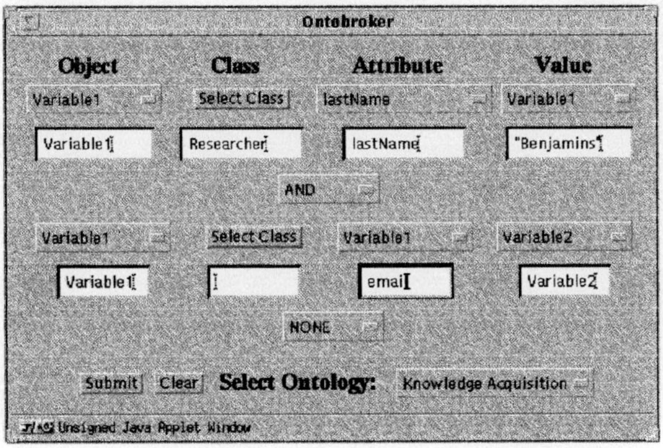

Fig. 1. The tabular query interface of Ontobroker.

664

manner. This requirement is met by a presentation scheme based on Hyperbolic Geometry: classes in the center are depicted with a large circle, whereas classes at the border of the surrounding circle are only marked with a small circle (see Figure 2). The visualization techniques allows a quick navigation to classes far away from the center as well as a closer examination of classes and their vicinity.

Knowledge contained in the WWW is generally formulated using HTML. Therefore, we developed an extension to the HTML syntax to enable the ontological annotation of web pages. Currently, the W3C is developing the *Resource Description Framework* (RDF). This format will be used to add meta information to documents, i.e. to include semantical information about documents. Therefore, we developed a translator that generates RDF specifications from our annotations. Another possibility for stable web sources is to replace the annotation effort by deriving wrappers which extract this information. Such a wrapper can be used to directly derive the factual knowledge that is used by the inference engine of Ontobroker.

References

1. Fensel, D., Decker, S., Erdmann, M., Studer, R.: Ontobroker: The Very High Idea. Proceedings of the 11th International Flairs Conference (FLAIRS-98), Sanibal Island, Florida, USA (1998) 131—135.
2. Friedman Noy, N. and Hafner, C. D.: The State of the Art in Ontology Design. AI Magazine, **18** (1997) 53—74.

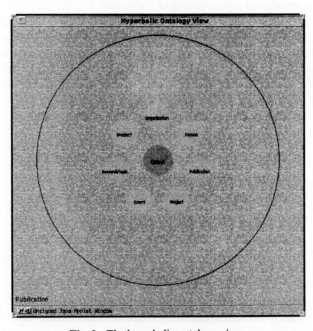

Fig. 2. The hyperbolic ontology view.

WAY: An Architecture for User Adapted Access to Z39.50 Servers Based on Intelligent Agents

Camino Fernández, Paloma Díaz, and Ignacio Aedo

e-mail: {camino,pdp}@inf.uc3m.es, aedo@ia.uc3m.es
DEI Laboratory. Department of Computer Science
Universidad Carlos III de Madrid
Butarque 15,E-28911 Leganés (Spain)

The work presented in this poster is based on the combination of three well-known paradigms of Computer Science applied to Digital Libraries: User Adaptive Interfaces, Information Retrieval and Intelligent Agents. Its objective is to define a model providing intelligent information access by means of an adaptive user interface. The model, called WAY (see figure 1), is supported by a web-based architecture and counts on the help of intelligent agents in charge of studying the user characteristics in terms of previous behaviours, in order to provide an adapted interface and to guide the user's searching process through the servers available in the net. This model is currently being implemented in java using RMI (Remote Method Invocation) technology.

Concerning user adaptive interfaces, what our model proposes is to offer a different initial interface for each type of user. These initial interfaces will be defined according to the users classification, taking into account where the user is accessing the system from. Once the user begins to interact with a specific interface, it will go on changing depending on the actions performed by the user in two ways: the preferences shown explicitly by the user -selected options in the configuration of the interface- and the preferences shown implicitly -by systematic actions. The following examples illustrate these ideas:

- The type of user: in a university library environment, the possible types could be students, teachers and library staff, all of them with quite different goals and needs.
- The user mother tongue: if the user is connecting from Germany, he/she is likely to prefer a German interface.
- The user preferences: there are people who still prefer textual environments although their computers allow a good performance of visual ones.
- The user repeated actions: in a university, students usually are more interested in books than in journals, unlike teachers, whose main research tools are papers.

The user will be asked no questions, but a *User Interface Agent* will be in charge of finding out the kind of interface which best fits that single user, creating a user *Profile* for further accesses from the same user. Of course, the user will always be able to change any of the decisions taken by the agent if they do not satisfy him/her.

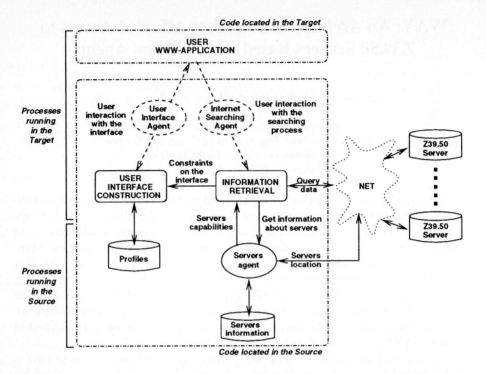

Fig. 1. WAY model

Concerning intelligent information access, an *Internet Searching Agent* will be in charge of guiding the user in the searching process by anticipating the user next step. For instance, when a user does not find what he/she was looking for in a particular server, his/her next step will be to search other servers. By the time the user tries to do so, the system will have anticipated the user and will have looked for the servers containing information that fit the user request and will have ordered and presented them to the user, beginning with the one that contains more related information.

Although WAY is a general model for accessing information, what we are presenting here is one of its possible applications to digital libraries and, more precisely, to servers implementing the Z39.50 standard, as it is becoming a broadly accepted information retrieval protocol specification that is being implemented by more and more libraries each day. To keep updated information about the Z39.50 servers, the *Servers Agent* is designed. This agent does not interact directly with the user. Its task is to keep updated information about which and where are the Z39.50 servers in the net. To do so, this agent has two main sources: the implementors page at the Z39.50 Maintenance Agency (http://lcweb.loc.gov/z3950/agency/) and the results obtained from web-searchers. Once the servers are located, this agent keeps update information about them: access controls, data bases, supported syntax, implemented services, etc.

ARIADNE - Digital Library Architecture

Nuno Maria, Pedro Gaspar, Nuno Grilo, António Ferreira, Mário J. Silva

FCUL
Faculdade de Ciências da Universidade de Lisboa,
Campo Grande, 1700 Lisboa, Portugal
info@ui.icat.fc.ul.pt

Abstract. We describe our approach for acquiring, preserving, organizing and disseminating information in a digital library of news publications.

Overview

The digital publishing group at the Informatics Department of FCUL studies new paradigms for processing heterogeneous information in organizations, combining multiple information processing technologies under a common framework. In our current project, ARIADNE, developed jointly with Público, S.A.[2], a national daily newspaper, we are building a new digital publishing infrastructure where all the information used and produced by journalists is organized in a common database. From the information in this digital library, we generate publications in digital format.

A main concern of the project is to build and maintain a large multimedia data repository, holding various collections of documents, from newsfeeds to newspaper articles, to databases of people, places and events. For some of the collections we only keep meta-data of various forms (from links to indexes and classification schemes).

We find that some of the new publications we are developing are taking us into a new publishing paradigm where the notion of edition disappears. The same information item is reformatted and published in multiple forms, and accessed as part of information collections that do not constitute publications in the usual sense. As a result, we are studying robust forms for classifying this information so it may be reused in the future and ways to preserve its current presentation and organization.

Organizing topic collections is another investigation topic associated with the preservation of information [1]. We need to provide the means, not only to view information at a later time, but also to find it. To achieve this ARIADNE has its own search engine combining information retrieval techniques with relational queries.

ARIADNE also supports personalized publication using information filtering based on dynamic user profiles. These are updated as a result of the data mining of logged accesses and user specified preferences. With this scheme, we intend to track user preferences as they change over time. In our architecture, a user profile maps a reader into one of a set of presentation styles (or templates). Publication editors define these

668

styles to match typical profiles, which are identified among the publications' readership.

Finally, we are developing a payment scheme for billing the use of our information services. In our publishing system, access to recent news is free. However, the use of all other services will be charged. These services include searches on our indexes and collections and notifications sent by user created information agents.

Architecture

The architecture of ARIADNE is based on large multimedia data repository, which holds various collections of documents, newspaper articles, databases of readers and authors, places and events. For some collections, namely external publications, we only keep metadata and links for the articles.

The global architecture and the main information flow are shown in the figure. Several sources, including news agencies feeds, articles created for the paper edition of *Público* and external publications provide news items to the ARIADNE repository. Each article received is submitted to a preprocessing stage, where its meta-data is extracted. The articles and news feeds are then converted into a common format based on the Extended Markup Language - XML, and archived. Editions of electronic publications are built on a second stage selecting a group of articles archived in the collections repository and packing them into presentations (or editions). This process finishes by converting the XML sources to HTML, making articles viewable from the current generation of web browsers.

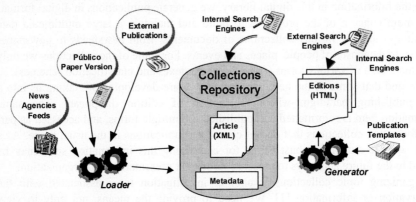

References

1. Maria, N., Gaspar, P., Ferreira A., Silva, M.: Information Preservation in ARIADNE, Proceedings of the 6th DELOS Workshop, Tomar, Portugal (1998);
2. Público On-line, http://www.publico.pt;

Facts and Myths of Browsing and Searching in a Digital Library

K.F. Tan[1], M.Wing[1], N. Revell1, G.Marsden[1], C. Baldwin[2], R. MacIntyre[3], A. Apps[3], K.D. Eason[4], and S. Promfett[4]

[1]School of Computing Science, Middlesex University, Bounds Green Road,
London N11 2NQ, United Kingdom
{kok1, michael47, n.revell, gary1}@mdx.ac.uk
[2]SuperJournal Information Design & Management, Broom, Hinksey Hill,
Oxford OX15BH, United Kingdom
c.baldwin@dial.pipex.com
[3]Manchester Computing, University of Manchester, Oxford Road, Manchester M13 9PL,
United Kingdom
{zzsupjrm, ann.apps}@mcc.ac.uk
[4]Department of Human Sciences, Loughborough University, Loughborough, Leicestershitre
LE11 3TU UK, United Kingdom
{K.D.Eason, s.m.pomfrett}@lboro.ac.uk

1 Introduction

In recent times, there has been increased interest in the querying of digital libraries (DLs). This is due in part to the development of the WWW, which enables easy access to both centralised and distributed digital library sources. The majority of published works on querying DLs are associated with information retrieval (IR), also known as digital querying. Information retrieval techniques are popular with querying DLs due to their flexibility in querying semi-structured data. In contrast, database querying of DLs has been largely ignored until only recent years. The key aspects of database querying of DLs involve the integration of database querying with browsing or navigating techniques to query semi-structured data. Our interest lies in developing the relatively limited database query facilities currently available to users of DLs, and a key stage in this process is to define what kinds of searching and browsing typical users would like to perform.

2 Focus of the poster

In this poster we will present the planning of an analysis of user browsing and searching strategies in the SuperJournal[1] digital library (SJDL). The browse and search strategies suggested for the analysis are derived from the navigational strategies for a database (see table 1) proposed by Canter, Rivers and Storrs. This

---

[1] SuperJournal is a project funded by the Joint Information Systems Committee (JISC) of the Higher Education Funding Councils, as part of its Electronic Libraries Programme (eLib).

derivation of browse and search strategies (for a DL) from the navigational strategies (of a database) will serve to highlight the similarities and differences between browsing/searching in DLs and databases. The proposed analysis is based on the activity logfiles of users of the SJDL, which are logged as ASCII files and are converted to SPSS files for statistical analysis purposes. These logfiles represent over two years worth of digital library browse and search activities.

The three aims for the analysis of user browse and search strategies are as follows:

- To define and verify the browse and search strategies used by SJDL users (e.g. Scanning, browsing and etc).
- To identify the browse and search features utilised in each of the browse and search strategies (e.g. cueing and full text search).
- To identify the internal and external factors which affect SJDL user browse and search strategies (e.g. User's mental models and physical environment settings).

3 Basic conceptual framework

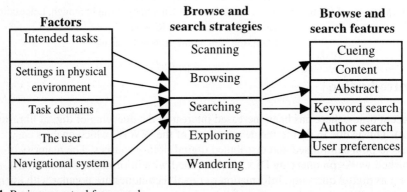

Fig. 1. Basic conceptual framework

This framework[2] allows analysis of the influence of the factors, such as intended tasks and task domains, on the browse and search strategies chosen by SJDL users. The chosen browse and search strategies will determine the type of browse and search features utilised. The features listed in figure 1 are selected examples from identified browse and search features in SuperJournal application.

4 Conclusion and further work

The proposed analysis presented in this poster will be used to define desirable extensions to the Object Query Language (OQL) that will allow typical digital library browsing or searching capability. A long term aim of the project is to design algorithm to support typical browsing and querying of digital libraries.

---

[2] The concept for the framework is derived from HUSAT's conceptual framework of user behavior in SuperJournal.

New Media Showcase

Michael Kreyche

New Media Services, Kent State University, PO BOX 1590, Kent OH 44242-0001
mkreyche@kent.edu

New Media Services is a relatively new unit of Kent State University Libraries and Media Services that provides technological and pedagogical support for instruction. Working closely with faculty, teaching assistants, and academic support staff, New Media Services supplies research, design, and production services and is engaged with a variety of technologies that support the Digital Library. Four types of projects are described here to illustrate the range of applications of new media technology.

Digital Text

The "Stater Archive" (http://www.library.kent.edu/stater) is a full text archive of Kent State University's student newspaper. The Archive presently covers a period of five and a half years (from 1990 to 1996) and consists of a collection of SGML files converted (perhaps "salvaged" is a more descriptive term) from newspaper production files using a combination of batch text processing utilities and custom interactive editing software. The resulting files have been validated against a DTD written specifically for this application. Currently, a Web-based interface passes queries to a search engine and translates the SGML text to HTML for display within the browser. A disadvantage of this technique is the significant server overhead required to perform the necessary conversion for each request. This database is an excellent testbed for experimenting with the emerging XML/XSL standards. Eventually these technologies will provide a more refined delivery for the database, moving formatting tasks from the server to an advanced browser.

Efficient, practical delivery of page images for issues prior to 1990 that only exist in paper or microform is being explored using the FlashPix image format. Full-page scans in this format are displayed in different resolutions from a single file. A reasonably sized window can display either an image of the full page at a resolution sufficiently high to make headlines readable at a glance, or a zoomed-in portion of the page for reading individual articles.

Bibliographic Instruction

A Web-based tutorial (http://www.library.kent.edu/ntl) is being used on a large scale this year at Kent State University to provide instruction to first-year students in the use of online library databases. Just as the Web has become a tremendous tool for doing library research, it is likewise an exciting instructional medium, and it is only natural to combine the these two uses of the Web. The tutorial incorporates HTML from actual database interfaces, so a student sees and interacts with screens that are identical in appearance with those in the database, though the functionality has been modified to serve the instructional purposes of the tutorial, and the operation of the database engines is only simulated. When the student understands the point being made and performs the desired action, the tutorial proceeds to the next step; if the student makes mistake, the tutorial provides corrective feedback instead of permitting the student to wander off on a tangent.

Virtual Exhibits

Two approaches are being used used to create digital exhibits with virtual reality techniques. The first uses photographic images to record exhibits that have been created in a physical space (http://www.kent.edu/museum/exh.htm). When images are stitched together into panoramas, virtual visitors are able to pan and zoom in on exhibits much as if they are actually present in the museum. When the images are in FlashPix format, the detail that can be shown is remarkable. Besides enabling visitors to see and explore exhibits that they are otherwise unable to visit, this technique preserves exhibits indefinitely in a convenient format. The other technique, a prototype for which funding is being sought, would create a true virtual exhibit of individual pieces from four different museums without ever physically mounting them in the same time and place.

Instructional Web Sites

The Microbiology Learning Center (http://www.kent.edu/microbiology) is an example of a Web site that is designed to support undergraduate instruction. It combines reference materials, an online discussion forum, and other materials such as lecture notes and a syllabus to support a basic microbiology course taught by a group of professors on different campuses. Funded by the OhioLINK library consortium, the Web site includes still shots and video clips demonstrating laboratory techniques and slide images of various organisms. A special feature of the Web site is an interactive virtual laboratory in which students perform a series of tests on samples of bacteria in order to identify them.

Creating a Collaborative Task-Specific Information Retrieval System

Aggis Simaioforidis, Jussi Karlgren, Anna-lena Ereback

Information and Language Engineering, SICS
Box 1263, S-164 29 Kista, Sweden
{aggis, jussi, annalena}@sics.se
http://www.sics.se/diglib/Sthlm123

1   Drawbacks with the systems of today

Systems for information access today work well for some tasks, but are not suitable for general purpose usage. Our contention is no systems can be. Information seeking behavior is manyfold and varying, and viable systems for information access will have to select among many different methods, designs, and underlying information analysis technology to cover all combinations of user preferences, background, task type, and domain variation.

Specifically, systems today are specification oriented. The typical way to interact is to specify the information need by a number of topical terms. The system retrieves a set of retrieved documents. This set is inspected, some documents are selected for further inspection. The system may allow the user to modify the set of search terms until the inspected documents are satisfactory, and finally some of the retrieved and inspected documents are selected for delivery. The standard approach has its limitations, many of which have to do with the rather narrow channels of information from the user to the system. The user is restricted to provide sets of terms, and these convey topical information only.

2   Stockholm123

In project Stockholm123 we address some of the above limitations by enriching the information given to system by the user. The project task is finding a restaurant for a meal using a local online business telephone directory and general internet search tools. Our interface provides the two information services in parallel in two browser frames. The phone directory is organized in a disjunctive hierarchy, and consists practically only of contact information. While the information is reliable enough, to make an informed choice of restaurant one needs more information, such as reviews, recommendations, menus, pictures, or commercial advertments to complete the picture. The other frame - in the current setup it is connected to Digital's Altavista service - provides rich information, but is rather low on precision.

In general, a useful way of improving a problematic information access situation is to request help from a trusted and experienced acquaintance, explain our task, and hope that acquaintance has previous experiences with similar information needs. Our system does the equivalent: we request of the user to describe themselves and what their information need is. We then find previous users with similar profiles and similar searches. While the user runs the original search through the information source retrieval systems, previous potentially relevant searches are presented along with the search results. These previous searches can be modified to suit the current search better, and if one of them, or the original searches provide useful results, they can be saved in the search database together with a short note giving a description of the result. The search, the description, the profile are all used in a weighted match for new incoming searches.

3 Current Work

Our system is but a first running specification. Most modules are make-shift, and while none of the components are faked, all are simplified. We are currently in the design phase, not the firming up phase. Surprisingly enough, the system surpises by providing to-the point matches and retrieval results at times. Quite often, at present it does not. While the technical end of retrieval is interesting in itself and will take a fair amount of work to perform, at present we are more concerned about the effectiveness of the concept of asynchronous collaborative search. We are currently investigating a number of hypotheses, more or less in the order shown below:

- Users are willing to provide personal information to an information service.
- Users understand the idea of saving and retrieving searches.
- Previous searches will be useful to improve new ones.
- Personally matched collaborative searches will improve search quality.
- Inference modules will be able to create useful generalizations from the information the users provide themselves.
- Users will be willing to provide the extra effort for what they get.

3.1 Integrity Issues

We performed a questionnaire study with a few subjects, and found, not surprisingly, that the attitudes vary. We varied the layout of the profile definition form to get a less threatening format, and found that this increased the amount of information elicited. We seem to be able to elicit sufficient information for our purposes.

3.2 Clarity Issues

Our second design question is if the interface functionality is perspicuous. Will the user understand what the recommended searches are? To investigate this, we are currently performing think-aloud evaluations and retooling the interface according to our results.

EULER:
An EU 'Telematics for Libraries' Project

Michael Jost[1] and Anna Brümmer[2]

[1] FIZ Karlsruhe, Dept. Math. & Comput. Sci.,
Franklinstr. 11, D-10587 Berlin, Germany, jo@zblmath.fiz-karlsruhe.de
[2] NetLab, Lund University Library,
P.O. Box 3, S-22100 Lund, Sweden, Anna.Brummer@lub.lu.se

Introduction

Since April 1998 the European Commission is funding the EULER project (European Libraries and Electronic Resources in Mathematical Sciences) in the framework of the 'Telematics for Libraries' sector from the Telematics Applications programme.

Main goal of EULER is to integrate different, electronically available information resources in the field of mathematics. EULER aims to construct a "digital library mathematics" from existing heterogeneous sources.

Starting Point and Goals of the Project

The following existing publications-related information resources on mathematics will be covered by the EULER service:

- scientific literature databases
- library OPACs and document delivery services
- electronic journals from academic publishers
- archives of preprints and grey literature
- quality controlled subject information gateways on the Internet
- robot-generated indexes of other relevant Internet resources

These resources are considered to be the most frequently used when conducting searches for scientific results and ongoing developments in the field of mathematics – today the user have to search them one by one. The intention of the EULER project is to offer a "one-stop-shopping site" for users interested in mathematics. Thus, one single strictly user-oriented, integrated networked based access point will be developed, the EULER service. A common user interface, available on the World Wide Web, will allow a homogeneouse access to all integrated information types. Only one search will be needed to generate a broad range of (mixed) hits, irrespective of type of resource.

The integration approach has to take into consideration the requirements of the different information providers. Participating institutions will still be autonomous in deciding on their scientific and organizational policies, while at the same time providing a common access strategy to their information services. The foremost requirement to achieve such an aim is to choose and apply suitable standards, formats and protocols.

Technical Approach and Work Plan

The integration approach makes use of common resource descriptions based on the Dublin Core (DC) element set and access to those descriptions via the Z39.50 protocol. Technically, all information providers will produce DC metadata for their resources and offer them as distributed databases, which are located at the providers' sites. The central "EULER Engine" will query these databases parallely via Z39.50 and perform result set merging and presentation formatting.

The main objectives of the project correspond to a set of workpackages:

An initial **Requirements Analysis** workpackage conducts a final discussion and definition of user requirements. Additionally, tasks on revision of methodologies and standard developments monitoring will ensure the openness of EULER approaches with respect to other developments.

The **Resource Adaptation** workpackage will build the basic set of EULER metadata databases that are finally accessible from the EULER Engine. This will be done by using DC as "switching language". The participants will reach concensus on a common DC format, and map their current information to this joint format, thus creating individual EULER (DC) databases.

The **EULER Engine Implementation** workpackage – carried out in parallel to the Resource Adaptation workpackage – will design and implement the EULER Engine. This includes both the user interfaces and the interfaces to the partners metadata databases and other selected Internet resources.

During the **Evaluation and Demonstration** workpackage - carried out after the release of the EULER Engine (beta version) - selected groups of users will start system evaluation. The workpackage intends to measure the system suitability and scalability and the satisfaction level of users with the service.

The last workpackage is **Information Dissemination and Exploitation Preparations.** Relevant reports and demonstrations of project's results will be made publically available on the World Wide Web. The final exploitation plan for EULER services and other project results will consider commercial exploitation for future operation of EULER services and transfer of EULER results other subject domains.

The EULER Consortium

The eight main project partners are: FIZ Karlsruhe (Dept. Math. & Comput. Sci., Berlin) (Coordinator), The European Mathematical Society, Technische Universität Berlin, Cellule de Coordination Documentaire Nationale pour les Mathématiques, NetLab, Lund University Library, Staats- und Universitätsbibliothek Göttingen, Centrum voor Wiskunde en Informatica, Amsterdam, Università degli Studi di Firenze.

EULER online

More information and expanded project descriptions are available from http://www.emis.de/projects/EULER/.
These pages will be updated constantly and reflect the state of the project.

A Virtual Community Library:
SICS Digital Library Infrastructure Project

Andreas Rasmusson, Tomas Olsson and Preben Hansen

Swedish Institute of Computer Science (SICS), Box 1263, SE-164 29 Kista, Sweden
{ara, tol, preben}@sics.se

1 Introduction

In this project[1], we aim to create an agent-based digital library architecture for a Virtual Community Library (VCL) where each user has a personal library and, at the same time, is part of a larger community. The community is dynamically composed of the users' personal libraries and, through intermediators, other digital libraries.

We want to stress the fact that the users participate in a large dynamic decentralised community where they continually interact with each other. Being a part of a community means that each user can benefit from the work put into the other libraries. For example, by obtaining documents through search queries or recommendations using social filtering, but also by getting help to organise the personal library.

In the VCL, we try to combine the best aspects of the WWW, the library and the personal library. For example, ease to publish documents, personal information space, decentralised control of the document collection and ability to search for documents.

We have currently implemented two prototypes of the system, one for the personal library and one for visualising the information spread between the users.

2 Agent Architecture

The foundation for the VCL is an agent architecture where the users are represented by self-interested agents. This is an open-ended knowledge system, which supports creation, inferring, manipulation and sharing of knowledge about information objects ("metadata"), and supports (enables automatisation of) interaction between agents pertaining to the information and knowledge management related business processes.

Interaction (compatibility) with other systems in a number of formats and protocols will be investigated, such as Z39.50, MARC, DIENST, Dublin Core, BibTeX, etc. [1], [2]. Many existing bibliographic formats are ambiguous or limited in the way they represent knowledge. This introduces difficulties when the information is to be used in machine-machine conversations (in contrast to human-machine). In our architecture,

---

[1] See http://www.sics.se/isl/diglib

emphasis is put on handling translations between partially incomplete, incoherent or incrementally developed ontologies and particular collections of knowledge.

The work is to be based on software-agent research and platforms developed in the SICS Intelligent Systems Laboratory.

3 Personal Library

A user is represented by a personal library agent. By emphasising that the information put into it is relevant to the individual users we address the problem that users will rarely bother to register information they themselves have no interest in. Classification of information by end-users usually introduces the problem of having non-librarians doing classification according to the best of their own knowledge. This makes it harder to develop usage-conventions in classifications. Hence, we still need librarians that classify larger collections to get homogeneous usage-conventions.

Within the information architecture, no library has any special status as keeping complete, correct or authoritative information. Each digital library is autonomous and free to negotiate which other libraries it depends on to find new information. However, large cohesive collections (institutions) should still be "influential" in defining authoritative descriptions of objects since they are more often consulted for information than a single-user personal library.

4 Information Dissemination and Retrieval

By seeing our digital library not just as a static entity but as a dynamic virtual community we strive to get properties of real communities. In real communities, information is spread in a number of ways, such as by looking in somebody's personal library, asking or telling other persons about something or searching in a database. The control of the information flow is decentralised to the individuals of the community and they can retrieve information both actively (by asking or looking) and passively (by being told). We implement active retrieval as explicitly formed search queries and we implement passive retrieval as decentralised social filtering based on trust [3], which is built on the interactions between personal recommender agents performing content-based filtering. Hence, we try to combine the advantages of both filtering techniques.

References

1. Library of Congress: Metadata, Dublin Core and USMARC: A Review of Current Efforts. MARBI Discussion Paper no. 99, Library of Congress, January 21 (1997)
2. Heery, R.: Review of Metadata Formats. In: Program, Vol. 30, No. 4 (1996) 345-373
3. Olsson, T.: Decentralised Social Filtering based on Trust. In: The Working Notes of the AAAI-98 Recommender Systems Workshop, Madison, Wisconsin (1998)

Digital Libraries:
Information Broker Roles in Collaborative Filtering

Annika Waern, Mark Tierney, Åsa Rudström,
Jarmo Laaksolahti and Torben Mård

Swedish Institute of Computer Science,
Box 1263, SE-164 29 Kista, Sweden
{annika, mark, asa, jarmo, torben}@sics.se

The main goal of the EdInfo project [1] is to utilize human *information brokers*, or editors, as a resource in adaptive information systems. An information broker can be any of the following:

- The dedicated expert that collects and potentially reviews literature within a restricted area of interest;
- The journalist that produces articles with specific reader groups in mind;
- The librarian that organizes incoming information and directs readers to various sources;
- The professional information broker, that processes specific information requests, seeks for appropriate information sources, and produces summaries of the obtained information.

The common characteristic of these roles is that the information broker has some kind of understanding of what his or her customers want, and is willing to adapt to these needs. Information brokers collect information from various sources, evaluate its relative importance and then choose whether to include the information as it is, disregard it, summarize it, or perhaps rewrite or illustrate it differently than in the original source.

Many existing information services build upon user profiles, e.g. news services such as CNN Custom News. Users are allowed to explicitly set up their profiles by selecting a set of categories and subcategories that fit their interests. However useful, this approach gives rise to a number of problems. Firstly, the available categories might not fit the users' real interests and preferences. Secondly, the categorization may have to change if a new need occurs, or a new type of information is added, but then all users must change their profiles to adhere to the new categorization. Finally, it is likely that users seldom change their profiles once they are set up, so it is not certain that the profile really reflects the user's true interests.

Individual user adaptation provides a way to deal with these problems, since it can provide user-defined categorizations that are automatically or semi-automatically maintained by learning from the user's actions with the system. But in order to introduce individual user adaptation, we must impose at least two additional tasks on information brokers:

1. to maintain the rules for stereotypic adaptation, used in user profiles;
2. to structure the information in a way that allows for these rules to be applicable.

The essential source of information necessary for these tasks is *feedback* from users, both in terms of which profiles they set up, and how they use the information they obtain. Since this information in itself is of imminent value for information brokers, we believe that they will accept the addition of these tasks. Nevertheless, a definite requirement is that the tasks are made as simple as possible; we cannot assume that information brokers have any particular interest in the details of the algorithms for user modeling.

ConCall is an agent-based system that implements the EdInfo ideas. The system supports the collection, filtering and browsing of conference and workshop calls, but could just as well be used for calls for participation in seminars, courses, etc. Using ConCall, the user (an individual researcher) can review calls and set up reminders for deadlines. To avoid uninteresting calls, the user sets up a filter to retrieve a personal selection of calls and organize them in a personal manner. This filter is maintained by semi-automatic means. The service is accessed over the web. Reminders are received by email or over the GSM network. The first version of the ConCall service has been implemented and is currently under experimental evaluation.

In ConCall, human editors take part in the filtering and classification process of domain data. To achieve this, the system uses "buzzwords" for information filtering and structuring. "Buzzwords" are used to annotate individual pieces of information, similar to keywords except they are not bound to any formal or informal ontology. A "buzzword" is just as likely to surface into the system originating from a user as from the editor. The editor uses the "buzzwords" to annotate calls, which are then filtered according to the preferences of the users. Users may also set up their own set of filtering rules using their own "buzzwords" for a second level of filtering or ordering. These user-defined words are provided as feedback to the editor who can react to trends or new topics of interest by incorporating the new words. The purpose of using "buzzwords" instead of keywords is to allow for a more flexible and self-adjusting body of classification words.

Acknowledgement

The EdInfo project is funded by the Swedish research institute for information technology (SITI AB) and the Swedish board for technical development (NUTEK).

References

1. Höök, K, Rudström, Å., and Waern, A. (1997) Edited Adaptive Hypermedia: Combining Human and Machine Intelligence to Achieve Filtered Information. In Milosavljevic, Brusilovsky, Moore, Oberlander and Stock (Eds.), proceedings of the *Flexible Hypertext Workshop*. Macquarie Computing Report No. C/TR97-06, Macquarie University, Australia. Available at http://www.sics.se/~kia/papers/edinfo.html

Virtual Reality and Agents in a Digital Library

Guadalupe Muñoz, Ignacio Aedo, Paloma Díaz

Departamento de Informática. Universidad Carlos III de Madrid
C/Butarque 15, 28911 Leganés (Spain)
E-mail: {lupe@inf, aedo@ia, pdp@inf }.uc3m.es
http://peterpan.uc3m.es

The objective of this poster is to present the digital library VILMA, (Virtual Intelligent Library using Multi-Agent Systems). A digital library has been described as a federated structure that provides humans both intellectual and physical access to the huge and growing world-wide networks of information encoded in multimedia digital formats. VILMA will provide physical access through its intelligent agents and will ease intellectual one using virtual reality for its interface. VILMA architecture (see figure 1) should be as flexible as possible because its environment is a big network, with users accessing it from different machines and protocols.

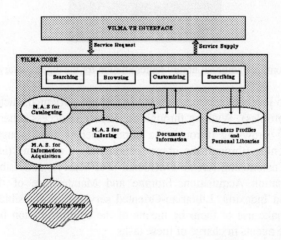

Fig. 1. VILMA architecture: Simplified diagram of the main modules in the digital library.

The most efficient way to achieve modularity, flexibility and scalability is distributing little tasks among many specialised agents [1]. If we use a set of intelligent agents for the library's architecture instead of a main program to control it, we will not need to update a main program each time we enlarge the library. These Multi-Agent Systems (M.A.S.) will be in charge of the main funcionalities in VILMA such as information retrieval from the world wide web according to readers and librarian requests and document cataloguing and indexing to include the obtained information in the proper database. To accomplish these tasks, they will have to communicate among themselves, coordinate their activities to determine organisational structure amongst a given group of agents and to allocate tasks and resources, and negotiate to solve conflicts.

Also, an interface based on virtual reality provides a friendly environment for the user as shown in [2]. This interface is based on the traditional library metaphor to make easier its manipulation. It is the intermediate between readers and the information stored in the digital library. In each VILMA virtual room, the user will be able to use the different library's functionalities by means of executing the underlying software agents through this interface. The whole library is represented as a building (see figure 2). The inner side is divided in three floors and all of them in two rooms, one of them is a hall, and the other is the main room. Floors are communicated through a lift. Each room will offer one of the library services.

Fig. 2. VILMA front: A traditional library representation for the digital library interface.

There are two levels of services in VILMA: Reader-Oriented, such as Subscribing (to keep users profiles), Walking through the library to access other services (using Virtual Reality), Browsing (through the library shelves and through a hierarchical structure), Searching (through the library catalogues), Consulting (ask for advice to the librarian), Customising (create a personal user library); and, Librarian-Oriented, such as Information Acquisition, Storage and Maintenance of the Information, Cataloguing, and Indexing. Librarian-Oriented services are invisible for the reader. This one will make use of them by means of the communication between the user interface and the agents in charge of these tasks.

References

1. Birmingham, W., Drabenstott, K., Frost, C., Warner, A. and Wills, K.,: The University of Michigan Digital Library: This is Not Your Father's Library. In *Proceedings of the Digital Library 94 Conference (DL'94)*. Schnase, J. L., Leggett, J. J., Furuta, R. K., Metcalfe, T. (eds.), 19-21, June 1994, College Station, Texas, U.S.A., pp. 53-59.

2. Muñoz, G., Layunta, J., Aedo, I. and Díaz, P.: A VR interface for the digital library VILMA. To appear in *Proceedings of the Fifth World Conference on Human Choice and Computers,* Geneva, Switzerland, 1998.

The European Schoolnet
An Attempt to Share Information and Services

Charlotte A. Linderoth[1], Anders Bandholm[1], Birte Christensen-Dalsgaard[1],
and Gertrud Berger[2]

[1] UNI-C
Olof Palmes Alle 38
DK-8200 Aarhus N, Denmark
[2] LUB Netlab
Dag Hammarskjlds v. 2D
SE-221 00 Lund, Sweden

Abstract. The European Schoolnet is a network of networks, created
for schools in Europe. Among the objectives for the EUN initiative is to
establish and test a shared repository of educational resources based on a
distributed model. The unity will be established through use of protocols
like Z39.50 for simultaneous search of heterogeneous databases and on
defining core metadata elements to be filled out by all participants.

1 Introduction

The European Schoolnet (EUN) is lead by an organisation consisting of representatives from all the Ministries of Education in Europe. The objective is
among others to share knowledge regarding Information and Communication
Technology. One of the tasks, therefore, is to initiate the EUN resource network.

The EUN resource network [1] is driven by a combination of national initiatives
and a central organisation. It is based on the idea that content and services will
grow primarily from the initiatives and needs of the users. New services and
content are initiated locally, and information on its existence propagates upwards
to (or is harvested by) the national and official servers, thereby becoming part
of the resources of the EUN platform.

An important task is to create a logical structure and ensure the collaboration
of national content/service providers to establish an entry to and a coherent
view of a multitude of services and information. The approach taken by EUN to
achieve this homogeneous appearance is to define interoperability in terms of

 - protocols (e.g. Z39.50) and exchange formats to be followed for the material
   to be visible via the EUN platform, and
 - a set of mandatory and optional metadata describing the learning resources.

The collaboration with teachers, students and publishers to test ideas and procedures and to get feed-back will have a high priority. Also questions related to
multilingual and multicultural aspects will be addressed.

---

[1] EUN can be accessed at: http://www.eun.org

2 Metadata Structure

The work on defining a metadata structure is based on international initiatives. The starting point is the existing standards and on-going initiatives such as Dublin Core [2], European projects (e.g. Ariadne [3]) and American projects (e.g. IMS [4], and Learning Object). These initiatives are closely related to Resource Description Framework, the Warwick Framework, and World Wide Web Consortium.

The EUN metadata model [5], is based on the 15 Dublin Core elements and extended with subelements relevant due to potential commercial aspects and the learning situation. New sub-elements now are: Approver, Date metadata last modified), Price Code, Release (metadata scheme), Requirements (software and hardware), Role, Security, Size, Use Rights, User Level and Version Number.

An important task for the EUN work will be to define mandatory elements and through user trial to test their adequateness. It is important to strike the right balance between a full description allowing specialised searches and few elements, which maximises the chance that authors will actually fill in the required metadata. The obligatory elements are envisioned to be situation and content specific, i.e. the required metadata for a learning module may be different from metadata for a document, and the description given to copyrighted material for sale from a publisher will be different from free material. However, to enable the user to search across all these resources, a common core of elements is identified.

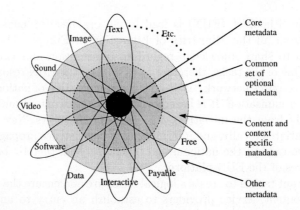

Fig. 1. A core set of elements for all types of matarial will have to be identified. The use and the appropriateness of metadata, mandatory as well as optional, will be tested in the learning environment

---

[2] Dublin Core: http://www.lub.lu.se/cgi-bin/nmdc.pl
[3] Ariadne: http://ariadne.unil.ch/
[4] Instructional Management System:http://www.imsproject.org/
[5] The full paper can be found at:http://www.eun.org/publications/metadata/

The Document Management System Saros Mezzanine and the New Product AGORA as Key Component in a Digital Library Architecture at Göttingen University Library

Frank Klaproth, Norbert Lossau

Lower Saxony State- and University Library, Göttingen DigitizationCenter (GDZ)
D- 37070 Göttingen, Germany
http://www.sub.uni-goettingen.de/GDZ
{klaproth, lossau}@mail.sub.uni-goettingen.de

Abstract. Current publications are more and more available in electronic form. Nevertheless there is still a clear predominance of printed material within library holdings. In order to facilitate online access to these information the Center for Digitization at Göttingen University Library was initiated as innovative service center for digitization work and techniques, financially supported by the German Research Foundation (DFG) and the Ministry of Culture of the Federal State of Lower Saxony. Setting up a Document-Management-System (DMS) as key component for the digital library architecture is one of the overall goals for the Center. Starting with Saros Mezzanine, a traditional EDMS for companies from FileNet, we present now, as result of a collaboration with the Satz-Rechen-Zentrum (SRZ) company in Berlin, a comfortable system named AGORA. The article gives a brief overview over development and functionality of the new DMS for digital libraries, AGORA.

1. Introduction

The large amount of digitized material, the problems of persistent URLs, the variety of library materials (monographs, journals etc. with multidimensional hierarchies), the requirement for describing them with various metadata (technical, structural, bibliographic) and the lack of complete existing solutions leads to the development of the web accessible AGORA system.

2. The new DMS AGORA and its Functionality

In the focus of nearly all functions (object import, metadata import/export, delivering objects to the user as online/offline or printed version) of AGORA is a relational database (RDB). The model for the database was developed at the Göttingen University Library under the aspect of minimizing metadata redundancy, optimizing the SQL queries and extensibility of the model itself. With other words a scalable object oriented model. It is possible to use the model with most of the known RDBs on the market, naturally independent of the underlying operation system.

As administrator of the AGORA system you have a administration tool – "a GUI of the RDB model" plus extended possibilities to manage special import/export jobs. This key application for the administrator is a MS Windows program at this moment, but will be additionally available as a Java version in the future. The administration tool gets all needed information out of the RDB (metadata database) and use a comfortable graphical browser to view and alter the complex hierarchy and the images of digitized literature. The jobs you can manage with this tool are:

1. **Import scanned images:** The scanned images (in TIF format) can be selected in a integrated directory browser. Only the location in the existing file structure will be picked up and the pointer to the image file is set. The files will remain in their original place.

2. **Import structured metadata:** In connection with the scanned images a document description file exists. A collection of images is described with this XML/RDF structured file. The document description contains information about bibliography, sequences (correlation between logical and physical pages; type of pagination, etc.) and technical properties (resolution, file format, etc.) of the related image collection. The import module parses these XML/RDF structure and place the metadata in the RDB. Full or partial updates of metadata can be done because of the object oriented nature of the RDB model in conjunction with the use of the RDF scheme in the document description file.

3. **Export structured metadata:** In the global concept of the Digital Library of Göttingen and other digital libraries in Germany (Distributed Digital Research Library) there should exist a interface for exchange of information between and across these libraries. The XML/RDF structured file can be accessed with internal and external search engines. A gather process over the exported XML/RDF structured metadata should give a proof of the existing electronic documents in the single digital library.

4. **Batch convert images:** The user offen does not want to get the original image as TIFF, but a more compressed version or a file format supported by a standard web browser without additional plugins. Therefore and for performance reason a converting module exists. Esp. if the institution, which is using AGORA, runs a proxy server then the administrator can produce GIF, PNG, JPEG, PDF – files "on a mouse click" for the normal web access.

5. **Generate WWW pages:** The concept for a web site using with AGORA is based on working with HTML templates. The web site layout and structure can be changed in a very easy but powerfull way. The templates come with some predefined tags but additional ones can be implemented. The administrator can create semi dynamic HTML pages. They are produced on demand of the administrator out of the context in the RDB and do not be created on the fly during a client session. On the other hand results of some search queries are produced on

the fly because of the changing contents. All queries over the WWW interface are processed through Java servlets. All standard web browser can access and use the web interface of AGORA without activating Java support on the client side. Besides the programs are portable to all platforms and web server for which the Java Virtual Machine and the support for servlets exists.

Esp. for search and retrieval of and work with fulltext documents the Göttingen University Library is using the DMS Saros Mezzanine. AGORA will provide a interface to the extended capabilities of this DMS. The unique ID of every checked in (imported) document in Saros Mezzanine will be equalized with the AGORA system. Every image or image set respectively and fulltext document can be accessed through the online catalog via the reference of the unique ID. A stable URL can be provided.

In the next stage AGORA will provide a "electronic book trolley", user accounting, ordering of CDRs over the web and controlled printing on demand

Electronic Roads in the Information Society

Costas Zervos[1], Stathis Panis[2], Dionysis Dionysiou[3], Michalis Dionysiou[3],
Constantinos Pattichis[1], Andreas Pitsillides[1], George Papadopoulos[1], Antonis
Kakas[1], and Christos Schizas[1],

[1] University of Cyprus, Department of Computer Science, P.O.Box 537
CY 1678 Nicosia, Cyprus
{czervos, pattichi, cspitsil, george, antonis, schizas} @cs.ucy.ac.cy
[2] Cyprus Telecommunications Authority, Telecommunications Street, P.O.Box 4929
CY 1396 Nicosia, Cyprus
panis@cytanet.com.cy
[3] Minisrty of Education and Culture
Nicosia, Cyprus
dennis@logos.cy.net, michalid@cs.ucy.ac.cy

The objective of this study is to investigate an approach for dynamic construction of Electronic Roads. We envision Electronic Roads spanning a virtual multidimensional space, a distributed digital information repository, comprising primarily of video data of cultural heritage. A visitor (user) will be able to travel in this multidimensional space along different, semantically related historical, geographical, economic or cultural paths.

Consider the following example. At a particular point in time our visitor (user) is located at a node of this multidimensional space and s/he has to decide how to proceed with his/her journey. A cluster of nearest neighbours is computed and presented to the user based on the current node but also the most recently visited nodes in order to postulate as to which semantic path the visitor is actually following. Even though the *next* node along this path has precedence the user will have the option to override this, thus migrating to a different path.

The building block of the system is the *information unit,* which consists of the actual data (e.g. segment of video, image, sound or text) with an attached metadata index. All information units are elementary in granularity. That is, there is no hierarchical structure. The repository of information can be viewed as a pool of information units. There is of course a tradeoff as to what will be precisely the level of granularity, i.e. how elementary the information units will be. The more elementary the information units are the more flexibility the system has to adapt dynamically to the user needs, but of course the overall set of activities incur more overhead. On the other hand, the more coarse grain the information units are the easier it is to retrieve them and combine them but flexibility is limited.

The structure of the *metadata index* is central to the system design. The metadata index would therefore consist of four principal entries one for each subspace.

1. The date the information unit refers to.
2. The (x, y, z) coordinate the information unit refers to.

3. The location of the information unit in the Economy space.
4. The location of the information unit in the Cultural space.

In addition the metadata index contains data about media type (e.g. voice, video, text), size, location (e.g. IP address), and quality of service considerations (e.g. real-time, loss tolerant).

Information units are combined to form composite *knowledge units*. These knowledge units are the nodes in the traveler's path. The composite knowledge units themselves contain an *knowledge unit index* which is produced from the fusion of the indexes of the underlying information units. In essence each entry in this index pin-points the exact location of the attached data/pointers to information units along the path the entry corresponds to. An example could illustrate the case better.

Assume that we have a virtual space with information units that refer to the cultural heritage of the island of Cyprus. One could navigate (travel) through this space along many directions but for now let us assume there are only four subspaces.

1. Historical/Chronological Path.
2. Geographical/Topological Path.
3. Path through the Economy.
4. Path through Culture.

A *coordination agent* now based on a user "query" and taking into consideration the network and the user profiles, locates several of the elementary information units, composes them into a knowledge unit, and presents this to the user as the result of the "query". The "query" itself could be replaced by the instruction of the user to move to the next node in order to tie this paradigm to the notion of a journey.

The construction of the Electronic Road is made possible by the calculation of the nearest neighbors of the knowledge unit. The nearest neighbors can be computed from the knowledge unit indexes since their entries correspond to the location of each knowledge unit in the particular subspace. Currently the Euclidean distance is the metric used although more complicated evaluation methods are investigated. If we confine the traveler to travel only in one subspace, the only metric relevant is the metric of the subspace itself. On the other hand if we allow the traveler to cross subspace boundaries it means that the distance metric will be a weighted sum of the metrics in each subspace with the weights summing up to 1. The idea is that the higher the relevance of the subspace to the trip the higher the weight.

A thematic prototype for the cultural heritage of Cyprus encompassing the system architecture of Electronic Roads introduced in this work is currently being developed.

The Technical Chamber of Greece Digital Library
The Vision of a Special Organisation to Save and
Disseminate Its Information Work
Through the Network

Katerina Toraki[1], Sarantos Kapidakis[2]

[1] Documentation and Information Unit, Technical Chamber of Greece,
toraki@tee.gr
[2] Institute of Computer Science, Foundation for Research and Technology - Hellas, Greece
sarantos@ics.forth.gr

This presentation discusses the creation of a digital library which contains scientific work produced by the Technical Chamber of Greece and disseminated to its members through post or library services. The Technical Chamber of Greece (TEE) is the technical consultant to the Government as well as the professional organisation of greek engineers (numbering more than 60.000). Among TEE activities, it conducts studies and organizes various meetings on technical and related aspects, like architecture, town planning, environment, information technology, chemical engineering, naval architecture, civil engineering and so on.

It publishes three professional periodicals : the weekly information bulletin "Enimerotiko Deltio" which is sent free to all members and contains news, comments and activities of TEE, the bimonthly journal Technika Chronika, containing studies, reports and articles on general technical subjects and the scientific publication Technika Chronika, published in five separate sections addressed to the various engineering fields, with scientific and research articles in Greek including an extended summary in English. In addition, TEE publishes scientific and technical books and translations of foreign specifications.

All above works are used heavily by engineers as well as by other scientists and students. They are disseminated through the Documentation and Information Unit of TEE in Athens as well as the libraries of its 15 regional sections connected to a network through a virtual library system.

The Data Bank of TEE is an information system, which provides online access by subscription to a great amount of information and services interesting engineers, such as engineers' registry, rewards, firms data, cost of products and services, bibliographical information, legislation, electronic mail, competitions, TEE activities.

Although the scientific production of TEE is high and attracts the interest of a large number of interested parties, there is a great demand from engineers all over the country not only to get informed on what' s on in technical fields in Greece and what is the participation of TEE but also to get that primary information resources on his/her desk, without having to visit one of its libraries.

A pilot TEE digital library has already been created in a computer of TEE with the cooperation of the ICS-FORTH, using the Dienst software. The electronic address of the digital library is: http://www.central.tee.gr/dlib. It contains in digital form scientific work produced by TEE, aiming to serve primarily its members all over the country but also any other interested in technical aspects. The documents that TEE hold include material mainly in greek, but in english as well.

More specifically, the library contains the periodicals published by TEE, the proceedings of meetings and the reports produced by working groups and scientific committees of TEE as well as other miscellaneous works. Besides these, the digital library will eventually contain other collective work of general interest conducted by TEE. As an example, the work conducted in the 70's on the traditional places and buildings in Greece, with photos and designs from particular buildings is presented here. All this work is kept now in paper files in the library of Athens and is not easily accessible by the end-users. Among the benefits of the digital library are saving of physical space, promotion through the Internet, dissemination and awareness, ease of access, search and retrieval, availability.

During the pilot phase, separate contacts with people working at TEE have taken place in order to get the digital material. It has been noticed that the greatest difficulty is to organise and manage the collection of the various scientific works in digital form. The production of above works and the organisation of meetings are responsibility of different people referring to different members of the Executive Committe of TEE. The need for coordination and integration is stressed in order to achieve the best results. A technical problem with word processing during data entry and compatibility with Unix environment has been solved. Some other issues to be taken into consideration are the cooperation with the computer department, the familiarity of library staff with the new type of application, the management and maintenance of the service.

A very important issue is to make the digital library an element of the integrated information system of TEE. One way to achieve this task is to link the records of the bibliographic database to the relevant resources of the digital library using the Unimarc tag 856. Some examples are presented here.

The special support required by the organisation is necessary in order to ensure the continuous operation of the digital library. The successful operation in Athens could lead to the extension of the application to corresponding work produced at the regional sections and which is much less accessible by engineers, especially in the rest of the country. This task will complement the virtual library system of TEE operating with the cooperation and coordination of all its libraries.

Used-Centered Design of Adaptive Interfaces for Digital Libraries

T. Gavrilova*, A. Voinov**

*St.Petersburg State Technical University, gavr@fn.csa.ru;
** Institute for High Performance Computing,
St.Petersburg, Russia, avv@ipa.rssi.ru

Abstract. An approach to account for various user's characteristics, such as professional status, physiological and psychological pecularities in both a Digital Library and any other adaptive system, addressed to an "end-user", is described. This approach is based, first, on a battery of tests to formally measure user's characteristics and, second, on a method of statistical mapping of these factors onto the appropriate adjustable characteristics of the adaptive system.

Introduction

One of the objectives of digital libraries is to present information to a maximally broad scope of users. These users are *individuals* and differ in many aspects, from professional and educational status up to very subtle socio-cultural peculiarities. Given a static volume of data without any ability to metamorphize its presentation one could observe that these data are understood differently and even inadequately by different groups of users. There are many approaches to adaptive architectures of Digital Libraries. Most of them, following the lines of Machine Learning, pay much attention to tracking of user-application interaction and forecasting his/her behavior and expectation. Such a purely empirical approach does not impose any hypothesis about *what* such a human user could be.

User Model

This poster presents another approach to user modelling that can also be efficiently implemented for digital libraries applications. The focus is made on analysis and evaluation of the *third party* personal user's features. This means that the system takes into account not only the empirical track of user's interaction with the system, but also some other information, accumulated from the sources which are out of the scope of given concrete system. This information comprises:

Demographic factors such as age, gender, first language, place of birth, social and cultural peculiarities; *Professional factors* which tie such user's features as position, professional experience, computer skills into integral «portrait» of his/her expertise; *Physiological factors* which include reaction, workability, attention, etc.; *Psychological factors* which can be defined through the two dominant strata: *communicative* stratum (*perception, understanding, clarity, usability, handiness*) and *cognitive* stratum (*personal cognitive style, locus of control* and *logical mentality*). It should be emphasized, that each of these classes of factors enumerates only those factors, which could be automatically registered and processed. The way of such registering is evident for such characteristics as demographic and professional ones. For those factors, which are related to the psychology and physiology, a battery of special *tests* and *questionnaires*, designed for automatical presentation to the users and processing, is proposed.

The final set of characteristics could be symbolically represented by a formal structure, which could be called *in that case* "User Model":

```
UM:
    demographic:
        age:                    young | medium | old,
        education:              higher | medium | none,
        ...................
    professional:
        experience:             value₁
        ...................
    psychological:
        assertiveness: high | medium | low
        ...................
```

Interface Model

Analogously to the way of formalization of user's characteristics a similar "bookkeeping" could be performed for a representative set of applications of interest, which interface is searched to be adaptive to user's peculiarities.

In that way *Interface Model* is also defined as a formal frame structure. The most important components of the IM are those of *control* (metaphor, types of dialog and interaction dynamics), *design* (e.g. overall layout of application screen), *navigation* and *help*.

An accordance between the UM and the IM may be either drawn from some theoretical considerations, rooted in human studies, or estimated though a series of experiments under a sample of subjects.

The idea of such an experiment concludes not only in a search of statistical dependence between two formally measured sets of parameters, but in a specific *method* of measuring of *real* user's productivity in a concrete interface environment. This method is derived from some modern approach for experimentally-psychological investigation of user's workability, stress-tolerance etc, introduced in the Russian school of psychology, founded by Vygotsky and Leontiev.

Pilot sample of respondents consisting of 22 students and tutors are in process.

Preliminary results of experiment, showing some statistical correspondence between the IM and the UM parameters will be presented. These issues are worth further investigation.

A New Method for Segmenting Newspaper Articles

B. Gatos [1], N. Gouraros [1], S. Mantzaris [1], S. Perantonis [2],
A. Tsigris [1], P. Tzavelis [1] and N. Vassilas [2]

[1] Lambrakis Press S.A., 10 Heyden Str,
104 34 Athens, Greece
atsigris@dolnet.gr
[2] Institute of Informatics and Telecommunications,
National Research Center "Demokritos",
15310 Athens, Greece
sper@estia.iit.nrcps.ariadne-t.gr

Digital preservation of old newspapers contributes greatly to the historical register of a country's social, political and economical events. At the same time, newspaper preservation is an imperative necessity because of the fast paper deterioration and difficulty in tracing the overwhelming amount of information. Lambrakis Press S.A. owns a large collection of newspapers and periodicals that consists of 1,300,000 pages and covers a time period from 1890 up to date. This material is divided into 600,000 A2 pages, 500,000 A3 tabloid and 200,000 A4 pages approximately. Our team is working on all aspects of the transformation procedure from the printed material to an accessible digital archive (verification and quality control, digitization, cataloguing, search and retrieval, design and content presentation). The final digital documents form the foundation of our digital library.

Preservation and processing of this precious material can be achieved by focusing on a series of problems related to the digitization of the printed material, such as: image enhancement by noise removal, isolation of newspaper articles by document understanding techniques (segmentation - labeling). The successful tackling of these problems allows the subsequent efficient cataloguing by employing OCR, full text retrieval and information extraction techniques along with manual indexing.

In our paper we will present the results of our research associated with the stage of segmentation of the various regions - the image consists of - as well as the identification of text regions which have to be separated from other regions, i.e. figures, drawings or line regions. The main region segmentation techniques are based on two fundamental approaches: firstly, on the smearing and labeling of regions [1-2], and secondly on the image profiling in various directions [3-4]. Both techniques have not been successful in achieving newspaper segmentation because of the haphazard lay out of newspaper articles and their very close contact. Furthermore, the first approach results in great computational cost. Aiming at a solution of these particular problems accruing from the newspaper segmentation, we suggest a new technique based on horizontal and vertical image projections which provides a quick region segmentation as well as identification of text areas.

The proposed technique consists of three main stages: a) the calculation of horizontal and vertical smoothed profiling of the image, b) the indication of the various image regions using the local minima of the horizontal and vertical profiles and c) the indication of text regions by analyzing the FFT of the horizontal projections of segmented regions. More precisely, during the first stage, the image is projected horizontally and vertically using for each point the information obtained from the application of a mask whose dimensions depend on the approximate average of letter size. The result of this process is the projection of an image block in a massive rectangular region. Because newspaper images usually have clear vertical segments, we first process the vertical projections and secondly we get horizontal projections at the vertical extracted zones. During the second stage, the local minima of horizontal and vertical projections are indicated and they correspond to several segments into which the image can be divided horizontally and vertically. Horizontal neighboring segments are grouped together due to the existence of foreground pixels between the segments. During the last stage of our method, for each located area the horizontal projections are used. By analyzing their FFT we determine dominant frequencies which are used for identification of text areas as well as for the labeling of text segments according to their letter sizes. We identify text areas by defining a threshold at the dominant frequency amplitude. The letter size is provided by calculating the value of the dominant frequency which corresponds to the average distance between two successive lines.

The testbed is a collection of images from the newspaper "TO VIMA" published by Lambrakis Press S.A. from 1922 to 1970. The suggested method has already been applied with great success even in cases where text regions and graphs co-exist in an especially noisy environment.

References

1. Maier, M., Porinelli, R.: Separating Graphic Objects in Written Texts. Advances in Image Processing and Pattern Recognition (1986)
2. Kasturi, R., Bow, S., El-Masri, W., Shah, J., Gattiker, J., Mokate, U.: A System for Interpretetion of Line Drawings, Vol. 12. IEEE Trans. On Patt. Anal. And Mach. Intell., (1990) 978–991
3. Verikas, A., Bachauskene, M., Vilunas, S., Skaisgiris, D.: Adaptive Character Recognition System, Vol. 13. Pattern Recognition Letters, (1992) 207–212
4. Lettera, Maier, M., Paoli, C.: Character Recognition in Office Automation, Advances in Image Processing and Pattern Recognition, eds V. Cappellini and R. Marconi, Elsvier Science Publishers B. V., North-Holland, (1986) 191–197

Broadway, a Case-Based Browsing Advisor for the Web

Michel Jaczynski and Brigitte Trousse

INRIA Sophia Antipolis, AID Research Group, 2004 routes des Lucioles,
06902 Sophia Antipolis, France
{Michel.Jaczynski, Brigitte.Trousse}@inria.sophia.fr

Extended Abstract

The World Wide Web (WWW) is an hypermedia of heterogeneous and dynamic documents, frequently referred to be the world wide digital library. This virtual space is growing more and more every day, offering to the user a huge amount of data. Two kinds of tasks can be handled to locate a relevant document through this space: *querying* and *browsing*. Querying is appropriate when the user has a clear goal which should usually be expressed through a list of keywords. Different servers on the WWW (such as Yahoo, Lycos, Altavista) can be then used to retrieve matching documents based on their indexing capability. Browsing is well suited when the user cannot express his goal explicitly or when query formulation by keywords is not adequate. Then, the user must navigate through this space, moving from one node to another, looking for a relevant document. These two tasks can be mixed so that querying gives a list of reasonable starting points for browsing.

However, the huge size and the structure of this space make difficult the indexing of the documents required by querying access methods and could disorient the user during a browsing session. This poster focuses on the assistance given to a group of users during their browsing session, and more precisely on the design of a *browsing advisor or recommendation system*. A browsing advisor is able to follow the user during a browsing session to infer his goal, and then must advise him of potentially relevant documents to visit next. Three main approaches for recommendation computation can be distinguished: content-based recommendation, profile-similarity based recommendation and behaviour-similarity based recommendation. Our approach corresponds to the third one. In addition, we claim as others that a particular state of the navigation (current document and/or an *instantaneous* navigation description) is not sufficient to compute relevant advice. In order to better infer the user's implicit intent during browsing, we want to consider past visited documents and their access order in a time-extended situation. As for us, a time-extended situation represents not only the current state of the observed navigation but also its past sequence of events. Other works have proposed browsing advisors but they do not satisfy our requirements. Thus, we propose a browsing advisor, named Broadway (http://www.inria.fr/aid/broadway), based on the Case-Based Reasoning (CBR) paradigm. In CBR, a case basically represents a problem situation and the solution that has been applied. The first step of the reasoning is the retrieval through indexes of relevant cases which are somehow similar, or partially match the current problem situation. The goals of others steps are mainly the reuse of the past solution by adaptation and the learning of this new experience in the memory for future reuse. Broadway uses CBR to learn from users'navigations the set of relevant cases, which can be reused to improve and to keep updated the recommendation process. The use of CBR is based on the following hypothesis: *if two users with similar profiles went through a similar sequence of documents, they might have similar browsing intent, so that we can advise one user of the documents evaluated as relevant by the other one.* The evaluations are given by users throw a toolbar inserted in each visited HTML page (cf. Fig. 1).

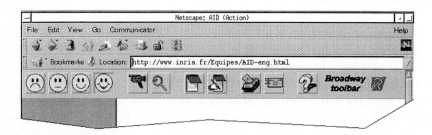

Fig. 1. The toolbar is inserted at the top of each page and can be hidden or displayed

This poster describes Broadway, our browsing advisor written in the object-oriented Java™ programming language using our toolbox Broadway*tools (cf. this book) for collaborative information searching systems. Broadway has a distributed architecture based on Java Remote Method Invocation and HTTP protocols, and follows users on any sites on Web thanks to a proxy module. It uses navigational cases that reference precise experiences extracted from navigations and indexed by time-extended situations [1]. The case-based reasoner embedded in Broadway computes the list of recommendations by reusing past cases and learns from new navigations. The recommendations are displayed asynchronously to users during their navigations. Finally, we describe some evaluation results of a first experimentation with Broadway and the originality of our work compared to related ones [2].

References

1. M. Jaczynski. A Framework for the Management of Past Experiences with Time-Extended Situations. In *Proceedings of the 6th International Conference on Information and Knowledge Management (CIKM'97)*, ACM Press, pages 32–39, Las Vegas, 1997.
2. M. Jaczynski and B. Trousse. WWW Assisted Browsing by Reusing Past Navigations from a Group of Users. In *Proceedings of 4th European Workshop on Case-Based Reasoning (EWCBR98)*, volume 1488 of Lecture Notes in Artificial Intelligence, Springer Verlag, pages 160–171, Dublin, 1998.

A Digital Library Model for the Grey Literature of Academic Institutes

V. Chrissikopoulos*, D. Georgiou**, N. Koziris***, K. Toraki****, P. Tsanakas***

* Dept of Informatics, University of Piraeus, chris@unipi.gr
** Dept. of ECE, University of Thrace
*** Dept. of ECE, National Technical University of Athens, {panag,nkoziris}@cs.ntua.gr
**** Technical Chamber of Greece, toraki@tee.gr

1. Introduction

A great amount of scientific work carried out at universities, is being disseminated through non-commercially published types of literature, the so-called Grey literature, like dissertations, internal technical reports, teaching material, deliverables of research projects etc. The systematic storage, processing and dissemination of the intellectual work produced in the Greek higher education institutions is an objective which can be achieved with the use of new information and communication technologies.

A digital library model for the Grey literature of the Greek higher education is proposed, based on the DIENST architecture, leading to an integrated, distributed digital library system. The system will allow the easy and fast entry, access and location of primary information contained and produced in any participating institution. The technical and organisational issues related to the design and implementation of such a system are presented.

2. System Skeleton

The presentation is based on the study of the ARTEMIS system (Interacademic Digital Library System for Greek Grey Literature), delivered as part of the Greek Academic Libraries project. The kernel of the proposed library system is a distributed database management system, supporting the following system and user level applications:

Local applications

- Local *library management systems* to handle submitted queries, in order to retrieve the requested material from the local databases. Such systems support a common gateway interface (CGI) to interact with the http server, and communicate with other relative servers. These local management systems organize the locally stored data in categories, using different keys, and build indexes to facilitate searches including free-text search and retrieval. The indexing data are forwarded to the central management system, which handles queries with results distributed all over the library net.
- *Data entry applications* to update the local databases in every node (university) of the distributed system. Authorized users use these applications only. They fill in the appropriate forms for each entry, and update the local database.

- *Office automation applications* to support the organization of the stored material in each local database. Documents should be created and stored in standard format (postscript, pdf).

Core Applications

- *Administrative applications* for the central management of the distributed library system. The proposed model is based on a central system that keeps track of data stored in each library node. Multiple search keys and indexes for every document are gathered from the corresponding nodes. Every local library management system is responsible for organizing (i.e. indexing) its material. The central system organizes hierarchically and disseminates the necessary information to all nodes, so that any local queries can be efficiently forwarded to the corresponding nodes. Non-local transactions are consistent, since all nodes are regularly being updated with the necessary data (keys, indexes, synonyms, terms) from the central system. In addition, a list of all subscribers is being kept together with user statistics (such as library subscription fees, number of retrievals per doc etc). Checking for users id and privileges during every library transaction and access to data, from any node ensures security.

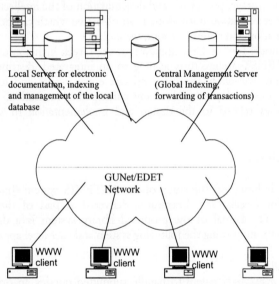

Local Server for electronic documentation, indexing and management of the local database

Central Management Server (Global Indexing, forwarding of transactions)

GUNet/EDET Network

WWW client   WWW client   WWW client

All library applications interact with and support the open architecture protocol for digital libraries, DIENST, which is currently used from a wide network of university libraries around the world. DIENST is based on HTTP and gives the possibility of manipulating a distributed library management system over different Internet nodes using WWW based applications. The protocol is based on HTTP. The adoption of DIENST in the proposed library system ensures the portability of applications to every library node.

Finally, users from any Internet node can search the library contents by submitting a query to any of the local library nodes, through the WWW interface. Their search is based on composite keys (topic, index terms, authors, etc) using Boolean forms or free text content similarity properties. The text search mechanism covers both Greek and English languages aiming to the highest possible precision and recall rates.

Cross-Language Web Querying:
The EuroSearch Approach

Martin Braschler[1], Carol Peters[2], Eugenio Picchi[3], and Peter Schäuble[1]

[1]EuroSpider Information Technology AG, Schaffhauserstr. 18,
CH-8006 Zurich, Switzerland
[2]Istituto di Elaborazione della Informazione (IEI-CNR), Via S. Maria 46, Pisa, Italy
[3]Istituto di Linguistica Computazionale (ILC-CNR), Via della Faggiola 32, Pisa, Italy

1   Introduction

Initially comprising services from Italy (Arianna), Spain (Olé) and Switzerland (EuroSpider), EuroSearch[1] will provide a multilingual searching functionality. Each national site is responsible for maintaining and operating a search service for its own languages, so that the needs of distinct language communities can be catered for by native speakers of that language. The languages covered are currently French, German, Italian and Spanish, plus also English. Differences in the partners' document collections and indexing mechanisms have led to the implementation of different search strategies, depending on the collection to be queried. The cross-language search component of EuroSearch thus consists of an integration of lexicon- and corpus-based search mechanisms and two distinct types of searching will be activated:

- query translation using a multilingual lexicon; enhanced by an experimental corpus-based mechanism
- similarity thesaurus technology.

2   Why is CLIR Difficult?

Cross-Language Information Retrieval (CLIR) remains a difficult task. One reason is simply the cost of existing linguistic resources, such as dictionaries. Allowing the user to formulate free text queries also means the vocabulary covered must typically be large to avoid user frustration. This criterion may be difficult to meet if special terminology is involved. Translation ambiguities are also hard to resolve, especially if little or no context is available because the queries are very short. Moreover, queries are often not well-formed sentences, which can make syntactic analysis impossible. This makes using methods developed for automatic machine translation problematic.

3   Lexicon-based Technology

The EuroSearch Multilingual Lexicon, developed by CNR, will consist of a core general language vocabulary plus the most significant terms used in Web queries and documents. The pivot language concept has been adopted to facilitate the insertion of

[1] EuroSearch (LE-8303) began in January 1998. Industrial partners are Italia On-Line - Pisa (Coordinator), CINET - Barcelona, EuroSpider Information Technology - Zurich; academic members are the Italian National Research Council (CNR) - Pisa, and Dortmund University. For more information, see http://eurosearch.iol.it.

additional languages. This decision has implied a trade-off between the higher level of precision provided by using separate bilingual dictionaries for each pair of languages treated against the costs of constructing and maintaining such a (potentially) high number of dictionaries. The lexicon has been designed to facilitate mapping through the pivot language and semantic indicators are assigned to polysemous words to permit interactive sense disambiguation. However, a lexicon-based query translation has clear limits. We will thus also be implementing an experimental methodology which expands the terms in a query by associating a vocabulary of significantly related terms extracted from an archive of comparable documents; this vocabulary is then translated together with the query term. In this way, we provide a relevance ranking of our results (documents containing a higher proportion of the correlated vocabulary are ranked higher) and query terms not found in the multilingual lexicon are searched by looking for a significant presence of their associated vocabulary.

4   Similarity Thesaurus Technology

The similarity thesaurus approach used by the EuroSpider translation server is based on ideas originally developed for query expansion in monolingual Information Retrieval. A multilingual similarity thesaurus contains entries that link terms in one language (L1) to a list of "similar" terms in another language (L2), each assigned with a value giving an estimate of similarity. This estimate of similarity is based on statistical coocurrence, i.e. basically how often the terms cooccur in similar texts taken from training data. The process for calculating a thesaurus is fully automatic. A similarity thesaurus that provides a mapping from terms in language L1 to similar terms in language L2 allows a query formulated by the user to be transferred into the target language by substituting the query terms with some of their counterparts most similar to the overall query concept. A distinctive property of this approach is that the target language query produced is not really a translation of the user's search request, but a reformulation containing terms that are likely to retrieve documents relevant to the user's information needs ("pseudo-translation").

5   Advantages/Disadvantages

Apart from being driven by the need to cater efficiently for different kinds of document collections (general-purpose and domain specific) indexed in different ways, employing two different approaches to the cross-language task also gives us an excellent opportunity to evaluate the pros and cons of both strategies. While query translation is fast, the development of a suitable multilingual lexicon is both expensive and time-consuming and it is impossible to guarantee exhaustive vocabulary coverage. The latter problem can be amended by corpus-based approaches, such as the similarity thesaurus, which use sufficiently large training collections. Downsides are potentially erroneous translations stemming from unsuitable or too little training data and the computational complexity often present in such approaches. The two approaches are integrated within Eurosearch project through the development of common translation server interfaces and data exchange formats; this has the advantage of facilitating future extensions of the Eurosearch components.

Interaction Design in Digital Libraries

Organiser: Dr. Constantine Stephanidis

Institute of Computer Science (ICS)
Foundation for Research and Technology - Hellas (FORTH)
Science and Technology Park of Crete
GR - 71110 Heraklion, Crete, Greece
Tel: +30 - 81 - 391741
Fax: +30 - 81 - 391740
email: cs@ics.forth.gr

Abstract. In recent years, the field of Human-Computer Interaction (HCI) has made significant advances, penetrating an increasing number and range of computer-mediated human activities. In this context, interaction design has become a critical component of advanced interactive applications and telematic services as well as an increasingly complex challenge to meet.

This panel is concerned with interaction design in the domain of Digital Libraries (DL) and aims to bring together individuals interested in the inter-relationships between HCI and DL, to exchange experience, to advance an understanding and to promote common ground regarding the design, development and deployment of interactive DL services that meet the diverse abilities, skills, requirements, and preferences of individual users.

In particular, the panel seeks to broadly address and discuss a number of related themes, including:

- how interaction with DL services can be designed so as to meet the desirable levels of quality in use;
- alternative approaches to the development of user interfaces to DLs that exhibit task aware, co-operative and intelligent behaviour;
- development of an understanding of how user interface software technologies (e.g. user modelling components, knowledge based user interface development toolkits, etc) can be integrated into architectural models for DLs.

Panellists
- Dr. Constantine Stephanidis, FORTH-ICS, GREECE (chair)
- Prof. David Benyon, Napier University, UK
- Dr. Mark Maybury, MITRE Corporation, USA
- Dr. Daniel Dardailler, W3C/WAI, FRANCE

Beyond Navigation as Metaphor

David Benyon

Computing dept., Napier University, 219 Colinton road, Edinburgh, EH14 1LD

Abstract With the development of large information spaces such as digital libraries, the notion of user navigation through such spaces has gained prominence. The popular view of navigation is that it is a conscious, goal directed activity in which someone is trying to reach a destination. Such a view of navigation is essentially individualistic, objectivist and cognitive. A semiotic analysis of space recognises that there are many different views of space and that space is a subjectively defined concept. There is a context to space which needs to be communicated, negotiated and understood between people. More than just space, there is the idea of place. People produce or construct their places at different times and there is a knock on effect from one place to another. In this paper some implications of taking this different view of information space are explored.

Introduction

With the development of large information spaces such as digital libraries, the notion of user navigation through such spaces has gained prominence [3]. If we take the concept of navigation metaphorically, then we begin with notions of sea faring and the navigation of ships and boats. It would be fair to say that navigation is also now extended to navigation on land and in space and more generally to be the activity of finding ones way throughout an environment. In architecture, the term 'wayfinding' is preferred (and used synonymously with the term 'navigation'). Passini ([14], p154) defines wayfinding as, "a person's ability, both cognitive and behavioural, to reach spatial destinations." He bases his conception on Downs and Stea [5] who see wayfinding as composed of four steps: orienting oneself in the environment, choosing the correct route, monitoring this route, and recognizing that the destination has been reached.

Such a view of navigation is essentially individualistic, objectivist and cognitive and there has been much work on how people develop 'cognitive maps' of their environment which enables them to find their way to a specific location. Early studies of environments such as those conducted by Lynch, culminating in the classic 'The Image of the City' [12] identified features of the environments; edges, paths, nodes, districts and landmarks. Lynch's aim in trying to specify the basic, discrete units of (urban) space have had a significant impact on urban planning and design, but whether they can act as the basis of an understanding of what people do in such spaces is another matter.

In direct opposition to 'The Image of the City', 'The City and the Sign' [7] presents a number of views from urban semioticians that highlight the limitations of the Lynchian and cognitive perspective. The crucial thing missing form the traditional geographies is the failure to appreciate how environments are*conceived* by people as opposed to simply *perceived* by people. Ledrut [10] indicates the importance of this by arguing that if we accept the objective identification of landmarks, districts and so forth, this does not distinguish between humans finding their way and animals moving through a maze. The environment is not simply some physical structure to which humans must adapt. People play a role in producing the space, through their activities and practice. This view is strongly re-inforced by Lefebvre [11] in his 'The Production of Space' and others in a post-modern tradition; geographers such as Soja [15] and de Certeau (e.g. 'Walking in the City', [4]), feminist writers such as Massey [13] and semioticians such as Barthes (writing on urban semiotics, [1]) and Eco (writing on architectural semiotics, [6]).

The cognitive approach to geography leaves the use that people make of their environment out of the analysis. This is not to say that all studies of cognitive mapping and all the analysis provided by cognitive geographies needs to be thrown away. Only that the social construction and the ideological impact of space needs to be considered also. So, Gottdiener [8] can comment that 'In the case of [shopping] malls...on the one hand the mall is the materialization of the retailers intention to sell consumer goods...on the other hand, the mall is the physical space within which individuals come to a participate in a certain type of urban ambience'. And Barthes [1] 'that two neighbourhoods are adjoining, if we rely on the map...while, from the moment when they receive two different significations, they are radically separated in the image of the city'. It is these differences which are ignored by the objectivist tradition of the analysis of space.

The semiotic analysis of space recognises that there are many different views of space and that space is a subjectively defined concept. We recognize that we as people negotiate a shared understanding of space. There is a context to space which needs to be communicated, negotiated and understood between people. More than just space, there is the idea of place. People produce or construct their places at different times and there is a knock on effect from one place to another.

For example, a group of academics had a meeting in the meeting room. This space became a place for them to have a meeting, but only because no-one else had booked it. If they had had the Christmas party in the meeting room it would have become a different place for that period, and if the party were too noisy, the offices nearby would no longer be work places for their occupants. The city centre retains it's physical structure but changes from a shopping place during the day to a place where gangs hang out at night. The gangs have notions of 'their' space which would not be recognised by the shoppers.

With these ideas navigation (as opposed to wayfinding) includes a number of activities which occur in space and which people are willing to agree are sorts of navigation. Thinking about space also leads us to think that virtual spaces, or information spaces, may be like physical ones or they may not be.

We can, then distinguish navigation from wayfinding. Clearly people navigate *through* places, so navigation is not always directed towards a destination. I might be going camping in the highlands and so I navigate through Glasgow. Someone might be trying to get away from something - e.g. a football crowd. In this case navigation is away from a place, looking for somewhere safe. Away from the geographical space and towards a social space - i.e. a space for safety.

Different people see things differently. The shoppers and the gangs see street corners in different ways. There are different conceptions of landmarks, districts, etc. depending on race, gender and social group. The ship's captain can see many different landmarks in the ebb and flow of a river than the novice. A climber might tell me about a landmark but I may totally fail to see it.

There is little objectivity in the physical world. Can you really measure the length of a coastline? But you can certainly navigate it. Is the drunk navigating his way home really engaged in a conscious activity? If I drive past my turning on the way home, or make some other 'expert slip' am I conscious? It seems that navigation can be unconscious.

In considering navigation of information space as a metaphor, then, we must be careful not to load ourselves with too much of the metaphor's baggage. Similarly we need to be careful about how previous analyses of the phenomena may have missed important aspects. To quote from Barthes [1] again writing on understanding the urban; 'The city is a discourse and this discourse is truly a language: the city speaks to its inhabitants, we speak our city....The real scientific leap will be realised when we speak of a language of the city without metaphor.'

In a similar vein we may argue that 'Navigation of Information Space' is not (just) a metaphor, it is a paradigm shift. Navigation of Information Space is a new paradigm for thinking about HCI, just as Direct Manipulation was a new paradigm in the 1980s. Shifting the paradigm changes the way you think about things. Computers still compute even though we have an object-oriented paradigm instead of one based on functional decomposition. It happens that people believe that thinking about computing as OO helps us to develop better systems. In this approach, then, we seek the 'real scientific leap' by emptying Navigation of Information Space of its metaphorical meaning so that the real meaning can emerge. If you were to ask people what their image is of people using computers today, they would describe a person looking at a VDU. This image is important because it means that we see people outside the computer, looking in onto the world of information, trying to access systems, trying to find things out. But if you ask those people about the image of other activities such as driving, shopping, or having a meeting, they will describe people as inside the activity, in a social environment, part of and surrounded by the various objects the are using. It is this change from seeing the person outside the information space to seeing the person inside the information space that is the important change of view.

Activity and Information Space

By adopting the concept of an information space, we immediately set up a correspondence with something that is not an information space. We call this the activity space - the space of 'real world' activities (or at least the space of physical action). In order to undertake activities in the activity space, people need access to information. Thus the information space is intrinsically linked with the activity space.

As humans we live, work and relax in information spaces. At one level of description all our multifarious interactions with the experienced world are effected through the discovery, exchange, organisation and manipulation of information. Information spaces are not the province of computers. They are central to our everyday experience. Finding your way through an airport, a hotel or a city involves travelling though the activity space, using an information space. Paper documents represent another type of information space. Users will get quite different information from books, from newspapers and from magazines. Similarly they will find various information in timetables, guides and maps. Interacting with other people involves sharing some activities in an information space.

Our purpose — as information system designers — is to design and develop structures and procedures which will make information available to people which will help people to undertake their activities; to help them plan, control and monitor their undertakings. People undertake some activities using some artefact(s) (thus activities are always mediated by artefacts). Activities are processes which make use of artefacts within the system and are triggered by some events. This system (or activity space) has a boundary, outside of which the activities can be considered to have little or no influence. Events may arise from inside the system or from outside (Figure 1). A system is a coherent set of interdependent components which exists for some purpose, has some stability and can usefully be viewed as a whole. As illustrated below, such systems consist of people, artefacts, processes and the activities which are undertaken as a result of events.

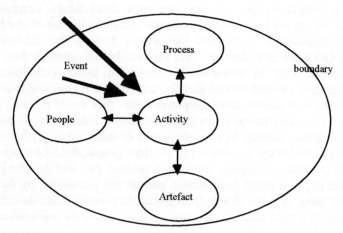

Fig. 1   The components of a system; an activity space

709

Each of these systems also has an information system, the purpose of which is to help plan, control, monitor and maintain the activity space. The information system may be informal (for example, casual conversation), or it may be formalised to a greater or lesser extent.

The information system (or information space) is a system which has a similar structure to the activity system. The important difference is that it uses information artefacts to represent relevant features of the activity system. Users of the information system engage in various activities by performing various processes on the information artefacts — such as selecting items of interest, calculating totals, looking at pictures, etc.. The information space uses signs, structured into information artefacts to represent (certain aspects) of the activity space. This is illustrated in Figure 2.

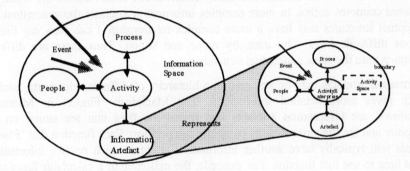

Fig. 2   The Information Space

Information Artefacts

The concept of an information space can now be understood by appealing to the notion of an information system - people, processes, events, activities and information artefacts. An information artefact is 'any artefact whose purpose is to allow information to be stored, retrieved, and possibly transformed' [9]. Interactive devices such as spreadsheets, word processors, and e-mail systems are clearly examples of information artefacts, but so are non-interactive devices like tables, documents and musical scores. An information artefact consists of two levels of description; a conceptual level provides some abstraction of the experienced world and a perceptual level provides a view, or viewport onto that structure. Thus a paper train timetable is one information artefact providing information about train journeys and a talking timetable is another [2].

All information artefacts employ various symbols, structured in some fashion, and provide functions to manipulate the symbols (whether conceptually or physically). From these symbols people are able to derive information. Thus every information artefact constrains and defines an information space - the symbols, structure and functions which enable people to store, retrieve and transform information.

We have posited the existence of two spaces; the activity space and the information space. In the activity space people undertake actions — they drink coffee, travel to Edinburgh, buy clothes and so on. To undertake these activities they use information and carry out activities in the information space. For example, to drink some coffee, I might see a sign, KENCO, which exists in the activity space. I need to locate a button (so undertake an information space activity), press the button (in the activity space), take the coffee (in the activity space) and so on. To do these things I have perceived and interpreted various information artefacts that rely on culturally determined signalling conventions (K-E-N-C-O spells KENCO. KENCO is a sign for coffee because KENCO make coffee).

Information artefacts have a conceptual structure and one or more viewports onto that structure. In the case of simple signs such as KENCO the conceptual and perceptual sides of the information artefact are tightly coupled. The letters denote the word, but the word connotes coffee. In more complex information artefacts the conceptual and perceptual structures may have a more complex relationship. I can view my files in various different ways - by date, by name and so on. Thus there are different viewports onto the same conceptual structure.

Information artefacts may be arranged in a hierarchy of different viewports, each of which gives more detailed information. The Macintosh 'Finder' or Microsoft 'Windows' are information artefacts that reveal the files that are stored on the computer and the functions that the computer can perform. Each function that 'Finder' reveals will typically have another information artefact which reveals information about how to use that function. For example, the existence of a calculator function is revealed by a menu item or icon labelled 'Calculator' (Figure 3). The calculator display in turn reveals more information about the calculator's functions by using a layout which looks very like the layout of a 'traditional' hand-held calculator, and which includes icons for specific functions such as '+', '-', '*' etc. These specific functions are not explained any further by information artefacts; instead the user is expected to know that (for example) '*' means 'multiply', and the user is expected to understand the effects of the multiply function without any further help. The calculator icon information artefact allows the user to double click in order to open the calculator. The icons on the calculator itself behave very differently if double clicked.

When we consider an information artefact, we need to distinguish between two levels of description. We need to consider both the information that the artefact presents to us and the way in which the information is presented. More formally, we need a conceptual description (or conceptual model) of the information in the artefact and a description of the perceptual display (or perceptual model) of that artefact. For example, we could have a conceptual model of a clock as a device which represents time in hours and minutes. This conceptual model could have a variety of perceptual displays, such as an analog clock face, a digital clock face, or a speaking clock. Different viewports enable different tasks to be performed more or less easily.

An information artefact abstracts certain aspects of an object or device and then employs some perceptual device to reveal that abstraction to the user. In a well designed information artefact, the abstraction which is chosen highlights the important features of the object or device. Ideally, the abstraction should also be closely related to concepts that the user already knows about, and the perceptual device used to reveal the conceptualisation should capitalise on the user's existing knowledge. For example, the Macintosh 'Calculator' offers similar operations, and uses a similar layout, to that of a familiar pocket calculator.

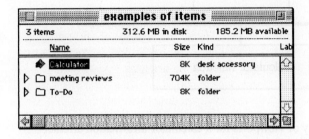

Fig. 3 Hierarchical viewports onto information structures: the Macintosh Finder reveals the calculator icon; launching the calculator reveals another interface.

An information artefact consists of:

- a conceptualisation of objects in the experienced world which has the purpose of revealing some information about the underlying objects to some users (and possibly allowing changes to be made).
- a viewport which provides access to that conceptualisation and which employs a method of presentation from which the user may derive information (and if necessary provides means for making changes).

Just as there may be several levels of viewport onto the same underlying structure, so there may be different viewports at the same level. The same information can be presented in different ways; some methods of presentation may hide certain information altogether, or they may make it quicker and easier to discover some kinds of information than others. The telephone network can be viewed in terms of subscribers who have a name, address, exchange and telephone number. The viewport onto this is usually provided by a telephone book which lists the relevant information. The telephone book presents the data in alphabetical order of subscriber name which affects the usability of this view - so searching for a particular number, not knowing the subscriber's name, becomes a nearly impossible task. Other viewports onto this structure (e.g. the 'Directory Enquiries' or the 'Call Tracing' viewport) enable other goals to be achieved.

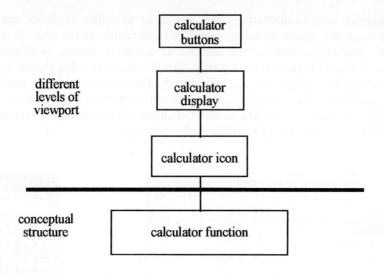

Fig. 4 Illustrating a hierarchy of viewports for a calculator information artefact

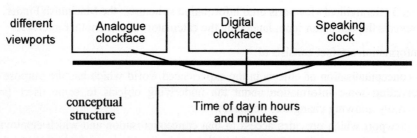

Fig. 5 Illustrating different viewports at the same level of abstraction

A train timetable could be presented on paper or as a talking timetable. The different methods of presentation may look very different, but since the underlying structure of the information is the same many aspects of the different information displays will also be the same. A talking timetable typically gives only a summary of the departure time from one major station and the arrival time at the main destination (i.e. it hides some information), whereas a paper timetable usually gives times at the intermediate stops. With a talking timetable it can take substantially longer to find out when the evening trains leave, since the times are usually read in sequence – i.e. it is harder to discover some kinds of information.

We have seen that an information artefact consists of a conceptualisation of some object(s) in the experienced world which has the purpose of revealing some information about the underlying object(s) for some users and a viewport which provides access to that conceptualisation and displays the actual data from which the user may derive information. However, whenever we create a perceptual display (a viewport) it then becomes an object in the experienced world (the activity space). Consequently it may have its own information artefact designed to reveal information about the display. This leads to the hierarchical arrangement described above.

The fact that there can be multiple levels of information artefacts, each built upon the others is important. The process may be seen as follows. Some designers recognise something about the experienced world. They choose to conceptualise the structure of this in a particular way and develop a conceptual model. In order to access this conceptualisation, various viewports are created. Each viewport reveals something about the underlying structure and it is this combination of viewport and conceptual structure which we call an information artefact. The viewports can now be considered in a similar fashion. We recognise that the viewports are part of the experienced world. Accordingly we can conceptualise the viewport and provide a view onto that conceptual structure. This produces another information artefact.

In theory this can continue indefinitely with information artefacts being created on top of one another revealing different aspects of the underlying experienced world. In practice, users tend to specialise in a particular level of discourse about information artefacts and lower levels effectively disappear from their experienced world. For example, one view of the world of computers deals with the physical arrangement of files on discs, with the workings of disc access times and transfer rates, memory allocation and so on. For most of us such a view is not experienced, instead it is presented to us through information artefacts such as computer operating systems. The graphical user interfaces which are so ubiquitous provide another view onto the operating system and so the experienced world for us is one of dragging icons, double clicking and using menus to issue commands. The car mechanic experiences a different world from the driver. The surgeon experiences a different world from the patient. Recognising these different levels of information artefact is important in order to establish a shared level of abstraction within which we can discuss our needs and concerns.

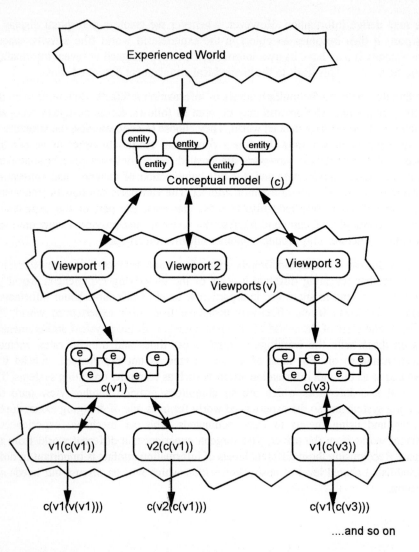

Fig. 6 When we create viewports they become part of the activity space

Conclusion

With this conception, navigation in information space is exactly the activities which people undertake in the information space. Navigation in information space means manipulating the information artefacts, moving between levels of viewport and between different viewports. When using a word processor, for example, the actual typing of the document's contents is not an information space activity, but as soon as the user looks at the text and sets about to reposition the cursor, change the font, or select a menu item, so they step immediately into the information space. In the information space they must perceive and interpret the information artefacts so that they can achieve their activity space goals.

As information space designers, we need to consider how people will interpret the information artefacts; how they will conceive the underlying domain from their perceptions of the form and function of the viewports. Eco [6] comments that in architecture, architectural objects are not there primarily to communicate, they are there to function. Thus a roof is clearly intended to keep out the rain and a doorway functions to let people go into or out of a building. In a similar way my word processor provides various functions to format my text. But by recognising that these are information artefacts, we recognise that their form (the viewport that we provide onto the conceptual structure) denotes their function. Recognising something as a roof allows the person to get shelter from the rain, recognising something as a doorway allows us to get into the building and recognising 'Font...' allows us to format our text.

In producing information spaces, designers create information artefacts to denote functions. But once people enter the information space they interpret not just the primary function of the information artefact. They will make other connotations about the culture, history and ideology that surrounds, and is defined by, that space. The full meaning of, and activities undertaken with, information artefacts are not determined by the designer: they are produced by the users. We need, then, to populate our information spaces with information artefacts that enable and encourage people to understand the activity space. We do that by facilitating navigation in the information space.

Acknowledgment

Many of the ideas presented in this paper have arisen as a result of discussions with other members of the PERSONA project (Personal and Social Navigation of Information Space) and we would like to acknowledge their input. The project is funded by the EC under contract 25637.

References

1. Barthes, R. (1986) Semiology and the Urban in Gottdiener, M. and Lagopoulos, A. Ph. (Eds.) (1986) *The City and the Sign*. Columbia University Press, New York

2. Benyon, D. R., Green, T. R. G. and Bental, D. (1998)*Conceptual Modelling for Human Computer Interaction, using ERMIA* Springer, London

3. Benyon, D. R. and H k, K. (1997) Navigation in Information Space. In S. Howard, J. Hammond, and G. Lindegaard (eds.), *Human-Computer Interaction, INTERACT 97,* Chapman & Hall.

4. de Certeau, M. (1993) Walking in the City In During, S. (Ed.) *The Cultural Studies Reader*, Routledge, London

5. Downs, R. & Stea, D. (1973). "Cognitive Representations", in Downs, R. & Stea, D (eds.), *Image and Environment*, Chicago: Aldine (79-86).

6. Eco, U. (1986) Function and Sign: Semiotics of Architecture in Gottdiener, M. and Lagopoulos, A. Ph. (Eds.) (1986) *The City and the Sign*. Columbia University Press, New York

7. Gottdiener, M. and Lagopoulos, A. Ph. (Eds.) (1986) *The City and the Sign*. Columbia University Press, New York

8. Gottdiener, M. Recapturing the Center: A semiotic analysis of shopping malls In Gottdiener, M. and Lagopoulos, A. Ph. (Eds.) (1986) *The City and the Sign*. Columbia University Press, New York

9. Green, T. R. G. and Benyon, D. R. (1996) The skull beneath the skin; Entity-relationship modelling of Information Artefacts. *International Journal of Human-Computer Studies* 44(6) 801-828

10. Ledrut, R. (1986) Chapter 5 In Gottdiener, M. and Lagopoulos, A. Ph. (Eds.) (1986) *The City and the Sign*. Columbia University Press, New York

11. Lefebvre, H. (1991) *The Production of Space* Blackwell

12. Lynch, K. (1960) *The Image of the City*. MIT press, Cambridge, MA

13. Massey, D. (1996) *Space, Place and Gender* Blackwell, Oxford

14. Passini, *Wayfinding in Architecture*

15. Soja, E. (1993) History: geography: modernity. In During, S. (Ed.)*The Cultural Studies Reader*, Routledge, London

User Interaction in Digital Libraries: Coping with Diversity through Adaptation

Constantine Stephanidis, Demosthenes Akoumianakis and Alex Paramythis

Institute of Computer Science
Foundation for Research and Technology-Hellas
Science and Technology Park of Crete
P.O. Box 1385, GR-71110, Heraklion, Crete, Greece
{cs, demosthe, alpar}@ics.forth.gr

Abstract. User interface adaptations can be used to address several user interaction challenges in the development of digital library systems. To this end, this paper: (a) examines some of the intrinsic characteristics of digital library systems; (b) identifies some of the key Human-Computer Interaction (HCI) challenges; and (c) develops an argumentation for adaptations in digital library systems. By drawing parallels to recent work in HCI research into adaptable and adaptive user interaction, the paper illustrates potential areas in which user interface adaptation can provide a useful technique for advancing the quality of human interaction with a digital library system.

Keywords. digital libraries, user interface adaptation, unified interface development

1 Introduction

Digital Libraries (DL) are complex and advanced forms of information systems which extend and augment their physical counterparts by amplifying existing resources and services and enabling development of new kinds of human problem solving and expression. Their complexity arises from the data-rich domain of discourse as well as the extended demands for multi-disciplinary input, involving collaboration support, digital document preservation, distributed database management, hypertext, information filtering, etc. In addition, a broad range of non-technical issues, such as ethics and intellectual property rights, add to the complication that is normally associated with their development, maintenance and practice.

In the recent past, several organisational, institutional, national and trans-national efforts have been devoted to the development of digital library (DL) systems to accommodate requirements across a range of application areas, such as cultural heritage [30], [16], statistical literacy [15], multilingual document access [27], [21], bibliographic searching [24], etc. Projects such as the above provide an illustrative account of technical challenges and new opportunities offered by digital libraries.

In this paper we are concerned with the exploration of an additional dimension pertaining to the development of digital libraries. Specifically, we aim to address the human-computer interaction (HCI) related challenges that predominate large information spaces and underpin the development of digital library systems. The normative perspective adopted is that, despite the broad and diverse range of technological competencies required by digital library systems and applications (e.g. advanced data access and retrieval mechanisms, distributed systems, interoperability, etc.), HCI remains a critical success factor that needs to be carefully planned and integrated into a project's life cycle.

The interest in HCI and the study of the related issues in the context of a digital library system stems from certain characteristics of this type of information system that pose important (and sometimes unique) challenges for both communities. In the recent literature there is an increasing recognition of several of these challenges [29], [42], [28] and a few research initiatives (see April 1995 and April 1998 issues of Communications of the ACM) have pursued activities at the dichotomy of the two scientific disciplines. In this paper, we will be concerned with some additional insights, aiming to shed light into the aspects of automatic adaptation and how they can be used to improve the usability of digital library systems. In the recent past, the requirement for adaptation in digital library systems has been repeatedly identified as a core research challenge to be addressed by future R&D in this area [25], [8], [1].

The paper is structured as follows. The next section highlights some of the HCI challenges posed by digital library systems. Then, we discuss how user interface adaptation may cater for some of these challenges and draw upon recent practice and experience to elaborate on the premises of adaptable and adaptive systems, as well as how the available design wisdom can be applied in the domain of digital libraries. The paper concludes with a summary and a preliminary account of joint developments that would mutually benefit both the digital libraries and the HCI communities.

2   HCI challenges posed by Digital Library systems

Digital libraries as a new form of information system have distinctive characteristics that introduce several HCI challenges. In this section, an attempt is made to reveal and briefly elaborate on some of these challenges with the view to provide a rationale for articulating the argumentation about user interface adaptation in the next section.

The first HCI challenge that arises in the context of a digital library is that of coping with diversity. Elements of diversity may be identified along many different dimensions:

(a) *The users* - A major source of diversity are the users themselves. Differences in their abilities, skills, requirements and preferences, as well as differences attributed to differing cultural backgrounds and domain-specific levels of expertise, make it necessary for any system intended for "global" use to go far beyond the illusive assumptions made in addressing the requirements of the non-existent "average" user. In particular, such differences, which may exist between categories of end-users, but also between individual users, require different and, sometimes, even conflicting design decisions to be made. Aspects of the interaction with a DL that might be affected are, for example, the level and type of support provided to users for navigation in the information space, the nature and extent of facilities that assist users in retrieving, filtering, clustering, and classifying information, etc.

(b) *The information content - An equally important source of diversity in the context of DLs* is the nature and extent of the information content itself. Both navigation / browsing and searching in a DL are largely affected by the size of the DL, the structure / classification of the information therein, whether multimedia data is present or not, the semantic correlation between different portions / items in the DL, etc. It is evident that all of the above constitute factors that need to be taken into account in designing the interaction between users and the DL.

(c) *The context of use* - Treating diversity at the levels of the end-user population and information content is not sufficient in itself, if one does not also take into account the context within which users interact with DLs. For example, it is of great importance in designing the interaction whether the user is accessing the system solely to retrieve information, or the user intends to provide additional information, based on what is already available; or, whether the DL is accessed from an insecure computing environment, or from a secure terminal that can guarantee the accuracy and integrity of communicated data; or, even, whether access is made through a private terminal, or a public information terminal.

(d) *The technology platform* - The software and hardware environment through which the user accesses a DL is yet another source of diversity. Graphical capabilities and interaction norms of the underlying operating system, the availability of, or necessity for, input / output devices, the specific architecture of the system, etc., all contribute to the delineation of a multitude of requirements on the DL, as far as independence from, and appropriateness for, a platform are concerned.

An added challenge, when it comes to designing interaction in DLs, is the fact that the "interface" and "application" portions of a DL are very closely interrelated, as is often the case with most categories of information systems. Therefore, it is important that any approach to addressing diversity in the design of a DL system, strives to facilitate and support the user both in conceiving the system as a single information entity, made up of numerous information artefacts, as well as in attaining high quality access to. and control over, the system.

In addition to the above, HCI challenges arise from the very nature of digital libraries as evolutionary community-oriented information resources. In particular, the long life-cycles that digital libraries are usually associated with, as well as their evolutionary nature as community-wide information resources introduce the compelling requirement for scaleable HCI, incremental design and design reuse; attributes that are still loosely addressed by prevalent HCI frameworks and currently available user interface development tools and technologies. Finally, additional challenges are encountered when one considers the integration and interoperability issues for different digital libraries. In this context, multi-lingual access is pertinent, especially for transnational digital libraries. Moreover, the distribution of federated digital libraries across the network creates new virtual spaces, new capabilities for human problem solving and new opportunities for expression. Designing systems to facilitate these targets challenges traditional HCI and calls for the application of more developmental approaches towards the construction of new frameworks to support access by wide audiences, global exchanges and understanding.

Obviously, the above non-exhaustive properties of digital libraries do not simply call for a suitable mix of HCI design techniques, but also signify a paradigm shift that has more general implications on the design of computer-mediated human activities. HCI will increasingly need to provide the means for addressing such novel requirements by suitably applying, revising and extending the existing design wisdom so as to meet the emerging usability challenges. In the remainder of the paper, we focus on one technique, namely user interface adaptation and discuss how recent advances in the area of adaptable and adaptive interaction in HCI can be employed to facilitate increased usability of digital library systems and a new insight into the challenges identified earlier on. In this endeavour, we draw upon examples and design cases in which user interface adaptation has been a prime design objective. Our intention is to rationalise the need for adaptable and adaptive interaction in the context of digital libraries and extend recent practice and experience to this effect.

3   Coping with diversity through adaptation

3.1   User interface adaptation

There exists today a considerable amount of mainstream HCI work that has addressed the issue of user interface adaptations [14], in the form of either adaptability or adaptivity [33]. Some of the early attempts to construct adaptable systems are OBJECT-LENS [23], BUTTONS [26], Xbuttons [34]. All these systems allow the user to modify certain aspects of their interactive behaviour, while working with them. More recently, the AURA project (Adaptable User Interfaces for Reusable Applications) of the ESPRIT-II Programme of the European Commission has investigated thoroughly the issue of adaptability [22] and the underlying architectural abstractions for adaptable systems. Adaptability has also been the chief objective in the development of the PODIUM system [36].

In addition to the above research efforts towards adaptability, a number of systems have been developed to investigate the "complementary" technique of adaptivity. The state of the art in adaptive user interfaces includes OPADE [13], AIDA [11], UIDE [41], as well as the results of several projects at national and international levels, such as AID [9] and FRIEND21 [32]. In addition to the above architectures for adaptable and/or adaptive user interfaces, there have been a few other proposals which, however, are more narrow in scope.

A more recent approach towards adaptable and adaptive HCI is embodied in the notion of *unified interface development*, which has been introduced to practically support the concept of *User Interfaces for All* [37], which constitutes a specialisation of the "Design for All" principle in the HCI domain [38]. The guiding principles of *User Interfaces for All* (UI4All) are that:

a) considerations for all potential target user categories and usage contexts are taken into account early on in the design process, resulting in a multitude of alternative interaction artefacts, each of them meeting different sets of requirements, and

b) suitable development techniques and tools are employed to allow for the different design artefacts to coexist in the final interface, and to control their availability to the end-user, based on the interaction context.

3.2   Adaptation in Unified Interface Development

Unified User Interface Development [40], [35], [2] has been defined as an appropriate vehicle for realising the goal of *User Interfaces for All*. In particular, Unified User Interface Development (U^{2}ID) is based on the notions of:

a) polymorphic task hierarchies (any task may have an arbitrary number of *alternative* instantiation styles and sub-task *decomposition*);

b) unified user interface specification (tools are employed to generate the implementation of the interface from specifications; the implemented user interface allows for the coexistence and concurrent availability of the multiple instantiation styles and decomposition); and,

c) dynamic interface adaptations (at run-time, dedicated assessment and decision mechanisms select the appropriate -combinations of- styles to make available to the user).

Adaptation in U^{2}ID is a multi-faceted process, which can be analysed along three main axes: the "timing" of adaptation; the level of interaction at which it is applied (i.e. physical, syntactic or semantic); and, the type of information considered in deciding appropriate adaptations.

As far as the "timing" of adaptations is concerned, one can identify two complementary classes: adaptation decisions driven from knowledge available at start-up, i.e. prior to the initiation of interaction (e.g. user profile, platform profile, usage context); and, adaptation decisions drawn upon knowledge derived at run-time (e.g. through interaction monitoring, inspection of the computing environment). The former adaptation behaviour in an interface is termed *adaptability* and reflects the capability on the part of the interface to automatically tailor itself to the initial interaction requirements, as these are shaped by the information available to the interface. The latter adaptation behaviour is termed *adaptivity* and refers to the capability on the part of the interface to dynamically derive further knowledge about the user, the usage context, etc., and use that knowledge in order to further modify itself to better suit the revised interaction requirements.

The second axis of analysis of adaptation in U^{2}ID concerns the level of interaction at which adaptations are applied. In particular, U^{2}ID does not pose any constraints in this respect, making it possible to design and effect adaptations at all three levels of interaction:

a) at the *semantic* level of interaction (e.g., by employing different metaphors to convey the functionality and facilities of the underlying system);

b) at the *syntactic* level of interaction (e.g., by de/activating alternative dialogue patterns, such as, for example, "object-function" versus "function-object" interaction sequencing); and,

c) at the *lexical* level of interaction (e.g., grouping and spatial arrangement of interactive elements, modification of presentation attributes).

The third main axis of analysis concerns the type of information being considered when deciding upon adaptations. Once again, U^2ID does not pose any restrictions on the breadth and depth of information that can be utilised. Exemplary categories of information that can be employed include: design constraints, as these are defined by user characteristics (abilities, skills, requirements, preferences, expertise, cultural background, etc.), platform characteristics (e.g., terminal capabilities, input/output devices, etc.), task requirements (e.g., urgency, criticality, error-proneness, sequencing), etc. Furthermore, information that can only be acquired during interaction can equally participate in the decision process (e.g., identifying the user's inability to successfully complete a task, inferring the user's goal / intention, detecting modifications to the run-time environment).

3.3   Practice and experience

The *unified interface development* method has been applied in several application domains in the context of collaborative research and development work. Initially, it was validated in two application domains, in the context of the TIDE-ACCESS project (see Acknowledgements). Subsequently, the *unified interface development* method was used to design a unified browser for Web-based interaction with metropolitan information systems. The system, developed in the context of the ACTS-AVANTI project (see Acknowledgements) was targeted for the population at large, including people with disabilities (blind users and users with severe or mild motor impairments) [39]. In what follows, we provide a brief account of the latter effort for purposes of illustration of the points raised thus far.

The AVANTI information system comprises five main modules (see Figure 1): (i) a collection of multimedia databases which are accessed through a common communication interface (Multimedia Database Interface - MDI); (ii) the User Modelling Server (UMS), which maintains and updates individual user profiles, as well as user stereotypes; (iii) the Content Model (CM), which retains a meta-description of the information available in the system; (iv) the Hyper-Structure Adaptor (HSA), which adapts the information content, according to user characteristics; and, (v) the User Interface component (browser), which is capable of tailoring itself to individual users.

Following U^2ID, the AVANTI browser has been designed and developed with a (single) unified user interface, which comprises alternative interaction components, appropriate for different target user categories. This single design artefact may have multiple instantiations during initiation of interaction (adaptability), in order to ensure accessibility for a wide range of users. Moreover, each interface instance is continuously enhanced at run-time (adaptivity), in order to provide high-quality of interaction to all potential users.

In the AVANTI browser, adaptability is based on "static" user characteristics known prior to interaction (e.g. user abilities, requirements), and assumed to remain unchanged within a single interaction session. Adaptivity, on the other hand, is based on dynamic user characteristics and interaction states that are detected at run-time (e.g. high error rate, inability to complete a task). Adaptations in both cases concern the syntactic and lexical levels of interaction.

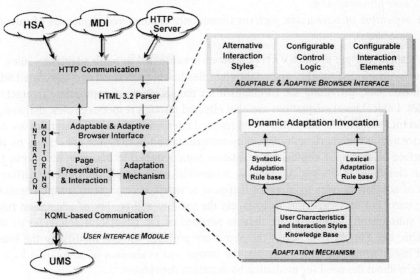

Fig. 1. The architecture of the AVANTI browser [39].

The "static" user characteristics that serve as the basis for adaptability, were selected during an initial requirements analysis phase. They include:

(i)   physical abilities, i.e., whether the user is able-bodied, blind or motor-impaired;
(ii)   the language of the user (the system supports English, Italian and Finnish);
(iii) familiarity of the user with the Web and the AVANTI system itself;
(iv)   the overall interaction target: speed, ease of use, accuracy, error prevention; and,
(v)   user preferences regarding specific aspects of the application and the interaction.

The selection of the above characteristics was made so as to ensure that adequate knowledge exists for the system to cater for a wide range of users, taking into account not only possible disabilities, but also characteristics that differentiate individual users (who may in general belong to the same broad category) between each other. In the prototype version of the system, these characteristics are either acquired through an initial "questionnaire" session, or retrieved from smart-cards (users have different, personal smart-cards containing their individual profiles). It should be noted, that although these characteristics are termed "static", they are not all assumed to remain unchanged "permanently". In fact, it is foreseen that future versions of the system will detect and record changes in these characteristics over time, thus causing different adaptations to be effected in the user interface, in terms of adaptability. The dynamic user characteristics and interaction states that are taken into account for adaptivity (also derived from the requirements analysis phase) concern:

(i)   *user familiarity* with specific tasks (capability to successfully initiate and complete certain tasks);

(ii) *ability to navigate* (move from one document to another in a consistent way);

(iii) *error rate*;

(iv) *disorientation* (defined as inability to cope with the current state of the system);

(v)   *user idle time*; and,

(vi) *repetition of interaction patterns* (commonly encountered sequences of interaction steps).

Adaptation logic in the AVANTI browser is expressed through adaptation rules. A set of syntactic adaptability and adaptivity rules has been defined and associated with each user task, providing the mechanism for the selection of appropriate interaction styles. Lexical level adaptations are also effected through respective rules, that assign different values to the attributes of the realised interaction objects. These rules are not hard-wired in the interface; rather, they are maintained in files that are read in by the interface at start-up. Keeping the adaptation logic external to the interface allows for great flexibility in the system, making it possible, for example, to: develop different sets of adaptation rules to cater for different or new user categories, usage contexts, etc.; carry out user experiments to assess the validity and quality of adaptation rules and subsequently modify them; disable portions of the adaptation behaviour of the system; etc. Furthermore, all of the above are possible without modifying the interface itself, which, in turn, facilitates the design and evaluation of adaptation by experts, without the need for mediation by interface developers.

3.3.1   Adaptability in the AVANTI browser

The AVANTI browser exhibits several adaptability capabilities, some of which will be briefly elaborated in this section. Upon start-up, and based on static user knowledge, the system determines several aspects of the interactive behaviour to be exhibited. Thus, for instance, an "ordinary" user will be presented with a conventional interface such as that illustrated in Figure 2a. For a more experienced user, the system augments the interactive behaviour by providing additional elements (see Figure 2b) such as the *overview pane* that replicates the links in the current page, various *feedback mechanisms* (e.g. convey availability of bookmarks) as well as *buttons* to represent *links*.

Augmented interaction facilities are also evident in the case of motor impaired users (see Figure 2c). Here, the interface provides an additional *toolbar for window management*, while interaction with the interface is managed through *scanning* of interaction elements (including image maps) and suitable interaction techniques for specific interaction tasks (e.g. the virtual keyboard of Figure 2d intended to facilitate text editing).

In addition to the above visual alternatives, the AVANTI browser can also adapt to non-visual modalities in case that the user is blind. At this point, it is important to iterate that the above examples of adaptability utilise knowledge that is available prior to any interaction. Such knowledge is usually available in user models encoded explicitly, either in the user information server (UMS), or in a smart card.

3.3.2   Adaptivity in the AVANTI browser

Adaptivity in the AVANTI browser complements adaptability and aims to augment the run-time interactive behaviour of the system, based on interaction monitoring and dynamic updates in the interface. In contrast with adaptability, therefore, adaptivity relies on the availability of dynamic user information that is collected through monitoring and processed by a dedicated component, namely the user modelling server. Figure 3 depicts several examples of adaptive behaviour. Figure 3a illustrates the response of the interface upon detection of the fact that the user seems incapable of completing the task of selecting a link from the "link bar". Alternatively, in Figure 3b the same dialogue is augmented with guidance for the case that a user seems to be unable to comprehend its use. Finally, in Figure 3c, the interface offers to the user a list from which a previously visited document can be selected and loaded.

During the design stage of the AVANTI browser, it was found that certain categories of adaptations exist, which were applicable in a large number of interaction tasks. These adaptations are not specific to Web browsing, and can be expected to be equally common in other application domains. The main adaptation categories identified include:

(i)   adaptive provision of explicit feedback, either during task performance (interim feedback), or after task completion (completion feedback);

(ii)   adaptive requests for confirmation, which may belong to one of two types: either a brief request for explicit approval before the system carries out an action, or a more elaborate explanation of the possible consequences or side effects of the action, in conjunction with the request for approval;

(iii)   adaptive guidance, which provides help for the completion of a task (e.g., the sequencing of actions, the types of data required in each field), when, for example, there is evidence that the user is unable to complete this task;

(iv)   adaptive prompting, which provides information concerning the initiation and successful completion of a specific task, when, for example, there is evidence that the user is unable to initiate this task.

3.4.   Towards an architectural abstraction for adaptable and adaptive interfaces

The employment of U^2ID in the AVANTI project offered valuable insight into interface adaptation in general. The knowledge acquired and the principles verified in the design and development of the adaptable and adaptive AVANTI browser can easily be generalised and reused in different application domains. This section provides a brief overview of the architectural underpinnings of employing U^2ID in practice, as well as a reflection on how the suggested model could be utilised to support user interface adaptation in digital library systems.

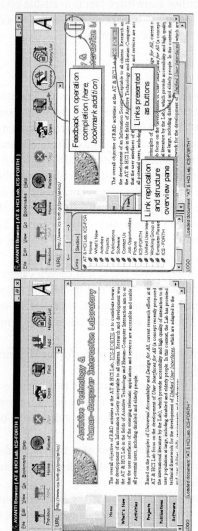

(a) A conventional instance of the interface

(b) Adaptations for an experienced user

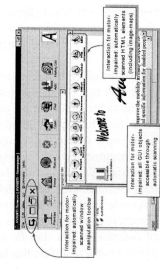

(c) Scanning in the interface

(d) Example of a virtual keyboard for text editing

Fig. 2. Examples of adaptability in the AVANTI browser

727

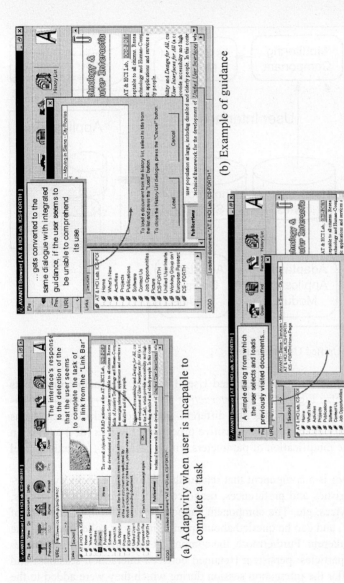

(a) Adaptivity when user is incapable to complete a task

(b) Example of guidance

(c) Adaptive preview of previously visited locations

Fig. 3. Examples of adaptive behaviour in the AVANTI browser

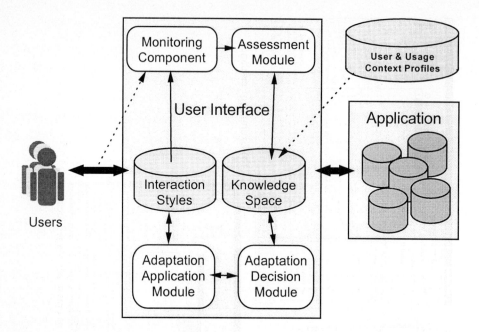

Fig. 4. Architecture of a Unified User Interface

Starting from the architecture of a Unified User Interface, six main components can be identified (see also Figure 4). The *interaction styles repository* stores alternative, implemented instantiation styles for different interaction tasks. Mechanisms offered by the repository enable context sensitive processing towards (de-) activation of styles, as well as the modification of parameters within each style (for lexical level adaptations).

The *knowledge space* is a component that retains the knowledge of the system regarding user characteristics and preferences, usage context, platform characteristics, availability of I/O devices, etc. The component supports the addition, or removal of knowledge "particles", and can be queried about specific items, or collectively on the knowledge contained therein. Furthermore, the component supports two different lifetimes for knowledge particles: persistent (retained between interaction sessions) and transient (discarded after the interaction session during which they were added to the knowledge space). Although there are no specific requirements as far as knowledge representation is concerned, it is necessary that "set" (multi-valued) attributes are supported.

The *adaptation decision* module draws upon the knowledge in the knowledge space to arrive at decisions regarding what adaptations are required at any given point in time. In particular, the component decides upon and communicates decisions regarding style availability and (de-) activation, as well as lexical level attributes of the interaction. The functional requirements of the adaptation decision module are that: it monitors modifications made in the knowledge space and acts upon them (by going through the adaptation logic and identifying the possible modifications triggered by the knowledge updates); it communicates any modifications in the actual adaptations to the adaptation application module (see below); and, finally, it can be queried about the current state of any specific (category of) syntactic or lexical level adaptation. Other than the above, there are no specific requirements in terms of what approach to decision making is employed. In the recent past, we have experimented with alternatives to decision making including preference-based frameworks [3], [4] and utility-based models [19], [20].

The *adaptation application* module undertakes the task of "managing" the interface by applying dialogue control. More specifically, it is responsible for applying different policies in how adaptations are actually introduced into the system, and how the user is made aware of them. Furthermore, it is responsible for enabling the user to control adaptations, by selectively allowing or disallowing, and modifying them, or by refining the policy according to which they are applied.

The *monitoring* component is responsible for observing user interaction with the system, and detecting possible changes in the computing environment (e.g., availability of I/O devices, inter-operations with other applications or system components , etc.) The information collected by the monitoring component is communicated to the assessment module (see below), where it is further processed. An advanced incarnation of the monitoring component could also incorporate facilities that would allow for pre-processing (grouping, filtering, transformations, etc.) of the collected data, before it is communicated further.

Finally, the *assessment* module is responsible for dynamically identifying changes in the characteristics of the users, and the state of interaction. In doing so, it utilises the existing knowledge in the knowledge space, and, more importantly, the information communicated by the monitoring component. Any inferences derived are communicated to the knowledge space, thus becoming themselves part of the system's knowledge. As is the case with the rest of the modules in the *unified user interface* architecture, it is possible to use any of the existing alternative technologies for the development of the assessment module.

The major distinction between the architectural abstraction of Figure 4 and other architectural models for user interface software, such as MVC [17], or PAC [12] is that the former emphasises detailed functional roles and well defined communication protocols amongst the various components driving the adaptation process. Thus, the *unified interface* architecture is orthogonal to such models, provided that they are suitably enhanced to facilitate adaptation-oriented goals.

The employment of the interface architecture outlined above in a digital library is a rather straightforward task, since it is, for the most part, orthogonal to the overall architecture of a digital library system. The major design decision concerning user interface adaptation that needs to be made in this context is the distribution of the different adaptation components of the user interface, taking into account the related distribution of the DL components. Assuming a typical client-server approach, it is possible to have all the aforementioned user interface components at the client side (this would be the case, for example, if a dedicated, domain-aware front-end to the DL was employed), or, on the opposite extreme, to have all the components on the server side (this might be necessary, if the DL employed a thin-client interface, e.g., if it was Web-based). Naturally, any intermediate solution can also be applied, depending on the operational and functional requirements of the DL system.

The orthogonality between the user interface and the DL architectures is mainly due to the fact that existing, or proposed DL architectures advocate a clear separation between the information content, the retrieval mechanisms and the user interface [5], [10], [31], [43]. Even in those approaches where the interface is tightly coupled to the DL architecture (e.g. [7]), it is possible to combine the two architectures by "plugging" the adaptation components into the overall framework. The latter is possible thanks to the restricted interaction of these components with the functional core of the DL. Figure 5 depicts graphically some of the possible approaches to the employment of the proposed architecture in DL systems.

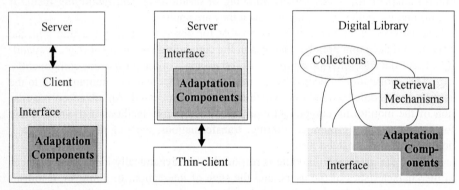

Fig. 5. Alternatives to building user interface adaptation into DL systems

4   The design space of adaptation in the context of Digital Libraries

Having reviewed the *unified interface development* framework and its employment for user interface adaptation, this section attempts to draw parallels with the domain of digital libraries. Our intention is to sketch a roadmap for user interface adaptation in digital library systems and to briefly elaborate on the design space of such adaptations. In the context of digital libraries, adaptation may be employed to facilitate a variety of design goals. Examples of prominent targets include *flattening the interaction hierarchy* and *anchoring users in stable contexts* [29]. In general, adaptations can be envisaged at several levels of the user interaction with a digital library system.

First of all, adaptation may be used to facilitate the presentation of interactive and non-interactive elements of the interface. Attributes that are subject to adaptation include size, colour combinations, font family and size, placement, grouping, etc. Adaptations at this level may also relate to physical elements of an interface, such as initiation, interim and completion feedback, as well as topology (e.g., horizontal, vertical) of container objects. In addition, the use of multimodal representations and suitable interaction techniques, engaging combinations of user modalities (e.g., vision and auditory) constitute another area where adaptations may prove very useful.

Secondly, adaptations may address the interaction syntax. This entails determining and engaging the user in a suitable sequence of interaction steps required for the successful and efficient completion of a task. Indicative adaptations at this level include: adaptive requests for confirmation, selection of suitable command order (e.g., object-function versus function-object syntax), alternative function activation modes (e.g., explicit versus implicit activation), multiple levels of help or guidance, etc. In addition, several techniques may be used to augment navigation and facilitate performance targets (e.g., effectiveness, efficiency and satisfaction). For example, structured overviews [18], link bars (see the AVANTI examples), frames, tables and other tools for guided navigation may help reduce the need for backtracking in the page structure and thereby improving efficiency. Moreover, additional toolbars, such as the window management toolbar of the AVANTI system, may be used to anchor users in stable contexts. This would minimise disorientation and distraction and would allow users to focus their cognitive resources on the task at hand, rather than the system's navigation.

Thirdly, adaptations may be targeted at the *interaction semantics*. This relates to what the user perceives as the prevailing interactive embodiment of the computer (e.g., desktop, book, rooms), as well as the functionality that should be available. Adaptations at this level mainly concern the metaphor(s) used to embody different functional properties of the system. Metaphor in user interfaces to digital library systems may be either embedded in the interface, or characterise the overall interactive environment. For instance, using a metaphor to develop a suitable visualisation of a collection of related articles is an example of embedding metaphor in the user interface. In contrast, developing an interface which allows the user to interact with the digital library through book- rather than desktop-related concepts such as table of contents, chapters, index, paragraph, etc., implies using metaphor to characterise the overall interactive embodiment of the computer. Adaptation may be used not only to select and instantiate suitable interactive metaphors for different users and tasks, but also to individualise interaction.

It is important to note at this point that the capability to adapt a specific aspect of interaction, does not necessarily imply the necessity, or, for that matter, the *usefulness* of doing so. Rather, each such adaptation capability should be treated as a tool in accommodating specific design problems (diversity being amongst the most prominent ones), and should be treated with care, as exaggerations in the employment of adaptations could significantly compromise the usability, user-friendliness and overall acceptability of the system.

5 Summary and conclusions

This paper has developed an argumentation for user interface adaptation in the context of digital library systems. To this effect, some of the HCI challenges posed by digital libraries were briefly elaborated upon; moreover, methods for utilising adaptability and adaptivity were described, in order to facilitate access to, and ensure the usability of, digital library systems by diverse user groups. Specifically, it was pointed out how the existing wisdom in the area of adaptable and adaptive interfaces could be transferred and applied in digital libraries. For purposes of illustration, we reviewed examples of user interface adaptations as implemented in the AVANTI browser. In addition, we presented an architectural model detailing the software components in a *unified interface* that drive and facilitate adaptation.

The practical value of the above treatment to the digital library community is multi-faceted. First of all, the architectural model of the *unified interface* concept provides a novel account and a functional view of the underlying building blocks needed to support adaptable and adaptive interaction. This architectural model may be suitably specialised or enhanced to facilitate user interface adaptations in a digital library system. The scope of these adaptations could vary to accommodate semantic, syntactic or lexical aspects of a user interface. The examples from the AVANTI browser illustrate how this could be attained.

In the future, it is expected that user interface adaptation will become a prominent target in digital library research and development efforts. Though the issues identified in this paper will continue to pose challenges, additional ones are likely to emerge as digital libraries become evolutionary information repositories in communities of users. In this context, organisational and social aspects of digital libraries will complement accessibility, usability and performance targets, thus extending the scope and nature of adaptations and necessitating a range of collaborative and reciprocal efforts between the DL and the HCI communities.

In conclusion, it is important to iterate that the *capability* of any interactive system to adapt a specific aspect of interaction, does not necessarily imply the *necessity*, or, for that matter, the *usefulness* of doing so. This is no different in the area of digital libraries. It follows, therefore, that any adaptation capability should be treated as a tool in accommodating specific design problems, and should be treated with care, as exaggerations in the employment of adaptations could significantly compromise the usability, user-friendliness and overall acceptability of the system.

Acknowledgements

The development of the *unified user interface development* approach has been supported through collaborative research and development projects, partially funded by the European Commission. These projects are:

The TIDE-ACCESS TP1001 project (Development Platform for Unified Access to Enabling Environments) of the European Commission (DG XIII). The ACCESS consortium comprised the following organisations: CNR-IROE (Italy) - Prime contractor; ICS-FORTH (Greece); University of Hertforshire (UK); University of Athens (Greece); NAWH (Finland); VTT (Finland); Hereward College (UK); RNIB (United Kingdom); Seleco (Italy); MA Systems and Control (UK); PIKOMED (Finland).

The ACTS-AVANTI AC042 project (Adaptable and Adaptive Interaction in Multimedia Telecommunications Applications) of the European Commission (DG XIII). The partners of the AVANTI consortium are: ALCATEL Italia - Siette division (Italy) - Prime contractor; IROE-CNR (Italy); ICS-FORTH (Greece); GMD (Germany); VTT (Finland); University of Sienna (Italy); TECO Systems (Italy); STUDIO ADR (Italy); MA Systems and Control (UK).

References

1. Angre, P.: Research topics for Social Aspects of Digital Libraries. UCLA-NSF Social Aspects of Digital Libraries Workshop, UCLA, February 15-17, 1996. Available on-line at: http://www.gslis.ucla.edu/DL/agre.html.
2. Akoumianakis, D., Savidis, A., Stephanidis, C.: Encapsulating intelligent interactive behaviour in unified user interface artefacts. In: Interacting with Computers, Special Issue on The Realities of Intelligent Interface Technology (1998, accepted for publication).
3. Akoumianakis, D., Stephanidis, C.: Knowledge-based support for user-adapted interaction design. In: Expert Systems with Applications: An international journal, 12-1 (1997) 225-245.
4. Akoumianakis, D., Stephanidis, C.: Supporting user-adapted interface design: The USE-IT System. In: Interacting with Computers, 9-2 (1997) 73-104.
5. Arms, W. Y.: Key Concepts in the Architecture of the Digital Library. In: D-Lib Magazine (July 1995).
6. Benyon, D., Murray, D.: Adaptive Systems: from intelligent tutoring to autonomous agents. In: Knowledge-Based Systems, 6-4 (1993) 197-219.
7. Birmingham, W. P.: An Agent-Based Architecture for Digital Libraries. In: D-Lib Magazine (July 1995).
8. Borgman, C. L., Bates, M. J., Cloonan, M. V., Efthimiadis, E. N., Gilliland-Swetland, A. J., Kafai, Y. B., Leazer, G. H., Maddox, A. B.: Final Report. UCLA-NSF Social Aspects of Digital Libraries Workshop, UCLA, February 15-17, 1996. Available on-line at: http://www.gslis.ucla.edu/DL/UCLA_DL_Report.html
9. Browne, P. D.: Experiences from the AID project. In: Schneider-Hufschmidt, M., Kuhme, T., Mallinowski, U. (eds.): Adaptive User Interfaces. Elsevier Science Publishers B.V, Amsterdam, North-Holland (1993) 69-78.
10. Corporation for National Research Initiatives: Digital Object Architecture Project. Available on-line at: http://www.cnri.reston.va.us/doa.html.
11. Cote-Munoz, A. H.: AIDA: An Adaptive System for Interactive Drafting and CAD Applications. In: Schneider-Hufschmidt, M., Kuhme, T., Mallinowski, U. (eds.): Adaptive User Interfaces. Elsevier Science Publishers B.V, Amsterdam, North-Holland (1993) 225-240.
12. Coutaz, J.: Architecture models for interactive software: Failures and trends. In: Cocton, G. (ed): Engineering for Human-Computer Interaction. Elsevier Science Publishers B.V, Amsterdam, North-Holland, (1990) 473-490.
13. de Carolis, B., de Rosis, F.: Modeling Adaptive Interaction of OPADE by Petri Nets. In: SIGCHI, 26-2 (1994) 48-52.
14. Dieterich, H., Malinowski, U., Kuhme, T., Schneider-Hufschmidt, M.: State of the Art in Adaptive User Interfaces. Adaptive User Interfaces: Principles and Practice. In: Schneider-Hufschmidt, M., Kuhme, T., Malinowski, U. (eds.): Adaptive User Interfaces. Elsevier Science Publishers B.V, Amsterdam, North-Holland (1993) 13-48.

734

15. Dippo, C.: FedStats promotes Statistical Literacy. In: Communications of the ACM, 41-4 (1998) 58-60.
16. Gladney, H., Mintzer, F., Schiattarella, F., Bescos, J., Treu, M.: Digital access to Antiquities. In: Communications of the ACM, 41-4 (1998) 49-57.
17. Glodberg, A., Robson, D.: Smalltalk-80: The Interactive Programming Environment, Addison-Wesley Publishing, Inc. (1984).
18. Greene S., Marchionini G., Plaisant C., Shneiderman B.: Previews and overviews in digital libraries: designing surrogates to support visual information seeking. Technical Report CS-TR-3838, UMIACS-TR-97-73. University of Maryland (1997).
19. Karagiannidis, C., Koumbis, A., Stephanidis, C.: Modeling Decisions in Intelligent User Interfaces. In: International Journal of Intelligent Systems, 12 (1997) 753-762.
20. Karagiannidis, C., Koumbis, A., Stephanidis C.: Adaptation in IMMPS as decision making process. In: Computer Standards and Interfaces, 18 (1997) 509-514.
21. Klavans, J., Schauble, P.: NSF-EU Multilingual information access. In: Communications of the ACM, 41-4 (1998) 69.
22. Koller, F.: A demonstrator based investigation of adaptability. In: Schneider-Hufschmidt, M., Kuhme, T., Mallinowski, U. (eds.): Adaptive User Interfaces. Elsevier Science Publishers B.V, Amsterdam, North-Holland (1993) 183-196.
23. Lai, K., Malone, T.: Object Lens: A Spreadsheet for Co-operative Work. In: Proceedings of the Conference on CSCW. ACM Press, New York (1988) 115-124.
24. Leong, M. K., Cao, L., Lu, Y.: Distributed Chinese Bibliographic Searching. In: Communications of the ACM, 41-4 (1998) 66-68.
25. Lynch, C., Hector, G. M.: Interoperability, Scaling, and the Digital Libraries Research Agenda. Workshop Report, IITA Digital Libraries Workshop, May 18-19, 1995.
26. MacLean, A., Carter, K., Lovstrand, L., Moran, T.: User-Tailorable Systems: Pressing the Issues with Buttons. In: Proceedings of CHI'90. ACM Press, New York (1990) 175-182.
27. Maeda, A., Datrois, M., Fujita, T., Sakaguchi, T., Sugimoto, S., Tabata, K.: Viewing Multilingual Documents on Your Local Web Browser. In: Communications of the ACM, 41-4 (1998) 64-65.
28. Marchionini G.: Digital Library Research and Development. In: Kent A. (ed.): Encyclopaedia of Library and Information Science (in press).
29. Marchionini G., Plaisant C., Komlodi A.: Interfaces and Tools for the Library of Congress National Digital Library Program. To appear in: International Journal of Information Processing and Management. CS-TR-3872, UMIACS-TR-98-09, CLIS-TR-97-07, University of Maryland (1997). Available on-line:ftp://ftp.cs.umd.edu/pub/hcil/Reports-Abstracts-Bibliography/3872HTML/3872.html.
30. Moen, W.: Accessing distributed Cultural Heritage Information. In: Communications of the ACM, 41-4 (1998) 45-48.
31. Nurnberg, P. J., Furuta, R., Leggett, J. L., Shipman, F. M.: Digital Libraries: Issues and Architectures. In: Proceedings of Digital Libraries '95, The Second Annual Conference on the Theory and Practice of Digital Libraries, Austin, Texas, USA, June 11-13.
32. Okada, K.: Adaptation by task intention identification. In: FRIEND 21 Conference Proceedings, Institute for Personalised Information Environment, Japan, 1994.
33. Opperman, R.: Adaptively supported adaptability. In: International Journal of Human-Computer Studies, 40 (1994) 455-472.
34. Robertson, G., Henderson, D., Card, S.: Buttons as First Class Objects on an Xdesktop. In: Proceedings of UIST '91. ACM Press, New York (1991) 35-44.
35. Savidis A., Paramythis A., Akoumianakis D., Stephanidis C.: Designing user-adapted interfaces: the unified design method for transformable interactions. In: Proceedings of ACM

Conference on Designing Interactive System: Processes, Methods and Techniques (DIS '97), Amsterdam, The Netherlands, 18-20 August, 1997. ACM Press (1997) 323-334.

36.Sherman, H., E., Shortliffe, H., E.: A User-Adaptable Interface to predict Users' Needs. In: Schneider-Hufschmidt, M., Kuhme, T., Mallinowski, U. (eds.): Adaptive User Interfaces. Elsevier Science Publishers B.V, Amsterdam North-Holland (1993) 285-315.

37.Stephanidis, C.: Towards User Interfaces for All: Some Critical Issues. In: Proceedings of HCI International '95, Panel Session "User Interfaces for All - Everybody, Everywhere, and Anytime", Tokyo, Japan, 9-14 July 1995, 137-142.

38.Stephanidis, C.: Design for All in Human-Computer Interaction. In: European Telematics: Advancing the Information Society Conference, Session "Human-Computer Interfaces - Imagining the Interfaces of the Future", Barcelona, Spain, 4-7 February 1998.

39.Stephanidis, C., Paramythis, A., Sfyrakis, M., Stergiou, A., Maou, N., Leventis, A., Paparoulis, G., Karagianidis, C.: Adaptable and Adaptive User Interfaces for Disabled Users in AVANTI Project. In: Trigila, S., Mullery, A., Campolargo, M., Vanderstraeten, H., Mampaey, M. (eds.): Proceedings of the 5th International Conference on Intelligence in Services and Networks (IS&N '98), "Technology for Ubiquitous Telecommunication Services", Antwerp, Belgium, 25-28 May 1998. Lecture Notes in Computer Science, Vol. 1430. Springer-Verlag Haidelberg Germany (1998) 153-166.

40.Stephanidis, C., Savidis, A., Akoumianakis, D.: Unified Interface Development: Tools for Constructing Accessible and Usable User Interfaces. Tutorial no. 13, HCI International Conference '97. San Francisco, USA, 23-29 August, 1997.

41.Sukaviriya, P., Foley, J.: Supporting Adaptive Interfaces in a knowledge-based user Interface Environment. In: Gray, W. D., Hefley, W. E., Murray, D. (eds.): Proceedings of the 1993 International Workshop on Intelligent User Interfaces, Orlando, FL. ACM Press, New York (1993) 107-114

42.van House, N. A.: User Needs Assessment and Evaluation for the UC Berkeley Electronic Environmental Library Project: a Preliminary Report. In: Proceedings of Digital Libraries '95, The Second Annual Conference on the Theory and Practice of Digital Libraries, Austin, Texas, USA, June 11-13, 1995.

43.Yuan, Y., Roehrig, S., Sirbu, M.: Service Models, Operational Decisions and Architecture of Digital Libraries. In: Proceedings of Digital Libraries '95, The Second Annual Conference on the Theory and Practice of Digital Libraries, Austin, Texas, USA, June 11-13, 1995.

Metadata and Content-Based Approaches to Resource Discovery

Organisers:

Thomas Baker

Visiting Faculty, Computer Science & Information Management
Programme School of Advanced Technologies
Asian Institute of Technology
P.O. Box 4, Klong Luang, 12120 Thailand
tbaker@cs.ait.ac.th

Judith Klavans

Director, CRIA - Center for Research on Information Access
Department of Information Services
Columbia University
535 West 114th Street, New York, NY 10027, USA
klavans@cs.columbia.edu

Abstract. Researchers in multilingual information retrieval and natural language processing are making progress on algorithms for guessing what a text is about and for translating queries between languages; some day we may have reliable programs for recognizing musical melodies or the content of images. In contrast, researchers in metadata focus more on seeking consensus on the meanings of categories for describing resources; on finding ways to allow simple schemas to interoperate with complex ones; and on designing frameworks for managing the messy equivalencies between metadata models in different fields and languages. Do the two perspectives form a continuum? What problems do they solve best? For resource discovery, what is the best balance between human and machine?

Panellists

- Stuart Weibel (OCLC), co-founder and primus inter pares of the Dublin Core Workshop Series, participant in the EU-NSF WG on Metadata.
- Peter Schauble (ETH), co-leader of the EU-NSF WG on Multilingual Information Access, designer of numerous multilingual retrieval systems.
- Judith Klavans (Columbia), co-leader of the EU-NSF WG on Multilingual Information Access, researcher in natural language processing, director of the Center for Research in Information Access.

- Thomas Baker (GMD and AIT), co-leader of the EU-NSF WG on Metadata, coordinator of the WG for Dublin Core in Multiple Languages.
- Carl Lagoze (Cornell), co-leader of the EU-NSF WG on Distributed Indexing, co-inventor of the Warwick Framework, participant in Dublin Core.
- Someone else from IR or NLP.

Architectures and Services
for Cultural Heritage Information

Organiser: Prof. Panos Constantopoulos

Institute of Computer Science (ICS)
Foundation for Research and Technology - Hellas (FORTH)
Science and Technology Park of Crete
GR - 71110 Heraklion, Crete, Greece
Tel: +30 - 81 - 391634
Fax: +30 - 81 - 391601
email: panos@ics.forth.gr

Abstract. The electronic processing of cultural heritage information involves stages of acquisition/production, storage, indexing, use/exploitation and transfer. The value of information is compounded by usage and association to other information. It is thus important to ensure the linking of information from disparate sources or held in different systems, access according to multiple viewpoints and needs, and exchange among different systems and user groups. Key issues are the selection of architectures that ensure interoperability and the development of services that support the recording, safeguarding, scientific study and promotion of cultural heritage, including artifacts and information sources. This panel will address these issues with a view towards the shaping of a DL domain.

Biographical note: Panos Constantopoulos is professor of Computer Science at the University of Crete and head of the Information Systems and Software Technology Division at the Institute of Computer Science, Foundation for Research and Technology-Hellas. His current research interests include multimedia information systems, conceptual modelling, information retrieval and decision support.

Federated Scientific Data Repositories for the Environment Towards Global Scalable Management of Environmental Information: How Useful Will They Be? What Is Their Potential Impact? Shall We Save the Environment?

Catherine Houstis[1]

[1] Institute of Computer Science, Foundation for Research and Technology - Hellas, Science and Technology Park of Crete, Vassilika Vouton, P.O. Box 1385, GR 711 10, Heraklion, Crete, Greece
housti@csi.forth.gr

Abstract. We are currently witnessing a proliferation of the Internet, the World Wide Web, and new distributed systems technologies. The idea of federated scientific data repositories, built from organizationally and geographically distributed units, is becoming an area of increasing interest to both scientists and authorities. The general public could benefit from them as well with appropriate access. Such a development would pave the way towards global sharing and combination of environmental information, thereby promoting co-operation among scientists and considerably supporting environmental information management and decision making. From a technical perspective, building federated scientific repositories involves confronting problems such as heterogeneity, distribution, integration, knowledge, authentication, appropriate interfaces and performance. From an organizational perspective it involves Inter-disciplinary co-operation, cross-organizational management, as well as important legal and economic issues. Within the computer science arena solutions exist to each of the technical problems, but their integration is still elusive. Notably, the organizational problems that have to be addressed at the management level may prove far more challenging. So, given that the ingredients exist, how are we to proceed? And will such an effort be worthwhile? In the end shall we save the environment?

1. Aims

This panel aims to bring together a complementary group of practitioners and researchers from a range of fields with a common interest in open systems accessed via the Internet and WWW constructing federated scientific data repositories. The intention is to facilitate the exchange of ideas between those working on the general problems of data and component integration and those with specific practical problems to solve or experiences to offer. The panel will thus be of interest not only to computer engineers and scientists, but also to representatives of various environmental organizations, state authorities as well as information market economies. The specific goals of the panel are:

- to identify those factors - technological, managerial, economical and political – which impede the creation of federated scientific repositories;
- to compare support for projects pursuing the idea of federated scientific repositories in Europe, the US and Japan;
- to identify any new co-operation models that will emerge from improving communication and interaction among scientific repositories; and
- to draw a road map of projected future developments, to aid the development of strategies for deploying virtual enterprises

2.   Panel Format

The panel will consist of several invited speakers from different scientific disciplines, including an economist and a politician. After a brief "scene-setting" presentation, the panel body will be requested to elaborate on a set of themes concerning the creation of federated scientific repositories. During the panel discussion, the floor will be open for anyone to participate

3.   Bibliographical note

Catherine Houstis is an associate professor of Computer Science at the University of Crete and a research associate in the distributed systems division at the Institute of Computer Science –Foundation for Research and Technology-Hellas. She is leading a project on Data Management and Data Visualization for supporting Coastal Zone management for the Mediterranean Sea. Her current research interests includes issues related to open distributed systems architectures for environmental information.

Preservation and Access: Two Sides of the Same Coin

Pieter J.D.Drenth

Chairman European Commision on Preservation and Access.

1. Introduction

The number of conferences, meetings and publications on digital and electronic information over the past years has increased exponentially. Digital records seem to replace to a large extent the classical paper collections and paper records, and concern about availability and accessibility of paper material seem to vanish in the shining light of the explosion of present day's electronic communication and digitization developments.

Let us bring in some realism. In a recent interview in Der Spiegel Klaus Dieter Lehmann, the director of the Deutsche Bibliothek, the German deposit library, mentioned under the appropriate heading Books do have advantages" that of the 300.000 acquisitions per year only 2-3000, that is less than 1%, are in digital form. It is obvious that if such a large proportion of large libraries is still in paper format concern for this type of material does not reflect a quaint preference for an old fashioned and outdated medium.

2. The ECPA

An organization which is concerned with the preservation and acccess of our collective memory in all its forms is the European Commission on Preservation and Access, and it is a privilege for me as its chairman to present to the conference the aims and objectives and some of the past and future activites of this commission. The ECPA was established in 1994 by a group of librarians, archivists and scholars out of concern for the fate of millions of books and documents threatened by acidification and embrittlement in Europe. It has been clear right from the start that activities aimed at saving the printed and written heritage will have to take place in the context of general policies for preservation and access.

The ECPA was modelled after its elder sister, the American CPA, which has been successfully active for some fifteen years in raising public awareness of preservation issues and getting the problem on the agenda of politicians and decision-makers. The ECPA intends to be a European platform for similar activities, bringing together information and stimulating discussion and exchange of experience of all those involved in preservation our intellectual and cultural heritage. Its aim is to foster, develop and support in Europe collaboration among libraries, archives and allied organizations, in order to ensure the preservation of the published and documentary record in all formats and to provide enhanced access to the cultural and intellectual heritage'

The fourteen members of the Commission represent academies and learned societies, universities, libraries, archives and the world of publishing. The members and their institutions have committed themselves to promote this unique European initiative, and will actively support ECPA projects, acting as intermediate between European and national or regional level. The Secretariat is housed in the Royal Netherlands Academy of Arts and Sciences since May 1995. The ECPA works in close collaboration with other related institutions in this field, including UNESCO, EU (DG X and XIII), the U.S. CPA, IFLA, ICA, LIBER, the Open Society, and others.

As far as ECPS's achievements are concerned the following brief overview can be given:

(1) Communication.
Early in 1996 the ECPA created a website (the European Center for Preservation Activities, EPIC), offering information on preservation activities in Europe. The site contains addresses, news items, information on conferences, workshops and publications, links to other relevant sites and current contents of books, journals and newsletters. The site also contains a discussion list for preservation professionals. The list serves an important function as a news bulletin, and has over 200 subscribers in some 40 countries.
Sponsored by DG X (Raphael Programme) EPIC now includes a Preservation Map of Europe", bringing together basic information on preservation activities in (at present 24) European countries (http://www.knaw.nl/ecpa/ecpatex/map). A fully searchable database was developed that can be consulted over the Internet. A printed directory is available as well.
Again funded by DG X a virtual exhibition on damage to library and archive materials was developed. The presentation aimes at the non-specialist. The project was publicized among libraries, archives and scholarly associations, who are encouraged to create links, and to use the material as a basis to offer their own information (http:/www.knaw.nl/ecpa/expo.htm). Cooperation is sought with institutions that can contribute additional chapters, for instance on photographs and modern information carriers.

(2) Conferences and workshops.

In 1996 the ECPA organized in a conference in Leipzig, together with die Deutsche Bibliothek on the theme Choosing to preserve'. About 160 participants from 30 European countries gathered for three days to discuss preservation policies and activities.

Furthermore, a number of training workshops were held at the Marburger Archivschule, in cooperation with LIBER and ICA: in 1996 a workshop on training needs, in 1997 a summer school on preservation management, to be followed by similar workshops in London and Budapest.

One of the outcomes of the workshops was that there was a clear need for preservation management guidelines. Staff of the Information Science department at the University of Loughborough were contracted to write such guidelines.

(3) Publications.

Part of ECPA's responsibility is to publish on preservation and to optimally desseminate such publications. Since 1997 ECPA and the U.S. CPA agreed to combine their publication programmes, and to act as co-publishers or distributors of each other's reports. ECPA also agreed with UNESCO to act as a distributing agent for a selection of their RAMP (Records and Archives Management Programme) studies. The publications of ECPA include a report on training for preservation (ECPA, 1997), a book on the Leipzig Conference Choosing to preserve' (De Lusenet, 1997), a translation of a German research report on digitization as a method for preservation' (Weber, 1997), a publication on dangers threatening scientific collections in archives and libraries (Beentjes et al. 1997), and a study on digitization of historical pictural collections for the Internet (Ostrow, 1998). Earlier ECPA had published a report on mass-deacidification (Porck, 1996), a report on preservation in Russia (Kislovskaya, 1996) and the report on the European Register of Microform Masters (EROMM).

The ECPA further regards it essential that basic information on preservation is translated into national languages, in order to raise awareness and to enable training at national levels. In this connection various articles and reports have been translated into a number of Eastern European languages.

Many of these activities are intended to support the efforts of professionals in the field to find solutions for the massive problem of preservation of paper collections. But it is just as essential to involve those who benefit most from optimal access to the preserved material, the scientists and the scholars, into the debate. This is the group which ECPA tries to reach in the years to come, and the above mentioned exhibition is one example of these efforts. Their recommendations about priorities for preservation and the format in which the information should be preserved are indispensible. Of course, the decisions about such matters lie with the keepers, but there is no doubt that the judgements and ideas of the users can help them reach the best decision in every case.

The name of the Commission as well as the title of this presentation deliberately unifies the two concepts preservation and acces. They are two sides of the same coin. Preservation is only important if the preserved material can be used, and, therefore, will remain accessible. Without access and use preservation of books and papers is pointless. At the same time, continued use of these materials also contributes to its ruination. Accessibility, therefore, requires a permanent effort for its preservation.

3. Endangered paper

We just spoke of documentary record in all formats'. This implies that the questions the Commission tries to raise relate to the preservation of all information, whether this is printed on paper, stored on microfilm, or in digital form. However, the ECPA was established primarily out of concern for paper materials, and the focus in ECPA's work has been on the large amount of relatively recent (primarily the previous and present century) records which are threatened by acidification and embrittlement. And the figures are stunning: In the US the estimate of books endangered by embrittlement is somewhere between 70 and 80 million volumes. Similarly, for the research libraries in former Western Germany an estimate of 40 million volumes has been made, some 18 million of which are too brittle to be saved through mass conservation techniques, while over 20% (or 600 kilometers) of archive material badly needs treatment. Some 60 kilometer of documents in the Dutch State archives needs to be treated by de-acidification or substitution. Comparable or even worse numbers can no doubt be found for other countries. Moreover, it is hardly a comfort if these figures do not exist in certain countries; it simply means that they have not been recorded systematically. Reports at a meeting of the IBM Foundation in Rome in 1993 (Eclipse of the Memory"), and the IFLA Conference in Barcelona that same year were similarly pessimistic. It is clear that libraries and archives around the world are facing one of the great epidemics of modern times: a massive loss of written and printed carriers of our collective memory, which we need to understand the past and to make decisions about the future. And there are certainly not enough time and resources to save all the materials that are at risk.

For the responsible keepers", the librarians and archivists, these figures are all too well known. They constantly witness the ravages of time in their collections. But unfortunately the users - the scientists and scholars - often underestimate the scope and the urgency of the need for preservation work. In hearing about paper preservation" they think primarily in terms of mediaeval manuscripts, precious editions and old documents. They do not realize that the danger of getting lost concerns a substantial part of the comparatively recent written record. Even scholars and scientists who depend on fairly recent material for their research are not sufficiently aware that a large part of this is now crumbling away. Certainly outsiders find it difficult to conceive the scale of the problem.

4. Options

In trying to cope with the difficulties described above libraries and archives have a number of options, including the following:

a. Keep the material, refrain from taking measures to preserve it and let the decay take its course. For a number of books and papers this unfortunately will be the only option, given the costs of saving everything which is endangered. The pace of the decaying process can be slackened at most by careful handling, proper control of climate conditions etc.

b. De-acidification of the papers and books. At best, however, this measure only serves to stop further deterioration, but it does not return the pages into their original status. And for much of the endangered material for which the brittling process has progressed to far mass de-acidification would no longer be of any avail. For other papers and books, however, it may be a helpful measure. Anyway, new books and journals could be printed as much as possible on de-acidified paper, and the promotion and encouragement of the use of acid-free paper is an important objective. In a survey among European publishers some years ago very little enthusiasm or sometimes even ignorance was found with respect to the possibilities and standards of permanent paper.

c. Restoration of the materials. This includes all efforts to restore damaged books and papers to the initial and predetermined state. It will be clear that the procedures involved are often costly in terms of time and personnel and financial resources. Obviously this option will not be useful for the majority of written materials, and can be applied only in rare and special cases.

d. Paper splitting. This is a technically advanced procedure of splitting the pages into two separate sheets, which are prepared with a plastic layer and then pasted together again. In a number of places this procedure is commercially practiced and larger quantities of books and journals han be handled this way, but the costs are still substantial: between 3 and 10 US$ per book.

e. Transference of information. For millions of books and papers that are beyond the stage of physical restoration (that is, if they fall apart at the touch) and still contain information which deserves to be saved, there is only one solution left : transference to another medium. Basically there are two options. filming and digitization.

Filming, and particular microfilming is a very popular option and is used in almost every country. The weaknesses and strengths of microfilming are known, and there are well established microfilming standards. Since many large scale microfilming projects have been initiated, the need for coordination and the formation of a bibliographic database became apparent. Stimulated by the International Program' of the Commission on Preservation and Access in the US such a database has been formed. The European Register of Microform Masters (EROMM) serves as an important source of information for those working on microfilming in Europe.

Let us now turn to the second transference option, digital storage.

5. Digitization 'the' solution?

Not only is there a poor understanding of the nature and scope of the problem just described, particularly among the users', but it is also striking that once it is described and made clear those concerned display an unrealistic optimism about the way it could be solved. In the digital age a high-tech solution should be within easy reach, as is often thought and said. All university libraries and national archives have to do is to scan all their material, digitize it and put it on a computer disc; an obvious option for the present generation of Internet scholars. Why bother with clumsy micro-films or expensive restoration?

However, the enthousiastic high tech adherent overlooks a couple of things.

First of all, he often has an overoptimitic view on the longevity of digital material. In spite of the sophistication of the present day electronic communication and storage systems and their world wide and immediate access we will be lucky if digital information can be read 20 years after its storage. Even if the carrier of the information can be kept in good condition for half a century or more there remains the problem that equipment and software get outdated much more rapidly. The need for preservation and access strategies with respect to the electronic information is certainly not less pressing than with information stored on paper.

Secondly, there is the cost factor: the costs of digitization at present would be several times higher than micro-filming, and this certainly will increase with the required conversion and transmission of the electronic data in the future.

Thirdly, even the most fanatic computer devotee cannot deny nor neglect the problems of inaccessibility and incompatibility of the various systems in use. Unsolvable difficulties in the exchange of data and files can and do bring despair to many a scholar, archivist or librarian who had hopefully turned to electronic record keeping.

So, in spite of the exciting possibilities of the new media and the fundamental changes in the process of publishing and record keeping which they bring about, as long as we do not have standards for storage and transmission, and as long as digitized information has to be converted every so many years to remain accessible, we are far from preserving the threatened information for eternity if transformed in digitized format. At the moment it is merely incorrect to regard digitization as a simple way to store documents safely once and for all.

6. Digital libraries

This brings us to the topic of this conference digital libraries', consisting of digital books and journals. Can and should they replace the classical libraries? And if so. under what conditions?

A working group of the Academia Europaea recently organized two conferences, in Stockholm and Darmstadt, on the impact of eletronic publishing and communication on the Academic Community, during which this question was given extensive attention (Butterworth, 1998).

First, with respect to electronic journals, it was acknowledged that traditional publishing suffers from a number of impediments and inconveniences, including the time lag, unwieldy procedures, ever increasing expenses, and the consequences of paper decay. Some hold the optimistic view that through the use of e-mail and the publication of preprints on the Internet (Paul Ginsparg, 1998) or purely electronic journals (e.g. Steve Harnad's Psycholoquy, Harnad & Hemus, 1998) most of these obstacles can be avoided.

Others are not so sure. First of all, most of the time and effort is caused by the review and refereeing system, and most scientists want to keep this. They want to be able to trust the quality and relevance of what is offered in the journals. They do not want to receive ripe and green' and to have to make own judgements, neither do they consider the adjudgement of quality to be a democratic process which can be decided through general internet disputes.

Secondly, it is not certain that electronic journals will be less expensive in the long run, if one takes into account that here it is the scholars and scientists in stead of the professional publishers who have to do the administrative work, and that the refereeing system will not be abolished. Also the day may not be far away that one has to pay for the derivation of information: some form of pay per view.

In the third place, there still are quite some practical and procedural difficulties which have to be solved in order for this medium to be a worthy replacement of (part of) the classical journals. Most of these have to do with lack of compatibility, lack of standardization and lack of access and availability.

In other words, electronic journals offer innovative and challenging opportunities, including new search facilities, better service facilities, increased rapidity of publication, opportunities for addition, commenting and deletion according to one's own wishes, etc., but it questionable at this moment whether the academic world, as far as the scholarly journals are concerned, should put all its eggs in the one electronic basket.

A similar type of reasoning is applicable on the question of the raison d'etre' of electronic viz ů viz classical libraries. Again, we speak of revolutionary and innovative opportunities, but probably even of survival. Libraries will survive as a useful and used asset only if fully integrated into the information society; otherwise they will be progressively marginalized and be replaced by commercial services, more attractive but less profound and solid", as the former Director General of DG XII, Paolo Fasella, stated (see Drenth, 1998, p.151). He further suggested to extend the idea developed under the 3d and 4th Framework Programme of the EC, namely the creation of a European virtual digitized library, based on mutual access to national libraries through a telematic network.

On the other hand, also with respect to electronic libraries there are many unanswered questions and unsolved problems. At the same Academia Europaea conference in Stockholm Meadows presented an analysis of the essential requirements of a library, and raised the question how many of these can be fulfilled by an electronic library (Meadows, 1998): People come to the library for help, publications should be placed in careful order in order for the customer to find wat he or she is looking for, publications should be well looked after so that they remain available for future users, the users obey the copy right regulations, users hope to find information from very long ago, which requires long time saving. He concludes that it is not so easy for electronic libraries to meet these requirements.

In addition, problems of costs and payment arise, although difficult to predict as yet. These costs certainly will increase if larger commercial companies move in, expecting return upon their investments.

There is a further difficulty, which is also mentioned by Meadows, and that is the almost inherent paradox of electronic information that needs to be kept up to date as well as to be retrieved regularly. The updating and constant improvement of the technical qualities of the information require continuous amendment and improvement of both the hardware and the software. And that is exactly the weakness of the system, since the user cannot keep up and will be annoyed with these changes.

Some of the problems pertaining to electronic journals apply in the case of electronic libraries as well. Availability, compatibility and access are often problematic. Standardization is still far away. The definition of what is a publication is not always easy: first pre-print? which version? what about later versions? Legal issues with respect to copy rights and other intellectual property rights are not easy to solve, and first publication disputes are likely to increase. An interesting social-political question is whether the electronic library system creates a further split between the haves' and the have-nots' (this applies also internationally, e.g. with respect to economically less developed versus more developed countries), or whether it just will decrease such contrasts, since the access to information will be easened and democratized.

In view of the present state of affairs it may be wise to join with Meadows in assuming that in the coming decades there will be a need for an hybrid library, a combination of both paper-based and electronic library. The question, therefore, will not be how and when the latter will take over, but rather how parallel services can be kept intact, and for which user needs either of the two models fits best.

I would like to express my appreciation to the secretary of ECPA, Yola de Lusenet, for her input and suggestions during the preparation of this paper.

References

1. G. Beentjes, M. Herweijer, Y. de Lusenet, K. Scheper en P. Witkamp, (1997), Weten geweten gewist. Bedreigde wetenschappelijke collecties in archieven en bibliotheken. Amsterdam: ECPA.

2. I. Butterworth (ed.)(1998), The impact of electronic publishing on the academic community. London/Miami: Portland Press.

3. P.J.D. Drenth (1998), Discussion session 5. In: I. Butterworth (ed.), The impact of electronic publishing on the academic community. London/Miami: Portland Press. Pp. 149-151.

4. P. Ginsparg (1998), Electronic research archives for physics. In: I. Butterworth (ed.), The impact of electronic publishing on the academy community. London/Miami: Portland Press. Pp. 32-43.

5. S. Harnad & M. Hemus, (1998), All or none: no stable hybrid or half-way solutions for launching the learned periodical literature into the post-Gutenberg galaxy. In: I. Butterworth (ed.), The impact of electronic publishing on the academic community. London/Miami: Portland Press. Pp. 18-27.

6. G. Kislovskaya (1996), Preservation challenges in a changing political climate; a report from Russia. Amsterdam: ECPA.

7. J. Meadows (1998), the development of digital libraries. In: I. Butterworth (ed.), The impact of electronic publishing on the academic community. London/Miami: Portland Press. Pp. 18-27.

8. Y. de Lusenet (ed.)(1997), Choosing to Preserve. Towards a cooperative strategy for long-term access to the intellectual heritage. Amsterdam: ECPA.

752

9. S.E. Ostrow (1998), Digitizing historical pictorial collections for the Internet. Amsterdam: ECPA.

10. H.J. Porck (1996), Mass acidification, an update of possibilities and limitations. Amsterdam: ECPA.

11. H. Weber & M. Dφrr (1997), Digitization as a method of preservation? Amsterdam: ECPA.

Access Versus Holdings: The Paradox of the Internet

Derek Law

King's College London

It is the purpose of this paper to argue that librarians have been blinded to its basic flaws by the gaudiness of the Internet and that we are confusing sources and resources. The Internet shows none of the features required for scholarly communication and whether or not we believe this will change, we should be developing models which offer electronic services as a viable and reliable resource.

Although the Internet is of some age in the dog years which pass for computing time, the World Wide Web is relatively new, with the first web browser dating only from 1994. In the four years after that it achieved a phenomenal acceptance, in what Paul Evan Peters called the largest mass migration in human history. It was adopted by fifty million users in fifty months. Radio took 38 years to gain such an audience and television some thirteen years. Currently it has some seventy million users. And yet it lacks the important elements of sustainability necessary for scholarship:
- Permanence
- Availability
- Accessibility

One of the unremarked triumphs of librarianship in the last forty years is that we have created a system which allows the researcher reliably and persistently to identify and retrieve any document published anywhere in the world. This has been a long term project which is a bedrock for scholarship. The Web, on the other hand, is in fact a four year old experiment, not a robust service. Not for nothing is it called the World Wide Wait. Not for nothing has a Dilbert cartoon appeared noting that all the time saved through automation and computers in the last fifty years has been entirely outweighed by people sitting in front of pc's waiting for web pages to load. A variety of issues reflect the very real difficulties of the Web for scholarship.

Identifiers and Naming.

The continuity of citation is central scholarship. In a print on paper world we take it for granted that a scholarly paper can cite Vesalius, Lister or Suzanne Bakker and that other scholars or libraries can trace and find these publications or data. That stability does not exist on the Internet where there is a basic need to reference objects as they move and change over time and place. Rather resignedly we simply not the impermanence of URLs. Nor is their any consistency over who may name objects since it appears that anyone can. This in turn removes one of our marks of quality. Authorship, ownership and impartiality are easily disguised. Worse, there is no expectation of who will maintain naming over time. It is our experience that libraries, even national libraries are as guilty as anyone else in having created a fluidity that sits uneasily with scholarship. Commercial publishers have created Digital Object Identifiers, but it is not at all clear that they are usable in the very substantial area of primary sources and grey literature.

Metadata.

This appears to be under better control by our profession as the Dublin Core now involves Europe, USA and the Pacific Rim. But there is still basic work to be done on how to describe new genres of multimedia and how to describe new services. What kind of record are we to create for a changing and dynamic resource. We also need to describe the terms and conditions of use and at present these vary between locations, between user groups and over time. For example, an electronic textbook may be licensed to be available only to first year anatomy students in the summer semester.

Authentication.

This is important for electronic commerce, but there are no good ways of proving membership of the data club when away from home. This is perhaps no more than irritating. More importantly once membership is established through some form of individual log-on, are we willing to give up the anonymity of the user? Most libraries consider it a matter of professional ethics not to reveal who has used what library material, unless a criminal offence has been committed. Some users, particularly those working with pharmaceutical companies, regard their library use as commercially sensitive. Are we really willing to cede this anonymity to gain access to electronic data?

Distributed Search and Indexing.

This remains a very big issue with a great deal still to be done technically. Web indexing systems are breaking down as their architecture collapses under the weight of data. A simple quite specific search will frequently produce over a million hits, listed in no discernible order. There were 320 million web pages on the Internet in May 1998, of which no more than 34% are searched by the best search engine – and there is no readily available way of discovering which 34%!

Rights Management Systems.

These are being designed largely at the behest of commercial organisations in ways which mirror the power and needs of the entertainment industry. And yet from the scholarly perspective there are at least three major areas of philosophic contention.

- Privacy. As mentioned above, the right to anonymity is both an academic requirement and has been an obligation from the library to its users. Not only is such privacy under threat, there is the further possibility that usage information could be sold on to third parties as marketing information.

- Preservation. Publishers have never had a responsibility to preserve their publications, yet we have no general legal deposit for electronic publications, even if we had a definition of what constitutes an electronic publication. As publishers typically lease rather than sell electronic data, such material must be considered at risk. In any case the technology for preserving electronic material is far from robust. Who is to preserve what remains a major, undecided issue.

- Fair Use. The concept of fair use for private study and research is an important one. Yet rights management systems which prevent general browsing take away that right. Commercial publishers feel it inappropriate to an electronic environment; scholars might beg to differ.

Network Topology.

In Europe, at least since the time of the first Bangemann Report this has been assumed to be a matter for the commercial marketplace. Yet scholarship, unlike commercial markets, is both global and goes into uneconomic areas. Problems arise at both extremes of need. On the one hand high technology scholarship demands very high bandwidth computing at the leading edge of technology. Yet the report on the (in academic terms) quite modest Ten-34 Project to link European Research Networks found that such links were not available commercially. At the other end of the spectrum, the commercial marketplace will not put adequate technology into non-commercial markets. That is to say that there are large parts of the world where networks and network services will lag impossibly if left to purely commercial motives.

Preservation and Archiving of Electronic Information.

This is commonly acknowledged to be one of the hardest of areas to resolve for all stakeholders, one fraught with technical, legal and operational problems. Some technical preservation centres have been running for over twenty-five years. They have produced no magic solutions and little comfort in proving that the technical problems are very difficult and very expensive to resolve. Some progress is being made on electronic legal deposit where useful dialogue has opened up with the publishers. But it must constantly be re-emphasised that much of the material we will wish to preserve is non-commercial. Nor is it self-evident who should conduct the preservation. The national libraries might manage the process but it seems safe to assume that issues of institutional continuity will be even more important than in the paper environment, where company take-overs and bankruptcies, incompetence, indifference and even malice have put many historic collections at risk over the years.

Instructional Media, Courseware and new media.

Libraries need to rethink their roles and mission in relation to electronic material. This applies both to external material and to internally produced material. In the case of external material librarians must consider not just purchasing licences to make titles available (or ignoring them while departments make the purchases). We would argue that they must consider the relative costs and merits of remote access, local mirroring, consortial purchasing and so on. And this must sensibly involve the total cost including network charges. Even for "free" sites such as pre-print archives it is important to establish whether the archive has a more appropriate European mirror site which turns it from a variably available source into a reliable resource, saving the organisation many hours of waiting for screens to load. In terms of access how far should library staff surf the web to catalogue and record useful sites or e-journals and start to provide information on what is available rather than what is possessed.

Internally the Library has to clarify its role in relation to electronic information. Is it the institutional provider and/or archive for all instructional material created locally? If so, how far does the remit extend? Does it include, for example, collaborative data analysis and its records or knowledge representation and its re-use? Even if the library is not meant to cover this type of activity does it or should it have a role in ensuring that standards are met by the organisation as a whole for issues ranging from standards used to intellectual property rights.

The new media require a major redefinition of the library's role. Even if the outcome is to leave the libraries role as it was, at least the organisation will have ensured that it has a series of policies and responsibilities in place for dealing with electronic material.

Scholarly Communication.

There is a real threat of what has been called cybercolonialism, the overt or covert preference for one set of resources over another. This is compounded by our own willingness to confuse sources and resources. As an example of this it is worth examining a language neutral discipline such as mathematics and comparing the treatment of major and very longstanding east European journals from universities such as Cracow or Warsaw. This will appear in European gateway sites but not North American ones. This problem is worsened by an increasingly common practice – often fostered by search engines – of preferring to use American websites. These may provide better or richer sources but if slow to the point of unavailability for much of the European day are in truth inadequate resources or services.

Two key issues are standards for version control and mirror sites. Originators of data, jealous of its quality are often unwilling to entrust it to third parties without prolonged negotiation. And yet mirror sites are a very economic method of improving network performance. An obvious solution is a set of standards or kite-marking to indicate the quality of potential mirror hosts. This would reassure not only the data supplier but also the data – user, who must at present also rest uncertain of the version of the document which is available.

It is also regrettable that the debate on electronic publishing has been so dominated by the STM commercial model. STM publishing while undeniably important represents only a fraction of the annual acquisitions of most universities. Even in scientific libraries significant quantities of non-commercial material or small learned society material are acquired and this may be expected to grow in an electronic arena. And yet it is not self-evident that systems and practices designed for electronic commerce sit comfortably with the needs of scholarly discourse. Yet at present very little thought is being given as to how we support the scholarly infrastructure of the small learned society or the science and medicine of developing countries.

There is a further category of material at risk, what Clifford Lynch of CNI has called endangered content. Computer Science, a discipline founded and maintained on a non-printed tradition has reached a point where its pioneers are retiring and dying. As a discipline it has only just begun to realise how much of its common heritage it may need and may already have lost. Great efforts are now being made to salvage this position. It illustrates perfectly that in an electronic environment new thought must be given to how we record and locate a discipline. We cannot wait for paper archives to arrive on the death of great men, nor are laboratory books now the only source of laboratory data. A complete reappraisal is needed of how primary research data and even the e-mail of scientists, of bulletin boards and discussion groups is to be maintained to show the traceable path on which science depends.

Network Topology.

As already remarked, the United States becomes a virtual country for most of Europe in the afternoon, as the bandwidth clogs and slows with traffic. It is claimed that costs are dropping and so we can simply buy more bandwidth. It is more likely that the UK experience is typical. For the UK academic community, the cost per bit of international traffic halves each year - but the traffic trebles, inexorably increasing the bill to a point where restraint has to be applied. It has been interesting to see the reaction to this in Australia where costs are passed on directly to universities. In 1998/9 Australian Vice-Chancellors have introduced scheme in which hits on non-Australian web-sites will be charged at twice the rate of local web-sites. This clearly recognises the distinction between sources and resources and aims to manage traffic in sensible ways. We may expect others to follow this model.

Although Australian universities have adopted a model for managing network topology it is not clear whether that model has any theoretical underpinning. We would then wish to suggest that the current model of unbridled access to the anarchy of the Internet is not the only or the best model for managing electronic resources. Intranets and/or regional networks are being created which form more appropriate boundaries for electronic resources. As the cost of filestore drops very quickly it can often be shown to be economic – not least of time – to mirror resources on the local network. Further, the ease of access to electronic resources allows us to revisit the issue of access versus holdings strategies – where access has held sway for some time as a professional dogma – and argue that holdings strategies may again be appropriate in an electronic environment. When managing information, what organisations have never done is line all employees or students up (at least metaphorically) at the start of the financial year, give them one thousand guilders and told them to acquire anything they liked that might help with their work. Instead they have identified the material relevant to the work of the organisation, collected as much of it as they could in one place, employed professional information specialists to manage it and make it available, and arranged controlled access to the information which cannot be held locally for those who can show they require it. This does not prevent individuals using other channels from public libraries to bookshops for any other information they choose. We would then argue that this model of the library provides a perfect paradigm for the management of networked resources.

LIBRARY CORE ACTIVITY	INTRANET CORE ACTIVITY
Acquisition	Resource Discovery
Collection Building	Local Fileservers and Mirrors
Classification	Knowledge Management
Preservation	Long-term Data Sinks
Inter-Lending and Document Supply	Controlled Internet Access
User Instruction	User Instruction

We would contend that there has been an all too ready acceptance of the Internet. Its undoubtedly huge impact on the availability of current information has dazzled us to its flaws as a medium for scholarly communication. It is important to revisit the information needs of our organisations and of scholarship and to re-interpret them in the light of the possibilities and limitations of networks. The model proposed above then describes how in a local context we can take control of the environment and use it positively, acting collectively to meet institutional need.

The Human Factors in Digital Library Development

Professor Andrew McDonald

Director of Information Services
University of Sunderland
Chester Road Library
Chester Road
Sunderland SR1 3SD
United Kingdom
andrew.mcdonald@sunderland.ac.uk

Abstract.
In developing successful digital libraries there are considerable human resource challenges for our institutions, library management and library staff. There is growing evidence from a number of research projects and from the experience of library managers that the management culture and attitudes required for digital libraries are quite different than those appropriate for print-based libraries. The critical human, cultural and organisational factors needed to create the environment in which digital delivery can be effective and sustained are explored. These include the cultural and organisational shifts in parent institutions; new service culture and values in the library; changes in organisational structure and management style in the library; and the effect of the digital library on service staff. Digital libraries need digital librarians who possess particular skills, knowledge and experience and these may be very different from those required of the "analogue" librarian. Regrettably, the importance of human factors in digital library development is often underestimated in relation to the technological and information challenges involved.

Key words: Human factors, digital libraries, digital librarians, library management, organisational culture, service culture and values, library staff

Introduction

We have considerable experience of electronic information within Information Services at the University of Sunderland. We provide one of the largest and most heavily-used electronic information networks in the sector with something like 155 databases and 3,500 electronic journals available on campus. We have just launched the UK's first City-wide networked electronic information service with 1,500 full-text journals made available in the University, City College and the public library, and potentially all around our Learning City of Sunderland. We have also created digital databases of examination papers, module guides and reading lists (that is when we can get them out of the academic community!), and we have plans to create more digital content of local history and archival material.

We are particularly interested in the human factors necessary for effective and sustainable digital library development and we are engaged in a couple of relevant research projects funded by the EU and The British Library Research and Innovation Centre.

A few interesting points emerge from this experience. Despite all the research and all that has been written, it has to be said that we are very much at the *start of the electronic adventure*. There are *no established rules* for the development of the digital library and we must admit, at least to ourselves, that are all really *making it up as we go along* [1]. Indeed, some even argue that the digital library does not exist, but it seems clear to me that I am managing a hybrid library service which has both "analogue" and digital components and that this mixed economy is likely to persist for the foreseeable future.

Human Factors in Digital Library Development

Many people in the library world believe that electronic and digital library developments can be grafted onto print-oriented libraries, and that the management culture developed to deliver print-based library services is equally appropriate to the digital library. However, there is growing evidence that different attitudes and a different management culture are required to facilitate successful digital library developments.

I should like to pose a number of questions. What makes a digital librarian (or cybrarian or even cyberpunk librarian as they are less flatteringly referred to); what are the skills and attributes required of the digital librarian; what is the management culture needed for effective digital library development; and in what way is the digital culture different from the print-based environment? This is largely based on our British Library Research and Innovation Centre project in which we are investigating the key human and cultural factors within the institution, amongst library managers and library staff. There are clearly other important stakeholders too, not least the users of our services and the suppliers of information, but these are not the primary focus of our current research.

It is perhaps inevitable that all the other factors involved in digital library development receive much greater attention than the human factors, and many of these will be discussed during this conference. They include communications and information technology; money; legal obstacles; digital content creation; bibliographic control; quality control; and continuity of access and preservation. There is also the whole question of information landscapes and gateways, and enough acronyms to keep the most enthusiastic librarian happy!

Digital Librarians and Institutions

Digital libraries need digital librarians. As Hastings and Tennant observed in their excellent article "it is more important that digital librarians possess particular personal qualities (which are innate) rather than specific technical expertise (which can be learned) [1]. They suggest that the digital librarian requires certain distinctive personal qualities and present a challenging list which could form the basis of the job description of the future:

"Digital librarians must thrive on change. They should read constantly (but selectively) and experiment endlessly. They need to love learning, be able to self-teach, and be inclined to take risks. And they must have a keen sense of both the potentials and pitfalls of technology.

Any individual with those qualities (or some measure of them) is an excellent candidate to forge new methods for accomplishing the age-old mission of libraries to select, acquire, organise, provide access to, and preserve the intellectual and artistic record of humanity. We are after all making it up as we go along. We need professionals who don't need a lot of guidance or hand-holding. We need individuals with imagination and foresight and the ability to make their vision a reality."

Turning to our organisations, Davis, Scammell and Hall remind us that the digital environment is very different from the print-oriented culture [2]:

"it has always been recognised that some shifts in culture, both for libraries and other stakeholders in information, were crucial if electronic libraries were to make a real difference".

Project Aims and Methodology

The objectives of our research project into effective digital library development are:

to survey the experience and perceptions of library managers and staff
to identify the key human resource factors involved, and
to define the critical success factors and constraints.

This is intended to assist in the planning and development of digital libraries and to "empower" managers to achieve the necessary culture shift. It will also inform the training and education of library and information professionals.

The partners, in what we see very much as a cross-sectoral issue, are Education *for* Change Ltd. (consulting, research, project management in education, libraries, information systems and information management), Gateshead MBC Public Libraries and Arts Service and Information Services at the University of Sunderland. Although primarily focused on libraries in the UK, we have looked at good practice in Europe and the States, and we are well aware that there is much to learn from digital private sector companies too.

Following a consultative exercise, a questionnaire survey and an extensive literature review, we have organised successful practitioner workshops in which library managers from all sectors have exchanged experience about the key human factors involved in their digital library projects. As a result, we will report on successful models, teasing out the important human resource factors for the institution, the service culture, library management and library staff.

Although our project is only six months old, a number of interesting themes have already emerged.

The Parent Institution

The role of our parent institution is a particularly interesting one. Some suggest that success can only be achieved with the full support and strategic commitment of the institution, whilst others believe that change happens almost despite the parent organisation. It seems that change can effectively be driven top-down or bottom-up, but it seems that a number of library managers have found themselves in the latter position more often than the former!

Some institutions have the benefit from an Information Strategy but many of these strategies focus erroneously on technology and communications issues and very few explicitly address the crucial human factors which underpin effective strategic development.

A number of influential factors have been raised. These include managerial vision and leadership; management style and the way in which decisions are made and communicated; the structure of the organisation and the extent to which different parts of the organisation work together, particularly the integration of personnel management with strategic planning; and, of course, the overall level of resourcing.

It is clear that an effective digital organisation is very different from an analogue one. Whilst some institutions, particularly in the private sector, have adapted quickly to this new challenge, others have struggled to "learn" how to become a successful organisation in the digital age. Ironically, it is suggested that universities are amongst the slowest learning organisations!

Service Culture and Values

The digital library has a different "culture" from the traditional library service. One can only speculate as to whether the "cultural shift" involved is a prerequisite of digital library development or whether there is a "cultural lag" and change follows as a result of the introduction of digital services. Numbers of managers have commented that the latter is the case in libraries!

Ferguson & Bunge suggest that digital librarians should develop new service values in addition to our "timeless" values of equity of access, personal service and meeting user needs [3]. In the digital age, they say that the emphasis should be upon integrating technologies and maintaining holistic computer environments; on making technology work for all; on delivering core services through networks; and on collaborating across administrative lines. They seem to be stressing the importance of delivering electronic information to all those who require it by exploiting communications and information technology and by breaking down unhelpful departmental barriers.

Library Staff

As one might expect, much has emerged from our investigation into the key factors affecting library staff. We are just as interested in the ways in which library managers can actively facilitate the development of the digital library, both in terms of organisational structures and management style, as in the effect of the digital library on service staff. This goes well beyond the predictable need for additional staff training and development although it has become clear that training groups of staff together for change, team working and skills development is a very useful approach.

Different staff attitudes, skills, abilities and motivation are all seen as crucial, and this challenges traditional ways of selecting staff and the type of qualifications and experience required. New forms of structure, organisation and operation are needed and staff often assume greater responsibility and more flexible working arrangements. In one way, the digital library is more centralised in its operation but in another it can be more decentralised in the delivery of services. There are questions for managers in the way in which they lead change and innovation since both of these have a profound effect on staff.

The IMPEL project has revealed the considerable social and organisational impact of electronic libraries on the staff who work in them [4]. These include changes in workload; concerns about effectiveness in work, job satisfaction; job security; the importance of technical expertise and confidence with IT; and certain feelings of isolation from both colleagues and users.

We have not concentrated on the other stakeholders involved. However, we have become aware that whilst our users have become empowered to access all sorts of electronic information easily, some remain dubious and even frightened of the electronic age and many retain their strong "emotional" ties to print on paper.

Job Specification for the Digital Librarian

It seems that the skills, knowledge and experience required to be a digital librarian are very different from those required of the "analogue" librarian. Indeed, one can speculate about the person specification for the post of a digital librarian which might read something like this:

We require a professional who has the skills and experience to turn our vision for a digital library into a reality. You should be imaginative and thrive on taking risks and change; you must be independent and flexible; you will read constantly and experiment endlessly; and you should love learning and be self-teaching. You will have an understanding of the potentials and pitfalls of communications and information technology to achieve the digital library. Above all you must have an understanding of the human factors involved.

In our experience at Sunderland, it has become very difficult to recruit staff to communication and information technology posts who have the necessary mix of information, networking and people skills. This is certainly true in relation to the salaries we are able to pay in libraries! It is interesting to note that successful digital librarians have often been self-starters who have picked up the relevant skills and training as they have gone along rather than through any formal qualifications in communications and information technology. We also badly need professionals who can think across the traditional sectors of library provision and I am reassured that some library schools are encouraging this approach.

On the other hand, it is probably true to say that many of the qualities are just as relevant to digital as analogue library managers and, since most of us continue to manage hybrid libraries, they are really the generic skills required be effective managers in today's library and information services.

Our Digital Future

Even after a few months of our research project, we have discovered a whole range of human factors which are important in creating the environment in which digital delivery can be effective and sustained. There are considerable human resource challenges for our institutions, library management and our staff.

However, in contemplating our digital future, we must be careful not to be too prescriptive. Many librarians have told us their electronic libraries work well but they don't really know why! We must avoid simply responding to the short-lived difficulties of today's technological challenges. Technology is changing fast and we know, for example, that the digital library of tomorrow will be more interactive than that of today. We should not discard our traditional skills since it is likely that we shall need the skills of both analogue *and* digital librarians for many years to come.

Libraries continue to be a network of social places which are trusted and accessible to individuals of all ages and to communities throughout the country. We provide access to a rich and diverse range of materials and information, including digital sources, and we also provide serviced equipment and supportive staff. Libraries are one place where the information have-nots in society can access electronic sources. Librarians are crucial for supporting learning and assisting people in accessing information, and we are developing new roles in the digital age as advisers and navigators through the maze of information available electronically.

Electronic information is a great leveller and users can increasingly retrieve the information they require from home and new "places" as well as traditional libraries. Libraries could lose their "monopoly" of information provision in their particular organisations and they run the risk of becoming displaced by other service providers. Digital TV, cable and satellite channels, the BBC and Microsoft will all become increasingly important in the delivery of electronic information and learning materials to users when and where they require it.

However, our research project has identified the critical human factors involved in developing successful digital libraries, both in the academic and public sector. An understanding of these human, cultural and organisational factors, together the necessary technology and funding, will assist library managers in grasping the nettle and developing effective, high-quality digital information services. In this way libraries, and the digital librarians who manage them, can retain their justifiable position at centre stage in the Information Society.

References

1. Hastings, K and Tennant, R. How to build a digital librarian. Digital Library Research & Development. University of California, D-Lib Magazine, November 1996
2. Davis, C, Scammell, A and Hall, M. eLib: Changing the lightbulb - er , the Culture. Ariadne July, 1997 (http://www.ariadne.ac.uk/issue10/cultural)
3. Ferguson, CD & Bunge, CA. The shape of services to come: values-based versus reference service for the largely digital library. College & Research Libraries, 58 (3) May 1997, pp 252-65
4. Edwards, C Walton, G & Day, JM Impel project: the impact on people of electronic libraries. Aslib Proceedings 47(9) September 1995 pp 203-208
5. Batt, C. Cutting edge. Public Library Journal 9(4) Jul/Aug 1994, pp 7-10
6. Breaks, M. Wake up! Professional development. Proceedings of the UK Office for Library Networking Conference, April 2-5, 1992. Edited by J.W.T. Smith. London: Meckler, 1993 pp 144-150
7. Busch, NJ. Leadership and change: an interview with Amy Owen. Library Administration and Management 9(2) Spring 1995, pp 73-76
8. Corrall, S. Academic libraries in the information society. New Library World 96(1120) 1995, pp 35-42
9. Davis, C. Organizational influences on the university electronic library. Information Processing and Management 33(3) 1997, pp 377-392
10. Day, J M, Walton, G and Edwards. The culture of convergence. International Journal of Electronic Library Research 1(1) March 1997
11. Dougherty, RM & Dougherty, A. The academic library: a time of crisis change and opportunity. Journal of Academic Librarianship 18 (6) January 1993, pp 342-357
12. Forster, J. Netskills: training users of the electronic library. Library Technology News (20) Nov/Dec 1995, pp 1-4
13. Gallimore, A. A public library IT strategy for the millennium. Journal of Librarianship and Information Science 28(3) September 1996, pp 149-157
14. Garrod, P. Skills for the new professional. Library Technology 1(5) November 1996, pp 99-100
15. Human resource management and the digital library. International Journal of Electronic Library Research 1(1), March 1997
16. Klemperer, K. & Chapman, S. Digital libraries: a selected resource guide. Information Technology and Libraries 16(3) 1997, pp 126-131
17. Long, LM. Academic reference librarians: under the microscope. Reference Librarian (54) 1996 pp 21-17
18. Matson, LD & Bronski DJ. Do digital libraries need librarians. Online 21(6) November 1, 1997, pp 87
19. Probst, LK. Libraries in an environment of change: changing roles, responsibilities, and perception in the information age. Journal of Library Administration 22 (2/3) 1996, pp 7-20

20. Rice-Lively, ML & Racine, JD. The role of academic librarians in the era of information technology. Journals of Librarianship 23(1) January 1997, pp 31-41
21. Sandlian, P. Visioning the future of the digital library. Library Trends 45(4) 1997, pp 582-584
22. St. Clair, G. The digital librarian. Journal of Academic Librarianship 23(2) March 1997, pp 79
23. Steel, C. Virtual professions and digital libraries: the lessons of 1996. Information Management Report, January 1997, pp 1-8
24. Tennant, R. Digital libraries. Library Journal 123(3) February 15, 1998, pp 102
25. The librarian and the library user: what the future holds. Electronic Library 15(1), February 1997, pp 15-22
26. Travica, B. Organizational aspects of the virtual/digital library: a survey of academic libraries. Proceedings of the ASIS Annual Meeting 34 1997 pp 149-161
27. Walter, VA. Becoming digital: policy implications for youth library services. Library Trends 45(4) 1997, pp 585-601
28. Walton, G, Edwards, C & Day, J. Training needs for staff competencies in a quality library service: relevance of the IMPEL project. European Research Libraries Cooperation 5(4) 1995, pp 389-400
29. Wilson, J. Enter the cyberpunk librarian: future directions in cyberspace. Library Review 44(8) 1995, pp 63-72

Digital Information Management Within Modern Library Systems, Consortia and e-journals

Friedrich W. Froben

speaker of the Friedrich-Althoff-Konsortium of scientific libraries in Berlin/Brandenburg

Dept. Physics, Free University Berlin, Germany

Arnimallee 14, 14195 Berlin

froben@physik.fu-berlin.de

1.   Introduction - from paper to online

In our modern world of fast changing technology, let us look back for a minute and remember the beginning of communication. Not so long ago, only language was available for interaction and only memory for storage. Few years ago - relatively speaking - the print culture started, first on stone and later on papyrus, that was around 1900 years ago, it was possible to write, to read, to store and to register. Most likely, this helped to promote and spread our culture, literature, philosophy, medical and natural science, but also technical and human mistakes.

Today, one of the interesting questions is, whether the digital information, the new superhighway of fast data transfer will help to develop new values of our society, restore some of the old values, or if the new information will only be used to promote injustice. As long as libraries existed, remember the Alexandra library in old Egypt, they are always centres of information, of study, storage and innovation. Now their role is changing to using modern technology, to the distribution of knowledge via digital data networks and we will discuss some of this new role and its advantages and disadvantages (1-4).

2.   Consortia - goals, advantages and disadvantages

Consortium is one of this modern words, there are consortia for constructions, for banking, of airlines... and for libraries - a larger unit of libraries to coordinate acquisition and to cooperate in many aspects. In this context, the consortium is thought to cooperate for joint access to online material, mainly e-journals. It is thought as a framework for the scientific libraries and allows individual members to participate in contracts with publishers or agents.

The idea of the consortium in respect to online journals is: If at least one member is a subscriber of a journal, then all participating libraries have full access to the electronic versions of this journal. The only problem is the license fee and license principles have to be developed. If the fee is affordable then it is an advantage, the disadvantage is that the libraries pay for access only, they do not get something heavy to put on the shelf and store. The new role of libraries is sometimes difficult to understand for an old fashioned bookworm - and enough problems remain unsolved, like storage of electronic material for centuries, interlibrary loan, technical problems of speed, easy access and different formats for different publishers to mention a few.

3. The budget dilemma and the price spiral

One of the reasons for library consortia is of cause the financial situation. The budget of most libraries went up for many years in accord to the growing book and journal market. 50 years ago, 40% of the budget went into books, only 40% into journals and the rest was used for binding, infrastructure etc. With increasing publication volume, mostly in the journal market both in number of journals and in pages, the budget percentage for journals increased in expense of books. Today, with appr. 5% of the journals online, this fast increasing number and the possible, easy access via the Internet, could help to relieve the situation.

The price increase during the last 20 years was not linear but indeed can be considered as a price spiral. To illustrate this in an example, the table gives a spotlight of the development, typical for STM journals from 5 different publishers. As you see prices and pages are coupled, but differently (5,6).

Journal/Pub.		pages	price	price/page
Journal Chem. Phys.	1976	11.000	800,--	0.073
AIP	1986	14.700	2.000,--	0.136
	1996	21.730	4.500,--	0.207
	in 1998		6.400,--	
Appl. Physics	1976	1.000	480,--	0.48
Springer	1986	1.660	1.400,--	0.84
	1996	2.570	4.000,--	1.56
	in 1998		5.500,--	
Ann. of Physics	1976	4.050	1.020,--	0.252
Academic Press	1986	3.500	2.160,--	0.617
	1996	3.750	3.000,--	0.80
	in 1998		4.500,--	
Nature	1976	4.700	$ 40,--	0.008
	1986	4.700	125,--	0.026
	1996	3.500	235,--	0.067
	in 1998		270,--	
Surface Science	1976	4.880	1.450,--	0.30
Elsevier	1986	9.280	5.380,--	0.58
	1996	12.100	17.300,--	1.43
	in 1998		21.800,--	

Nowadays, many publishers double journal prices within ~5 years and sometimes they even consider price increases of more than 20% per year. This is something libraries can no longer afford, because their budget remained constant during the last years or went down. The dilemma is a decrease of information in the library and only mainstream information available. Therefore consortia, to assign research fields to specific members, and keep the sum of information at a high standard.

4.   License principles

To help discussions with publishers it is very important to formulate general principles and try to avoid some of the problems that endanger the electronic form of publication (7,8). These dangers include:

a. noncompability of technical standards
b. neglect of the user need for access to information independent of the provider
c. threatening of the right to copy and to interlibrary loan used in the printed   world
d. barriers for storage of digital material by the user
e. high charges for electronic access
f. connection of non cancellation clauses with online access

Accepted principles for license contracts include:
a. access to electronic material for all authorized users
b. licenses shall permit "fair use" for all noncommercial, educational, scientific purpose including viewing, downloading and printing
c. allow to make print, fax or e-mail copies for non commercial interlibrary lending
d. permanent access to information
e. access from different computing platforms and network environment in acceptable format and speed
f. cooperation to develop search engines and alerting functions independent of specific publishers
g. cooperation for uniform access without password or ID via Z39.50 and metadata and DOI usage.
h. low prices for online access only - without printed version, to reflect the much lower cost of the e-material production.

5.   The scientist - producer and user of information and the publisher

The scientists get money form universities and research funds for teaching and research. Their international reputation depends on talks at international conferences, publishing papers in peer review journals and individual contacts. Most of the results gotten by a group of graduate students, postdocs and senior researchers are send to a publisher , in many cases in electronic form, and free of charge. The manuscripts undergo the redactional procedure including refereeing and go to the printer or could

774

be put directly into the net. Each publisher is handling the manuscripts differently and supplies the articles in different electronic format if online versions exist. For each journal or at least for each publisher the access to the articles is different, for each a different license has to be negotiated, sometimes an individual ID and password, the format is different, the addons also. Sometimes references can be followed further, sometimes there is an alerting function, all these goodies are under development and the producer of the information - the scientist - has to pay through his library to get all the information back he needs for further publications.

Now, with the described price spiral the system is broad to the point, where it does not work anymore. Now, new models have to be developed to get better access to the information and to redistribute the costs.

6. The Friedrich Althoff Consortium of scientific libraries in Berlin/Brandenburg

The idea of the consortium was developed in 1996, with regular meetings of representitives from about 15 libraries, including the 6 Universities, libraries from the Helmholtz Association like the Hahn-Meitner-Institut, the Geo-Research Institute Potsdam, the Max-Delbróck-Centre, the Weierstrass Institut for Mathematics, the National-Material-Labs and some Instituts of the Max-Planck-Society. It is thought as a legal body to represent the members and to negotiate with publishers. Every member has the right to participate in contracts with publishers. Officially the consortium was founded end of 1997 and named after Friedrich Althoff, one of the most interesting Prussian civil servant at the turn of the century.

Friedrich Theodor Althoff, born 1862 in Dinslaken, died 1908 in Berlin, law student at Neuwied, Cologne and Bonn (9-11). Law professor at Strasbourg. Since 1871 at the ministry of Education in Berlin, he became head of the department for higher education in 1897. Under his leadership the University Berlin was enlarged from 38 to 81 Institutes. He was responsible for the appointment of famous scientists like Harnack, Planck, Nernst or Koch, for the development and enlargement of the medical school "Charitı", for the new botanical garden in Dahlem and the famous Dahlem project - an idea to establish a German Oxford in the outskirts of Berlin, with led to the foundation of the "Kaiser-Wilhelm Gesellschaft" now named Max-Planck-Gesellschaft".

In respect to libraries he founded the first library professorship 1886 in Gφttingen, started among others an uniform Catalogue-system 1892, founded a commission for incunable 1904 and established the interlibrary load system in Prussia. All the years he fought for more money for the libraries - and he got it. Without him libraries in Germany would not have been so important at the beginning of the century. His name is a obligation for the consortium today, because he also believed in the independence of research and teaching, independent of government, religion, political parties and commerce.

7. Contracts with publishers

One of the most difficult parts are contracts with publishers, because the publications are produced or distributed in very different form.
1. The scientist writing his paper or report puts the material on a server available free of charge to everyone.
2. Professional societies start to think about consortia contracts and in some cases the annual price increase might be affordable for the libraries.
3. The commercial publishers - and unfortunately they are the most important ones in this game - cause the most serious problems, because their price increase is too high.

Following the license principles there remain some different models for a solution.
1. Only table of content (TOCs) are available for the user, no printed journals, but article delivery on demand. Most of the scientist are not yet ready for this dramatic change and believe in their own paper journal.
2. For all members of a consortium, electronic access to all journals is possible and the consortium gets one print version for archiving. The problem of this possibility is in the base price for the consortia holdings.

The situation now and maybe also in 1999 is how to handle the problem in the fast changing world. We, the scientists, we the libraries, maybe also the publishers need an experimental transition phase and we need an agreement for a constant price level for electronic articles, or at least a maximum price increase of 5% per year. Also publishers should be able to learn that the situation might lead to a pitfall if no sensible agreement can be reached.

8. Future developments - towards e-journals?

At large the situation is somewhat frustrating. On one side the publisher, he is still convinced that he is doing the right thing publishing more material every year at an annual price increase of around 15%. On another side the scientist, he is convinced that he has to publish more and faster to keep up in the international ranking game and to get enough money to support his research. And let us not forget the libraries because they sit on the least comfortable chair, they have not enough money to buy all the material their users, the scientists, want and need for information and they have not enough money to satisfy the publishers either.

The only way out, seems to establish a new method of publication: an e-journal with a different business background. The question is, looking into journal publishing, how high is the cost for the journal without printing and without distribution, is it 80% or only 50% of the cost for the printed journal with online version. All other procedures of the journal production mechanism stay the same, and for sure it has to be highly prestigious and peer review. To use all the potential of electronic publishing every article can be published as soon as it is ready and indexed with metadata and classified by a persistent identification system, the digital object identifier, DOI (12).

A possible finance model could include page charges, pay per view and subscriptions. It is hoped that some of these new electronic journals will be born within the near future with and without prestiges publishers.

9.   Sum up and thanks

Future information within the digital library environment is only possible using online media and requires consortia solutions. For this purpose it is essential to establish a close cooperation between scientists as producer and user of information, libraries and publishers worldwide.

But online media alone are not enough to satisfy all information needs. To be able to pay for printed information too, online access has to be easy, fast and not expensive.

To guaranty this complex information, new financial models and new possibilities for realisation must be developed. These initiatives are one of the goals for digital information management.

My thanks to discussion partners from libraries, publishers and to the Global-Info" project for financial support.

10.   References

1.   Digital Libraries, N.R. Adam et al. eds. Lecture Notes in Computer Science 1082, Springer 1996
2.   C. Peters et al. eds.: Research and Advanced Technology for Digital Libraries, Lecture Notes in Computer Science 1324, Springer 1997
3.   D-lib magazine //www.dlib.org
4.   J.J. Branin and M. Case Notices of the AMS 45 (1998) p. 475-486
5.   H.H. Barschall Physics Today July 1988, p. 56-59
6.   Newsletter on serials pricing issues, M. Tuttle ed. //www.lib.unc.edu/prices
7.   Licensing Principles, Tilbury Univ. Library //cwis.kub.nl/~dbi/cwis/licprinc.htm
8.   International   Coalition   of   Library   Consortia //www.library.yale.edu/consortia/statement.html
9.   B. vom Brocke in: Bildungspolitik in Preussen zur Zeit des Kaiserreichs p. 9-118, Klett-Cotta, Stuttgart, 1980
10.   A. Sachse: Friedrich Althoff und sein Werk E.S. Mittler, Berlin, 1928
11.   R.L. Lischke, Friedrich Althoff Sigma, Berlin, 1990
12.   DOI: The Digital Object Identifier System //www.doi.org

METU-Emar: An Agent-Based Electronic Marketplace on the Web[*]

Asuman Dogac, Ilker Durusoy, Sena Arpinar, Esin Gokkoca, Nesime Tatbul, and Pinar Koksal

Software Research and Development Center
Dept. of Computer Eng.
Middle East Technical University
06531, Ankara, Turkey
asuman@srdc.metu.edu.tr

Abstract. In this paper, we describe a scenario for a distributed marketplace on the Web where resource discovery agents find out about resources that may want to join the marketplace and electronic commerce is realized through buying agents representing the customers and the selling agents representing the resources like electronic catalogs.

We propose a possible architecture which is based on the emerging technologies and standards. In this architecture, the resources expose their metadata using Resource Description Framework (RDF) to be accessed by the resource discovery agents and their content through Extensible Markup Language (XML) to be accessed by the selling agents by using Document Object Model (DOM). The marketplace contains Document Type Definitions (DTDs) and a dictionary of synonyms to be used by the buying agents to help the customer to specify the item s/he wishes to purchase. Distribution infrastructure is CORBA and Web on which the buying and selling agents find out about each other using Trading Object Services. The modifications necessary to the proposed architecture considering only the available technology are also discussed.

1 Introduction

Electronic commerce is a generic term that encompasses numerous information technologies and services used to implement business practices ranging from customer service to inter-corporation coordination. One of the most common instances of electronic commerce is the exchange of goods and services over the Internet. However, the electronic commerce services that are established so far are still far from being mature. There is no real integration of the available underlying technologies, and the provided services lack many important but also more challenging features.

[*] This work is partially being supported by Middle East Technical University, the Graduate School of Natural and Applied Sciences, Project Number: AFP-97-07.02.08 and by the Scientific and Technical Research Council of Turkey, Project Number: 197E038

One such feature is the automation of a marketplace on the Web through agents. For such a marketplace, there is a need for a facility which enables the semantic interoperability of resources on the Web so that buyers are able to reach the sellers that can meet their needs and vice versa. In this respect, the currently emerging standards like RDF and DTDs sound very promising. Furthermore, after the resources are discovered, the process of interaction between buyers and sellers (resources), that is commerce, should be automated. In other words, a virtual marketplace on the Web should be created which not only makes buyers and sellers meet but also helps the exchange of goods between them through negotiations. Intelligent software agent and workflow technologies are the means through which this automation can be achieved.

With these considerations in mind, we envision a scenario for an electronic marketplace on the Web. The distribution infrastructure of the marketplace is CORBA and Web. The marketplace, in addition to resource discovery agents, contains templates of buying and selling agents, pointers to the Document Type Definitions (DTDs), trader objects implemented through Trading Object Service and an intelligent dictionary of synonyms.

In this scenario, resource discovery agents working in the background discover resources. If a resource is willing to join the marketplace, the marketplace creates a selling agent workflow template for the resource and registers it with the trader. However if the resource already has a selling agent, that one is registered. If there are any related buying agents already in the marketplace when the selling agent is registered, the trader makes the selling agent aware of this buying agent.

When a customer specifies a service or an item s/he wishes to purchase from the marketplace, a buying agent workflow template is created for the customer. The customer may not know the right term (used in DTD) to use for the item, therefore an intelligent dictionary of synonyms is used for this purpose. For example, consider a computer shop using a computer DTD in describing its service. If a customer wants to buy a CPU and uses the term "Processor" and if "CPU" is the term used in DTD, then dictionary of synonyms is to match the word "Processor" with "CPU". The buying agent contacts the marketplace and obtains a form for the customer to specify the properties of the item s/he wants to buy which contains the names and types of the properties of the item. Such a form which is created using the information in the related DTD, is necessary since the customer may not know in advance all the properties of the item.

The buying agent gets the filled form containing the values or ranges for the properties of the item from the customer along with the criteria that s/he wishes to be optimized in the negotiation phase and the required parameters. The buying agent negotiates with the related selling agents to realize the transaction. A comparative analysis of the available alternatives can also be presented to the customer by the buying agent if the customer wishes so.

The rest of this paper describes the related technologies and an architecture for realizing this scenario. Section 2 summarizes the technologies that can be used as building blocks in implementing the proposed scenario. Section 3 describes the architecture and discusses its feasibility and the advantages. In Section 4 related work is presented and the conclusions are given in Section 5.

2 Related Technologies

In this section we briefly summarize the advanced technologies and emerging standards which constitute the building blocks of the proposed architecture. In this respect, current distribution infrastructures, Trading Object Service, agent technology, workflow agents, Knowledge Query and Manipulation Language (KQML), Resource Description Framework (RDF), Extensible Markup Language (XML), Document Type Definition (DTD), and Document Object Model (DOM) are covered.

2.1 Distribution Infrastructure

Web itself and the distributed object platforms like CORBA or Active X/DCOM provide a distribution infrastructure. It is possible to use the Web (HTTP, HTML and Java) in conjunction with an object-oriented "communication bus" following Common Object Request Broker Architecture's (CORBA) Object Request Brokers (CORBA 2.0 and IIOP). Indeed, these sets of technologies constitute the basis of some of the major electronic commerce platforms like Netscape ONE (Open Network Environment), Oracle's NCA (Network Computing Architecture), IBM's CommercePoint and Sun and JavaSoft's Java Electronic Commerce Framework [17].

Using CORBA 2.0 and IIOP with Web rather than using Web alone provides the following advantages [16]:

1. In Web, method invocation is realized through HTTP and Common Gateway Interface (CGI) protocol. When this HTTP/CGI layer is replaced by CORBA, since CORBA allows clients to directly invoke methods on a server, a lot of overhead is avoided. Furthermore, any IDL defined method on the server can be invoked and typed parameters can be passed instead of just strings.
2. With CGI, a new instance of a program must be started every time an applet invokes a method on the server. With CORBA, the same server object receives successive calls from the client and preserves the state between these invocations.
3. CGI is a stateless protocol, that is, CGI does not maintain information from one form to the next. Therefore, hidden fields within a form are used to maintain state on the client side. CORBA maintains the state between client invocations avoiding this overhead, too.
4. CGI creates a bottleneck because it has no way to distribute the incoming requests across multiple processes and processors. CORBA ORBs on the other hand can create as many server objects as necessary. These server objects can run on multiple servers to provide load balancing for incoming client requests.

5. With CORBA, Java clients and applets can invoke a wide variety of IDL defined operations on the server. In contrast, HTTP clients are restricted to a limited set of operations.
6. CORBA provides a rich set of distributed object services that augment Java, including trader, transactions, security, naming and persistence.

It should be noted that, like HTTP, CORBA's IIOP uses Internet as the backbone. This means that both IIOP and HTTP can run on the same networks.

As a summary, CORBA in conjunction with Web seems to be a very promising infrastructure for electronic commerce applications.

2.2 Trading Object Service

The OMG Trading Object Service [20] facilitates the offering and the discovery of instances of services of particular types. A trader is an object that supports the Trading Object Service in a distributed environment. It can be viewed as an object through which other objects can advertise their capabilities and match their needs against advertised capabilities. Advertising a capability or offering a service is called "export". Matching against needs or discovering services is called "import". Export and import facilitate dynamic discovery of, and late binding to, services.

To export, an object gives the trader a description of a service together with the location of an interface at which that service is available. To import, an object asks the trader for a service having certain characteristics. The trader checks against the service descriptions it holds and responds the importer with the location of the selected service's interface. The importer is then able to interact with the service.

Due to the sheer number of service offers that will be available worldwide, and the differing requirements that users of a trading service will have, it is inevitable that a trading service will be split up and that the service offers will be partitioned. Traders in different partitions interact with each other to answer the needs of a client.

2.3 Agent Technology

Agents are programs that perform specific tasks on behalf of their users. Agents are distinguished from other types of software because they are independent entities capable of completing complex assignments without intervention, rather than as tools that must be manipulated by a user.

The fundamental properties of software agents are as follows [22]:

Autonomy: Agents operate without the direct intervention of humans or others, and have some kind of control over their actions and internal state.
Social ability: Agents interact with other agents (and possibly with humans) via some kind of agent communication language.

Reactivity: Agents perceive their environment, (which may be the physical world, a user via a graphical user interface, a collection of other agents, the Internet, or perhaps all of these combined), and respond in a timely fashion to changes that occur in it.

Pro-activeness: Agents do not simply act in response to their environment, they are able to exhibit goal-directed behavior by taking the initiative.

The agents can be made more intelligent with the following additional properties:

Rationality: Agents select actions that follow from knowledge and goals.

Adaptivity: Agents are able to modify knowledge and behavior based on experience.

Collaboration: Agents can plan and execute multi-agent problem solving.

An earlier example of a software agent for electronic commerce is ShopBot [7] which is a domain-independent comparison-shopping agent. Given the home pages of several online stores, ShopBot automatically learns how to shop at these vendors. Learning process involves extracting product descriptions from home pages. This is not an easy problem because home pages may vary in format and also contain other information like advertisements and links to other sites. After learning, ShopBot is able to visit over a dozen of software vendors, extract product information, and summarize the results for the user. Preliminary results show that ShopBot enables users to both find superior prices and substantially reduce Web shopping time. ShopBot relies on a combination of heuristic search, pattern matching, and inductive learning techniques.

Yet ShopBot has several limitations. It works only on home pages that have a searchable index. It expects product descriptions to start on a fresh line. Furthermore, ShopBot heavily relies on HTML. If a vendor provides information exclusively by embedding graphics or using Java, ShopBot will be unable to handle that vendor. More importantly ShopBot shopper's performance is linear in the number of vendors it accesses which is not acceptable given the number of resources on the Web.

2.4 Workflow Agents

Coupling agent technology with workflow systems seems to be a very promising research direction since these technologies nicely complement each other. The resultant "intelligent workflow" will not only have the properties of intelligent agents like being reactive, intelligent and adaptive but also will define an agent consisting of processing steps with data and control flow among them. However, to be used in agent construction, the current workflow technology must be improved in several directions including better support for ad hoc workflows and modifications at run time as well as truly distributed enactment service [5,6].

2.5 Knowledge Query and Manipulation Language (KQML)

One of the requirements for software agents to interact and interoperate effectively is a common communication language (*social ability property*). KQML [8] is an agent communication language and a protocol developed by the Knowledge Sharing Effort (KSE) Consortium. It has been developed both as a message format and a message-handling protocol to support run-time knowledge sharing among agents which may have different content languages. It is a communication language which expresses communicative acts and it is different from the content language which expresses facts about the domain. The aim of KQML is to support computer programs in identifying, connecting with and exchanging information with other programs.

KQML language consists of three main layers: the content layer, the message layer, and the communication layer. The content layer contains the actual content of the message in the program's own representation language. This layer enables KQML to carry any message written in any representation language. The communication layer encodes a set of lower level communication parameters to the message like the identity of the sender and recipient and a unique identifier associated with the communication. The message layer is the core of KQML and determines the kinds of interactions one can have with a KQML-speaking agent. It identifies the protocol to be used to deliver the message and supplies a performative which the sender attaches to the content (such as that it is an assertion, a query, a command, or any set of known performatives). The performatives comprise a substrate on which to develop higher-level models of inter-agent interaction such as contract nets and negotiation. The set of performatives defined by KSE is extensible. A group of agents may agree on to use additional performatives if they agree on their interpretation and the protocol associated with each. The message layer also includes optional features which describe the content language, the ontology, and some type of description of the content. These features make it possible for KQML implementations to analyze, route and properly deliver messages even though their content is inaccessible.

Following are the main advantages of KQML as an agent communication language:

- KQML messages are declarative, simple, readable and extensible,
- Since KQML has a layered structure and since KQML messages are unaware of the content of the message they carry, KQML can easily be integrated with other system components,
- KQML imposes no restrictions about the transport protocol and the content language.

In addition to these, KQML has the potential to enhance the capabilities and functionality of large-scale integration and interoperability efforts in communication and information technology such as OMG's CORBA, as well as in application areas like electronic commerce [8].

2.6   Resource Description Framework (RDF)

As ShopBot's limitations given in Section 2.3 clearly demonstrated, there is a need for machine understandable information on the Web. An emerging solution to letting automated agents surf the Web is to provide a mechanism which allows a more precise description of the resources that are available on the Web [11]. The Resource Description Framework (RDF) [21] by the World Wide Web Consortium (W3C) is a standard for metadata that provides interoperability between applications that exchange machine-understandable information on the Web.

RDF [21] defines both a data model for representing RDF metadata, and an XML-based syntax for expressing and transporting metadata. RDF is a model for representing named properties and their values. These properties serve both to represent attributes of resources and to represent relationship between resources. The RDF data model is syntax independent way of representing RDF expressions and in [21], three representations of the model are given, that is, representation as 3-tuples, as a graph and in XML. In 3-tuple representation, a property is a three tuple consisting of the resource being described, a property name or type, and a value. A collection of property triples describing the same resource is called an *assertions*. In graph representation, the resources being described and the values describing them are nodes in a directed graph, with the edges being labelled by the property names. An RDF statement can itself be the target node of an arc (i.e., the value of some property) or the source node of an arc (i.e., it can have properties). In these cases, the original property (i.e., the statement) must be reified; that is, converted into nodes and arcs. Reified properties are drawn as a single node with several arcs emanating from it representing the resource, property name and value [13].

It is clear that RDF will provide the much needed information for the agent technologies working on the Web. Agents can use RDF not only for describing their capabilities and negotiating the terminologies used in communication, but also the other resources on the Web.

2.7   Extensible Markup Language (XML) and Document Type Definitions (DTDs)

World Wide Web Consortium's (W3C) Extensible Markup Language (XML) [19] defines a simple subset of SGML (the Standard Generalized Markup Language). Unlike HTML, which defines a fixed set of tags, XML allows the definition of customized markup languages with application specific tags [14]. That is, XML provides support for the representation of data in terms of attribute/value pairs with user defined tags.

XML differs from HTML in three major respects [2]:

1. Information providers can define new tag and attribute names at will.
2. Document structures can be nested to any level of complexity.
3. Any XML document can contain an optional description of its grammar for use by applications that need to perform structural validation.

Document Type Definitions (DTD) which are defined for user groups provide a formal definition of documents for that group, that is, they define what names can be used for elements, where they may occur and how they all fit together in an XML file.

2.8 Document Object Model (DOM)

W3C's Document Object Model (DOM) [18] defines an object-oriented API for HTML and XML documents which a Web client can present to programs that need to process the documents [14]. DOM represents a document as a hierarchy of objects with proper inheritance relationship among them, called nodes, which are derived (by parsing) from a source representation of a document (HTML or XML). In other words, the DOM object classes represent generic components of a document, and hence define a document object meta model. The major DOM classes are: Node, Document, Element, Attribute, Text, Processing Instruction, and Comment. The representation of a Web page in terms of objects makes it easy to associate code with the various subcomponents of the page. For example, Document object has a "documentType" method which returns DTD for XML documents (and "null" for HTML and XML documents without DTDs) and a "getElementsByTagName" method which produces an enumerator that iterates over all Element nodes within the document whose "tagName" matches the input name provided. Thus DOM provides a general means for applications to access and traverse documents written in HTML and XML without having themselves to perform complex parsing.

3   METU-EMar Architecture

A possible architecture realizing the scenario given in Section 1 that uses the technology summarized in Section 2 is described in the following (Figure 1):

PHASE I: The resource discovery agents working in the background find out about the resources providing products and services. If the resources want to join the marketplace, the marketplace provides them a template workflow of a selling agent. If the resource already has a selling agent, this one is registered to selling trader through Trading Object Service.

We expect resources to expose their semantics by using the Resource Description Framework (RDF) [12] and the Extensible Markup Language (XML) [19]. As briefly summarized in Section 2.6, RDF defines both a data model for representing RDF metadata, and an XML-based syntax for expressing and transporting the metadata.

Since resources use RDF to expose their metadata, the resource discovery agents do not need intelligence in extracting information from the resources. However, they do have other properties of agents like being autonomous, reactive and proactive.

The buying and the selling agents which are autonomous, reactive and proactive with negotiation ability, should be defined as workflows since they consist

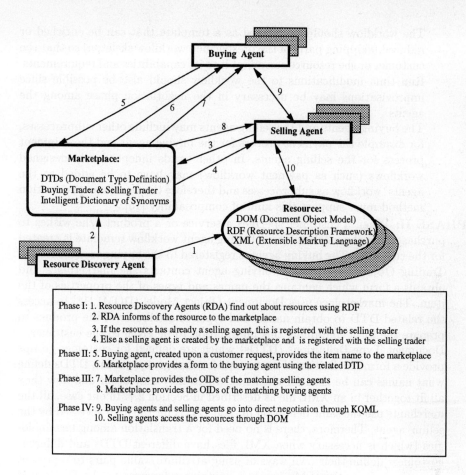

Fig. 1. The Architecture of METU-EMar

of processing steps with data and control flow among them communicating with resources, with the customer and among themselves. A workflow system to be used in modelling a buying or a selling agent should have the following properties:

- The scheduler of these workflows must be truly distributed in the sense that the workflow should be able to execute in any node of the network without consulting to a top level central control [5, 6]. This is essential since the domain of the workflow contains all the Web resources registered to the marketplace. Also, since the distribution infrastructure is CORBA, these resources must have an ORB. It should be noted that it is possible for different ORBs to communicate through IIOP.

  The other components of the workflow, like the history management used for logging and recovery purposes, should also be handled in a distributed way to exploit the advantages brought by a distributed scheduler [9].

- The workflow should be defined as a template that can be enriched or reduced (skipping parts of the prespecified workflow skeleton) so that the customer or the resource can adapt it to its capabilities and requirements. Run time modifications to the workflow should also be possible since improvisations may be necessary in the negotiation phase among the agents.
- The buying agents and the selling agents may include other subprocesses, for example the payment process for the buying agent and the shipment process for the selling agents. In other words independently designed workflows (such as payment workflow) may have to be added to the agents' workflow as subprocesses and therefore the workflow specification method must support this kind of composability [15].

PHASE II: When a customer specifies a service or a product s/he wishes to purchase from the marketplace, a buying agent workflow template is created for the customer. The buying agent is registered to the buying trader through Trading Object Service. The buying agent contacts the marketplace and obtains a form which contains the names and types of the properties of the item. The marketplace uses Document Object Model (DOM) [18] to access the related DTD to obtain names and types of attributes of the product to prepare the form containing this information to be given to the customer.

Document Type Definitions (DTDs) which are defined for customer groups provide a formal definition of documents for that group, that is, DTDs define what names can be used for elements, where they may occur and how they all fit together in an XML file as described in Section 2.7. In our case, all the merchants use the same definition in their DTDs for the item accessed by the selling agent. Therefore, there is no need for a translation among terminologies (which is necessary when XML files have different DTDs and different customers define their own ways of using attribute/value pairs to represent the same information). Marketplace contains references to the DTDs and uses the Document Object Model to access and manipulate parsed DTDs as a collection of objects.

Different names can be provided for the same product by the customers, in other words, the customers may not know the standard terms used in DTDs. Therefore, a dictionary of synonyms is necessary in the marketplace. This dictionary of synonyms may be implemented to contain some intelligence in the sense that whenever an item or service is not found in the dictionary, the customer may be asked to provide synonyms and these terms can be added to the dictionary for later use.

PHASE III: The buying agents and the selling agents find out about each other through the related trader objects. Having two trader objects (buying and selling) makes the process symmetric, that is, both buying objects and selling objects can locate all the related agents as soon as they join the marketplace. A buying agent may contact all related selling agents, to determine a buying strategy. For example, if a selling agent with a bargaining facility is already giving a lower price than a selling agent without a negotiation facility, the second is eliminated. Such a strategy is also possible for the selling agents. In other words, the buying and selling agents are playing a game where each is trying to satisfy its goal. The buying agents are on the customers' side and the selling agents are on the resources' side.

PHASE IV: The buying agents go in direct negotiation with selling agents provided by the marketplace. In this respect, RDF is used in encoding resources and query capabilities and KQML [10] is used to communicate RDF among agents.

The buying and selling agents in the marketplace act autonomously, that is, once released in the marketplace, they negotiate and make decisions on their own, without requiring customer intervention. They are proactive in contacting the other interested agents and reactive to the changes in the marketplace like new agents.

The resources should provide semantic information about their content to the selling agent. In this respect, the resources should be defined in XML. DOM is used by the selling agents in processing XML pages to obtain specific product data, like the price of the product. The selling agents should be authorized to invoke certain applications at the resource to obtain the bargaining strategy and its parameters which implies that the resources should provide this information through a standard interface. The negotiation strategies as described in [3] can be used in the negotiation phase. Several parameters can be specified, like the desired date to sell (buy) the item, desired price, lowest (highest) acceptable price and a decay function if the agent wants to decrease (increase) the price over its given time frame. However there is a need for more solid bargaining algorithms [1].

When CORBA and Web is used as the distribution infrastructure, all the agents in the system can be implemented as CORBA objects. Document Object Model defines its interfaces already in IDL which makes it possible to access the resources as CORBA objects, too. Furthermore, using CORBA as the infrastructure provides the opportunity to use OMG's Trading Object Service as a part of the marketplace. The selling agents of the resources as well as the buying agents can be registered to the related trader objects through the "Register" interface of this service and the buying agents find out about the selling agents through the "Lookup" interface and vice versa. Trading Object Service is distributed in the sense that several traders can be linked through the "Link" interface and can be searched depending on the prespecified policies.

As an extension to this scenario, the buying agent can be activated from an application program through the API of the buying agent. Note that the application might itself be a workflow. In this case, the application program should be designed to be able to fill in the form produced by the marketplace.

3.1 Feasibility

The technological requirement of the architecture proposed is the semantic interoperability of the Web resources. The building blocks for this, although have already been defined or are being defined mostly as standards, are at their infancy.

For example, work is underway to define XML-based data exchange formats in both the chemical and the health care communities. A number of industry groups defined SGML DTDs for their documents (e.g. the US Defense Department, which requires much of its documentation to be submitted according to SGML DTDs)[14]. A large US project aims to define specific attribute names for specific elements in computer industry that can possibly be implemented through XML DTDs [4].

The architecture we describe requires the DTDs for the user groups to be available. Note that since RDF assertions use properties defined in the schemas, i.e., DTDs, the use of RDF also depends on the availability of standard DTDs. Until the standard DTDs become available and the RDFs start using these schemas, there is a need for the following modifications in METU-EMar architecture in realizing the proposed scenario:

1. The resource discovery agents utilize machine understandable information (RDF) and therefore can not be implemented easily when the standard vocabulary (DTDs) used by RDF is not available. In this case, resource discovery agents should either be more intelligent or include heuristic techniques to understand the content of the resources.
2. When XML files have different DTDs (i.e., different users define their own ways of using attribute/value pairs to represent the same information), there is a need for a mechanism to identify associations among the terminologies of the XML files. This can be achieved through a translation mechanism between terminologies. This translation is also needed in the negotiation phase among the buying and the selling agents.

Also as stated previously, more solid bargaining algorithms must be developed [1] to better exploit the scheme described.

3.2 Advantages

It is clear that in a marketplace as large as the one provided by the Web, the service provided by the proposed architecture is invaluable. It will not only help to locate better opportunities for both the buyers and the sellers but it will also save a lot of their time in negotiations. In other words, the proposed marketplace aims to find the best conditions for its clients and help to overcome the limitations of direct communications between customers and suppliers. The marketplace enables the customers to reach various suppliers whose existence they are unaware of and hence it would be impossible for them to reach otherwise. Symmetrically, the marketplace also gives the suppliers the chance to contact to a much wider range of customers.

4 Related Work

One of the earliest examples of an electronic marketplace is Kasbah [3] where users create autonomous agents that buy and sell goods on their behalf in the marketplace. Kasbah's selling agents are pro-active, they contact interested parties (namely, buying agents) and negotiate with them to find the best deal. A selling agent is autonomous in that, once released into the marketplace, it negotiates and makes decisions on its own, without requiring user intervention. Marketplace's job is to facilitate interaction between the agents by letting buying and selling agents know each other and by ensuring that they speak a common language and use a common terminology to describe the goods.

Kasbah has a simple prototype implemented in CLOS using Harequin Lisp to test the basic concepts of negotiation. In Kasbah, all agents are locally built and thus are made to communicate via a predefined set of methods.

A CORBA based electronic broker (OFFER) is described in [1]. The business model consists of suppliers, customers and electronic brokers (e-broker). Suppliers and e-brokers offer services which can be accessed over the Internet and which are procured by customers. The interfaces of these services are described in OMG's Interface Definition Language (IDL). Therefore, there is a need in establishing an interface standard on which all suppliers of a certain product category agree.

Suppliers offer an e-catalog to the customer; suppliers can also register with the e-broker. The e-broker can either maintain its own database of registered e-catalogs or it can use services of an Object Trader implemented through Trading Object Services of OMG. Hence, a customer can search for a service either directly in the catalog of a supplier or can use the e-broker to search in all the e-catalogs of all the suppliers which are registered with this broker. An IDL interface is specified for the e-catalogs and for the e-broker which they should conform. The electronic broker described supports search in underlying catalogs and it provides a centralized marketplace with the possibility to use an auction mechanism to buy or sell goods.

5 Conclusions

The Internet is revolutionizing commerce. However, closed markets that cannot use each other's services, incompatible applications and frameworks that can not interoperate or build upon each other are hampering the progress of electronic commerce [17].

The need for semantic interoperability of the resources on the Web resulted in a series of standardization efforts from the World Wide Web Consortium. In this paper, we present an electronic market that exploits these standards as well as some other emerging technologies like workflow agents. The realization of this architecture depends on the availability of DTDs for different user groups. We also present the modifications to the architecture when DTDs are not available.

References

1. Bichler, M., Beam, C., Segev, A., "Offer: A Broker-centered Object Framework for Electronic Requisitioning", in Proc. of Intl. IFIP Working Conference: Trends in Electronic Commerce, Hamburg, Germany, June 1998.

2. Bosak, J., "XML, Java, and the Future of the Web", http://sunsite.unc.edu/pub/sun-info/standards/xml/why/xmlapps.html.
3. Chavez, A., Maes, P., "Kasbah: An Agent Marketplace for Buying and Selling Goods", Proc. of the First Intl. Conference on the Practical Application of Intelligent Agents and Multi-Agent Technology, London, UK, April 1996, http://agents.www.media. mit.edu:80/groups/agents/Publications/kasbah-paam96.ps.
4. Danish, S., Personal Communication.
5. Dogac, A., Gokkoca, E., Arpinar, S., Koksal, P., Cingil, I., Arpinar, B., Tatbul, N., Karagoz, P., Halici, U., Altinel, M., "Design and Implementation of a Distributed Workflow Management System: METUFlow", in [6].
6. Dogac, A., Kalinichenko, L., Ozsu, T., Sheth, A., (Edtrs.), "Advances in Workflow Management Systems and Interoperability", Springer-Verlag, 1998.
7. Doorenbos, R. B., Etzioni, O., Weld, D. S., "A Scalable Comparison-Shopping Agent for the World- Wide Web", ACM Agents '97 Conference, 1997.
8. Finin, T., Labrou, Y., Mayfield, J., "KQML as an agent communication language", in Jeffery M. Bradshaw, editor, Software Agents, MIT Press, 1995.
9. Koksal, P., Arpinar, S., Dogac, A., "Workflow History Management", ACM Sigmod Record, Vol. 27, No. 1, March 1998.
10. Labrou, Y., Finin, T., "A Proposal for a new KQML Specification", Report TR-97-03, Computer Science and Electrical Engineering Department, University of Maryland Baltimore County. Available on-line as http://www.cs.umbc.edu/~jklabrou/-publications/tr9703.ps.
11. Lassila, O., "RDF Metadata and Agent Architectures", http://www.objs.com/-workshops/ws9801/papers/paper056.html.
12. Lassila, O., Swick, R. R. "Resource Description Framework (RDF) Model and Syntax", Working Draft, World Wide Web Consortium. Available on-line as http://www.w3.org/TR/WD-rdf-syntax/.
13. Manola, F., "Towards a Web Object Model", http://www.objs.com/OSA/wom.htm.
14. Manola, F., "Towards a Richer Web Object Model", ACM Sigmod Record, Vol. 27, No. 1, March 1998.
15. Muth, P., Weissenfels, J., Weikum, G., "What Workflow Technology Can Do for Electronic Commerce", in Current Trends in Database Technology, Dogac, A., Khosrowpour, M., Ozsu, T., Ulusoy, O., (Edtrs.), Idea Group Publishing, 1998.
16. Orfali, R., Harkey, D., "The Essential Client/Server Programming with JAVA and CORBA", John Wiley, 1997.
17. Tanenbaum, J. M., "Eco System: An Internet Commerce Architecture", IEEE Computer, Vol. 30, No. 5, May 1997.
18. Document Object Model (DOM), http://www.w3.org/DOM/.
19. Extensible Markup Language (XML), http://www.w3.org/XML/.
20. OMG's Trading Object Service. OMG Document orbos/96-05-06, Version 1.0.0, May 10, 1996.
21. Resource Description Framework (RDF), http://www.w3.org/Metadata/RDF/.
22. Woolridge, M., Jennings, N, "Intelligent Agents- Theory and Practice", Knowledge Engineering Journal, June 1995.

Electronic Commerce for Software

Tsuneo Ajisaka

Wakayama University, Wakayama 640-8510 Japan
ajisaka@sys.wakayama-u.ac.jp

Abstract. Since software is electronic itself, the features of electronic commerce to be highlighted in case software is its domain can be discussed comparing with other tangible kinds of merchandise. Several spectra of e-commerce are firstly investigated in terms of largely two types of software and its distribution, i.e., shrink-wrapped package software and custom software developed by contract. E-commerce for software is basically service- or process- oriented, in which a brokering service for software packages or components is particular. The architectures of the business-to-business software e-commerce, or the Software CALS, are discussed next. Business, logical, and physical architectures are investigated in terms of their structure and components, services, and data models. Middleware engineering for the UI, communication, and data servers will be one of the most important agenda for the deployment of software e-commerce.

1 Introduction

Software is the only category of merchandise that can be fully processed by electronic commerce. Of course software is on the same line with other kinds of goods in many features of e-commerce particularly in ordering, billing, and payment mechanisms and related security issues. However, there is an essential and apparent difference between software and other tangible kinds of goods, that is, software itself is electronic and does not need any physical (off-line) distribution to complete a trade.

It means not only the final distribution of a self-contained software product but also intermediate transactions of software components and services to assemble them can be carried on solely within an e-commerce system. Moreover, in the software e-commerce system, both business information services and engineering services can be interacted each other and provide a seamless platform to facilitate both trading and developing software. It is again because of the self-applicability of software, that is, a thing and the information about the thing are both digital if and only if the thing is software.

This paper discusses mainly the architectures for the software e-commerce system that has above mentioned characteristics, after some clarifications about the features of e-commerce in case software is its domain.

2   Types of Software and E-Commerce

The area of e-commerce is very broad from architectural to security issues, and from technical to economic or legal issues. In this section, several spectra of e-commerce are investigated in terms of largely two types of software and its distribution. A summary is shown in Table 1.

Table 1. E-Commerce features and software types

	Package Software	Custom Software
Marketplace design & advertisement	important as other kinds of goods	less important
ordering, billing, & payment	important as other kinds of goods	less frequent
security for cash flow (incl. d-cash)	important as other kinds of goods	less important
security for business/engr. info.	mostly unconcerned	vitally important
rights management	needed to prevent illegal copy when network distr.	less important (needed for contents used)
trial use	efficient as marketing campaign	needed for component brokering
software sommelier	as retailer's business	as electronic catalog vendor
service supplier	possible for content centered software	possible for remote exec. & test
communication	mostly unconcerned	same as workflow support or CSCW system

2.1   Shrink-wrapped package software

This kind of software is for end users, i.e. consumers, either in companies or at home. Many technical and strategic issues of e-commerce needed to consider for this kind of software are therefore common with other kinds of goods, for example,

- design of electronic marketplaces,
- advertisement both by push and pull technologies,
- ordering, billing, and payment mechanisms (including digital cash) and related security issues.

On the other hand, some features are specific even to the software for consumers:

- Vendors can provide free trial-use (down-graded) products just by putting them on a web-accessible directory. It may be an efficient way of marketing campaign with virtually no distribution cost.
- Since a vast number of packages are there in many marketplaces, people may want the service of searching, evaluating, and selecting a product best fit for their requirements. This may be a brokering service specific to this domain, that is called a 'software sommelier' [1].
- The user does not necessarily need a shrink-wrapped package and disc media, and even manual books. Program code and documents can be delivered through the network, while the mechanism of charging and preventing illegal copy must be considered.
- Moreover, the user is interested not in the program code but in the useful services provided by the program. It suggests the possibility of a business using an e-commerce system that supplies not software products but services through the network. This framework may be easier to expect for content (common data) centered software rather than processing centered software. Specifications and pricing models for atomic services and their combinations should be considered for this kind of business framework.

2.2   Custom software developed by contract

Business-to-business e-commerce, or the Software CALS (Continuous Acquisition and Life-cycle Support; Commerce At Light Speed), supports this kind of software. Marketplace design and advertisement are less important. Instead, electronic catalog vendors, i.e. another kind of software sommeliers for enterprise software acquirers may join in the e-commerce system. It reflects the recent trend of software development, i.e component based development using the COTS (commercial off-the-shelf software), that may be more efficient than the older style of two-party contract.

While ordering, billing, and payment occur less frequently, more frequent electronic communication, negotiation, and agreements should be supported in every business and development stage. In this sense, a b-to-b e-commerce system has the same functional aspects as a business process/workflow support or CSCW (computer supported cooperative work) system being used by multiple companies. Security issues are thus vital, mainly for authentication to access the confidential information about the software development in a group, rather than for secure money flows or rights management.

The next section will concentrate on the architectures of this kind of e-commerce system.

From the software engineering point of view, embedded software should be recognized as a different type other than the above two. However, it is not likely

---

[1] The author has firstly heard this word from Hitoshi Tadaumi of NTT and Masahiro Kikuta of Synergy Incubate.

to distribute over an e-commerce system because this type of software is tightly coupled with a certain hardware equipment.

3 Architectures for Software E-Commerce

Several aspects are there in the architectural discussion of software e-commerce. They are pivoted by the component types of an architecture. If the roles that participate in a business are chosen as the component types, the architecture describes a business model and a business process. On the other hand, a technical architecture is composed by software components (logical/external or physical/internal) and associated services or functions.

An architecture is represented by using a network diagram in general. The nodes of the diagram are components of the architecture. The arcs represent relationships in general, but in case of architecture, they are the services provided or requested by a component to another. In many cases, a service needs the models of information or data on which the service should have effects. Thus, in order to talk about an architecture, the structure and components, services, and data models should be considered simultaneously.

The rest of this section describes the business and technical architectures of software e-commerce, and the services and data models involved in the software e-commerce architectures. Table 2 summarizes the aspects in terms of the technical items.

Table 2. Architectures in diffrent aspects

	Business architecture	Logical architecture	Physical architecture
components	roles of organizations participating in a commerce	abstract middleware modules	available software components
services	business process (SLCP) activities	system & internal interfaces	UI operations & internal procedure calls
data models	document types identification	common data interchange formats & repository schema	

3.1 Business Architecture

A typical business architecture of software e-commerce is shown in Figure 1. The components of this architecture represents the roles of the organizations that participate in a software commerce [2].

---

[2] This architecture is designed by reference to some example architectures originally developed in 1996 – 1997 by a group of the Technical Committee for Software CALS

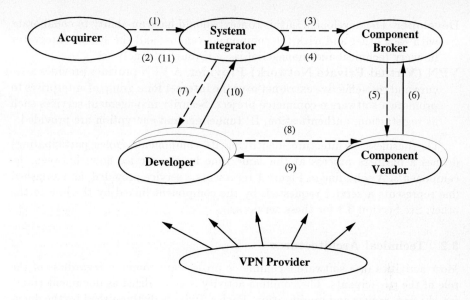

Fig. 1. A typical business architecture

Acquirer A software e-commerce project is kicked off by an acquirer submitting its requirements description and RFP (request for proposal) on its web page and/or sending it using a mailing list.

System Integrator Several system integrators may respond to the RFP submitted by the acquirer. The system integrator ordered by the acquirer is responsible for providing and maintaining the final product by coordinating component brokers, component vendors, and developers. A system integrator may be a virtual enterprise (joint venture) cooperated by multiple companies.

Component Broker A component broker is a software sommelier for custom software development, maybe in a specific application domain. It is able to investigate, evaluate, and select software components best fit for the acquirer's requirements and the design specification developed by the system integrator.

Component Vendor A component vendor develops and provides software components, maybe in a specific application domain. It maintains the components and their electronic catalogs as well. It also has an ability to test their components embedded in custom software through the network.

under INSTAC/JSA (Information Technology Research and Standardization Center in Japanese Standards Association) and by another group of the Software CALS Consortium sponsored by IPA (Information-technology Promotion Agency, Japan). The author has been a steering member of the INSTAC SCALS-TC and chair of the working group (WG6) of the TC for SCALS architecture.

Developer The developers in this context should have an ability to collaborate with each other and with the component vendors and the system integrator in every technical and managerial issue through the network.

VPN (Virtual Private Network) Provider A VPN provider provides a secure and cost-effective extra-net over the Internet for a group of enterprises to promote a software e-commerce project. Security management services such as registration, authentication, IP tunneling, and encryption are provided.

The business architecture identifying its components (roles participating) defines a business process at the same time by the service flows between the components. A solid line in Figure 1 represents a service provided, and a dashed line represents a service requested, by the component linked by the line to the other. See Section 3.3 for these services.

3.2 Technical Architectures

Most activities in a software e-commerce project are common regardless of the role of the participants. The common activity is generalized as document transfer, sharing, review and modification. Each activity is distinguished by the document type to be handled in the activity, for example, RFP, proposal, contract, design documents, process management reports, test reports, question and answer sheet, etc. All management documents and most of technical products (artifacts; software configuration items) are handled by the generalized common activity. Only exception is executable code that should be evaluated not by review but by the behavior when it runs [3].

The common activity may be supported by a logical architecture shown in Figure 2. This is pretty simple, but if you try to refine it any further, it will be a detailed design rather than an architecture, that should give a style of a system identifying its large components and their connections. The information repository, for example, may have sub-components managing artifacts, configuration data, and schema to define configurations. Identifying the components of this level, the connections among these components and the connections between a sub-component and the adapter become much more complicated than before and it makes difficult to understand the basic style to realize the common activity.

A typical and rapidly feasible physical architecture [4] may be constructed by assigning COTS and some customized software to each component of the logical architecture:

- a web browser with dialog functions for the user interface,
- for the adapter, an HTTP (Hyper Text Transfer Protocol) server with some service procedures hooked on the CGI (Common Gateway Interface)
- for the information repository, various data bases or file systems already existing and having been used in each organization, that may be only a feasible choice for most organizations.

---

[3] There is an approach called clean room approach in which code as well as specification documents should be thoroughly and statically reviewed until the final delivery.

[4] It is based on the discussion in the INSTAC SCALS-TC/WG6.

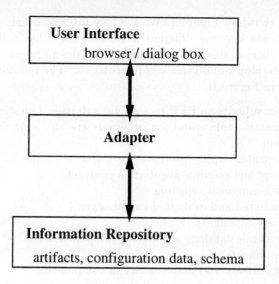

Fig. 2. The logical architecture supporting the common activity

The web-based interfaces are so widely disseminated that they should be the first candidate for the cost-effective user interface. While they may be fairly good tools for information presentation and navigation, their lack of a logical structuring framework leaves much work to the part of the adapter, for example, searching, assembling, and storing data to and from the information repository.

A specific adapter is necessary to support an EC-based software development assembling distributed executable components. A current solution is middleware for component communication such as the CORBA (Common Object Request Broker Architecture) of the OMG (Object Management Group) using the IIOP (Inter-ORB Inter-Operability Protocol) [1], Microsoft's DCOM (Distributed Component Object Model) with ActiveX [2], and Sun's RMI (Remote Method Invocation) for Java with Java Beans [3]. The main issue after introducing the middleware of this kind is to assure interconnections between the middleware and the web system, between the middleware and the repository, and between different middleware [5].

3.3 Services

The services produced and consumed within and along with a software e-commerce system are grouped in three categories according to their field of work. The first group of services are effective in the business process, or software life cycle process (SLCP) [4], that is a human process supported by the system. Example

---

[5] The Software CALS Consortium mentioned before has made experiments for several combinations of such interconnections.

activities were shown in Figure 1. We are here interested only in the activities having interactions between different parties. Many other activities closed to each party are there in SLCP, for example, activities to prepare documents, select partners, develop responsible components, etc. The following services were enumerated as in Figure 1:

1. The acquirer submits an RFP to a public web page. Questions and answers, and preliminary applications for proposals are also sent through the electronic system.
2. System integrators apply proposals in response to the RFP. The selected integrator and the acquirer negotiate a contract.
3. Request for component selection.
4. Report of selected and evaluated components.
5. Research for components.
6. Provide electronic catalogs of software components.
7. Specify components.
8. Request for delivery and maintenance of components.
9. Provide components and remote test facilities.
10. Deliver responsible parts of software.
11. Deliver the final product.

These external (from the support system's point of view) services are carried on by combining system functions. The second group of services are those identified on the surface of the system's user interface such as data storing, data searching, message handling, etc. In order to design this service group, detailed analysis is needed on a scenario describing how an external service is decomposed to utilize a series of system functions and how the results of the used system functions are reorganized to form the overall result for the original external service.

The third group of services are provided from an internal component of the system to another in order to implement the system functions. Interconnection of distributed repositories, and the interface services of the adapter connecting it to the web system and data bases are the examples of this kind of service of the program component level. Pluggable interfaces for different components are ideal, while it is rather difficult to define a generic, simple and useful service group because of existing legacy subsystems. The 'CORBA services' [1] with the encapsulation technique may be a good reference for this area, although it is not so simple.

3.4 Data Models

One of the key factors of the business-to-business software e-commerce system is data sharing, that is at the same time the objective of the system to achieve efficient development and delivery of software. There are two approaches to speak the same language about the data to be shared.

The first is the common data interchange formats to be used in various management and technical aspects. This approach is advantageous in that any existing data store subsystem can continue to be used with the adapter transforming the legacy data to a common interchange format. CDIF (CASE Data Interchange Format) [5] is the leading standard particularly for diagrammatic design documents. Other documents including various specification descriptions, status reports, and even message sheets being exchanged frequently can be written in the framework of SGML (Standard Generalized Markup Language) [6] or XML (Extensible Markup Language) [7]. Commerce languages describing software components may join this arena too [6].

The second approach to facilitating data sharing is introducing a common information repository. This is applicable and may be more efficient than the first because the transformation adapter is not required, when a project is rather free from legacy data and legacy subsystems. However, it is not often the case, that is proved by the current status of PCTE (Portable Common Tool Environment) [8]. In this situation, this approach can shift to provide not a whole repository system but common data schema to represent the contents of the repository with a schema transformation adapter [7].

4 Concluding Remarks

Middleware engineering will become more and more important both for developing software components to be used in software e-commerce and for developing the software e-commerce system itself. Most application software in general have rather small segments to provide the specific core functions of the software depending on each application objective. The larger peripheral parts of the software can therefore be prepared as generic common middleware that is applicable to a wide range of application programs.

Middleware functions are classified in the three:

- data store/access/management,
- communication between multiple (the same or different type of) core functions, and
- user interface functions.

They are coincident with the three logical components identified in Figure 2, and also with the three (data, control, and user interface) integration capabilities for CASE environments (the toaster model) [9], while they are not only for software e-commerce systems or CASE environments but generally for component based application software. Middleware components must have clear boundaries

---

[6] INSTAC SCALS-TC/WG7 (component based development; chaired by Mikio Aoyama) is working on a language called SCL for compact description of software components in terms of commerce information (purchase/licensing/support conditions) as well as run-time environment, design specification, and usage guidelines.

[7] The author's research group is developing a data modeling system called PRISM (Portable Repository Interfaces supporting Semantic Modularity), with which a data model is decomposed in three aspects, that is, structure, constraint, and schema definitions, for more flexible and less procedural data modeling.

(interfaces) to assure interoperability. We believe that a micro-scopic semantic analysis [10] will rationalize this issue.

In a broader sense, software includes not only computer software but also various electronic media contents. Software engineering will be more content-directed as information processing becomes more popularized. Additional functions are required to the system supporting content-directed software e-commerce, for example, watermarking and other IPR technologies, per-click purchases with micro pricing/payment, etc.

Acknowledgements

The author would like to thank the members of the INSTAC SCALS-TC and the Software CALS Consortium for their work and demonstartions in the committee. Specific contributions to this paper are commented in each footnote.

References

1. OMG: Formal Documentation, http://www.omg.org/corba/.
2. S. Robinson, A. Krasilshchikov: ActiveX Magic: An ActiveX Control and DCOM Sample Using ATL, 1997,
   http://www.microsoft.com/workshop/components/activex/magic.asp.
3. Sun microsystems: Java Computing, http://www.sun.com/java/.
4. ISO/IEC: International Standard 12207 – Information Technology – Software Life Cycle Processes, 1995.
5. EIA/CDIF: Understanding between modelling tools, http://www.cdif.org/.
6. ISO/IEC: International Standard 8879 – Standard Generalized Markup Language (SGML), 1986.
7. The World Wide Web Consortium: Extensible Markup Language (XML), http://www.w3.org/XML/.
8. ISO/IEC: International Standard 13719-1 – Portable Common Tool Environment (PCTE) Abstract Specification, 1995.
9. ECMA and NIST: Reference Model for Frameworks of Software Engineering Environments, Technical Report ECMA TR/55 and NIST Special Publication 500-201, 1993.
10. T. Ajisaka: The Software Quark Model: a Universal Model for CASE Repositories, *Information and Software Technology*, Vol.38, No.3, pp.173–180, Elsevier Science, 1996.

RainMaker: Workflow Execution Using Distributed, Interoperable Components

Santanu Paul, Edwin Park, David Hutches, and Jarir Chaar

IBM T. J. Watson Research Center
P. O. Box 704
Yorktown Heights, NY 10598
{santanu, esp, hutches, jarir}@watson.ibm.com

Abstract. As individuals and enterprises interconnect via wide area networks, workflows that span them seamlessly will become increasingly valuable. It is likely that heterogeneous participants - humans, applications, organizations - that are physically dispersed over such networks will share workflows that cut across organizational and geographic boundaries. We address the problem of designing a *distributed workflow infrastructure* that supports such scenarios in the presence of heterogeneous workflow systems and components. We present *RainMaker*, a workflow framework based on a service requestor/service provider execution model. RainMaker defines a core set of abstract interfaces that can be implemented by distributed workflow components. Together, the RainMaker execution model and interfaces provide a foundation for the interoperability of workflow systems and components.

1. Introduction

The traditional use of workflow systems has been in the design, execution, and management of process-driven applications common to enterprises such as banks and insurance companies. Examples of such applications include loan application and claims processing (Figure 1). Commercial workflow systems of today allow business processes to be described and automated as *workflows*. Workflow systems help eliminate expensive document flows, exploit parallelism among process steps, and minimize delays inherent to manual document routing. They also help enterprises track the status of ongoing workflows, thus improving organizational responsiveness.

Fig. 1. Business Loan Approval Workflow

A typical workflow system integrates a wide variety of services. A specification tool allows designers to describe workflows relevant to the enterprise. A workflow server manages the execution of multiple workflow instances, assigns work generated by workflows to organizational resources in an efficient manner, and tracks the progress of assigned work. The resources that do work on behalf of the workflow server include humans, applications, or other workflow servers. In today's commercial workflow systems, the interactions between workflow servers and resources are proprietary, and the default design assumption is that these resources are *within the scope of authority of the workflow system* (Figure 2). In effect, the design of existing workflow systems predates concerns of *interoperability* among *heterogeneous* workflow systems and resources.

As individuals and organizations get connected via wide area networks such as the Internet, it is evident that workflows no longer need to be confined within enterprises. In fact, it should be possible for participants dispersed over such networks to team up and share workflows among themselves. For workflows to cross organizational and geographic boundaries seamlessly, the monolithic design assumptions of current workflow systems will have to be abandoned. Any distributed workflow infrastructure must squarely address issues such as heterogeneity of workflow components, decentralized workflow execution, workflow system interoperability, and low-cost workflow participation. Our work with RainMaker explores the potential of the Internet to enable workflow execution via distributed, interoperable workflow components that reside across this global infrastructure. It examines the requirements and implications of such workflow execution, and describes a framework by which it might be realized. The objective is to enable new kinds of workflows involving dispersed individuals, multiple organizations, scattered network resources, and heterogeneous workflow components.

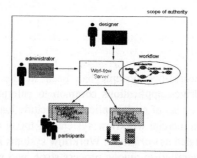

Fig. 2. Design of Current Workflow Systems

This paper is organized as follows. Section 2 describes the requirements for a distributed workflow infrastructure. Section 3 describes RainMaker, a framework that can serve as the basis for a distributed workflow infrastructure. Section 4 discusses related work, and finally, Section 5 presents our conclusions.

2. Requirements for a Distributed Workflow Infrastructure

In this section, we present concrete scenarios of workflow execution across wide area networks and some of the important considerations in designing an infrastructure to support such scenarios.

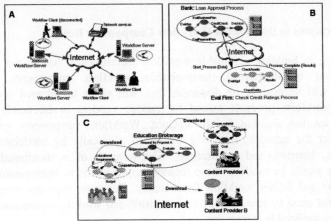

Fig. 3. Distributed Workflow Scenarios

2.1. Workflow Scenarios

Consider a virtual team of IT consultants from different, geographically dispersed organizations, working on a project that is coordinated via a workflow. The consultants may be mobile and intermittently connected to the network. Irrespective of location, the project leader may want to modify or track the workflow at any time. Similarly, irrespective of location, specific work assigned to consultants must appear on their respective heterogeneous computing devices - desktops, laptops, Personal Digital Assistants - in a timely manner (Figure 3A). A distributed workflow infrastructure must thus automatically route work from workflows to participants over a global network and return the results from participants to workflows.

Next, recall the example of the *BusinessLoanApproval* workflow running on a bank's workflow server (Figure 1). The *CreditCheck* step may itself be a nested workflow that is delegated to a credit evaluation firm with a different workflow server (i.e. a product from a different vendor). During execution, the bank's server would notify the firm's server to start an instance of its local *CheckCreditRatings* workflow. On completion of the subworkflow, the bank's server would continue with its suspended workflow (Figure 3B). With global connectivity, it should be possible to enable such *peer-to-peer* workflow operation between heterogeneous servers.

Finally, as business-to-business interactions increase on the Internet, it is likely that workflows may be downloaded for just-in-time execution. *Downloadable* workflows make sense especially in cases where pre-installing and maintaining workflows is not cost effective. Consider an education brokerage service on the Internet (Figure 3C) that specializes in locating custom education services [Hama96]. In a plausible scenario, the

EducationBrokerage workflow downloads a *RequirementsGathering* subworkflow to the client organization and requests its execution. Next, the *EducationBrokerage* workflow downloads the requirements gathered to content providers along with a *RequestForProposal* subworkflow that the latter must execute to create the proposal. At the end, the brokerage compares all the proposals received and notifies the client.

2.2 Considerations in Distributed Workflow Components Design

The challenge in building a scalable workflow infrastructure lies in the design and implementation of distributed, interoperable workflow components. Workflow components will necessarily be disparate; they will either be adapted from existing proprietary workflow products owned by various vendors or be newly developed specifically for the distributed infrastructure. Workflow components will also be dispersed over the network; they will be owned physically by participants such as organizations, humans, and applications. The purpose of a distributed workflow infrastructure would be to allow these disparate components to interoperate over wide area networks and deliver workflow functionality. However, there are some important constraints that must be respected by such a distributed workflow infrastructure. These constraints are outlined in this section.

2.2.1 Heterogeneity of Workflow Specification Languages
As a practical matter, a wide variety of languages are used in the *specification* of workflows. These languages have different formalisms and operational semantics. The existence of multiple workflow specification languages is unlikely to go away either by convention or mandate. Reasons for this include the proprietary concerns of individual vendors that have committed themselves to specific languages in their products. Also, as increasingly diverse domains are mapped into the context of workflow, it becomes increasingly unlikely that the workflow specification needs of these domains (e.g., insurance, banking, healthcare, manufacturing, and telecommunications) will be satisfied via a common specification language. It is thus necessary that workflow developers have freedom in choosing multiple workflow specification languages in defining their applications, and yet be able to participate in the distributed workflow infrastructure.

2.2.2 Heterogeneity and Autonomy of Participants
To support workflow execution across a distributed infrastructure, the execution model must allow workflows to *invoke* the services of various workflow participants. Participants will be heterogeneous: humans, applications, business objects, and workflow systems are regularly invoked during the course of workflow execution. It is thus imperative that a distributed workflow infrastructure address issues of how participants can be invoked independent of their implementation. Third-party providers or developers of business objects and applications should be able to *workflow-enable* their components and plug them as participants into the distributed workflow infrastructure.

A participant in a heterogeneous workflow infrastructure must also be assumed to be autonomous. Autonomy implies that the participant is entirely responsible for work that happens within its specific scope of authority. Such a scope of authority, which the participant can exercise both in terms of its internal mechanisms and the uniform, external view it presents to workflows, is needed in a distributed workflow infrastructure to ensure privacy, security, and scalability. The degree of autonomy required or enforced by any given participant may vary depending on the needs of applications, nevertheless, a reasonable assertion is that each participant's need for autonomy will increase as the distributed workflow infrastructure grows to incorporate increasingly heterogeneous components. It is simply not possible to build a scalable workflow infrastructure based on a single, global scope of authority.

2.2.3 Workflows and Participants: Service Requestors and Service Providers

As seen above, there are essentially two kinds of components involved in workflow execution: *workflows* and *participants*. In this context, workflow execution across a distributed infrastructure may best be viewed in terms of *service requestors* and *service providers. Workflows act as service requestors. Participants such as humans, applications, and organizations act as service providers to workflows.* The delineation of the notions of service requestor and service provider results in a clear separation of the responsibilities associated with them. Workflows are responsible for 'workflow routing', which involves coordinating the scheduling and routing of work among various service providers. The workflow is also responsible for managing the flow of data and control among service providers, as well as for dealing with service provider failures and exceptions. A workflow is responsible *only* for the management of its process, and has no jurisdiction over service providers invoked during the course of its execution.

On the other hand, service providers are responsible for managing the execution of work requests sent to them by various workflows. For a service provider to function meaningfully in a distributed workflow infrastructure, the services it provides must be shareable among multiple, heterogeneous workflows which act as clients of those services. It is within the scope of authority of the service provider to bind a service request to a specific implementation. Service providers should also have discretion with respect to how requests to use their services are handled. For example, a service provider may delegate subtasks to other service providers, refuse to service certain requests, or forward requests to other service providers.

3. RainMaker Workflow Infrastructure

This section describes RainMaker, a workflow framework that consists of a workflow execution model and a core set of interfaces that can be implemented by distributed, heterogeneous workflow components. The workflow execution model captures the runtime relationships between workflow components in an implementation-independent manner. RainMaker distills the fundamental design abstractions in workflow systems and captures them as interfaces. Implementors of workflow components can use these interfaces to guarantee interoperability of their components and yet maintain control over implementation details.

3.1 RainMaker Workflow Execution Model

Workflows are instances of long running applications that model the execution of a process. During the execution of a workflow a number of service providers - humans, applications, organizations, other workflow systems - are invoked to perform the steps in the workflow. For example, a step may be a request to a human service provider, an invocation of an available application, or an invocation to another workflow server to run a workflow on behalf of the requesting workflow.

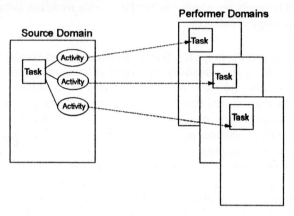

Fig. 4. Execution Model

The RainMaker workflow execution model can be described using four fundamental concepts (Figure 4). The basic unit of work in this model is the *Task*, which represents a long running computation. Each Task executes within a certain scope of authority or domain that owns the Task. A Task can be simple, in which case it is indivisible, and can be executed completely within the domain in which it is created. A Task can also be a workflow, in which case it generates *Activities*, which represent the steps in the workflow. Actual execution of these Activities is delegated out over time to external service provider domains, defined as *Performers* in this model. The domain of the workflow Task is called a *Source*, or a service requestor. Once a Performer receives a request from a Source, it creates a Task within its scope of authority or domain to service the request.

Fig. 5. Task States

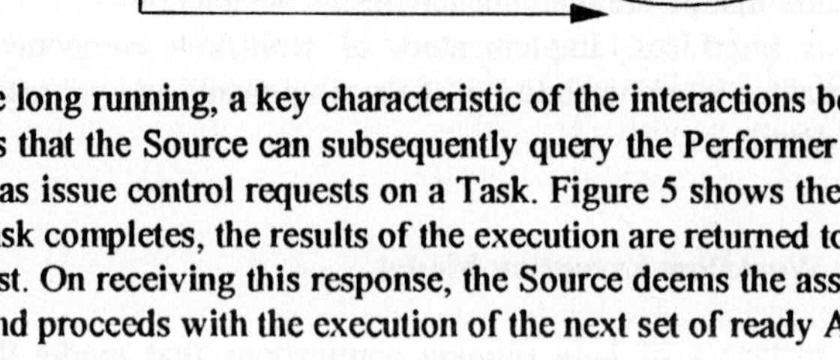

Since Tasks are long running, a key characteristic of the interactions between a Source and a Performer is that the Source can subsequently query the Performer about the status of a Task as well as issue control requests on a Task. Figure 5 shows the lifecycle of any Task. After the Task completes, the results of the execution are returned to the Source that initiated the request. On receiving this response, the Source deems the associated Activity to be completed and proceeds with the execution of the next set of ready Activities.

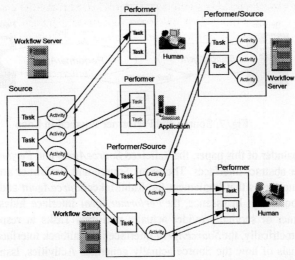

Fig. 6. Recursive behavior of service providers

The key observation that lies at the core of the RainMaker model is that workflow execution is essentially based on the *principle of delegation*. The Source (the workflow domain) is the *delegator* responsible for coordinating the order in which work is *delegated* to specific Performers (the service provider domains), which act as *delegatees*. However, once work has been delegated to a service provider, the latter has complete authority over how the work is actually implemented. As seen above, a Task can be simple or it can be a workflow; and it is within the scope of authority of the Performer to decide that. The Source merely interacts with the abstract notion of Task on the Performer, it has no knowledge of its internal implementation on the Performer. This is an application of the composite design pattern [Gamma94] , and allows complete privacy and late-binding of Tasks to their implementation on the Performer. This execution model has the recursive property that a Performer can choose to bind an incoming Task request from a Source to a workflow implementation, and itself act as a Source for other downstream Performers (Figure 6).

3.2 RainMaker Interfaces

Based on the execution model described in the previous section, RainMaker defines a set of abstract interfaces that represent the principal components of a workflow system. In this section, we describe these interfaces in detail and demonstrate how they can be used. The core RainMaker interfaces that help support the execution model are:

- *PerformerAgent:* An abstract interface that is implemented by Performers on the network. The interface provides mechanisms for delegating, controlling, and querying Tasks on the Performer.
- *SourceAgent:* An abstract interface implemented by Sources on the network. It provides a callback mechanism for Performers to return the results of Tasks to Sources.

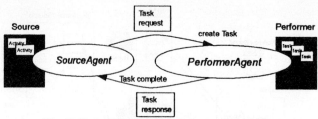

Fig. 7. Source and Performer Interaction Loop

For the remainder of this paper, the italicized *SourceAgent* and *PerformerAgent* refer to the RainMaker abstract interfaces. The terms Source and Performer are used generically to refer to components that implement the RainMaker *SourceAgent* and *PerformerAgent* interfaces respectively. In essence, the *PerformerAgent* interface hides the internals of how a Performer or service provider actually performs Tasks in response to the Task requests. Symmetrically, the *SourceAgent* interface is a callback interface implemented to hide the internals of how the Source actually generates Activities, issues Task requests, and handles responses from Performers. The interfaces also describe control mechanisms by which Tasks can be suspended, resumed, and aborted; and query mechanisms by which their status can be tracked. The asynchronous interaction loop between Sources and Performers is shown in Figure 7.

3.2.1 PerformerAgent

The *PerformerAgent* interface represents any generic Performer or service provider on the network. The following methods are defined in the interface:

1. createTask(SourceAgent source, ActivityID activityid, TaskRequest taskreq): Task requests are sent to a Performer by invoking this method. The source argument describes to the Performer the origin of the request; it is a reference to the Source that can be used as a callback handle by the Performer once the Task is completed. The activityid argument is a unique reference to the Activity that is being delegated to the Performer. It is returned with the results to the Source after the Task is completed. This is needed by the Source to identify the callback with the appropriate Activity within its domain. The taskreq parameter is a service-specific data structure that contains information about the type of Task requested and the necessary parameters needed to create an instance of the Task. RainMaker does not mandate the content of taskreq and leaves it to specific implementations. Consequently, the TaskRequest type may be based on standardized Task types that are understood by domain-specific Sources and Performers (such service standards will hopefully emerge in vertical domains such as insurance, manufacturing, banking, healthcare, etc). Alternately, it can be based on private agreements between specific Sources and Performers. The method returns a unique TaskID to the caller which can be used subsequently for tracking and controlling this Task.

2. abortTask(TaskID taskid): A Task executing on a Performer can be aborted by an invocation of this method. The semantics of abort is that the Task is forced into an ABORTED state by the Performer. In the handling of abort requests RainMaker does not require that Performers be stateful or that Task implementations be

transactional. It is left as a quality of service issue that lies outside the scope of the basic workflow framework.

3. `suspendTask(TaskID taskid)`: A Task executing on a Performer can be suspended by an invocation of this method. The semantics of suspend is that the Task is forced into a SUSPENDED state by the Performer.

4. `resumeTask(TaskID taskid)`: A previously suspended Task on a Performer can be resumed by an invocation of this method. The semantics of suspend is that the Task is returned to a RUNNING state by the Performer.

5. `queryTask(TaskID taskid)`: The status of a Task on a Performer can be requested via this method. Service-independent state information (NOT STARTED, RUNNING, SUSPENDED, ABORTED, COMPLETED) is returned as a result of this call. Service-specific state information may also be returned as part of the result.

6. `listTasks()`: The Tasks within a Performer can be listed by an invocation of this method. This can be used to monitor the workload on a Performer.

7. `listTaskDefinitions()`: The capabilities of a Performer can be listed using this method. It can be used by Sources to discover Performers of interest. Note that if a trading service for Performers is available, the same capabilities would be visible via a trading service browser.

3.2.2 SourceAgent

The SourceAgent interface provides a callback mechanism for Performers to communicate with Sources. The following methods are defined in the interface:

1. completedTask(PerformerAgent performer, ActivityID activityid, TaskResponse taskresp): Task responses are sent back to a Source by invoking this method. The performer argument describes to the Source the origin of the response; it is a reference to the Performer that performed the Task. The activityid argument is returned with the Task response to the Source. This is needed by the Source to identify the callback with the appropriate Activity within its domain. The `taskresp` parameter is a service-specific data structure that contains the results of the Task execution. As with `taskreq`, RainMaker does not mandate the content of `taskresp` and leaves it to specific implementations.

2. `refusedTask(PerformerAgent performer, ActivityID activityid)`: Since Performers are autonomous, they may elect not to service a Task request. This method allows a Performer to notify the Source about its inability to service the request.

3. `forwardedTask(PerformerAgent performer, ActivityID activityID, PerformerAgent newperformer, TaskID taskid)`: This method provides a mechanism for a Performer to forward a Task request, if permitted, to another Performer based on its knowledge of the latter's capabilities and notify the Source accordingly. The forwarding itself can occur using the standard `createTask()` method on the latter Performer. The identity of the latter Performer and the TaskID returned by it are returned to the Source using this method.

4. `seekPermissionToStartTask(PerformerAgent performer, ActivityID activityID)`: This method allows a Performer to seek the Source's permission when it is ready to start a Task requested earlier by the Source. If the return value of this call is true, then the Performer actually starts the Task; else it simply aborts the Task.

3.3 RainMaker Applicability

In this section, we show how the RainMaker interfaces and workflow execution model can be applied. The purpose is to demonstrate the wide range of distributed, interoperable components that can be built using the RainMaker infrastructure.

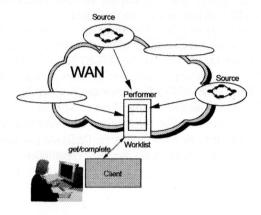

Fig. 8. Worklists as Performers

3.3.1 Human Performers

The *PerformerAgent* interface is versatile and can support a wide range of service provider behaviors. Human participants constitute the most important class of service providers in any workflow environment. The classic representation of a human participant in a workflow system is via the *worklist*; worklists are persistent queues similar to email inboxes through which work is assigned to human participants. In RainMaker terms, a Worklist is a Performer on the network that represents a human participant. Various Sources can send Task requests to a Worlist Performer. Task requests, in turn, generate WorkItem requests that are surfaced to the human participant through the *Worklist* interface. The *Worklist* interface permits humans (or any worklist client application) 'pull' access to WorkItem requests (Figure 8). Effectively, the *Worklist* interface offers a mechanism for asynchronous exchange of requests between workflows and humans. Sources can continue to post Task requests to a Worklist Performer even when the human is disconnected from the network. When the human reconnects with the Worklist, the *Worklist* interface enables access to stored WorkItem requests from his or her Worklist client application. The following methods form the core of the *Worklist* interface:

- getWorklistIndex(): The method returns a list of WorkItem descriptions of currently waiting WorkItem requests. It is used by worklist client applications as a refresh mechanism.
- getWorkItem(WorkItemID wid): This method returns a WorkItemRequest.
- completedWorkItem(WorkItemID wid, WorkItemResponse wresp): This method signals to the Worklist that a WorkItem has been completed by the human participant.

The relationship between a Worklist client and its Worklist is shown in Figure 9. The dotted arrows indicate that once a Task request is downloaded to the client, the human can work in a disconnected mode if the Task request contains all information needed to perform it, and no network accesses for data or applications are required.

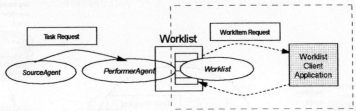

Fig. 9. Using the Worklist Interface

In RainMaker, the Worklist is only one of many possible modes of interaction possible between a Performer and the human or application that owns it. It is conceivable that a Performer entity on the network and its owner may communicate via other metaphors such as *push* and *publish/subscribe*, and possibly over cellular and wireless networks. Such implementations would fit naturally into the RainMaker framework, and would extend the reach of workflows beyond traditional client platforms such as desktops and laptops to nontraditional client platforms such as PDAs.

3.3.2 Heterogeneous Application Performers

Heterogeneous applications can be plugged into the distributed workflow infrastructure via 'adapters' that implement the *PerformerAgent* interface (Figure 10). Independently developed, heterogeneous database servers, printer servers, email gateways, fax gateways, legacy applications, etc can be cheaply incorporated into the workflow infrastructure using this mechanism.

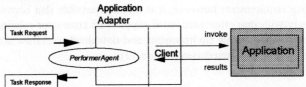

Fig. 10. Application Performers

3.3.3 Peer-to-Peer Workflow Execution

The *PerformerAgent* interface can also be implemented by gateways to heterogeneous workflow systems. Peer-to-peer execution of workflows that reside on heterogeneous workflow systems is a necessary prerequisite for the automation of inter-organizational processes. Sources and Performers can be used to model such peer-to-peer behavior. Any workflow system that wishes to make its internal workflow scripts accessible to other workflow systems or Sources can implement the *PerformerAgent* interface. Sources can then use the listTaskDefinitions() method to inspect the capabilities of the workflow system and use the createTask() method to request workflow execution. The *SourceAgent* and *PerformerAgent* abstractions hide the implementation details -

812

including the heterogeneity of their workflow specification languages - of the participating workflow systems (Figure 11).

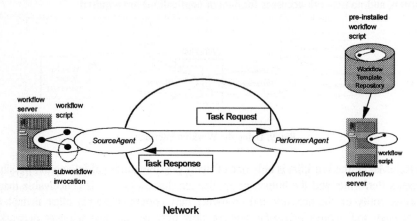

Fig. 11. Peer-to-peer workflows

3.3.4 Downloadable Workflow Execution

Since the implementation of TaskRequest is left completely open to specific Sources and Performers, it can be used to download workflow scripts as well. Consider the downloadable workflow scenario where a Source delegates a (sub) workflow execution to a Performer, and as a part of the Task request, sends it the script for the workflow itself. This is feasible in the RainMaker infrastructure, as long as the Performer domain has the environment needed to execute scripts sent to it from the Source domain. This is admittedly a strong requirement; however, it is entirely possible that organizations that partner very closely with one other (dedicated supplier or contractor relationships) may actually implement homogeneous environments and download workflow scripts to each other for just-in-time workflow execution (Figure 12).

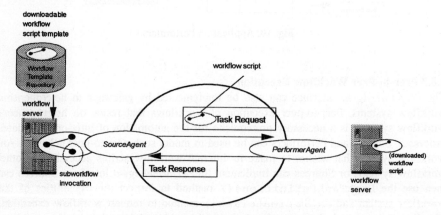

Fig. 12. Downloadable workflow execution

3.3.5 Role Management

Roles are an important feature in workflow systems. Based on their capabilities, participants can be grouped into roles, and Task requests can be issued to roles instead of individual participants for the purposes of efficiency. Various policies can be used to determine how Task requests are issued to roles and how they are retracted. For example, in many workflow systems, identical work items can be assigned to members of a role, and after *any* one of them starts working on it, it is retracted from the worklists of others. RainMaker avoids committing itself to any specific policy for Task request and retraction based on roles; however, an important hook for implementing various role-based policies is provided via the seekPermissiontoStartTask() method on the *SourceAgent* interface, which is used by Performers to check with the Source before actually starting a Task.

3.3.6 Source Heterogeneity

A key characteristic of RainMaker is that the definition of the *SourceAgent* interface is generic enough to support a wide range of semantics, and can embody workflows described in any arbitrary workflow specification language. Any component capable of generating Task requests, regardless of the means whereby these requests are generated, qualifies as a Source; and can implement the *SourceAgent* interface. RainMaker thus allows heterogeneous workflows to be plugged into a distributed workflow infrastructure cheaply, and these workflows can invoke the services of available Performers using standard mechanisms.

3.4 Considerations in RainMaker Design

The RainMaker infrastructure is minimalist in its approach; it defines interactions between core workflow components and avoids mandating specific behaviors for Sources and Performers. However, for real workflows to make use of RainMaker, a collection of related services need to be available. In this section, we explore some of these services and issues pertaining to them. In keeping with our overall design philosophy, these services are perceived as relating to RainMaker, but not part of it.

3.4.1 Trading Service for Performers

Sources need to locate Performers on the distributed workflow infrastructure. While the designer of a workflow may designate a Performer during specification, he might instead specify a Performer role , the resolution to a specific Performer fitting that role being deferred until workflow execution. This can be very useful because it allows for late-binding of Activities to Performers on the network.

A trading service offers a meaningful way for Performers to register and advertise their service capabilities. In any application domain where RainMaker may be applied, it is reasonable to expect that a name space of standardized task or service types will either be available or eventually emerge by consensus. A view of this trading service of Performers should be available to the workflow designer; an interface to it should be available to Sources at execution time to retrieve automatically handles to Performers. CORBA-based implementations of RainMaker could utilize the CORBA Trading Services for this purpose.

While simple trading services may work well with *standardized service types*, they will break down in the face of new and non-standardized services that innovative Performers may provide. In such situations, *standardized descriptions of services* will be necessary. The problem of service mediation had been explored in distributed computing to allow new service types to be *discovered* via the use of standardized Service Description Languages [Merz94]. This is an area of future research in the context of RainMaker. The listTaskDefinitions() method on the *PerformerAgent* interface offers a hook for retrieving capabilities based on such service description languages.

3.4.2 Failure Handling and Compensations

Much workflow research in recent years has focused on the transactional aspects of workflows [Rus94, Al96, Ley95]. The basic objective has been to ensure the recoverability of workflows, since workflows are long-running applications that can execute over days or weeks or months. Flat ACIDic transactions do not work for such applications; workflow researchers have thus borrowed concepts from nested transactions, sagas, and spheres of compensation to address the needs of workflows.

The distribution of Tasks, as proposed in RainMaker, alters the picture significantly. If Source workflows are to execute across wide area networks, the autonomy of Performers and their non-proximity to each other and to the Source itself must be taken as a given. A Source attempting to recover must request for compensations from Performers. RainMaker takes the view that a compensation is like any other Task (Figure 13). This is reasonable because the meaning of a compensation can be understood only in the context of a specific application or service; there is no general-purpose semantics for compensation. For example, *reserve* and *cancel* are both meaningful Task types that can be handled by a *Hotel Service* Performer. This Performer is authoritative in terms of what compensation means within the context of hotel services, and how to provide it. The Source for its part understands the semantics of both *reserve* and *cancel*, the semantic relationship between them, and how to invoke them. RainMaker is thus *service-neutral*; it does not claim to know the semantics or implementations of services provided by Performers and their compensations, and hence does not distinguish between regular Tasks and 'compensation' Tasks. In this context, long-running *conversations* between autonomous network entities that engage in business transactions are of interest [Dan97].

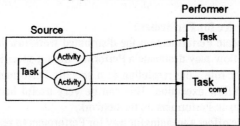

Fig. 13. Compensations as ordinary Tasks

Since compensations are like other tasks, a Performer must describe its compensation capabilities on the trading service as well. Once a Task has been requested of a Performer, any subsequent request for a compensation (if available), would be bound by the terms and conditions of the original request. This in turn leads to issues related to description of *terms and conditions*, their enforcement on the part of the Performer, and their nonrepudiability on the part of the Source, all of which are open questions left for future research.

3.4.3 Security

For workflows to run across wide area networks and especially across organizations, multiple security concerns must be addressed. First, an authentication mechanism must exist to validate the identity of both Source and Performer domains. This would allow basic functions such as Worklist access and Performer invocation to be done in a secure fashion only by authorized users or components. Second, access control rights need to be described and enforced in a scalable fashion to control access to methods on Performers and Sources. Third, the integrity and privacy of Task requests and responses exchanged between Sources and Performers should be maintained. Finally, support for nonrepudiability and enforcement of terms and conditions is needed. We are currently exploring these issues by drawing from the state-of-practice in distributed systems security. Many of these problems can be easily alleviated in the case of workflows between trusted parties by setting up private channels (Intranets or Extranets) between the participant individuals and organizations.

3.5 RainMan System

Using the RainMaker framework and interfaces, we have designed RainMan, a prototype distributed, object-oriented workflow system written in Java, that can support a broad range of workflows on the Internet [Paul97b]. The system has been designed as a loosely-coupled collection of independent, lightweight services on the network. Process management, activity distribution, directory services, worklist management, and application management are all treated as independent services that work together to deliver workflow functionality.

The architecture of RainMan consists of a *runtime environment*, a collection of distributed services implemented as Java applications, and *user interface components*, implemented as Java applets and used by workflow users to interact with the runtime system and executing workflows. To facilitate low cost, Internet-based workflow participation, the ongoing implementation of RainMan uses open standards and Web-browser based user interface components.

4 Related Work

The Workflow Management Coalition (WfMC) - an industry-wide consortium of workflow system vendors formed in 1993 - has defined a set of interfaces to enable workflow system interoperability [WfMC]. Our research stems from the realization that the WfMC standard is unsuitable for workflow execution using distributed, interoperable components. The standard assumes that a workflow server is a monolithic entity that centralizes a wide range of workflow-related services; this is a result of the WfMC's clear bias towards designing a standard to suit the needs of current commercial workflow products. The negative implications of the WfMC standard for distributed workflow execution are well-understood and have been discussed in detail elsewhere [Schul96,

Paul97a]. For example, the standard requires the workflow server to host worklists on behalf of all its participants. Since worklists are hidden within the workflow server and not externally addressable, tasks can be sent only to worklists that reside in the same workflow server. Thus, to participate in multiple heterogeneous workflows, a participant must have a worklist maintained separately inside each workflow server, connect to them explicitly, and *pull* tasks from all of them. This is not a scalable solution, especially if one is to participate in a large number of workflows on the Internet, use thin clients or PDAs, or operate in a disconnected mode. Of current interest is the Workflow RFP issued by the OMG in May 1997 [OMGwf97]; we expect that the submissions made in response to this RFP will address the needs of distributed workflow execution more realistically.

There is a growing body of research in the area of workflow systems, aside from work occurring in the standards bodies. An interesting model of workflow execution that can decentralize both workflow coordination and activity execution has been proposed in the context of the Arjuna project [Ranno97]. This execution model decentralizes workflow coordination by installing 'task controller' objects in different domains that coordinate with each other to deliver workflow routing functionality. While RainMaker and Arjuna share a belief in the importance of distributed workflow components, our work places greater emphasis on the interoperability of *disparate* workflow components, and less emphasis on decentralized coordination. The issue of decentralized process enactment in the domain of software development has been addressed in OZ [BenSh94]. The premise of decentralized domains is the same in RainMaker; however, the OZ project emphasizes *collaborative steps* between independent, dispersed processes as a design requirement, and requires that a common process modeling formalism be used across domains. RainMaker does not address collaborative process steps and does not mandate common modeling formalisms; instead, it emphasizes interoperability between *fully autonomous* Performers with *heterogeneous* formalisms via standardized object interfaces. The issues of reliable messaging and interoperability between workflow servers and applications in a client-server framework have been discussed in [Schus97]. Programming workflows as active objects using a class libraries approach within a nested-transactional environment has been explored in [Papa97].

5 Conclusions

RainMaker is an attempt to design and implement a distributed workflow infrastructure based on interoperable, heterogeneous components that can be deployed within and across organizational boundaries. This is a relevant and important problem as individuals and organizations rapidly become interconnected. This interconnectivity can be exploited to enable workflows on a much wider scale at a relatively low cost. It can also be used to introduce workflow technology to emerging application areas such as virtual enterprises and electronic commerce.

RainMaker defines a core set of abstract interfaces that represent the essential components of a workflow infrastructure. The contribution of RainMaker lies in the clean separation of responsibilities between the domains of workflows (that can be implemented using workflow specification languages or mechanisms) and service providers (that represent humans, legacy applications, organizations, and workflow

817

systems). An inviolable design principle is that participants in a distributed workflow infrastructure will be heterogeneous and autonomous.

RainMaker defines an execution model of asynchronous task creation, control, and query that can be used by workflow components to interact with one another. This execution model is ideally suited to workflows and other long running applications that need to delegate tasks to various autonomous service provider domains. Service provider domains themselves may implement their tasks as workflows, allowing workflow computation to extend recursively across such domains. The RainMaker interfaces enable developers and service providers, including owners of legacy workflow systems, to build and deploy pluggable, workflow-enabled components (Figure 14).

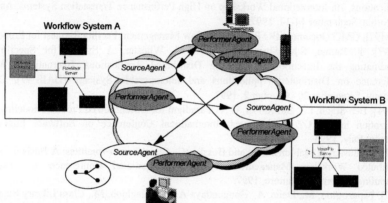

Fig. 14. A distributed infrastructure of heterogeneous, interoperable workflow components

Using RainMaker, we have implemented RainMan, a distributed workflow system prototype written in Java. The system consists of a collection of independent, lightweight components and services. We are using RainMan to experiment with a range of interesting features such as dynamic workflow modification, disconnected participation, and workflow participation via Personal Digital Assistants.

References

[Silver95]: Bruce Silver, The BIS Guide to Workflow Software, BIS Strategy Decisions, One Longwater Circle, Norwell, MA 02061, 1995.
[WfMC]: Workflow Management Coalition, *http://www.aiai.ed.ac.uk/WfMC*
[Hama96]: Hamalainen, M., Whinston, A.B., and Vishik, S., Electronic Markets for Learning: Education Brokerages on the Internet, CACM, Vol. 39, Number 6, June 1996.
[Gamma94]: Gamma, E., Helm, R., Johnson, R., and Vlissides, J., Design Patterns, Addison-Wesley, 1994.
[Merz94]: Merz, M., Muller, K., and Lamersdorf, W., Service Trading and Mediation in Distributed Computing Systems, International Conference on Distributed Computing Systems, 1994.
[Schul96]: Schulze, W., Bohm, M., and Meyer-Wegener, K., Services of Workflow Objects and Workflow Meta-objects in OMG compliant Environments, OOPSLA Workshop on Business Objects Design and Implementation, 1996.
[Paul97a]: Paul, S., Park, E., and Chaar, J., Essential Requirements for a Workflow Standard, OOPSLA Workshop on Business Objects Design and Implementation, October 6th, 1997, *http://www.tiac.net/users/jsuth/oopsla97/santanu.html*

[Paul97b]: Paul, S., Park, E., and Chaar, J., RainMan: A Workflow System for the Internet, USENIX Symposium on Internet Technologies & Systems, Monterrey, California, 7-11 December, 1997. (To appear)

[Rus94]: M. Rusinkiewicz and A. Sheth, Specification and Execution of Transactional Workflows, In W. Kim, Editor, Modern Database Systems: The Object Model, Interopreability and Beyond, ACM Press, 1994.

[Al96]: G. Alonso, D. Agrawal, A. El Abbadi, M. Kamath, R. Gunthor, and C. Mohan, Advanced Transactional Models in Workflow Contexts, In Proceedings of ICDE, 1996.

[Ley95]: Frank Leymann, Supporting Business Transactions via Partial Backward Recovery in Workflow Management, in Proceedings of BTW'95, Dresden, Germany, 1995, Springer Verlag.

[Dan97]: Asit Dan and Francis Parr, The Coyote Approach to Network Centric Service Applications, 7th International Workshop on High Performance Transaction Systems, Asilomar, California, September 14-17, 1997.

[OMGwf97]: OMG Document BO RFP2, Workflow Management Facility Request for Proposal.

[Ranno97]: F. Ranno, S.K. Shrivastava and S.M. Wheater, A System for Specifing and Coordinating the Execution of Reliable Distributed Applications, International Working Conference on Distributed Applications and Interoperable Systems (DAIS'97), Cottbus, Germany, September 30 - October 2, 1997.

[BenSh94]: Ben-Shaul, I.Z. and Kaiser, G., A Paradigm for Decentralized Process Modeling and its Realization in the OZ Environment, International Conference on Software Engineering, Sorrento, Italy, 1994.

[Schus97]: Schuster, H., Jablonski, S., and Bussler, C., Client/Server Qualities: A Basis for Reliable Distributed Workflow Management Systems, International Conference on Distributed Computing Systems, Baltimore, 1997.

[Papa97]: Papazoglou, M., Delis, A., Bouguettaya A., and Haghjoo, M., Class Library Support for Workflow Environments and Applications, IEEE Transactions on Computers, Vol. 46, No. 6, June 1997.

Design Criteria for a Virtual Market Place (ViMP)

S. Field, C. Facciorusso, Y. Hoffner, A. Schade, and M. Stolze

IBM Research Division, Zurich Research Laboratory, CH-8803 Rüschlikon,
Switzerland
sif,cfa,yho,san,mrs@zurich.ibm.com

Abstract. This paper considers the requirements customers and providers have from a virtual insurance market place, and proposes a set of
desirable features to satisfy them. A design implementing these features
is proposed, based on a logical structuring of the information needed to
support the dialogue between providers and customers. The applicability
of this design for market places trading products other than insurance
is discussed, and further research to consider the particular features of
business services is suggested.

1 Introduction

1.1 Virtual Market Places

The organisation and desirable features of electronic market places can be determined from a study of the requirements of the principal parties involved:
the prospective customers and the product or services providers. Rather than
attempt to generalise these requirements for all possible market places at the
outset, we present a study of the particular requirements for a virtual insurance
market place in Section 2.

Insurance and other financial services products are well suited to being sold
electronically, as they are in effect purchases of a promise, in the form of a contract, which can be successfully described in detail electronically (as compared
with physical goods, where pictures on the Internet are a poor substitute for
seeing and touching the real thing).

Section 3 describes the desirable features of a virtual insurance market place,
and proposes a design for their realisation, while Section 4 considers the extent
to which these requirements and features can be applied to market places which
trade products and services other than insurance.

2 Insurance Market Place Requirements

2.1 Customer Requirements of an Electronic Insurance Market Place

From a customer point of view, there is a clear attraction to being able to shop
electronically in one place, and purchase more than one product from different

providers, or compare multiple offers which may satisfy the customer's requirements to varying degrees. What do customers require of an electronic insurance market place?

C1 *A recognised point of entry:* Customers want a point of entry to the market place which is easy to find, such as a single, recognisable and well-advertised, URL on the Internet.

C2 *Choice for the customer:* Customers would like a market place to give them access to wide variety of insurance products offered by a large number of insurance companies. Whilst insurance is an important purchase (it is compulsory in many cases, e.g. car insurance), it deals with matters which most people do not wish to spend much time discussing: accidents, illness, disability, financial and physical risk. It is therefore something many customers wish to purchase quickly and efficiently, if possible at a single location.

C3 *An audited and regulated market place:* Purchase of a financial product such as insurance requires the purchaser to place considerable trust in the provider. For most insurances, payment for coverage is made in advance, and all that is received is a promise of cover, in the form of a contract. For this reason, financial services is a highly regulated sector of most economies, where government agencies regulate the sale of financial products within their spheres of control. This provides a degree of protection for customers which must also be reflected in any electronic market place in which financial products are sold.

C4 *Supply necessary information only once:* Customers would prefer to specify their requirements, and provide information only once. This requirement is relatively easy to satisfy for market places dealing with simple products such as books or CDs, where the customer's requirements are simply stated, and once a purchase decision has been made, further information (such as delivery and payment details) can be provided to the selected provider. With insurance, the customer's requirements are not always so easy to translate into a set of suitable offers without a considerable exchange of information between customer and prospective insurance providers [1]. In addition, insurance companies typically require a considerable amount of information from customers before they are prepared to put a detailed offer before them. A major attraction for customers visiting an insurance market place is therefore the consolidation of the information exchange which must take place between them and each provider into a single dialogue with the market place.

C5 *Facilitate product selection — receive only relevant offers:* Customers wish to be able to express preferences concerning their requirements, and therefore filter the large volume of possible offers available, concentrating on those offers which most closely match their requirements.

C6 *Protect confidential information:* For many classes of insurance, an applicant must provide personal information to the insurer (e.g. name, address, date of birth) before receiving an offer or quotation. Consumers wish to be assured that personal information will be treated confidentially, and may be particularly concerned when being asked to divulge personal information to an Internet-based market place representing more than one company.

C7 *Only provide personal data when necessary:* Customers are often reluctant to divulge personal information before a level of confidence has been established between them and the providers in the market place. This suggests that providers should demonstrate to the customer that they have an understanding of the customer's requirements, and that they are likely to be able to offer something relevant, before they require the customer to provide detailed personal information.

C8 *Explore offer feature space:* Insurance products are complex, with different offers containing subtle variations in coverage and features. There are often additional, priced options for the customer to consider. Customers therefore wish to be able to compare the features of offered products, and make the tradeoff between the prices and available features of competing insurance policies.

C9 *Interruptible long-life sessions:* The purchase of an insurance or other financial product is often a long-term financial decision. Customers do not wish to be forced to make a quick purchase decision, and in some countries the law requires financial services providers to give customers time to reconsider purchase decisions (e.g. the Financial Services Act in the United Kingdom). There is therefore a need for a market place to allow the customer to suspend a dialogue before it has reached a conclusion, and return to it at a later stage.

C10 *Reward for loyalty:* Customers may wish to be rewarded for making multiple purchases from a single provider, either during a single visit to the market place, or over a period of time.

C11 *Protection from direct access:* Customers may not wish to be bothered by unsolicited email, and would not wish their identity to be made available to all providers in a market place.

2.2 Provider Requirements of an Electronic Insurance Market Place

Why should an insurance company choose to join an electronic market place, alongside competitors, when it is quite capable of advertising and selling its products electronically from its own internet site? Of course, there is nothing to preclude an insurer from doing both, the electronic equivalent of a farm having a shop to serve local callers while also selling produce at the local market. Critical mass is the main driver in the success of a market place — and this requires a reasonable population of both customers and providers.

P1 *A well-visited market place:* Insurers will be more inclined to join a market place if they believe that it will be visited by many potentially profitable customers. As customers are more prepared to visit a market place if it is populated by many insurers (see C2 above), insurers must therefore accept the necessity of joining market places alongside their competitors. Once a certain critical mass is achieved, the fact that competitors are there can become an incentive to join in itself.

P2 *Provide complete and dynamic control of the advertising:* Insurance companies wish to retain control of their presence in the market place. This means being able to add new products, withdraw old ones, or modify existing ones. Changes to a product may include alteration of the premium calculation, the underwriting or marketing criteria applied to it, or changes to its terms, conditions or benefits. Traditionally, the calculation of insurance premiums has been based on mathematical models, associating historic claims behaviour of a population with application form details, translated into the application of a simple algorithm to a set of rating tables. As this methodology has been common among insurers it has been possible with some classes of business such as car insurance, to apply a common algorithm (known as a rating engine) to rating tables specific to individual products. This has made the sharing of pricing information on a common platform (e.g. in an insurance broker's office, or an Internet market place such as InsWeb [2], InsureMarket [3], and Screentrade [4]) feasible. However, more recently, there has been a trend among insurers towards applying more complex models which rate applicants as individuals rather than as members of larger populations [5]. Insurers no longer wish their premium calculation to be tied to a common algorithm, considering their freedom to calculate premiums as they wish an essential tool with which to control the profitability of a portfolio.

P3 *Protect commercially sensitive information and business processes:* As mentioned in P2 above, the premium calculation has become a commercially sensitive business process for many classes of insurance. There is a desire to keep this process, and information relating to it, within the insurer's organisational boundary, while allowing the market place access to them where necessary.

P4 *Allow integration and exploitation of legacy systems:* Much of the information about policies required for the market place will already be stored in existing applications and databases, in support of other sales channels employed by insurers. To avoid wasteful replication of this information, insurers wish to reuse such existing information and processes when providing offers via the market place.

P5 *An audited and regulated market place:* Insurance is a regulated business in most economies, and reputable insurers will wish to see that competition in an electronic market place is free and fair, and that regulations are complied with by all participants. Auditing will help to ensure that disputes are dealt with fairly.

P6 *Avoid unnecessary interaction with customers:* Insurers wish to apply their own underwriting and marketing criteria to customers, with some filtering of applicants taking place before any lengthy dialogue with them is entered. This will help to minimise the expense of handling customer enquiries via the market place, and avoid triggering costly back-office processes unnecessarily.

P7 *Allow provider and product differentiation and specialisation:* Insurers do not wish their products to be treated as commodities, compared merely on price. The benefits of choosing one or another insurer are difficult to compare at the time of purchase, and for many classes of insurance, customers hope that they will never receive the benefits (i.e. make a claim). Compulsory insurances, such as car insurance, tend to be similarly packaged by insurers because they are shaped by legislation, and whilst insurers often offer options around the basic cover, electronic comparison makes it easiest to focus on premium. Insurers would like their corporate branding and product features to be compared in addition to premium.

P8 *Allow for human intervention in the decision process:* Whilst mathematical models play an increasing role in the insurance underwriting process (see P2 above), there may still be circumstances in which insurers wish to involve expert underwriters in the process of deciding whether to put one or more offers to a customer, and with what terms and conditions. The market place must therefore allow an insurer to take time in deciding how to respond to a customer request for a quotation.

P9 *Special customer treatment:* Insurers may wish to tailor offers for individual customers. For example they may wish to treat existing or former customers differently according to their previous policy history.

3 Desirable Features of a Virtual Insurance Market Place

This section proposes a number of key features which bring together many of the requirements of both customers and providers as described above. Not all of the requirements can be reconciled with each other, and a certain amount of compromise, either among the requirements of the customer or the provider, or between them, must be achieved.

For example, among the customer requirements are conflicting desires to restrict provision of personal information, yet receive a wide variety of offers from insurers. On the provider side, insurers want control over the advertising process, and to protect commercially sensitive information, yet they wish to join a market which will be well-visited, which requires them to share the market place with competitors. Customers want easy comparison among competing products, while insurers want to maximise product differentiation.

The eight features described below represent a reasonable compromise across the set of requirements described in Section 2, which we believe will result in a market place which is attractive to both insurers and prospective customers, thus maximising the possibility of achieving the critical mass necessary for the success of the market place. The connection between the features and the requirements described in Section 2 is indicated in parentheses.

3.1 Centralised Point of Entry

Given that insurers are, in principle, prepared to consider joining a market place which will also be inhabited by competitors, both customers and insurers share an interest in the market place being easy to locate. Insurers wish to maximise the number of prospective customer who visit the market place (P1) provided that they can influence which ones they conduct a dialogue with (P6). Customers want a "one-stop shop". (C1, C2). Both customers and insurers have an interest in a market place which can be regulated (C3, P5). Whilst a centralised point of entry is not a prerequisite for monitoring and regulation, it certainly makes provision of this facility easier.

A single entry point, in the form of a home page on the Internet, is therefore proposed, to represent the interests of all of the market place participants.

3.2   Standardised Dialogue

The customer wishes to obtain offers from across the market (C2), while providing information about their requirements and risk profile just once (C4). Whilst this would appear to be in conflict with the insurers desire to control the dialogue with the customer (P3), some compromise on the part of the insurer would appear to be necessary if a well-visited market place is to be achieved (P1). If a "one to many" dialogue is to be consolidated as a single conversation from the customer's point of view, then some agreement concerning how questions are asked of the customer, must be achieved among the insurers. This could take the form of agreeing common application forms (such as already exist to a certain extent in the US with the Accord organisation), or an agreement to construct application forms from a common pool of questions (e.g. the use of a common data dictionary by members of Polaris/CLMI in the UK). The former would simplify the task of implementing the dialogue with the customer, at the cost of reduced control over that dialogue by the insurers, while the latter requires the development of an interface which can dynamically construct forms from the data dictionary, depending on the stage of the dialogue, and the information requirements of those insurers which are still party to it.

Further complications arise concerning the extent to which insurers should be allowed to impose validation rules at the point of data entry. Whilst this is preferable to validation on submission, difficulties arise if two or more insurers require contradictory validation rules. A two stage approach is proposed whereby simple validation, which can be agreed by all insurers, can be performed at the point of data entry, but with provision for individual insurers to apply further validation rules on receipt of completed forms.

A standardised dialogue is also in conflict with the insurers' requirement to project their own branded image (P7). The dialogue between an insurer and prospective customer represents an opportunity to convey brand and image which is in danger of being lost in the case where the dialogue is standardised across the different market place providers. Opportunities must therefore be found during the dialogue process for differences among insurers to be presented to the customer. This may take the form of presenting company and product logos, or indicating to the customer which questions on a dynamically constructed form are being asked by which insurers.

3.3 Two-Way Selection Process

Both customers and insurers wish to be able to make selections. Customers wish to be able to specify requirements, in terms of desirable product features, and restrict the offers they receive to those which most closely satisfy those requirements (C5). Insurers wish to be able to apply their own marketing and underwriting criteria to control which products are offered to prospective customers, and to avoid unnecessary processing of applications from unsuitable customers (P6). This suggests that the dialogue between customer and insurers should be bi-directional, whereby each is able to specify requirements of the other, while providing descriptive information against which the requirements of the other party can be matched (see Figure 1).

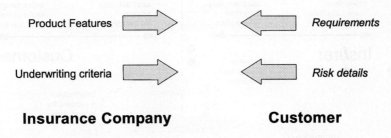

Fig. 1. Bi-directional exchange of information

A consequence of this bi-directional exchange of information is the need for a symmetric match-making process, whereby a selection is only made if the requirements of each party are successfully matched with the descriptive information provided by the other (see Figure 2).

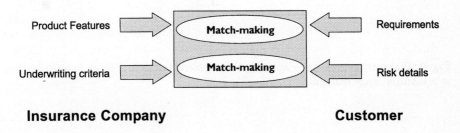

Fig. 2. The symmetric match-making process

3.4 Gradual Selection Process

Both customers and insurers share a common desire to stage the selection process. Customers do not wish to divulge personal data until they have confidence that disclosure of such information would be worthwhile (C7), while insurers wish to avoid unnecessary interaction with unsuitable customers (P6). Insurers also have a desire to protect commercially sensitive information (P3). A gradual selection process would therefore allow both customers and insurers to build trust in each other while providing for the possibility that either party can withdraw from the process at any stage during the dialogue.

Taken with the desire for a two-way selection process (3.3 above) within the context of standardised dialogue (3.2 above), we can propose a scheme which allows for the gradual transition in a dialogue from less to more detail and complexity, and from less to more sensitive and personal information (Figure 3).

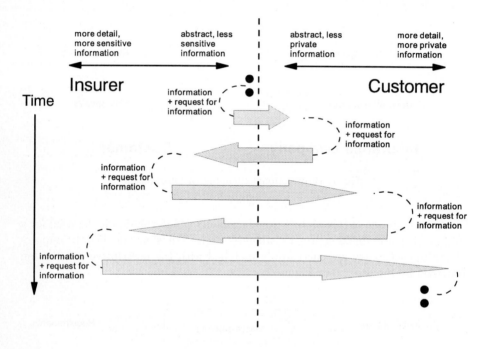

Fig. 3. Dialogue progression — going from the general to the specific and more sensitive in a multiple stage dialogue

3.5 Distributed Market Place

Insurers wish to control the advertising process (P2), while retaining some parts of the quotation process within their organisational boundary, for both confidentiality (P3) and efficiency (P4) reasons. This, together with the desire to be able to handle prospective customers on an individual basis (P9, C10), suggests the need for a market place which is distributed among its participants, rather than centralised in a single location. Whilst this is of primary benefit to the insurers, it can be used to provide the basis for implementing the sophisticated, gradual selection process via a standardised dialogue (3.2, 3.3 and 3.4 above), to the benefit of all parties.

The gradual selection process (described in 3.4 above) shows how the dialogue can be structured so that earlier stages avoid the need to request, and reveal, sensitive information, on the part of both the customer and the insurer. This suggests that the earlier stages are least likely to involve processes which the insurers wish to keep within their systems, and can therefore take place in an environment shared with other insurers. The subject matter of the dialogue at this stage is more likely to centre on establishing whether insurers have products likely to be suitable to the customer, whether the customer is interested in dealing with those insurers, and whether the insurers are interested in obtaining further information from the customer with a view to putting forward an insurance quotation. Later stages of the dialogue involve more sensitive information and processes, which insurers will wish to control inside their organisational boundaries.

The staged dialogue illustrated in Figure 3 can therefore be implemented across a network, whereby the earlier stages take place in an environment common to all insurers in the market place (which could also be the single entry point specified in 3.1 above), while the later stages are distributed among the systems environments of each insurer. The symmetrical match-making system, described in 3.3 above, is required to handle each stage of the dialogue, the first stage being handled in the common environment, with subsequent stages being handled by match-makers belonging to the insurers, in parallel. The "high level" results of the first level of match-making are presented to the customer, who can decide which "high level" offers are worthy of a further exchange of information. A form to obtain information and requirements sufficient to satisfy the needs of the next level of match-making can then be presented to the user, and submitted once it has been completed. The process is repeated with increasing levels of detail as a series of coordinated "dialogue exchanges" between the customer and individual insurers (Figure 4).

Each "dialogue exchange" terminates in one of three circumstances:

1. The customer chooses not to continue the exchange in between stages of match-making.
2. All products or services considered by the exchange fail the symmetrical match-making process at a subsequent stage, with the consequence that a more detailed offer is not returned to the customer for selection.
3. Sufficient stages of symmetrical match-making have been passed, and sufficient information has been gathered, to enable the insurer to put forward one or more insurance quotations which match the customer's requirements, and satisfy the insurer's marketing and underwriting criteria.

The result from the customer's perspective is a dialogue which progresses from asking for high level requirements and non-personal information to more detailed requirements and more private information, while giving the customer the ability, at each stage of the dialogue, to determine with whom it should

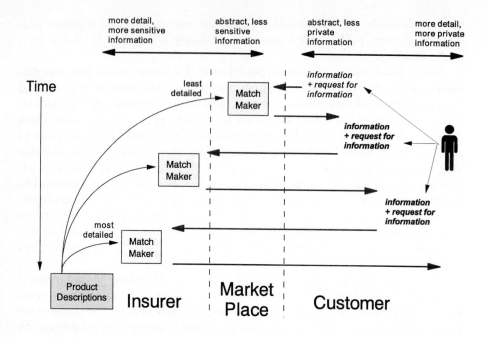

Fig. 4. Phased dialogue implementation across a distributed market place

be conducted. Eventually, a set of offers compatible with the customer's stated requirements, is received.

From the insurer's perspective, sensitive information such as rating tables, pricing algorithms, and detailed underwriting criteria, can be kept to later stages of the dialogue, which can be processed within the insurer's own systems environment. This gives the insurer complete control over this part of the process, enabling the insurer to reuse processes already encoded within existing systems. This more detailed, and also more costly, stage will only be invoked if the dialogue has progressed beyond the earlier stages (i.e. passed successive match-making stages), which can be used by the insurer to filter out unwanted customers, and to target products towards desirable customers.

3.6 Flexible Catalogue

The series of dialogues between the customer and the insurers finishes with a set of insurance quotations being delivered to the customer. The customer wishes to be able to explore and compare these offers (C8), and the insurers wish to be able to differentiate their products from each other (P7). These requirements suggest the need for a catalogue tool which can be used by the customer to explore and compare the feature space of the quotations. Whilst price comparison is important, the catalogue should allow the customer to compare coverages, features and options, ideally providing visual support for the tradeoff between more expensive, feature-rich products, and cheaper, simpler ones, and a more detailed matching between offered product features and the customer's own needs.

This requirement of yet more match-making prompts the question - what is the difference between the match-making which takes place at each stage of the dialogue, and the proposed match-making in the flexible catalogue? The former is a series of "hard constraints" expressed by the customer based on his or her initial requirements, in order to narrow down the search space to manageable proportions. The customer may only become aware of some requirements in the light of reviewing the features of a set of competing offers. The flexible catalogue enables the customer to express these new requirements, which are more likely to take the form of "soft constraints", used to rank rather than filter the offers, all of which match the customer's initial requirements.

As with the standardised dialogue (3.2 above), where a common language was needed to define information requirements common to insurers, a flexible catalogue requires that the providers conform to a common language, this time with which to describe common product information, such as prices, terms and condition, features and priced options.

3.7 Security and Trust Features

The desire of both customers and insurers to protect confidential information and processes (C6, P3) requires that information transmitted between them is properly protected. The distributed architecture, with its single entry point and coordinated dialogue, enables the market place to act as a trusted third party on behalf of all insurers. As membership of the market place can be controlled, certain guarantees can be given by the market place to prospective customers. For example, assurances can be given that all advertising insurers are authorised to transact business in a given geography. The market place could also be used to act as an agent on behalf of the customers, protecting customers' electronic identities from the insurers (C11).

3.8 Long-Life Sessions

Both customers and insurers want to be able to take time, the customers in the final purchase decision (C9), and the insurers, sometimes, in the underwriting process (P8). The market place therefore needs to be able to allow the customer to break a session, and resume it without losing information previously sent and received. This is particularly important once offers have been received, when the customer may wish to take time to compare them with offers obtainable from other channels (e.g. direct telephone, brokers, sales agents). Insurers will wish to be able to put a "sell by" date on a quotation, indicating to the customer that the quotation remains available to the customer until that date has passed.

3.9 ViMP Implementation

The features discussed earlier have been implemented in a prototype system known as the Virtual Market Place (ViMP), which has been used to create a demonstration market place for car insurance. The dialogue and the flexible catalogue are part of a Java applet, delivered to the customer via the market place's home page, and the distributed market place has been developed using Java (JDK 1.1.5) on a CORBA-compliant platform [6] (Iona's OrbixWeb 2.0.1 [7]). Additional tools have been designed and built to support the insurer in the process of product design, and the staged advertising of product features and marketing and underwriting criteria. CORBA connections were also developed to a pricing engine, and a vehicle database to enable accurate identification of the customer's car. In addition to the car insurance prototype, ViMP has also been applied to a number of other classes of insurance with success, to test the extent to which the design and implementation can be generalised.

4 Summary

We have shown how an analysis of the requirements of both customers of, and providers to, an electronic insurance market place can lead to the derivation of a set of desirable features, which can in turn drive many of the key design criteria. Figure 5 below summarises the relationship between the requirements on both sides and the desirable features in the centre. A question which remains to be considered is — to what extent are the same requirements and derived features relevant to market places dealing with products and services other than insurance?

Other financial services, such as bank accounts, loans, mortgages, credit card applications, investment funds and pensions, have similar properties. Their markets tend to be regulated by government agencies, and their purchase tends to involve an exchange of sensitive information on the customer's side, and some constraints (either self-imposed, or legislation imposed) on the provider side. There is often a gap between the way customers express requirements and providers describe products, which needs to be bridged with a dialogue, and the products themselves are often complex. The major desirable features of a standardised one-to-many dialogue with a gradual, two-way selection process across a distributed market place would therefore appear to fit financial services other than insurance equally well.

If one considers simpler, more commodity-like products, such as books, CDs or hi-fi equipment, one would expect that the ease with which they can be described and matched would render many of the proposed design criteria unnecessary. The need for a standardised dialogue is reduced if requirements can be simply stated, and the use of personal data is no longer part of the selection process (though it may need to be given to the provider by the customer for payment and delivery purposes once a purchase decision has been made). However, there is sometimes a benefit in conducting a staged dialogue when the customer's expression of requirements differs substantially from the way products are typically described. For example, purchasers of hi-fi are interested in how their favourite type of music will sound in their living room, whereas products are often described in terms of technical information such as wattage output

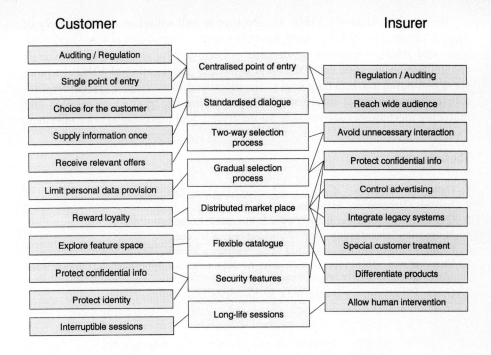

Fig. 5. Derivation of design criteria from requirements

and CD sampling rates. A provider with a large range of similar products may wish to use the two-way gradual selection process to guide the customer towards the most suitable products. Applying a market place with the features described in Section 3 could therefore result in substantially improved customer service compared with many of today's Internet shopping malls.

A business-to-business market place is also unlikely to involve an exchange of personal data, and where such a market place is used among regular business partners to process regular orders, such as buying and selling components, a simpler solution than the one proposed here is likely to suffice. However, there may be a desire on the purchasers side to stage the dialogue in order not to reveal commercially sensitive information unnecessarily. Where the product is more complex, for example a service which one business might perform for another, we believe that the two-way gradual selection process will be of considerable benefit in ensuring that the requirements of both parties in a business relationship are satisfied. Such a business service market place could be used to bring together the semi-autonomous entities which form a virtual enterprise. An analysis of the requirements of the members of such a partnership, and the ways in which service offerings should be described, would be necessary to determine how well the ViMP architecture described here would fit this rather different kind of market place.

We conclude that the ViMP architecture is well suited to a wide variety of market places, particularly those where the space of products is large and complex, and where the search space can be narrowed by a symmetric exchange of information between customers and providers. Application of ViMP to more service-oriented markets may lead to the identification of further system requirements. In particular, it remains to be seen whether the product description and matching mechanisms are suitable for describing and matching service offerings.

References

1. Haller, M.: Sicherheit durch Versicherung? Herbert Lang, Bern (1975)
2. InsWeb Corporation: http://www.insweb.com
3. Quicken InsureMarket: http://www.insuremarket.com
4. Misys plc (Screentrade): http://www.screentrade.com
5. Field, S.: Postcode Underwriting. The Insurance Times (May 3, 1995)
6. The Common Object Request Broker: Architecture and Specification. Object Management Group and X/Open (1992)
7. Orbix: Programmer's Guide. Iona Technologies Ltd., Dublin (1993)

Intellectual Property Rights and the Global Information Network

Nikos K. Lakoumentas[1], Emmanuel N. Protonotarios[1]

[1] National Technical University of Athens,
Department of Electrical and Computer Engineering, Telecommunications Laboatory,
Heroon Polytechniou 9, GR-15773 Athens, Greece
nickl@telecom.ntua.gr, protonot@softlab.ntua.gr

Abstract. By digitizing copyright works and other protected objects, many benefits for the users arise, especially by simplifying the access, however, for the rights owners it can represent both an opportunity and a threat. Materials can be distributed speedily on the networks, and new markets are opened up, but there is also the danger of loss of sales through unauthorized use and exploitation of these same materials. There are different legal aspects and technologies, which cope with Intellectual Property Rights on the Global Information Network.

1 Introduction

Intellectual property rights (IPRs) have been essential to providing security and trust with respect to investment and trade in ideas and cultural activities by guaranteeing commercial returns. The growing importance of intellectual content in the global information infrastructure-global information society (GII-GIS) means that such rights are crucial for the development of electronic commerce. Yet, the digital nature of the content and the availability of new technologies make it relatively easy to circumvent many controls, owing to the possibility of making exact duplicates. At the same time, new technologies (digital watermarking, encryption) can help protect against rights violations. In a number of cases, the private sector has made significant progress in agreeing to common standards for the protection of IPRs in new multimedia goods and services, like Digital Libraries. Through the TRIPS (Trade Related Aspects of Intellectual Property Rights) and recent WIPO agreements on intellectual property rights, governments have also made progress in agreeing to common international standards of protection: it is important for the development of electronic commerce that countries move rapidly to implement these agreements in national legislation.

Intellectual Property Rights (IPR's), which include patents, copyright, trade marks, know-how, design rights and moral rights, continue to be of increasing value to businesses. For many they are one of the most valuable assets.

IPRs are intangible since they are the result of and attach to creativity. They are not goods, nor does one global law protect them.

The Global Information Network (Internet) is intangible too. It exists as a result of a global network of computers but it is not one system. It is not controlled by one entity, it is not subject to one law and it is not in one place. The Internet is, however, one of the most valuable marketing and distribution channels in the world. At the same time it is by its global nature, full of risks.

2 Legal Aspects of IPRs on the Global Information Network

2.1 Patents and Copyrights

In most countries an invention cannot be patented if it has already been published or put into the public domain. It is arguable that by e-mailing details of an invention or by discussing an idea on a bulletin board or user group network, you may be destroying the opportunity of protecting your idea by patent.

You can patent an idea, but you can only copyright the expression of an idea. In fact in most countries copyright protection arises automatically upon reducing the idea to written form (paper or electronic). Copyright gives the owner the right to prevent copying without permission.

In the paper world we tend to have some control over copyright material in that it is usual to limit copying by the use of copyright notices, contractual terms and the use or threat of use of litigation.

In cyberspace the situation is complex. As soon as you put copyright material on a computer and make it available for browsing on the Internet you impliedly consent to limited copying. If you have a Web site then any material on it will be automatically copied in the course of browsing and further copied on downloading to hard drive, disk or printed material. It is suggested that any copyright material on a Web page should be accompanied by a notice stipulating the terms of use.

A further extension of a copyright notice is the click-wrap contract. This is a set of terms and conditions relating to the use of IPR's in on-line material and data. Click-wrap contracts also include terms and conditions as to payment, delivery, warranties and liabilities, all relating to the on-line supply of goods and services.

A click-wrap contract usually appears on screen at the point of access to a Web page or Internet service and has to be scrolled or read through before a customer may proceed further. Often the click-wrap contracts asks the customer to signify acceptance or rejection of the terms and conditions by clicking on an appropriate on-screen button, thereby unwrapping the rest of the Web page or services - hence the term "click-wrap".

2.2 Digitized Material

The digitization of material in cyberspace reduces all information into binary digits (bits) of data and one advantage of the Internet - the globalization of data - is at the same time a disadvantage. This is because data may be manipulated, misused, misdirected and mismanaged at a greater speed over greater distances and with greater consequences than in the paper world.

The European Union now has two Directives, which impact upon data. The first is the Database Directive, which creates two tier proprietary rights in databases - seventy years copyright protection in valuable selected and highly researched databases and fifteen years sui generis protection in simple lists and compilations of data. Second is the Data Protection Directive, which regulates the collection, storage, retrieval, use and transmission of data relating to individuals.

2.3 Trade Marks and Domain Names

There is an international treaty and there are national laws relating to the registration and use of trade marks and service marks. There is, however, no legislation and no international regulation of Internet domain names. A domain name is the unique identifier which each individual or business is allocated when obtaining a presence on the Internet (e.g. harrods.com, hobsonaudley.co.uk and mcdonalds.com).

Initially all domain names were allocated from the United States on a first come first served basis with the entities name being followed by the word in ".com". Early applicants were given ".com" irrespective of their country of origin and without regard to conflict with well known brands, merchandising names or trade marks.

mcdonalds.com was obtained by a journalist as an exercise to prove the failings of the system. McDonalds the food chain objected but had to purchase the domain name of the journalist who gave the purchase money to charity.

Most large companies have tried to protect their names and brands by registering them as both domain names as well we trade marks. This is an expensive exercise however, because to obtain maximum protection they need to register trade marks and domain names in almost every country.

2.4 Dispute Resolution

Whether protecting IPR's on the Internet or regulating Cybertrade, one of the problematic areas is the multi-jurisdictional nature of cyberspace. In order to establish which law applies in a dispute and in the absence of any agreement between the parties, the law where the contract is made will be deemed to apply. But how do you decide where the contract is made? Is it where the seller has his computer, is it where the Internet service provider is based, is it where the person accessing the service Web site is based or in the case of IPR infringement, is it where the infringement takes place? In an IPR infringement case it is likely that the plaintiff will bring an action based on the law of the country where his IPRs are protected. If the infringement is of copyright then since most countries are members of the Berne Convention which provides international protection for copyright, the plaintiff will be reasonably secure, but not all countries enforce copyright as well as others. If there is infringement of a Greek patent or Greek registered trade mark and if the infringement takes place outside Greece, the IPRs are unprotected unless they are also registered in the country where infringement takes place. This is, of course, the same situation as would occur in the paper world, although the potential for mass multi-jurisdictional infringement is greater over the Internet.

3 Copyright Management Technologies

There has been a great deal of activity on the part of technology vendors, copyright stakeholders (publishers, authors, collecting societies), academic institutions and libraries, to develop copyright management technologies for controlling access to and usage of materials.

The potential benefits are considerable. Copyright owners gain the facility to collect and distribute fees, and are, therefore, more willing to give permission for the electronic use of their materials. Libraries can track what items are being used and thereby manage their collections more efficiently, and are able to implement accounting and billing mechanisms to recover costs. Users are informed of copyright ownership and the terms and conditions of access.

However, the development of electronic copyright management systems (ECMS) can pose many problems too. From the user's point of view, a complex system requiring registration and passwords, linked to pay-per-use charging mechanisms may deter use. It is clear that there will be a considerable overhead involved in implementing an ECMS and it may, therefore, not be appropriate for content which is not of high intrinsic value. Furthermore, there is the issue of privacy when a system may track and report to libraries and copyright owners what individual users are reading and printing. If the user's privacy is to be maintained then the technology should enable the user to be authorized but to keep his or her identity anonymous. There are also legal problems raised by ECMS. Firstly, ECMS are, at present, not protected under law and, therefore, there is nothing to prevent someone from developing the tools to circumvent such systems. Secondly, ECMS are not designed to accommodate copyright exceptions like fair use, which allow users free access to materials for research and private study in a library. If this provision is to be maintained in a digital environment, should free access be restricted to the location of the library or should remote access to the library be possible?

Copyright management technologies can be grouped in different categories, and some systems may involve a combination of the different technologies.

- Document security and post-control techniques, which ensure control over the distribution of works. Techniques such as the encryption (scrambling) and decryption of objects to prevent unauthorized access; verification to prove the origin of a work; authentication to prove the work has not changed; attachment of a copyright notice to a document and the use of concealed information (labeling or watermarking), which can be used to determine ownership and the source.

- Tracking and recording document usage: the technologies employed include mechanisms for controlling access, user identification and authentication, metering use and, if necessary, charging for use.
- Document identification and digital object identifiers (DOI): work is underway in Europe and the USA to develop a standardized system of identifier codes, which can be used for marking and tracking use of documents.
- Secure billing and payment systems: The number of technology vendors offering or developing ECMS tools for electronic commerce on the Internet has increased. In most cases, the documents or objects are held on the publishers' own servers, but the Internet billing system allows access through registration, user identification and credit checking. The pay-as-you-use approach is based on various payment schemes: credit cards/institutional or personal accounts/electronic cash.
- Rights management tools: these are administrative support systems required by libraries (and publishers) to manage electronic permissions requests, chasers and the electronic licenses which are the result of the successful negotiation.

4   Epilogue

It is the instantaneous global nature of the Internet which is its greatest appeal and yet this is at the same time a threat to IPR protection and enforcement. IPR's will need to be diligently protected and enforced in order to maintain their value as a business asset.

But, maybe, the biggest challenge that cyberspace poses for authors and publishers is not how to strengthen copyright law, but how to reinvent their business models so that they figure out how to provide content that will interest potential customers on terms that these consumers find acceptable. It may be far more important to protect revenues than to protect bits, although it may take some farsightedness to look beyond very strong encryption as a way to protect copyrighted materials in digital networked environments. And protecting revenues may mean giving away some content in order to attract customers for other content or for services that people interested in such content would find desirable. Digital networked environments will provide authors with many new opportunities to make their works available to the public.

References

1. Bond, R., B.A., Notary Public Partner, Hobson Audley Hopkins & Wood Solicitors, London, UK: Intellectual Property Rights and the Internet (1997)
2. Ramsden A.: Copyright Management Technologies: The key to unlocking digital works? Ariadne, The Web Version, Issue 10, (1997)

3. Samuelson P.: On Authors' rights in cyberspace: Questioning the need for new international rules on authors' rights in cyberspace. First Monday, Peer-Reviewed Journal on the Internet (1997)
4. World Intellectual Property Organization (WIPO): Copyright Treaty
5. World Trade Organization (WTO): Agreement on Trade-Related Aspects of Intellectual Property Rights

NetBazaar: Networked Electronic Markets for Trading Computation and Information Services

J. Sairamesh and C. Codella

IBM T. J. Watson Research
Yorktown Heights
New York, NY, 10598
email: jramesh@watson.ibm.com

Abstract. In this paper, we present the design and implementation of NetBazaar, which is a distributed, federated electronic trading system (Marketplace) for buying and selling network resources and services and information products and services distributed across the Internet. The trading system provides mechanisms for suppliers to advertise information about their services and attribute-value pairs, and for consumers to query for information about service offerings by the suppliers. In addition, the trading system offers services to perform the trades on behalf of the consumers or it offers the consumers with a list of suppliers to contact. In order to recover costs and profit, the trading system charges a small fee to the suppliers and consumers for every trade that occurs. The charges could vary depending on the complexity of the trade, such as the overheads of payment, transaction and contract enforcement. Net-Bazaar has been designed to support a variety of business models, pricing and market mechanisms, searching and matching algorithms, fast negotiation mechanisms for a high volume of trades, and distributed access for consumers and suppliers to the trading system. An initial version of NetBazaar has been implemented using CORBA and Java components.

Keywords: Electronic Marketplace, Distributed Markets, Searching and Matching, Pricing, Product Differentiation, Industrial Organization

1 Introduction

With the rapidly emerging technologies for e-commerce over the Internet and with the decreasing costs of computation and communication, we envision that in the coming decades, commerce over the Internet will become a large part of the human economy. We also envision that buying and selling information goods will steadily move towards increasing automation where computer (software agents)[1] mediated price setting and trading of resources and services will become commonplace. We also expect that in such electronic economies, sellers

---

[1] Software agents working on behalf of the humans, and making decisions based on criteria specified by the humans.

of services will compete vigorously than ever before, leading them to differentiate themselves as much possible based on value added services[9, 12, 4], and intermediaries such as trading systems will find a niche in bringing suppliers closer to the consumers and in providing trusted marketplaces[3].

The Internet already has become home to many electronic marketplaces, but most of these are simple web-based solutions, and owned mostly by the suppliers themselves and very few by intermediaries. Consumers, through the web browsers access the marketplaces and purchase products of interest. Owners of these marketplaces advertise a variety of products offered by the various suppliers. The advertising and updating of product information is still done manually in most cases by the owners, except for a few like the on-line airline travel reservation systems[2], the updates are done in an automated fashion. These marketplaces will soon evolve to provide some level of automation for product updates by suppliers distributed across the Internet.

Not very distant in the future, these marketplaces will begin to interact with each other in order to aggregate products, thereby creating networked marketplaces, where negotiations not only happen between consumers and suppliers via the trading systems in an automated fashion, but also between trading systems owned by different organizations. Very little work has been done to understand the nature of these interactions and contracts among various trading systems or intermediaries. These interactions will facilitate the aggregation of product bundles[3] and creation of new product bundles customized to the demands of the consumers. An example is the aggregation of network service bundles, which would involve trading among various markets integrated vertically[3]. Another example is the aggregation of information products from various information marketplaces.

In this paper, we present NetBazaar, which is a distributed, federated marketplace architecture for trading different types of products and services, which include **soft goods** such as network services, information products, computational resources, energy products and others, and **hard-goods:** (or physical goods) such as books, CDs, automobiles parts, computer hardware and others. In this marketplace, trades are done by the trading system on behalf of suppliers and consumers. The trading system acts as a *trusted* intermediary, which provides mechanisms for suppliers to advertise their products and attributes of products at the trading system, and for the consumers to query the trading system in order to search for and match with the right set of suppliers. The trading system can either perform the trade on behalf of the consumers and provide services to manage the transactions and service contracts, or it can simply provide the consumers with a list of suppliers to contact. Some of these suppliers could be other marketplaces (e.g. auction sites), and therefore consumers just need their contact addresses to interact with these suppliers (or providers) directly.

NetBazaar has similarities and dissimilarities from the traditional stock and

---

[2] Travelocity: www.travelocity.com

[3] Network Services over the Internet are provided by a collection of network providers who are integrated vertically.

commodities trading systems[8] (e.g. Nasdaq). Among the dissimilarities, the following are noteworthy: (a) Information services/goods and network services have many more parameters other than just price and quantity, which describe the products and services. These parameters will influence the consumer bids and selection of suppliers, the trading mechanisms and price setting by the trading system and suppliers; (b) NetBazaar has been designed to support federation among trading systems owned by various organizations. The trading sites, owned by different organizations, have specific contracts to query and interact among each other. The interaction is primarily for business reasons. The main idea behind federation is the linking of trading systems to share information and perform trades on behalf of each other. Keeping this in view, we have built a flexible framework to support different levels of federation depending on the market structure[9, 10] (vertical or horizontal integration). The trading system, in order to recover costs and profit, implements a variety of charging policies based on the complexity of the trade and the overheads involved in managing the transaction and service contracts.

A version of the trading system is currently operational, and its design and implementation is based on CORBA[4] and Java components. Using this trading system, we plan to investigate various business models (market hierarchies and non-hierarchies)[9, 10], pricing and market mechanisms, advanced trading policies, secure and efficient payment and banking to handle a large volume of transactions, and service contracts for reserving services in the future. NetBazaar has also been designed to study pricing and resource allocation in computational markets[5], where several issues such as price setting by the competing suppliers and intermediaries, market dynamics[11], impact of information delay and partial information on consumers and suppliers decision making.

Several fundamental technologies are already in place fueling a variety of designs for buying and selling both physical and electronic goods. Some of these include: E-cash and payment (e.g. First Virtual, CyberCash, OpenMarket, VeriFone, and IC Verify), secure transactions and communication (e.g. SET, S-HTTP, SSL), middleware brokering (e.g. Web, CORBA, DCOM and Java based platforms), and distributed transaction processing. In addition to these services and technologies an advanced set of services to facilitate interaction among marketplaces is required, and some of these include the following: mechanisms and algorithms for searching and matching suppliers in networked electronic marketplace, pricing of products and service bundles, advanced trading mechanisms, and support for service contract management and enforcement. In this paper, we present the design of these services for networked marketplaces. We motivate our work via two example economies in section 2. Using the example economies, we present the design requirements of NetBazaar in section 3. In section 4, we present the NetBazaar architecture, and in section 5, we present the implementation of NetBazaar and current status of our work.

---

[4] Common Object Request Broker Architecture. A standard specified by the Object Management Group (OMG): http://www.omg.org.
[5] These are markets for network bandwidth and server resources: processing and storage.

2 Examples of two market economies

In this section, we describe two kinds of markets: one of them is for trading network services (e.g bandwidth services) over the Internet, and the other for trading information products and services. We present simple models of economic interaction among the various players in each of the markets. Using these examples, we present our motivation in designing advanced trading systems.

2.1 Network Services Economy

The network services economy over the current Internet consists mainly of the following three players: Backbone ISPs or NSPs who offer backbone services to local ISPs and consumers (businesses); local ISPs who offer Internet access services to consumers (homes and small businesses)[6]; consumers who select ISPs (local or backbone) based on services offerings, reputation of the services, quality and the price. With the emerging differentiated services over the Internet, a whole range of network qualities of service will be offered to support a variety of applications[13, 12], and this will create a need for a marketplace to search for the right set of suppliers on behalf of the consumers.

Consider the following simple market structure for network services in the future: local ISPs buy resources (network bandwidth and buffers) along one or more routes from backbone ISPs. The local ISPs then offer one or more qualities of service to the consumers (homes or small businesses). ISPs aggregate consumer demand in the form of network traffic and route the traffic to the backbone ISPs, which then forward traffic to the specified destinations. Consumers[7] will have a choice in selecting one or more ISPs based on quality and price offerings for bandwidth services along the requested source-destination pairs. Given a model of this kind, the local ISPs can take a risk in reserving bandwidth along routes in advance from the backbone ISPs, and they can profit by aggregating the consumer demand and by providing value added services to lock their consumers. Depending the consumer demand, pricing can be static or dynamic in order to recover costs and make profit.

The current Internet houses about 5000 ISPs, of which about 40 of them are backbone ISPs offering access services to various consumer types. In the past the backbone ISPs were connected via public access points (public NAPs), which provided trusted cross-over points for network traffic, but more recently, private NAPs are being established between the backbone ISPs with detailed service contracts. We envision that a marketplace is bound to naturally emerge for establishing connectivity and peer-to-peer networking among the backbone

---

[6] Large business have enough resources to connect directly to backbone ISPs for reasons of performance and better security and other value added services based on the needs of the business

[7] Mainly businesses in need of network access and services.

ISPs. In such a marketplace, each ISP would advertise its services across the Internet to attract potential customers (whether they are homes, businesses or other ISPs). The marketplace can offer more information to ISPs (local and backbone) for better connectivity and performance to their consumers.

There is a thrust by the network providers to provide differentiated transport services over the Internet for performance critical applications such as video, voice and data. In the near future, they will provide different qualities of service, priority services, and other transport mechanisms end-to-end to support real-time and non-real time applications. For end-to-end Quality of Service (QoS), the providers will allocate bundles of resources to guarantee some level of performance (statistical guarantees)[1, 2, 13]. With multiple providers offering a multitude of qualities of services, it is natural for one or more intermediaries to find a niche in matching the application QoS requirements to the offerings of the network providers.

With the emerging enabling technologies for setting up virtual paths and networks dynamically (dynamic VPNs and SVCs[8]), the reservation of bandwidth will done on demand, and markets for bandwidth will become commonplace, and intermediaries will find a niche in providing various kinds of bandwidth services such as futures contracts (e.g. reserving bandwidth in the future) on network services and value added services (for security, reliability and performance). The example economic scenario given above motivates the design of NetBazaar to handle a variety of consumer queries, and to provide a trading facility for network services.

2.2 Information Economy

In this subsection, we motivate the requirements for NetBazaar by describing a simple information economy for information products and services. The economy consists of three kinds of players. The first kind are the Information suppliers, who provide information items and services to the consumers. The information items could include a book or a collection of books or documents based on the specific tastes of the consumer. If the item is in its electronic form, then it could be provided in various formats to the consumer depending on the consumer needs and willingness to pay. If the item is in its physical form, then either a hardbound or a paper-back version can be provided. For multimedia information items such as a video-movie or a collection of images, the costs for transport and presentation could be high depending on the costs for bandwidth.

The second kind are the consumers, who wish to purchase information items from suppliers. Consumers select suppliers based prices and services offered. Consumer selection of suppliers is based not just on the information content (precision and recall of the delivered items), but also their costs and qualities of service. For example, a consumer, interested in purchasing information items from suppliers selects suppliers based on price, format of the information item

---

[8] VPN stands for Virtual Private Networks, and SVC stands for Shared Virtual Circuits

(ex: postscript, hypertext, text or some other media) and quality of service (such as immediate delivery or late delivery)[14, 15, 16, 4].

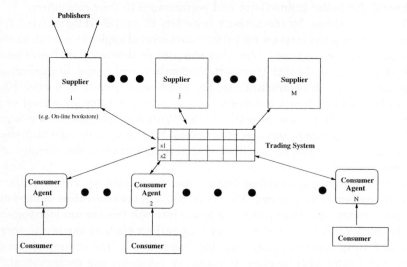

Fig. 1. Example of an Information Economy

The third kind are the brokers (intermediaries), who aggregate and transform information products and services to a variety of consumers depending on their preferences and tastes. The broker could offer a wide variety of services such as bulletin boards, directory, information storage and delivery, cataloging, searching, and retrieval[16]. An example of a simple broker that provides searching, matching and simple filtering services is shown in figure 1. The broker, which is more like a trading system[9] provides the consumers with price of an information item (e.g. books) or a collection of information items. The trading system performs the trade on behalf of each consumer. We assume for now that the consumers knows about the books (e.g authors name and title of book) they want from the trading system.

The trading system selects the cheapest supplier which has a copy of the information item. The consumer is notified of the cost of the book and the cost of the shipping charges, and the trade is performed. If the book is in its physical form, then the delivery time could take one or more days, but if the book is in its electronic form, then the delivery could be done within minutes or within hours depending on the transport charges, network congestion and the size (in bytes) of the book. The suppliers, shown in the figure 1 are on-line book stores selling physical and electronic versions of the books. We assume for now that the suppliers have access to all the books from the various publishers.

Over the Internet, examples of such intermediaries include the on-line book

---

[9] In this paper, we use trading system and trading site interchangeably.

stores such as: Amazon[10], Barnes and Nobles[11], and others. Currently, they sell books in their physical form and not in their electronic form, and so the delivery time is in the order of days. Other examples include the on-line CD stores, such as BargainFinder and Firefly[12] provide search and matchmaking services to consumers looking for music CDs. They not only provide a list of cheap CDs, but also recommend new CDs and provide other value added services. Intermediaries like Broadcast.com[13] provide customized and regular broadcast video and audio of news and other events to homes and businesses. With more bandwidth, they should be able to provide customized programming to consumers, though this is still in the distant future.

3   Design considerations

With the emerging new markets for Information and Network Services (e.g. Network bandwidth, bundling of information goods/services) products over the Internet, a need for flexible marketplace design is essential for new and emerging business models, new pricing/market mechanisms and advanced trading services. Keeping this in view, our main design considerations for NetBazaar are the following:

- Distributed, federated Trading platform for Intranets and Internets. Within an organizational boundary over the Internet, the trading system is distributed in order to provider speedy access to consumers and suppliers located across the Internet, but trading across the administrative or organizational domains involves some form of inter-trading contracts or business models for establishing extranet links between the trading sites. The business reasons for such a contract can be many fold depending on the structure of the markets: vertically and horizontally integrated markets.
- Support for a variety of market and pricing models: The market models could range from simple advertising of prices to consumers and price updates from suppliers to more sophisticated bidding and auctioning mechanisms to support a variety of many-to-many interactions among the consumers and suppliers.
- Distributed searching and matching: searching over a large collection of service information. In order to facilitate this, the following are required: language for the consumers to query the trading system, collection of interfaces for suppliers to advertise their products/services and attribute-value pairs.
- Dynamic updates of prices and service properties: In a large distributed marketplace, one of the fundamental requirements is the mechanism to automatically update prices and properties of services by the suppliers. This is crucial to the consumers and the trading system, as they make decisions based on price and available supply of the resources.

---

[10] http://www.amazon.com
[11] http:www.barnesandnobles.com
[12] http://bf.ctar.ac.com/bf and http://www.agentsinc.com
[13] http://www.broadcast.com

– Negotiations and service contracts: For supporting various kinds of trades among the consumer bids and supplier offers, the trading system should provide a framework to support a variety of negotiation algorithms or matching algorithms. In addition, it should provide a framework for futures contracts for consumers who want services reserved in advance. For example, for reserving network resources or bandwidth ahead of time from providers, the trading system should provide a framework for futures contracts and pricing.
– Secure transactions, payment and banking services: The trading system has to keep track of every transaction that has been done on behalf of the consumers and suppliers. The payment must be done in a secure manner across the Internet. For a large volume of transactions, new payment mechanisms have to be developed to reduce the overheads.

In figure 2, we show a block diagram of the trading system, and we list the main services offered by the trading system.

4 Architecture

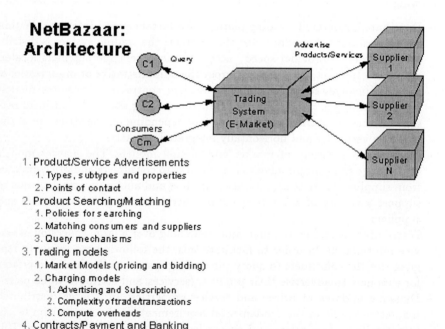

Fig. 2. Trading System: Architecture

Based on the requirements from the example economies, the key components in our architecture, as shown in figure 3, are the following:

- Distributed search, query and yellow pages services: for this we chose the
OMG trading services (CORBA). The OMG Trading services specifies a
query language for consumers to query for information about suppliers. The
consumers specify a base service type, a list of constraints on the attributes
of the service type and a set of policies for the trading system to execute on
its behalf. Some of these policies are the following:
  - Search policies (cost, depth of search and performance)
  - Matching policies
  - Negotiation policies
  - Trading policies
  - Pricing and Charging policies
  - Payment policies
- Naming Service: The naming service is used by the trading sites within
an organization to advertise their interfaces and properties of the trading
servers. Some of these properties could include the current load the server,
location of the server and other details. The naming service is based on the
extended naming service of IBM's component broker service.
- Notification Service: The trading system uses the notification service to update the consumers and suppliers of trades that happen in the future. In
addition, the notification and event services are used for asynchronous communication among the trading sites and other asynchronous events related
to service contracts and transaction management[5].
- Transaction Service: This service is required to keep track of all the trades
that happen on behalf at the trading site on behalf of the consumers and
suppliers. The transaction management system handles the ACID properties
when multiple tasks are updating the information about the suppliers at the
database.
- Repository Services: The middle-ware layer provides an ODBC interface to
the underlying repository to store information about the various service types
and service properties.
- Security, Payment and Banking Services: This is a very important feature of
the trading system, where consumers request the trading system to perform
the trade on its behalf and finish the payment with it preferred bank.

4.1 Trading Service Component

The main trading component is the OMG CORBA Trading service[14] which
provides a glue between customers and service providers[15]. The OMG Trading
service is analogous to a distributed yellow-pages service, and it not a system
for buying and selling services or commodities. We are using this component to
build a marketplace (or a real trading system) for trading network services and
information products. The OMG Trading service provides a simple framework to

---

[14] This is an adopted OMG Standard: http://www.omg.org
[15] Service providers wish to advertise their collection of resources.

NetBazaar: Design and Implementation

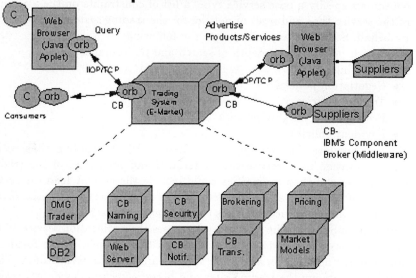

Fig. 3. Trading System: Design and Implementation

advertise and query for information about services and resources in a distributed fashion. The OMG trading service provides the following:

- A query language for clients (or importers) to import information from a trading system about suppliers based on some criteria.
- An interface for suppliers to register and advertise information about their objects and their properties[16].
- Distributed search policies to search for information about suppliers in a network of trading systems.
- A distributed search and match service in a federated system of trading sites.
- A proxy service to access the *legacy* service objects into the trading system. The proxy can be used to access service objects from LDAP[17] and DNS[18].

In figure 4, we show a simple block-diagram of the trading system. The suppliers post information about their services their properties, and consumers query the trading site for information about suppliers based on some criteria. The consumers can request the trading system to perform the trade on its behalf if the trading site finds the appropriate supplier. If a collection of suppliers match

---

[16] Properties are simply name-value pairs. Properties have modes such as read-only, mandatory or both.

[17] Light Weight Directory Access Protocol

[18] Domain Name Service

the consumers criteria, then the cheapest among the list of the suppliers will be selected.

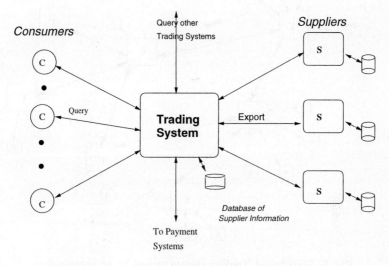

Fig. 4. Trading System

4.2 Federated Trading Service

Depending on the administrative boundaries, trading systems can cooperate if they belong to the same organization or they could establish contracts among themselves to search each others information spaces for products and services. In such a setting, trading systems forward consumer queries to other trading systems for information about suppliers.

A decentralized model of the trading system is shown in figure 5 and figure 6. In the figure 5, one organization owns all the trading sites. This organization could be a single firm or a collection of firms loosely coupled. In figure 6, the trading sites are owned by different organizations, but for business reasons, they are connected together to trade services on behalf of each other. In this model, there is an explicit service contract established among the trading systems (or entities).

In order perform a distributed search, each trading site has to keep information about other trading sites or contact the naming service to find them when needed. Each trading site establishes a link with one or more trading sites, and client queries are forwarded along these links to other trading sites. Links could cross domain boundaries managed by different administrators, providing a federated system of trading service to consumers and suppliers (see figure 6). To facilitate distributed trading owned by one organization or by a loosely coupled cooperative organizations, semantics of the keywords describing the service

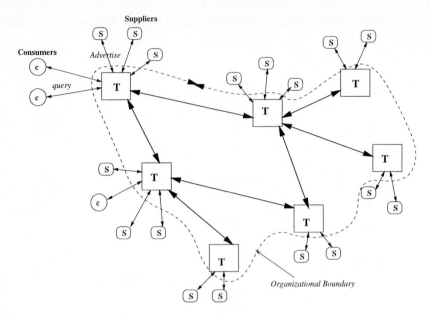

Fig. 5. Distributed Trading system owned by an organization

types and attributes by the suppliers have to be agreed upon by the trading organizations, and made a standard among the participating organizations. For example, consider many network trading system providing trading services to ISPs of various kinds and consumers. For the trading sites to interact, the keywords describing the network service types, subtypes, and the attribute names (Bandwidth classes, QoS parameters and so on) have to be standardized or accepted among the trading systems.

4.3 Product Advertisements

Suppliers who wish to use the trading system can advertise their products and services and their attribute-value pairs to the trading system via their export interfaces. Suppliers within a domain have access to the export interface of a trading system, which registers and authenticates new suppliers and provides a certificate for future updates by the registered suppliers. The export interface lets suppliers specify the high level service types or base service types (e.g. Network Service or ISP service or New Service), and a list of attribute value pairs describing the service types, and a contact address or an object reference.

Every time a supplier does an update of its prices and its service properties, it uses its unique certificate to access the trading system. The trading system provides services to delete and add new service types and properties by the suppliers. Based on the market organization of applications such as network services and information products, the trading site takes a percentage cut from

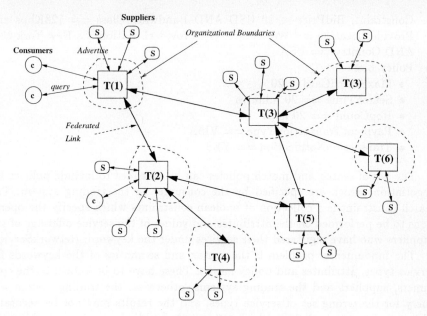

Fig. 6. Federated Trading System

the suppliers for matching consumers to their products. The suppliers **trust** the trading system to perform the right matching.

4.4 Searching and Matching

A consumer query consists of a service type (domain of search) , a list of constraints to select the appropriate service offers from the set of offerings, and a list of policies that the consumer asks the trading system to execute. The constraint language is given in detail in [7]. The constraints are simply boolean expressions. The consumer search constraints include the following: the depth and breath of the search by submitting *search cards* or *scoping policies* along with the query. This will instruct the trading site to stop the search when the search card criteria are met. For example, a *max-search-card* scoping policy which will indicate to the trading site the maximum upper bound of offers to be searched. Another example is *max-match-card*, which is the maximum upper bound of matched offers to be ordered. *Hop-count* policy is yet another example which limits the query to a certain depth in the network of trading systems. Consumers have a lot of flexibility in specifying to the trading system the kind information to look for and what filters to place on the matched offers. A detailed list of consumer search and match preferences is given in [7].

An example of a search criteria and the search polices are as follows by a consumer to the trading system:

- ServiceType: NetworkService

- Constraint: BidPrice $<$ 20 USD AND BandwidthClass $==$ 128Kbps and ProviderLocation $==$ Westchester OR ProviderLocation $==$ New York City AND Country $==$ USA
- Policy List
  - MaxSearchCard $=$ 20
  - SearchTime $==$ 20 minutes
  - HopCount $==$ 20 hops
  - PaymentTransactionType $==$ VISA
  - TransactionNotification $==$ YES

The list of search and match policies can be *extended* to include policies for negotiation, which are specified by the consumer to the trading system. The search constraint is a collection of boolean constraints which specify the operations to be performed on the attributes and values of the service offerings of the suppliers who have registered their services under the keyword: NetworkService.

The fundamental problem is the syntax and semantics of the keywords for service types, attributes and policy names. These have to be known to the consumers, suppliers and the trading systems, otherwise, the trading system will query for the wrong set of service types, and the results may not be accurate. This calls for standards based bodies to set the public keywords describing the service types. However, private marketplaces can set their own keywords and metadata describing the service types, but in an open market, a common set of keywords need to be defined and made available to all consumers and suppliers.

For humans accessing the trading system, the pull-down menus of a Web browser, for example, can hide the details of the keywords to be used in the search queries, but for the suppliers who will be sending in their updates automatically, the keywords have to be well understood.

4.5 Fast Negotiations

Negotiations are done by the trading system on behalf of the consumers. The overheads for negotiation are charged to the consumers. Negotiations could involve very complex transactions and service contracts and management, and these services are providing value add over the searching and matching. A simple policy could be "take-it-or-leave-it" policy for the consumers, who would just look at the bulletin board and make decisions as to whether the prices and attributes of products offered are within their interests. Consumers and suppliers can employ software agents who will work on their behalf to post the bids and offers to the trading system. These are analogous to the traders representing consumers and suppliers in the stock market or in the securities trading systems.

For more sophisticated negotiations, market models such as bidding and auctioning and other price setting mechanisms can be employed. For consumers interested in buying , for example, network bandwidth services in advanced, futures contracts and the corresponding negotiation mechanisms can be implemented. The services and products offered by the suppliers. For example, a consumer might want to buy bandwidth services between New York and Los Angeles for

6 hours between the times 9.00 A.M and 3.00 P.M 5 days ahead of the day the consumer plans to place the order.

4.6 Payment Mechanisms and Infrastructure

The completion of a transaction in the trading system involves payment for services. This will require some bookkeeping, payment authorization and clearing mechanisms. The payment infrastructure and mechanisms might be considered to some extent independent of the core of the trading system. Similar to the service contracts, they are an essential component of the trading system, in that they enable the actual trading to take place.

The architecture and implementation of the payment infrastructure have a few major goals: 1. Security; 2. Scalability in terms of customers and transactions that can be handled; 3. Operation in real time; and 4. Ability to operate with various payment mechanisms such as e-cash, credit cards, etc. The goals mentioned in 2 and 3 are essential. They will provide the trading system with the ability to trade both traditional e-commerce goods (e.g., cars, books, houses, etc.) and computational services such as access to databases, web access, I/O, storage, cpu time etc. Current banking infrastructures are centralized and particular to specific payment protocols. They would fail in the near future to cover the needs for network commerce due to scaling and real-time issues which they are not designed to handle[6].

The key assumption for the NetBazaar design is that in the future a large volume of transactions per minute will be executed at the trading system(e.g millions)[19], and the overhead can be substantial for authentication, verification and payment. Therefore we need to come up with some payment mechanism that is scalable, i.e., we have to keep minimal information for verification, and we can't heavily depend on the trading system for verification of payment and service provision as they would be a bottleneck for the real-time operation of the system.

5 Implementation and Work in Progress

The trading system has been implemented using IBM's CORBA and Java based middle-ware components. The middleware services are provided by IBM's Component Broker (CB) distributed object application server. The middleware services run on top of Windows NT and UNIX (AIX). The repository and transaction services have interface drivers to DB2. A number of trading servers were run to test the distributed query processing and search mechanisms. Though our current system is CORBA based, we plan to implement this using Java components (Enterprise Java Beans) and enterprise Java technologies. The following are the key components of the implementation:

---

[19] One can question this rate of transactions to be to high, but with increasing automation and with a large number of applications, the volume of trades for network services combined with the requests for information products could be very high.

- CB OMG Trading service
- CB Naming service
- CB Transaction service
- CB security service
- CB Notification service

The clients to this system can be Java applets distributed across the network. The clients have to be registered at the trading system. The registration process is done through the naming service, which uses DCE security service to authenticate clients. The clients of the trading system are the consumers, suppliers and other trading systems.

The OMG Trading service is implemented using the Component Broker's middleware services layer (e.g. ORB and others). The OMG trading service specifies an interface repository for the storage of service information (service objects) and their properties. The repository interface is supported by an underlying database, which is DB2. In addition, the repository interface is used to keep logs of all the trades that happen. The CB transaction service is being used to update supplier information, and to manage the active service contracts.

For accounting purposes and to perform debits and credits of consumer and supplier accounts, we have designed a banking system, which is a collection of bank servers, which provide accounts to the consumers and suppliers. The bank plays a role of keeping consumer and supplier accounts, and performing authorized debits on behalf of the trading system and suppliers.

For supporting asynchronous interactions among the consumers, suppliers and the trading system, we provide notification services. These services for example are used to acknowledge the service contracts among the trading entities. We also use the notification to support futures contracts on services, where the trades happen sometime in the future. Consumers are notified as soon as they happen.

To support inter-operability among trading systems implemented over different ORBs, we have also implemented a medium-weight trading system using JavaIDL (Sun's ORB) and other Java components (e.g. JDBC, Beans and others). We are currently evaluating various query processing, searching and matching algorithms given that there is underlying market-model and business model for interaction among the trading entities. Queries submitted by trading sites to other trading sites are charged based on the type of query and the service requested. We are currently exploring various charging policies based on subscription, volume of queries and the complexity of the queries.

We are currently implementing simple markets for selling computational resources and information resources. The consumers and suppliers are software programs which have utility functions implemented in them to post bids and offers. The consumers select suppliers based on price, quantity and quality offered. An example of the kinds of consumer preferences is given in figure 7. Suppliers simply post information on the prices of the computational resources (per unit prices). They also post the prices for the various levels of QoS offered; the quality in this case is the QoS at the packet level in a packet network.

Consumer and Supplier Utility Functions

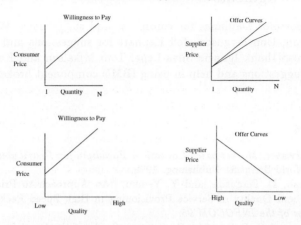

Fig. 7. Consumer preferences

6 Conclusion

The evolving, disparate marketplaces over the Internet will at some point need to interact in order to share and aggregate services and products so that consumers can benefit from product bundles. There is much debate over the roles of intermediaries and functionality of these intermediaries, very little has been done in understanding the potential interactions that will occur among the intermediaries to create networked electronic marketplaces for various vertically and horizontally integrated industries. In the coming years, much work needs to done to understand the federated nature of interactions that could occur among the various intermediaries for aggregating and bundling goods (soft and hard) and services.

In this paper we presented the design and architecture of NetBazaar, which is a distributed marketplace or a trading system for trading soft services such as network bandwidth and information products. In this marketplace, trades are done on behalf of suppliers and consumers. Suppliers advertise their products and attributes of products at the trading system, and consumers request the trading system to search for and match the right set of suppliers. The trading system can either perform the trade on behalf of the consumers and handle the transactions, or provide the consumers with the contact addresses of the suppliers and let the consumers negotiate on their own. Our design of the trading system is general enough to provide a marketplace for hard (physical) commodities.

A version of the trading system is currently operational, and its design and implementation is based on CORBA and Java components. Our goal is to use this trading system to investigate various business models, pricing and matching algorithms, complex trading mechanisms, payment and banking, and service contracts. NetBazaar is also designed to be used as a testbed to study the dynamics of computational markets in a realistic setting with information delays and other frictional effects.

7 Acknowledgments

We thank Apostolos Dailianas for comments and suggestions. We also thank Anant Jhingran, Don Ferguson, Jeff Kephart for suggestions and ideas to this project. We also thank Ignacio Silva-Lepe, Tom Mikalsen and Katherine Betz for valuable suggestions and help in using IBM's component broker middleware services.

References

1. Scott Clearwater, *Market based Control: A Paradigm for Distributed Resource Allocation*, World Scientific Publishing, 1995.
2. J. Sairamesh, D. Ferguson, and Y. Yemini, "An Approach to Pricing, Optimal Allocation and Quality of Service Provisioning in High Speed Packet Networks," *Proceedings of the INFOCOM'95.*
3. J. P. Bailey and Y. Bakos, "An Exploratory Study of the Emerging Role of Electronic Intermediaries," *International Journal of Electronic Commerce*, Vol. 1, No. 3, Spring 1997.
4. J. Sairamesh and J. Kephart, "Dynamics of Price and Quality Differentiation in Information and Computation Markets," *Proceedings of the ICE-98*, October 25-28, 1998.
5. C. Codella et. al, "Event Management and Advanced Notification Services," *IBM Research Report*, RC 20947, 1995.
6. A. Dailianas et. al, "Reliable and Efficient Payment and Banking Services for Distributed Trading Systems," *in preparation*, 1998.
7. OMG Services, "Trading Object Service Specification," *OMG Specification*, 1997.
8. S. M. H. Wallman, "Technology takes to Securities Trading," *IEEE Spectrum*, February 1997.
9. J. Tirole, "The Theory of Industrial Organization," The MIT Press, Cambridge, Massachusetts, 1995.
10. Oz Shy, "Industrial Organization: Theory and Applications," The MIT Press, Cambridge, Massachusetts, 1996.
11. J. Kephart, J. Hanson and J. Sairamesh, "Price-war dynamics in a Free-Market Economy of Software Agents" *proceedings of the Alife'98 conference*, 1998.
12. H. Varian, "Differential Pricing and Efficiency," *First Monday Journal*, 1998.
13. J. K. Mackie-Mason and H. R. Varian, "Pricing the Internet," *Second International Conference on Telecommunication Systems Modelling and Analysis* pp: 378-393, Nashville, Tennesse, March, 1994.
14. J. J. Gabszewicz and J.F. Thisse, "Price Competition, Quality and Income Disparities," *Journal of Economic Theory*, 20, 340-359, 1979.
15. A. Shaked and J. Sutton, "Multiproduct firms and market structure," *RAND Journal of Economics*, Vol 21, No. 1, Spring 1990.
16. J. Sairamesh, D. Ferguson, C. Nikolaou and Y. Yemini, "Economic Framework for Pricing and Charging in Digital Libraries,", *http://www.dlib.org*, Dlib Magazine, February issue, 1996.

The Shift Towards Electronic Commerce: Market Transformation and Employment Impact

Panayotis Miliotis[1], Angeliki Poulymenakou[2], Georgios Doukidis[3]

[1] Athens University of Economics and Business, Patission 76 Street, 104 34 Athens, Greece
http://www.heltrun.aueb.gr

[2] Athens University of Economics and Business, Patission 76 Street, 104 34 Athens, Greece
akp@aueb.gr
http://www.heltrun.aueb.gr

[3] Athens University of Economics and Business, Patission 76 Street, 104 34 Athens, Greece
gjd@aueb.gr
http://www.heltrun.aueb.gr

Abstract. Electronic commerce is a technology enabled market phenomenon having an increasing impact in how markets are changing. Electronic markets are in a transition characterized by the entrance of strong market players promoting concentration of market activity, and by a slower move, compared to early predictions, towards open electronic markets. Market change has significant impact on the levels, sources and nature of employment. The types of firms that will survive or enter in the emerging market places will affect the *sources of employment* in the market, while the nature of knowledge and skills required within electronic market places will affect the *types of employment* that will be offered in the future. This paper provides an understanding regarding future employment conditions by tracing the processes of market change and by providing a detailed explanation of the underlying rationale for these changes. Furthermore, a link has been developed between business transformation phenomena incurred by market change and transformation of the nature and types of work. The analysis model used to discuss specific changes to jobs and skills is applied illustratively to the case of the commerce sector.

Introduction

The notion of electronic markets has come to denote the context where any human activity with an attributable economic impact takes place when buyers and sellers interact and transact supported by information and communication technologies. The study of electronic markets and their effects on economies and societies is closely linked with the study of the technologies that make them possible.

In this paper we examine the relationship among market transformation phenomena induced by electronic commerce, business re-organization activities and the impact these have on the nature, sources and types of employment in electronic markets.

1   Market Characteristics

The use of information and communication technologies is assuming an increasingly pervasive role in shaping current market conditions. Global competition, decreasing product development cycles, flexible manufacturing systems and dramatic increases in the number and variety of products and services available to the consumer (Fisher et al, 1994) are some of the key issues characterizing current market conditions. Both challenges and opportunities are steadily rising not only for suppliers of goods and services but also for other types of business organizations.

A persistent challenge for enterprises is the continuous quest for strategies and means allowing the reduction of costs related to the entire value chain. Amongst other strategies, the exploitation of information technology has been identified as a key enabler in this area (Porter and Millar, 1985). IT exploitation has moved from the support of localized and isolated processes to enterprise-wide systems offering cost reductions through the integrated support of business operations and further than that into the areas of business process change, support for inter-firm collaboration and the creation of new businesses (Venkatraman in Scott-Morton, 1991).

Challenges rise also from the increasing complexities associated with the accurate prediction of the level of demand for products and services (Fisher et al, 1994). Causes, though, are rooted deeper: in essence, industry "has built and converted more production capacity than is required to meet even peak demand" (Ackoff, 1987, p.473). Ackoff suggests that the determination of market behavior requires more than the manipulation of marketing variables – this approach 'has reached its limits'. Further development and growth requires the study of consumer activity and attitudes from a behavioral perspective. This, in turn, requires the adequate supply of a critical resource: consumer related information.

The emergence of electronic commerce has opened new horizons in meeting both these challenges, particularly the second. Interaction and transaction over electronic means allows the development of new products and services, the establishment of a whole new set of ways of developing and maintaining a customer base, the set-up of new types of inter-organizational cooperation, and ultimately, the development of new types of markets and industries. These developments lead inevitably to restructuring of intra- as well as inter-organizational processes. The most prominent case is that of marketing activities where personalized, one-to-one marketing techniques have evolved in conjunction with internet based sales. More pervasive changes occur in the deployment and management of information technology and systems within and across enterprise boundaries. These changes can be attributed both to the 'push' of new technologies (e.g. the implementation of intranet based systems) but also to the 'pull' of market and industry trends (e.g. the deployment of Efficient Consumer Response programs in the food retail sector) (Coopers &Lybrand , 1996; ECR Europe, 1998).

2 Electronic markets

2.1 The Evolution of Electronic Markets

Two basic mechanisms for coordinating the flow of materials through the value chain have been recognized: *markets,* coordinating multiple buyers and sellers, and *hierarchies* supporting coordination within the firm as well as across an industry value chain. Although information and communication technologies are making both markets and hierarchies more efficient, it is argued (Malone *et al*, 1987), that the overall trend is proportionately towards more market coordination. The basic argument to support this prediction is that markets are communication intensive structures and, as the information cost to run the market decreases, more efficient market structures will emerge. Information is a critical resource for coordination in markets; it supports tasks such as selecting suppliers, establishing contracts, scheduling activities, controlling resources and tracking performance in monetary and other terms.

The evolution of electronic markets can be best described by reference to and comparison with the traditional value chain:

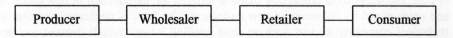

Each step of the above value chain incurs a significant cost for the final value of the product. Replacing one or more steps by systems acting as electronic counterparts requires not only complex inter-organizational systems, but also bargaining procedures among the stakeholders almost from a zero basis. Thus the most effective, although simple way to cut cost is to bypass as many of the above steps in the value chain as possible by supplying information directly to the consumer and by setting up appropriate transaction and delivery mechanisms.

This logic, which leads to a single source market, can in principle contribute to final product price reductions for the consumer. However, cost reductions achieved through reduced operation cost in single source markets could be offset by two factors: (1) restricted choice for the consumer, who is discouraged by the risk of being locked into one supplier, and (2) inability of the producer/ manufacturer to reach out a mass market either due to internal operational inefficiencies, or due to insufficient access to distribution channels. Usually small firms with limited resources are those who suffer the most.

Hence there are pressures for overcoming the above inefficiencies of single source markets by having them develop into more open electronic markets. However this transition is not straightforward as single source markets, wherever they emerge, show strength in market share and cost effectiveness. The move towards open electronic markets is complicated by two factors: (1) fast reaction to consumers' demand in an open market requires highly coordinated processes that can only be achieved through tight electronic linkages between firms - they prefer networks with few suppliers that they treat as their partners, and (2) firms are very skeptical of giving up their single source sales channels as this will lead to their profit margin erosion; thus they will not move until such time as a virtual market has been created with enough participants to threaten their market position (Benjamin & Wigand, 1995).

2.2 The Role of Intermediaries in Electronic Markets

The changes introduced to the economics of channels of trade through electronic commerce have been the topic of intense debate recently. Before embarking onto a presentation of the main analyses and their projected impact, we need to draw the reader's attention to the following fact: for business-to-business electronic commerce our observations and data can be based on actual results as this side of EC has had the time to evolve through actual use. For business to consumer electronic commerce, the analyses and suggestions are far more speculative in nature since they are based on initial indications for the behavior of a market that has not yet captured more than a small fraction of the trade in this area. However, most surveys project a rapid growth for this channel of trade in the near future (Economist, 1997).

Behind firms' involvement in electronic commerce, we can identify two generic motivators: the need to improve efficiency in business activity through the reduction of cost, and the need to create new demand through the introduction of new products and services and the attraction of new customers. The latter is particularly evident in traditional commerce sectors such as food retailing where overall demand has not risen for years and internal competition has intensified (ECR Europe Newsletter, 1998).

Electronic commerce allows essentially the networking of players in an industry value chain from the producer to the consumer. This networking creates capabilities with significant effects for the structure of markets.

First, the position of all intermediaries between the manufacturer/producer and the consumer is threatened as the manufacturer can now reach the consumer directly.*The issue that emerges is whether it makes sense for manufacturers to do so, in which cases and under what conditions.* An intermediary is thought of as the external party to a transaction between the producer and the consumer, responsible for reconciling their, often conflicting, interests. Intermediaries may also enter the chain as independent parties linking the producer to the wholesaler, the wholesaler to the retailer and the retailer to the customer. Finally, producers, wholesalers and the retailers may choose to carry out distribution on their own thus bypassing any remaining intermediaries 'downstream' to the consumer.

Traditionally, the value adding activities of intermediaries included market search and evaluation services for their customers. Intermediaries are well placed for assessing needs and proceeding to respective product matching. Risk reduction due to consumer uncertainty and product distribution and delivery complete the list of possible intermediary customer assistance. On the part of the producer, the intermediary creates and disseminates product information, influences the consumer purchases and reduces the cost of distribution through transaction scale economies.

The elimination of some or all intermediaries in an industry value chain is a means for reducing costs accrued along the value chain. *The question is who benefits for this cost reduction- it is not necessarily the consumer.*

One possible scenario enabled by electronic commerce is the *disappearance from the value chain of any retailer intermediation*. The wholesaler bypasses the retailer through the development of order and delivery systems that offer convenient search and content information services to the client. An example of a successful value chain of this form is the Internet-based Amazon bookstore (Kotha, 1998). The added value of this 24 hour ordering system is the search engine for the book catalogue (by key word, author, special interest, etc.) allowing for information intensive product browsing. This case illustrates how commercial activity regarding a physical object, books, turns through electronic commerce into a form of *'product-plus-service'* type of trade. The consumer is no longer offered simply the physical goods over new channels of trade, but an integrated package containing the actual goods as well as services related to information on the goods as well as him/herself (e.g. notifying readers/customers of new book arrivals based on book subject and profile of reader interests).

Another possibility is that *the manufacturer chooses to conduct business directly with the consumer*. In this case the producer delivers and bills the customer. Normally the delivery can be physical, over the traditional logistics or online over the Internet for intangible goods.

The response of retailers to Electronic Commerce scenarios that leave them out of the value chain may be *the consolidation of their position as the primary channel for reaching consumers*. Retailers may rework their physical distribution systems via arranging for products to be shipped directly from the manufacturer to the consumer. The consumers may still be with the impression that they have purchased the product from the retailer, paid the retailer and received the goods from the retailer. The retailer in effect still "owns" the relationship with the consumer.

The service sector provides also useful insights on how commerce could be arranged in the future. The integration of 'product-plus-service' in electronic retailing may gain insight from current transformations to service delivery over electronic channels. In the case of a service, the traditional value chain included the service supplier who reached the consumer through the service retailer. In an Electronic Commerce scenario *the service retailer may be by-passed by the service supplier*. In this case, the service retailers can *remain in business if they capitalize on their existing relationship with the customer*. If their position is strong enough they may make a strategic decision to represent those service suppliers who do not sell directly to the consumer. This is achieved by possessing and adding value to information along the transactional chain. The current trend for service retailers is to use the Internet to convince customers that they are still in a position to guide them through the multitude of services to the one that best suits their needs.

An example of this scenario is the presence of mutual fund companies on the Internet. Traditionally, although such companies create products and manage the financial portfolios behind them, banks often conduct the actual sale of mutual funds to customers adding value to the transaction by offering at the same time loans and investment advise. By entering the Internet, mutual fund companies are able to sell directly to consumers. Banks, however, may still be able to take advantage of their relationship with customers and use the Internet to convince them that it is able to meet their financial needs timely and effectively.

Intermediaries do have certain unique competencies that are difficult to replace by electronic operations. Nevertheless, their sustained existence will depend on how well they exploit in-depth knowledge they have in particular aspects of commercial operations (knowledge of market segments, comparative characteristics of products, particular features of customers) in terms of *converting them to information based services over electronic means*. Given the appropriate consolidation actions on the part of the intermediaries, they evolve into *cybermediaries* in the Internet era. They may take, among others (Perales, 1998), one of the following forms:

- *Directories and Search Services:* Directory service intermediaries help consumers to locate producers through systems that offer web site categorization and structured internet navigation (e.g. topic oriented search as in "The All-Internet Shopping Directory", or technical and evaluative information about products as in Jeff Frohwein's ISDN Technical Page);
- *Publishers:* Web sites offering access to online newspapers or magazines (e.g. Information Week). Publishers become intermediaries by offering news and information producers links through advertising or product listings related to their content and charging for this service on a flat fee or transaction basis;
- *Financial intermediaries:* Such intermediaries are necessary in an Electronic Commerce environment as all sale and purchase transactions require some means of making and authorizing payments. Such systems may take the form of cash payments (Digicash) or credit authorization by major credit card companies such as Visa. These financial intermediaries, already using technologies such as EDI and participating in systems such as SWIFT, may charge on the basis of transactions, thus absorbing the risk associated with money flows.

Bacos (1991) argues that an important competitive strategy for intermediaries in electronic marketplaces is to achieve economies of scope and scale in their activities. He identifies four elements in such strategies (1) building substantial systems in terms of size, complexity, initial investment required, and number of participants; (2) building systems that are complex so that learning through them can lower the cost of subsequent system development; (3) achieving economies of scope in development expertise, sharing of operational costs and data collection (as data collected through system operation becomes an asset in itself); and (4) achieving a large number of network participants. The elements of this strategy favor firms that are strong in performance and customer base and wealthy in terms of resources. *In fact, intermediation in an electronic market may be a key enabler for a firm in capitalizing in its technology and systems development expertise, existing networks and customer base.*

The development of electronic markets and the reorganization undergoing businesses to respond to new market conditions restructures jobs in firms and places new skill requirements. A detailed description of these phenomena is supplied in section 4.

3 Electronic Commerce and Business Re-Organization: Exploiting Information Flow Across Virtual Value Chains

Electronic commerce offers cost reduction opportunities beyond the reduction or redistribution of players in the value chain. EC impacts on firms' transaction costs by lowering coordination costs (Malone *et al*, 1987). IT enabled improvements in coordination within and across organizations have four distinct dimensions: (1) organizational efficiency improvements through the simplification of transactions between buyers and sellers; (2) acceleration of the flow through the production-distribution system; (3) intensification in the use of factors of production, and (4) intensification in the use of information flowing across the value chain (Rayport & Sviokla, 1995).

Numerous cases reflect the rationale presented above. Inland Steel allow customers to access their internal systems to place orders and track steel shipments; DEC provide on-line catalogue and ordering service (Malone *et al*, 1989); Dell, Compaq and Gateway allow customers to configure and order their computers on-line thus reducing product specificity as well as inventory costs (IMRG, 1998).

In this section we focus on the impact of extensive changes in the availability and exploitation of information flowing across industry value chains, as a result of extensive use of advanced information technologies. Our argument is that the intensification in the use of information across the value chain in electronic markets changes business processes for firms participating in such markets, and thus changes jobs and skills associated with these processes.

3.1 Exploiting the Information Flow from Producer to Consumer

Changes in the ways information is supplied to the consumer about products and services has far reaching implications for the structure and behavior of markets.Bacos (1991) argues that systems creating and supporting electronic markets have distinct characteristics that, from an economic perspective, transform value creation mechanisms in industry value chains. One of them is that *such systems can reduce customer's search costs for obtaining information about products or services as well as suppliers' costs of communicating this information to consumers.* Bacos differentiates between commodity markets, where products are identical and buyers select sellers that offer the lowest total cost (one factor of which is the cost of searching the market), and differentiated markets, which are the majority, and which involve a variety of product offerings and more complex search mechanisms since buyers consider both product price and product characteristics in selecting a seller.

Electronic commerce intensifies product differentiation since any type of good can now be supplied within a 'product-plus-service' package. We can now provide an explanation for this trend based on Bacos' analysis: electronic market systems make the distribution of information far more efficient thus making comparison shopping far cheaper for consumers. *Where price is the only differentiation for products offered, more expensive products are now pushed out of the market.*

In differentiated markets search costs are incurred as buyers are attempting to locate products with desirable characteristics as well as price. The provision of cheap and easy to access to product and price information reduces sellers' ability to take advantage of buyers' search costs. In cases where previously product quality information was impossible to be obtained without buying the product (e.g. legal or medical services), electronic market systems undermine monopolistic price situations. In general price information is considered as the most threatening for seller's profits: for example, ticket prices are complicated to determine in computerized reservation systems in the airline industry in an effort to discourage price comparisons. Product differentiation intensifies through electronic market systems (e.g. frequent flyer programs in the airline industry). Finally, systems that act as intermediaries in these markets, such as American Airlines' SABRE claim some of the gain buyers have through reduced search costs in the form of user fees for the system (Dahl, 1991).

Information flow across traditional value chains has been treated as a means for supporting value-adding activities, rather than as a value adding element in itself. In electronic markets this situation changes fundamentally. The focus is now new services delivered to the customer based on information captured along value chain activities. The case of Federal Expressinternet based system which allows customers to track the progress of package delivery is illustrative. Value thus created for the customer increases customer loyalty in a context of intense competition. This paradigm can inform similar initiatives in other industry sectors. Rayport & Sviokla (1995) propose three stages for the adoption of information value adding initiatives in electronic market. In the first, *visibility,* the use of large scale information systems integrating internal operations allows firms to 'see' these operations far more effectively while preparing them for linkages in a virtual value chain. In the*mirroring* stage, firms reflect physical activities into a virtual market environment (e.g. using CAD technology and videoconferencing turns product design from a physical to a virtual value chain activity). Finally, firms *establish new customer relationships* drawing on information they extract from the virtual value chain - a prime example is DEC's internet system automating the interface between the sales function and the customer.

The changes in the information offered on products and services in an electronic market, the manner in which products 'packaged' with information are promoted, offered and delivered over networks, and the ways in which information flowing across value chains can be exploited to develop new customer services, require new skills and capabilities for those handling these processes in today's' organizations. These issues are discussed in section 4.

3.2   Exploiting the Information Flow from Consumer to Producer

Information technology is a major lever in the quest for improvements in organisational efficiency. Reducing the time and cost parameters associated with business operations is achieved through systems that automate and integrate business processes. (Scott-Morton, 1991; Applegate*et al*, 1996). IT, however, has uses beyond the management of complex and highly dependent tasks. It offers opportunities for the restructuring of business operations to create value for customers (Venkatraman in Scott-Morton, 1991). Such opportunities include the reduction of response times through the creation of cross-functional links that speed up the flow of material through the value chain, and the customization of products according to customer requirements. The ever increasing choice offered to buyers in all types of product and service markets intensifies the need to enrich them by value adding services. To achieve these goals, companies turn to re-think the way their supply chains are set-up and managed. The sharing and exploitation of information flowing across processes becomes a critical activity. Optimal delivery of basic and customized services to the buyer, requires the set-up of *demand driven models for supply chain management*. This implies the reversal of flow of information, which now is fed 'backwards' from the consumer to the producer/manufacturer. The reverse information flows through networks that link players along the supply chain operating on EDI or internet based technological infrastructures. Perpetual inventory tacking, automatic product replentishment, and optimization of distribution are thus enabled. Flexible production systems exploit technologies such as POS systems in retailing that supply data allowing demand driven forecasts of production (Kalakota & Whinston, 1996). Therefore, supply chain management involves the integration of internal systems as well as the networking of systems across organizational boundaries.

The new conception of supply chain management transforms the organization of production, marketing and promotion activities, the order-deliver cycle, and the management of the IT infrastructure in organizations. Significant changes are also introduced to financial controlling mechanisms. Ability to develop and operate effective network based information systems becomes critical. The section that follows discusses how these changes transform the nature of work and the skills required to carry out the aforementioned business processes.

4 Impact on Employment and the Transformation of Jobs and Skills: The Case of the Commerce Sector

The extensive changes to ways in which firms and markets operate in today's environments, punctuated by distinct changes in the way technology is employed by all kinds of organizations, has significant effects on the nature work being carried out in them and on the availability of employment in various industry sectors. We discuss these phenomena in this section using as an illustrative example the case of the commerce sector. Our analysis has not focused on producing quantitative measures related to the extent to which jobs will be created or will disappear in this sector. Quantification at this stage can only be based on indications from trends. Our particular interest lies in the ways in which particular jobs and work in general will be transformed in the sector; the manner in which the analysis has been performed may also serve as a model for producing similar analyses for other industry sectors.

In order to examine how Electronic Commerce affects the *job content* of working individuals, we need first to consider the impact of the technological aspect of Electronic Commerce initiatives. From this perspective Electronic Commerce can be seen as *a new form of information technology in the workplace*. Computerization in organizations usually goes through successive eras during which an increasing sophistication and pervasiveness of the role that technology plays can be observed. Three eras are normally identified: the *automation* period (batch processing, 'back office' applications), the *information* period (value adding applications, real time processing) and the *transformation* period (systems that change the nature of business) (Scott-Morton, 1991).

Seen in perspective, the eras of computerization identified above correspond to a steady rise in skill levels among workers as they take away routine and repetitive tasks and they provide a far richer information basis to work (Beirne & Ramsay, 1992). Specifically, job content changes depend on the nature of IT solutions introduced in the workplace where the distinction is drawn between algorithmic and 'non-standard' use of technology. Most technologies may suit both modes of use, making this distinction an issue of social choice. Such choice affects the degree of resulting change in work and is characterized by the emergence of:
- dedicated staff (operators of the particular technology, e.g. operators of the web site);
- centralization of the function supported by the particular technology (and thus separation from other work in the enterprise);
- changes in the standardization of work ranging from routinization, to addition of complementary tasks resulting in learning.

In order to assess the degree to which the above phenomena occur in the case of Electronic Commerce applications, we review below changes to the nature and forms of work introduced by such applications. Our assessment is based on changes introduced to the main *functions* within the commerce value chain. Such functions make up the *task profiles* of employees in the commerce sector. In some cases however, particularly within small commerce firms where job differentiation is low, an entire function, or even a number of them fall within the work brief of a single individual.

4.1 Business Functions and Job Transformation

In an Electronic Commerce environment the main commerce functions (quotation, order, picking and packing, shipping, delivery, billing, payment) are transformed as follows:
- ***Product promotion***: Electronic Commerce enables companies to promote their products through the use of digital media (multimedia, 3D graphics, video, music, voice). This possibility leads to a series of changes in the nature of work performed by people involved in promotion as well as in the way enterprises operate. Promotion personnel, will not be affected by the introduction of Electronic Commerce technology, as the majority of electronic stores will operate in parallel with the physical ones. However, the need for electronic promotion particularly through the Internet will lead to a new type of position - that of the *web promoter*. Web promoters design and publish product advertisement campaigns over the internet, and manage the electronic interaction with prospective clients. Therefore,

web promoters are required to have extra qualifications such as specialized knowledge on web technologies and web page design. Moreover, such promoters need to have detailed insights into similar activities of competitor firms. Finally, web promoters need a detailed understanding of the processes related to personalized, one-to-one marketing enabled through the information captured on the consumer in the course of an electronic transaction;

- *Sales*: Electronic sales are now part of business-to-business and business-to-consumer *applications*. The opportunities offered for electronic sales, lead a small part of the existing personnel to shift towards *electronic selling*. This type of sales personnel experience a number of changes in the nature of their work: selling is turning from a one-to-one interaction to a broadcast activity of product related information over electronic media, to the consumer market. Sales personnel become responsible for keeping the information supporting electronic sales up-to-date, for 'posting' information of new products and offers, for monitoring level of sales activities, and for communicating electronically with consumers as part of sales and after sales support. It may be true, that fewer sales people may be needed to promote and sell the products of an enterprise, yet the traditional responsibilities of a sales person will shift focus as all the exchange of information will be carried out electronically. On-line interactivity - supported also by intelligent systems-gives information and gathers information from clients based on their responses to options on offer. Sales people need to analyze data and segment client niches in order to give customers product information that matches their preferences. This broadening of the role of the sales person is derived entirely from the additional capabilities provided by Electronic Commerce;

- *Order preparation and delivery:* Electronic commerce creates additional demand for product delivery services as a vast range of physical goods usually delivered at the cashier's desk need now to be transported to client's location. This introduces changes to work procedures related to order preparation and product delivery. The operator of the Electronic Commerce application becomes involved in checking incoming orders and transmitting them to the warehouse. Then stock keepers prepare the orders and the company's distribution service delivers the goods. Retailers often do not have access to a distribution service and thus higher demand for such services leads to recruitment of extra personnel. Current practice has proved that companies may also opt for outsourcing of the delivery processes to specialized distribution enterprises (e.g. courier services). A task within this function that is fundamentally transformed is the distribution of intangible goods, as this kind of goods can be distributed directly to consumers through the network. This is directly related to changes in the role of intermediaries in the industry value chain as discussed in the sections above;

- *Payment:* Electronic Commerce supports a set of methods (EDI, Smart Cards, Credit Cards, electronic cash, Internet Banking, Home Banking etc.) that facilitate electronic payments. In cases where a virtual store replaces a physical point of sale or operates in parallel with a physical store, a new work role is expected to arise. This new task is related to the auditing and control of electronic transactions. Knowledge on electronic payment systems using EDI, smart card, web and a host of other technologies will be required to audit the payment system and check all financial transactions. In the absence of appropriate legal and regulatory frameworks for the financial aspects of electronic the issuance of invoices as well as other documents related to financial transactions and their dispatch to the warehouse in order to be filed with the orders is still necessary. Electronic financial transactions need also to be reconciled with internal financial systems where the trend is now to have them integrated within systems that support the full range of a firm's business processes. The essence of these combined changes is reflected in the exchange of information and facilitation of payments made and received by the accounting officer. With respect to *accounts payable*, extensive data entry requirements are now replaced by invoice verification and approval before it automatically feeds into the accounting system of the company. Payments will be facilitated via the transmission of Electronic Fund Transfer request (EFT), or through Electronic Data Interchange (EDI) payment order message to the bank. Internal accounting systems can be automatically updated. In a similar manner, the payroll process is settled. With respect to *accounts receivable,* electronic invoicing is automatic and instantaneous while it also bridges buyer and seller accounting systems in the case of business to business transactions. Finally, *general ledger accounting changes* through the integration of all the activities encompassed in the order-sale cycle which will automatically initiate the necessary accounting postings to internal systems. *The accounting officer may no longer need to control consistency manually and therefore emphasis in this profession is shifted towards the improvement of financial reporting and management activities.*

4.2   New Task Arrangements

New task arrangements for employees within an Electronic Commerce environment are expected to place emphasis on three generic types of activities:

*   *managing product promotion and marketing and monitoring competitors*: an inclusion to all sales related tasks, where the electronic 'presence' of the store as well as electronic orders processing will force sales personnel to gauge both consumer reactions to promotion and products, and competitor activity in Electronic Commerce (e.g. 'surfing' the Internet to obtain information on competitive product qualities and alternative product promotion patterns). These activities are also candidates for *teleworking* arrangements (CEC, 1997);
*   *managing the communication between the enterprise and its customers and suppliers:* on the retail side, affected functions include inventory and distribution, where the functional and geographical independence from the sales location will lead to the promotion of *outsourcing.* This trend, with the emergence of specialist firms, may spread to the wholesale sector where currently the employment situation is less volatile compared to retail;
*   *managing the information and communication technology infrastructure:* ensuring appropriate performance of technical systems is emerging as a key issue. Speed of communication, response time, on-line and other types of user support are some of the concerns here. Another important issue concerns the definition of appropriate

and relevant management reporting on the basis of information held and processed within corporate systems.

Having identified the nature of changes brought by Electronic Commerce to work tasks, we now turn to address the following question: how extensive will these changes be in the commerce sector? Electronic Commerce applications (e.g. electronic stores) appear to follow two basic trends:

- *replacing* existing operations, and
- *operating* in parallel within existing business practices and functions.

In the cases where Electronic Commerce applications *replace traditional operations* (e.g. a store folds up because a virtual one takes its place) a lot of professions will disappear or be replaced by new ones. The professions that deal with the sales, office administration, and auxiliary work (cleaning or store security) are practically eliminated. In contrast, warehouse (stock keepers) and product distribution staff that will be maintained as their role continues to be significant in virtual enterprises.

There is the possibility that many enterprises will require existing personnel to transfer to different work functions in order to capitalize on their enterprise-specific experience. Two types of transfer are possible:

- *from one traditional function to another*, for example, the number of employees working in distribution will be potentially increased by incoming personnel from the sales department;
- *from traditional work functions to new ones,* for example to positions related to the management and operation of the electronic environment (e.g. computer operators, system administrators, database and information officers, and accountants).

The transformation of the role and nature of the work performed by certain employees can only be made possible if employees acquire the necessary skills to cope with new work requirements.

It is anticipated, however, that at least in the first instance commerce companies will opt to operate both electronically and manually (using the existing methods and practices). The impact of Electronic Commerce in such cases is not as intensive as in the eventuality discussed above because change is restricted to the professions related to the functions of the new applications. In this case, the need for management and operation of applications, the warehouse and the distribution will maintain a steady demand for employees.

Finally, new types of managers will be required within the new work environments. These will be generalists, able to operate on a cross-functional basis, in less defined and more volatile types of organization. The managers of the future will need to replace ability to control with the ability to facilitate and to be able to forge new partnerships inside and across businesses (IMRG, 1998).

5 Conclusions and directions for future work

Electronic markets are in a transition characterized by the entrance of strong market players promoting concentration of market activity, and by a slower move, compared to early predictions, towards open electronic markets. As a result of changes in the market structure, the sources of employment change. The extent to which intermediaries will contribute to the establishment of open electronic markets as opposed to strong single source markets will determine to a large extent the redistribution of sources of employment. In this paper we have examined a number of possible intermediation scenarios to establish an understanding of emerging as well as disappearing sources of employment. The impact on employment has been discussed then from the perspective of changes to the nature of work inside business functions, as well as from the perspective of where today's' employees will find themselves working in the future.

Changes to the nature of work inside business functions has been discussed with reference to significant changes we have identified to the use of information flowing from the producer to the consumer, and vice versa, across the value chain. First, the trend towards intense product differentiation in electronic markets is based on the capabilities offered by technology to convert product characteristics into information conveyed to the consumer, and to anchor services supplied in conjunction with the product on such information. Packaging 'products plus services' (explained in the previous section) and offering them through electronic networks introduces fundamental changes in marketing and sales functions which in turn impact on the nature of work and the skills required to carry out these activities. Likewise, the information flowing in both physical and virtual value chain operations is exploited to deliver new types of service for the customer. Finally, supply chain management is increasingly becoming demand driven, which implies a reversal of information flowing across the value chain from the consumer to the producer. These changes require a re-configuration of the notion of customer service, as well as a re-conceptualization of the internal structure of value chain processes. New capabilities and skills are required to handle these changes.

The changes to the content of work discussed in this paper provide strong evidence that job transformation resulting from Electronic Commerce will be extensive. The question to tackle next is whether this transformation is actually expected to have an *enskilling* or *deskilling* potential. In this situation we need to draw a distinction between *job enlargement* (adding similar tasks) and *job enrichment* (adding different job elements such as control). A related issue is whether job transformation will result on average in increased task ranges for workers coupled by reduced areas of control. (Daniel, 1987). There is a need for further research, based in an in-depth study of specific Electronic Commerce cases, where the following variables will be considered (Beirne & Ramsay, 1992):

- management values and objectives;
- product markets and their characteristics;
- labor markets and their characteristics;
- organizational size and structure;
- employer's attitudes and behavior;
- labor costs (and related financial incentives to adopt technology);
- labor inputs to work (quality);
- pre-existing task structures and occupational control.

In-depth study of the issues presented in this paper requires empirical research which is industry specific in nature. The discussion in this paper has been informed by studies already in progress in commerce sector (Doukidis *et al* 1998), while market and business transformation issues have been reviewed in a number of sectors among which are the grocery (Terpsidis et al, 1998) and public administration sectors (Pergioudakis et al, 1998).

References

1. Ackoff R.L. (1987) OR: A post-mortem. Operational Research, 35, 471-474.
2. Applegate L.M., McFarlan F.W., McKenney J.L. (1996) Corporate information systems management. Irwin
3. Bacos Y. (1991) A strategic analysis of electronic marketplaces. MIS Quarterly, September, 295-310.
4. Beirne M., Ramsay H. (1992) IT and workplace democracy. Routledge, London.
5. Benjamin R., Wigand R. (1995) Electronic markets and virtual value chains on the information superhighway. Sloan Management Review, Winter, 62-72.
6. CEC (1997) Status report on European Teleworkin. DG-XIII.
7. Coopers & Lybrand (1996) European value chain analysis study. Final report, ECR Europe Publications.
8. Dahl J. (1991) Agents rankle airlines with fare checking programs. Wall Street Journal, May 20, P.B1.
9. Daniel W. (1987) Workplace industrial relations and technical change. Francis Pinter, London.
10. Doukidis G., Poulymenakou A., Terpsidis J., Themistokleous M., Miliotis P. (1998) The impact of the development of electronic commerce on the employment situation in European commerce. Study to be published by CEC, DGV.
11. Economist (1997) Electronic Commerce: In search of the perfect market. May 10th.
12. ECR Europe (1998) Working together – A strategic imperative? Coopers & Lybrand ECR Center of Excellence, The Netherlands.
13. ECR Europe Newsletter (1998) Creating a new partnership with the consumer: A new dimesion of ECR.ECR Europe Hamburg Conference Report, Spring 1998,6-7.
14. Fisher M.L., Hammond J.H., Obermeyer W.R., Raman A. (1994) Making supply meet demand in an uncertain world. Harvard Business Review, May-June, 83-93.
15. IMRG (1998) Electronic commerce in Europe: An action plan for the marketplace. June 1998, London. www.imrg.org.
16. Kalakota R., Whinston A.B. (1996) Frontiers in electronic commerce. Addison-Wesley.
17. Kotha S. (1998) Competing on the internet: The case of Amazon.com. European Management Journal, 16(2), 212-222.
18. Malone T.W., Yates J., Benjamin R.I. (1987) Electronic markets and electronic hierarchies. Communications of the ACM, 30(6), 484-497.

19. Malone T.W., Yates J., Benjamin R.I. (1989) The logic of electronic markets. Harvard Business Review, May-June, 166-170.
20. Perales N. (1998) Exchange costs as determinants of electronic markets.Electronic Markets, 8(1), 3-6
21. Pergioudakis V., Miliotis P., Doukidis G. (1998) Electronic public procurement: From the international experience to the reality of the Mediteranean region. Proceedings of European Conference In Information systems, Marseilles, June 1998.
22. Rayport J.F., Sviokla J.J. (1995) Exploiting the virtual value chain. Harvard Business Review, November-December, 75-85.
23. Scott-Morton M. (ed)(1991) The corporation in the 90's: IT and organizational transformation. Oxford University Press.
24. Terpsidis J., Doukidis G., Zarogianni V., Manikas K., Poulymenakou A., Miliotis P. (1998) The role of information systems within Efficient Consumer Response (ECR): Towards a maturity model of engagement. Proceedings of the 11th International Bled Electronic Commerce Conference, Bled, Slovenia, June 1998.

The Coyote Project:
Framework for Multi-party E-Commerce

Asit Dan, Daniel Dias, Thao Nguyen, Marty Sachs, Hidayatullah Shaikh,
Richard King and Sastry Duri

IBM Research Division, T.J. Watson Research Center

P.O. Box 704, Yorktown Heights, NY 10598

Abstract: The Internet provides the opportunity for quickly setting up deals between businesses for promoting each other's products, and to jointly offer new services. Specification and enforcement of such deals stretch traditional transaction processing concepts in several directions since they involve independent businesses with their own internal processes. First, the greater variability in response time in business to business interaction creates a need for asynchronous and event-driven processing, in which correct handling of reissued and cancelled requests is critical. Second, a new transaction processing paradigm is required that supports different views of a **unit of business** for all participants, i.e., service providers as well as end consumers. Between any two interacting parties, there may be several related interactions dispersed in time, creating a **long running conversation**. This paper describes our approach (Coyote) to solving these problems including use of a service contract for specifying the rules of interaction across businesses, and directly generating code for enforcement of the contract. We finally describe the architecture and a prototype of a system which implements the Coyote concepts.

1. Introduction

The ubiquity in network connectivity promises electronic commerce in every walk of life, e.g., shopping, entertainment, education, etc. The client merely connects via an access device to the network, i.e., to a long running service application, and performs business transactions, e.g., creating and modifying a travel plan, checking the status of a purchase request, accepting discount offers, etc. Many such commerce activities may actually span multiple autonomous business organizations. For example, when a client makes a purchase request for an item, he may receive a *business deal* in the form of receiving a discount on another product, perhaps from a different business organization. Figure 1.

1 illustrates one of many such possible deals:

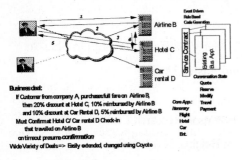

Figure 1.1: Multi-party electronic commerce

If a customer from company A purchases full fare on Airline B, then the customer receives a 20% discount at Hotel C, half of which is reimbursed to Hotel C by Airline B; The customer also receives a 10% discount at Car Rental D, half of which is reimbursed to Car Rental D by Airline B. During check-in at Hotel C and/or Car Rental D the customer must confirm that he/she travelled on Airline B; if there is a timeout during confirmation, successful confirmation is assumed.

It is easy to imagine a wide variety of business deals across multiple business organizations with different terms and conditions, in order to promote each other's products and to provide an improved set of services to a customer. For example, a university enrolment may entitle a student to a discount in a book store; a Broadway ticket may offer a discount at a restaurant, etc. In such cases, there may be concomitant payment between the businesses, transparent to the client. Even between a single selling organization and a single buying organization, many different deals are possible, e.g., *an airline ticket purchased from the Airline A by the customers from the organization B is refundable until 24 hours prior to the date of arrival.* To facilitate spontaneous electronic commerce, deals need to be constructed and implemented quickly, reflecting the dynamic nature of the marketplace. Deals may also promote customer loyalty and ensure guaranteed services across organizations.

Lack of a suitable application development platform, however, hinders quick implementation of such deals on a larger scale. Taken in its entirety, each such business deal is a ***distributed long running application spanning multiple autonomous business organizations [1,2].*** Specification and enforcement of such deals stretch traditional strict transaction processing concepts in several directions. First, transactions spanning multiple independent organizations may need to address enforcement of pairwise legal agreements and **service contracts**. Second, a new transaction processing paradigm is required that supports different views of a **unit of business** for all participants, i.e., service providers as well as end consumers. There may be several related interactions between any two interacting parties dispersed in time, creating a **long running conversation**. Achieving global data consistency across the businesses participating in a contract is not possible, both because of the length of time which may be involved in a conversation (which precludes locking the internal resources of a business for the duration of the conversation) and because each business has its own internal processes which generally cannot be synchronized with the processes of other businesses, precluding use of a two-phase commit process across the businesses. Instead, persistent records of business actions must to be kept at each business to aid in recovery, auditing, etc. The greater variability in response time for network computing creates a need for asynchronous and event-driven processing, in which correct handling of reissued and cancelled requests is critical.

We illustrate shortly that conventional technologies do not address the requirements of the above types of applications. As a result, currently it requires a long time to set up electronic business operations across organizations. To alleviate some of these problems, standard Electronic Data Interchange (EDI) messages representing service requests and replies have been defined (e.g., Purchase order (PO), Request for Quote (RFQ)) [3]. Some of these are unique to specific industry segments; others have industry-specific variants. In addition, further agreements (referred to as Implementation Conventions, and complex trading partner agreements) are needed before such EDI messages can be exchanged across business applications. Finally, note that building long running, stateful distributed applications, taking into account various state dependent exception handling, and rollback/compensation of previous operations, etc., is always a challenging task. Erroneous (and, in the worst case, malicious) implementation of application components by a business partner can adversely affect the businesses of other partners.

We now outline the Coyote approach and contrast this approach with earlier models in the next two subsections. In Section 2, we describe the key elements of a service contract. We present the details of the overall application structure and illustrate the associated execution flow in Section 3. Subsequently, we describe the Coyote server environment along with details of the some of the services in Section 4. Finally, a summary and concluding remarks appear in Section 5.

1.1 Coyote Approach

The Coyote (Cover YOurself Transaction Environment) approach recognizes the key features of a multiparty e-commerce application, i.e., *long running, event driven, compensation based business interactions*, and advocates development of service applications as autonomous business processes that interact with other business processes via formally defined rules of engagement. It advocates a clear separation of states across businesses as well as a separation of *internal and external business processes* within an organization. The rules of external interaction and externally visible states are defined as a *service contract* [1,2]. The semantics of such external interaction are well defined, such that there is no ambiguity across businesses as to what each message may mean, what actions are allowed, and what responses are expected at any point during long running interactions (also referred to as *conversations*). A service contract acts both as a guideline for interaction across businesses and also as an enforcement mechanism for guaranteeing proper interaction. Furthermore, at the contract level there is no specification of internal processes of the businesses that may introduce unnecessary dependency or close coupling across businesses. For example, when a customer returns a previously purchased product to the selling organization, there is no need to specify what the selling organization may do with the returned item (e.g., send back to the producer, reshelve the item, etc.).

At the semantic level all messages are assumed to be committed and, hence, cannot be rolled back. In contrast, traditional distributed business applications embrace a

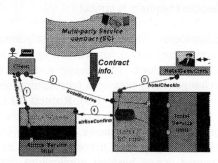

Figure 1.2: Coyote Approach

distributed transaction model, where each application component runs under a transaction monitor so that the application components can participate in a two-phase commit protocol [4,5]. Note that such traditional models of distributed application development not only introduce close dependencies across software systems in different businesses, but are also inadequate to model long running interactions. Under the Coyote approach the business interactions are modelled after common business practice, i.e., cancellation and/or compensation of previous requests.

Another important aspect of the Coyote approach is to provide an application development and execution environment for *long running, event-driven compensation-based business interactions*. The overall business application is built from code segments that capture internal business processes and the service contract(s). Figure 1.2 illustrates the development of a multiparty e-commerce application for the earlier mentioned business deal. There are three parties (i.e., client, Hotel and Airline) participating in this deal. (The Car rental agency is not shown in the Figure.) The client for this deal can be a travel agency that makes reservations on behalf of its customers.

To implement this deal the client, Airline and Hotel companies generate deal-specific code from this joint deal specification. The generated code on each side also connects to the corresponding internal processes. As part of this deal, the client makes a reservation on both the Airline and Hotel companies (actions 1 & 2). As illustrated, each reservation operation has two components: the contract specific code maintaining the state of the interaction and invocation of the reservation service implementation in the Hotel and Airline companies, respectively. At a later point, the customer flies via the Airline, and subsequently checks in at the Hotel (action 3). The Hotel, in turn, as specified in the contract, confirms with the Airline (action 4) that the end-client has indeed travelled via the Airline participating in this deal.

Figure 1.3 illustrates the use of the Coyote framework in a general business setting, where different organizations provide different services as well as receive services from other business organizations. A single business process may interact with many different business partners, where the interactions are specified via one or more service contracts. The Coyote server in each of the business nodes (which can be suppliers, manufacturers, agencies, warehouse owners, etc.) facilitates development and execution of its overall business processes. The services provided by a business organization can be invoked either directly by an end-user (e.g., through the web) or by a service application in another business, where allowable interactions are defined

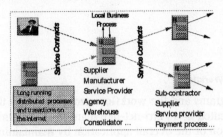

Figure 1.3: Generic Business service application mod

via a service contract.

1.2 Related work

Both transaction processing and providing the support for distributed applications, have been active areas of research and development for many years. In the area of transaction processing, the focus has been on extending the ACID transaction model to capture dependencies across many atomic steps of a long running transactional application [6-10]. In contrast to Coyote, the focus in supporting distributed applications has been on middleware for gluing together independently developed application components to build complex but synchronous applications within a single business organization. The CORBA IDL [11] provides the interface of an application component that encapsulates some business logic. The programmer is freed from various system resource management issues (e.g., application scalability, thread allocation, runtime allocation of system nodes to an application component, etc.). However, the programmer has to still understand the overall semantics and make sure the sequence of calls to an application component is meaningful (e.g., that it is a valid sequence of operations on an object). In the current e-commerce context, where different application components are created and managed by different organizations, the programmers in various organizations have to cooperate in creating a meaningful application. Service contracts that formally define not only the interfaces and method signatures, but also the rules of interaction, allow the application development process in various organizations to be decoupled.

Workflow systems provide support for definition and execution of long running applications [12,8,9]. Typically, the execution of an application step may also require the participation of a specific user or a member of a group. The application steps may

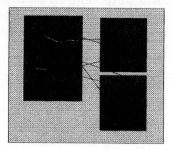

Figure 1.4: Building a Service Flow from Workflo

be developed separately as individual programs and the workflow process defines the sequence in which the steps are to be executed in a Petri-net-like manner. At runtime, the workflow monitor co-ordinates execution of the overall application by maintaining the state of the overall execution flow, maintaining the output data of the previous application steps, selecting the next application step or steps to be invoked, and invoking these application steps by passing appropriate input data. While workflow is an important technology for modelling many business processes within an organization, it may be inadequate for supporting distributed applications capturing multi-party business deals. First, irrespective of the application component programming model, a Coyote-like framework is needed for specification of the service contract, and the generation of the code in each organization that deals with service contracts and, in turn, invokes the corresponding internal business processes. Second, appropriate interaction (i.e., conversation) semantics need to be defined that both decouple the individual internal business processes, and yet allow cancellation of earlier, committed operations.

One implication of the above point is that, at any time in a conversation, a business partner may be allowed to issue many possible service requests, rather than a fixed, small set of operations. Therefore, the set of possible invocation sequences is very large, and a Petri-net like definition may not be appropriate. This is illustrated in the Petri-net of Figure 1.
4, where each node represents the operations performed in a business organization. When transition 1 on Node A fires, it triggers actions 2 on both nodes B and C in parallel. Depending on the responses from nodes B and C, action 3 on node A is triggered. Since there are many possible responses from nodes B and C, other actions on node A may need to be triggered instead of action 3. Action 3 then triggers actions 4 on nodes B and C, and so on. Since the number of possible action sequences is large, representing them in a Petri-net model, and therefore, in a workflow model, becomes complex. Generally speaking, the next service request issued by a partner as well as the set of requests accepted by the other partner depend on the conversation history. In the absence of a global workflow monitor spanning multiple organizations, the conversation history needs to be passed around. (Note that the individual

application steps are not aware of the global execution steps.) Therefore, the workflow and other business processing implementation infrastructures need to be extended to manage long running conversational states across businesses as further illustrated in Section 3.

2. Coyote Multi-party Service Contract

As discussed in section 1.1, the contract is a high-level description of the interaction between two or more business partners (parties to the contract). The contract contains two kinds of information. The first is a machine-readable description of the computer-to-computer interactions between the parties that supports the overall application. It concerns those aspects of the application which each party must agree to and that are enforceable by the Coyote system. The second is the usual human-readable legal language that is part of any business-to-business contract and includes those aspects of the agreement which must be enforced by person to person contact rather than by the computer systems. This project is concerned with the machine-readable section, which we now describe in more detail and which is what we mean when we refer to the contract.

The contract is written in a language from which code can be directly generated. We have selected XML [13] as the contract specification language and are developing a graphical tool that can be used to assist in generating the XML contract. After agreement by all parties, the XML contract can then be turned into code at each of the Coyote servers. In our prototype, the contract is used to generate a service-contract object (SCO) at each party to the contract. During any information exchange between two parties, each party effectively communicates with the SCO at the other party. The SCOs provide interfaces to the application program at each party to the contract. The application program in turn communicates with the individual party's internal processes.

A particular transaction under the contract is a single long-running conversation. We refer to this as a particular instantiation of the contract. An application causes the conversation to be initiated, which results in assignment of a conversation ID and in creation of the necessary SCOs at the various parties. For example, in a contract between a travel agent and an airline, a conversation would be initiated when a traveller asks the travel agent for reservations for a particular trip. All interactions about that trip between the traveller and the travel agent and between the travel agent and the airline would then be associated with that particular conversation, which would remain active until the traveller checks in with the airline for the final segment of the trip (or perhaps longer, if settlement of the travel agent's commission does not take place until later). All activity logging would be labelled with the conversation ID to ensure proper error recovery, and for auditing on a conversation basis. The complete flow of requests and replies through the SCOs to the internal business processes is described in section 3.

As indicated earlier, a contract may involve more than two parties. For example, in

```
Identification
Overall properties
Communication proper
Security/Authentication
Role
Actions
    ⚬ Method signatures    ⚬ Glob
    ⚬ Semantics            Imple
    ⚬ Responsiveness
Constraints & sequenc
State transition logic
Compensation rules
Error handling
Legal aspects
```

Figure 2.1: Elements of a Ser

the multiparty application described in Section 1.1, travellers would be serviced by a travel agent which has entered into a 3-party contract with the airline and the hotel. The combined discount would be provided to the traveller when checking out of the hotel. In addition to defining the normal set of actions for making and servicing reservations, the contract would also define actions used between the airline and the hotel for confirming that the traveller met the conditions for receiving the combined discount, for settling the shares of the discount contributed by the airline and the hotel, and for settling the travel agent's commission.

In summary, the service contract defines the properties of each party to the contract that must be made visible to the other parties to the contract. These properties include action definitions for each party as a server, communication protocol definitions, security/authentication definitions, and others.

2.1 Elements of multi-party service contract

The primary elements of the contract are shown in Figure 2.1.

Identification: The identification section assigns a name to the contract and provides the names of each of the parties to the contract.

Overall properties: Overall properties are those attributes of the contract that apply to the contract as a whole and all instantiations of it. Included are the contract duration, permitted number of instantiations, maximum lifetime of a single conversation, default maximum permitted time from a request to receipt of the results of the request, and the name of an outside arbitrator which may mediate resolution of any apparent contract violations.

Communication properties: The communication-properties section provides the information necessary for each party to communicate with all the others. Each party is identified by its name and the information needed for person-to-person communications (mailing address, telephone number, and email address).   An authentication code, typically a public-key certificate, is also provided by each party for security and authentication purposes. The communication protocol is described with all necessary parameters such as IP address, service name, port numbers, etc. The message format rules and security mode are also included.

Security/Authentication: The following levels of security are provided (in order from strongest to weakest): nonrepudiation, authentication, encryption, and none. The security mode can be selected for the initial exchange during contract instantiation, all messages, and some messages. The initial and message security modes are specified in the communication properties of the contract and apply to all parties. If the initial security specification is omitted, the initial security mode is "none". If the message security specification is omitted, the message security mode is "selective", in which case, the security specification is included in the definition of each action which requires security above "none". Non-repudiation both proves who sent a message and prevents later repudiation of the contents of the message. It is based on public-key cryptography. To support non-repudiation, the contract must include the public-key certificate for each party. The corresponding private key for each party, of course, is private to each party and does not appear in the contract. The public-key certificate can be obtained from any recognized certification authority. There is no requirement that all parties to a contract use the same certification authority.

Role: The contract can be formulated in terms of generic roles such as *&airlineco* and *&hotelco*. These roles can then be assigned to specific parties at the time the contract is instantiated as a particular conversation.

Actions: An action is a specific request which a party, acting as a client, can issue to a party acting as a server. Examples of actions are *purchase, reserve_hotel,* and *query_status.* For each party to the contract that can act as a server, the contract specifies an action menu, which is a list of permissible actions and various properties of each action. Action properties include its name, parameter definitions, means by which the server will return its results (e.g. callback), whether the action is cancellable, the name of the cancellation method, and maximum permitted response time.

Constraints and sequencing rules: Constraints are various conditions which must be satisfied for individual actions. For example, the action *reserve_hotel* might be accompanied by a rule stating the latest time to cancel the reservation. Sequencing rules state the permissible order of actions on a given server. For example, a *cancel_reservation* action cannot be invoked until after the *reserve_hotel* action has been invoked.

State transition logic: When an action is performed, the state associated with the action (and hence the state of the contract) changes. The contract defines additional changes of variables and parameters which take place following the completion or failure of an action. For example, the price of an item may change as the result of an action. Additionally, a single action on one party may result in invocation of actions on other parties to the contract as well as invocation of local actions. In the above multi-party example, a check-in at a hotel causes the hotel to contact the airline involved in the contract for confirmation that the traveller flew on that airline.

Compensation rules: Compensation rules state any conditions relating to the cancellation of previously-invoked actions. As mentioned above, the properties of an action include whether it is cancellable and, if so, the name of the cancellation method. Cancellation groups can be defined in which a group of actions can be cancelled with a single request.

Error handling: Error conditions and methods to be called when they occur are identified. Maximum response times are stated and the number of retries and time-out recovery actions defined. Application-level errors (e.g. no room at the hotel) are identified and recovery actions defined. An outside arbitrator is identified as mentioned above.

Legal aspects: Legal aspects are any and all conditions which are typically defined in a legal contract such as handling of disputes and other exceptional conditions. An example in the context of Coyote is what is to be done if one of the servers is not reachable via the network after a specified amount of time. Another example is rules for premature termination of the contract such as when it is allowed and the penalties which might have to be paid.

3. Coyote Application Development and Flow Through the System

In this section we outline the key aspects of creating a Coyote application, and describe the flow through a Coyote-based system. Illustrated in Figure 3.1 is a Coyote-based node, which gets inbound requests from clients; these clients could be end users or business partners. The client's requests ultimately trigger business logic at this node. The business logic may require calls to business processes or pre-existing services at that node, such as workflow processes, enterprise resource planning (ERP) applications, Enterprise JavaBeans[14] based services, or other applications. Access to such existing applications is provided by so-called connectors, or by encapsulating the applications in objects with methods provided to invoke these applications. In order to provide the requested function, services from subcontracted service providers may also be needed; these are provided by outbound requests to those service providers, as illustrated in the figure. Both the inbound and outbound requests are specified and enforced by service contracts, as described in Section 2.

There are two main parts to creating a Coyote application: (i) writing a service contract between the parties involved in the application, and (ii) writing the business logic for the actions to be taken in response to requests from clients, as specified in the service contract. The service contract is written in a higher-level language, as outlined in Section 2. A code generator transforms the service contract specification into code which enforces the contract. In an object implementation[2], this code is referred to as the service contract object (SCO). From each service contract, code is generated at each site based on whether that party functions as a server, a client, or both. The service contract objects corresponding to contracts with clients are referred to as Server Side Contract Objects (SSCO), and those corresponding to contracts with service providers (relative to this Coyote server) are referred to as Client Side Contract Objects (CSCO). The contract objects enforce the specifications of the contract, such as checking if an inbound request is allowable, and checking whether its parameters match the request signature defined in the contract; if so, the appropriate method or function in the business logic is invoked, as described in more detail later.

The business logic consists of methods which either execute the required functions at this node or invoke the required services from an existing application or other subsystem. The business logic also uses Coyote services to make outbound calls to remote services.

We now outline the flow through a Coyote node. While we describe the flow primarily in the context of an object implementation, a similar flow applies to other implementations. Referring to Figure 3.1, an inbound request first goes through a transport security layer, as specified in the service contract. For example, the Secure Socket Layer (SSL) can be used for transport security. Next, depending on the transport protocol and format (as specified in the service contract), a message adapter

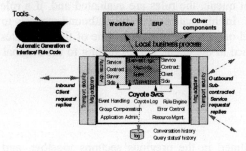

Figure 3.1: Coyote Execution Flow

layer transforms the request, i.e., extracts and transforms the parameters, and calls the service contract object. For example, the transport could be IIOP (Internet Inter-Orb protocol) [11], which in a CORBA [11] implementation of Coyote would result in using CORBA services to call the SSCO; or the transport could be MQSeries[15], with a message adapter; or it could be EDI (Electronic Data Interchange) [3], on top of HTTP[16], requiring a message adapter. As a specific instance, the transport protocol specified in OBI (Open Buying on the Internet)[17], is EDI over HTTP.

From the message adapter, the SSCO is invoked. First, application-level security, as specified in the service contract, is enforced, including authentication and provisions for non-repudiation [18]. Following this, the aspects of the contract related to the action requested are enforced. This includes determining whether the client is allowed to invoke the requested function, or whether the request is valid at this point in the conversation between the client and this server. For instance, a cancel request is only valid after an order.

Next, the underlying (core) Coyote services, shown in Figure 3.1, are invoked; the request is time-stamped and logged for audit trail purposes, and for supporting queries of the state of a client-server conversation; it is then placed in an event queue. If the request is specified in the contract to be asynchronous, a (synchronous) acknowledgement is sent back to the client that the request has been received. When the request is processed from the event queue, the internal method corresponding to the action in the contract is invoked. This method may invoke existing applications, such as workflow processes, ERP applications or other back-end applications.

In order to satisfy the incoming request, the application may need to make requests to service providers, as illustrated in Figure 3.1. For instance, if the node is an agency (e.g., a travel agency) on the Web, outgoing requests to its service providers (e.g. airline, hotel, etc.) would need to be made. This is done using Coyote services and the CSCO. Rules are attached to the outbound service request, in order to specify what to do when responses come back from the service providers. For instance, an all-or-nothing rule specifies that a specific method at this node is to be called if all the requests to a set of service providers are successful; if any are unsuccessful, cancel requests would be sent to all other service providers that were successful in the initial request, and a specified failure method would be called at this node. Responses from service providers are placed in the event queue, the rules are evaluated and, if a rule fires, the appropriate method is invoked. In this manner, several outbound requests to service providers can be made in parallel or serially. Eventually, one of the responses specified in the service contract is returned to the client, corresponding to the original client request.

4. Coyote Architecture

In this section, we pull the pieces outlined in the previous sections together, and describe the overall Coyote architecture and components. Figure 4.1 illustrates the Coyote server and application components and how they fit together. The top of Figure 4.1 shows the two main elements in building a Coyote application, as outlined in Section 3: (i) the definition of the service contract, and (ii) the development of the business logic. Graphical tools are provided to assist in defining and developing these two elements. A contract template is provided, and the graphical tool assists in generating a specific contract from the template. As illustrated on the left side of Figure 4.1, from the resulting service contract, a code generation tool generates the Client-side and Server-Side Contract Objects (see also Section 3).

The contract and the business logic are registered independently with a Business

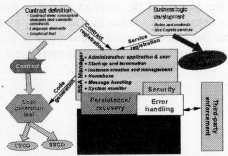

Figure 4.1: Coyote server environment

Services Application (BSA) manager. The BSA manager provides various application and user services for a Coyote system. These services, shown in the middle of Figure 4.1, include application and user administration, start-up and termination, contract instance creation and management, home-base, which supports interaction with an end user, message handling, and the system monitor. They are described in Section 4.1.

The Coyote run-time services, shown at the bottom of Figure 4.1, are the core system services on which the higher-level functions are built. They include event handling, handling of asynchronous requests and replies, conversation management (i.e. correlation of inbound and outbound requests), compensation, thread management, and performance management and are described in Section 4.2.

The persistence and recovery component provides persistence of conversation state and recovery from failures of nodes and components. Conversation persistence is provided by time-stamping and logging incoming and outgoing requests and responses in stable storage. This log is used for providing responses to queries of conversation state, for audit trail purposes, and for re-creation of conversation state. It is replayed during recovery to re-create the states of the open conversations. Recovery also involves interaction with clients and service providers to receive pending responses for determining the status of ongoing actions, and to issue any cancellation actions which may be required.

The error-handling component handles time-out and other soft errors during run time (while persistence and recovery are focused on "hard" system failures). Error handling is based on contract-defined rules as described in Section 2. As shown in Figure 4.1, error handling may involve the outside arbitrator in order to perform third-party enforcement when an error is likely to involve violation of the contract terms.

The security component handles security and authentication according to rules specified in the contract. It applies the required security to each outgoing message and tests each incoming message. The security and authentication rules have been discussed earlier (Section 2).

4.1 Coyote Server - BSA Manager

The BSA manager provides administrative services for a Coyote system. In this section we will outline some of the key functions of the BSA Manager.

Service registration: Once a Coyote application has been written it has to be announced to the BSA manager. This is done via a service registration tool. The service registration tool splits the business logic into actions and the user is prompted to associate replies, cancellation methods, etc. with each one of these actions.

Contract registration and automatic code generation: The contract, once written, is to be registered with the BSA managers of all the involved parties. This is done via a contract registration tool. This tool collects information for mapping actions to business logic methods from the administrator and then feeds this information along with the contract and the service registration information to the Automatic Code Generator, which in turn generates the contract objects (SSCO, CSCO or both).

User administration: This basically involves registering the client information with the BSA Manager. This information includes attributes like name, userid, public-key, contact information and privileges. This information is used at runtime for user authentication, callbacks etc.

Service instance creation and management: It is the job of the BSA Manager to create service instances for the clients who are using the services. This is *Server Service Instance Creation* and involves instantiating a BSA object whenever a client wants to start a conversation. When a BSA wants to utilize a remote service the BSA manager instantiates a CSCO object for it.

Startup and termination of the system: Startup involves bringing up dependencies like ORB[11] and Enterprise JavaBeans server and calling the recovery manager which in turn activates the "active conversation" objects. Termination involves gracefully passivating the conversation objects. Startup and termination are done via administrative screens.

Multiprotocol support: The BSA Manager has support for IIOP, MQ and HTTP. A custom protocol handler can easily be plugged in.

Home-base services: This is essentially a proxy for a web browser end-client, in order to maintain the state of a conversation with an end-client so that a client can reconnect and continue in a conversation where he left off. The BSA manager provides a series of conversation query functions.

System monitoring: The BSA manager has system monitoring functions which detect failures and invoke recovery actions. Tools are available for viewing and querying the trace information.

4.2 Coyote Run-time Services

To invoke services on a Coyote application server, the client (either an end user or an application) first needs to identify and authenticate itself with the BSA manager. Then the client requests the BSA manager to create a new BSA instance to start a new conversation or activate an existing BSA instance to resume a previously started conversation. Each BSA instance, depicted in Figure 4.2, is a version of the Coyote application server that has been customized to a particular client via a service contract. It is created specifically to serve that client and maintains the entire history of the client's conversation with the server until the conversation is terminated. Following are the main components or objects in each BSA instance, as shown in Figure 4.2, as well as the services that each offers:

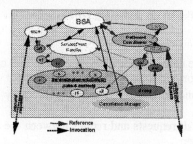

Figure 4.2: Coyote Runtime Services

- The BSA Implementation consists of a **Service Implementation** (SI) object and rule objects (r1 and r2). The SI embodies the business logic of the Coyote application server and contains methods to execute inbound service requests from clients as well as methods to handle responses from remote service providers. The rule objects are used to trigger appropriate methods in the SI to handle different outcomes of the outbound requests to the remote service providers. In addition, there may be application-specific objects (A and B). The BSA implementation is defined by the Coyote application developer. The remaining components discussed below are provided by the Coyote framework or generated from the service contracts.

- A **Service Event Handler** (SEH) is provided by the Coyote framework to support event driven asynchronous request/reply execution. An event is generated for each inbound request from clients or response from external service providers. Each event is attached with rules and delivered to an event queue. The events are processed serially by the SEH which tests each rule and fires an appropriate method in SI to handle the event.

- The **Outbound Coordinator Object** (OCO) is a Coyote framework object that provides many important services to the SI, including:
  - Supplying CSCO references to SI to invoke remote services;
  - mapping outbound requests to inbound requests;
  - creating outbound groups to help SI manage outbound requests;
  - providing a query interface to allow SI to find out state of outbound requests or groups.

- The **Cancellation Manager** (CM) is a Coyote framework object that offers cancellation services. The SI can use these services to cancel an inbound or outbound requests, outbound groups or an entire conversation.

- The **CSCO** is generated from the service contract between the Coyote application server and its remote service providers. It offers the following services to SI:
  - Time-stamping and logging all outbound requests and replies for audit trail;
  - passing service requests to the remote service providers;

- responding to queries from the SI on outbound requests;
- providing time-out services.

- The **SSCO** is generated from the service contract with a client and can differ from one BSA instance to another. It provides many services to the client, particularly:
  - enforcing the terms and conditions of the service contract by performing a variety of checking;
  - time-stamping and logging all requests and replies between the client and the server for audit trail purposes;
  - passing client requests to the SI by generating an event and delivering the event to the SEH;
  - providing a query service to allow clients to find out the status of past requests.

5. Summary and Conclusions

In this paper we have described the Coyote concepts for multi-party electronic commerce, and outlined the design of the Coyote framework for defining and implementing inter-business deals on the Internet. A key concept in Coyote is the multi-party service contract, which specifies the rules of engagement between the parties, including the inter-business actions which can be performed, the responsiveness criteria for each action, error handling for time-outs and other conditions, the application level security required for each action, compensation rules for cancelling prior actions, and so on. We have described the creation of a Coyote application, which essentially consists of defining the service contract and business logic corresponding to actions in the contract; graphical tools are provided to assist in both these aspects of application development. From the higher level specification of the service contract(s), contract objects are automatically generated, which enforce the contract and invoke the corresponding business logic. We have outlined the Coyote framework, composed of a Business Services Application (BSA) manager, which is primarily for application and user administration, a run-time environment, which is an event-driven rule-based system, and other components for persistence, recovery, error handling and security.

We have implemented a prototype Coyote system. The prototype has a Java-CORBA based Coyote framework for most of the components outlined earlier, including the BSA manager, the run-time system, simple error handling, and automatic code generation from the service contract specification. Additional work is ongoing on recovery, security and third-party authentication. We are in the process of porting the framework to an Enterprise JavaBeans [14] environment. We have also put together several sample applications, including one similar to the example in Section 1, an OBI-like [17] flow, and tie-in to workflow and other sub-systems.

Our longer term objective in Coyote is that of spontaneous business-to-business electronic commerce. To this end, we are extending the Coyote concepts to registration of service contracts with trading services, negotiation of terms and conditions in the contract, followed by instantiation of the contract objects and tie-in to existing applications. Our Coyote prototype is a first step in this direction.

Acknowledgements: We would like to thank Francis Parr for his active participation at the early stage of the project in defining the concepts, Arun Iyengar for his participation in defining the security and third-party aspects of the Coyote framework, and Nagui Halim for his vision, support and encouragement.

References

1. A. Dan, and F. N. Parr, "*The Coyote Approach for Network Centric Business Service Applications: Conversational Service Transactions, a Monitor, and an Application Style*," **HPTS Workshop**, Asilomar, CA, Sept. 1997.
2. A. Dan, and F. N. Parr, "*An Object implementation of Network Centric Business Service Applications: (NCBSAs): Conversational Service Transactions, a Service Monitor and an Application Style*," **OOPSLA Business Object Workshop**, Atlanta, GA, Sept. 1997.
3. **Electronic Commerce Resource Guide**, http://www.premenos.com
4. *Customer Information Control System/ Enterprise Systems Architecture (CICS/ESA), IBM, 1991.*
5. *J. Gray, and A. Reuter ``Transaction Processing: Concepts and Techniques," Morgan Kaufmann Publishers, 1993.*
6. *H. Garcia-Molina, and K. Salem, ``SAGAS," Proc. of ACM SIGMOD Conf., 1987, pp. 249--259.*
7. *P. Attie, M. P. Singh, A. Sheth, M. Rusinkiewicz, ``Specifying and Enforcing Intertask Dependencies", VLDB 1993, pp. 134-145.*
8. *G. Alonso, D. Agrawal, A. El Abbadi, M. Kamath, R. Gunthor and C. Mohan, ``Advanced Transaction Models in Workflow Contexts" In 12th ICDE, New Orleans, Lousiana, Feb. 1996.*
9. *Y. Breitbart, A. Deacon, H. Schek, A. Sheth and G. Weikum, ``Merging Application Centric and Data Centric Approaches to Support Transaction-Oriented Multi-System Workflows", ACM SIGMOD Record, 22(3), Sept. 1993.*
10. *A. Biliris, S. Dar, N. Gehani, H. V. Jagadish, K. Ramamritham, ``ASSET: A System for Supporting Extended Transactions", Proc. ACM SIGMOD 1994, pp. 44-54.*
11. **Object Management Group (OMG),** *http://www.omg.org*
12. *FlowMark, SBOF-8427-00, IBM Corp., 1996.*
13. **XML 1.0 Proposed Recommendation**, *http://www.w3c.org.*
14. **Enterprise JavaBeans Specification**, http://www.javasoft.com/products/ejb
15. *MQSeries: An Introduction to Messaging and Queuing, IBM publication no. G511-1908*
16. **HTTP/1.1 Specification**, http://www.w3c.org
17. **The Open Buying on the Internet (OBI) Consortium**, *http://www.openbuy.org/*
18. **RSA Data Security**, *Frequently Asked Questions About Today's Cryptography 3.0, http://www.rsa.com/rsalabs/newfaq*

MarketNet: Using Virtual Currency to Protect Information Systems

Y. Yemini, A. Dailianas, D. Florissi

Department of Computer Science, Columbia University,
450 Computer Science Bldg.
New York, NY 10027
{yemini, apostolo, df}@cs.columbia.edu

Abstract. This paper describes novel market-based technologies for systematic, quantifiable and predictable protection of information systems against attacks. These technologies, incorporated in the MarketNet system, use currency to control access to information systems resources and to account for their use. Clients wishing to access a resource must pay in currency acceptable to the domain that owns it. An attacker must thus pay to access the resources used in an attack. Therefore, the opportunities to attack and the damage that can be caused are strictly limited by the budget available to the attacker. A domain can control its exposure to attacks by setting the prices of critical resources and by limiting the currency that it makes available to potential attackers. Currency carries unique identifiers, enabling a domain to pinpoint the sources of attacks. Currency also provides a resource-independent instrumentation to monitor and correlate access patterns and to detect intrusion attacks through automated, uniform statistical analysis of anomalous currency flows. These mechanisms are resource-independent, and admit unlimited scalability for very large systems consisting of federated domains operated by mutually distrustful administrations. They uniquely establish quantifiable and adjustable limits on the power of attackers; enable verifiable accountability for malicious attacks; and admit systematic, uniform monitoring and detection of attacks.

1 Introduction

Protecting large-scale information systems remains an elusive challenge of ever-growing importance and complexity. Exposure to insecurities and the opportunities available to attackers are increasing with the growth in the range of resources, scale, complexity, and operations management practices of different domain administrations. Current information systems enable attackers to pursue virtually unlimited attempts to compromise a system; they involve ad-hoc instrumentation to monitor resource access and manual correlation of these access logs to detect intrusion; and they leave attackers completely unaccountable to abuses and crimes that they commit.

Rapid changes in technologies increase the vulnerability to attackers. First, at present protection technologies are specialized to each component. A minor insecurity in a new component can propagate substantial exposure to other components. Thus, insecurities can be formed non-monotonically; i.e., a system that is secure can be rendered insecure by the addition of a single component. Second, the combinatorics of interactions between new components and existing ones increases exponentially, creating ample possible insecurities. Third, in the absence of a unifying security architecture it is practically impossible for component vendors, or domain administrations to accomplish a coordinated protection.

Domain administrations are thus increasingly exposed to security risks and are unable to control, bound or even assess this exposure. They require expert manual labor to monitor and correlate access anomalies and detect an attack, typically through off-line non-real-time processes completed hours or days after the attack has been completed. And even when an attack is detected, identifying the source accountable for it can be virtually impossible and requires complex ad-hoc collaborations of multiple expert police forces.

MarketNet uses market-based mechanisms to provide a novel approach to the protection of large-scale information systems. In MarketNet, resources are instrumented to use currency for access control and monitoring. Clients must pay resource managers, using appropriate currency and prices, to gain access to respective resources. An attacker is limited by its budget in gaining access to resources and in creating damage. A domain administration can control access to its resources and establish quantifiable limits on its exposure to attacks by adjusting prices of critical resources and controlling the availability of currency to potential sources of attacks.

Currency flows provide uniform resource-independent instrumentation to monitor and correlate access patterns and to detect anomalies. This enables the development of uniform resource-independent intrusion-detection mechanisms entirely based on the statistics of currency flows. Intrusion-detection can be thus automated and accomplished in real-time with an attack. Furthermore, currency carries unique identifiers. A domain maintains full accountability of the entities to which currency has been allocated. A domain can account for sources of each access to its resources. In particular, once an attack has been identified a domain can establish verifiable proof of accountability in tracing its sources.

MarketNet mechanisms are structured to admit unlimited scalability and enable protection among mutually distrustful domains organized in a large scale federated system. These protection mechanisms, furthermore, are entirely independent of the underlying resources and can thus be retrofitted into an existing system with minor adaptation of its components.

This paper provides an overview of the MarketNet architecture, mechanisms and operations.

2 MarketNet architecture and mechanisms

2.0 MarketNet Architecture

MarketNet introduces a distributed protection middleware infrastructure, the Resource Access Layer (**RAL**), overlaid on existing infrastructure (Figure 1). RAL includes several mechanisms. Resource managers are responsible to set the price for a resource, collect payments for its access and deposit revenues with the bank server of the respective domain. Client managers are responsible to manage client budget, obtain pricing information and pass respective payments required to access services used by the client. Bank servers provide accounting, clearing and monitoring of currency flows. Price directories provide pricing information. These mechanisms are depicted in Figure 1 below.

In a typical scenario, depicted in Figure 1, a client belonging to domain X wishes to access a resource belonging to domain Y. The client needs to first obtain currency acceptable to domain Y. The client manager obtains respective pricing information and issues a request to the bank server of domain X to provide it with currency for domain Y. The bank server of domain X must obtain currency issued by domain Y and credit the account of domain Y with a respective central bank for this amount. The two domain bank servers pursue secure transactions with the central bank to accomplish this. Once the client manager obtains respective currency from its bank server, it can proceed to execute accesses to the service. Each access will incur a payment collected by the server manager.

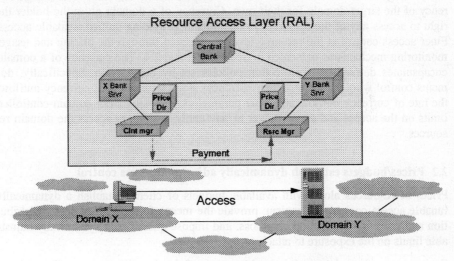

Figure 1: Overall Architecture of MarketNet

It is important to note several salient features of this architecture.
• The RAL mechanisms provide incremental extensions of existing components and systems.
• The client and resource managers provide uniform (i.e., resource independent) and minimal extensions of existing software components to control access.
• All transactions involving currency flows between managers and their bank servers and between bank servers are secured through encryption and authentication.
• The overheads involved in converting currency among domains and in allocating currency to a client can be minimized through caching of currency. For example, the bank server of domain X can cache sufficient currency of domain Y in anticipation of requests by clients in its domain.
• Once a client obtains currency, the payment to resource managers involves very minimal overhead.

Thus, the RAL provides in effect a distributed secure access management kernel that is independent of underlying resources.

2.1 Currency domains organize global protection

Resources and clients in MarketNet are organized in currency domains. Resources include physical resources such as CPU cycles, storage, bandwidth, I/O devices, or sensors as well as higher-level software services such as file storage, name service, database, or web service. A currency domain establishes access protection for a group of resources. It provides administrative infrastructure for imposing domain-level protection policies covering pricing of critical resources, assignment of budgets to internal clients, limitation of access by external domains, monitoring access to detect intrusion attacks and activating responses to attacks.

Domains use special currency to provide unified, scalable access to their services. The currency is uniquely identified by a *currency ID*. This establishes full accountability in the use of resources by tracing access to resources back to the holder of the currency. To gain access to the resources in a domain, clients first have to exchange currency of the target domain for their own. Currency of a domain gives the holder the right to access any of the resources in the domain, providing unified, scalable access. Finer access control at the resource level is achieved through the pricing and usage-monitoring mechanisms presented in Sections 2.2 and 2.4. The currency of a domain encapsulates domain-level protection policies set by the domain. Specifically, domains control who can acquire their currency, along with the total currency outflow, the rate of currency outflow and other parameters, imposing strict domain-controlled limits on the access and attack power of any entity wishing to access the domain resources.

2.2 Prices/budgets establish dynamically adjustable access control

Prices of resources along with available budgets of clients establish a dynamically tunable access control mechanism; provide the means for optimized load redistribution and graceful degradation upon loss; and impose quantifiable dynamically adjustable limits on the exposure to attackers.

Each resource in a domain is priced in terms of the domain currency. This price is advertised in respective price directories of the RAL. Prices are dynamically updated to reflect various operation parameters such as access control policies and changing demand for a resource. The combination of prices and budgets available to clients provides a fine granularity, dynamically adjustable access control mechanism. Limiting access to a specific set of clients can be achieved by raising the prices to higher levels, guaranteeing that only qualified clients (those that have sufficient budget) can access them. Furthermore, currency identifiers enable additional price discrimination techniques. Budget and price discrimination can achieve a continuous spectrum of limits imposed on the use of a resource, based on the source domain of a request.

The pricing mechanism can also be used to reflect resource unavailability due to congestion or loss. A loss of a resource reduces the supply, thus automatically causing clients to redirect their demands to backup replicas. Reduced availability results in rising prices of the replicated resources. Rising prices create a natural selection process where applications automatically adapt to resource availability and obtain access to alternate resources according to their intrinsic priority captured by their budget. High-priority clients can apply their budget to continue and obtain high QoS, while low priority clients are priced-out. Thus a loss results in graceful selective degradation of services that optimizes the balance between available resources and demands.

Furthermore, prices can force the operation of resources within a "*desirable*" region of operation. The *desirable* region of operation is resource-dependent, and in general refers to the region of operation specified by the resource manager, where specific QoS constraints or other considerations are satisfied (e.g., the average incoming rate to a switch should be controlled to provide low delays and loss). Assume the purpose of attacking a resource is to move it to an "undesirable" region of operation. Then the price of the resource should reflect its reluctance to operate in that region. Should the attacker or coalition of attackers desire to sustain the attack, they would see a continuously increasing price to access the resource, forcing them to exhaust their budget at an increasing rate to sustain the attack. The pricing mechanism in this case provides a means to convert a "fixed" budget (belonging to a specific client or a coalition of clients potentially residing in different domains), to a much lower "effective" budget. Knowledge of the specific pricing policy can provide analytical upper bounds on the duration of attacks achievable by given collective budgets.

2.3 Setting Quantified Limits on The Power of Attackers

MarketNet limits the power of attackers by their available budget. An attacker can gain access to resources only to the extent that his budget permits it. Furthermore, with each access required for an attack, the remaining budget and with it the power of the attacker decreases.

Thus, *enforcement* of budgets (i.e., guarantees that no client or application can spend more than their budget) is a very powerful tool for limiting attacks and damages. MarketNet pursues hierarchical budget enforcement by organizing network entities (i.e., resources, clients, or subdomains) in hierarchically nested domains; each domain has a bank that controls the budget usage of the entities inside the domain. For example, in the figure to the right, the budget of a user in domain **A** is controlled by the bank of this domain, the budget of the entire domain **A** is controlled by the domain **X** bank, and the budget of the domain **X** is controlled by the central bank. Even if an intruder conquers the **A** bank, his/her budget (and power of attack) cannot 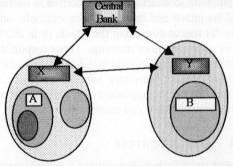 exceed the budget for the whole **A** domain. Similarly, even if the **X** bank is conquered the amount of damage the intruder can do is limited by the **X** budget, enforced by the central bank. Moreover, an intruder that conquered the **X** domain is not only limited in its power to attack other domains outside the scope of **X**, but also in its ability to attack interior domains. For example, to access any resources of the nested domain **A**, the intruder must still obtain sufficient currency of **A**. The amount of currency of **A** maintained in the bank of **X**, or made available to it, is strictly controlled by **A**.

The total exposure of a domain to external attacks is thus limited by the total budget that it maintains in external domains as well as the rate at which it accepts payments for services from external clients. A domain can tune both parameters to control its exposure.

Exchanges of currency between domains are performed by the banks at the outermost enclosing domains. For example, a client from domain **A** that wishes to access services of **B** needs to pursue an exchange conducted between the **X** bank and **Y** bank.

This restriction is imposed for scalability and authentication reasons. Organization of resources in currency domains provides the means to scaleably limit the spread of faults or attacks and localizes their effects. For example, assume an intruder has conquered the whole **X** domain. Once any domain detects this, the information can be rapidly propagated to other domains and the currency of **X** can be declared invalid until appropriate action is taken to restore normal operation of the **X** domain.

2.4 Monitoring, detection and response to intrusion attacks

Current intrusion monitoring, detection and response mechanisms depend on specific resource details. They require specialized instrumentation to monitor resource access data, ad-hoc manual techniques to correlate this data and identify attack patterns and specialized response mechanisms that depend on the resource.

In contrast, currency provides a uniform -- resource independent -- instrumentation to monitor resource access. This enables one to use standard statistical correlation techniques to automatically analyze currency flows and to identify anomalous patterns of access. Currency IDs, the unique identifiers carried by currency, establish accountability for the use of resources by enabling one to determine the entity responsible for given resource accesses. The combination of resource access monitoring, and correlation of access and entities through currency IDs is used to identify and isolate attack sources.

Once an attack has been identified, currency IDs are used to identify and isolate the source of the attack, without affecting the operation of users in legal domains. The responses to attacks can be specified in uniform response policies, based on the nature of the attack and its source. For example, one can disable access to certain resources by the source domain of the attack, or in extreme cases isolate the source domain from any access to other domains. These responses can be deployed rapidly in all currency domains by the domain attacked to prevent similar attacks on other domains. This entire process, currently handled through complex and slow manual clearing processes can be accomplished automatically in real time isolating an attacker and limiting the damage that it can cause.

3 Attack Sources

MarketNet is designed to detect, react to, and prevent attacks to systems. The goal of this section is to clearly define what are the sources of attack to computer systems and what MarketNet can do in each case.

3.1 Vulnerability of the MarketNet Infrastructure

A system is as safe as the protection subsystem it uses. The natural question is therefore how safe the MarketNet infrastructure is itself and how does it prevent undesirable protection leaks. There are two potential attacks of interest: (1) circumvention of MarketNet, (2) tempering with the MarketNet infrastructure.

Figure 1 illustrates how the Resource Access Layer (RAL) middleware introduced by MarketNet is overlaid on existing infrastructure. What if an attacker decides to manipulate resources by circumventing the MarketNet APIs? For example, a process may decide to directly allocate memory at a particular node using the OS API. MarketNet should encompass such allocations, which may otherwise undermine or lower its own allocations. Therefore a crucial task in the MarketNet infrastructure is to enforce that resource manipulations may only happen via well-defined MarketNet APIs. The system that installs MarketNet must disable any "back-door" APIs that may enable attackers to directly manipulate resources.

Another option is to use the MarketNet infrastructure itself to attack. The best way to accomplish this is to tamper with the protocols and processes to gain illegitimate access to resources. The most obvious case of such attacks is to abuse bugs in the implementations. This is a problem with any software system and we are using sophisticated Software Engineering technology that minimizes such bugs.

More peculiar to MarketNet is to counterfeit, duplicate, or steal money. For example, some agent may discover a way of generating money that looks legal either from scratch or by duplicating money already in the system. Alternatively, it may attack the communication channels to acquire digital money in transit. Illegitimate wealth can become a security threat for any system relying on MarketNet for security. The protocols in MarketNet outlined in Section 4.1 are designed to virtually eliminate the possibility of such occurrences.

3.2 The Power of Wealth in MarketNet

Money concentration, even if legitimate, is undesirable due to the potential attack power it represents. Rich agents constitute a potential attack threat. They are also prone to attacks by intruders who are attracted by the attack power they would gain by taking over the rich agents.

The owner of a popular resource or service will accumulate unbound wealth over time if the resource generates revenues in excess of its operational costs. One option would be to impose restrictions on the wealth a single agent can accumulate. This would limit the power of any single entity to attack, but it would also reduce the incentive of resource managers to provide services. An alternative is to impose restrictions on the rate at which the accumulated wealth can be used to purchase other resources or services. This is made possible by the intervention of the banking infrastructure in the transactions between clients and resource managers.

3.3 Abusive Consumption of Resources

Another potential attack is to abuse consumption of resources. It may take place in multiple ways. Firstly, one may simply conquer the resource and use it without paying dues or even profiting by re-selling services. Such situation must be prevented at all costs by enforcing that only MarketNet APIs can be used to access and manipulate resources.

Secondly, an agent may acquire cheaper or even nominal access to resources and either use them or re-sell them for profit. The MarketNet APIs prevent such situations by requesting immediate payment for resource consumption.

3.4 Non-for-profit Attacks

Some attackers are willing to disrupt or deny services to other users even when they do not profit directly from the attack. Open systems are susceptible to such attacks, and have proven particularly vulnerable to them. Part of the reason is that there is no uniform and scalable way to protect against them. The famous denial-of-service attack is a good example of this category of attacks. The goal of such an attack is to bring down some service or resource by overloading it with requests for service, (e.g., requests for access to web sites, consumption of memory cache or processor cycles). Other users perceive the resource or service as unavailable or unable to deliver the expected performance.

Non-for-profit attacks usually manifest themselves in two ways. The first form of attack is to overload resources in the system, like in the denial-of-service case. MarketNet uses its price adjustment mechanism to cope with such situations. Increases in demand force prices to go up and eventually the attacker will run out of budget. The effectiveness of this mechanism may be emphasized if discriminatory pricing is used. This mechanism has been outlined in Section 2.2

The second form of non-for-profit attack is to sabotage MarketNet itself. For example, an agent may start destroying MarketNet money passing through a given device. Since the volume of transactions is proportional to the amount of currency transferred between client and resource managers, it is apparent that money destruction would severely reduce the utilization of the system. An alternative way to reduce system utilization would is to overload MarketNet processes such as the bank server, by issuing ever-increasing requests for currency exchanges. This difficult problem needs further investigation. Two issues should be pointed out with respect to such attacks in MarketNet: (1) malicious destruction of information is an issue orthogonal to MarketNet. For example an eavesdropper can easily alter or drop information in transit independent of *what* this information might be; and (2) the liability established through currency identifiers significantly alleviates the problem, first by identifying the source of attack and second by providing the means to isolate it.

4 Bounds on attack power

Money is synonymous with attack power in MarketNet. It is important to quantify precisely what is the attack power of an agent or domain. In the case of a particular agent such as a server, its accumulated wealth represents its power of attack. A domain policy may force donation of excesss wealth as discussed in the previous section. This section quantifies the attack power of a domain.

The attack power of a domain is the sum of two components: (1) surplus in the trade balance with other domains and (2) domain wealth. The trade balance is the difference between the in flowing money to the domain and the out flowing money to other domains. The domain wealth is the summation of these differences from the time the domain started up to the current time. Both measures are a function of the revenues that services offered by the domain can generate and the number of customers they attract.

What can one do to bound the attack? Domain policies can enforce the bounds on trade flows and consequently limit the accumulation of wealth. For example, one may force a domain to always balance in flow and out flow. Ideally, a zero trade balance will force domains to not accumulate wealth. Another policy could be that the domain must convert excess wealth in some special currency where the transaction is logged. For example, a domain may be forced to convert revenues to dollars.

Another protection is the price mechanism in MarketNet. Attacks to resources will increase the demands for services and consequently increase prices. Eventually the domain budget finishes and the attack is contained.

Let us now consider the situation when a domain launches an attack to some other domain. It may operate according to the domain policies but still attack. It may change its patterns of expenditure so that it balances its trade, but the out flow of money is directed to attack. In this case, the power to attack is really a function of the domain wealth plus the revenues its resources may generate. This situation can only be contained issuing an embargo against the domain that will discourage or forbid other domains from acquiring resources that belong to the malicious domain. Such decisions may be issued by the central bank.

5 An Example: The Worm Attack

In this section we take as an attack example the famous "worm attack" (9) and show how MarketNet would have reacted to it. The purpose of the worm was to spread itself, i.e., to break into systems, install and locally run itself. To achieve this goal it exploited flaws in utility programs based on BSD-derived versions of Unix. The worm program eventually spread itself to thousands of machines around the Internet, and disrupted normal activities and Internet connectivity for many days. The disruption was caused by the worm's heavy use of system resources in order to break to other systems. The worm was not destructive in nature, i.e., it did not delete user files or try to cause other such disruptions, but it has to be noticed that if its intention were to do so, nothing would have prevented it.

The worm spread using three techniques:

1. Exploiting a bug in the *gets* standard C I/O library used by the finger daemon (*fingerd*). The *gets* call takes input to a buffer without doing any bounds checking. The worm would overran the buffer and rewrite the stack frame, allowing it to gain control in the target machine and install and execute itself locally.

2. Using the *debug* option in *sendmail* servicing the SMTP port. This feature enables testers to run programs on remote machines to display the state of the remote mail system without sending mail or establishing a login connection.

3. Guessing passwords and exploiting trust between hosts. Once present in a system the worm would try to guess user passwords, break into their accounts and exploit trust between hosts (e.g., hosts found in /etc/hosts.equiv and /.rhosts) to remotely execute into those systems as well. Password guessing is a computationally very intensive operation using a big portion of the system resources.

Using any of the above methods, the worm would successfully spread without leaving any trace of where it came from.

MarketNet can protect against several features of worm-like attacks:

1. The prospective attacker would have to pay to use *sendmail* or *fingerd*, leaving an unforgeable trace of the originator of the attack.

2. Using system resources is not free. To perform password guessing the process would involve heavy system resource utilization. Monitoring of the budget usage at the conquered account domain would soon trigger alarms due to the unusual behavior.

Furthermore, the amount of damage (e.g., overloading system resources) the process can achieve is limited by the budget available to it. Notice that we make a worst-case assumption, namely that the intruder manages to use the budget available to the account for using the system resources. Mechanisms to impose restrictions on the budget available to processes are currently under investigation in MarketNet.

MarketNet protects systems without eliminating software bugs. It assumes that software bugs are always very likely to exist and creates a layer of protection that is independent of the correctness of software.

The worm attack is one of the most difficult attacks to handle and shows some of the limitations of MarketNet. These limitations are not particular to MarketNet. The limitations under consideration stem form the fact that software implementation bugs may allow intruders to impersonate legal users of systems and therefore gain the same privileges the legal user would have. We are currently investigating how MarketNet can efficiently react in the following scenarios:

Assume that the worm had destructive intentions. Budget enforcement along with usage monitoring in MarketNet would limit the scope and the extent of the damage. We are currently investigating price discrimination techniques that may be able to limit such attacks by making resources very expensive when the process does not normally use it. For example, deletion of files would be very expensive for unknown processes, which will not have enough money for the attack.

In a worm-like attack, the attacker manages to impersonate the owner of an account. Even when this happens, it should not be equivalent to getting hold of the budget of the conquered account. One of the mechanisms to break this equivalence is usage monitoring. Abnormal access patterns can be restricted providing adjustable limits on the amount of damage a malicious or faulty processes can cause. A second mechanism under investigation is the separation of budgets available on a per process and/or per task basis. The tradeoff in this case is protection level vs. ease of use of the system.

6   Conclusions

Market-based technologies can provide an effective solution to the protection of information systems. MarketNet develops unified, systematic market-based technologies to provide scalable and tunable access control for large multi-domain networked systems. These technologies enable unified monitoring and correlated analysis of resource access to detect intrusion attacks, isolate the sources of attacks and respond quickly to control its damages. MarketNet develops mechanisms to protect critical network services, based on their quantifiable value to users, and assure their continuous availability through failures or attacks based on user's priority.

In summary, some of the key ideas in MarketNet are the following:

• Currency is used to provide unified, scaleable, resource-independent access control to resources and services and account for their use.

• Resources and clients are organized in currency domains. Each domain has its own currency. Clients wishing to access a resource must pay in currency acceptable to the domain that owns the resource. A domain has full control over its exposure to attacks, by controlling access to its resources through several parameters: the price of a resource; the budget allocated to a given client; and the rate at which currency is provided to a given client.

• Organization in currency domains can limit the spread of faults and attacks.

• The power of attacks is limited by the budget available to the attacker and by the price of resources.

• Currency carries unique unforgeable identifiers that can be monitored and traced back to the holder. Currency identifiers establish verifiable accountability on the use of resources.

• Currency provides a resource-independent instrumentation to monitor and correlate access patterns and to detect intrusion attacks through automated, uniform statistical analysis of anomalous currency flows.

• Prices are dynamic. They can be used to fine tune access control to resources. They provide the means for optimized load redistribution and graceful degradation upon loss, and impose quantifiable dynamically adjustable limits on the exposure to attackers.

These mechanisms are resource-independent, and admit unlimited scalability for very large systems consisting of federated domains operated by mutually distrustful administrations

References

1. Clearwater, S., editor. "*Market-based Control of Distributed Systems*," World Scientific Press, 1996.

2. Dailianas, A., and Y. Yemini "*A Protocol for Secure Financial Transactions*," Paper in Preparation.

3. Hull, J. C. "Options, Futures, and Other Derivatives," third edition, Prentice Hall.

4. Kurose, J., M. Schwartz, and Y. Yemini "*A Microeconomic Approach to Optimization of Channel Access Policies in Multiaccess Networks*," Proc. Of the 5th International Conference on Distributed Computer Systems, Denver, Colorado, 1995.

5. MacKie-Mason, J., and H. Varian "*Economic FAQs About the Internet*," in The Journal of Economic Perspectives, vol. 8, no. 3, pp. 75-96, 1994. Reprinted (with revisions) in Internet Economics, J. Bailey and L. McKnight, eds. Cambridge, MIT Press, 1996.

6. MacKie-Mason, J., and H. Varian "*Pricing the Internet*," in B. Kahin and J. Keller, editors, Public Access to the Internet, ACM, Boston, Massachusetts, May 1993.

7. Sairamesh, J., D. Ferguson, and Y. Yemini "*An Approach to Pricing, Optimal Allocation and Quality of Service Provisioning in High-speed Packet Networks*," in Proc. of the Conference on Computer Communications, Boston, Massachusetts, April 1995.

8. Schneier, B. "*Applied Cryptography*," second edition, John Wiley & Sons, pp. 139-147.

9. Spafford, E. *"The Internet Worm Incident,"* Technical Report CSD-TR-933, Department of Computer Sciences, Purdue University, Sept. 19, 1991.

10. Walsh, W., M. Wellman, P. Wurman, and J. MacKie-Mason *"Some Economics of Market-Based Distributed Scheduling,"* In Proc. of the 8th International Conference on Distributed Computing Systems (ICDCS-98), Amsterdam, the Netherlands, May 1998.

11. Yemini, Y. *"Selfish Optimization in Computer Networks,"* Proc. of the 20th IEEE Conference on Decision and Control, pp. 281-285, San Diego, CA., Dec. 1981.

CiBIT: Biblioteca Italiana Telematica
A Digital Library for the Italian Cultural Heritage

Eugenio Picchi, Lisa Biagini, Davide Merlitti

Istituto di Linguistica Computazionale, CNR, Via della Faggiola 32, Pisa, Italy

1   Introduction

The primary objective of the CiBIT digital library is the widest possible diffusion of information on Italian art, literature and history. The aim of CiBIT is to allow scholars and other interested users throughout the world to access and study multimedia documentation (voice and image data are also included) containing all kinds of information on and describing different aspects of Italian culture. The following main areas of artistic and cultural interest are covered: philology, literature, linguistics, medieval and modern history, legal history, musicology.

The intention is to make the CiBIT service available to students and scholars in university libraries and research institutes, in the first place, but also in libraries serving the general public. Main aims of the project are to allow users throughout the world (through Internet) to access and consult Italian cultural data, and to provide them with a series of sophisticated tools to process and analyse the textual material in various ways.

2   CiBIT query system

The CiBIT query system, which is based on that of the DBT system[1], has been completely developed in JAVA so that it can be used by all existing WEB browsers and can operate on all kinds of hardware and software platforms. Java applets have been implemented to provide the same level of functionality as the stand-alone DBT system. A multiserver middleware engine automatically selects the best host site depending on the particular requirements of a given query. The CiBIT digital library can be accessed through the consultation of a single text, of a set of texts, or of an entire corpus. Relevant subsets of texts in a corpus can be defined dynamically using the bibliographic data associated with the texts.

Main access functions. The query system employed by CiBIT has been implemented not only as a general purpose search engine but also to meet the particular needs of scholars in the field of the humanities. Thus in addition to basic search functions, the user also has the following search and retrieval options available:

---

[1] CiBIT has adopted the query system of the DBT textual database system developed at the Istituto di Linguistica Computazionale (ILC-CNR), Pisa as its starting point. For more information on the DBT and other text processing procedures developed at ILC-CNR, see http://www.ilc.pi.cnr.it/dbt/index.htm.

- retrieval of ordered concordances for all occurrences of the keyword(s) searched (sorted alphabetically on the word immediately preceding or following the keyword, as specified by the user);
- application of common text processing statistical functions such as the Mutual Information Index (e.g. the identification of significant correlations between words);
- retrieval of contrastive text analyses;
- access to critical textual annotations;
- access to multimedia data (e.g. images and sound in the original source text - manuscripts or oral versions - or iconographs).

In addition, users can intervene on single texts (not over an entire corpus but on particularly significant texts) in order to enrich them with additional information. This type of textual annotation can consist of labels identifying chosen hypertextual paths or linguistic classifications (e.g. lexical, grammatical and morphosyntactic labels) which can be then exploited by appropriate search and analysis functions of the system.

3 System Architecture

The system will have a fully distributed system architecture, connecting multiple CiBIT-DBT servers transparently to the users. CiBIT runs on the DBT-NET client-server system, which is structured in three levels. The client level consists of a Java applet while on the server side there is a server module and a gateway written in Object Pascal and C, respectively. The server and the gateway are both 32bit multi-thread Windows applications on an Intel32 platform. Client-server communication is through the DBT protocol over TCP.

The gateway mediates the client-server dialog distributing the service in order to balance the load to the server over the machines available at any one time. In this way, it is possible to overcome the limitation posed by Java applets that can connect only with the machine from which they have been downloaded.

Whereas a query session will consist of a number of client queries and server responses, the client-server connection is maintained only for the duration of a single query/response. The status for the execution of an entire session is maintained principally by the server. The continuity of a session is guaranteed by the server identifying the client on each query.

4 How to Access CiBIT

CiBIT is currently implemented in an experimental version and is under test by the institutes belonging to the Consortium. However, once the testing stage is completed, the intention is to make the CiBIT digital library service publicly available, free of charge. Users from anywhere in the world will be able to access, browse and search archives containing a wealth of information on Italian literature, art and history. A user-friendly interface and on-line helps will guide them in their choice of material and in the use of the query functions.

The ERCIM Technical Reference Digital Library

Stefania Biagioni[1], Josè Luis Borbinha[2], Reginald Ferber[3], Preben Hansen[4],
Sarantos Kapidakis[5], Laszlo Kovacs[6], Frank Roos[7], Anne-Marie Vercoustre[8]

[1]IEI-CNR, Via S. Maria 46, 56126 Pisa, Italy
[2]INESC, Rua Alves Redol, 9, Lisbon, Portugal
[3]GMD-IPSI, Dolivostr. 15, D-64293 Darmstadt, Germany
[4]SICS, S-164 28 Kista, Sweden
[5]ICS-FORTH, Vassilika Vouton, GR-71110 Heraklion, Crete, Greece
[6]SZTAKI, H-1518 Budapest, Hungary
[7]CWI, Kruislaan 413, NL-1098 SJ Amsterdam, The Netherlands
[8]INRIA, Domaine de Voluceau, Rocquencourt, France

1 Introduction

Within the context of the DELOS[1] Working Group, eight institutions of the
European Research Consortium for Informatics and Mathematics (ERCIM) are
currently collaborating on the installation of an ERCIM Technical Reference Digital
Library (ETRDL). The aim is to implement and test a prototype infrastructure for
networked access to a distributed multi-format collection of technical documents
produced by ERCIM members. The collection is managed by a set of interoperating
servers, based on the Dienst system developed by a US consortium led by Cornell
University and adopted by NCSTRL (Networked Computer Science Technical
Reference Library). Pilot server sites have already been set up at half of the 14
ERCIM national labs. Servers are expected to be installed at the other centres soon.
The aim is to assist ERCIM scientists to make their research results immediately
available world-wide and provide them with appropriate on-line facilities to access the
technical documentation of others working in the same field. Public access to this
reference service is provided through Internet.

2 Common User Interface

In addition to the basic service provided by the DIENST system, some additional
functionalities are being implemented in the ETRDL common user interface in order
to meet the particular needs of the European IT scientific community. An author
submission form has been included to facilitate the insertion of new documents by the
users themselves. The service can be accessed through the DELOS Web site.
Extending the Metadata Set. Dienst provides services to store both documents and
their metadata. Retrieval is based on the registered metadata. Dienst accepts a small
set of metadata but can be configured to handle additional elements. We are now
implementing an extension to the current configuration of the Dienst system in order
to increase retrieval options. The additional data fields are compatible with the

[1]For more information on the activities of the DELOS Working Group on Digital Library
related research issues (ESPRIT - LTR No. 21057), see http: www.iei.pi.cnr.it/DELOS/.

906

Dublin Core (DC) metadescription standard. The Dienst code has thus been modified to enable the new fields to be indexed and searched.

Common Classification Scheme. One set of extensions are fields for the ACM Computing Classification, for the AMS Mathematics Subject Classification, and for free keywords. For submission and retrieval, users can browse the classifications, mark selected keywords and insert them in the appropriate fields. Authors should enter terms from at least one classification; they can also use all three fields. Searches are performed on all three fields by default, but may be restricted to single fields. Problems caused by the adoption of multiple classification schemes are being studied.

3 Multilingual Interface

Multilinguality is an issue of strategic importance for the European scientific community. The first activities of the ETRDL in this area are aimed at (i) implementing an interface capable of handling multiple languages and (ii) providing very basic functionalities for cross-language querying.

Multilingual Access and Browsing. Each national site is responsible for localisation, i.e. implementation of local site user interfaces (also) in the national language as well as English: one of the tasks of the group will be to investigate problems involved in rendering the Dublin Core element set multilingual. Documents are tagged for language and character code switching mechanisms are provided for the local display and printing of non-Latin-1 languages (Hungarian and Greek in our collection). However, it is agreed that UNICODE must be adopted eventually in order to fully internationalise the system.

Cross-language Querying. In the short term a simple form of cross-language querying will use controlled keyword (ACM/AMS) terms. All documents in the ETRDL, in whatever language, classified using this scheme, can thus be searched. Authors are also requested to include an abstract in English, which makes English free term searching over documents in any language also possible. INESC has developed an LDAP service with a multilingual repository for the ACM and AMS classification systems, which is integrated in the ETRDL system. This multilingual service makes cross-language querying in local languages possible. In the longer term, other methods for cross-language querying which enable the user of the DL service to retrieve texts composed or indexed in one language via a query formulated in another will be investigated.

4 Gateway to Z39.50

The Z39.50 protocol enables access to library data; adopted by the EU Librarians Programme, it will be the official protocol for search and retrieval in European libraries. A Z39.50 access to Dienst has been developed at FORTH and will be integrated in the ETRDL service.

Acknowledgments. ETRDL is a collaborative effort between a number of ERCIM Institutes. Many ERCIM scientists and technicians have been involved in the setting up of the experimental technical reference service. In particular, we should mention: Barbara Lutes (GMD-IPSI); Jacob Mauroidis, Giorgos Sapunjis, Panagiotis Alexakos, Gregory Karvounarakis (ICS-FORTH); Maria Bruna Baldacci, Carlo Carlesi, Donatella Castelli, Carol Peters (IEI-CNR); Mario Loffredo and Giuseppe Romano (CNUCE-CNR); Paula Viana, Nuno Freire, João Fernandes and João Ferreira (INESC).

NAIST Digital Library

Hideki Sunahara, Rei (Suzuki) Atarashi, Toru Nishimura,
Masakazu Imai, and Kunihiro Chihara*

Nara Institute of Science and Technology,
8916-5, Takayama, Ikoma, Nara 630-0101, Japan

Introduction

NAIST Digital Library provides practical library services for faculties, students and staffs of Nara Institute of Science and Technology. Operation of this system is started in April 1996[1]. The system mainly consists of the database system including electronic books, journals, magazines, NAIST technical reports, etc., the digital video library system, the browser system, the information retrieval system. Our system allows users to browse electronic books, journals, transactions, and magazines through networks. In addition, the video browser is also provided.

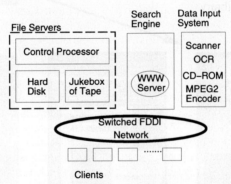

Fig. 1. System Overview

System Overview

Fig. 1 shows the overview of our current system. File servers have a capacity of storing library data of totally 5TB. A hierarchical storage works as UNIX file systems. Furthermore, files on the servers will migrate to the suitable storage according to frequency of access to them.

The library search engine enables users to easily obtain what they need in the library database. This search engine works as WWW server. Fig. 2 shows an example what you can actually get from **NAIST Digital Library**.

The Data Input System generates data for digital library with scanners, OCR softwares, CD-ROM drives, and MPEG-2 encoders.

Provided Services

A current system provides following services.

* suna@wide.ad.jp, ray@itc.aist-nara.ac.jp, nisimura@itc.aist-nara,ac.jp, imai@is.aist-nara.ac.jp, chihara@is.aist-nara.ac.jp

908

- search function includes bibliographical information search and whole text search.
- E-mail based notification of new arrival information which includes the pre-registered keywords by users.
- digital video library with 4Mbps MPEG-2 stream data.

Research Topics

We are developing new services for digital libraries including following topics: content based information retrieval function for video data[2], search advise agents with thesaurus, data structures for digital libraries, administration/management mechanisms for peta bytes class file servers.

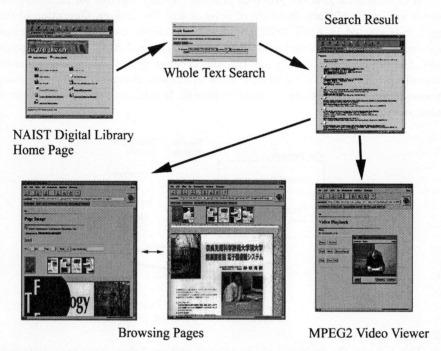

Search Result

Whole Text Search

NAIST Digital Library
Home Page

Browsing Pages   MPEG2 Video Viewer

URL: http://dlw3.aist-nara.ac.jp/
Fig. 2. Example of Browsing NAIST Digital Library

References

1. Rei Suzuki, Hideki Sunahara, Masakazu Imai, Kunihiro Chihara, "Building Digital Library Systems – NAIST Challenge –," Proceedings of International Symposium on Research, Development and Practice in Digital Libraries 1997 (ISDL'97), pp.28–31, Nov. 1997.
2. Yukiko Kawasaki, Rei Suzuki, Hideki Sunahara, "NAIST Digital Video Library: Tools for Restructuring Video Data for the Content Based Information Retrieval - A Representative Image of Shot Concept for the Internet," in this Proceedings, Sep. 1998.

Author Index

Springer
and the
environment

At Springer we firmly believe that an
international science publisher has a
special obligation to the environment,
and our corporate policies consistently
reflect this conviction.
We also expect our business partners –
paper mills, printers, packaging
manufacturers, etc. – to commit
themselves to using materials and
production processes that do not harm
the environment. The paper in this
book is made from low- or no-chlorine
pulp and is acid free, in conformance
with international standards for paper
permanency.

Springer

Lecture Notes in Computer Science

For information about Vols. 1–1420

please contact your bookseller or Springer-Verlag

Vol. 1460: G. Quirchmayr, E. Schweighofer, T.J.M. Bench-Capon (Eds.), Database and Expert Systems Applications. Proceedings, 1998. XVI, 905 pages. 1998.

Vol. 1461: G. Bilardi, G.F. Italiano, A. Pietracaprina, G. Pucci (Eds.), Algorithms – ESA'98. Proceedings, 1998. XII, 516 pages. 1998.

Vol. 1462: H. Krawczyk (Ed.), Advances in Cryptology - CRYPTO '98. Proceedings, 1998. XII, 519 pages. 1998.

Vol. 1463: N.E. Fuchs (Ed.), Logic Program Synthesis and Transformation. Proceedings, 1997. X, 343 pages. 1998.

Vol. 1464: H.H.S. Ip, A.W.M. Smeulders (Eds.), Multimedia Information Analysis and Retrieval. Proceedings, 1998. VIII, 264 pages. 1998.

Vol. 1465: R. Hirschfeld (Ed.), Financial Cryptography. Proceedings, 1998. VIII, 311 pages. 1998.

Vol. 1466: D. Sangiorgi, R. de Simone (Eds.), CONCUR'98: Concurrency Theory. Proceedings, 1998. XI, 657 pages. 1998.

Vol. 1467: C. Clack, K. Hammond, T. Davie (Eds.), Implementation of Functional Languages. Proceedings, 1997. X, 375 pages. 1998.

Vol. 1468: P. Husbands, J.-A. Meyer (Eds.), Evolutionary Robotics. Proceedings, 1998. VIII, 247 pages. 1998.

Vol. 1469: R. Puigjaner, N.N. Savino, B. Serra (Eds.), Computer Performance Evaluation. Proceedings, 1998. XIII, 376 pages. 1998.

Vol. 1470: D. Pritchard, J. Reeve (Eds.), Euro-Par'98: Parallel Processing. Proceedings, 1998. XXII, 1157 pages. 1998.

Vol. 1471: J. Dix, L. Moniz Pereira, T.C. Przymusinski (Eds.), Logic Programming and Knowledge Representation. Proceedings, 1997. IX, 246 pages. 1998. (Subseries LNAI).

Vol. 1473: X. Leroy, A. Ohori (Eds.), Types in Compilation. Proceedings, 1998. VIII, 299 pages. 1998.

Vol. 1474: F. Mueller, A. Bestavros (Eds.), Languages, Compilers, and Tools for Embedded Systems. Proceedings, 1998. XIV, 261 pages. 1998.

Vol. 1475: W. Litwin, T. Morzy, G. Vossen (Eds.), Advances in Databases and Information Systems. Proceedings, 1998. XIV, 369 pages. 1998.

Vol. 1476: J. Calmet, J. Plaza (Eds.), Artificial Intelligence and Symbolic Computation. Proceedings, 1998. XI, 309 pages. 1998. (Subseries LNAI).

Vol. 1477: K. Rothermel, F. Hohl (Eds.), Mobile Agents. Proceedings, 1998. VIII, 285 pages. 1998.

Vol. 1478: M. Sipper, D. Mange, A. Pérez-Uribe (Eds.), Evolvable Systems: From Biology to Hardware. Proceedings, 1998. IX, 382 pages. 1998.

Vol. 1479: J. Grundy, M. Newey (Eds.), Theorem Proving in Higher Order Logics. Proceedings, 1998. VIII, 497 pages. 1998.

Vol. 1480: F. Giunchiglia (Ed.), Artificial Intelligence: Methodology, Systems, and Applications. Proceedings, 1998. IX, 502 pages. 1998. (Subseries LNAI).

Vol. 1481: E.V. Munson, C. Nicholas, D. Wood (Eds.), Principles of Digital Document Processing. Proceedings, 1998. VII, 152 pages. 1998.

Vol. 1482: R.W. Hartenstein, A. Keevallik (Eds.), Field-Programmable Logic and Applications. Proceedings, 1998. XI, 533 pages. 1998.

Vol. 1483: T. Plagemann, V. Goebel (Eds.), Interactive Distributed Multimedia Systems and Telecommunication Services. Proceedings, 1998. XV, 326 pages. 1998.

Vol. 1484: H. Coelho (Ed.), Progress in Artificial Intelligence – IBERAMIA 98. Proceedings, 1998. XIII, 421 pages. 1998. (Subseries LNAI).

Vol. 1485: J.-J. Quisquater, Y. Deswarte, C. Meadows, D. Gollmann (Eds.), Computer Security – ESORICS 98. Proceedings, 1998. X, 377 pages. 1998.

Vol. 1486: A.P. Ravn, H. Rischel (Eds.), Formal Techniques in Real-Time and Fault-Tolerant Systems. Proceedings, 1998. VIII, 339 pages. 1998.

Vol. 1487: V. Gruhn (Ed.), Software Process Technology. Proceedings, 1998. VIII, 157 pages. 1998.

Vol. 1488: B. Smyth, P. Cunningham (Eds.), Advances in Case-Based Reasoning. Proceedings, 1998. XI, 482 pages. 1998. (Subseries LNAI).

Vol. 1490: C. Palamidessi, H. Glaser, K. Meinke (Eds.), Principles of Declarative Programming. Proceedings, 1998. XI, 497 pages. 1998.

Vol. 1493: J.P. Bowen, A. Fett, M.G. Hinchey (Eds.), ZUM '98: The Z Formal Specification Notation. Proceedings, 1998. XV, 417 pages. 1998.

Vol. 1495: T. Andreasen, H. Christiansen, H.L. Larsen (Eds.), Flexible Query Answering Systems. IX, 393 pages. 1998. (Subseries LNAI).

Vol. 1497: V. Alexandrov, J. Dongarra (Eds.), Recent Advances in Parallel Virtual Machine and Message Passing Interface. Proceedings, 1998. XII, 412 pages. 1998.

Vol. 1498: A.E. Eiben, T. Bäck, M. Schoenauer, H.-P. Schwefel (Eds.), Parallel Problem Solving from Nature – PPSN V. Proceedings, 1998. XXIII, 1041 pages. 1998.

Vol. 1499: S. Kutten (Ed.), Distributed Computing. Proceedings, 1998. XII, 419 pages. 1998.

Vol. 1501: M.M. Richter, C.H. Smith, R. Wiehagen, T. Zeugmann (Eds.), Algorithmic Learning Theory. Proceedings, 1998. XI, 439 pages. 1998. (Subseries LNAI).

Vol. 1503: G. Levi (Ed.), Static Analysis. Proceedings, 1998. IX, 383 pages. 1998.

Vol. 1504: O. Herzog, A. Günter (Eds.), KI-98: Advances in Artificial Intelligence. Proceedings, 1998. XI, 355 pages. 1998. (Subseries LNAI).

Vol. 1508: S. Jajodia, M.T. Özsu, A. Dogac (Eds.), Advances in Multimedia Information Systems. Proceedings, 1998. VIII, 207 pages. 1998.

Vol. 1510: J.M. Zytkow, M. Quafafou (Eds.), Principles of Data Mining and Knowledge Discovery. Proceedings, 1998. XI, 482 pages. 1998. (Subseries LNAI).

Vol. 1513: C. Nikolaou, C. Stephanidis (Eds.), Research and Advanced Technology for Digital Libraries. Proceedings, 1998. XV, 912 pages. 1998.

Vol. 1514: K. Ohta,, D. Pei (Eds.), Advances in Cryptology – ASIACRYPT'98. Proceedings, 1998. XII, 436 pages. 1998.

Vol. 1516: W. Ehrenberger (Ed.), Computer Safety, Reliability and Security. Proceedings, 1998. XVI, 392 pages. 1998.